Webster's II
Children's
Dictionary

Houghton Mifflin Company

Boston • New York

Printed in the U.S.A.

Library of Congress Cataloging-in-Publication Data

Webster's II children's dictionary
     p.   cm.
    Rev. ed. of: Webster's II new Riverside children's dictionary. © 1984.
    Summary: A dictionary for elementary school students featuring word histories, synonym paragraphs, a spelling table, and a reference appendix with maps and tables.
    ISBN 0-395-84825-3 (pbk.)
    1. English language—Dictionaries, Juvenile. [1. English language—Dictionaries.] I. Webster's II new Riverside children's dictionary. II. Title: Webster's 2nd children's dictionary. III. Title: Webster's second children's dictionary.
PE1628.5.W363   1997
423—DC20   96-21176
                                 CIP

For information about this and other Houghton Mifflin trade and reference books and multimedia products, visit The Bookstore at Houghton Mifflin on the World Wide Web at http://www.hmco.com/trade/.

"quickly" are adverbs.

ad·verb (ad′vûrb′) ☐*noun, plural* **adverbs**

adversary *noun* Someone on the opposite side in a war or contest: *She is my adversary in the election for class president.*
ad·ver·sar·y (ad′vər ser′ē) ☐*noun, plural* **adversaries**

adversity *noun* Great misfortune; hardship: *The people suffered through many adversities during the war.*
ad·ver·si·ty (ad vûr′si tē) ☐*noun, plural* **adversities**

advertise *verb* To bring to the attention of the public: *That store advertises bicycles on television.*
ad·ver·tise (ad′vər tīz′) ☐*verb* **advertised, advertising, advertises**

advertisement *noun* A public announcement about something. An advertisement may be used to sell a product, find or offer work, or find or offer a service.
ad·ver·tise·ment (ad′vər tīz′mənt *or* ad-vûr′tis mənt) ☐*noun, plural* **advertisements**

advice *noun* Opinion about what to do: *I always follow my father's advice.*
ad·vice (ad vīs′) ☐*noun*

advisable *adjective* Worth doing; sensible: *It is advisable to go to the doctor if you feel sick.*
ad·vis·a·ble (ad vī′zə bəl) ☐*adjective*

advise *verb* **1.** To give advice to: *He advised me to save the money I made.* **2.** To notify; inform: *She advised us she would be late.*
ad·vise (ad vīz′) ☐*verb* **advised, advising, advises**

adviser *or* **advisor** *noun* Someone who gives advice.
ad·vis·er *or* **ad·vi·sor** (ad vī′zər) ☐*noun, plural* **advisers** *or* **advisors**

advocate *verb* To speak in favor of; recommend; urge: *The mayor advocated increasing the size of the police force.* ☐*noun* Someone who speaks in favor of something.
ad·vo·cate (ad′və kāt′) ☐*verb* **advocated, advocating, advocates** ☐*noun* (ad′və kit), *plural* **advocates**

adz *or* **adze** *noun* A tool that looks like an ax with its blade set at an angle. It is used for shaping logs and other heavy pieces of wood.
adz *or* **adze** (adz) ☐*noun, plural* **adzes**

aerial *noun* An antenna for radio or television.
aer·i·al (âr′ē əl) ☐*noun, plural* **aerials**

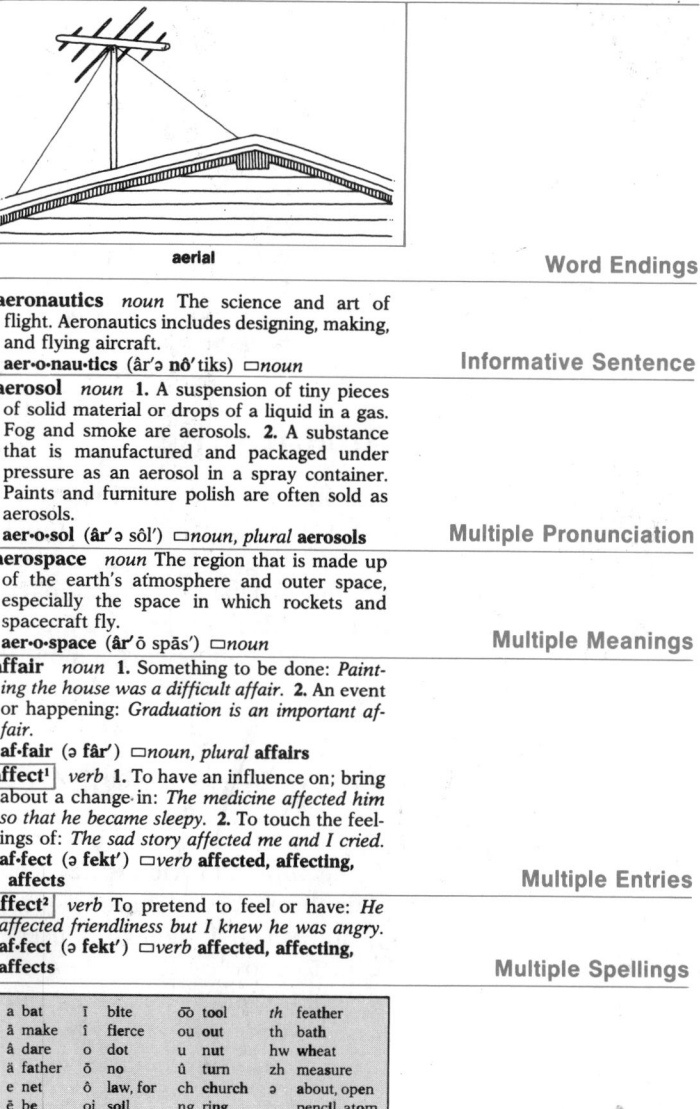

aerial

aeronautics *noun* The science and art of flight. Aeronautics includes designing, making, and flying aircraft.
aer·o·nau·tics (âr′ə nô′tiks) ☐*noun*

aerosol *noun* **1.** A suspension of tiny pieces of solid material or drops of a liquid in a gas. Fog and smoke are aerosols. **2.** A substance that is manufactured and packaged under pressure as an aerosol in a spray container. Paints and furniture polish are often sold as aerosols.
aer·o·sol (âr′ə sôl′) ☐*noun, plural* **aerosols**

aerospace *noun* The region that is made up of the earth's atmosphere and outer space, especially the space in which rockets and spacecraft fly.
aer·o·space (âr′ō spās′) ☐*noun*

affair *noun* **1.** Something to be done: *Painting the house was a difficult affair.* **2.** An event or happening: *Graduation is an important affair.*
af·fair (ə fâr′) ☐*noun, plural* **affairs**

affect¹ *verb* **1.** To have an influence on; bring about a change in: *The medicine affected him so that he became sleepy.* **2.** To touch the feelings of: *The sad story affected me and I cried.*
af·fect (ə fekt′) ☐*verb* **affected, affecting, affects**

affect² *verb* To pretend to feel or have: *He affected friendliness but I knew he was angry.*
af·fect (ə fekt′) ☐*verb* **affected, affecting, affects**

Illustrations

Word Endings

Informative Sentence

Multiple Pronunciation

Multiple Meanings

Multiple Entries

Multiple Spellings

Short Pronunciation Key

Your Guide to the Dictionary

Entry Words

Your dictionary is made up of a long list of words. There are thousands of words in it—from *abacus* to *zucchini*. Each word in the list is called an *entry word* and is printed in **heavy black type.** You will find information after each entry word. The entry word and the information after it make up the *entry*. Here are two entries from your dictionary. What are the entry words for each entry?

> **backboard** *noun* A board to which the basket is attached in basketball.
> **back·board** (**bak'**bôrd') □*noun, plural* **backboards**
> **backbone** *noun* **1.** The series of jointed bones in the back; spine. The backbone is the main support of the body of human beings and many animals. **2.** Strength of character: *It took backbone to be a pioneer.*
> **back·bone** (**bak'**bōn') □*noun, plural* **backbones**

Guidewords

Now that you know how words are listed in your dictionary, you are on your way to locating words quickly. To make this task even easier, you can use the *guidewords* that are at the top of almost every page in your dictionary. Open your dictionary to any page and notice the two words in **heavy black type** at the top of the page. These two words are called *guidewords*. Guidewords show the first and last entry words on the page. They help guide you to the entry you are looking for.

Entry Words with One Definition

People often use dictionaries to find out what words mean. They read the *definition*, or the explanation of the exact meaning of the word. In your dictionary, definitions are given in short sentences or phrases. Simple, clear language is used so you can easily find out what you want to know.

Many entry words have only one meaning. Read the definition for *faucet*. What is a faucet? What is it used for? The definition answers these questions quickly and simply.

> **faucet** *noun* A device with a handle for controlling the flow of liquid from a pipe or container.
> **fau·cet** (**fô'**sit) □*noun, plural* **faucets**

A definition is often followed by a colon (:) and a sentence or phrase in *italic type* that includes the entry word. The sentence or phrase is helpful in two ways. First, it shows how the word may be used in a sentence. Second, a sentence or phrase can provide the context, or clues you can use to figure out the meaning of the word.

Multiple Meanings

You probably know that some words have more than one meaning. In fact, one word may have many meanings. The word *go*, for example, has eight meanings; *bad* has seven meanings; and *run* has more than twenty meanings.

When a word has multiple meanings, each meaning is numbered. The most common meaning is number 1. The next most common meaning is number 2, and so on. Read all the meanings for *basket*. Then put the sentences below in order from the most common meaning to the least common.

    a. Our team won the game by four <u>baskets</u>.
    b. My mother hung the <u>basket</u> on the garage so we could practice for the basketball game.
    c. We used twigs from a grapevine to make a <u>basket</u>.

> **basket** *noun* **1.** A container made of woven twigs, grasses, or strips of wood. **2.** A metal hoop with an open net hanging from it, used in basketball. **3.** A goal scored in basketball by throwing the ball through this hoop. **bas·ket** (bas′kit) ◻*noun, plural* **baskets**

Synonyms

By now you have probably noticed that the meanings for entry words may be given in the form of sentences, phrases, or single words. A word that means almost the same thing as another word is called a *synonym*. Single-word definitions are synonyms.

Synonyms can help you understand the meaning of a word. For example, you may not know what *resolution* means, but its synonym, *promise*, is familiar to you; therefore, your understanding of the synonym *promise* helps you understand one meaning of *resolution*.

Your dictionary shows synonyms in three ways. Synonyms for an entry word may appear as a one-word meaning within the entry. In addition, synonyms may be highlighted in synonym boxes in which they are explained and used in sample sentences. Look at the entry and synonym box for *victory*. What synonym can you find in the entry? What synonyms are shown in the synonym box?

victory *noun* The winning of a battle, contest, or struggle; triumph.
vic·to·ry (**vik′**tə rē) □*noun, plural* **victories**

> *SYNONYMS:* **victory, conquest, triumph**
>
> These nouns mean the winning of a battle, contest, or struggle: *Being elected mayor was the greatest victory of her political career. The doctor developed a vaccine that was responsible for the conquest of polio. That famous general has many military triumphs to his credit.*

Word Histories and Multiple Entries

Some of the words in your dictionary are very new words. For example, the dictionary your grandparents had when they were children probably didn't have the words *computer* or *laser* in it. Other words are very old words that have changed over time. Many words, both old and new, have interesting histories. Your dictionary presents many of these word histories in Word History boxes.

Do you know how the word *sandwich* came to be used? Read the Word History for *sandwich* below. How did inventing the sandwich help the Earl?

> *WORD HISTORY:* **sandwich**
>
> The *sandwich* was named after the fourth Earl of Sandwich. The earl was fond of gambling at cards and is said to have invented the sandwich so that he would not have to leave the game to eat a regular meal.

Some words have different origins, yet these words are spelled the same and often sound the same. However, their meanings may be very different. In your dictionary, these words have separate, numbered entries such as *duck*[1] and *duck*[2]. When you see such entries, you will know that these words have very different histories.

How Words Are Used

You may have noticed these labels in most dictionary entries: *noun, pronoun, verb, adjective, adverb, conjunction, preposition,* and *interjection.* These labels tell you how the entry word may be used in a sentence, that is, its part of speech. The part of speech label is in *italic type* and appears before the meanings for that part of speech. When there is more than one part of speech you will see an open rectangle (□) before the next part of speech. The following table defines the parts of speech and shows how they are used.

Part of Speech	Function	Examples
Noun	names a person, place, thing, or idea	Magazines and books about freedom were piled on Myra's shelf in the den.
Pronoun	stands for a noun	She took the vase even though it was his.
Verb	expresses action or state of being	The children felt anxious when they lost their mother in the supermarket.
Adjective	describes a noun	The huge, silvery fish leaped out of the cold, clear stream.
Adverb	describes a verb, adjective, or other adverb	The very large dog ran downstairs and quickly ate his dinner.
Conjunction	joins words or groups of words	Betsy and Lee went to the town meeting, but the others stayed home.
Preposition	shows a relation between a noun or pronoun and another word	The record was in the jacket on the shelf over the couch.
Interjection	shows a strong feeling	Ouch, you stepped on my foot!

Inflected Forms

Identical twins juggled oranges.

It may surprise you to learn that only one word in the sentence above is an entry word in your dictionary. Do you know which one?

Words with endings, such as *-s*, *-es*, *-ed*, *-ing*, *-er* and *-est*, are known as *inflected forms*. Words with these endings are not usually listed as entry words. To find the meanings of these words, you need to locate the base word. Sometimes the spelling of a base word changes when an ending is added. A *y* may be changed to *i*, the final consonant may be doubled, or a silent *e* may be dropped before an ending.

Your dictionary lists inflected forms of a word at the very end of an entry. You will find inflected forms for noun plurals, verb tenses, and adjectives and adverbs that show comparison.

Special Phrases

Read the following sentence and tell what it means.

> Mark was on pins and needles about taking the bicycle skills test.

You know that Mark is not a human pincushion! *On pins and needles* is a special phrase in which knowing the meaning of each word does not always lead to understanding the meaning of the whole phrase. Mark was not sitting on real pins and needles. Rather, he was nervous and anxious.

The English language includes many special phrases. Your dictionary explains them under the entry word that seems most important in the phrase. *On pins and needles* is found in the entry for *pin*. Special phrases are presented near the end of the entry.

Your dictionary explains other phrases that may also have unexpected meanings. These phrases contain a verb and one or two other short words. The meaning of phrases such as *break down*, *bawl out*, *bring up*, and *let down* can be found by looking up the entry for the verb in each phrase.

The Pronunciation Key

The way a word is pronounced is called its *pronunciation*. Your dictionary provides a code to help you figure out the pronunciation of words. You will find the pronunciation of entry words in parentheses () after the meanings in the entry. The code uses letters of the alphabet, special marks, and special symbols to stand for sounds. Each letter, mark, or symbol stands for one sound.

Look at the pronunciation key on page B-20. Just as a key helps you unlock a door, this key will help you unlock the sounds of letters in a word. It shows all the letters, marks, and symbols that stand for the sounds of every word listed in your dictionary. The left column shows the code for a sound while the right column gives you an example of a familiar word that contains that sound. You can easily locate the part of the word that contains the familiar sound because it is printed in **heavy black type**. You read the pronunciation key like this:

> a stands for the sound of *a* as in the word *bat*
> b stands for the sound of *b* as in the word *best*

You will also find a shorter form of the pronunciation key at the bottom of almost every right-hand page in the A to Z word list of your dictionary.

a	bat	ī	bite	ōō	tool	th	feather
ā	make	î	fierce	ou	out	th	bath
â	dare	o	dot	u	nut	hw	wheat
ä	father	ō	no	û	turn	zh	measure
e	net	ô	law, for	ch	church	ə	about, open
ē	be	oi	soil	ng	ring		pencil, atom
i	dip	oo	look	sh	shade		circus

More Help Pronouncing Words

You may have already noticed that the pronunciation of many words is divided into parts. These parts are called *syllables*. You will find the entry word divided into syllables in **heavy black type** after the meanings are given. Syllables are separated by dots.

> **banquet** *noun* A large, formal dinner, usually given for a special occasion.
> **ban·quet** (**bang′**kwit) □*noun, plural* **banquets**

Using Accent Marks

People do not talk like machines. They will accent some syllables more than others. In your dictionary the syllable or syllables to be accented are printed in **heavy black type** within the pronunciation. The accented syllable also has an *accent mark* (′) after it. All words with more than one syllable have accent marks in their pronunciations.

Some longer words will have two kinds of accent marks. These words have a syllable in heavy black type with a strong accent mark and one or more syllables in regular type with a lighter accent mark (′). Look at the pronunciation for *television:* **tel′** ə vizh′ ən.

Words that Sound Alike and Words that Look Alike

Look at the pictures below. There is one word that names each picture. What is that word? The word is *bow*.

Homographs

Bow has three separate entries. You know that words with separate entries have different histories. The entry words have different meanings even though they are spelled the same.

Words that are spelled the same but have different meanings are called *homographs*. Homographs may sometimes have different pronunciations. Is *bow* always pronounced the same way? When you are reading entries for homographs, always check to see if the pronunciations are the same.

Homophones

Suppose you came to class just in time to hear your teacher ask: "What happens after the (dō) rises?" Without knowing what your teacher is talking about, you might see two very different pictures in your mind.

Words like *dough* and *doe* are homophones. Homophones are pronounced the same way although they can be spelled differently. Homophones also have different meanings. You need to use the clues in the sentence, or the words around the homophone, to figure out which homophone is being used.

Two Ways to Say the Same Thing

When you see two pronunciations for an entry word connected by the word *or* in italic type, you will know that either pronunciation is acceptable. Neither one is more correct than the other. The pronunciation that is given first is usually the most common. However, you may choose the pronunciation you prefer.

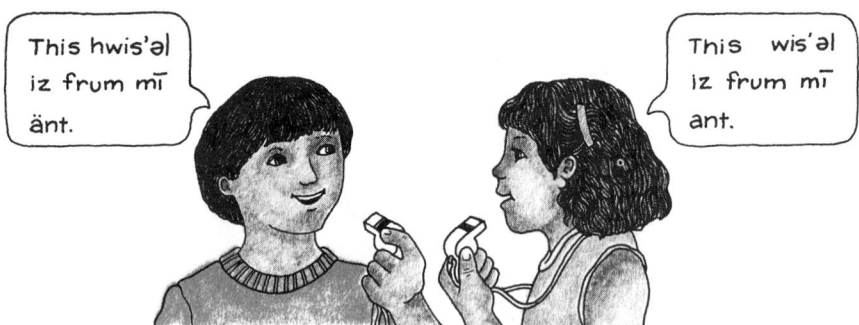

Learning to Use the Spelling Table

To use your dictionary easily you will need to know how to spell the words you want to find. The Spelling Table on pages B–16 to B–19 will help you. The Spelling Table looks something like the pronunciation key. The left column lists the sound a letter represents. You already know these sounds from working with the pronunciation key. The middle column lists the ways the sound may be spelled. The right column gives an example of a word that has the sound spelled with those letters. Look at the first sound represented. You read the Spelling Table like this:

If the sound is *a*, it might be spelled with an
a as in cat, or
ai as in plaid, or
al as in half, or
au as in laugh

To spell a word you can use the following method for each sound you hear in the word. Suppose you wanted to spell a word that sounds like *num*, but you found no entry for *num*. The next thing you should do is turn to the Spelling Table and look for the letters that spell the sound of *n*.

n	gn
	kn
	n
	nn
	pn

You might start looking for your word in the dictionary by looking up each of the letters or combinations for the *n* sound. When you do, you find only a few words that start with *gn* and *pn*. None of those words is correct. There are no words starting with *nn*, so that combination is removed from your list. Therefore, you would look for combinations of the *num* sound that start with *n* or *kn*.

Words Spelled in More than One Way

Most of the words you use every day can only be spelled in one way. However, there are some words that can be spelled correctly in more than one way. Your dictionary lists more than one correct spelling this way:

coconut or **cocoanut**   *noun* The large, round nut of a tropical palm tree. A coconut has sweet white meat and a hollow center filled with a sweet, milky liquid.
co·co·nut or **co·coa·nut** (kō′kə nut′) □*noun, plural* **coconuts** or **cocoanuts**

The spelling that appears first is the most common spelling. Both spellings of the words are usually pronounced the same.

Sometimes an alternate spelling of an entry is listed as a separate entry. When this happens the definition appears only in the entry for the most common spelling. Which is the most common spelling of the following entries?

ameba   *noun* A very small animal that has only one cell. The shape of an ameba is always changing.
a·me·ba (ə mē′bə) □*noun, plural* **amebas**
amoeba   *noun* Another spelling for **ameba**.
a·moe·ba (ə mē′bə) □*noun, plural* **amoebas**

There are two things to remember when you come across a word with two spellings. First, try to use the most common spelling of the word. Second, do not use two different spellings for a word in the same paragraph or story.

Prefixes and Suffixes

Can you explain the meanings of *fair*, *unfair*, *unfairly*, and *unfairness*? You know that one meaning of *fair* is "not favoring one side more than another." The letters *un-*, *-ly*, and *-ness* have meanings too. You can find their meanings in the dictionary.

> **un-** A prefix that means: **1.** Not; the opposite of: *unhappy.* **2.** To do the opposite of: *unlock.* **3.** Lack of: *unemployment.*

Un- is a prefix. A prefix is a syllable or group of syllables joined to the beginning of a base word that changes the meaning of the base word. Adding a prefix usually does not change the spelling of a base word.

> un- + fair = unfair, meaning "not fair"

Irregular Verbs and Irregular Plurals

Your dictionary can help you locate and spell irregular verbs. Irregular verbs do not form the past tense by adding *-ed* as regular verbs do. The past tense of an irregular verb looks very different from the present tense.

> I <u>strike out</u> when I'm nervous.
> Yesterday, I <u>struck out</u> with the bases loaded.

The verb forms of *strike* are listed at the end of that entry. You will also find a separate entry for the past tense of an irregular verb. Look up *struck* in your dictionary. Notice that you have to go to the main entry, *strike*, for the definition.

strike *verb* **1.** To hit: *His head struck the floor when he fell.* **2.** To indicate the time by sounding: *The clock struck five.* **3.** To make an impression on: *The idea struck her as silly.* **4.** To come upon; discover: *strike oil.* **5.** To stop work in order to get better working conditions: *The union struck for higher pay.*
□*noun* **1.** An act of striking; hit. **2.** A stopping of work by employees in order to get better working conditions. **3.** A valuable discovery: *a gold strike.* **4.** A baseball pitch that the batter swings at and misses or that passes into the area that is over home plate and between the batter's knees and armpits.
strike (strīk) □*verb* **struck, struck** or **stricken, striking, strikes** □*noun, plural* **strikes**

struck *verb* The past tense and a past participle of **strike:** *He struck the gong with a mallet.*
struck (strŭk) □*verb*

One familiar irregular plural is *children*, meaning more than one child. Look at the entry for *child*. The plural form of a noun is listed at the end of the entry.

> **child** *noun* **1.** A young girl or boy. **2.** A son or daughter:
> *She is an only child.* —See Synonyms at **descendant.**
> **child** (chīld) □*noun, plural* **children**

Check your dictionary if you are unsure of the correct form for any noun or verb.

Spelling Table

SOUND	SPELLING	EXAMPLE
a	a	cat
	ai	plaid
	al	half
	au	laugh
ā	a	ate
	ai	aid
	ay	play
	ea	steak
	ei	vein
	eig	reign
	eigh	eight
	ey	they
â	a	dare
	ae	aerospace
	ai	hair
	e	there
	ea	pear
	ei	their
ä	a	father
	ah	ah
	al	palm
	e	sergeant
	ea	heart
b	b	bib
	bb	rubber
	pb	cupboard
ch	c	cello
	ch	chill
	tch	patch
	ti	question
	tu	creature
d	d	did
	ed	sailed
	dd	ladder
	ld	could

SOUND	SPELLING	EXAMPLE
e	a	any
	ai	said
	ay	says
	e	set
	ea	head
	ie	friend
	u	bury
ē	ay	quay
	e	be
	ea	heap
	ee	feet
	ei	seize
	eo	people
	ey	turkey
	i	piano
	ie	relieve
	oe	amoeba
	y	very
f	f	first
	ff	ruffle
	gh	cough
	lf	calf
	ph	physical

SOUND	SPELLING	EXAMPLE
g	g	get
	gg	egg
	gh	ghost
	gu	guest
	gue	catalogue
gz	x	exact
h	h	he
	wh	who
hw	wh	what
i	a	manage
	e	enough
	ee	been
	i	in
	ia	carriage
	o	women
	u	business
	ui	building
	y	myth
ī	ai	aisle
	ay	kayak

	eigh	height
	ey	eye
	i	white
	ie	tie
	igh	night
	is	isle
	uy	buy
	y	my
	ye	dye

SOUND	SPELLING	EXAMPLE
î	e	mere
	ea	ear
	ee	deer
	ei	weird
	ie	fierce
j	d	individual
	dg	fudge
	di	soldier
	dj	adjust
	g	gem
	ge	page

	gg	exaggerate
	j	just
k	c	catch
	cc	occur
	ch	school
	ck	track
	k	keep
	lk	walk
ks	x	six
kw	qu	quiet
l	l	low
	ll	cellar
m	lm	calm
	m	move
	mb	lamb
	mm	hammer
	mn	hymn

SOUND	SPELLING	EXAMPLE
n	gn	gnat
	kn	know
	n	not
	nn	banner
	pn	pneumonia
ng	n	sink
	ng	ring
	ngue	tongue
o	a	want
	o	hot
ō	eau	bureau
	ew	sew
	o	note

	oa	coat
	oe	toe
	oh	oh
	oo	brooch
	ou	shoulder
	ough	thorough
	ow	low
	owe	owe
ô	a	call
	al	talk
	au	caught
	aw	awful
	o	for
	oa	abroad
	ough	fought
oi	oi	noise
	oy	toy
ou	ou	our
	ough	bough
	ow	cow

SOUND	SPELLING	EXAMPLE
oo	o	woman
	oo	wood
	ou	would
	u	pull
ōō	eu	maneuver
	ew	few
	ieu	lieutenant
	o	move
	oe	canoe
	oo	food
	ou	group
	ough	through
	u	flute
	ue	true
	ui	fruit
p	p	pen
	pp	pepper

r	r	run
	rh	rhythm
	rr	arrange
	wr	write
s	c	center
	ce	mice
	ps	psychology
	s	serve
	sc	science
	ss	mass

SOUND	SPELLING	EXAMPLE
sh	ce	ocean
	ch	machine
	ci	special
	s	sugar
	sc	conscience
	sh	shop
	si	mansion
	ss	mission
	ti	attention
t	ed	joked
	ght	light
	t	ten
	tt	litter
th	th	thin
<u>th</u>	th	there
	the	breathe
u	o	done
	oe	does
	oo	flood
	ou	double
	u	nut
yoo	u	pure
yo͞o	eau	beauty
	eu	feud
	ew	few
	iew	view

	u	mute
	ue	cue
	you	you
	yu	yule

SOUND	SPELLING	EXAMPLE
û	ear	learn
	er	serve
	ir	skirt
	or	work
	our	journey
	ur	burn
v	f	of
	v	very
w	o	one
	w	warm
	wh	when
y	i	million
	y	year
z	s	rise
	ss	scissors

	x	xylophone
	z	zero
	zz	drizzle
zh	ge	garage
	s	measure
	si	vision
	z	azure
ə	a	sofa
	ai	certain
	e	recent
	ea	sergeant
	i	pencil
	ie	ancient
	o	lemon
	ou	famous
	u	circus

Pronunciation Key

	as in
a	bat
ā	day, make
â	dare
ä	father
b	best
ch	church
d	date
e	net
ē	be
f	farm
g	get
h	hand
hw	wheat
i	dip
ī	bite
î	fierce
j	just
k	kite
kw	quite
l	let
m	meat
n	not
ng	ring
o	dot
ō	no
ô	for, law

	as in
oi	soil
ou	out
oo	look
o͞o	tool
p	pat
r	rap
s	sit
sh	shade
t	toe
th	think
t͟h	then
u	nut
û	turn
v	very
w	well
y	year
yo͞o	pure
yoo	use
z	zero
zh	measure
ə	about, open, pencil, atom, circus
'	after a syllable with the strongest stress
'	after a syllable with the second strongest stress

Your Dictionary of English

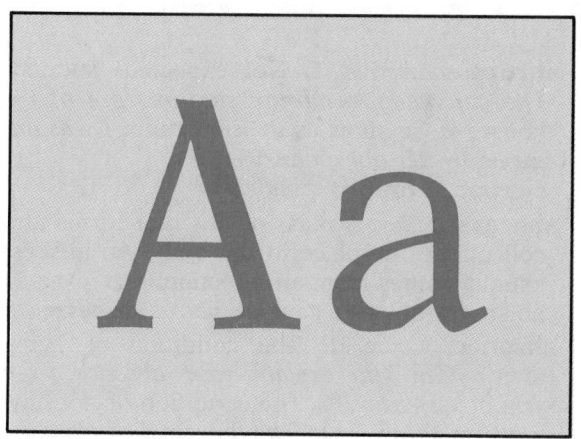

ANCIENT GREEK

The letter **A** has evolved from many forms of ancient writing. One of the earliest known examples is the Greek character shown above, which dates from almost 3000 years ago. Over the years, artists and designers have created their own versions of the English letter **A**. Some of the more common examples seen today are shown below.

$A\alpha$ $\mathcal{A}\alpha$	$\mathbf{Aa}\,\mathbf{Aa}$	$\mathsf{Aa}\,\mathsf{Aa}$	$\mathrm{Aa}\,\mathrm{Aa}$	$\mathcal{A}a\,\mathscr{A}a$
HANDWRITING	CALLIGRAPHY	MODERN SANS SERIF	MODERN SERIF	SCRIPT

a or **A**   *noun* The first letter of the English alphabet.
a or **A** (ā) □*noun, plural* **a's** or **A's**

a   *indefinite article* **1.** Any: *A baseball is round.* **2.** One: *Don't make a sound.* **3.** A kind of: *Carrots are a vegetable.* **4.** Each; every: *I visit my grandparents once a week.*
a (ə *or* ā) □*indefinite article*

abacus   *noun* An old-fashioned calculator used especially for adding and subtracting. It is made up of a frame on which beads slide back and forth.
ab·a·cus (ăb′ə kəs) □*noun, plural* **abacuses**

abacus

abandon   *verb* **1.** To leave for good; desert: *The crew abandoned the sinking ship.* **2.** To give up completely: *He had to abandon the idea of buying a new car.*
a·ban·don (ə băn′dən) □*verb* **abandoned, abandoning, abandons**

abbey   *noun* A building or set of buildings where nuns or monks live.
ab·bey (ăb′ē) □*noun, plural* **abbeys**

abbreviate   *verb* To make shorter by leaving out letters: *You can abbreviate "Street" to "St."*
ab·bre·vi·ate (ə brē′vē āt′) □*verb* **abbreviated, abbreviating, abbreviates**

abbreviation   *noun* A short way of writing a word or group of words: *"Mr." is an abbreviation for "Mister."*
ab·bre·vi·a·tion (ə brē′vē ā′shən) □*noun, plural* **abbreviations**

abdicate   *verb* To give up power in a formal way: *The king abdicated and his son became king.*
ab·di·cate (ăb′di kāt′) □*verb* **abdicated, abdicating, abdicates**

abdomen   *noun* **1.** In human beings and other mammals, the front part of the body from below the chest to about where the legs join. The stomach, the intestines, and other important organs are in the abdomen. **2.** The section of the body that is located behind the thorax of an insect.
ab·do·men (ăb′də mən *or* ăb dō′mən) □*noun, plural* **abdomens**

abide　*verb* To put up with; bear: *She can't abide loud music.*
　abide by To agree to follow; obey: *You must abide by your father's decision.*
　a·bide (ə **bīd′**) □*verb* **abided, abiding, abides**

ability　*noun* The power or skill to do something: *Ants have the ability to carry objects heavier than themselves. She has great ability as a dancer.*
　a·bil·i·ty (a **bil′**i tē) □*noun, plural* **abilities**

able　*adjective* Having the power or skill to do something: *Beavers are able to build dams. She is an able car mechanic.*
　a·ble (ā′bəl) □*adjective* **abler, ablest**

aboard　*adverb* On, onto, or in a ship, train, airplane, or other vehicle: *I climbed aboard the bus as soon as it stopped.*
　a·board (ə **bôrd′**) □*adverb*

abolish　*verb* To put an end to; do away with: *The school abolished the football program.*
　a·bol·ish (ə **bol′**ish) □*verb* **abolished, abolishing, abolishes**

aborigine　*noun* A member of a group of people who were the first to have lived in a particular region.
　ab·o·rig·i·ne (ab′ə **rij′**ə nē) □*noun, plural* **aborigines**

abound　*verb* To be plentiful: *Deer abound in the forest.*
　a·bound (ə **bound′**) □*verb* **abounded, abounding, abounds**

about　*preposition* **1.** Of or having to do with; concerning: *It's a movie about a creature from outer space.* **2.** Near in time to: *She is going to call about noon.* **3.** All around: *We looked all about the house but couldn't find the book.* □*adverb* **1.** Nearly; approximately: *There were about twenty people in the store.* **2.** Around: *We looked about for a gas station.*
　a·bout (ə **bout′**) □*preposition* □*adverb*

above　*adverb* In or to a higher place or position; overhead: *Look at the clouds above.* □*preposition* Over or higher than: *The helicopter was flying just above the buildings. A corporal is above a private.*
　a·bove (ə **buv′**) □*adverb* □*preposition*

abreast　*adverb* Side by side: *We walked to class two abreast.*
　a·breast (ə **brest′**) □*adverb*

abroad　*adverb* In or to a foreign country: *We traveled abroad to France.*
　a·broad (ə **brôd′**) □*adverb*

abrupt　*adjective* **1.** Not expected; sudden: *The car made an abrupt stop in front of my house.* **2.** So short as to seem rude: *I was annoyed by her abrupt answer.*
　a·brupt (ə **brupt′**) □*adjective*

abscess　*noun* A mass of pus that forms and collects at one place in the body. An abscess usually comes from an infection.
　ab·scess (ab′ses′) □*noun, plural* **abscesses**

absence　*noun* **1.** The condition of being away: *Can you explain your absence from school yesterday?* **2.** The condition of not having something; lack: *The flowers died from the absence of rain.*
　ab·sence (ab′səns) □*noun, plural* **absences**

absent　*adjective* Not present; away: *Five students are absent today.*
　ab·sent (ab′sənt) □*adjective*

absent-minded　*adjective* Not paying attention to what is going on; forgetful: *The absent-minded boy is always losing his glasses.*
　ab·sent-mind·ed (ab′sənt **mīn′**did) □*adjective*

absolute　*adjective* **1.** Complete; total: *You must tell the absolute truth.* **2.** Not limited in any way: *The queen has absolute power.*
　ab·so·lute (ab′sə lo͞ot′) □*adjective*

absolutely　*adverb* **1.** Completely; entirely: *She told us to be absolutely silent.* **2.** Without any doubt; positively: *It was absolutely the best movie I ever saw.*
　ab·so·lute·ly (ab′sə **lo͞ot′**lē *or* ab′sə lo͞ot′lē) □*adverb*

absorb　*verb* **1.** To take in or soak up: *A sponge absorbs liquid.* **2.** To take the full attention of: *The movie absorbed us.*
　ab·sorb (ab **sôrb′** *or* ab **zôrb′**) □*verb* **absorbed, absorbing, absorbs**

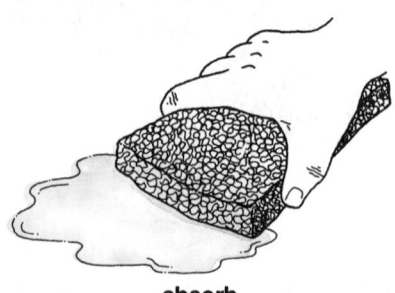

absorb

absorption　*noun* The act or process of absorbing: *Thick towels have good absorption.*
　ab·sorp·tion (ab **sôrp′**shən *or* ab **zôrp′**shən) □*noun*

abstain *verb* To keep oneself from doing something: *He had to abstain from playing baseball until his broken ankle healed.*
ab·stain (ab stān′) □*verb* **abstained, abstaining, abstains**

abstract *adjective* Expressing a quality that is not connected with a specific person or thing. "Love" and "hatred" are abstract words because they do not refer to a specific person or thing.
ab·stract (**ab′**strakt′ *or* ab **strakt′**) □*adjective*

absurd *adjective* Very silly; ridiculous: *The dog looked absurd wearing a sweater.*
ab·surd (ab **sûrd′** *or* ab **zûrd′**) □*adjective*

absurd

abundance *noun* A supply that is more than enough; a great amount: *The farm produced an abundance of corn this year.*
a·bun·dance (ə **bun′**dəns) □*noun*

abundant *adjective* In great amounts; plentiful: *We had abundant food for the picnic.*
a·bun·dant (ə **bun′**dənt) □*adjective*

abuse *verb* **1.** To put to bad or wrong use: *He abused the privilege of staying up late by complaining when it was time to go to bed.* **2.** To treat in a bad or cruel way: *He abused his bicycle by leaving it out in the rain.*
□*noun* **1.** Bad or wrong use: *The people hated the king for his abuse of power.* **2.** Bad or rough treatment: *The old car got a lot of abuse.* **3.** Rude and insulting language: *The children had to listen to the old man's abuse.*
a·buse (ə **byōōz′**) □*verb* **abused, abusing, abuses** □*noun* (ə **byōōs′**), *plural* **abuses**

abyss *noun* A very deep and large hole in the earth.
a·byss (ə **bis′**) □*noun, plural* **abysses**

academy *noun* **1.** A school for a special kind of study: *a music academy; a military academy.* **2.** A private high school.

a·cad·e·my (ə **kad′**ə mē) □*noun, plural* **academies**

accelerate *verb* To increase in speed: *The sled accelerated as it slid down the hill.*
ac·cel·er·ate (ak **sel′**ə rāt′) □*verb* **accelerated, accelerating, accelerates**

acceleration *noun* An increase in speed; faster movement: *You can feel the acceleration of the airplane as it takes off.*
ac·cel·er·a·tion (ak sel′ə **rā′**shən) □*noun*

accelerator *noun* Something that increases speed. In a car the accelerator is a pedal on the floor.
ac·cel·er·a·tor (ak **sel′**ə rā′tər) □*noun, plural* **accelerators**

accent *noun* **1.** More force or stronger tone of voice given to a syllable or syllables of a word. The accent is on the first syllable in "funny"; it is on the second syllable in "alone." **2.** A mark used to show that a syllable has an accent. In this dictionary the darker mark (′) is used for the syllable that has the most force. The lighter mark (′) is used to show a syllable with an accent that is not quite so strong. For example, the pronunciation of the word "accent" has two accents: (**ak′**sent′). **3.** A style of speech or pronunciation that shows the speaker comes from a particular country or part of a country: *an English accent; a southern accent.*
□*verb* To pronounce a syllable in a word with more force or a stronger tone: *You accent the first syllable of the word "berry."*
ac·cent (**ak′**sent′) □*noun, plural* **accents** □*verb* **accented, accenting, accents**

accept *verb* **1.** To take something that is offered: *accept a gift; accept an apology.* **2.** To say yes to; agree to: *accept an invitation.* **3.** To think of as true; believe: *The teacher accepted my excuse.*
ac·cept (ak **sept′**) □*verb* **accepted, accepting, accepts**

acceptable *adjective* Good enough to be accepted; satisfactory: *Your homework assignment is acceptable but it isn't excellent.*
ac·cept·a·ble (ak **sep′**tə bəl) □*adjective*

a bat	ī bite	ōō tool	th feather
ā make	î fierce	ou out	th bath
â dare	o dot	u nut	hw wheat
ä father	ō no	û turn	zh measure
e net	ô law, for	ch church	ə about, open
ē be	oi soil	ng ring	pencil, atom
i dip	oo look	sh shade	circus

acceptance *noun* **1.** The act of taking something that is offered: *She went up on the stage for the acceptance of the prize.* **2.** The condition of being accepted; approval: *My plan to get a summer job had my father's acceptance.*
ac·cept·ance (ak **sep′**təns) □*noun, plural*
acceptances

acceptance

access *noun* **1.** A way to get into or reach a place: *The dirt road is the only access to the lake.* **2.** The means to get or reach something: *You need special permission to have access to the library after school.*
ac·cess (**ak′**ses′) □*noun, plural* **accesses**

accessory *noun* **1.** An extra item that goes with and improves a main item. *Air conditioners and radios are accessories in cars.* **2.** Someone who helps another person carry out a crime.
ac·ces·so·ry (ak **ses′**ə rē) □*noun, plural* **accessories**

accident *noun* **1.** Something bad or unlucky that happens without being expected: *an automobile accident.* **2.** Something that happens without being planned or expected: *Finding the money was a lucky accident.*
ac·ci·dent (**ak′**si dənt) □*noun, plural* **accidents**

accidental *adjective* Happening without being planned or expected: *He didn't mean to lose the key; it was accidental.*
ac·ci·den·tal (ak′si **den′**təl) □*adjective*

acclaim *verb* To greet with great approval: *Everyone acclaimed the doctor who discovered a vaccine against polio.*
□*noun* Enthusiastic praise or approval: *The movie star was greeted with acclaim.*
ac·claim (ə **klām′**) □*verb* **acclaimed, acclaiming, acclaims** *noun*

accommodate *verb* **1.** To have room for; hold: *The car accommodates six people.* **2.** To

provide with a place to stay or sleep: *The hotel can accommodate 1,000 people.* **3.** To do a favor for; help out: *I accommodated her by feeding her dog when she was away.*
ac·com·mo·date (ə **kom′**ə dāt′) □*verb*
accommodated, accommodating, accommodates

accommodation *noun* **1.** A help or favor: *He came earlier than usual as an accommodation to me.* **2. accommodations** A place to stay or sleep: *I found accommodations at a hotel.*
ac·com·mo·da·tion (ə kom′ə **dā′**shən) □*noun, plural* **accommodations**

accompaniment *noun* **1.** Something that goes along with something else: *Many people serve applesauce as an accompaniment to pork chops.* **2.** Music that is played to go along with singing, dancing, or other music: *I sang while she played an accompaniment on the piano.*
ac·com·pa·ni·ment (ə **kum′**pə ni mənt) □*noun, plural* **accompaniments**

accompaniment

accompany *verb* **1.** To go along with: *Will you accompany me when I go to the store?* **2.** To happen along with: *Fever often accompanies a cold.* **3.** To play an accompaniment for: *He played the violin and I accompanied him on the piano.*
ac·com·pa·ny (ə **kum′**pə nē) □*verb*
accompanied, accompanying, accompanies

accomplice *noun* Someone who helps another person commit a crime.
ac·com·plice (ə **kom′**plis) □*noun, plural* **accomplices**

accomplish *verb* To finish after setting out to do; complete: *She accomplished all her homework in two hours.*
ac·com·plish (ə **kom′**plish) □*verb*
accomplished, accomplishing, accomplishes

accomplishment *noun* **1.** The act of finishing what one has set out to do; completion:

The accomplishment of painting the house took one week. **2.** Something that has been done with success: *Getting the highest mark in the class was a great accomplishment for him.* **3.** A skill that has been learned well: *Dancing and skiing are two of his accomplishments.*
ac·com·plish·ment (ə kom′plish mənt)
▢*noun, plural* **accomplishments**

accord *noun* Agreement; harmony: *Their feelings about the movie are in accord with mine.*
▢*verb* To be in agreement; agree: *Her version of how the accident happened does not accord with her sister's.*
   of one's own accord Without assistance or suggestions from anybody else: *She cleaned her room of her own accord.*
ac·cord (ə kôrd′) ▢*noun* ▢*verb* **accorded, according, accords**

> *WORD HISTORY:* **accord**
>
> The verb *accord* comes from a Latin verb that literally meant "to bring heart to heart." The Latin verb also meant "to agree."

according to *preposition* **1.** On the authority of: *According to her, grandfather called at exactly noon.* **2.** In agreement with; in keeping with: *I built the model ship according to the directions.*
ac·cord·ing to (ə kôr′ding) ▢*preposition*

accordion *noun* A musical instrument with a keyboard, buttons, bellows, and metal reeds. The sound is created when the player operates the bellows to force air through the reeds.
ac·cor·di·on (ə kôr′dē ən) ▢*noun, plural* **accordions**

accordion

account *noun* **1.** A written or spoken description: *All the students will give an account of what they did during vacation.* **2.** A record of

money spent or received: *a bank account. I keep an account of the money I make washing cars.* **3.** Importance; value: *When the experiment failed the scientist thought all his work was of little account.*
▢*verb* To believe to be: *She accounts him a generous person.*
   account for To give a reason for; explain: *I want you to account for your bad behavior.*
   on account of Because of: *The game was postponed on account of rain.*
ac·count (ə kount′) ▢*noun, plural* **accounts**
▢*verb* **accounted, accounting, accounts**

accountant *noun* Someone who keeps or inspects the money records of a business or a person.
ac·count·ant (ə koun′tənt) ▢*noun, plural* **accountants**

accumulate *verb* To gather together; collect: *We accumulated a large stack of old magazines. Leaves were accumulating on the lawn.*
ac·cu·mu·late (ə kyōō′myə lāt′) ▢*verb* **accumulated, accumulating, accumulates**

accumulation *noun* **1.** The act of accumulating: *The accumulation of her stamp collection took 50 years.* **2.** Something accumulated; collection: *an accumulation of old newspapers.*
ac·cu·mu·la·tion (ə kyōō′myə lā′shən)
▢*noun, plural* **accumulations**

accuracy *noun* The condition of being correct and exact: *When you add numbers you must check the accuracy of your answers.*
ac·cu·ra·cy (ak′yər ə sē) ▢*noun*

accurate *adjective* Free from errors; correct; exact: *an accurate description; a clock that is always accurate.*
ac·cu·rate (ak′yər it) ▢*adjective*

accusation *noun* A statement that a person has done something wrong.
ac·cu·sa·tion (ak′yōō zā′shən) ▢*noun, plural* **accusations**

accuse *verb* To state that someone has done something wrong: *She accused me of stealing.*
ac·cuse (ə kyōōz′) ▢*verb* **accused, accusing, accuses**

a bat	ī bite	ōō tool	th feather
ā make	î fierce	ou out	th bath
â dare	o dot	u nut	hw wheat
ä father	ō no	û turn	zh measure
e net	ô law, for	ch church	ə about, open
ē be	oi soil	ng ring	pencil, atom
i dip	oo look	sh shade	circus

accustom *verb* To make familiar by practice, use, or habit: *We had to accustom ourselves to the hot weather when we moved to Florida.*
ac·cus·tom (ə kus′təm) □*verb* **accustomed, accustoming, accustoms**

accustomed *adjective* Usual; familiar: *My sister and I sat in our accustomed places at the kitchen table.*

accustomed to Familiar with; used to: *I am not accustomed to staying up so late.*
ac·cus·tomed (ə kus′təmd) □*adjective*

ace *noun* **1.** A playing card with one mark in the center. An ace is the highest card in most card games. **2.** Someone who is outstanding at something: *She is an ace at golf.* —See Synonyms at **expert.**
ace (ās) □*noun, plural* **aces**

ache *verb* **1.** To feel a steady pain: *My head aches.* **2.** To want very much: *She was aching to see her friend who had moved away.*
□*noun* A steady pain.
ache (āk) □*verb* **ached, aching, aches**
□*noun, plural* **aches**

achieve *verb* **1.** To accomplish something: *She achieved her goal of making the swimming team.* **2.** To get as a result of one's own effort: *He achieved fame as a scientist.*
a·chieve (ə chēv′) □*verb* **achieved, achieving, achieves**

achievement *noun* **1.** An outstanding act or accomplishment: *It was a great achievement to land an astronaut on the moon.* **2.** The act of doing something with skill and effort: *Work hard for the achievement of your goals.*
a·chieve·ment (ə chēv′mənt) □*noun, plural* **achievements**

acid *noun* A chemical substance that can join with a base to form water and a salt. An acid can turn blue litmus paper red.
□*adjective* **1.** Sharp, sour, or biting to the taste: *Lemons are an acid fruit.* **2.** Sharp in manner: *She made some acid comments about my brother that made me angry.*
ac·id (as′id) □*noun, plural* **acids** □*adjective*

acknowledge *verb* **1.** To admit or agree that something is true: *She acknowledged her error.* **2.** To recognize the authority or position of: *We all acknowledged her as the best player on the team.* **3.** To say that one has received something: *I acknowledged my aunt's birthday present with a letter.*
ac·knowl·edge (ak nol′ij) □*verb* **acknowledged, acknowledging, acknowledges**

acknowledgment *noun* The act of acknowledging.
ac·knowl·edg·ment (ak nol′ij mənt) □*noun, plural* **acknowledgments**

acne *noun* A skin condition in which the oil glands of the skin become infected and form pimples.
ac·ne (ak′nē) □*noun*

acorn *noun* The nut of an oak tree.
a·corn (ā′kôrn′) □*noun, plural* **acorns**

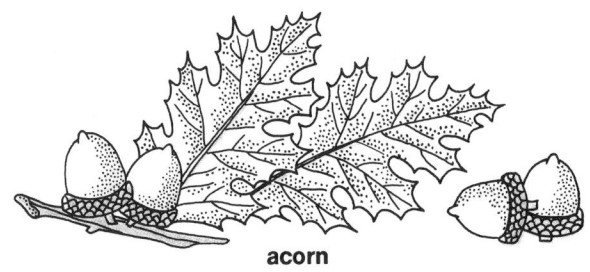

acorn

acquaint *verb* To make familiar: *Please acquaint me with everyone in your class.*
ac·quaint (ə kwānt′) □*verb* **acquainted, acquainting, acquaints**

acquaintance *noun* **1.** A person one knows but not very well: *We have many acquaintances around town.* **2.** A knowledge of something: *I have some acquaintance with French but do not speak it very well.*
ac·quaint·ance (ə kwān′təns) □*noun, plural* **acquaintances**

acquire *verb* To get as one's own; gain: *I acquired a liking for sailing.*
ac·quire (ə kwīr′) □*verb* **acquired, acquiring, acquires**

acquit *verb* To declare not guilty: *The jury acquitted the prisoners of the crime.*
ac·quit (ə kwit′) **acquitted, acquitting, acquits.**

acre *noun* A unit for measuring land equal to 43,560 square feet or 4,840 square yards.
a·cre (ā′kər) □*noun, plural* **acres**

acreage *noun* Land as measured in acres.
a·cre·age (ā′kər ij) □*noun*

acrobat *noun* Someone who is skilled in performing on a trapeze, walking a tightrope, and tumbling.
ac·ro·bat (ak′rə bat′) □*noun, plural* **acrobats**

across *preposition* **1.** To or from the other side of: *walk across the street.* **2.** On the other side of; beyond: *I could see the buildings across the river.*

□*adverb* From one side to the other: *The yard is 50 feet across.*
a·cross (ə **krôs′**) □*preposition* □*adverb*

act *noun* **1.** Something that is done; deed; action: *a courageous act; a foolish act.* **2.** The process of doing something: *We were caught in the act of taking the cookies.* **3.** A main division of a play or other dramatic work: *The play has three acts.* **4.** A law: *an act of Congress.* □*verb* **1.** To do something: *She acted quickly to rescue the child from the burning house.* **2.** To conduct oneself; behave: *She was screaming and acting like a baby.* **3.** To perform on television, in a movie, or on a stage.
act (akt) □*noun, plural* **acts** □*verb* **acted, acting, acts**

action *noun* **1.** The activity, process, or fact of doing something. **2.** Something that is done; act: *a kind and friendly action.* **3.** Battle; combat: *He was wounded in action.*
ac·tion (**ak′**shən) □*noun, plural* **actions**

activate *verb* To set in operation: *Press this button to activate the computer.*
ac·ti·vate (**ak′**tə vāt′) □*verb* **activated, activating, activates**

active *adjective* **1.** Moving about much of the time; full of action: *an active child.* **2.** In operation or in action: *an active volcano.*
ac·tive (**ak′**tiv) □*adjective*

activity *noun* **1.** The condition of being active; action: *There was a lot of activity in the playground.* **2.** Something to do or to be done: *What is your favorite outdoor activity?*
ac·tiv·i·ty (ak **tiv′**i tē) □*noun, plural* **activities**

actor *noun* A person who acts in plays, motion pictures, or on television or radio.
ac·tor (**ak′**tər) □*noun, plural* **actors**

actress *noun* A woman or girl who acts in plays, motion pictures, or on television or radio.
ac·tress (**ak′**tris) □*noun, plural* **actresses**

actual *adjective* Existing in fact; real: *The story is about an actual event and not one the writer made up.*
ac·tu·al (**ak′**chōo əl) □*adjective*

actually *adverb* In fact; really: *Did you actually see him break the window?*
ac·tu·al·ly (**ak′**chōo ə lē) □*adverb*

acute *adjective* **1.** Sharp and intense: *an acute pain in the stomach.* **2.** Sharp and keen: *Many animals have an acute sense of smell.*
a·cute (ə **kyōot′**) □*adjective*

acute angle *noun* An angle that is smaller than a right angle. It measures between zero and ninety degrees.

ad *noun* An advertisement.
ad (ad) □*noun, plural* **ads**

A.D. An abbreviation for the Latin words *anno Domini,* which mean "in the year of the Lord." "A.D." is used in giving dates after the birth of Jesus. For example, A.D. 500 means five hundred years after the birth of Jesus.

adamant *adjective* Not willing to change one's mind: *My mother was adamant about not letting me go on the fishing trip.*
ad·a·mant (**ad′**ə mənt) □*adjective*

WORD HISTORY: **adamant**
The Greek word that *adamant* comes from means "a very hard metal" and "a diamond." The word was applied to persons as inflexible as a hard stone or piece of metal. The word *diamond* comes from the same Greek word as *adamant.*

Adam's apple *noun* The lump at the front of a person's throat made by the larynx.
Ad·am's apple (**ad′**əmz) □*noun*

adapt *verb* To adjust or become adjusted to fit different conditions: *I adapted quickly to my new school.*
a·dapt (ə **dapt′**) □*verb* **adapted, adapting, adapts**

add *verb* **1.** To find the sum of two or more numbers: *If you add 2 and 4, you get 6.* **2.** To put something more in, on, or next to: *We added a porch to the house.* **3.** To say or write something more: *He said good-by and added that he would call tomorrow.*
add (ad) □*verb* **added, adding, adds**

addend *noun* Any one of a set of numbers that are to be added. In 2 + 4 = 6, the numbers 2 and 4 are addends.
ad·dend (**ad′**end′ *or* ə **dend′**) □*noun, plural* **addends**

addict *noun* Someone who has developed a need to have something harmful, as drugs.
ad·dict (**ad′**ikt) □*noun, plural* **addicts**

a	bat	ĭ	bite	ōō	tool	*th*	feather
ā	make	î	fierce	ou	out	th	bath
â	dare	o	dot	u	nut	hw	wheat
ä	father	ō	no	û	turn	zh	measure
e	net	ô	law, for	ch	church	ə	about, open
ē	be	oi	soil	ng	ring		pencil, atom
i	dip	oo	look	sh	shade		circus

addition   *noun*   **1.** The process of finding the sum of two or more numbers. An example of addition is 3 + 7 + 2 = 12. **2.** The act of adding one thing to another: *The addition of curtains made the room look better.* **3.** Something that is added: *built an addition to the school.*

   in addition or **in addition to** Also; besides: *In addition to washing the dishes every night, I also have to take out the garbage.*
ad·di·tion (ə **dish′** ən) □*noun, plural* **additions**

additional   *adjective*   Added; extra: *The boss said he needed additional workers to get the job done on time.*
ad·di·tion·al (ə **dish′** ə nəl) □*adjective*

address   *noun*   **1.** The house number, street name, city, state, and zip code where a person lives, works, or receives mail. **2.** The information on an envelope or other piece of mail that shows where mail is going to or is sent from. **3.** A formal speech: *I heard the President's address on the radio.*
□*verb* **1.** To write the house number, street name, city, state, and zip code on mail: *I have to address the invitations to the party.* **2.** To speak to or give a speech to: *The mayor addressed the city council.*
ad·dress (ə **dres′** *or* **ad′** res′) □*noun, plural* **addresses** □*verb* (ə **dres′**) **addressed, addressing, addresses**

adenoids   *plural noun*   Growths at the back of the nose, above the throat. When adenoids are swollen, it is often difficult to breathe and speak.
ad·e·noids (**ad′** ə noidz′) □*plural noun*

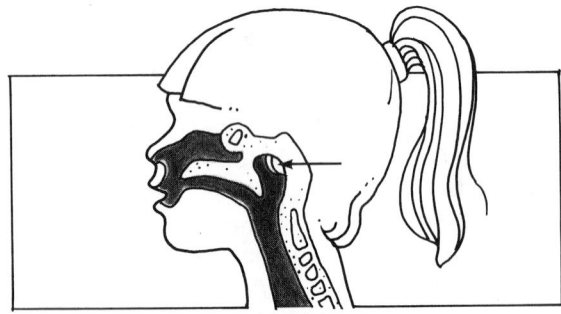

adenoids

adept   *adjective*   Very good at something: *She is the most adept rider in the class.*
a·dept (ə **dept′**) □*adjective*

adequate   *adjective*   As much as is needed; enough: *We have an adequate supply of food for the weekend.*
ad·e·quate (**ad′** i kwit) □*adjective*

adhere   *verb*   To hold fast; stick: *The wallpaper adheres to the wall.*
ad·here (ad **hîr′**) □*verb* **adhered, adhering, adheres**

adhesive   *noun*   Something that sticks or makes things stick: *Glue and paste are adhesives.*
□*adjective* Able to stick to something; sticky: *adhesive tape.*
ad·he·sive (ad **hē′** siv) □*noun, plural* **adhesives** □*adjective*

adios   *interjection*   A word used to express farewell.
a·di·os (ä′dē **ōs′** *or* ad′ē **ōs′**) □*interjection*

adjacent   *adjective*   Next to; near: *The baseball field is adjacent to the school.*
ad·ja·cent (ə **jā′** sənt) □*adjective*

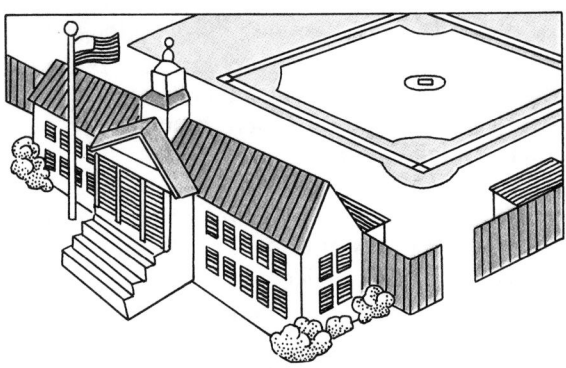

adjacent

adjective   *noun*   A word that describes a noun. In the sentence "The old truck smashed into the big tree" the adjectives are "old" and "big."
ad·jec·tive (**aj′** ik tiv) □*noun, plural* **adjectives**

adjoin   *verb*   To be next to: *My sister's bedroom adjoins mine.*
ad·join (ə **join′**) □*verb* **adjoined, adjoining, adjoins**

adjourn   *verb*   To stop and plan to continue at another time: *We adjourned the meeting until next week. The court adjourned for lunch.*
ad·journ (ə **jûrn′**) □*verb* **adjourned, adjourning, adjourns**

adjust   *verb*   **1.** To change in order to make right or better: *adjust a television picture. The bicycle seat adjusts to different heights.* **2.** To become used to; adapt: *I quickly adjusted to life in the city.*

ad·just (ə **just′**) □*verb* **adjusted, adjusting, adjusts**

adjustment *noun* **1.** The act of changing to make right or better: *Dad had to make some adjustments to the motor of the washing machine.* **2.** The act of getting used to something. **ad·just·ment** (ə **just′**mənt) □*noun, plural* **adjustments**

administer *verb* **1.** To be in charge of; manage: *The principal administers the school.* **2.** To give or deal out: *The nurse administered first aid to the child. Courts administer justice.* **ad·min·is·ter** (ad **min′**i stər) □*verb* **administered, administering, administers**

administration *noun* **1.** The act of managing a company, business, or other organization; management: *He has a lot of experience in the administration of a large company.* **2.** The people who manage a business, organization, or government: *The school administration includes the principal, assistant principal, and teachers.* **3. Administration** The President of the United States, the Vice President, the Cabinet officers, and the departments they are in charge of. **4.** The period of time during which a government is in power. **ad·min·is·tra·tion** (ad min′i **strā′**shən) □*noun, plural* **administrations**

admiral *noun* An officer of high rank in the United States Navy. There are four ranks of admirals: fleet admiral, admiral, vice admiral, and rear admiral. **ad·mi·ral** (**ad′**mər əl) □*noun, plural* **admirals**

admiration *noun* A feeling of pleasure, respect, and approval: *We all felt admiration for the beautiful song she wrote.* **ad·mi·ra·tion** (ad′mə **rā′**shən) □*noun*

admire *verb* **1.** To look at or think of with pleasure, respect, and approval: *I admired his new car.* **2.** To feel respect for: *Don't you admire her bravery?* **ad·mire** (ad **mīr′**) □*verb* **admired, admiring, admires**

admission *noun* **1.** The act of allowing to enter or join: *Have you applied for admission to college?* **2.** The price charged or paid to enter a place: *The admission to the circus was two dollars.* **3.** A statement that something is true; confession: *She made the admission that she had broken the dish.* **ad·mis·sion** (ad **mish′**ən) □*noun, plural* **admissions**

admit *verb* **1.** To say that something is true, usually in a reluctant manner: *I admitted that I lost the money.* **2.** To accept and take in: *The hospital admitted the accident victim.* **ad·mit** (ad **mit′**) □*verb* **admitted, admitting, admits**

SYNONYMS: **admit, concede, confess**

These verbs mean to say that something is true, especially when one feels one has to: *I had to admit that I had lied. After the argument she conceded that I was right. The student confessed that he had lost the book.*

---

admittance *noun* Permission or right to enter; entrance: *The sign said "No admittance."* **ad·mit·tance** (ad **mit′**əns) □*noun*

adobe *noun* **1.** A brick made of clay and straw dried and hardened in the sun. **2.** A building made of these bricks. **a·do·be** (ə **dō′**bē) □*noun, plural* **adobes**

WORD HISTORY: **adobe**

Adobe was borrowed from Spanish. The Spanish word comes from an Arabic phrase that means "the brick."

adobe

adolescent *noun* A boy or girl who is older than a child but not yet an adult; teen-ager. **ad·o·les·cent** (ad′ə **les′**ənt) □*noun, plural* **adolescents**

a	bat	ī	bite	ōō	tool	*th*	feather
ā	make	î	fierce	ou	out	th	bath
â	dare	o	dot	u	nut	hw	wheat
ä	father	ō	no	û	turn	zh	measure
e	net	ô	law, for	ch	church	ə	about, open
ē	be	oi	soil	ng	ring		pencil, atom
i	dip	oo	look	sh	shade		circus

adopt *verb* **1.** To take someone else's child and by law make that child one's own: *They adopted two children.* **2.** To take and use as one's own: *He adopted his older brother's style of walking.*
a·dopt (ə dopt′) □*verb* **adopted, adopting, adopts**

adoption *noun* **1.** The act of adopting: *The adoption of the new program meant that everyone had to work harder.* **2.** The condition of being adopted: *The two brothers were given up for adoption.*
a·dop·tion (ə dop′shən) □*noun, plural* **adoptions**

adore *verb* To love and admire greatly: *He adores his grandparents.*
a·dore (ə dôr′) □*verb* **adored, adoring, adores**

adorn *verb* To decorate with something beautiful: *They adorned the royal robes with embroidery and precious stones.*
a·dorn (ə dôrn′) □*verb* **adorned, adorning, adorns**

adrift *adverb* and *adjective* Drifting or floating without direction: *The empty canoe was adrift in the water.*
a·drift (ə drift′) □*adjective* and *adverb*

adult *noun* **1.** Someone who is fully grown; grownup. **2.** A plant or animal that is fully grown.
□*adjective* Fully grown: *An adult elephant is the largest land animal.* —See Synonyms at **mature.**
a·dult (ə dult′ *or* ad′ult′) □*noun, plural* **adults** □*adjective*

advance *verb* **1.** To move forward: *The line of cars advanced down the highway.* **2.** To make or help make progress; improve: *Scientists do experiments to advance our knowledge of the world.* **3.** To raise or rise in rank or position; promote or be promoted: *He advanced to be the head of the company.* **4.** To put forward; offer: *The detective advanced a new theory to explain the facts.* **5.** To pay money ahead of time: *Will you advance me a dollar until I get my allowance?*
□*noun* **1.** A movement forward: *We made a quick advance up the hill.* **2.** Money paid ahead of time: *I got an advance on my salary.* **3. advances** Efforts to win someone's favor or friendship: *She made the first advances to make up after our quarrel.*
ad·vance (ad vans′) □*verb* **advanced, advancing, advances** □*noun, plural* **advances**

SYNONYMS: advance, proceed, progress
These verbs mean to move forward: *The army advanced to the frontier. The parade proceeded through town. We watched the climbers progress steadily up the mountain.*

---

advancement *noun* **1.** A forward step; progress: *I made great advancements in school this year.* **2.** A move ahead in position; promotion: *a job with a good opportunity for advancement.*
ad·vance·ment (ad vans′mənt) □*noun, plural* **advancements**

advantage *noun* Something that is helpful or useful: *His height was an advantage when he played basketball.*
   take advantage of 1. To put to good use: *He told us to take advantage of the nice weather by going outside to play.* **2.** To treat or use unfairly: *She is always taking advantage of her little sister.*
ad·van·tage (ad van′tij) □*noun, plural* **advantages**

advantageous *adjective* Giving an advantage or extra help: *The treaty is advantageous to both countries.*
ad·van·ta·geous (ad′van tā′jəs) □*adjective*

adventure *noun* **1.** An activity that involves danger and risk: *He experienced many adventures exploring in the jungle.* **2.** An unusual or exciting experience: *Our first trip to the zoo was an adventure.*
ad·ven·ture (ad ven′chər) □*noun, plural* **adventures**

adventurous *adjective* **1.** Willing to take chances: *The adventurous group set out to climb to the top of the mountain.* **2.** Full of danger or excitement: *an adventurous journey to the South Pole.*
ad·ven·tur·ous (ad ven′chər əs) □*adjective*

SYNONYMS: adventurous, bold, daring
These adjectives mean willing to take chances: *They made an adventurous journey into the jungle. She was injured during a bold rescue attempt. Climbing the mountain was a daring feat.*

---

adverb *noun* A word that modifies a verb, an adjective, or another adverb. Adverbs usually tell when, where, and how and give information about time, place, manner, or degree. In the sentence "I got out of bed very late and ate my breakfast too quickly," "very," "too," and

"quickly" are adverbs.
ad·verb (**ad′**vûrb′) □*noun, plural* **adverbs**

adversary *noun* Someone on the opposite side in a war or contest: *She is my adversary in the election for class president.*
ad·ver·sar·y (**ad′**vər ser′ē) □*noun, plural* **adversaries**

adversity *noun* Great misfortune; hardship: *The people suffered through many adversities during the war.*
ad·ver·si·ty (ad **vûr′**si tē) □*noun, plural* **adversities**

advertise *verb* To bring to the attention of the public: *That store advertises bicycles on television.*
ad·ver·tise (**ad′**vər tīz′) □*verb* **advertised, advertising, advertises**

advertisement *noun* A public announcement about something. An advertisement may be used to sell a product, find or offer work, or find or offer a service.
ad·ver·tise·ment (ad′vər **tīz′**mənt *or* ad-**vûr′**tis mənt) □*noun, plural* **advertisements**

advice *noun* Opinion about what to do: *I always follow my father's advice.*
ad·vice (ad **vīs′**) □*noun*

advisable *adjective* Worth doing; sensible: *It is advisable to go to the doctor if you feel sick.*
ad·vis·a·ble (ad **vī′**zə bəl) □*adjective*

advise *verb* **1.** To give advice to: *He advised me to save the money I made.* **2.** To notify; inform: *She advised us she would be late.*
ad·vise (ad **vīz′**) □*verb* **advised, advising, advises**

adviser *or* **advisor** *noun* Someone who gives advice.
ad·vis·er *or* **ad·vi·sor** (ad **vī′**zər) □*noun, plural* **advisers** *or* **advisors**

advocate *verb* To speak in favor of; recommend; urge: *The mayor advocated increasing the size of the police force.* □*noun* Someone who speaks in favor of something.
ad·vo·cate (**ad′**və kāt′) □*verb* **advocated, advocating, advocates** □*noun* (**ad′**və kit), *plural* **advocates**

adz *or* **adze** *noun* A tool that looks like an ax with its blade set at an angle. It is used for shaping logs and other heavy pieces of wood.
adz *or* **adze** (adz) □*noun, plural* **adzes**

aerial *noun* An antenna for radio or television.
aer·i·al (**âr′**ē əl) □*noun, plural* **aerials**

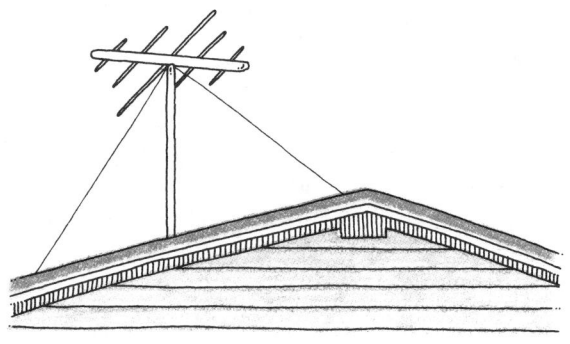

aerial

aeronautics *noun* The science and art of flight. Aeronautics includes designing, making, and flying aircraft.
aer·o·nau·tics (âr′ə **nô′**tiks) □*noun*

aerosol *noun* **1.** A suspension of tiny pieces of solid material or drops of a liquid in a gas. Fog and smoke are aerosols. **2.** A substance that is manufactured and packaged under pressure as an aerosol in a spray container. Paints and furniture polish are often sold as aerosols.
aer·o·sol (**âr′**ə sôl′) □*noun, plural* **aerosols**

aerospace *noun* The region that is made up of the earth's atmosphere and outer space, especially the space in which rockets and spacecraft fly.
aer·o·space (**âr′**ō spās′) □*noun*

affair *noun* **1.** Something to be done: *Painting the house was a difficult affair.* **2.** An event or happening: *Graduation is an important affair.*
af·fair (ə **fâr′**) □*noun, plural* **affairs**

affect¹ *verb* **1.** To have an influence on; bring about a change in: *The medicine affected him so that he became sleepy.* **2.** To touch the feelings of: *The sad story affected me and I cried.*
af·fect (ə **fekt′**) □*verb* **affected, affecting, affects**

affect² *verb* To pretend to feel or have: *He affected friendliness but I knew he was angry.*
af·fect (ə **fekt′**) □*verb* **affected, affecting, affects**

a	bat	ī	bite	o͞o	tool	*th*	feather
ā	make	î	fierce	ou	out	th	bath
â	dare	o	dot	u	nut	hw	wheat
ä	father	ō	no	û	turn	zh	measure
e	net	ô	law, for	ch	church	ə	about, open
ē	be	oi	soil	ng	ring		pencil, atom
i	dip	oo	look	sh	shade		circus

affection *noun* A loving feeling: *He has great affection for his parents.*
af·fec·tion (ə fek'shən) □*noun, plural* **affections**

affectionate *adjective* Having or showing love or affection: *an affectionate hug.*
af·fec·tion·ate (ə fek'shə nit) □*adjective*

affirmative *adjective* Saying that something is so; indicating "yes": *an affirmative answer.*
af·firm·a·tive (ə fûr'mə tiv) □*adjective*

afflict *verb* To cause pain or trouble to: *He is afflicted by bad eyesight.*
af·flict (ə flikt') □*verb* **afflicted, afflicting, afflicts**

affliction *noun* **1.** Pain or sorrow: *The fire caused great affliction.* **2.** A cause of pain or trouble: *The flu is a common affliction.*
af·flic·tion (ə flik'shən) □*noun, plural* **afflictions**

affluent *adjective* Having a lot of money; wealthy: *an affluent family.*
af·flu·ent (af'lōō ənt) □*adjective*

afford *verb* **1.** To be able to pay for: *Can you afford a new sled?* **2.** To give; provide: *Weekends afford me a chance to stay up late.*
af·ford (ə fôrd') □*verb* **afforded, affording, affords**

afire *adjective* and *adverb* On fire; burning: *The house was afire. I set the logs afire.*
a·fire (ə fīr') □*adjective* and *adverb*

afloat *adjective* and *adverb* Floating on a liquid or in the air: *a ship afloat on the sea.*
a·float (ə flōt') □*adjective* and *adverb*

afoot *adjective* and *adverb* **1.** On foot; walking: *He made his journey afoot.* **2.** In the process of happening: *Something strange is afoot.*
a·foot (ə foot') □*adjective* and *adverb*

afraid *adjective* **1.** Filled with fear; frightened: *Are you afraid of dogs?* **2.** Filled with regret; sorry: *I'm afraid I can't go with you.*
a·fraid (ə frād') □*adjective*

African *noun* Someone who was born or lives in Africa.
□*adjective* Of Africa or the Africans.
Af·ri·can (af'ri kən) □*noun, plural* **Africans** □*adjective*

African American *noun* An American who has African ancestors.
African American □*noun, plural* **African Americans**

aft *adverb* Toward or near the rear of a ship: *He went aft to take the tiller.*
aft (aft) □*adverb*

after *preposition* **1.** In a place or order following: *He stood after me in line.* **2.** At a later time than; following: *After lunch I'm going swimming.* **3.** Past the hour of: *ten minutes after two.* **4.** In search or pursuit of: *The men were running after the thief.*
□*adverb* **1.** At a later time; afterward: *forever after.* **2.** Behind: *He came running after.*
□*conjunction* Following the time that: *You can rest after we get home.*
af·ter (af'tər) □*preposition* □*adverb* □*conjunction*

afternoon *noun* The part of the day from noon until sunset.
af·ter·noon (af'tər nōōn') □*noun, plural* **afternoons**

afterward *adverb* At a later time: *We raked the leaves and afterward we relaxed.*
af·ter·ward (af'tər wərd) □*adverb*

afterwards *adverb* Another spelling for **afterward.**
af·ter·wards (af'tər wərdz) □*adverb*

again *adverb* Once more; another time: *He telephoned yesterday and again today.*
a·gain (ə gen') □*adverb*

against *preposition* **1.** So as to come into contact with: *He banged his knee against the desk.* **2.** In opposition to: *It is against the rules to talk in class.* **3.** In a direction opposite to: *It is hard to swim against the current.*
a·gainst (ə genst') □*preposition*

agate *noun* **1.** A stone that is a type of quartz and is striped with different colors. **2.** A playing marble that is made of or looks like agate.
ag·ate (ag'it) □*noun, plural* **agates**

agate

age *noun* **1.** The amount of time a person, plant, animal, or thing has lived or existed: *His age is seven. What is the age of that house?* **2.** A particular period of time when some special thing is important: *the space age.* **3.** A long time: *We haven't seen my uncle in ages.*
□*verb* **1.** To grow old. **2.** To cause to become

or appear old: *Grief over his wife's tragic death aged him suddenly.*
age (āj) ▢*noun, plural* **ages** ▢*verb* **aged, aging, ages**

aged *adjective* **1.** Having lived for a long time; old: *an aged man.* **2.** Of the age of: *He has a child aged two.*
ag·ed (**ā′** jid *for sense 1;* ājd *for sense 2*) ▢*adjective*

agency *noun* A business or organization that acts for another person or business: *The employment agency found a job for me.*
a·gen·cy (**ā′** jən sē) ▢*noun, plural* **agencies**

agent *noun* **1.** A person or group that handles business for another: *We bought our house from a real estate agent.* **2.** A means by which something is done or caused: *Chlorine bleach is a cleaning agent.*
a·gent (**ā′** jənt) ▢*noun, plural* **agents**

aggravate *verb* **1.** To make worse: *He aggravated his arm injury by throwing the ball.* **2.** To irritate; annoy: *Her constant complaints aggravate her teacher.*
ag·gra·vate (**ag′** rə vāt′) ▢*verb* **aggravated, aggravating, aggravates**

aggression *noun* A hostile action undertaken without cause: *The army could not check the enemy's aggression.*
ag·gres·sion (ə **gresh′** ən) ▢*noun, plural* **aggressions**

aggressive *adjective* **1.** Quick to attack or start a fight: *He is an aggressive boy who often quarrels with his friends.* **2.** Full of energy; active: *an aggressive salesman.*
ag·gres·sive (ə **gres′** iv) ▢*adjective*

aghast *adjective* Shocked by something terrible or wrong: *I was aghast when I saw him kick the dog.*
a·ghast (ə **gast′**) ▢*adjective*

agile *adjective* Capable of moving quickly and easily: *An athlete needs to be agile.*
ag·ile (**aj′** əl) ▢*adjective*

agile

agility *noun* The ability to move quickly and easily: *an acrobat's agility.*
a·gil·i·ty (ə **jil′** i tē) ▢*noun*

agitate *verb* **1.** To shake or stir: *The storm agitated the sea.* **2.** To upset the mind or feelings of; disturb: *The bad news agitated her.*
ag·i·tate (**aj′** i tāt′) ▢*verb* **agitated, agitating, agitates**

ago *adjective* and *adverb* In the past: *We lived in Kansas four years ago.*
a·go (ə **gō′**) ▢*adjective* and *adverb*

agony *noun* Great pain of body or mind; suffering: *I'm in agony from my broken arm.*
ag·o·ny (**ag′** ə nē) ▢*noun, plural* **agonies**

agree *verb* **1.** To have the same opinion: *He hated the movie and I agreed.* **2.** To say "yes"; consent: *I agreed to stay for supper.*
 agree with To be good for: *The hot dog did not agree with me.*
a·gree (ə **grē′**) ▢*verb* **agreed, agreeing, agrees**

agreeable *adjective* **1.** Pleasant; pleasing: *an agreeable person.* **2.** Willing to say "yes": *He was agreeable to the change in our plans.*
a·gree·a·ble (ə **grē′** ə bəl) ▢*adjective*

agreement *noun* **1.** The condition of agreeing: *My parents are in agreement on what color to paint the house.* **2.** An understanding between two or more people or groups: *The countries made an agreement to stop the war.*
a·gree·ment (ə **grē′** mənt) ▢*noun, plural* **agreements**

agricultural *adjective* Of farms or farming: *We live in an agricultural region.*
ag·ri·cul·tur·al (ag′ri **kul′** chər əl) ▢*adjective*

agriculture *noun* The science and business of farming.
ag·ri·cul·ture (**ag′** ri kul′chər) ▢*noun*

ahead *adverb* and *adjective* **1.** At or to the front: *He ran ahead of me. There is a bad hole in the road ahead.* **2.** In advance: *Phone ahead for tickets.* **3.** Onward; forward: *I went ahead with the work.*
a·head (ə **hed′**) ▢*adverb* and *adjective*

a bat	ī bite	o͞o tool	*th* feather
ā make	î fierce	ou **out**	th bath
â dare	o dot	u nut	hw **wh**eat
ä father	ō no	û turn	zh measure
e net	ô law, for	ch **ch**urch	ə about, open
ē be	oi soil	ng ring	pencil, atom
i dip	oo look	sh shade	circus

aid   *verb* To help or assist: *We aided the rescue workers.*
□*noun* **1.** Help; assistance: *financial aid to help pay tuition.* **2.** Something that helps or is helpful: *A map is a useful aid on a hike.*
aid (ād) □*verb* **aided, aiding, aids** □*noun, plural* **aids**

aide   *noun* A helper; assistant.
aide (ād) □*noun, plural* **aides**

AIDS   *noun* A serious disease that attacks and greatly weakens the body's immunity. AIDS is caused by a virus.
AIDS (ādz) □*noun*

ail   *verb* **1.** To be ill; feel sick: *He is ailing.* **2.** To cause pain or trouble to: *What ails you?*
ail (āl) □*verb* **ailed, ailing, ails**

ailment   *noun* An illness or sickness that may last a long time.
ail·ment (āl′mənt) □*noun, plural* **ailments**

aim   *verb* **1.** To point or direct one thing at another: *He aimed the gun at the target.* **2.** To have a purpose or goal: *He aims to be a doctor.*
□*noun* **1.** The act of pointing or directing one thing at another: *His aim was bad and he missed the target.* **2.** A purpose; goal.
aim (ām) □*noun, plural* **aims** □*verb* **aimed, aiming, aims**

ain't   A contraction of "am not," "is not," "are not," "have not," and "has not." *Ain't* is not usually considered to be standard English.
ain't (ānt)

air   *noun* **1.** The mixture of gases that surrounds the earth. The two main gases in air are nitrogen and oxygen. **2.** Fresh air that is moving: *I opened the window to let in some air.* **3.** The open space above the earth; sky. **4.** A simple melody; tune. **5.** A look, style, or manner: *He walked and spoke with a carefree air.* **6. airs** Manners used to make oneself seem better than others: *He put on airs because he won the spelling contest.*
□*verb* **1.** To let fresh air in: *air a room.* **2.** To talk about: *She aired her complaints.*
  on the air Broadcasting or being broadcast: *The program is on the air at noon.*
air (âr) □*noun, plural* **airs** □*verb* **aired, airing, airs**

air conditioner   *noun* A machine that cools and cleans the air in a room or other enclosed place.
air con·di·tion·er (kən dish′ə nər) □*noun*

aircraft   *noun* A machine that is made for flying. Airplanes, helicopters, and gliders are all aircraft.
air·craft (âr′kraft′) □*noun, plural* **aircraft**

airfield   *noun* A field where aircraft can take off and land.
air·field (âr′fēld′) □*noun, plural* **airfields**

air force   *noun* The branch of a country's military forces that is equipped with aircraft.

airline   *noun* A company whose business is to carry passengers and cargo in airplanes.
air·line (âr′līn′) □*noun, plural* **airlines**

airmail   *adjective* For or of mail sent by aircraft: *an airmail letter.*
air·mail (âr′māl′) □*adjective*

air mail   *noun* Mail that is sent by aircraft.

airman   *noun* Someone of the lowest rank in the United States Air Force.
air·man (âr′mən) □*noun, plural* **airmen**

airplane   *noun* A machine that is heavier than air but is able to fly. It has wings and is driven by propellers or jet engines.
air·plane (âr′plān′) □*noun, plural* **airplanes**

airport   *noun* A place with runways where aircraft can land and take off. An airport has buildings for passengers and for storing and repairing aircraft.
air·port (âr′pôrt′) □*noun, plural* **airports**

airship   *noun* An aircraft that is lighter than air, can be steered, and has engines.
air·ship (âr′ship′) □*noun, plural* **airships**

airtight   *adjective* So tight that no air or other gases can get in or out. Many foods come in jars with airtight seals.
air·tight (âr′tīt′) □*adjective*

airy   *adjective* With air moving freely: *an airy room.*
air·y (âr′ē) □*adjective* **airier, airiest**

aisle   *noun* A narrow passage through which one may walk, as between rows of seats in a theater or between counters in a store.
aisle (īl) □*noun, plural* **aisles**

ajar   *adjective* and *adverb* Partly open: *I left the door ajar.*
a·jar (ə jär′) □*adjective* and *adverb*

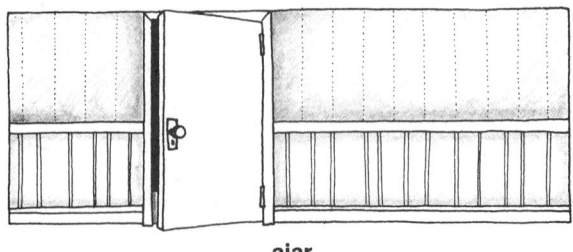

ajar

akimbo *adjective* and *adverb* With the hands on the hips and the elbows bent outward.
a·kim·bo (ə **kim′** bō) □*adjective* and *adverb*

akimbo

akin *adjective* **1.** Belonging to the same family; related. **2.** Of the same sort; similar: *Pity is akin to love.*
a·kin (ə **kin′**) □*adjective*

alarm *noun* **1.** Sudden fear caused by a feeling of danger: *The noise in the woods made me shake with alarm.* **2.** A warning that danger is near: *The soldier sent out an alarm that the enemy was approaching the fort.* **3.** A bell, buzzer, or other signal sounded to warn people of danger or to wake them up: *a fire alarm. I set the alarm on my clock.*
□*verb* To fill with fear; frighten: *The explosion alarmed the child.*
a·larm (ə **lärm′**) □*noun, plural* **alarms**
□*verb* **alarmed, alarming, alarms**

alas *interjection* A word used to express sorrow, regret, or grief.
a·las (ə **las′**) □*interjection*

albatross *noun* A large sea bird with webbed feet, a hooked beak, and very long wings.
al·ba·tross (**al′** bə trôs′) □*noun, plural* **albatrosses**

album *noun* **1.** A book with blank pages in which collections of photographs, stamps, or other things may be kept. **2.** A long-playing phonograph record.
al·bum (**al′** bəm) □*noun, plural* **albums**

alchemy *noun* Chemistry as practiced in the Middle Ages. People who practiced alchemy tried to find a way to turn common metals into gold and to find a magic substance that would keep people young forever.
al·che·my (**al′** kə mē) □*noun*

alcohol *noun* A liquid that is clear, has no color or taste, evaporates rapidly, and catches fire quickly. Alcohol is contained in wine, beer, whiskey, some kinds of medicine, and in many other products.
al·co·hol (**al′** kə hôl′) □*noun, plural* **alcohols**

alcoholic *adjective* Of or containing alcohol: *an alcoholic drink.*
□*noun* Someone who suffers from alcoholism.
al·co·hol·ic (al′kə **hô′**lik) □*adjective* □*noun, plural* **alcoholics**

alcoholism *noun* A disease in which people cannot control how much alcohol they drink.
al·co·hol·ism (**al′** kə hô liz′əm) □*noun*

alcove *noun* A small room that opens on a larger one.
al·cove (**al′** kōv′) □*noun, plural* **alcoves**

WORD HISTORY: **alcove**

Alcove comes from an Arabic phrase that means "the vault" and "a vaulted room." A vaulted room is one with an arched ceiling.

---

alder *noun* A tree or shrub similar to a birch that grows in cool, damp places.
al·der (**ôl′** dər) □*noun, plural* **alders**

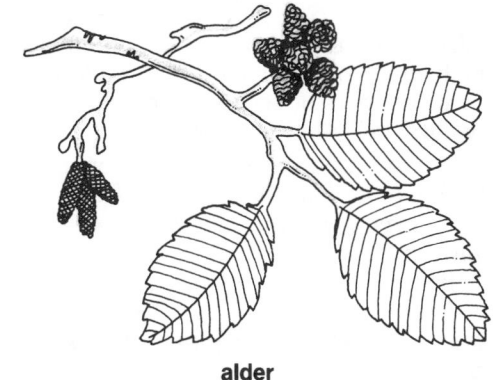

alder

ale *noun* An alcoholic drink made of malt and hops.
ale (āl) □*noun, plural* **ales**

a bat	ī bite	ōō tool	*th* feather
ā make	î fierce	ou out	th bath
â dare	o dot	u nut	hw wheat
ä father	ō no	û turn	zh measure
e net	ô law, for	ch church	ə about, open
ē be	oi soil	ng ring	pencil, atom
i dip	oo look	sh shade	circus

alert *adjective* **1.** Quick to understand: *an alert mind.* **2.** Watching carefully: *an alert guard.*
□*verb* To warn or make aware of approaching danger: *The smoke alerted us to the fire.*
□*noun* A signal of danger.
a·lert (ə **lûrt′**) □*adjective verb* **alerted, alerting, alerts** □*noun, plural* **alerts**

alfalfa *noun* A plant with purple flowers and leaves that look like clover. Alfalfa is grown as food for cattle and other animals.
al·fal·fa (al **fal′**fə) □*noun*

algae *plural noun* Water plants, such as seaweed, that do not have roots, stems, or leaves.
al·gae (**al′**jē) □*plural noun*

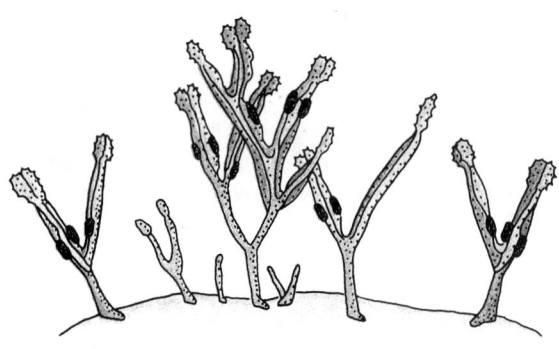

algae

algebra *noun* A branch of mathematics in which letters or other symbols are used to represent numbers or sets of numbers.
al·ge·bra (**al′**jə brə) □*noun*

alias *noun* A name assumed to conceal one's identity: *The British writer Charles Lamb wrote essays using the alias Elia.*
□*adverb* Also known as; otherwise named: *The police arrested Bob Jones, alias Bob Smith, for the robbery.*
a·li·as (**ā′**lē əs) □*noun, plural* **aliases**
□*adverb*

alibi *noun* **1.** A claim by a person that he or she was somewhere else when a crime was committed: *His alibi is that he was out of town when the bank was robbed.* **2.** An excuse: *She has a good alibi for not doing her homework.*
al·i·bi (**al′**ə bī′) □*noun, plural* **alibis**

alien *adjective* Of or from another country; foreign: *alien customs.*
□*noun* Someone who lives in one country but is a citizen of another country; foreigner.
a·li·en (**āl′**yən *or* **ā′**lē ən) □*adjective* □*noun, plural* **aliens**

alienate *verb* To make someone hostile or unfriendly: *Her rude behavior alienated her friends.*
al·ien·ate (**āl′**yə nāt′ *or* **ā′**lē ə nāt′) □*verb* **alienated, alienating, alienates**

alight¹ *adjective* **1.** Lighted up: *His face was alight with hope.* **2.** On fire; burning: *The bonfire is alight.*
a·light (ə **līt′**) □*adjective*

alight² *verb* **1.** To come down; land: *A bird alighted on the roof.* **2.** To get off or down: *He alighted from his horse.*
a·light (ə **līt′**) □*verb* **alighted** or **alit, alighting, alights**

align *verb* To bring into a straight line: *Let's align the books on the shelf.*
a·lign (ə **līn′**) □*verb* **aligned, aligning, aligns**

alike *adjective* Having a close resemblance; similar: *The two pictures are much alike.*
□*adverb* In the same way or manner: *Mary and her mother walk and talk alike.*
a·like (ə **līk′**) □*adjective* □*adverb*

alimentary canal *noun* The tube in the body in which food is taken and digested, and from which wastes are expelled.
al·i·men·ta·ry canal (al′ə **men′**tə rē) □*noun*

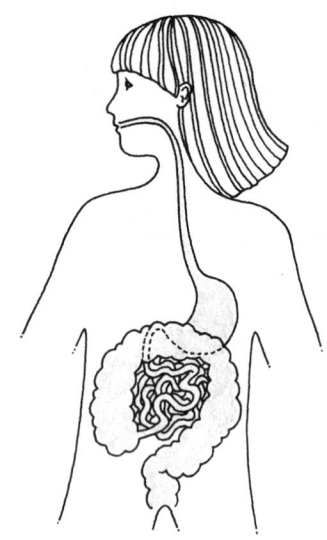

alimentary canal

alimony *noun* Money that must be paid regularly by one spouse to support the other during or after a divorce or legal separation.
al·i·mo·ny (**al′**ə mō′nē) □*noun*

alive *adjective* **1.** Having life; living: *The injured man is unconscious but still alive.* **2.** In

existence or operation; active: *Her hopes of winning the contest are still alive.*
a·live (ə **līv′**) □*adjective*

all *adjective* **1.** The whole quantity or amount of: *She ate all the pudding.* **2.** Each one of: *All her friends came to the party.*
□*pronoun* **1.** Each and every one: *All aboard were drowned.* **2.** Everything: *All is lost.*
□*adverb* Entirely; completely: *She is all alone.*
all (ôl) □*adjective* □*pronoun* □*adverb*

Allah *noun* The name of God in Islam.
Al·lah (**al′**ə *or* **ä′**lə) □*noun*

allege *verb* To declare without definite proof: *Four witnesses alleged that she was the robber.*
al·lege (ə **lej′**) □*verb* **alleged, alleging, alleges**

allegiance *noun* Loyal and faithful devotion to a person, group, or idea.
al·le·giance (ə **lē′**jəns) □*noun, plural* **allegiances**

allergic *adjective* Having an allergy: *She is allergic to cats.*
al·ler·gic (ə **lûr′**jik) □*adjective*

allergy *noun* An unpleasant physical reaction to certain foods, plants, animals, or other things that are harmless to most people.
al·ler·gy (**al′**ər jē) □*noun, plural* **allergies**

alley *noun* **1.** A narrow street or passage between buildings. **2.** A long, smooth, narrow lane down which bowling balls are rolled.
al·ley (**al′**ē) □*noun, plural* **alleys**

alliance *noun* An agreement by two or more persons, groups, or nations to join together and work for a common purpose.
al·li·ance (ə **lī′**əns) □*noun, plural* **alliances**

alligator *noun* A large reptile with sharp teeth and strong jaws. Alligators look like crocodiles but have a shorter, wider snout.
al·li·ga·tor (**al′**i gā′tər) □*noun, plural* **alligators**

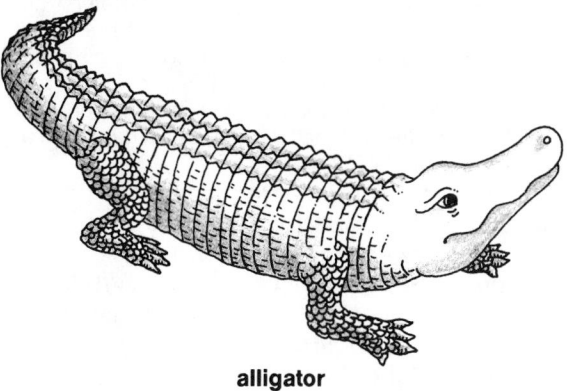

alligator

allot *verb* To give as a part or share: *The teacher allotted several hours a week to reviewing grammar.*
al·lot (ə **lot′**) □*verb* **allotted, allotting, allots**

allow *verb* **1.** To let do or happen; permit: *My parents allow me to stay up late on weekends.* **2.** To let have: *The teacher allowed me extra time to finish the test.*
al·low (ə **lou′**) □*verb* **allowed, allowing, allows**

allowance *noun* A sum of money given at regular times: *Each child has an allowance of fifty cents a week.*
make allowance for To take into account; consider: *We made allowance for traffic by leaving early.*
al·low·ance (ə **lou′**əns) □*noun, plural* **allowances**

alloy *noun* A metal made by melting together two or more different metals. Brass, bronze, and pewter are alloys.
al·loy (**al′**oi *or* ə **loi′**) □*noun, plural* **alloys**

all right *adjective* **1.** Satisfactory but not excellent; average: *His work is all right, but it could be better.* **2.** Not sick or injured; well: *I was afraid she was hurt, but she's all right.*
□*adverb* Very well; yes: *All right, I'll come.*

ally *verb* To join or unite for a special purpose: *a small country that allied with another against the enemy.*
□*noun* A person or country that has joined with another for a special purpose: *The teacher was her ally in the campaign against cheating.*
al·ly (ə **lī′**) □*verb* **allied, allying, allies**
□*noun* (**al′**ī′ *or* ə **lī′**), *plural* **allies**

almanac *noun* A book published once a year containing facts and information on many different subjects. Some almanacs are arranged like calendars and give facts about weather, tides, the moon, the stars, and the sun.
al·ma·nac (**ôl′**mə nak′) □*noun, plural* **almanacs**

almond *noun* **1.** An oval, edible nut with a soft, light-brown shell. **2.** A tree on which almonds grow.

a	bat	ī	bite	ōō	tool	*th*	feather
ā	make	î	fierce	ou	out	th	bath
â	dare	o	dot	u	nut	hw	wheat
ä	father	ō	no	û	turn	zh	measure
e	net	ô	law, for	ch	church	ə	about, open
ē	be	oi	soil	ng	ring		pencil, atom
i	dip	oo	look	sh	shade		circus

al·mond (ä′mənd *or* am′ənd) □*noun, plural* **almonds**

almond

almost *adverb* Nearly but not quite: *I have almost finished the book.*
al·most (ôl′mōst) □*adverb*

aloft *adverb* **1.** Above the earth; in or into the air: *The swallows soared aloft.* **2.** High on the masts and rigging of a sailing ship: *The sailor climbed aloft.*
a·loft (ə lôft′) □*adverb*

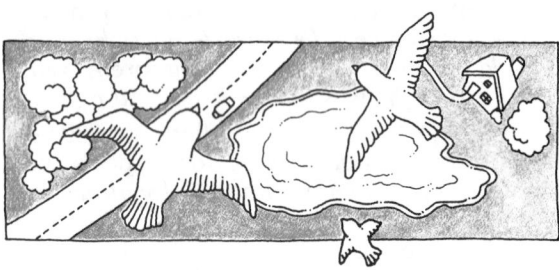

aloft

aloha *interjection* A word used to express greetings and farewell.
a·lo·ha (ä lō′hä′) □*interjection*

alone *adjective* Without anyone or anything else: *She is alone in the house. The noise alone is enough to frighten her.*
□*adverb* Without help: *I can do it alone.*
   leave alone or **let alone** To keep from bothering or interrupting: *Leave him alone while he reads.*
a·lone (ə lōn′) □*adjective* □*adverb*

along *preposition* In a line with the length of: *The parade marched along the main street.*
□*adverb* **1.** Forward; ahead: *The truck moved along fast.* **2.** As a companion: *Bring your sister along to the party.*
a·long (ə lông′) □*preposition* □*adverb*

alongside *preposition* By the side of: *cars parked alongside the curb.*
□*adverb* At the side: *a ship with a tugboat alongside.*

a·long·side (ə lông′sīd′) □*preposition* □*adverb*

aloof *adjective* Cool, distant, and not very friendly: *Her aloof manner angers people.*
□*adverb* At a distance; apart: *She remained aloof as the others argued.*
a·loof (ə loof′) □*adjective* □*adverb*

aloud *adverb* With the voice: *She read the story aloud to the children.*
a·loud (ə loud′) □*adverb*

alpaca *noun* **1.** A South American animal with long, silky wool. **2.** The wool of the alpaca.
al·pac·a (al pak′ə) □*noun, plural* **alpacas**

alpaca

alphabet *noun* A set of letters or other symbols used to write the different sounds of a language.
al·pha·bet (al′fə bet′) □*noun, plural* **alphabets**

WORD HISTORY: **alphabet**

The word *alphabet* is a combination of *alpha* and *beta*, the names of the first two letters of the Greek alphabet. The alphabet was invented by the Phoenicians about 3,000 years ago. The Greeks adopted the Phoenician alphabet, and the Romans borrowed it from the Greeks. English is written with the Roman version of the alphabet.

---

alphabetical *adjective* Arranged in the order of the letters of the alphabet.
al·pha·bet·i·cal (al′fə bet′i kəl) □*adjective*

already *adverb* By this or that time: *When I arrived, she had already left.*
al·read·y (ôl red′ē) □*adverb*

also *adverb* In addition; too: *She is a painter and also a musician.*
al·so (ôl′sō) □*adverb*

altar *noun* A table or a raised place used in religious ceremonies.
al·tar (ôl′tər) □*noun, plural* **altars**

altar

alter *verb* To make or become different: *We altered our plans because of the weather. He altered the pants by making the legs shorter.* —See Synonyms at **change.**
al·ter (ôl′tər) □*verb* **altered, altering, alters**

alternate *verb* **1.** To take turns, changing back and forth: *Day alternates with night.* **2.** To pass back and forth, as between conditions: *His mood alternates between happiness and sadness.*
□*adjective* **1.** Happening in turns; one after the other: *We had alternate days of rain and sunshine.* **2.** Every other; every second: *She telephones her grandparents on alternate weekends.* **3.** In place of another: *The road was blocked off, so we took an alternate route.*
□*noun* Someone or something that takes the place of another; substitute.
al·ter·nate (ôl′tər nāt′) □*verb* **alternated, alternating, alternates** □*adjective* (ôl′tər nit) □*noun* (ôl′tər nit), *plural* **alternates**

alternating current *noun* An electric current that flows first in one direction, then in the opposite direction, at regular intervals.

alternative *noun* **1.** A choice between two or more things or ways of doing things: *The man had the alternative of going by bus or by train.* **2.** One of two or more things or ways of doing things that can be chosen: *He chose the first alternative and went by bus.*
al·ter·na·tive (ôl tûr′nə tiv) □*noun, plural* **alternatives**

although *conjunction* Even though: *She won't drink, although she is thirsty.*
al·though (ôl thō′) □*conjunction*

altimeter *noun* An instrument that measures altitude.
al·tim·e·ter (al tim′i tər) □*noun, plural* **altimeters**

altitude *noun* Vertical height measured from sea level or from the surface of the earth: *The plane flew at an altitude of 30,000 feet.* —See Synonyms at **height.**
al·ti·tude (al′ti tōōd′ *or* al′ti tyōōd′) □*noun, plural* **altitudes**

alto *noun* **1.** The lowest singing voice of a woman or a man's highest singing voice. **2.** A singer who has an alto voice. **3.** A musical instrument with the same range as an alto.
al·to (al′tō) □*noun, plural* **altos**

altogether *adverb* **1.** Completely; entirely: *She is altogether wrong.* **2.** With everything included or counted: *Altogether there are ten pupils in the class.* **3.** On the whole; considering everything: *Altogether she had a good time.*
al·to·geth·er (ôl′tə geth′ər) □*adverb*

aluminum *noun* An element that is a lightweight, silver-white metal. It is used for making such things as pots and pans, kitchen foil, tools, and airplanes.
a·lu·mi·num (ə lōō′mə nəm) □*noun*

always *adverb* **1.** On every occasion; every single time: *She always leaves for work at eight o'clock.* **2.** At all times; forever: *They will always be friends.*
al·ways (ôl′wāz *or* ôl′wiz) □*adverb*

am *verb* The first person singular present tense of **be:** *I am glad to be here.*
am (am) □*verb*

a.m. or **A.M.** An abbreviation that means the time between midnight and noon: *Breakfast is served at 8:00 a.m.*

amateur *noun* Someone who does something for pleasure and does not get paid: *The actors in the play are amateurs.*
am·a·teur (am′ə chər *or* am′ə tər) □*noun, plural* **amateurs**

a	bat	ī	bite	ōō	tool	*th*	feather
ā	make	î	fierce	ou	out	th	bath
â	dare	o	dot	u	nut	hw	wheat
ä	father	ō	no	û	turn	zh	measure
e	net	ô	law, for	ch	church	ə	about, open
ē	be	oi	soil	ng	ring		pencil, atom
i	dip	oo	look	sh	shade		circus

amaze *verb* To fill with surprise; astonish: *The speed of the jet plane amazed us.*
a·maze (ə māz′) ▫*verb* **amazed, amazing, amazes**

amazement *noun* Great surprise or wonder; astonishment: *She was filled with amazement at the magician's tricks.*
a·maze·ment (ə māz′mənt) ▫*noun*

ambassador *noun* An official of the highest rank who goes to another country to represent his or her own country or government.
am·bas·sa·dor (am bas′ə dər) ▫*noun, plural* **ambassadors**

amber *noun* A light or brownish-yellow material that looks like stone. Amber is a hardened fossil resin from ancient pine trees and is used for making jewelry.
am·ber (am′bər) ▫*noun*

ambiguous *adjective* Having two or more possible meanings: *She listened to what he asked and gave an ambiguous answer.*
am·big·u·ous (am big′yo͞o əs) ▫*adjective*

ambition *noun* A strong desire to succeed at something: *Her ambition is to be a scientist.*
am·bi·tion (am bish′ən) ▫*noun, plural* **ambitions**

ambitious *adjective* **1.** Eager for success, fame, money, or power: *an ambitious worker.* **2.** Requiring much effort or skill to succeed: *They have an ambitious plan to build an electric car in shop class.*
am·bi·tious (am bish′əs) ▫*adjective*

ambulance *noun* A vehicle that is used to convey people who are sick or hurt to a hospital.
am·bu·lance (am′byə ləns) ▫*noun, plural* **ambulances**

ambush *noun* **1.** A surprise attack made from a place of hiding. **2.** The place of hiding from which an ambush is made.
▫*verb* To attack from an ambush: *The soldiers ambushed the enemy patrol.*
am·bush (am′bo͞osh′) ▫*noun, plural* **ambushes** ▫*verb* **ambushed, ambushing, ambushes**

ameba *noun* A very small animal that has only one cell. The shape of an ameba is always changing.
a·me·ba (ə mē′bə) ▫*noun, plural* **amebas**

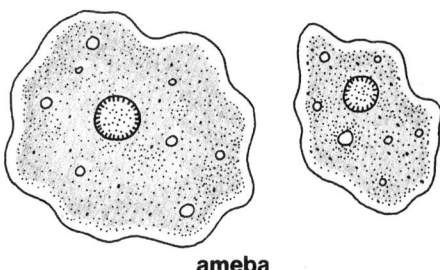

ameba

amen *interjection* A word that occurs at the end of a prayer and that is used to express agreement.
a·men (ā′men′ *or* ä′men′) ▫*interjection*

amend *verb* To change for the better; improve: *The teacher told him to amend his behavior in class.*
a·mend (ə mend′) ▫*verb* **amended, amending, amends**

amendment *noun* A change in a law or in an official document: *an amendment to the Constitution.*
a·mend·ment (ə mend′mənt) ▫*noun, plural* **amendments**

amends *plural noun* **make amends** To make up for an insult, injury, or wrong: *She made amends for her rudeness by apologizing.*
a·mends (ə mendz′) ▫*plural noun*

America *noun* **1.** The United States of America. **2.** North America. **3.** South America. **4. Americas** North America, Central America, and South America.
A·mer·i·ca (ə mer′i kə) ▫*noun, plural* **Americas**

American *noun* **1.** Someone who was born in or is a citizen of the United States. **2.** Someone who was born in North America, Central America, or South America.
▫*adjective* **1.** Of the United States or its people. **2.** Of North America, Central America, or South America or their peoples.
A·mer·i·can (ə mer′i kən) ▫*noun, plural* **Americans** ▫*adjective*

American English *noun* The English language as it is used in the United States.

American Indian *noun* A Native American.

amiable *adjective* Good-natured and friendly; pleasant: *He is an amiable person who makes friends easily.*
a·mi·a·ble (ā′ mē ə bəl) □*adjective*

amid *preposition* In the middle of; among.
a·mid (ə mid′) □*preposition*

amigo *noun* A friend.
a·mi·go (ə mē′ gō) □*noun, plural* **amigos**

amiss *adjective* Not proper or right; wrong: *Her expression told me something was amiss.*
a·miss (ə mis′) □*adjective*

ammonia *noun* **1.** A gas that is made up of nitrogen and hydrogen and has a strong smell and no color. **2.** A solution of ammonia and water.
am·mo·nia (ə mōn′ yə) □*noun*

ammunition *noun* Materials, such as bullets, explosives, bombs, or grenades, that can be fired from a gun or weapon or can explode.
am·mu·ni·tion (am′yə nish′ ən) □*noun*

amnesia *noun* A loss of memory caused by a shock, a brain injury, or an illness.
am·ne·sia (am nē′ zhə) □*noun*

amoeba *noun* Another spelling for **ameba.**
a·moe·ba (ə mē′ bə) □*noun, plural* **amoebas**

among *preposition* **1.** In the company of; with: *We were glad to be among friends.* **2.** With a portion to each of: *The chores were shared among the four of them.* **3.** Between one and another of: *There is often quarreling among the four sisters.* **4.** In the group of: *Swimming and skating are among my favorite sports.*
a·mong (ə mung′) □*preposition*

amount *noun* **1.** The total of two or more quantities; sum: *The amount of the bill was $50.* **2.** Quantity: *She has a great amount of patience.*
□*verb* To add up in total: *The check for dinner amounted to $10.*
a·mount (ə mount′) □*noun, plural* **amounts**
□*verb* **amounted, amounting, amounts**

amphibian *noun* One of a group of animals with smooth, moist skin. Amphibians have gills and live in water when they are young. Later they develop lungs and breathe air. Frogs and toads are amphibians.
am·phib·i·an (am fib′ē ən) □*noun, plural* **amphibians**

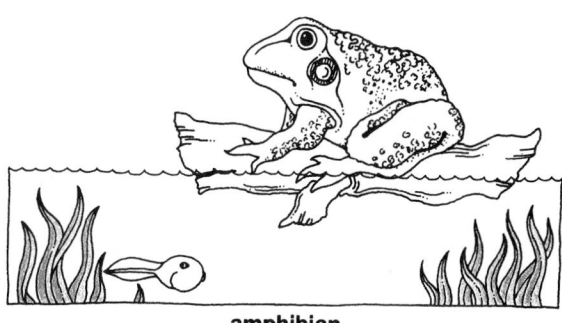
amphibian
A frog

amphibious *adjective* Able to live both on land and in water: *The salamander is an amphibious animal.*
am·phib·i·ous (am fib′ē əs) □*adjective*

amphitheater *noun* An oval or round structure with an open space in the center and rows of seats rising gradually outward all around.
am·phi·the·a·ter (am′fə thē′ə tər) □*noun, plural* **amphitheaters**

ample *adjective* **1.** Generously sufficient; abundant: *I allowed ample time to get to school.* **2.** Of large size; roomy: *a cabin with ample room for six people.*
am·ple (am′pəl) □*adjective* **ampler, amplest**

ample

amplify *verb* **1.** To add to; expand: *The policeman amplified his report with more details.* **2.** To make louder by electrical or mechanical means: *The singer's voice was amplified during the concert.*

a bat	ī bite	ōō tool	*th* feather
ā make	î fierce	ou out	th bath
â dare	o dot	u nut	hw wheat
ä father	ō no	û turn	zh measure
e net	ô law, for	ch church	ə about, open
ē be	oi soil	ng ring	pencil, atom
i dip	oo look	sh shade	circus

am·pli·fy (am′plə fī′) ▭*verb* **amplified, amplifying, amplifies**

amputate   *verb* To cut off part of: *amputated a finger.*
am·pu·tate (am′pyoo tāt′) ▭*verb* **amputated, amputating, amputates**

amuse   *verb* **1.** To hold someone's attention in a pleasant or agreeable way: *She amused us with adventure stories.* **2.** To cause to laugh or smile: *The new toy amused the child.*
a·muse (ə myōōz′) ▭*verb* **amused, amusing, amuses**

SYNONYMS: **amuse, divert, entertain**

These verbs mean to hold someone's attention in a pleasant or agreeable way: *The visit to the zoo amused the children. The old man diverted us all afternoon with his funny stories. We were all entertained by the clown's tricks.*

---

amusement   *noun* **1.** The condition of being amused: *We laughed in amusement at his jokes.* **2.** Something that provides enjoyment or entertainment: *His favorite amusement in the winter is skiing.*
a·muse·ment (ə myōōz′mənt) ▭*noun, plural* **amusements**

an   *indefinite article* A form of **a** used before words beginning with a vowel or with an *h* that is not pronounced: *an apple; an elephant; an ice-cream cone; an orange; an umbrella; an hour.*
an (ən *or* an) ▭*indefinite article*

anaconda   *noun* A large, nonpoisonous snake of South America that coils around and crushes its prey.
an·a·con·da (an′ə kon′də) ▭*noun, plural* **anacondas**

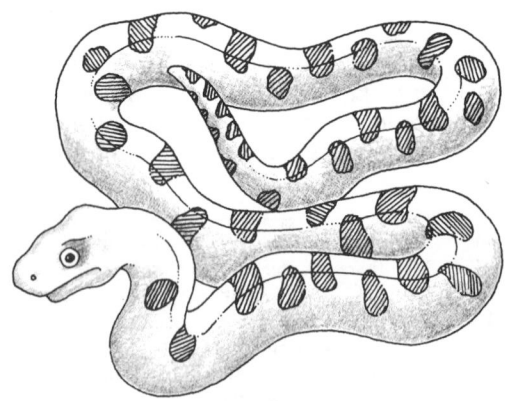

anaconda

analysis   *noun* The separation of something into its basic parts to find out what it contains or is made of: *An analysis of the water showed that it contained chemical pollutants.*
a·nal·y·sis (ə nal′i sis) ▭*noun, plural* **a·nal·y·ses** (ə nal′i sēz′)

analyze   *verb* **1.** To separate something into its basic parts to find out what it contains or is made of: *They analyzed the ore and found iron in it.* **2.** To examine in detail: *We analyzed our plan to see why it had failed.*
an·a·lyze (an′ə līz′) ▭*verb* **analyzed, analyzing, analyzes**

anatomy   *noun* **1.** The scientific study of the structure of animals and plants. **2.** The structure of an animal or plant: *We studied the anatomy of the butterfly in science class.*
a·nat·o·my (ə nat′ə mē) ▭*noun, plural* **anatomies**

ancestor   *noun* A person from whom one is descended.
an·ces·tor (an′ses′tər) ▭*noun, plural* **ancestors**

SYNONYMS: **ancestor, forefather**

These nouns mean a person from whom one is descended: *Her ancestors came to America from Italy over a hundred years ago. Her forefathers were among the first pioneers in Oregon.*

---

anchor   *noun* A heavy weight that is dropped from a rope or chain to keep a ship from floating away.
▭*verb* To hold or be held in place by means of an anchor: *The sailors anchored the ship in the harbor.*
an·chor (ang′kər) ▭*noun, plural* **anchors** ▭*verb* **anchored, anchoring, anchors**

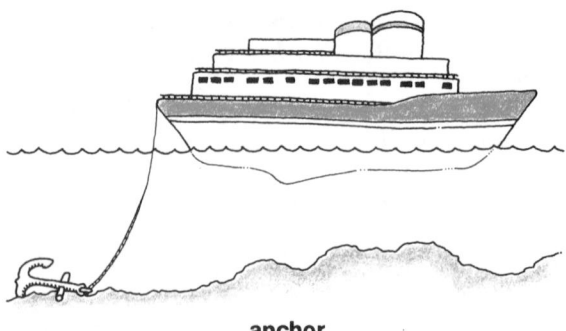

anchor

ancient   *adjective* **1.** Very old: *an ancient typewriter.* **2.** Of times long past, especially before

A.D. 500: *ancient Rome.*
an·cient (ān′shənt) □*adjective*

and *conjunction* **1.** Together with: *She and her daughter were here.* **2.** As well as: *I paint and sew.* **3.** Added to; plus: *Two and two make four.*
and (ənd *or* ən *or* and) □*conjunction*

andiron *noun* One of a pair of metal supports for holding logs in a fireplace.
and·i·ron (and′ī′ərn) □*noun, plural* **andirons**

andiron
A pair of andirons

anecdote *noun* A short account of an interesting or amusing event.
an·ec·dote (an′ik dōt′) □*noun, plural* **anecdotes**

anemia *noun* A condition in which the body has too few red blood cells.
a·ne·mi·a (ə nē′mē ə) □*noun*

anesthetic *noun* A substance, such as a drug, that causes the body or part of the body to be unable to feel pain, heat, cold, or touch.
an·es·thet·ic (an′is **thet′**ik) □*noun, plural* **anesthetics**

anew *adverb* Over again; once more: *begin anew.*
a·new (ə nōō′ *or* ə nyōō′) □*adverb*

angel *noun* **1.** A heavenly being who serves as an attendant and messenger of God. **2.** Someone who is considered especially kind, good, or pleasant.
an·gel (ān′jəl) □*noun, plural* **angels**

WORD HISTORY: **angel**

Angel comes from a Greek word meaning "a messenger." In Jewish and Christian writing the Greek word was used to mean "a messenger from God."

---

anger *noun* A strong feeling of hostility, as from the belief that one has been treated badly: *He showed his anger by shouting at me.* □*verb* To make or become angry: *Her constant complaining angered her mother.*
an·ger (ang′gər) □*noun* □*verb* **angered, angering, angers**

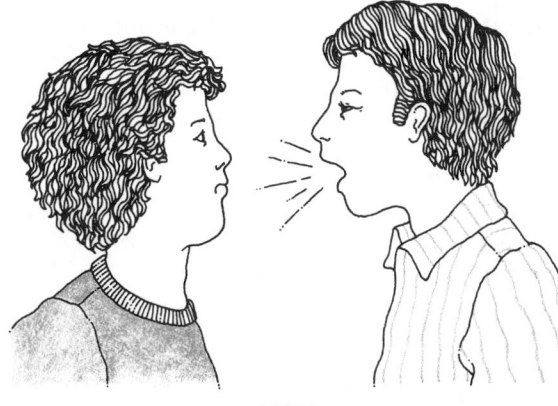

anger

angle *noun* **1.** The space between two lines or two surfaces that meet. **2.** A way of looking at something; point of view: *studying every angle of the problem.* □*verb* To bend or move at an angle: *The street angles sharply to the right.*
an·gle (ang′gəl) □*noun, plural* **angles** □*verb* **angled, angling, angles**

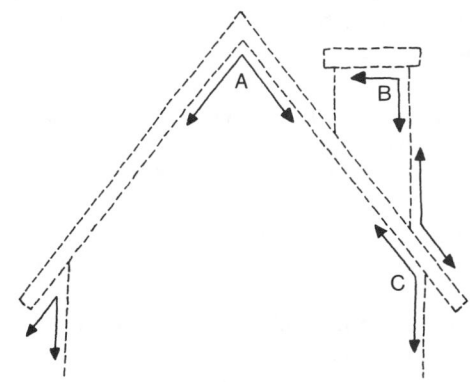

angle
(A) acute, *(B)* right, *(C)* obtuse

a	bat	ī	bite	ōō	tool	*th*	feather
ā	make	î	fierce	ou	out	th	bath
â	dare	o	dot	u	nut	hw	wheat
ä	father	ō	no	û	turn	zh	measure
e	net	ô	law, for	ch	church	ə	about, open
ē	be	oi	soil	ng	ring		pencil, atom
i	dip	oo	look	sh	shade		circus

angry *adjective* **1.** Feeling or showing anger: *I was angry at her for telling my secret.* **2.** Red, sore, and painful: *He had an angry sore that would not heal.*
an·gry (ang′ grē) □*adjective* **angrier, angriest**

anguish *noun* Very great pain or suffering of body or mind.
an·guish (ang′ gwish) □*noun*

animal *noun* A living thing that is not a plant. Animals can usually move from place to place, and they eat plants or other animals as food. Human beings, ants, fish, birds, and elephants are animals.
an·i·mal (an′ ə məl) □*noun, plural* **animals**

animosity *noun* Strong hatred; ill will: *The looks on their faces showed their animosity.*
an·i·mos·i·ty (an′ə mos′i tē) □*noun*

ankle *noun* The joint connecting the foot and the leg.
an·kle (ang′ kəl) □*noun, plural* **ankles**

anklet *noun* A short sock that reaches just above the ankle.
an·klet (ang′ klit) □*noun, plural* **anklets**

annex *verb* To add something to something else: *The state annexed the island off its coast.* □*noun* A building or structure that is added to another: *the new library annex.*
an·nex (ə neks′) □*verb* **annexed, annexing, annexes** □*noun* (an′ eks′), *plural* **annexes**

annihilate *verb* To destroy completely: *The eruption of the volcano annihilated the village.*
an·ni·hi·late (ə nī′ə lāt′) □*verb* **annihilated, annihilating, annihilates**

anniversary *noun* The return each year of the date on which an event happened: *a wedding anniversary.*
an·ni·ver·sa·ry (an′ə vûr′ sə rē) □*noun, plural* **anniversaries**

announce *verb* To make known: *The governor announced that he would not run for office again.*
an·nounce (ə nouns′) □*verb* **announced, announcing, announces**

announcement *noun* Something that has been announced; a public statement or notice: *a newspaper announcement of a sale.*
an·nounce·ment (ə nouns′ mənt) □*noun, plural* **announcements**

announcer *noun* Someone who introduces programs, reads news, or presents commercials on radio or television.
an·nounc·er (ə noun′ sər) □*noun, plural* **announcers**

annoy *verb* To make someone angry or impatient: *His teasing annoyed his sister.*
an·noy (ə noi′) □*verb* **annoyed, annoying, annoys**

SYNONYMS: **annoy, bother, pester**

These verbs mean to make someone angry or impatient: *The child's rude behavior annoyed the teacher. The music bothered him while he was trying to study. The boy pestered his mother with questions while she was cooking.*

---

annoyance *noun* **1.** Someone or something that annoys: *The sound of the airplanes was an annoyance during the outdoor concert.* **2.** The feeling of being annoyed: *She expressed her annoyance that I had kept her waiting.*
an·noy·ance (ə noi′ əns) □*noun, plural* **annoyances**

annual *adjective* **1.** Happening or done every year; yearly: *Our school has an annual picnic in June.* **2.** For or in one year: *an annual salary of $30,000.*
an·nu·al (an′ yoo əl) □*adjective*

anonymous *adjective* **1.** From or by a person whose identity is not known: *an anonymous phone call.* **2.** From or by a person whose name is kept secret: *The wealthy woman made an anonymous gift to the hospital.*
a·non·y·mous (ə non′ə məs) □*adjective*

another *adjective* **1.** Some other; different: *He has another edition of that book.* **2.** One more; additional: *Have another piece of cake.* **3.** Of the same kind as; equal to: *He thinks he's another George Washington.*
□*pronoun* **1.** An additional one: *I finished my soda and ordered another.* **2.** A different one: *This dress doesn't fit; give me another.*
an·oth·er (ə nuth′ ər) □*adjective* and *pronoun*

answer *noun* **1.** Something said or written in return to a question or statement: *My answer is "yes." She sent an answer to my letter.* **2.** A solution to a problem: *The answers to the puzzle are on a different page.*
□*verb* **1.** To speak or write in return to a question or statement: *She answered "no" to all my questions.* **2.** To act in response to a signal: *She answered the phone on the second ring.* **3.** To correspond to; match: *He answers to the description the police gave.*
an·swer (an′ sər) □*noun, plural* **answers** □*verb* **answered, answering, answers**

ant *noun* An insect that lives with others of
the same kind in large colonies.
ant (ant) ☐*noun, plural* **ants**

ant

antagonism *noun* Unfriendly or hostile feeling: *There was antagonism between the farmers and those who lived in town.*
an·tag·o·nism (an **tag′**ə niz′əm) ☐*noun*

antagonize *verb* To earn the antagonism of:
If you want his help, don't antagonize him.
an·tag·o·nize (an **tag′**ə nīz′) ☐*verb*
  antagonized, antagonizing, antagonizes

antarctic *adjective* Of, at, or near the South
Pole.
  ☐*noun* **the Antarctic** The south polar region.
ant·arc·tic (ant **ärk′**tik *or* ant **är′**tik)
  ☐*adjective* ☐*noun*

anteater *noun* An animal that feeds on ants
and other insects. It has no teeth, a long snout,
and a long, sticky tongue that it uses to catch
its food.
ant·eat·er (ant′ ē′tər) ☐*noun, plural* **anteaters**

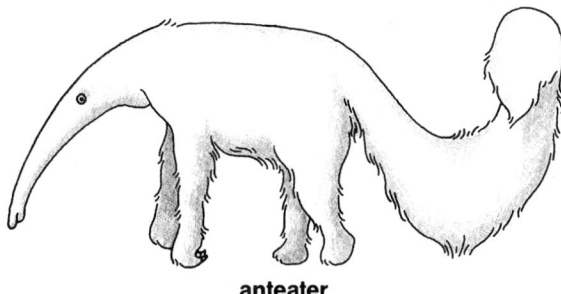

anteater

antelope *noun* **1.** A horned animal of Africa
and Asia. It looks like a deer but is related to
the goat. **2.** The pronghorn.

an·te·lope (an′tə lōp′) ☐*noun, plural*
  antelope or **antelopes**

antenna *noun* **1.** *plural* **antennae** One of a
pair of long, thin feelers on the head of an
animal. Insects and lobsters have antennae.
2. *plural* **antennas** An aerial for sending or receiving radio and television signals.
an·ten·na (an ten′ə) ☐*noun, plural*
  an·ten·nae (an ten′ē) and **antennas**

antenna
Antennae of a butterfly

anthem *noun* A song of loyalty, devotion, or
praise: *"The Star-Spangled Banner" is the national anthem of the United States.*
an·them (an′thəm) ☐*noun, plural* **anthems**

anther *noun* The part of the stamen of a
flower that produces pollen.
an·ther (an′thər) ☐*noun, plural* **anthers**

anther

a bat	ī bite	ōō tool	*th* feather
ā make	î fierce	ou out	th bath
â dare	o dot	u nut	hw wheat
ä father	ō no	û turn	zh measure
e net	ô law, for	ch church	ə about, open
ē be	oi soil	ng ring	pencil, atom
i dip	oo look	sh shade	circus

anthology *noun* A collection of poems, articles, or stories by different authors.
an·thol·o·gy (an **thol′**ə jē) □*noun, plural* **anthologies**

anthracite *noun* A kind of coal that is hard and makes little smoke when it burns.
an·thra·cite (**an′**thrə sīt′) □*noun*

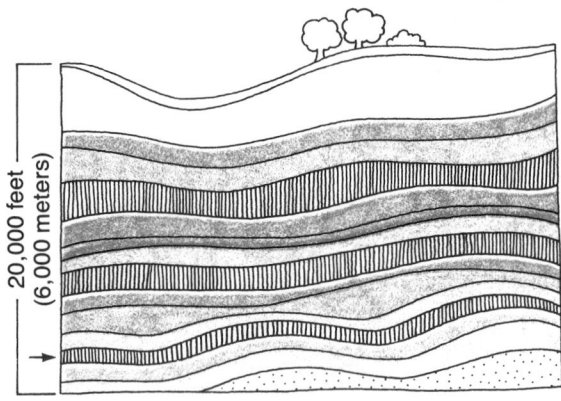

anthracite
Beneath the surface of the earth

antibiotic *noun* A substance produced by certain molds or bacteria that can kill or slow the growth of germs that cause disease.
an·ti·bi·ot·ic (an′ti bī **ot′**ik) □*noun, plural* **antibiotics**

antibody *noun* A substance produced in the blood of human beings and animals that destroys or weakens germs.
an·ti·bod·y (**an′**ti bod′ē) □*noun, plural* **antibodies**

anticipate *verb* To look forward to; expect: *We had not anticipated such a big audience.*
an·tic·i·pate (an **tis′**ə pāt′) □*verb* **anticipated, anticipating, anticipates**

anticipation *noun* The act of anticipating; expectation: *He smiled in anticipation of a fine dinner.*
an·tic·i·pa·tion (an tis′ə **pā′**shən) □*noun, plural* **anticipations**

antidote *noun* A substance, especially a medicine, that acts against the harmful effects of a poison.
an·ti·dote (**an′**ti dōt′) □*noun, plural* **antidotes**

antique *noun* Something made a long time ago: *This rocking chair is an early American antique.*
□*adjective* Of times long ago; ancient: *an antique music box.*

an·tique (an **tēk′**) □*noun, plural* **antiques**
□*adjective*

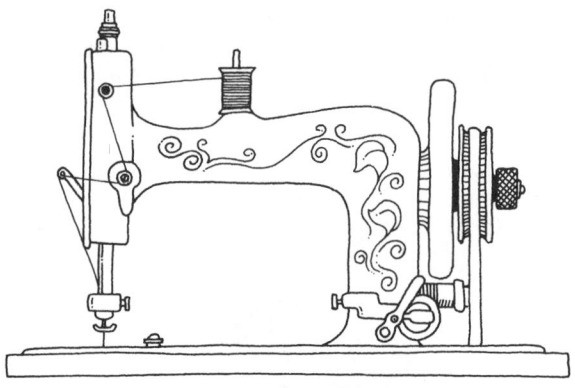

antique
An antique sewing machine

antiseptic *noun* A substance that destroys harmful bacteria or stops them from growing. Alcohol is an antiseptic.
an·ti·sep·tic (an′ti **sep′**tik) □*noun, plural* **antiseptics**

antiseptic

antitoxin *noun* An antibody that can protect a person against certain diseases.
an·ti·tox·in (an′ti **tok′**sin) □*noun, plural* **antitoxins**

antler *noun* One of the two bony growths on the head of a deer or related animal. Antlers grow each year and are shed at the end of a season.
ant·ler (**ant′**lər) □*noun, plural* **antlers**

antonym *noun* A word that means the opposite of another word. For example, "hot" is the antonym of "cold."
an·to·nym (**an′**tə nim′) □*noun, plural* **antonyms**

anvil   *noun* A heavy block of iron or steel with a smooth, flat top on which metals are hammered and shaped.
an·vil (**an′**vil) □*noun, plural* **anvils**

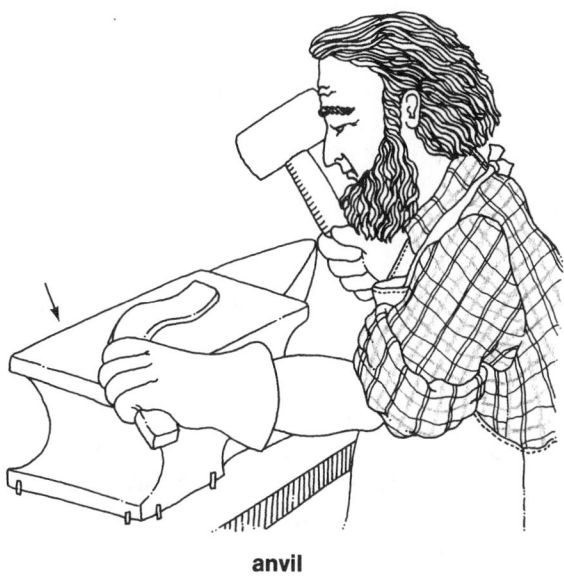
anvil

anxiety   *noun* **1.** An uneasy feeling about what might happen; worry: *Darkness increased our anxiety about their safety.* **2.** Eager desire: *My anxiety to succeed made me work hard.*
anx·i·e·ty (ang **zī′**i tē) □*noun, plural* **anxieties**

anxious   *adjective* **1.** Uneasy about what might happen; worried: *Being alone in the big city made us anxious.* **2.** Filled with eager desire: *I was anxious to begin working.*
anx·ious (**angk′**shəs) □*adjective*

any   *adjective* **1.** One out of three or more: *Take any piece you want.* **2.** Every: *Any friend would do the same to help.* **3.** Some: *Is there any milk?* **4.** Much: *He doesn't need any strength to read a book.*
□*pronoun* **1.** Any person or persons: *Are there any here who think so?* **2.** Anything: *Did you buy fruit? No, I didn't buy any.*
□*adverb* At all: *He doesn't feel any better.*
an·y (**en′**ē) □*adjective* □*pronoun* □*adverb*

anybody   *pronoun* Any person; anyone: *Has anybody called you today?*
an·y·bod·y (**en′**ē bod′ē) □*pronoun*

anyhow   *adverb* In any case; anyway: *The store was closed, but it was too late to shop anyhow.*
an·y·how (**en′**ē hou′) □*adverb*

anyone   *pronoun* Any person; anybody: *Has anyone seen the dog today?*
an·y·one (**en′**ē wun′) □*pronoun*

anyplace   *adverb* To, in, or at any place; wherever: *I can go anyplace I want.*
an·y·place (**en′**ē plās′) □*adverb*

anything   *pronoun* Any thing whatever: *I'll cook anything you want to eat.*
□*adverb* At all: *Her dress isn't anything like mine.*
an·y·thing (**en′**ē thing′) □*pronoun* □*adverb*

anytime   *adverb* At any time whatever: *You may go to the movies anytime you want.*
an·y·time (**en′**ē tīm′) □*adverb*

anyway   *adverb* At any rate; anyhow: *I was very tired but I went to the meeting anyway.*
an·y·way (**en′**ē wā′) □*adverb*

anywhere   *adverb* **1.** To, in, or at any place: *They can travel anywhere they want to.* **2.** At all: *Before I was anywhere near him, he ran away.*
an·y·where (**en′**ē hwâr′ *or* **en′**ē wâr′) □*adverb*

aorta   *noun* The largest artery of the body. It begins at the left ventricle of the heart and carries blood to all the organs of the body except the lungs.
a·or·ta (ā **ôr′**tə) □*noun, plural* **aortas**

apart   *adverb* **1.** Away from each other in time or space: *The runners began the race five minutes apart. Those cities are about ten miles apart.* **2.** In or into separate parts; to pieces: *His old car was falling apart.*
a·part (ə **pärt′**) □*adverb*

apart from   *preposition* Other than; besides: *Apart from her work, she has very few interests.*

apartment   *noun* A room or set of rooms to live in. An apartment is often in a building that has other apartments in it.
a·part·ment (ə **pärt′**mənt) □*noun, plural* **apartments**

apathy   *noun* Lack of feeling or interest: *We listened to the dull speech with apathy.*
ap·a·thy (**ap′**ə thē) □*noun*

a	bat	ī	bite	o͞o	tool	*th*	feather
ā	make	i	fierce	ou	out	th	bath
â	dare	o	dot	u	nut	hw	wheat
ä	father	ō	no	û	turn	zh	measure
e	net	ô	law, for	ch	church	ə	about, open
ē	be	oi	soil	ng	ring		pencil, atom
i	dip	oo	look	sh	shade		circus

ape   *noun* A large animal that has no tail and is related to the monkeys. Gorillas, chimpanzees, and orangutans are apes.
□*verb* To imitate the actions of; mimic: *The boy apes his brother's way of walking.*
ape (āp) □*noun, plural* **apes** □*verb* **aped, aping, apes**

ape

aphid   *noun* A small insect that sucks juices from plants.
a·phid (ā′fid *or* af′id) □*noun, plural* **aphids**

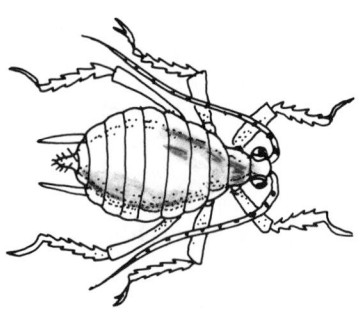

aphid

apiece   *adverb* To or for each one; each: *Stamps cost 20¢ apiece.*
a·piece (ə pēs′) □*adverb*

apologize   *verb* To say one is sorry; make an apology: *I apologized for losing my temper.*
a·pol·o·gize (ə pol′ə jīz′) □*verb* **apologized, apologizing, apologizes**

apology   *noun* A statement that one is sorry for something: *I made an apology to my piano teacher for being late.*
a·pol·o·gy (ə pol′ə jē) □*noun, plural* **apologies**

Apostle   *noun* One of the twelve original disciples of Christ.
A·pos·tle (ə pos′əl) □*noun, plural* **Apostles**

apostrophe   *noun* A punctuation mark (′) that: **1.** Shows that one or more letters or figures have been left out of a word: *aren't* for *are not.* **2.** Shows possession or ownership: *Tom's hat.* **3.** Is used in writing the plural of numbers and letters: *two 100's; four A's.*
a·pos·tro·phe (ə pos′trə fē) □*noun, plural* **apostrophes**

appall   *verb* To fill with horror and amazement; dismay: *The news about the earthquake appalled them.*
ap·pall (ə pôl′) □*verb* **appalled, appalling, appalls**

apparatus   *noun* Something that is used to do or perform a certain task: *Hoses are part of the apparatus of firefighters.*
ap·pa·ra·tus (ap′ə rā′təs *or* ap′ə rat′əs) □*noun, plural* **apparatus** *or* **apparatuses**

apparel   *noun* Clothing; attire: *a store that sells women's apparel.*
ap·par·el (ə par′əl) □*noun*

apparent   *adjective* **1.** Easily seen or understood; obvious: *Her scar was apparent even though she wore make-up. It was apparent to me that he was lying.* **2.** Appearing to be true or real even though it may not be: *His size was an apparent advantage, but the smaller boy was really stronger.*
ap·par·ent (ə par′ənt) □*adjective*

apparently   *adverb* As far as one can tell: *The concert is apparently going to start late.*
ap·par·ent·ly (ə par′ənt lē) □*adverb*

appeal   *verb* **1.** To make a strong or urgent request, especially for help or sympathy: *They appealed to the governor for food and shelter.* **2.** To be attractive or interesting: *The idea appeals to her.*
□*noun* **1.** A strong or urgent request: *During the flood the governor made an appeal for food and clothing.* **2.** The power of attracting: *The circus has great appeal for children.*
ap·peal (ə pēl′) □*verb* **appealed, appealing, appeals** □*noun, plural* **appeals**

appear   *verb* **1.** To come into view; be seen: *A truck appeared at the top of the hill.* **2.** To have the appearance of: *The boy appeared happy enough.* **3.** To come before the public: *He has appeared in many movies.*
ap·pear (ə pîr′) □*verb* **appeared, appearing, appears**

appearance *noun* **1.** The act of coming into view: *The soldiers were startled by the sudden appearance of the enemy.* **2.** The way someone or something looks: *She hid her anger under a cheerful appearance.* **3.** The act of coming before the public: *It has been many years since her last appearance in a movie.*
ap·pear·ance (ə pîr′ əns) □*noun, plural*
appearances

appease *verb* To satisfy: *I appeased the bully by giving him half of my allowance.*
ap·pease (ə pēz′) □*verb* **appeased,
appeasing, appeases**

appendicitis *noun* A painful swelling or inflammation of the appendix.
ap·pen·di·ci·tis (ə pen′di sī′tis) □*noun*

appendix *noun* **1.** A section at the end of a book that gives additional information such as charts, tables, and lists. **2.** A thin, closed tube that is attached to the large intestine.
ap·pen·dix (ə pen′ diks) □*noun, plural*
appendixes

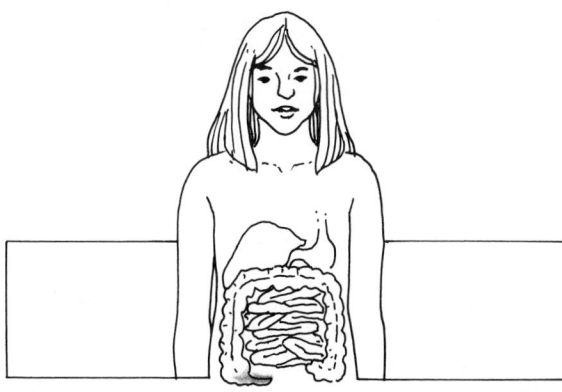
appendix
In the body

appetite *noun* **1.** A desire for food. **2.** A desire: *He has a great appetite for work.*
ap·pe·tite (ap′i tīt′) □*noun, plural* **appetites**

applaud *verb* To show approval of, especially by clapping the hands.
ap·plaud (ə plôd′) □*verb* **applauded,
applauding, applauds**

applause *noun* Approval shown especially by clapping the hands.
ap·plause (ə plôz′) □*noun*

apple *noun* A firm, rounded, edible fruit with red, green, or yellow skin.
ap·ple (ap′ əl) □*noun, plural* **apples**

apple
Fruit and tree

appliance *noun* A small machine, as a vacuum cleaner, used to do a household task.
ap·pli·ance (ə plī′ əns) □*noun, plural*
appliances

appliance

application *noun* **1.** The act of laying on or spreading: *the application of polish to the chair.* **2.** The act of putting into action; use: *the application of information to solve a problem.* **3.** A request, as for a job: *She made an application for the position.*

a	bat	ī	bite	ōō	tool	*th*	feather
ā	make	î	fierce	ou	out	th	bath
â	dare	o	dot	u	nut	hw	wheat
ä	father	ō	no	û	turn	zh	measure
e	net	ô	law, for	ch	church	ə	about, open
ē	be	oi	soil	ng	ring		pencil, atom
i	dip	oo	look	sh	shade		circus

ap·pli·ca·tion (ap'li **kā'**shən) □*noun, plural* **applications**

apply *verb* **1.** To spread: *He sanded the wood and then applied paint.* **2.** To put into action; use: *To stop the car you must apply the brakes.* **3.** To cause to work or do with care and attention: *She applied herself to playing the violin.* **4.** To have to do with; concern: *This rule applies to you.* **5.** To make a request, especially for employment, acceptance, or admission: *She applied for a job.*
ap·ply (ə **plī'**) □*verb* **applied, applying, applies**

apply

appoint *verb* To name for an office, duty, or position; designate: *The governor appointed her to the committee.*
ap·point (ə **point'**) □*verb* **appointed, appointing, appoints**

appointment *noun* **1.** The act of appointing to an office, duty, or position: *The appointment of a new chairman will be announced today.* **2.** An office, duty, or position to which a person has been appointed: *She accepted the appointment as conductor of the orchestra.* **3.** An arrangement to meet with someone at a particular time and place; engagement: *I have an appointment to play tennis.*
ap·point·ment (ə **point'**mənt) □*noun, plural* **appointments**

appraise *verb* To set a value on: *The expert appraised the painting at $500.*
ap·praise (ə **prāz'**) □*verb* **appraised, appraising, appraises**

appreciate *verb* **1.** To recognize the worth or importance of: *She thought no one appreciated her work.* **2.** To be grateful for: *We appreciate your kindness.*

ap·pre·ci·ate (ə **prē'**shē āt') □*verb* **appreciated, appreciating, appreciates**

> *SYNONYMS:* **appreciate, prize, value**
> These verbs mean to recognize the worth or importance of: *We appreciate good food. All citizens prize their freedom. He values accuracy more than speed.*

appreciation *noun* **1.** The act of recognizing the worth or importance of something: *an appreciation of music.* **2.** Gratitude: *He expressed his appreciation with a gift.*
ap·pre·ci·a·tion (ə **prē'**shē **ā'**shən) □*noun*

apprehend *verb* To take into custody; arrest: *The police apprehended the thief after a chase.*
ap·pre·hend (ap'ri **hend'**) □*verb* **apprehended, apprehending, apprehends**

apprehend

apprehension *noun* **1.** Fear of what might happen: *Going to a new school filled me with apprehension.* **2.** Capture or arrest.
ap·pre·hen·sion (ap'ri **hen'**shən) □*noun, plural* **apprehensions**

apprentice *noun* Someone who learns a skill or trade by working for a skilled worker.
ap·pren·tice (ə **pren'**tis) □*noun, plural* **apprentices**

approach *verb* **1.** To come near or nearer to: *We approached the town by car. Spring is approaching.* **2.** To bring up a request or plan: *I approached the boss for a raise.*
□*noun* **1.** The act of approaching: *Birds fly south at the approach of winter.* **2.** A way of dealing or working with someone or something: *We tried a new approach to the problem.* **3.** A way of reaching a place; access: *The only approach to the house is a dirt road.*

ap·proach (ə prōch′) ☐*verb* **approached, approaching, approaches** ☐*noun, plural* **approaches**

appropriate *adjective* Suitable for a certain person, place, or event; proper: *A bathing suit is appropriate for swimming.*
ap·pro·pri·ate (ə prō′prē it) ☐*adjective*

approval *noun* **1.** Favorable opinion: *She showed her approval with a smile.* **2.** Permission or consent: *I have her approval for my project.*
ap·prov·al (ə prōo′vəl) ☐*noun, plural* **approvals**

approve *verb* **1.** To have a favorable opinion of: *My parents don't approve of my playing football.* **2.** To give permission or consent to: *The town council approved the mayor's budget.*
ap·prove (ə prōov′) ☐*verb* **approved, approving, approves**

approximate *adjective* Almost exact or accurate: *The approximate height of the tree is 100 feet.*
ap·prox·i·mate (ə prok′sə mit) ☐*adjective*

apricot *noun* A juicy, yellowish, edible fruit that looks like a small peach.
ap·ri·cot (ap′ri kot′ *or* ā′pri kot′) ☐*noun, plural* **apricots**

apricot

April *noun* The fourth month of the year. April has 30 days.
A·pril (ā′prəl) ☐*noun*

WORD HISTORY: **April**

The name *April* comes from a Latin word, whose exact origin is unknown. All of the names of the months originated in Latin.

---

apron *noun* A garment worn over the front of the body and tied around the waist to keep a person's clothes clean.
a·pron (ā′prən) ☐*noun, plural* **aprons**

apt *adjective* **1.** Having or showing a tendency; likely: *If you're not careful when you do your homework, you're apt to make mistakes.* **2.** Quick to learn or understand; bright: *an apt student.*
apt (apt) ☐*adjective*

aptitude *noun* **1.** A natural ability or talent: *She has an aptitude for music.* **2.** The ability to learn or understand quickly: *He is a student of great aptitude.*
ap·ti·tude (ap′ti tōod′ *or* ap′ti tyōod′) ☐*noun, plural* **aptitudes**

aquarium *noun* **1.** A tank, glass bowl, or other container filled with water in which fish, water animals, and water plants are kept. **2.** A building in which collections of fish, water animals, and water plants are kept and shown.
a·quar·i·um (ə kwâr′ē əm) ☐*noun, plural* **aquariums**

aquarium

aqueduct *noun* A large pipe or channel that carries water a long distance.
aq·ue·duct (ak′wi dukt′) ☐*noun, plural* **aqueducts**

Arab *noun* **1.** Someone who was born or lives in Arabia. **2.** A member of any of the various Arabic-speaking peoples of Asia and Africa. ☐*adjective* Of Arabia or the Arabs.
Ar·ab (ar′əb) ☐*noun, plural* **Arabs** ☐*adjective*

a bat	ī bite	ōo tool	*th* feather
ā make	î fierce	ou out	th bath
â dare	o dot	u nut	hw wheat
ä father	ō no	û turn	zh measure
e net	ô law, for	ch church	ə about, open
ē be	oi soil	ng ring	pencil, atom
i dip	oo look	sh shade	circus

Arabian *adjective* Having to do with Arabia or its people.
▢*noun* Someone who was born or lives in Arabia.
A·ra·bi·an (ə rā′ bē ən) ▢*adjective* ▢*noun,* plural **Arabians**

Arabic *noun* The language of the Arabs.
▢*adjective* Of the Arabs or their language.
Ar·a·bic (ar′ə bik) ▢*noun* ▢*adjective*

Arabic numeral *noun* One of the numerical figures 1, 2, 3, 4, 5, 6, 7, 8, 9, and 0.

arbitrary *adjective* Based on wishes, opinions, or feelings and not on law or reason: *An arbitrary decision is often unfair.*
ar·bi·trar·y (är′bi trer′ē) ▢*adjective*

arbitrate *verb* To make a decision that settles an argument: *The coach arbitrated the argument between the two players.*
ar·bi·trate (är′bi trāt′) ▢*verb* **arbitrated, arbitrating, arbitrates**

arbitration *noun* The process of settling a dispute by having an outside person listen to both sides and make a decision.
ar·bi·tra·tion (är′bi trā′shən) ▢*noun,* plural **arbitrations**

arbor *noun* A shaded place formed by trees or bushes or by vines growing on frames.
ar·bor (är′bər) ▢*noun,* plural **arbors**

arc *noun* **1.** A part of a curve, especially of a circle. **2.** Something that is curved: *She bent the wire into an arc.*
arc (ärk) ▢*noun,* plural **arcs**

arch *noun* **1.** A curved structure that supports the weight of the material on top of it. Arches often form the tops of doorways and windows. **2.** Something that is curved like an arch: *the arch of a rainbow.*
▢*verb* To form an arch; curve: *She arched her eyebrows in surprise.*
arch (ärch) ▢*noun,* plural **arches** ▢*verb* **arched, arching, arches**

arch

archaeologist *noun* Someone who practices archaeology.
ar·chae·ol·o·gist (är′kē ol′ə jist) ▢*noun,* plural **archaeologists**

archaeology *noun* The scientific study of the way of life and activities of people of ancient times. Archaeologists dig up the ruins of buildings and study the tools, pottery, weapons, and household items that are found there.
ar·chae·ol·o·gy (är′kē ol′ə jē) ▢*noun*

archer *noun* Someone who shoots with a bow and arrows.
arch·er (är′chər) ▢*noun,* plural **archers**

archery *noun* The sport or skill of shooting with a bow and arrows.
arch·er·y (är′chə rē) ▢*noun*

architect *noun* Someone who designs buildings and supervises their construction.
ar·chi·tect (är′ki tekt′) ▢*noun,* plural **architects**

architecture *noun* **1.** The profession or skill of designing and planning buildings. **2.** A style or method of building: *Roman architecture.*
ar·chi·tec·ture (är′ki tēk′chər) ▢*noun*

arctic *adjective* Of, at, or near the North Pole; far north.
▢*noun* **the Arctic.** The north polar region.
arc·tic (ärk′tik *or* är′tik) ▢*adjective* ▢*noun*

are *verb* **1.** The second person singular present tense of **be:** *You are wrong.* **2.** The first, second, and third person plural present tense of **be:** *We are cold. You are all invited. They are tired.*
are (är) ▢*verb*

area *noun* **1.** A section or region, as of land: *We live on the coast in a fishing area.* **2.** A space set aside for a particular use: *a dining area.* **3.** The measure of a surface: *The area of our garden is 20 square feet.* **4.** A field or range of study, interest, or activity: *That subject is in the area of general science.*
ar·e·a (âr′ē ə) ▢*noun,* plural **areas**

area code *noun* A set of three numbers given to each telephone area in the United States and used to call from one part of the country to another.

arena *noun* An enclosed area used for sports events and entertainments such as circuses and concerts.
a·re·na (ə rē′nə) ▢*noun,* plural **arenas**

aren't Contraction of "are not."
aren't (ärnt *or* är′ ənt)

argue *verb* **1.** To have a quarrel or disagreement: *They have been arguing about money.* **2.** To give reasons for or against: *My mother argued against buying a new car.*
ar·gue (är′gyōō) ▢*verb* **argued, arguing, argues**

argument *noun* **1.** A quarrel or disagreement: *They had an argument about who would cut the grass.* **2.** A reason given for or against something: *His argument for staying home was that he could work better there.*
ar·gu·ment (är′gyə mənt) ▢*noun, plural* **arguments**

arid *adjective* Having little or no rainfall; dry: *an arid desert.*
ar·id (ar′id) ▢*adjective*

arise *verb* **1.** To get up; rise: *He arose from his seat.* **2.** To move upward; ascend: *Smoke arose from the campfire.* **3.** To come into being; appear: *When the chance arose, he took it.*
a·rise (ə riz′) ▢*verb* **arose, arisen, arising, arises**

aristocracy *noun* **1.** A class of people who have a high position in society because of birth, title, or rank. Kings, queens, princes, princesses, dukes, and duchesses all belong to the aristocracy. **2.** A group of people who are thought to be superior because of their ability, intelligence, or wealth.
ar·is·toc·ra·cy (ar′i **stok′**rə sē) ▢*noun, plural* **aristocracies**

aristocrat *noun* Someone who belongs to the aristocracy.
a·ris·to·crat (ə **ris′**tə krat′) ▢*noun, plural* **aristocrats**

arithmetic *noun* **1.** The study of numbers and their use in addition, subtraction, multiplication, and division. **2.** The act of adding, subtracting, multiplying, or dividing.
a·rith·me·tic (ə **rith′**mə tik) ▢*noun*

ark *noun* **1.** The large ship built by Noah that saved him, his family, and two of every animal from the great flood which God sent to punish the people of the world. **2.** The cabinet in a synagogue in which the Torah is kept.
ark (ärk) ▢*noun, plural* **arks**

arm[1] *noun* **1.** The part of the body between the shoulder and the hand. **2.** Something shaped or used like an arm: *the arms of a chair; an arm of the sea.*
arm (ärm) ▢*noun, plural* **arms**

arm[2] *noun* A weapon that can be used in war or for defense. Guns and missiles are arms.

▢*verb* **1.** To supply with weapons: *They armed the soldiers for the battle.* **2.** To supply with something that protects or strengthens: *She left for the hike armed with insect spray.*
arm (ärm) ▢*noun, plural* **arms** ▢*verb* **armed, arming, arms**

armada *noun* A big fleet of warships.
ar·ma·da (är mä′də) ▢*noun, plural* **armadas**

armadillo *noun* A burrowing animal whose body has a bony covering that looks like armor. Armadillos live in South America and southern North America.
ar·ma·dil·lo (är′mə **dil′**ō) ▢*noun, plural* **armadillos**

armadillo

armament *noun* **1.** Weapons and war supplies. **2.** All the military forces and war equipment of a country.
ar·ma·ment (är′mə mənt) ▢*noun, plural* **armaments**

armchair *noun* A chair with supports on the sides for a person's arms.
arm·chair (ärm′châr′) ▢*noun, plural* **armchairs**

armistice *noun* A temporary stop in fighting agreed to by both sides in a war; truce.
ar·mi·stice (är′mi stis) ▢*noun, plural* **armistices**

armor *noun* **1.** A heavy covering, usually made of metal, worn to protect the body in battle. **2.** A protective covering, such as the

a bat	ī bite	ōō tool	*th* feather
ā make	î fierce	ou out	th bath
â dare	o dot	u nut	hw wheat
ä father	ō no	û turn	zh measure
e net	ô law, for	ch church	ə about, open
ē be	oi soil	ng ring	pencil, atom
i dip	oo look	sh shade	circus

hard shell of a turtle or the metal plates on a warship.
ar·mor (är′mər) □*noun*

armored *adjective* Covered with or having armor: *an armored car.*
ar·mored (är′mərd) □*adjective*

armory *noun* A place where military weapons are stored.
ar·mor·y (är′mə rē) □*noun, plural* **armories**

armpit *noun* The hollow part under the arm at the shoulder.
arm·pit (ärm′pit′) □*noun, plural* **armpits**

army *noun* **1.** A large group of soldiers organized and trained to fight on land. **2.** A large group of people organized for a purpose: *It took an army of men to paint the large house.*
ar·my (är′mē) □*noun, plural* **armies**

aroma *noun* A pleasant smell; fragrance: *the aroma of bread just out of the oven.*
a·ro·ma (ə rō′mə) □*noun, plural* **aromas**

arose *verb* The past tense of **arise:** *Problems with the car arose last week.*
a·rose (ə rōz′) □*verb*

around *preposition* **1.** So as to surround, enclose, or encircle: *She put her arms around the baby.* **2.** On or to all sides of: *a tree with flowers around it.* **3.** Here and there in: *The reporter traveled around the state.* **4.** In the neighborhood of; near: *He arrived around noon.* **5.** On or to the other side of: *We drove around the mountain.*
□*adverb* **1.** Here and there; all over: *Come to the library and I'll take you around.* **2.** In a circle: *The students gathered around to talk to the teacher.* **3.** In the neighborhood; nearby: *He hung around and watched.* **4.** In or toward the opposite position or direction: *She turned around quickly and ran.*
a·round (ə round′) □*preposition* □*adverb*

arouse *verb* **1.** To awaken from sleep. **2.** To stir up; excite: *The movie aroused a lively discussion.*
a·rouse (ə rouz′) □*verb* **aroused, arousing, arouses**

arrange *verb* **1.** To put in proper order: *Arrange these words alphabetically.* **2.** To prepare for; plan: *Mother will arrange a dinner for eight.* **3.** To adapt a piece of music for instruments or voices other than those for which it was originally written.
ar·range (ə rānj′) □*verb* **arranged, arranging, arranges**

arrangement *noun* **1.** The act of putting in order: *The arrangement of the tables for the party took time.* **2.** The way or style in which things are arranged; order: *an alphabetical arrangement of names.* **3.** A group of things that have been arranged: *a flower arrangement.* **4.** A plan; preparation: *We made arrangements to go to Europe.*
ar·range·ment (ə rānj′mənt) □*noun, plural* **arrangements**

arrangement

array *noun* An orderly arrangement or display: *soldiers in battle array; a store with a wide array of shoes.*
□*verb* To put in order: *The lieutenant arrayed the troops for the attack.*
ar·ray (ə rā′) □*noun, plural* **arrays** □*verb* **arrayed, arraying, arrays**

array

arrest *verb* To seize and hold by authority of the law: *The police arrested the thief.*
□*noun* The act of seizing and holding by authority of the law.
ar·rest (ə rest′) □*verb* **arrested, arresting, arrests** □*noun, plural* **arrests**

arrival *noun* **1.** The act of arriving: *We waited at the airport for the arrival of the movie*

star. **2.** Someone or something that has arrived: *The hotel was full of new arrivals.*
ar·ri·val (ə rī′vəl) ▢*noun, plural* **arrivals**

arrive *verb* **1.** To come to a place: *They arrived by train.* **2.** To reach or come to a goal: *They tried to arrive at an agreement.*
ar·rive (ə rīv′) ▢*verb* **arrived, arriving, arrives**

arrogant *adjective* Having or showing a feeling of superiority; too proud.
ar·ro·gant (ar′ə gənt) ▢*adjective*

arrow *noun* **1.** A thin, straight shaft that is shot from a bow and has a sharp point at one end. **2.** Something shaped like an arrow.
ar·row (ar′ō) ▢*noun, plural* **arrows**

arrowhead *noun* The pointed tip of an arrow.
ar·row·head (ar′ō hed′) ▢*noun, plural* **arrowheads**

arrowhead

arsenal *noun* A building where weapons and ammunition are made or stored.
ar·se·nal (är′sə nəl) ▢*noun, plural* **arsenals**

arsenic *noun* A strong poison that has no taste, is white in color, and is used to kill weeds, rats, and insects.
ar·se·nic (är′sə nik) ▢*noun*

arson *noun* The crime of intentionally setting fire to buildings or other property.
ar·son (är′sən) ▢*noun*

art *noun* **1.** The use of the imagination to create something, such as a painting, musical composition, or poem. **2.** Works of art, such as paintings, sculpture, or drawings: *His art is on display at the museum.* **3.** A practical skill; craft: *the art of cooking.* **4.** An ability learned by experience: *the art of making friends.*
art (ärt) ▢*noun, plural* **arts**

art
Sculpture

artery *noun* **1.** Any of the tubes that carry blood from the heart to all parts of the body. **2.** A channel or main road: *The river was a major artery between the two towns.*
ar·ter·y (är′tə rē) ▢*noun, plural* **arteries**

arthritis *noun* Painful swelling of a joint of the body.
ar·thri·tis (är thrī′tis) ▢*noun*

artichoke *noun* The flower of a plant that looks like a thistle and is covered with thick, leafy scales. It is eaten as a vegetable.
ar·ti·choke (är′ti chōk′) ▢*noun, plural* **artichokes**

artichoke

a bat	ī bite	o͞o tool	*th* feather
ā make	i fierce	ou out	th bath
â dare	o dot	u nut	hw wheat
ä father	ō no	û turn	zh measure
e net	ô law, for	ch church	ə about, open
ē be	oi soil	ng ring	pencil, atom
i dip	oo look	sh shade	circus

article *noun* **1.** A written composition in a newspaper, magazine, or book: *Have you read the article on the war in the evening newspaper?* **2.** A section or item of a written document, such as a treaty or contract: *an article of the Constitution.* **3.** A particular thing; object: *A couch is an article of furniture.* **4.** A word, such as English *a, an,* or *the,* that modifies and limits a noun. *A* and *an* are indefinite articles. *The* is the definite article.
ar·ti·cle (**är′**ti kəl) □*noun, plural* **articles**

articulate *adjective* Able to express oneself clearly and effectively: *The senator was an articulate speaker.*
□*verb* To express clearly and effectively: *He articulated the feelings of the group.*
ar·tic·u·late (är **tik′**yə lit) □*adjective* □*verb* (är **tik′**yə lāt′) **articulated, articulating, articulates**

artificial *adjective* **1.** Made by human effort, not by nature; not natural: *artificial pearls.* **2.** Not genuine, honest, or real; insincere: *She gave an artificial smile.*
ar·ti·fi·cial (är′tə **fish′**əl) □*adjective*

artillery *noun* **1.** Large, heavy guns or cannons that are supported on carriages. **2.** The part of an army that uses artillery.
ar·til·ler·y (är **til′**ə rē) □*noun*

artist *noun* Someone who practices an art, such as painting or music.
art·ist (**är′**tist) □*noun, plural* **artists**

artist
A musician

artistic *adjective* Of or having to do with art or artists: *Her sculpture was popular in artistic circles.*
ar·tis·tic (är **tis′**tik) □*adjective*

as *adverb* **1.** To the same degree; equally: *He is as clever as you are.* **2.** For example: *large animals, as elephants.*
□*conjunction* **1.** To or in the same degree that: *happy as can be.* **2.** In the same way that: *Do as she tells you.* **3.** At the same time that; while: *She smiled as we met.* **4.** For the reason that; because: *He cooked dinner, as he was hungry.*
□*pronoun* **1.** That; who; which: *I received the same letter as you did.* **2.** A fact that: *The sun is hot, as everyone knows.*
□*preposition* **1.** In the same manner as; like: *The three left the room as one.* **2.** In the role or function of: *Father works as a firefighter.*
as (az *or* əz) □*adverb* □*conjunction* □*pronoun* □*preposition*

asbestos *noun* A gray mineral that does not burn. Asbestos fibers can be woven into fireproof material.
as·bes·tos (as **bes′**təs) □*noun*

ascend *verb* To go, move, or climb upward: *The balloon ascended slowly in the air. The hikers ascended the mountain.*
as·cend (ə **send′**) □*verb* **ascended, ascending, ascends**

ascend

ascent *noun* The act of going, moving, or climbing upward: *the ascent of smoke from the chimney; planned an ascent of the mountain.*
as·cent (ə **sent′**) □*noun, plural* **ascents**

ascertain *verb* To find out; make sure: *We ascertained that the house had not been damaged by the flood.*
as·cer·tain (as′ər **tān′**) □*verb* **ascertained, ascertaining, ascertains**

ash¹ *noun* The grayish, solid material left after something has burned completely: *The*

ashes of the campfire were completely cold.
ash (ash) □*noun, plural* **ashes**

ash² *noun* A tree that has leaves with many leaflets and strong, tough wood that is often used for making baseball bats.
ash (ash) □*noun, plural* **ashes**

ashamed *adjective* **1.** Feeling shame or guilt: *She was ashamed that she had lied.* **2.** Not wanting or willing to do something because of fear of being shamed: *He was ashamed to admit that a little girl had knocked him down.*
a·shamed (ə shāmd′) □*adjective*

ashore *adverb* On or to the shore: *The sailors stepped ashore on the island.*
a·shore (ə shôr′) □*adverb*

Asian *noun* Someone born or living in Asia. □*adjective* Of Asia or the Asians.
A·sian (ā′zhən *or* ā′shən) □*noun, plural* **Asians** □*adjective*

aside *adverb* **1.** To or toward one side: *She stepped aside so the children could pass.* **2.** In reserve for a special purpose or use: *He put some money aside to buy a new suit.*
a·side (ə sīd′) □*adverb*

ask *verb* **1.** To put a question to: *Her mother asked her why she was crying.* **2.** To seek an answer to: *The more questions you ask, the more you learn.* **3.** To make a request: *I asked for another hamburger.* **4.** To seek information about; inquire: *If you get lost, ask the way.* **5.** To invite: *Why don't we ask them for dinner?*
ask (ask) □*verb* **asked, asking, asks**

askew *adjective* and *adverb* Out of line; crooked: *Her hat is askew. She hung the picture askew.*
a·skew (ə skyoō′) □*adjective* and *adverb*

askew

asleep *adjective* **1.** Not awake; sleeping: *She was asleep when the phone rang.* **2.** Without

feeling; numb: *My hand is asleep.*
□*adverb* Into a condition of sleep: *He fell asleep quickly after the long hike.*
a·sleep (ə slēp′) □*adjective* □*adverb*

asparagus *noun* **1.** A plant grown for its young, tender green stalks. **2.** The stalks of the asparagus, eaten as a vegetable.
as·par·a·gus (ə spar′ə gəs) □*noun*

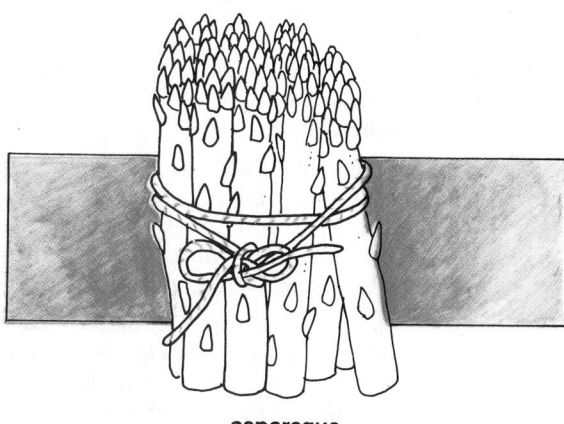

asparagus

aspect *noun* **1.** An element or side, as of a situation or idea: *We considered every aspect of our plan before we decided to go ahead.* **2.** Appearance to the mind or eye; look: *The sober black dress gave her a serious aspect.*
as·pect (as′pekt′) □*noun, plural* **aspects**

aspen *noun* A poplar tree with leaves that flutter in the lightest breeze.
as·pen (as′pən) □*noun, plural* **aspens**

asphalt *noun* A thick, sticky, brownish-black substance that is found in natural deposits or made by refining petroleum. It is mixed with sand and gravel and used to pave roads.
as·phalt (as′fôlt′) □*noun*

aspiration *noun* A strong desire to achieve something, especially something important.
as·pi·ra·tion (as′pə rā′shən) □*noun, plural* **aspirations**

aspirin *noun* **1.** A drug used to reduce fever and ease pain. **2.** A tablet of aspirin.
as·pi·rin (as′pə rin) □*noun, plural* **aspirins**

a	bat	ī	bite	oō	tool	*th*	feather
ā	make	î	fierce	ou	out	th	bath
â	dare	o	dot	u	nut	hw	wheat
ä	father	ō	no	û	turn	zh	measure
e	net	ô	law, for	ch	church	ə	about, open
ē	be	oi	soil	ng	ring		pencil, atom
i	dip	oo	look	sh	shade		circus

assassin *noun* A murderer, especially one who kills a person of political importance.
as·sas·sin (ə **sas′**in) □*noun, plural* **assassins**

assassinate *verb* To murder in a sudden attack, usually for political reasons: *They tried to assassinate the President.*
as·sas·si·nate (ə **sas′**ə nāt′) □*verb* **assassinated, assassinating, assassinates**

assassination *noun* The act of assassinating.
as·sas·si·na·tion (ə sas′ə **nā′**shən) □*noun, plural* **assassinations**

assault *noun* A violent attack: *The guerrillas made an assault on the enemy camp.*
□*verb* To make an assault on; attack violently.
as·sault (ə **sôlt′**) □*noun, plural* **assaults**
□*verb* **assaulted, assaulting, assaults**

assemble *verb* **1.** To bring or come together: *The teachers assembled the students in the auditorium. The campers assembled in the parking lot.* **2.** To fit or put together the parts of: *I assembled the jigsaw puzzle.* —See Synonyms at **gather.**
as·sem·ble (ə **sem′**bəl) □*verb* **assembled, assembling, assembles**

assembly *noun* **1.** A group of persons gathered together for a particular purpose or reason: *a school assembly.* **2.** Often **Assembly** A group or body of lawmakers that make up the lower house of a legislature in some states of the United States. **3.** The act of fitting or putting together a number of parts to make up a complete object: *The assembly of the model airplane took a long time.*
as·sem·bly (ə **sem′**blē) □*noun, plural* **assemblies**

assert *verb* **1.** To state or declare strongly and positively; claim: *The woman asserted that she had not stolen the necklace.* **2.** To show the existence of: *He asserted his independence by refusing to go to the party.*
as·sert (ə **sûrt′**) □*verb* **asserted, asserting, asserts**

assess *verb* **1.** To estimate the value of for taxation: *assessed the property at $12,000.* **2.** To charge or tax: *assessed each member of the club fifty cents.*
as·sess (ə **ses′**) □*verb* **assessed, assessing, assesses**

asset *noun* **1.** Something that is useful or valuable: *Her smile is her best asset.* **2. assets** All of the objects and property owned by a person, business, or group that are worth money: *Her assets include a house and a car.*
as·set (**as′**et′) □*noun, plural* **assets**

assign *verb* **1.** To give out; allot: *The teacher assigned the homework for tomorrow.* **2.** To appoint: *We were assigned to the entertainment committee.* **3.** To fix: *The mayor will assign a day for the parade.*
as·sign (ə **sīn′**) □*verb* **assigned, assigning, assigns**

assignment *noun* **1.** Something assigned: *Her assignment was to bring the cake.* **2.** The act of assigning or of being assigned: *His assignment to the school committee surprised everyone.*
as·sign·ment (ə **sīn′**mənt) □*noun, plural* **assignments**

assist *verb* To help; aid: *We assisted Dad with the marketing.*
as·sist (ə **sist′**) □*verb* **assisted, assisting, assists**

assistance *noun* Help; aid: *I asked for their assistance drawing up a new schedule.*
as·sis·tance (ə **sis′**təns) □*noun*

assistant *noun* Someone who assists: *My uncle is an assistant to the President.*
□*adjective* Helping: *an assistant editor.*
as·sis·tant (ə **sis′**tənt) □*noun, plural* **assistants**

associate *verb* **1.** To bring together in one's mind; connect: *I associate spring with flowers.* **2.** To join as a friend, member, or partner: *She associates with women who have the same interests.*
□*noun* A friend, member, or partner: *a business associate.*
as·so·ci·ate (ə **sō′**shē āt′) □*verb* **associated, associating, associates** □*noun* (ə **sō′**shē it), *plural* **associates**

association *noun* **1.** A group of people joined together for a particular purpose: *I belong to several business associations.* **2.** A partnership or friendship: *He had a close association with the governor.* **3.** A connection in the mind between thoughts, feelings, or ideas: *What associations does the word "food" bring to your mind?*
as·so·ci·a·tion (ə sō′sē **ā′**shən) □*noun, plural* **associations**

assortment *noun* A collection of different kinds of persons or things; variety: *an assortment of flowers.*

as·sort·ment (ə **sôrt′** mənt) □*noun, plural* **assortments**

assume *verb* **1.** To take for granted; suppose: *He assumed the train would be on time.* **2.** To take upon oneself; undertake: *He assumed responsibility for his sister.* **3.** To take for oneself: *The king assumed the right to arrest those who opposed him.*
as·sume (ə **soōm′**) □*verb* **assumed, assuming, assumes**

assumption *noun* **1.** The act of assuming: *her assumption of responsibility.* **2.** Something that is assumed: *My assumption that it would snow today was wrong.*
as·sump·tion (ə **sump′** shən) □*noun, plural* **assumptions**

assurance *noun* **1.** A statement that is meant to make someone feel certain or sure: *He gave me his assurance that he would return the book.* **2.** Belief in one's own ability; confidence: *Practice gave me the assurance to play the violin in public.*
as·sur·ance (ə **shoor′** əns) □*noun, plural* **assurances**

assure *verb* **1.** To say positively; declare: *I can assure you that we will be home early.* **2.** To make certain or sure; guarantee: *He checked the jacket to assure that no buttons were missing.*
as·sure (ə **shoor′**) □*verb* **assured, assuring, assures**

aster *noun* A plant with purple, white, or pink flowers that look like daisies.
as·ter (**as′** tər) □*noun, plural* **asters**

aster

asterisk *noun* A symbol (*) used in printing or writing to tell the reader that more information can be found somewhere else on the page.
as·ter·isk (**as′** tə risk′) □*noun, plural* **asterisks**

> **WORD HISTORY: asterisk**
>
> The word *asterisk* comes from a Greek word that means ''little star.''

asteroid *noun* One of thousands of small heavenly bodies that revolve around the sun, mostly between Mars and Jupiter.
as·ter·oid (**as′** tə roid′) □*noun, plural* **asteroids**

asthma *noun* A disease that causes coughing and makes it difficult to breathe.
asth·ma (**az′** mə) □*noun*

astonish *verb* To surprise greatly; amaze: *Her generous gift astonished me.*
as·ton·ish (ə **ston′** ish) □*verb* **astonished, astonishing, astonishes**

astonishment *noun* Great surprise; amazement: *The audience looked with astonishment at the juggler's tricks.*
as·ton·ish·ment (ə **ston′** ish mənt) □*noun*

astound *verb* To fill with sudden wonder; astonish: *Our success completely astounded him.*
a·stound (ə **stound′**) □*verb* **astounded, astounding, astounds**

astray *adverb* Away from the right path or direction: *One of the lambs has gone astray. She was led astray by bad advice.*
a·stray (ə **strā′**) □*adverb*

astride *preposition* With one leg on each side of: *The boy sat astride the branch of the tree.*
a·stride (ə **strīd′**) □*preposition*

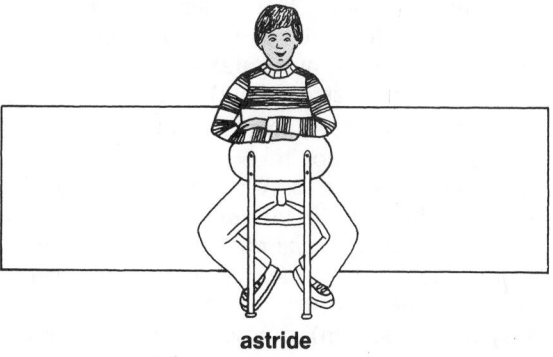

astride

a	bat	ī	bite	oō	tool	*th*	feather
ā	make	î	fierce	ou	out	th	bath
â	dare	o	dot	u	nut	hw	wheat
ä	father	ō	no	û	turn	zh	measure
e	net	ô	law, for	ch	church	ə	about, open
ē	be	oi	soil	ng	ring		pencil, atom
i	dip	oo	look	sh	shade		circus

astrology *noun* The study of the influence that the stars and planets are believed to have on events and on people's lives.
as·trol·o·gy (ə strol'ə jē) □*noun*

astronaut *noun* Someone who is trained to fly in a spacecraft.
as·tro·naut (as'trə nôt') □*noun, plural* **astronauts**

> *WORD HISTORY:* **astronaut**
>
> The word *astronaut* is a compound of a Greek word that means "star" and a Greek word that means "sailor."

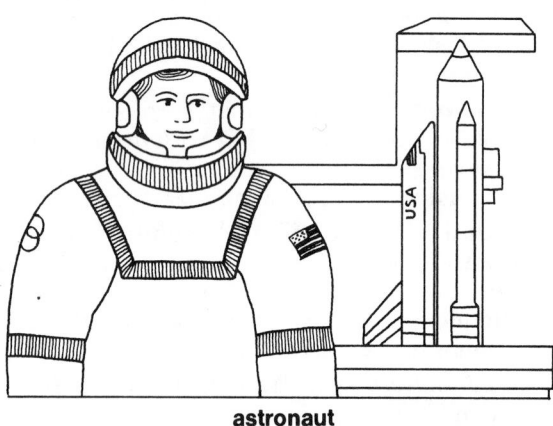

astronaut

astronomer *noun* Someone who is skilled in astronomy.
as·tron·o·mer (ə stron'ə mər) □*noun, plural* **astronomers**

astronomy *noun* The scientific study of heavenly bodies such as the sun, moon, planets, stars, comets, and galaxies.
as·tron·o·my (ə stron'ə mē) □*noun*

asylum *noun* **1.** An institution for the care of people who cannot take care of themselves: *an orphan asylum.* **2.** A place of protection or safety; shelter: *His library was an asylum where he could escape the noise.* **3.** Protection offered by a government to a political refugee from another country.
a·sy·lum (ə sī'ləm) □*noun, plural* **asylums**

at *preposition* **1.** In the location or position of: *She's at home. The line forms at the rear.* **2.** In a condition of: *The two countries were at war.* **3.** To or toward the direction of: *Look at me.* **4.** Near or on the time of: *I go to sleep at ten.* **5.** To the extent or amount of: *I bought the dress at a very low price.*
at (at *or* ət) □*preposition*

ate *verb* The past tense of **eat**: *We ate lunch at home.*
ate (āt) □*verb*

athlete *noun* Someone who is trained for and takes part in sports or physical exercises that require skill, strength, and speed. Baseball players and gymnasts are athletes.
ath·lete (ath'lēt') □*noun, plural* **athletes**

athletic *adjective* **1.** Of or for athletes or athletics: *The school built a new athletic building.* **2.** Physically strong and muscular.
ath·let·ic (ath let'ik) □*adjective*

athletics *noun* The activities engaged in by athletes; sports: *Athletics are an important part of our school's program.*
ath·let·ics (ath let'iks) □*noun*

atlas *noun* A book of maps.
at·las (at'ləs) □*noun, plural* **atlases**

atmosphere *noun* **1.** The gas that surrounds a body in space, especially the air that surrounds the earth. **2.** The air or climate of a place: *the damp atmosphere of a swamp.* **3.** A general feeling or mood: *the busy atmosphere of a big city.*
at·mos·phere (at'mə sfir') □*noun, plural* **atmospheres**

atmospheric *adjective* Of, in, or from the atmosphere: *atmospheric pressure.*
at·mos·pher·ic (at'mə sfer'ik) □*adjective*

atoll *noun* A coral island that forms a partial or complete ring around a lagoon.
at·oll (at'ôl' *or* ā'tôl') □*noun, plural* **atolls**

atoll

atom *noun* The smallest unit of a chemical element, consisting of a nucleus surrounded by electrons.
at·om (at'əm) □*noun, plural* **atoms**

atomic *adjective* **1.** Of an atom. **2.** Of or using nuclear energy: *an atomic power plant.*
a·tom·ic (ə tom'ik) □*adjective*

atomic bomb *noun* A bomb whose explosion releases atomic energy.

atomic energy   *noun* Energy that is released as a result of reactions in the nuclei of atoms.

atop   *preposition* On top of: *a little house atop the hill.*
a·top (ə **top´**) □*preposition*

attach   *verb* **1.** To join one thing or another: *We attached a ribbon to the box.* **2.** To bind by love or loyalty: *She is very attached to her family.* **3.** To add: *He attached his signature to the contract.*
at·tach (ə **tach´**) □*verb* **attached, attaching, attaches**

SYNONYMS: attach, connect, fasten

These verbs mean to join one thing to another: *I attached a headlight to my bicycle. Will you connect the hose to the faucet? She fastened the sign to the fence post.*

---

attachment   *noun* **1.** Something that is attached, as to a machine; accessory: *The vacuum cleaner has several attachments.* **2.** Love, affection, or loyalty: *She felt a strong attachment for her friend.*
at·tach·ment (ə **tach´**mənt) □*noun, plural* **attachments**

attack   *verb* **1.** To set upon with violent force: *The dog attacked the mailman. The troops attacked at dawn.* **2.** To speak or write about in an unfriendly way: *The candidates attacked each other in the debate.* **3.** To be harmful to; afflict: *Beetles attacked the rose bushes.* **4.** To begin work on with energy: *She attacked the problem as soon as she reached the office.* □*noun* **1.** The act of attacking: *We were ready for the enemy's attack.* **2.** A sudden occurrence of a disease: *I had an attack of asthma.*
at·tack (ə **tak´**) □*verb* **attacked, attacking, attacks** □*noun, plural* **attacks**

attain   *verb* **1.** To get, do, or bring about by effort; achieve: *She attained confidence through practice.* **2.** To come to through time or growth; reach: *He attained the age of 80.*
at·tain (ə **tān´**) □*verb* **attained, attaining, attains**

attempt   *verb* To make an effort; try: *The child attempted to ride the bicycle.* □*noun* **1.** An effort or try: *He made an attempt to fix the car.* **2.** An attack; assault: *An attempt was made on the governor's life.*
at·tempt (ə **tempt´**) □*verb* **attempted, attempting, attempts** □*noun, plural* **attempts**

attend   *verb* **1.** To be present at: *All the teachers attended the meeting.* **2.** To stay or go with in order to serve; wait upon: *Many knights attended the king.* **3.** To take care of: *Doctors attended the victims of the fire.*
at·tend (ə **tend´**) □*verb* **attended, attending, attends**

attendance   *noun* **1.** The act of being present: *His attendance at the play was unexpected.* **2.** The persons or number of persons present: *an attendance of 500 at the concert.*
at·ten·dance (ə **ten´**dəns) □*noun*

attention   *noun* **1.** Thinking, watching, or listening carefully: *Pay attention to what the teacher says.* **2.** Consideration; notice: *Your interesting idea has come to our attention.*
at·ten·tion (ə **ten´**shən) □*noun*

attic   *noun* The space in a house just under the roof.
at·tic (**at´**ik) □*noun, plural* **attics**

attire   *noun* Clothing; apparel: *tennis attire.* —See Synonyms at **dress.**
at·tire (ə **tīr´**) □*noun*

attitude   *noun* A way of thinking or feeling about someone or something; point of view: *What is your attitude toward education?*
at·ti·tude (**at´**i tood´ *or* **at´**i tyood´) □*noun, plural* **attitudes**

attorney   *noun* Someone appointed to act for another in legal matters; lawyer.
at·tor·ney (ə **tûr´**nē) □*noun, plural* **attorneys**

attract   *verb* To draw or pull to oneself or itself: *A magnet attracts nails. Her funny hat attracted attention.*
at·tract (ə **trakt´**) □*verb* **attracted, attracting, attracts**

attraction   *noun* **1.** The act or power of attracting: *His charm was his main attraction.* **2.** Something or someone that attracts: *The cathedral is one of the town's attractions.*
at·trac·tion (ə **trak´**shən) □*noun, plural* **attractions**

attractive   *adjective* Pleasing to the eye, mind, or senses: *She wore an attractive dress.*
at·trac·tive (ə **trak´**tiv) □*adjective*

a	bat	ī	bite	o͞o	tool	th	feather
ā	make	î	fierce	ou	out	th	bath
â	dare	o	dot	u	nut	hw	wheat
ä	father	ō	no	û	turn	zh	measure
e	net	ô	law, for	ch	church	ə	about, open
ē	be	oi	soil	ng	ring		pencil, atom
i	dip	oo	look	sh	shade		circus

attribute *verb* To think of as caused by: *We attribute air pollution partly to cars.*
□*noun* A quality that belongs to a person or thing; characteristic: *Among the man's attributes are honesty and courage.*
at·trib·ute (ə **trib**′yo͞ot) □*verb* **attributed, attributing, attributes** □*noun* (**at**′rə byo͞ot′), *plural* **attributes**

auction *noun* A public sale of goods or property to the person who bids the largest amount of money.
□*verb* To sell at an auction: *He auctioned off his house with all its furnishings.*
auc·tion (**ôk**′shən) □*noun, plural* **auctions** □*verb* **auctioned, auctioning, auctions**

audible *adjective* Loud enough to be heard: *an audible whisper.*
au·di·ble (**ô**′də bəl) □*adjective*

audience *noun* **1.** The people gathered together to see and hear a performance such as a play, movie, or concert. **2.** The readers, listeners, or viewers reached by a book, radio broadcast, or television program. **3.** A formal hearing or conference: *an audience with the prime minister.*
au·di·ence (**ô**′dē əns) □*noun, plural* **audiences**

auditorium *noun* A large room or building used to hold public gatherings.
au·di·to·ri·um (ô′di **tôr**′ē əm) □*noun, plural* **auditoriums**

auger *noun* A tool for boring holes.
au·ger (**ô**′gər) □*noun, plural* **augers**

August *noun* The eighth month of the year. August has 31 days.
Au·gust (**ô**′gəst) □*noun*

WORD HISTORY: **August**

The month of *August* was named by the Roman emperor Augustus. He named it after himself.

---

auk *noun* A black and white sea bird with a thick body and short wings. Auks live along northern shores.
auk (ôk) □*noun, plural* **auks**

auk

aunt *noun* **1.** The sister of one's father or mother. **2.** The wife of one's father's or mother's brother.
aunt (ant *or* änt) □*noun, plural* **aunts**

auricle *noun* **1.** The external part of the ear. **2.** One of two chambers of the heart that receives blood from a vein.
au·ri·cle (**ôr**′i kəl) □*noun, plural* **auricles**

Australian *noun* Someone who was born in or is a citizen of Australia.
□*adjective* Of Australia or its people.
Aus·tra·lian (ô **strāl**′yən) □*noun, plural* **Australians** □*adjective*

authentic *adjective* Not copied or counterfeit; genuine: *an authentic antique.*
au·then·tic (ô **then**′tik) □*adjective*

author *noun* Someone who writes a book, story, article, or play.
au·thor (**ô**′thər) □*noun, plural* **authors**

authority *noun* **1.** The power and right to order, act, decide, and enforce laws or rules: *The parents had authority over their children.* **2.** Someone who has authority: *School authorities decided to order new books.* **3.** A source of correct or expert information: *an authority on American history.*
au·thor·i·ty (ə **thôr**′i tē) □*noun, plural* **authorities**

authorize *verb* **1.** To give authority to: *The mayor authorized them to form a committee.* **2.** To give official permission for; approve: *He authorized the collection of an automobile tax.*
au·thor·ize (**ô**′thə rīz′) □*verb* **authorized, authorizing, authorizes**

auto *noun* An automobile.
au·to (**ô**′tō) □*noun, plural* **autos**

autobiography *noun* The story of a person's life written by himself or herself.
au·to·bi·og·ra·phy (ô′tō bī **og**′rə fē) □*noun, plural* **autobiographies**

autograph *noun* A signature, especially of a famous person.
□*verb* To write one's signature on or in.
au·to·graph (**ô**′tə graf′) □*noun, plural* **autographs** □*verb* **autographed, autographing, autographs**

automatic *adjective* **1.** Working, moving, or acting without the control of a human being: *an automatic washing machine.* **2.** Done or produced by the body without thought or control: *Breathing is automatic.*
□*noun* A device or machine, especially a firearm, that is entirely or partly automatic.

au·to·mat·ic (ô'tə **mat'**ik) ▭*adjective* ▭*noun*, *plural* **automatics**

automation *noun* The automatic operation or control of a machine, process, or system that takes the place of human labor.
au·to·ma·tion (ô'tə **mā'**shən) ▭*noun*

automobile *noun* A passenger vehicle that usually has four wheels and is moved by an engine that usually uses gasoline; car.
au·to·mo·bile (ô'tə mə **bēl'**) ▭*noun, plural* **automobiles**

automobile

autumn *noun* The season of the year between summer and winter; fall.
au·tumn (ô'təm) ▭*noun, plural* **autumns**

auxiliary *adjective* Giving help or support: *Our sailboat has an auxiliary motor.*
▭*noun* **1.** Someone or something that helps; aid: *The microphone is an auxiliary to the human voice.* **2.** An organization that is part of a larger one: *an auxiliary of volunteer nurses.*
aux·il·ia·ry (ôg **zil'**yə rē) ▭*adjective* ▭*noun, plural* **auxiliaries**

available *adjective* **1.** Capable of being had or obtained: *The curtains are available in three colors.* **2.** Ready or present to be used: *Four people are available to do the jobs.*
a·vail·a·ble (ə **vā'**lə bəl) ▭*adjective*

avalanche *noun* A large mass of snow, ice, earth, or rocks that falls or slides down the side of a mountain.
av·a·lanche (**av'**ə lanch') ▭*noun, plural* **avalanches**

ave. An abbreviation for **avenue**.

avenue *noun* A wide street or road.
av·e·nue (**av'**ə nōō' *or* **av'**ə nyōō') ▭*noun, plural* **avenues**

average *noun* A number found by dividing the sum of two or more quantities by the number of quantities. The average of 1, 3, 5, and 7 is 4, since $1 + 3 + 5 + 7 = 16 \div 4 = 4$.
▭*verb* **1.** To find the average of: *We averaged our living expenses for the month.* **2.** To have as an average: *The temperature in December averaged 30 degrees.*
▭*adjective* **1.** Being an average: *Our average*

speed was 45 miles an hour. **2.** Not out of the ordinary; usual: *She was of average height.*
av·er·age (**av'**ər ij *or* **av'**rij) ▭*noun, plural* **averages** ▭*verb* **averaged, averaging, averages** ▭*adjective*

avert *verb* **1.** To turn away or aside: *She averted her face from his stare.* **2.** To keep from happening; prevent: *He had to drive off the road to avert an accident.*
a·vert (ə **vûrt'**) ▭*verb* **averted, averting, averts**

aviation *noun* The science, business, or operation of aircraft.
a·vi·a·tion (ā'vē **ā'**shən) ▭*noun*

aviator *noun* Someone who flies an aircraft; pilot.
a·vi·a·tor (**ā'**vē ā'tər) ▭*noun, plural* **aviators**

aviator

avocado *noun* A tropical American fruit with leathery green or blackish skin, smooth, yellowish-green pulp, and a large seed. The pulp of the avocado is often eaten in salads.
av·o·ca·do (av'ə **kä'**dō) ▭*noun, plural* **avocados**

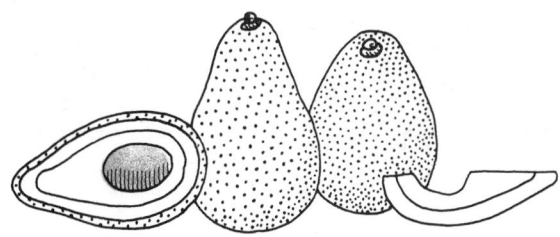

avocado

a	bat	ī	bite	ōō	tool	*th*	feather
ā	make	î	fierce	ou	out	th	bath
â	dare	o	dot	u	nut	hw	wheat
ä	father	ō	no	û	turn	zh	measure
e	net	ô	law, for	ch	church	ə	about, open
ē	be	oi	soil	ng	ring		pencil, atom
i	dip	oo	look	sh	shade		circus

avoid *verb* To keep away from: *We left early to avoid traffic.*
a·void (ə **void'**) □*verb* **avoided, avoiding, avoids**

await *verb* **1.** To wait for: *He awaited her phone call.* **2.** To be waiting or ready for: *A big dinner awaits him at home.*
a·wait (ə **wāt'**) □*verb* **awaited, awaiting, awaits**

awake *verb* To rouse from sleep; wake up: *The siren awoke me in the middle of the night.* □*adjective* Not asleep: *The noise kept him awake.*
a·wake (ə **wāk'**) □*verb* **awoke, awaked, awaking, awakes** □*adjective*

awaken *verb* To wake up; awake: *The clatter outside awakened me.*
a·wak·en (ə **wā'**kən) □*verb* **awakened, awakening, awakens**

award *verb* **1.** To give as being needed or deserved; grant: *The committee awarded him the prize for the best experiment.* **2.** To give by legal or governmental decision: *The judge awarded money to the victim of the accident.* □*noun* **1.** Something given for special quality or performance. **2.** Something given by legal or governmental decision.
a·ward (ə **wôrd'**) □*verb* **awarded, awarding, awards** □*noun, plural* **awards**

award

aware *adjective* Being conscious; knowing: *He is not really aware of his faults.*
a·ware (ə **wâr'**) □*adjective*

away *adverb* **1.** At or to a distance: *a school three miles away.* **2.** In or to a different place or direction: *Don't run away.* **3.** From one's presence or possession: *Her mother gave her old coat away.* **4.** Out of existence: *The music died away.* **5.** All the time; without stopping:

She worked away at her job. **6.** At once; immediately: *Fire away!*
□*adjective* **1.** Absent: *He's away from his desk.* **2.** At a distance: *The store is only a few miles away.*
a·way (ə **wā'**) □*adverb* □*adjective*

awe *noun* A feeling of wonder and fear mixed together with deep respect: *We looked with awe at the king.*
□*verb* To fill with awe: *The size of the mountain awed everyone.*
awe (ô) □*noun* □*verb* **awed, awing, awes**

awful *adjective* **1.** Inspiring awe: *the awful power of a king.* **2.** Very bad or unpleasant; terrible: *an awful pain; awful weather.* **3.** Very great: *She did an awful lot of work.*
aw·ful (ô'fəl) □*adjective*

awfully *adverb* **1.** Very: *He did seem awfully upset.* **2.** Very badly: *He behaved awfully in front of his mother's guests.*
aw·ful·ly (ô'fə lē *or* ô'flē) □*adverb*

awhile *adverb* For a short time: *I waited awhile, but he never came.*
a·while (ə **hwīl'** *or* ə **wīl'**) □*adverb*

awkward *adjective* **1.** Not graceful; clumsy: *She is too awkward with a pen to draw well.* **2.** Not natural, as in speech or behavior: *He became shy and awkward whenever he saw her.* **3.** Difficult to move, handle, or manage: *an awkward bundle to carry.* **4.** Causing embarrassment: *an awkward silence.*
awk·ward (ôk'wərd) □*adjective*

awl *noun* A pointed tool that is used to make small holes especially in wood or leather.
awl (ôl) □*noun, plural* **awls**

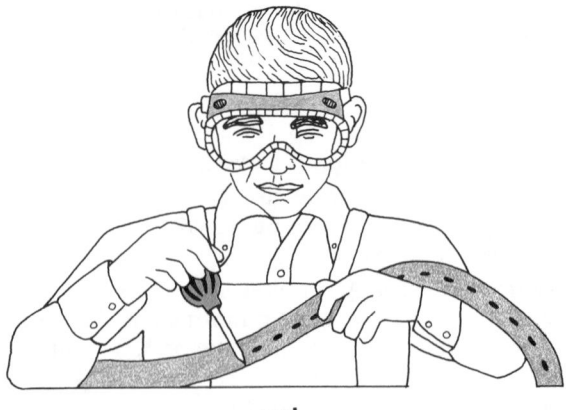

awl

awning *noun* A cover of canvas, plastic, or other material that looks like a roof and is set up over a window or door as protection from the sun and rain.

awn·ing (ô′ning) ▢*noun, plural* **awnings**

awoke *verb* The past tense of **awake:** *We awoke early to start on our trip.*

a·woke (ə wōk′) ▢*verb*

ax or **axe** *noun* A chopping or cutting tool that has a head with a sharp blade fixed on a long handle.

ax or **axe** (aks) ▢*noun, plural* **axes**

axis *noun* A straight line around which an object turns or may be imagined to turn: *The earth's axis passes through the North Pole and the South Pole.*

ax·is (ak′sis) ▢*noun, plural* **ax·es** (ak′sēz′)

axle *noun* A bar or shaft on which a wheel or set of wheels turns.

ax·le (ak′səl) ▢*noun, plural* **axles**

aye or **ay** *adverb* Yes: *Aye, sir.*

▢*noun* **1.** A vote of "yes." **2.** Someone who votes "yes": *The ayes have it; the town will get a new school.*

aye or **ay** (ī) ▢*adverb* ▢*noun, plural* **ayes**

azalea *noun* A shrub with cluster of flowers that are usually pink, red, or white.

a·zal·ea (ə zāl′yə) ▢*noun, plural* **azaleas**

azure *noun* A light to medium blue, like that of the sky on a clear day.

▢*adjective* Light to medium blue.

az·ure (azh′ər) ▢*noun, plural* **azures** ▢*adjective*

a	bat	ī	bite	o͞o	tool	*th*	feather
ā	make	î	fierce	ou	out	th	bath
â	dare	o	dot	u	nut	hw	wheat
ä	father	ō	no	û	turn	zh	measure
e	net	ô	law, for	ch	church	ə	about, open
ē	be	oi	soil	ng	ring		pencil, atom
i	dip	oo	look	sh	shade		circus

ANCIENT GREEK

The letter **B** has evolved from many forms of ancient writing. One of the earliest known examples is the Greek character shown above, which dates from almost 3,000 years ago. Over the years, artists and designers have created their own versions of the English letter **B.** Some of the more common examples seen today are shown below.

Bb Bb   **Bb Bb**   Bb Bb   Bb Bb   *Bb Bb*

HANDWRITING   CALLIGRAPHY   MODERN SANS SERIF   MODERN SERIF   SCRIPT

---

b or **B** *noun* The second letter of the English alphabet.
  b or **B** (bē) ▢*noun, plural* **b's** or **B's**

baa *noun* The sound made by a sheep.
  ▢*verb* To make this sound.
  baa (ba *or* bä) ▢*noun, plural* **baas** ▢*verb* **baaed, baaing, baas**

babble *verb* **1.** To make sounds that have no meaning: *The baby babbled softly.* **2.** To talk a long time about something that is not interesting: *She babbled on and on about the game.* **3.** To make a low, gurgling sound: *water babbling in the fountain.*
  ▢*noun* **1.** A confused mixture of sounds: *the babble of voices in the playground.* **2.** A low, gurgling sound.
  bab·ble (bab′əl) ▢*verb* **babbled, babbling, babbles** ▢*noun, plural* **babbles**

babe *noun* A baby; infant.
  babe (bāb) ▢*noun, plural* **babes**

baboon *noun* A large African monkey with a long face.
  ba·boon (ba boon′) ▢*noun, plural* **baboons**

baboon

baby *noun* **1.** A very young child. **2.** The youngest member of a family. **3.** A childish person.
  ▢*verb* To treat like a baby.
  ba·by (bā′bē) ▢*noun, plural* **babies** ▢*verb* **babied, babying, babies**

baby-sit *verb* To take care of a child when the parents are not at home.
  ba·by-sit (bā′bē sit′) ▢*verb* **baby-sat, baby-sitting, baby-sits**

baby sitter *noun* Someone who baby-sits.

bachelor *noun* A man who has not married.
  bach·e·lor (bach′ ə lər *or* **bach′**lər) ▢*noun, plural* **bachelors**

back *noun* **1.** The part of the human or animal body that is along the spine. **2.** The side of something that is opposite the front: *the back of the building.*
  ▢*adverb* **1.** To a direction opposite the front: *She leaned back in her chair.* **2.** To a former place or time: *They went back home.*
  ▢*adjective* **1.** Opposite the front: *the back door.* **2.** Old; past: *She keeps back issues of the magazines.*
  ▢*verb* **1.** To move or cause to move backward: *She backed slowly away from the snake. Mom backed the car into the parking place.* **2.** To give support to: *All his friends backed him for class president.*
  back (bak) ▢*noun, plural* **backs** ▢*adverb* ▢*adjective* ▢*verb* **backed, backing, backs**

backboard *noun* A board to which the basket is attached in basketball.

back·board (**bak′**bôrd′) ☐*noun, plural* **backboards**

backbone *noun* **1.** The series of jointed bones in the back; spine. The backbone is the main support of the body of human beings and many animals. **2.** Strength of character: *It took backbone to be a pioneer.*
back·bone (**bak′**bōn′) ☐*noun, plural* **backbones**

background *noun* **1.** The part of a scene that is at the back: *Hills were painted in the background.* **2.** A person's past experience and training: *Pilots have the right background to be astronauts.*
back·ground (**bak′**ground′) ☐*noun, plural* **backgrounds**

backhand *noun* A stroke in tennis and other games made with the back of the hand facing forward.
back·hand (**bak′**hand′) ☐*noun, plural* **backhands**

backhand

backward *adverb* **1.** Toward the back: *She looked backward when she heard someone calling her.* **2.** With the back first: *wearing a hat backward.* **3.** In reverse order: *The teacher called the roll backward.*
☐*adjective* **1.** Directed toward the back: *a backward look.* **2.** Behind others in development: *a backward region.*
back·ward (**bak′**wərd) ☐*adverb* ☐*adjective*

backwards *adverb* Another spelling for **backward.**
back·wards (**bak′**wərdz) ☐*adverb*

bacon *noun* The salted and smoked meat from the back and sides of a pig.
ba·con (**bā′**kən) ☐*noun*

bacteria *plural noun* Tiny plants that can be seen only with a microscope. Some bacteria cause diseases.
bac·te·ri·a (bak tîr′ē ə) ☐*plural noun*

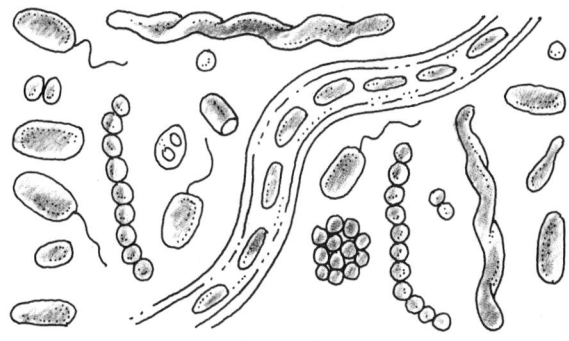

bacteria
Several kinds of bacteria

bad *adjective* **1.** Not good; *a bad movie.* **2.** Not favorable or convenient: *a bad time to call.* **3.** Disagreeable; unpleasant: *bad news.* **4.** Incorrect; improper: *bad manners.* **5.** Morally evil; naughty: *a bad boy.* **6.** In poor health: *He is feeling bad today.* **7.** Sorry: *I feel bad about the accident.*
bad (bad) ☐*adjective* **worse, worst**

badge *noun* Something worn to show that a person has a certain rank, position, or job.
badge (baj) ☐*noun, plural* **badges**

badger *noun* A furry animal that has short legs and lives underground.
☐*verb* To annoy; bother: *We badgered him till he told us the whole story.*
badg·er (**baj′**ər) ☐*noun, plural* **badgers**
☐*verb* **badgered, badgering, badgers**

badger

a	bat	ī	bite	o͞o	tool	*th*	feather
ā	make	î	fierce	ou	out	th	bath
â	dare	o	dot	u	nut	hw	wheat
ä	father	ō	no	û	turn	zh	measure
e	net	ô	law, for	ch	church	ə	about, open
ē	be	oi	soil	ng	ring		pencil, atom
i	dip	oo	look	sh	shade		circus

badly *adverb* **1.** In a bad way: *He drives badly.* **2.** Very much; greatly: *badly hurt.*
bad·ly (**bad′**lē) □*adverb*

badminton *noun* A game in which players use light rackets to hit a small rubber and plastic object back and forth over a high net.
bad·min·ton (**bad′**min′tən) □*noun*

WORD HISTORY: **badminton**

The word *badminton* comes from the name of a duke's estate in England. The game seems to have been first played on the Badminton estate.

---

baffle *verb* To be too hard for someone to understand or solve: *The riddle baffled us all.*
baf·fle (**baf′**əl) □*verb* **baffled, baffling, baffles**

bag *noun* **1.** A container made of paper, cloth, plastic, or leather. **2.** The amount that a bag holds: *We shared a bag of peanuts.*
bag (bag) □*noun, plural* **bags**

bagel *noun* A chewy roll baked in the shape of a ring.
ba·gel (**bā′**gəl) □*noun, plural* **bagels**

baggage *noun* The suitcases and bags that a traveler carries.
bag·gage (**bag′**ij) □*noun*

baggy *adjective* Fitting loosely: *baggy trousers.*
bag·gy (**bag′**ē) □*adjective* **baggier, baggiest**

bagpipe *noun* A musical instrument made of a leather bag and four pipes. A player blows air into the bag and then forces the air through the pipes by squeezing the bag.
bag·pipe (**bag′**pīp′) □*noun, plural* **bagpipes**

bagpipe

bail¹ *noun* Money given to a court to set free an arrested person until a trial takes place. The money is returned when the person appears for the trial.
□*verb* To set free by giving bail.
bail (bāl) □*noun* □*verb* **bailed, bailing, bails**

bail² *verb* To take water out of a boat: *We bailed out the leaky canoe with a can.*
bail (bāl) □*verb* **bailed, bailing, bails**

bail

bait *noun* Something that attracts or lures.
□*verb* **1.** To put bait on: *We baited our fishhooks with worms.* **2.** To tease in a mean way: *The bullies baited the small child by calling him names.*
bait (bāt) □*noun, plural* **baits** □*verb* **baited, baiting, baits**

bake *verb* **1.** To cook in an oven with dry heat: *We baked a cake. The rolls baked quickly.* **2.** To harden or dry by heating: *He baked the clay bowl in a kiln.*
bake (bāk) □*verb* **baked, baking, bakes**

baker *noun* Someone who bakes or sells bread, rolls, pastries, and cookies.

bakery *noun* A place where bread, rolls, pies, and cookies are baked or sold.
bak·e·ry (**bā′**kə rē) □*noun, plural* **bakeries**

baking powder *noun* A powder used to make breads and cakes rise as they are cooked.

baking soda *noun* A white powder used in cooking and in medicine.

balance *noun* **1.** An instrument for weighing things. **2.** A condition in which amounts, weights, forces, or power are equal: *The number of boys and girls in the class is in balance: fifteen boys and fifteen girls.* **3.** Steadiness: *The skater lost her balance and fell.* **4.** Something

that is left over: *She spent the balance of the evening reading.*
□*verb* To hold in a steady position: *The seal balanced the ball on its nose.*
bal·ance (bal′əns) □*noun, plural* **balances** □*verb* **balanced, balancing, balances**

balance

balcony *noun* **1.** A platform that juts out from the side of a building. **2.** A platform that juts out over the main floor of a theater or auditorium.
bal·co·ny (bal′kə nē) □*noun, plural* **balconies**

bald *adjective* **1.** Having little or no hair on the head. **2.** Without natural covering: *a bald mountain top.* —See Synonyms at **bare.**
bald (bôld) □*adjective* **balder, baldest**

bald eagle *noun* A North American eagle with a white head. It is the national emblem of the United States.

bald eagle

bale *noun* A large, tightly wrapped bundle: *a bale of hay.*
bale (bāl) □*noun, plural* **bales**

balk *verb* **1.** To stop and refuse to go on: *The horse balked at the river's edge.* **2.** To keep from happening: *His plans were balked.*
balk (bôk) □*verb* **balked, balking, balks**

ball¹ *noun* **1.** Something round: *a ball of yarn.* **2.** A round object used in games: *a tennis ball.* **3.** Baseball or some other game played with a ball. **4.** A pitch in baseball that the batter does not swing at and is not thrown over home plate between the batter's knees and shoulders.
ball (bôl) □*noun, plural* **balls**

ball² *noun* A large, formal party for dancing.
ball (bôl) □*noun, plural* **balls**

ballad *noun* A poem or song that tells a story.
bal·lad (bal′əd) □*noun, plural* **ballads**

ballast *noun* Heavy material carried in a vehicle to keep it steady.
bal·last (bal′əst) □*noun*

ball bearing *noun* A bearing in which the moving part turns on rolling steel balls.

ballerina *noun* A woman or girl who dances ballet.
bal·le·ri·na (bal′ə rē′nə) □*noun, plural* **ballerinas**

ballet *noun* A kind of dancing with formal jumps, turns, and poses. A ballet often tells a story.
bal·let (ba lā′ *or* bal′ā′) □*noun, plural* **ballets**

ballet
Ballet dancers

a	bat	ī	bite	ōō	tool	*th*	feather
ā	make	î	fierce	ou	out	th	bath
â	dare	o	dot	u	nut	hw	wheat
ä	father	ō	no	û	turn	zh	measure
e	net	ô	law, for	ch	church	ə	about, open
ē	be	oi	soil	ng	ring		pencil, atom
i	dip	oo	look	sh	shade		circus

balloon   *noun* A bag filled with air or another gas. Large balloons lift passengers and loads into the air. Small balloons are used as toys.
  □*verb* To puff out like a balloon: *The sail ballooned in the wind.*
  bal·loon (bə loon′)   □*noun, plural* **balloons**
  □*verb* **ballooned, ballooning, balloons**

ballot   *noun* A piece of paper or other object used to cast a vote in an election.
  bal·lot (bal′ət)   □*noun, plural* **ballots**

> *WORD HISTORY:* **ballot**
>
> The word *ballot* comes from an Italian word that means "little ball." Little balls were dropped into a container to register votes—white for "aye" and black for "nay."

ball-point pen   *noun* A pen with a small rolling metal ball for its writing point.
  ball-point pen (bôl′ point′)   □*noun*

ballroom   *noun* A large room for dancing.
  ball·room (bôl′ room′ *or* bôl′ room′)   □*noun, plural* **ballrooms**

balsa   *noun* A light, strong wood obtained from a tropical American tree.
  bal·sa (bôl′ sə)   □*noun*

balsam   *noun* A fir tree of North America.
  bal·sam (bôl′ səm)   □*noun, plural* **balsams**

bamboo   *noun* A tall grass that has hollow, woody stems that are used to make poles, furniture, and many other objects.
  bam·boo (bam boo′)   □*noun, plural* **bamboos**

ban   *verb* To forbid by law or decree: *The principal banned skating in the playground.*
  □*noun* An official order or decree that forbids something.
  ban (ban)   □*verb* **banned, banning, bans** □*noun, plural* **bans**

banana   *noun* A curved fruit with sweet, soft flesh and a yellow peel.
  ba·na·na (bə nan′ə)   □*noun, plural* **bananas**

band¹   *noun* **1.** A strip of material that binds or ties: *The box was fastened with metal bands.* **2.** A stripe of color or material: *the white and black bands on a zebra's coat.*
  band (band)   □*noun, plural* **bands**

band²   *noun* **1.** A group of people or animals acting together: *a band of criminals.* **2.** A group of musicians who play together.
  □*verb* To gather in a group: *The citizens banded together to protest the school's closing.*

band (band)   □*noun, plural* **bands** □*verb* **banded, banding, bands**

bandage   *noun* A strip of cloth used to bind or cover a wound.
  □*verb* To cover or bind with a bandage.
  band·age (ban′ dij)   □*noun, plural* **bandages** □*verb* **bandaged, bandaging, bandages**

bandanna   *noun* A large, brightly colored handkerchief, often worn around the neck.
  ban·dan·na (ban dan′ə)   □*noun, plural* **bandannas**

bandit   *noun* A robber; outlaw.
  ban·dit (ban′ dit)   □*noun, plural* **bandits**

bang   *noun* A loud, sharp noise: *The balloon popped with a bang.*
  □*verb* **1.** To make a loud, sharp noise: *The screen door banged shut.* **2.** To strike or hit with force: *She banged her knee against the leg of the table.*
  bang (bang)   □*noun, plural* **bangs** □*verb* **banged, banging, bangs**

bangs   *plural noun* Hair cut straight across the forehead.
  bangs (bangz)   □*plural noun*

banish   *verb* **1.** To force someone officially to leave a country: *The king banished his dishonest brother.* **2.** To drive away: *The happy song banished our gloom.*
  ban·ish (ban′ ish)   □*verb* **banished, banishing, banishes**

banister   *noun* The railing along a staircase.
  ban·is·ter (ban′ i stər)   □*noun, plural* **banisters**

banjo   *noun* A musical instrument with a round body, a neck with frets, and five strings that are plucked.
  ban·jo (ban′ jō)   □*noun, plural* **banjos** or **banjoes**

banjo

bank[1] *noun* **1.** The sloping ground next to a river or lake. **2.** A pile or heap: *a snow bank.* □*verb* To form into a bank.
bank (bangk) □*noun, plural* **banks** □*verb* **banked, banking, banks**

bank[2] *noun* **1.** A place where people's money is kept and money is lent for a charge. **2.** A small container used for saving money.
□*verb* **1.** To put in a bank: *She banked most of her wages.* **2.** To have an account at a certain bank.
bank (bangk) □*noun, plural* **banks** □*verb* **banked, banking, banks**

WORD HISTORY: bank[2]

In Italy during the Middle Ages financial dealings were carried out on a bench or counter in an open market. The word *bank* at first simply meant "a bench" and then "a place where money could be exchanged, lent, or borrowed."

---

banker *noun* A manager of a bank.
bank·er (bang′kər) □*noun, plural* **bankers**

bankrupt *adjective* Unable to pay one's debts.
□*verb* To make bankrupt.
bank·rupt (bangk′rupt′) □*adjective* □*verb* **bankrupted, bankrupting, bankrupts**

banner *noun* A small flag or piece of cloth that has words or a design on it.
□*adjective* Outstanding: *a banner year for apple growers.*
ban·ner (ban′ər) □*noun, plural* **banners** □*adjective*

banquet *noun* A large, formal dinner, usually given for a special occasion.
ban·quet (bang′kwit) □*noun, plural* **banquets**

banquet

baptism *noun* The act of dipping in or sprinkling with water as part of the ceremony of receiving someone into the Christian Church.
bap·tism (bap′tiz′əm) □*noun, plural* **baptisms**

baptize *verb* To cause to undergo baptism.
bap·tize (bap tīz′ *or* bap′tīz′) □*verb* **baptized, baptizing, baptizes**

bar *noun* **1.** A straight piece of wood or metal that is longer than it is wide: *bars on a prison window.* **2.** A solid, rectangular block: *a bar of soap.* **3.** An obstacle: *Lack of education is often a bar to success.* **4.** A narrow marking: *The bars on a soldier's sleeve show that he has served overseas.* **5.** One of the vertical lines drawn across a musical staff to mark the end of a measure. **6.** A musical measure. **7.** The legal profession. **8.** A counter where alcoholic drinks and sometimes food are served.
□*verb* **1.** To close and fasten with a bar: *bar a door.* **2.** To keep out; exclude: *The law bars dogs from supermarkets.*
bar (bär) □*noun, plural* **bars** □*verb* **barred, barring, bars**

barb *noun* A sharp point that is aimed backward from the main point: *The fishhook had a barb.*
barb (bärb) □*noun, plural* **barbs**

barbarian *noun* Someone who is a member of an uncivilized people.
bar·bar·i·an (bär bâr′ē ən) □*noun, plural* **barbarians**

WORD HISTORY: barbarian

Barbarian comes from a Greek word that means "foreign." To the Greeks the word resembled the strange sounds in the languages spoken by non-Greeks.

---

barbecue *noun* **1.** An open fireplace used for cooking meat, usually outdoors. **2.** An outdoor meal cooked on a barbecue.
□*verb* To cook on a barbecue.
bar·be·cue (bär′bi kyo͞o′) □*noun, plural* **barbecues** □*verb* **barbecued, barbecuing, barbecues**

a bat	ī bite	o͞o tool	*th* feather
ā make	î fierce	ou out	th bath
â dare	o dot	u nut	hw wheat
ä father	ō no	û turn	zh measure
e net	ô law, for	ch church	ə about, open
ē be	oi soil	ng ring	pencil, atom
i dip	oo look	sh shade	circus

> *WORD HISTORY:* **barbecue**
>
> Before the Europeans colonized the New World, the Indians of the Caribbean Sea had invented a way of cooking meat and fish. They placed the food on a framework of sticks over a fire and smoked, grilled, or roasted it. Their word for the framework of sticks eventually became the English word *barbecue.*

barbed wire *noun* Strands of wire having sharp barbs.

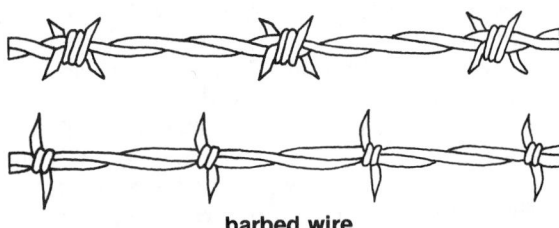

barbed wire

barber *noun* Someone whose work is cutting hair and shaving beards.
bar·ber (bär′ bər) □*noun, plural* **barbers**

> *WORD HISTORY:* **barber**
>
> The word *barber* was borrowed from French. The French word is derived from the Latin word for ''beard.''

bare *adjective* **1.** Without a covering; naked: *bare feet; a bare tabletop.* **2.** Empty: *a cupboard with bare shelves.* **3.** Just enough; meager: *She earns a bare living.*
□*verb* To uncover: *The dog bared its teeth.*
bare (bâr) □*adjective* **barer, barest** □*verb* **bared, baring, bares**

> *SYNONYMS:* **bare, bald, naked**
>
> These adjectives mean without the normal or natural covering: *a bare arm, a bare tree; a bald head, bald hills; a naked baby, naked branches of a tree.*

bareback *adjective* On a horse's bare back: *a bareback rider.*
□*adverb* Without a saddle: *riding a horse bareback.*
bare·back (bâr′ bak′) □*adjective* □*adverb*

barefoot *adjective* Lacking covering for the feet.
□*adverb* Without shoes on: *running barefoot on the grass.*
bare·foot (bâr′ foot′) □*adjective* □*adverb*

barely *adverb* Only just; hardly: *barely enough room.*
bare·ly (bâr′ lē) □*adverb*

bargain *noun* **1.** An agreement; deal: *We made a bargain to take turns cleaning our room.* **2.** Something offered or bought at a low price.
□*verb* To argue over a price to be paid: *bargained with the salesman.*
bar·gain (bär′ gin) □*noun, plural* **bargains**
□*verb* **bargained, bargaining, bargains**

barge *noun* A boat with a flat bottom, used to carry freight: *a river barge.*
barge (bärj) □*noun, plural* **barges**

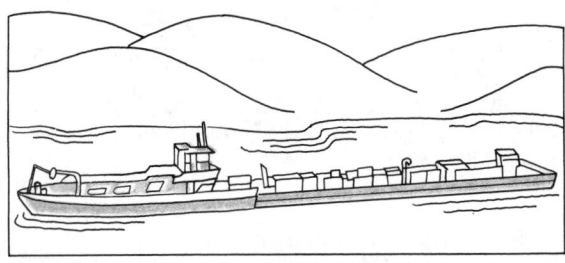

barge

baritone *noun* **1.** A man's singing voice higher than a bass and lower than a tenor. **2.** A singer with such a voice.
bar·i·tone (bar′ i tōn) □*noun, plural* **baritones**

bark¹ *noun* The short, loud sound made by dogs and certain other animals.
□*verb* To make such a sound.
bark (bärk) □*noun, plural* **barks** □*verb* **barked, barking, barks**

bark² *noun* The outer covering of the trunk and branches of a tree.
□*verb* To scrape the skin from: *He fell and barked his knee on the sidewalk.*
bark (bärk) □*noun, plural* **barks** □*verb* **barked, barking, barks**

barley *noun* A plant that bears seeds that are used as food and in making beer.
bar·ley (bär′ lē) □*noun*

barn *noun* A farm building used for storing grain and hay and for sheltering livestock.
barn (bärn) □*noun, plural* **barns**

barnyard *noun* The yard around a barn.
barn·yard (bärn′ yärd′) □*noun, plural* **barnyards**

barometer *noun* An instrument that measures the pressure of the air. It is used to predict changes in the weather.

ba·rom·e·ter (bə **rom′**i tər) □*noun, plural*
barometers

baron *noun* A British nobleman of the lowest
rank.
bar·on (**bar′**ən) □*noun, plural* **barons**

baroness *noun* **1.** The wife or widow of a
baron. **2.** A woman with the rank of a baron.
bar·on·ess (**bar′**ə nis) □*noun, plural*
baronesses

barracks *plural noun* A building or group of
buildings where soldiers live: *His barracks is
very cold and drafty. The barracks were built
ten years ago.*
bar·racks (**bar′**əks) □*plural noun*

barracuda *noun* A tropical sea fish with a
long, narrow body and very sharp teeth.
bar·ra·cu·da (bar′ə **koo′**də) □*noun, plural*
barracudas or **barracuda**

barrel *noun* **1.** A large wooden container
with curved sides. **2.** The metal tube of a gun.
bar·rel (**bar′**əl) □*noun, plural* **barrels**

barren *adjective* Not able to produce offspring, fruit, or other growing things: *a barren
cow; barren soil.*
bar·ren (**bar′**ən) □*adjective*

barrette *noun* A clip for holding the hair.
bar·rette (bə **ret′**) □*noun, plural* **barrettes**

barricade *noun* A fence or other structure
set up to block a way.
□*verb* To close off or block with a barricade.
bar·ri·cade (**bar′**i kād′) □*noun, plural*
barricades □*verb* **barricaded, barricading,
barricades**

barricade

barrier *noun* Something that blocks passage:
The disabled truck was a barrier to traffic.
bar·ri·er (**bar′**ē ər) □*noun, plural* **barriers**

barter *verb* To trade one thing for another
without using money: *The fur trappers bartered animal skins for food.*

□*noun* The act of bartering.
bar·ter (**bär′**tər) □*verb* **bartered, bartering,
barters** □*noun*

base¹ *noun* **1.** The lowest part: *the base of the
mountain.* **2.** A part on which something rests:
the base of the statue. **3.** The main part of
something: *The sauce has a cream base.* **4.** A
starting place; headquarters. **5.** One of the
four corners of the infield in baseball. **6.** A
chemical substance that combines with an
acid to make a salt.
□*verb* To place on a base or foundation: *The
writer based the novel on actual events.*
base (bās) □*noun, plural* **bases** □*verb*
based, basing, bases

base² *adjective* **1.** Not honorable; mean: *a
base trick.* **2.** Not of great value: *Iron is a base
metal.*
base (bās) □*adjective* **baser, basest**

baseball *noun* **1.** A game played with a bat
and ball by two teams of nine players each.
Runs are scored when a player is able to go
around and touch all four bases. **2.** The ball
used in this game.
base·ball (**bās′**bôl′) □*noun, plural* **baseballs**

basement *noun* The lowest floor of a building, often below ground.
base·ment (**bās′**mənt) □*noun, plural*
basements

bases *noun* The plural of **basis.**
ba·ses (**bā′**sēz′) □*noun*

bashful *adjective* Embarrassed with strangers; shy: *a bashful child.*
bash·ful (**bash′**fəl) □*adjective*

bashful

a bat	ī bite	oo tool	*th* feather
ā make	î fierce	ou out	th bath
â dare	o dot	u nut	hw wheat
ä father	ō no	û turn	zh measure
e net	ô law, for	ch church	ə about, open
ē be	oi soil	ng ring	pencil, atom
i dip	oo look	sh shade	circus

basic *adjective* Forming the main part of something; fundamental: *basic ingredients; a basic understanding.*
□*noun* Basic knowledge or skills: *learning the basics of cooking.*
ba·sic (**bā′**sik) □*adjective* □*noun, plural* **basics**

basin *noun* **1.** A round, shallow bowl for holding liquids. **2.** A place filled with still water: *a boat basin.* **3.** The land that is drained by a large river.
ba·sin (**bā′**sən) □*noun, plural* **basins**

basis *noun* The part on which other parts rest; foundation: *the basis of his theory.*
ba·sis (**bā′**sis) □*noun, plural* **bases**

bask *verb* To rest and enjoy warmth: *The girls basked in the sun.*
bask (bask) □*verb* **basked, basking, basks**

basket *noun* **1.** A container made of woven twigs, grasses, or strips of wood. **2.** A metal hoop with an open net hanging from it, used in basketball. **3.** A goal scored in basketball by throwing the ball through this hoop.
bas·ket (**bas′**kit) □*noun, plural* **baskets**

basketball *noun* **1.** A game played by two teams of five players each who try to throw a large ball through a raised basket. **2.** The ball used in this game.
bas·ket·ball (**bas′**kit bôl′) □*noun, plural* **basketballs**

bass¹ *noun* Any of several North American fishes caught for food or sport.
bass (bas) □*noun, plural* **bass** or **basses**

bass² *noun* **1.** The lowest singing voice of a man. **2.** A singer who has such a voice.
bass (bās) □*noun, plural* **basses**

bassoon *noun* A musical instrument with a long wooden body. It makes a low, deep tone when the player blows into the curved metal mouthpiece.
bas·soon (bə soon′) □*noun, plural* **bassoons**

bassoon

baste¹ *verb* To sew with large, loose stitches: *She basted the lining to the jacket.*
baste (bāst) □*verb* **basted, basting, bastes**

baste² *verb* To pour melted fat or other liquid over roasting food: *baste a chicken.*
baste (bāst) □*verb* **basted, basting, bastes**

baste

bat¹ *noun* A wooden or metal club used to hit the ball in games such as baseball.
□*verb* To hit with a bat: *She batted the ball high into the air.*
bat (bat) □*noun, plural* **bats** □*verb* **batted, batting, bats**

bat² *noun* A flying animal with a furry body and thin, leathery wings.

bat

batch *noun* A group of things made or put together: *a batch of brownies.*
batch (bach) □*noun, plural* **batches**

bath *noun* **1.** The act of washing the body in water. **2.** The water used for a bath: *She ran a*

bath for her little sister. **3.** A bathroom.
bath (bath) ▢*noun, plural* **baths**

bathe *verb* **1.** To give or take a bath: *Dad is bathing the baby.* **2.** To seem to pour over; flood: *The porch was bathed in sunlight.* **3.** To go swimming.
bathe (bā*th*) ▢*verb* **bathed, bathing, bathes**

bathing suit *noun* A garment worn for swimming.

bathroom *noun* A room with a sink, toilet, and a bathtub or shower.
bath·room (bath′ro̅o̅m′ *or* bath′room′) ▢*noun, plural* **bathrooms**

bathtub *noun* A tub to bathe in.
bath·tub (bath′tub′) ▢*noun, plural* **bathtubs**

baton *noun* **1.** A thin stick used by an orchestra leader. **2.** A stick twirled by a drum major or majorette.
ba·ton (bə ton′) ▢*noun, plural* **batons**

battalion *noun* A large group of soldiers organized as a unit.
bat·tal·ion (bə tal′yən) ▢*noun, plural* **battalions**

batter¹ *verb* To strike again and again with heavy blows: *Waves battered the little boat.*
bat·ter (bat′ər) ▢*verb* **battered, battering, batters**

batter² *noun* A baseball player who is batting.
bat·ter (bat′ər) ▢*noun, plural* **batters**

batter³ *noun* A mixture of flour, eggs, and milk or water. Batter is fried or baked to make pancakes, biscuits, and cakes.
bat·ter (bat′ər) ▢*noun, plural* **batters**

battery *noun* **1.** A small, sealed container with chemicals inside it that make or store electricity. **2.** A group of things or people that do something together: *a battery of guns.*
bat·ter·y (bat′ər ē) ▢*noun, plural* **batteries**

battle *noun* A fight or struggle: *armies fighting a battle; a battle between chess players.*
▢*verb* To fight; struggle: *Our soldiers battled the enemy troops all night.*
bat·tle (bat′əl) ▢*noun, plural* **battles** ▢*verb* **battled, battling, battles**

battle-ax *or* **battle-axe** *noun* A heavy ax with a broad head, once used as a weapon.
bat·tle-ax *or* **bat·tle-axe** (bat′əl aks′) ▢*noun, plural* **battle-axes**

battlefield *noun* A place where a battle is fought or has been fought.
bat·tle·field (bat′əl fēld′) ▢*noun, plural* **battlefields**

battlement *noun* A wall along the top of a tower or castle with openings for soldiers to shoot through.
bat·tle·ment (bat′əl mənt) ▢*noun, plural* **battlements**

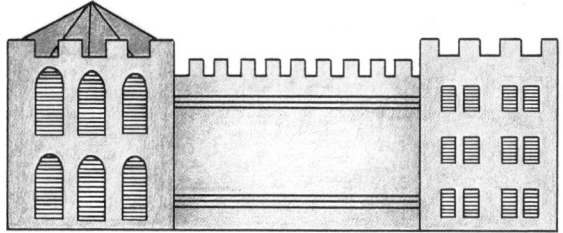
battlement

battleship *noun* A large, heavy warship.
bat·tle·ship (bat′əl ship′) ▢*noun, plural* **battleships**

bawl *verb* To cry loudly: *The frightened child bawled for help.*
▢*noun* A loud cry or shout.
   bawl out To scold: *The coach bawled him out for being late for practice.*
bawl (bôl) ▢*verb* **bawled, bawling, bawls** ▢*noun, plural* **bawls**

bay¹ *noun* A broad part of a sea or lake partly surrounded by land.
bay (bā) ▢*noun, plural* **bays**

bay² *adjective* Reddish-brown: *a bay horse.*
bay (bā) ▢*adjective*

bay³ *noun* The long, deep barking or howling of a dog.
▢*verb* To bark with long, deep cries.
bay (bā) ▢*noun, plural* **bays** ▢*verb* **bayed, baying, bays**

bayonet *noun* A blade attached to the end of a rifle.
bay·o·net (bā′ə nit *or* bā′ə net′) ▢*noun, plural* **bayonets**

WORD HISTORY: **bayonet**

The word *bayonet* comes from the name of the French city Bayonne, where the weapon was first made.

---

a	bat	ĭ	bite	o͝o	tool	*th*	feather
ā	make	î	fierce	ou	out	th	bath
â	dare	o	dot	u	nut	hw	wheat
ä	father	ō	no	û	turn	zh	measure
e	net	ô	law, for	ch	church	ə	about, open
ē	be	oi	soil	ng	ring		pencil, atom
i	dip	oo	look	sh	shade		circus

bayou *noun* A stream that moves slowly through a marsh.
bay·ou (bī′ o͞o *or* bī′ ō) ◻*noun, plural* **bayous**

bazaar *noun* **1.** A market made up of shops and stalls. **2.** A fair or sale, usually held to raise money: *a church bazaar.*
ba·zaar (bə zär′) ◻*noun, plural* **bazaars**

B.C. The abbreviation for "Before Christ." It is used to name a particular year before the birth of Christ: *We learned that 400 B.C. is 250 years earlier than 150 B.C.*

be *verb* **1.** To exist; live: *There was once a young man who wanted to be an explorer.* **2.** To occupy a certain position: *My shoes are in the closet.* **3.** To take place; occur: *When is the meeting?* **4.** Used as a linking verb: *They were exhausted. A poodle is a dog. That pillow was mine.* **5.** Used as a helping verb to indicate the nature or time of an action: *We were talking quietly. I was taken by surprise. You are to go home immediately.*
be (bē) ◻*verb*

Inflected Forms of the Verb *Be*		
PRESENT TENSE		
	1st Person	2nd Person	3rd Person
singular	**am**	**are**	**is**
plural	**are**	**are**	**are**
PRESENT PARTICIPLE		
	1st Person	2nd Person	3rd Person
	being	**being**	**being**
PAST PARTICIPLE		
	1st Person	2nd Person	3rd Person
	been	**been**	**been**
PAST TENSE		
	1st Person	2nd Person	3rd Person
singular	**was**	**were**	**was**
plural	**were**	**were**	**were**

beach *noun* A shore of sand or pebbles next to a body of water.
◻*verb* To pull or drive onto a shore: *beached the canoe.*
beach (bēch) ◻*noun, plural* **beaches** ◻*verb* **beached, beaching, beaches**

beacon *noun* A light or fire used to guide or warn.
bea·con (bē′ kən) ◻*noun, plural* **beacons**

bead *noun* **1.** A small, round piece of hard material with a hole in it through which a string can be pulled: *a bracelet of glass beads.* **2.** A small, round object: *beads of sweat.*
bead (bēd) ◻*noun, plural* **beads**

beagle *noun* A small hunting dog with a smooth coat and drooping ears.
bea·gle (bē′ gəl) ◻*noun, plural* **beagles**

beak *noun* The hard mouth parts of a bird.
beak (bēk) ◻*noun, plural* **beaks**

beak

beaker *noun* A deep container having a wide mouth and sometimes a lip for pouring.
beak·er (bē′ kər) ◻*noun, plural* **beakers**

beam *noun* **1.** A long, sturdy piece of wood or metal. Beams are used to support floors and ceilings. **2.** A ray of light.
◻*verb* **1.** To send off light: *A full moon beamed forth from the clouds.* **2.** To smile widely: *She beamed with happiness.*
beam (bēm) ◻*noun, plural* **beams** ◻*verb* **beamed, beaming, beams**

bean *noun* **1.** A rounded seed of a plant related to peas or clover, often eaten as a vegetable: *lima beans.* **2.** A seed that is like a bean: *coffee beans.*
bean (bēn) ◻*noun, plural* **beans**

bear¹ *verb* **1.** To hold up; support: *That tree branch can't bear your weight.* **2.** To carry: *The card bears a message.* **3.** To put up with: *My grandmother can't bear loud noises.* **4.** To produce; yield: *trees that bear fruit.* **5.** To give birth to: *She has borne four children.*
bear (bâr) ◻*verb* **bore, borne, bearing, bears**

bear

bear² *noun* A large, powerful animal with shaggy fur.
bear (bâr) □*noun, plural* **bears**

beard *noun* **1.** The hair on a man's face. **2.** Something, such as the tuft of hair on a goat's chin, that looks like a beard.
beard (bîrd) □*noun, plural* **beards**

beard

bearing *noun* **1.** The way a person acts, stands, and moves: *the proud bearing of a champion.* **2.** A part on a machine that holds a moving part and allows it to move smoothly. **3.** Connection in thought or meaning: *Her question had no bearing on the subject we were discussing.* **4. bearings** Sense of direction: *We lost our bearings in the forest.*
bear·ing (bâr′ing) □*noun, plural* **bearings**

beast *noun* **1.** An animal, especially a large animal with four feet. **2.** A cruel person.
beast (bēst) □*noun, plural* **beasts**

beat *verb* **1.** To hit or strike again and again: *In the old days, people beat carpets to get out the dust. The waves beat against the shore.* **2.** To move up and down; flap: *The hawk beat its wings and soared off.* **3.** To pound heavily; throb: *His heart beat very fast as he got up to speak.* **4.** To mix rapidly: *beat eggs.* **5.** To win against: *Our team always beats your team.* — See Synonyms at **defeat**.
□*noun* **1.** A stroke or blow made again and again: *the beat of a drum.* **2.** A throb of the heart. **3.** The basic unit of time in music: *Count four beats to each measure.* **4.** A regular route: *a police officer's beat.*
beat (bēt) □*verb* **beat, beaten** or **beat, beating, beats** □*noun, plural* **beats**

beaten *verb* A past participle of **beat**: *Their team hasn't beaten us yet.*
□*adjective* **1.** Defeated. **2.** Much traveled: *beaten paths.*
beat·en (bēt′ən) □*verb* □*adjective*

beautiful *adjective* Very pleasing to the senses: *a beautiful face; beautiful music.*
beau·ti·ful (byoo′tə fəl) □*adjective*

SYNONYMS: **beautiful, handsome, lovely, pretty**

These adjectives mean pleasing to the senses, especially having an appearance that is appealing to look at: *a beautiful painting; a handsome suit; a lovely child; a pretty dress.*

---

beauty *noun* **1.** A quality that makes someone or something pleasing to look at or listen to: *the beauty of a summer morning.* **2.** Someone or something that is beautiful.
beau·ty (byoo′tē) □*noun, plural* **beauties**

beaver *noun* A furry animal with a broad, flat tail, and large front teeth. Beavers gnaw down trees to build dams and homes in rivers and ponds.
bea·ver (bē′vər) □*noun, plural* **beavers**

beaver

became *verb* The past tense of **become**: *He became head of the company.*
be·came (bi kām′) □*verb*

because *conjunction* For the reason that: *He ate because he was hungry.*
be·cause (bi kôz′) □*conjunction*

because of *preposition* On account of: *He was absent from school because of illness.*

beckon *verb* To signal with the head or hand: *She beckoned us to follow her.*
beck·on (bek′ən) □*verb* **beckoned, beckoning, beckons**

a	bat	ī	bite	oo	tool	*th*	feather
ā	make	î	fierce	ou	out	th	bath
â	dare	o	dot	u	nut	hw	wheat
ä	father	ō	no	û	turn	zh	measure
e	net	ô	law, for	ch	church	ə	about, open
ē	be	oi	soil	ng	ring		pencil, atom
i	dip	oo	look	sh	shade		circus

become *verb* **1.** To grow or come to be: *Tadpoles become frogs.* **2.** To look good on: *That new coat becomes you.*
   become of To happen to: *What has become of your old playmates?*
be·come (bi kum′) □*verb* **became, become, becoming, becomes**

becoming *adjective* Attractive; pleasing: *a becoming dress.*
be·com·ing (bi kum′ing) □*adjective*

bed *noun* **1.** A piece of furniture used to rest or sleep on. **2.** A place for sleeping or resting: *The chickens sat on a bed of straw.* **3.** A small piece of land for growing things: *a bed of flowers.* **4.** A bottom or supporting part: *a bed of cement under a house.*
□*verb* To provide with a place to sleep: *He bedded his horse in the barn.*
bed (bed) □*noun, plural* **beds** □*verb* **bedded, bedding, beds**

bedding *noun* Sheets, blankets, and other coverings for a bed.
bed·ding (bed′ing) □*noun*

bedroom *noun* A room for sleeping.
bed·room (bed′rōōm′ *or* bed′room′) □*noun, plural* **bedrooms**

bedspread *noun* A top covering for a bed.
bed·spread (bed′spred′) □*noun, plural* **bedspreads**

bedtime *noun* The time when a person goes to bed.
bed·time (bed′tīm′) □*noun, plural* **bedtimes**

bee *noun* A winged insect that gathers pollen and nectar from flowers. Some bees sting.
bee (bē) □*noun, plural* **bees**

beech *noun* A tree with light-gray bark, strong wood, and small, good-tasting nuts.
beech (bēch) □*noun, plural* **beeches**

beef *noun* The meat of a steer, bull, or cow.
beef (bēf) □*noun*

beefsteak *noun* A slice of beef for broiling or frying.
beef·steak (bēf′stāk′) □*noun, plural* **beefsteaks**

beehive *noun* A place where a swarm of bees lives.
bee·hive (bē′hīv′) □*noun, plural* **beehives**

been *verb* The past participle of **be:** *Where have you been all afternoon?*
been (bin) □*verb*

beer *noun* An alcoholic drink made from malt and hops.
beer (bîr) □*noun, plural* **beers**

beeswax *noun* The wax made by honeybees to build their honeycombs.
bees·wax (bēz′waks′) □*noun*

beet *noun* A plant with a thick, rounded root. A kind of beet with red roots is eaten as a vegetable. Another kind with white roots is used to make sugar.
beet (bēt) □*noun, plural* **beets**

beetle *noun* An insect that has hard, glossy front wings that fold over its back.
bee·tle (bēt′əl) □*noun, plural* **beetles**

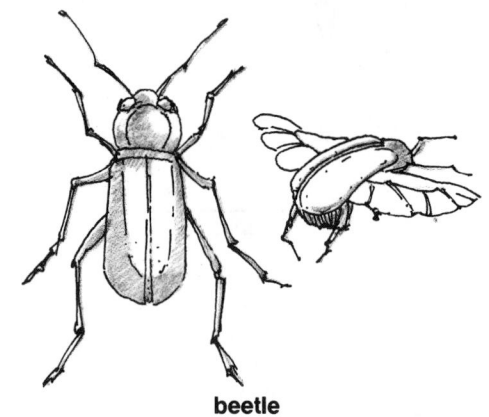

beetle

befall *verb* To happen to: *A strange adventure befell the children.*
be·fall (bi fôl′) □*verb* **befell, befallen, befalling, befalls**

before *adverb* Earlier; previously: *Have you two met before?*
□*preposition* **1.** Earlier than: *She got here before me.* **2.** In front of: *Stand before the window.*
□*conjunction* In advance of the time when: *Think hard before you decide.*
be·fore (bi fôr′) □*adverb* □*preposition* □*conjunction*

beforehand *adverb* Ahead of time: *I only heard about the party an hour beforehand.*
be·fore·hand (bi fôr′hand′) □*adverb*

beg *verb* **1.** To ask for in a humble way: *He begged for forgiveness.* **2.** To ask for as charity: *The poor man had to beg for food.*
beg (beg) □*verb* **begged, begging, begs**

began *verb* The past tense of **begin:** *He began his homework after supper.*
be·gan (bi gan′) □*verb*

beggar *noun* A very poor person who lives by begging.
beg·gar (beg′ər) □*noun, plural* **beggars**

begin *verb* **1.** To have as a starting point: *The parade begins at the firehouse.* **2.** To do the first part of: *He began the jigsaw puzzle but didn't finish it.*
be·gin (bi **gin′**) □*verb* **began, begun, beginning, begins**

SYNONYMS: **begin, commence, start**
These verbs mean to have as a starting point: *School begins at 8 o'clock. The program commenced with a speech by the principal. I always start breakfast with a glass of orange juice.*

---

beginner *noun* Someone who is just learning to do something: *a tennis class for beginners.*
be·gin·ner (bi **gin′**ər) □*noun, plural* **beginners**

beginning *noun* **1.** The first part. **2.** The time when something begins: *Today is the beginning of summer.*
be·gin·ning (bi **gin′**ing) □*noun, plural* **beginnings**

begonia *noun* A plant with brightly colored flowers and leaves.
be·go·nia (bi **gōn′**yə) □*noun, plural* **begonias**

begun *verb* The past participle of **begin**: *The flowers have begun to blossom.*
be·gun (bi **gun′**) □*verb*

behalf *noun* Interest; support: *Your parents will act in your behalf.*
  in behalf of or **on behalf of** In the interest of; for: *She accepted the trophy on behalf of her team.*
be·half (bi **haf′**) □*noun*

behave *verb* **1.** To act or perform in a certain way: *The children behaved badly because they were tired.* **2.** To act properly: *You can come with us if you promise to behave.*
be·have (bi **hāv′**) □*verb* **behaved, behaving, behaves**

behavior *noun* A way of acting; conduct.
be·hav·ior (bi **hāv′**yər) □*noun*

behead *verb* To cut someone's head off.
be·head (bi **hed′**) □*verb* **beheaded, beheading, beheads**

beheld *verb* The past tense and past participle of the verb **behold**: *He beheld the beauty of the northern lights.*
be·held (bi **held′**) □*verb*

behind *preposition* **1.** At the back of: *Hide behind the armchair.* **2.** Later than: *The bus was behind schedule.* **3.** Less advanced than: *He is behind the other students in arithmetic.* **4.** In support of: *Those who were behind the bill worked hard to get it passed.*
□*adverb* **1.** At the back: *sneaking up from behind.* **2.** In the place from which others are departing or have departed: *the children who stayed behind.* **3.** Slower or later than others: *behind in his homework.*
be·hind (bi **hīnd′**) □*preposition* □*adverb*

behold *verb* To look at; see: *People stopped to behold the queen's coach.*
be·hold (bi **hōld′**) □*verb* **beheld, beholding, beholds**

beige *noun* A very light shade of brown.
□*adjective* Of the color beige.
beige (bāzh) □*noun* □*adjective*

being *noun* **1.** A living creature. **2.** Existence: *When did the United States come into being?*
be·ing (**bē′**ing) □*noun, plural* **beings**

belated *adjective* Late or too late; tardy: *She sent a belated birthday present to my brother.*
be·lat·ed (bi **lā′**tid) □*adjective*

belfry *noun* A tower or a space in a tower where bells are hung.
bel·fry (**bel′**frē) □*noun, plural* **belfries**

WORD HISTORY: **belfry**
The word *belfry* has no connection with the word *bell*. Its origin is not certain, but probably *belfry* goes back to a Greek phrase that refers to a movable tower used in war for attacking a city.

belfry

a bat	ī bite	ōō tool	*th* feather
ā make	î fierce	ou out	th bath
â dare	o dot	u nut	hw wheat
ä father	ō no	û turn	zh measure
e net	ô law, for	ch church	ə about, open
ē be	oi soil	ng ring	pencil, atom
i dip	oo look	sh shade	circus

belief *noun* **1.** A thing or idea that is considered to be true: *a belief in God.* **2.** A strong opinion or expectation: *It is my belief that he will come to the party.*
be·lief (bi lēf′) □*noun, plural* **beliefs**

believe *verb* **1.** To accept as true or real: *He believes in Santa Claus.* **2.** To think or suppose: *I believe she's already left.*
be·lieve (bi lēv′) □*verb* **believed, believing, believes**

SYNONYMS: **believe, figure, think**

These verbs mean to accept as true or real: *Do you believe in ghosts? I figured she wouldn't come. I think she is telling the truth.*

WORD HISTORY: **believe**

The word *believe* is a very old word. It originally meant "to consider something to be valuable," or "to be pleased with something." *Believe* is related to the word *love.*

---

bell *noun* **1.** A hollow piece of metal that is shaped like a cup. It makes a ringing sound when struck. **2.** Something that makes a ringing sound, such as a door bell.
bell (bel) □*noun, plural* **bells**

belligerent *adjective* Fighting or eager to fight: *a belligerent bully.*
bel·lig·er·ent (bə lij′ər ənt) □*adjective*

bellow *verb* To make a loud roaring noise: *The angry bull bellowed.*
□*noun* A loud roar.
bel·low (bel′ō) □*verb* **bellowed, bellowing, bellows** □*noun, plural* **bellows**

bellows *plural noun* A simple air pump, often used for making fires burn hotter.
bel·lows (bel′ōz) □*plural noun*

belly *noun* **1.** The front part of the body between the chest and thighs; abdomen. **2.** The stomach. **3.** A deep, bulging part of something: *the belly of the ship.*
□*verb* To swell; bulge: *The sails bellied in the wind.*
bel·ly (bel′ē) □*noun, plural* **bellies** □*verb* **bellied, bellying, bellies**

belong *verb* **1.** To have a proper place: *The milk belongs in the refrigerator.* **2.** To be owned by: *This ring belonged to my grandmother.* **3.** To be a member of: *She belongs to several clubs.*
be·long (bi lông′) □*verb* **belonged, belonging, belongs**

belongings *plural noun* The things a person owns; possessions.
be·long·ings (bi lông′ings) □*plural noun*

beloved *adjective* Dearly loved: *a beloved friend.*
□*noun* Someone who is greatly loved.
be·lov·ed (bi luv′id *or* bi luvd′) □*adjective* □*noun*

below *adverb* **1.** In or to a lower place: *looking down at the river below.* **2.** Lower on a scale than zero: *a temperature of 25° below.*
□*preposition* **1.** Underneath; beneath: *the ground below us.* **2.** Lower than: *below freezing.*
be·low (bi lō′) □*adverb* □*preposition*

belt *noun* **1.** A band or strap worn around the waist to hold up clothing or for decoration. **2.** A region; area: *the farm belt.* **3.** A band that goes around wheels or pulleys.
belt (belt) □*noun, plural* **belts**

bench *noun* **1.** A long seat: *a park bench.* **2.** A sturdy table on which to work: *a carpenter's bench.* **3.** A judge in a law court: *The prisoner approached the bench.*
□*verb* To remove or keep a player from a game: *The coach benched him for the week.*
bench (bench) □*noun, plural* **benches** □*verb* **benched, benching, benches**

bend *verb* **1.** To make or become curved or crooked: *He bent the nail by hitting it wrong. Willow branches bend in the wind.* **2.** To move part of the body lower: *She bent down to pet the kitten.*
□*noun* A bent part: *a bend in the road.*
bend (bend) □*verb* **bent, bending, bends** □*noun, plural* **bends**

bend

beneath *preposition* Below; under: *sleeping beneath the tree.*

□*adverb* Below; underneath: *a bedspread with a blanket beneath.*
be·neath (bi **nēth′**) □*preposition* □*adverb*

benefit *noun* Something that is good or helpful: *The new hospital will be a great benefit to the city.*
□*verb* **1.** To be helpful to: *A new coat of paint would benefit the room.* **2.** To receive help: *I benefited from his good advice.*
ben·e·fit (**ben′**ə fit) □*noun, plural* **benefits**
□*verb* **benefited, benefiting, benefits**

bent *verb* The past tense and past participle of **bend:** *You have bent the nail.*
□*adjective* **1.** Not in a straight line; curved: *a bent key.* **2.** Determined: *She is bent on winning the race.*
bent (bent) □*verb* □*adjective*

beret *noun* A soft, round, flat cap.
be·ret (bə **rā′**) □*noun, plural* **berets**

beret

berry *noun* A small, juicy fruit with many seeds.
ber·ry (**ber′**ē) □*noun, plural* **berries**

berth *noun* **1.** A small bed or bunk: *a berth on a train.* **2.** A space for a ship to dock.
berth (bûrth) □*noun, plural* **berths**

beseech *verb* To ask in an earnest or pleading way: *They beseeched him to release the prisoner.*
be·seech (bi **sēch′**) □*verb* **besought** or **beseeched, beseeching, beseeches**

beside *preposition* At the side of: *the yard beside the school.*
be·side (bi **sīd′**) □*preposition*

besides *adverb* In addition: *I don't like basketball, and besides I'm too short.*
□*preposition* In addition to; other than: *What sports do you like besides tennis?*
be·sides (bi **sīdz′**) □*adverb* □*preposition*

besiege *verb* To surround in order to capture: *The enemy besieged the town.*
be·siege (bi **sēj′**) □*verb* **besieged, besieging, besieges**

besought *verb* A past tense and past participle of **beseech:** *We besought his mercy.*
be·sought (bi **sôt′**) □*verb*

best *adjective* **1.** Most excellent: *the best fried chicken; the best athlete.* **2.** The largest: *the best part of an hour.* **3.** Closest; favorite: *my best friend.*
□*adverb* **1.** In the most excellent way: *I work best in the morning.* **2.** In the highest degree; most: *What color do you like best?*
□*noun* **1.** The most excellent person or persons: *Even the best of us make mistakes.* **2.** The most possible: *Do your best.*
best (best) □*adjective* □*adverb* □*noun*

bet *noun* An agreement between two people that the one who makes the wrong guess about something will give money or something of value to the one who is right.
□*verb* **1.** To assert with or as if with a bet: *He bet that whales aren't fish, and he won. I bet we have a test today.* **2.** To risk on a bet: *He bet five dollars.*
bet (bet) □*noun, plural* **bets** □*verb* **bet, betting, bets**

betray *verb* To be disloyal to: *He betrayed his country by giving secrets to the enemy.*
be·tray (bi **trā′**) □*verb* **betrayed, betraying, betrays**

better *adjective* **1.** More excellent or suitable: *He is a better runner than his brother.* **2.** Improved in condition or health: *Do you feel better?*
□*adverb* In a more excellent or suitable way: *This pen writes better.*
□*noun* Someone or something that is superior: *This drawing is the better of the two.*
bet·ter (**bet′**ər) □*adjective* □*adverb* □*noun, plural* **betters**

between *preposition* **1.** In the time or space separating: *a valley between two ridges; the time between 3 and 4 o'clock.* **2.** After a comparison of: *a choice between two desserts.*

a	bat	ī	bite	oo	tool	*th*	feather
ā	make	î	fierce	ou	out	th	bath
â	dare	o	dot	u	nut	hw	wheat
ä	father	ō	no	û	turn	zh	measure
e	net	ô	law, for	ch	church	ə	about, open
ē	be	oi	soil	ng	ring		pencil, atom
i	dip	oo	look	sh	shade		circus

3. Linking: *a highway between the two cities.*
4. Engaged in by; involving: *an argument between two drivers.*
□*adverb* In the time or space separating: *two towns with a winding road between.*
be·tween (bi **twēn′**) □*preposition* □*adverb*

beverage *noun* A liquid for drinking.
bev·er·age (**bev′**ər ij) □*noun, plural* **beverages**

beware *verb* To watch out for: *Beware of the dog!*
be·ware (bi **wâr′**) □*verb*

bewilder *verb* To confuse very much: *The complicated instructions bewildered the child.* —See Synonyms at **confuse.**
be·wil·der (bi **wil′**dər) □*verb* **bewildered, bewildering, bewilders**

bewitch *verb* **1.** To cast a spell over: *The magician bewitched the king and turned him into a statue.* **2.** To charm; delight: *The adorable child bewitched the whole family.*
be·witch (bi **wich′**) □*verb* **bewitched, bewitching, bewitches**

beyond *preposition* **1.** On the far side of: *The lake is just beyond those trees.* **2.** Farther than: *Can you count beyond ten?* **3.** Outside the limit of: *beyond control.*
□*adverb* Farther away: *explore our solar system and the vast space beyond.*
be·yond (bē **ond′** *or* bi **yond′**) □*preposition* □*adverb*

bias *noun* A strong feeling for or against something without enough reason: *Some people have a bias against foreigners.*
bi·as (**bī′**əs) □*noun, plural* **biases**

Bible *noun* **1.** The Old Testament, the sacred book of the Jews. **2.** The Old Testament and the New Testament, which together make up the sacred book of the Christians.
Bi·ble (**bī′**bəl) □*noun, plural* **Bibles**

WORD HISTORY: **Bible**

The Bible is a collection of many different works written down at different times. The word *Bible* comes from a Greek word that means "the books."

Biblical or **biblical** *adjective* Of or relating to the Bible.
Bib·li·cal or **bib·li·cal** (**bib′**li kəl) □*adjective*

biceps *noun* The large muscle at the top of the arm.
bi·ceps (**bī′**seps′) □*noun, plural* **biceps**

bicker *verb* To argue over unimportant things: *bicker over who will wash the dishes.*
bick·er (**bik′**ər) □*verb* **bickered, bickering, bickers**

bicuspid *noun* A tooth that has two points.
bi·cus·pid (bī **kus′**pid) □*noun, plural* **bicuspids**

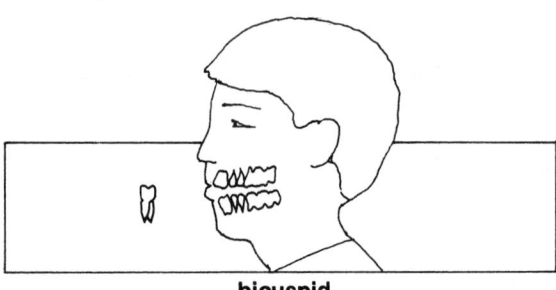

bicuspid

bicycle *noun* A vehicle that has two wheels. It is moved forward by pushing two pedals with the feet and is steered by turning the handlebars.
□*verb* To ride a bicycle.
bi·cy·cle (**bī′**si kəl) □*noun, plural* **bicycles** □*verb* **bicycled, bicycling, bicycles**

bid *verb* **1.** To tell someone to do something; command: *The librarian bid us be quiet.* **2.** To say when greeting or leaving: *The clerk bids us good morning every day.* **3.** To offer to pay a certain price: *I bid $25 for his collection of baseball cards.*
□*noun* An offer of a certain price: *a bid of $100 for the painting.*
bid (bid) □*verb* **bid, bidding, bids** □*noun, plural* **bids**

bidding *noun* A command or request: *She washed the dishes at her mother's bidding.*
bid·ding (**bid′**ing) □*noun, plural* **biddings**

bide *verb* **bide one's time** To wait for the right moment.
bide (bīd) □*verb* **bided, biding, bides**

big *adjective* **1.** Of considerable size; large: *a big animal; the biggest house.* **2.** Important: *a big game.*
big (big) □*adjective* **bigger, biggest**

SYNONYMS: **big, great, large**

These adjectives mean of considerable size: *She gets a big allowance. The farm covered a great tract of land. A large crowd filled the stadium.*

---

bike *noun* A bicycle.
bike (bīk) □*noun, plural* **bikes**

bile   *noun* A bitter liquid made by the liver. It helps the body digest fats.
bile (bīl) □*noun*

bill[1]   *noun* **1.** A written statement of money owed for things bought or work done: *a doctor's bill.* **2.** A piece of paper money: *a five-dollar bill.* **3.** A poster or public sign. **4.** A proposal for a new law: *Congress passed the bill.* □*verb* To send a statement of money owed: *The school billed me for the lost library book.*
bill (bil) □*noun, plural* **bills** □*verb* **billed, billing, bills**

bill[2]   *noun* The hard, projecting mouth parts of a bird.
bill (bil) □*noun, plural* **bills**

billboard   *noun* A large board for displaying advertising posters.
bill·board (bil′bôrd′) □*noun, plural* **billboards**

billfold   *noun* A small folding case for holding paper money or cards; wallet.
bill·fold (bil′fōld′) □*noun, plural* **billfolds**

billiards   *plural noun* A game played on a cloth covered table in which points are scored by using a long stick called a cue to hit three solid balls against one another.
bil·liards (bil′yərdz) □*plural noun*

billion   *noun* One thousand million; 1,000,000,000.
bil·lion (bil′yən) □*noun, plural* **billions**

billow   *noun* A great wave or swelling mass of something: *Billows of smoke rose from the burning building.*
□*verb* To rise or swell in billows: *Smoke billowed from the campfire.*
bil·low (bil′ō) □*noun, plural* **billows** □*verb* **billowed, billowing, billows**

billow

bin   *noun* An enclosed space for storing grain or other items.
bin (bin) □*noun, plural* **bins**

bind   *verb* **1.** To tie up; fasten: *He bound the pile of magazines with string.* **2.** To wrap a bandage around: *bind a wound.* **3.** To unite: *The friends were bound by common interests.* **4.** To fasten pages together between covers: *bind a book.*
bind (bīnd) □*verb* **bound, binding, binds**

bind

binoculars   *plural noun* A device that consists of two small telescopes joined together and that is used to make distant objects seem closer and larger.
bi·noc·u·lars (bə nok′yə lərz) □*plural noun*

biography   *noun* A written history of someone's life.
bi·og·ra·phy (bī og′rə fē) □*noun, plural* **biographies**

biology   *noun* The study of plants and animals and their origin, growth, structure, and distribution.
bi·ol·o·gy (bī ol′ə jē) □*noun*

birch   *noun* A tree with hard wood and smooth bark that peels off easily.
birch (bûrch) □*noun, plural* **birches**

bird   *noun* An animal that lays eggs and has feathers and wings. Most birds can fly.
bird (bûrd) □*noun, plural* **birds**

birth   *noun* **1.** The beginning of a life: *The baby weighed six pounds at birth.* **2.** A beginning; origin: *the birth of a friendship.*
birth (bûrth) □*noun, plural* **births**

a	bat	ī	bite	ōō	tool	*th*	feather
ā	make	i	fierce	ou	out	th	bath
â	dare	o	dot	u	nut	hw	wheat
ä	father	ō	no	û	turn	zh	measure
e	net	ô	law, for	ch	church	ə	about, open
ē	be	oi	soil	ng	ring		pencil, atom
i	dip	oo	look	sh	shade		circus

birthday   *noun* **1.** The day on which someone is born. **2.** The anniversary of this day.
birth·day (bûrth′dā′) ☐*noun, plural* **birthdays**

birthmark   *noun* A mark present on the skin at birth.
birth·mark (bûrth′märk′) ☐*noun, plural* **birthmarks**

birthmark

birthplace   *noun* The place where someone was born.
birth·place (bûrth′plās′) ☐*noun, plural* **birthplaces**

biscuit   *noun* A small roll or cake of baked dough.
bis·cuit (bis′kit) ☐*noun, plural* **biscuits**

WORD HISTORY: **biscuit**

Biscuit comes from an old French word that means ''cooked twice.''

---

bishop   *noun* **1.** A Christian clergyman of high rank. **2.** A chess piece that can move only in a diagonal line.
bish·op (bish′əp) ☐*noun, plural* **bishops**

bison   *noun* A large animal of western North America that has a humped back and a large shaggy head.
bi·son (bī′sən *or* bī′zən) ☐*noun, plural* **bison**

bit[1]   *noun* **1.** A small piece or amount: *The bottle fell and broke into bits. It didn't help a bit.* **2.** A short time: *Please stay a bit.*
    a bit Slightly; somewhat: *I am a bit worried.*
bit (bit) ☐*noun, plural* **bits**

bit[2]   *noun* **1.** A pointed part of a tool used for drilling holes. **2.** A metal piece on a bridle that fits into a horse's mouth.
bit (bit) ☐*noun, plural* **bits**

bit

bit[3]   *verb* The past tense of **bite:** *The dog bit the mailman.*
bit (bit) ☐*verb*

bite   *verb* **1.** To cut or tear with the teeth: *She bit off the end of the hot dog.* **2.** To pierce the skin with fangs, a stinger, or teeth: *A snake bit him. That dog bites!* **3.** To cause a sharp pain to: *The cold wind bit his face.* **4.** To take bait: *The fish aren't biting today.*
☐*noun* **1.** A wound that comes from biting. **2.** An amount of food taken into the mouth at one time. **3.** A sharp pain; sting.
bite (bīt) ☐*verb* **bit, bitten, biting, bites** ☐*noun, plural* **bites**

bitter   *adjective* **1.** Tasting sharp or unpleasant: *a bitter medicine.* **2.** Full of or causing pain, resentment, or hatred: *a bitter wind; bitter tears; bitter enemies.*
bit·ter (bit′ər) ☐*adjective* **bitterer, bitterest**

bituminous coal   *noun* A soft coal that burns with a smoky flame.
bi·tu·mi·nous coal (bi tōō′mə nəs) ☐*noun*

black   *noun* **1.** The darkest of all colors. **2.** Often **Black** A member of a race of people having brown to black skin.
☐*adjective* **1.** Having the darkest of all colors: *black ink.* **2.** Often **Black** Of or belonging to a race of people having brown to black skin: *Black history.* **3.** Without light; dark.
black (blak) ☐*noun, plural* **blacks** ☐*adjective* **blacker, blackest**

blackberry   *noun* An edible black berry that grows on a thorny plant.

black·ber·ry (blak′ber′ē) ▫*noun, plural* **blackberries**

blackbird *noun* Any of several birds that have mostly black feathers.
black·bird (blak′bûrd′) ▫*noun, plural* **blackbirds**

blackboard *noun* A hard board for writing on with chalk.
black·board (blak′bôrd′) ▫*noun, plural* **blackboards**

blacken *verb* To make or become black: *Smoke from the factory blackened the sky. The sky blackened before the storm.*
black·en (blak′ən) ▫*verb* **blackened, blackening, blackens**

blackmail *verb* To try to force a person to pay something by threatening to tell a secret. ▫*noun* An act of blackmailing.
black·mail (blak′māl′) ▫*verb* **blackmailed, blackmailing, blackmails** ▫*noun*

WORD HISTORY: **blackmail**

In the border counties of England and Scotland about 400 years ago robber chiefs used to force the inhabitants to give them money. If the local people refused to pay, the chiefs would plunder their property. The payment was known as "black mail," which means "black tax." The current sense of the word *blackmail* developed from this practice.

---

blacksmith *noun* Someone who makes things out of iron, such as horseshoes.
black·smith (blak′smith′) ▫*noun, plural* **blacksmiths**

black widow *noun* A black spider. The female has a red mark and a poisonous bite.

bladder *noun* A small structure like a bag in the body. It stores urine.
blad·der (blad′ər) ▫*noun, plural* **bladders**

blade *noun* **1.** The flat, sharp part of a tool that cuts: *a knife blade.* **2.** A leaf of grass. **3.** A broad, flat part: *the blade of an oar.*
blade (blād) ▫*noun, plural* **blades**

blame *verb* **1.** To consider guilty or responsible: *She blamed me for starting the fight.* **2.** To find fault with: *You're afraid of snakes, and I don't blame you.* ▫*noun* Responsibility for something wrong: *I took the blame for losing the money.*
blame (blām) ▫*verb* **blamed, blaming, blames** ▫*noun*

blank *adjective* **1.** Without writing or decoration on it: *blank paper.* **2.** Without expression or ideas: *a blank stare.*
▫*noun* **1.** An empty space: *Write your answers in the blanks after the questions.* **2.** A form with empty spaces to be written in: *an application blank for a job.* **3.** A cartridge containing gunpowder but no bullet.
blank (blangk) ▫*adjective* **blanker, blankest** ▫*noun, plural* **blanks**

blanket *noun* **1.** A covering of soft, thick cloth, used on a bed to keep a person warm. **2.** A thick cover: *a blanket of snow.*
▫*verb* To cover with a blanket.
blank·et (blang′kit) ▫*noun, plural* **blankets** ▫*verb* **blanketed, blanketing, blankets**

blare *noun* A loud, shrill sound: *the blare of a horn.*
▫*verb* To make a loud, shrill sound: *The trumpets blared.*
blare (blâr) ▫*noun, plural* **blares** ▫*verb* **blared, blaring, blares**

blast *noun* **1.** A strong gust of wind or air. **2.** A loud noise: *the blast of a car horn.* **3.** An explosion.
▫*verb* **1.** To blow up with explosives: *They blasted the trees to make room for the new road.* **2.** To destroy or ruin.
blast off To move into flight propelled by rockets: *The spaceship will blast off at noon.*
blast (blast) ▫*noun, plural* **blasts** ▫*verb* **blasted, blasting, blasts**

blast

a	bat	ī	bite	ŏŏ	tool	th	feather
ā	make	î	fierce	ou	out	th	bath
â	dare	o	dot	u	nut	hw	wheat
ä	father	ō	no	û	turn	zh	measure
e	net	ô	law, for	ch	church	ə	about, open
ē	be	oi	soil	ng	ring		pencil, atom
i	dip	oo	look	sh	shade		circus

blaze¹   *noun* **1.** A burning fire or flame. **2.** A bright light: *the blaze of a spotlight.*
□*verb* **1.** To burn with a bright flame: *The forest fire blazed for two days.* **2.** To send out a bright light.
blaze (blāz) □*noun, plural* **blazes** □*verb* **blazed, blazing, blazes**

SYNONYMS: **blaze¹, gleam, shine**
These verbs mean to send out a bright light: *The child's eyes blazed in delight. A flashlight gleamed in the darkness. The sun was shining all day.*

---

blaze²   *noun* A mark made on a tree to show where a trail is.
□*verb* To put marks on or along: *We blazed a trail through the woods.*
blaze (blāz) □*noun, plural* **blazes** □*verb* **blazed, blazing, blazes**

bldg. An abbreviation of **building.**

bleach   *verb* To make or become lighter or white: *He bleached the laundry by adding chlorine. Her hair bleaches in the sun.*
□*noun* A substance used for bleaching.
bleach (blēch) □*verb* **bleached, bleaching, bleaches** □*noun, plural* **bleaches**

bleachers   *plural noun* Benches for people to sit on at outdoor events.
bleach·ers (blē′chərz) □*plural noun*

bleak   *adjective* **1.** Gloomy; dreary: *a bleak, lonely life.* **2.** Cold and bare: *a bleak hillside.*
bleak (blēk) □*adjective* **bleaker, bleakest**

bled   *verb* The past tense and past participle of **bleed:** *She cut her toe and it bled.*
bled (blĕd) □*verb*

bleed   *verb* **1.** To lose blood: *My nose is bleeding.* **2.** To lose sap or liquid.
bleed (blēd) □*verb* **bled, bleeding, bleeds**

blemish   *noun* Something, such as a mark, that spoils appearance or quality: *The wet glass left a blemish on the desk.*
□*verb* To spoil the appearance or quality of: *A low grade in English blemished his report card.*
blem·ish (blĕm′ish) □*noun, plural* **blemishes** □*verb* **blemished, blemishing, blemishes**

blend   *verb* **1.** To mix together thoroughly: *Blend the milk and eggs.* **2.** To have a color that goes well with another: *The brown sofa blends well with the rug.*
□*noun* A smooth mixture: *The sauce is a blend of mustard and cream.*

blend (blend) □*verb* **blended, blending, blends** □*noun, plural* **blends**

bless   *verb* **1.** To make holy: *The bishop blessed the new church.* **2.** To ask God's favor for: *The woman blessed the little children.* **3.** To grant good fortune to: *She has always been blessed with good health.*
bless (bles) □*verb* **blessed** or **blest, blessing, blesses**

blessing   *noun* **1.** A prayer for God's favor or to thank God. **2.** A wish for success; approval: *He devoted himself to music with his parents' blessing.* **3.** Something that brings happiness: *The child is a blessing to her grandparents.*
bless·ing (bles′ing) □*noun, plural* **blessings**

blew   *verb* The past tense of **blow:** *He blew up the balloon.*
blew (blo͞o) □*verb*

blight   *noun* A disease that withers or kills plants.
blight (blīt) □*noun, plural* **blights**

blimp   *noun* An airship that resembles a large balloon and can be steered and can carry things.
blimp (blimp) □*noun, plural* **blimps**

blimp

blind   *adjective* **1.** Not able to see. **2.** Depending on instruments and not on eyes: *The pilot made a blind landing in the fog.* **3.** Without reason or good sense: *blind faith.* **4.** Closed at one end: *a blind alley.*
□*noun* Something that shuts out light: *window blinds.*
□*verb* **1.** To make unable to see: *The dazzling snow temporarily blinded him.* **2.** To cause to lose good judgment: *His love blinded him to her faults.*
blind (blīnd) □*adjective* **blinder, blindest** □*noun, plural* **blinds** □*verb* **blinded, blinding, blinds**

blindfold   *verb* To cover the eyes of.
□*noun* A piece of cloth put over the eyes to keep someone from seeing.

blind·fold (blīnd′fōld′) □*verb* **blindfolded, blindfolding, blindfolds** □*noun, plural* **blindfolds**

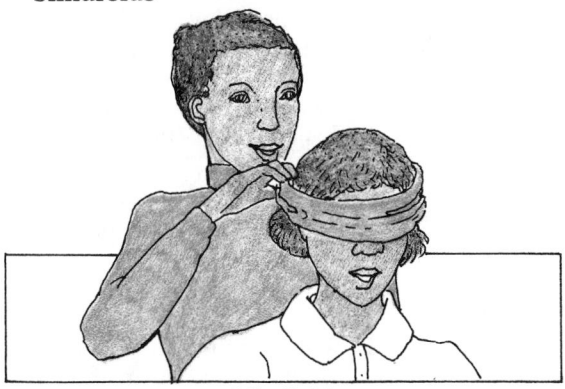

blindfold

blindness *noun* The condition of not being able to see.
blind·ness (blīnd′nis) □*noun*

blink *verb* **1.** To close and open the eyes quickly: *She blinked in the bright sunlight.* **2.** To flash off and on: *The weak flashlight kept blinking.*
blink (blingk) □*verb* **blinked, blinking, blinks**

bliss *noun* Great happiness or joy.
bliss (blis) □*noun*

blister *noun* A small sore on the skin that is filled with fluid: *The tight shoes gave him blisters.*
□*verb* To form a blister: *His skin blistered from the sunburn.*
blis·ter (blis′tər) □*noun, plural* **blisters** □*verb* **blistered, blistering, blisters**

blizzard *noun* A heavy snowstorm with strong winds.
bliz·zard (bliz′ərd) □*noun, plural* **blizzards**

bloat *verb* To cause to swell: *Eating too much bloated the dog's stomach.*
bloat (blōt) □*verb* **bloated, bloating, bloats**

blob *noun* A soft lump: *a blob of paint.*
blob (blob) □*noun, plural* **blobs**

block *noun* **1.** A solid piece of hard material: *a building made of stone blocks.* **2.** Something that gets in the way of other things: *The fallen tree caused a block in the flow of the stream.* **3.** An area in a city or town with streets on all four sides. **4.** The length of one side of a city block: *The bus stops two blocks from my house.* **5.** A group of connected things: *a block of tickets.*
□*verb* To be in the way of: *A guard blocked*

the entrance.
block (blok) □*noun, plural* **blocks** □*verb* **blocked, blocking, blocks**

blockade *noun* The closing off of an area to keep people and supplies from going in or out. □*verb* To close off with a blockade: *The ships blockaded the enemy's ports.*
block·ade (blo kād′) □*noun, plural* **blockades** □*verb* **blockaded, blockading, blockades**

blockhouse *noun* A fort built of heavy timbers or other sturdy material.
block·house (blok′hous′) □*noun, plural* **block·hous·es** (blok′hou′ziz)

blond or **blonde** *adjective* **1.** Having light-colored hair and pale skin: *a blond boy; a blonde girl.* **2.** Light in color: *blond wood.*
□*noun* Someone with light-colored hair and pale skin.
blond or **blonde** (blond) □*adjective* **blonder, blondest** □*noun, plural* **blonds** or **blondes**

blood *noun* **1.** The red liquid that the heart pumps through the body. Blood carries oxygen throughout the body, and it carries away waste materials. **2.** Ancestry; kinship: *Brothers and sisters are related by blood.*
in cold blood Without being sorry; cruelly: *He killed the stranger in cold blood.*
blood (blud) □*noun, plural* **bloods**

bloodhound *noun* A large dog with drooping ears, a wrinkled face, and a keen sense of smell.
blood·hound (blud′hound′) □*noun, plural* **bloodhounds**

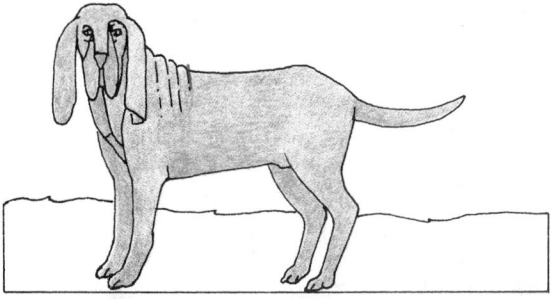

bloodhound

a	bat	ī	bite	o͞o	tool	th	feather
ā	make	î	fierce	ou	out	th	bath
â	dare	o	dot	u	nut	hw	wheat
ä	father	ō	no	û	turn	zh	measure
e	net	ô	law, for	ch	church	ə	about, open
ē	be	oi	soil	ng	ring		pencil, atom
i	dip	oo	look	sh	shade		circus

bloodshed *noun* The loss of blood or life by killing or wounding: *The police captured the robbers without bloodshed.*
blood·shed (blŭd′shĕd′) □*noun*

bloodstream *noun* The blood flowing through a living body.
blood·stream (blŭd′strēm′) □*noun*

bloodthirsty *adjective* Eager to cause or see bloodshed: *a bloodthirsty villain.*
blood·thirst·y (blŭd′thûr′stē) □*adjective*
bloodthirstier, bloodthirstiest

blood vessel *noun* Any of the tubes in the body through which blood circulates.

bloody *adjective* **1.** Bleeding or covered with blood: *bloody bandages.* **2.** Marked by much bloodshed: *a bloody battle.*
blood·y (blŭd′ē) □*adjective* **bloodier,**
bloodiest

bloom *noun* **1.** A flower. **2.** The time or condition of flowering: *The cherry trees are in bloom now.*
□*verb* To bear flowers; blossom.
bloom (blōōm) □*noun, plural* **blooms** □*verb*
bloomed, blooming, blooms

blossom *noun* **1.** A flower. **2.** The time or condition of flowering: *The apple trees are in blossom.*
□*verb* **1.** To bear flowers; bloom. **2.** To grow and develop: *The boy blossomed into a tall, strong young man.*
blos·som (blŏs′əm) □*noun, plural* **blossoms**
□*verb* **blossomed, blossoming, blossoms**

blot *noun* **1.** A stain or spot: *a blot of ink.* **2.** Something that spoils beauty or perfection: *One bad grade left a blot on his record.*
□*verb* **1.** To spot or stain: *The ink spilled and blotted the letter.* **2.** To soak up: *She blotted up the water with a cloth.*
blot (blŏt) □*noun, plural* **blots** □*verb*
blotted, blotting, blots

blotch *noun* A large, irregular spot or blot.
□*verb* To mark with spots: *The rash blotched his face.*
blotch (blŏch) □*noun, plural* **blotches**
□*verb* **blotched, blotching, blotches**

blotter *noun* A piece of thick paper used to soak up wet ink.
blot·ter (blŏt′ər) □*noun, plural* **blotters**

blouse *noun* A loose shirt, usually worn by women or girls.
blouse (blous *or* blouz) □*noun, plural*
blouses

blow¹ *verb* **1.** To be in motion: *The wind blew all night.* **2.** To move by means of a current of air: *The balloon blew across the field.* **3.** To send out a current of air: *Blow out the candles.* **4.** To make a noise by forcing air through: *blow a whistle.* **5.** To shape by forcing air into or through: *blow bubbles.* **6.** To destroy or break by an explosion: *The bomb blew the house apart.*
   blow up 1. To fill with air or gas: *blow up a bicycle tire.* **2.** To make larger: *blow up a photograph.* **3.** To get angry.
blow (blō) □*verb* **blew, blown, blowing,**
blows

blow² *noun* **1.** A hard hit with a fist or weapon. **2.** A sudden shock or misfortune: *Losing the game was a blow to the team.*
blow (blō) □*noun, plural* **blows**

blower *noun* A device that creates a flow of air: *Blowers keep air moving in the tunnel.*
blow·er (blō′ər) □*noun, plural* **blowers**

blown *verb* The past participle of **blow**: *The wind has blown the snow into drifts.*
blown (blōn) □*verb*

blowtorch *noun* A small torch that can give off a hot flame and is used for melting metal and burning off old paint.
blow·torch (blō′tôrch′) □*noun, plural*
blowtorches

blowtorch

blubber *noun* The thick layer of fat under the skin of whales and some other sea animals.
blub·ber (blŭb′ər) □*noun*

blue *noun* The color of the sky on a clear day.
□*adjective* **1.** Of the color blue. **2.** Gloomy; sad: *She felt blue because her dog was sick.*

blue (bloo) ▢*noun, plural* **blues** ▢*adjective* **bluer, bluest**

blueberry *noun* A round, juicy, edible blue berry that grows on a bush.
blue·ber·ry (bloo′ber′ē) ▢*noun, plural* **blueberries**

bluebird *noun* A North American bird with a blue back and a red breast.
blue·bird (bloo′bûrd′) ▢*noun, plural* **bluebirds**

bluegrass *noun* A grass with bluish stems, grown on lawns and pastures.
blue·grass (bloo′gras′) ▢*noun*

blue jay *noun* A North American bird that has a crest on its head and blue feathers.

bluejay

blue jeans *plural noun* Pants made out of sturdy blue cloth; dungarees.

blueprint *noun* A design for a building or machine, with white lines on blue paper.
blue·print (bloo′print′) ▢*noun, plural* **blueprints**

blues *plural noun* **1.** A kind of slow, sad jazz music. **2.** Low spirits; sadness: *I get the blues when I'm all alone.*
blues (blooz) ▢*plural noun*

bluff¹ *verb* To try to fool others by pretending to have, do, or be something: *He said he was a great tennis player, but he was only bluffing.* ▢*noun* Something that is pretended in order to fool others.
bluff (bluf) ▢*verb* **bluffed, bluffing, bluffs** ▢*noun, plural* **bluffs**

bluff² *noun* A steep cliff or river bank.
bluff (bluf) ▢*noun, plural* **bluffs**

bluff

blunder *noun* A foolish mistake: *She made a blunder when she lost her keys.* ▢*verb* **1.** To make a foolish mistake: *I blundered when I said that Maine was next to Ohio.* **2.** To move in a clumsy way: *He blundered through the darkened room.*
blun·der (blun′dər) ▢*noun, plural* **blunders** ▢*verb* **blundered, blundering, blunders**

blunderbuss *noun* An old type of gun with a wide muzzle, used to shoot at close range without aiming carefully.
blun·der·buss (blun′dər bus′) ▢*noun, plural* **blunderbusses**

blunt *adjective* **1.** Having an edge or point that is not sharp: *a blunt pencil.* **2.** Very direct and frank: *a blunt answer.* ▢*verb* To make less sharp: *You'll blunt the scissors if you use it to cut cardboard.*
blunt (blunt) ▢*adjective* **blunter, bluntest** ▢*verb* **blunted, blunting, blunts**

blur *verb* To make or become less clear: *Fog blurred the tops of the hills. Her vision blurred as she became sleepy.* ▢*noun* Something that is not clear: *The hummingbird's wings were a blur.*
blur (blûr) ▢*verb* **blurred, blurring, blurs** ▢*noun, plural* **blurs**

blurt *verb* To say suddenly and without thinking: *He blurted out the secret.*
blurt (blûrt) ▢*verb* **blurted, blurting, blurts**

a bat	ī bite	oo tool	*th* feather
ā make	î fierce	ou out	th bath
â dare	o dot	u nut	hw wheat
ä father	ō no	û turn	zh measure
e net	ô law, for	ch church	ə about, open
ē be	oi soil	ng ring	pencil, atom
i dip	oo look	sh shade	circus

blush *verb* To become red in the face from embarrassment or shame.
□*noun* A reddening of the face from embarrassment or shame.
blush (blush) □*verb* **blushed, blushing, blushes** □*noun, plural* **blushes**

bluster *verb* **1.** To blow in violent gusts: *The wind blustered against the windows.* **2.** To make loud boasts or threats: *He blustered that he could run faster than all of us.*
□*noun* **1.** A noisy, gusty wind. **2.** Loud boasts or threats.
blus·ter (blus′tər) □*verb* **blustered, blustering, blusters** □*noun, plural* **blusters**

blvd. An abbreviation for **boulevard.**

boa constrictor *noun* A large snake of tropical America. It coils itself around the animals it eats and suffocates them.
boa con·stric·tor (bō′ə kən strik′tər) □*noun, plural* **boa constrictors**

boar *noun* A wild pig with a thick coat of dark bristles.
boar (bôr) □*noun, plural* **boars** or **boar**

board *noun* **1.** A flat, long piece of sawed wood: *I made a raft out of boards.* **2.** A flat piece of material used for a special purpose: *a game board; a bulletin board.* **3.** Regular meals served for pay: *The hotel offers room and board.* **4.** A group of persons who run or manage something: *a school board.*
□*verb* **1.** To cover with boards: *board up a broken window.* **2.** To get regular meals for pay: *They board at the school.* **3.** To go onto a ship, train, or other vehicle: *board a bus.*
board (bôrd) □*noun, plural* **boards** □*verb* **boarded, boarding, boards**

boast *verb* **1.** To speak with too much pride about oneself: *He boasted that he was smarter than everyone else.* **2.** To be proud of having: *The town boasts a fine zoo.*
□*noun* Talk that is too full of pride in oneself: *his foolish boasts about how talented he is.*
boast (bōst) □*verb* **boasted, boasting, boasts** □*noun, plural* **boasts**

> *SYNONYMS:* **boast, brag, crow**
> These verbs mean to speak with too much pride about oneself: *She boasted that she could beat anyone at Ping-Pong. He's always bragging about how smart he is. You shouldn't crow just because you got an A on the test.*

boat *noun* **1.** A small open vessel for traveling on water. **2.** A ship.
□*verb* To travel by boat.
boat (bōt) □*noun, plural* **boats** □*verb* **boated, boating, boats**

bob *noun* A quick up-and-down motion: *I gave a bob of my head to show I heard her.*
□*verb* To move up and down with quick motions: *The rubber ball bobbed on the water.*
bob (bob) □*noun, plural* **bobs** □*verb* **bobbed, bobbing, bobs**

bobbin *noun* A spool that holds thread or yarn. Some bobbins are used in sewing machines.
bob·bin (bob′in) □*noun, plural* **bobbins**

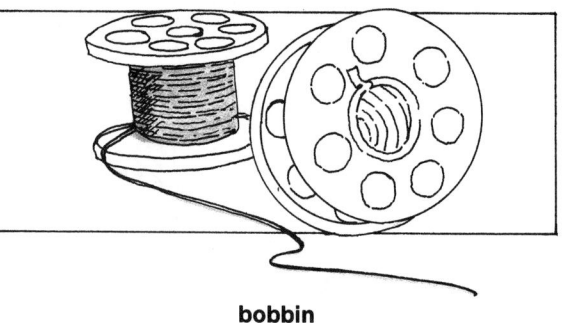

bobbin

bobcat *noun* A wildcat of North America with reddish-brown fur and a short tail.
bob·cat (bob′kat′) □*noun, plural* **bobcats**

bobolink *noun* An American songbird with black, white, and tan feathers.
bob·o·link (bob′ə lingk′) □*noun, plural* **bobolinks**

bobsled *noun* A long racing sled with two sets of runners, a steering wheel, and brakes.
bob·sled (bob′sled′) □*noun, plural* **bobsleds**

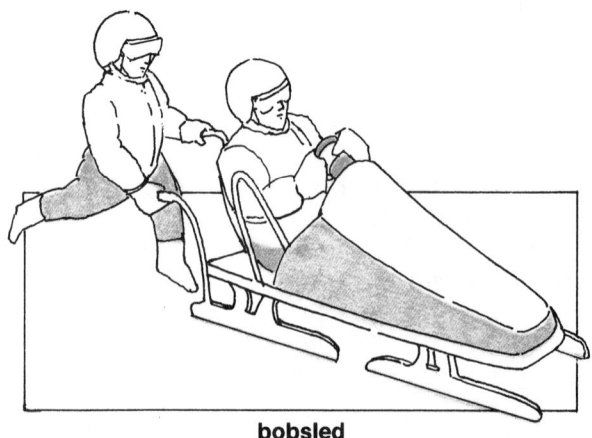

bobsled

bobwhite *noun* A plump brown and white bird of North America having a call that sounds like its name.

bob·white (bob **hwīt'**) □*noun, plural* **bobwhites**

bode *verb* To be a sign or omen of: *The captain's worried face boded trouble.*
bode (bōd) □*verb* **boded, boding, bodes**

bodily *adjective* Of or in the body: *The heart is a bodily organ.*
bod·i·ly (**bod'** ə lē) □*adjective*

body *noun* **1.** All of the physical structure of a person or animal: *Exercise strengthens the body.* **2.** A dead person or animal. **3.** The main part: *the body of a car.* **4.** A mass of something: *a body of water; a celestial body.*
bod·y (**bod'** ē) □*noun, plural* **bodies**

bodyguard *noun* One or more persons who protect someone.
bod·y·guard (**bod'** ē gärd') □*noun, plural* **bodyguards**

bog *noun* A soft, wet area of land; marsh. □*verb* To get stuck or cause to get stuck: *The wagon bogged down in the mud.*
bog (bôg) □*noun, plural* **bogs** □*verb* **bogged, bogging, bogs**

boil¹ *verb* **1.** To reach or cause to reach a temperature where bubbles form and steam is given off: *The water is boiling. Boil some milk for cocoa.* **2.** To cook or be cooked in boiling liquid: *I boiled some eggs.* □*noun* The condition of boiling: *Bring the mixture to a boil.*
boil (boil) □*verb* **boiled, boiling, boils** □*noun*

boil² *noun* A painful swelling on the skin, filled with pus.
boil (boil) □*noun, plural* **boils**

boiler *noun* **1.** A large tank for heating or boiling water. Boilers run engines and heat buildings. **2.** A large pot for boiling liquids.
boil·er (**boi'** lər) □*noun, plural* **boilers**

boiling point *noun* The temperature at which a liquid starts to boil. The boiling point of water is 100 degrees Celsius, or 212 degrees Fahrenheit.

bold *adjective* **1.** Showing or needing courage: *bold mountain climbers; a bold plan of rescue.* **2.** Not polite; rude. —See Synonyms at **adventurous.**
bold (bōld) □*adjective* **bolder, boldest**

boll *noun* The rounded seed pod of the cotton plant.
boll (bōl) □*noun, plural* **bolls**

boll weevil *noun* A beetle that damages cotton plants.

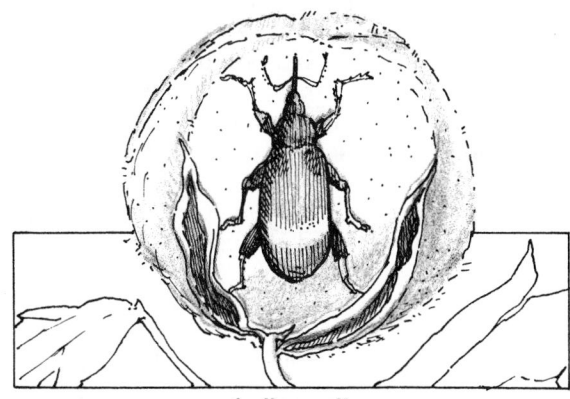

boll weevil

bolster *noun* A long, narrow pillow or cushion. □*verb* To keep from falling; support: *Steel beams bolstered the ceiling.*
bol·ster (**bōl'** stər) □*noun, plural* **bolsters** □*verb* **bolstered, bolstering, bolsters**

bolt *noun* **1.** A rod or pin used to hold things together. A bolt has grooves cut around it so that a nut may be screwed onto it. **2.** A rod that slides to fasten a door. **3.** The part of a lock that is turned by a key. **4.** A flash of lightning. **5.** A sudden dash: *We made a bolt for the bus.* **6.** A large roll of cloth or paper. □*verb* **1.** To fasten or lock with a bolt: *bolt a door.* **2.** To dash away suddenly: *The deer bolted off in fright.* **3.** To swallow quickly: *She bolted her breakfast and ran off.*
bolt (bōlt) □*noun, plural* **bolts** □*verb* **bolted, bolting, bolts**

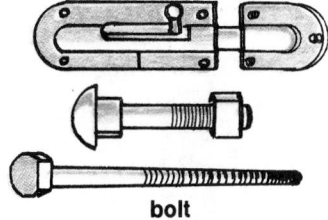

bolt
Three kinds of bolts

a bat	ī bite	o͞o tool	th feather
ā make	i fierce	ou out	th bath
â dare	o dot	u nut	hw wheat
ä father	ō no	û turn	zh measure
e net	ô law, for	ch church	ə about, open
ē be	oi soil	ng ring	pencil, atom
i dip	oo look	sh shade	circus

bomb *noun* A weapon consisting of a container filled with a material that can explode. A bomb is dropped or thrown on something to destroy it.
□*verb* To attack with a bomb.
bomb (bom) □*noun, plural* **bombs** □*verb* **bombed, bombing, bombs**

bombard *verb* **1.** To attack with bombs or heavy gunfire. **2.** To attack with words: *Reporters bombarded the mayor with questions.*
bom·bard (bom **bärd′**) □*verb* **bombarded, bombarding, bombards**

bomber *noun* An airplane used to drop bombs.
bomb·er (**bom′** ər) □*noun, plural* **bombers**

bond *noun* **1.** Something that binds or unites: *a prisoner's iron bonds; a strong bond of love.* **2.** A certificate issued by a government or a company in exchange for a loan of money. The bond is a promise that the money will be paid back with interest.
bond (bond) □*noun, plural* **bonds**

bondage *noun* The condition of being a slave; slavery.
bond·age (**bon′** dij) □*noun*

bone *noun* One of the hard pieces of the skeleton of an animal that has a backbone.
□*verb* To remove the bones of: *I boned the fish and broiled it.*
bone (bōn) □*noun, plural* **bones** □*verb* **boned, boning, bones**

bonfire *noun* A large outdoor fire.
bon·fire (**bon′** fīr′) □*noun, plural* **bonfires**

bonnet *noun* **1.** A hat with a wide brim and ribbons that tie under the chin. **2.** A headdress made of feathers worn by Native Americans.
bon·net (**bon′** it) □*noun, plural* **bonnets**

bonnet

bonus *noun* Something extra in addition to what is usual or expected: *The boss gave all the employees a $50 bonus for Christmas.*
bo·nus (**bō′** nəs) □*noun, plural* **bonuses**

> **WORD HISTORY:**   **bonus**
>
> *Bonus* is a borrowing of a Latin word that means "good."

---

bony *adjective* **1.** Of, like, or full of bones: *a bony piece of meat.* **2.** Very thin; gaunt.
bon·y (**bō′** nē) □*adjective* **bonier, boniest**

boo *interjection* A word used to scare, surprise, or indicate disapproval.
□*verb* To say "boo" as a sign of disapproval: *The fans booed the opposing team.*
boo (bōō) □*interjection* □*verb* **booed, booing, boos**

book *noun* **1.** A set of pages with writing or printing that are fastened together between covers. **2.** A set of blank pages fastened together between covers: *an address book.* **3.** A main division of a bigger written or printed work: *a book of the Bible.*
□*verb* To arrange for ahead of time: *Dad booked plane tickets for our vacation.*
book (book) □*noun, plural* **books** □*verb* **booked, booking, books**

bookcase *noun* A piece of furniture with shelves for holding books.
book·case (**book′** kās′) □*noun, plural* **bookcases**

bookkeeper *noun* Someone who keeps the financial records of a business.
book·keep·er (**book′** kē′pər) □*noun, plural* **bookkeepers**

booklet *noun* A small book that usually has paper covers.
book·let (**book′** lit) □*noun, plural* **booklets**

boom¹ *noun* **1.** A deep, hollow sound, as that of an explosion: *the boom of a cannon.* **2.** A time of sudden or rapid growth: *The town had a boom after the railroad was built.*
□*verb* **1.** To make a deep, hollow sound: *The waves boomed along the shore.* **2.** To grow suddenly or rapidly: *Business is booming.*
boom (bōōm) □*noun, plural* **booms** □*verb* **boomed, booming, booms**

boom² *noun* A long pole that stretches out the bottom of a sail or that holds an object being lifted by a derrick.
boom (bōōm) □*noun, plural* **booms**

WORD HISTORY: **boom²**

The word *boom*, meaning "a long pole," comes from a Dutch word that originally meant "a tree" or "a pole." *Boom* is related to the English word *beam*, which also once meant "a tree," but which more commonly referred to a piece of timber used for building houses or ships.

boomerang *noun* A flat, curved piece of wood that can be thrown so that it returns to the thrower. Boomerangs are used as weapons by the native people of Australia.
boo·mer·ang (bōō′mə rang′) □*noun, plural* **boomerangs**

boon *noun* A blessing; benefit: *The warm coat was a boon to me during the winter.*
boon (bōōn) □*noun, plural* **boons**

boost *verb* To lift by pushing from below: *He boosted me onto the horse.*
□*noun* A push upward or ahead: *Give me a boost into the saddle.*
boost (bōōst) □*verb* **boosted, boosting, boosts** □*noun, plural* **boosts**

boost

boot *noun* A kind of shoe, usually made of leather or rubber, that covers the foot and ankle and often part of the leg.
□*verb* To kick: *She booted the soccer ball.*
boot (bōōt) □*noun, plural* **boots** □*verb* **booted, booting, boots**

booth *noun* 1. A small enclosed compartment: *a telephone booth.* 2. A stand or stall for selling or displaying goods: *a ticket booth.*
booth (bōōth) □*noun, plural* **booths** (bōōz or bōōths)

border *noun* 1. The line where one thing ends and another begins: *The mountains form the border between the two countries.* 2. A strip along an edge: *a border of lace on the hem.*
□*verb* 1. To be next to: *Mexico borders the United States.* 2. To put a border on: *She bordered the skirt with a ruffle.*
bor·der (bôr′dər) □*noun, plural* **borders** □*verb* **bordered, bordering, borders**

bore¹ *verb* 1. To make by drilling or digging: *I bored a hole in the stone.* 2. To make a hole in: *The carpenter bored the wood.*
bore (bôr) □*verb* **bored, boring, bores**

bore² *verb* To make tired or restless by failing to interest or by being dull: *Listening to the same story again bored me.*
□*noun* Someone or something that is dull and tiresome: *The play was a bore.*
bore (bôr) □*verb* **bored, boring, bores** □*noun, plural* **bores**

bore³ *verb* The past tense of **bear¹**: *She bore the tray in her hands.*
bore (bôr) □*verb*

born *adjective* 1. Brought into being or existence: *He was born on Valentine's Day.* 2. By birth or natural ability: *a born singer.*
born (bôrn) □*adjective*

borne *verb* A past participle of **bear¹**: *She has borne three children.*
borne (bôrn) □*verb*

borough *noun* 1. A town that governs itself, found in some parts of the United States. 2. One of the five divisions of New York City.
bor·ough (bûr′ō) □*noun, plural* **boroughs**

borrow *verb* 1. To take something from someone else with the understanding that it will be given back or replaced later: *I borrowed money from my friend.* 2. To take and use as one's own: *I borrowed his ideas.*
bor·row (bor′ō *or* bôr′ō) □*verb* **borrowed, borrowing, borrows**

bosom *noun* The front part of the human chest; breast: *She clasped the child to her bosom.*

a	bat	ī	bite	ōō	tool	th	feather
ā	make	î	fierce	ou	out	th	bath
â	dare	o	dot	u	nut	hw	wheat
ä	father	ō	no	û	turn	zh	measure
e	net	ô	law, for	ch	church	ə	about, open
ē	be	oi	soil	ng	ring		pencil, atom
i	dip	oo	look	sh	shade		circus

□*adjective* Very dear and close: *bosom friends.*
bos·om (booz′ əm) □*noun, plural* **bosoms**
□*adjective*

bosom

boss *noun* Someone who makes decisions and supervises other people.
□*verb* To be or act as the boss of: *She wouldn't let her brother boss her around.*
boss (bôs) □*noun, plural* **bosses** □*verb* **bossed, bossing, bosses**

botany *noun* The scientific study of plants.
bot·a·ny (bot′ə nē) □*noun*

both *adjective* One and the other; the two: *Both dresses were pretty.*
□*pronoun* The one and the other: *Both of the boys were late. We were both tired.*
□*conjunction* **Both** is used before two words or phrases connected by **and** to show that the two are included and to give special importance to this fact: *Her friends include both boys and girls.*
both (bōth) □*adjective* □*pronoun* □*conjunction*

bother *verb* **1.** To give trouble to; annoy. **2.** To take the trouble: *Don't bother to close the window.* —See Synonyms at **annoy.**
□*noun* Someone or something that annoys or worries: *His questions were a bother.*
both·er (both′ ər) □*verb* **bothered, bothering, bothers** □*noun, plural* **bothers**

bottle *noun* A container, usually made of glass, with a narrow neck that can be closed with a cap or cork.
□*verb* To place in a bottle.
bot·tle (bot′ əl) □*noun, plural* **bottles** □*verb* **bottled, bottling, bottles**

bottom *noun* **1.** The lowest part of something: *the bottom of the mountain.* **2.** The low-

est surface; underside: *The bottom of the glass was wet.* **3.** The land under a body of water: *the bottom of the sea.* **4.** The source or cause: *How can we get to the bottom of the problem?*
bot·tom (bot′ əm) □*noun, plural* **bottoms**

bough *noun* A large branch of a tree.
bough (bou) □*noun, plural* **boughs**

bought *verb* The past tense and past participle of **buy:** *They bought a new car. I have bought two new suits.*
bought (bôt) □*verb*

boulder *noun* A large round rock.
boul·der (bōl′ dər) □*noun, plural* **boulders**

boulevard *noun* A broad city street.
boul·e·vard (bool′ə värd′) □*noun, plural* **boulevards**

bounce *verb* **1.** To spring back after striking a surface: *The ball bounced on the sidewalk.* **2.** To cause to bounce: *He bounced the ball against the wall.*
□*noun* A bounding movement; spring.
bounce (bouns) □*verb* **bounced, bouncing, bounces** □*noun, plural* **bounces**

bound¹ *verb* **1.** To jump; leap: *He bounded over the fence and ran away.* **2.** To spring back after hitting a surface; bounce: *The ball bounded off the truck and rolled down the street.*
□*noun* A jump; leap.
bound (bound) □*verb* **bounded, bounding, bounds** □*noun, plural* **bounds**

bound

bound² *noun* A boundary; limit: *His imagination knew no bounds.*
□*verb* To lie along or be the boundary of: *Hills bounded the town on all sides.*

bound (bound) □*noun, plural* **bounds**
□*verb* **bounded, bounding, bounds**

bound³ *verb* The past tense and past participle of **bind**: *He bound the pens together with string. We have bound the package with a ribbon.*
□*adjective* **1.** Certain; sure: *We are bound to have hot weather soon.* **2.** Being under obligation; obliged: *I am bound by my promise not to tell anyone.* **3.** Enclosed in a cover or binding: *a bound book.*
bound (bound) □*verb* □*adjective*

bound⁴ *adjective* On the way; headed: *They are bound for Europe.*
bound (bound) □*adjective*

boundary *noun* A dividing line between one place or thing and another; border: *A river formed the boundary between the two states.*
bound·a·ry (boun′də rē *or* boun′drē)
□*noun, plural* **boundaries**

boundless *adjective* **1.** Without any known limits; infinite: *the boundless regions of outer space.* **2.** Very great; tremendous: *He had boundless enthusiasm for the idea.*
bound·less (bound′lis) □*adjective*

bounty *noun* **1.** Generosity in giving: *The charity thanked the donors for their bounty.* **2.** Something produced in great abundance: *the bounty of a good harvest.* **3.** A reward given by a government for killing an animal that is a pest.
boun·ty (boun′tē) □*noun, plural* **bounties**

bouquet *noun* A bunch of flowers.
bou·quet (bō kā′ *or* bōō kā′) □*noun, plural* **bouquets**

bout *noun* **1.** A contest: *a boxing bout.* **2.** A period of time: *a long bout of cold weather.*
bout (bout) □*noun, plural* **bouts**

bow¹ *noun* **1.** A weapon for shooting arrows. It is made of a curved piece of wood or plastic with a string stretched tightly from one tip to the other. **2.** A knot tied in loops: *He tied the ribbon in a bow.* **3.** A slender stick with horsehair stretched from end to end, used to play a stringed instrument such as a violin.
bow (bō) □*noun, plural* **bows**

bow² *verb* **1.** To bend the body, head, or knee in greeting, respect, or worship: *They bowed to the king.* **2.** To give in; yield: *They refused to bow to his wishes.*
□*noun* The act of bending the body, head, or knee.
bow (bou) □*verb* **bowed, bowing, bows**

□*noun, plural* **bows**

bow³ *noun* The front part of a ship or boat.
bow (bou) □*noun, plural* **bows**

bowels *plural noun* **1.** The tube in the body into which food from the stomach passes; intestines. **2.** The deepest parts of something: *drilling for oil in the bowels of the earth.*
bow·els (bou′əlz *or* boulz) □*plural noun*

bower *noun* A quiet place that is shaded by leafy trees, bushes, or vines; arbor.
bow·er (bou′ər) □*noun, plural* **bowers**

bowl¹ *noun* **1.** A round, hollow dish or container: *a soup bowl.* **2.** The curved, hollow part of an object: *the bowl of a spoon.*
bowl (bōl) □*noun, plural* **bowls**

bowl² *verb* **1.** To play the game of bowling. **2.** To take a turn or roll a ball in bowling.
bowl (bōl) □*verb* **bowled, bowling, bowls**

bowlegged *adjective* Having legs that curve outward at or below the knee.
bow·leg·ged (bō′leg′id) □*adjective*

bowling *noun* A game in which a heavy ball is rolled down a wooden alley to knock down wooden pins at the other end.
bowl·ing (bō′ling) □*noun*

bowstring *noun* A string connecting the two ends of a shooting bow.
bow·string (bō′string′) □*noun, plural* **bowstrings**

box¹ *noun* **1.** A container made of a stiff material, such as cardboard or wood, that has four sides, a bottom, and often a lid or cover. **2.** Something shaped or closed in like a box: *a theater box.*
□*verb* To put or pack in a box: *She boxed the books and mailed them.*
box (boks) □*noun, plural* **boxes** □*verb* **boxed, boxing, boxes**

box² *verb* **1.** To fight with the fists as a sport. **2.** To hit or slap with the fist or open hand: *You should never box a person's ears.*
□*noun* A blow with the fist or open hand: *a box on the ear.*

a bat	ī bite	ōō tool	*th* feather
ā make	î fierce	ou out	th bath
â dare	o dot	u nut	hw wheat
ä father	ō no	û turn	zh measure
e net	ô law, for	ch church	ə about, open
ē be	oi soil	ng ring	pencil, atom
i dip	oo look	sh shade	circus

box (boks) □*verb* **boxed, boxing, boxes**
□*noun, plural* **boxes**

boxcar *noun* A railway car that is closed on all sides and is used to carry freight.
box·car (boks′kär′) □*noun, plural* **boxcars**

boxer[1] *noun* Someone who fights with the fists.
box·er (bok′sər) □*noun, plural* **boxers**

boxer[2] *noun* A medium-sized dog with a short coat and a square face.
box·er (bok′sər) □*noun, plural* **boxers**

boxing *noun* The sport of fighting an opponent with the fists.
box·ing (bok′sing) □*noun*

box office *noun* A booth where tickets are sold at a theater, an auditorium, or a stadium.

boy *noun* A male child who has not yet become a man.
boy (boi) □*noun, plural* **boys**

boycott *noun* The refusal of a group of people to use, buy from, or deal with a store, company, person, or nation. A boycott is often used as a way of protesting or of forcing a change.
□*verb* To take part in a boycott against: *We boycotted the company to protest the way it treated its employees.*
boy·cott (boi′kot′) □*noun, plural* **boycotts**
□*verb* **boycotted, boycotting, boycotts**

boyfriend *noun* A special male companion or sweetheart.
boy·friend (boi′frend) □*noun, plural* **boyfriends**

boyhood *noun* The time of being a boy: *He spent his boyhood in the city.*
boy·hood (boi′hood′) □*noun, plural* **boyhoods**

boyish *adjective* Of, like, or suitable for a boy: *a boyish smile; a boyish trick.*
boy·ish (boi′ish) □*adjective*

Boy Scout *noun* A member of an organization for boys that help develop outdoor skills and good character.

brace *noun* **1.** A device that holds two or more parts together or that helps to support something: *He wore a brace on his leg after he had polio.* **2. braces** An arrangement of wires and bands used for straightening a person's teeth. **3.** A handle used to hold and turn the bit of a drill. **4.** A pair: *a brace of pigeons; a brace of horses.*
□*verb* **1.** To support or strengthen: *brace a floor with timbers; propped a board against the sagging wall to brace it.* **2.** To prepare for something difficult or unpleasant: *He braced himself for the hostile questions they were sure to ask.* **3.** To fill with energy or strength; refresh: *The cold shower braced him after a tiring day.*
brace (brās) □*noun, plural* **braces** □*verb* **braced, bracing, braces**

bracelet *noun* A band or chain worn around the wrist as an ornament.
brace·let (brās′lit) □*noun, plural* **bracelets**

bracket *noun* **1.** A support that is fastened to a wall to hold up something, such as a shelf. **2.** Either of the symbols [ ], used to enclose letters, words, or numerals in written or printed material. **3.** A group or category: *The first race is for swimmers in the 9-to-12 age bracket.*
brack·et (brak′it) □*noun, plural* **brackets**

brag *verb* To praise oneself or the things one owns: *She bragged about her apartment.* —See Synonyms at **boast.**
brag (brag) □*verb* **bragged, bragging, brags**

braggart *noun* A person who brags or boasts a lot.
brag·gart (brag′ərt) □*noun, plural* **braggarts**

braid *verb* To weave three or more strands together: *He braided his daughter's hair in a pigtail.*
□*noun* A strip, as of hair, that has been made by braiding.
braid (brād) □*verb* **braided, braiding, braids** □*noun, plural* **braids**

Braille *or* **braille** *noun* A system of writing and printing in which blind people use the sense of touch to read different patterns of raised dots representing letters, words, numbers, and punctuation marks.
Braille or **braille** (brāl) □*noun*

WORD HISTORY: **Braille**
Louis Braille was a French musician and teacher of the blind who was blind himself. He invented the system of writing and printing with raised dots that is called *Braille* today.

---

brain *noun* **1.** The large mass of gray nerve tissue inside the skull of an animal with a backbone. The brain is the center of thinking, feeling, learning, and remembering. **2. brains** Intelligence: *She has plenty of brains.*
□*verb* To hit hard on the head.

brain (brān) □*noun, plural* **brains** □*verb*
brained, braining, brains

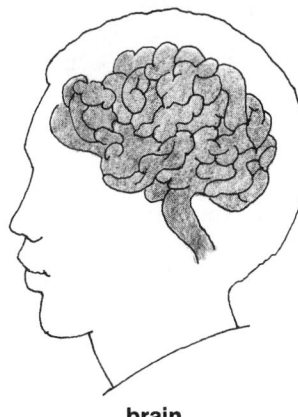

brain

brake *noun* A device that can stop or slow down the motion of a vehicle, wheel, or machine.
□*verb* To slow down or stop by using a brake: *He braked the car as he neared the corner.*
brake (brāk) □*noun, plural* **brakes** □*verb* **braked, braking, brakes**

bramble *noun* A prickly plant or shrub such as the blackberry or raspberry.
bram·ble (bram′bəl) □*noun, plural* **brambles**

bran *noun* The outer covering of grains such as wheat, rye, and oats. Bran is sifted out when flour is made and is used in some cereals and breads and in animal foods.
bran (bran) □*noun*

branch *noun* **1.** One of the parts that grow out from the trunk or limbs of a tree or shrub. **2.** A part that is a division of a larger thing: *the legislative branch of government; my father's branch of the family.*
□*verb* To divide or spread into branches: *The road branches near the gas station.*
branch (branch) □*noun, plural* **branches** □*verb* **branched, branching, branches**

brand *noun* **1.** A make, kind, or type: *a new brand of crackers.* **2.** A mark burned into the skin of cattle to show who owns them.
□*verb* To mark with a brand: *The farmer branded his calves.*
brand (brand) □*noun, plural* **brands** □*verb* **branded, branding, brands**

brand-new *adjective* Completely new; not used.
brand-new (brand′noo′ *or* brand′nyoo′) □*adjective*

brass *noun* **1.** A yellowish metal that contains copper and zinc. **2.** Often **brasses** The group of musical instruments that includes the trumpet, trombone, French horn, and tuba.
brass (bras) □*noun, plural* **brasses**

brat *noun* A nasty or spoiled child.
brat (brat) □*noun, plural* **brats**

brave *adjective* Having or showing courage; able to overcome fear or pain.
□*noun* A Native American warrior.
□*verb* To face in a courageous way: *She braved the current to rescue the swimmers.*
brave (brāv) □*adjective* **braver, bravest** □*noun, plural* **braves** □*verb* **braved, braving, braves**

> *SYNONYMS:* **brave, courageous, gallant**
> These adjectives mean having or showing courage: *a brave soldier; a courageous rescue; a gallant effort to put out the fire.*

brave

bravery *noun* The quality of being brave; courage.
brav·er·y (brā′və rē *or* brāv′rē) □*noun*

breach *noun* A hole in something solid: *Water came through the breach in the dam.*

a	bat	ī	bite	oo	tool	*th*	feather
ā	make	î	fierce	ou	out	th	bath
â	dare	o	dot	u	nut	hw	wheat
ä	father	ō	no	û	turn	zh	measure
e	net	ô	law, for	ch	church	ə	about, open
ē	be	oi	soil	ng	ring		pencil, atom
i	dip	oo	look	sh	shade		circus

□*verb* To make a hole in; break through: *Our army breached the enemy's defenses.*
breach (brēch) □*noun, plural* **breaches**
□*verb* **breached, breaching, breaches**

bread   *noun* **1.** A food made from flour or meal mixed with water or milk and baked in an oven. **2.** The things one needs to stay alive: *She earned her daily bread by singing at weddings and parties.*
bread (bred) □*noun, plural* **breads**

breadth□*noun* The distance from side to side; width: *What is the breadth of this room?*
breadth (bredth) □*noun, plural* **breadths**

break   *verb* **1.** To crack, split, or burst into two or more pieces: *She broke the mirror when she dropped it. China breaks easily.* **2.** To crack a bone of: *She broke her leg.* **3.** To damage or become damaged: *The boy broke the toy train. The clock broke and couldn't be fixed.* **4.** To fail to keep or follow: *He broke his promise.* **5.** To appear or come about suddenly: *Applause broke out in the audience.* **6.** To put a stop to; end: *He is trying to break the habit of biting his nails.* **7.** To do better than; go beyond: *She broke the record for the mile.* **8.** To make or become known: *Who will break the news to the family? The story broke in all the newspapers.* **9.** To force one's way: *The bull broke out of the barn.*
□*noun* **1.** A broken place; opening, crack, or gap: *a break in the pipe.* **2.** A pause or rest: *We took a break for dinner.* **3.** An attempt to force one's way out: *a jail break.* **4.** A sudden change: *a break in the weather.* **5.** An unexpected event: *She got a lucky break.*
  break down To fail to work properly: *The truck broke down on the road.*
  break in To enter by force: *A thief broke in and stole my camera.*
  break up To bring or come to an end: *He broke up the quarrel. The friendship broke up.*
break (brāk) □*verb* **broke, broken, breaking, breaks** □*noun, plural* **breaks**

breakdown   *noun* A failure to work properly: *the breakdown of a car on the road.*
break·down (brāk′doun′) □*noun, plural* **breakdowns**

breaker   *noun* A wave that breaks into foam when it reaches shore.
break·er (brā′kər) □*noun, plural* **breakers**

breakfast   *noun* The first meal of the day.
break·fast (brek′fəst) □*noun, plural* **breakfasts**

WORD HISTORY: breakfast

Breakfast is so called because you break your fast when you eat the first meal of the day. In other words, you eat nothing when you are asleep at night, and in the morning you begin to eat again.

breast   *noun* **1.** The front part of the body from the neck to the abdomen; chest. **2.** A gland in a female mammal that produces milk.
breast (brest) □*noun, plural* **breasts**

breastbone   *noun* The bone in the center of the breast to which the ribs are attached.
breast·bone (brest′bōn′) □*noun, plural* **breastbones**

breath   *noun* **1.** The air that is taken into the lungs and forced out when one breathes. **2.** The ability to breathe easily: *He had to stop running and get his breath.* **3.** The act of breathing. **4.** A slight breeze: *Not a breath of air was stirring on that hot day.*
breath (breth) □*noun, plural* **breaths**

breathe   *verb* **1.** To take in and force out air from the lungs. **2.** To say in a quiet way; whisper: *Don't breathe a word of what I said.*
breathe (brēth) □*verb* **breathed, breathing, breathes**

breathless   *adjective* **1.** Out of breath: *She was breathless after the race.* **2.** Holding the breath because of fear, excitement, or interest: *We were breathless as we watched the firemen race into the burning house.*
breath·less (breth′lis) □*adjective*

breathtaking   *adjective* Very exciting; thrilling: *a breathtaking view.*
breath·tak·ing (breth′tā′king) □*adjective*

bred   *verb* The past tense and past participle of **breed:** *We bred ponies for sale. They have bred cattle for years.*
bred (bred) □*verb*

breeches   *plural noun* Short trousers that are fastened at or just below the knees.
breech·es (brich′iz) □*plural noun*

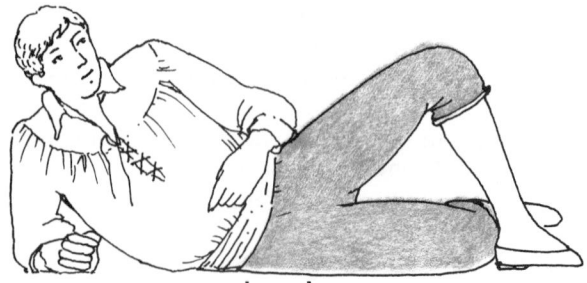

breeches

breed *verb* **1.** To produce offspring: *Flies breed rapidly.* **2.** To grow or raise: *My brother breeds horses.*
□*noun* A particular type or variety of animal or plant that has been produced from a selected group of parents.
breed (brēd) □*verb* **bred, breeding, breeds** □*noun, plural* **breeds**

breeding *noun* The way a person has been brought up; training: *Their manners show good breeding.*
breed·ing (brē′ding) □*noun*

breeze *noun* A gentle movement of air.
□*verb* To move quickly and easily: *He breezed through the house singing.*
breeze (brēz) □*noun, plural* **breezes** □*verb* **breezed, breezing, breezes**

brew *verb* **1.** To make beer or ale by soaking, boiling, and fermenting malt and hops. **2.** To make by soaking, boiling, or mixing: *She brewed some strong tea.* **3.** To think up; plan or plot: *He brewed a scheme for making money quickly.* **4.** To begin to take form: *A hurricane is brewing.*
□*noun* A drink made by brewing.
brew (brōo) □*verb* **brewed, brewing, brews** □*noun, plural* **brews**

briar *noun* Another spelling for **brier.**
bri·ar (brī′ər) □*noun, plural* **briars**

bribe *noun* Money or something else valuable that is offered or given to make a person do something dishonest: *The thief offered the policeman a bribe to let him go.*
□*verb* To offer or give a bribe to: *She tried to bribe the reporter to change his story.*
bribe (brīb) □*noun, plural* **bribes** □*verb* **bribed, bribing, bribes**

brick *noun* A block of clay that has been baked by the sun or in an oven until hard. Bricks are used for building and for paving.
brick (brik) □*noun, plural* **bricks**

bride *noun* A woman who is about to be married or who has just been married.
bride (brīd) □*noun, plural* **brides**

bridegroom *noun* A man who is about to be married or who has just been married.
bride·groom (brīd′ grōom′) □*noun, plural* **bridegrooms**

bridge *noun* **1.** Something built across a river, railroad track, or road so that people or vehicles can cross from one side to the other. **2.** The upper bony part of the human nose. **3.** A platform above the main deck of a ship

from which the officer in charge controls the ship.
□*verb* To build a bridge over or across: *Workers bridged the river.*
bridge (brij) □*noun, plural* **bridges** □*verb* **bridged, bridging, bridges**

bridle *noun* The straps, bit, and reins that fit over a horse's head and are used for control.
□*verb* **1.** To put a bridle on: *He bridled his own horse.* **2.** To control: *He tried to bridle his anger.*
bri·dle (brī′dəl) □*noun, plural* **bridles** □*verb* **bridled, bridling, bridles**

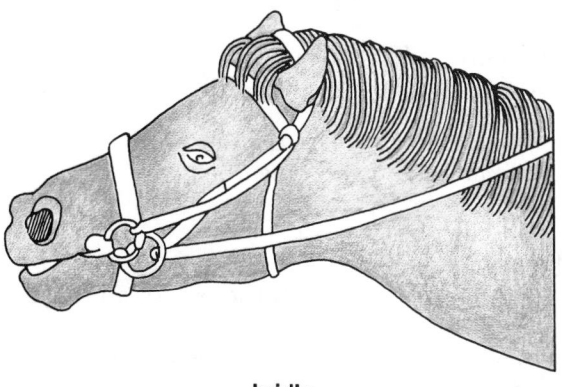

bridle

brief *adjective* Short in time or length: *a brief speech; a brief letter.*
□*verb* To give detailed instructions, information, or advice to: *The lawyer briefed his client before the trial.*
brief (brēf) □*adjective* **briefer, briefest** □*verb* **briefed, briefing, briefs**

brier *noun* A thorny plant or bush, especially a rosebush with prickly stems.
bri·er (brī′ər) □*noun, plural* **briers**

brig *noun* **1.** A sailing ship with two masts and square sails. **2.** A prison on a ship.
brig (brig) □*noun, plural* **brigs**

brigade *noun* **1.** A large army unit that usually has two or more regiments. **2.** A group of persons organized for a special purpose: *My uncle belongs to the fire brigade.*
bri·gade (bri gād′) □*noun, plural* **brigades**

a bat	ī bite	ōo tool	*th* feather
ā make	î fierce	ou out	th bath
â dare	o dot	u nut	hw wheat
ä father	ō no	û turn	zh measure
e net	ô law, for	ch church	ə about, open
ē be	oi soil	ng ring	pencil, atom
i dip	oo look	sh shade	circus

bright *adjective* **1.** Giving off much light: *A bright moon shone through the clouds.* **2.** Vivid or strong in color: *a clear bright red; the bright colors of a beach ball.* **3.** Smart; clever: *a bright girl; a bright idea.* **4.** Happy; cheerful: *a bright, smiling face.* —See Synonyms at **cheerful.**
bright (brīt) □*adjective* **brighter, brightest**

SYNONYMS: **bright, brilliant, radiant**

These adjectives mean giving off much light: *A bright sun shone through the trees. She wore a brilliant diamond. Thousands of candles in the church spread a radiant light.*

---

brilliant *adjective* **1.** Full of light; very bright: *a brilliant star; brilliant diamonds.* **2.** Magnificent; splendid: *the brilliant life at the court of the king.* **3.** Very high in intelligence or ability: *He is a brilliant actor.* —See Synonyms at **bright.**
bril·liant (bril′yənt) □*adjective*

brim *noun* **1.** A rim or upper edge: *He filled the bowl to the brim.* **2.** The part of a hat that stands out from the crown.
□*verb* To be or seem to be full to the brim: *His eyes were brimming with tears.*
brim (brim) □*noun, plural* **brims** □*verb*
 brimmed, brimming, brims

brine *noun* Water that contains a large amount of salt and is used to preserve or pickle foods.
brine (brīn) □*noun*

bring *verb* **1.** To take or carry along with oneself: *Please bring me a newspaper. He brought his son to the party.* **2.** To cause to happen or come: *The accident brought death to many. The movie brought tears to her eyes.*
 bring up To take care of and educate; rear: *Her grandparents brought her up.*
bring (bring) □*verb* **brought, bringing,**
 brings

brink *noun* **1.** The upper edge of a high or steep place: *The girl looked over the brink of the cliff.* **2.** The very edge; verge: *on the brink of a discovery.*
brink (bringk) □*noun, plural* **brinks**

brisk *adjective* **1.** Fast and lively: *a brisk run in the park.* **2.** Fresh and keen; sharp: *The wind was brisk and cold.*
brisk (brisk) □*adjective* **brisker, briskest**

bristle *noun* A short, coarse, stiff hair: *Hog bristles are often used to make brushes.*
□*verb* **1.** To raise the bristles stiffly: *The dog*

bristled and growled. **2.** To stand up straight and stiff like bristles: *The tips of his mustache bristled.*
bris·tle (bris′əl) □*noun, plural* **bristles**
 □*verb* **bristled, bristling, bristles**

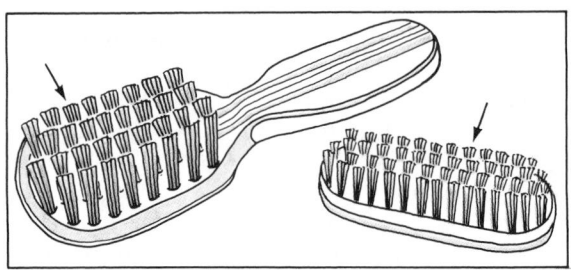

bristle

British *adjective* Of Great Britain, its people, or their language.
□*plural noun* **British** The people of Great Britain.
Brit·ish (brit′ish) □*adjective* □*plural noun*

brittle *adjective* Hard and likely to break: *brittle bones; brittle glass ornaments.*
brit·tle (brit′əl) □*adjective* **brittler, brittlest**

broad *adjective* **1.** Large from side to side; wide: *Five of us could sit on the broad couch.* **2.** Covering a wide range; having few limits: *He has a broad understanding of the subject.* **3.** Clear and open: *I saw the accident in broad daylight.*
broad (brôd) □*adjective* **broader, broadest**

broadcast *verb* **1.** To send out over radio or television: *The station will broadcast the governor's speech.* **2.** To make widely known: *She broadcast the secret all over town.*
□*noun* Something that is sent out by radio or television; a radio or television program.
broad·cast (brôd′kast′) □*verb* **broadcast** or
 broadcasted, broadcasting, broadcasts
 □*noun, plural* **broadcasts**

brocade *noun* A rich cloth with a raised pattern woven into it.
bro·cade (brō kād′) □*noun, plural* **brocades**

broccoli *noun* A plant with dark green stalks and flower buds that are eaten as a vegetable.
broc·co·li (brok′ə lē) □*noun*

broil *verb* **1.** To cook directly under or over heat: *broil a steak on the grill.* **2.** To become very hot: *We broiled in the sun.*
broil (broil) □*verb* **broiled, broiling, broils**

broiler *noun* A pan, rack, or part of a stove for broiling foods.
broil·er (broi′lər) □*noun, plural* **broilers**

broke The past tense of **break:** *My sister broke her ankle.*
broke (brōk) □*verb*

broken *verb* The past participle of **break:** *The windshield was broken in the accident.*
□*adjective* **1.** Not whole; in pieces: *a broken cup.* **2.** Not working properly; out of order: *a broken radio.* **3.** Not kept: *a broken promise.*
bro·ken (brō′kən) □*verb* □*adjective*

bronchial tube *noun* One of the tubes in the lungs that form branches of the windpipe.
bron·chi·al tube (brong′kē əl) □*noun*

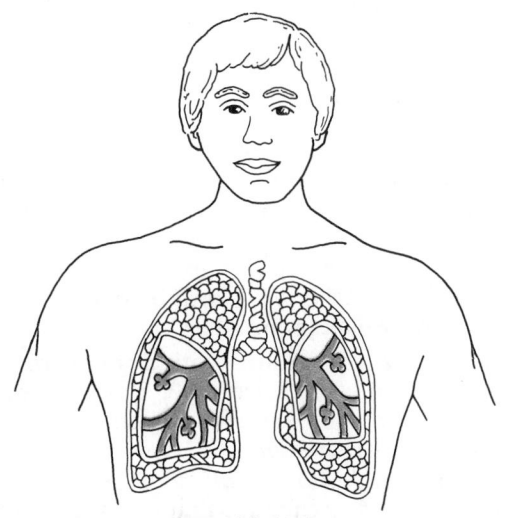

bronchial tube

bronchitis *noun* An illness caused by an infection or swelling of the bronchial tubes. People who have bronchitis may have a severe cough.
bron·chi·tis (brong kī′tis) □*noun*

bronco *noun* A small wild or partly tamed horse of western North America.
bron·co (brong′kō) □*noun, plural* **broncos**

bronze *noun* **1.** A hard metal made of copper and tin. **2.** A yellowish brown color.
□*adjective* Yellowish brown.
□*verb* To make or become the color of bronze: *The sun bronzed her face.*
bronze (bronz) □*noun, plural* **bronzes**
□*adjective* □*verb* **bronzed, bronzing, bronzes**

brooch *noun* A pin that is worn as an ornament and fastens with a clasp.
brooch (brōch *or* brooch) □*noun, plural* **brooches**

brood *noun* A group of young birds that are hatched from eggs laid at the same time.
□*verb* **1.** To sit on eggs so they will hatch. **2.** To worry or think about for a long time: *He brooded over the job he had lost.*
brood (brood) □*noun, plural* **broods** □*verb* **brooded, brooding, broods**

brook *noun* A small freshwater stream.
brook (brook) □*noun, plural* **brooks**

broom *noun* **1.** A tool that has a long handle with straw bristles or a brush at one end, used for sweeping. **2.** A shrub with yellow flowers, small leaves, and many straight, slender branches.
broom (broom *or* broom) □*noun, plural* **brooms**

broth *noun* A thin soup made by boiling fish, meat, or vegetables in water.
broth (brôth) □*noun, plural* **broths** (brôths *or* brôthz)

brother *noun* A boy or man who has the same parents as another person.
broth·er (bruth′ər) □*noun, plural* **brothers**

brotherhood *noun* **1.** Close feeling or friendship among a group; fellowship. **2.** A group of men who are united in an organization or club.
broth·er·hood (bruth′ər hood′) □*noun, plural* **brotherhoods**

brotherhood

brother-in-law *noun* **1.** The brother of one's husband or wife. **2.** The husband of one's sister. **3.** The husband of the sister of one's husband or wife.
broth·er-in-law (bruth′ər in lô′) □*noun, plural* **brothers-in-law**

a	bat	ī	bite	oo	tool	*th*	feather
ā	make	î	fierce	ou	out	th	bath
â	dare	o	dot	u	nut	hw	wheat
ä	father	ō	no	û	turn	zh	measure
e	net	ô	law, for	ch	church	ə	about, open
ē	be	oi	soil	ng	ring		pencil, atom
i	dip	oo	look	sh	shade		circus

brotherly *adjective* Of or appropriate to a brother; warm and friendly: *brotherly love.*
broth·er·ly (bru*th*′ ər lē) □*adjective*

brought *verb* The past tense and past participle of **bring**: *She brought a book with her. I have brought all the tools I need.*
brought (brôt) □*verb*

brow *noun* **1.** The part of the face between the eyes and the line of the hair; forehead. **2.** One of the two arches of hair above the eyes; eyebrow.
brow (brou) □*noun, plural* **brows**

brown *noun* The color of chocolate and coffee.
□*adjective* Of the color brown.
□*verb* To make or become brown: *She browned the onions in butter.*
brown (broun) □*noun, plural* **browns**
□*adjective* **browner, brownest** □*verb*
browned, browning, browns

brownie *noun* **1.** A small imaginary creature who is supposed to do helpful deeds while people sleep. **2.** A small, chewy chocolate cake that often has nuts in it. **3. Brownie** A girl who is a member of the junior division of the Girl Scouts.
brown·ie (brou′ nē) □*noun, plural* **brownies**

browse *verb* To look at or read in a casual way: *browse through a magazine.*
browse (brouz) □*verb* **browsed, browsing, browses**

browse

bruise *noun* **1.** An injury that leaves a bluish or blackish mark on the skin but does not break the skin. **2.** An injury to the outside of a fruit or vegetable caused by dropping or rough handling.
□*verb* To make or receive a bruise on: *The fall bruised her knees.*
bruise (brōōz) □*noun, plural* **bruises** □*verb*
bruised, bruising, bruises

brunette *adjective* Having hair that is dark or dark brown in color.
□*noun* Someone with hair that is dark or dark brown in color.
brunette (brōō **net**′) □*adjective* □*noun, plural* **brunettes**

brush¹ *noun* **1.** A tool for scrubbing, grooming, or applying liquids. A brush is usually made of bristles attached to a hard back or a handle. **2.** The act of using a brush: *Give the suit a good brush to remove the lint.* **3.** A light touch in passing: *I felt the brush of his coat as he went by.*
□*verb* **1.** To clean, polish, sweep, or groom with a brush: *She brushed her hair.* **2.** To put on or take off with a brush: *He brushed on some paint.* **3.** To give a light touch in passing: *Her hand just brushed his arm.*
brush (brush) □*noun, plural* **brushes** □*verb*
brushed, brushing, brushes

brush² *noun* **1.** An area with a thick growth of shrubs and small trees. **2.** Branches and twigs that have broken off or been cut off.
brush (brush) □*noun*

Brussels sprouts *plural noun* The edible buds of a kind of cabbage that grow on a thick stalk and look like small heads of cabbage.
Brus·sels sprouts (brus′ əlz) □*plural noun*

brutal *adjective* Cruel and harsh like a brute; savage: *a brutal attack.*
bru·tal (brōō′ təl) □*adjective*

brute *noun* **1.** An animal other than a human being; beast. **2.** A cruel and harsh person.
brute (brōōt) □*noun, plural* **brutes**

bubble *noun* A thin film of liquid that is shaped like a ball and has air or gas trapped inside it: *a soap bubble. My soda was full of bubbles.*
□*verb* To form or rise in bubbles: *The soup bubbled on the stove.*
bub·ble (bub′ əl) □*noun, plural* **bubbles**
□*verb* **bubbled, bubbling, bubbles**

buck *noun* A male deer, rabbit, or antelope.
□*verb* **1.** To leap upward and forward suddenly with the head down: *The mule bucked and kicked.* **2.** To go, work, or struggle against: *The small car bucked a strong wind on the bridge.*
buck (buk) □*noun, plural* **bucks** □*verb*
bucked, bucking, bucks

bucket *noun* A round, open container with a handle, used for carrying such things as water, coal, and sand; pail.
buck·et (buk′it) □*noun, plural* **buckets**

buckle *noun* **1.** A clasp used to fasten one end of a belt or strap to the other. **2.** A bend, bulge, or twist: *The frost caused a buckle in the road.*
□*verb* **1.** To fasten with a buckle. **2.** To bend, bulge, or twist: *The floor buckled under the weight of the piano.*
    buckle down To begin to work hard: *He buckled down to the task and made progress.*
buck·le (buk′əl) □*noun, plural* **buckles**
□*verb* **buckled, buckling, buckles**

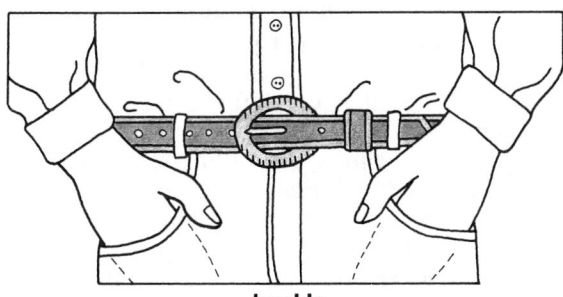
buckle

buckskin *noun* A soft, strong, yellow leather made from the skins of deer or sheep.
buck·skin (buk′skin′) □*noun, plural* **buckskins**

buckwheat *noun* A plant with seeds that are often ground into flour.
buck·wheat (buk′hwēt′ *or* buk′wēt′) □*noun*

bud *noun* A small swelling on a plant that contains a flower, stem, or leaves that have not yet developed.
□*verb* To form or produce buds: *The trees bud in the spring.*
bud (bud) □*noun, plural* **buds** □*verb* **budded, budding, buds**

Buddha *noun* The title of a religious leader who lived in India about 2,500 years ago.
Bud·dha (boō′də) □*noun*

WORD HISTORY: **Buddha**
The title *Buddha* means "the Enlightened One."

Buddhism *noun* The religion that is based on the teachings of Buddha.
Bud·dhism (boō′diz′əm) □*noun*

buddy *noun* A close friend; pal.
bud·dy (bud′ē) □*noun, plural* **buddies**

budge *verb* To move or cause to move slightly: *He didn't budge when I called him. The strong men could not budge the door.*
budge (buj) □*verb* **budged, budging, budges**

budget *noun* A plan for how money will be spent. A household budget must include rent, food, and clothing.
□*verb* To plan in advance how to spend money: *She budgeted $50 for food this week.*
bud·get (buj′it) □*noun, plural* **budgets**
□*verb* **budgeted, budgeting, budgets**

buff *noun* **1.** A soft, thick, yellowish leather made from the skin of a buffalo, elk, or ox. **2.** A yellowish tan color.
□*adjective* Yellowish tan.
□*verb* To polish or shine: *I buffed my fingernails to a bright shine.*
buff (buf) □*noun, plural* **buffs** □*adjective*
□*verb* **buffed, buffing, buffs**

buffalo *noun* **1.** An animal, the bison of North America. **2.** An African or Asian animal with curved, spreading horns; water buffalo.
buf·fa·lo (buf′ə lō′) □*noun, plural* **buffaloes** or **buffalos** or **buffalo**

buffalo

buffet *noun* **1.** A piece of furniture that has a flat top from which food may be served and drawers and shelves for holding china, silverware, and table linens. **2.** A meal at which guests may serve themselves from food set out on a table or buffet.
buf·fet (bə fā′ *or* boō fā′) □*noun, plural* **buffets**

a	bat	ī	bite	oō	tool	*th*	feather
ā	make	î	fierce	ou	out	th	bath
â	dare	o	dot	u	nut	hw	wheat
ä	father	ō	no	û	turn	zh	measure
e	net	ô	law, for	ch	church	ə	about, open
ē	be	oi	soil	ng	ring		pencil, atom
i	dip	oo	look	sh	shade		circus

bug   *noun*   **1.** Any of a group of insects with mouth parts used for sucking. Some bugs have no wings, and some have four wings. **2.** An insect, such as a cockroach, beetle, or spider, that resembles a true bug. **3.** A germ that causes a disease: *the flu bug.* **4.** A fault in a machine or a system: *There are still some bugs in the motor, but they can be fixed.*
□*verb* To hide a microphone in for listening in on conversations: *The police bugged the gangster's house.*
bug (bug) □*noun, plural* **bugs** □*verb*
bugged, bugging, bugs

buggy   *noun* A small, light carriage pulled by a horse.
bug·gy (bug′ē) □*noun, plural* **buggies**

bugle   *noun* A brass musical instrument that resembles a trumpet. Bugles are used in the army and navy to sound signals.
bu·gle (byōō′gəl) □*noun, plural* **bugles**

bugler   *noun* Someone who plays a bugle.
bu·gler (byōō′glər) □*noun, plural* **buglers**

build   *verb*   **1.** To make or form by putting parts or materials together; construct: *Let's build a house near the river. The state built a system of roads.* **2.** To make or form little by little; develop: *He built his argument on facts.*
□*noun* The way a person or thing is shaped or put together: *a man with a sturdy build.*
build (bild) □*verb* **built, building, builds**
□*noun, plural* **builds**

SYNONYMS: **build, construct, erect**
These verbs mean to make or form by putting parts or materials together: *The children built a clubhouse. I constructed a model airplane. We were watching the workers erect the building.*

build

building   *noun*   **1.** Something that is built as a shelter, as a gathering place, or for storage.

Houses, stores, churches, and garages are buildings. **2.** The business or work of putting up or constructing structures such as buildings, railways, ships, and bridges.
build·ing (bil′ding) □*noun, plural* **buildings**

built   *verb* The past tense and past participle of **build**: *We built a cottage at the beach. My uncle has built a very big art collection.*
built (bilt) □*verb*

bulb   *noun*   **1.** A rounded underground plant part from which a new plant grows. Tulips, daffodils, and onions grow from bulbs. **2.** A rounded part of something: *the bulb of a thermometer.* **3.** A rounded glass lamp that fits into an electrical socket: *a light bulb.*
bulb (bulb) □*noun, plural* **bulbs**

bulge   *noun* A rounded part that swells out: *The peach made a bulge in her pocket.*
□*verb* To swell beyond the usual size: *Her pockets bulged with coins.*
bulge (bulj) □*noun, plural* **bulges** □*verb*
bulged, bulging, bulges

bulk   *noun*   **1.** Great size, volume, or mass: *The truck's bulk made it look clumsy.* **2.** The largest part; greatest portion: *The bulk of the book was interesting.*
bulk (bulk) □*noun*

bull   *noun*   **1.** The full-grown male of cattle. **2.** The male of certain other large animals, such as the elephant.
bull (bool) □*noun, plural* **bulls**

bulldog   *noun* A dog with short hair, a thick body, short legs, a large head, and strong, square jaws.
bull·dog (bool′dôg′) □*noun, plural* **bulldogs**

bulldozer   *noun* A large, powerful tractor with a heavy metal blade in front. It is used for moving earth, rocks, and small trees.
bull·doz·er (bool′dō′zər) □*noun, plural* **bulldozers**

bullet   *noun* A piece of metal made to be shot from a small gun such as a pistol or rifle.
bul·let (bool′it) □*noun, plural* **bullets**

bulletin   *noun*   **1.** A short public announcement that gives the latest news: *a weather bulletin.* **2.** A small magazine or pamphlet published by an organization: *Our school bulletin appears once a month.*
bul·le·tin (bool′i tin) □*noun, plural* **bulletins**

bullfight   *noun* A performance in which a person fights a bull in an arena. Bullfights are popular in Spain, Mexico, and some parts of South America.
bull·fight (bool′fīt′) □*noun, plural* **bullfights**

bullfrog   *noun* A large frog with a loud, deep croak.
bull·frog (**bool′** frôg′) ▢*noun, plural* **bullfrogs**

bull's-eye   *noun* **1.** The small circle at the center of a target. **2.** A shot that hits in that small circle.
bull's-eye (**boolz′ī**′) ▢*noun, plural* **bull's-eyes**

bully   *noun* Someone who likes to pick fights with or tease smaller and weaker people.
▢*verb* To use strength or threats to get what one wants: *He bullied her into going to the store for him.*
bul·ly (**bool′** ē) ▢*noun, plural* **bullies** ▢*verb* **bullied, bullying, bullies**

bumblebee   *noun* A large, hairy bee that flies with a humming sound.
bum·ble·bee (**bum′** bəl bē′) ▢*noun, plural* **bumblebees**

bump   *verb* **1.** To knock or strike: *She bumped into the door. He bumped his elbow on the door.* **2.** To move with jerks and jolts: *The car bumped down the lane.*
▢*noun* **1.** A knock, blow, or jolt: *The cars came together with a bump.* **2.** A swelling; lump: *The mosquito bite left a bump on my arm.*
bump (**bump**) ▢*verb* **bumped, bumping, bumps** ▢*noun, plural* **bumps**

bumper   *noun* A metal bar attached to the front and back of a car, bus, or truck to protect it from being damaged if it is hit.
▢*adjective* Very large: *There should be a bumper crop of corn this year.*
bump·er (**bum′** pər) ▢*noun, plural* **bumpers** ▢*adjective*

bun   *noun* **1.** A small bread roll. Many buns are sweet and have raisins, nuts, or spices. **2.** A roll of hair worn at the back or on the top of a woman's head.
bun (**bun**) ▢*noun, plural* **buns**

bunch   *noun* **1.** A group of similar things that are growing, fastened, or placed together: *a bunch of lettuce; a bunch of roses; a bunch of pencils.* **2.** A group of people: *He is the smartest of the bunch.*
▢*verb* To gather together in a bunch: *She bunched up the paper into a ball.*
bunch (**bunch**) ▢*noun, plural* **bunches** ▢*verb* **bunched, bunching, bunches**

bundle   *noun* **1.** A number of objects tied or wrapped together: *a bundle of old magazines.* **2.** A package; parcel: *We made up birthday bundles for the children.*
▢*verb* To tie, wrap, or package together: *I bundled up the old clothes.*
bun·dle (**bun′** dəl) ▢*noun, plural* **bundles** ▢*verb* **bundled, bundling, bundles**

bungalow   *noun* A small house or cottage that is one story high.
bun·ga·low (**bung′** gə lō′) ▢*noun, plural* **bungalows**

WORD HISTORY: bungalow

Bungalow comes from a word that literally means "house in the Bengal style." Bengal is a region in northeast India.

---

bunk   *noun* A narrow bed that is often built in against a wall.
bunk (**bungk**) ▢*noun, plural* **bunks**

Bunsen burner   *noun* A small burner used in a laboratory. A Bunsen burner produces a very hot flame by using a mixture of gas and air.
Bun·sen burner (**bun′** sən) ▢*noun*

WORD HISTORY: Bunsen burner

The *Bunsen burner* is named after Robert Bunsen, the German chemist who invented it about 100 years ago.

Bunsen burner

a	bat	ī	bite	ōō	tool	*th*	feather
ā	make	î	fierce	ou	out	th	bath
â	dare	o	dot	u	nut	hw	wheat
ä	father	ō	no	û	turn	zh	measure
e	net	ô	law, for	ch	church	ə	about, open
ē	be	oi	soil	ng	ring		pencil, atom
i	dip	oo	look	sh	shade		circus

bunt   *verb* To bat a baseball lightly so that it rolls slowly and does not go very far.
□*noun* A ball that has been bunted.
bunt (bunt) □*verb* **bunted, bunting, bunts**
□*noun, plural* **bunts**

buoy   *noun* **1.** A float used to mark dangerous places in a body of water to show where boats may safely go. **2.** A ring made of a material that floats and worn to keep a person from sinking in water.
buoy (bōō′ē *or* boi) □*noun, plural* **buoys**

buoy

bur   *noun* A seed or other plant part with a rough, prickly covering.
bur (bûr) □*noun, plural* **burs**

burden   *noun* **1.** Something that is carried; load: *The man carried a heavy burden of coal to the cellar.* **2.** Something that is hard to bear: *His debts were a great burden to him.*
bur·den (bûr′dən) □*noun, plural* **burdens**

burden

bureau   *noun* **1.** A chest of drawers; dresser. **2.** An office for a particular kind of business: *a news bureau.* **3.** A department of a government: *the Federal Bureau of Investigation.*
bu·reau (byoor′ō) □*noun, plural* **bureaus**

burglar   *noun* Someone who breaks into a house or other place in order to steal.
bur·glar (bûr′glər) □*noun, plural* **burglars**

burial   *noun* The act of placing a dead body in a grave, the sea, or a tomb.
bur·i·al (ber′ē əl) □*noun, plural* **burials**

burlap   *noun* A coarse cloth woven of thick fibers of hemp, jute, or flax. Burlap is used to make bags, sacks, curtains, and wrappings.
bur·lap (bûr′lap′) □*noun*

burn   *verb* **1.** To set on fire or be on fire: *They burned all his old letters. The newspapers burned in the fireplace.* **2.** To hurt, damage, or destroy with fire or heat: *She burned her fingers while ironing.* **3.** To be hurt, damaged, or destroyed by fire, heat, or chemicals: *The barn burned to the ground.* **4.** To feel or cause to feel hot: *Her face burned with fever. The food burned his mouth.* **5.** To use as fuel: *Our furnace burns gas.* **6.** To make or produce by fire, heat, or chemicals: *The spark burned a hole in his sleeve.*
□*noun* Damage or an injury caused by burning.
burn (bûrn) □*verb* **burned** *or* **burnt, burning, burns** □*noun, plural* **burns**

burner   *noun* The part of a stove top on which a pot or pan may be heated.
burn·er (bûr′nər) □*noun, plural* **burners**

burnt   *verb* A past tense and a past participle of **burn**: *I burnt my finger.*
burnt (bûrnt) □*verb*

burr   *noun* Another spelling for **bur**.
burr (bûr) □*noun, plural* **burrs**

burro   *noun* A small donkey used for riding or carrying loads.
bur·ro (bûr′ō) □*noun, plural* **burros**

burrow   *noun* A hole, tunnel, or opening dug in the ground by a small animal such as a rabbit or mole.
□*verb* **1.** To dig a hole, tunnel, or opening in the ground: *Moles have been burrowing in my garden.* **2.** To search as if burrowing: *He burrowed in his suitcase for his slippers.*
bur·row (bûr′ō) □*noun, plural* **burrows**
□*verb* **burrowed, burrowing, burrows**

burst   *verb* **1.** To break open or cause to break open suddenly: *The tire hit a nail and*

burst. Flood water can burst dams. **2.** To come in or go out suddenly: *He burst into the house without knocking.* **3.** To be or seem to be full enough to break open: *The bag was bursting with apples.*
□*noun* A sudden outbreak or rush: *a burst of anger; a burst of speed.*
burst (bûrst) □*verb* **burst, bursting, bursts** □*noun, plural* **bursts**

bury *verb* **1.** To place a dead body in a grave, the sea, or other place. **2.** To put in the ground and cover with earth: *Dogs often bury bones.* **3.** To hide as if by burying: *He buried his face in his hands.*
bur·y (ber′ē) □*verb* **buried, burying, buries**

bus *noun* A long vehicle with seats for many passengers. Most buses travel on regular routes.
□*verb* To send or go by bus: *The town buses children to school.*
bus (bus) □*noun, plural* **buses** or **busses** □*verb* **bused** or **bussed, busing** or **bussing, buses** or **busses**

bush *noun* A woody plant that is smaller than a tree and has many branches; shrub.
bush (bŏosh) □*noun, plural* **bushes**

bushel *noun* A unit used in the United States to measure grain, fruit, vegetables, and other dry foods. A bushel is equal to 4 pecks or 32 dry quarts.
bush·el (boosh′əl) □*noun, plural* **bushels**

bushy *adjective* Thick and spreading like a bush: *a bushy tail; bushy hair.*
bush·y (boosh′ē) □*adjective* **bushier, bushiest**

business *noun* **1.** The work a person does to earn a living; job or occupation: *Her business is selling shoes.* **2.** A company, such as a store or factory, that buys or sells goods or services: *She sold her father's business when he died.* **3.** Buying and selling; trade: *Business is bad this year.* **4.** Something that concerns or interests: *What he told me is not your business.*
busi·ness (biz′nis) □*noun, plural* **businesses**

bust *noun* A sculpture of a person's head, shoulders, and the upper part of the chest.
bust (bust) □*noun, plural* **busts**

bust

bustle *verb* To hurry and move around in a busy and excited way: *She bustled around cleaning the house before the party.*
□*noun* Busy, excited activity: *There is a great deal of bustle in the kitchen when I give a party.*
bus·tle (bus′əl) □*verb* **bustled, bustling, bustles** □*noun*

busy *adjective* **1.** Having plenty to do; active: *The busy mother of four children.* **2.** Crowded with activity: *We had a busy day at school.* **3.** In use: *Her telephone was busy when he called.*
□*verb* To make, get, or keep busy: *She busied herself with some sewing.*
bus·y (biz′ē) □*adjective* **busier, busiest** □*verb* **busied, busying, busies**

busy

a	bat	ī	bite	ŏŏ	tool	*th*	feather
ā	make	î	fierce	ou	out	th	bath
â	dare	o	dot	u	nut	hw	wheat
ä	father	ō	no	û	turn	zh	measure
e	net	ô	law, for	ch	church	ə	about, open
ē	be	oi	soil	ng	ring		pencil, atom
i	dip	oo	look	sh	shade		circus

but *conjunction* **1.** On the contrary: *These are not fruits but vegetables.* **2.** Yet; nevertheless: *She was thought to be poor, but she had money.*
□*adverb* Only; merely: *He saw her but a minute ago.*
□*preposition* **1.** Except: *Everyone but me was invited to the party.* **2.** Other than: *He told us nothing but lies.*
but (but) □*conjunction* □*adverb* □*preposition*

butcher *noun* Someone who cuts and sells meat.
butch·er (booch′ ər) □*noun, plural* **butchers**

> *WORD HISTORY:* **butcher**
>
> The word *butcher* was borrowed from French in the Middle Ages. It is derived from the French word for "male goat." Apparently a butcher was originally someone who sold goat meat.

butler *noun* The chief male servant in a household.
but·ler (but′ lər) □*noun, plural* **butlers**

butt¹ *noun* Someone who is the target of jokes and teasing: *The little girl was the butt of her sister's jokes.*
butt (but) □*noun, plural* **butts**

butt² *verb* To hit or push with the head or horns: *The goat butted the fence.*
□*noun* A push or blow with the head or horns.
butt (but) □*verb* **butted, butting, butts**
□*noun, plural* **butts**

butt³ *noun* **1.** The thicker end of something such as a tool or weapon: *the butt of a rifle.* **2.** An end that is left over: *a cigarette butt.*
butt (but) □*noun, plural* **butts**

butter *noun* **1.** A soft, yellow fat that is made by churning cream or milk and is used as food. **2.** A spread that is smooth like butter: *apple butter; peanut butter.*
□*verb* To spread butter on.
but·ter (but′ ər) □*noun, plural* **butters** □*verb* **buttered, buttering, butters**

buttercup *noun* A flower that is shaped like a cup and has shiny yellow petals.
but·ter·cup (but′ ər kup′) □*noun, plural* **buttercups**

butterfly *noun* An insect with four large wings that are often brightly colored.
but·ter·fly (but′ ər flī′) □*noun, plural* **butterflies**

buttermilk *noun* The sour liquid that remains after butter has been churned.
but·ter·milk (but′ ər milk′) □*noun*

butternut *noun* The oily nut of a North American tree that is related to the walnut.
but·ter·nut (but′ ər nut′) □*noun, plural* **butternuts**

butterscotch *noun* A flavoring or a candy made from brown sugar and butter.
but·ter·scotch (but′ ər skoch′) □*noun*

buttocks *plural noun* The rounded part of the body on which a person sits; rump.
but·tocks (but′ əks) □*plural noun*

button *noun* **1.** A round disk or knob sewn onto clothing as a fastener or as an ornament. **2.** A knob that is turned or pushed to cause something, such as a doorbell, to work.
□*verb* To fasten with buttons.
but·ton (but′ ən) □*noun, plural* **buttons**
□*verb* **buttoned, buttoning, buttons**

buttress *noun* Something that is built against a wall to support or strengthen it.
□*verb* To support or strengthen with or as if with a buttress: *He buttressed his argument with facts.*
but·tress (but′ ris) □*noun, plural* **buttresses**
□*verb* **buttressed, buttressing, buttresses**

buttress

buy *verb* To pay money to get; purchase.
□*noun* A bargain: *His stereo was a real buy.*
buy (bī) □*verb* **bought, buying, buys**
□*noun, plural* **buys**

buyer *noun* Someone who buys; customer.
buy·er (bī′ ər) □*noun, plural* **buyers**

buzz *verb* **1.** To make a low, humming sound like that of a bee: *A fly buzzed around the horse.* **2.** To be full of activity and talk: *The town buzzed with excitement.* **3.** To fly an airplane low over: *The pilot buzzed his friend's house.*
□*noun* A low, humming sound: *the buzz of a mosquito. An excited buzz went through the theater.*

buzz (buz) ▢*verb* **buzzed, buzzing, buzzes**
▢*noun, plural* **buzzes**

buzzard *noun* A large bird with dark feathers, broad wings, and a head without feathers. A buzzard is a kind of vulture.
buz·zard (buz′ərd) ▢*noun, plural* **buzzards**

buzzer *noun* An electrical device that makes a buzzing sound as a signal.
buzz·er (buz′ər) ▢*noun, plural* **buzzers**

by *preposition* **1.** Through the action of: *The poem was written by my sister.* **2.** With the help or use of: *We crossed the ocean by ship.* **3.** According to: *We always play by the rules.* **4.** Next to; close to: *a lamp by the table.* **5.** In the period of; during: *working by night and sleeping by day.* **6.** In the measure or amount of: *They sell gasoline by the liter.* **7.** Not later than: *You must be here by noon.* **8.** Up to and beyond; past: *A car drove by the house.*
▢*adverb* **1.** Up to, alongside, and past: *The train whizzed by.* **2.** In the neighborhood: *Do you live close by?*
by (bī) ▢*preposition* ▢*adverb*

bygone *adjective* Gone by; past: *the bygone days of the blacksmith.*
by·gone (bī′gôn′) ▢*adjective*

bypass *noun* A road that passes around a city. ▢*verb* To go or send around by bypass.

by·pass (bī′pas) ▢*noun, plural* **bypasses**
▢*verb* **bypassed, bypassing, bypasses**

by-product *noun* Something useful that is the result of making or doing something else: *Phonograph records are made from a by-product of oil.*
by-prod·uct (bī′prod′əkt) ▢*noun, plural* **by-products**

bystander *noun* Someone who is present when something happens but does not take part in the action.
by·stand·er (bī′stand′ər) ▢*noun, plural* **bystanders**

byte *noun* The amount of computer memory needed to store a single letter, number, or punctuation mark.
byte (bīt) ▢*noun, plural* **bytes**

a	bat	ī	bite	o͞o	tool	th	feather
ā	make	î	fierce	ou	out	th	bath
â	dare	o	dot	u	nut	hw	wheat
ä	father	ō	no	û	turn	zh	measure
e	net	ô	law, for	ch	church	ə	about, open
ē	be	oi	soil	ng	ring		pencil, atom
i	dip	oo	look	sh	shade		circus

The letter **C** has evolved from many forms of ancient writing. One of the earliest known examples is the Greek character shown above, which dates from almost 3,000 years ago. Over the years, artists and designers have created their own versions of the English letter **C**. Some of the more common examples seen today are shown below.

Cc Cc	Cc Cc	Cc Cc	Cc Cc	Cc Cc
HANDWRITING	CALLIGRAPHY	MODERN SANS SERIF	MODERN SERIF	SCRIPT

c or **C** *noun* The third letter of the English alphabet.
c or **C** (sē) ▫*noun, plural* **c's** or **C's**

C An abbreviation for **Celsius.**

cab *noun* **1.** An automobile that carries passengers for a charge; taxicab. **2.** A one-horse carriage that carries passengers. **3.** A compartment for the operator or driver of a train, truck, crane, or other machine.
cab (kab) ▫*noun, plural* **cabs**

cab
Of a truck

cabbage *noun* A vegetable with a round head of overlapping green or reddish leaves.
cab·bage (kab′ij) ▫*noun, plural* **cabbages**

cabin *noun* **1.** A small, simply built house; hut: *a log cabin.* **2.** A room for a passenger or crew member on a ship or boat. **3.** The space for passengers in an aircraft.
cab·in (kab′in) ▫*noun, plural* **cabins**

cabinet *noun* **1.** A case or cupboard with doors and compartments or shelves for storing or showing objects: *a file cabinet.* **2.** Often **Cabinet** A group of people chosen by the head of a government to serve as advisers and to be in charge of important departments of state.
cab·i·net (kab′ə nit) ▫*noun, plural* **cabinets**

cable *noun* **1.** A thick, strong rope made of twisted wire or fiber. **2.** A bundle of protected wires that carry electric current. **3.** A message sent by a cable under the ocean.
▫*verb* To telegraph a message by cable.
ca·ble (kā′bəl) ▫*noun, plural* **cables** ▫*verb* **cabled, cabling, cables**

cable television or **cable TV** *noun* A system for transmitting television programs by means of a special cable. People must pay a fee to receive cable television.

caboose *noun* The last car on a freight train. The train crew eat and sleep in the caboose.
ca·boose (kə bo͞os′) ▫*noun, plural* **cabooses**

cacao *noun* A tropical American tree whose seeds are used to make chocolate and cocoa.
ca·ca·o (kə kä′ō *or* kə kā′ō) ▫*noun*

cackle *verb* **1.** To make the harsh, broken cry of a hen that has just laid an egg. **2.** To laugh with a cackling sound.
▫*noun* **1.** The harsh, broken cry of a hen. **2.** A sound like a hen's cackle.
cack·le (kak′əl) ▫*verb* **cackled, cackling, cackles** ▫*noun, plural* **cackles**

cactus *noun* A plant that has thick stems covered with spines. Cactuses grow especially in hot, dry places.

cac·tus (kak′təs) □*noun, plural* **cactuses** or **cac·ti** (kak′tī′)

cactus

cadet *noun* A student at a military or naval academy who is training to be an officer.
ca·det (kə det′) □*noun, plural* **cadets**

café *noun* A small restaurant.
ca·fé (ka fā′) □*noun, plural* **cafés**

cafeteria *noun* A restaurant in which customers wait on themselves.
caf·e·te·ri·a (kaf′i tîr′ē ə) □*noun, plural* **cafeterias**

caffeine *noun* A slightly bitter, stimulating substance found in coffee, tea, and some soft drinks. Too much caffeine can keep a person awake.
caf·feine (kaf′ēn′) □*noun*

cage *noun* **1.** A structure that has bars or screens and is used to keep or carry birds and animals. **2.** Something that looks like a cage: *a cage for the cashier at the movie theater.*
□*verb* To put or keep in a cage.
cage (kāj) □*noun, plural* **cages** □*verb* **caged, caging, cages**

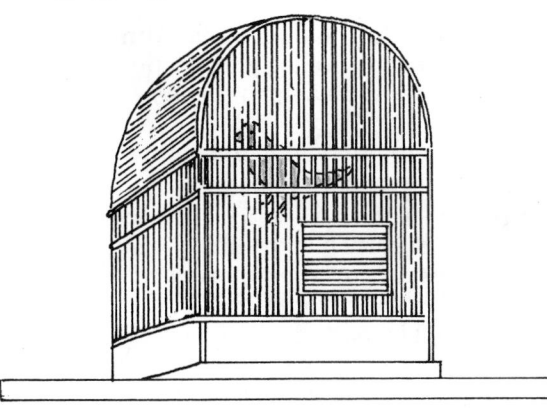

cage

cake *noun* **1.** A mixture of flour, sugar, liquid, eggs, and other ingredients, that is baked and sometimes covered with icing. **2.** A food mixture that is baked or fried in a usually flat shape: *fish cakes.* **3.** A solid, shaped mass of something: *a cake of soap.*
□*verb* To become or form into a hardened mass: *Dried mud had caked on his new shoes.*
cake (kāk) □*noun, plural* **cakes** □*verb* **caked, caking, cakes**

calamity *noun* Something that causes great misfortune and suffering; disaster: *The earthquake was a calamity that killed thousands.*
ca·lam·i·ty (kə lam′i tē) □*noun, plural* **calamities**

calcium *noun* A silvery metallic element that is found in substances such as bone or shells.
cal·ci·um (kal′sē əm) □*noun*

calculate *verb* **1.** To find out an answer or result by using mathematics: *We calculated our profits by adding up our sales.* **2.** To figure out: *They calculated that they needed at least another hour.* **3.** To plan deliberately; intend: *The letter was calculated to arouse our curiosity.*
cal·cu·late (kal′kyə lāt′) □*verb* **calculated, calculating, calculates**

calculation *noun* The act or result of calculating: *My father checked my calculations.*
cal·cu·la·tion (kal′kyə lā′shən) □*noun, plural* **calculations**

calculator *noun* A machine that automatically solves arithmetic problems.
cal·cu·la·tor (kal′kyə lā′tər) □*noun, plural* **calculators**

calendar *noun* A chart showing each month, week, and day of the year.
cal·en·dar (kal′ən dər) □*noun, plural* **calendars**

calf¹ *noun* **1.** A young cow or bull. **2.** A young whale, seal, or elephant. **3.** Leather made from the skin of a calf.
calf (kaf) □*noun, plural* **calves**

calf² *noun* The fleshy back part of the leg between the knee and the ankle.
calf (kaf) □*noun, plural* **calves**

a bat	ī bite	o͞o tool	*th* feather
ā make	î fierce	ou out	th bath
â dare	o dot	u nut	hw wheat
ä father	ō no	û turn	zh measure
e net	ô law, for	ch church	ə about, open
ē be	oi soil	ng ring	pencil, atom
i dip	oo look	sh shade	circus

calico *noun* A cotton cloth printed with a brightly colored design.
□*adjective* **1.** Made of calico: *a calico blouse.* **2.** Having spots of a different color: *a calico cat.*
cal·i·co (**kal′**i kō) □*noun, plural* **calicoes** or **calicos** □*adjective*

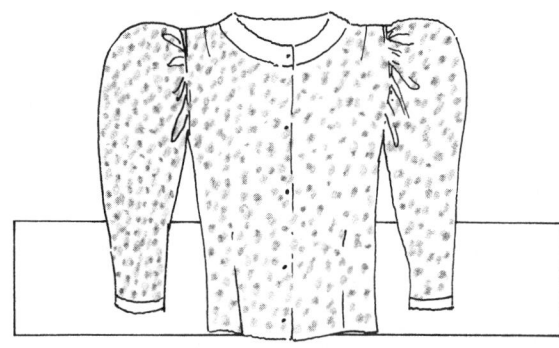
calico

call *verb* **1.** To say or speak in a loud voice: *She called his name last.* **2.** To send for; summon: *Call an ambulance right away!* **3.** To give a certain name: *Let's call the kitten Mischief.* **4.** To telephone: *Call your mother tomorrow.* **5.** To make a short visit: *Let's call on them soon.* —See Synonyms at **name.**
□*noun* **1.** A shout or loud cry: *a call for help.* **2.** The usual cry of a bird or animal. **3.** An act of calling on the telephone: *Did I get any calls while I was out?* **4.** A short visit: *We made a call on my uncle.*
call (kôl) □*verb* **called, calling, calls**
□*noun, plural* **calls**

callus *noun* A hard, thick area of skin that usually forms on the hands or feet.
cal·lus (**kal′**əs) □*noun, plural* **calluses**

calm *adjective* **1.** Not excited; quiet: *She remained calm during the argument.* **2.** Not moving; still: *a calm sea.*
□*noun* A condition of quiet or stillness: *the calm of the lake after a storm.*
□*verb* To make or become calm: *Her speech calmed the restless crowd. Stop shouting and calm down.*
calm (käm) □*adjective* **calmer, calmest**
□*noun, plural* **calms** □*verb* **calmed, calming, calms**

calorie *noun* **1.** A unit for measuring the amount of heat in something. **2.** A unit for measuring the amount of energy in food: *An apple has about one hundred calories.*
cal·o·rie (**kal′**ə rē) □*noun, plural* **calories**

calves *noun* The plural of **calf.**
calves (kavz) □*noun*

came *verb* The past tense of **come:** *She came to our house last summer.*
came (kām) □*verb*

camel *noun* An animal with a long neck and one or two humps. Camels live in northern Africa and western Asia. They are used for riding and carrying loads.
cam·el (**kam′**əl) □*noun, plural* **camels**

camera *noun* A device that can take photographs or motion pictures. A camera usually consists of a box having a lens that lets in light and records a picture on film.
cam·er·a (**kam′**ər ə *or* **kam′**rə) □*noun, plural* **cameras**

camouflage *noun* An appearance that hides or disguises people, animals, or things with colors and patterns that make them look like their surroundings.
□*verb* To hide or disguise by using camouflage: *We camouflaged the cannon by covering it with the branches of a tree.*
cam·ou·flage (**kam′**ə fläzh′) □*noun* □*verb* **camouflaged, camouflaging, camouflages**

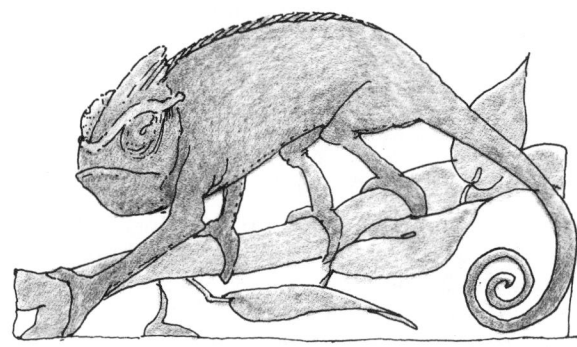
camouflage
A chameleon uses camouflage for protection

camp *noun* An outdoor area with tents or cabins for people to live and sleep in.
□*verb* To live in a camp: *We camped next to a brook.*
camp (kamp) □*noun, plural* **camps** □*verb* **camped, camping, camps**

campaign *noun* A series of actions for achieving a particular result: *a military campaign. The new governor thanked all the people who worked on his campaign.*
□*verb* To take part in a campaign.
cam·paign (kam **pān′**) □*noun, plural* **campaigns** □*verb* **campaigned, campaigning, campaigns**

camper *noun* **1.** Someone who camps out-doors. **2.** A car or trailer specially designed for camping or long trips.
camp·er (**kam′**pər) □*noun, plural* **campers**

campfire *noun* An outdoor fire for cooking or for keeping people warm.
camp·fire (**kamp′**fīr′) □*noun, plural* **campfires**

campfire

camphor *noun* A white, strong-smelling sub-stance used in medicine, in making plastics, and to keep away moths.
cam·phor (**kam′**fər) □*noun*

campus *noun* The buildings of a university, college, or school.
cam·pus (**kam′**pəs) □*noun, plural* **campuses**

can¹ *verb* **1.** To know how to: *She can skate well.* **2.** To be able to: *Green plants can make their own food.* **3.** To have permission to: *She said we can borrow her car.*
can (kan *or* kən) □*verb*

can² *noun* **1.** An airtight metal container for foods or liquids. **2.** A large container, usually with a lid: *a garbage can.*
□*verb* To preserve food in a sealed container: *They can plums and peaches every summer.*
can (kan) □*noun, plural* **cans** □*verb* **canned, canning, cans**

Canadian *noun* Someone who was born in or is a citizen of Canada.
□*adjective* Of Canada or the people of Canada.
Ca·na·di·an (kə **nā′**dē ən) □*noun, plural* **Canadians** □*adjective*

canal *noun* A body of water that is dug to connect two or more points. Canals are used for travel, shipping, and to irrigate or drain an area.
ca·nal (kə **nal′**) □*noun, plural* **canals**

canary *noun* **1.** A yellow songbird that is popular as a pet. **2.** A light, bright yellow color.
ca·nar·y (kə **nâr′**ē) □*noun, plural* **canaries**

cancel *verb* **1.** To put an end to or give up: *cancel an appointment.* **2.** To mark a postage stamp or check to show that it may no longer be used.
can·cel (**kan′**səl) □*verb* **canceled, canceling, cancels**

cancel

cancer *noun* A disease in which some cells of the body grow too rapidly, destroying healthy tissues and organs.
can·cer (**kan′**sər) □*noun, plural* **cancers**

candidate *noun* Someone who seeks or is nominated for a prize, honor, or office: *She is a candidate for mayor.*
can·di·date (**kan′**di dāt′) □*noun, plural* **candidates**

WORD HISTORY: **candidate**

Candidate comes from a Latin word meaning "dressed in white." In ancient Rome candidates for public office wore white togas.

candle *noun* A solid stick of wax or tallow formed around a wick or string that is burned to give light or heat.
can·dle (**kan′**dəl) □*noun, plural* **candles**

candlestick *noun* Something that holds a candle.
can·dle·stick (**kan′**dəl stik′) □*noun, plural* **candlesticks**

candy *noun* A sweet food made from sugar or syrup, often mixed with fruit, nuts, or fla-voring.
can·dy (**kan′**dē) □*noun, plural* **candies**

cane *noun* **1.** A stick used to help in walking. **2.** A hollow, woody stem of a grass plant such

a	bat	ī	bite	o͞o	tool	*th*	feather
ā	make	î	fierce	ou	out	th	bath
â	dare	o	dot	u	nut	hw	wheat
ä	father	ō	no	û	turn	zh	measure
e	net	ô	law, for	ch	church	ə	about, open
ē	be	oi	soil	ng	ring		pencil, atom
i	dip	oo	look	sh	shade		circus

as bamboo. Cane is often used to make furniture. **3.** A plant with a hollow, woody stem: *sugar cane.*
cane (kān) □*noun, plural* **canes**

cannibal *noun* Someone who eats human flesh.
can·ni·bal (kan′ə bəl) □*noun, plural* **cannibals**

cannon *noun* A large gun mounted on wheels or on a heavy base.
can·non (kan′ən) □*noun, plural* **cannons** or **cannon**

cannonball *noun* A heavy ball fired from a cannon.
can·non·ball (kan′ən bôl′) □*noun, plural* **cannonballs**

cannot Can not.
can·not (kan′ot′ *or* ka **not**′)

canoe *noun* A light, narrow boat that is pointed at the ends and moved with paddles. □*verb* To travel in or paddle a canoe.
ca·noe (kə nōō′) □*noun, plural* **canoes** □*verb* **canoed, canoeing, canoes**

canopy *noun* A covering that is usually made of fabric and hangs over a bed, entrance, or throne.
can·o·py (kan′ə pē) □*noun, plural* **canopies**

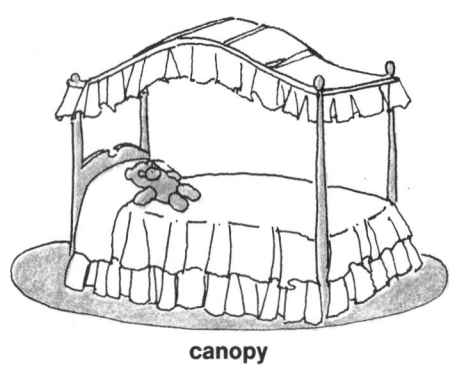

canopy

can't Contraction of "can not."
can't (kant *or* känt)

cantaloupe *noun* A melon with sweet, orange flesh and a rough rind.
can·ta·loupe (kan′tə lōp′) □*noun, plural* **cantaloupes**

WORD HISTORY: cantaloupe

Cantaloupe is named after Cantalupo, an estate near Rome where the fruit was first grown in Europe.

---

canteen *noun* **1.** A container for carrying drinking water or other liquids. **2.** A store in a school, factory, or office where food and beverages are sold.
can·teen (kan tēn′) □*noun, plural* **canteens**

canvas *noun* **1.** A heavy, coarse cloth used for making such things as tents and sails. **2.** A piece of canvas stretched on a frame and used for an oil painting.
can·vas (kan′vəs) □*noun, plural* **canvases**

canyon *noun* A deep valley with steep cliffs on both sides and often a stream running through it.
can·yon (kan′yən) □*noun, plural* **canyons**

cap *noun* **1.** A close-fitting covering for the head. Some caps have no brims. **2.** A cover that looks like or fits like a cap: *a bottle cap.* **3.** A small amount of explosive powder wrapped in paper. □*verb* To cover with or as if with a cap: *A storm capped the mountain with snow.*
cap (kap) □*noun, plural* **caps** □*verb* **capped, capping, caps**

capable *adjective* Having the ability or skill for something: *He was a capable teacher. She is capable of winning the spelling contest.*
ca·pa·ble (kā′pə bəl) □*adjective*

capacity *noun* The amount that can be held: *This jug has a capacity of five quarts.*
ca·pac·i·ty (kə pas′i tē) □*noun, plural* **capacities**

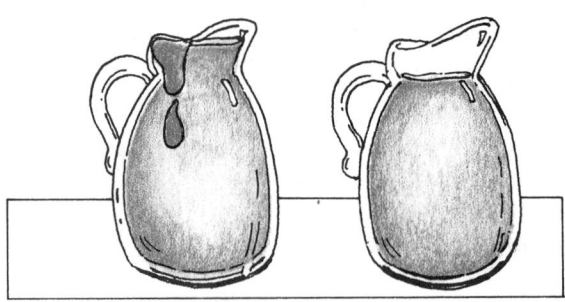

capacity

cape[1] *noun* A piece of clothing with no sleeves that is worn loosely over the shoulders.
cape (kāp) □*noun, plural* **capes**

cape[2] *noun* A point of land extending into the sea or other body of water.
cape (kāp) □*noun, plural* **capes**

capital *noun* **1.** A city where the government of a state or country is located. **2.** Money or property that is invested to produce more money. **3.** A capital letter.

□*adjective* **1.** Most important; chief: *a capital city.* **2.** Calling for a penalty of death: *capital punishment.*
cap·i·tal (kap′i təl) □*noun, plural* **capitals** □*adjective*

WORD HISTORY: **capital**

Capital comes from the Latin word meaning "a head."

---

capitalize *verb* **1.** To begin with a capital letter: *Capitalize proper nouns.* **2.** To write or print in capital letters.
cap·i·tal·ize (kap′i təl īze′) □*verb* **capitalized, capitalizing, capitalizes**

capitalism *noun* An economic system in which goods are produced for profit, labor is performed for wages, and the means of production, such as factories or land, are owned by private persons rather than by the state.
cap·i·tal·ism (kap′i təl iz′əm) □*noun*

capital letter *noun* A letter, such as A, B, or C, written or printed in a size larger than the same smaller letter, such as a, b, or c.

capitol *noun* **1. Capitol** The building in Washington, D.C., occupied by the Congress of the United States. **2.** The building in which a state legislature meets.
cap·i·tol (kap′i təl) □*noun, plural* **capitols**

capsize *verb* To turn bottom side up: *The boat capsized in the storm.*
cap·size (kap′sīz′ *or* kap **sīz**′) □*verb* **capsized, capsizing, capsizes**

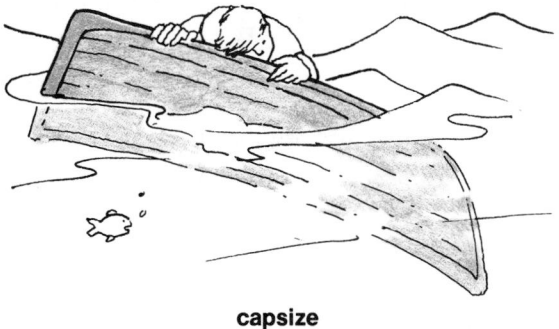

capsize

capsule *noun* **1.** A small container holding a dose of medicine. After it is swallowed whole, the capsule dissolves in the stomach. **2.** A place on a spacecraft for the crew.
cap·sule (kap′səl) □*noun, plural* **capsules**

captain *noun* **1.** The leader of a group: *the captain of the team.* **2.** The officer in charge of

a ship. **3.** An Army, Air Force, or Marine Corps officer ranking above a first lieutenant. **4.** A Navy officer ranking above a commander.
cap·tain (kap′tən) □*noun, plural* **captains**

caption *noun* A title or explanation that goes with a picture.
cap·tion (kap′shən) □*noun, plural* **captions**

captive *adjective* Held prisoner; not free: *a captive tiger.*
□*noun* A prisoner: *The captives were put in a room with bars on the windows.*
cap·tive (kap′tiv) □*adjective* □*noun, plural* **captives**

capture *verb* **1.** To get hold of; seize: *capture a wild animal.* **2.** To hold the attention of: *The movie captured my interest.*
□*noun* The act of capturing: *The robbers fled to avoid capture.*
cap·ture (kap′chər) □*verb* **captured, capturing, captures** □*noun, plural* **captures**

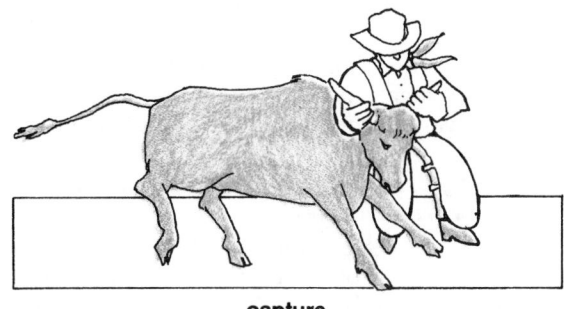

capture

car *noun* **1.** An automobile. **2.** A vehicle with wheels that moves along rails or tracks: *the dining car of a train.*
car (kär) □*noun, plural* **cars**

caramel *noun* **1.** A brown syrup made by melting sugar, used to color and flavor foods. **2.** A chewy, soft candy flavored with caramel.
car·a·mel (kar′ə məl *or* kär′məl) □*noun, plural* **caramels**

carat *noun* A unit of weight for diamonds, rubies, and other precious stones. Another way of spelling this word is **karat**.
car·at (kar′ət) □*noun, plural* **carats**

a bat	ī bite	o͞o tool	*th* feather
ā make	i fierce	ou out	th bath
â dare	o dot	u nut	hw wheat
ä father	ō no	û turn	zh measure
e net	ô law, for	ch church	ə about, open
ē be	oi soil	ng ring	pencil, atom
i dip	oo look	sh shade	circus

caravan *noun* A group of people or vehicles traveling together: *a caravan of merchants traveling across the desert; a caravan of trucks and jeeps.*
car·a·van (kăr′ə van′) □*noun, plural* **caravans**

caravan

carbohydrate *noun* A substance, such as starch or sugar, made up of carbon, hydrogen, and oxygen. Carbohydrates are made by green plants.
car·bo·hy·drate (kär′bō hī′drāt′) □*noun, plural* **carbohydrates**

carbon *noun* A chemical element found in all living things. Coal and charcoal have large amounts of carbon, and diamonds are pure carbon in crystal form.
car·bon (kär′bən) □*noun*

carbon dioxide *noun* A gas without color or odor, consisting of carbon and oxygen. Carbon dioxide is formed when animals breathe and when any fuel containing carbon burns.
carbon di·ox·ide (dī ok′sīd′) □*noun*

carbon monoxide *noun* A poisonous gas that has no color or odor and forms when a substance that contains carbon does not burn completely. Fumes from the exhaust pipe of a car contain carbon monoxide.
carbon mo·nox·ide (mə nok′sīd′) □*noun*

carburetor *noun* A part of a gasoline engine that mixes the gasoline with air to form a mixture that will burn properly.
car·bu·re·tor (kär′bə rā′tər) □*noun, plural* **carburetors**

carcass *noun* The dead body of an animal.
car·cass (kär′kəs) □*noun, plural* **carcasses**

card *noun* **1.** A small, thin piece of stiff paper or plastic. Cards are used to carry a greeting or give information: *a library card; a birthday card.* **2.** One of a pack of cards marked with numbers, pictures, and designs. They are used to play games.
card (kärd) □*noun, plural* **cards**

cardboard *noun* A stiff, heavy paper made by pressing layers of paper pulp together.
card·board (kärd′bôrd) □*noun*

cardinal *noun* **1.** An official of the Roman Catholic Church whose rank is next below that of the Pope. **2.** A North American songbird that has bright red feathers and a crest on its head.
□*adjective* Of greatest or first importance; chief; foremost: *the cardinal point in her speech.*
car·di·nal (kär′dən əl) □*noun, plural* **cardinals** □*adjective*

cardinal number *noun* A number used in counting that tells how many: *3, 11, and 412 are cardinal numbers.*

care *noun* **1.** A feeling of worry or concern: *We were free from care on our vacation.* **2.** Serious attention: *You should do your work with more care.* **3.** Protection or charge; keeping: *in the care of a nurse.*
□*verb* **1.** To be interested or concerned: *She doesn't care what happens.* **2.** To wish for; want: *Would you care to dance?* **3.** To like: *He doesn't care for music.*
care (kâr) □*noun, plural* **cares** □*verb* **cared, caring, cares**

career *noun* The kind of work or occupation that a person chooses to do through life: *He chose teaching as a career.*
ca·reer (kə rîr′) □*noun, plural* **careers**

carefree *adjective* Without worries or responsibilities: *a carefree holiday.*
care·free (kâr′frē′) □*adjective*

careful *adjective* Taking time to think before acting: *I am always careful when crossing a street.*
care·ful (kâr′fəl) □*adjective*

SYNONYMS: **careful, cautious**

These adjectives mean taking one's time in order to avoid danger or error: *If you had been careful you wouldn't have spilled the paint. Always be cautious when riding your bicycle.*

---

careless *adjective* **1.** Not taking care or paying close attention: *a careless worker; a careless mistake.* **2.** Done or made without care:

They did a careless job that was full of mistakes.
care·less (kâr′lis) □*adjective*

caress *noun* A gentle touch that shows love or affection.
□*verb* To touch in a way that shows fondness or love.
ca·ress (kə res′) □*noun, plural* **caresses**
□*verb* **caressed, caressing, caresses**

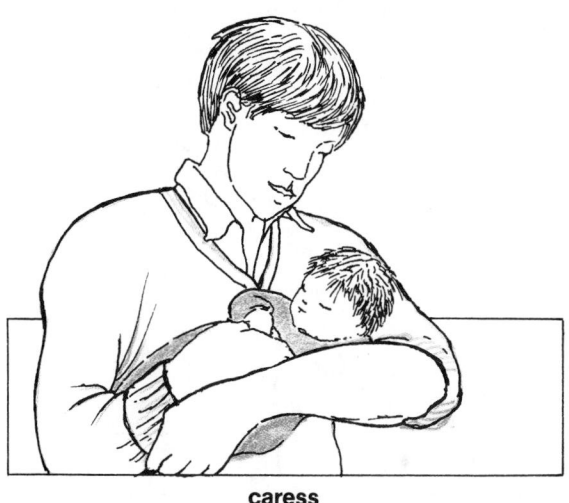

caress

caretaker *noun* Someone who has the job of taking care of property that belongs to another.
care·tak·er (kâr′ tā′kər) □*noun, plural* **caretakers**

cargo *noun* The freight carried by a ship, airplane, or other vehicle.
car·go (kär′ gō) □*noun, plural* **cargoes** or **cargos**

caribou *noun* A large deer of northern North America. Both the males and the females have large, spreading antlers.
car·i·bou (kar′ə bōō′) □*noun, plural* **caribou** or **caribous**

carnation *noun* A flower with a spicy smell. Carnations can be red, pink, or white.
car·na·tion (kär nā′shən) □*noun, plural* **carnations**

carnival *noun* An outdoor show that has rides, games, and other entertainment.
car·ni·val (kär′nə vəl) □*noun, plural* **carnivals**

carnivorous *adjective* Feeding on the flesh of other animals: *A weasel is a carnivorous animal.*
car·ni·vor·ous (kär niv′ər əs) □*adjective*

carol *noun* A song of joy or praise: *Christmas carols.*
□*verb* To sing with great joy.
car·ol (kar′əl) □*noun, plural* **carols** □*verb* **caroled, caroling, carols**

carp *noun* An edible fish that lives in fresh water.
carp (kärp) □*noun, plural* **carp** or **carps**

carpenter *noun* Someone who builds or repairs things that are made of wood.
car·pen·ter (kär′ pən tər) □*noun, plural* **carpenters**

carpenter

carpet *noun* **1.** A thick, heavy covering for a floor, usually made of a woven fabric. **2.** Something that covers a surface like a carpet: *a carpet of grass.*
□*verb* To cover with a carpet: *We carpeted the den.*
car·pet (kär′ pit) □*noun, plural* **carpets** □*verb* **carpeted, carpeting, carpets**

carriage *noun* **1.** A passenger vehicle that has four wheels and is pulled by horses. **2.** A small vehicle for a baby that is pushed along by a person. **3.** A movable part of a machine that holds or carries another part. The carriage of a typewriter holds a piece of paper and moves back and forth.
car·riage (kar′ij) □*noun, plural* **carriages**

carrier *noun* Someone or something that carries things: *A truck is a freight carrier.*
car·ri·er (kar′ē ər) □*noun, plural* **carriers**

a	bat	ī	bite	ōō	tool	*th*	feather
ā	make	î	fierce	ou	out	th	bath
â	dare	o	dot	u	nut	hw	wheat
ä	father	ō	no	û	turn	zh	measure
e	net	ô	law, for	ch	church	ə	about, open
ē	be	oi	soil	ng	ring		pencil, atom
i	dip	oo	look	sh	shade		circus

carrot *noun* A plant having a long, orange root that is eaten as a vegetable.
car·rot (kar′ət) □*noun, plural* **carrots**

carry *verb* **1.** To move from one place to another: *She carried the baby into the house.* **2.** To keep or have with oneself: *Did you carry your wallet?* **3.** To hold up; support: *Don't stand on the table; it can't carry your weight.* **4.** To have for sale: *That store carries brown eggs.* **5.** To bring forward and add a number in the next column of figures. **6.** To cause to continue: *carry a joke too far.*
car·ry (kar′ē) □*verb* **carried, carrying, carries**

cart *noun* **1.** A vehicle that has two wheels and is used to carry people or goods. **2.** A small, light vehicle with wheels that can be pushed by hand: *a grocery cart.*
□*verb* To move in or as if in a cart: *We carted the empty bottles to the store.*
cart (kärt) □*noun, plural* **carts** □*verb* **carted, carting, carts**

cart

cartilage *noun* A tough, white substance that is attached to bones near the joints and helps to hold them in position.
car·ti·lage (kär′təl ij) □*noun*

carton *noun* A cardboard box made in different sizes and used to hold goods, liquids, and other objects.
car·ton (kär′tən) □*noun, plural* **cartons**

cartoon *noun* **1.** A sketch or drawing that shows people or events in a way that is funny. **2.** A movie made up of such drawings. **3.** A comic strip.
car·toon (kär to͞on′) □*noun, plural* **cartoons**

> **WORD HISTORY: cartoon**
>
> *Cartoon* comes from a French word that originally meant "cardboard." (*Carton* comes from the same French word.) Later the French word was also used for a drawing made on cardboard. The modern English word *cartoon* refers to a sketch on any kind of paper.

cartridge *noun* **1.** A small case that holds gunpowder and a bullet. **2.** A small container that holds something, such as film for a camera or tape for a tape recorder.
car·tridge (kär′trij) □*noun, plural* **cartridges**

cartwheel *noun* **1.** The wheel of a cart. **2.** A somersault in which the arms and legs are spread like the spokes of a wheel.
cart·wheel (kärt′hwēl′ *or* kärt′wēl′) □*noun, plural* **cartwheels**

cartwheel

carve *verb* **1.** To slice or cut into pieces: *carve a turkey.* **2.** To make by cutting: *carve a statue.*
carve (kärv) □*verb* **carved, carving, carves**

cascade *noun* A small waterfall.
□*verb* To fall in a cascade: *Water cascaded over the rocks.*
cas·cade (kas kād′) □*noun, plural* **cascades** □*verb* **cascaded, cascading, cascades**

case[1] *noun* **1.** An example of something: *Her spelling errors are a case of carelessness.* **2.** A situation or state of affairs: *In such a case there is nothing you can do.* **3.** An instance of illness or injury: *a case of the mumps.* **4.** Something that is to be decided in a court of law: *a murder case.*
in any case No matter what happens: *In any case, you should lock the car.*
in case of If there should be: *In case of bad weather, the game will be postponed.*
case (kās) □*noun, plural* **cases**

case[2] *noun* A box or container for holding things: *a packing case; a camera case.*
case (kās) □*noun, plural* **cases**

cash *noun* Money in the form of bills or coins: *Did you pay cash for the bicycle?*
□*verb* **1.** To give cash for: *The bank will cash*

my check. **2.** To get cash for: *I cashed my check at the bank.*
cash (kash) □*noun* □*verb* **cashed, cashing, cashes**

cashew *noun* The curved, edible nut of a tropical American tree.
cash·ew (kash′o͞o) □*noun, plural* **cashews**

cashier *noun* Someone whose job is taking care of money in a bank, store, or other business.
cash·ier (ka shîr′) □*noun, plural* **cashiers**

cashier

cashmere *noun* A fine, soft wool obtained from a goat of Asia.
cash·mere (kazh′mîr′ *or* kash′mîr′) □*noun*

cask *noun* A barrel used to hold liquids.
cask (kask) □*noun, plural* **casks**

casket *noun* **1.** A box in which a dead person is buried; coffin. **2.** A small box.
cas·ket (kas′kit) □*noun, plural* **caskets**

casserole *noun* A heavy dish in which food is baked and served.
cas·se·role (kas′ə rōl′) □*noun, plural* **casseroles**

cassette *noun* **1.** A case that holds film and is loaded into a camera. **2.** A case that holds magnetic tape and is loaded into some things, such as a typewriter, tape recorder, or video recorder.
cas·sette (kə set′) □*noun, plural* **cassettes**

cast *verb* **1.** To throw or hurl: *cast a fishing line.* **2.** To cause to fall upon something; throw off: *The lamp cast shadows on the wall.* **3.** To form by pouring a soft material into a mold so it will harden: *The artist cast the statue in bronze.* **4.** To give; deposit: *cast my vote for president.* **5.** To pick for a part in a play: *The teacher cast me as the villain in the school play.*
□*noun* **1.** The act of throwing: *made a cast*

with the fishing line. **2.** The actors in a play: *The movie had a cast of thousands.* **3.** A stiff bandage, usually made of gauze coated with plaster: *My broken leg was in a cast for two months.* **4.** Something that is formed in a mold: *a plaster cast of a face.*
cast (kast) □*verb* **cast, casting, casts**
□*noun, plural* **casts**

castanets *plural noun* A rhythm instrument consisting of two wooden or ivory hollow shells that are struck together to make a sharp click.
cas·ta·nets (kas′tə nets′) □*plural noun*

castanet

cast iron *noun* A hard, brittle form of iron made by pouring molten iron into a mold.

castle *noun* **1.** A large fort or group of buildings strong enough to resist attack. In the Middle Ages castles were built with thick walls and sometimes were surrounded by a deep ditch filled with water. **2.** A playing piece in chess; rook.
cas·tle (kas′əl) □*noun, plural* **castles**

casual *adjective* Not planned or prepared for: *a casual visit.*
cas·u·al (kazh′o͞o əl) □*adjective*

casualty *noun* Someone who is killed or injured in an accident or in war.
cas·u·al·ty (kazh′o͞o əl tē) □*noun, plural* **casualties**

a	bat	ī	bite	o͞o	tool	*th*	feather
ā	make	i	fierce	ou	out	th	bath
â	dare	o	dot	u	nut	hw	wheat
ä	father	ō	no	û	turn	zh	measure
e	net	ô	law, for	ch	church	ə	about, open
ē	be	oi	soil	ng	ring		pencil, atom
i	dip	oo	look	sh	shade		circus

cat   *noun* **1.** A small, furry animal with sharp claws, whiskers at each side of the mouth, and usually a long tail. Cats are kept as pets or for catching rats and mice. **2.** A large animal related to the cat, such as the lion, tiger, leopard, or wildcat.
cat (kat) ☐*noun, plural* **cats**

catalog or **catalogue**   *noun* A list, often in alphabetical order, that has a short description of each item: *Every item the store sells is printed in its catalog.*
☐*verb* To make a list of: *I cataloged all my books.*
cat·a·log or **cat·a·logue** (kat′əl ôg′ *or* kat′əl og′) ☐*noun, plural* **catalogs** or **catalogues**
☐*verb* **cataloged** or **catalogued, cataloging** or **cataloguing, catalogs** or **catalogues**

cataract   *noun* **1.** A large, high waterfall. **2.** A large flood or downpour of water.
cat·a·ract (kat′ə rakt′) ☐*noun, plural* **cataracts**

catastrophe   *noun* A sudden and terrible disaster: *The flood was a catastrophe that killed hundreds.*
ca·tas·tro·phe (kə tas′trə fē) ☐*noun, plural* **catastrophes**

catbird   *noun* A dark-gray songbird that makes a sound like the mewing of a cat.
cat·bird (kat′bûrd′) ☐*noun, plural* **catbirds**

catch   *verb* **1.** To take hold of someone or something that is moving: *catch a ball.* **2.** To capture: *The police caught the robbers.* **3.** To come upon suddenly; surprise: *She caught me watching TV instead of studying.* **4.** To be in time for: *I just caught the last bus.* **5.** To become stuck or lodged: *A bone caught in her throat.* **6.** To become entangled: *Her blouse caught on the fence.* **7.** To become ill with: *catch the flu.* **8.** To attract: *The fancy car caught my attention.* **9.** To take in especially by seeing or hearing: *I caught sight of her leaving school.* **10.** To begin to burn: *The dry wood caught quickly.*
☐*noun* **1.** The act of getting hold of: *The outfielder made a great catch.* **2.** Something that holds or secures: *the catch on a screen door.* **3.** An amount of something caught: *They brought home a large catch of fish.* **4.** A game of throwing a ball back and forth between two or more people. **5.** A hidden condition: *The question seemed so easy that I thought there must be a catch to it.*
catch (kach) ☐*verb* **caught, catching, catches** ☐*noun, plural* **catches**

catch

catcher   *noun* **1.** Someone or something that catches. **2.** A baseball player who stands behind home plate to catch the ball thrown by the pitcher.
catch·er (kach′ər) ☐*noun, plural* **catchers**

category   *noun* A division or group in a class of things: *Science books are in a separate category from books of poems.*
cat·e·go·ry (kat′ə gôr′ē) ☐*noun, plural* **categories**

category

cater   *verb* To provide with food and services: *The restaurant caters lunches and dinners.*
ca·ter (kā′tər) ☐*verb* **catered, catering, caters**

caterpillar   *noun* The larva of a butterfly or moth after hatching from an egg. Caterpillars are often covered with hair or bristles.
cat·er·pil·lar (kat′ər pil′ər) ☐*noun, plural* **caterpillars**

catfish   *noun* A fish having no scales and feelers that look like whiskers around its mouth.

cat·fish (**kat′**fish′) □*noun, plural* **catfish** or **catfishes**

catfish

cathedral *noun* A very large church.
ca·the·dral (kə **thē′**drəl) □*noun, plural* **cathedrals**

Catholic *adjective* Of or belonging to the Roman Catholic Church.
□*noun* A member of the Roman Catholic Church.
Cath·o·lic (**kath′**ə lik) □*adjective* □*noun, plural* **Catholics**

catsup *noun* Another spelling of **ketchup**.
cat·sup (**kat′**səp *or* **kech′**əp) □*noun, plural* **catsups**

cattail *noun* A tall plant that grows in wet places. It has a long stalk of tiny, fuzzy brown flowers.
cat·tail (**kat′**tāl′) □*noun, plural* **cattails**

cattle *plural noun* Animals, such as cows and bulls, that have horns and hoofs and are raised for meat or milk.
cat·tle (**kat′**əl) □*plural noun*

caught *verb* The past tense and past participle of **catch**: *We caught the thief.*
caught (kôt) □*verb*

cauliflower *noun* A vegetable with a rounded head of small whitish flowers.
cau·li·flow·er (**kô′**li flou′ər) □*noun*

cause *noun* **1.** Someone or something that makes something happen: *A campfire was the cause of the forest fire.* **2.** A goal or ideal that a person supports: *We should all work for the cause of peace.*
□*verb* To be the cause of; make happen: *War causes suffering and destruction.*
cause (kôz) □*noun, plural* **causes** □*verb* **caused, causing, causes**

caution *noun*. **1.** Great care to avoid trouble or danger: *Use caution when you cross a busy street.* **2.** A warning against trouble or danger: *gave us a caution about playing with matches.*
□*verb* To urge to be careful: *She cautioned us not to play in the street.*
cau·tion (**kô′**shən) □*noun, plural* **cautions** □*verb* **cautioned, cautioning, cautions**

cautious *adjective* Showing caution; careful: *He is always cautious when he drives.* —See Synonyms at **careful**.
cau·tious (**kô′**shəs) □*adjective*

cavalry *noun* Soldiers who fight on horseback or in armored vehicles.
cav·al·ry (**kav′**əl rē) □*noun, plural* **cavalries**

cave *noun* A hollow area in the earth or in the side of a hill or mountain.
□*verb* **cave in** To fall in; collapse: *The roof caved in because of the weight of the snow.*
cave (kāv) □*noun, plural* **caves** □*verb* **caved, caving, caves**

cavern *noun* A large cave.
cav·ern (**kav′**ərn) □*noun, plural* **caverns**

cavity *noun* **1.** A hollow or hole. **2.** A hollow place in a tooth, usually caused by decay.
cav·i·ty (**kav′**i tē) □*noun, plural* **cavities**

caw *noun* The loud, hoarse cry of a crow.
□*verb* To make this sound.
caw (kô) □*noun, plural* **caws** □*verb* **cawed, cawing, caws**

CD An abbreviation for **compact disk**.

CD-ROM *noun* A compact disk whose information can be read but not erased by the user.
CD-ROM (**sē′dē′rom′**) □*noun, plural* **CD-ROMs**

cease *verb* To bring or come to an end; stop: *He worked for hours without ceasing.*
cease (sēs) □*verb* **ceased, ceasing, ceases**

cedar *noun* An evergreen tree that has reddish wood with a pleasant smell.
ce·dar (**sē′**dər) □*noun, plural* **cedars**

ceiling *noun* **1.** The inside upper surface in a room. **2.** The distance from the earth to the lowest clouds: *The ceiling was only 100 feet in the heavy fog.* **3.** The greatest or upper limit:

a	bat	ī	bite	ōō	tool	*th*	feather
ā	make	î	fierce	ou	out	th	bath
â	dare	o	dot	u	nut	hw	wheat
ä	father	ō	no	û	turn	zh	measure
e	net	ô	law, for	ch	church	ə	about, open
ē	be	oi	soil	ng	ring		pencil, atom
i	dip	oo	look	sh	shade		circus

The government put a ceiling on gasoline prices.
ceil·ing (sē′ling) □*noun, plural* **ceilings**

celebrate *verb* **1.** To honor or mark with festivities or by acting in a special way: *We celebrated New Year's Eve by staying up until midnight.* **2.** To perform a religious ceremony: *The priest celebrated Mass.*
cel·e·brate (sel′ə brāt′) □*verb* **celebrated, celebrating, celebrates**

celebration *noun* **1.** The act of celebrating: *the celebration of their wedding anniversary.* **2.** A party or other activity in honor of a special occasion or event: *a birthday celebration.*
cel·e·bra·tion (sel′ə brā′shən) □*noun, plural* **celebrations**

celebrity *noun* A famous person.
ce·leb·ri·ty (sə leb′ri tē) □*noun, plural* **celebrities**

celery *noun* A plant with edible, crisp, whitish or green stems.
cel·er·y (sel′ər ē) □*noun*

cell *noun* **1.** A small room for one person, as in a monastery or prison: *a monk's cell; a jail cell.* **2.** The smallest part of a living plant or animal. A cell has a very thin membrane that encloses a substance called protoplasm and a small central mass called a nucleus. All living plants and animals are made up of cells. **3.** A small part of an object or substance: *the cells of a honeycomb.* **4.** A container holding chemicals that produce electricity.
cell (sel) □*noun, plural* **cells**

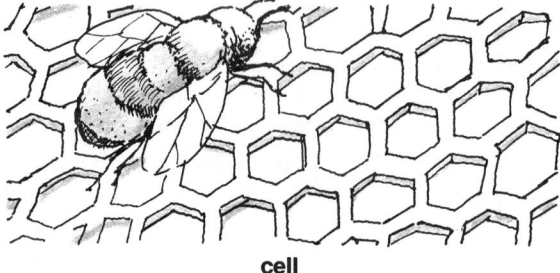
cell
Cells of a honeycomb

cellar *noun* An underground room or set of rooms under a building where things are stored.
cel·lar (sel′ər) □*noun, plural* **cellars**

cello *noun* A musical instrument that is similar to but much larger than a violin and has a deeper tone. It is held between the knees when played.
cel·lo (chel′ō) □*noun, plural* **cellos**

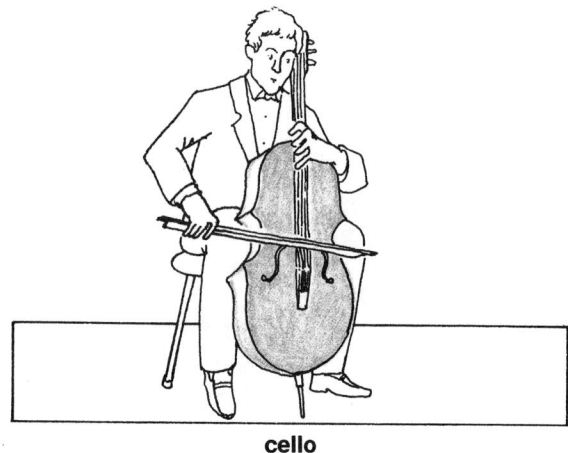
cello

cellophane *noun* A thin, clear material made from wood pulp and used as a wrapping.
cel·lo·phane (sel′ə fān′) □*noun*

cellulose *noun* A substance that forms the cell walls of plants and trees. It is used to make paper, cloth, plastics, and explosives.
cel·lu·lose (sel′yə lōs′) □*noun*

Celsius scale *noun* Celsius scale is the official name for the centigrade temperature scale on which the freezing point of water is 0 degrees and the boiling point is 100 degrees.

cement *noun* **1.** A mixture of powders made from clay and limestone, to which water is added to form a paste. When cement dries, it becomes hard like stone. It is used as a building material, to make sidewalks and streets, and to hold bricks and stones together. **2.** A material, such as glue, that hardens to hold things together.
□*verb* To join or cover with cement: *He cemented together pieces of the vase. The town is going to cement all the dirt paths in the park.*
ce·ment (si ment′) □*noun, plural* **cements**
□*verb* **cemented, cementing, cements**

cemetery *noun* A place where the dead are buried; graveyard.
cem·e·ter·y (sem′i ter′ē) □*noun, plural* **cemeteries**

census *noun* An official count of the people living in a country or district. A census may also gather information about the age, sex, and occupation of each person.
cen·sus (sen′səs) □*noun, plural* **censuses**

cent *noun* A coin of the United States and Canada; penny. One hundred cents equal one dollar.
cent (sent) □*noun, plural* **cents**

centennial *noun* A 100th anniversary.
▢*adjective* Having to do with a 100th anniversary: *a centennial year; a centennial celebration.*
cen·ten·ni·al (sen ten′ē əl) ▢*noun, plural* **centennials** ▢*adjective*

center *noun* **1.** A point that is the same distance from every point of a circle or sphere; the exact middle. **2.** The middle point, place, or part of something: *There was a round table in the center of the room.* **3.** A place where many things or activities are gathered together: *a business center; a sports center.* **4.** A main or principal person or thing: *She is always the center of attention.* **5.** A player on a team who has the middle position: *He plays center on the basketball team.*
▢*verb* To place in or at the center: *We centered the picture over the fireplace.*
cen·ter (sen′tər) ▢*noun, plural* **centers**
▢*verb* **centered, centering, centers**

centigrade *adjective* Having 100 degrees between the freezing and boiling points of water. The centigrade thermometer shows 0 degrees as the temperature at which water freezes and 100 degrees as the temperature at which water boils.
cen·ti·grade (sen′ti grād′) ▢*adjective*

centigram *noun* A unit of weight in the metric system equal to 1/100 gram.
cen·ti·gram (sen′ti gram′) ▢*noun, plural* **centigrams**

centimeter *noun* A unit of length in the metric system equal to 1/100 meter.
cen·ti·me·ter (sen′ti mē′tər) ▢*noun, plural* **centimeters**

centipede *noun* An animal that has a long, flat body and many pairs of legs.
cen·ti·pede (sen′ti pēd) ▢*noun, plural* **centipedes**

centipede

central *adjective* **1.** At or near the center: *The clock tower is in the central part of town.* **2.** Most important; main; chief: *The central office is in New York City.*
cen·tral (sen′trəl) ▢*adjective*

century *noun* A period of one hundred years: *The United States has been in existence for more than two centuries.*

cen·tu·ry (sen′chər ē) ▢*noun, plural* **centuries**

ceramics *plural noun* The art of making dishes, cups, and other containers out of clay baked at a high temperature.
ce·ram·ics (sə ram′iks) ▢*plural noun*

ceramics

cereal *noun* **1.** The seeds of certain grasses, such as wheat, oats, corn, or rice, used as food. **2.** A food made from the seeds of such plants: *Bran is my favorite cereal, but my sister prefers oatmeal.*
ce·re·al (sîr′ē əl) ▢*noun, plural* **cereals**

ceremonial *noun* A ceremony.
cer·e·mo·ni·al (ser′ə mō′ne əl) ▢*noun, plural* **ceremonials**

ceremony *noun* **1.** A formal act or series of acts performed on a special occasion: *Everyone in the small town attended the wedding ceremony.* **2.** Very polite or formal behavior: *The queen greeted the ambassador with great ceremony.*
cer·e·mo·ny (ser′ə mō′nē) ▢*noun, plural* **ceremonies**

certain *adjective* **1.** Positive; sure: *I'm certain that I closed the windows.* **2.** Agreed upon; settled: *We meet at a certain time every day.* **3.** Not named but known; some: *Certain ani-*

a	bat	ī	bite	oo	tool	*th*	feather
ā	make	î	fierce	ou	out	th	bath
â	dare	o	dot	u	nut	hw	wheat
ä	father	ō	no	û	turn	zh	measure
e	net	ô	law, for	ch	church	ə	about, open
ē	be	oi	soil	ng	ring		pencil, atom
i	dip	oo	look	sh	shade		circus

mals hibernate in winter.
cer·tain (**sûr′** tən) ▢*adjective*

SYNONYMS: **certain, positive, sure**

These adjectives mean having no doubt: *I'm certain I added the numbers correctly. Are you positive that she's coming? She is sure that the party is this weekend.*

---

certainly   *adverb* Without a doubt; surely or definitely: *She will certainly want to help her sister.*
cer·tain·ly (**sûr′** tən lē) ▢*adverb*

certainty   *noun* The condition of being certain or sure: *There is no certainty that the plane will land on time.*
cer·tain·ty (**sûr′** tən tē) ▢*noun, plural* **certainties**

certificate   *noun* An official document that gives information. A birth certificate states the date and place of birth of a person.
cer·tif·i·cate (sər **tif′** i kit) ▢*noun, plural* **certificates**

chain   *noun* **1.** A row of connected rings or loops, usually made of metal. Most chains are used to hold or fasten things. **2.** A series of connected or related things: *a chain of mountains; a chain of hamburger restaurants.* ▢*verb* To hold or fasten with a chain: *He chained his bike to a tree.*
chain (chān) ▢*noun, plural* **chains** ▢*verb* **chained, chaining, chains**

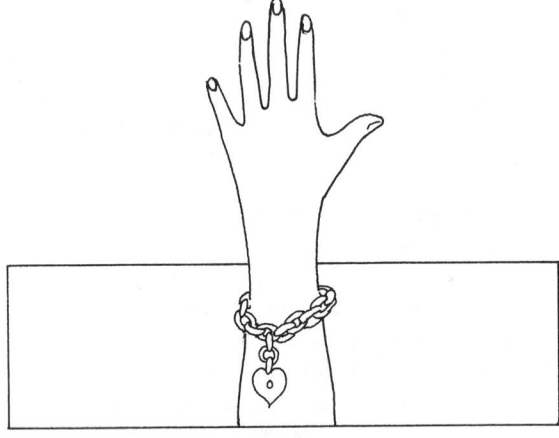

chain

chair   *noun* A piece of furniture on which a person sits. A chair usually has a back, seat, and legs. Some chairs have arms.
chair (châr) ▢*noun, plural* **chairs**

chairman   *noun* A man in charge of a meeting, committee, or other group.
chair·man (**châr′** mən) ▢*noun, plural* **chairmen**

chairperson   *noun* A person in charge of a meeting, committee, or other group.
chair·per·son (**châr′** pûr′sən) ▢*noun, plural* **chairpersons**

chairwoman   *noun* A woman in charge of a meeting, committee, or other group.
chair·wom·an (**châr′** woom′ən) ▢*noun, plural* **chairwomen**

chalk   *noun* **1.** A soft mineral made up mostly of tiny fossil seashells. **2.** A piece of this substance used especially for writing or drawing on a blackboard.
chalk (chôk) ▢*noun, plural* **chalks**

challenge   *noun* **1.** A call to take part in a contest or fight to see who is better: *Their team accepted our challenge to another game.* **2.** Something that demands great effort and skill: *The science project was a real challenge for her.*
▢*verb* **1.** To call to take part in a contest or fight. **2.** To order a person to stop and prove who he or she is.
chal·lenge (**chal′** ənj) ▢*noun, plural* **challenges** ▢*verb* **challenged, challenging, challenges**

challenge

chamber   *noun* **1.** A private room, especially a bedroom. **2.** A hall where lawmakers meet: *the Senate chamber.* **3.** A body of lawmakers: *The House of Representatives is the lower chamber of Congress.* **4.** An enclosed space in a plant or animal body: *There are four chambers in the heart of a human being.* **5.** The place in a gun where a bullet is put.

cham·ber (**chām′** bər) □*noun, plural* **chambers**

chameleon *noun* A small lizard that can change its color quickly in order to blend in with its surroundings.
cha·me·leon (kə **mēl′** yən) □*noun, plural* **chameleons**

WORD HISTORY: chameleon

Chameleon comes from a Greek word that means ''lion on the ground.''

---

champion *noun* Someone or something that wins first place in a game or contest: *My team is the champion in swimming.*
cham·pi·on (**cham′** pē ən) □*noun, plural* **champions**

champion

championship *noun* The title or position of champion: *He won the boxing championship last year.*
cham·pi·on·ship (**cham′** pē ən ship′) □*noun, plural* **championships**

chance *noun* **1.** The happening of things by luck or accident: *I met her on the street by chance.* **2.** The possibility that something will happen: *She has a good chance of winning the spelling contest.* **3.** A good opportunity: *Have you had a chance to see that new movie yet?* **4.** A risk: *Don't take chances on your bicycle.* —See Synonyms at **opportunity.**
□*verb* **1.** To happen by accident: *I chanced to see them at the ballgame.* **2.** To risk: *You chance losing your money if you gamble.*
□*adjective* Happening by accident: *a chance meeting.*
chance (chans) □*noun, plural* **chances**
□*verb* **chanced, chancing, chances**
□*adjective*

chancellor *noun* A high official of the head of a government. Chancellor is the title of the prime minister of certain European countries.
chan·cel·lor (**chan′** sə lər) □*noun, plural* **chancellors**

chandelier *noun* A light fixture that hangs from the ceiling and has several branches for holding lights.
chan·de·lier (shan′də **lîr′**) □*noun, plural* **chandeliers**

change *verb* **1.** To make or become different: *Why did you change your mind? The weather can change suddenly in Florida.* **2.** To replace with another: *He changed the subject. Can you change a dollar for me?* **3.** To put fresh clothing or coverings on: *change a bed.*
□*noun* **1.** The act or result of changing: *a change in plans.* **2.** Something that is put in place of something else: *I brought a change of clothes in case we went swimming.* **3.** The money returned when the amount given in payment is more than the amount owed. **4.** Coins: *I don't have any change.*
change (chānj) □*verb* **changed, changing, changes** □*noun, plural* **changes**

SYNONYMS: **change, alter, vary**

These verbs mean to make or become different: *We had to change our vacation plans. The tailor altered the pants to make them shorter. We decided to vary the program by adding some music.*

change

a bat	ī bite	o͞o tool	*th* feather
ā make	î fierce	ou out	th bath
â dare	o dot	u nut	hw wheat
ä father	ō no	û turn	zh measure
e net	ô law, for	ch church	ə about, open
ē be	oi soil	ng ring	pencil, atom
i dip	oo look	sh shade	circus

channel *noun* **1.** The deepest part of a river or harbor through which ships can pass. **2.** A body of water that connects two larger bodies. **3.** A band of radio waves used for broadcasting or communicating: *a television channel.* **4.** A long groove.
□*verb* To form a channel in or through something: *The river had channeled a canyon through the rock.*
chan·nel (chan′əl) □*noun, plural* **channels**
□*verb* **channeled, channeling, channels**

chant *noun* **1.** A song. **2.** Words said over and over again in a definite rhythm.
□*verb* **1.** To sing a chant. **2.** To call out as a chant: *The crowd chanted her name until she appeared on stage.*
chant (chant) □*noun, plural* **chants** □*verb* **chanted, chanting, chants**

Chanukah *noun* A Jewish festival that comes in December or late November and lasts eight days.
Cha·nu·kah (hä′nŏŏ kä′) □*noun*

WORD HISTORY: **Chanukah**

Chanukah comes from a Hebrew word that means "dedication." In 164 B.C. the Temple in Jerusalem had to be dedicated again after a Greek king had used the altar for a pagan sacrifice. Chanukah celebrates this event.

---

chaos *noun* Great confusion; disorder: *When the battle was over the city was in chaos.*
cha·os (kā′os) □*noun*

chap¹ *verb* To make or become rough, dry, and cracked: *My hands always chap in the winter. His lips were chapped by the wind and sun.*
chap (chap) □*verb* **chapped, chapping, chaps**

chap² *noun* A man or boy; fellow.
chap (chap) □*noun, plural* **chaps**

chapel *noun* **1.** A small church. **2.** A room or place for worship.
chap·el (chap′əl) □*noun, plural* **chapels**

chaplain *noun* A clergyman for a school, prison, military unit, or other group.
chap·lain (chap′lən) □*noun, plural* **chaplains**

chaps *plural noun* Heavy leather coverings worn over pants by cowboys to protect their legs.
chaps (chaps) □*plural noun*

chaps

chapter *noun* **1.** A main division of a book. **2.** A local branch of a club or other group.
chap·ter (chap′tər) □*noun, plural* **chapters**

character *noun* **1.** The combination of qualities that makes one person or thing different from another: *the noisy, busy character of a large city.* **2.** A character is judged by the way a person thinks, talks, and acts. **3.** Moral strength; honesty: *a woman of character.* **4.** A person in a book, story, play, or movie. **5.** Someone who is different, odd, and often funny: *My brother is a real character.* **6.** A symbol, such as a letter of the alphabet, used in writing or printing.
char·ac·ter (kar′ik tər) □*noun, plural* **characters**

characteristic *noun* A special feature or quality that makes someone or something different from others: *Honesty is her chief characteristic.* —See Synonyms at **quality.**
□*adjective* Showing a special feature or identity: *the zebra's characteristic stripes.*
char·ac·ter·is·tic (kar′ik tər **is**′tik) □*noun, plural* **characteristics** □*adjective*

characterize *verb* **1.** To describe the character or qualities of; portray: *He characterized her as a kind person.* **2.** To be a characteristic or quality of: *Strength and hardness characterize steel.*
char·ac·ter·ize (kar′ik tə rīz′) □*verb* **characterized, characterizing, characterizes**

charade *noun* **1.** A word presented in the form of a riddle or silent action. **2. charades** A game in which players act out a word or

phrase for the other players to guess at.
cha·rade (shə **rād′**) □*noun, plural* **charades**

charades

charcoal   *noun* A black material made mostly of carbon and produced by heating wood or other plant or animal matter. Charcoal is used as fuel and for drawing.
char·coal (**chär′** kōl′) □*noun*

charge   *verb* **1.** To ask as payment. **2.** To put off paying for something, with an arrangement to pay later: *Are you going to pay for this now, or do you want to charge it to your account?* **3.** To rush at or into with force: *The cavalry charged the enemy and led the attack.* **4.** To accuse; blame: *He charged her with theft.* **5.** To put or take electrical energy into a battery.
□*noun* **1.** The amount asked or made as payment: *There is no charge for this service.* **2.** Care; supervision; control: *The lions are in the keeper's charge. She is in charge of the refreshments.* **3.** An accusation: *a charge of treason.* **4.** An attack: *an infantry charge.*
charge (chärj) □*verb* **charged, charging, charges** □*noun, plural* **charges**

charge account   *noun* An arrangement in which a customer receives goods or services and pays for them at a later time.

chariot   *noun* A two-wheeled vehicle pulled by horses. In ancient times chariots were used in battles, races, and parades.
char·i·ot (**char′**ē ət) □*noun, plural* **chariots**

charity   *noun* **1.** Good will or kindness toward others. **2.** Money or help given to the needy. **3.** A group that is organized to help the poor or needy.
char·i·ty (**char′**i tē) □*noun, plural* **charities**

charm   *noun* **1.** The power to please or delight: *The cottage was small but had a lot of charm.* **2.** A magic spell, act, or saying: *The witch's charm put everyone to sleep.* **3.** An object that is thought to have magic power: *a lucky charm.* **4.** A small ornament worn on a necklace or bracelet.
□*verb* To please or delight: *He charmed everyone who met him.*
charm (chärm) □*noun, plural* **charms** □*verb* **charmed, charming, charms**

charm

charming   *adjective* Very pleasing; delightful: *a charming person; a charming house.*
charm·ing (**chär′** ming) □*adjective*

chart   *noun* **1.** A paper giving information in the form of graphs and tables. **2.** A map for sailors showing the coast, water depth, and other information.
□*verb* **1.** To make a chart of: *The captain charted a new course for the ship.* **2.** To draw up or lay out a plan for.
chart (chärt) □*noun, plural* **charts** □*verb* **charted, charting, charts**

charter   *noun* A written document that gives certain rights and privileges. A charter is given by a ruler or a government to a person, group, or organization.
char·ter (**chär′** tər) □*noun, plural* **charters**

a	bat	ī	bite	oo	tool	*th*	feather
ā	make	î	fierce	ou	out	th	bath
â	dare	o	dot	u	nut	hw	wheat
ä	father	ō	no	û	turn	zh	measure
e	net	ô	law, for	ch	church	ə	about, open
ē	be	oi	soil	ng	ring		pencil, atom
i	dip	oo	look	sh	shade		circus

chase *verb* **1.** To go quickly after and try to catch: *The sheriff chased the robbers.* **2.** To drive away: *We chased the dog off the lawn.* □*noun* The act of chasing.
  chase (chās) □*verb* **chased, chasing, chases** □*noun, plural* **chases**

chasm *noun* A deep crack in the earth's surface.
  chasm (kaz′əm) □*noun, plural* **chasms**

chat *verb* To talk in a friendly way: *We chatted about our plans for the summer.* □*noun* A friendly talk.
  chat (chat) □*verb* **chatted, chatting, chats** □*noun, plural* **chats**

chatter *verb* **1.** To talk fast about unimportant things: *He is always chattering on about sports.* **2.** To make quick, rattling noises: *Our teeth chattered in the cold.* □*noun* **1.** Unimportant talk. **2.** Quick, rattling sounds: *the chatter of machines.*
  chat·ter (chat′ər) □*verb* **chattered, chattering, chatters** □*noun, plural* **chatters**

chauffeur *noun* Someone who drives a car for pay.
  chauf·feur (shō′fər *or* shō fûr′) □*noun, plural* **chauffeurs**

cheap *adjective* **1.** Low in price; inexpensive: *The coat was cheap because it had a small tear.* **2.** Charging low prices: *a cheap hotel.* **3.** Of low or poor quality: *a cheap toy that will break easily.* **4.** Not willing to spend or give money; stingy.
  cheap (chēp) □*adjective* **cheaper, cheapest**

cheat *verb* To deal with or act in a dishonest way: *cheat on a test; cheat an old woman of her savings.* □*noun* Someone who cheats.
  cheat (chēt) □*verb* **cheated, cheating, cheats** □*noun, plural* **cheats**

check *verb* **1.** To stop; hold back: *He tried to check his tears.* **2.** To test, examine, or compare to make sure something is right or in good condition: *Check the car before your trip.* **3.** To mark with a sign showing something has been noted or is correct. **4.** To leave something to be kept: *Check your coat at the door.* □*noun* **1.** A stop; halt: *Darkness put a check on the baseball game.* **2.** A test to make sure something is right: *The crew made a check of the plane before taking off.* **3.** A mark showing that something has been noted or is correct. **4.** A written order to a bank to pay money from an account: *pay the bill with a check.* **5.** A ticket given in return for something that has been left: *a baggage check.* **6.** A bill at a restaurant. **7.** A pattern of squares: *a shirt with checks.*
  check (chek) □*verb* **checked, checking, checks** □*noun, plural* **checks**

check

checkerboard *noun* A board for playing checkers and chess divided into 64 squares of two alternating colors.
  check·er·board (chek′ər bôrd′) □*noun, plural* **checkerboards**

checkers *plural noun* A game played by two players with twelve pieces each. Players take turns trying to capture or block each other's pieces.
  check·ers (chek′ərz) □*plural noun*

checkup *noun* A test to find out the condition of a person or thing.
  check·up (chek′up′) □*noun, plural* **checkups**

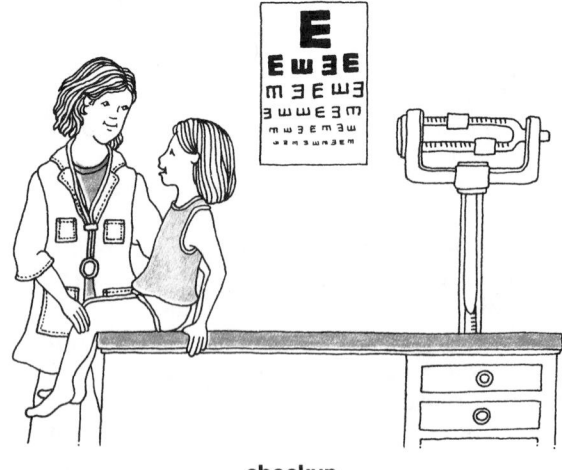

checkup

cheek *noun* The part of the face on either side below the eye.
  cheek (chēk) □*noun, plural* **cheeks**

cheer *verb* **1.** To shout in happiness, praise, or encouragement: *The crowd cheered the players.* **2.** To make or become happier: *The joke cheered us up.*
□*noun* **1.** A shout of happiness, praise, or encouragement. **2.** Good spirits; gaiety.
cheer (chîr) □*verb* **cheered, cheering, cheers** □*noun, plural* **cheers**

cheer

cheerful *adjective* **1.** In good spirits; happy. **2.** Causing a happy feeling: *a cheerful room.*
cheer·ful (chîr′fəl) □*adjective*

SYNONYMS: **cheerful, bright, happy**

These adjectives mean being in or showing good spirits: *He has a cheerful smile. She is a bright, energetic child. It was a beautiful day for a picnic and everyone was happy.*

---

cheese *noun* A solid food made by separating the curds from milk.
cheese (chēz) □*noun, plural* **cheeses**

cheetah *noun* A spotted wild cat of Africa and southern Asia.
chee·tah (chē′tə) □*noun, plural* **cheetahs**

chef *noun* A head cook of a restaurant.
chef (shef) □*noun, plural* **chefs**

chemical *adjective* Of or used in chemistry. □*noun* A substance produced by or used in chemistry.
chem·i·cal (kem′i kəl) □*adjective* □*noun, plural* **chemicals**

chemist *noun* Someone who is an expert in chemistry. `
chem·ist (kem′ist) □*noun, plural* **chemists**

chemistry *noun* The scientific study of substances to see what they are made of, what characteristics they have, and how they combine with other substances.
chem·is·try (kem′i strē) □*noun*

cherish *verb* To care for or think of tenderly; hold dear: *She loved and cherished her sister.*
cher·ish (cher′ish) □*verb* **cherished, cherishing, cherishes**

cherish

cherry *noun* **1.** A small, round red fruit with a hard pit. **2.** A bright red color.
cher·ry (cher′ē) □*noun, plural* **cherries**

chess *noun* A game played on a chessboard by two players having sixteen pieces each. Each player has a king, and the object of chess is to put the other player's king into a position in which it can no longer move in any direction.
chess (ches) □*noun*

chess

a	bat	ī	bite	ōō	tool	*th*	feather
ā	make	î	fierce	ou	out	th	bath
â	dare	o	dot	u	nut	hw	wheat
ä	father	ō	no	û	turn	zh	measure
e	net	ô	law, for	ch	church	ə	about, open
ē	be	oi	soil	ng	ring		pencil, atom
i	dip	oo	look	sh	shade		circus

chessboard *noun* A game board with sixty-four squares in two alternating colors, used in playing chess and checkers.
chess·board (ches′bôrd′) □*noun, plural* **chessboards**

chest *noun* **1.** The upper front part of the body between the neck and the stomach. **2.** A strong box with a lid: *a tool chest.* **3.** A piece of furniture with drawers.
chest (chest) □*noun, plural* **chests**

chestnut *noun* **1.** A sweet-tasting brown nut that grows inside a prickly bur. **2.** A tree on which chestnuts grow. **3.** A reddish-brown color.
chest·nut (ches′nut′) □*noun, plural* **chestnuts**

chew *verb* To grind or crush with the teeth.
chew (choo) □*verb* **chewed, chewing, chews**

chewing gum *noun* Gum for chewing, usually sweetened.

Chicano *noun* An American who was born in Mexico or whose ancestors were from Mexico.
Chi·ca·no (chi kä′nō) □*noun, plural* **Chicanos**

chick *noun* A young chicken or bird.
chick (chik) □*noun, plural* **chicks**

chickadee *noun* A small North American bird with gray, black, and white feathers.
chick·a·dee (chik′ə dē′) □*noun, plural* **chickadees**

chicken *noun* **1.** A large bird raised for its eggs or as food; hen or rooster. **2.** The meat of this bird.
chick·en (chik′ən) □*noun, plural* **chickens**

chicken pox *noun* A disease in which the skin breaks out in spots and fever occurs.

chief *noun* Someone with the highest rank: *the chief of police.*
□*adjective* **1.** Highest in rank: *the chief accountant on the staff.* **2.** Most important: *What is your chief responsibility as the teacher's assistant?*
chief (chēf) □*noun, plural* **chiefs** □*adjective*

chiefly *adverb* **1.** Mainly; mostly: *The ship is made chiefly of steel.* **2.** Above all; especially: *She is chiefly concerned about the safety of the students in our school.*
chief·ly (chēf′lē) □*adverb*

chieftain *noun* The leader of a tribe or clan.
chief·tain (chēf′tən) □*noun, plural* **chieftains**

child *noun* **1.** A young girl or boy. **2.** A son or daughter: *She is an only child.* —See Synonyms at **descendant.**

child (chīld) □*noun, plural* **children**

childhood *noun* The condition or time of being a child.
child·hood (chīld′hood′) □*noun, plural* **childhoods**

childish *adjective* Of or typical of a child: *It is childish to play silly jokes on people.*
child·ish (chīl′dish) □*adjective*

children *noun* The plural of **child.**
chil·dren (chil′drən) □*noun*

chili *noun* A hot spice made from the pods of a red pepper.
chil·i (chil′ē) □*noun, plural* **chilies**

chill *noun* **1.** An unpleasant coldness: *a chill in the air.* **2.** A feeling of cold from illness or fear: *The scary movie sent chills up my spine.* □*verb* To make or become cold: *Dad chilled the tea in the refrigerator.*
chill (chil) □*noun, plural* **chills** □*verb* **chilled, chilling, chills**

chill

chilly *adjective* **1.** Fairly cold: *a chilly fall day.* **2.** Not friendly: *a chilly greeting.* —See Synonyms at **cold.**
chill·y (chil′ē) □*adjective* **chillier, chilliest**

chime *noun* **1. chimes** A set of bells or pipes that make musical sounds. **2.** A musical sound made by chimes: *the chime of the church bells.* □*verb* To ring with a musical sound: *The church bells chime every hour.*
chime (chīm) □*noun, plural* **chimes** □*verb* **chimed, chiming, chimes**

chimney *noun* A hollow, upright structure that carries away the smoke from a fireplace or furnace.
chim·ney (chim′nē) □*noun, plural* **chimneys**

chimpanzee *noun* A small African ape with dark hair.

chim·pan·zee (chim′pan **zē′** *or* chim **pan′**zē)
□*noun, plural* **chimpanzees**

chin   *noun* The front of the lower jaw.
□*verb* To hang from a bar and pull oneself up with the arms until the chin is level with the bar.
chin (chin) □*noun, plural* **chins** □*verb*
chinned, chinning, chins

china   *noun* **1.** A fine, hard, usually white pottery made from clay. **2.** Dishes, cups, and other objects made from china.
chi·na (**chī′**nə) □*noun*

chinchilla   *noun* A small South American animal that looks like a squirrel. Chinchillas have soft, pale-gray fur.
chin·chil·la (chin **chil′**ə) □*noun, plural* **chinchillas**

Chinese   *noun* **1.** Someone who was born in or is a citizen of China. **2.** The language spoken in China.
□*adjective* Of China, the Chinese, or their language.
Chi·nese (chī **nēz′**) □*noun, plural* **Chinese**
□*adjective*

chink   *noun* A narrow crack: *Water dripped through the chink in the wall.*
chink (chingk) □*noun, plural* **chinks**

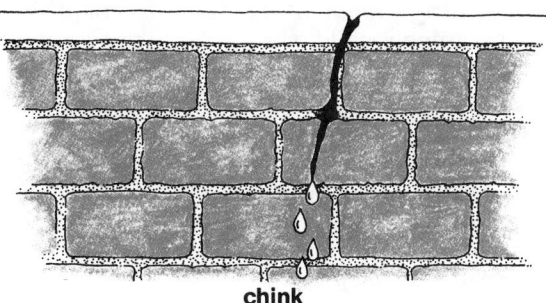
chink

chip   *noun* **1.** A small piece that has been cut or broken off: *a chip of ice.* **2.** A mark left when a small piece is broken off: *a chip in the glass.* **3.** A microchip.
□*verb* To break off a piece by hitting or cutting: *I chipped the rim of the cup.*
chip (chip) □*noun, plural* **chips** □*verb*
chipped, chipping, chips

chipmunk   *noun* A small North American animal that is like a squirrel and has dark stripes on its back.
chip·munk (**chip′**mungk′) □*noun, plural* **chipmunks**

chirp   *noun* A short, high sound such as that made by a bird or a cricket.

□*verb* To make such a sound.
chirp (chûrp) □*noun, plural* **chirps** □*verb*
chirped, chirping, chirps

chisel   *noun* A metal tool that is used to cut or shape wood, stone, or metal.
chis·el (**chiz′**əl) □*noun, plural* **chisels**

chivalry   *noun* The qualities that an ideal knight should have, including honor, courtesy, and being helpful to the weak.
chiv·al·ry (**shiv′**əl rē) □*noun*

chlorine   *noun* A greenish-yellow, poisonous gas that is one of the chemical elements. Compounds of chlorine are used to purify water.
chlo·rine (**klôr′**ēn′) □*noun, plural* **chlorines**

chlorophyll   *noun* A green substance in the leaves of plants that helps plants make sugar from elements in air and water.
chlo·ro·phyll (**klôr′**ə fil) □*noun*

chocolate   *noun* **1.** A food made from roasted and ground cacao beans. **2.** A sweet drink made with chocolate: *hot chocolate.* **3.** A candy made with chocolate. **4.** A dark brown color.
choc·o·late (**chô′**kə lit *or* **chôk′**lit) □*noun, plural* **chocolates**

choice   *noun* **1.** The act of choosing: *We had to make a choice between the two movies.* **2.** The right or chance to choose: *He gave us the choice of going to the ball game or to the beach.* **3.** Someone or something chosen: *He is my choice for class secretary.* **4.** A number of things to choose from: *a wide choice of foods.*
□*adjective* Of fine quality: *choice fruits.*
choice (chois) □*noun, plural* **choices**
□*adjective* **choicer, choicest**

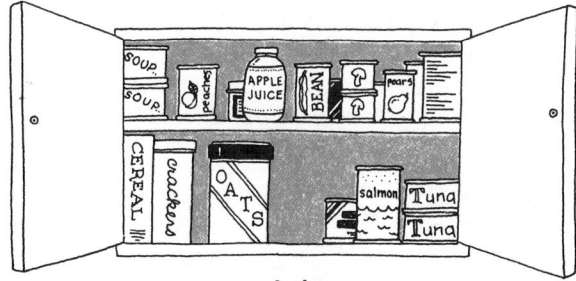
choice

a bat	ī bite	ōō tool	*th* feather
ā make	î fierce	ou out	th bath
â dare	o dot	u nut	hw wheat
ä father	ō no	û turn	zh measure
e net	ô law, for	ch church	ə about, open
ē be	oi soil	ng ring	pencil, atom
i dip	oo look	sh shade	circus

choir   *noun* A group of singers that perform together, often in a church.
choir (kwīr) ☐*noun, plural* **choirs**

choke   *verb* **1.** To stop or block the breathing of: *The tight collar was choking him.* **2.** To be unable to breathe normally: *He choked on a chicken bone.* **3.** To hold back; stop: *choke back laughter.* **4.** To fill up; clog: *Leaves choked the garden drain.*
choke (chōk) ☐*verb* **choked, choking, chokes**

choose   *verb* **1.** To pick from a group: *Which book did you choose?* **2.** To decide or prefer: *I'll go to the dance if I choose.*
choose (chōōz) ☐*verb* **chose, chosen, choosing**

SYNONYMS: **choose, pick, select**

These verbs mean to take one from a group: *Have you chosen the movie you want to go see? Will you help me pick a dress to wear to the dance? The teacher selected me for the biggest part in the school play.*

---

chop   *verb* **1.** To cut by hitting with a sharp tool: *chop down a tree with an ax.* **2.** To cut into little pieces: *He chopped celery for the salad.*
☐*noun* **1.** A quick, short blow. **2.** A small cut of meat that often includes part of a rib: *a pork chop.*
chop (chop) ☐*verb* **chopped, chopping, chops** ☐*noun, plural* **chops**

chopsticks   *plural noun* A pair of thin sticks used as eating tools especially in certain Asian countries.
chop·sticks (chop′stiks) ☐*plural noun*

chord   *noun* A combination of three or more musical notes sounded at the same time.
chord (kôrd) ☐*noun, plural* **chords**

chore

chore   *noun* A small job: *One of my chores is taking out the garbage.*
chore (chôr) ☐*noun, plural* **chores**

chorus   *noun* **1.** A group of singers or dancers who perform together. **2.** A part of a song repeated after each verse.
☐*verb* To sing or speak together.
cho·rus (kôr′əs) ☐*noun, plural* **choruses** ☐*verb* **chorused, chorusing, choruses**

chose   *verb* The past tense of **choose:** *He chose a card to send to his aunt.*
chose (chōz) ☐*verb*

chosen   *verb* The past participle of **choose:** *She was chosen to represent the class.*
chos·en (chō′zən) ☐*verb*

chowder   *noun* A thick soup made with clams or fish and vegetables.
chow·der (chou′dər) ☐*noun, plural* **chowders**

Christ   *noun* Jesus, the founder of the Christian religion.
Christ (krīst) ☐*noun*

christen   *verb* **1.** To baptize and receive into a Christian church. **2.** To give a name to at baptism: *The priest christened the baby "Jane."*
chris·ten (kris′ən) ☐*verb* **christened, christening, christens**

christening   *noun* A ceremony for baptizing and naming a child.
chris·ten·ing (kris′ə ning) ☐*noun, plural* **christenings**

Christian   *noun* Someone who believes in Jesus Christ or does what he taught.
☐*adjective* **1.** Believing in Christ or his teachings. **2.** Of Christ, Christianity, or Christians.
Chris·tian (kris′chən) ☐*noun, plural* **Christians** ☐*adjective*

Christianity   *noun* The religion of Christians.
Chris·ti·an·i·ty (kris′chē an′i tē) ☐*noun*

Christmas   *noun* A holiday on December 25 that celebrates the birth of Christ.
Christ·mas (kris′məs) ☐*noun, plural* **Christmases**

Christmas tree   *noun* An evergreen tree, decorated to celebrate Christmas.

chromium   *noun* A hard, gray metal that is one of the chemical elements. Chromium can be polished to a bright shine.
chro·mi·um (krō′mē əm) ☐*noun*

chrysanthemum   *noun* A round flower with many closely clustered petals.
chry·san·the·mum (kri **san**′thə məm) ☐*noun, plural* **chrysanthemums**

chrysanthemum

chubby   *adjective* Round and plump.
chub·by (**chub′ē**) □*adjective* **chubbier,
chubbiest**

chubby

chuckle   *verb* To laugh quietly.
□*noun* A quiet laugh.
chuck·le (**chuk′əl**) □*verb* **chuckled,
chuckling, chuckles** □*noun, plural* **chuckles**
chum   *noun* A good friend.
chum (**chum**) □*noun, plural* **chums**
chunk   *noun* A thick piece; lump: *a chunk of
watermelon.*
chunk (**chungk**) □*noun, plural* **chunks**
church   *noun* **1.** A building for religious worship. **2.** A group of people with the same religious beliefs: *We belong to the Protestant
Church.*
church (**chûrch**) □*noun, plural* **churches**

WORD HISTORY: **church**

Church comes from a Greek word meaning "of the
Lord."

---

churn   *noun* A container in which cream is
beaten to make butter.
□*verb* **1.** To beat cream in a churn to make
butter. **2.** To move violently; swirl: *The water*

churned behind the motorboat.
churn (**chûrn**) □*noun, plural* **churns** □*verb*
churned, churning, churns

churn

chute   *noun* A long passage through which
things can be dropped or slid: *a mail chute.*
chute (**shoōt**) □*noun, plural* **chutes**
cider   *noun* Juice pressed from apples and
used as a drink or to make vinegar.
ci·der (**sī′dər**) □*noun, plural* **ciders**

cider

cigar   *noun* A roll of tobacco leaves used for
smoking.
ci·gar (**si gär′**) □*noun, plural* **cigars**
cigarette   *noun* A small roll of chopped tobacco leaves that are wrapped in thin paper
for smoking.

a	bat	ī	bite	oō	tool	*th*	feather
ā	make	î	fierce	ou	out	th	bath
â	dare	o	dot	u	nut	hw	wheat
ä	father	ō	no	û	turn	zh	measure
e	net	ô	law, for	ch	church	ə	about, open
ē	be	oi	soil	ng	ring		pencil, atom
i	dip	oo	look	sh	shade		circus

cig·a·rette (sĭg′ə **rĕt′** or **sĭg′**ə rĕt′) □*noun,* plural **cigarettes**

cinder *noun* A piece of partly burned coal or wood.
cin·der (sĭn′dər) □*noun,* plural **cinders**

cinnamon *noun* A reddish-brown spice made from the bark of a tropical tree.
cin·na·mon (sĭn′ə mən) □*noun*

circle *noun* **1.** A curve that is closed. Every point on the curve is at the same distance from a point called the center. **2.** Something that has the shape of a circle: *We stood in a circle.* **3.** A group of people having the same interests: *a circle of friends.*
□*verb* **1.** To form a circle around: *Circle the correct number.* **2.** To move in a circle around: *We circled the town to avoid traffic.*
cir·cle (sûr′kəl) □*noun,* plural **circles** □*verb* **circled, circling, circles**

circuit *noun* **1.** A moving or going around: *The runners made two circuits of the track.* **2.** A path through which electricity can flow. A light switch closes an electric circuit.
cir·cuit (sûr′kĭt) □*noun,* plural **circuits**

circular *adjective* Of or shaped like a circle; round: *The bus takes a circular route around the city.*
□*noun* A printed announcement given out to many people.
cir·cu·lar (sûr′kyə lər) □*adjective* □*noun,* plural **circulars**

circulate *verb* To move or send around: *Blood circulates through the body. The fan circulated the air in the room.*
cir·cu·late (sûr′kyə lāt′) □*verb* **circulated, circulating, circulates**

circulation *noun* **1.** Movement from place to place or person to person: *The circulation of air kept us cool.* **2.** The movement of blood through the blood vessels: *Exercise helps your circulation.*
cir·cu·la·tion (sûr′kyə lā′shən) □*noun,* plural **circulations**

circumference *noun* **1.** The outside edge of a circle. **2.** The distance around the edge of something: *We were surprised to learn that the circumference of the field is 300 yards.*
cir·cum·fer·ence (sər kŭm′fər əns) □*noun,* plural **circumferences**

circumstance *noun* A condition, fact, or event that goes along with and affects something else: *Rainy weather and darkness were*

two circumstances that helped to cause the car accident.
cir·cum·stance (sûr′kəm stăns′) □*noun,* plural **circumstances**

circus *noun* A colorful show put on by clowns, acrobats, and trained animals.
cir·cus (sûr′kəs) □*noun,* plural **circuses**

citizen *noun* **1.** Someone who is a member of a country, either by birth or by choosing to become a member. **2.** Someone who lives in a city or town: *the citizens of Boston.*
cit·i·zen (sĭt′i zən) □*noun,* plural **citizens**

citizenship *noun* The duties and rights of a citizen.
cit·i·zen·ship (sĭt′i zən shĭp′) □*noun*

citrus *noun* A tree that grows in warm climates and bears oranges, lemons, limes, grapefruits, or similar fruits.
cit·rus (sĭt′rəs) □*noun*

city *noun* A place where many people live and work. Cities are larger than towns.
cit·y (sĭt′ē) □*noun,* plural **cities**

civil *adjective* **1.** Of or having to do with a citizen or citizens: *Voting is a civil right.* **2.** Not related to military or church activities: *Thanksgiving Day is a civil holiday.* **3.** Having or showing good manners; polite: *He is always civil even when he is in a rush.* —See Synonyms at **courteous.**
civ·il (sĭv′əl) □*adjective*

civilian *noun* Someone who is not in the armed forces.
ci·vil·ian (sĭ vĭl′yən) □*noun,* plural **civilians**

civilization *noun* A condition in which people have reached a very high level of development in art, science, religion, and government.
civ·i·li·za·tion (sĭv′ə lĭ zā′shən) □*noun,* plural **civilizations**

civilize *verb* To change from a primitive way of life to a more highly developed one: *Can we civilize people just by teaching them to read and write?*
civ·i·lize (sĭv′ə līz′) □*verb* **civilized, civilizing, civilizes**

civil war *noun* A war between groups of people within one country.

clad *adjective* Clothed; covered: *Dancers clad in bright colors entertained the crowd with a comical dance. The knight was clad in armor.*
clad (klăd) □*adjective*

claim *verb* **1.** To ask for something one owns or deserves: *She claimed her lost mittens at the*

principal's office. **2.** To say that something is true: *He claimed that he saw her take the book.*
□*noun* **1.** A demand for something one owns or deserves. **2.** A statement that something is true. **3.** Something, such as a piece of land, that has been claimed.
claim (klām) □*verb* **claimed, claiming, claims** □*noun, plural* **claims**

clam *noun* A water animal with a soft body inside a shell that has two parts hinged together. Many clams are used as food.
clam (klam) □*noun, plural* **clams**

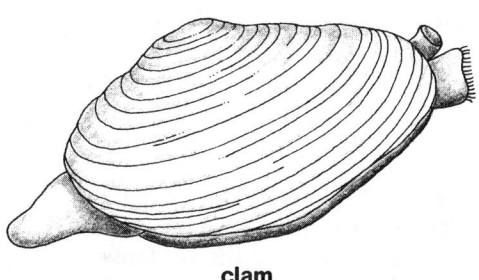

clam

clamp *noun* A device used for gripping or keeping things together.
□*verb* To hold together with a clamp: *We clamped the two boards together.*
clamp (klamp) □*noun, plural* **clamps** □*verb* **clamped, clamping, clamps**

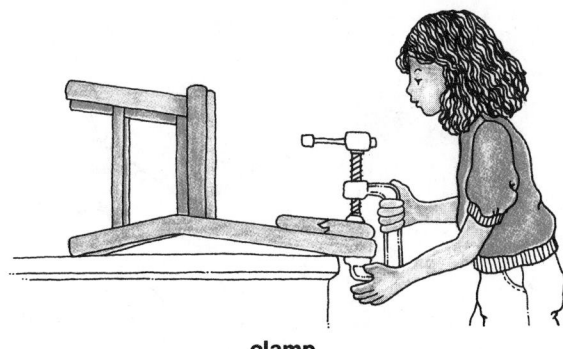

clamp

clan *noun* A group of families that claim to be related to the same ancestor.
clan (klan) □*noun, plural* **clans**

clap *verb* **1.** To hit the hands together quickly and loudly: *The audience clapped at the end of the concert.* **2.** To strike with an open hand: *He clapped his friend on the back.*
□*noun* **1.** A loud, sudden noise: *a clap of thunder.* **2.** A slap.
clap (klap) □*verb* **clapped, clapping, claps** □*noun, plural* **claps**

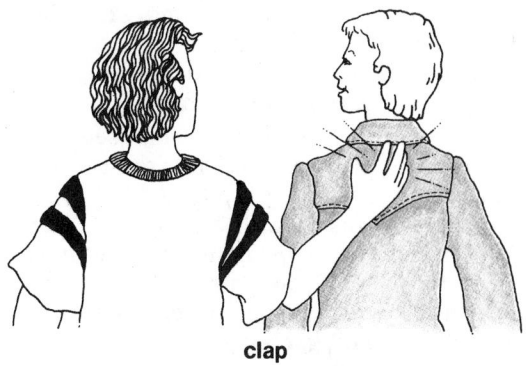

clap

clarify *verb* To make something clear or easier to understand: *Her explanation clarified the problem.*
clar·i·fy (klar′i fī′) □*verb* **clarified, clarifying, clarifies**

clarify

clarinet *noun* A musical instrument shaped like a tube and played by blowing into the mouthpiece and covering holes or pressing keys.
clar·i·net (klar′i net′) □*noun, plural* **clarinets**

clarity *noun* Clearness: *He described the person with great clarity.*
clar·i·ty (klar′i tē) □*noun*

clash *verb* **1.** To come together with a loud, harsh noise: *Their swords clashed.* **2.** To disagree strongly: *The boys clashed over who would use the sled first.*

a	bat	ī	bite	o͞o	tool	*th*	feather
ā	make	i	fierce	ou	out	th	bath
â	dare	o	dot	u	nut	hw	wheat
ä	father	ō	no	û	turn	zh	measure
e	net	ô	law, for	ch	church	ə	about, open
ē	be	oi	soil	ng	ring		pencil, atom
i	dip	oo	look	sh	shade		circus

□*noun* **1.** A loud, harsh sound. **2.** A strong disagreement.

clash (klăsh) □*verb* **clashed, clashing, clashes** □*noun, plural* **clashes**

clasp *noun* **1.** A buckle or hook used to hold two objects or parts together: *the clasp on a bracelet.* **2.** A strong grasp or hold.
□*verb* **1.** To fasten with a clasp. **2.** To grasp tightly: *She clasped my hand as we went down the stairs.* —See Synonyms at **hold.**

clasp (klăsp) □*noun, plural* **clasps** □*verb* **clasped, clasping, clasps**

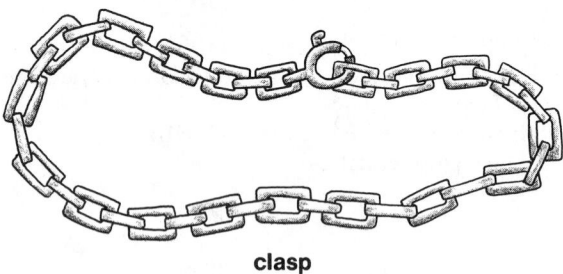

clasp

class *noun* **1.** A group of objects or people alike in some way: *a class of animals; people in the middle class of a society.* **2.** A group of students learning together in the same classroom. **3.** A quality or grade: *She's an athlete of the first class.*
□*verb* To put into a class: *I would class that book as a novel.*

class (klăs) □*noun, plural* **classes** □*verb* **classed, classing, classes**

classic *adjective* Thought to be of the highest quality: *a classic book.*
□*noun* A poem, painting, or other work of art thought to be of the highest quality.

clas·sic (klăs′ĭk) □*adjective* □*noun, plural* **classics**

classical *adjective* **1.** Of the art, writings, and way of life of ancient Greece and Rome: *classical languages; classical sculpture.* **2.** Of music that follows a standard or traditional form and is very different from popular and folk music.

clas·si·cal (klăs′ĭ kəl) □*adjective*

classification *noun* An arrangement in classes or kinds: *The classification of books is according to their subject.*

clas·si·fi·ca·tion (klăs′ə fĭ kā′shən) □*noun, plural* **classifications**

classify *verb* To sort into classes or groups: *We classified the books as we unpacked them.*

clas·si·fy (klăs′ə fī′) □*verb* **classified, classifying, classifies**

classmate *noun* A member of the same class in school.

class·mate (klăs′māt′) □*noun, plural* **classmates**

classroom *noun* A room in a school where classes are held.

class·room (klăs′rōōm′ *or* klăs′rōŏm′) □*noun, plural* **classrooms**

clatter *verb* To make a noisy, rattling sound: *The dishes clattered as he piled them up.*
□*noun* A noisy, rattling sound.

clat·ter (klăt′ər) □*verb* **clattered, clattering, clatters** □*noun*

clause *noun* A part of a sentence that contains a subject and a verb. In the sentence "We left when the clock struck ten," "We left" is a **main clause** because it can stand alone and does not depend on another clause for its meaning. "When the clock struck ten" is a **dependent clause** because its meaning depends on the main clause of the sentence.

clause (klôz) □*noun, plural* **clauses**

claw *noun* **1.** A sharp, curved nail on the toe of an animal or bird. **2.** One of the pincers of a lobster or crab.
□*verb* To scratch with the claws or hands: *The cat clawed the rug.*

claw (klô) □*noun, plural* **claws** □*verb* **clawed, clawing, claws**

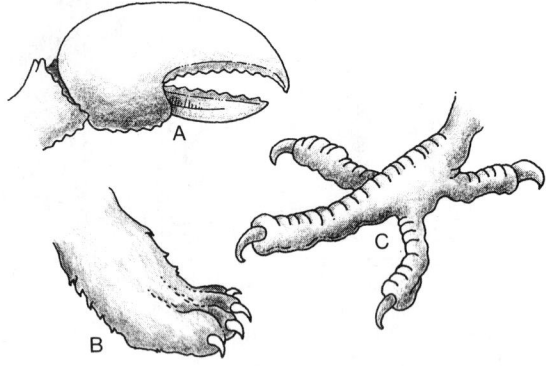

claw
(A) lobster, *(B)* cat, *(C)* hawk

clay *noun* A firm, fine kind of earth that can be shaped and then hardened by heat to make bricks and pottery.

clay (klā) □*noun, plural* **clays**

clean *adjective* **1.** Free from dirt: *clean clothes.* **2.** Free from wrongdoing; innocent: *a clean record.* **3.** Complete; total: *a clean break.*
□*adverb* Completely: *cutting clean through the rope.*

□*verb* To get rid of dirt or clutter: *I must clean up the house after the party.*
clean (klēn) □*adjective* **cleaner, cleanest** □*adverb* □*verb* **cleaned, cleaning, cleans**

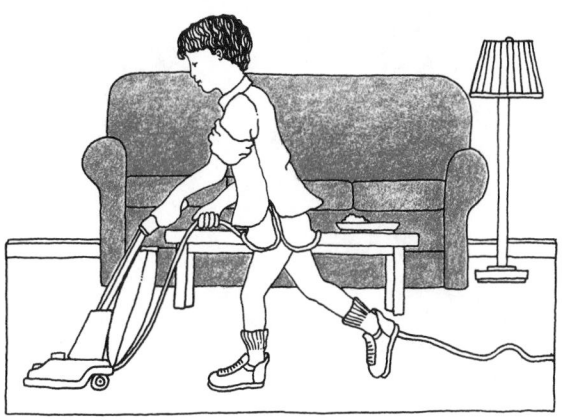

clean

cleaner *noun* **1.** A person or business whose job is to clean: *I took my skirts to the cleaner.* **2.** A machine or substance used in cleaning.
clean·er (klēn′ ər) □*noun, plural* **cleaners**

cleanliness *noun* The condition of being clean.
clean·li·ness (klen′ lē nis) □*noun*

cleanly *adjective* Always neat and clean: *a cleanly person.*
clean·ly (klen′ lē) □*adjective* **cleanlier, cleanliest**

cleanse *verb* To make clean: *The nurse cleansed the wound.*
cleanse (klenz) □*verb* **cleansed, cleansing, cleanses**

cleanser *noun* A material or liquid used for cleaning: *a kitchen cleanser.*
clean·ser (klen′ zər) □*noun, plural* **cleansers**

clear *adjective* **1.** Free from anything that darkens or blocks: *a clear sky; a clear road.* **2.** Easily seen through: *clear water.* **3.** Easily seen, heard, or understood: *a clear warning.* □*adverb* In a clear way: *Speak loud and clear.* □*verb* **1.** To make or become clear: *Clear the way. The air cleared slowly after the fire.* **2.** To get rid of; remove: *They cleared away the dishes.* **3.** To pass by or over without touching: *The airplane barely cleared the mountain top.*
clear (klîr) □*adjective* **clearer, clearest** □*adverb* □*verb* **cleared, clearing, clears**

clearing *noun* An area of land where there are no trees.
clear·ing (klîr′ ing) □*noun, plural* **clearings**

clearly *adverb* **1.** In a clear way; plainly: *Speak clearly.* **2.** Without doubt: *Clearly, we must act now.*
clear·ly (klîr′ lē) □*adverb*

cleaver *noun* A tool with a heavy, broad blade for cutting meat.
cleav·er (klē′ vər) □*noun, plural* **cleavers**

clef *noun* A printed mark on a musical scale that tells the pitch for each line and space.
clef (klef) □*noun, plural* **clefs**

clef
Above: treble clef
Below: bass clef

clench *verb* **1.** To close tightly: *clench one's fist.* **2.** To grip tightly: *The child clenched his father's hand.*
clench (klench) □*verb* **clenched, clenching, clenches**

clench

clergy *noun* Ministers, priests, and rabbis.
cler·gy (klûr′ jē) □*noun, plural* **clergies**

a	bat	ī	bite	ōō	tool	*th*	feather
ā	make	i	fierce	ou	out	th	bath
â	dare	o	dot	u	nut	hw	wheat
ä	father	ō	no	û	turn	zh	measure
e	net	ô	law, for	ch	church	ə	about, open
ē	be	oi	soil	ng	ring		pencil, atom
i	dip	oo	look	sh	shade		circus

clergyman   *noun* A member of the clergy.
cler·gy·man (klûr′ jē mən) □*noun, plural*
clergymen

clerk   *noun* **1.** Someone who works in an office and keeps records and other papers in order. **2.** Someone who sells things in a store.
clerk (klûrk) □*noun, plural* **clerks**

clever   *adjective* Having or showing a quick
mind; smart: *a clever student; a clever idea.*
clev·er (klev′ər) □*adjective* **cleverer,**
cleverest

click   *noun* A short, sharp sound.
□*verb* **1.** To make such a sound: *The padlock*
clicked as it opened. **2.** To press down and release a button on a computer mouse.
click (klik) □*noun, plural* **clicks** □*verb*
clicked, clicking, clicks

client   *noun* Someone who uses the services
of another person: *Lawyers give advice to their*
clients.
cli·ent (klī′ ənt) □*noun, plural* **clients**

cliff   *noun* A high, steep slope of earth or
rock.
cliff (klif) □*noun, plural* **cliffs**

climate   *noun* The usual weather a place has
all year: *The west coast has a mild, rainy cli-*
mate.
cli·mate (klī′ mit) □*noun, plural* **climates**

climax   *noun* The highest or most exciting
point: *The climax of the story comes when the*
hero kills the dragon and rescues the princess.
cli·max (klī′ maks) □*noun, plural* **climaxes**

climb   *verb* To go or move upward: *Her tem-*
perature climbed. The vines climbed the brick
wall. The fireman climbed quickly up the lad-
der. —See Synonyms at **rise.**
□*noun* The act of climbing.
climb (klīm) □*verb* **climbed, climbing,**
climbs □*noun, plural* **climbs**

climb

cling   *verb* To hold tight; stick: *Mud clung to*
their shoes. Country people often cling to old
customs and beliefs.
cling (kling) □*verb* **clung, clinging, clings**

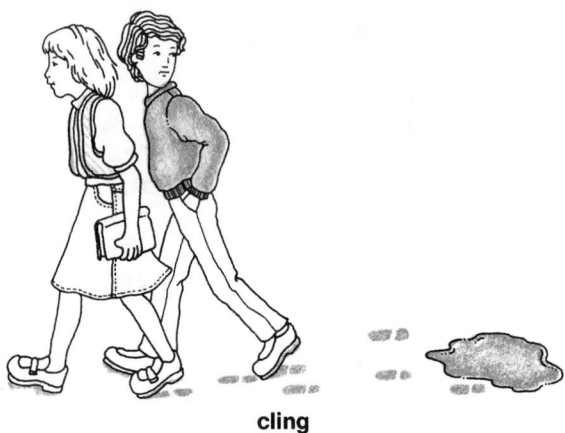

cling

clinic   *noun* A place that gives medical help to
people not staying in the hospital.
clin·ic (klin′ ik) □*noun, plural* **clinics**

clip¹   *verb* To cut; trim: *He clipped the hedge.*
□*noun* A rate of moving: *walking at a fast clip.*
clip (klip) □*verb* **clipped, clipping, clips**
□*noun, plural* **clips**

clip²   *noun* An object used to hold things together: *a paper clip.*
□*verb* To hold together with a clip: *I clipped*
the papers together.
clip (klip) □*noun, plural* **clips** □*verb*
clipped, clipping, clips

clipper   *noun* **1.** A tool for clipping: *a nail*
clipper. **2.** A fast sailing ship.
clip·per (klip′ ər) □*noun, plural* **clippers**

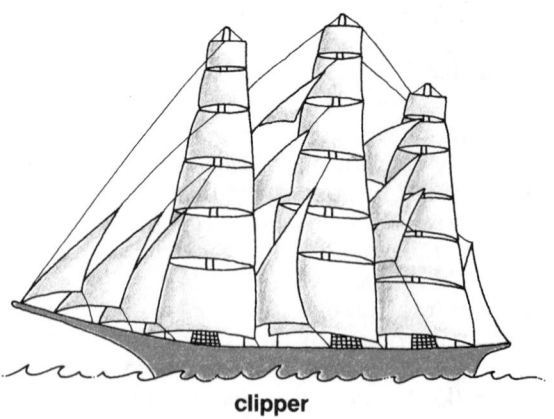

clipper

clipping   *noun* A piece cut from a newspaper
or magazine.
clip·ping (klip′ ing) □*noun, plural* **clippings**

cloak *noun* A loose piece of outer clothing, usually without sleeves.
□*verb* To cover up; hide: *Snow cloaked the fields.*
cloak (klōk) □*noun, plural* **cloaks** □*verb* **cloaked, cloaking, cloaks**

clock *noun* An instrument that tells the time. Some clocks have a face with numerals and moving hands. Other clocks show the time directly in numerals.
□*verb* To measure the time or speed of: *I clocked the runners in the mile race.*
clock (klok) □*noun, plural* **clocks** □*verb* **clocked, clocking, clocks**

clockwise *adverb* In the same direction as the moving hands of a clock: *Turn the dial clockwise.*
□*adjective* Moving in the same direction as the hands of a clock.
clock·wise (klok′wīz′) □*adverb* □*adjective*

clockwise

clog *verb* To block up: *Many cars clogged the highway.*
clog (klog) □*verb* **clogged, clogging, clogs**

clog

close *adjective* **1.** Near in space or time: *Our house is close to the park.* **2.** Near within a family or in relationship: *close friends.* **3.** Without enough fresh air: *a close, stuffy room.* **4.** Almost even or equal: *a close contest.*

□*verb* **1.** To shut: *Please close the window. The store closes at seven o'clock.* **2.** To bring or come to an end: *He closed his speech with a joke.* **3.** To pull or come together: *It took several stitches to close the rip.*
□*noun* An ending: *The class came to a close.*
close (klōs) □*adjective* **closer, closest** □*verb* (klōz) **closed, closing, closes** *noun* (klōz)

closet *noun* A small room for hanging clothes or storing supplies.
clos·et (kloz′it) □*noun, plural* **closets**

clot *noun* A soft, thickened lump: *a blood clot.*
□*verb* To form into clots: *The blood on the cut clotted and formed a scab.*
clot (klot) □*noun, plural* **clots** □*verb* **clotted, clotting, clots**

cloth **1.** Material made by weaving or knitting fibers together: *a dress of cotton cloth.* **2.** A piece of cloth.
cloth (klôth) □*noun, plural* **cloths** (klô*th*z or klôths)

clothe *verb* To put clothes on: *She fed and clothed the children.*
clothe (klō*th*) □*verb* **clothed, clothing, clothes**

clothes *plural noun* Things that are worn to cover the body: *Shirts and dresses are clothes.* —See Synonyms at **dress.**
clothes (klōz or klō*th*z) □*plural noun*

clothing *noun* Things that are worn to cover the body; clothes. —See Synonyms at **dress.**
cloth·ing (klō′*th*ing) □*noun*

cloud *noun* **1.** A large white or gray mass of very small drops of water or tiny pieces of ice floating in the sky. **2.** A floating mass that is like a cloud: *a cloud of flies.*
□*verb* To cover or become covered with clouds: *Fog clouded the hills. The sky clouded over before the storm.*
cloud (kloud) □*noun, plural* **clouds** □*verb* **clouded, clouding, clouds**

cloudy *adjective* **1.** Full of clouds: *cloudy skies.* **2.** Not clear: *cloudy water.*
cloud·y (kloud′ē) □*adjective* **cloudier, cloudiest**

a	bat	ī	bite	o͞o	tool	*th*	feather
ā	make	î	fierce	ou	out	th	bath
â	dare	o	dot	u	nut	hw	wheat
ä	father	ō	no	û	turn	zh	measure
e	net	ô	law, for	ch	church	ə	about, open
ē	be	oi	soil	ng	ring		pencil, atom
i	dip	o͞o	look	sh	shade		circus

clove¹ *noun* A dried flower bud of a tropical plant, used as a spice.
clove (klōv) ◻*noun, plural* **cloves**

clove² *noun* One section of a garlic bulb.
clove (klōv) ◻*noun, plural* **cloves**

clover *noun* A plant with leaves made up of three leaflets and small flowers growing in round, tight clusters.

clover

clown *noun* Someone in a circus who performs tricks and tells jokes to make people laugh.
◻*verb* To perform as or act like a clown: *Stop clowning around.*
clown (kloun) ◻*noun, plural* **clowns** ◻*verb* **clowned, clowning, clowns**

clown

club *noun* **1.** A heavy stick with one thick end, used as a weapon. **2.** A stick used to hit a ball in certain games: *a golf club.* **3.** A playing card marked with a black figure that looks like a clover leaf. **4.** A group of people who meet together to do the same thing: *a hiking club.*
◻*verb* To hit with a club.
club (klub) ◻*noun, plural* **clubs** ◻*verb* **clubbed, clubbing, clubs**

clue *noun* Something that helps to solve a problem or mystery.
clue (klōō) ◻*noun, plural* **clues**

clump *noun* **1.** A thick group or cluster: *a clump of bushes.* **2.** A heavy, dull sound: *We heard the clump of footsteps on the stairs.*
◻*verb* To walk with a heavy, dull sound: *clump around in boots.*
clump (klump) ◻*noun, plural* **clumps** ◻*verb* **clumped, clumping, clumps**

clumsy *adjective* Awkward in moving or acting; not graceful: *He is a clumsy man who is always dropping things.*
clum·sy (klum′zē) ◻*adjective* **clumsier, clumsiest**

clumsy

clung *verb* The past tense and past participle of **cling**: *He clung to a rock ledge.*
clung (klung) ◻*verb*

cluster *noun* A number of things growing or grouped close together: *The factory consisted of a cluster of buildings.*
◻*verb* To gather or grow in clusters: *We all clustered near the television.*
clus·ter (klus′tər) ◻*noun, plural* **clusters** ◻*verb* **clustered, clustering, clusters**

clutch *verb* To hold tightly: *She clutched the baby in her arms.*
◻*noun* **1.** A tight hold or grip. **2.** A part of a machine that is used to connect and disconnect the motor that makes the machine work.
clutch (kluch) ◻*verb* **clutched, clutching, clutches** ◻*noun, plural* **clutches**

clutter *noun* Things scattered about in a messy way: *a clutter of shoes and hangers on the bottom of the closet.*
◻*verb* To scatter things about in a messy way: *He cluttered up the basement with tools.*

clut·ter (klut′ər) ☐*noun* ☐*verb* **cluttered, cluttering, clutters**

cm. An abbreviation for **centimeter.**

coach *noun* **1.** A large, closed carriage pulled by horses. **2.** A bus or a railroad passenger car. **3.** A less expensive section of seats on a train, airplane, or bus. **4.** Someone in charge of a team. **5.** Someone who gives private lessons: *an acting coach.*
☐*verb* To teach or train: *coach a basketball team.*
coach (kōch) ☐*noun, plural* **coaches** ☐*verb* **coached, coaching, coaches**

coal *noun* **1.** A black mineral taken from the ground and used as a fuel. **2.** A glowing or burned piece of hard fuel.
coal (kōl) ☐*noun, plural* **coals**

coarse *adjective* **1.** Not smooth; rough: *coarse cloth.* **2.** Made up of large parts: *coarse gravel.* **3.** Rude; crude: *Everyone dislikes coarse language.*
coarse (kôrs) ☐*adjective* **coarser, coarsest**

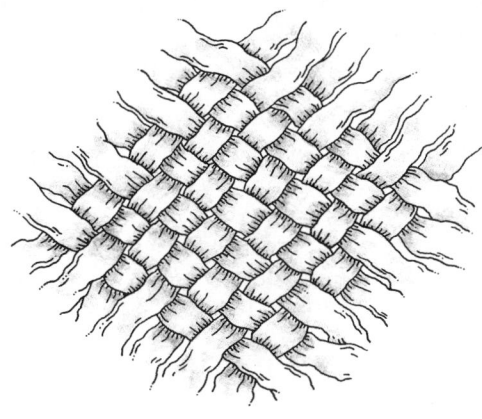

coarse

coast *noun* The land touching or near the sea.
☐*verb* To move along without any power: *The sled coasted down the side of the hill.*
coast (kōst) ☐*noun, plural* **coasts** ☐*verb* **coasted, coasting, coasts**

coastal *adjective* On, along, or near a coast.
coast·al (kō′stəl) ☐*adjective*

coast guard *noun* A military group that guards the coast of a country and helps boats and ships in trouble.

coastline *noun* The shape or outline of a coast.
coast·line (kōst′līn′) ☐*noun, plural* **coastlines**

coat *noun* **1.** A piece of outer clothing with sleeves. **2.** The fur of an animal: *a dog's shaggy coat.* **3.** A thin layer: *a coat of paint.*
☐*verb* To cover with a thin layer: *The candy was coated with chocolate.*
coat (kōt) ☐*noun, plural* **coats** ☐*verb* **coated, coating, coats**

coating *noun* A layer spread over a surface: *a coating of polish.*
coat·ing (kō′ting) ☐*noun, plural* **coatings**

coat of arms *noun* The design on a shield that shows the symbols of a family or organization.
coat of arms ☐*noun, plural* **coats of arms**

coax *verb* To try in a gentle way to persuade: *He coaxed the shy girl into taking a part in the play.*
coax (kōks) ☐*verb* **coaxed, coaxing, coaxes**

cob *noun* The center part of an ear of corn on which the kernels grow.
cob (kob) ☐*noun, plural* **cobs**

cobalt *noun* A hard, brittle metal that is one of the chemical elements. It is used in making steel and paint.
co·balt (kō′bôlt′) ☐*noun*

cobbler *noun* Someone who makes or repairs shoes.
cob·bler (kob′lər) ☐*noun, plural* **cobblers**

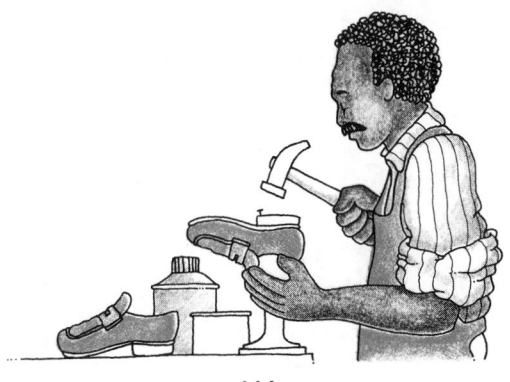

cobbler

cobblestone *noun* A round stone once used to pave streets.

a	bat	ī	bite	ōō	tool	*th*	feather
ā	make	î	fierce	ou	out	th	bath
â	dare	o	dot	u	nut	hw	wheat
ä	father	ō	no	û	turn	zh	measure
e	net	ô	law, for	ch	church	ə	about, open
ē	be	oi	soil	ng	ring		pencil, atom
i	dip	oo	look	sh	shade		circus

cob·ble·stone (kob′əl stōn′) ☐*noun, plural* **cobblestones**

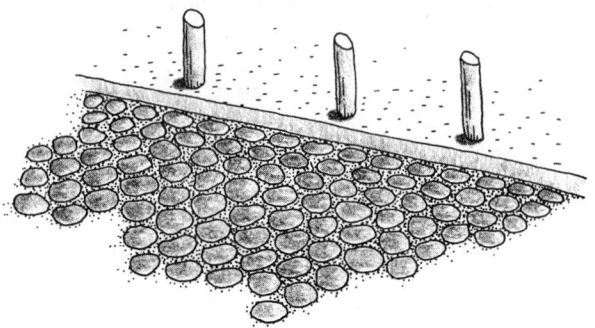

cobblestone

cobra *noun* A poisonous snake of Asia or Africa that can spread out the skin of its neck to form a flattened hood.
co·bra (kō′brə) ☐*noun, plural* **cobras**

cobweb *noun* A spider's web.
cob·web (kob′web′) ☐*noun, plural* **cobwebs**

cock *noun* **1.** An adult male chicken; rooster. **2.** The male of other birds.
☐*verb* To pull back the hammer of a gun so that it can be fired.
cock (kok) ☐*noun, plural* **cocks** ☐*verb* **cocked, cocking, cocks**

cockatoo *noun* A large Australian parrot that has a crest.
cock·a·too (kok′ə tōo′) ☐*noun, plural* **cockatoos**

cockle *noun* A small sea animal having a hinged shell that is shaped like a heart.
cock·le (kok′əl) ☐*noun, plural* **cockles**

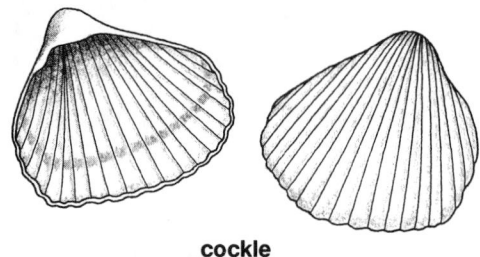

cockle
Cockleshell

cockpit *noun* The part of an airplane where the pilot sits.
cock·pit (kok′pit′) ☐*noun, plural* **cockpits**

cockroach *noun* A brown insect with a long, flat body, often found in kitchens.
cock·roach (kok′rōch′) ☐*noun, plural* **cockroaches**

cocky *adjective* Too sure of oneself; conceited: *She has become very cocky since she won the tennis match.*
cock·y (kok′ē) ☐*adjective* **cockier, cockiest**

cocoa *noun* **1.** A powder made from roasted and ground cacao seeds. **2.** A drink made with cocoa and milk or water.
co·coa (kō′kō′) ☐*noun*

coconut or **cocoanut** *noun* The large, round nut of a tropical palm tree. A coconut has sweet white meat and a hollow center filled with a sweet, milky liquid.
co·co·nut or **co·coa·nut** (kō′kə nut′) ☐*noun, plural* **coconuts** or **cocoanuts**

cocoon *noun* A case of silky strands made by a caterpillar to protect itself while it turns into a butterfly or moth.
co·coon (kə kōon′) ☐*noun, plural* **cocoons**

cod *noun* An edible fish of northern waters of the Atlantic Ocean.
cod (kod) ☐*noun, plural* **cod** or **cods**

code *noun* **1.** A system of signals or symbols used to send messages. **2.** A collection of laws or rules: *It is against the building code to block stairways.*
☐*verb* To put into a code: *He coded the message so that the spies could not understand it.*
code (kōd) ☐*noun, plural* **codes** ☐*verb* **coded, coding, codes**

coffee *noun* **1.** A dark-brown drink made from the ground, roasted seeds of a tropical tree. **2.** The beans of the coffee tree.
cof·fee (kô′fē) ☐*noun*

coffin *noun* A box in which a dead person is buried.
cof·fin (kô′fin) ☐*noun, plural* **coffins**

coil *noun* **1.** A loop or series of loops made by winding something around and around a center. **2.** Something wound in such a shape: *a coil of wire.*
☐*verb* To wind into a coil: *coil a rope.*
coil (koil) ☐*noun, plural* **coils** ☐*verb* **coiled, coiling, coils**

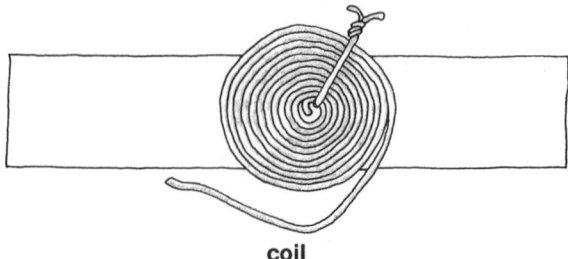

coil

coin *noun* A piece of flat, round metal used as money.
□*verb* **1.** To make coins from metal: *The United States government coins money.* **2.** To make up: *coin a new word.*
coin (koin) □*noun, plural* **coins** □*verb* **coined, coining, coins**

coincide *verb* **1.** To be in the same place: *The river and the state border coincide.* **2.** To happen at the same time: *My birthday coincides with Easter this year.*
co·in·cide (kō'in **sīd'**) □*verb* **coincided, coinciding, coincides**

coincidence *noun* The unplanned happening of two events at the same time: *It was a coincidence that we were both reading the same book.*
co·in·ci·dence (kō **in'**si dəns) □*noun, plural* **coincidences**

coke *noun* A solid black fuel made by heating coal with almost no air present.
coke (kōk) □*noun*

cold *adjective* **1.** Having a low temperature: *cold soda; a cold day.* **2.** Feeling no warmth; chilly: *I felt cold after I got out of the pool.* **3.** Not friendly: *their cold greeting made it clear that I was not welcome.*
□*noun* **1.** A lack of heat. **2.** A common sickness that causes sneezing, coughing, and a running nose.
cold (kōld) □*adjective* **colder, coldest** □*noun, plural* **colds**

SYNONYMS: **cold, chilly, cool**

These adjectives mean having a low temperature: *Would you like a cold drink? It's chilly outside. I wanted to go swimming but the water is too cool.*

---

cold-blooded *adjective* Having a body temperature that changes as the surrounding air or water becomes colder or warmer. Fish and snakes are cold-blooded animals.
cold-blood·ed (kōld' blud'id) □*adjective*

coliseum *noun* A large stadium or building used for sports events and shows.
col·i·se·um (kol'i **sē'** əm) □*noun, plural* **coliseums**

collage *noun* A picture made by gluing different materials onto a surface.
col·lage (kə **läzh'**) □*noun, plural* **collages**

collapse *verb* **1.** To fall down suddenly: *One of our old chairs collapsed when I sat on it.*

2. To fold together: *The tent collapses for easy storage.*
□*noun* The act of collapsing.
col·lapse (kə **laps'**) □*verb* **collapsed, collapsing, collapses** □*noun, plural* **collapses**

collapse

collar *noun* **1.** A band around the neck of a coat, dress, or shirt. **2.** A leather or metal band for the neck of an animal.
col·lar (kol'ər) □*noun, plural* **collars**

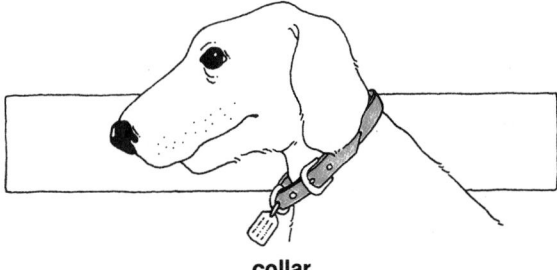

collar

collarbone *noun* A bone between the shoulder blade and the breastbone.
col·lar·bone (kol'ər bōn') □*noun, plural* **collarbones**

collect *verb* **1.** To bring or come together; gather: *He collects butterflies. Dust collected in the deserted house.* **2.** To pick up and take away: *collect garbage.* **3.** To receive payment for: *collect taxes.* —See Synonyms at **gather.**
col·lect (kə **lekt'**) □*verb* **collected, collecting, collects**

a bat	ī bite	o͞o tool	*th* feather
ā make	î fierce	ou out	th bath
â dare	o dot	u nut	hw wheat
ä father	ō no	û turn	zh measure
e net	ô law, for	ch church	ə about, open
ē be	oi soil	ng ring	pencil, atom
i dip	oo look	sh shade	circus

collection *noun* **1.** The act of collecting: *Trash collection is every Friday.* **2.** A group of things gathered or kept together: *a stamp collection.*
col·lec·tion (kə lek′shən) □*noun, plural* **collections**

collector *noun* Someone or something that collects: *a stamp collector.*
col·lec·tor (kə lek′tər) □*noun, plural* **collectors**

college *noun* A school attended after high school.
col·lege (kol′ij) □*noun, plural* **colleges**

collide *verb* To strike together violently; crash: *Two cars collided at the corner.*
col·lide (kə līd′) □*verb* **collided, colliding, collides**

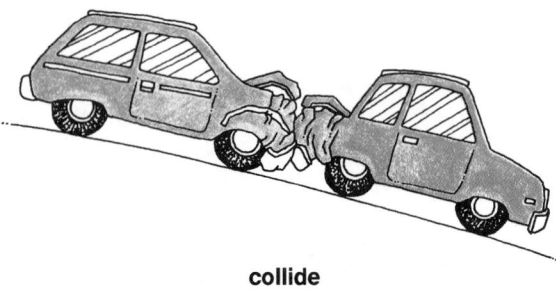

collide

collie *noun* A large dog with long hair and a narrow face.
col·lie (kol′ē) □*noun, plural* **collies**

collie

collision *noun* The act of colliding; crash.
col·li·sion (kə lizh′ən) □*noun, plural* **collisions**

colon¹ *noun* A punctuation mark (:) used to introduce a list, explanation, or quotation.
co·lon (kō′lən) □*noun, plural* **colons**

colon² *noun* The lower part of the large intestine.
co·lon (kō′lən) □*noun, plural* **colons**

colonel *noun* A military officer who ranks above a major and below a general.
colo·nel (kûr′nəl) □*noun, plural* **colonels**

colonial *adjective* **1.** Of or having colonies: *a colonial empire.* **2.** Often **Colonial** Having to do with the thirteen original American colonies.
co·lo·ni·al (kə lō′nē əl) □*adjective*

colonist *noun* Someone who lives in a colony.
col·o·nist (kol′ə nist) □*noun, plural* **colonists**

colony *noun* **1.** A group of people who leave their native country and settle in another place. **2.** A territory that is ruled by a country that is far away from it: *India once was a British colony.* **3.** A group of animals or plants living closely together: *a colony of wasps.*
col·o·ny (kol′ə nē) □*noun, plural* **colonies**

color *noun* **1.** The property that makes it possible to see a difference between two things, such as a red apple and a green apple, that are similar or identical in all other ways. **2.** The way the skin looks: *She has a healthy color.*
□*verb* To give color to: *She colored her nails with polish.*
col·or (kul′ər) □*noun, plural* **colors** □*verb* **colored, coloring, colors**

colorful *adjective* **1.** Full of color: *She wore a colorful dress.* **2.** Exciting to the imagination: *a colorful story.*
col·or·ful (kul′ər fəl) □*adjective*

coloring *noun* **1.** The way something or someone is colored. **2.** A substance used to give color: *food coloring.*
col·or·ing (kul′ər ing) □*noun, plural* **colorings**

colt *noun* A young horse, especially a male.
colt (kōlt) □*noun, plural* **colts**

column *noun* **1.** A long, thin, upright structure that supports or decorates a building. **2.** Something long and upright like a column: *a column of smoke.* **3.** A narrow vertical section of printed words on a page. **4.** An article that appears regularly in a newspaper or magazine. **5.** A long line or row: *a column of marchers in a parade.*
col·umn (kol′əm) □*noun, plural* **columns**

column

combination

comb *noun* **1.** A device having teeth, made of metal, plastic, or other hard material and used to arrange or fasten the hair. **2.** A red strip of flesh on the head of a rooster or other bird. □*verb* **1.** To arrange hair or fur with a comb. **2.** To look everywhere in: *Pirates combed the area looking for the hidden treasure.*
comb (kōm) □*noun, plural* **combs** □*verb* **combed, combing, combs**

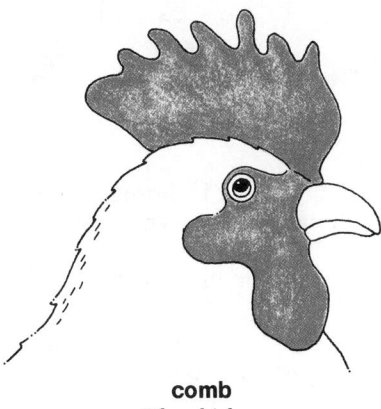

comb
Of a chicken

combat *noun* A fight or battle: *a soldier injured in combat.*
□*verb* To fight or struggle against: *The new drug combats influenza.*
com·bat (kəm **bat'** *or* **kom'**bat') □*noun* (**kom'**bat), *plural* **combats** □*verb* **combated, combating, combats**

combination *noun* **1.** Something made by combining: *Pancakes and maple syrup make a delicious combination.* **2.** A series of numbers or letters used to open a lock.
com·bi·na·tion (kom'bi **nā'**shən) □*noun, plural* **combinations**

combine *verb* To bring or come together; join: *He combined apples and bananas to make a fruit salad. Hydrogen and oxygen combine to form water.*
com·bine (kəm **bīn'**) □*verb* **combined, combining, combines**

combustion *noun* The process of burning.
com·bus·tion (kəm **bus'**chən) □*noun, plural* **combustions**

come *verb* **1.** To move toward: *Come here, please.* **2.** To arrive at a place or result: *I came to the meeting late. They came to an agreement.* **3.** To exist or occur: *June comes after May.* **4.** To be from: *He comes from Boston.*
come (kum) □*verb* **came, come, coming, comes**

comedian *noun* Someone who makes other people laugh by telling jokes or doing funny things.
co·me·di·an (kə **mē'**dē ən) □*noun, plural* **comedians**

comedy *noun* A play or movie that is funny or has a happy ending.
com·e·dy (**kom'**i dē) □*noun, plural* **comedies**

comet *noun* A glowing, heavenly body in the shape of a ball with a bright center that travels around the sun and often develops a long, bright tail that points away from the sun.
com·et (**kom'**it) □*noun, plural* **comets**

a bat	ī bite	ōō tool	*th* feather
ā make	î fierce	ou out	th bath
â dare	o dot	u nut	hw wheat
ä father	ō no	û turn	zh measure
e net	ô law, for	ch church	ə about, open
ē be	oi soil	ng ring	pencil, atom
i dip	oo look	sh shade	circus

comfort *verb* To soothe someone in a time of grief or pain: *comfort a frightened child.*
□*noun* **1.** A pleasant feeling of content that is without pain or worry. **2.** Something or someone that gives this feeling: *Hot chocolate is a comfort on a very cold day.*
com·fort (kŭm′fərt) □*verb* **comforted, comforting, comforts** □*noun, plural* **comforts**

WORD HISTORY: **comfort**
The word *comfort* comes from a Latin word that means "to strengthen."

---

comfortable *adjective* **1.** Giving comfort: *a comfortable bed.* **2.** Feeling comfort; at ease: *I feel comfortable in the new school.*
com·fort·a·ble (kŭmf′tə bəl *or* kŭm′fər tə bəl) □*adjective*

comic *adjective* Funny; amusing: *a comic character.*
□*noun* **1.** Someone who is funny; comedian. **2. comics** Comic strips.
com·ic (kŏm′ĭk) □*adjective* □*noun, plural* **comics**

comical *adjective* Causing laughter; funny: *a circus clown's comical stunts.*
com·i·cal (kŏm′ĭ kəl) □*adjective*

comic book *noun* A booklet of comic strips.

comic strip *noun* A series of drawings that tells a story or part of a story.

comic strip

comma *noun* A punctuation mark (,) used to separate things or ideas in a sentence.
com·ma (kŏm′ə) □*noun, plural* **commas**

command *verb* **1.** To give orders to: *The teacher commanded us to follow her.* **2.** To have control or authority over: *The general commanded a large army.*

□*noun* **1.** An order or direction: *He gave us the command to begin.* **2.** The power to give orders: *The captain was in command of the whole crew.* **3.** The ability to control or use: *He has command of a foreign language.*
com·mand (kə mănd′) □*verb* **commanded, commanding, commands** □*noun, plural* **commands**

SYNONYMS: **command, direct, order**
These verbs mean to give instructions or orders to: *The general commanded the soldiers to march. The teacher directed the students to form a single line. The boss had to order the men to get back to work.*

command

commander *noun* **1.** Someone in charge; leader. **2.** A navy officer who ranks next below a captain.
com·mand·er (kə măn′dər) □*noun, plural* **commanders**

commandment *noun* A command; order.
com·mand·ment (kə mănd′mənt) □*noun, plural* **commandments**

commence *verb* To begin; start: *The teacher arrived and the lesson commenced.* —See Synonyms at **begin.**
com·mence (kə mĕns′) □*verb* **commenced, commencing, commences**

commencement *noun* A graduation ceremony on the day in which students receive their diplomas from a school.
com·mence·ment (kə mĕns′mənt) □*noun, plural* **commencements**

comment *noun* A note or remark that gives an opinion or explains something: *I wanted to know her comments on the movie.*
□*verb* To make a comment: *He commented that my spelling had improved.*

com·ment (kom′ent′) ☐*noun, plural* **comments** ☐*verb* **commented, commenting, comments**

commerce *noun* The buying and selling of goods; trade.
com·merce (kom′ərs) ☐*noun*

commercial *adjective* Having to do with business: *The book was a commercial success and made lots of money.*
☐*noun* An advertisement on television or radio.
com·mer·cial (kə mûr′shəl) ☐*adjective*
☐*noun, plural* **commercials**

commission *noun* **1.** A group of people chosen to study, decide, or do something: *The president named a commission to study ways to reduce air pollution.* **2.** The act of doing something: *the commission of a crime.* **3.** Money paid for work done: *His commission was twenty cents for every box of cookies he sold.* **4.** The rank of a military officer.
☐*verb* **1.** To give someone a certain position or task: *commission an artist to paint a portrait.* **2.** To appoint someone to the rank of an officer in the military.
com·mis·sion (kə mish′ən) ☐*noun, plural* **commissions** ☐*verb* **commissioned, commissioning, commissions**

commissioner *noun* Someone who is in charge of a department of the government.
com·mis·sion·er (kə mish′ə nər) ☐*noun, plural* **commissioners**

commit *verb* **1.** To do or perform: *commit a crime.* **2.** To pledge: *She committed herself to working for a better world.*
com·mit (kə mit′) ☐*verb* **committed, committing, commits**

commitment *noun* A pledge or promise to do something: *I made a commitment to be on time for every rehearsal.*
com·mit·ment (kə mit′mənt) ☐*noun, plural* **commitments**

committee *noun* A group of people chosen to do a particular job: *I am on the committee that is planning the school dance.*
com·mit·tee (kə mit′ē) ☐*noun, plural* **committees**

commodity *noun* Something that can be bought and sold: *wheat, corn, and other farm commodities.*
com·mod·i·ty (kə mod′i tē) ☐*noun, plural* **commodities**

common *adjective* **1.** Belonging to all: *common interests.* **2.** Happening often; usual: *Rain is common in April.* **3.** Average; ordinary:

The sparrow is a common bird.
☐*noun* An area of land that belongs to or that is used by the community as a whole.
in common Shared together: *Bicycling is one of the interests we have in common.*
com·mon (kom′ən) ☐*adjective* **commoner, commonest** ☐*noun, plural* **commons**

commonplace *adjective* Ordinary; usual: *Palm trees are commonplace in Florida.*
com·mon·place (kom′ən plās′) ☐*adjective*

common sense *noun* Good judgment that is the result of experience rather than instruction.

commonwealth *noun* A nation or state governed by the people: *The United States is a commonwealth.*
com·mon·wealth (kom′ən welth′) ☐*noun, plural* **commonwealths**

commotion *noun* A noisy and disorderly confusion: *The fight caused a commotion.*
com·mo·tion (kə mō′shən) ☐*noun, plural* **commotions**

communicate *verb* **1.** To make known; express: *A baby must learn how to communicate its needs.* **2.** To pass along or exchange thoughts, feelings, or information: *We can communicate over long distances by using the telephone.*
com·mu·ni·cate (kə myōō′ni kāt′) ☐*verb* **communicated, communicating, communicates**

communication *noun* **1.** The exchange of thoughts, feelings, or information: *Communication was hard in the noisy hall.* **2. communications** A system for the sending and receiving of messages, as by telephone or radio.
com·mu·ni·ca·tion (kə myōō′ni kā′shən) ☐*noun, plural* **communications**

communion *noun* **1.** The act of sharing feelings or thoughts. **2. Communion** A Christian religious ceremony that is celebrated in memory of the last meal of Jesus with his apostles before his death.
com·mun·ion (kə myōōn′yən) ☐*noun, plural* **communions**

a	bat	ī	bite	o͞o	tool	*th*	feather
ā	make	î	fierce	ou	out	th	bath
â	dare	o	dot	u	nut	hw	wheat
ä	father	ō	no	û	turn	zh	measure
e	net	ô	law, for	ch	church	ə	about, open
ē	be	oi	soil	ng	ring		pencil, atom
i	dip	oo	look	sh	shade		circus

communism *noun* A social system in which factories, farms, and other property are owned by everyone in common.
com·mu·nism (kom′yə niz′əm) ▢*noun*

communist *noun* Someone who believes in communism or belongs to a political party that supports communism.
com·mu·nist (kom′yə nist) ▢*noun, plural*
communists

community *noun* **1.** A group of people living in the same area: *The whole community came out to watch the fireworks on the Fourth of July.* **2.** The area in which a group of people live: *a small community by the river.*
com·mu·ni·ty (kə myōō′ni tē) ▢*noun,*
plural **communities**

commute *verb* To travel to and from work or school: *My mother commutes to her job in the city by bus.*
com·mute (kə myōōt′) ▢*verb* **commuted,**
commuting, commutes

compact[1] *adjective* **1.** Packed together tightly; dense: *a firm, compact mass of snow.* **2.** Taking up a small amount of space: *a compact kitchen.*
▢*noun* **1.** A small case for face powder. **2.** An automobile that is smaller than the standard size.
com·pact (kəm pakt′) ▢*adjective* ▢*noun*
(kom′pakt′), *plural* **compacts**

compact[2] *noun* An agreement: *We made a compact to be friends forever.*
com·pact (kom′pakt) ▢*noun, plural*
compacts

compact disk *noun* A small plastic disk on which information and computer programs can be stored. Compact disks are read using lasers.
com·pact disk (kom′pakt disk) ▢*noun,*
plural **compact disks**

companion *noun* Someone who is often with another person; friend.
com·pan·ion (kəm pan′yən) ▢*noun, plural*
companions

companionship *noun* The relationship of companions; friendship.
com·pan·ion·ship (kəm pan′yən ship′)
▢*noun, plural* **companionships**

company *noun* **1.** Visitors or guests: *We are expecting company for dinner.* **2.** Companionship. **3.** A business organization: *The company has sales offices in five cities.*
com·pa·ny (kum′pə nē) ▢*noun, plural*
companies

comparative *adjective* **1.** Based on or making a comparison: *He did a comparative study of taxes in the two countries.* **2.** Measured in relation to something else: *Next to the sun, the earth is a comparative dwarf.*
▢*noun* The form of an adjective or adverb that is used to express the idea of "more." The comparative of *old* is *older* and the comparative of *bad* is *worse.*
com·par·a·tive (kəm par′ə tiv) ▢*adjective*
▢*noun, plural* **comparatives**

compare *verb* **1.** To say that something is similar: *The poet compared the still pond to a large mirror.* **2.** To study the differences and similarities: *We compared the skeletons of cats and frogs.*
com·pare (kəm pâr′) ▢*verb* **compared,**
comparing, compares

comparison *noun* **1.** The act of comparing: *My parents made a comparison of all the different cars before deciding which one to buy.* **2.** Similarity: *There's no comparison between those two players.*
com·par·i·son (kəm pâr′i sən) ▢*noun, plural*
comparisons

compartment *noun* A separate section: *My desk has compartments for letters, bills, and stationery.*
com·part·ment (kəm pärt′ment) ▢*noun,*
plural **compartments**

compartment

compass *noun* **1.** An instrument used to show directions. A compass has a magnetic needle that always points to the north. **2.** An instrument for drawing circles or measuring distances. It is made up of two pieces joined together at the top. One piece ends in a point and the other holds a pencil.
com·pass (kum′pəs) ▢*noun, plural*
compasses

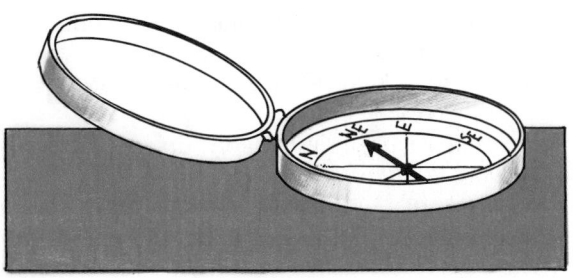

compass

compassion *noun* A feeling of understanding and sympathy for another's suffering or misfortune, mixed with a desire to help.
com·pas·sion (kəm **pash′** ən) ▢*noun*

compel *verb* To force; drive: *The rain compelled us to go indoors. Only lack of money will compel him to work.*
com·pel (kəm **pel′**) ▢*verb* **compelled, compelling, compels**

compete *verb* To take part in a contest: *Our soccer team competed for the championship.*
com·pete (kəm **pēt′**) ▢*verb* **competed, competing, competes**

competition *noun* **1.** The act of taking part in a contest. **2.** A contest: *State fairs have baking competitions.*
com·pe·ti·tion (kom′pi **tish′** ən) ▢*noun,* **plural competitions**

competitive *adjective* Of or decided by competition: *competitive sports.*
com·pet·i·tive (kəm **pet′** i tiv) ▢*adjective*

competitor *noun* A person or group that competes with another person or group; rival: *Those two drug stores are competitors.*
com·pet·i·tor (kəm **pet′** i tər) ▢*noun, plural* **competitors**

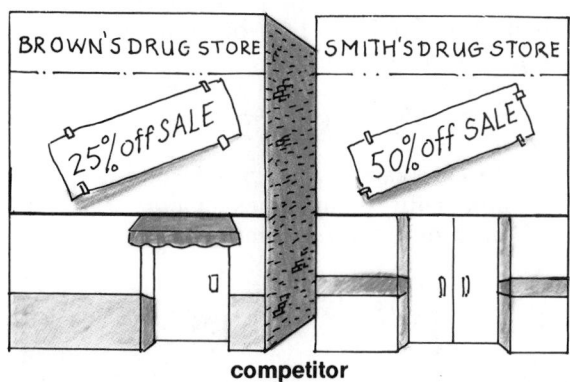

competitor

complacent *adjective* Too satisfied with oneself: *The winning runner became so compla-*

cent that he lost his next race.
com·pla·cent (kəm **plā′** sənt) ▢*adjective*

complain *verb* To say that something is not satisfactory: *He complained that the soup was cold. We complained about the noise that our neighbors made.*
com·plain (kəm **plān′**) ▢*verb* **complained, complaining, complains**

complaint *noun* **1.** A statement that one is unhappy or not satisfied: *He did all his chores without a complaint.* **2.** A cause for complaining: *If the job is finished on time, you should have no complaint.* **3.** A formal accusation or protest.
com·plaint (kəm **plānt′**) ▢*noun, plural* **complaints**

complement *noun* Something that completes or makes something better: *The silk scarf was a perfect complement to her dress.* ▢*verb* To make complete or better: *That sweater complements your skirt nicely.*
com·ple·ment (kom′plə mənt) ▢*noun, plural* **complements** ▢*verb* **complemented, complementing, complements**

complete *adjective* **1.** Not lacking anything; whole: *a complete deck of cards.* **2.** Thorough; perfect: *a complete surprise.* —See Synonyms at **whole**.
▢*verb* **1.** To add what is missing: *Complete the sentence with the correct word.* **2.** To finish; end: *Can you complete the assignment before lunch?* —See Synonyms at **end**.
com·plete (kəm **plēt′**) ▢*adjective* ▢*verb* **completed, completing, completes**

completely *adverb* Totally; entirely: *Be completely honest.*
com·plete·ly (kəm **plēt′** lē) ▢*adverb*

completion *noun* **1.** The act of completing: *The completion of the job took two weeks.* **2.** The condition of being completed: *bring the project to completion.*
com·ple·tion (kəm **plē′** shən) ▢*noun, plural* **completions**

complex *adjective* **1.** Made up of many parts: *a complex machine.* **2.** Difficult to understand or do: *complex problems in arithmetic.*

a bat	ī bite	o͞o tool	*th* feather
ā make	î fierce	ou out	th bath
â dare	o dot	u nut	hw wheat
ä father	ō no	û turn	zh measure
e net	ô law, for	ch church	ə about, open
ē be	oi soil	ng ring	pencil, atom
i dip	oo look	sh shade	circus

com·plex (kəm **pleks′** *or* **kom′**pleks′)
□*adjective*

Find the answer:
2 × 3 + 10 ÷ 5 = ?

complex
An equation

complexion *noun* **1.** The natural look and color of a person's skin: *a healthy complexion.* **2.** The general appearance or nature of something: *The new star changed the complexion of the play.*
com·plex·ion (kəm **plek′**shən) □*noun, plural* **complexions**

complexity *noun* **1.** The condition of being complex: *The complexity of his instructions confused me.* **2.** Something that is complex.
com·plex·i·ty (kəm **plek′**si tē) □*noun, plural* **complexities**

complicate *verb* To make something hard to understand or do: *The foreign words complicated the message.*
com·pli·cate (**kom′**pli kāt′) □*verb* **complicated, complicating, complicates**

complicated *adjective* Not easy to understand or do: *complicated directions.*
com·pli·ca·ted (**kom′**pli kā′tid) □*adjective*

complication *noun* A difficulty or obstacle.
com·pli·ca·tion (**kom′**pli **kā′**shən) □*noun, plural* **complications**

compliment *noun* Something good said to show praise or admiration: *She received many compliments for the sweater she made.*
□*verb* To say something that shows praise or admiration: *I complimented the cook for the tasty dinner.*
com·pli·ment (**kom′**plə mənt) □*noun, plural* **compliments** □*verb* **complimented, complimenting, compliments**

complimentary *adjective* **1.** Expressing praise: *complimentary remarks.* **2.** Given free: *complimentary tickets to the circus.*
com·pli·men·ta·ry (kom′plə **men′**tə rē *or* kom′plə **men′**trē) □*adjective*

compose *verb* **1.** To make up; form: *Our class is composed of thirty pupils.* **2.** To write; create: *compose a poem.* **3.** To make calm or controlled: *He was not able to compose himself after the accident.*
com·pose (kəm **pōz′**) □*verb* **composed, composing, composes**

composer *noun* Someone who composes musical works.
com·pos·er (kəm **pō′**zər) □*noun, plural* **composers**

composite *adjective* Made up of different parts: *a composite picture.*
com·pos·ite (kəm **poz′**it) □*adjective*

composition *noun* **1.** The act of composing: *The composition of the symphony took many years.* **2.** A musical work. **3.** A short story or essay: *She wrote a composition for English class.* **4.** The parts that form something: *Do you know the composition of air?*
com·po·si·tion (kom′pə **zish′**ən) □*noun, plural* **compositions**

composure *noun* A calm manner; self-control: *Anger made her lose her composure.*
com·po·sure (kəm **pō′**zhər) □*noun*

compound *noun* **1.** A word made by combining two or more words or word parts: *The word "fireman" is an example of a compound.* **2.** A substance formed by the chemical combination of two or more elements: *Water is a compound of hydrogen and oxygen.*
□*adjective* Made up of two or more things: *"Homework" is a compound word.*
com·pound (**kom′**pound′) □*noun, plural* **compounds** □*adjective* (**kom′**pound′)

comprehend *verb* To understand: *Do you comprehend the reasons for his decision?*
com·pre·hend (kom′pri **hend′**) □*verb* **comprehended, comprehending, comprehends**

comprehension *noun* The act or power of understanding.
com·pre·hen·sion (kom′pri **hen′**shən) □*noun, plural* **comprehensions**

compress *verb* **1.** To press together. **2.** To make smaller in size by or as if by pressing together or squeezing.
□*noun* A soft pad that is put against a wound or injury: *She put a cold compress on his sore leg.*
com·press (kəm **pres′**) □*verb* **compressed, compressing, compresses** □*noun* (**kom′**pres′),□*plural* **compresses**

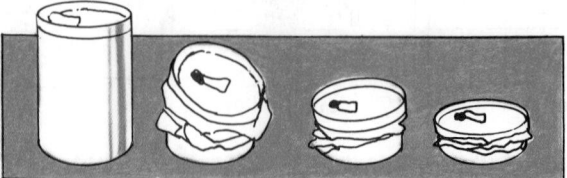

compress

comprise *verb* To be composed of; include: *The United States comprises fifty states.*
com·prise (kəm **prīz′**) □*verb* **comprised, comprising, comprises**

compromise *noun* A settlement of a disagreement in which each side gives up some of its demands.
□*verb* To reach an agreement by having each side give up certain demands.
com·pro·mise (kom′prə mīz′) □*noun, plural* **compromises** □*verb* **compromised, compromising, compromises**

compute *verb* To work out by mathematics; calculate: *We computed how long it would take to walk across the country.*
com·pute (kəm **pyo͞ot′**) □*verb* **computed, computing, computes**

computer *noun* An electronic machine that can solve complicated problems quickly, store information, and control other machinery.
com·put·er (kəm **pyo͞o′**tər) □*noun, plural* **computers**

comrade *noun* A companion who shares one's activities.
comrade (kom′rad′) □*noun, plural* **comrades**

concave *adjective* Curved inward like the inside of a bowl.
con·cave (kon **kāv′** *or* kon′kāv′) □*adjective*

concave

conceal *verb* To keep from being seen or known; hide: *He concealed the letter in a book. I tried to conceal my fear under a smile.* —See Synonyms at **hide.**
con·ceal (kən **sēl′**) □*verb* **concealed, concealing, conceals**

concede *verb* To admit that something is true: *He conceded that he was wrong.* —See Synonyms at **admit.**
con·cede (kən **sēd′**) □*verb* **conceded, conceding, concedes**

conceited *adjective* Too proud of oneself or one's abilities: *The conceited boy expected*

everyone to admire him.
con·ceit·ed (kən **sē′**tid) □*adjective*

concentrate *verb* **1.** To keep one's attention on something: *It was hard to concentrate because of the noise.* **2.** To gather together in one place: *The guests at the party were concentrated at the refreshment table.* **3.** To make thicker or stronger: *Fruit juice is concentrated and sold in cans.*
con·cen·trate (kon′sən trāt′) □*verb* **concentrated, concentrating, concentrates**

concentration *noun* Close attention: *Concentration is important when you are reading.*
con·cen·tra·tion (kon′sən **trā′**shən) □*noun*

concept *noun* A general idea: *the basic concepts of time and space.*
con·cept (kon′sept′) □*noun, plural* **concepts**

conception *noun* A mental picture; idea: *Do you have any conception of what it would be like to travel in a submarine?*
con·cep·tion (kən **sep′**shən) □*noun, plural* **conceptions**

concern *verb* **1.** To have to do with: *This is my business and it doesn't concern you.* **2.** To worry: *She was concerned that she would be late for school.*
□*noun* **1.** Something that belongs to or has to do with one: *Her concern was to get her homework finished on time.* **2.** Serious care or interest: *The sick man was grateful for his friend's concern.* **3.** A business; firm.
con·cern (kən **sûrn′**) □*verb* **concerned, concerning, concerns** □*noun, plural* **concerns**

concerning *preposition* About; regarding: *I asked a question concerning the exam.*
con·cern·ing (kən **sûr′**ning) □*preposition*

concert *noun* A performance of music: *He is going to give a concert next week.*
con·cert (kon′sərt) □*noun, plural* **concerts**

concerto *noun* A piece of music that is written for one or more instruments accompanied by an orchestra.
con·cer·to (kən **cher′**tō) □*noun, plural* **concertos**

a bat	ī bite	o͞o tool	*th* feather
ā make	i fierce	ou out	th bath
â dare	o dot	u nut	hw wheat
ä father	ō no	û turn	zh measure
e net	ô law, for	ch church	ə about, open
ē be	oi soil	ng ring	pencil, atom
i dip	oo look	sh shade	circus

conch *noun* A tropical sea animal with a large spiral shell.
conch (kongk *or* konch) □*noun, plural* **conchs** *or* **conches**

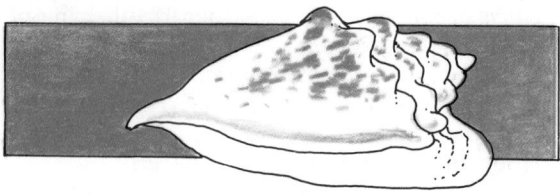

conch

concise *adjective* Expressing much in a few words; brief and clear: *She gave us concise instructions.*
con·cise (kən **sīs'**) □*adjective*

conclude *verb* **1.** To bring or come to an end: *The teacher concluded the lesson and dismissed the class.* **2.** To think over and decide: *After hearing my excuse, she concluded that I was telling the truth.* —See Synonyms at **end.**
con·clude (kən **klood'**) □*verb* **concluded, concluding, concludes**

conclusion *noun* **1.** The end of something: *the conclusion of a book.* **2.** A decision made after careful thought: *I can't reach a conclusion until I know all the facts.*
con·clu·sion (kən **kloo'**zhən) □*noun, plural* **conclusions**

concrete *noun* A building material made of cement, pebbles, sand, and water. Concrete becomes hard when it dries. Buildings and sidewalks can be made from concrete.
con·crete (kon'krēt' *or* kon **krēt'**) □*noun*

concussion *noun* **1.** A violent shaking. **2.** An injury, especially to the brain, caused by a hard blow.
con·cus·sion (kən **kush'** ən) □*noun, plural* **concussions**

condemn *verb* **1.** To be strongly against: *My parents condemn wasting food.* **2.** To give a punishment to a person judged to be guilty: *The judge condemned the thief to four years in prison.* **3.** To declare no longer fit for use: *The city condemned the old building.*
con·demn (kən **dem'**) □*verb* **condemned, condemning, condemns**

condensation *noun* **1.** The process of changing from a gas to a liquid or a solid. **2.** A shortened form of something: *a condensation of a novel.*
con·den·sa·tion (kon'den **sā'** shən) □*noun, plural* **condensations**

condense *verb* **1.** To change from a gas to a liquid or solid: *Steam condenses to water when cooled.* **2.** To make thicker or more dense: *Milk is condensed by boiling away most of its water.* **3.** To shorten: *He condensed the book into a newspaper article.*
con·dense (kən **dens'**) □*verb* **condensed, condensing, condenses**

condition *noun* **1.** The way something or someone is: *a bicycle in good condition; a sick person in poor condition.* **2.** Something necessary; requirement: *Being a good swimmer is one of the conditions for being a lifeguard.* **3.** Often **conditions** Circumstances: *tried to improve working conditions at the factory.*
□*verb* **1.** To put into good condition: *condition oneself for a race.* **2.** To adapt; accustom: *Living in the city has conditioned us to sleep through all kinds of noise.*
con·di·tion (kən **dish'** ən) □*noun, plural* **conditions** □*verb* **conditioned, conditioning, conditions**

condor *noun* A large bird of the mountains of California and South America.
con·dor (kon'dôr') □*noun, plural* **condors**

condor

conduct *verb* **1.** To lead; guide: *She conducted the visitors on a tour of the city.* **2.** To manage: *They conduct a class for beginners.* **3.** To act as a path for; transmit: *Wire conducts electricity well.* **4. conduct oneself** To behave; act.
□*noun* The way a person acts; behavior.
con·duct (kən **dukt'**) □*verb* **conducted, conducting, conducts** □*noun* (kon'dukt')

conductor *noun* **1.** Someone who conducts: *Who is the conductor of the school orchestra?* **2.** Someone who collects fares on a bus or train. **3.** Something that provides an easy path for the flow of heat, electricity, or other forms of energy.
con·duc·tor (kən **duk'**tər) □*noun, plural* **conductors**

cone *noun* **1.** A solid object that has a circular, flat base and is pointed at the other end. **2.** Something shaped like a cone: *an ice-cream cone.* **3.** A fruit in the form of a cluster of overlapping scales that grows on a pine or other evergreen tree. A cone contains the seeds of the tree.
cone (kōn) □*noun, plural* **cones**

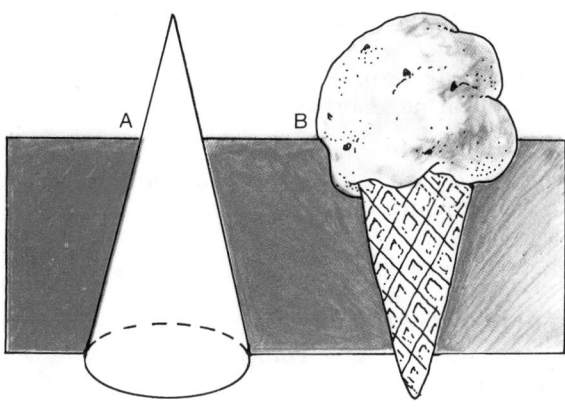

cone
(A) a diagram, *(B)* an ice-cream cone

confederacy *noun* **1.** A group of people or countries joined together for a common purpose: *a confederacy of tribes of Native Americans.* **2. Confederacy** The eleven southern states that left the United States in 1860 and 1861.
con·fed·er·a·cy (kən fed′ər ə sē) □*noun, plural* **confederacies**

confederate *adjective* **1.** Belonging to a confederacy. **2. Confederate** Of the Confederacy: *the Confederate flag.*
□*noun* **1.** Someone who helps another keep a secret or commit a crime. **2.** A member of a confederacy. **3. Confederate** Someone who supported the Confederacy.
con·fed·er·ate (kən fed′ər it) □*adjective*
□*noun, plural* **confederates**

confederation *noun* A confederacy.
con·fed·er·a·tion (kən fed′ə rā′shən) □*noun, plural* **confederations**

confer *verb* **1.** To take part in a conference; discuss together: *The teachers conferred about their student.* **2.** To give; award: *They conferred a medal on the winner of the competition.*
con·fer (kən fûr′) □*verb* **conferred, conferring, confers**

conference *noun* A meeting to discuss something: *a business conference.*

con·fer·ence (kon′fər əns) □*noun, plural* **conferences**

confess *verb* **1.** To say that one has committed a crime or done something bad: *confess to a crime.* **2.** To say that something is true: *I must confess I don't want to go to that party.* **3.** To tell one's sins to God or to a priest. —See Synonyms at **admit.**
con·fess (kən fes′) □*verb* **confessed, confessing, confesses**

confession *noun* An act of confessing: *His confession will help catch the other criminals who took part in the robbery.*
con·fes·sion (kən fesh′ən) □*noun, plural* **confessions**

confetti *noun* Small pieces of colored paper that are made to be thrown at celebrations: *We threw confetti at the bride and groom.*
con·fet·ti (kən fet′ē) □*noun*

confetti

confide *verb* To tell or share a secret with someone: *I always confide in my best friend. She confided her fears to her mother.*
con·fide (kən fīd′) □*verb* **confided, confiding, confides**

confidence *noun* **1.** A feeling of faith in oneself: *She has confidence in her ability to solve the problem.* **2.** Trust or faith: *The candidate won the voters' confidence.* **3.** Faith or trust that someone will keep a secret: *She told me the winner's name in confidence.*

a	bat	ī	bite	ōō	tool	*th*	feather
ā	make	î	fierce	ou	out	th	bath
â	dare	o	dot	u	nut	hw	wheat
ä	father	ō	no	û	turn	zh	measure
e	net	ô	law, for	ch	church	ə	about, open
ē	be	oi	soil	ng	ring		pencil, atom
i	dip	oo	look	sh	shade		circus

con·fi·dence (kon′fi dəns) □*noun, plural* **confidences**

SYNONYMS: **confidence, faith, trust**

These nouns mean a complete belief in the trustworthiness of another: *She said she would help me, and I have confidence in her. You shouldn't put your faith in him because he's unreliable. I asked my mother's advice because I have trust in her judgment.*

---

confident *adjective* **1.** Having confidence; feeling sure: *I am confident that he will pass the test.* **2.** Showing confidence or assurance: *He had a confident smile on his face.*
con·fi·dent (kon′fi dənt) □*adjective*

confidential *adjective* Secret; private: *I received the information in a confidential letter that arrived last week.*
con·fi·den·tial (kon′fi den′shəl) □*adjective*

confine *verb* To keep from moving freely; hold in: *He was confined to the house for a week. Several people were confined to jail after the riot.*
con·fine (kən fīn′) □*verb* **confined, confining, confines**

confine

confirm *verb* **1.** To show or prove to be true: *The governor confirmed the report that he would run for President.* **2.** To consent to: *The Senate confirmed her appointment to the court.* **3.** To admit as a full member of a church or synagogue: *How old was your brother when he was confirmed?*
con·firm (kən fûrm′) □*verb* **confirmed, confirming, confirms**

confirmation *noun* **1.** The act of confirming. **2.** A ceremony in which a person is made a full member of a church or synagogue. **3.** Something that confirms: *He asked for a confirmation of his plane reservation.*
con·fir·ma·tion (kon′fər mā′shən) □*noun, plural* **confirmations**

confiscate *verb* To take something away by authority: *The government confiscated the stolen documents.*
con·fis·cate (kon′fi skāt′) □*verb* **confiscated, confiscating, confiscates**

conflict *noun* **1.** Long fighting; warfare: *armed conflict between the two countries.* **2.** A disagreement: *The two reports on the accident are in conflict.*
□*verb* To be different; clash: *What he did conflicts with what he said.*
con·flict (kon′flikt′) □*noun, plural* **conflicts**
□*verb* (kən flikt′) **conflicted, conflicting, conflicts**

conform *verb* To follow a rule or standard: *If you don't conform to the rules, you will receive a penalty.*
con·form (kən fôrm′) □*verb* **conformed, conforming, conforms**

conformity *noun* **1.** Agreement as in nature or form: *You should always act in conformity with your beliefs.* **2.** Action that is in agreement with an authority, rule, or standard.
con·form·i·ty (kən fôr′mi tē) □*noun*

confront *verb* **1.** To come face to face with, especially in opposition: *He confronted the man who had lied to him.* **2.** To meet or cause to meet: *A serious problem confronts us.*
con·front (kən frunt′) □*verb* **confronted, confronting, confronts**

confuse *verb* **1.** To mix up: *The two signs have confused me so that I don't know which road to follow.* **2.** To mistake for someone or something else: *It is easy to confuse one twin with another.*
con·fuse (kən fyōōz′) □*verb* **confused, confusing, confuses**

SYNONYMS: **confuse, bewilder, puzzle**

These verbs mean to cause to be unsure in the mind: *The directions to her house were so long they confused me. The sudden change in plans bewildered many of the students. Tell me if the instructions for assembling the toy puzzle you.*

confuse

confusion *noun* **1.** An act of confusing: *You can avoid confusion by spelling correctly.* **2.** The condition of being confused: *In my confusion I took the wrong road.*
con·fu·sion (kən **fyoo**′ zhən) □*noun, plural* **confusions**

congratulate *verb* To praise someone for something the person has done or for a pleasant or fortunate event: *We congratulated her for her brilliant performance.*
con·grat·u·late (kən **grach**′ə lāt′) □*verb* **congratulated, congratulating, congratulates**

congratulations *plural noun* An expression used to praise or congratulate: *We shouted our congratulations to the runners as they crossed the finish line.*
con·grat·u·la·tion (kən grach′ə **lā**′ shən) □*plural noun* **congratulations**

congregate *verb* To gather together; assemble: *The people congregated to watch the parade.*
con·gre·gate (**kong**′ gri gāt′) □*verb* **congregated, congregating, congregates**

congregation *noun* A gathering of people, as a group assembled for religious worship.
con·gre·ga·tion (kong′grə **gā**′ shən) □*noun, plural* **congregations**

congress *noun* **1.** A group of people who make laws in a republic. **2. Congress** The United States Senate and House of Representatives.
con·gress (**kong**′ gris) □*noun, plural* **congresses**

congressman *noun* A member of the United States Congress, especially of the House of Representatives.
con·gress·man (**kong**′ gris mən) □*noun, plural* **congressmen**

congresswoman *noun* A woman who is a member of the United States Congress.
con·gress·wom·an (**kong**′ gris woom′ən) □*noun, plural* **congresswomen**

conjunction *noun* **1.** A word used to connect words or groups of words in a sentence. *If, or, but,* and *and* are conjunctions. **2.** A combination or association: *The local police worked in conjunction with the state police.*
con·junc·tion (kən **jungk**′ shən) □*noun, plural* **conjunctions**

connect *verb* **1.** To join or fasten together: *They connected the gas pipe to our house.* **2.** To plug into an electrical circuit: *Please connect the radio.* —See Synonyms at **attach** and **join.**
con·nect (kə **nekt**′) □*verb* **connected, connecting, connects**

connect

connection *noun* **1.** The act of connecting: *This tool makes connection of the antenna easy.* **2.** A relationship: *the connection between the moon and the tides.* **3.** Something that connects: *We had a bad telephone connection.*
con·nec·tion (kə **nek**′ shən) □*noun, plural* **connections**

a bat	ī bite	oo tool	th feather
ā make	î fierce	ou out	th bath
â dare	o dot	u nut	hw wheat
ä father	ō no	û turn	zh measure
e net	ô law, for	ch church	ə about, open
ē be	oi soil	ng ring	pencil, atom
i dip	oo look	sh shade	circus

conquer *verb* To defeat or overcome: *Our soldiers conquered the enemy army. He tried to conquer his fear.*
con·quer (**kong′**kər) □*verb* **conquered, conquering, conquers**

conqueror *noun* Someone who conquers.
con·quer·or (**kong′**kər ər) □*noun, plural* **conquerors**

conquest *noun* **1.** The act of conquering: *Our conquest of certain diseases has been successful.* **2.** Something conquered: *Spain made many conquests in the Americas.* —See Synonyms at **victory.**
con·quest (**kon′**kwest′ *or* **kong′**kwest′) □*noun, plural* **conquests**

conscience *noun* An inner feeling that tells a person right from wrong.
con·science (**kong′**shəns) □*noun, plural* **consciences**

conscientious *adjective* Showing or done with thought and care: *a conscientious worker who is never late.*
con·sci·en·tious (kon′shē **en′**shəs) □*adjective*

conscious *adjective* **1.** Able to see, feel, hear, and know what is happening: *She is badly hurt but still conscious.* **2.** Capable of seeing or noticing; aware: *He was conscious of his mistakes.* **3.** Done with awareness; intentional: *Will you please make a conscious effort to write clearly.*
con·scious (**kon′**shəs) □*adjective*

consecutive *adjective* Following in order without a break or interruption: *four consecutive rainy days.*
con·sec·u·tive (kən **sek′**yə tiv) □*adjective*

consent *verb* To give permission; agree: *She consented to let him go on the field trip.* □*noun* Permission; agreement: *The king gave his consent to his daughter's marriage.*
con·sent (kən **sent′**) □*verb* **consented, consenting, consents** □*noun*

consequence *noun* **1.** Something that happens as a result of another action or condition; effect: *What were the consequences of your decision?* **2.** Importance: *That is a matter of no consequence to me.*
con·se·quence (**kon′**si kwens′) □*noun, plural* **consequences**

consequently *adverb* As a result; therefore: *I took my time and, consequently, I was late.*
con·se·quent·ly (**kon′**si kwent′lē) □*adverb*

conservation *noun* The careful use and protection of natural elements and resources: *a*

need for the conservation of oil.
con·ser·va·tion (kon′sər **vā′**shən) □*noun*

conservative *adjective* Tending to be against change; favoring traditional values. □*noun* Someone who is conservative.
con·serv·a·tive (kən **sûr′**və tiv) □*adjective* □*noun, plural* **conservatives**

conserve *verb* To use carefully, without waste: *Try to conserve your energy on a very hot day.*
con·serve (kən **sûrv′**) □*verb* **conserved, conserving, conserves**

consider *verb* **1.** To think over: *I'm considering your offer.* **2.** To regard as; believe to be: *I consider him an excellent pianist.*
con·sid·er (kən **sid′**ər) □*verb* **considered, considering, considers**

considerate *adjective* Thoughtful of others: *a considerate and polite hostess.*
con·sid·er·ate (kən **sid′**ər it) □*adjective*

consideration *noun* **1.** Careful thought: *Let's give the new idea consideration.* **2.** Thoughtful concern for other people: *He shows no consideration for his neighbor's feelings.*
con·sid·er·a·tion (kən sid′ə **rā′**shən) □*noun*

considering *preposition* In view of: *Considering their ages, they did a good job of cleaning the garage.*
con·sid·er·ing (kən **sid′**ər ing) □*preposition*

consist *verb* To be made up: *A year consists of twelve months.*
con·sist (kən **sist′**) □*verb* **consisted, consisting, consists**

consistency *noun* **1.** The degree of how stiff, thick, or firm something is: *He mixed clay and water to the consistency of thick cream.* **2.** The ability to stay with the same ideas or actions: *His behavior has no consistency; first he does one thing and then the opposite.*
con·sis·ten·cy (kən **sis′**tən sē) □*noun, plural* **consistencies**

consistent *adjective* **1.** Staying always with the same actions or ideas: *Consistent habits for studying make a good student.* **2.** In agreement: *What she says now is not consistent with what she said before.*
con·sist·ent (kən **sis′**tənt) □*adjective*

consolation *noun* **1.** Comfort during a time of sorrow or disappointment. **2.** Something that gives consolation: *The doll seemed to be the little girl's only consolation.*
con·so·la·tion (kon′sə **lā′**shən) □*noun*

console¹ *verb* To comfort during a time of disappointment or sorrow: *We tried to console her when she lost her puppy.*
con·sole (kən **sōl′**) □*verb* **consoled, consoling, consoles**

console² *noun* A cabinet that contains a radio, record player, or a television set and is designed to stand on the floor.
con·sole (**kon′** sōl′) □*noun, plural* **consoles**

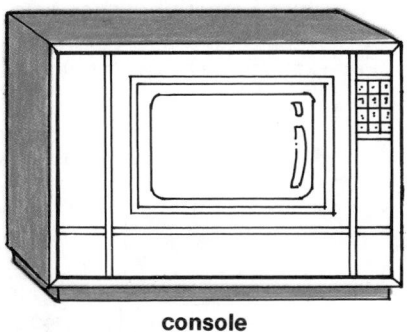
console

consonant *noun* A letter of the alphabet that is not a vowel. For example, the letters *b, c, d, f,* and *g* are consonants.
con·so·nant (**kon′** sə nənt) □*noun, plural* **consonants**

conspicuous *adjective* Attracting attention; easy to notice: *He was wearing a gaudy, conspicuous tie.*
con·spic·u·ous (kən **spik′** yōo əs) □*adjective*

conspicuous

conspiracy *noun* **1.** The act of planning in secret with others to do something that is against the law. **2.** An agreement among those who conspire.
con·spir·a·cy (kən **spîr′** ə sē) □*noun, plural* **conspiracies**

conspire *verb* To plan together secretly with others to do something wrong or against the law: *The outlaws conspired to rob the bank.*
con·spire (kən **spīr′**) □*verb* **conspired, conspiring, conspires**

constable *noun* A member of a police force in a town or village.
con·sta·ble (**kon′** stə bəl) □*noun, plural* **constables**

constant *adjective* **1.** Staying the same; not changing: *a constant speed of 40 miles an hour.* **2.** Without interruption; continuous: *a patient needing constant care.*
con·stant (**kon′** stənt) □*adjective*

constellation *noun* A group of stars that is thought to look like an animal, a person, or an object.
con·stel·la·tion (kon′stə **lā′** shən) □*noun, plural* **constellations**

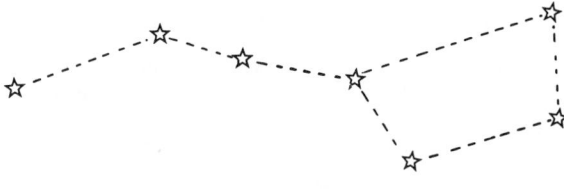
constellation
The Big Dipper

constitute *verb* To make up: *Twelve months constitute a year.*
con·sti·tute (**kon′** sti tōot′ *or* **kon′** sti tyōot′) □*verb* **constituted, constituting, constitutes**

constitution *noun* **1.** A set of laws or a plan under which a government or social group is organized. **2. the Constitution** The written constitution of the United States. **3.** The make-up or nature of someone or something: *a boy with a strong constitution.*
con·sti·tu·tion (kon′sti tōo′ shən *or* kon′sti tyōo′ shən) □*noun, plural* **constitutions**

constitutional *adjective* Of or according to a constitution: *a constitutional right; a constitutional government.*
con·sti·tu·tion·al (kon′sti tōo′ shə nəl *or* kon′sti tyōo′ shə nəl) □*adjective*

a	bat	i	bite	ōo	tool	*th*	feather
ā	make	î	fierce	ou	out	th	bath
â	dare	o	dot	u	nut	hw	wheat
ä	father	ō	no	û	turn	zh	measure
e	net	ô	law, for	ch	church	ə	about, open
ē	be	oi	soil	ng	ring		pencil, atom
i	dip	oo	look	sh	shade		circus

constrict   *verb* To make or become smaller or narrower: *When his throat muscles constricted, he choked.*
con·strict (kən **strikt′**) □*verb* **constricted, constricting, constricts**

construct   *verb* To build or put together: *The company is constructing four new houses.*
—See Synonyms at **build** and **make.**
con·struct (kən **strukt′**) □*verb* **constructed, constructing, constructs**

construction   *noun* **1.** The act of constructing: *A new building is under construction.* **2.** Something that is put together; a structure: *That skyscraper is a construction of steel and glass.*
con·struc·tion (kən **struk′**shən) □*noun, plural* **constructions**

constructive   *adjective* Serving a useful purpose; helpful: *constructive suggestions to improve our work.*
con·struc·tive (kən **struk′**tiv) □*adjective*

consult   *verb* To go to for information or advice: *consult a doctor; consult a dictionary to check a spelling.*
con·sult (kən **sult′**) □*verb* **consulted, consulting, consults**

consume   *verb* **1.** To eat or drink. **2.** To use up: *Big cars consume a lot of fuel.* **3.** To destroy by burning: *Flames consumed the old house.*
con·sume (kən **so͞om′**) □*verb* **consumed, consuming, consumes**

consumer   *noun* Someone who buys and uses goods and services.
con·sum·er (kən **so͞o′**mər) □*noun, plural* **consumers**

consumption   *noun* The act of consuming: *Consumption of the right kind of food will help to keep you healthy.*
con·sump·tion (kən **sump′**shən) □*noun*

contact   *noun* **1.** The act of touching: *This glue should not come in contact with your skin.* **2.** The condition or fact of being in touch: *The two ships kept radio contact.*
□*verb* **1.** To come into contact with; touch: *We felt our boat contact the sandy beach.* **2.** To get in touch with; communicate with: *He contacted me by telephone.*
con·tact (**kon′**takt′) □*noun, plural* **contacts**
□*verb* **contacted, contacting, contacts**

contact lens   *noun* A small, thin plastic lens worn directly on the eye in order to correct poor vision.

contagious   *adjective* Easily spread by contact: *a contagious disease.*
con·ta·gious (kən **tā′** jəs) □*adjective*

contain   *verb* **1.** To have within itself; hold: *The box contains sugar.* **2.** To be made up of: *A gallon contains four quarts.* **3.** To hold back; restrain: *Please try to contain your enthusiasm.*
con·tain (kən **tān′**) □*verb* **contained, containing, contains**

container   *noun* Something, such as a box or jar, used to hold something else.
con·tain·er (kən **tā′**nər) □*noun, plural* **containers**

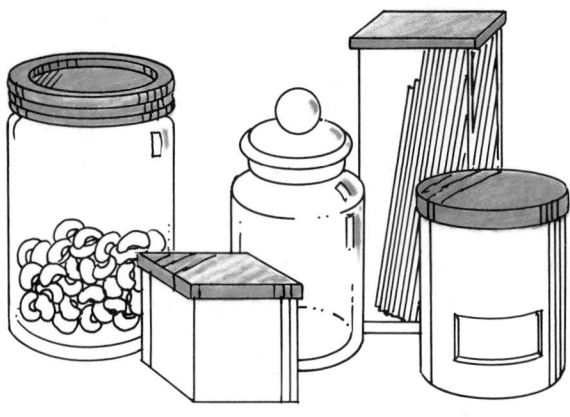

container
Several types of containers

contaminate   *verb* To make impure by mixing; pollute: *Many of our rivers have been contaminated by garbage.*
con·tam·in·ate (kən **tam′**ə nāt′) □*verb* **contaminated, contaminating, contaminates**

contaminate

contemporary   *adjective* Living or happening in the same period of time: *The American Revolution and the French Revolution were* *contemporary events.*

□*noun* Someone living at the same time as another: *Benjamin Franklin and George Washington were contemporaries.*
con·tem·po·rar·y (kən **tem′**pə rer′ē)
□*adjective* □*noun, plural* **contemporaries**

contempt *noun* A feeling that someone or something is of little value or worthless; scorn: *He has contempt for anyone who cheats.*
con·tempt (kən **tempt′**) □*noun*

contend *verb* 1. To fight or struggle: *We had to contend with rain and fog on our hiking trip.* 2. To compete: *The runners in this race are contending for a gold medal.* 3. To argue or claim: *She contends that she is the best speller in the class.*
con·tend (kən **tend′**) □*verb* **contended, contending, contends**

content¹ *noun* 1. Often **contents** Something that is inside a container: *I emptied the contents of my purse onto the table.* 2. Often **contents** The information that is contained in a book, letter, film, or other kind of communication.
con·tent (**kon′**tent′) □*noun, plural* **contents**

content² *adjective* Pleased with what one has or is; satisfied: *She is content with that answer to her question.*
□*noun* A feeling of happiness or satisfaction: *He sat in complete content by the fire.*
□*verb* To make content; satisfy: *The good dinner contented him.*
con·tent (kən **tent′**) □*adjective* □*noun*
□*verb* **contented, contenting, contents**

contented *adjective* Satisfied with things as they are; content: *a contented kitten sleeping in the sun; a contented person who enjoys her work.*
con·tent·ed (kən **ten′**tid) □*adjective*

contest *noun* 1. A race, game, or other competition: *a beauty contest.* 2. A struggle or fight: *the contest between France and Spain for territory in the New World.*
con·test (**kon′**test′) □*noun, plural* **contests**

contestant *noun* Someone who takes part in a contest; competitor.
con·test·ant (kən **tes′**tənt) □*noun, plural* **contestants**

continent *noun* One of the seven main land masses of the earth. The continents are Africa, Antarctica, Asia, Australia, Europe, North America, and South America.
con·ti·nent (**kon′**tə nənt) □*noun, plural* **continents**

continual *adjective* Not interrupted or broken; steady: *the continual noise of the traffic in a big city; the dog's continual barking.*
con·tin·u·al (kən **tin′**yoo əl) □*adjective*

continue *verb* 1. To go on without stopping: *The rain continued for days. The scientists continued their research.* 2. To begin again after stopping: *He continued the story after dinner.*
con·tin·ue (kən **tin′**yoo) □*verb* **continued, continuing, continues**

continuous *adjective* Going on without interruption or break: *a continuous supply of fresh air in the mine.*
con·tin·u·ous (kən **tin′**yoo əs) □*adjective*

contour *noun* The shape or outline of something: *the contour of the American coast.*
con·tour (**kon′**toor′) □*noun, plural* **contours**

contour

contract *noun* An agreement between two or more persons or groups to do or not to do something.
□*verb* 1. To make or become smaller in length, width, or size: *Muscles contract in the cold.* 2. To make by means of a contract: *contract for a new house.*
con·tract (**kon′**trakt′) □*noun, plural*
contracts □*verb* (kən **trakt′** *or* **kon′**trakt′)
contracted, contracting, contracts

a	bat	ī	bite	oo	tool	th	feather
ā	make	i	fierce	ou	out	th	bath
â	dare	o	dot	u	nut	hw	wheat
ä	father	ō	no	û	turn	zh	measure
e	net	ô	law, for	ch	church	ə	about, open
ē	be	oi	soil	ng	ring		pencil, atom
i	dip	oo	look	sh	shade		circus

contraction *noun* **1.** The act of contracting: *the contraction of stomach muscles in digestion.* **2.** A shortened form of a word or pair of words. For example, *aren't* is a contraction of *are not.*
con·trac·tion (kən **trak′** shən) ▢*noun, plural* **contractions**

contradict *verb* To say the opposite of: *She contradicted what she had said earlier.*
con·tra·dict (kon′trə **dikt′**) ▢*verb* **contradicted, contradicting, contradicts**

contradiction *noun* An act of contradicting or of being contradicted: *That story is a contradiction of the story you told us the day before yesterday.*
con·tra·dic·tion (kon′trə **dik′** shən) ▢*noun, plural* **contradictions**

contralto *noun* **1.** The lowest woman's singing voice. **2.** A singer who has such a voice.
con·tral·to (kən **tral′** tō) ▢*noun, plural* **contraltos**

contrary *adjective* **1.** Completely different; opposite: *The two brothers have contrary points of view about conservation.* **2.** Stubborn and opposed to others: *He is the most contrary child in the class.*
▢*noun* Something that is opposite: *I think the contrary of his statement is true.*
con·tra·ry (kon′ trer′ē; *also* kən **trâr′** ē *for adjective sense 2*) ▢*adjective* ▢*noun, plural* **contraries**

contrast *verb* **1.** To compare in order to show differences: *The story contrasts rich people and poor people.* **2.** To show differences when a comparison is made: *Sugar contrasts with salt.*
▢*noun* A great difference: *the contrast between summer and winter.*
con·trast (kən **trast′**) ▢*verb* **contrasted, contrasting, contrasts** ▢*noun* (**kon′** trast′), *plural* **contrasts**

contribute *verb* To give or supply; donate: *He contributed money to several charities.*
con·trib·ute (kən **trib′** yoŏt) ▢*verb* **contributed, contributing, contributes**

contribution *noun* **1.** The act of contributing: *the contribution of clothes for the needy.* **2.** Something contributed: *He gave a contribution of $50.*
con·tri·bu·tion (kon′tri byoŏ′ shən) ▢*noun, plural* **contributions**

control *verb* **1.** To have authority over; direct: *The ancient Romans controlled a large empire.* **2.** To hold in check: *He couldn't control his laughter.*
▢*noun* **1.** Authority or power: *The foreman has control over the workers.* **2.** Something that restrains; check: *She showed great control over her temper.* **3.** An instrument or device used to operate or regulate a machine.
con·trol (kən **trōl′**) ▢*verb* **controlled, controlling, controls** ▢*noun, plural* **controls**

control tower *noun* A high tower at an airport where workers observe and direct the landing and taking off of aircraft.

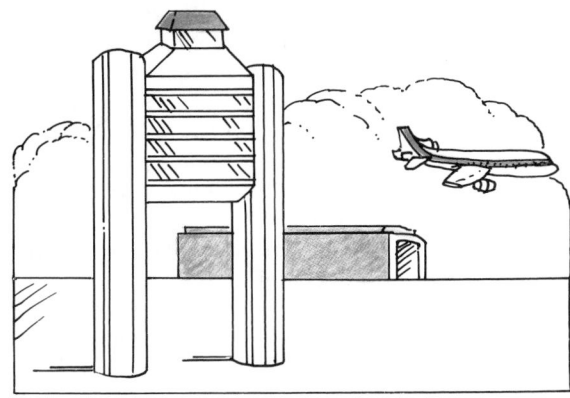
control tower

controversial *adjective* Causing or able to cause controversy: *a controversial rule.*
con·tro·ver·sial (kon′trə **vûr′** shəl) ▢*adjective*

controversy *noun* **1.** Argument; disagreement: *The location of the new park caused a lot of controversy.* **2.** Dispute; quarrel: *He was involved in a controversy with the mayor.*
con·tro·ver·sy (kon′ trə vûr′sē) ▢*noun, plural* **controversies**

convenience *noun* **1.** Comfort or ease: *the convenience of running water.* **2.** Something that gives comfort or ease: *We rely on modern conveniences such as toasters and washing machines.*
con·ven·ience (kən **vēn′** yəns) ▢*noun, plural* **conveniences**

convenient *adjective* Easy to reach or use; handy: *She put the supplies on a convenient shelf. They live in a house that is convenient to the school.*
con·ven·ient (kən **vēn′** yənt) ▢*adjective*

SYNONYMS: **convenient, handy, nearby**
These adjectives mean easy to reach: *Where is the most convenient place to put the telephone? We keep a flashlight handy in case the lights go out. I bought some eggs at a nearby grocery store.*

convenient

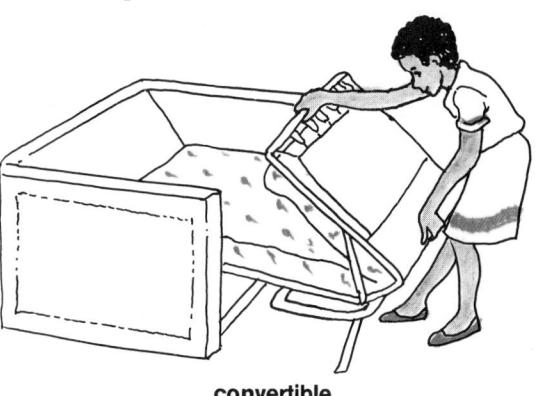

convertible

convent   *noun* A building that a group of nuns lives in.
con·vent (**kon′** vənt) □*noun, plural* **convents**

convention   *noun* **1.** A formal meeting of a group of people for a particular purpose: *a political convention.* **2.** A usual way of acting or of doing something; custom: *Shaking hands when you meet someone is a convention.*
con·ven·tion (kən **ven′** shən) □*noun, plural* **conventions**

conventional   *adjective* Following accepted practice or customs: *a conventional greeting.*
con·ven·tion·al (kən **ven′** shə nəl) □*adjective*

conversation   *noun* An informal talk in which people share ideas and feelings.
con·ver·sa·tion (kon′vər **sā′** shən) □*noun, plural* **conversations**

converse   *verb* To talk informally with another. —See Synonyms at **talk.**
con·verse (kən **vûrs′**) □*verb* **conversed, conversing, converses**

conversion   *noun* The act of changing or being changed: *the conversion of water to ice; the conversion of the attic into a bedroom.*
con·ver·sion (kən **vûr′** zhən) □*noun, plural* **conversions**

convert   *verb* **1.** To change into something else: *Many palaces have been converted into museums.* **2.** To convince a person to adopt a new religion or belief.
con·vert (kən **vûrt′**) □*verb* **converted, converting, converts**

convertible   *adjective* Able to be changed into something else: *A convertible sofa can be made into a bed.*
□*noun* An automobile with a top that can be folded back or taken off.

con·vert·i·ble (kən **vûr′** tə bəl) □*adjective*
□*noun, plural* **convertibles**

convex   *adjective* Curving outward: *The outside of a bowl is convex.*
con·vex (kon **veks′** *or* **kon′** veks) □*adjective*

convey   *verb* **1.** To take or carry from one place to another: *The Alaskan pipeline conveys oil.* **2.** To make known; communicate: *No words can convey my feelings.*
con·vey (kən **vā′**) □*verb* **conveyed, conveying, conveys**

convict   *verb* To prove that someone is guilty: *The court convicted him of robbing the bank.* □*noun* Someone who has been proven guilty of a crime and sent to jail.
con·vict (kən **vikt′**) □*verb* **convicted, convicting, convicts** □*noun* (**kon′** vikt′), *plural* **convicts**

conviction   *noun* **1.** The act of proving that someone is guilty: *The trial of the bank robber resulted in a conviction.* **2.** A strong feeling or belief about something: *It is my conviction that she is telling the truth.*
con·vic·tion (kən **vik′** shən) □*noun, plural* **convictions**

convince   *verb* To persuade someone to believe or do something: *I convinced him that I was right. He convinced me to buy a new car.*
con·vince (kən **vins′**) □*verb* **convinced, convincing, convinces**

a	bat	ī	bite	o͞o	tool	*th*	feather
ā	make	î	fierce	ou	out	th	bath
â	dare	o	dot	u	nut	hw	wheat
ä	father	ō	no	û	turn	zh	measure
e	net	ô	law, for	ch	church	ə	about, open
ē	be	oi	soil	ng	ring		pencil, atom
i	dip	o͝o	look	sh	shade		circus

cook *verb* **1.** To get food ready for eating by using heat: *You can cook vegetables by boiling or steaming.* **2.** To be cooked: *The steak will cook in a few minutes.*
□*noun* Someone who cooks.
cook (kŏok) □*verb* **cooked, cooking, cooks** □*noun, plural* **cooks**

cookie or **cooky** *noun* A small, sweet cake, usually flat.
cook·ie or **cook·y** (kŏok′ē) □*noun, plural* **cookies**

cool *adjective* **1.** Not very warm or very cold: *cool weather; cool milk.* **2.** Not excited; calm: *She stayed cool when everyone else was shouting.* **3.** Not friendly or warm: *a cool hello.* —See Synonyms at **cold.**
□*verb* To make or become less warm: *The breeze cooled us. Let the soup cool.*
□*noun* The state or quality of being cool: *the cool of the evening; the cool of the forest.*
cool (kŏol) □*adjective* **cooler, coolest** □*verb* **cooled, cooling, cools** □*noun*

coop *noun* A cage or pen for small animals: *a chicken coop.*
□*verb* To put or shut in a coop or other closed space.
coop (kŏop) □*noun, plural* **coops** □*verb* **cooped, cooping, coops**

cooperate *verb* To work or act together: *We can clean this campsite up quickly if we all cooperate.*
co·op·er·ate (kō ŏp′ə rāt′) □*verb* **cooperated, cooperating, cooperates**

cooperate

cooperation *noun* The act of working together: *The cooperation of the students got the job done quickly.*
co·op·er·a·tion (kō ŏp′ə rā′shən) □*noun*

coordinate *verb* To work or cause to work together well or efficiently: *Your brain coordinates your body's movements.*
co·or·di·nate (kō ôr′dən āt′) □*verb* **coordinated, coordinating, coordinates**

cope *verb* To struggle with or handle successfully: *She coped with the emergency alone.*
cope (kōp) □*verb* **coped, coping, copes**

copilot *noun* The second pilot or assistant pilot of an airplane.
co·pi·lot (kō′pī′lət) □*noun, plural* **copilots**

copper *noun* **1.** A reddish-brown metallic element that is a good conductor of heat and electricity. **2.** A reddish-brown color.
□*adjective* Reddish brown.
cop·per (kŏp′ər) □*noun* □*adjective*

copperhead *noun* A poisonous reddish-brown snake of the eastern United States.
cop·per·head (kŏp′ər hed′) □*noun, plural* **copperheads**

copperhead

copy *noun* **1.** Something that is made to look like something else; a reproduction or duplicate: *two copies of the letter.* **2.** One of a number of things that have been printed at the same time: *The library has two copies of that book.*
□*verb* **1.** To make a copy of: *He copied the diagram by tracing it.* **2.** To follow as a model or example; imitate: *She copies everything her big sister does.*
cop·y (kŏp′ē) □*noun, plural* **copies** □*verb* **copied, copying, copies**

coral *noun* A hard substance made up of the skeletons of tiny sea animals. Some kinds are used to make jewelry.
cor·al (kôr′əl) □*noun*

coral snake *noun* A poisonous snake of the southern United States that is marked with red, yellow, and black bands.

cord *noun* **1.** A strong string or thin rope that is made of a number of smaller strings twisted together. **2.** An electric wire that is covered with protecting material and has a plug at one or both ends. **3.** A part of the body that is like a cord: *the spinal cord.* **4.** A unit of measure for cut firewood. A cord of wood is equal to a stack that is 4 feet high, 4 feet wide, and 8 feet long, or 128 cubic feet.
cord (kôrd) ▢*noun, plural* **cords**

cordial *adjective* Cheerful and friendly; sincere: *a cordial greeting.*
cor·dial (kôr′jəl) ▢*adjective*

corduroy *noun* A heavy cotton cloth with a smooth surface of raised ridges. It is usually used for making clothes.
cor·du·roy (kôr′də roi′) ▢*noun*

core *noun* **1.** The tough center part of an apple, pear, and some other fruits. The seeds of the fruit are in the core. **2.** The central or most important part of something: *the core of the problem.*
▢*verb* To cut out the core of: *Peel and core the apples before you cook them.*
core (kôr) ▢*noun, plural* **cores** ▢*verb* **cored, coring, cores**

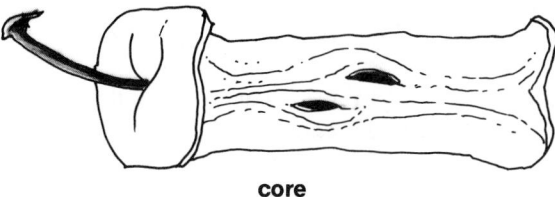

core

cork *noun* **1.** The light, soft outer bark of a kind of oak tree. It is used to make bottle stoppers, rafts, floor covering, and other things. **2.** A stopper for a bottle or jar made from cork.
▢*verb* To stop up with a cork: *cork a bottle.*
cork (kôrk) ▢*noun, plural* **corks** ▢*verb* **corked, corking, corks**

corkscrew *noun* A tool or device used to pull corks out of bottles.
cork·screw (kôrk′skrōō′) ▢*noun, plural* **corkscrews**

corn *noun* **1.** A tall plant that has large ears with many kernels. Corn is grown as food for people and animals. **2.** The ears or kernels of the corn plant.
corn (kôrn) ▢*noun*

corn bread *noun* A bread made with cornmeal.

corncob *noun* The tough center part of an ear of corn, on which the kernels grow.
corn·cob (kôrn′kob′) ▢*noun, plural* **corncobs**

cornea *noun* The transparent outer covering of the eyeball that covers the iris and pupil.
cor·ne·a (kôr′nē ə) ▢*noun, plural* **corneas**

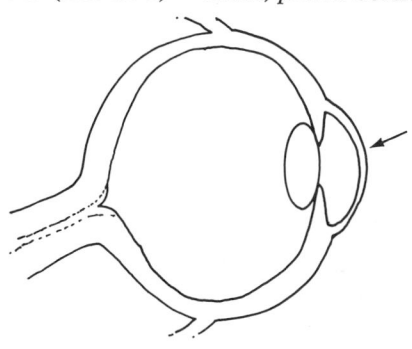

cornea

corner *noun* **1.** The place where two surfaces or lines meet: *the corner of a table; the corner of the room.* **2.** The place where two roads or streets meet: *The drugstore is at the corner of Elm Street and Main Street.*
▢*verb* To place or force into a difficult position or situation: *The cat cornered the mouse.*
cor·ner (kôr′nər) ▢*noun, plural* **corners**
▢*verb* **cornered, cornering, corners**

cornet *noun* A brass musical instrument that resembles a trumpet.
cor·net (kôr net′) ▢*noun, plural* **cornets**

cornmeal *noun* Ground dried corn kernels.
corn·meal (kôrn′mēl′) ▢*noun*

coronation *noun* The act or ceremony of crowning a king, queen, or other monarch.
cor·o·na·tion (kôr′ə nā′shən) ▢*noun, plural* **coronations**

corporal *noun* An officer in the United States Army or Marine Corps. A corporal ranks above a private and below a sergeant.
cor·po·ral (kôr′pər əl *or* kôr′prəl) ▢*noun, plural* **corporals**

corporation *noun* A business or other organization formed by a group of people and

a bat	ī bite	ōō tool	*th* feather
ā make	î fierce	ou out	th bath
â dare	o dot	u nut	hw wheat
ä father	ō no	û turn	zh measure
e net	ô law, for	ch church	ə about, open
ē be	oi soil	ng ring	pencil, atom
i dip	oo look	sh shade	circus

allowed by law to act as a single person.
cor·po·ra·tion (kôr′pə rā′shən) □*noun, plural*
corporations

corps *noun* **1.** A section of the armed forces
having a special function: *the medical corps.*
2. A group of people acting or working together: *a large corps of scientists.*
corps (kôr) □*noun, plural* **corps** (kôrz)

corpse *noun* A dead human body.
corpse (kôrps) □*noun, plural* **corpses**

corpuscle *noun* A cell of the body that can
move about freely. Red and white blood cells
are corpuscles.
cor·pus·cle (kôr′pus′əl) □*noun, plural*
corpuscles

corral *noun* A place with a fence around it
that is used for keeping cattle or horses.
□*verb* To put or drive into a corral: *Dogs often
help to corral sheep.*
cor·ral (kə ral′) □*noun, plural* **corrals**
□*verb* **corralled, corralling, corrals**

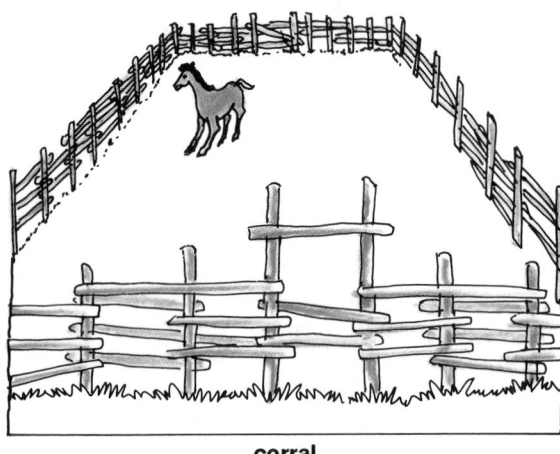
corral

correct *verb* **1.** To remove mistakes from: *I
checked my spelling and corrected the errors.*
2. To mark the errors in: *The teacher corrected
our papers.* **3.** To make something right by
changing or adjusting: *Eyeglasses correct poor
vision.*
□*adjective* **1.** Free from error; accurate: *a correct answer.* **2.** Following rules; proper: *correct behavior.*
cor·rect (kə rekt′) □*verb* **corrected,
correcting, corrects** □*adjective*

correction *noun* **1.** The act of correcting:
*Correction of the final tests took the teacher a
long time.* **2.** Something put in place of a mistake or error: *The corrections on the final tests
are in red.*

cor·rec·tion (kə rek′shən) □*noun, plural*
corrections

correspond *verb* **1.** To be in agreement;
match: *Her selfish actions do not correspond
with her unselfish words.* **2.** To be similar or
the same: *The eyelids correspond to the shutter
of a camera.* **3.** To write and send letters: *I still
correspond with the friends I made last summer.*
cor·re·spond (kôr′i spond′) □*verb*
corresponded, corresponding, corresponds

correspondence *noun* **1.** Agreement, similarity, or likeness: *There may be little correspondence between the spelling of a word and
its pronunciation.* **2.** Communication by writing and sending letters.
cor·re·spond·ence (kôr′i spon′dəns) □*noun,
plural* **correspondences**

correspondent *noun* **1.** Someone to whom
one writes regularly. **2.** Someone hired by a
newspaper or television station to report on
news in distant places.
cor·re·spond·ent (kôr′i spon′dənt) □*noun,
plural* **correspondents**

corridor *noun* A narrow hallway or passage
in a building, that often has rooms opening
onto it.
cor·ri·dor (kôr′i dər) □*noun, plural*
corridors

corrode *verb* To wear away gradually: *Rust is
corroding the old car.*
cor·rode (kə rōd′) □*verb* **corroded,
corroding, corrodes**

corrupt *adjective* Capable of being bribed;
dishonest: *a corrupt judge.*
□*verb* To make dishonest; bribe: *The smug-
gler tried to corrupt the captain of the ship.*
cor·rupt (kə rupt′) □*adjective* □*verb*
corrupted, corrupting, corrupts

corsage *noun* A small bouquet of flowers
worn by a woman, usually at the shoulder.
cor·sage (kôr säzh′) □*noun, plural* **corsages**

corset *noun* A tight undergarment worn by
women to shape the waist and hips.
cor·set (kôr′sit) □*noun, plural* **corsets**

cosmetic *noun* A preparation, such as powder or lotion, used to beautify some part of the
body.
cos·met·ic (koz met′ik) □*noun, plural*
cosmetics

cosmic *adjective* Of the universe, especially
the heavens as distinguished from the earth.
cos·mic (koz′mik) □*adjective*

cost *noun* **1.** The amount paid or charged for a purchase. **2.** Something given up as a loss or penalty: *The battle was won at the cost of many lives.*
□*verb* **1.** To have as a price: *The new car cost more than we expected.* **2.** To cause the loss of: *The strike cost him his job.*
cost (kôst) □*noun, plural* **costs** □*verb* **cost, costing, costs**

costly *adjective* Having a high price; expensive: *costly jewelry.*
cost·ly (kôst′lē) □*adjective* **costlier, costliest**

costume *noun* **1.** Clothing that is typical of a certain place, group of people, or period of history: *Kilts are part of the national costume of Scotland.* **2.** Clothing worn when playing a part or dressing up in disguise: *We had to wear costumes to the ball.*
cos·tume (kôs′ tōōm′ *or* kôs′ tyōōm′) □*noun, plural* **costumes**

costume
National costume of Scotland

cot *noun* A narrow bed, usually made of canvas stretched over a folding frame.
cot (kot) □*noun, plural* **cots**

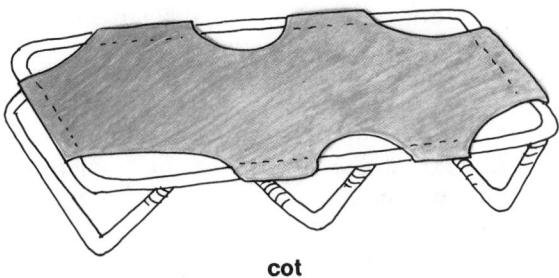
cot

cottage *noun* A small house, especially one that is used as a summer home.
cot·tage (kot′ij) □*noun, plural* **cottages**

cottage cheese *noun* A soft white cheese that has a mild flavor and is made of the curds of skim milk.

cotton *noun* **1.** A tall plant that has seeds covered with soft, fluffy white fibers. **2.** Cloth or thread made from these fibers.
cot·ton (kot′ ən) □*noun*

cotton

cotton gin *noun* A machine that separates the cotton fibers from the seeds.

cottontail *noun* An American rabbit with a short, fluffy white tail.
cot·ton·tail (kot′ ən tāl) □*noun, plural* **cottontails**

cottontail

cottonwood *noun* A tree that has seeds with white tufts that look like cotton.

a	bat	ī	bite	ōō	tool	*th*	feather
ā	make	î	fierce	ou	out	th	bath
â	dare	o	dot	u	nut	hw	wheat
ä	father	ō	no	û	turn	zh	measure
e	net	ô	law, for	ch	church	ə	about, open
ē	be	oi	soil	ng	ring		pencil, atom
i	dip	oo	look	sh	shade		circus

cot·ton·wood (kŏt′ən wŏŏd′) □*noun, plural* **cottonwoods**

couch *noun* A piece of furniture on which two or more persons can sit; sofa.
couch (kouch) □*noun, plural* **couches**

cougar *noun* A large wild cat.
cou·gar (kŏŏ′gər) □*noun, plural* **cougars**

cough *verb* To force air from the lungs in a sudden, noisy way.
□*noun* **1.** The act or sound of coughing. **2.** An illness that causes much coughing.
cough (kôf) □*verb* **coughed, coughing, coughs** □*noun, plural* **coughs**

could *verb* The past tense of **can:** *We could tell that she was unhappy.*
could (kŏŏd) □*verb*

couldn't Contraction of "could not."
couldn't (kŏŏd′nt)

council *noun* **1.** A group of persons brought together to discuss or settle a problem or question. **2.** A group of people chosen to make laws or rules: *the town council.*
coun·cil (koun′səl) □*noun, plural* **councils**

counsel *noun* **1.** Advice; guidance: *He listened to bad counsel and got into worse trouble.* **2.** A lawyer or group of lawyers: *the counsel for the defense.*
□*verb* To give advice: *We counseled him to refuse the offer.*
coun·sel (koun′səl) □*noun, plural* **counsels** □*verb* **counseled, counseling, counsels**

counselor *noun* Someone who advises or guides; adviser.
coun·sel·or (koun′sə lər *or* koun′slər) □*noun, plural* **counselors**

count[1] *verb* **1.** To find the total number of; add up: *Count the number of dishes on the table.* **2.** To list or say numbers in order: *Count up to 100.* **3.** To take account of; include: *There are ten people here, counting me.* **4.** To be important: *Hurry up because every minute counts.*
□*noun* The total number reached by counting: *The official count was 50.*
count (kount) □*verb* **counted, counting, counts** □*noun, plural* **counts**

count[2] *noun* A European nobleman.
count (kount) □*noun, plural* **counts**

countdown *noun* The act of counting backward to zero to indicate how much time is left until the beginning of an event: *The countdown for the launching of the rocket will begin at noon.*

count·down (kount′doun′) □*noun, plural* **countdowns**

counter *noun* **1.** A narrow table on which things are sold or food is served. **2.** A small disk or other object used in some games to keep score.
count·er (koun′tər) □*noun, plural* **counters**

counterclockwise *adverb* In a direction opposite to the direction in which a clock's hands move: *Turn the lid of the jar counterclockwise.*
□*adjective* Moving in a counterclockwise direction: *The dog was running in a counterclockwise circle.*
coun·ter·clock·wise (koun′tər klŏk′wīz) □*adverb* □*adjective*

counterclockwise

counterfeit *verb* To make a copy of something in order to fool or cheat people: *The two men were arrested for counterfeiting hundred-dollar bills.*
□*adjective* Made as a copy in order to fool or cheat people.
□*noun* Something that has been counterfeited: *The painting is a counterfeit.*
coun·ter·feit (koun′tər fit) □*verb* **counterfeited, counterfeiting, counterfeits** □*adjective* □*noun, plural* **counterfeits**

counterpart *noun* Someone or something that closely resembles another in characteristics or function: *The President of the United States is the counterpart of the Prime Minister of Canada.*
coun·ter·part (koun′tər pärt′) □*noun, plural* **counterparts**

countess *noun* **1.** The wife of a count. **2.** A woman with a rank equal to that of a count.

count·ess (koun′tis) ▢*noun, plural*
countesses

country *noun* **1.** All the people who live under a single independent government; nation or state: *The President spoke to the country.* **2.** The territory occupied by such a group of people. **3.** The land away from cities and large towns: *a drive in the country.* **4.** An area of land; region.
coun·try (kun′trē) ▢*noun, plural* **countries**

countryman *noun* A person from one's own country.
coun·try·man (kun′trē mən) ▢*noun, plural*
countrymen

countryside *noun* The land away from cities and towns.
coun·try·side (kun′trē sīd′) ▢*noun*

countrywoman *noun* A woman from one's own country.
countrywoman (kun′trē woom′ən) ▢*noun,*
plural **countrywomen**

county *noun* One of the divisions of a state or country.
coun·ty (koun′tē) ▢*noun, plural* **counties**

couple *noun* **1.** Two things of the same kind; pair. **2.** A man and a woman who are married, engaged, or partners in a dance.
▢*verb* To join together.
cou·ple (kup′əl) ▢*noun, plural* **couples**
▢*verb* **coupled, coupling, couples**

coupon *noun* A ticket that can be exchanged for a gift or money.
cou·pon (kōō′pon *or* kyōō′pon) ▢*noun,*
plural **coupons**

courage *noun* The ability to face danger or hardship without fear; bravery.
cour·age (kûr′ij) ▢*noun*

courageous *adjective* Having or showing courage; brave. —See Synonyms at **brave.**
cou·ra·geous (kə rā′jəs) ▢*adjective*

course *noun* **1.** Forward or onward movement; progress: *the course of history.* **2.** A direction taken: *The airplane was on a direct course to Hawaii.* **3.** A way of acting or behaving: *Our best course is to wait until it stops snowing before we leave.* **4.** A series of classes in a particular subject: *a history course.* **5.** An area used for races or other sports: *a golf course.* **6.** A dish or other part of a meal: *Chicken was the main course.*
     of course Without a doubt; certainly: *Of course I'm coming.*
course (kôrs) ▢*noun, plural* **courses**

court *noun* **1.** A courtyard. **2.** An area that is marked off for certain games: *a tennis court.* **3.** The attendants and advisers of a monarch or other ruler. **4.** A place where trials or other legal proceedings are held.
▢*verb* **1.** To try to win the favor of. **2.** To try to win the love or approval of.
court (kôrt) ▢*noun, plural* **courts** ▢*verb*
courted, courting, courts

courteous *adjective* Considerate toward others; polite.
cour·te·ous (kûr′tē əs) ▢*adjective*

courtesy *noun* **1.** Polite or thoughtful behavior: *She treated her guests with courtesy.* **2.** A polite act.
cour·te·sy (kûr′ti sē) ▢*noun, plural*
courtesies

SYNONYMS: **courteous, civil, polite**

These adjectives mean having or showing good manners: *She is always courteous to the teachers. A civil person is always considerate of the feelings of others. It is not polite to leave the table before everyone has finished dinner.*

---

courthouse *noun* A building in which trials and other legal proceedings are held.
court·house (kôrt′hous′) ▢*noun, plural*
courthouses

courtyard *noun* An open space surrounded by walls or buildings.
court·yard (kôrt′yärd) ▢*noun, plural*
courtyards

courtyard

a	bat	ī	bite	ōō	tool	*th*	feather
ā	make	î	fierce	ou	out	th	bath
â	dare	o	dot	u	nut	hw	wheat
ä	father	ō	no	û	turn	zh	measure
e	net	ô	law, for	ch	church	ə	about, open
ē	be	oi	soil	ng	ring		pencil, atom
i	dip	oo	look	sh	shade		circus

cousin *noun* A child of one's aunt or uncle.
cous·in (kuz′ən) □*noun, plural* **cousins**

cove *noun* A small sheltered bay.
cove (kōv) □*noun, plural* **coves**

cove

cover *verb* **1.** To spread over or upon: *He covered the baby with a blanket. Snow covered the yard.* **2.** To deal with; include: *The book covered the Civil War.* **3.** To travel over: *We covered 500 miles on our trip.* **4.** To guard or defend: *One soldier ran ahead and the others covered him.* **5.** To hide or conceal: *She tried to cover up what really happened.*
□*noun* **1.** Something that covers another thing: *Please put the cover on the pot.* **2.** Something that protects or hides: *a book cover.*
cov·er (kuv′ər) □*verb* **covered, covering, covers** □*noun, plural* **covers**

covered wagon *noun* A large wagon covered with canvas stretched over hoops and pulled by horses or oxen.

covering *noun* Something that covers: *We put plastic covering on the sofa.*
cov·er·ing (kuv′ər ing) □*noun, plural* **coverings**

cow *noun* **1.** The fully grown female of cattle. **2.** The female of some other large animals, such as the elephant or moose.
cow (kou) □*noun, plural* **cows**

coward *noun* Someone who lacks courage or is easily frightened.
cow·ard (kou′ərd) □*noun, plural* **cowards**

cowardice *noun* Lack of courage.
cow·ard·ice (kou′ər dis) □*noun*

cowardly *adjective* Lacking courage or showing fear.
cow·ard·ly (kou′ərd lē) □*adjective*

cowboy *noun* A man who takes care of cattle on a ranch.
cow·boy (kou′boi′) □*noun, plural* **cowboys**

cowgirl *noun* A woman who takes care of cattle on a ranch.
cow·girl (kou′gûrl′) □*noun, plural* **cowgirls**

coyote *noun* A kind of wolf that lives in the western parts of North America.
coy·o·te (kī ō′tē *or* kī′ōt′) □*noun, plural* **coyotes**

cozy *adjective* Snug and comfortable: *We felt cozy sitting by the fire.*
co·zy (kō′zē) □*adjective* **cozier, coziest**

cozy

crab *noun* An animal that lives in water and has a broad, flat body covered with a tough shell. Its front legs have large claws.
crab (krab) □*noun, plural* **crabs**

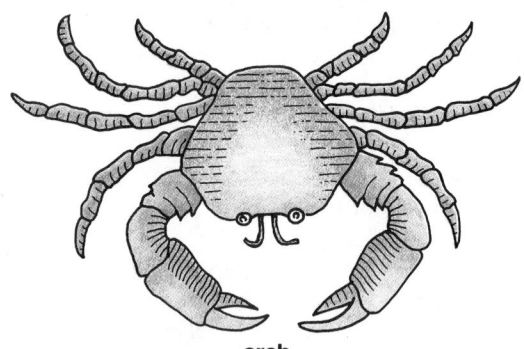

crab

crab apple *noun* A small, sour fruit that is used to make jelly.

crabby *adjective* Always complaining; irritable or grouchy.
crab·by (krab′ē) □*adjective* **crabbier, crabbiest**

crack *noun* **1.** A small break or opening: *There is a crack in the dish.* **2.** A sharp, snapping sound: *a crack of thunder.* **3.** A sharp blow: *a crack on the head.*
□*verb* **1.** To break or split suddenly and with

a sharp sound: *We cracked the walnuts.* **2.** To break without separating; split: *I cracked the window when I banged into it.* **3.** To make a sharp, snapping sound: *Thunder cracked overhead.* **4.** To strike sharply: *She cracked her knee on the table.*
crack (krak) □*noun, plural* **cracks** □*verb* **cracked, cracking, cracks**

cracker *noun* A thin, crisp biscuit.
crack·er (krak′ər) □*noun, plural* **crackers**

crackle *verb* To make slight, sharp, snapping sounds: *The fire crackled in the fireplace.*
□*noun* The act or sound of crackling: *the crackle of crushed paper.*
crack·le (krak′əl) □*verb* **crackled, crackling, crackles** □*noun, plural* **crackles**

cradle *noun* A small bed for a baby, usually set on rockers.
□*verb* To hold closely: *She cradled the baby in her arms.*
cra·dle (krād′əl) □*noun, plural* **cradles** □*verb* **cradled, cradling, cradles**

craft *noun* **1.** A special skill or ability: *a work requiring great craft.* **2.** An occupation, skill, or trade: *the carpenter's craft.* **3.** *plural* **craft** A boat, aircraft, or spacecraft.
craft (kraft) □*noun, plural* **crafts**

craftsman *noun* A worker skilled in doing or making something with the hands.
crafts·man (krafts′mən) □*noun, plural* **craftsmen**

crag *noun* A steep rock that juts out of a cliff or mountain.
crag (krag) □*noun, plural* **crags**

crag

cramp *noun* A sharp, painful contraction of a muscle.
cramp (kramp) □*noun, plural* **cramps**

cranberry *noun* A sour, shiny red berry that grows in wet places. Cranberries are used to make sauce, jelly, and juice.

cran·ber·ry (kran′ber′ē) □*noun, plural* **cranberries**

crane *noun* **1.** A large bird with a long neck, long legs, and a long bill. Cranes live near water. **2.** A large machine with a long arm that is used for lifting heavy objects.
□*verb* To stretch or strain for a better view: *I had to crane my neck to see the stage.*
crane (krān) □*noun, plural* **cranes** □*verb* **craned, craning, cranes**

crank *noun* **1.** A device that has a handle or a rod for making a part of a machine turn: *the crank on a pencil sharpener.* **2.** Someone who is very irritable or cross. **3.** Someone whose ideas are considered odd or strange.
□*verb* To start or operate with a crank.
crank (krangk) □*noun, plural* **cranks** □*verb* **cranked, cranking, cranks**

crash *noun* **1.** A sudden, loud noise like that of things hitting one another: *a crash of thunder.* **2.** A violent collision: *a plane crash.*
□*verb* **1.** To make a sudden, loud noise: *Thunder crashed overhead.* **2.** To strike or collide violently and with noise: *The bicycle crashed into a telephone pole.*
crash (krash) □*noun, plural* **crashes** □*verb* **crashed, crashing, crashes**

crate *noun* A large box made of slats of wood: *The furniture was delivered in crates.*
□*verb* To pack into a crate.
crate (krāt) □*noun, plural* **crates** □*verb* **crated, crating, crates**

crater *noun* A bowl-shaped depression or low place in the ground.
cra·ter (krā′tər) □*noun, plural* **craters**

crawl *verb* **1.** To move forward with the body close to the ground: *The baby crawled across the room.* **2.** To go forward slowly: *Cars crawled down the street.* **3.** To be covered with crawling things: *The yard was crawling with ants.*
□*noun* **1.** A very slow pace: *Traffic slowed to a crawl.* **2.** A swimming stroke in which arm strokes alternate and the legs kick rapidly.
crawl (krôl) □*verb* **crawled, crawling, crawls** □*noun*

a bat	ī bite	ōō tool	*th* feather
ā make	î fierce	ou out	th bath
â dare	o dot	u nut	hw wheat
ä father	ō no	û turn	zh measure
e net	ô law, for	ch church	ə about, open
ē be	oi soil	ng ring	pencil, atom
i dip	oo look	sh shade	circus

crayfish *noun* An animal that looks like a small lobster and lives in fresh water.
cray·fish (krā′fish′) □*noun, plural* **crayfish** or **crayfishes**

crayon *noun* A stick of colored wax or chalk used for drawing.
cray·on (krā′on′ *or* krā′ən) □*noun, plural* **crayons**

crazy *adjective* **1.** Suffering from mental illness; insane. **2.** Not sensible; foolish: *It was crazy to wear a heavy coat in this heat.* **3.** Full of enthusiasm: *I'm crazy about jazz.*
cra·zy (krā′zē) □*adjective* **crazier, craziest**

crazy

creak *verb* To make a sharp or harsh squeaking sound: *The floor creaked when I walked on it.*
□*noun* A sharp or harsh squeaking sound.
creak (krēk) □*verb* **creaked, creaking, creaks** □*noun, plural* **creaks**

cream *noun* **1.** The yellowish part of milk that contains fat. Cream can be separated from milk and is used in cooking and to make butter. **2.** A substance, such as a lotion, that looks like cream: *shaving cream.* **3.** The best part of something: *the cream of the crop.* **4.** A pale yellow color.
□*verb* **1.** To apply cream to. **2.** To beat or stir until soft and smooth: *cream butter and eggs together.*
cream (krēm) □*noun, plural* **creams** □*verb* **creamed, creaming, creams**

crease *noun* A mark or line made by folding: *slacks with a sharp crease.*
□*verb* To make or become creased, folded, or wrinkled: *I creased the pages when I closed the book.*
crease (krēs) □*noun, plural* **creases** □*verb* **creased, creasing, creases**

crease

create *verb* **1.** To cause to exist: *The novelist created many memorable characters.* **2.** To make happen; cause: *Her mistake created a lot of trouble.*
cre·ate (krē āt′) □*verb* **created, creating, creates**

creation *noun* **1.** The act of creating: *the creation of a new computer.* **2.** Something invented or produced by a person's intelligence or imagination: *The writer feels that his new novel is his greatest creation.*
cre·a·tion (krē ā′shən) □*noun, plural* **creations**

creative *adjective* Having the ability to create things: *a creative artist.*
cre·a·tive (krē ā′tiv) □*adjective*

creator *noun* **1.** Someone who creates: *She is the creator of the new television show.* **2. Creator** God.
cre·a·tor (krē ā′tər) □*noun, plural* **creators**

creature *noun* A living person or animal.
crea·ture (krē′chər) □*noun, plural* **creatures**

credit *noun* **1.** Belief in the truth or accuracy of something: *He gives too much credit to idle gossip.* **2.** Honor; praise: *She did all the work and should get the credit.* **3.** A system of buying things and paying for them later: *They bought a car on credit.*
□*verb* To believe; trust: *I credit her explanation of why she was late.*
cred·it (kred′it) □*noun, plural* **credits** □*verb* **credited, crediting, credits**

credit card *noun* A card given out by a company that allows a person to buy on credit.

creed *noun* A statement of the beliefs or principles held by a person or group: *Their creed* *includes a belief in God.*

creed (krēd) ▫*noun, plural* **creeds**

creek   *noun* A small stream.
   creek (krēk *or* krik) ▫*noun, plural* **creeks**

creep   *verb* **1.** To move slowly or cautiously with the body close to the ground; crawl: *We crept up the stairs.* **2.** To have a tingling sensation, as if covered with crawling things: *The strange sound made my flesh creep.* **3.** To grow along the ground or by clinging to a wall or other surface: *ivy creeping up the stone wall.* ▫*noun* **the creeps** A feeling of fear and disgust as if things were crawling on one's skin.
   creep (krēp) ▫*verb* **crept, creeping, creeps** ▫*noun*

creep

crepe paper   *noun* Thin, crinkled paper.
   crepe paper (krāp) ▫*noun*

crept   *verb* The past tense and past participle of **creep**: *The dog crept under the sofa.*
   crept (krept) ▫*verb*

crescent   *noun* The shape of the moon when only a quarter of it can be seen.
   cres·cent (kres′ənt) ▫*noun, plural* **crescents**

crescent

crest   *noun* **1.** A tuft of feathers on a bird's head. **2.** A band of feathers on top of a warrior's helmet. **3.** The top of something, such as a mountain or a wave.
   crest (krest) ▫*noun, plural* **crests**

crew   *noun* **1.** All the persons who operate a boat, ship, or aircraft. **2.** A group of people who work together: *He works on a crew that*

repairs roads.

crew (krōō) ▫*noun, plural* **crews**

crib   *noun* **1.** A baby's bed that is enclosed on four sides. **2.** A small building for storing corn or other grain. **3.** A rack or trough from which cattle or horses eat.
   crib (krib) ▫*noun, plural* **cribs**

cricket[1]   *noun* An insect that looks like a small, dark grasshopper. The male makes a chirping sound by rubbing the front wings together.
   crick·et (krik′it) ▫*noun, plural* **crickets**

crick·et[2]   *noun* An outdoor game for two teams of eleven players each that is played with bats, a ball, and wickets. Cricket is popular in England.
   crick·et (krik′it) ▫*noun*

cricket

crime   *noun* **1.** An action or activity that is against the law or a failure to do what the law requires. **2.** A disgraceful or wrong act: *It's a crime to spread gossip.*
   crime (krīm) ▫*noun, plural* **crimes**

criminal   *noun* Someone who has committed a crime.
   ▫*adjective* Having to do with crime: *a criminal act; a criminal lawyer.*

a bat	ī bite	ōō tool	*th* feather
ā make	î fierce	ou out	th bath
â dare	o dot	u nut	hw wheat
ä father	ō no	û turn	zh measure
e net	ô law, for	ch church	ə about, open
ē be	oi soil	ng ring	pencil, atom
i dip	oo look	sh shade	circus

crim·i·nal (**krim′**ə nəl) □*noun, plural*
criminals □*adjective*

SYNONYMS: **criminal, illegal, unlawful**

These adjectives mean having to do with crime:
*Robbery is a criminal act. It is illegal to drive a car
without a license. The man was accused of fraud
and other unlawful activities.*

crimson *noun* A bright purplish-red color.
□*adjective* Bright purplish red.
crim·son (**krim′**zən *or* **krim′**sən) □*noun*
□*adjective*

cringe *verb* **1.** To shrink back in fear: *He
cringed when she frowned and spoke in an angry voice.* **2.** To act in a humble manner:
*Everyone cringed and bowed in the presence of
the haughty prince.*
cringe (krinj) □*verb* **cringed, cringing,
cringes**

crin·kle *verb* To make wrinkles in: *I crinkled
the newspaper.*
crin·kle (**kring′**kəl) □*verb* **crinkled,
crinkling, crinkles**

cripple *noun* A person or animal that cannot
move normally because some part of the body
is injured or defective.
□*verb* **1.** To injure so as to make useless: *The
car accident crippled him.* **2.** To make helpless
or useless: *The flood crippled the town.*
crip·ple (**krip′**əl) □*noun, plural* **cripples**
□*verb* **crippled, crippling, cripples**

crisis *noun* **1.** A turning point in the course
of a disease when the patient either improves
or gets worse. **2.** A time of danger or difficulty: *There was a crisis in the city when the
electric power failed.*
cri·sis (**krī′**sis) □*noun, plural* **crises**

crisp *adjective* **1.** Pleasantly dry and hard:
crisp toast. **2.** Not wilted or limp; fresh: *crisp
lettuce.* **3.** Cool and refreshing; bracing: *a crisp
breeze.* **4.** Brief and clear: *She gave a crisp answer to his question.*
crisp (krisp) □*adjective* **crisper, crispest**

crisscross *verb* **1.** To mark with a pattern of
crossing lines: *We could see where animal
tracks crisscrossed in the snow.* **2.** To move
back and forth across: *Airplanes crisscrossed
the sky overhead.*
□*noun* A pattern of crossing lines.
□*adjective* Crossing one another: *the crisscross lines of a puzzle.*
criss·cross (**kris′**krôs′) □*verb* **crisscrossed,**

crisscrossing, crisscrosses □*noun, plural*
crisscrosses □*adjective*

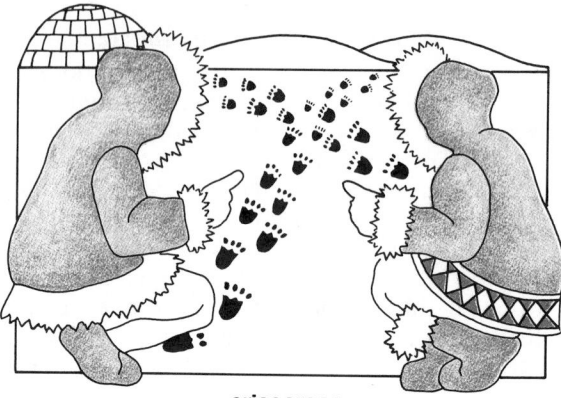

crisscross

critic *noun* Someone whose job is judging
books, plays, and other artistic efforts.
crit·ic (**krit′**ik) □*noun, plural* **critics**

critical *adjective* **1.** Of or having to do with
criticism or a critic: *She writes critical reviews
of books.* **2.** Likely to find fault or disapprove:
She is critical of everything I do. **3.** Very serious or dangerous: *The patient is in critical condition.*
crit·i·cal (**krit′**i kəl) □*adjective*

criticism *noun* **1.** The act of making judgments about the good and bad qualities of
things. **2.** A critical or disapproving comment:
Her criticisms of the play upset the actors.
crit·i·cism (**krit′**i siz′əm) □*noun, plural*
criticisms

criticize *verb* **1.** To judge whether something
is good or bad: *I won't criticize the book until
I've read it all.* **2.** To find something wrong
with: *He's always criticizing me.*
crit·i·cize (**krit′**i sīz) □*verb* **criticized,
criticizing, criticizes**

croak *noun* A low, hoarse sound, such as that
made by a frog or crow.
□*verb* To make this sound.
croak (krōk) □*noun, plural* **croaks** □*verb*
croaked, croaking, croaks

crochet *verb* To make something by connecting loops of thread with a hooked needle: *crochet a sweater.*
cro·chet (krō **shā′**) □*verb* **crocheted,
crocheting, crochets**

crocodile *noun* A large reptile with thick
skin, sharp teeth, and long, narrow jaws that
live in wet, tropical places.
croc·o·dile (**krok′**ə dīl′) □*noun, plural*
crocodiles

crocus *noun* A small garden plant with purple, yellow, or white flowers that bloom early in spring.
cro·cus (krō′kəs) □*noun, plural* **crocuses**

crook *noun* **1.** A bent or curved part: *the crook of his arm.* **2.** A dishonest person; thief: *The crook stole my purse.*
crook (krook) □*noun, plural* **crooks**

crooked *adjective* **1.** Not straight; bent or curved: *a crooked road; a crooked nose.* **2.** Not honest: *a crooked card player.*
crook·ed (krook′id) □*adjective*

crop *noun* **1.** Plants grown to be used as food or to make various products: *We raised a large crop of corn.* **2.** A group of persons or things appearing at one time: *There is a large crop of new teachers in our school this year.* **3.** A pouch in the neck of a bird where food is stored and partially digested. **4.** A short whip used in horseback riding.
□*verb* To cut off the tops or ends of; trim: *The sheep cropped the grass.*
crop (krop) □*noun, plural* **crops** □*verb*
cropped, cropping, crops

crop

croquet *noun* An outdoor game in which each player uses a large mallet to hit a wooden ball along the ground through a series of wickets.
cro·quet (krō kā′) □*noun*

cross *noun* **1.** An upright post with a horizontal bar at the top or near the top. **2. Cross** The cross upon which Christ was crucified. **3.** Something shaped like a cross: *I wear a gold cross on a chain around my neck.* **4.** The result of combining two things: *This dog is a cross between a poodle and a terrier.*
□*verb* **1.** To go to the other side of: *cross a street.* **2.** To meet and pass beyond each other:

The two highways cross at the state line. **3.** To draw a line across: *Cross your t's.* **4.** To place one thing over another so as to cross: *He sat down and crossed his legs.*
□*adjective* **1.** Lying or placed across: *I'll wait for you at the cross street near the bank.* **2.** In a bad mood: *Why is she so cross today?*
cross (krôs) □*noun, plural* **crosses** □*verb*
crossed, crossing, crosses □*adjective*

crossbow *noun* A weapon for shooting arrows or darts. A crossbow has a bow fixed across a wooden stock which directs the arrow or dart.
cross·bow (krôs′bō′) □*noun, plural* **crossbows**

cross-eyed *adjective* Having one or both eyes turned in toward the nose.
cross-eyed (krôs′īd′) □*adjective*

crossing *noun* **1.** The place where two or more things cross; intersection. **2.** A place at which a street, railroad, river, or other route may be crossed: *There is a crossing and a traffic light in front of the school.*
cross·ing (krô′sing) □*noun, plural* **crossings**

crossroad *noun* **1.** A road that crosses another road. **2. crossroads** A place where two or more roads meet: *There is a gas station at the crossroads.*
cross·road (krôs′rōd′) □*noun, plural* **crossroads**

crossword puzzle *noun* A puzzle in which one is given clues to words that are to be fitted into numbered squares, one letter to a square. Words cross through one another and may be read across or down.
cross·word puzzle (krôs′wûrd′) □*noun*

crotch *noun* **1.** The point at which a branch grows out from the trunk or from another branch of a tree. **2.** The point at which a person's legs branch off from the body.
crotch (kroch) □*noun, plural* **crotches**

crouch *verb* To stoop low with the legs bent; squat.
crouch (krouch) □*verb* **crouched, crouching, crouches**

a bat	ī bite	ǒǒ tool	*th* feather
ā make	î fierce	ou out	th bath
â dare	o dot	u nut	hw wheat
ä father	ō no	û turn	zh measure
e net	ô law, for	ch church	ə about, open
ē be	oi soil	ng ring	pencil, atom
i dip	oo look	sh shade	circus

crow¹ *noun* A large, glossy black bird with a harsh, hoarse call.
crow (krō) □*noun, plural* **crows**

crow² *noun* The loud cry of a rooster.
□*verb* **1.** To utter the loud cry of a rooster. **2.** To make a cry of delight: *We crowed when our team won the game.* **3.** To boast; brag: *They crowed about their success.* —See Synonyms at **boast.**
crow (krō) □*noun, plural* **crows** □*verb* **crowed, crowing, crows**

crowbar *noun* A bar of iron or steel that is bent slightly at one end and is used as a lever for lifting or prying.
crow·bar (krō′bär′) □*noun, plural* **crowbars**

crowd *noun* A large number of people gathered together: *A crowd was gathering outside the football stadium.*
□*verb* **1.** To fill with many people or things: *People crowded into the bus. Shoppers crowded the store.* **2.** To press tightly; cram: *I crowded my clothes in the small suitcase.*
crowd (kroud) □*noun, plural* **crowds** □*verb* **crowded, crowding, crowds**

crown *noun* **1.** A covering for the head, often made of gold and set with jewels, worn by kings and queens. **2.** The top part of something: *the crown of a person's head.* **3.** The part of a tooth that is above the gums.
□*verb* To make someone king or queen by placing a crown on the person's head.
crown (kroun) □*noun, plural* **crowns** □*verb* **crowned, crowning, crowns**

crow's-nest *noun* A small platform located near the top of a ship's mast, used by sailors for seeing long distances.
crow's-nest (krōz′nest′) □*noun, plural* **crow's-nests**

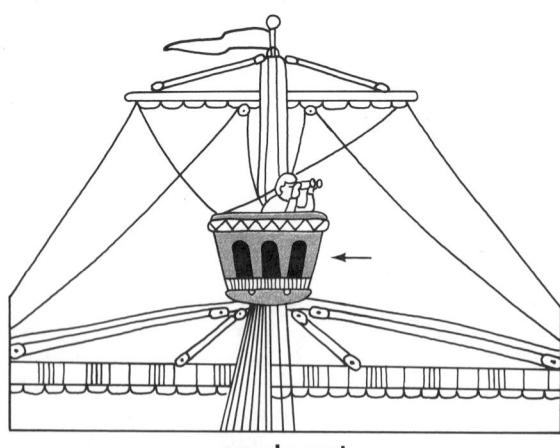
crow's-nest

crucial *adjective* Of the greatest importance: *He had to make a crucial decision about which college to attend.*
cru·cial (krōō′shəl) □*adjective*

crucifix *noun* A cross with the figure of Christ on it.
cru·ci·fix (krōō′sə fiks′) □*noun, plural* **crucifixes**

crucifixion *noun* **1.** The act of crucifying someone. **2. Crucifixion** The death of Christ on the Cross.
cru·ci·fix·ion (krōō′sə fik′shən) □*noun, plural* **crucifixions**

crucify *verb* To put a person to death by nailing or tying to a cross.
cru·ci·fy (krōō′sə fī′) □*verb* **crucified, crucifying, crucifies**

crude *adjective* **1.** In a raw or natural state: *crude rubber.* **2.** Not done or made with skill: *We built a crude table that was very shaky.* **3.** Not polite or considerate: *She said it was crude to eat with one's fingers.*
crude (krōōd) □*adjective* **cruder, crudest**

crude

cruel *adjective* **1.** Liking to cause pain or suffering: *The cruel man kicked the dog.* **2.** Causing suffering; painful: *a cruel disappointment.*
cru·el (krōō′əl) □*adjective* **crueler, cruelest**

cruelty *noun* **1.** The quality of being ready to cause pain to others: *He was known all over town for his cruelty to animals.* **2.** A cruel act or remark.
cru·el·ty (krōō′əl tē) □*noun, plural* **cruelties**

cruise *verb* **1.** To sail from place to place: *We cruised up the coast of California.* **2.** To travel about from place to place: *Police cars cruise the streets.*
□*noun* A sea voyage for pleasure: *We are going on a cruise to Puerto Rico.*
cruise (krōōz) □*verb* **cruised, cruising, cruises** □*noun, plural* **cruises**

cruiser   *noun* **1.** A fast warship that is smaller than a battleship and has fewer guns. **2.** A police car.
cruis·er (**kroo′**zər) □*noun, plural* **cruisers**

crumb   *noun* A tiny piece of food, especially bread: *Clean the crumbs off the table.*
crumb (krum) □*noun, plural* **crumbs**

crumble   *verb* **1.** To break into pieces or crumbs: *I crumbled bread to feed the birds.* **2.** To fall into small pieces: *The old stone walls were slowly crumbling away.*
crum·ble (**krum′**bəl) □*verb* **crumbled, crumbling, crumbles**

crumple   *verb* To crush out of shape; crease or wrinkle: *Try not to crumple my clean suit.*
crum·ple (**krum′**pəl) □*verb* **crumpled, crumpling, crumples**

crunch   *verb* To chew with a noisy or cracking sound: *He crunched a piece of celery.*
□*noun* A cracking sound: *You could hear the crunch of our boots on the snow.*
crunch (krunch) □*verb* **crunched, crunching, crunches** □*noun, plural* **crunches**

crusade   *noun* **1.** **Crusade** Any of the military expeditions that European Christians undertook in the 11th, 12th, and 13th centuries to take the Holy Land from the Moslems. **2.** A campaign or fight for a cause: *a crusade for women's rights.*
□*verb* To take part in a crusade.
cru·sade (kroo **sād′**) □*noun, plural* **crusades** □*verb* **crusaded, crusading, crusades**

crusader   *noun* Someone who takes part in a crusade.
cru·sad·er (kroo **sā′**dər) □*noun, plural* **crusaders**

crush   *verb* **1.** To press or squeeze with enough force to break or injure: *I crushed the eggshell.* **2.** To grind or pound into very fine bits: *crush rocks into powder.* **3.** To put down or destroy: *crush a rebellion.*
□*noun* **1.** A dense crowd of people in motion: *There was a crush at the entrance to the movie theater.* **2.** A sudden, strong liking for another: *She has a crush on my brother.*
crush (krush) □*verb* **crushed, crushing, crushes** □*noun, plural* **crushes**

crust   *noun* **1.** The hard outer surface of a loaf of bread. **2.** The shell of a pie or other pastry. **3.** A hard outer layer or covering: *There was a crust of snow on the lawn.*
□*verb* To cover or become covered with a crust: *The pond was crusted over with ice.*
crust (krust) □*noun, plural* **crusts** □*verb* **crusted, crusting, crusts**

crustacean   *noun* One of a group of animals with two pairs of antennae and a body that has a hard outer covering. Most crustaceans live in the water. Lobsters, crabs, and shrimps are crustaceans.
crus·ta·cean (kru **stā′**shən) □*noun, plural* **crustaceans**

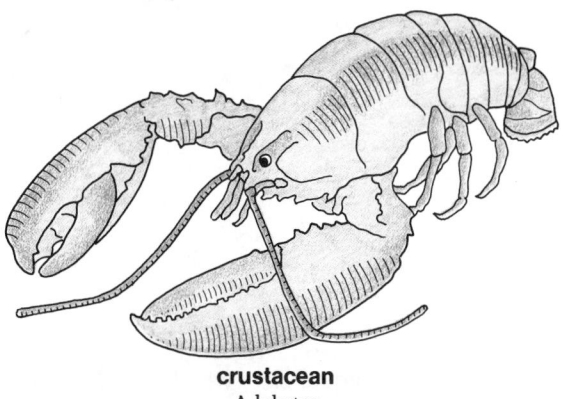
crustacean
A lobster

crutch   *noun* A support, often one of a pair, used to help a lame or injured person.
crutch (kruch) □*noun, plural* **crutches**

cry   *verb* **1.** To shed tears; weep: *He cried when his cat ran away. She cried for joy.* **2.** To call loudly; shout: *He cried out to attract their attention.*
□*noun* **1.** A loud call; shout: *We heard his cries for help.* **2.** A fit of weeping: *She had a long cry after her dog died.* **3.** The characteristic sound of an animal: *the cry of a coyote.*
cry (krī) □*verb* **cried, crying, cries** □*noun, plural* **cries**

crystal   *noun* **1.** A solid substance with sides and angles that naturally form a regular pattern. **2.** A piece of quartz or other transparent mineral. **3.** A clear glass of high quality that is used to make vases, drinking glasses, and other objects. **4.** The glass cover over the dial of a clock or watch.
crys·tal (**kris′**təl) □*noun, plural* **crystals**

a	bat	ī	bite	oo	tool	*th*	feather
ā	make	î	fierce	ou	out	th	bath
â	dare	o	dot	u	nut	hw	wheat
ä	father	ō	no	û	turn	zh	measure
e	net	ô	law, for	ch	church	ə	about, open
ē	be	oi	soil	ng	ring		pencil, atom
i	dip	oo	look	sh	shade		circus

cub   *noun* A young bear, wolf, or lion.
   cub (kub) ▢*noun, plural* **cubs**

cub
A lion cub

cube   *noun* **1.** A solid figure having six flat, square sides of equal size, which meet at right angles. **2.** Something shaped like a cube: *a cube of sugar.* **3.** The result of multiplying a number by itself twice. The cube of 2 is 2 × 2 × 2, or 8.
   ▢*verb* To cut or form into cubes: *We cubed slices of bread to make stuffing for the turkey.*
   cube (kyoob) ▢*noun, plural* **cubes** ▢*verb* **cubed, cubing, cubes**

cubic   *adjective* **1.** Having the shape of a cube. **2.** Having a volume equal to a cube whose edge is a certain length: *a cubic foot.*
   cu·bic (kyoo′bik) ▢*adjective*

Cub Scout   *noun* A member of the junior division of the Boy Scouts.

cuckoo   *noun* A bird with grayish feathers and a call that sounds like its name. It lays its eggs in the nests of other birds.
   cuck·oo (koo′koo) ▢*noun, plural* **cuckoos**

cuckoo

cucumber   *noun* A long vegetable with green skin and white flesh. They grow on vines and are eaten in salads or made into pickles.
   cu·cum·ber (kyoo′kum′bər) ▢*noun, plural* **cucumbers**

cud   *noun* Food that has been swallowed by a cow, sheep, or other animal, and then brought up to the mouth to be chewed again.
   cud (kud) ▢*noun, plural* **cuds**

cue¹   *noun* A word, sound, or other signal to a performer to begin a speech or movement: *The sound of the door slamming was the actress's cue to faint.*
   ▢*verb* To give a person a cue.
   cue (kyoo) ▢*noun, plural* **cues** ▢*verb* **cued, cuing, cues**

cue²   *noun* A long, tapered stick used to strike a ball in billiards or pool.
   cue (kyoo) ▢*noun, plural* **cues**

cuff¹   *noun* A band or fold of cloth at the bottom of a sleeve or trouser leg.
   cuff (kuf) ▢*noun, plural* **cuffs**

cuff²   *verb* To strike with the hand; slap: *She cuffed me on the head for talking back to her.*
   ▢*noun* A blow or slap.
   cuff (kuf) ▢*verb* **cuffed, cuffing, cuffs** ▢*noun, plural* **cuffs**

culprit   *noun* Someone who is guilty of doing something wrong or illegal.
   cul·prit (kul′prit) ▢*noun, plural* **culprits**

cultivate   *verb* **1.** To prepare and use land for growing plants. **2.** To develop by study or teaching: *She reads to cultivate her mind.*
   cul·ti·vate (kul′tə vāt′) ▢*verb* **cultivated, cultivating, cultivates**

cultivate

cultural   *adjective* Having to do with culture: *a town that offers many cultural activities.*
   cul·tur·al (kul′chər əl) ▢*adjective*

culture *noun* **1.** Acquaintance with the arts, history, literature, and other areas of learning: *His interest in opera and drama shows that he is a man of great culture.* **2.** The customs, beliefs, arts, and institutions of a group of people: *We studied the culture of ancient Greece.* **3.** Development of the mind or body through special training.
cul·ture (**kul′**chər) □*noun, plural* **cultures**

cunning *adjective* Very clever in tricking or deceiving others: *a cunning scheme; a cunning person.*
□*noun* The act or condition of being cunning: *The fox is an animal of great cunning.*
cun·ning (**kun′**ing) □*adjective* □*noun*

cup *noun* **1.** A small, open container, usually with a handle, that is used for drinking liquids. **2.** Something with the shape of a cup: *The team received a gold cup for winning the championship.*
□*verb* To form something to look like a cup: *She cupped her hands and I put all the marbles into them.*
cup (kup) □*noun, plural* **cups** □*verb* **cupped, cupping, cups**

cupboard *noun* A closet with shelves for storing dishes, food, or other items.
cup·board (**kub′**ərd) □*noun, plural* **cupboards**

cupcake *noun* A small cake that is baked in a pan shaped into one or more cups.
cup·cake (**kup′**kāk′) □*noun, plural* **cupcakes**

curb *noun* **1.** A rim of stone or concrete along the edge of a road or sidewalk. **2.** Something that stops or holds back: *a curb on spending.*
□*verb* To hold back or keep under control: *I tried to curb my anger.*
curb (kûrb) □*noun, plural* **curbs** □*verb* **curbed, curbing, curbs**

curd *noun* A thick substance that separates from milk when it turns sour. Curds are used to make cheese.
curd (kûrd) □*noun, plural* **curds**

cure *noun* A treatment or medicine that gets rid of a disease or fixes a bad condition: *Rest and fluids are the best cure for a cold.*
□*verb* **1.** To bring back to good health: *The pills cured me of a sore throat.* **2.** To get rid of: *My apology cured her anger.* **3.** To preserve food by drying, salting, smoking, or by other means.
cure (kyoor) □*noun, plural* **cures** □*verb* **cured, curing, cures**

curfew *noun* A fixed time at night when one must be indoors: *I have a 10 p.m. curfew on weekends.*
cur·few (**kûr′**fyoo) □*noun, plural* **curfews**

curiosity *noun* **1.** A desire to know or learn: *My curiosity made me open the package.* **2.** Something unusual or remarkable: *The store sells antiques and other curiosities.*
cu·ri·os·i·ty (kyoor′ē **os′**i tē) □*noun, plural* **curiosities**

curious *adjective* **1.** Eager to learn or know: *a curious child who is always asking questions.* **2.** Unusual or strange: *I don't know what that curious gadget is used for.*
cu·ri·ous (**kyoor′**ē əs) □*adjective*

curl *verb* To twist or form into rings or coils: *Will you help me curl my hair? Smoke curled from the chimney.*
□*noun* **1.** A ring or coil of hair. **2.** Something with a spiral or coiled shape: *a curl of smoke.*
curl (kûrl) □*verb* **curled, curling, curls** □*noun, plural* **curls**

curly *adjective* Having curls or tending to curl: *curly hair.*
curl·y (**kûr′**lē) □*adjective* **curlier, curliest**

currant *noun* **1.** A small, sour, red or blackish berry that grows on a prickly bush. Currants are used for making jelly. **2.** A small raisin without seeds, used mostly in baking.
cur·rant (**kur′**ənt) □*noun, plural* **currants**

currant

currency *noun* The form of money that a country circulates.

a bat	ī bite	oo tool	*th* feather
ā make	î fierce	ou out	th bath
â dare	o dot	u nut	hw wheat
ä father	ō no	û turn	zh measure
e net	ô law, for	ch church	ə about, open
ē be	oi soil	ng ring	pencil, atom
i dip	oo look	sh shade	circus

cur·ren·cy (kûr′ən sē) □*noun, plural* **currencies**

current *adjective* Belonging to the present time: *current events. What is your current address?*
□*noun* **1.** Liquid or gas that is moving: *a current of air; the current of a river.* **2.** A flow of electricity through a wire or cord.
cur·rent (kûr′ənt) □*adjective* □*noun, plural* **currents**

curriculum *noun* All the courses of study offered at a school or college.
cur·ric·u·lum (kə rik′yə ləm) □*noun, plural* **curriculums**

curse *noun* **1.** An appeal to God to bring evil or harm to someone. **2.** A word or group of words expressing great anger or hatred. **3.** Something that causes great evil or harm: *Poverty and disease are two of the greatest curses of humanity.*
□*verb* **1.** To call down a curse on a person. **2.** To bring harm or trouble to: *Poor eyesight has cursed him since he was a child.* **3.** To swear: *It is very rude to curse or use bad language.*
curse (kûrs) □*noun, plural* **curses** □*verb* **cursed, cursing, curses**

cursor *noun* A pointer on a computer screen that shows where information will appear when entered or where an action will take place. The cursor can be moved using a keyboard or a computer mouse.
cur·sor (kûr′sər) □*noun, plural* **cursors**

curtain *noun* **1.** A piece of cloth hung at a window. **2.** A large piece of cloth hung across the front of a stage. **3.** Something that acts as a screen or cover: *The mountain was hidden by a curtain of fog.*
cur·tain (kûr′tən) □*noun, plural* **curtains**

curtsy *noun* A way of showing respect by bending one's knees and lowering the body.
□*verb* To make a curtsy.
curt·sy (kûrt′sē) □*noun, plural* **curtsies** □*verb* **curtsied, curtsying, curtsies**

curve *noun* **1.** A line or surface that bends smoothly and continuously. **2.** Something shaped like a curve: *a curve in the road.*
□*verb* To move in or have the shape of a curve: *The river curves around the base of the mountain.*
curve (kûrv) □*noun, plural* **curves** □*verb* **curved, curving, curves**

cushion *noun* A pad or pillow with a soft filling, used to sit, rest, or lie on.
□*verb* **1.** To supply with a cushion: *cushion a chair.* **2.** To soften a shock or blow: *The mound of snow cushioned my fall.*
cush·ion (koosh′ən) □*noun, plural* **cushions** □*verb* **cushioned, cushioning, cushions**

custard *noun* A dessert, similar to pudding, that is made of eggs, milk, sugar, and flavoring.
cus·tard (kus′tərd) □*noun, plural* **custards**

custodian *noun* **1.** Someone in charge of something: *the custodian of the building.*
cus·to·di·an (ku stō′dē ən) □*noun, plural* **custodians**

custody *noun* **1.** The act of taking care of someone or something: *I left my dog in the custody of my cousin.* **2.** The condition of being held by police or under guard: *The suspect was in the custody of the police.*
cus·to·dy (kus′tə dē) □*noun*

custody

custom *noun* **1.** Something people do that is widely accepted or has become a tradition: *Eating turkey on Thanksgiving is a popular custom.* **2.** Something a person usually does; habit: *It is his custom to read the newspaper during breakfast.* **3.** **customs** A tax that must be paid on things brought into a country that were bought outside that country.
cus·tom (kus′təm) □*noun, plural* **customs**

customary *adjective* According to custom or habit; usual: *We sat in our customary places at the dinner table.*
cus·tom·ar·y (kus′tə mer′ē) □*adjective*

customer *noun* Someone who buys goods or services: *The clerk in the store could only help one customer at a time.*

cus·tom·er (kus′tə mər) ◻*noun, plural* **customers**

cut *verb* **1.** To go through or into with something sharp: *I cut my finger with the knife. Will you cut the grass?* **2.** To shape or divide with a sharp instrument: *cut a pie.* **3.** To shorten or trim: *cut the bushes. Dad cut my allowance.* **4.** To remove; eliminate: *We cut two days off our trip.*
◻*noun* **1.** A slit, wound, or other opening made by cutting. **2.** A reduction; decrease: *a cut in pay; a cut in prices.*
cut (kut) ◻*verb* **cut, cutting, cuts** ◻*noun, plural* **cuts**

cute *adjective* **1.** Delightfully pretty; charming: *a cute baby.* **2.** Clever; devious: *a cute trick.*
cute (kyo͞ot) ◻*adjective* **cuter, cutest**

cuticle *noun* The strip of hardened skin at the base of a fingernail or toenail.
cu·ti·cle (kyo͞o′ti kəl) ◻*noun, plural* **cuticles**

cutlass *noun* A short, heavy sword with a curved blade.
cut·lass (kut′ləs) ◻*noun, plural* **cutlasses**

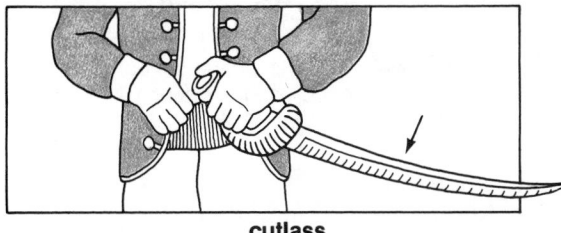
cutlass

cutter *noun* **1.** A worker whose job is to cut material, such as cloth, glass, or stone. **2.** A tool or machine for cutting: *a cookie cutter.*
cut·ter (kut′ər) ◻*noun, plural* **cutters**

cutting *noun* **1.** A part cut off from a main body: *She has a newspaper cutting about the game.* **2.** A stem, leaf, or twig cut from a plant and placed in sand, soil, or water to form roots and develop into a new plant.
◻*adjective* **1.** Used for cutting: *a cutting blade.* **2.** Mean and insulting: *a cutting remark.*
cut·ting (kut′ing) ◻*noun, plural* **cuttings** ◻*adjective*

cycle *noun* An event or series of events that is repeated regularly: *the yearly cycle of the seasons.*
◻*verb* To ride a bicycle or motorcycle: *I cycled to the beach.*
cy·cle (sī′kəl) ◻*noun, plural* **cycles** ◻*verb* **cycled, cycling, cycles**

cyclone *noun* A violent rotating wind storm, such as a tornado.
cy·clone (sī′klōn) ◻*noun, plural* **cyclones**

cylinder *noun* A hollow or solid object shaped like a tube or pipe: *Paper towels come rolled around a cardboard cylinder.*
cyl·in·der (sil′ən dər) ◻*noun, plural* **cylinders**

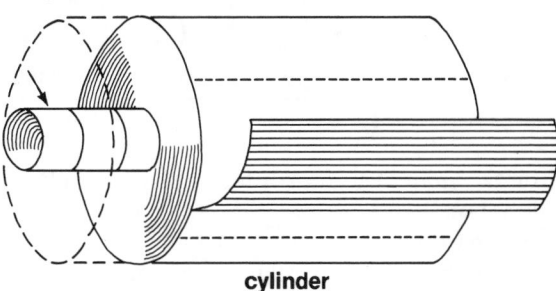
cylinder

cymbal *noun* A brass musical instrument that is shaped like a plate. The cymbal is sounded by being struck against another cymbal or with a drumstick.
cym·bal (sim′bəl) ◻*noun, plural* **cymbals**

cypress *noun* **1.** An evergreen tree that has small needles that look like scales. **2.** The wood of a cypress tree.
cy·press (sī′prəs) ◻*noun, plural* **cypresses**

czar *noun* An emperor of Russia.
czar (zär) ◻*noun, plural* **czars**

czarina *noun* The wife of a czar.
cza·ri·na (zä rē′nə) ◻*noun, plural* **czarinas**

a bat	ī bite	o͞o tool	*th* feather
ā make	î fierce	ou out	th bath
â dare	o dot	u nut	hw wheat
ä father	ō no	û turn	zh measure
e net	ô law, for	ch church	ə about, open
ē be	oi soil	ng ring	pencil, atom
i dip	oo look	sh shade	circus

ANCIENT GREEK

The letter **D** has evolved from many forms of ancient writing. One of the earliest known examples is the Greek character shown above, which dates from almost 3,000 years ago. Over the years, artists and designers have created their own versions of the English letter **D**. Some of the more common examples seen today are shown below.

Dd *Dd*	**Dd Dd**	Dd Dd	**Dd** Dd	*Dd Dd*
HANDWRITING	CALLIGRAPHY	MODERN SANS SERIF	MODERN SERIF	SCRIPT

d or **D** *noun* The fourth letter of the English alphabet.
d or **D** (dē) □*noun, plural* **d's** or **D's**

dab *verb* **1.** To touch lightly: *She dabbed the cut with a damp cloth.* **2.** To put on with light strokes: *dabbed powder on her face.*
□*noun* A very small amount of something: *a dab of butter.*
dab (dab) □*verb* **dabbed, dabbing, dabs**□*noun, plural* **dabs**

dabble *verb* **1.** To splash in and out of water playfully: *We dabbled our feet in the swimming pool.* **2.** To work at something without interest or seriousness: *She dabbled at the guitar but quickly lost interest.*
dab·ble (dab′əl) □*verb* **dabbled, dabbling, dabbles**

dabble

dachshund *noun* A small dog with a long body, drooping ears, and very short legs.

dachs·hund (däks′hŏont′ *or* daks′hŏond′) □*noun, plural* **dachshunds**

> *WORD HISTORY:* **dachshund**
> The word *dachshund* comes from the German name for the dog, which means "badger hound." This breed of dog was once used for hunting badgers.

dad *noun* Father.
dad (dad) □*noun, plural* **dads**

daddy *noun* Father.
dad·dy (dad′ē) □*noun, plural* **daddies**

daddy longlegs *noun* An animal that has a small, round body and eight long, slender legs. It looks much like a spider.
daddy long·legs (lông′legz′) □*noun, plural* **daddy longlegs**

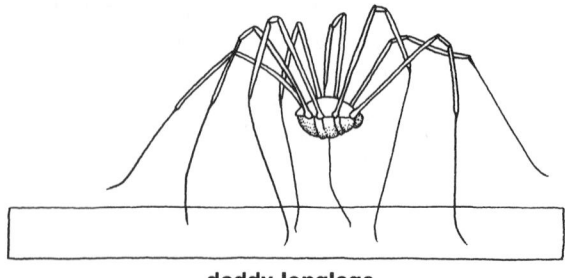

daddy longlegs

daffodil *noun* A plant with long, narrow leaves and yellow or white flowers.
daf·fo·dil (daf′ə dil) □*noun, plural* **daffodils**

dagger *noun* A short, pointed weapon with sharp edges, used like a knife.
dag·ger (dag′ər) □*noun, plural* **daggers**

daily *adjective* Done, appearing, or happening every day: *a daily newspaper; a daily bath.* □*adverb* Every day: *She telephones her best friend daily.* □*noun* A newspaper published every day.
dai·ly (dā′lē) □*adjective* □*adverb* □*noun, plural* **dailies**

dainty *adjective* Very fine and delicate: *a dainty necklace; a dainty teacup.*
dain·ty (dān′tē) □*adjective* **daintier, daintiest**

dairy *noun* **1.** A place where milk and cream are prepared or made into butter and cheese. **2.** A business that makes or sells milk, cream, butter, and cheese. **3.** A farm that produces milk and milk products.
dai·ry (dâr′ē) □*noun, plural* **dairies**

dais *noun* A raised platform for a throne, a speaker, or group of special guests.
da·is (dā′is) □*noun, plural* **daises**

daisy *noun* A plant with flowers that have white, pink, or yellow petals around a yellow center.
dai·sy (dā′zē) □*noun, plural* **daisies**

WORD HISTORY: daisy

The word *daisy* comes from two old English words that mean "day's eye." Originally the name *daisy* belonged to a tiny European flower with white petals around a yellow center. The plant was probably called "day's eye" because it folds its petals at night and opens them again in the morning with the sun, like an eye that sleeps and wakes.

---

dale *noun* A valley.
dale (dāl) □*noun, plural* **dales**

Dalmatian *noun* A dog that has a smooth white coat with small black spots.
Dal·ma·tian (dal mā′shən) □*noun, plural* **Dalmatians**

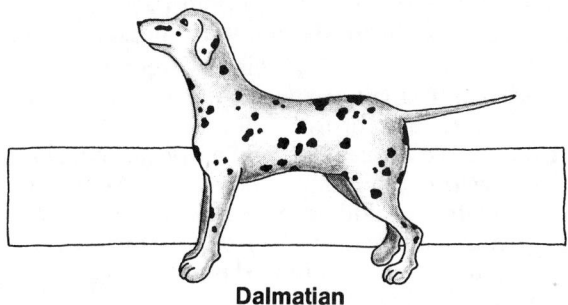

Dalmatian

dam *noun* A wall built across a river or stream to control the level of the water. □*verb* To control with a dam.
dam (dam) □*noun, plural* **dams** □*verb* **dammed, damming, dams**

damage *noun* Harm or injury that makes something less useful or valuable: *The fire caused a lot of damage to the adjoining stores.* —See Synonyms at **harm.** □*verb* To harm or injure: *The cat damaged the chair with its claws.*
dam·age (dam′ij) □*noun, plural* **damages** □*verb* **damaged, damaging, damages**

dame *noun* **1. Dame** A title of honor in England given to a woman for some worthwhile accomplishment. It is equal to a knight's title of "Sir." **2.** A lady or wife.
dame (dām) □*noun, plural* **dames**

damn *verb* **1.** To describe as being very bad: *The reviewers damned the new book.* **2.** To curse or swear at.
damn (dam) □*verb* **damned, damning, damns**

damp *adjective* Slightly wet; moist: *a cold, damp day. Wipe the table with a damp cloth.* □*noun* Slight wetness; moisture.
damp (damp) □*adjective* **damper, dampest** □*noun*

dampen *verb* **1.** To make moist or wet: *dampen a sponge.* **2.** To lower or lessen: *Losing the contest dampened my mood.*
damp·en (dam′pən) □*verb* **dampened, dampening, dampens**

dance *verb* **1.** To move the body or parts of the body in time to music. **2.** To move or jump about actively or with excitement: *After she won the tennis match she danced up and down in happiness.* □*noun* **1.** A special set of steps and motions, usually done in time to music. **2.** A party at which people dance.
dance (dans) □*verb* **danced, dancing, dances** □*noun, plural* **dances**

dancer *noun* Someone who dances.
dan·cer (dan′sər) □*noun, plural* **dancers**

a	bat	ī	bite	ōō	tool	*th*	feather
ā	make	î	fierce	ou	out	th	bath
â	dare	o	dot	u	nut	hw	wheat
ä	father	ō	no	û	turn	zh	measure
e	net	ô	law, for	ch	church	ə	about, open
ē	be	oi	soil	ng	ring		pencil, atom
i	dip	oo	look	sh	shade		circus

dandelion *noun* A plant with bright yellow flowers and leaves with ragged edges.
dan·de·li·on (dan′dəl ī′ən) □*noun, plural* **dandelions**

WORD HISTORY: **dandelion**

Dandelion comes from an old French phrase that means "lion's tooth." The French probably called the plant by this name because its leaves have sharp edges like teeth.

---

dandruff *noun* Small white pieces of dead skin that fall from the scalp.
dan·druff (dan′drəf) □*noun*

dandy *noun* **1.** A man who is very fussy about his clothing. **2.** Something very good of its kind: *Her new sled is a dandy.*
dan·dy (dan′dē) □*noun, plural* **dandies**

danger *noun* **1.** The chance or threat of something harmful happening: *She warned them of the danger of playing in the street.* **2.** Something that threatens safety: *Bears in the forest are a danger to campers.*
dan·ger (dān′jər) □*noun, plural* **dangers**

SYNONYMS: **danger, hazard, risk**

These nouns mean the chance or threat of something harmful happening: *The children are aware of the danger of cars when they ride their bicycles. The large pile of newspapers is a fire hazard. She took a big risk by swimming alone where the water was very deep.*

---

dangerous *adjective* Able or likely to cause harm: *Playing with matches is dangerous.*
dan·ger·ous (dān′jər əs) □*adjective*

dangle *verb* To hang loosely and swing: *The broken telephone wire dangled from the pole.*
dan·gle (dang′gəl) □*verb* **dangled, dangling, dangles**

dare *verb* **1.** To be brave enough to do or try to do something; have courage for: *He dared to swim across the lake.* **2.** To challenge: *I dare you to try and catch me.*
□*noun* A challenge: *I took his dare to jump over the fence.*
dare (dār) □*verb* **dared, daring, dares** □*noun, plural* **dares**

daring *adjective* Willing to take chances; bold: *a daring mountain climber.* —See Synonyms at **adventurous.**
□*noun* Great courage; bravery: *a rescue mis-*

sion requiring great skill and daring.
dar·ing (dâr′ing) □*adjective* □*noun*

daring

dark *adjective* **1.** With very little light or with no light: *We came home late to a dark house.* **2.** Dim or gray rather than bright: *a dark winter day.* **3.** Close to black or brown in color: *dark hair.*
□*noun* **1.** Lack of light: *Sometimes people are afraid of the dark.* **2.** Night; nightfall.
dark (därk) □*adjective* **darker, darkest** □*noun*

darken *verb* To make or become dark or darker: *Rain clouds darkened the sky.*
dark·en (där′kən) □*verb* **darkened, darkening, darkens**

darkroom *noun* A room in which photographs are developed and printed, usually in total darkness.
dark·room (därk′rōōm′) □*noun, plural* **darkrooms**

darling *noun* A dearly loved person.
□*adjective* **1.** Loved very much: *my darling husband.* **2.** Very charming and attractive; cute: *a darling kitten.*
dar·ling (där′ling) □*noun, plural* **darlings** □*adjective*

darn *verb* To mend by making stitches with yarn or thread across a hole: *darn socks.*
darn (därn) □*verb* **darned, darning, darns**

dart *noun* **1.** A thin, pointed weapon that looks like a small arrow. **2. darts** A game in which darts are thrown at a target.
□*verb* **1.** To move suddenly and quickly: *The dog darted in front of the car.* **2.** To shoot out or send forth suddenly: *The snake darted its tongue at us. She darted a frown at me.*
dart (därt) □*noun, plural* **darts** □*verb* **darted, darting, darts**

dash   *verb* **1.** To move with sudden speed: *He dashed out of the room.* **2.** To hit or throw with force: *Waves dashed against the rocks.* **3.** To destroy; wreck: *Losing the game dashed the team's hope of winning the championship.*
□*noun* **1.** A quick run or rush: *We made a dash for the bus.* **2.** A short, fast race: *I ran in the 50-yard dash.* **3.** A small amount: *a dash of salt.* **4.** A punctuation mark (—) used to set off part of a sentence from the rest or to show a pause or break in a sentence. A dash is also used to show that a word or letters in a word have been left out.
dash (dash) □*verb* **dashed, dashing, dashes** □*noun, plural* **dashes**

dash

dashboard   *noun* The panel behind the steering wheel in an automobile. The dashboard has instruments and dials that show if the automobile is working properly, and how much gasoline, oil, and water are in it.
dash·board (dash′bôrd′) □*noun, plural* **dashboards**

data   *plural noun* Facts; information: *He doesn't have enough data to solve the math problem.*
da·ta (dā′tə *or* dat′ə) □*plural noun*

date¹   **1.** The time when something happened or will happen: *My date of birth is May 27, 1965.* **2.** An appointment to meet someone or be somewhere: *I made a date to go fishing with my cousin.* **3.** The person with whom one has the appointment: *Who is your date for the school dance?*
□*verb* **1.** To mark with a date: *date a letter.* **2.** To come from or belong to a certain period of time: *an old car that dates from the 1930's.*
  out of date No longer in use or fashion: *She wore a short coat that is out of date.*
  up to date 1. In style; modern: *His suit is up to date.* **2.** Up to the present time: *Our information is up to date.*
date (dāt) □*noun, plural* **dates** □*verb* **dated, dating, dates**

date²   *noun* The sweet fruit of a kind of palm tree.
date (dāt) □*noun, plural* **dates**

daughter   *noun* A female child.
daugh·ter (dô′tər) □*noun, plural* **daughters**

daughter-in-law   *noun* The wife of a person's son.
daugh·ter-in-law (dô′tər in lô′) □*noun, plural* **daughters-in-law**

dawn   *noun* **1.** The first light that shows in the morning; daybreak. **2.** The first appearance; beginning: *the dawn of civilization.*
□*verb* **1.** To begin to grow light in the morning: *We stayed up all night and saw the day dawn.* **2.** To become clear or plain: *It dawned on him that he wouldn't finish the job on time.*
dawn (dôn) □*noun, plural* **dawns** □*verb* **dawned, dawning, dawns**

day   *noun* **1.** The time between sunrise and sunset. **2.** The period that includes one day and one night. A day has twenty-four hours. **3.** One of the seven divisions of the week. **4.** The part of a day spent in work or other activity: *Our school day ends at four o'clock.* **5.** A period or time: *The scientist spoke about the days when dinosaurs walked the land.*
day (dā) □*noun, plural* **days**

daybreak   *noun* The time each morning when light first shows; dawn.
day·break (dā′brāk′) □*noun, plural* **daybreaks**

day care center   *noun* A school that takes care of children who are too young for nursery school or kindergarten. Many parents who work during the day leave their children in day care centers.

daydream   *noun* The act of wishing or thinking about pleasant things that one would like to happen: *I had a daydream of becoming a famous movie star.*

a bat	ī bite	oo tool	*th* feather
ā make	î fierce	ou out	th bath
â dare	o dot	u nut	hw wheat
ä father	ō no	û turn	zh measure
e net	ô law, for	ch church	ə about, open
ē be	oi soil	ng ring	pencil, atom
i dip	oo look	sh shade	circus

□*verb* To think about something pleasant or desirable: *My teacher said I should stop daydreaming in class and pay more attention.*
day·dream (dā′drēm′) □*noun, plural* **daydreams** □*verb* **daydreamed, daydreaming, daydreams**

daylight *noun* **1.** The light of day; daytime. **2.** Dawn; daybreak.
day·light (dā′līt′) □*noun*

daytime *noun* The time between dawn and dark; day.
day·time (dā′tīm′) □*noun*

daze *verb* To confuse or stun; puzzle: *The punch dazed the boxer so that he didn't remember where he was.*
□*noun* A confused condition: *I was in a daze after the car accident.*
daze (dāz) □*verb* **dazed, dazing, dazes** □*noun, plural* **dazes**

dazzle *verb* To make blind or nearly blind for a short time with too much bright light: *The sunlight dazzled her, and she covered her eyes.*
daz·zle (daz′əl) □*verb* **dazzled, dazzling, dazzles**

de– A prefix that means: **1.** To do the reverse of; undo: *decode.* **2.** To remove: *defrost.* **3.** To make lower; reduce: *decline.*

deacon *noun* **1.** An officer of a church who helps the minister. **2.** A clergyman ranking below a priest in some churches.
dea·con (dē′kən) □*noun, plural* **deacons**

dead *adjective* **1.** No longer alive or living: *dead flowers; a dead tree.* **2.** Without any feeling; numb: *My leg felt dead from sitting on it.* **3.** No longer used or needed: *a dead language that nobody speaks anymore.* **4.** No longer working or operating: *The telephone is dead.* **5.** Complete; total: *dead silence.* **6.** Exact; sure: *She is a dead shot with a bow and arrow.*
□*noun* **1.** People who have died: *After the battle the soldiers buried their dead.* **2.** The darkest, coldest, or most quiet part: *the dead of night.*
□*adverb* **1.** Completely; absolutely: *dead tired.* **2.** Straight; directly: *The next town is dead ahead about 10 miles down the road.*
dead (ded) □*adjective* **deader, deadest** □*noun* □*adverb*

deaden *verb* To make weak or dull: *The doctor gave me a pill to deaden the pain.*
dead·en (ded′ən) □*verb* **deadened, deadening, deadens**

deadline *noun* A set time by which something must be completed: *The deadline for my science project is next Tuesday.*
dead·line (ded′līn′) □*noun, plural* **deadlines**

deadly *adjective* **1.** Causing or capable of causing death: *deadly poison; a deadly weapon.* **2.** Dangerous or violent enough to kill: *deadly enemies.*
□*adverb* Completely; absolutely: *I could tell she was deadly serious.*
dead·ly (ded′lē) □*adjective* **deadlier, deadliest** □*adverb*

deaf *adjective* **1.** Not being able to hear well or to hear at all. **2.** Not willing to listen: *The teacher was deaf to my excuses.*
deaf (def) □*adjective* **deafer, deafest**

deafen *adjective* To make deaf: *The noise deafened him.*
deaf·en (def′ən) □*verb* **deafened, deafening, deafens**

deal *verb* **1.** To have to do with; be about: *I'm reading a book that deals with plants and flowers.* **2.** To behave toward: *The coach deals fairly with all the players on the team.* **3.** To do business; trade: *a store that deals in parts for automobiles.* **4.** To give or deliver: *She dealt me a blow on the head.* **5.** To hand out cards to players in a card game.
□*noun* An agreement or bargain: *We made a deal to buy the neighbor's sailboat.*
a good deal or **a great deal** A large amount: *He spends a good deal of time studying.*
deal (dēl) □*verb* **dealt, dealing, deals** □*noun, plural* **deals**

dealt *verb* The past tense and past participle of **deal:** *The television show dealt with the American Revolution.*
dealt (delt) □*verb*

dear *adjective* Loved and cherished; beloved: *She is my dearest friend.*
□*noun* A person one likes or is grateful to: *He is such a dear for helping me.*
□*interjection* A word used to express dismay or surprise: *Oh, dear! Dear me!*
dear (dîr) □*adjective* **dearer, dearest** □*noun, plural* **dears** □*interjection*

dearly *adverb* Very much; greatly: *He dearly wants to go to the circus.*
dear·ly (dîr′lē) □*adverb*

death *noun* **1.** The end of life: *The forest fire was responsible for many deaths.* **2.** The ending or destruction of something: *Our history*

class was about the death of the Roman Empire.
death (deth) □*noun, plural* **deaths**

debate   *noun* A discussion of the arguments for or against something: *There was much debate in town about building a new library.*
□*verb* **1.** To discuss arguments for or against something: *The city council debated whether or not to raise taxes.* **2.** To consider carefully before deciding: *We debated whether we should go to the zoo or to the ballgame.*
de·bate (di **bāt′**) □*noun, plural* **debates**
□*verb* **debated, debating, debates**

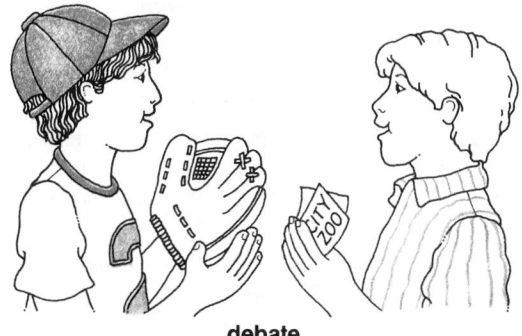

debate

debt   *noun* **1.** Something that is owed to another: *I had to borrow money from my brother, but I'll repay the debt next week. I owe everyone who helped me a debt of thanks.* **2.** The condition of owing: *She is in debt because she bought a new car.*
debt (det) □*noun, plural* **debts**

debtor   *noun* Someone who owes something to another.
debt·or (**det′**ər) □*noun, plural* **debtors**

decade   *noun* A period of ten years.
dec·ade (**dek′**ād′) □*noun, plural* **decades**

decanter   *noun* An ornamental glass bottle used to hold liquids, especially wine.
de·cant·er (di **kan′**tər) □*noun, plural* **decanters**

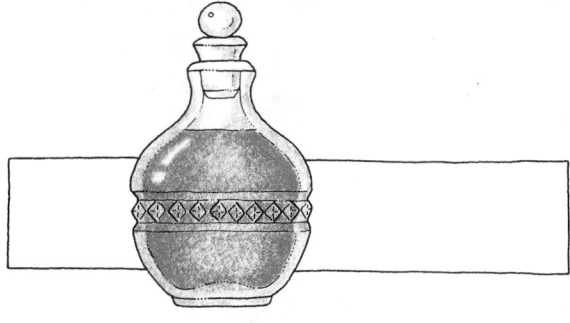

decanter

decay   *verb* To rot or cause to become rotten: *The wet lumber began to decay. Sugar can decay your teeth.*
□*noun* The slow rotting of animal or plant matter: *tooth decay.*
de·cay (di **kā′**) □*verb* **decayed, decaying, decays** □*noun, plural* **decays**

deceased   *adjective* No longer living; dead: *Her parents are deceased.*
□*noun* **the deceased** A dead person or persons.
de·ceased (di **sēst′**) □*adjective* □*noun*

deceit   *noun* The act or practice of deceiving: *The salesman was guilty of deceit when he told us the used car was in perfect condition.*
de·ceit (di **sēt′**) □*noun, plural* **deceits**

deceive   *verb* To make a person believe something that is not true: *He broke the window and then tried to deceive his father by telling him he didn't know how it got broken.*
de·ceive (di **sēv′**) □*verb* **deceived, deceiving, deceives**

December   *noun* The 12th and last month of the year. December has thirty-one days.
De·cem·ber (di **sem′**bər) □*noun, plural* **Decembers**

WORD HISTORY: **December**

December comes from a Latin word meaning "the tenth month" because it was the tenth month in the Roman calendar.

---

decent   *adjective* **1.** Being correct or proper: *It was not decent to lie to your friend.* **2.** Good enough; sufficient: *My grades are not excellent but they are decent.*
de·cent (**dē′**sənt) □*adjective*

deceptive   *adjective* Intended or likely to deceive: *He tried to hide his disappointment with a deceptive smile.*
de·cep·tive (di **sep′**tiv) □*adjective*

decide   *verb* **1.** To make up one's mind: *He decided to become a teacher.* **2.** To judge or settle: *The jury decided in favor of the accused men.* —See Synonyms at **judge.**

a bat	ī bite	ōō tool	*th* feather
ā make	î fierce	ou out	th bath
â dare	o dot	u nut	hw wheat
ä father	ō no	û turn	zh measure
e net	ô law, for	ch church	ə about, open
ē be	oi soil	ng ring	pencil, atom
i dip	oo look	sh shade	circus

de·cide (di **sīd′**) □*verb* **decided, deciding, decides**

deciliter *noun* A unit of volume in the metric system equal to ¹/₁₀ of a liter.
dec·i·li·ter (des′ə lē′tər) □*noun, plural* **deciliters**

decimal *noun* **1.** A numeral in the decimal system of numbers. **2.** A numeral based on 10, used in expressing a decimal fraction. □*adjective* Of or based on 10: *The United States has a decimal system of money.*
dec·i·mal (des′ə məl) □*noun, plural* **decimals** □*adjective*

decimal fraction *noun* A fraction in which the denominator is 10 or a power of 10. In the decimal system of numbers, 29/100 would be written .29 and 29/1000 would be written .029.

decimal point *noun* A period placed before a decimal fraction. The periods in .29 and .029 are decimal points.

decimeter *noun* A unit of length in the metric system equal to ¹/₁₀ of a meter.
dec·i·me·ter (des′ə mē′tər) □*noun, plural* **decimeters**

decipher *verb* **1.** To decode: *decipher a secret message.* **2.** To make out the meaning of something that is difficult to understand: *I never decipher her handwriting.*
de·ci·pher (di **sī′**fər) □*verb* **deciphered, deciphering, deciphers**

decision *noun* An act of result of deciding: *I asked my parents if I could go to summer camp but they haven't made a decision yet.*
de·ci·sion (di sizh′ən) □*noun, plural* **decisions**

decisive *adjective* **1.** Having the power to settle or decide something: *a decisive victory that ended the war.* **2.** Showing or marked by determination and firmness: *She's a decisive person who knows what she wants.*
de·ci·sive (di sī′siv) □*adjective*

deck *noun* **1.** One of the floors of a boat or ship. **2.** A set of playing cards. □*verb* To decorate or adorn: *We decked the house with lights and holly at Christmas.*
deck (dek) □*noun, plural* **decks** □*verb* **decked, decking, decks**

declaration *noun* A formal statement or announcement: *a declaration of war.*
dec·la·ra·tion (dek′lə **rā′**shən) □*noun, plural* **declarations**

Declaration of Independence *noun* A statement, made on July 4, 1776, declaring the thirteen American colonies independent of Great Britain.

declare *verb* **1.** To state strongly: *He declared that nothing could make him change his mind.* **2.** To announce officially; make known: *declare war.*
de·clare (di **klâr′**) □*verb* **declared, declaring, declares**

decline *verb* **1.** To refuse, especially politely: *I declined their invitation to dinner.* **2.** To become less or weaker; decrease: *The store owner says sales declined again this month.* □*noun* A slow lessening or weakening: *a decline in prices; a decline in health.* —See Synonyms at **reject.**
de·cline (di **klīn′**) □*verb* **declined, declining, declines** □*noun, plural* **declines**

decode *verb* To change something written in code into ordinary language; decipher.
de·code (dē **kōd′**) □*verb* **decoded, decoding, decodes**

decompose *verb* To decay; rot: *Dead trees and plants decompose quickly in the jungle.*
de·com·pose (dē′kəm **pōz′**) □*verb* **decomposed, decomposing, decomposes**

decorate *verb* **1.** To make more attractive or beautiful; adorn: *decorate a Christmas tree.* **2.** To give a medal to: *The general decorated the soldier for bravery.*
dec·o·rate (dek′ə rāt′) □*verb* **decorated, decorating, decorates**

decorate

decoration *noun* **1.** The act of decorating: *The decoration of the house was finished in an hour.* **2.** Something that decorates: *Balloons were used as decorations for the party.* **3.** A medal, badge, or ribbon given as an honor.

dec·o·ra·tion (dek′ə **rā′** shən) □*noun, plural* **decorations**

decoration

decorator *noun* Someone who chooses the paint, wallpaper, and furnishings for the inside of a building.
dec·o·ra·tor (**dek′** ə rā′tər) □*noun, plural* **decorators**

decoy *noun* **1.** A model of a duck or other bird used by hunters to attract wild birds or animals. **2.** Someone who leads another person into danger or a trap: *The soldier walked ahead as a decoy for the enemy.*
□*verb* To lure into danger or a trap: *We tried to decoy the dog away from the garbage cans.*
de·coy (**dē′** koi′ *or* di **koi′**) □*noun, plural* **decoys** □*verb* (di **koi′**) **decoyed, decoying, decoys**

decrease *verb* To make or become less: *She decreased the price of all the dresses in the store. The store's sales have decreased.*
□*noun* **1.** The act of decreasing: *The sudden decrease in temperature was a result of the storm.* **2.** The amount by which something decreases: *There was a decrease of four in the number of students entering the first grade this year.*
de·crease (di **krēs′**) □*verb* **decreased, decreasing, decreases** □*noun* (**dē′** krēs′ *or* di **krēs′**), *plural* **decreases**

decree *noun* An official order; law: *The governor put out a decree that allowed many stores to open on Sunday.*
□*verb* To settle or decide by decree: *The President decreed that all government offices should close for the holiday.*
de·cree (di **krē′**) □*noun, plural* **decrees** □*verb* **decreed, decreeing, decrees**

dedicate *verb* To set apart for a special use or purpose: *She dedicated her life to teaching.*
ded·i·cate (**ded′** i kāt′) □*verb* **dedicated, dedicating, dedicates**

dedication *noun* The act of dedicating: *The mayor came to the dedication of the new library.*
ded·i·ca·tion (ded′i **kā′** shən) □*noun, plural* **dedications**

deduct *verb* To take away one amount from another: *The store deducted five dollars from the price of the coat because it was dirty.*
de·duct (di **dukt′**) □*verb* **deducted, deducting, deducts**

deduction *noun* Something that is deducted or subtracted: *The salesman gave us a deduction of two dollars on the book.*
de·duc·tion (di **duk′** shən) □*noun, plural* **deductions**

deed *noun* **1.** Something done; act; action: *Helping the lost child was a good deed.* **2.** A legal document that shows who owns a certain piece of property.
deed (dēd) □*noun, plural* **deeds**

deep *adjective* **1.** Going far down from the top or the surface: *a deep hole; a deep lake.* **2.** Going far in from the front to the back: *a deep closet.* **3.** Extreme or intense: *He fell into a deep sleep.* **4.** Hard to understand: *This science book is too deep for me.* **5.** Dark and rich in color: *a deep blue.* **6.** Low in pitch: *a deep voice.*
□*adverb* Far down or into: *We dug deep looking for water.*
□*noun* The ocean; sea.
deep (dēp) □*adjective* **deeper, deepest** □*adverb* □*noun*

deepen *verb* To make or become deep or deeper: *deepen a hole.*
deep·en (**dē′** pən) □*verb* **deepened, deepening, deepens**

deer *noun* An animal that has hoofs and chews a cud. Deer can run very fast. Most male deer have antlers.
deer (dîr) □*noun, plural* **deer**

a bat	ī bite	ōō tool	th feather
ā make	î fierce	ou out	th bath
â dare	o dot	u nut	hw wheat
ä father	ō no	û turn	zh measure
e net	ô law, for	ch church	ə about, open
ē be	oi soil	ng ring	pencil, atom
i dip	oo look	sh shade	circus

deface *verb* To spoil the appearance of: *Children defaced the wall with markers.*
de·face (di **fās'**) □*verb* **defaced, defacing, defaces**

deface

defeat *verb* To win a victory over; overcome: *Our army defeated the enemy in battle.*
□*noun* **1.** The condition of being defeated. **2.** The loss of a contest: *Our baseball team has suffered four defeats in a row.*
de·feat (di **fēt'**) □*verb* **defeated, defeating, defeats** □*noun, plural* **defeats**

> **SYNONYMS: defeat, beat, triumph**
> These verbs mean to win a victory over: *She always defeats me at checkers. Do you think you can beat me in a race? It was a close baseball game but our team triumphed in the end.*

defect *noun* A flaw, shortcoming, or weakness: *The new car doesn't run because of a defect in the engine.*
de·fect (dē'**fekt'** *or* di **fekt'**) □*noun, plural* **defects**

defective *adjective* Having a defect or flaw: *The washing machine is defective and can't be used.* —See Synonyms at **imperfect.**
de·fec·tive (di **fek'**tiv) □*adjective*

defend *verb* **1.** To keep safe from attack or harm: *The army defended the city.* **2.** To argue or speak in support of: *She was accused of stealing and hired a lawyer to defend her in court.*
de·fend (di **fend'**) □*verb* **defended, defending, defends**

> **SYNONYMS: defend, protect, safeguard**
> These verbs mean to keep safe from attack or harm: *Soldiers defended the town from the enemy attack. All the students were given a vaccine to protect them against the flu. It's up to you to safeguard your little brother from the bully.*

defense *noun* **1.** The act of defending: *Soldiers ready to fight in defense of their country.* **2.** Something that defends: *People built a wall around the fort as a defense against attack.* **3.** A team or part of a team that tries to stop the opposing team from scoring.
de·fense (di **fens'**) □*noun, plural* **defenses**

defensive *adjective* Protecting from attack: *a defensive wall.*
de·fen·sive (di **fen'**siv) □*adjective*

defer[1] *verb* To put off until a later time; delay: *The meeting was deferred because of the storm.*
de·fer (di **fûr'**) □*verb* **deferred, deferring, defers**

defer[2] *verb* To give in to and accept the judgment or opinion of another: *He deferred to his mother's judgment and did not take the job.*
de·fer (di **fûr'**) □*verb* **deferred, deferring, defers**

defiance *noun* Outright refusal to obey authority: *The workers showed their defiance by slowing down.*
de·fi·ance (di **fī'**əns) □*noun*

deficiency *noun* **1.** A lack of something that is needed or important: *Her health suffered because of a vitamin deficiency.* **2.** The amount lacking; shortage: *We discovered a deficiency of $50 in the club treasury.*
de·fi·cien·cy (di **fish'**ən sē) □*noun, plural* **deficiencies**

define *verb* **1.** To give the exact meaning or meanings of: *A dictionary defines words.* **2.** To describe or tell exactly: *My father defined what he wanted me to do when I cleaned the garage.*
de·fine (di **fīn'**) □*verb* **defined, defining, defines**

definite *adjective* Known with certainty; clear: *Is it definite that she will be there?*
def·i·nite (**def'**ə nit) □*adjective*

definite article *noun* The word **the,** used to introduce a noun or noun phrase: *The phone is ringing. The teacher asked me a question.*

definition *noun* An explanation of the exact meaning or meanings of a word or phrase.
def·i·ni·tion (def'ə **nish'**ən) □*noun, plural* **definitions**

deform *verb* To spoil the shape or appearance of: *The fruit was deformed because of the drought.*
de·form (di **fôrm'**) □*verb* **deformed, deforming, deforms**

defrost *verb* To make or become free of ice or frost; thaw: *defrost a refrigerator.*
de·frost (dē **frôst**′) ☐*verb* **defrosted, defrosting, defrosts**

deft *adjective* Quick and skillful: *You need deft fingers to play the piano.*
deft (deft) ☐*adjective* **defter, deftest**

deft

defy *verb* To go against openly; oppose: *He defied his mother and stayed out late.*
de·fy (di **fī**′) ☐*verb* **defied, defying, defies**

degrade *verb* To lower in rank, standing, or character; bring shame or disgrace upon: *You degrade yourself by lying and cheating.*
de·grade (di **grād**′) ☐*verb* **degraded, degrading, degrades**

degree *noun* **1.** A step in a process or course of action: *She learned to swim by degrees.* **2.** Amount or extent: *To what degree do you want to become a lawyer?* **3.** One of the equal units into which a temperature scale is divided: *She is ill and has a temperature of 100 degrees.* **4.** A unit for measuring arcs of a circle or angles: *A square has four angles of 90 degrees.*
de·gree (di **grē**′) ☐*noun, plural* **degrees**

deity *noun* A god or goddess.
de·i·ty (dē′i tē) ☐*noun, plural* **deities**

dejected *adjective* Sad or depressed: *She felt dejected after failing the test.*
de·ject·ed (di **jek**′tid) ☐*adjective*

delay *verb* **1.** To put off until a later time; postpone: *We delayed our vacation for a week.* **2.** To cause to be late: *Snow delayed the bus.*
☐*noun* **1.** The act of delaying or being delayed. **2.** An instance of being delayed: *There was a delay before I could see the doctor.*
de·lay (di **lā**′) ☐*verb* **delayed, delaying, delays** ☐*noun, plural* **delays**

delegate *noun* Someone chosen to speak and act for another person or for a group; representative: *The governor appointed her as his delegate to the conference.*
☐*verb* To choose a person as a delegate: *He delegated me to meet the train.*
del·e·gate (**del**′i gāt′ *or* **del**′i git) ☐*noun, plural* **delegates** ☐*verb* (**del**′i gāt′) **delegated, delegating, delegates**

delegation *noun* A person or persons chosen to represent another: *A delegation of Russian diplomats met with the President.*
del·e·ga·tion (del′ə **gā**′shən) ☐*noun, plural* **delegations**

deliberate *adjective* **1.** Done or said on purpose: *a deliberate lie.* **2.** Not hurried or quick: *a deliberate choice.*
☐*verb* To give careful thought to before deciding: *She deliberated whether or not to go on a cruise.*
de·lib·er·ate (di **lib**′ər it) ☐*adjective* ☐*verb* (di **lib**′ə rāt′) **deliberated, deliberating, deliberates**

delicacy **1.** The condition or quality of being delicate: *great delicacy of workmanship.* **2.** A very special food: *Certain kinds of fish eggs are thought to be a delicacy by some people.*
del·i·ca·cy (**del**′i kə sē) ☐*noun, plural* **delicacies**

delicate *adjective* **1.** Very finely made: *delicate lace.* **2.** Pleasing to the senses: *food with a delicate flavor; a delicate perfume.* **3.** Having a soft, pale tint: *a very delicate pink.* **4.** Requiring or needing great skill: *a delicate negotiation.* **5.** Easily spoiled or broken; fragile: *delicate china.* **6.** Very sensitive: *delicate weather instruments.*
del·i·cate (**del**′i kit) ☐*adjective*

delicatessen *noun* A store that sells foods that are ready to eat. Cheeses, salads, smoked meats, sandwiches, and pastries are sold in a delicatessen.
del·i·ca·tes·sen (del′i kə **tes**′ən) ☐*noun, plural* **delicatessens**

delicious *adjective* Very pleasing to the taste and smell. —See Synonyms at **tasty.**
de·li·cious (di **lish**′əs) ☐*adjective*

a bat	ī bite	ōō tool	*th* feather
ā make	î fierce	ou out	th bath
â dare	o dot	u nut	hw wheat
ä father	ō no	û turn	zh measure
e net	ô law, for	ch church	ə about, open
ē be	oi soil	ng ring	pencil, atom
i dip	oo look	sh shade	circus

delight *noun* Great pleasure; joy: *He greeted his old friend with delight.*
□*verb* To please greatly: *The new bicycle delighted her.*
de·light (di **līt'**) □*noun, plural* **delights**
□*verb* **delighted, delighting, delights**

delight

delightful *adjective* Giving delight; very pleasing: *I spent a delightful day at the beach.*
de·light·ful (di **līt'** fəl) □*adjective*

delirious *adjective* **1.** Out of one's senses: *The high fever made the patient delirious.* **2.** Wildly excited: *She was delirious with joy when she won the race.*
de·lir·i·ous (di **lîr'** ē əs) □*adjective*

deliver *verb* **1.** To carry and give out; distribute: *Our milkman delivers butter and eggs in addition to milk.* **2.** To send against; throw: *I delivered a punch that knocked the bully down.* **3.** To give or utter: *deliver a speech.*
de·liv·er (di **liv'** ər) □*verb* **delivered, delivering, delivers**

deliver

delivery *noun* **1.** The act of delivering: *Delivery of the new couch is scheduled for Tuesday.* **2.** A manner of speaking or singing.
de·liv·er·y (di **liv'** ə rē) □*noun, plural* **deliveries**

delta *noun* A mass of sand, mud, and soil that settles at the mouth of a river.
del·ta (**del'** tə) □*noun, plural* **deltas**

> *WORD HISTORY:* **delta**
>
> The word *delta* comes from the name of the fourth letter in the Greek alphabet. The capital letter *delta* is written as a triangle, the shape of many river deltas.

demand *verb* **1.** To ask for very strongly: *The miners demanded safer working conditions.* **2.** To need or require: *This job demands long hours.*
□*noun* **1.** A very strong request: *a demand for an answer.* **2.** The condition of being needed or wanted very much: *Seats for the basketball game are in great demand.*
de·mand (di **mand'**) □*verb* **demanded, demanding, demands** □*noun, plural* **demands**

democracy **1.** A form of government in which the power belongs to the people, who exercise their power through representatives they have elected. **2.** A country with this kind of government: *The United States of America is a democracy.*
de·moc·ra·cy (di **mok'** rə sē) □*noun, plural* **democracies**

democrat *noun* **1.** Someone who believes in and supports democracy. **2.** **Democrat** Someone who is a member of the Democratic Party.
dem·o·crat (**dem'** ə krat') □*noun, plural* **democrats**

democratic *adjective* **1.** Of, like, or for a democracy: *a democratic government.* **2.** Based on the idea of equal rights for all: *The Bill of Rights is a democratic statement.* **3.** **Democratic** Of the Democratic Party.
dem·o·crat·ic (dem'ə **krat'** ik) □*adjective*

Democratic Party *noun* One of the two main political parties of the United States.

demolish *verb* To tear down completely; wreck: *The tornado demolished all the buildings on Main Street.*
de·mol·ish (di **mol'** ish) □*verb* **demolished, demolishing, demolishes**

demon *noun* **1.** An evil spirit; devil. **2.** Someone with great energy or enthusiasm for a par-

ticular thing: *a demon for work.*
de·mon (dē′mən) ▢*noun, plural* **demons**

demonstrate *verb* **1.** To show clearly: *She demonstrated her ability to drive a car.* **2.** To show, operate, or explain: *An apple falling to the ground demonstrates the law of gravity.* **3.** To take part in a parade or rally to protest or demand something: *The students demonstrated for a new dormitory.* —See Synonyms at **prove.**
dem·on·strate (dem′ən strāt′) ▢*verb* **demonstrated, demonstrating, demonstrates**

demonstration *noun* **1.** The act of showing, operating, or explaining: *a demonstration of the law of gravity; a demonstration of a new car.* **2.** A parade or rally to protest or demand something: *a demonstration against the war.*
dem·on·stra·tion (dem′ən strā′shən) ▢*noun, plural* **demonstrations**

den *noun* **1.** The home of a wild animal; lair. **2.** A small room for study or relaxing. **3.** A unit of about eight Cub Scouts.
den (den) ▢*noun, plural* **dens**

denial *noun* The act of denying: *He made a quick denial of the accusation.*
de·ni·al (di nī′əl) ▢*noun, plural* **denials**

denim *noun* **1.** A heavy cotton cloth used for work clothes and sport clothes. **2. denims** Overalls or trousers made of denim.
den·im (den′im) ▢*noun, plural* **denims**

WORD HISTORY: **denim**

The word *denim* comes from the French phrase *serge de Nîmes*, which means "serge of Nîmes." Nîmes is a town in France.

denim
Denims

denomination *noun* **1.** An organized religious group: *The Protestant church is made*

up of many different denominations. **2.** A unit in a system of money: *A dollar and a nickel are different denominations of money in the United States.*
de·nom·i·na·tion (di nom′ə nā′shən) ▢*noun, plural* **denominations**

denominator *noun* The number written below the line in a fraction. In the fraction ½, 2 is the denominator.
de·nom·in·a·tor (di nom′ə nā′tər) ▢*noun, plural* **denominators**

denote *verb* **1.** To mean exactly; signify: *The word "chair" denotes a piece of furniture on which a person sits.* **2.** To be a sign of; indicate: *Frost denotes the coming of winter.*
de·note (di nōt′) ▢*verb* **denoted, denoting, denotes**

denounce *verb* To show or express very strong lack of approval of: *The people denounced the dictator.*
de·nounce (di nouns′) ▢*verb* **denounced, denouncing, denounces**

dense *adjective* Packed closely together; thick: *a dense forest.*
dense (dens) ▢*adjective* **denser, densest**

density *noun* The condition of being dense: *The density of the fog was so great that we could not see the car ahead of us.*
den·si·ty (den′si tē) ▢*noun, plural* **densities**

dent *noun* A hollow place in a surface, usually caused by a blow or pressure: *This can of peaches has a lot of dents in it.*
▢*verb* To make a dent in: *The hail dented the tin roof.*
dent (dent) ▢*noun, plural* **dents** ▢*verb* **dented, denting, dents**

dental *adjective* **1.** Of or for the teeth: *a dental x-ray.* **2.** Having to do with the work of a dentist: *a busy dental office.*
den·tal (den′təl) ▢*adjective*

dentine *noun* The hard part of a tooth underneath the outer enamel.
den·tine (den′tēn′) ▢*noun*

dentist *noun* A doctor who treats people's teeth. A dentist cleans teeth, pulls teeth when

a	bat	ī	bite	ōō	tool	*th*	feather
ā	make	î	fierce	ou	out	th	bath
â	dare	o	dot	u	nut	hw	wheat
ä	father	ō	no	û	turn	zh	measure
e	net	ô	law, for	ch	church	ə	about, open
ē	be	oi	soil	ng	ring		pencil, atom
i	dip	oo	look	sh	shade		circus

necessary, fills cavities, and does other work related to the teeth and mouth.
den·tist (**den′** tist) ▢*noun, plural* **dentists**

dentist

deny *verb* **1.** To say that something is not true: *I denied the charge of stealing.* **2.** To refuse to give: *He denied the request for extra time.*
de·ny (di **nī′**) ▢*verb* **denied, denying, denies**

depart *verb* **1.** To go away; leave: *Your train departs at noon.* **2.** To change from the usual course or way; vary: *The teacher departed from the lesson plan and announced a surprise test.*
de·part (di **pärt′**) ▢*verb* **departed, departing, departs**

department *noun* A separate division of an organization that has a special purpose or function: *the shoe department of a large store.*
de·part·ment (di **pärt′** mənt) ▢*noun, plural* **departments**

department store *noun* A large store that sells many kinds of goods.

departure *noun* The act of departing: *The plane's departure was on schedule.*
de·par·ture (di **pär′** chər) ▢*noun, plural* **departures**

depend *verb* **1.** To be affected or determined: *Whether or not we arrive on time depends on the traffic.* **2.** To be certain about; trust: *I depend on you to be on time for the meeting.* **3.** To rely on for support: *He depended on his parents until he got a job.*
de·pend (di **pend′**) ▢*verb* **depended, depending, depends**

dependable *adjective* Trustworthy; reliable: *a dependable friend; dependable transportation.*
de·pend·a·ble (di **pen′** də bəl) ▢*adjective*

dependence *noun* The condition of being dependent: *the dependence of crops upon the weather.*
de·pend·ence (di **pen′** dəns) ▢*noun*

dependent *adjective* **1.** Relying on someone or something else: *Plants are dependent on the sun for their growth.* **2.** Determined by something or someone else: *The outcome is dependent upon our cooperation.*
▢*noun* Someone who depends on another for support.
de·pend·ent (di **pen′** dənt) ▢*adjective*
▢*noun, plural* **dependents**

depict *verb* To show by using words, drawings, or pictures: *This book depicts life in the country.*
de·pict (di **pikt′**) ▢*verb* **depicted, depicting, depicts**

deposit *verb* **1.** To put down; lay down: *She deposited the package on the chair.* **2.** To place money in a bank.
▢*noun* **1.** An amount of money in a bank or ready to be put in a bank. **2.** An amount of money given as part of a full payment: *I made a deposit of ten dollars.* **3.** A mass of material that builds up by a natural process.
de·pos·it (di **poz′** it) ▢*verb* **deposited, depositing, deposits** ▢*noun, plural* **deposits**

depot *noun* A railroad or bus station.
de·pot (**dē′** pō) ▢*noun, plural* **depots**

depress *verb* **1.** To press down: *depress the brake pedal.* **2.** To make gloomy or sad: *The bad weather depressed me.*
de·press (di **pres′**) ▢*verb* **depressed, depressing, depresses**

depression *noun* **1.** An unhappy state of mind: *His long illness caused his depression.* **2.** An area that is lower than its surroundings; hollow: *a depression in the road.* **3.** A time when business is bad and many people are out of work.
de·pres·sion (di **presh′** ən) ▢*noun, plural* **depressions**

deprive *verb* To keep or prevent from having or doing: *The dictator deprived the people of their right to vote.*
de·prive (di **prīv′**) ▢*verb* **deprived, depriving, deprives**

dept. An abbreviation for **department**.

depth *noun* **1.** The distance from top to bottom: *the depth of a well.* **2.** The distance from front to back: *the depth of a shelf.* **3.** Deep learning, thought, or feeling: *a person of great depth.*
depth (depth) ☐*noun, plural* **depths**

deputy *noun* Someone appointed to assist or act in the place of another: *a sheriff's deputy.*
dep·u·ty (dep′yə tē) ☐*noun, plural* **deputies**

derby *noun* **1.** A man's stiff felt hat with a rounded top and a narrow, curved brim. **2.** An annual race for three-year-old horses.
der·by (dûr′be) ☐*noun, plural* **derbies**

derive *verb* To get or receive from a source: *She derives great satisfaction from her work. The word "algebra" is derived from Arabic.*
de·rive (di rīv′) ☐*verb* **derived, deriving, derives**

derrick *noun* **1.** A large machine for lifting and moving heavy objects. It has a long, movable arm with pulleys and cables and is connected to the base of an upright beam that doesn't move. **2.** A tall framework that supports the equipment used to drill an oil well.
der·rick (der′ik) ☐*noun, plural* **derricks**

WORD HISTORY: **derrick**

The word *derrick* comes from the last name of a hangman who lived in England about 300 years ago. The hangman was so well-known that his name became used as a term for "a gallows." Later a machine for lifting came to be known as a *derrick* because it looked somewhat like a gallows.

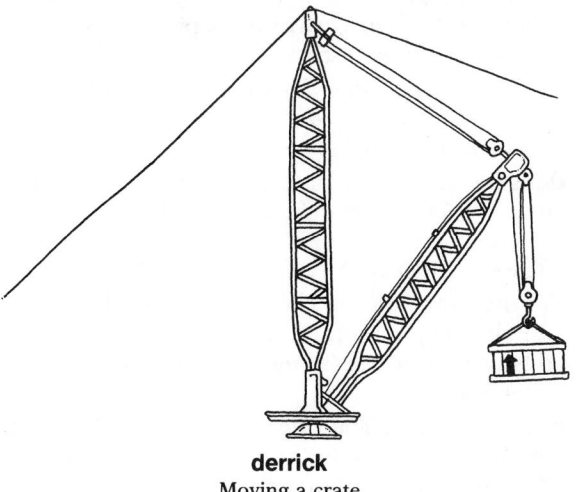

derrick
Moving a crate

descend *verb* **1.** To move from a higher to a lower place or position; go or come down:

They descended the mountain. The balloon descended slowly. **2.** To come down or along from a source or origin: *The necklace descended from mother to daughter.* —See Synonyms at **fall.**
de·scend (di send′) ☐*verb* **descended, descending, descends**

descendant *noun* A person or animal that comes from a certain parent or ancestor: *That horse is a descendant of champions.*
de·scen·dant (di sen′dənt) ☐*noun, plural* **descendants**

SYNONYMS: **descendant, child, offspring**

These nouns mean a person or animal that comes from a certain parent or ancestor: *She is a descendant of the first people who settled in this valley. I am my parents' only child. Both of these puppies are the offspring of my collie.*

---

descent *noun* **1.** The act of descending: *He made a descent by parachute.* **2.** A downward slope: *a hill with a sharp descent.* **3.** Family origin: *She is of Canadian descent.*
de·scent (di sent′) ☐*noun, plural* **descents**

describe *verb* To give an account of in words: *Please describe how the accident happened.*
de·scribe (di skrīb′) ☐*verb* **described, describing, describes**

description *noun* **1.** The act of describing: *Her description of the accident was upsetting.* **2.** An account in words describing something: *a poster with a description of the outlaw.* **3.** A kind or variety; sort: *There were people of every description at the auction.*
de·scrip·tion (di skrip′shən) ☐*noun, plural* **descriptions**

descriptive *adjective* Giving a description; describing: *a descriptive booklet about the museum.*
de·scrip·tive (di skrip′tiv) ☐*adjective*

desegregate *verb* To put an end to the forced separation of races in public schools and other facilities.

a	bat	i	bite	oo	tool	*th*	feather
ā	make	î	fierce	ou	out	th	bath
â	dare	o	dot	u	nut	hw	wheat
ä	father	ō	no	û	turn	zh	measure
e	net	ô	law, for	ch	church	ə	about, open
ē	be	oi	soil	ng	ring		pencil, atom
i	dip	oo	look	sh	shade		circus

de·seg·re·gate (dē seg′ri gāt′) □*verb*
desegregated, desegregating, desegregates

desert¹　*noun* A dry region that is usually covered with sand and has few or no plants.
□*adjective* Without people: *a desert island.*
des·ert (dez′ərt) □*noun, plural* **deserts**
□*adjective*

desert²　*verb* To leave or abandon: *The soldier deserted his post.* —See Synonyms at **abandon.**
de·sert (di zûrt′) □*verb* **deserted, deserting, deserts**

deserve　*verb* To be worthy of: *He deserves a reward.* —See Synonyms at **merit.**
de·serve (di zûrv′) □*verb* **deserved, deserving, deserves**

design　*verb* **1.** To prepare a plan for something, especially by sketching or drawing: *Who designed the new shopping center?* **2.** To plan or intend to use for a special purpose: *Playgrounds are designed for children.*
□*noun* **1.** A drawing or sketch showing how something is to be made: *He showed us the design for our new house.* **2.** An arrangement of lines, figures, or objects into a pattern.
de·sign (di zīn′) □*verb* **designed, designing, designs** □*noun, plural* **designs**

designate　*verb* **1.** To point out; show: *A marker designated the highest point of the flood.* **2.** To call by a name or title. **3.** To choose; appoint: *We designated the class president as our representative.*
des·ig·nate (dez′ig nāt′) □*verb* **designated, designating, designates**

designate

designated hitter　*noun* A baseball player who bats instead of the pitcher.

desirable　*adjective* Worthy of being desired: *a desirable location.*
de·sir·a·ble (di zīr′ə bəl) □*adjective*

desire　*verb* To wish or long for; want: *Our country desires peace.*
□*noun* A wish or longing: *a strong desire for freedom.*
de·sire (di zīr′) □*verb* **desired, desiring, desires** □*noun, plural* **desires**

desk　*noun* A piece of furniture with a flat or sloping top used for writing or reading. A desk usually has drawers.
desk (desk) □*noun, plural* **desks**

desolate　*adjective* **1.** Without people; deserted: *a desolate island.* **2.** Lonely and sad: *a lost child with a desolate expression.*
des·o·late (des′ə lit) □*adjective*

despair　*noun* Lack of all hope.
□*verb* To lose all hope: *I despaired of ever passing the course.*
des·pair (di spâr′) □*noun, plural* **despairs** □*verb* **despaired, despairing, despairs**

desperate　*adjective* **1.** Being in a situation without hope and ready to do anything: *The escaped criminal became desperate when he was cornered by the police.* **2.** Having an urgent need: *was desperate for money because she had lost her job.* **3.** Almost hopeless; very bad: *They were in a desperate position many miles from help.*
des·per·ate (des′pər it) □*adjective*

desperation　*noun* A reckless feeling that comes from losing all hope: *Desperation made him jump from the burning building.*
des·per·a·tion (des′pə rā′shən) □*noun*

despise　*verb* To look down on with scorn; hate: *I despise liars.*
de·spise (di spīz′) □*verb* **despised, despising, despises**

despite　*preposition* In spite of: *I went swimming despite the cold water.*
de·spite (di spīt′) □*preposition*

dessert　*noun* The last part of a lunch or dinner: *Ice cream and fruit were served for dessert.*
des·sert (di zûrt′) □*noun, plural* **desserts**

destination　*noun* The place to which someone is going or something is sent.
des·ti·na·tion (des′tə nā′shən) □*noun, plural* **destinations**

destiny　*noun* The fate or fortune of a person or thing. Destiny is thought of as decided or determined ahead of time.
des·ti·ny (des′tə nē) □*noun, plural* **destinies**

destroy　*verb* To ruin completely; wipe out: *The locusts destroyed the crops last year.*

de·stroy (di **stroi′**) ☐*verb* **destroyed, destroying, destroys**

destroyer *noun* A fast warship that carries guns, torpedoes, and other weapons.
de·stroy·er (di **stroi′** ər) ☐*noun, plural* **destroyers**

destruction *noun* **1.** The act of destroying: *They plan to use dynamite for the destruction of the old bridge.* **2.** Serious harm or damage: *The tornado caused great destruction.*
de·struc·tion (di **struk′** shən) ☐*noun*

destructive *adjective* Causing destruction: *a destructive flood.*
de·struc·tive (di **struk′** tiv) ☐*adjective*

detach *verb* To separate or disconnect: *I detached the nozzle from the hose.*
de·tach (di **tach′**) ☐*verb* **detached, detaching, detaches**

detail *noun* **1.** A small or less important part or item: *The details of the faces are not clear in the photograph.* **2.** Lengthy treatment of particular items: *Tell me the plans for the holiday but don't go into detail.* **3.** A small group of persons given a special duty or mission.
☐*verb* To tell or relate very precisely: *He detailed each step of the routine.*
de·tail (di **tāl′** or **dē′** tāl′) ☐*noun, plural* **details** ☐*verb* (di **tāl′**) **detailed, detailing, details**

detain **1.** To make late; delay: *She was detained by traffic.* **2.** To keep in custody; confine: *detained the suspect for questioning.*
de·tain (di **tān′**) ☐*verb* **detained, detaining, detains**

detect *verb* To notice or find the presence of: *This device can detect the presence of smoke in a house.*
de·tect (di **tekt′**) ☐*verb* **detected, detecting, detects**

detective *noun* Someone, usually a police officer, whose work is getting information about crimes and trying to solve them.
de·tec·tive (di **tek′** tiv) ☐*noun, plural* **detectives**

deter *verb* To prevent from doing something; discourage: *Bad weather deterred us from bicycling to town.*
de·ter (di **tûr′**) ☐*verb* **deterred, deterring, deters**

detergent *noun* A cleaning powder or liquid used instead of soap. Detergents are used especially for cleaning oily, greasy, or very dirty surfaces or materials.

de·ter·gent (di **tûr′** jənt) ☐*noun, plural* **detergents**

determination *noun* **1.** The act of coming to a decision: *The photograph helped in the determination of the winner of the horse race.* **2.** A strong and firm purpose: *He has the determination to overcome all the obstacles to success.*
de·ter·mi·na·tion (di **tûr′**mə **nā′**shən) ☐*noun, plural* **determinations**

determine *verb* **1.** To decide or settle: *The judges will determine which dog is the champion.* **2.** To be the cause of; influence: *Climate determines the way that people live in different parts of the world.* **3.** To find out; establish: *Scientists have determined that there is no life on the moon.*
de·ter·mine (di **tûr′** min) ☐*verb* **determined, determining, determines**

determined *adjective* Showing a firm purpose: *a determined effort to win the race.*
de·ter·mined (di **tûr′** mined) ☐*adjective*

determiner *noun* A word that modifies a noun and that can occupy the position before another adjective modifying the same noun. Some of the determiners are: *a, an, the, my, his, our, this, that, each, every, several, first, second, hundred,* and *some.*
de·ter·min·er (di **tûr′** mə nər) ☐*noun, plural* **determiners**

detest *verb* To dislike strongly; hate: *I detest bats.*
de·test (di **test′**) ☐*verb* **detested, detesting, detests**

detour *noun* A road or path used while another is out of use or being repaired.
☐*verb* To cause to take a detour: *The police detoured all buses and heavy trucks away from the center of town.*
de·tour (dē′ toor′) ☐*noun, plural* **detours** ☐*verb* **detoured, detouring, detours**

detract *verb* To make less pleasing or valuable: *The scratches detracted from the value of the used car.*
de·tract (di **trakt′**) ☐*verb* **detracted, detracting, detracts**

a	bat	ī	bite	ō͞o	tool	*th*	feather
ā	make	i	fierce	ou	out	th	bath
â	dare	o	dot	u	nut	hw	wheat
ä	father	ō	no	û	turn	zh	measure
e	net	ô	law, for	ch	church	ə	about, open
ē	be	oi	soil	ng	ring		pencil, atom
i	dip	o͞o	look	sh	shade		circus

devastate *verb* To destroy completely; ruin: *Fire devastated the town hall.*
dev·as·tate (**dev′**ə stāt′) ◻*verb* **devastated, devastating, devastates**

develop *verb* **1.** To come or cause to come into being or action; grow: *A tadpole develops into a frog. Using a dictionary will develop your vocabulary.* **2.** To treat a photographic film, plate, or print with chemicals so that the picture can be seen.
de·vel·op (di **vel′**əp) ◻*verb* **developed, developing, develops**

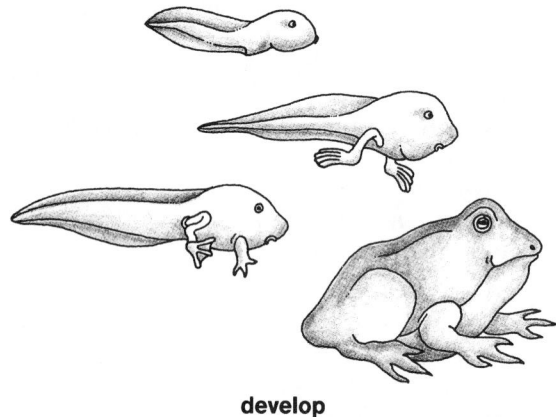
develop

development *noun* **1.** The act of developing: *The development of a hairy caterpillar into a butterfly seems to be a miracle.* **2.** An event or happening: *watched for new developments in the case.* **3.** A group of buildings or houses built in a similar style, usually by the same builder.
de·vel·op·ment (di **vel′**əp mənt) ◻*noun,* **plural developments**

device *noun* Something that is made, designed, or used for a special purpose: *A pulley is a useful device for lifting heavy weights.*
de·vice (di **vīs′**) ◻*noun, plural* **devices**

devil *noun* **1.** Often **Devil** An evil spirit believed to be the ruler of Hell. **2.** Someone who is wicked or has a bad temper.
dev·il (**dev′**əl) ◻*noun, plural* **devils**

devise *verb* To form or arrange in the mind; plan: *He devised a better method for producing steel.*
de·vise (di **vīz′**) ◻*verb* **devised, devising, devises**

devote *verb* To give one's time, attention, or effort to someone or some purpose.
de·vote (di **vōt′**) ◻*verb* **devoted, devoting, devotes**

devoted *adjective* **1.** Affectionate: *devoted parents.* **2.** Faithful; loyal: *a devoted friend.*
de·vot·ed (di **vōt′**id) ◻*adjective*

devotion *noun* Loyal feeling; loyalty: *devotion to one's country.*
de·vo·tion (di **vō′**shən) ◻*noun*

devour *verb* To swallow or eat up eagerly: *The hungry bears devoured the food.*
de·vour (di **vour′**) ◻*verb* **devoured, devouring, devours**

devout *adjective* **1.** Deeply religious: *a devout nun.* **2.** Sincere; earnest: *a devout wish for your success.*
de·vout (di **vout′**) ◻*adjective*

dew *noun* Small drops of water that condense from the air and collect on a surface, usually during the night.
dew (dōō or dyōō) ◻*noun, plural* **dews**

dewlap *noun* A loose fold of skin that hangs from the neck of cattle and certain other animals.
dew·lap (**dōō′**lap′ or **dyōō′**lap′) ◻*noun, plural* **dewlaps**

dexterous *adjective* **1.** Skillful in the use of the hands, body, or mind. **2.** Skillfully done.
dex·ter·ous (**dek′**stər əs) ◻*adjective*

WORD HISTORY: **dexterous**

In ancient times people thought that the right side was connected with good luck and the left side with bad luck. *Dexterous* comes from the Latin word that means "on the right side." The Latin word came also to mean "skillful," because if you were skillful it meant that the gods liked you and gave you good luck.

---

dia. An abbreviation for **diameter.**

diabetes *noun* A disease in which the level of sugar in the blood is too high.
di·a·be·tes (dī′ə **bē′**tis or dī′ə **bē′**tēz) ◻*noun*

diacritical mark *noun* Any of different marks added to a letter or letters, used to show a certain kind of pronunciation. The long mark over the *i* in the pronunciation of *"bite"* (bīt) is a diacritical mark.
di·a·crit·i·cal mark (dī′ə **krit′**i kəl) ◻*noun*

diagnosis *noun* The act of examining persons or animals and studying their symptoms to find out what is wrong with them.
di·ag·no·sis (dī′əg **nō′**sis) ◻*noun, plural* **di·ag·no·ses** (dī′əg **nō′**sēz′)

diagonal *adjective* Having a slanting direction.

diagram 177 diary

□*noun* A line that goes from one corner to the opposite corner of a rectangle or square.
di·ag·o·nal (dī ag′ ə nəl) □*adjective* □*noun, plural* **diagonals**

diagram *noun* A plan or drawing that shows how something works: *a diagram of the model airplane.*
□*verb* To draw or show by a diagram.
di·a·gram (dī′ ə gram′) □*noun, plural* **diagrams** □*verb* **diagrammed, diagramming, diagrams**

dial *noun* **1.** A part on the face of an instrument that is marked with numbers or figures. It has pointers that move and show the measurements to be read or chosen. Clocks, meters, and telephones have dials. **2.** A disk or knob that tunes in a radio or television set to a particular station.
□*verb* To control or choose by means of a dial: *He dialed the emergency number.*
di·al (dī′ əl) □*noun, plural* **dials** □*verb* **dialed, dialing, dials**

dial

dialect *noun* A variety of a language spoken in particular places or parts of a country or by particular groups of people. Dialects usually differ in the pronunciation of certain words, in the way certain words are used, or in what certain words mean.
di·a·lect (dī′ ə lekt′) □*noun, plural* **dialects**

dialogue *noun* A conversation between two or more people.
di·a·logue (dī′ ə lôg′) □*noun, plural* **dialogues**

dial tone *noun* A sound in a telephone receiver that goes on without a break when the receiver is lifted. It tells the user that a call can be dialed.

diameter *noun* A straight line that goes through the center of a circle or other round

figure or object from one side to the other.
di·am·e·ter (dī am′ i tər) □*noun, plural* **diameters**

diamond *noun* **1.** A mineral that is a crystal form of carbon and is the hardest of all known substances. Diamonds are used for cutting and grinding in industry. They are also polished, cut, and used as jewels. **2.** A playing card marked with a red figure (♦) that is formed with four equal sides. **3. diamonds** The suit of cards marked with this figure. **4.** The infield in baseball.
di·a·mond (dī′ mənd *or* dī′ ə mənd) □*noun, plural* **diamonds**

diaper *noun* A soft cloth or other material that is folded and fastened around a baby to serve as underpants.
di·a·per (dī′ ə pər *or* dī′ pər) □*noun, plural* **diapers**

diaphragm *noun* A wall of muscle that separates the chest from the abdomen. The diaphragm forces air into and out of the lungs.
di·a·phragm (dī′ ə fram′) □*noun, plural* **diaphragms**

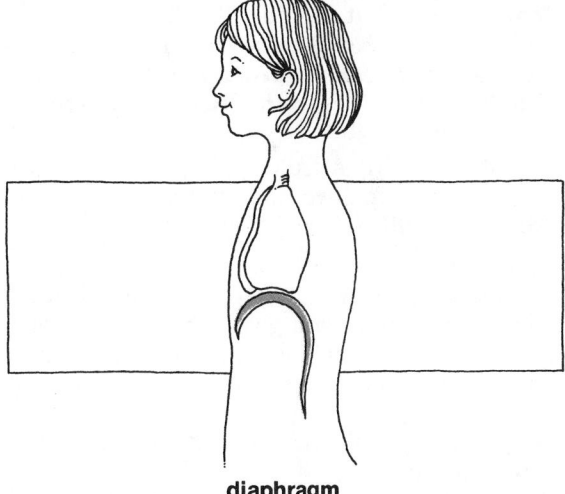

diaphragm

diary *noun* A daily record of a person's own experiences and thoughts.
di·a·ry (dī′ ə rē) □*noun, plural* **diaries**

a	bat	ī	bite	ōō	tool	*th*	feather
ā	make	î	fierce	ou	out	th	bath
â	dare	o	dot	u	nut	hw	wheat
ä	father	ō	no	û	turn	zh	measure
e	net	ô	law, for	ch	church	ə	about, open
ē	be	oi	soil	ng	ring		pencil, atom
i	dip	oo	look	sh	shade		circus

dice *plural noun* Small cubes marked on each side with from one to six dots. Dice are used to play many different games.
□*verb* To cut into small cubes: *We diced vegetables for the soup.*
dice (dīs) □*plural noun* □*verb* **diced, dicing, dices**

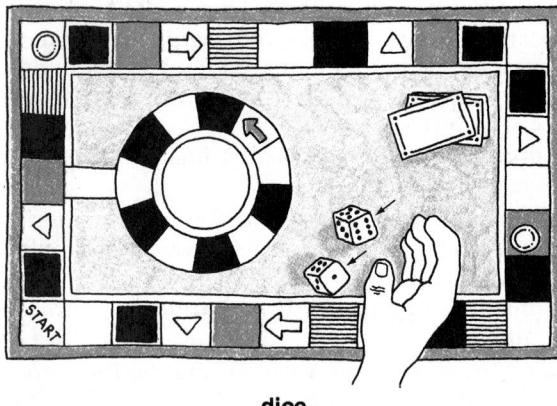

dice

dictate *verb* **1.** To say or read aloud so that another person can write down or a machine can record what is said: *She dictates most of her letters to her secretary.* **2.** To order with authority: *He cannot dictate to us.*
dic·tate (dik′tāt′) □*verb* **dictated, dictating, dictates**

dictator *noun* A ruler who has complete power over the government of a country.
dic·ta·tor (dik′tā′tər) □*noun, plural* **dictators**

dictionary *noun* A book in which the words of a language are arranged in alphabetical order, with information given about each word. This dictionary includes the spelling, the pronunciation, and the meaning or meanings of each word.
dic·tion·ar·y (dik′shə ner′ē) □*noun, plural* **dictionaries**

did *verb* The past tense of **do**: *She did a good job.*
did (did) □*verb*

didn't (did′ənt) Contraction of "did not."

die[1] *verb* **1.** To stop living: *The plants died during the drought.* **2.** To become weak: *The noise of the explosion died down.* **3.** To want very much: *I'm dying for a glass of lemonade.*
die (dī) □*verb* **died, dying, dies**

die[2] *verb* **1.** A metal device for stamping designs on coins, making raised patterns on paper, or cutting and shaping metal or leather.

2. One of a pair of dice.
die (dī) □*noun, plural* **dies** *for sense 1* and **dice** *for sense 2*

diesel engine *noun* An engine that burns oil in its cylinders. The oil is burned by the heat of air compressed in the cylinders.
die·sel engine (dē′zəl) □*noun*

WORD HISTORY: **diesel engine**

The *diesel engine* is named after Rudolf Diesel, the German engineer who invented it.

---

diet *noun* **1.** The usual food and drink taken in by a person or animal: *A good diet will supply the vitamins that your body needs.* **2.** Special foods eaten for medical reasons or to gain or lose weight.
□*verb* To eat and drink special foods, especially to lose weight.
di·et (dī′it) □*noun, plural* **diets** □*verb* **dieted, dieting, diets**

differ *verb* **1.** To be unlike in form, quality, or amount: *His habits differ from mine.* **2.** To have another opinion of; disagree: *They differed over a political matter.*
dif·fer (dif′ər) □*verb* **differed, differing, differs**

difference *noun* **1.** The condition of being different: *the difference between right and wrong.* **2.** The amount of being different: *a difference of three feet in our measurements.* **3.** A disagreement: *We made up our differences.* **4.** The amount left after one number is subtracted from another: *The difference between 6 and 9 is 3.*
dif·fer·ence (dif′ər əns *or* dif′rəns) □*noun, plural* **differences**

different *adjective* **1.** Not being the same; unlike: *The penguin is different from most other birds.* **2.** Separate or distinct: *Different people like different things.*
dif·fer·ent (dif′ər ənt *or* dif′rənt) □*adjective*

difficult *adjective* **1.** Not easy to do, understand, or solve: *a difficult task; a difficult problem.* **2.** Hard to please or manage: *He is a difficult person.*
dif·fi·cult (dif′i kult′) □*adjective*

SYNONYMS: **difficult, hard, tough**

These adjectives mean not easy to do, understand, or solve: *Learning how to ice-skate can be difficult. She found it hard to make out what the old man was saying. That was a tough arithmetic test.*

---

difficulty *noun* **1.** The condition of being difficult: *the difficulty of the science exam.* **2.** Something that is difficult: *the difficulties of his job.*
dif·fi·cul·ty (dif′i kul′tē) □*noun, plural* **difficulties**

dig *verb* **1.** To break up, turn over, or take away earth with a tool, hands, or paws. **2.** To make by digging: *dig a tunnel under the river.* **3.** To get by digging: *dig for gold.*
dig (dig) □*verb* **dug, digging, digs**

digest *verb* To change food into simple substances that can be used by the body.
□*noun* A shortening or summary of a written work: *a digest of the book.*
di·gest (di **jest′** *or* dī **jest′**) □*verb* **digested, digesting, digests**

digestible *adjective* Able to be be digested: *digestible food.*
di·gest·i·ble (di **jes′**tə bəl *or* dī **jes′**tə bəl) □*adjective*

digestion *noun* The process of digesting.
di·ges·tion (di **jes′**chən *or* dī **jes′**chən) □*noun*

digestive *adjective* Of, helping, or active in the digestion of food.
di·ges·tive (di **jes′**tiv *or* dī **jes′**tiv) □*adjective*

digestive system *noun* The alimentary canal together with certain other organs of the body, such as the liver and pancreas, that produce substances needed for digestion.

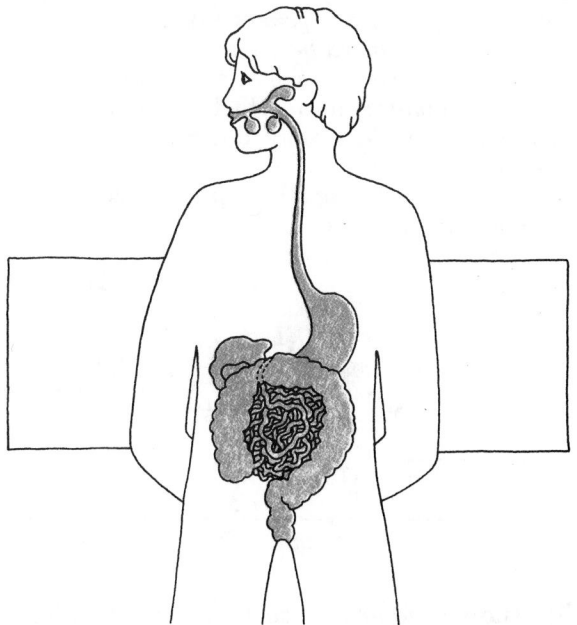

digestive system

digit *noun* **1.** A finger or toe. **2.** One of the numerals 1, 2, 3, 4, 5, 6, 7, 8, 9, and sometimes 0.
di·git (dij′it) □*noun, plural* **digits**

dignified *adjective* Having or showing dignity; serious and stately: *The judge always behaves in a dignified manner.*
dig·ni·fied (dig′nə fīd′) □*adjective*

dignity *noun* The condition of being worthy or honorable: *the rights and dignity of a citizen.*
dig·ni·ty (dig′ni tē) □*noun*

dike *noun* A wall or dam that is built to hold back water and prevent flooding.
dike (dīk) □*noun, plural* **dikes**

dilapidated *adjective.* Being in a state of poor repair or almost ruined: *a dilapidated car with no fenders.*
di·lap·i·dat·ed (di **lap′**i dā′tid) □*adjective*

diligent *adjective* Working hard and carefully: *a diligent student.*
dil·i·gent (dil′ə jənt) □*adjective*

dilute *verb* To make thinner or weaker by adding a liquid.
di·lute (di **loot′** *or* dī **loot′**) □*verb* **diluted, diluting, dilutes**

dim *adjective* **1.** Having cr giving little light: *the dim light of a candle.* **2.** Not clear: *the dim outline of the castle in the distance.* **3.** Not sharp or keen: *dim eyesight.*
□*verb* To make or become dim: *She dimmed the headlights.*
dim (dim) □*adjective* **dimmer, dimmest** □*verb* **dimmed, dimming, dims**

dime *noun* A coin of the United States or Canada worth ten cents.
dime (dīm) □*noun, plural* **dimes**

> **WORD HISTORY:** **dime**
>
> The word *dime* comes from a Latin word meaning ''tenth.'' A dime is one tenth of a dollar.

dimension *noun* The measure of the length, width, or height of something.
di·men·sion (di **men′**shən) □*noun, plural* **dimensions**

a	bat	ī	bite	ŏŏ	tool	*th*	feather
ā	make	î	fierce	ou	out	th	bath
â	dare	o	dot	u	nut	hw	wheat
ä	father	ō	no	û	turn	zh	measure
e	net	ô	law, for	ch	church	ə	about, open
ē	be	oi	soil	ng	ring		pencil, atom
i	dip	oo	look	sh	shade		circus

diminish   *verb* To make or become smaller or less: *The drought diminished the food supply.*
di·min·ish (di **min**′ish) □*verb* **diminished, diminishing, diminishes**

diminutive   *adjective* Of very small size; tiny.
di·min·u·tive (di **min**′yə tiv) □*adjective*

dimple   *noun* A small hollow in the flesh of the body, as in the cheek or chin.
dim·ple (dim′pəl) □*noun, plural* **dimples**

dimple

din   *noun* Loud, confusing noise: *the din of traffic in the city.*
□*verb* To cause to understand something by repeating it over and over: *The teacher dinned the dates of the battles into our heads.*
din (din) □*noun* □*verb* **dinned, dinning, dins**

dine   *verb* To eat dinner: *We usually dine at seven.*
dine (dīn) □*verb* **dined, dining, dines**

diner   *noun* **1.** Someone who is eating a meal. **2.** A railroad car in which meals are served. **3.** A small restaurant often resembling a railroad car.
din·er (dī′nər) □*noun, plural* **diners**

dinghy   *noun* A small boat, especially a rowboat.
din·ghy (ding′ē) □*noun, plural* **dinghies**

dinghy

dingy   *adjective* Dirty or soiled: *the tramp's dingy clothes.*
din·gy (din′jē) □*adjective* **dingier, dingiest**

dining room   *noun* A room used for eating meals.

dinner   *noun* **1.** The main meal of the day, served at noon or in the evening. **2.** A formal meal in honor of a person or a special occasion: *I am planning to give a dinner for the governor next month.*
din·ner (din′ər) □*noun, plural* **dinners**

dinosaur   *noun* One of many kinds of reptiles that lived millions of years ago. Some dinosaurs were the largest land animals that have ever lived.
di·no·saur (dī′nə sôr′) □*noun, plural* **dinosaurs**

WORD HISTORY: **dinosaur**

The word *dinosaur* is a compound of two Greek words, one meaning "terrible" and the other meaning "lizard."

---

diocese   *noun* A church district under the direction of a bishop.
di·o·cese (dī′ə sis) □*noun, plural* **dioceses**

dip   *verb* **1.** To put briefly into a liquid: *I dipped my hand into the water to see if it was cold.* **2.** To go into water and come out quickly: *We dipped in the pond to cool off.* **3.** To lower and raise in salute: *The soldier dipped the flag to the general.* **4.** To go down; sink: *The sun dipped below the horizon.*
□*noun* **1.** A brief plunge or swim. **2.** A liquid or soft mixture into which something is dipped. **3.** A sudden slope downward: *a dip in the road.*
dip (dip) □*verb* **dipped, dipping, dips** □*noun, plural* **dips**

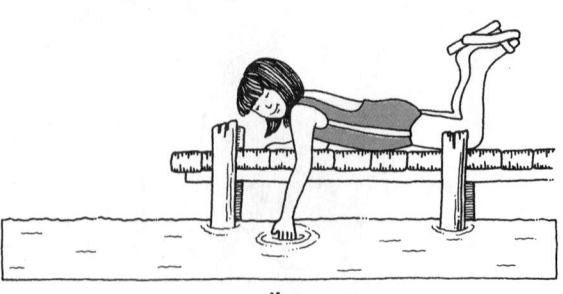

dip

diphthong   *noun* A speech sound beginning with one vowel sound and moving to another within the same syllable. In the word "boy" *oy* is a diphthong.

diph·thong (**dif′** thông′ *or* **dip′** thông′)
□ *noun, plural* **diphthongs**

diploma *noun* A document given to a person showing that he or she graduated from a school or college or finished a course of study.
di·plo·ma (di **plō′** mə) □ *noun, plural* **diplomas**

WORD HISTORY: diploma

Diploma comes from a Greek word that means literally "something folded double."

---

diplomat *noun* Someone who is appointed to represent his or her country in its relations with other countries.
dip·lo·mat (**dip′** lə mat′) □ *noun, plural* **diplomats**

dipper *noun* A cup with a long handle for scooping up liquids.
dip·per (**dip′** ər) □ *noun, plural* **dippers**

direct *verb* **1.** To manage or control: *The principal directs the activities of the school.* **2.** To instruct, order, or command: *The teacher directed me to collect the books.* **3.** To aim, point, or guide to: *A sign directed us to the library.* —See Synonyms at **command**.
□ *adjective* **1.** Going or lying in a straight way or line: *This street is a direct route into town.* **2.** Straightforward; honest: *I gave her a direct answer.*
□ *adverb* In a straight line; directly: *This plane flies direct to Atlanta from Houston.*
di·rect (di **rekt′** *or* dī **rekt′**) □ *verb* **directed, directing, directs** □ *adjective* □ *adverb*

direct current *noun* An electric current that does not change its direction of flow.

direction *noun* **1.** Control, management, and guidance. **2.** An instruction or command telling the way to act or to do something: *gave the direction to begin; followed the directions for building a model.* **3.** The line or course along which someone or something points, faces, or moves: *We drove in the direction of the town.*
di·rec·tion (di **rek′** shən *or* dī **rek′** shən)
□ *noun, plural* **directions**

directly *adverb* **1.** In a direct line; straight: *This road leads directly into town.* **2.** Exactly: *Her feelings about the movie are directly opposite to mine.* **3.** Without delay; at once: *I will see you directly after the meeting.*
di·rect·ly (di **rekt′** lē *or* dī **rekt′** lē) □ *adverb*

director *noun* Someone who manages, controls, or guides something: *He was the director of the play.*
di·rec·tor (di **rek′** tər *or* dī **rek′** tər) □ *noun, plural* **directors**

directory *noun* A list of names, addresses, or other information: *a telephone directory.*
di·rec·to·ry (di **rek′** tə rē *or* dī **rek′** tə rē)
□ *noun, plural* **directories**

dirigible *noun* A large airship with a motor and a steering mechanism.
dir·i·gi·ble (**dîr′** ə jə bəl *or* di **rij′** ə bəl)
□ *noun, plural* **dirigibles**

dirt *noun* **1.** Earth or soil: *We raked the dirt in the flower bed.* **2.** Mud, grease, or other filthy material that soils: *Her hands were covered with dirt.*
dirt (dûrt) □ *noun*

dirty *adjective* Not clean; soiled: *dirty laundry.*
□ *verb* To make or become soiled: *Don't dirty your new dress.*
dirt·y (**dûr′** tē) □ *adjective* **dirtier, dirtiest**
□ *verb* **dirtied, dirtying, dirties**

dis- A prefix that means: **1.** Not; the opposite of: *disadvantage.* **2.** To do the opposite of: *disagree.*

disable *verb* To make weak or unable; cripple: *The broken leg disabled her for months.*
dis·a·ble (dis **ā′** bəl) □ *verb* **disabled, disabling, disables**

disable

a	bat	ī	bite	oo	tool	*th*	feather
ā	make	î	fierce	ou	out	th	bath
â	dare	o	dot	u	nut	hw	wheat
ä	father	ō	no	û	turn	zh	measure
e	net	ô	law, for	ch	church	ə	about, open
ē	be	oi	soil	ng	ring		pencil, atom
i	dip	oo	look	sh	shade		circus

disadvantage *noun*   **1.** Something that makes it harder to do something: *His lack of education was a disadvantage when he looked for a job.*   **2.** Damage or harm: *Not studying will be to your disadvantage.*
dis·ad·van·tage (dis′əd **van′**tij) □*noun, plural* **disadvantages**

disagree *verb*   **1.** To fail to agree; differ: *Our answers to the problem disagreed.*   **2.** To have a different opinion: *We disagreed on which movie to see.*
dis·a·gree (dis′ə **grē′**) □*verb* **disagreed, disagreeing, disagrees**

disagreement *noun* A difference of opinion; quarrel: *We had a disagreement over who was going to walk the dog.*
dis·a·gree·ment (dis′ə **grē′**mənt) □*noun, plural* **disagreements**

disappear *verb*   **1.** To pass out of sight: *The car disappeared over the hill.*   **2.** To pass from existence: *The snow disappeared overnight.*
dis·ap·pear (dis′ə **pîr′**) □*verb* **disappeared, disappearing, disappears**

disappearance *noun* The act or an example of disappearing: *No one could explain the stranger's sudden disappearance.*
dis·ap·pear·ance (dis′ə **pîr′**əns) □*noun, plural* **disappearances**

disappoint *verb* To fail to satisfy the hopes or wishes of: *His poor performance disappointed his friends.*
dis·ap·point (dis′ə **point′**) □*verb* **disappointed, disappointing, disappoints**

disappointment *noun*   **1.** The feeling of being disappointed: *He tried to hide his disappointment at not making the football team.*   **2.** A person or thing that disappoints: *The circus was a disappointment.*
dis·ap·point·ment (dis′ə **point′**mənt) □*noun, plural* **disappointments**

disapproval *noun* A feeling of not liking or of being against something: *She showed her disapproval with a frown.*
dis·ap·prov·al (dis′ə **proo′**vəl) □*noun*

disapprove *verb* To have a feeling of being against something: *She disapproves of gambling.*
dis·ap·prove (dis′ə **proov′**) □*verb* **disapproved, disapproving, disapproves**

disaster *noun* Something that causes great destruction or misfortune, such as a flood or forest fire.
dis·as·ter (di **zas′**tər) □*noun, plural* **disasters**

> **WORD HISTORY: disaster**
>
> In the Middle Ages people believed that calamities on Earth were caused by the evil influence of the stars and planets. This helps to explain the origin of *disaster*. The word *disaster* was formed from a Latin prefix that means "unfavorable" and a Greek word for "star."

disbelief *noun* A refusal to believe: *She felt disbelief when she won first prize.*
dis·be·lief (dis′bi **lēf′**) □*noun*

disc *noun* A phonograph record.
disc (disk) □*noun, plural* **discs**

discard *verb* To throw away: *He discarded the broken radio.*
dis·card (dis **kärd′**) □*verb* **discarded, discarding, discards**

discard

discharge *verb*   **1.** To release; dismiss: *He discharged the workers when the job was finished.*   **2.** To remove passengers or cargo; unload: *The truck discharged its cargo at the rear of the store.*   **3.** To fire or shoot: *discharge a gun.*   **4.** To let flow or give off: *This pipe discharges waste into the sewer.*
□*noun* The act of discharging: *an honorable discharge from the army.*
dis·charge (dis **chärj′**) □*verb* **discharged, discharging, discharges** □*noun* (**dis′**chärj′) □*plural* **discharges**

disciple *noun* Someone who believes in and spreads the teachings of a leader.
dis·ci·ple (di **sī′**pəl) □*noun, plural* **disciples**

discipline *noun*   **1.** Training of the mind, body, or character: *It requires discipline to become a great athlete.*   **2.** Orderly behavior that results from training and obedience to rules: *The students were praised for their discipline.*   **3.** Punishment.

□*verb* **1.** To train through practice and teaching: *a disciplined artist.* **2.** To punish in order to control: *He disciplined the unruly students by keeping them after class.*
dis·ci·pline (**dis′**ə plin) □*noun* □*verb*
disciplined, disciplining, disciplines

disc jockey *noun* Someone who chooses and plays phonograph records for a radio station or discotheque.

disc jockey

disclose *verb* To make known: *Please don't disclose my secret.*
dis·close (dis **klōz′**) □*verb* **disclosed, disclosing, discloses**

disco *noun* A discotheque.
dis·co (**dis′**cō) □*noun, plural* **discos**

disconnect *verb* To break the connection of or between: *I disconnected the radio by pulling out the plug.*
dis·con·nect (dis′kə **nekt′**) □*verb*
disconnected, disconnecting, disconnects

discontented *adjective* Not happy or satisfied: *He was discontented with his job.*
dis·con·tent·ed (dis′kən **ten′**tid) □*adjective*

discontinue *verb* To bring to an end; stop: *He discontinued his guitar lessons.*
dis·con·tin·ue (dis′kən **tin′** yōo) □*verb*
discontinued, discontinuing, discontinues

discotheque *noun* A club where people dance to recorded music.
dis·co·theque (**dis′**kə tek′) □*noun, plural*
discotheques

discount *noun* An amount that is subtracted from the full or regular price: *I bought the book at a 25 percent discount.*
dis·count (**dis′**kount′) □*noun, plural*
discounts

discourage *verb* **1.** To cause to lose hope or enthusiasm: *Failing the swimming test discouraged her.* **2.** To try to stop: *She discouraged me from trying out for the team.*
dis·cour·age (di **skûr′**ij) □*verb* **discouraged, discouraging, discourages**

discourteous *adjective* Lacking courtesy: *a discourteous child.* —See Synonyms at **rude.**
dis·cour·te·ous (dis **kûr′**tē əs) □*adjective*

discover *verb* To find or come upon something for the first time: *Who discovered America? Dad discovered that one of his books was missing.*
dis·cov·er (di **skuv′**ər) □*verb* **discovered, discovering, discovers**

discover

discovery *noun* **1.** The act of discovering: *When did Balboa's discovery of the Pacific Ocean take place?* **2.** Something discovered: *The vaccine against polio was a great medical discovery.*
dis·cov·er·y (di **skuv′**ə rē) □*noun, plural* **discoveries**

discriminate *verb* To treat people differently and often badly because of their color, religion, sex, or age.
dis·crim·i·nate (di **skrim′**ə nāt′) □*verb*
discriminated, discriminating, discriminates

discrimination *noun* Behavior marked by unfairness or injustice toward others because

a bat	ī bite	ōō tool	*th* feather
ā make	î fierce	ou out	th bath
â dare	o dot	u nut	hw wheat
ä father	ō no	û turn	zh measure
e net	ô law, for	ch church	ə about, open
ē be	oi soil	ng ring	pencil, atom
i dip	oo look	sh shade	circus

of color, religion, sex, or age.
dis·crim·in·a·tion (di skrim′ə nā′shən)
▢*noun*

discuss *verb* To talk over with: *I discussed my book report with the teacher.*
dis·cuss (di **skus′**) ▢*verb* **discussed, discussing, discusses**

discussion *noun* A serious talk about something: *a discussion about current events.*
dis·cus·sion (di **skush′**ən) ▢*noun, plural* **discussions**

disease *noun* A condition that does not let the body or the mind function normally; sickness; illness.
dis·ease (di **zēz′**) ▢*noun, plural* **diseases**

disgrace *noun* **1.** A loss of honor or good name; shame: *He was in disgrace for lying.* **2.** A cause of shame or dishonor: *You are a disgrace to your family.*
▢*verb* To cause shame or dishonor to: *Your behavior has disgraced the entire school.*
dis·grace (dis **grās′**) ▢*noun, plural* **disgraces** ▢*verb* **disgraced, disgracing, disgraces**

disguise *noun* Something that changes or hides a person's appearance: *The robber wore dark glasses and a hat as a disguise.*
▢*verb* **1.** To change the appearance of in order to look like someone or something else: *I disguised myself as a ghost at Halloween.* **2.** To hide; conceal: *She tried to disguise her disappointment by smiling.*

disguise

disgust *verb* To cause a strong and sickening dislike in: *The filth disgusted me.*
▢*noun* A feeling of strong dislike that makes a person feel sick.

dis·gust (dis **gust′**) ▢*verb* **disgusted, disgusting, disgusts**

dish *noun* **1.** A flat or shallow container for holding or serving food. **2.** Food prepared in a special way: *Roast beef is her favorite dish.*
▢*verb* To put in a dish; serve: *He dished out the vegetables.*
dish (dish) ▢*noun, plural* **dishes** ▢*verb* **dished, dishing, dishes**

dish

dishonest *adjective* Not honest: *a dishonest person.*
dis·hon·est (dis **on′**ist) ▢*adjective*

dishonor *noun* Loss of honor or good name; shame: *His is in dishonor since he was convicted of the theft.*
▢*verb* To bring shame upon; disgrace: *He dishonored himself by cheating.*
dis·hon·or (dis **on′**ər) ▢*noun* ▢*verb* **dishonored, dishonoring, dishonors**

dishwasher *noun* A machine that washes dishes, pots, and glasses.
dish·wash·er (**dish′**wosh′ər) ▢*noun, plural* **dishwashers**

disinfect *verb* To destroy germs that can cause disease: *disinfect a cut.*
dis·in·fect (dis′in **fekt′**) ▢*verb* **disinfected, disinfecting, disinfects**

disintegrate *verb* To break into many separate pieces: *The plane disintegrated when it crashed.*
dis·in·te·grate (dis **in′**ti grāt′) ▢*verb* **disintegrated, disintegrating, disintegrates**

disinterested *adjective* Free from selfish interest; impartial: *A good judge should be disinterested.*
dis·in·ter·est·ed (dis **in′**tri stid *or* dis **in′**tə res′tid) ▢*adjective*

disk *noun* **1.** A thin, flat, round object, such as a phonograph record or coin. **2.** A thin, flat, round magnetic plate on which information and computer programs can be stored. **3.** A compact disk.

disk (disk) □*noun, plural* **disks**

disk drive   *noun*   The unit on a computer that reads information from a computer disk and that can write information to the disk.

diskette   *noun*   A small portable computer disk that is used to store information; floppy disk.

disk·ette (di **sket′**) □*noun, plural* **diskettes**

disk jockey   *noun*   An announcer who plays recorded music, especially on the radio.

dislike   *verb*   To have a feeling of not liking: *He dislikes doing chores around the house.* □*noun* A feeling of not liking: *a dislike of horror movies.*

dis·like (dis **līk′**) □*verb* **disliked, disliking, dislikes** □*noun*

dislocate   *verb*   To put or force a bone out of joint: *dislocate a shoulder.*

dis·lo·cate (**dis′**lō kāt′) □*verb* **dislocated, dislocating, dislocates**

dislodge   *verb*   To move or force out of position: *The boat was stuck on the reef and we couldn't dislodge it.*

dis·lodge (dis **loj′**) □*verb* **dislodged, dislodging, dislodges**

disloyal   *adjective*   Not loyal; unfaithful: *She would never be disloyal to her brother.*

dis·loy·al (dis **loi′**əl) □*adjective*

dismal   *adjective*   Causing gloom; dreary: *a cold, dismal day.*

dis·mal (**diz′**məl) □*adjective*

dismantle   *verb*   To take apart: *We had to dismantle the refrigerator to get it down the stairs.*

dis·man·tle (dis **man′**təl) □*verb* **dismantled, dismantling, dismantles**

WORD HISTORY: **dismal**

In the Middle Ages some days were considered lucky and some unlucky. People referred to the unlucky days by two Latin words that meant "evil days." The Latin words eventually became the English word *dismal.*

---

dismay   *verb*   To cause to lose courage or confidence in the face of danger or trouble: *She was dismayed at having to find a new job.* □*noun* A loss of courage or confidence in the face of danger or trouble: *We were filled with dismay when the car broke down.*

dis·may (dis **mā′**) □*verb* **dismayed, dismaying, dismays** □*noun*

dismiss   *verb*   To cause or allow to leave; send away: *The teacher dismissed the class.*

dis·miss (dis **mis′**) □*verb* **dismissed, dismissing, dismisses**

dismount   *verb*   To get off or down: *dismount a horse.*

dis·mount (dis **mount′**) □*verb* **dismounted, dismounting, dismounts**

disobedient   *adjective*   Failing or refusing to obey: *a disobedient child.*

dis·o·be·di·ent (dis′ə **bē′**dē ənt) □*adjective*

disobey   *verb*   To fail or refuse to obey: *He would never disobey his father.*

dis·o·bey (dis′ə **bā′**) □*verb* **disobeyed, disobeying, disobeys**

disorder   *noun*   Lack of order; confusion: *papers thrown in disorder on the floor.*

dis·or·der (dis **ôr′**dər) □*noun*

dispatch   *verb*   To send off quickly: *She dispatched a message to her boss.* □*noun* A written message or report: *The reporter sent a dispatch to his paper.*

dis·patch (di **spach′**) □*verb* **dispatched, dispatching, dispatches** □*noun, plural* **dispatches**

dispense   *verb*   To give out; distribute: *The nurse dispensed the medicine.*

dis·pense (di **spens′**) □*verb* **dispensed, dispensing, dispenses**

disperse   *verb*   To move or scatter in different directions: *The police dispersed the crowd. The crowd dispersed quickly.*

dis·perse (di **spûrs′**) □*verb* **dispersed, dispersing, disperses**

displace   *verb*   **1.** To put out of the usual place: *The flood displaced all the people who lived along the river.* **2.** To take the place of: *Robots are displacing people in factories.*

dis·place (dis **plās′**) □*verb* **displaced, displacing, displaces**

display   *verb*   To put on view; show: *The stores are displaying summer clothes.* □*noun* A public showing or exhibition: *We*

a	bat	ī	bite	ōō	tool	th	feather
ā	make	î	fierce	ou	out	th	bath
â	dare	o	dot	u	nut	hw	wheat
ä	father	ō	no	û	turn	zh	measure
e	net	ô	law, for	ch	church	ə	about, open
ē	be	oi	soil	ng	ring		pencil, atom
i	dip	oo	look	sh	shade		circus

saw *an interesting display at the museum.*
— See Synonyms at **show.**
   dis·play (di **splā′**) ☐*verb* **displayed,**
displaying, displays ☐*noun, plural* **displays**

display

displease *verb* To cause annoyance to: *His laziness displeased her.*
   dis·please (dis **plēz′**) ☐*verb* **displeased,**
displeasing, displeases

disposal *noun* The act of throwing something away: *The town takes care of the disposal of garbage.*
   dis·pos·al (di **spō′**zəl) ☐*noun*

dispose *verb* **dispose of** To get rid of: *How do you plan to dispose of your old clothes?*
   dis·pose (di **spōz′**) ☐*verb* **disposed,**
disposing, disposes

disposition *noun* A person's nature or attitude: *He has a cheerful disposition.*
   dis·po·si·tion (dis′pə **zish′**ən) ☐*noun, plural*
dispositions

dispute *verb* **1.** To question the truth of: *He disputed my story of what happened.* **2.** To quarrel or argue: *The children disputed over who would ride the pony first.*
   ☐*noun* A quarrel; argument.
   dis·pute (di **spyoot′**) ☐*verb* **disputed,**
disputing, disputes ☐*noun, plural* **disputes**

disqualify *verb* To make or declare unfit: *The judges disqualified her entry because it was late.*
   dis·qual·i·fy (dis **kwol′**ə fī′) ☐*verb*
disqualified, disqualifying, disqualifies

disregard *verb* To pay no attention to: *He disregarded the bully's insults.*
   ☐*noun* Lack of attention to or respect for something: *His behavior shows a disregard for other people's feelings.*

dis·re·gard (dis′ri **gärd′**) ☐*verb* **disregarded,**
disregarding, disregards ☐*noun*

disrespectful *adjective* Impolite; rude: *Don't be disrespectful to your elders.*
   dis·re·spect·ful (dis′ri **spekt′**fəl) ☐*adjective*

disrupt *verb* To throw into confusion; upset: *An argument disrupted the game.*
   dis·rupt (dis **rupt′**) ☐*verb* **disrupted,**
disrupting, disrupts

dissatisfied *adjective* Not pleased; discontented: *Mom was dissatisfied with the way I cleaned my room.*
   dis·sat·is·fied (dis **sat′**is fīd′) ☐*adjective*

dissect *verb* To cut apart or separate in order to examine: *dissect a frog.*
   dis·sect (di **sekt′** *or* dī **sekt′**) ☐*verb*
dissected, dissecting, dissects

dissolve *verb* **1.** To mix or become mixed into a liquid: *Dissolve the pill in a glass of orange juice. Sugar dissolves in hot liquids.* **2.** To break up; end: *We dissolved the meeting.*
   dis·solve (di **zolv′**) ☐*verb* **dissolved,**
dissolving, dissolves

distance *noun* The length of the space between two things or points: *What is the distance from your house to school?*
   dis·tance (dis′**təns**) ☐*noun, plural* **distances**

distant *adjective* **1.** Far away in space or time; not near: *a distant city; the distant future.* **2.** Not friendly: *Why is she so distant toward you?*
   ☐*adverb* At or to a distance; away: *Our house is a mile distant from the school.*
   dis·tant (dis′**tənt**) ☐*adjective* ☐*adverb*

distill *verb* To make a liquid pure by heating it until it becomes a vapor and then cooling it until it becomes a liquid again.
   dis·till (di **stil′**) ☐*verb* **distilled, distilling,**
distills

distinct *adjective* **1.** Not the same; different: *Even though they are twins they have distinct personalities.* **2.** Easily perceived by the senses; clear: *What is that distinct odor?* **3.** Very definite: *Her schoolwork shows a distinct improvement.*
   dis·tinct (di **stingkt′**) ☐*adjective*

distinction *noun* **1.** The act of making a difference between things: *The teacher treats all the students without distinction.* **2.** Something that makes one different; difference: *The color is the only distinction between these two coats.* **3.** Excellence; superiority: *a writer of distinction.*

dis·tinc·tion (di **stingk′**shən) □*noun, plural* **distinctions**

distinction

distinctive *adjective* Marking or showing a difference from others: *The two teams wore distinctive uniforms.*
dis·tinc·tive (di **stingk′**tiv) □*adjective*

distinguish *verb* **1.** To make different; set apart: *His red hair distinguishes him from his brother.* **2.** To know or see clearly the difference between two things: *Can you distinguish robins from sparrows?* **3.** To hear or see clearly; make out: *I could see the car coming but I couldn't distinguish who was driving.* **4.** To make oneself well known: *She distinguished herself by her scientific research.*
dis·tin·guish (di **sting′**gwish) □*verb* **distinguished, distinguishing, distinguishes**

distort *verb* To bend or twist out of the usual shape: *The curved mirror distorted their faces.*
dis·tort (di **stôrt′**) □*verb* **distorted, distorting, distorts**

distort

distract *verb* To draw away the attention of: *The movie distracted me from my problems.*
dis·tract (di **strakt′**) □*verb* **distracted, distracting, distracts**

distraction *noun* Something that draws away the attention of someone: *The television was a distraction when I was trying to read.*
dis·trac·tion (di **strak′**shən) □*noun, plural* **distractions**

distress *noun* **1.** Great grief or suffering; misery; sorrow: *The quarrel caused me great distress.* **2.** Serious danger or trouble: *a ship in distress.*
□*verb* To cause grief or suffering: *My poor grades distressed my parents.*
dis·tress (di **stres′**) □*noun* □*verb* **distressed, distressing, distresses**

distribute *verb* **1.** To give something out in shares: *He distributed paper and pencils to the students.* **2.** To spread out; scatter: *We distributed fertilizer over the grass.* **3.** To put into groups; sort: *The post office distributes mail.*
dis·trib·ute (di **strib′**yo͞ot) □*verb* **distributed, distributing, distributes**

distribution *noun* The act of distributing: *The distribution of the prizes was the climax of the program.*
dis·tri·bu·tion (dis′trə **byo͞o′**shən) □*noun, plural* **distributions**

district *noun* A part of a larger area marked out for a special purpose: *a school district.*
dis·trict (**dis′**trikt) □*noun, plural* **districts**

disturb *verb* **1.** To make uneasy, upset, or nervous: *Losing her purse disturbed her greatly.* **2.** To upset or change the arrangement of: *Don't disturb the papers on the desk.* **3.** To break in upon; interrupt: *The phone call disturbed our dinner.*
dis·turb (di **stûrb′**) □*verb* **disturbed, disturbing, disturbs**

disturbance *noun* **1.** The act of disturbing: *He closed his door so he could study without disturbance.* **2.** Something that disturbs: *The radio was a disturbance when I was trying to sleep.*

a	bat	ī	bite	o͞o	tool	th	feather
ā	make	î	fierce	ou	out	th	bath
â	dare	o	dot	u	nut	hw	wheat
ä	father	ō	no	û	turn	zh	measure
e	net	ô	law, for	ch	church	ə	about, open
ē	be	oi	soil	ng	ring		pencil, atom
i	dip	oo	look	sh	shade		circus

dis·turb·ance (di **stûr′**bəns) □*noun, plural* **disturbances**

ditch *noun* A long, narrow trench dug in the ground.
ditch (dich) □*noun, plural* **ditches**

dive *verb* **1.** To plunge headfirst into water: *He dived into the pool.* **2.** To plunge downward at a steep angle: *The plane dived out of the sky.* **3.** To go, move, or drop suddenly and quickly: *We dived for cover when the thunder started.* □*noun* **1.** A headfirst plunge into water. **2.** A sudden downward plunge: *The wind stopped and the kite went into a dive.*
dive (dīv) □*verb* **dived** or **dove, diving, dives** □*noun, plural* **dives**

dive

diver *noun* **1.** Someone who dives. **2.** Someone who works or explores underwater with special equipment that lets a person breathe and stay underwater for a while.
di·ver (dī′vər) □*noun, plural* **divers**

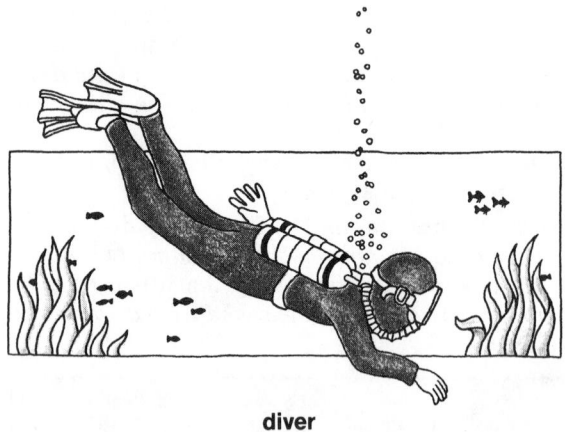

diver

diverse *adjective* Of several or many kinds; different: *We met people of diverse backgrounds at the United Nations.*
di·verse (di **vûrs′**) □*adjective*

diversion *noun* **1.** A change in the direction in which something moves: *A diversion of traffic to a side road was necessary so the main road could be repaired.* **2.** Something that relaxes or amuses: *Swimming and sailing are my favorite diversions.* **3.** Something that draws the attention to another direction: *The enemy created a diversion with a surprise attack from the rear.*
di·ver·sion (di **vûr′**zhən) □*noun, plural* **diversions**

diversion

diversity *noun* Difference; variety: *There is a great diversity of opinion as to where to build the new city hall.*
di·ver·si·ty (di **vûr′**si tē) □*noun, plural* **diversities**

divert *verb* **1.** To change the direction in which something moves: *Police diverted traffic while the road was being repaired.* **2.** To draw the attention to another direction: *The noise in the street diverted me from my homework.* **3.** To amuse or entertain: *I read a story to divert the children.* —See Synonyms at **amuse**.
di·vert (di **vûrt′**) □*verb* **diverted, diverting, diverts**

divide *verb* **1.** To separate or become separated into parts, groups, or branches; split: *divide a watermelon into slices. The river divides here.* **2.** To separate into parts that are against each other: *The argument divided the two friends.* **3.** To separate from; cut off: *A wall divides their yard from ours.* **4.** To give out in parts or shares: *We sold lemonade and divided the money we made.* **5.** To find out how many times a number contains another number: *12 divided by 2 is 6.* —See Synonyms at **separate**.
di·vide (di **vīd′**) □*verb* **divided, dividing, divides**

divide

dividend *noun* **1.** A number that is to be divided: *When you divide 12 by 2, the dividend is 12.* **2.** Money that is earned by a company as profit and shared among the owners.
div·i·dend (**div′**i dend′) □*noun, plural* **dividends**

divine *adjective* **1.** Of or from God or a god: *divine love.* **2.** Sacred; holy: *divine worship.*
di·vine (di **vīn′**) □*adjective*

divisible *adjective* Able to be divided: *The number 6 is divisible by 2, 3, and 6.*
di·vis·i·ble (di **viz′**ə bəl) □*adjective*

division *noun* **1.** The act of dividing or the state of being divided: *The teacher organized the division of the class into three groups.* **2.** One of the parts into which something is divided: *She works in the division of the company responsible for advertising.* **3.** Something that divides or separates: *The fence forms a division between the two pieces of property.* **4.** The process of dividing one number by another. **5.** An army unit that is made up of a number of battalions.
di·vi·sion (di **vizh′**ən) □*noun, plural* **divisions**

divisor *noun* The number by which another number is to be divided: *When you divide 12 by 2, the divisor is 2.*
di·vi·sor (di **vī′**zər) □*noun, plural* **divisors**

divorce *noun* The legal ending of a marriage. □*verb* To end a marriage legally.
di·vorce (di **vôrs′**) □*noun, plural* **divorces** □*verb* **divorced, divorcing, divorces**

dizzy *adjective* Having a feeling that one is spinning and about to fall.
diz·zy (**diz′**ē) □*adjective* **dizzier, dizziest**

do *verb* **1.** To perform; carry out. **2.** To act; behave: *She won't do as she is told.* **3.** To bring about or produce: *a rumor that did a great deal of harm.* **4.** To work on in order to prepare, arrange, or put in order: *Who will do the dishes?* **5.** To figure out; solve: *Do all the arithmetic problems on this page.* **6.** To be good enough; be adequate: *These shoes won't do for running.* **7.** To work at for a living: *What do you do?* **8.** To get along; manage: *She will do very well in business.* **9.** Used to form the present or past tense in a question or negative sentence: *Did you go shopping yesterday? I don't want any cake.* **10.** Used for emphasis: *Do take care.* **11.** Used as a substitute for a verb mentioned previously: *She swims as fast as he does.*
do (dōō) □*verb* **did, done, doing, does**

Doberman pinscher *noun* A large dog with a smooth black or brown coat.
Do·ber·man pin·scher (**dō′**bər mən **pin′**shər) □*noun, plural* **Doberman pinschers**

docile *adjective* Easy to manage or train: *a docile child.*
doc·ile (**dos′**əl) □*adjective*

dock¹ A platform extending into the water where ships may tie up to load and unload. □*verb* **1.** To come up to a dock: *Ocean liners dock with the help of tugboats.* **2.** To join two or more spacecraft together while in space.
dock (dok) □*noun, plural* **docks** □*verb* **docked, docking, docks**

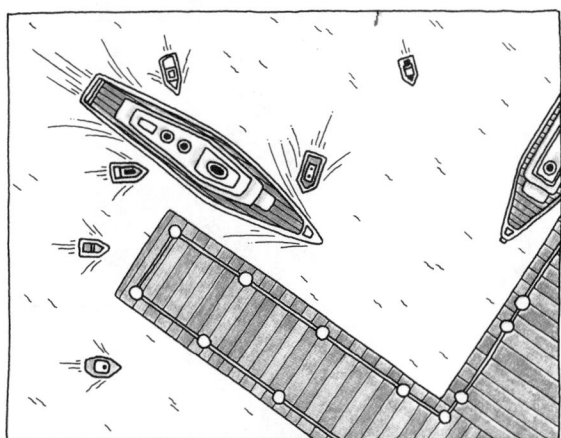

dock

a	bat	ī	bite	ōō	tool	*th*	feather
ā	make	î	fierce	ou	out	th	bath
â	dare	o	dot	u	nut	hw	wheat
ä	father	ō	no	û	turn	zh	measure
e	net	ô	law, for	ch	church	ə	about, open
ē	be	oi	soil	ng	ring		pencil, atom
i	dip	oo	look	sh	shade		circus

dock²   *verb* **1.** To take part off: *Your pay will be docked if you are late.* **2.** To cut off the end of: *The veterinarian docked the horse's tail.*
dock (dok) ▢*verb* **docked, docking, docks**

doctor   *noun* **1.** Someone who is trained and licensed to treat diseases and injuries. A surgeon, a dentist, and a veterinarian are all doctors. **2.** Someone who has the highest degree that a university gives.
doc·tor (dŏk′tər) ▢*noun, plural* **doctors**

doctrine   *noun* A belief or set of beliefs: *the doctrine of human rights.*
doc·trine (dŏk′trĭn) ▢*noun, plural* **doctrines**

document   *noun* An official paper that can be used to give information or proof of something. A birth certificate and a driver's license are documents.
doc·u·ment (dŏk′yə mənt) ▢*noun, plural* **documents**

dodge   *verb* **1.** To avoid by moving quickly out of the way: *I dodged the book she threw at me. I dodged when he tried to tag me.* **2.** To avoid by being clever or cunning: *He dodged the question by changing the subject.*
dodge (dŏj) ▢*verb* **dodged, dodging, dodges**

dodo   *noun* A large bird that is now extinct. It had a heavy body and short wings and was not able to fly.
do·do (dō′dō) ▢*noun, plural* **dodoes** or **dodos**

dodo

doe   *noun* **1.** A female deer. **2.** The female of some other animals, such as the rabbit or antelope.
doe (dō) ▢*noun, plural* **does**

does   *verb* The third person singular present tense of **do:** *He does his homework every night.*
does (dŭz) ▢*verb*

doesn't Contraction of "does not."
does·n't (dŭz′ənt)

dog   *noun* An animal that is related to wolves and foxes. There are many breeds of dogs.
▢*verb* To follow closely: *The little girl dogged her mother's footsteps all over the house.*
dog (dôg) ▢*noun, plural* **dogs** ▢*verb* **dogged, dogging, dogs**

dogwood   *noun* A tree that blooms in spring and has small greenish flowers surrounded by white or pink leaves that look like petals.
dog·wood (dôg′wŏod′) ▢*noun, plural* **dogwoods**

doily   *noun* A small, fancy mat of lace, paper, or other material placed under something, such as a dish or vase, for decoration or protection.
doi·ly (doi′lē) ▢*noun, plural* **doilies**

dol. An abbreviation for **dollar.**

doll   *noun* A toy that is made to look like a human being.
doll (dŏl) ▢*noun, plural* **dolls**

dollar   *noun* A unit of money equal to 100 cents in the United States and Canada.
dol·lar (dŏl′ər) ▢*noun, plural* **dollars**

> **WORD HISTORY: dollar**
> The word *dollar* comes from the German *taler,* which is short for *Joachimstaler,* a silver coin once minted in the German town of Joachimstal.

dolphin   *noun* **1.** A sea animal that has a snout shaped like a beak. Dolphins are related to whales. **2.** A large, brightly colored ocean fish.
dol·phin (dŏl′fĭn) ▢*noun, plural* **dolphins**

dolphin

domain   *noun* All the lands under the control of a ruler or government: *the king's domain.*
do·main (dō mān′) ▢*noun, plural* **domains**

dome *noun* A roof in the shape of a hemisphere.
dome (dōm) □*noun, plural* **domes**

domestic *adjective* **1.** Of or having to do with a home, household, or family life: *domestic tasks.* **2.** Not wild; tame: *The cat is a domestic animal.* **3.** Of or having to do with one's own country: *The President makes important decisions in both domestic and foreign affairs.*
do·mes·tic (də mes′tik) □*adjective*

domesticate *verb* To train to live with and be useful to human beings; tame: *domesticate animals.*
do·mes·ti·cate (də mes′ti kāt′) □*verb* **domesticated, domesticating, domesticates**

dominant *adjective* Most important or powerful: *The chairman is the dominant person at this meeting. The dominant color in that design is red.*
dom·i·nant (dom′ə nənt) □*adjective*

dominate *verb* To control, govern, or rule by will or strength: *a country that dominated its less powerful neighbors.*
dom·i·nate (dom′ə nāt′) □*verb* **dominated, dominating, dominates**

dominion *noun* All lands under the control of one ruler or government; domain.
do·min·ion (də min′yən) □*noun, plural* **dominions**

Dominion Day *noun* A Canadian national holiday observed on July 1 that celebrates the establishment of Canada as a united country.

domino *noun* **1.** One of a set of small, thin blocks or tiles that is divided in half and marked with from 1 to 6 dots. **2. dominoes** A game played with a set of these blocks.
dom·i·no (dom′ə nō) □*noun, plural* **dominoes** or **dominos**

domino

donate *verb* To contribute: *He donated a painting to the museum.*

do·nate (dō′nāt′) □*verb* **donated, donating, donates**

donation *noun* A gift or contribution: *a donation to charity.*
do·na·tion (dō nā′shən) □*noun, plural* **donations**

done *verb* The past participle of **do**: *You have done a good job.*
□*adjective* **1.** Completely finished: *Thank goodness that my chores are done.* **2.** Cooked enough: *Is the turkey done?*
done (dun) □*verb* □*adjective*

donkey *noun* An animal that is related to the horse, but smaller and with longer ears.
don·key (dong′kē) □*noun, plural* **donkeys**

donor *noun* One who gives or contributes something: *a donor to charity; a blood donor.*
do·nor (dō′nər) □*noun, plural* **donors**

don't Contraction of "do not."
don't (dōnt)

doom *noun* A terrible fate, especially death. □*verb* To come to an unhappy end: *The criminal was doomed to life in prison.*
doom (do͞om) □*noun, plural* **dooms** □*verb* **doomed, dooming, dooms**

door *noun* **1.** A movable part that is used to open or close an entrance to a room, building, or vehicle. **2.** A doorway: *Don't stand in the door, I'm coming through!*
door (dôr) □*noun, plural* **doors**

doorbell *noun* A bell or buzzer outside a door.
door·bell (dôr′bel′) □*noun, plural* **doorbells**

doorstep *noun* A step leading up to an outside door.
door·step (dôr′step′) □*noun, plural* **doorsteps**

doorway *noun* The entrance to a room or building where a door may be placed.
door·way (dôr′wā′) □*noun, plural* **doorways**

dope *noun* **1.** A very stupid person. **2.** A narcotic drug, especially heroin. **3.** Information: *I've got the dope on the new principal.*
dope (dōp) □*noun, plural* **dopes**

a bat	ī bite	o͞o tool	th feather
ā make	î fierce	ou out	th bath
â dare	o dot	u nut	hw wheat
ä father	ō no	û turn	zh measure
e net	ô law, for	ch church	ə about, open
ē be	oi soil	ng ring	pencil, atom
i dip	oo look	sh shade	circus

dormant *adjective* Not active for a period of time: *a dormant volcano.*
dor·mant (dôr′ mənt) □*adjective*

dormitory *noun* A building containing many bedrooms. College students often live in dormitories.
dor·mi·to·ry (dôr′ mi tôr′ ē) □*noun, plural* **dormitories**

dormouse *noun* A small animal that has brown or gray fur and looks like a squirrel. The dormouse sleeps during the day and is active at night.
dor·mouse (dôr′ mous′) □*noun, plural* **dor·mice** (dôr′ mīs′)

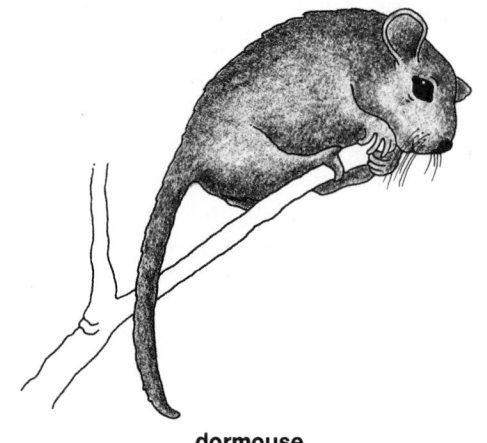

dormouse

dose *noun* The amount of medicine taken at one time: *a dose of cough syrup.*
dose (dōs) □*noun, plural* **doses**

dot *noun* A small, rounded spot or mark: *She's wearing a white blouse with red dots.*
□*verb* **1.** To mark with a dot or dots: *Dot your i's.* **2.** To be scattered here and there: *Dandelions dotted the lawn.*
dot (dot) □*noun, plural* **dots** □*verb* **dotted, dotting, dots**

dote *verb* To show too much affection: *a spoiled child whose parents dote on him.*
dote (dōt) □*verb* **doted, doting, dotes**

double *adjective* **1.** Two times as much in size, strength, number, or amount: *a double scoop of ice cream.* **2.** Having two parts that are the same: *double doors.*
□*adverb* **1.** Two together: *They rode double on the bike.* **2.** In twos or in pairs: *His new glasses made him see double.*
□*noun* **1.** A number that is twice as much: *Six is the double of three.* **2.** Someone or something that looks like another. **3.** A hit in base-

ball that lets the batter get to second base safely.
□*verb* **1.** To make or become twice as great: *The boss doubled my salary.* **2.** To bend or fold over: *He doubled over in pain.* **3.** To hit a double in baseball.
dou·ble (dub′ əl) □*adjective* □*adverb* □*noun, plural* **doubles** □*verb* **doubled, doubling, doubles**

SYNONYMS: **double, duplicate, image**
These nouns mean someone or something that looks like another: *All of the actor's stunts in the movie were done by his double. I lost my key to the house so my father gave me a duplicate. She is the image of her grandmother.*

double
Double doors

double-cross *verb* To betray someone by not doing what was agreed on.
dou·ble-cross (dub′ əl krôs′) □*verb* **double-crossed, double-crossing, double-crosses**

double-header *noun* Two games played one after the other on the same day.
dou·ble-head·er (dub′ əl hed′ ər) □*noun, plural* **double-headers**

double play *noun* A play in baseball in which two runners are put out.

doubt *verb* To not be sure or certain about: *I doubt that he will come. She doubted that he was telling the truth.*
□*noun* **1.** A feeling of not being sure or certain: *I had doubts about making the team.* **2.** A state of not being sure or certain: *If you are in doubt about the spelling of a word, look in the dictionary.*
doubt (dout) □*verb* **doubted, doubting, doubts** □*noun, plural* **doubts**

doubtful *adjective* Having, showing, or causing doubt: *I'm doubtful that it will stop snowing by tomorrow.*
doubt·ful (dout′fəl) □*adjective*

dough *noun* A soft, thick mixture of flour, water or milk, and other ingredients that is used to make bread, pastry, and other baked goods.
dough (dō) □*noun, plural* **doughs**

doughnut *noun* A small, round cake made of sweetened dough fried in deep fat.
dough·nut (dō′nut′) □*noun, plural* **doughnuts**

dove¹ *noun* A bird related to the pigeon, having a plump body, short legs, and a cooing voice.
dove (duv) □*noun, plural* **doves**

dove

dove² *verb* A past tense of **dive:** *She dove into the lake.*
dove (dōv) □*verb*

down¹ *adverb* **1.** From a higher to a lower place: *They climbed down from the top of the ladder.* **2.** In or to a lower position or condition: *He sat down. Prices are coming down.*
□*preposition* **1.** From a higher to a lower place or position in or on: *Rain trickled down the panes of the window.* **2.** On a path or way through: *I saw her walking down the street.*
□*noun* Any of four plays in football during which a team must move the ball forward by at least ten yards. If it fails to do so, the other team gets possession of the ball.
□*verb* To bring or put down: *We downed our lunch and went out to play.*
down (doun) □*adverb* □*preposition* □*noun, plural* **downs** □*verb* **downed, downing, downs**

down² *noun* Fine, soft feathers, as on a newly hatched bird.
down (doun) □*noun*

downpour *noun* A heavy fall of rain.

down·pour (doun′pôr′) □*noun, plural* **downpours**

downpour

downright *adjective* Complete; thorough: *a downright lie.*
□*adverb* Thoroughly; absolutely: *He's downright crazy.*
down·right (doun′rīt′) □*adjective* □*adverb*

downstairs *adverb* **1.** Down the stairs: *He fell downstairs.* **2.** On or to a lower floor: *I left my glasses downstairs in the kitchen.*
down·stairs (doun′stârz′) □*adverb*

downstairs

downstream *adverb* In the direction in which a stream flows: *We swam downstream.*
down·stream (doun′strēm′) □*adverb*

a bat	ī bite	ōō tool	*th* feather
ā make	î fierce	ou out	th bath
â dare	o dot	u nut	hw wheat
ä father	ō no	û turn	zh measure
e net	ô law, for	ch church	ə about, open
ē be	oi soil	ng ring	pencil, atom
i dip	oo look	sh shade	circus

downtown *adverb* Toward or in the main or business part of a town or city: *We went downtown to the movies.*
□*adjective* Of the main or business part of a town or city: *a downtown restaurant.*
down·town (**doun′toun′**) □*adverb* □*adjective*

downward *adverb* From a higher to a lower place or condition: *The bird glided downward.*
□*adjective* Moving from a higher to a lower place or condition: *the downward flight of the plane.*
down·ward (**doun′wərd**) □*adverb* □*adjective*

downwards *adverb* Another spelling for **downward.**
down·wards (**doun′wərdz**) □*adverb*

dowry *noun* Money or property brought by a woman to her husband when she marries.
dow·ry (**dou′rē**) □*noun, plural* **dowries**

doz. An abbreviation for **dozen.**

doze *verb* To sleep lightly; nap: *I dozed during the long bus ride.*
doze (**dōz**) □*verb* **dozed, dozing, dozes**

dozen *noun* A group of twelve.
doz·en (**duz′ən**) □*noun, plural* **dozens** or **dozen**

Dr. An abbreviation for **doctor.**

drab *adjective* Not bright or cheerful; dull: *a drab room that needs a new coat of paint.*
drab (**drab**) □*adjective* **drabber, drabbest**

draft *noun* **1.** A current of air: *There is a cold draft coming from the open window.* **2.** A device for controlling the flow of air in a fireplace, furnace, and some stoves. **3.** A rough sketch, plan, or outline for something: *I wrote four drafts of my essay.* **4.** The selection of someone for a special job or duty: *Is your brother eligible for the draft?*
□*verb* **1.** To make a rough sketch, plan, or outline for something: *draft a speech.* **2.** To pick someone for a special job or duty: *They were drafted to help put the books away.*
□*adjective* Used for pulling loads: *Horses and mules are draft animals.*
draft (**draft**) □*noun, plural* **drafts** □*verb* **drafted, drafting, drafts** □*adjective*

draftsman *noun* Someone whose work is drawing plans or designs for buildings, machines, and other things.
drafts·man (**drafts′mən**) □*noun, plural* **draftsmen**

drag *verb* **1.** To draw or pull along slowly or with force: *We dragged the box of toys out of*
the closet. **2.** To move or go too slowly: *The boring movie dragged on.* **3.** To use nets or hooks to search the bottom of a river or lake: *They dragged the lake for the sunken boat.*
drag (**drag**) □*verb* **dragged, dragging, drags**

drag

dragon *noun* An imaginary monster that looks like a giant lizard with wings and claws.
drag·on (**drag′ən**) □*noun, plural* **dragons**

dragonfly *noun* A large insect with a long body and four narrow wings. Dragonflies eat other insects and live near water.
drag·on·fly (**drag′ən flī′**) □*noun, plural* **dragonflies**

drain *verb* **1.** To draw off slowly: *I drained the water from the bathtub.* **2.** To draw off liquid from: *Workmen drained the swamp.* **3.** To use up completely: *The long walk drained her strength.*
□*noun* **1.** A pipe, ditch, sewer, or other device for carrying away liquids. **2.** Something that uses up completely: *Working at night is a drain on her energy.*
drain (**drān**) □*verb* **drained, draining, drains** □*noun, plural* **drains**

drainage *noun* The act of draining off water or waste material: *The drainage of the swamp took two weeks.*
drain·age (**drā′nij**) □*noun*

drake *noun* A male duck.
drake (**drāk**) □*noun, plural* **drakes**

drama *noun* **1.** A story written for actors to perform on a stage; play. **2.** A situation in real life that has the excitement and interest of a play: *The trial was an exciting drama.*
dra·ma (**drä′mə** or **dram′ə**) □*noun, plural* **dramas**

dramatic *adjective* **1.** Of drama or the theater: *a dramatic actress.* **2.** Full of action and

excitement like a drama: *a dramatic rescue.*
dra·mat·ic (drə **mat′**ik) ▭*adjective*

dramatize *verb* **1.** To make something into a play: *The students dramatized a story they had read in class.* **2.** To do or see things in a dramatic way: *She said I should tell her exactly what happened and not dramatize anything.*
dram·a·tize (dram′ə tīz′) ▭*verb* **dramatized, dramatizing, dramatizes**

drank *verb* The past tense of **drink:** *I drank a glass of milk.*
drank (drangk) ▭*verb*

drape *verb* **1.** To cover or hang with cloth in loose folds: *The stadium was draped with colorful banners.* **2.** To arrange or hang cloth in folds: *She draped the veil over her head.*
▭*noun* Long, heavy curtains that hang in loose folds.
drape (drāp) ▭*verb* **draped, draping, drapes** ▭*noun, plural* **drapes**

drapery *noun* Long, heavy curtains; drapes.
drap·er·y (drā′pə rē) ▭*noun, plural* **draperies**

drastic *adjective* Extreme or severe: *Jail would be a rather drastic punishment for jaywalking.*
dras·tic (dras′tik) ▭*adjective*

draw *verb* **1.** To pull or haul: *At one time the army used mules to draw heavy loads.* **2.** To pull or take out; remove: *She drew a book from the shelf. I've drawn $50 from my bank account.* **3.** To move or cause to move in a given direction: *He drew me aside.* **4.** To make a picture or design with pen, pencil, chalk, or other similar object: *She drew an airplane. He draws well.* **5.** To cause or allow a current of air to pass: *The fireplace draws well.* **6.** To breathe in; inhale: *Draw a deep breath.*
▭*noun* **1.** The act of taking out and aiming a firearm: *The sheriff was quick on the draw.* **2.** A contest or game that ends in a tie.
draw (drô) ▭*verb* **drew, drawn, drawing, draws** ▭*noun, plural* **draws**

drawback *noun* Something that makes a situation or experience more difficult or unsatisfying: *The biggest drawback to my new job is that I have to work on Saturdays.*
draw·back (drô′bak′) ▭*noun, plural* **drawbacks**

drawbridge *noun* A bridge that can be raised or turned to one side. A drawbridge can be moved to permit tall boats to pass through. In past times the drawbridge of a castle was raised or moved to keep the enemy from crossing.
draw·bridge (drô′brij′) ▭*noun, plural* **drawbridges**

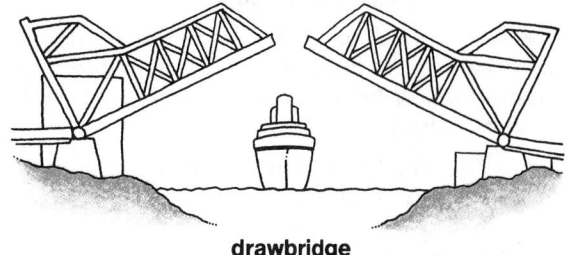

drawbridge

drawer *noun* A box that slides in and out of a piece of furniture such as a desk or table.
draw·er (drôr) ▭*noun, plural* **drawers**

drawing *noun* **1.** A picture or design made on a surface with a pen, pencil, chalk, or similar object. **2.** The choosing of a winning ticket, number, or chance in a lottery.
draw·ing (drô′ing) ▭*noun, plural* **drawings**

drawl *verb* To speak in a slow way.
▭*noun* A slow way of speaking: *a southern drawl.*
drawl (drôl) ▭*verb* **drawled, drawling, drawls** ▭*noun, plural* **drawls**

drawn *verb* The past participle of **draw:** *She has drawn many pictures of the house.*
drawn (drôn) ▭*verb*

dread *noun* A great fear of something: *She is filled with dread at the sight of a spider.*
▭*verb* To be frightened by: *He dreads flying in airplanes.*
▭*adjective* Causing fear: *a dread disease.*
dread (dred) ▭*noun, plural* **dreads** ▭*verb* **dreaded, dreading, dreads** ▭*adjective*

dreadful *adjective* **1.** Causing great fear; terrible: *a dreadful storm.* **2.** Very bad or unpleasant: *a dreadful toothache.*
dread·ful (dred′fəl) ▭*adjective*

dream *noun* **1.** A series of pictures or thoughts that a person has during sleep. **2.** Something like this that a person wishes for: *Her dream is to be a doctor.*

a	bat	ī	bite	ōō	tool	*th*	feather
ā	make	î	fierce	ou	out	th	bath
â	dare	o	dot	u	nut	hw	wheat
ä	father	ō	no	û	turn	zh	measure
e	net	ô	law, for	ch	church	ə	about, open
ē	be	oi	soil	ng	ring		pencil, atom
i	dip	oo	look	sh	shade		circus

□*verb* **1.** To have a dream while sleeping. **2.** To think of as possible: *I never dreamed I would get the highest grade in the class.*
dream (drēm) □*noun, plural* **dreams** □*verb* **dreamed** or **dreamt, dreaming, dreams**

dreamt   *verb* A past tense and past participle of **dream:** *I dreamt that I was in England. She has dreamt of her cousin every night this week.*
dreamt (dremt) □*verb*

dreary   *adjective* Gloomy or dismal: *a wet, dreary day; a dreary room.*
drear·y (drîr′ē) □*adjective* **drearier, dreariest**

dredge   *noun* A large machine that scoops or brings up mud, silt, or other material from the bottom of a body of water.
□*verb* To clean out or deepen the bottom of a channel or harbor.
dredge (drej) □*noun, plural* **dredges** □*verb* **dredged, dredging, dredges**

dregs   *plural noun* Small bits of material that settle to the botttom of a liquid: *coffee dregs.*
dregs (dregz) □*plural noun*

drench   *verb* To wet completely; soak: *The rain drenched us on the way home.*
drench (drench) □*verb* **drenched, drenching, drenches**

drench

dress   *noun* **1.** An outer garment worn by women and girls that usually has a top and skirt made in one piece. **2.** Clothing: *formal dress.*
□*verb* **1.** To put clothes on; clothe: *Dad dressed the baby. I dressed quickly.* **2.** To get something ready for cooking: *dress a turkey.* **3.** To clean and treat: *dress a wound.*
dress (dres) □*noun, plural* **dresses** □*verb* **dressed, dressing, dresses**

> **SYNONYMS:**   **dress, attire, clothes, clothing**
>
> These nouns mean articles worn to cover the body: *Long gowns and tuxedos are formal dress. She said a T-shirt and shorts are not the proper attire to wear to school. Her clothes were all wet from the rain. His clothing is very important to him.*

dresser   *noun* A piece of furniture that has drawers and often a mirror above it. It is used for storing clothes and other objects.
dress·er (dres′ər) □*noun, plural* **dressers**

dressing   *noun* **1.** A sauce for salads and some other foods. **2.** A seasoned mixture used to stuff poultry, fish, or meat. **3.** Medicine and bandages that are put on a wound.
dress·ing (dres′ing) □*noun, plural* **dressings**

drew   *verb* The past tense of **draw:** *He drew a picture.*
drew (drōō) □*verb*

dribble   *verb* **1.** To drip or cause to drip; trickle: *Milk dribbled down the baby's chin.* **2.** To move a ball along by bouncing or kicking it many times.
□*noun* A small quantity; drop: *A dribble of honey ran down the side of the jar.*
drib·ble (drib′əl) □*verb* **dribbled, dribbling, dribbles** □*noun, plural* **dribbles**

dribble

dried   *verb* The past tense and past participle of **dry:** *I dried the dishes before I went out.*
dried (drīd) □*verb*

drier¹   *noun* Another spelling for **dryer.**
dri·er (drī′ər) □*noun, plural* **driers**

drier²   *adjective* The comparative of **dry.**
dri·er (drī′ər) □*adjective*

driest   *adjective* The superlative of **dry.**
dri·est (drī′ist) □*adjective*

drift *verb* To carry or be carried along by a current of water or air: *Clouds drifted by.*
☐*noun* Something that has been carried along or piled up by a current of water or air: *drifts of snow.*
drift (drift) ☐*verb* **drifted, drifting, drifts**
☐*noun, plural* **drifts**

driftwood *noun* Wood floating in the water or washed ashore.
drift·wood (drift′ wood′) ☐*noun*

driftwood

drill *noun* **1.** A tool with a pointed end that is used to make holes in wood, rocks, plastic, or other solid materials. **2.** Training or teaching through frequent repetition and practice: *Our class has a daily drill in spelling.*
☐*verb* **1.** To make a hole with a drill. **2.** To train or teach by repeating something again and again: *The dancers were drilled until they mastered every step.*
drill (dril) ☐*noun, plural* **drills** ☐*verb* **drilled, drilling, drills**

drink *verb* **1.** To take liquid into the mouth and swallow: *I drink orange juice every morning.* **2.** To soak up; absorb: *Plants drink up water.* **3.** To take in an alcoholic beverage.
☐*noun* **1.** A liquid for drinking; beverage. **2.** A portion of a beverage: *a drink of water.* **3.** An alcoholic beverage.
drink (dringk) ☐*verb* **drank, drunk, drinking, drinks** ☐*noun, plural* **drinks**

drip *verb* To fall or let fall in drops: *Water dripped from the roof. He dripped glue on the chair.*
☐*noun* Liquid or moisture that falls in drops.
drip (drip) ☐*verb* **dripped, dripping, drips**
☐*noun, plural* **drips**

drive *verb* **1.** To steer or operate a car or other vehicle: *I drove the truck into the garage. Please drive carefully.* **2.** To carry in a vehicle: *I drove my sister to the bus station.* **3.** To put into and keep in motion: *a motor that was*
driven by electricity. **4.** To force someone into feeling or acting in a certain way: *Her questions drive me crazy.* **5.** To force; make penetrate: *Drive the nail into the wood.*
☐*noun* **1.** A ride or trip in a car or other vehicle: *It's only a short drive to school.* **2.** A road or driveway: *Park your car in the drive.* **3.** An organized effort: *a drive to raise money for charity.* **4.** A ball hit hard in a game: *She hit a drive over the fence.* **5.** A disk drive.
drive (drīv) ☐*verb* **drove, driven, driving, drives** ☐*noun, plural* **drives**

drive-in *noun* A restaurant, movie theater, or bank that customers can use without leaving their cars.
drive-in (drīv′ in′) ☐*noun, plural* **drive-ins**

drive-in

driver *noun* Someone who drives a car, truck, or other vehicle.
driv·er (drī′ vər) ☐*noun, plural* **drivers**

driveway *noun* A private road leading from a house or other building to the street.
drive·way (drīv′ wā′) ☐*noun, plural* **driveways**

drizzle *verb* To rain in gentle drops like mist.
☐*noun* A gentle rain like mist.
driz·zle (driz′ əl) ☐*verb* **drizzled, drizzling, drizzles** ☐*noun, plural* **drizzles**

dromedary *noun* A camel with one hump, used in northern Africa and southwestern Asia for riding and carrying loads.

a bat	ī bite	ōō tool	*th* feather
ā make	î fierce	ou out	th bath
â dare	o dot	u nut	hw wheat
ä father	ō no	û turn	zh measure
e net	ô law, for	ch church	ə about, open
ē be	oi soil	ng ring	pencil, atom
i dip	oo look	sh shade	circus

drom·e·dar·y (**drom′**ə der′ē) ☐*noun, plural* **dromedaries**

drone¹   *noun* A male bee.
drone (drōn) ☐*noun, plural* **drones**

drone²   *verb* **1.** To make a low, humming noise: *Airplanes droned overhead.* **2.** To talk in a boring, dull way: *The speaker droned on for a long time.*
☐*noun* A low, humming sound: *the drone of an engine.*
drone (drōn) ☐*verb* **droned, droning, drones** ☐*noun, plural* **drones**

drool   *verb* To let saliva dribble from the mouth.
drool (drōōl) ☐*verb* **drooled, drooling, drools**

droop   *verb* To bend or hang downward; sag: *The plants drooped because they needed water.*
droop (drōōp) ☐*verb* **drooped, drooping, droops**

droop

drop   *verb* **1.** To fall or let fall from a higher to a lower place: *The book dropped from his hand. She dropped her glasses.* **2.** To decrease; become less: *The temperature dropped five degrees overnight.* **3.** To leave out; omit: *You dropped the second "z" from the word "drizzle."* **4.** To put down or let out at a particular place; deliver: *He dropped me at school.* **5.** To put an end to; stop: *Let's drop the subject.* —See Synonyms at **fall**.
☐*noun* **1.** A tiny mass of liquid that usually has a round shape. **2.** Something that is shaped like this: *a cough drop.* **3.** A sudden fall or decrease: *a drop in temperature.* **4.** The distance between something and what is below it: *It's a long drop from the roof down to the ground.*
drop (drop) ☐*verb* **dropped, dropping, drops** ☐*noun, plural* **drops**

drought   *noun* A long period with little or no rain.
drought (drout) ☐*noun, plural* **droughts**

drove¹   *verb* The past tense of **drive**: *He drove the car carefully.*
drove (drōv) ☐*verb*

drove²   *noun* **1.** A number of cattle, sheep, or other animals being driven or moving as a group. **2.** A crowd: *Droves of people came to the parade.*
drove (drōv) ☐*noun, plural* **droves**

drown   *verb* **1.** To die in water for lack of air to breathe. **2.** To kill by keeping under water: *The flood drowned many animals.* **3.** To cover up a sound with a louder sound: *The siren drowned out his voice.*
drown (droun) ☐*verb* **drowned, drowning, drowns**

drowsy   *adjective* Partly asleep; sleepy.
drows·y (drou′ze) ☐*adjective* **drowsier, drowsiest**

drug   *noun* **1.** A substance that is used to treat or cure disease or pain. **2.** A substance that affects the nervous system and can become habit forming. Heroin and alcohol are drugs.
☐*verb* To give a drug to.
drug (drug) ☐*noun, plural* **drugs** ☐*verb* **drugged, drugging, drugs**

druggist   *noun* **1.** Someone who owns and runs a drugstore. **2.** A pharmacist.
drug·gist (drug′ist) ☐*noun, plural* **druggists**

druggist

drugstore   *noun* A store where medicines are sold. Drugstores may also sell magazines, cosmetics, and sometimes food.
drug·store (drug′stôr′) ☐*noun, plural* **drugstores**

drum *noun* **1.** A musical instrument that makes a sound when it is beaten. It consists of a hollow container, such as a tube, with material stretched tightly across an opening. **2.** A container shaped like a drum: *an oil drum.*
□*verb* **1.** To play a drum. **2.** To tap again and again: *He drummed his fingers on the table.* **3.** To force into by repeating: *She finally drummed the idea into his head.*
drum (drum) □*noun, plural* **drums** □*verb* **drummed, drumming, drums**

drum major *noun* Someone who leads a marching band.

drum majorette *noun* A girl who twirls a baton and marches with a band.
drum ma·jor·ette (mā′jə ret′) □*noun*

drumstick *noun* **1.** A stick for beating a drum. **2.** The lower part of the leg of a cooked fowl.
drum·stick (drum′stik′) □*noun, plural* **drumsticks**

drunk *verb* The past participle of **drink:** *We have drunk all the milk.*
□*adjective* Having had too much alcoholic liquor to drink.
□*noun* Someone who drinks too much alcoholic liquor.
drunk (drungk) □*verb* □*adjective* **drunker, drunkest** □*noun, plural* **drunks**

dry *adjective* **1.** Free from liquid or moisture; not wet or damp: *I changed into dry clothes.* **2.** Having little liquid or moisture: *the dry climate of the desert.* **3.** Not under water: *dry land.* **4.** Thirsty: *They were so dry that they drank a pitcher of lemonade.* **5.** Not interesting; dull: *a dry speech that bored everyone.*
□*verb* To make or become dry: *She told me to dry the dishes.*
dry (drī) □*adjective* **drier, driest** □*verb* **dried, drying, dries**

dry cell *noun* An electric cell in which the negative and positive poles are separated by a moist paste rather than a liquid.

dry-clean *verb* To clean clothes with chemicals rather than water.
dry-clean (drī′klēn′) □*verb* **dry-cleaned, dry-cleaning, dry-cleans**

dryer *noun* An appliance that removes moisture: *a hair dryer; a clothes dryer.*
dry·er (drī′ər) □*noun, plural* **dryers**

dual *adjective* Having or made up of two parts; double: *This helicopter has dual controls.*
du·al (dōō′əl *or* dyōō′əl) □*adjective*

duchess *noun* **1.** The wife or widow of a duke. **2.** A woman with a rank equal to that of a duke.
duch·ess (duch′is) □*noun, plural* **duchesses**

duck¹ *noun* **1.** A water bird with a broad, flat bill, short legs, and webbed feet. There are several different kinds of ducks. Some are raised for food. **2.** The meat of a duck, used as food.
duck (duk) □*noun, plural* **ducks**

duck² *verb* **1.** To lower the head or body quickly to avoid being hit or seen: *I ducked behind the fence so she wouldn't see me.* **2.** To push suddenly under water: *My sister swam around me and ducked me from behind.*
duck (duk) □*verb* **ducked, ducking, ducks**

duck

duckling *noun* A young duck.
duck·ling (duk′ling) □*noun, plural* **ducklings**

duct *noun* A tube or pipe through which a liquid or air can flow.
duct (dukt) □*noun, plural* **ducts**

due *adjective* **1.** Owed as a debt; owing: *The rent is due.* **2.** Expected or supposed to arrive or be ready: *His bus is due at noon.*
□*noun* **1.** Something that is owed; something that must be given to another: *He earned the job through hard work, and you must give him his due.* **2. dues** A charge or fee paid by a person to a club or institution for the right of being a member.

a bat	ī bite	ōō tool	*th* feather
ā make	î fierce	ou out	th bath
â dare	o dot	u nut	hw wheat
ä father	ō no	û turn	zh measure
e net	ô law, for	ch church	ə about, open
ē be	oi soil	ng ring	pencil, atom
i dip	oo look	sh shade	circus

□*adverb* Directly; straight: *We drove due east.*
due (do͞o *or* dyo͞o) □*adjective* □*noun, plural*
dues □*adverb*

duel   *noun* A fight arranged ahead of time between two people armed with swords or pistols.
□*verb* To fight a duel.
du·el (do͞o′əl *or* dyo͞o′əl) □*noun, plural*
duels □*verb* **dueled, dueling, duels**

duet   *noun* A piece of music for two voices or two instruments.
du·et (do͞o et′ *or* dyo͞o et′) □*noun, plural*
duets

duet

dug   *verb* The past tense and past participle of **dig**: *We dug a well in the back yard.*
dug (dug) □*verb*

dugout   *noun* **1.** A boat or canoe made by hollowing out a log. **2.** A long, low shelter at the side of a baseball field for the players.
dug·out (dug′out′) □*noun, plural* **dugouts**

dugout

duke   *noun* A nobleman who has the next highest rank below a prince.
duke (do͞ok *or* dyo͞ok) □*noun, plural* **dukes**

dull   *adjective* **1.** Not having a sharp edge or point; blunt: *a dull knife.* **2.** Not exciting or interesting; boring: *a dull book.* **3.** Not bright or clear: *The old car is a dull brown.* **4.** Not

sharply or strongly felt: *a dull ache.* **5.** Slow to learn: *a dull student.*
□*verb* To make or become dull: *Cutting the cloth dulled the scissors.*
dull (dul) □*adjective* **duller, dullest** □*verb*
dulled, dulling, dulls

dumb   *adjective* **1.** Not able to speak; mute: *dumb with surprise.* **2.** Stupid or silly: *a dumb joke.*
dumb (dum) □*adjective* **dumber, dumbest**

dummy   *noun* **1.** A figure made to look like a human being. **2.** An object that looks like and takes the place of a real one: *The gun used in the play was a dummy.*
dum·my (dum′ē) □*noun, plural* **dummies**

dump   *verb* To let fall in a mass; unload: *The trucks dumped the gravel in the driveway.*
□*noun* A place where trash is dumped: *the town dump.*
dump (dump) □*verb* **dumped, dumping, dumps** □*noun, plural* **dumps**

dune   *noun* A hill of sand heaped up by the wind.
dune (do͞on *or* dyo͞on) □*noun, plural* **dunes**

dungaree   *noun* **1.** A sturdy blue cotton fabric. **2. dungarees** Overalls or pants made of this fabric; blue jeans.
dun·ga·ree (dung′gə rē′) □*noun, plural*
dungarees

dungeon   *noun* A dark, underground prison.
dun·geon (dun′jən) □*noun, plural* **dungeons**

duplicate   *noun* Something that is exactly like another: *She gave me a duplicate of my birth certificate.* —See Synonyms at **double.**
□*adjective* Exactly like another: *a duplicate key.*
□*verb* To make an exact copy of: *duplicate a letter.*
du·pli·cate (do͞o′pli kit *or* dyo͞o′pli kit)
□*noun, plural* **duplicates** □*adjective* □*verb*
(do͞o′pli kāt′ *or* dyo͞o′pli kāt′) **duplicated, duplicating, duplicates**

durable   *adjective* Able to stand wear and heavy use: *durable shoes.*
dur·a·ble (do͝or′ə bəl *or* dyo͝or′ə bəl)
□*adjective*

duration   *noun* The length of time during which something goes on or continues: *He stayed in the army for the duration of the war.*
du·ra·tion (do͝o rā′shən *or* dyo͝o rā′shən)
□*noun*

during   *preposition* **1.** Throughout the time of: *It rained hard every day during the month*

of June. **2.** At some time in: *My aunt telephoned us during dinner.*
dur·ing (**door′**ing *or* **dyoor′**ing) ▢*preposition*

dusk *noun* The time of evening just before darkness.
dusk (dusk) ▢*noun*

dust *noun* Matter in the form of tiny, dry particles.
▢*verb* To remove the dust from by wiping, brushing, or beating: *I dust the furniture every few days.*
dust (dust) ▢*noun* ▢*verb* **dusted, dusting, dusts**

dust

Dutch *noun* **1.** The people of the Netherlands. **2.** The language of the Netherlands.
▢*adjective* Of the Netherlands, its people, or their language.
Dutch (duch) ▢*noun* ▢*adjective*

duty *noun* **1.** Something that a person must or should do: *It was her duty as a citizen to vote.* **2.** A task or function: *Washing the dishes is one of my household duties.* **3.** A tax paid on goods brought into or taken out of a country.
du·ty (**doo′**tē *or* **dyoo′**tē) ▢*noun, plural* **duties**

dwarf *noun* **1.** A person, animal, or plant that is much smaller than normal. **2.** A tiny man in fairy tales who has magic powers.
▢*verb* To make seem small beside someone or something else: *The big tree dwarfed the shed.*
dwarf (dwôrf) ▢*noun, plural* **dwarfs** *or* **dwarves** ▢*verb* **dwarfed, dwarfing, dwarfs**

dwell *verb* To live in; reside.
dwell (dwel) ▢*verb* **dwelt** *or* **dwelled, dwelling, dwells**

dwelling *noun* A place to live in; residence.
dwell·ing (**dwel′**ing) ▢*noun, plural* **dwellings**

dwelt *verb* A past tense and past participle of **dwell.**
dwelt (dwelt) ▢*verb*

dwindle *verb* To grow less; become smaller: *Their supplies were dwindling away.*
dwin·dle (**dwin′**dəl) ▢*verb* **dwindled, dwindling, dwindles**

dye *noun* A substance that is used to give color to something.
▢*verb* To color with or become colored by a dye: *We dyed the tablecloth yellow.*
dye (dī) ▢*noun, plural* **dyes** ▢*verb* **dyed, dyeing, dyes**

dynamic *adjective* Full of energy; active; forceful: *He is a dynamic speaker.*
dy·nam·ic (dī **nam′**ik) ▢*adjective*

dynamite *noun* A powerful explosive.
▢*verb* To blow up with or as if with dynamite.
dy·na·mite (**dī′**nə mīt′) ▢*noun* ▢*verb* **dynamited, dynamiting, dynamites**

WORD HISTORY: **dynamite**

When *dynamite* was invented about 100 years ago, its inventor made up a name from the Greek word for "force."

---

dynamo *noun* An electric generator that produces direct current.
dy·na·mo (**dī′**nə mō′) ▢*noun, plural* **dynamos**

dynasty *noun* A line of rulers who belong to the same family.
dy·nas·ty (**dī′**nə stē) ▢*noun, plural* **dynasties**

a bat	ī bite	ōō tool	th feather
ā make	î fierce	ou out	th bath
â dare	o dot	u nut	hw wheat
ä father	ō no	û turn	zh measure
e net	ô law, for	ch church	ə about, open
ē be	oi soil	ng ring	pencil, atom
i dip	oo look	sh shade	circus

ANCIENT GREEK

The letter **E** has evolved from many forms of ancient writing. One of the earliest known examples is the Greek character shown above, which dates from almost 3,000 years ago. Over the years, artists and designers have created their own versions of the English letter **E**. Some of the more common examples seen today are shown below.

Ee Ee	**Ee Ee**	**Ee Ee**	**Ee Ee**	*Ee Ee*
HANDWRITING	CALLIGRAPHY	MODERN SANS SERIF	MODERN SERIF	SCRIPT

---

e or **E** *noun* The fifth letter of the English alphabet.
e or **E** (ē) □*noun, plural* **e's** or **E's**

each *adjective* Being one of two or more persons or things; every: *There was a chair at each end of the table.*
□*pronoun* Every one: *Each of the girls baked a cake.*
□*adverb* For or to each one; apiece: *The books cost a dollar each.*
each (ēch) □*adjective* □*pronoun* □*adverb*

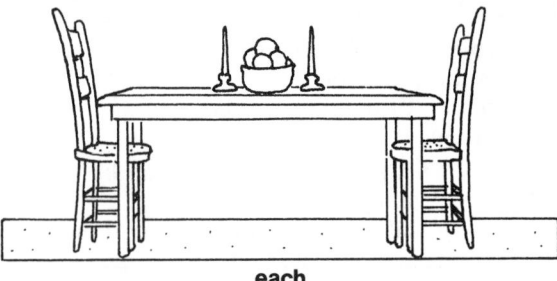

each

each other *pronoun* One another: *They looked at each other and smiled.*
eager *adjective* Wanting very much: *We were eager to see the play.*
ea·ger (ē′gər) □*adjective* **eagerer, eagerest**
eagle *noun* A large bird with a hooked bill and broad, strong wings. Eagles fly high and have very good eyesight.
ea·gle (ē′gəl) □*noun, plural* **eagles**
eaglet *noun* A young eagle.
ea·glet (ē′glit) □*noun, plural* **eaglets**

ear¹ *noun* **1.** The part of the body with which people and animals hear. **2.** The sense of hearing: *A musician needs a good ear.*
ear (îr) □*noun, plural* **ears**
ear² *noun* The part of a grain plant on which the seeds grow: *an ear of corn.*
ear (îr) □*noun, plural* **ears**
eardrum *noun* A layer of thin tissue that separates the middle and outer parts of the ear and that vibrates when sound waves strike it.
ear·drum (îr′drum′) □*noun, plural* **eardrums**

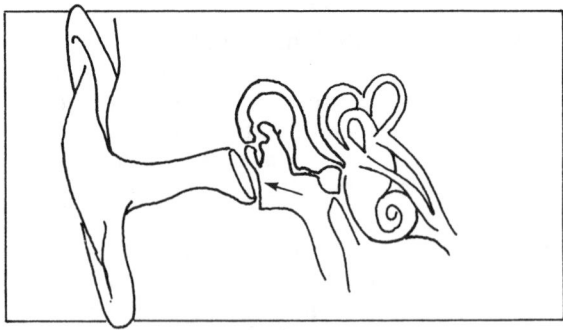

eardrum

earl *noun* A British nobleman.
earl (ûrl) □*noun, plural* **earls**
early *adjective* **1.** Of, at, or near the beginning: *We went out in the early afternoon.* **2.** Before the usual or expected time: *an early lunch.*
□*adverb* **1.** At or near the beginning: *We began working early in the day.* **2.** Before the

usual or expected time: *The bus arrived early.*
ear·ly (ûr′lē) □*adjective* **earlier, earliest**
□*adverb* **earlier, earliest**

earn *verb* **1.** To get in return for work: *She earned $100 a week.* **2.** To deserve or win by one's efforts: *He earned his good reputation.* —See Synonyms at **merit.**
earn (ûrn) □*verb* **earned, earning, earns**

earnest *adjective* Serious and sincere: *an earnest request for help.*
ear·nest (ûr′nist) □*adjective*

earnings *plural noun* Money earned in payment for work or as profit.
earn·ings (ur′ningz) □*plural noun*

earphone *noun* A device worn over the ear that carries sound to the ear.
ear·phone (îr′fōn′) □*noun, plural* **earphones**

earphone

earring *noun* A piece of jewelry worn on the ear.
ear·ring (îr′ring) □*noun, plural* **earrings**

earth *noun* **1.** Often **Earth** The planet on which human beings live. It is the fifth largest planet in the solar system. **2.** The surface of the land; ground: *The autumn leaves drifted to the earth.* **3.** Dirt; soil: *Plants grow quickly in good, rich earth.*
earth (ûrth) □*noun, plural* **earths**

earth

earthly *adjective* **1.** Of or from the earth rather than heaven: *Her earthly belongings were few.* **2.** Possible; practical: *There is no earthly reason for us to go.*
earth·ly (ûrth′lē) □*adjective*

earthquake *noun* A shaking of the earth caused by the movement of masses of rock far below the earth's surface.
earth·quake (ûrth′kwāk′) □*noun, plural* **earthquakes**

earthworm *noun* A common worm that lives in the ground and that has a body made up of many narrow parts shaped like rings.
earth·worm (ûrth′wûrm′) □*noun, plural* **earthworms**

ease *noun* Freedom from pain, trouble, strain, or hard work: *He can run long distances with ease.*
□*verb* **1.** To free from pain, worry, or hard work. **2.** To make less painful: *The pills eased her pain.* **3.** To move slowly and carefully: *I eased the heavy chair into place.*
ease (ēz) □*noun* □*verb* **eased, easing, eases**

easel *noun* A stand for holding a painting or displaying a sign or picture.
ea·sel (ē′zəl) □*noun, plural* **easels**

WORD HISTORY: **easel**

The word *easel* comes from a Dutch word meaning "donkey." An easel is like a donkey because it can carry something.

easel

a	bat	ī	bite	o͞o	tool	*th*	feather
ā	make	î	fierce	ou	out	th	bath
â	dare	o	dot	u	nut	hw	wheat
ä	father	ō	no	û	turn	zh	measure
e	net	ô	law, for	ch	church	ə	about, open
ē	be	oi	soil	ng	ring		pencil, atom
i	dip	oo	look	sh	shade		circus

easily *adverb* **1.** Without difficulty: *She found the store easily.* **2.** Without doubt; definitely: *He is easily the best tennis player in town.*
eas·i·ly (ē′zə lē) □*adverb*

east *noun* **1.** The direction in which the sun is seen rising in the morning. **2.** Often **East** A region in this direction. **3. the East** The part of the United States along or near the coast of the Atlantic Ocean. **4. the East** Asia and the lands near it; Orient.
□*adjective* **1.** Of, in, or toward the east: *the east branch of the railroad.* **2.** Coming from the east: *an east wind.*
□*adverb* In, from, or toward the east: *I walked east to the park.*
east (ēst) □*noun* □*adjective* □*adverb*

Easter *noun* A Christian holiday that celebrates Christ's return to life. Easter falls on the first Sunday after the first full moon on or after March 21.
Eas·ter (e′ster) □*noun*

eastern *adjective* **1.** Of, in, or toward the east: *eastern Mexico.* **2.** Coming from or lying toward the east: *the eastern border of the country.*
east·ern (ē′stərn) □*adjective*

eastward *adverb* To or toward the east: *He walked eastward down the hill.*
□*adjective* Moving to or toward the east: *the eastward flow of the current.*
east·ward (ēst′wərd) □*adverb* □*adjective*

easy *adjective* **1.** Not difficult to get or do; not hard: *It was easy to please her.* **2.** Free from worry, pain, or trouble: *She retired and had an easy life.* **3.** Not strict or severe: *He is an easy teacher.*
eas·y (ē′zē) □*adjective* **easier, easiest**

SYNONYMS: **easy, simple**
These adjectives mean not difficult to get or do: *It's easy to ride a bicycle. The test was easy. Painting the desk was a simple job. There is a simple solution to the problem.*

---

eat *verb* **1.** To take into the body by swallowing: *I ate a big dinner.* **2.** To have a meal: *Let's eat at a restaurant.* **3.** To destroy as if by eating; consume: *Rust ate away the car's fender.*
eat (ēt) □*verb* **ate, eaten, eating, eats**

eaten *verb* The past participle of **eat:** *He had eaten his dinner before we came.*
eat·en (ēt′ən) □*verb*

eaves *plural noun* The lower edge of a roof that juts out over the side of a building.
eaves (ēvz) □*plural noun*

eavesdrop *verb* To listen secretly to the private conversation of others.
eaves·drop (ēvz′drop′) □*verb* **eavesdropped, eavesdropping, eavesdrops**

WORD HISTORY: **eavesdrop**
The word *eavesdrop* originally referred to the space of ground beside a building where water dropped from the eaves. A person who stood in the eavesdrop to listen secretly to conversation taking place inside was said to be *eavesdropping*.

eavesdrop

ebb *verb* **1.** To flow away or out: *We went swimming after the tide began to ebb.* **2.** To fade; weaken: *Her energy ebbed as the hours passed.*
□*noun* The flowing out of the tide from the seashore: *The raft went out on the ebb of the tide.*
ebb (eb) □*verb* **ebbed, ebbing, ebbs** □*noun, plural* **ebbs**

ebony *noun* The hard, black wood of a tropical tree, used especially in making the black keys of pianos.
eb·on·y (eb′ə nē) □*noun, plural* **ebonies**

eccentric *adjective* Odd or unusual in appearance or behavior; strange: *an eccentric person who always put salt on ice cream.*
ec·cen·tric (ek sen′trik) □*adjective*

echo *noun* The repeating of a sound by the reflection of sound waves from a surface.
□*verb* To send back or repeat a sound in an echo: *Their calls for help echoed through the hills.*

ech·o (ek′ō) □*noun, plural* **echoes** □*verb*
echoed, echoing, echoes

echo

éclair *noun* An oblong pastry filled with custard or whipped cream and usually frosted with chocolate.
é·clair (ā klâr′) □*noun, plural* **éclairs**

eclipse *noun* The darkening of the moon or sun that happens when light coming from it is blocked. In an eclipse of the moon the earth casts a shadow as it passes between the sun and the moon. In an eclipse of the sun the moon blocks the light as it passes between the sun and the earth.
e·clipse (i klips′) □*noun, plural* **eclipses**

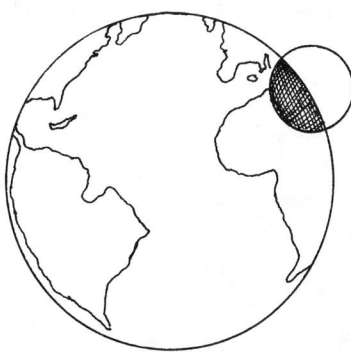

eclipse

ecology *noun* The study of living things in relation to each other and to their environment.
e·col·o·gy (ē kol′ə jē) □*noun*

economic *adjective* Of economics: *the government's economic policies.*

e·co·nom·ic (ē′kə **nom**′ik *or* ek′ə **nom**′ik) □*adjective*

economical *adjective* **1.** Careful about spending or using what one has; not wasteful. **2.** Working or operating with little waste: *a car with an economical engine.*
e·co·nom·i·cal (ē′kə **nom**′i kəl *or* ek′ə **nom**′i kəl) □*adjective*

SYNONYMS: **economical, frugal, thrifty**

These adjectives mean careful about spending or using what one has: *It was very economical to buy a small car that doesn't use a lot of gas. He was frugal with the paint. She is a thrifty shopper.*

---

economics *noun* The science that deals with money, goods, and services and how they are related to one another.
e·co·nom·ics (ē′kə **nom**′iks *or* ek′ə **nom**′iks) □*noun*

economize *verb* To lower expenses; save: *He economized by walking to work.*
e·con·o·mize (i kon′ə mīz′) □*verb*
economized, economizing, economizes

economy *noun* **1.** The way a country develops, divides up, and uses its money, goods, and services. **2.** The careful use of goods or money; thrift: *By practicing economy she was able to afford a vacation.*
e·con·o·my (i kon′ə mē) □*noun, plural* **economies**

ecstasy *noun* A state of very great happiness or delight.
ec·sta·sy (ek′stə sē) □*noun, plural* **ecstasies**

–ed¹ A suffix that forms the past tense and past participle of regular verbs: *leaked, hurried, spared.*

–ed² A suffix that forms adjectives: *a crested bird.*

eddy *noun* A current of water moving in a direction that is opposite to the direction of a main current; small whirlpool.
ed·dy (ed′ē) □*noun, plural* **eddies**

a	bat	ī	bite	ōō	tool	*th*	feather
ā	make	î	fierce	ou	out	th	bath
â	dare	o	dot	u	nut	hw	wheat
ä	father	ō	no	û	turn	zh	measure
e	net	ô	law, for	ch	church	ə	about, open
ē	be	oi	soil	ng	ring		pencil, atom
i	dip	oo	look	sh	shade		circus

edge   *noun* **1.** The line or place where something ends: *The house stood at the edge of a lake.* **2.** The cutting side of a tool: *the sharp edge of an ax.*
□*verb* **1.** To move slowly and gradually: *She edged toward the window.* **2.** To put or form an edge on: *She edged the skirt with ribbon.*
edge (ej) □*noun, plural* **edges** □*verb* **edged, edging, edges**

edge

edible   *adjective* Safe or fit to eat.
ed·i·ble (ed′ə bəl) □*adjective*

edict   *noun* An order or command given by someone in authority.
e·dict (ē′ dikt′) □*noun, plural* **edicts**

edit   *verb* To prepare for publication by checking, correcting, and revising: *Will you help edit the school newspaper?*
ed·it (ed′ it) □*verb* **edited, editing, edits**

edition   *noun* **1.** The entire number of copies of a book, newspaper, or magazine printed at one time. **2.** A single copy of an edition. **3.** The form in which a book is printed: *I have an illustrated edition of* Tom Sawyer.
e·di·tion (i dish′ ən) □*noun, plural* **editions**

editor   *noun* Someone who edits: *She became the editor of the newspaper.*
ed·i·tor (ed′ i tər) □*noun, plural* **editors**

editorial   *noun* An article in a newspaper or magazine or a statement on radio or television that gives the opinions of the editors or of the management.
□*adjective* Of an editor or the work of an editor: *an editorial opinion.*
ed·i·to·ri·al (ed′i tôr′ ē əl) □*noun, plural* **editorials** □*adjective*

educate   *verb* **1.** To give knowledge or training to; teach: *a teacher who educates the blind.*

2. To provide schooling for: *They spent a great deal of money to educate their children.*
ed·u·cate (ej′ə kāt′) □*verb* **educated, educating, educates**

education   *noun* **1.** The process of educating or being educated: *His education ended with high school.* **2.** The knowledge gained through education; learning: *She is a person of little education.*
ed·u·ca·tion (ej′ə kā′ shən) □*noun, plural* **educations**

educational   *adjective* **1.** Of education: *the city's educational system.* **2.** Giving education or knowledge: *an educational movie.*
ed·u·ca·tion·al (ej′ə kā′ shə nəl) □*adjective*

eel   *noun* A long, slippery fish that looks like a snake.
eel (ēl) □*noun, plural* **eels**

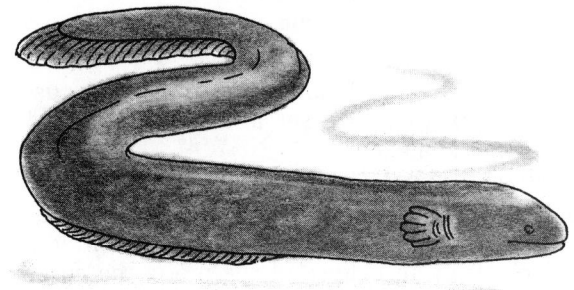

eel

eerie or **eery**   *adjective* Causing fear or dread: *We heard an eerie sound from the old barn.*
ee·rie or **ee·ry** (îr′ ē) □*adjective* **eerier, eeriest**

eerie

efface *verb* To remove by or as if by rubbing away from a surface: *The rock carvings were effaced by the action of the wind and the rain.*
ef·face (i **fās′**) □*verb* **effaced, effacing, effaces**

effect *noun* **1.** Something that is brought about by something else; result: *One effect of a cold is coughing.* **2.** The power to bring about a result; influence: *Her anger had no effect on them.*
□*verb* To bring about; cause: *The invention of the airplane effected many changes in travel.*
ef·fect (i **fekt′**) □*noun, plural* **effects** □*verb* **effected, effecting, effects**

effective *adjective* **1.** Able to bring about a desired result: *Window screens are effective in keeping out mosquitoes.* **2.** Being in force or operation: *an order that is effective immediately.*
ef·fec·tive (i **fek′**tiv) □*adjective*

efficient *adjective* Able to produce good results without wasting time, materials, or effort: *An efficient motor uses little fuel.*
ef·fi·cient (i **fish′**ənt) □*adjective*

effort *noun* **1.** The use of physical or mental energy to do something: *Building the new house took a great deal of effort.* **2.** A serious attempt; try: *She made an effort to be polite.*
ef·fort (**ef′**ərt) □*noun, plural* **efforts**

SYNONYMS: **effort, struggle, trouble**

These nouns mean the use of physical or mental energy to do something: *It isn't worth the effort to fix that old shed. Pulling the cart up the hill was quite a struggle. She took a great deal of trouble to find the books I needed.*

---

egg¹ *noun* **1.** A special cell formed in the body of a female animal from which a young animal develops. **2.** A rounded body with a hard shell that is produced by some animals and from which young animals hatch. **3.** The egg of a chicken, with its hard shell. The part inside the shell is used as food.
egg (eg) □*noun, plural* **eggs**

egg² *verb* To urge to action; encourage: *He egged me on to spend too much money.*
egg (eg) □*verb* **egged, egging, eggs**

eggbeater *noun* A kitchen utensil used for beating eggs or whipping and mixing foods.
egg·beat·er (**eg′**bē′tər) □*noun, plural* **eggbeaters**

eggnog *noun* A drink made of milk, beaten eggs, and sugar and often flavored with liquor: *On New Year's Day my father always makes eggnog.*
egg·nog (**eg′**nog′) □*noun*

eggplant *noun* A vegetable that has shiny purple skin and is shaped like a large egg.
egg·plant (**eg′**plant′) □*noun, plural* **eggplants**

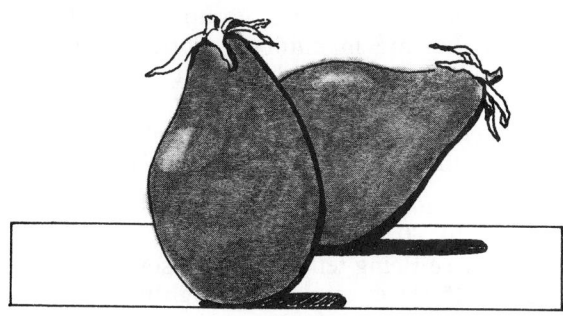

eggplant

egg roll *noun* A case consisting of a thin egg dough that has been filled with chopped vegetables and sometimes chopped fish or meat and then fried.

Egyptian *noun* **1.** Someone who was born in or is a citizen of Egypt. **2.** The language of the ancient Egyptians.
□*adjective* Of Egypt or the Egyptians.
E·gyp·tian (i **jip′**shən) □*noun, plural* **Egyptians** □*adjective*

eight *noun* A number equal to the sum of 7 + 1; 8.
□*adjective* Being one more than seven.
eight (āt) □*noun, plural* **eights** □*adjective*

eighteen *noun* A number equal to the sum of 10 + 8; 18.
□*adjective* Being one more than seventeen.
eight·een (ā′tēn′) □*noun, plural* **eighteens** □*adjective*

eighteenth *noun* **1.** In a group of people or things that are in numbered order, the one that matches the number eighteen. **2.** One of eighteen equal parts, written 1/18.
□*adjective* Coming after the seventeenth.

a	bat	ī	bite	ōō	tool	*th*	feather
ā	make	î	fierce	ou	out	th	bath
â	dare	o	dot	u	nut	hw	wheat
ä	father	ō	no	û	turn	zh	measure
e	net	ô	law, for	ch	church	ə	about, open
ē	be	oi	soil	ng	ring		pencil, atom
i	dip	oo	look	sh	shade		circus

eight·eenth (ā′tēnth′) □*noun, plural* **eighteenths** □*adjective*

eighth *noun* **1.** In a group of people or things that are in numbered order, the one that matches the number eight. **2.** One of eight equal parts, written ⅛.
□*adjective* Coming after the seventh.
eighth (ātth) □*noun, plural* **eighths**
□*adjective*

eightieth *noun* **1.** In a group of people or things that are in numbered order, the one that matches the number eighty. **2.** One of eighty equal parts, written ¹⁄₈₀.
□*adjective* Coming after the seventy-ninth.
eight·i·eth (ā′tē ith) □*noun, plural* **eightieths**

eighty *noun* A number equal to the product of 8 × 10; 80.
□*adjective* Being ten more than seventy.
eight·y (ā′tē) □*noun, plural* **eighties**
□*adjective*

either *adjective* **1.** One or the other; any one of two: *Take either apple.* **2.** One and the other; each: *She wore bracelets on either wrist.*
□*pronoun* One or the other: *Either of the coats will be warm enough.*
□*adverb* Likewise; also: *If you don't tell, we won't either.* The adverb **either** is only used following a negative statement.
□*conjunction* The conjunction **either** is used with **or** to present two alternatives: *Take either the apple or the grapes.*
ei·ther (ē′thər *or* ī′thər) □*adjective*
□*pronoun* □*adverb* □*conjunction*

either

eject *verb* **1.** To throw out with great force. **2.** To force to leave; drive out: *He was ejected from the meeting when he interrupted the speaker.*
e·ject (i jekt′) □*verb* **ejected, ejecting, ejects**

eke *verb* **1.** To earn with great effort: *He worked day and night to eke out a living for his family.* **2.** To add to with great strain or labor: *She eked out her small allowance by working at the library.*
eke (ēk) □*verb* **eked, eking, ekes**

elaborate *adjective* Worked out or made with careful attention and in great detail: *She made elaborate preparations for the party.*
□*verb* To work out with care and detail: *He elaborated on his plan.*
e·lab·o·rate (i lab′ər it) □*adjective* □*verb*
(i lab′ə rāt′) **elaborated, elaborating, elaborates**

elapse *verb* To go by; pass: *Years elapsed before she returned.*
e·lapse (i laps′) □*verb* **elapsed, elapsing, elapses**

elastic *adjective* Able to return to original shape after being stretched, squeezed, or pressed together: *Rubber is an elastic material.*
□*noun* A fabric or tape that stretches.
e·las·tic (i las′tik) □*adjective* □*noun, plural* **elastics**

elate *verb* To fill with joy or happiness: *The news of the victory elated all of us.*
e·late (i lāt′) □*verb* **elated, elating, elates**

elation *noun* A feeling of great joy or happiness.
e·la·tion (i lā′shən) □*noun*

elbow *noun* **1.** The joint or bend between the forearm and the upper arm. **2.** Something, such as a piece of pipe, that is bent like an elbow.
□*verb* To push or shove with the elbows: *They elbowed their way through the crowd.*
el·bow (el′bō) □*noun, plural* **elbows** □*verb* **elbowed, elbowing, elbows**

elder *adjective* A comparative of **old.**
□*noun* Someone who is older: *Children go to school; their elders go to work.*
el·der (el′dər) □*adjective* □*noun, plural* **elders**

elderly *adjective* Approaching old age: *an elderly woman with white hair.*
eld·er·ly (el′dər lē) □*adjective*

eldest *adjective* A superlative of **old.**
eld·est (el′dist) □*adjective*

elec. An abbreviation for **electric** and **electricity.**

elect *verb* **1.** To choose by voting: *The city elects a mayor every four years.* **2.** To make a choice; choose: *After careful thought, I elected to go to music school.*
e·lect (i **lekt′**) □*verb* **elected, electing, elects**

election *noun* **1.** The act of electing by voting. **2.** The fact of being elected by voting: *Her election to the board of directors caused great surprise.*
e·lec·tion (i **lek′**shən) □*noun, plural* **elections**

electric *adjective* Of, produced, or operated by electricity: *an electric current; an electric shock; an electric refrigerator.*
e·lec·tric (i **lek′**trik) □*adjective*

WORD HISTORY: **electric**

The word *electric* comes from a Greek word meaning "amber." When amber is rubbed, it becomes electrically charged and attracts light objects such as straw and small pieces of wood. The ancient Greeks noticed this property of amber over 2,000 years before electricity was first studied scientifically.

---

electrical *adjective* Electric: *an electrical engineer.*
e·lec·tri·cal (i **lek′**tri kəl) □*adjective*

electrician *noun* Someone who installs, repairs, or operates electrical equipment.
e·lec·tri·cian (i lek **trish′**ən) □*noun, plural* **electricians**

electricity *noun* **1.** A form of energy that can be sent through wires in a flow of tiny particles and can be used to produce light and heat and to run motors. **2.** Electric current: *The electricity was cut off by the storm.*
e·lec·tric·i·ty (i lek **tris′**i tē) □*noun*

electrode *noun* Any one of the parts that give off, collect, or control the flow of electricity in a battery or other electrical device.
e·lec·trode (i **lek′**trōd) □*noun, plural* **electrodes**

electromagnet *noun* A piece of iron that becomes a magnet when an electric current is passed through a wire wound around it.
e·lec·tro·mag·net (i lek′trō **mag′**nit) □*noun, plural* **electromagnets**

electron *noun* One of the smallest possible pieces of matter. Electrons are usually found in an atom outside the nucleus.
e·lec·tron (i **lek′**tron′) □*noun, plural* **electrons**

electronic *adjective* Of or having to do with electrons or electronics.
e·lec·tron·ic (i lek tron′ik) □*adjective*

electronics *noun* The study of electrons and their behavior and of electronic equipment, such as computers.
e·lec·tron·ics (i lek tron′iks) □*noun*

elegant *adjective* Showing good taste in appearance or manner: *an elegant gown.*
el·e·gant (el′i gənt) □*adjective*

element *noun* **1.** Any of the more than 100 basic materials from which all other things are made. Elements cannot be broken down into simpler substances by using chemicals. Gold and oxygen are elements. **2.** A basic part of which something is made up: *A willingness to work hard is one element of success.* **3.** A natural or preferred place or environment: *The jungle is the lion's element.* **4. elements** The forces of weather, such as rain, wind, and cold: *She felt the fury of the elements when she went out in the blizzard.*
el·e·ment (el′ə mənt) □*noun, plural* **elements**

elementary *adjective* Of or having to do with the basic or simplest parts of something: *an elementary grammar book.*
el·e·men·ta·ry (el′ə men′tə rē) □*adjective*

elementary school *noun* A school that includes the first six to eight years.

elephant *noun* A huge animal of Africa or Asia with two large curved tusks and a long trunk.
el·e·phant (el′ə fənt) □*noun, plural* **elephants**

elevate *verb* To raise to a higher place or position; lift up: *I put blocks of wood under the chair to elevate it.*
el·e·vate (el′ə vāt′) □*verb* **elevated, elevating, elevates**

elevation *noun* **1.** A raised place: *Our house is on a slight elevation above the highway.* **2.** Height, especially above the earth's surface or above sea level: *The helicopter flew at an elevation of 500 feet.* **3.** The act of elevating or

a bat	ī bite	ōō tool	*th* feather
ā make	î fierce	ou out	th bath
â dare	o dot	u nut	hw wheat
ä father	ō no	û turn	zh measure
e net	ô law, for	ch church	ə about, open
ē be	oi soil	ng ring	pencil, atom
i dip	oo look	sh shade	circus

the condition of being elevated: *His elevation to the presidency meant long hours and hard work.* —See Synonyms at **height.**
el·e·va·tion (el′ə **vā**′shən) ▢*noun, plural* **elevations**

elevation

elevator *noun* **1.** A platform or cage that can be raised or lowered to carry people or things from one level to another, as in a building or mine. **2.** A building for storing grain.
el·e·va·tor (el′ə vā′tər) ▢*noun, plural* **elevators**

eleven *noun* A number equal to the sum of 10 + 1; 11.
▢*adjective* Being one more than ten.
e·lev·en (i **lev**′ən) ▢*noun, plural* **elevens** ▢*adjective*

eleventh *noun* **1.** In a group of people or things that are in numbered order, the one that matches the number eleven. **2.** One of eleven equal parts, written 1/11.
▢*adjective* Coming after the tenth.
e·lev·enth (i **lev**′ənth) ▢*noun, plural* **elevenths** ▢*adjective*

elf *noun* A tiny, mischievous creature of folklore who is thought to have magical powers.
elf (elf) ▢*noun, plural* **elves**

elf

eligible *adjective* Suitable or qualified, as to hold a position: *He was eligible for a promotion.*
el·i·gi·ble (**el**′i jə bəl) ▢*adjective*

eliminate *verb* To get rid of; leave out or remove: *We must all work together to eliminate air pollution.*
e·lim·i·nate (i **lim**′ə nāt′) ▢*verb* **eliminated, eliminating, eliminates**

elk *noun* **1.** A large deer of North America. The male has large, branching antlers. **2.** The European moose.
elk (elk) ▢*noun, plural* **elk** or **elks**

ellipse *noun* A figure shaped like a narrow or flattened circle.
el·lipse (i **lips**′) ▢*noun, plural* **ellipses**

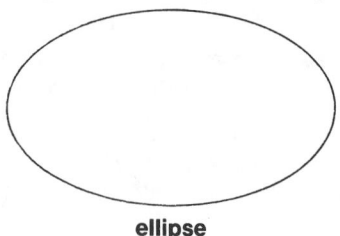
ellipse

elm *noun* A tall shade tree with arching or curving branches and strong, hard wood.
elm (elm) ▢*noun, plural* **elms**

elope *verb* To go or run away secretly in order to get married.
e·lope (i **lōp**′) ▢*verb* **eloped, eloping, elopes**

eloquent *adjective* Having or showing the ability to use words well and effectively: *an eloquent preacher.*
el·o·quent (**el**′ə kwənt) ▢*adjective*

else *adjective* **1.** Other; different: *Why don't you ask somebody else?* **2.** More; additional: *What else do you want?*
▢*adverb* **1.** In a different manner or place or at a different time: *How else should I have acted?* **2.** If not; otherwise: *Hurry, or else you will be late.*
else (els) ▢*adjective* ▢*adverb*

elsewhere *adverb* To or in a different place; somewhere else: *We went elsewhere for lunch.*
else·where (**els**′hwâr′ *or* **els**′wâr′) ▢*adverb*

elude *verb* To avoid or escape from, as by being daring and clever: *The fox eluded the dogs.*
e·lude (i **lōōd**′) ▢*verb* **eluded, eluding, eludes**

elves *noun* The plural of **elf.**
elves (elvz) ▢*noun*

emancipate *verb* To free, especially from slavery; liberate.
e·man·ci·pate (i **man′**sə pāt′) □*verb* **emancipated, emancipating, emancipates**

embankment *noun* A mound of earth or stone built to hold back water or support a road.
em·bank·ment (em **bangk′**mənt) □*noun*, *plural* **embankments**

embargo *noun* An order made by a government that forbids merchant ships to enter or leave its ports.
em·bar·go (em **bär′**gō) □*noun*, *plural* **embargoes**

embark *verb* **1.** To go on board a ship: *The sailors embarked at dawn.* **2.** To set out; make a start: *He embarked on a career as a painter.*
em·bark (em **bärk′**) □*verb* **embarked, embarking, embarks**

embarrass *verb* To cause to feel self-conscious or uncomfortable: *Her parents' remarks embarrassed her.*
em·bar·rass (em **bar′**əs) □*verb* **embarrassed, embarrassing, embarrasses**

embarrass

embarrassment *noun* The condition of being embarrassed: *He felt embarrassment when he spilled his soup on the table.*
em·bar·rass·ment (em **bar′**əs mənt) □*noun*, *plural* **embarrassments**

embassy *noun* The official home and offices of an ambassador.
em·bas·sy (**em′**bə sē) □*noun*, *plural* **embassies**

embed *verb* To set or fix firmly: *bricks that were embedded in sand.*
em·bed (em **bed′**) □*verb* **embedded, embedding, embeds**

embellish *verb* **1.** To make more beautiful by adding ornaments to: *She embellished the capital letters with loops and curling lines.* **2.** To add details to: *He embellished his story with poems and songs.*
em·bel·lish (em **bel′**ish) □*verb* **embellished, embellishing, embellishes**

ember *noun* A piece of glowing coal or wood, as from a fire that is dying down.
em·ber (**em′**bər) □*noun*, *plural* **embers**

embezzle *verb* To steal money or property that one is supposed to take care of as part of one's job: *The treasurer embezzled thousands of dollars from the company.*
em·bez·zle (em **bez′**əl) □*verb* **embezzled, embezzling, embezzles**

emblem *noun* An object or picture that represents something else; symbol: *The eagle is our national emblem.*
em·blem (**em′**bləm) □*noun*, *plural* **emblems**

emboss *verb* To decorate with a design that is raised: *The penny is embossed with a portrait of Lincoln.*
em·boss (em **bôs′**) □*verb* **embossed, embossing, embosses**

embrace *verb* **1.** To grasp or hold in the arms as a sign of affection; hug: *The father embraced his son.* **2.** To take up: *He embraced the life of a farmer.* **3.** To take in; include: *His knowledge embraces science and history.* □*noun* A hug.
em·brace (em **brās′**) □*verb* **embraced, embracing, embraces** □*noun*, *plural* **embraces**

embroider *verb* **1.** To decorate by making designs with a needle and thread: *She embroidered the blouse with butterflies.* **2.** To add made-up details to: *I think that he embroidered the story to make his own part seem more important.*
em·broi·der (em **broi′**dər) □*verb* **embroidered, embroidering, embroiders**

a bat	ī bite	o͞o tool	th feather
ā make	î fierce	ou out	th bath
â dare	o dot	u nut	hw wheat
ä father	ō no	û turn	zh measure
e net	ô law, for	ch church	ə about, open
ē be	oi soil	ng ring	pencil, atom
i dip	oo look	sh shade	circus

embroidery *noun* Decorative designs on cloth made with a needle and thread: *a blouse with delicate embroidery.*
em·broi·der·y (em **broi′**də rē) ▫*noun, plural* **embroideries**

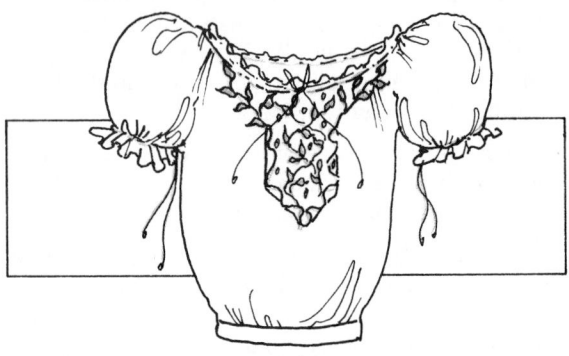

embroidery

embryo *noun* A plant or animal in a stage of development before birth.
em·bry·o (**em′**brē ō′) ▫*noun, plural* **embryos**

emerald *noun* **1.** A bright-green, clear stone that is used as a gem. **2.** A bright green. ▫*adjective* Bright green.
em·er·ald (**em′**ər əld) ▫*noun, plural* **emeralds** ▫*adjective*

emerge *verb* **1.** To come out or into view; appear: *The passengers emerged from the train.* **2.** To become known: *New ideas emerged as we discussed the plan.*
e·merge (i **mûrj′**) ▫*verb* **emerged, emerging, emerges**

emergency *noun* A serious situation that develops suddenly and calls for quick action.
e·mer·gen·cy (i **mûr′**jən sē) ▫*noun, plural* **emergencies**

emery *noun* A hard brown mineral that is used in powder form for grinding and polishing.
em·er·y (**em′**ə rē) ▫*noun, plural* **emeries**

emigrant *noun* Someone who leaves a country or region to settle in another: *Her grandparents were emigrants from Poland.*
em·i·grant (**em′**i grənt) ▫*noun, plural* **emigrants**

emigrate *verb* To leave a country or region and settle in another: *My parents emigrated from Europe to the United States.*
em·i·grate (**em′**i grāt′) ▫*verb* **emigrated, emigrating, emigrates**

eminent *adjective* Outstanding, as in character or rank; prominent: *an eminent artist.*
em·i·nent (**em′**ə nənt) ▫*adjective*

emissary *noun* A person who is sent on a mission as the representative or agent for someone else.
em·is·sar·y (**em′**i ser′ē) ▫*noun, plural* **emissaries**

emit *verb* To send or give out: *Fires emit smoke. The child emitted a happy giggle.*
e·mit (i **mit′**) ▫*verb* **emitted, emitting, emits**

emotion *noun* A strong feeling such as fright, rage, love, joy, or sorrow.
e·mo·tion (i **mō′**shən) ▫*noun, plural* **emotions**

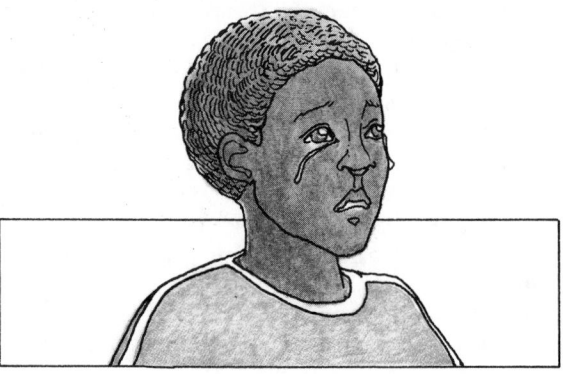

emotion

emotional *adjective* **1.** Of or having to do with emotion: *He suffered an emotional upset when his dog died.* **2.** Easily moved by emotion: *He is an emotional man who quickly becomes angry.* **3.** Arousing or expressing emotion: *An emotional argument will sometimes influence people.*
e·mo·tion·al (i **mō′**shə nəl) ▫*adjective*

emperor *noun* A man who rules an empire.
em·per·or (**em′**pər ər) ▫*noun, plural* **emperors**

emphases *noun* The plural of **emphasis.**
em·pha·ses (**em′**fə sēz′) ▫*noun*

emphasis *noun* **1.** Special importance given to something: *Her mother put an emphasis on neatness.* **2.** Special stress put on a particular syllable, word, or phrase: *The emphasis is on the first syllable in the word "happy."*
em·pha·sis (**em′**fə sis) ▫*noun, plural* **emphases**

emphasize *verb* To give emphasis to; stress: *He emphasized the importance of being fair.*
em·pha·size (**em′**fə sīz′) ▫*verb* **emphasized, emphasizing, emphasizes**

empire *noun* A group of countries or territories under one ruler or government.
em·pire (**em′**pīr′) ▫*noun, plural* **empires**

employ *verb* **1.** To provide with work that pays a salary or wages; hire: *Our plumber employs two assistants.* **2.** To make use of: *She employed a pair of scissors to cut the cloth.* □*noun* The condition of being employed: *His brother is in the employ of the railroad.*
em·ploy (em ploi′) □*verb* **employed, employing, employs** □*noun*

employee *noun* Someone who works for another person or an organization for wages: *How many employees does she have?*
em·ploy·ee (em ploi′ē) □*noun, plural* **employees**

employer *noun* A person or organization that employs people for wages: *Our employer is going to give us an extra holiday this year.*
em·ploy·er (em ploi′ər) □*noun, plural* **employers**

employment *noun* **1.** The act of employing or the condition of being employed: *The employment of airplanes sped up delivery.* **2.** Work that is paid for by an employer: *He found employment as a mechanic.*
em·ploy·ment (em ploi′mənt) □*noun, plural* **employments**

empress *noun* A woman who rules an empire.
em·press (em′pris) □*noun, plural* **empresses**

empty *adjective* **1.** Containing nothing: *an empty purse; an empty theater.* **2.** Lacking purpose, meaning, or interest: *an empty life; empty words.* □*verb* **1.** To make or become empty: *We emptied the box quickly. The room emptied when the meeting ended.* **2.** To remove from a container: *I emptied the money from my wallet.* **3.** To flow; discharge: *The brook empties into the river.*
emp·ty (emp′tē) □*adjective* **emptier, emptiest** □*verb* **emptied, emptying, empties**

SYNONYMS: **empty, vacant**

These adjectives mean not containing anything: *an empty box, an empty room; a vacant house, a vacant lot.*

---

emu *noun* A large bird of Australia that is very much like an ostrich.
e·mu (ē′myoo) □*noun, plural* **emus**

en– A prefix that forms verbs and means: **1.** To put into: *endanger.* **2.** To cause to be; make: *enable.* When *en–* is followed by *b, m,* or *p,* it becomes *em–: embed.*

–en¹ A suffix that forms verbs from adjectives and means "to make" or "to become": *weaken.*

–en² A suffix that forms adjectives from nouns and means "made of": *wooden.*

enable *verb* To give the means, ability, or opportunity to: *Training will enable you to find work.*
en·a·ble (en ā′bəl) □*verb* **enabled, enabling, enables**

enact *verb* **1.** To make into law: *Congress enacted a new tax bill.* **2.** To act out, as on a stage: *The students enacted a scene from the school play.*
en·act (en akt′) □*verb* **enacted, enacting, enacts**

enamel *noun* **1.** A smooth, hard substance that is baked onto the surface of metal, glass, or pottery to protect or decorate it. **2.** A paint that forms a hard, shiny surface when it dries. **3.** The hard, white outer layer of a tooth.
e·nam·el (i nam′əl) □*noun, plural* **enamels**

enchant *verb* **1.** To put under a magic spell; bewitch: *The whole village was enchanted by a wicked witch.* **2.** To delight completely; charm: *Her beautiful smile enchanted the children.*
en·chant (en chant′) □*verb* **enchanted, enchanting, enchants**

encircle *verb* **1.** To form a circle around; surround: *Flowers encircled the fountain.* **2.** To move in a circle around: *The earth encircles the sun.*
en·cir·cle (en sûr′kəl) □*verb* **encircled, encircling, encircles**

enclose *verb* **1.** To surround on all sides; close in: *A wall encloses the playground.* **2.** To put into the same envelope or package: *He enclosed a newspaper clipping in the letter he sent me last week.*
en·close (en klōz′) □*verb* **enclosed, enclosing, encloses**

encompass *verb* To encircle; surround.
en·com·pass (en kum′pəs) □*verb* **encompassed, encompassing, encompasses**

a bat	ī bite	ōō tool	*th* feather
ā make	î fierce	ou out	th bath
â dare	o dot	u nut	hw wheat
ä father	ō no	û turn	zh measure
e net	ô law, for	ch church	ə about, open
ē be	oi soil	ng ring	pencil, atom
i dip	oo look	sh shade	circus

encore *noun* **1.** A request by an audience for an additional performance. **2.** An additional performance given in response to applause.
en·core (ŏn'kôr') □*noun, plural* **encores**

encounter *verb* To come upon, especially unexpectedly: *I encountered an old friend on the street. We encountered many problems in finishing the job.*
□*noun* A meeting, especially an unexpected one: *Our encounter with the famous actor thrilled us.*
en·coun·ter (en koun'tər) □*verb* **encountered, encountering, encounters** □*noun, plural* **encounters**

encourage *verb* **1.** To give hope, courage, or confidence to; urge. **2.** To help bring about; create: *Rain encourages the growth of grass.*
en·cour·age (en kûr'ij) □*verb* **encouraged, encouraging, encourages**

encouragement *noun* Something that encourages: *Your kind words are an encouragement to me.*
en·cour·age·ment (en kûr'ij mənt) □*noun, plural* **encouragements**

encroach *verb* **1.** To take over the possessions of another by gradual or secret methods. **2.** To go beyond the usual boundaries or limits: *The ocean encroached upon the shore and washed away the path.*
en·croach (en krōch') □*verb* **encroached, encroaching, encroaches**

encumber *verb* **1.** To weigh down: *We were encumbered by our books, suitcases, and tennis rackets.* **2.** To prevent the progress of; hinder: *The program has been encumbered by a lack of money.*
en·cum·ber (en kum'bər) □*verb* **encumbered, encumbering, encumbers**

encyclopedia *noun* A book or set of books containing many articles on a wide variety of subjects and usually arranged in alphabetical order.
en·cy·clo·pe·di·a (en sī'klə pē'dē ə) □*noun, plural* **encyclopedias**

end *noun* **1.** The part where a thing begins or stops: *I grabbed one end of the stick.* **2.** The last part of something: *The war came to an end.* **3.** A purpose; goal: *Her children's happiness was the end toward which she worked.*
□*verb* To bring or come to an end: *The dinner ended the meeting. The concert ended with an encore.*

end (end) □*noun, plural* **ends** □*verb* **ended, ending, ends**

> **SYNONYMS: end, complete, conclude, finish**
>
> These verbs mean to bring or come to the last part of something: *My school day ends at 3 o'clock. We completed the game before it got dark. The assembly concluded with the singing of the school song. I didn't finish my homework assignment on time.*

end

endanger *verb* To put in danger: *Careless driving endangers lives.*
en·dan·ger (en dān'jər) □*verb* **endangered, endangering, endangers**

endeavor *verb* To make an earnest effort; try: *I endeavored to control my temper.*
□*noun* An earnest effort or attempt: *He made an endeavor to please his parents.*
en·deav·or (en dev'ər) □*verb* **endeavored, endeavoring, endeavors** □*noun, plural* **endeavors**

ending *noun* The last part; end: *a movie with a sad ending.*
end·ing (en'ding) □*noun, plural* **endings**

endless *adjective* **1.** Having or seeming to have no end: *We drove down an endless highway.* **2.** Joined at the ends; continuous: *an endless chain.*
end·less (end'lis) □*adjective*

endorse *verb* **1.** To sign one's name on the back of a check in order to receive the amount of money indicated on its front. **2.** To give public approval of; support openly: *Many famous scientists endorsed the new project.*
en·dorse (en dôrs') □*verb* **endorsed, endorsing, endorses**

endow *verb* **1.** To give property, income, or a source of income to: *A rich family endowed the hospital.* **2.** To equip with a talent or qual-

ity: *Nature endowed her with sharp hearing.*
en·dow (en **dou′**) ☐*verb* **endowed,
endowing, endows**

endurance *noun* The ability to withstand
strain, hardship, or use: *Running a marathon
is a test of endurance.*
en·dur·ance (en **dŏŏr′** əns *or* en **dyŏŏr′** əns)
☐*noun*

endurance

endure *verb* **1.** To put up with patiently;
bear: *When he broke his leg, he could hardly
endure the pain.* **2.** To continue to exist; last:
The building has endured for many centuries.
en·dure (en **dŏŏr′** *or* en **dyŏŏr′**) ☐*verb*
endured, enduring, endures

enemy *noun* **1.** Someone who hates or
wishes harm to another. **2.** A country that is at
war with another country. **3.** Something
harmful in its effects: *Fear is our worst enemy.*
en·e·my (**en′** ə mē) ☐*noun, plural* **enemies**

energetic *adjective* Having or showing energy; vigorous.
en·er·get·ic (en′ər **jet′** ik) ☐*adjective*

energy *noun* **1.** The ability, strength, or will
to work or act: *I lacked the energy to go shopping.* **2.** Power to move objects or do other
kinds of physical work. Electricity and heat
are sources of energy.
en·er·gy (**en′** ər jē) ☐*noun, plural* **energies**

enforce *verb* To make sure that a law or rule
is carried out or obeyed: *Police enforce traffic
laws.*
en·force (en **fôrs′**) ☐*verb* **enforced,
enforcing, enforces**

engage *verb* **1.** To employ; hire: *He engaged
a lawyer.* **2.** To take up and hold: *The play*

engaged her full attention. **3.** To take part; participate: *I'm too busy to engage in conversation
now.* **4.** To promise, especially to marry.
en·gage (en **gāj′**) ☐*verb* **engaged, engaging,
engages**

engaged *adjective* **1.** Busy: *He was engaged
in answering a letter.* **2.** Pledged to marry:
They have been engaged for a year.
en·gaged (en **gājd′**) ☐*adjective*

engagement *noun* **1.** The act of engaging or
the condition of being engaged. **2.** A promise
to marry. **3.** A promise to appear or meet at a
certain time; appointment: *a dinner engagement.*
en·gage·ment (en **gāj′** mənt) ☐*noun, plural*
engagements

engine *noun* **1.** A machine that uses energy
to make something run or move. **2.** A railroad
locomotive.
en·gine (**en′** jən) ☐*noun, plural* **engines**

WORD HISTORY: **engine**

Engine originally meant "human cleverness" and
came from a Latin word that also meant "cleverness." Later the word *engine* came to be used of
such products of human cleverness as a motor.

engine

engineer *noun* **1.** Someone who is trained in
engineering. **2.** Someone who runs a locomotive.
en·gin·eer (en′jə **nîr′**) ☐*noun, plural*
engineers

a	bat	ī	bite	ŏŏ	tool	*th*	feather
ā	make	î	fierce	ou	out	th	bath
â	dare	o	dot	u	nut	hw	wheat
ä	father	ō	no	û	turn	zh	measure
e	net	ô	law, for	ch	church	ə	about, open
ē	be	oi	soil	ng	ring		pencil, atom
i	dip	oo	look	sh	shade		circus

engineering　*noun* The use of scientific principles for the planning and building of structures such as bridges, engines, roads, or canals.
en·gi·neer·ing (en′jə **nîr′** ing) □*noun*

English　*noun* **1.** The language of Great Britain, the United States, Canada, Australia, and various other countries throughout the world. **2.** The people of England.
□*adjective* Of England, the English people, or the English language.
Eng·lish (**ing′** glish) □*noun* □*adjective*

English horn　*noun* A woodwind musical instrument that resembles the oboe but has a deeper tone.

engrave　*verb* **1.** To carve or cut into a surface: *The jeweler engraved my name on the spoon.* **2.** To fix firmly: *The sound of her laughter is engraved in my memory.*
en·grave (en **grāv′**) □*verb* engraved, engraving, engraves

engrave

engross　*verb* To take up all of; absorb: *The movie completely engrossed her attention.*
en·gross (en **grōs′**) □*verb* engrossed, engrossing, engrosses

engulf　*verb* To flow over and swallow up: *The island was engulfed by the flood.*
en·gulf (en **gulf′**) □*verb* engulfed, engulfing, engulfs

enhance　*verb* To make greater; improve: *Soft cushions enhanced the comfort of the chair.*
en·hance (en **hans′**) □*verb* enhanced, enhancing, enhances

enigma　*noun* Something that is hard to understand or explain.
e·nig·ma (i **nig′** mə) □*noun, plural* enigmas

enjoy　*verb* **1.** To get pleasure from: *We enjoyed our visit to the museum.* **2.** To have the use or benefit of: *She enjoys good health.*
en·joy (en **joi′**) □*verb* enjoyed, enjoying, enjoys

enjoyable　*adjective* Giving enjoyment: *an enjoyable trip.* —See Synonyms at **pleasant.**
en·joy·a·ble (en **joi′** ə bəl) □*adjective*

enjoyment　*noun* Pleasure; joy: *I cooked a fancy dinner for my own enjoyment.*
en·joy·ment (en **joi′** mənt) □*noun, plural* enjoyments

enlarge　*verb* To make or become larger: *My father enlarged the store. The town has enlarged in recent years.*
en·large (en **lärj′**) □*verb* enlarged, enlarging, enlarges

enlargement　*noun* **1.** The act of making or becoming larger. **2.** Something, such as a photograph, that has been enlarged: *We ordered three enlargements of our class picture.*
en·large·ment (en **lärj′** ment) □*noun, plural* enlargements

enlighten　*verb* To give wisdom or knowledge to: *The senator's speech enlightened us about the problems of government.*
en·light·en (en **līt′** ən) □*verb* enlightened, enlightening, enlightens

enlist　*verb* **1.** To join the armed forces: *She enlisted for two years in the navy.* **2.** To seek and gain the support or help of: *He enlisted his friends in cleaning the yard.*
en·list (en **list′**) □*verb* enlisted, enlisting, enlists

enormous　*adjective* Very large; huge: *an enormous factory; the enormous cost of a house.* —See Synonyms at **giant.**
e·nor·mous (i **nôr′** məs) □*adjective*

enough　*adjective* As many or as much as wanted or needed; sufficient: *There is enough food for four.*
□*adverb* To a satisfactory amount or degree: *My room is not neat enough.*
□*pronoun* An adequate quantity: *She had enough of everything.*
e·nough (i **nuf′**) □*adjective* □*adverb* □*pronoun*

enrage　*verb* To make very angry: *Lies enrage my mother.*
en·rage (en **raj′**) □*verb* enraged, enraging, enrages

enrich　*verb* To improve the quality of by adding something: *I decided to enrich the soil with fertilizer.*

en·rich (en **rich′**) ▢*verb* **enriched, enriching, enriches**

enroll *verb* To sign up; register: *They enrolled their children in a nearby school. My brother enrolled in college.*
en·roll (en **rōl′**) ▢*verb* **enrolled, enrolling, enrolls**

enrollment *noun* **1.** The act of enrolling: *College enrollment begins tomorrow.* **2.** The number enrolled: *Enrollment in the course will be 20.*
en·roll·ment (en **rōl′**mənt) ▢*noun, plural* **enrollments**

ensign *noun* **1.** A national flag displayed on ships and aircraft. **2.** An officer of the lowest rank in the U.S. Navy or Coast Guard.
en·sign (en**′**sən) ▢*noun, plural* **ensigns**

ensign

ensue *verb* To come after or follow as a result: *After the names of the winners were announced, a joyful celebration ensued.*
en·sue (en **sōō′**) ▢*verb* **ensued, ensuing, ensues**

ensure *verb* To make sure or certain; guarantee: *Careful driving ensures safety.*
en·sure (en **shoor′**) ▢*verb* **ensured, ensuring, ensures**

entangle *verb* To make tangled; snarl: *The kittens entangled themselves in the yarn.*
en·tan·gle (en **tang′**gəl) ▢*verb* **entangled, entangling, entangles**

entangle

enter *verb* **1.** To come or go in or into: *I entered without knocking. We entered the house.* **2.** To make a beginning in; take up: *entering the medical profession.* **3.** To become a member of; join: *She entered the army last fall.* **4.** To make a record of; inscribe: *We entered the names of the students in this book.*
en·ter (en**′**tər) ▢*verb* **entered, entering, enters**

enterprise *noun* An undertaking, especially one that is difficult or involves risk: *The new restaurant is her latest enterprise.*
en·ter·prise (en**′**tər prīz′) ▢*noun, plural* **enterprises**

entertain *verb* **1.** To hold the attention of; amuse: *She entertained us by playing the guitar.* **2.** To have as a guest: *I entertained a few friends for lunch.* **3.** To think about carefully; consider: *She refused to entertain the idea.* —See Synonyms at **amuse.**
en·ter·tain (en′tər **tān′**) ▢*verb* **entertained, entertaining, entertains**

entertainer *noun* Someone, such as a singer or dancer, who performs for an audience.
en·ter·tain·er (en′tər **tā′**nər) ▢*noun, plural* **entertainers**

entertainment *noun* **1.** Something that entertains: *The new mystery movie is first-class entertainment.* **2.** The act of entertaining: *We enjoyed the entertainment of our friends.* —See Synonyms at **recreation.**
en·ter·tain·ment (en′tər **tān′**mənt) ▢*noun, plural* **entertainments**

enthrall *verb* To hold as if under a magic spell; charm: *The beauty of his voice enthralled the audience.*
en·thrall (en **thrôl′**) ▢*verb* **enthralled, enthralling, enthralls**

enthusiasm *noun* Strong interest, admiration, or excitement: *I share his great enthusiasm for sailing.*
en·thu·si·asm (en **thōō′**zē az′əm) ▢*noun, plural* **enthusiasms**

enthusiastic *adjective* Full of enthusiasm; eager: *She is an enthusiastic basketball fan.*
en·thu·si·as·tic (en thōō′zē **as′**tik) ▢*adjective*

a bat	ī bite	ōō tool	*th* feather
ā make	î fierce	ou out	th bath
â dare	o dot	u nut	hw wheat
ä father	ō no	û turn	zh measure
e net	ô law, for	ch church	ə about, open
ē be	oi soil	ng ring	pencil, atom
i dip	oo look	sh shade	circus

entice   *verb* To attract by offering something that is desired; lure: *The promise of a large sum of money enticed him to reveal the secret.*
en·tice (en tīs′) □*verb* **enticed, enticing, entices**

entire   *adjective* **1.** With no part missing: *I read for the entire day. We painted the entire house.* **2.** Complete; total: *He gave his entire attention to the difficult task he had been assigned.* —See Synonyms at **whole.**
en·tire (en tīr′) □*adjective*

entirely   *adverb* Fully; completely: *I agree entirely.*
en·tire·ly (en tīr′lē) □*adverb*

entitle   *verb* **1.** To give a title to: *She entitled her article "Exploring New England."* **2.** To give a right or privilege to: *Your library card entitles you to borrow books.*
en·ti·tle (en tīt′əl) □*verb* **entitled, entitling, entitles**

entrance¹   *noun* **1.** The act of entering: *The clown made his entrance in a tiny car.* **2.** A door, gate, or passageway through which one enters. **3.** The permission or right to enter: *He was refused entrance to the meeting.*
en·trance (en′trəns) □*noun, plural* **entrances**

entrance²   *verb* To fill with delight or wonder; fascinate: *The beauty of the city entranced the tourists.*
en·trance (en trans′) □*verb* **entranced, entrancing, entrances**

entreat   *verb* To ask earnestly; beg: *I entreated my friend to help me.*
en·treat (en trēt′) □*verb* **entreated, entreating, entreats**

entrust   *verb* **1.** To give something in trust to: *She entrusted him with her jewels.* **2.** To give over to another with trust or confidence: *Should I entrust such a difficult task to him?*
en·trust (en trust′) □*verb* **entrusted, entrusting, entrusts**

entry   *noun* **1.** The act or right of entering: *My ticket gave me entry to the play.* **2.** A passage or opening that provides entrance: *The children squeezed through the narrow entry to the cave.* **3.** An item entered in a book, list, or record: *Do you make an entry in your diary every day?* **4.** Someone or something entered in a contest: *There were over 500 entries in the bike race.*
en·try (en′trē) □*noun, plural* **entries**

entry

enunciate   *verb* To pronounce or speak words: *Please enunciate clearly so we can understand what you are saying.*
e·nun·ci·ate (i nun′sē āt′) □*verb* **enunciated, enunciating, enunciates**

envelop   *verb* To enclose completely; wrap up: *Mist enveloped the distant mountains.*
en·vel·op (en vel′əp) □*verb* **enveloped, enveloping, envelops**

envelope   *noun* A flat paper wrapper with a gummed flap, used chiefly for mail.
en·ve·lope (en′və lōp′) □*noun, plural* **envelopes**

envious   *adjective* Feeling or showing envy: *He was envious of his friend's new sled.*
en·vi·ous (en′vē əs) □*adjective*

environment   *noun* The surroundings and conditions that affect the growth and development of living things: *The children grew up in a loving environment.*
en·vi·ron·ment (en vī′rən mənt) □*noun, plural* **environments**

envy   *noun* **1.** A feeling of resentment or unhappiness at another's good fortune, together with a strong desire to have it for oneself: *We were filled with envy when we saw his stamp collection.* **2.** Someone or something that makes one feel envy: *Her beautiful new dress is the envy of all her friends.*
□*verb* To feel envy toward or because of.
en·vy (en′vē) □*noun, plural* **envies** □*verb* **envied, envying, envies**

eohippus   *noun* A small, primitive horse that was the ancestor of the modern horse.
e·o·hip·pus (ē′ ō hip′əs) □*noun*

eon *noun* A very long period of time.
e·on (ē′on) ▫*noun, plural* **eons**

epic *noun* A long poem that tells about the adventures of heroes.
▫*adjective* **1.** Of or like an epic: *an epic hero.* **2.** Like something described in an epic; impressive: *Putting a man on the moon was an epic achievement.*
ep·ic (ep′ik) ▫*noun, plural* **epics** ▫*adjective*

epidemic *noun* An outbreak of disease that spreads rapidly and widely: *an epidemic of measles.*
ep·i·dem·ic (ep′i **dem**′ik) ▫*noun, plural* **epidemics**

episode *noun* An event or a series of related events in one's life, in a story, or in history: *There were six episodes in the serial.*
ep·i·sode (ep′i sōd′) ▫*noun, plural* **episodes**

epitaph *noun* A statement inscribed on a grave or tomb in memory of the dead person who is buried there.
ep·i·taph (ep′i taf′) ▫*noun, plural* **epitaphs**

epoch *noun* A particular period in history; era: *The launching of the satellite marked a new epoch in science.*
ep·och (ep′ək) ▫*noun, plural* **epochs**

equal *adjective* **1.** Being the same in size, amount, rank, degree, or capacity: *The three chairs are equal in height. One foot is equal to 12 inches.* **2.** Having the necessary strength or ability; capable: *She had worked all day and was not equal to a game of tennis.* —See Synonyms at **same.**
▫*noun* Someone or something that is equal to another: *As a scientist he has no equal.*
▫*verb* To be equal to: *A meter equals 39.37 inches.*
e·qual (ē′kwəl) ▫*adjective* ▫*noun, plural* **equals** ▫*verb* **equaled, equaling, equals**

equal

equality *noun* The condition of being equal: *All citizens have equality under the law.*
e·qual·i·ty (i **kwŏl**′i tē) ▫*noun*

equation *noun* A mathematical statement that two sets of values are equal. For example, $4 \times 2 = 8$ is an equation.
e·qua·tion (i **kwā**′zhən) ▫*noun, plural* **equations**

equator *noun* An imaginary line around the middle of the earth at an equal distance from the North and South Poles. The equator divides the earth into the Northern Hemisphere and the Southern Hemisphere.
e·qua·tor (i **kwā**′tər) ▫*noun, plural* **equators**

equator

equatorial *adjective* Of, at, or near the equator.
e·qua·to·ri·al (ē′kwə **tôr**′ē əl) ▫*adjective*

equilibrium *noun* Balance: *He extended his arms to keep his equilibrium as he walked on the log.*
e·qui·lib·ri·um (ē′kwə **lib**′rē əm) ▫*noun*

equinox *noun* Either of the times of the year in which the sun is exactly above the equator and day and night are almost equal in length. The equinoxes take place at about September 23 and March 21.
e·qui·nox (ē′kwə noks) ▫*noun, plural* **equinoxes**

equip *verb* To supply with what is needed or wanted: *The car is equipped with a radio.*
e·quip (i **kwip**′) ▫*verb* **equipped, equipping, equips**

a bat	ī bite	ōō tool	*th* feather
ā make	î fierce	ou out	th bath
â dare	o dot	u nut	hw wheat
ä father	ō no	û turn	zh measure
e net	ô law, for	ch church	ə about, open
ē be	oi soil	ng ring	pencil, atom
i dip	oo look	sh shade	circus

equipment *noun* The things needed or used for a particular purpose: *The school bought new sports equipment last year.*
e·quip·ment (i **kwip′**mənt) □*noun*

equivalent *adjective* Equal: *Sixteen ounces are equivalent to a pound.*
□*noun* Something that is equivalent: *a price that was the equivalent of a new bicycle.*
e·quiv·a·lent (i **kwiv′**ə·lənt) □*adjective*
□*noun, plural* **equivalents**

–er¹ A suffix that forms the comparative of adjectives and adverbs: *faster; bluer; drier.*

–er² A suffix that forms nouns: *foreigner; maker; speaker.*

era *noun* A period of history or of time: *a style that dates back to the era of the Old West.*
e·ra (**îr′**ə) □*noun, plural* **eras**

eradicate *verb* To remove every trace of; do away with: *a woman who worked all her life to eradicate poverty and injustice.*
e·rad·i·cate (i **rad′**i·kāt′) □*verb* **eradicated, eradicating, eradicates**

erase *verb* To remove by rubbing or wiping: *The teacher erased the blackboard.*
e·rase (i **rās′**) □*verb* **erased, erasing, erases**

erase

eraser *noun* Something used to erase marks, as those made by chalk or a pencil.
e·ras·er (i **rā′**sər) □*noun, plural* **erasers**

erect *adjective* Straight up; vertical: *The tree was still erect after the hurricane.*
□*verb* **1.** To build or construct; put up: *The town planned to erect a marble statue of a soldier as a war memorial.* **2.** To raise upright; set on end. —See Synonyms at **build.**

erect (i **rekt′**) □*adjective* □*verb* **erected, erecting, erects**

erect

ermine *noun* A weasel whose valuable fur is white in winter and brown for the rest of the year.
er·mine (**ûr′**min) □*noun, plural* **ermines** or **ermine**

erode *verb* To wear away bit by bit: *Water eroded the exposed rock.*
e·rode (i **rōd′**) □*verb* **eroded, eroding, erodes**

erosion *noun* The process of being worn away bit by bit: *Wind caused erosion of the soil.*
e·ro·sion (i **rō′**zhən) □*noun*

err *verb* To make a mistake: *It is only natural to err once in a while.*
err (**ûr**) □*verb* **erred, erring, errs**

errand *noun* A short trip taken to perform a task: *I went to the store on an errand.*
er·rand (**er′**ənd) □*noun, plural* **errands**

error *noun* **1.** Something that is wrong or incorrect; mistake: *He made an error in adding up the bill.* **2.** A mistake made by a fielder in baseball that allows a batter to get on base or a runner to advance.
er·ror (**er′**ər) □*noun, plural* **errors**

SYNONYMS: **error, mistake, slip**

These nouns mean something that is wrong or incorrect: *She made three subtraction errors on the test. You must be careful to avoid spelling mistakes. Take your time when you paint because we don't want any slips.*

erupt *verb* To burst forth suddenly and violently: *Flames erupted from the burning tanker.*
e·rupt (i **rupt′**) □*verb* **erupted, erupting, erupts**

erupt

escalator *noun* A moving stairway that takes people from one floor to another.
es·ca·la·tor (**es′**kə lā′tər) □*noun, plural* **escalators**

escapade *noun* A reckless action or adventure: *He was scolded for taking part in such a foolish escapade.*
es·ca·pade (**es′**kə pād′) □*noun, plural* **escapades**

escape *verb* To get free or clear; get away: *The elephant escaped from the hunter. The fugitive escaped capture.*
□*noun* **1.** The act of escaping: *The thief made his escape through the window.* **2.** A way of escaping: *A secret passage provided an escape from the locked room.*
es·cape (i **skāp′**) □*verb* **escaped, escaping, escapes** □*noun, plural* **escapes**

escort *noun* **1.** A person or group that goes along with another to give protection or show respect: *The President was given a police escort.* **2.** A man who acts as the companion of a woman, as at a social event: *Do you have an escort for the party?*
□*verb* To go with as an escort: *My brother is going to escort your sister to the dance.*
es·cort (**es′**kôrt′) □*noun, plural* **escorts**
   □*verb* (i **skôrt′**) **escorted, escorting, escorts**

Eskimo *noun* **1.** A member of a people of Arctic regions of North America and Asia. **2.** The language of the Eskimos.
□*adjective* Of the Eskimos or their language.

Es·ki·mo (**es′**kə mō′) □*noun, plural* **Eskimos** or **Eskimo** □*adjective*

esophagus *noun* The tube that connects the throat with the stomach.
e·soph·a·gus (i **sof′**ə gəs) □*noun*

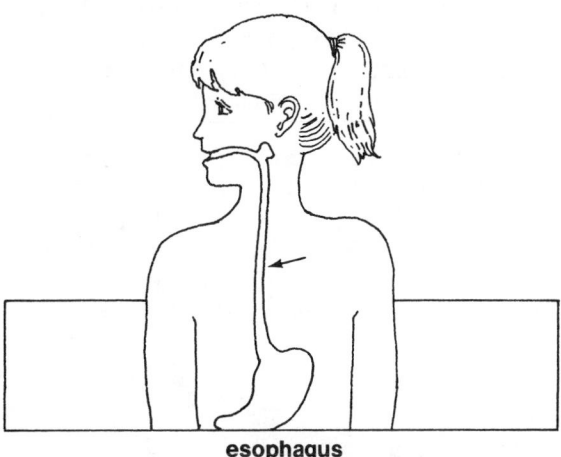

esophagus

especially *adverb* More than others; particularly: *He was especially careful when he crossed the street.*
es·pe·cial·ly (i **spesh′**ə lē) □*adverb*

espionage *noun* The practice of spying or of using spies to get secret information: *Do you think it is wrong for a government to engage in espionage?*
es·pi·o·nage (**es′**pē ə näzh′) □*noun*

essay *noun* A short piece of writing on a particular subject.
es·say (**es′**ā) □*noun, plural* **essays**

essence *noun* **1.** The basic or most important part of something: *The essence of democracy is freedom of speech.* **2.** The concentrated liquid form of a substance: *essence of peppermint.*
es·sence (**es′**əns) □*noun, plural* **essences**

essential *adjective* Very important; vital: *Exercise is essential to health.* —See Synonyms at **necessary.**
□*noun* A necessary thing: *Just bring your toothbrush and other essentials.*
es·sen·tial (i **sen′**shəl) □*adjective* □*noun, plural* **essentials**

a	bat	ī	bite	͞oo	tool	*th*	feather
ā	make	î	fierce	ou	out	th	bath
â	dare	o	dot	u	nut	hw	wheat
ä	father	ō	no	û	turn	zh	measure
e	net	ô	law, for	ch	church	ə	about, open
ē	be	oi	soil	ng	ring		pencil, atom
i	dip	oo	look	sh	shade		circus

-est A suffix that forms the superlative of adjectives and adverbs: *youngest; slowest.*

establish *verb* **1.** To set up; create: *establish a business.* **2.** To prove: *The trial established the fact that she was innocent.*
es·tab·lish (i **stab′**lish) ▫*verb* **established, establishing, establishes**

establishment *noun* **1.** The act of establishing. **2.** Something established, such as a business.
es·tab·lish·ment (i **stab′**lish mənt) ▫*noun*, *plural* **establishments**

estate *noun* **1.** A large piece of land with a large house. **2.** Everything owned by a person: *He left his estate to his daughter when he died.*
es·tate (i **stāt′**) ▫*noun*, *plural* **estates**

estate

esteem *verb* To think highly of: *I esteem you for your honesty.*
▫*noun* Respect; honor: *We had great esteem for his wisdom.*
es·teem (i **stēm′**) ▫*verb* **esteemed, esteeming, esteems** ▫*noun*

estimate *verb* To make a guess about; judge roughly: *The painter estimated that the job would take him two weeks.*
▫*noun* A rough guess.
es·ti·mate (**es′**tə māt′) ▫*verb* **estimated, estimating, estimates** ▫*noun* (**es′**tə mit), *plural* **estimates**

estimation *noun* An opinion; judgment: *In my estimation the movie is not very good.*
es·ti·ma·tion (es′tə **mā′**shən) ▫*noun*, *plural* **estimations**

etc. An abbreviation for **et cetera.**

et cetera And so forth: *Bring cups, napkins, et cetera, to the picnic.*
et cet·er·a (et **set′**ər ə)

WORD HISTORY: et cetera

Et cetera is borrowed from a Latin phrase that means "and the rest."

etch *verb* To make a drawing or design by cutting lines with acid on metal.
etch (ech) ▫*verb* **etched, etching, etches**

etch

eternal *adjective* **1.** Continuing forever: *Nature is eternal.* **2.** Seeming to last forever: *He bored us with his eternal preaching.*
e·ter·nal (i **tûr′**nəl) ▫*adjective*

eternity *noun* All of time without beginning or end.
e·ter·ni·ty (i **tûr′**ni tē) ▫*noun*, *plural* **eternities**

ether *noun* A liquid used to make people unconscious for medical operations.
e·ther (**ē′**thər) ▫*noun*, *plural* **ethers**

ethical *adjective* Agreeing with the rules or standards of right behavior: *An ethical person will always keep a promise.*
eth·i·cal (**eth′**i kəl) ▫*adjective*

ethnic *adjective* Of a group of people who share a common language and culture: *Has anyone ever counted all the ethnic groups living in the United States?*
eth·nic (**eth′**nik) ▫*adjective*

etiquette *noun* Rules that tell you how to behave: *It is good etiquette to stand up when you greet a guest.* —See Synonyms at **manners.**
et·i·quette (**et′**i kit) ▫*noun*

etymology *noun* The history of a word. An etymology traces a word and the parts of a word back to their earliest known forms and meanings.

et·y·mol·o·gy (et′ə **mol′**ə jē) □*noun, plural* **etymologies**

eucalyptus *noun* A tall tree that grows mostly in Australia. An oil with a strong smell is made from its leaves.
eu·ca·lyp·tus (yo͞o′kə **lip′**təs) □*noun, plural* **eucalyptuses**

European *noun* Someone who was born or lives in Europe.
□*adjective* Of Europe or its people.
Eu·ro·pe·an (yŏor′ə **pē′**ən) □*noun, plural* **Europeans** □*adjective*

evacuate *verb* To remove: *They evacuated everyone from the burning building.*
e·vac·u·ate (i **vak′**yo͞o āt′) □*verb* **evacuated, evacuating, evacuates**

evacuate

evade *verb* To avoid, especially by a trick or clever plan: *He evaded arrest by disguising himself.*
e·vade (i **vād′**) □*verb* **evaded, evading, evades**

evaluate *verb* To judge the value of: *The teacher will evaluate our progress at the end of the term.*
e·val·u·ate (i **val′**yo͞o āt′) □*verb* **evaluated, evaluating, evaluates**

evaporate *verb* To change from a liquid into a vapor or gas: *Puddles evaporate quickly in the sun.*
e·vap·o·rate (i **vap′**ə rāt′) □*verb* **evaporated, evaporating, evaporates**

evaporation *noun* The process of evaporating.
e·vap·o·ra·tion (i vap′ə **rā′**shən) □*noun*

eve *noun* The evening or day before a special day: *Christmas eve.*
eve (ēv) □*noun, plural* **eves**

even *adjective* **1.** Flat and smooth: *even ground.* **2.** At the same height or level: *The movie picture should be even with the top of the screen.* **3.** Not changing suddenly; steady: *an even speed.* **4.** Equal: *The score was even at the half.* **5.** Capable of being divided by two without a remainder: *14, 6, and 150 are even numbers.* —See Synonyms at **level.**
□*adverb* **1.** Yet; still: *Your room is even messier than before.* **2.** Though it seems unlikely: *Even dogs get colds.* **3.** Actually; indeed: *She is willing, even eager, to help.*
□*verb* To make or become even.
e·ven (ē′vən) □*adjective* □*adverb* □*verb* **evened, evening, evens**

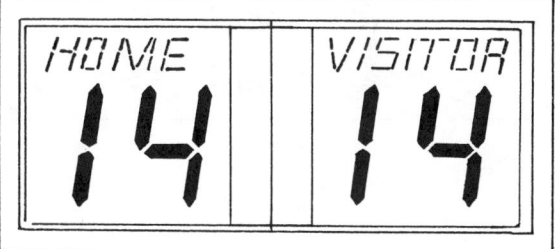

even

evening *noun* The time from around sunset until bedtime.
eve·ning (ēv′ning) □*noun, plural* **evenings**

event *noun* **1.** Something that happens; occurrence. **2.** One contest in a program of sports: *That swimmer is competing in three events.*
   in the event of In case of: *In the event of rain, the game will be postponed.*
e·vent (i **vent′**) □*noun, plural* **events**

eventual *adjective* Happening in the end: *The eventual cost of repairing the car was far more than we had expected.*
e·ven·tu·al (i **ven′**cho͞o əl) □*adjective*

ever *adverb* **1.** At all times: *A dog is ever faithful.* **2.** At any time: *Have you ever gone skiing?*

a bat	ī bite	o͞o tool	*th* feather
ā make	î fierce	ou out	th bath
â dare	o dot	u nut	hw wheat
ä father	ō no	û turn	zh measure
e net	ô law, for	ch church	ə about, open
ē be	oi soil	ng ring	pencil, atom
i dip	oo look	sh shade	circus

3. In any possible way: *How did you ever get here so fast?*
ev·er (ĕv′ər) ☐*adverb*

evergreen *adjective* Having green leaves or needles all year long: *Pines are evergreen trees.* ☐*noun* A tree or plant that stays green all year.
ev·er·green (ĕv′ər grēn′) ☐*adjective* ☐*noun, plural* **evergreens**

evergreen

every *adjective* Each without exception: *Every student was present.*
   every other Each second: *every other day.*
eve·ry (ĕv′rē) ☐*adjective*

everybody *pronoun* Each person without an exception: *If everybody helps, we'll get done quickly.*
eve·ry·bod·y (ĕv′rē bŏd′ē) ☐*pronoun*

everyday *adjective* Ordinary; usual: *everyday clothing.*
eve·ry·day (ĕv′rē dā′) ☐*adjective*

everyone *pronoun* Every person; everybody: *We spoke to everyone who was there.*
eve·ry·one (ĕv′rē wŭn′) ☐*pronoun*

everyplace *adverb* Everywhere: *I met interesting people everyplace I went.*
eve·ry·place (ĕv′rē plās′) ☐*adverb*

everything *pronoun* All things: *Everything was lost in the fire.*
eve·ry·thing (ĕv′rē thĭng′) ☐*pronoun*

everywhere *adverb* In all places: *I looked everywhere for my scarf.*
eve·ry·where (ĕv′rē hwâr′ *or* ĕv′rē wâr′) ☐*adverb*

evidence *noun* Something that furnishes proof: *The note that she pinned to the door was evidence that she had been there.*
ev·i·dence (ĕv′i dəns) ☐*noun*

evident *adjective* Easy to see or understand; obvious: *His grin made it evident that he was pleased.*
ev·i·dent (ĕv′i dənt) ☐*adjective*

evil *adjective* Morally bad; wicked: *an evil tyrant.*
☐*noun* Something wicked or harmful: *the evils of war.*
e·vil (ē′vəl) ☐*adjective* ☐*noun, plural* **evils**

evolution *noun* **1.** Slow, gradual development: *the evolution of democracy in Europe.* **2.** The scientific theory that all living things developed very slowly over millions of years from simpler forms of life.
ev·o·lu·tion (ĕv′ə lōō′shən) ☐*noun, plural* **evolutions**

evolve *verb* To develop gradually: *The horses we see today evolved from much smaller animals that existed long ago.*
e·volve (i vŏlv′) ☐*verb* **evolved, evolving, evolves**

ewe *noun* A female sheep.
ewe (yōō) ☐*noun, plural* **ewes**

ex– A prefix that means "former": *We listened to a speech by the ex-governor.*

exact *adjective* Accurate in every way: *an exact copy.*
ex·act (ig zăkt′) ☐*adjective*

exactly *adverb* Without any change or mistake; precisely: *Follow my directions exactly.*
ex·act·ly (ig zăkt′lē) ☐*adverb*

exaggerate *verb* To describe something as larger than it really is: *She always exaggerates the amount of work she has to do.*
ex·ag·ger·ate (ig zăj′ə rāt′) ☐*verb* **exaggerated, exaggerating, exaggerates**

exaggerate

exam *noun* An examination.
ex·am (ig zăm′) ☐*noun, plural* **exams**

examination   *noun* **1.** The act of examining: *A close examination of the butterfly showed that it had four wings.* **2.** A test.
ex·am·i·na·tion (ig zam′ə **nā**′shən) □*noun, plural* **examinations**

examine   *verb* **1.** To look at carefully; check: *The doctor examined the patient. We examined the used sailboat before we bought it.* **2.** To test the knowledge of: *The teacher examined the students in spelling.*
ex·am·ine (ig **zam**′in) □*verb* **examined, examining, examines**

example   *noun* **1.** Something that is singled out to show what other similar things are like: *Our teacher showed us an example of good handwriting.* **2.** A warning; lesson: *Let his punishment be an example to you.*
ex·am·ple (ig **zam**′pəl) □*noun, plural* **examples**

exasperate   *verb* To irritate or annoy: *Her foolish questions exasperated me.*
ex·as·per·ate (ig **zas**′pə rāt′) □*verb* **exasperated, exasperating, exasperates**

exasperation   *noun* Great irritation.
ex·as·per·a·tion (ig zas′pə **rā**′shən) □*noun*

excavate   *verb* **1.** To take out by digging: *excavated tons of dirt to make a cellar.* **2.** To make by digging: *excavate a tunnel.* **3.** To uncover by digging away: *archaeologists excavating an ancient city.*
ex·ca·vate (**eks**′kə vāt′) □*verb* **excavated, excavating, excavates**

excavate

exceed   *verb* To go beyond; surpass: *If you exceed the speed limit you are liable to get a ticket.*
ex·ceed (ek **sēd**′) □*verb* **exceeded, exceeding, exceeds**

excel   *verb* To be or do better than others: *She excels in swimming and debating.*
ex·cel (ek **sel**′) □*verb* **excelled, excelling, excels**

excellence   *noun* The quality of being excellent: *The excellence of the food soon attracted crowds to the small restaurant.*
ex·cel·lence (**ek**′sə ləns) □*noun*

excellent   *adjective* Of the highest quality; superior: *an excellent drawing.*
ex·cel·lent (**ek**′sə lənt) □*adjective*

except   *preposition* Not including: *She ate everything except her carrots.*
□*conjunction* But; only: *I'd come except I have to study.*
ex·cept (ek **sept**′) □*preposition* □*conjunction*

except

excepting   *preposition* Except: *Everyone excepting my mother helped with the dishes.*
ex·cept·ing (ek **sept**′ing) □*preposition*

exception   *noun* **1.** The fact of being left out: *He works every day, with the exception of Sunday.* **2.** Someone or something that is different from most others: *Most of us have had measles, but I am an exception.*
ex·cep·tion (ek **sep**′shən) □*noun, plural* **exceptions**

exceptional   *adjective* Unusual; outstanding: *an exceptional book.*
ex·cep·tion·al (ek **sep**′shə nəl) □*adjective*

excerpt   *noun* A passage taken out of a longer work.
ex·cerpt (**ek**′sûrpt) □*noun, plural* **excerpts**

a	bat	ī	bite	ōō	tool	*th*	feather
ā	make	î	fierce	ou	out	th	bath
â	dare	o	dot	u	nut	hw	wheat
ä	father	ō	no	û	turn	zh	measure
e	net	ô	law, for	ch	church	ə	about, open
ē	be	oi	soil	ng	ring		pencil, atom
i	dip	oo	look	sh	shade		circus

excess *noun* An amount that is more than usual or needed: *An excess of rain caused severe floods.*
□*adjective* Greater than the amount that is needed or normal: *excess fat.*
ex·cess (ek ses′ *or* ek′ses) □*noun, plural* **excesses** □*adjective*

excessive *adjective* Greater than necessary or normal: *He spends an excessive amount of time on the phone.*
ex·ces·sive (ek ses′iv) □*adjective*

exchange *verb* To give and get back; trade: *I exchanged the shirt for a smaller one.*
□*noun* **1.** An act of exchanging: *an exchange of letters.* **2.** A place where things are traded: *a stock exchange.* **3.** A central office where telephone calls are connected within a given area.
ex·change (eks chānj′) □*verb* **exchanged, exchanging, exchanges** □*noun, plural* **exchanges**

exchange

excite *verb* To arouse or stir up: *The close game excited the fans.*
ex·cite (ek sīt′) □*verb* **excited, exciting, excites**

excitement *noun* **1.** The condition of being excited. **2.** Something that excites: *the excitement of the holidays.*
ex·cite·ment (ek sīt′mənt) □*noun, plural* **excitements**

exciting *adjective* Causing excitement: *an exciting ride on a roller coaster.*
ex·cit·ing (ek sī′ting) □*adjective*

exclaim *verb* To speak out suddenly and loudly: *"Watch out!" she exclaimed.*
ex·claim (ek sklām′) □*verb* **exclaimed, exclaiming, exclaims**

exclamation *noun* Something said suddenly and loudly.
ex·cla·ma·tion (ek′sklə mā′shən) □*noun, plural* **exclamations**

exclamation point *noun* A mark of punctuation (!) used after an exclamation, as in "Help!"

exclude *verb* To keep or leave out: *He was excluded from the team because he was too young.*
ex·clude (ek sklo̅o̅d′) □*verb* **excluded, excluding, excludes**

exclude

exclusive *adjective* **1.** Not shared; complete: *exclusive ownership.* **2.** Admitting only some people and rejecting others: *an exclusive tennis club open only to members.*
ex·clu·sive (ek sklo̅o̅′siv) □*adjective*

excursion *noun* A short pleasure trip.
ex·cur·sion (ek skûr′zhən) □*noun, plural* **excursions**

excuse *verb* **1.** To pardon; forgive: *Please excuse me for being late.* **2.** To free from a duty: *He was excused from gym because he had a cold.* —See Synonyms at **pardon.**
□*noun* Something that serves to excuse; explanation.
ex·cuse (ek skyo̅o̅z′) □*verb* **excused, excusing, excuses** □*noun* (ek skyo̅o̅s′), *plural* **excuses**

execute *verb* **1.** To carry out; perform: *execute an order.* **2.** To put to death in accordance with a legal sentence: *execute a criminal.*
ex·e·cute (ek′si kyo̅o̅t′) □*verb* **executed, executing, executes**

execution *noun* **1.** The act of executing; performance. **2.** The act of putting to death.
ex·e·cu·tion (ek′si kyo̅o̅′shən) □*noun, plural* **executions**

executioner *noun* Someone who puts condemned prisoners to death.
ex·e·cu·tion·er (ek'si **kyōō'**shə nər) ▢*noun, plural* **executioners**

executive *noun* **1.** Someone who helps to manage and make decisions: *a business executive.* **2.** The branch of government that manages affairs of a country and sees that its laws are put into effect.
▢*adjective* Having to do with management and the making of decisions: *an executive committee.*
ex·ec·u·tive (eg **zek'**yə tiv) ▢*noun, plural* **executives** ▢*adjective*

exempt *verb* To free from a duty that others must do; excuse: *The government exempts churches from paying certain taxes.*
▢*adjective* Released from duty; excused: *She was exempt from helping with the dishes because of a broken arm.*
ex·empt (eg **zempt'**) ▢*verb* **exempted, exempting, exempts** ▢*adjective*

exercise

exert *verb* **1.** To bring into use: *exert one's strength.* **2.** To put oneself to a great effort: *He really had to exert himself to get his assignment finished on time.*
ex·ert (eg **zûrt'**) ▢*verb* **exerted, exerting, exerts**

exempt

exert

exemption *noun* An amount that is exempt from being taxed: *an exemption of $750.*
ex·emp·tion (ig **zemp'**shən) ▢*noun, plural* **exemptions**

exercise *noun* **1.** Use; practice: *the exercise of caution.* **2.** Activity done to train the body or mind: *running for exercise; a book of math exercises.* **3. exercises** A ceremony: *graduation exercises.*
▢*verb* **1.** To do or put through physical activity for the good of the body. **2.** To use: *All citizens should exercise their right to vote.*
ex·er·cise (ek'sər sīz') ▢*noun, plural* **exercises** ▢*verb* **exercised, exercising, exercises**

exertion *noun* Hard work.
ex·er·tion (eg **zûr'**shən) ▢*noun, plural* **exertions**

exhale *verb* To breathe out: *He exhaled a loud sigh.*
ex·hale (eks **hāl'**) ▢*verb* **exhaled, exhaling, exhales**

a	bat	ī	bite	ōō	tool	*th*	feather
ā	make	î	fierce	ou	out	th	bath
â	dare	o	dot	u	nut	hw	wheat
ä	father	ō	no	û	turn	zh	measure
e	net	ô	law, for	ch	church	ə	about, open
ē	be	oi	soil	ng	ring		pencil, atom
i	dip	oo	look	sh	shade		circus

exhaust   *verb* **1.** To use up: *exhaust a fuel sup-ply.* **2.** To make very tired; wear out: *Those stairs exhausted me.*
□*noun* The gases and other matter given off by an engine.
ex·haust (eg **zôst′**) □*verb* **exhausted, exhausting, exhausts** □*noun, plural* **exhausts**

exhaustion   *noun* The act of exhausting or the condition of being exhausted: *the exhaus-tion of our food supplies; worked to exhaus-tion.*
ex·haus·tion (eg **zôs′**chən) □*noun*

exhibit   *verb* **1.** To show; demonstrate: *She didn't exhibit any nervousness.* **2.** To put on display: *exhibit paintings.*
□*noun* Something exhibited: *an exhibit of Na-tive American rugs.*
ex·hib·it (eg **zib′**it) □*verb* **exhibited, exhibiting, exhibits** □*noun, plural* **exhibits**

exhibition   *noun* **1.** An act of exhibiting; dis-play: *Eating all the candy was an exhibition of his greed.* **2.** A public show: *We went to an exhibition of Japanese pottery at the museum.*
ex·hi·bi·tion (ek′sə **bish′**ən) □*noun, plural* **exhibitions**

exhilarate   *verb* To make cheerful or excited: *He was exhilarated by the news that he had won the prize.*
ex·hil·a·rate (eg **zil′**ə rāt′) □*verb* **exhilarated, exhilarating, exhilarates**

exile   *noun* **1.** Forced removal from one's country or home: *The punishment for disagree-ing with the king was exile.* **2.** Someone who has been forced to leave his country.
□*verb* To send into exile: *He was exiled to a remote village.*
ex·ile (**eg′**zīl *or* **ek′**sīl) □*noun, plural* **exiles** □*verb* **exiled, exiling, exiles**

exist   *verb* **1.** To be real: *Do witches exist?* **2.** To live: *Dinosaurs existed long ago.*
ex·ist (eg **zist′**) □*verb* **existed, existing, exists**

existence   *noun* **1.** The condition of being real. **2.** The fact of being alive: *Forest fires threaten the existence of many wild animals.*
ex·is·tence (eg **zis′**təns) □*noun, plural* **existences**

exit   *noun* **1.** A way out: *The building has a rear exit.* **2.** The act of leaving: *We made a rapid exit to avoid the crowds.*
□*verb* To depart: *We exited by the back door.*
ex·it (**eg′**zit *or* **ek′**sit) □*noun, plural* **exits** □*verb* **exited, exiting, exits**

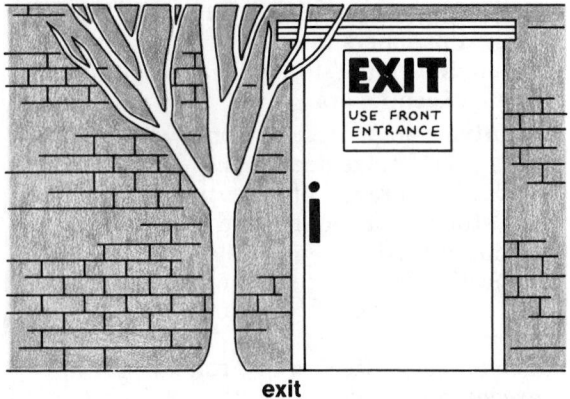

exit

exodus   *noun* A mass departure: *The bell was a signal for the exodus of workers from the mill.*
ex·o·dus (**ek′**sə dəs) □*noun*

exorbitant   *adjective* Going beyond reason-able limits: *We could not afford to eat in that restaurant because their prices were exorbitant.*
ex·or·bi·tant (ig **zôr′**bi tənt) □*adjective*

exotic   *adjective* Foreign; strange: *an exotic bird from a tropical country.*
ex·ot·ic (eg **zot′**ik) □*adjective*

exotic

expand   *verb* To make or become larger: *The city has expanded. She expanded her idea into an essay.*
ex·pand (ek **spand′**) □*verb* **expanded, expanding, expands**

expanse   *noun* A wide and open area: *an ex-panse of desert.*
ex·panse (ek **spans′**) □*noun, plural* **expanses**

expansion   *noun* **1.** The act of expanding or the condition of being expanded: *We made plans for the expansion of sales.* **2.** Something formed by expanding: *The book is an expan-sion of a short story.*

ex·pan·sion (ek **span′**shən) ☐*noun, plural* **expansions**

expect *verb* **1.** To regard as likely to happen: *I expect her to call tomorrow.* **2.** To consider as something proper or due: *The teacher expects you to do your best.* **3.** To suppose; think: *I expect you're tired.*
ex·pect (ek **spekt′**) ☐*verb* **expected, expecting, expects**

expectation *noun* The act or condition of expecting: *The messenger put out his hand in expectation of a tip.*
ex·pec·ta·tion (ek′spek **tā′**shən) ☐*noun, plural* **expectations**

expedition *noun* A long trip for exploring or studying something: *an expedition to study animal life in Australia.*
ex·pe·di·tion (ek′spi **dish′**ən) ☐*noun, plural* **expeditions**

expel *verb* To put or force out: *expel a student from school.*
ex·pel (ek **spel′**) ☐*verb* **expelled, expelling, expels**

expend *verb* **1.** To use up; consume: *How much time and effort did he expend on his science project?* **2.** To spend: *Over half of our tax money was expended on the new library.*
ex·pend (ik **spend′**) ☐*verb* **expended, expending, expends**

expense *noun* **1.** Cost; price. **2.** A reason or cause for spending money: *New clothes can be a heavy expense.*
ex·pense (ek **spens′**) ☐*noun, plural* **expenses**

expensive *adjective* Having a high price: *an expensive pair of shoes.*
ex·pen·sive (ek **spen′**siv) ☐*adjective*

experience *noun* **1.** Something that a person has done or lived through: *Tell us about your experiences in the war.* **2.** Knowledge or skill gained by practice: *She has the experience necessary to run a restaurant.*
☐*verb* To live through; undergo: *experience hunger.*
ex·pe·ri·ence (ek **spîr′**ē əns) ☐*noun, plural* **experiences** ☐*verb* **experienced, experiencing, experiences**

experiment *noun* A test to find out or prove something: *We did an experiment to show that light objects fall as fast as heavy ones.*
☐*verb* To do an experiment: *He experimented until he found the toughest paint for his boat.*

ex·per·i·ment (ek **sper′**ə mənt) ☐*noun, plural* **experiments** ☐*verb* **experimented, experimenting, experiments**

experiment

experimental *adjective* Of or based on experiments: *Doctors need experimental proof that a new drug is effective.*
ex·per·i·men·tal (ek sper′ə **men′**təl) ☐*adjective*

expert *noun* Someone who knows a lot about or is very good at doing something.
☐*adjective* Having or showing a lot of knowledge or skill: *an expert fisherman.*
ex·pert (**ek′**spûrt′) ☐*noun, plural* **experts** ☐*adjective*

SYNONYMS: **expert, ace, master**

These nouns mean someone who knows a lot about or is very good at doing something: *She is an expert at chess. He is an ace with computers. She worked hard at tennis until she became a master.*

---

expire *verb* To come to an end: *Your membership expires next month.*
ex·pire (ek **spīr′**) ☐*verb* **expired, expiring, expires**

explain *verb* **1.** To tell about in a way that is easy to understand: *She explained how an engine works.* **2.** To give a reason for: *Explain*

a	bat	ī	bite	oo	tool	*th*	feather
ā	make	î	fierce	ou	out	th	bath
â	dare	o	dot	u	nut	hw	wheat
ä	father	ō	no	û	turn	zh	measure
e	net	ô	law, for	ch	church	ə	about, open
ē	be	oi	soil	ng	ring		pencil, atom
i	dip	oo	look	sh	shade		circus

why you have not finished the assignment.
ex·plain (ek **splān'**) ☐*verb* **explained,**
explaining, explains

explanation *noun* **1.** The act of explaining.
2. A reason: *What is the explanation for his be-*
havior?
ex·pla·na·tion (ek'splə **nā'** shən) ☐*noun,*
plural **explanations**

explicit *adjective* Clearly stated: *explicit*
instructions.
ex·plic·it (ek **splis'** it) ☐*adjective*

explode *verb* **1.** To burst with a loud noise;
blow up: *The bombs exploded.* **2.** To burst
forth suddenly: *The captain exploded with an-*
ger at my careless mistake.
ex·plode (ek **splōd'**) ☐*verb* **exploded,**
exploding, explodes

exploit *noun* A daring act; deed: *Rescuing*
the puppy was a heroic exploit.
ex·ploit (**ek'** sploit') ☐*noun, plural* **exploits**

exploit

exploration *noun* The act of exploring: *the*
exploration of outer space.
ex·plo·ra·tion (ek'splə **rā'** shən) ☐*noun,*
plural **explorations**

explore *verb* **1.** To travel through an unfamiliar place for the purpose of discovery: *explore*
an unknown land. **2.** To look into closely: *The*
police are exploring the possibility that the sto-
len jewels may have been taken out of the
country.
ex·plore (ek **splôr'**) ☐*verb* **explored,**
exploring, explores

explorer *noun* Someone who explores.
ex·plor·er (ek **splôr'** ər) ☐*noun, plural*
explorers

explosion *noun* **1.** The act of breaking apart
with great force and noise: *the explosion of a*
firecracker. **2.** A sudden outbreak: *an explo-*
sion of laughter.

ex·plo·sion (ek **splō'** zhən) ☐*noun, plural*
explosions

explosive *noun* A substance that can explode. Dynamite is an explosive.
☐*adjective* Tending to explode: *an explosive*
chemical.
ex·plo·sive (ek **splō'** siv) ☐*noun, plural*
explosives ☐*adjective*

export *verb* To send goods to other countries
to be sold: *India exports tea.*
☐*noun* Something that is exported: *Automo-*
biles are a major Japanese export.
ex·port (ek **spôrt'**) ☐*verb* **exported,**
exporting, exports ☐*noun* (**ek'** spôrt'), *plural*
exports

expose *verb* **1.** To uncover; reveal: *The bud*
opened, exposing the petals that made up the
flower. **2.** To leave open to a certain action or
influence: *expose the film of a camera; expose*
oneself to criticism. **3.** To make known; disclose: *expose a secret.*
ex·pose (ek **spōz'**) ☐*verb* **exposed, exposing,**
exposes

expose

exposition *noun* A public show; exhibition:
an industrial exposition.
ex·po·si·tion (ek'spə **zish'** ən) ☐*noun, plural*
expositions

exposure *noun* **1.** The act of exposing or the
condition of being exposed: *suffered from ex-*
posure after being lost in the north woods.
2. The front or open side of a building or
room: *The house has a southern exposure.*
ex·po·sure (ek **spō'** zhər) ☐*noun, plural*
exposures

express *verb* **1.** To show; reveal: *Her face ex-*
pressed delight. **2.** To put into words: *Express*
your thoughts clearly.
☐*adjective* **1.** Clearly stated; definite: *an ex-*
press wish. **2.** Meant for fast travel or delivery:
an express train; express mail.
☐*noun* **1.** An express train or other vehicle.

2. A fast system for delivering goods and mail.
ex·press (ek **spres′**) ☐*verb* **expressed,
expressing, expresses** ☐*adjective* ☐*noun,
plural* **expresses**

express

expression *noun* **1.** An act of expressing: *the
expression of opinions; an expression of hope.*
2. A look that expresses a person's mood or
feeling: *a worried expression.* **3.** A common
word or saying: *"Time flies" is a familiar expression.*
ex·pres·sion (ek **spresh′** ən) ☐*noun, plural*
expressions

expressway *noun* A wide highway built for
direct, high-speed travel.
ex·press·way (ek **spres′** wā′) ☐*noun, plural*
expressways

extend *verb* **1.** To make longer; lengthen: *I
extended my vacation an extra week.* **2.** To
reach; stretch: *The mountains extend to the
north.* **3.** To offer: *extend greetings.*
ex·tend (ek **stend′**) ☐*verb* **extended,
extending, extends**

extend

extension *noun* **1.** The act of extending or
the condition of being extended: *the extension
of a deadline.* **2.** An addition: *a new extension
to the school building.* **3.** An extra telephone
linked with the main one.
ex·ten·sion (ek **sten′** shən) ☐*noun, plural*
extensions

extensive *adjective* Large; wide: *We did an
extensive review before the exam.*
ex·ten·sive (ek **sten′** siv) ☐*adjective*

extent *noun* The point to which something
extends: *She went to the greatest extent possible to help us. Do you know the extent of his
property?*
ex·tent (ek **stent′**) ☐*noun, plural* **extents**

exterior *adjective* Outer or outside: *an exterior wall.*
☐*noun* An outer part, surface, or appearance:
A composed exterior concealed his fear.
ex·te·ri·or (ek **stîr′** ē ər) ☐*adjective* ☐*noun,
plural* **exteriors**

exterior

exterminate *verb* To destroy completely: *We
exterminated the beetles in the garden.*
ex·ter·mi·nate (ek **stûr′** mə nāt′) ☐*verb*
exterminated, exterminating, exterminates

external *adjective* Of or for the outside or an
outer part: *an external layer.*
ex·ter·nal (ek **stûr′** nəl) ☐*adjective*

extinct *adjective* **1.** No longer in existence:
The dodo is an extinct bird. **2.** Not likely to

a	bat	ī	bite	ōō	tool	*th*	feather
ā	make	î	fierce	ou	out	th	bath
â	dare	o	dot	u	nut	hw	wheat
ä	father	ō	no	û	turn	zh	measure
e	net	ô	law, for	ch	church	ə	about, open
ē	be	oi	soil	ng	ring		pencil, atom
i	dip	oo	look	sh	shade		circus

erupt: *an extinct volcano.*
ex·tinct (ek **stingkt′**) □*adjective*

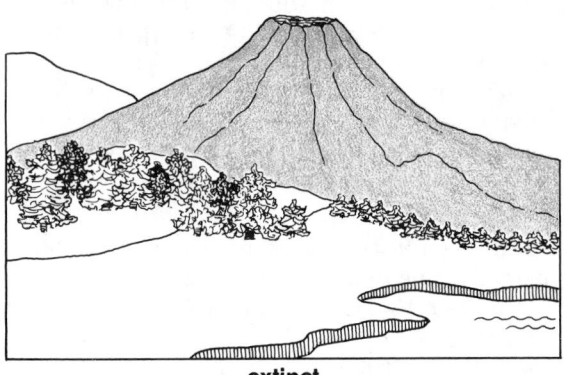

extinct

extinction *noun* Ending; destruction: *working for the extinction of poverty.*
ex·tinc·tion (ek **stingk′**shən) □*noun*

extinguish *verb* To put out: *extinguish a fire.*
ex·tin·guish (ek **sting′**gwish) □*verb*
extinguished, extinguishing, extinguishes

extinguisher *noun* A fire extinguisher.
ex·tin·guish·er (ek **sting′**gwi shər) □*noun,*
plural **extinguishers**

extol *verb* To praise highly: *She was extolled for her courage in the face of danger.*
ex·tol (ik **stōl′**) □*verb* **extolled, extolling, extols**

extra *adjective* More than what is usual or expected: *an extra helping.*
□*noun* Something additional: *a pizza with mushrooms and other extras.*
ex·tra (**ek′**strə) □*adjective* □*noun, plural*
extras

extract *verb* To take or pull out: *extract a tooth.*
□*noun* Something that is drawn out or extracted: *vanilla extract.*
ex·tract (ek **strakt′**) □*verb* **extracted, extracting, extracts** □*noun* (**ek′** strakt′),
plural **extracts**

extraordinary *adjective* Very remarkable; exceptional: *Light travels at an extraordinary speed.*
ex·traor·di·nar·y (ek **strôr′**dn er′ē)
□*adjective*

extravagance *noun* **1.** The spending of too much money: *His extravagance put them in debt.* **2.** Something extravagant.

extravagance (ek **strav′**ə gəns) □*noun,*
plural **extravagances**

extravagant *adjective* Spending or costing too much: *an extravagant expense.*
ex·trav·a·gant (ek **strav′**ə gənt) □*adjective*

extreme *adjective* **1.** Very great: *extreme heat.* **2.** Farthest: *the extreme end of town.* **3.** Drastic; severe: *an extreme penalty.*
□*noun* **1.** Either of two ends of a range: *the extremes of black and white.* **2.** The greatest or utmost degree: *He is polite in the extreme.*
ex·treme (ek **strēm′**) □*adjective* □*noun,*
plural **extremes**

extremely *adverb* Very; especially: *extremely happy.*
ex·treme·ly (ek **strēm′**lē) □*adverb*

extremity *noun* **1.** The farthest point: *the southern extremity of the island.* **2. extremities** A person's hands and feet.
ex·trem·i·ty (ek **strem′**i tē) □*noun, plural*
extremities

exult *verb* To be very joyful: *The king exulted when he learned that his enemies had been defeated.*
ex·ult (ig **zult′**) □*verb* **exulted, exulting, exults**

eye *noun* **1.** Either of a pair of round organs by which a person or animal sees. **2.** The colored part of the eye: *brown eyes.* **3.** A look or gaze: *casting a cold eye at her rival.* **4.** Ability to see. **5.** A loop or hole: *the eye of a needle.*
□*verb* To look at; watch.
eye (ī) □*noun, plural* **eyes** □*verb* **eyed, eyeing, eyes**

eye

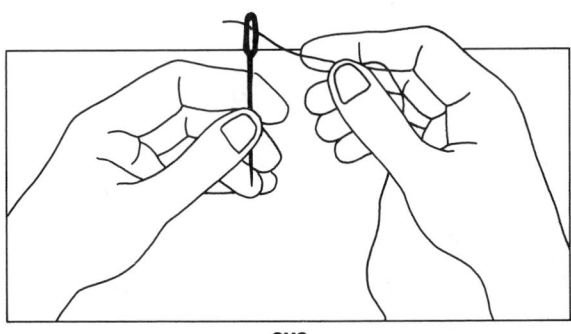

eye
Of a needle

eyeball *noun* The rounded ball that is the eye.
eye·ball (ī′bôl′) □*noun, plural* **eyeballs**

eyebrow *noun* The short hair growing on the ridge above each eye.
eye·brow (ī′brou′) □*noun, plural* **eyebrows**

eyeglasses *plural noun* A pair of lenses worn on a frame in front of the eyes to improve one's eyesight.
eye·glass·es (ī′glas′iz) □*plural noun*

eyelash *noun* **1.** A row of hairs along the edge of an eyelid. **2.** Any one of these hairs.
eye·lash (ī′lash′) □*noun, plural* **eyelashes**

eyelet *noun* A small hole for a lace or hook to fit through.
eye·let (ī′lit) □*noun, plural* **eyelets**

eyelid *noun* Either of a pair of folds of skin that can be closed over the eye.
eye·lid (ī′lid′) □*noun, plural* **eyelids**

eyesight *noun* The ability to see; vision.
eye·sight (ī′sīt′) □*noun*

eyetooth *noun* Either of the two pointed teeth in a person's upper jaw.
eye·tooth (ī′tooth′) □*noun, plural* **eyeteeth**

a bat	ī bite	oo tool	*th* feather
ā make	î fierce	ou out	th bath
â dare	o dot	u nut	hw wheat
ä father	ō no	û turn	zh measure
e net	ô law, for	ch church	ə about, open
ē be	oi soil	ng ring	pencil, atom
i dip	oo look	sh shade	circus

The letter **F** has evolved from many forms of ancient writing. One of the earliest known examples is the Greek character shown above, which dates from almost 3,000 years ago. Over the years, artists and designers have created their own versions of the English letter **F**. Some of the more common examples seen today are shown below.

HANDWRITING	CALLIGRAPHY	MODERN SANS SERIF	MODERN SERIF	SCRIPT

---

f or **F** *noun* The sixth letter of the English alphabet.
f or **F** (ef) ▢*noun, plural* **f's** or **F's**

F An abbreviation for **Fahrenheit.**

fable *noun* A story that teaches a lesson. The characters in many fables are talking animals.
fa·ble (fā′bəl) ▢*noun, plural* **fables**

fabric *noun* A material made by weaving or knitting; cloth.
fab·ric (fab′rik) ▢*noun, plural* **fabrics**

fabulous *adjective* Marvelous; fantastic: *fabulous wealth.*
fab·u·lous (fab′yə ləs) ▢*adjective*

face *noun* **1.** The front part of the head. **2.** An expression on the face: *a happy face.* **3.** The front or outer part of something: *the face of a building; a clock's face.*
▢*verb* **1.** To turn or have the face toward: *Face the front.* **2.** To deal with directly: *Let's face the facts.*
face (fās) ▢*noun, plural* **faces** ▢*verb* **faced, facing, faces**

facial *adjective* Of the face: *a facial expression.*
fa·cial (fā′shəl) ▢*adjective*

facility *noun* **1.** Skill without effort; ease: *He plays the piano with great facility.* **2.** Something provided for people to use: *The library facilities include a collection of records and tapes.*
fa·cil·i·ty (fə sil′i tē) ▢*noun, plural* **facilities**

fact *noun* Something that is known to be true or to have really happened.
fact (fakt) ▢*noun, plural* **facts**

factor *noun* **1.** Something that helps bring about a certain result: *Sheer luck was a factor in his success.* **2.** One of two or more numbers that when multiplied together form a product: *2 and 4 are factors of 8.*
fac·tor (fak′tər) ▢*noun, plural* **factors**

factory *noun* A building or group of buildings where things are made.
fac·to·ry (fak′tə rē) ▢*noun, plural* **factories**

factory

factual *adjective* Based on facts: *a factual report of the accident.*
fac·tu·al (fak′chōō əl) ▢*adjective*

faculty *noun* **1.** A power of the mind or body: *the faculties of speech and hearing.* **2.** A talent or skill. **3.** All the teachers of a school or college.
fac·ul·ty (fak′əl tē) ▢*noun, plural* **faculties**

fad *noun* Something that is very popular for a short time: *Purple lipstick was last year's fad.*
fad (fad) ▢*noun, plural* **fads**

fade *verb* **1.** To lose or cause to lose brightness or freshness: *Her jeans faded in the laundry.* **2.** To disappear slowly: *His smile faded when he looked at his report card.*
fade (fād) ☐*verb* **faded, fading, fades**

Fahrenheit *adjective* Of a temperature scale on which 32 degrees is the freezing point of water and 212 degrees is the boiling point.
Fahr·en·heit (far′ən hīt′) ☐*adjective*

WORD HISTORY: **Fahrenheit**

The *Fahrenheit* temperature scale was invented by Gabriel Fahrenheit, a German scientist who lived almost 300 years ago.

---

fail *verb* **1.** To not succeed: *She tried to jump across the puddle but failed.* **2.** To stop working or providing something: *The electric power failed.* **3.** To not help; let down: *Her friends failed her.* **4.** To become weaker: *The old dog's health was failing.* **5.** To get less than a passing grade in.
fail (fāl) ☐*verb* **failed, failing, fails**

failure *noun* **1.** The act or fact of failing. **2.** Someone or something that fails: *The new restaurant was a failure and soon closed.*
fail·ure (fāl′yər) ☐*noun, plural* **failures**

faint *adjective* **1.** Not clearly seen, felt, or heard; weak: *a faint light; a faint whisper.* **2.** Dizzy and weak.
☐*noun* A condition in which a person suddenly loses consciousness for a little while.
☐*verb* To fall into a faint.
faint (fānt) ☐*adjective* **fainter, faintest** ☐*noun, plural* **faints** ☐*verb* **fainted, fainting, faints**

fair¹ *adjective* **1.** Beautiful; attractive: *a fair princess.* **2.** Light in color: *fair skin.* **3.** Clear; not cloudy: *fair skies.* **4.** Not favoring one side more than another: *a fair judge; a fair share.* **5.** Average: *The movie was only fair.* **6.** Following the rules: *fair play.*
☐*adverb* In a fair way: *She doesn't play fair.*
fair (fâr) ☐*adjective* **fairer, fairest** ☐*adverb*

SYNONYMS: **fair¹, impartial, just**

These adjectives mean not favoring one person or side more than another: *Everyone agreed that the decision was fair. All the judges in the contest were impartial. The responsibility of a jury is to give a just verdict.*

fair

fair² *noun* **1.** A gathering for the buying and selling of goods; market. **2.** A large public show of farm or industrial products, often with entertainment and contests.
fair (fâr) ☐*noun, plural* **fairs**

WORD HISTORY: **fair²**

The word *fair²* meaning "a market" comes from a Latin word that means "a holiday."

---

fairly *adverb* **1.** In a fair manner: *treating students fairly.* **2.** Rather; somewhat: *fairly good grades.*
fair·ly (fâr′lē) ☐*adverb*

fairy *noun* A tiny imaginary being that has magical powers.
fair·y (fâr′ē) ☐*noun, plural* **fairies**

faith *noun* **1.** Confident belief; trust: *She had great faith in his honesty.* **2.** A religion: *people of different faiths.* —See Synonyms at **confidence.**
faith (fāth) ☐*noun, plural* **faiths**

faithful *adjective* **1.** Trustworthy; loyal: *faithful friends.* **2.** Accurate; exact: *a faithful copy.*
faith·ful (fāth′fəl) ☐*adjective*

fake *verb* **1.** To pretend: *She looked asleep, but she was faking.* **2.** To copy or make in order to deceive: *fake someone's signature.*
☐*noun* Someone or something that is not what it pretends to be: *That gun is a fake.*
☐*adjective* Not genuine; false: *fake money.*

a bat	ī bite	oo tool	*th* feather
ā make	î fierce	ou out	th bath
â dare	o dot	u nut	hw wheat
ä father	ō no	û turn	zh measure
e net	ô law, for	ch church	ə about, open
ē be	oi soil	ng ring	pencil, atom
i dip	oo look	sh shade	circus

fake (fāk) □*verb* **faked, faking, fakes**
□*noun, plural* **fakes** □*adjective*

fake

falcon   *noun*   A hawk with long wings and hooked claws. Hawks can be trained to hunt for small animals and birds.
fal·con (**fal′**kən *or* **fôl′**kən)   □*noun, plural* **falcons**

falcon

fall   *verb*   **1.** To drop or come down from a higher place: *She tripped and fell. Snow is falling.* **2.** To be wounded, killed, or defeated. **3.** To become lower: *The temperature has fallen ten degrees.* **4.** To pass from one condition to another; become: *fall asleep.* **5.** To come by chance: *fall into a trap.*
□*noun*   **1.** The act of coming down from a higher place: *a fall on the ice.* **2.** The season after summer; autumn. **3.** **falls** A waterfall. **4.** A decline; drop: *a fall in prices.* **5.** A collapse or defeat: *the fall of a government.*
fall (fôl) □*verb* **fell, fallen, falling, falls**
□*noun, plural* **falls**

SYNONYMS: **fall, descend, drop**

These verbs mean to drop or come down from a higher place: *The apples fell from the tree. The helicopter descended slowly. I dropped the glass.*

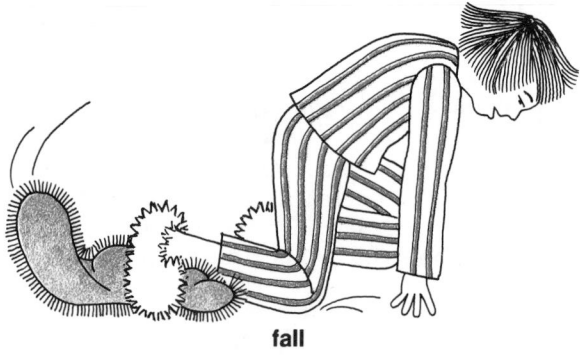

fall

fallen   *verb*   The past participle of **fall:** *Snow has fallen.*
fall·en (**fô′**lən)   □*verb*

fallout   *noun*   The radioactive dust that falls to the earth after a nuclear bomb is exploded.
fall·out (**fôl′**out′)   □*noun*

false   *adjective*   **1.** Not true or correct: *a false answer.* **2.** Not real; artificial: *false teeth.* **3.** Not to be trusted; insincere: *false promises.*
false (fôls)   □*adjective* **falser, falsest**

SYNONYMS: **false, incorrect, wrong**

These adjectives mean not true or correct: *The man gave the police a false name. Your answer is incorrect. I thought she was coming to visit today but I was wrong.*

falter   *verb*   To move or speak in an unsteady way.
fal·ter (**fôl′**tər)   □*verb* **faltered, faltering, falters**

fame   *noun*   The quality of being very well known.
fame (fām)   □*noun*

familiar   *adjective*   **1.** Often seen or heard: *People walking dogs are a familiar sight in the park.* **2.** Knowing something fairly well: *Are you familiar with this neighborhood?*
fa·mil·iar (fə **mil′**yər)   □*adjective*

family   *noun*   **1.** A parent or parents and their children. **2.** The children of a parent or parents: *raise a family.* **3.** A group of related persons; relatives. **4.** A group of related animals, plants, or other things: *Dogs, wolves, and foxes belong to the same animal family.*
fam·i·ly (**fam′**ə lē)   □*noun, plural* **families**

famine   *noun*   A very great shortage of food in an area.
fam·ine (**fam′**in)   □*noun, plural* **famines**

famous *adjective* Widely known: *a famous movie actor.*
fa·mous (**fā′**məs) ☐*adjective*

fan[1] *noun* **1.** A stiff piece of material that is waved back and forth to make air move in a cooling breeze. **2.** An electrical device with blades that turn fast and blow air.
☐*verb* To make air blow on or toward: *She fanned herself with a magazine.*
fan (fan) ☐*noun, plural* **fans** ☐*verb* **fanned, fanning, fans**

electric fan

fan

fan[2] *noun* Someone who loves something and follows it closely: *a sports fan; a fan of detective stories.*
fan (fan) ☐*noun, plural* **fans**

fanatic *noun* Someone who believes in or loves something so much that he or she does foolish things: *My uncle is a health fanatic and only eats raw food.*
fa·nat·ic (fə **nat′**ik) ☐*noun, plural* **fanatics**

fancy *noun* **1.** The ability to form pictures in the mind; imagination: *The story came from his fancy and was not based on fact.* **2.** An idea; notion: *a sudden fancy to run around the block.* **3.** A liking; fondness: *The child took a fancy to the kitten.*
☐*verb* **1.** To imagine: *He fancies himself a great singer.* **2.** To like; prefer: *She fancies quiet, polite boys.*
☐*adjective* Elaborate or special; fine: *fancy food; fancy clothes.*
fan·cy (**fan′**sē) ☐*noun, plural* **fancies** ☐*verb* **fancied, fancying, fancies** ☐*adjective* **fancier, fanciest**

fang *noun* A long, pointed tooth: *a snake's poisonous fangs.*
fang (fang) ☐*noun, plural* **fangs**

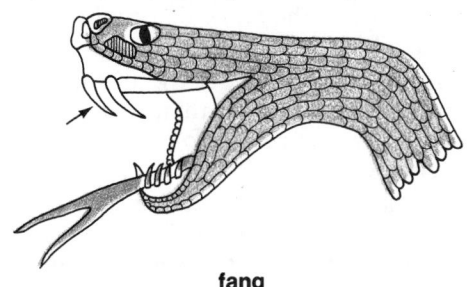

fang

fantastic *adjective* **1.** Very strange; weird: *fantastic shapes.* **2.** Very good; wonderful: *a fantastic game.*
fan·tas·tic (fan **tas′**tik) ☐*adjective*

fantasy *noun* **1.** Imagination; fiction: *Those ghost stories are pure fantasy.* **2.** A wishful story or picture in the mind.
fan·ta·sy (**fan′**tə sē) ☐*noun, plural* **fantasies**

far *adverb* **1.** To, from, or at a great distance: *young birds flying far from the nest.* **2.** To a certain distance, place, or time: *I painted the wall as far as I could reach.* **3.** Much: *far more interesting.*
☐*adjective* **1.** Distant: *a far country.* **2.** More distant: *the far side of the mountains.*
far (fär) ☐*adverb* **farther** or **further, farthest** or **furthest** ☐*adjective* **farther** or **further, farthest** or **furthest**

fare *noun* The price of a ride on a vehicle: *bus fare; plane fare.*
☐*verb* To get along; do: *He's faring well.*
fare (fâr) ☐*noun, plural* **fares** ☐*verb* **fared, faring, fares**

farewell *interjection* Good-by.
☐*noun* An expression of good wishes, used at parting.

a	bat	ī	bite	o͞o	tool	*th*	feather
ā	make	i	fierce	ou	out	th	bath
â	dare	o	dot	u	nut	hw	wheat
ä	father	ō	no	û	turn	zh	measure
e	net	ô	law, for	ch	church	ə	about, open
ē	be	oi	soil	ng	ring		pencil, atom
i	dip	oo	look	sh	shade		circus

fare·well (fâr **wel′**) ☐*interjection* ☐*noun,*
plural **farewells**

farm *noun* A piece of land where food crops
and animals are raised.
☐*verb* To raise food crops and animals.
farm (färm) ☐*noun, plural* **farms** ☐*verb*
farmed, farming, farms

farmer *noun* Someone who runs a farm.
farm·er (fär′mər) ☐*noun, plural* **farmers**

farming *noun* The work of running a farm.
farm·ing (fär′ming) ☐*noun*

far-sighted *adjective* Seeing distant things
more clearly than near things: *a far-sighted*
person who needs glasses to read.
far-sight·ed (fär′sī′tid) ☐*adjective*

farther *adverb* To a greater distance or extent: *He can throw the ball farther than I can.*
☐*adjective* More distant: *the farther side of the*
table.
far·ther (fär′thər) ☐*adverb* ☐*adjective*

farthest *adverb* To the greatest distance or
extent: *She walks farthest to school of all of us.*
☐*adjective* Most distant: *the farthest country.*
far·thest (fär′thist) ☐*adverb* ☐*adjective*

fascinate *verb* To attract and interest very
strongly: *The monkeys fascinated the child.*
fas·ci·nate (fas′ə nāt′) ☐*verb* **fascinated,**
fascinating, fascinates

fashion *noun* **1.** Way; manner: *Hold the*
brush in this fashion. **2.** A way of dressing, acting, or talking: *the latest fashion in hats.*
☐*verb* To make; form: *He fashioned a shelter*
out of a hollow log.
fash·ion (fash′ən) ☐*noun, plural* **fashions**
☐*verb* **fashioned, fashioning, fashions**

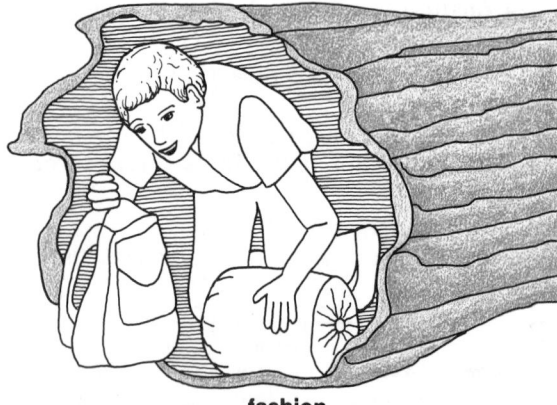

fashion

fashionable *adjective* In fashion; stylish:
fashionable new shoes.
fash·ion·a·ble (fash′ə nə bəl) ☐*adjective*

fast¹ *adjective* **1.** Acting or moving quickly: *a*
fast train; a fast runner. **2.** Running ahead of
the correct time: *That clock is fast.* **3.** Close;
faithful: *fast friends.*
☐*adverb* **1.** Quickly: *Don't eat so fast.*
2. Tightly; firmly: *The boat was held fast to the*
dock by a rope. **3.** Thoroughly; deeply: *He's*
fast asleep.
fast (fast) ☐*adjective* **faster, fastest** ☐*adverb*
faster, fastest

SYNONYMS: **fast¹, quick, rapid, speedy**
These adjectives mean acting or moving quickly:
She likes to drive a fast car. He was quick to answer
my question. The fireman made a rapid inspection
of the house. A speedy worker can finish the job in
an hour.

---

fast² *verb* To stop eating food or certain
foods: *Some religious people fast on holy days.*
☐*noun* A time of fasting.
fast (fast) ☐*verb* **fasted, fasting, fasts**
☐*noun, plural* **fasts**

fasten *verb* To make something hold or stick:
She fastened the corsage to her blouse. —See
Synonyms at **attach.**
fas·ten (fas′ən) ☐*verb* **fastened, fastening,**
fastens

fasten

fastener *noun* Something used to fasten
things together.
fas·ten·er (fas′ə nər) ☐*noun, plural*
fasteners

fat *noun* A soft white or yellow substance
found in the bodies of animals and in plants.
☐*adjective* Having much fat; plump or heavy.
fat (fat) ☐*noun, plural* **fats** ☐*adjective*
fatter, fattest

fatal *adjective* Causing death: *a fatal accident.*
fa·tal (fāt′ əl) □*adjective*

fate *noun* **1.** A power no one can control that is believed to decide everything that happens: *The outcome of the contest will be decided by fate.* **2.** An outcome or situation that comes about as though determined by fate; fortune.
fate (fāt) □*noun, plural* **fates**

father *noun* **1.** A male parent. **2.** **Father** God. **3.** A priest.
fa·ther (fä′ *th*ər) □*noun, plural* **fathers**

father-in-law *noun* The father of one's husband or wife.
fa·ther-in-law (fä′ *th*ər in lô′) □*noun, plural* **fathers-in-law**

fathom *noun* A unit of length equal to six feet: *The water was six fathoms deep.*
fath·om (fa*th*′ əm) □*noun, plural* **fathoms**

fatigue *noun* A feeling of being tired.
□*verb* To make tired; wear out: *The long journey fatigued her.*
fa·tigue (fə tēg′) □*noun* □*verb* **fatigued, fatiguing, fatigues**

fatten *verb* To make or become fat.
fat·ten (fat′ ən) □*verb* **fattened, fattening, fattens**

faucet *noun* A device with a handle for controlling the flow of liquid from a pipe or container.
fau·cet (fô′ sit) □*noun, plural* **faucets**

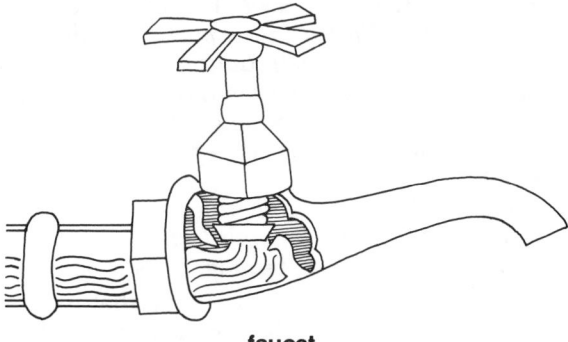

faucet

fault *noun* **1.** A bad quality; defect: *Always being late is one of his faults.* **2.** Responsibility for something that shouldn't have happened: *The traffic accident was the driver's fault.* **3.** A mistake; error.
fault (fôlt) □*noun, plural* **faults**

faun *noun* A Roman god of the woods and fields, part man and part goat.
faun (fôn) □*noun, plural* **fauns**

faun

favor *noun* **1.** An act that helps someone: *He did her a favor and carried her books.* **2.** Approval; acceptance: *Small cars are slowly gaining favor.* **3.** A little gift: *The children received paper hats and other party favors.*
□*verb* **1.** To be for; support: *Which candidate do you favor?* **2.** To look like; take after: *She favors her mother.* **3.** To treat in a careful way: *He's favoring his injured leg.*
fa·vor (fā′ vər) □*noun, plural* **favors** □*verb* **favored, favoring, favors**

favorable *adjective* **1.** Helping a plan or cause: *a favorable wind.* **2.** Approving or agreeing: *a favorable answer.*
fa·vor·a·ble (fā′ vər ə bəl) □*adjective*

favorite *noun* Someone or something liked best: *Wildflowers are my favorites.*
□*adjective* Liked best: *My favorite color is green.*
fa·vor·ite (fā′ vər it) □*noun, plural* **favorites** □*adjective*

fawn *noun* A young deer.
fawn (fôn) □*noun, plural* **fawns**

fear *noun* An unpleasant feeling caused by the nearness of danger or pain: *I felt fear when I looked down from the high window.*
□*verb* **1.** To be afraid of: *She feared being left alone.* **2.** To suspect unhappily: *I fear that you don't understand what I said.*
fear (fîr) □*noun, plural* **fears** □*verb* **feared, fearing, fears**

a	bat	ī	bite	o͞o	tool	*th*	feather
ā	make	î	fierce	ou	out	th	bath
â	dare	o	dot	u	nut	hw	wheat
ä	father	ō	no	û	turn	zh	measure
e	net	ô	law, for	ch	church	ə	about, open
ē	be	oi	soil	ng	ring		pencil, atom
i	dip	oo	look	sh	shade		circus

fearful *adjective* **1.** Feeling fear; afraid. **2.** Causing fear: *a fearful thunderstorm.*
fear·ful (fîr′fəl) □*adjective*

feast *noun* A large, fancy meal.
□*verb* To eat well: *We feasted on turkey.*
feast (fēst) □*noun, plural* **feasts** □*verb* **feasted, feasting, feasts**

feat *noun* An act that shows skill or daring.
feat (fēt) □*noun, plural* **feats**

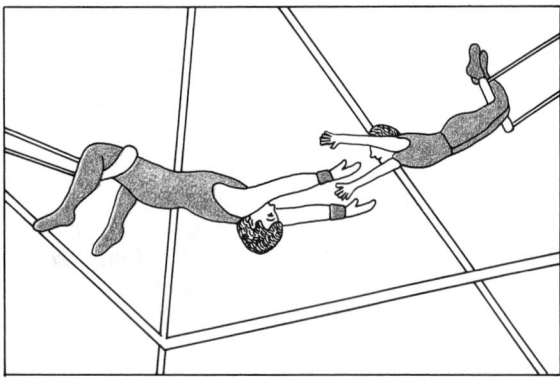

feat
Trapeze artists

feather *noun* One of the light growths that form the covering of the skin of birds.
feath·er (fe*th*′ər) □*noun, plural* **feathers**

feature *noun* **1.** An important part or quality: *The feature of the book I liked best was the pictures.* **2.** A part of the face. The nose, eyes, and forehead are features. **3.** A full-length movie. —See Synonyms at **quality.**
□*verb* To offer or present: *The circus features a famous acrobat.*
fea·ture (fē′chər) □*noun, plural* **features** □*verb* **featured, featuring, features**

February *noun* The second month of the year. February has 28 days except in leap year, when it has 29.
Feb·ru·ar·y (feb′rŏŏ er′ē) □*noun, plural* **Februarys**

WORD HISTORY: **February**

The name *February* comes from Latin. It was named after a feast of purifying.

---

fed *verb* The past tense and past participle of **feed:** *She fed the chickens.*
fed (fed) □*verb*

federal *adjective* **1.** Uniting different states under one authority: *The United States has a federal government.* **2.** Of the central government rather than the states: *The Post Office is a federal agency.*
fed·er·al (fed′ər əl) □*adjective*

fee *noun* A charge for a service or right: *The doctor's fee was $100.*
fee (fē) □*noun, plural* **fees**

feeble *adjective* Lacking strength; weak.
fee·ble (fē′bəl) □*adjective* **feebler, feeblest**

feed *verb* **1.** To give food to: *Feed the cat.* **2.** To give as food: *We feed lettuce to the turtles.* **3.** To eat: *Cows feed on hay.* **4.** To provide with material or fuel: *feed a furnace.*
□*noun* Food for animals or birds.
feed (fēd) □*verb* **fed, feeding, feeds** □*noun, plural* **feeds**

feed

feel *verb* **1.** To touch. **2.** To look for or find by touching: *He felt in his pocket for the key.* **3.** To seem to the touch: *Cotton feels soft.* **4.** To have a feeling: *He felt pain. She felt discouraged.* **5.** To hold an opinion; believe: *She feels that her answer was right.* —See Synonyms at **touch.**
□*noun* The way something seems when touched: *Silk has a smooth feel.*
feel (fēl) □*verb* **felt, feeling, feels** □*noun*

feeler *noun* A part of an animal that is used for feeling. An insect's antennae are feelers.
feel·er (fē′lər) □*noun, plural* **feelers**

feeling *noun* **1.** The ability to feel: *The cold made him lose feeling in his fingers.* **2.** A sensation or emotion: *a feeling of joy.* **3. feelings** The part of a person's mental and emotional nature that is strongly affected by another person's words or actions: *Her insulting comments hurt my feelings.* **4.** An opinion or belief.
feel·ing (fē′ling) □*noun, plural* **feelings**

feet *noun* The plural of **foot.**
feet (fēt) □*noun*

feign   *verb* To pretend: *feign illness.*
feign (fān) □*verb* **feigned, feigning, feigns**

fell¹   *verb* To cut down: *fell trees.*
fell (fel) □*verb* **felled, felling, fells**

fell
A felled tree

fell²   *verb* The past tense of **fall.**
fell (fel) □*verb*

fellow   *noun* **1.** A man or boy. **2.** A companion or associate.
fel·low (fel′ō) □*noun, plural* **fellows**

fellowship   *noun* Good feeling among members of a group; companionship.
fel·low·ship (fel′ō ship′) □*noun*

felt¹   *noun* A cloth made by pressing fibers together instead of weaving them.
felt (felt) □*noun, plural* **felts**

felt²   *verb* The past tense and past participle of **feel:** *He felt the radiator to see if it was hot.*
felt (felt) □*verb*

female   *adjective* Of or belonging to the sex that can give birth to young or produce eggs. □*noun* A female person or animal.
fe·male (fē′māl′) □*adjective* □*noun, plural* **females**

WORD HISTORY: female

The word *female* comes from a Latin word that means "little woman" or "girl." *Female* is not derived from the word *male.*

---

feminine   *adjective* Having to do with women or girls.
fem·i·nine (fem′ə nin) □*adjective*

fence   *noun* A structure set up around an area: *The yard is enclosed by a wooden fence.* □*verb* **1.** To surround or mark off with a fence. **2.** To fight with long, slender swords.
fence (fens) □*noun, plural* **fences** □*verb* **fenced, fencing, fences**

fencing   *noun* The sport of fighting with long, slender swords.
fenc·ing (fen′sing) □*noun*

fencing

fender   *noun* A metal guard above and around the wheel of a bicycle, automobile, truck, or other vehicle.
fen·der (fen′dər) □*noun, plural* **fenders**

ferment   *verb* To undergo or cause a chemical process in which the sugar in a liquid turns into alcohol and a gas: *The grape juice fermented and became wine.*
fer·ment (fər ment′) □*verb* **fermented, fermenting, ferments**

fern   *noun* A plant that has feathery leaves with many leaflets. Ferns have spores instead of flowers and seeds.
fern (fûrn) □*noun, plural* **ferns**

ferocious   *adjective* Very cruel and fierce: *ferocious animals.*
fe·ro·cious (fə rō′shəs) □*adjective*

ferret   *noun* An animal with yellowish or white fur that looks like a weasel. □*verb* To hunt; search: *The cat ferreted out the mouse.*
fer·ret (fer′it) □*noun, plural* **ferrets** □*verb* **ferreted, ferreting, ferrets**

Ferris wheel   *noun* A large, revolving wheel with seats hung from the rim in which people ride for fun.
Fer·ris wheel (fer′is) □*noun*

a bat	ī bite	o͞o tool	*th* feather
ā make	î fierce	ou out	th bath
â dare	o dot	u nut	hw wheat
ä father	ō no	û turn	zh measure
e net	ô law, for	ch church	ə about, open
ē be	oi soil	ng ring	pencil, atom
i dip	oo look	sh shade	circus

ferry *noun* A boat used to carry people and things across a narrow body of water.
□*verb* To carry in or take a ferry.
fer·ry (fer′ē) □*noun, plural* **ferries** □*verb*
  ferried, ferrying, ferries

fertile *adjective* **1.** Able to produce abundantly: *fertile soil.* **2.** Capable of having offspring, vegetation, or crops. **3.** Capable of developing into a complete plant or animal: *a fertile egg.*
fer·tile (fûr′təl) □*adjective*

fertilize *verb* **1.** To make fertile: *Bees help to fertilize flowers.* **2.** To use fertilizer on: *fertilize a garden with manure.*
fer·til·ize (fûr′təl īz′) □*verb* **fertilized, fertilizing, fertilizes**

fertilizer *noun* A substance that is added to soil to make it better for growing plants.
fer·til·iz·er (fûr′təl ī′zər) □*noun, plural* **fertilizers**

festival *noun* A day or time of celebrating; holiday.
fes·ti·val (fes′tə vəl) □*noun, plural* **festivals**

fetch *verb* To go and get; bring back: *I taught my dog to fetch sticks.*
fetch (fech) □*verb* **fetched, fetching, fetches**

fetter *noun* A chain attached to the ankles: *a prisoner in fetters.*
fet·ter (fet′ər) □*noun, plural* **fetters**

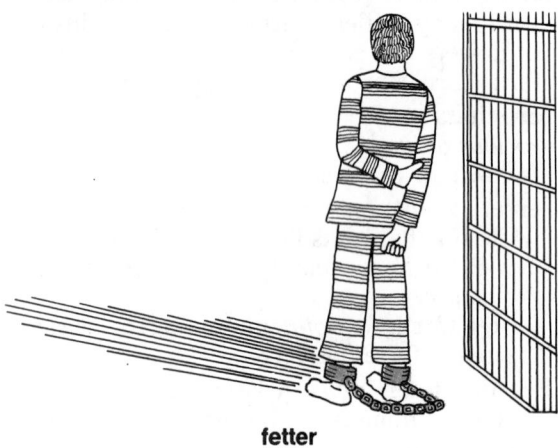

fetter

feud *noun* A long, bitter quarrel.
□*verb* To carry on a feud: *The two families feuded for years.*
feud (fyōod) □*noun, plural* **feuds** □*verb* **feuded, feuding, feuds**

fever *noun* A body temperature that is higher than normal.
fe·ver (fē′vər) □*noun, plural* **fevers**

few *adjective* Not many: *I only have a few pennies.*
□*noun* A small number: *Most wild elephants have been killed, but a few still exist.*
□*pronoun* A small number of persons or things: *Few were able to sleep that night.*
few (fyōo) □*adjective* **fewer, fewest** □*noun* □*pronoun*

fez *noun* A round felt cap with a high crown and no brim.
fez (fez) □*noun, plural* **fezzes**

fez

fiancé *noun* A man to whom a woman is engaged to be married.
fi·an·cé (fē′än sā′) □*noun, plural* **finacés**

fiancée *noun* A woman to whom a man is engaged to be married.
fi·an·cée (fē′än sā′) □*noun, plural* **fiancées**

fiber *noun* A long, thin strand: *Cotton fibers are spun to make thread.*
fi·ber (fī′bər) □*noun, plural* **fibers**

fiction *noun* **1.** Something imaginary: *His excuse was pure fiction.* **2.** Novels and short stories that tell about characters and events that are not real.
fic·tion (fik′shən) □*noun, plural* **fictions**

fictitious *adjective* Of or describing something that is not true or real; imaginary: *The events in that book are fictitious.*
fic·ti·tious (fik tish′əs) □*adjective*

fiddle *noun* A violin.
□*verb* To play the violin.
fid·dle (fid′əl) □*noun, plural* **fiddles** □*verb* **fiddled, fiddling, fiddles**

field *noun* **1.** A large area of open or cleared land. **2.** An area where a crop is grown or a resource is obtained: *a gold field.* **3.** An area of interest or work: *the field of teaching.*

□*verb* To catch or pick up a batted ball: *The pitcher fielded the baseball.*
field (fēld) □*noun, plural* **fields** □*verb* **fielded, fielding, fields**

fielder *noun* A baseball player who is out in the field instead of at bat.
field·er (fēl′dər) □*noun, plural* **fielders**

field glasses *plural noun* Binoculars for outdoor use.

field glasses

field trip *noun* A trip made by a class, as to a museum.

fierce *adjective* **1.** Wild and savage: *a fierce tiger.* **2.** Very strong; raging: *a fierce wind.* —See Synonyms at **intense.**
fierce (fîrs) □*adjective* **fiercer, fiercest**

fiesta *noun* A celebration or festival. Fiestas are held in Mexico and other Latin-American countries.
fi·es·ta (fē es′tə) □*noun, plural* **fiestas**

fife *noun* A small, high-pitched flute that is used in marching bands.
fife (fīf) □*noun, plural* **fifes**

fife

fifteen *noun* A number equal to the sum of 10 + 5; 15.
□*adjective* Being one more than fourteen.
fif·teen (fif′tēn′) □*noun, plural* **fifteens** □*adjective*

fifteenth *noun* **1.** In a group of people or things that are in numbered order, the one that matches the number fifteen. **2.** One of fifteen equal parts, written ¹/₁₅.
□*adjective* Coming after the fourteenth.
fif·teenth (fif′tēnth′) □*noun, plural* **fifteenths** □*adjective*

fifth *noun* **1.** In a group of people or things that are in numbered order, the one that matches the number five. **2.** One of five equal parts, written ¹/₅.
□*adjective* Coming after the fourth.
fifth (fifth) □*noun, plural* **fifths** □*adjective*

fiftieth *noun* **1.** In a group of people or things that are in numbered order, the one that matches the number fifty. **2.** One of fifty equal parts, written ¹/₅₀.
□*adjective* Coming after the forty-ninth.
fif·ti·eth (fif′tē ith) □*noun, plural* **fiftieths** □*adjective*

fifty *noun* A number that is equal to the product of 10 × 5; 50.
□*adjective* Being ten more than forty: *fifty pounds.*
fif·ty (fif′tē) □*noun, plural* **fifties** □*adjective*

fig *noun* A sweet fruit that has many small seeds. Figs grow on trees and shrubs in warm regions.
fig (fig) □*noun, plural* **figs**

fight *verb* **1.** To use the fists or weapons against an opponent: *The United States fought Japan in World War II.* **2.** To struggle against: *The tired child fought off sleep.* **3.** To quarrel or argue.
□*noun* **1.** A hard struggle; battle: *a fist fight; a fight for his life.* **2.** A quarrel or argument.
fight (fīt) □*verb* **fought, fighting, fights** □*noun, plural* **fights**

a bat	ī bite	o͞o tool	*th* feather
ā make	i fierce	ou out	th bath
â dare	o dot	u nut	hw wheat
ä father	ō no	û turn	zh measure
e net	ô law, for	ch church	ə about, open
ē be	oi soil	ng ring	pencil, atom
i dip	oo look	sh shade	circus

fighter *noun* **1.** A person or animal who fights. **2.** A boxer.
fight·er (fī′ tər) □*noun, plural* **fighters**

figurative *adjective* Using words in a way that is different from their ordinary or literal meanings. "She cried her eyes out" is a figurative expression.
fig·ur·a·tive (fig′ yər ə tiv) □*adjective*

figure *noun* **1.** A symbol that stands for a number. "1," "40," and "212" are figures. **2.** An amount given in numbers: *a population figure.* **3.** A picture or design. **4.** A form; shape: *The skirt suited her figure.* **5.** A person: *public figures.*
□*verb* **1.** To work out by using numbers: *Let's figure the cost of our lunch.* **2.** To believe; assume: *I figured we would take a bus.* —See Synonyms at **believe.**
   figure out To find out by thinking; solve: *Can you figure out how to get there?*
fig·ure (fig′ yər) □*noun, plural* **figures**
   □*verb* **figured, figuring, figures**

figurehead *noun* **1.** A person who seems to be the leader but has no real power. **2.** A carved figure on the bow of a ship.
fig·ure·head (fig′ yər hed′) □*noun, plural* **figureheads**

figurehead

figure of speech *noun* An expression in which words are used in a figurative way. "She's walking on air" is a figure of speech that means "She's very happy."

filament *noun* A fine wire or thread: *Electricity heats the filament in the light bulb.*
fil·a·ment (fil′ ə mənt) □*noun, plural* **filaments**

file¹ *noun* **1.** A container for keeping papers arranged in order. **2.** A collection of papers or other information arranged in order: *a file of newspaper clippings.* **3.** A line of people, animals, or things placed one behind the other.

□*verb* **1.** To put in a file. **2.** To send in; submit: *file a report.*
file (fīl) □*noun, plural* **files** □*verb* **filed, filing, files**

file² *noun* A tool with a rough surface, used for smoothing and scraping.
□*verb* To smooth, scrape, or grind down with a file: *file fingernails.*
file (fīl) □*noun, plural* **files** □*verb* **filed, filing, files**

file

filet *noun* Another spelling for **fillet.**
fi·let (fi lā′ *or* fil′ā′) □*noun, plural* **filets**

filing *noun* A small piece filed off.
fil·ing (fī′ ling) □*noun, plural* **filings**

fill *verb* **1.** To make or become full: *Fill the pot with water. The kitchen filled with smoke.* **2.** To take up the whole space of: *People filled the auditorium.* **3.** To give what is asked for; supply: *fill a grocery order.* **4.** To stop up or plug up: *fill a hole with cement.* **5.** To satisfy; fulfill: *fill a requirement.*
fill (fil) □*verb* **filled, filling, fills**

fillet *noun* A piece of meat or fish without bones or fat.
fil·let (fi lā′ *or* fil′ā′) □*noun, plural* **fillets**

filling *noun* Something used to fill a space: *a filling in a tooth; custard filling in a pie.*
fill·ing (fil′ ing) □*noun, plural* **fillings**

filly *noun* A young female horse.
fil·ly (fil′ ē) □*noun, plural* **fillies**

film *noun* **1.** A thin strip of material coated with a substance that changes when light hits it. Film is used in photography. **2.** A motion picture. **3.** A thin coating: *A film of grease covered the stove.*
□*verb* To make a motion picture of: *He filmed the rocket launching.*

film (f ilm) □*noun, plural* **films** □*verb*
filmed, filming, films

filter *noun* A device through which a liquid or air is passed in order to clean out dirt or other unwanted matter: *Her swimming pool has a charcoal filter.*
□*verb* **1.** To pass through a filter. **2.** To separate by a filter: *filter dust from the air.* **3.** To pass slowly: *The rain filtered through the soil.*
fil·ter (f il′tər) □*noun, plural* **filters** □*verb*
filtered, filtering, filters

filth *noun* Disgusting, dirty matter: *boots covered with mud and filth.*
filth (f ilth) □*noun*

filthy *adjective* Extremely dirty.
filth·y (f il′thē) □*adjective* **filthier, filthiest**

fin *noun* **1.** One of the thin parts that stick out from the body of a fish. They are used for swimming and for keeping balance. **2.** A part shaped or used like a fin.
fin (f in) □*noun, plural* **fins**

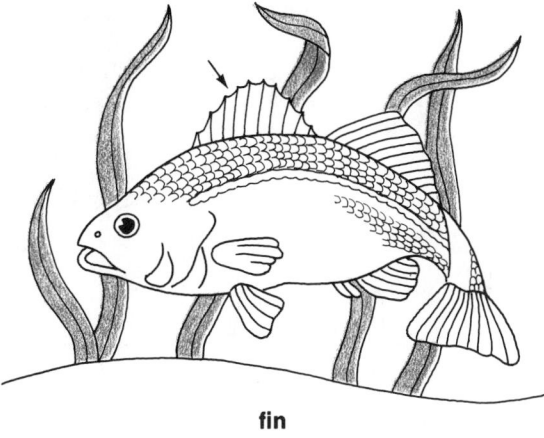

fin

final *adjective* **1.** Last: *final exams.* **2.** Not likely to change; definite: *My decision is final.*
—See Synonyms at **last¹.**
□*noun* **1.** The last game in a series of games. **2.** The last test of a school course or subject.
fi·nal (f ī′nəl) □*adjective* □*noun, plural*
finals

finally *adverb* At last: *Finally the train arrived.*
fi·nal·ly (f ī′nə lē) □*adverb*

finance *noun* **1.** The management and use of money. **2. finances** The money that a person, business, or government has.
□*verb* To provide money for: *They financed the new house with a loan from the bank.*
fi·nance (f i nans′ *or* f ī′nans′) □*noun, plural*

finances □*verb* **financed, financing, finances**

financial *adjective* Having to do with finance: *The newspaper has a section on financial news.*
fi·nan·cial (f i **nan′**shəl *or* f ī **nan′**shəl) □*adjective*

finch *noun* A bird with a short, thick bill. The cardinal, canary, and sparrow are finches.
finch (f inch) □*noun, plural* **finches**

find *verb* **1.** To come upon by accident: *He found a ball in the street.* **2.** To look for and discover: *find an answer; find out when a program starts.* **3.** To learn: *Today I found out that whales breathe air.* **4.** To get back; recover. **5.** To come to a decision and announce it: *The jury found him not guilty.*
□*noun* Something found.
find (f īnd) □*verb* **found, finding, finds**
□*noun, plural* **finds**

> **SYNONYMS: find, locate, spot**
>
> These verbs mean to look for and discover: *She helped me find my glasses. We couldn't locate his house. I spotted my friends at the other end of the playground.*

fine¹ *adjective* **1.** Very good; excellent: *a fine athlete.* **2.** Very thin or small: *fine threads; fine print.* **3.** In good health: *I'm feeling fine today.*
□*adverb* Excellently: *She's doing fine in school.*
fine (f īn) □*adjective* **finer, finest** □*adverb*

fine² *noun* An amount of money paid as a penalty for breaking a rule or law.
□*verb* To order to pay a fine.
fine (f īn) □*noun, plural* **fines** □*verb* **fined, fining, fines**

> **WORD HISTORY: fine²**
>
> The word *fine²* meaning "money paid as a penalty" comes from an old French word that means "end." In the Middle Ages this word was used to mean "the end of a case" or "money paid to settle a lawsuit."

a	bat	ī	bite	ōō	tool	*th*	feather
ā	make	î	fierce	ou	out	th	bath
â	dare	o	dot	u	nut	hw	wheat
ä	father	ō	no	û	turn	zh	measure
e	net	ô	law, for	ch	church	ə	about, open
ē	be	oi	soil	ng	ring		pencil, atom
i	dip	oo	look	sh	shade		circus

finger   *noun* Any one of the five parts that go outward from the hand. Sometimes the thumb is not counted as a finger.
□*verb* To handle or touch with the fingers: *She fingered the beads.*
fin·ger (f ĭng′gər) □*noun, plural* **fingers** □*verb* **fingered, fingering, fingers**

> *WORD HISTORY:*   **finger**
> The word *finger* comes from a very ancient Germanic word that literally means "one of five."

fingernail   *noun* The thin, hard layer at the end of each finger.
fin·ger·nail (f ĭng′gər nāl′) □*noun, plural* **fingernails**

fingerprint   *noun* A mark with many lines made by the tip of a finger. Because everyone's fingerprints are unique, they are used as a way of identifying people.
□*verb* To get the fingerprints of.
fin·ger·print (f ĭng′gər print′) □*noun, plural* **fingerprints** □*verb* **fingerprinted, fingerprinting, fingerprints**

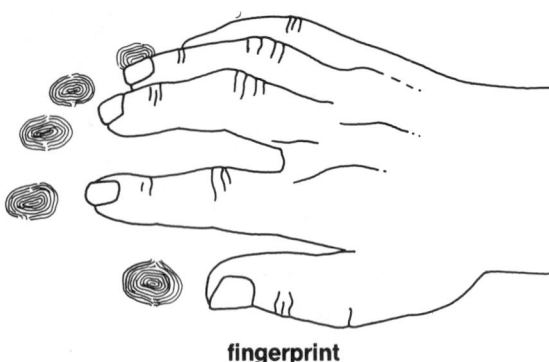
fingerprint

finish   *verb* **1.** To bring or come to an end: *When will you finish doing the dishes?* **2.** To use up: *finish the popcorn.* **3.** To treat the surface of: *We finished the desk with a clear varnish.* —See Synonyms at **end.**
□*noun* **1.** The end: *fight to the finish.* **2.** The final coating of a surface.
fin·ish (f ĭn′ish) □*verb* **finished, finishing, finishes** □*noun, plural* **finishes**

fir   *noun* An evergreen tree with small, flat needles.
fir (fûr) □*noun, plural* **firs**

fire   *noun* **1.** The flame, heat, and light given off when something burns. **2.** A burning that causes damage: *preventing forest fires.* **3.** Strong emotion: *words full of fire.* **4.** The

shooting of guns.
□*verb* **1.** To set on fire: *fire up the furnace.* **2.** To dismiss from a job. **3.** To stir up; excite: *The tales fired the child's imagination.* **4.** To shoot a gun: *fire a rifle.*
fire (f ĭr) □*noun, plural* **fires** □*verb* **fired, firing, fires**

firearm   *noun* A weapon that can be carried and is used for shooting, as a rifle or pistol.
fire·arm (f ĭr′ärm′) □*noun, plural* **firearms**

firecracker   *noun* A paper tube containing an explosive and a fuse, used to make noise during celebrations.
fire·crack·er (f ĭr′krak′ər) □*noun, plural* **firecrackers**

fire engine   *noun* A truck that carries equipment to fight fires.

fire escape   *noun* An outside flight of stairs attached to a building and used for escaping in case of fire.

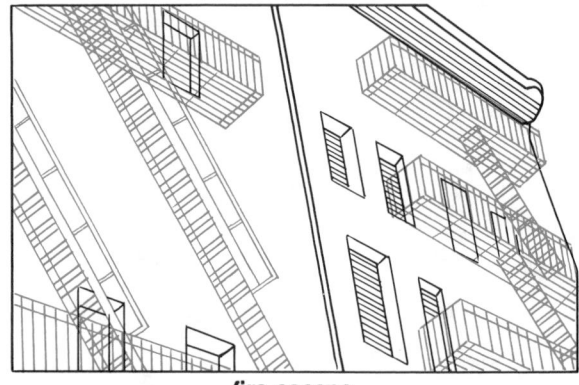
fire escape

fire extinguisher   *noun* A small device filled with chemicals that can be sprayed on a fire to put it out.

firefighter   *noun* Someone who fights fires.
fire·fight·er (f ĭr′fī′tər) □*noun, plural* **firefighters**

firefly   *noun* An insect that gives off a flashing light.
fire·fly (f ĭr′flī′) □*noun, plural* **fireflies**

firehouse   *noun* A building for fire engines and firefighters.
fire·house (f ĭr′hous′) □*noun, plural* **firehouses**

fireman   *noun* **1.** A firefighter. **2.** Someone who tends a fire in a furnace or steam engine.
fire·man (f ĭr′mən) □*noun, plural* **firemen**

fireplace   *noun* An opening in a chimney for holding a fire.

fire·place (fîr′ plās′) □*noun, plural*
fireplaces

fireproof *adjective* Designed not to burn: *a fireproof house.*
fire·proof (fîr′ pro͞of′) □*adjective*

fireside *noun* The area of a room around a fireplace.
fire·side (fîr′ sīd′) □*noun, plural* **firesides**

fireworks *plural noun* Firecrackers and other explosives that are used to make colorful displays at celebrations.
fire·works (fîr′ wûrks′) □*plural noun*

firm¹ *adjective* **1.** Not giving way to pressure: *a firm mattress.* **2.** Not changing; steady: *a firm belief.* **3.** Strong: *a firm grip.* —See Synonyms at **hard.**
firm (fûrm) □*adjective* **firmer, firmest**

firm² *noun* A company formed by two or more people who go into business together.
firm (fûrm) □*noun, plural* **firms**

first *adjective* Before any others: *first in line; the first President.*
□*adverb* **1.** Before any others: *You jump first.* **2.** For the first time: *I first met her when I was eight.*
□*noun* **1.** Someone or something that is first. **2.** The beginning: *At first the water was cold.*
first (fûrst) □*adjective* □*adverb* □*noun, plural* **firsts**

SYNONYMS: **first, initial, original**

These adjectives mean before any others: *Who was the first astronaut to walk on the moon? Our initial attempt to build a raft failed. Can you name the 13 original states of the United States?*

---

first aid *noun* Emergency help for an injured or sick person.

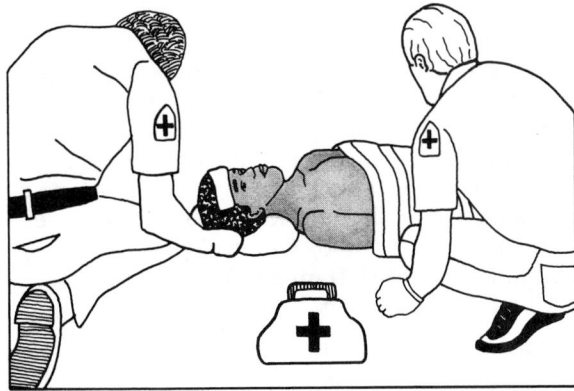

first aid

first-class *adjective* **1.** Of the best quality: *a first-class restaurant.* **2.** Of or for the best seats or rooms: *first-class tickets.*
□*adverb* With first-class seats or rooms: *flying first-class.*
first-class (fûrst′ klas′) □*adjective* □*adverb*

first-hand *adjective* Gotten from the original source: *first-hand information.*
first-hand (fûrst′ hand′) □*adjective*

fish *noun* An animal that lives in the water, has gills for breathing, and is usually covered with scales.
□*verb* **1.** To catch or try to catch fish. **2.** To search; hunt: *I fished in the purse for my keys.*
fish (fish) □*noun, plural* **fish** or **fishes**
□*verb* **fished, fishing, fishes**

fisherman *noun* Someone who fishes.
fish·er·man (fish′ ər mən) □*noun, plural* **fishermen**

fishery *noun* A place where fish are bred.
fish·er·y (fish′ ə rē) □*noun, plural* **fisheries**

fishing rod *noun* A long pole with a hook, line, and often a reel attached to it, used for catching fish.

fishy *adjective* **1.** Tasting or smelling of fish. **2.** Suspicious; doubtful: *His explanation sounded fishy to me.*
fish·y (fish′ ē) □*adjective* **fishier, fishiest**

fission *noun* The breaking up of the nucleus of an atom to release large amounts of energy.
fis·sion (fish′ ən) □*noun*

fist *noun* The hand closed tightly.
fist (fist) □*noun, plural* **fists**

fit¹ *verb* **1.** To be the proper size and shape: *The dress fits well.* **2.** To be suitable for: *That role just doesn't fit you.* **3.** To adjust; alter: *fit a suit.* **4.** To place snugly; insert: *She was able to fit all the socks into one drawer.* **5.** To equip; provide: *We fitted the campers with tents and sleeping bags.* —See Synonyms at **healthy.**
□*noun* The way something fits: *a perfect fit.*
□*adjective* **1.** Suitable; proper: *a fit reward.* **2.** Healthy: *looking fit.*
fit (fit) □*verb* **fitted, fitting, fits** □*noun, plural* **fits** □*adjective* **fitter, fittest**

a	bat	ī	bite	o͞o	tool	*th*	feather
ā	make	î	fierce	ou	out	th	bath
â	dare	o	dot	u	nut	hw	wheat
ä	father	ō	no	û	turn	zh	measure
e	net	ô	law, for	ch	church	ə	about, open
ē	be	oi	soil	ng	ring		pencil, atom
i	dip	oo	look	sh	shade		circus

fit² *noun* A sudden onset; attack: *a fit of laughter; a fit of asthma.*
fit (f it) □*noun, plural* **fits**

fit

five *noun* A number equal to the sum of 1 + 4; 5.
□*adjective* Being one more than four.
five (fīv) □*noun, plural* **fives** □*adjective*

fix *verb* **1.** To make stable or firm: *fix a stake in the ground.* **2.** To arrange definitely; settle: *fix a time to meet.* **3.** To direct steadily: *She fixed her eyes on the road ahead.* **4.** To place; put: *fix the blame.* **5.** To repair: *fix a broken doorknob.* **6.** To prepare: *fix dinner.*
□*noun* A difficult situation. —See Synonyms at **mend.**
fix (f iks) □*verb* **fixed, fixing, fixes** □*noun, plural* **fixes**

fixture *noun* Something fastened in place for permanent use: *The bathroom fixtures include a shower and a sink.*
fix·ture (f iks′chər) □*noun, plural* **fixtures**

flag *noun* A piece of cloth with a special design that is used as a symbol.
□*verb* To signal with or as if with a flag: *flag down a bus.*
flag (flag) □*noun, plural* **flags** □*verb* **flagged, flagging, flags**

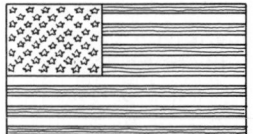 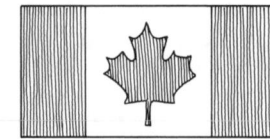

flag
Left: American; *Right:* Canadian

flair *noun* A natural talent: *a flair for languages.*
flair (flâr) □*noun, plural* **flairs**

flake *noun* A small, thin piece: *a soap flake.*
□*verb* To come off in flakes: *The old paint is flaking.*
flake (flāk) □*noun, plural* **flakes** □*verb* **flaked, flaking, flakes**

flame *noun* **1.** A glowing mass of light given off by a burning substance. **2.** Often **flames** The condition of burning: *The papers burst into flames.*
□*verb* **1.** To burn brightly. **2.** To glow fiercely: *His eyes flamed with resentment.*
flame (flām) □*noun, plural* **flames** □*verb* **flamed, flaming, flames**

flamingo *noun* A large, pink or red bird with a very long neck and legs.
fla·min·go (flə ming′gō) □*noun, plural* **flamingos** or **flamingoes**

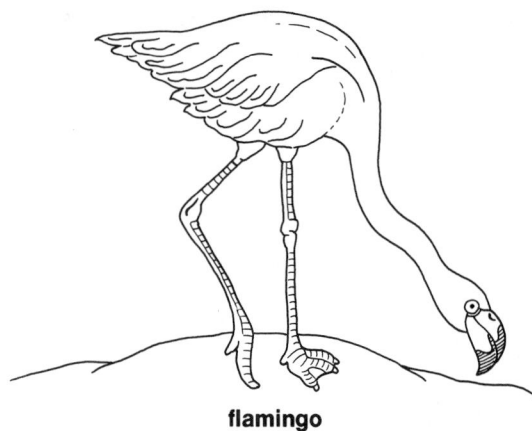

flamingo

flammable *adjective* Catching fire easily: *Gasoline is a flammable liquid.*
flam·ma·ble (flam′ə bəl) □*adjective*

flank *noun* The part between the hip and the ribs on either side of the body.
□*verb* To be at the side of: *Two guards flanked the doorway.*
flank (flangk) □*noun, plural* **flanks** □*verb* **flanked, flanking, flanks**

flannel *noun* **1.** A soft cloth made of cotton or wool. **2.** **flannels** Garments made of flannel.
flan·nel (flan′əl) □*noun, plural* **flannels**

flap *verb* **1.** To move up and down: *The hawk flapped its wings.* **2.** To wave loosely: *The flag flapped in the wind.*
□*noun* **1.** The sound or action of flapping: *the flap of the window shade.* **2.** A piece fastened at one edge and meant to fold over and cover something: *the flap of an envelope.*
flap (flap) □*verb* **flapped, flapping, flaps** □*noun, plural* **flaps**

flare *verb* **1.** To burn with a sudden flame: *The match flared up when I struck it.* **2.** To burst out with sudden feeling: *Tempers flared.*

3. To spread outward: *The pants flare at the bottom.*
□*noun* **1.** A sudden blaze of light. **2.** A fire used as a signal.
flare (flâr) □*verb* **flared, flaring, flares**
□*noun, plural* **flares**

flash *verb* **1.** To appear suddenly or for an instant: *The picture flashed on the screen. A warning light flashed at the corner.* **2.** To move rapidly.
□*noun* **1.** A sudden burst of light: *a flash of lightning.* **2.** An instant.
flash (flash) □*verb* **flashed, flashing, flashes**
□*noun, plural* **flashes**

flashlight *noun* An electric light powered by batteries and small enough to carry around.
flash·light (flash′lĭt′) □*noun, plural* **flashlights**

flask *noun* A small bottle.
flask (flask) □*noun, plural* **flasks**

flask
Three kinds of flasks

flat *adjective* **1.** Smooth; level: *flat land.* **2.** Lying stretched out: *flat on the ground.* **3.** Not deep; shallow: *a flat dish.* **4.** Having lost air: *a flat tire.* **5.** Without much flavor or interest: *food that tasted flat.* **6.** Downright; absolute: *a flat "no."* —See Synonyms at **level.**
□*noun* **1.** A flat surface. **2.** A flat tire.
flat (flat) □*adjective* **flatter, flattest** □*noun, plural* **flats**

flatcar *noun* A railroad car without sides or a roof.
flat·car (flat′kär′) □*noun, plural* **flatcars**

flatfish *noun* A fish that has a flat body with the eyes on the upper side.
flat·fish (flat′fĭsh′) □*noun, plural* **flatfish** or **flatfishes**

flatten *verb* To make or become flat or flatter.
flat·ten (flat′ən) □*verb* **flattened, flattening, flattens**

flatter¹ *verb* **1.** To try to please with compliments: *She flattered him by saying how strong and handsome he was.* **2.** To make more attractive than is actually true: *The photograph flatters her by making her look older than she really is.*
flat·ter (flat′ər) □*verb* **flattered, flattering, flatters**

flatter² □*adjective* The comparative of **flat.**
flat·ter (flat′ər) □*adjective*

flattery *noun* Insincere praise.
flat·ter·y (flat′ə rē) □*noun, plural* **flatteries**

flattest *adjective* The superlative of **flat.**
flat·test (flat′ist) □*adjective*

flavor *noun* **1.** A taste: *a chocolate flavor.* **2.** A special quality or charm.
□*verb* To give flavor to: *We flavored the cookies with ginger.*
fla·vor (flā′vər) □*noun, plural* **flavors** □*verb* **flavored, flavoring, flavors**

flavoring *noun* Something added to a food or beverage to give flavor.
fla·vor·ing (flā′vər ing) □*noun, plural* **flavorings**

flaw *noun* A defect: *a flaw in a diamond; flaws in his character.*
□*verb* To spoil; mar.
flaw (flô) □*noun, plural* **flaws** □*verb* **flawed, flawing, flaws**

flax *noun* **1.** A plant that has blue flowers and seeds from which linseed oil is made. **2.** The fibers from the stems of this plant, from which linen is made.
flax (flaks) □*noun*

flea *noun* A small, jumping insect that lives on the bodies of animals and human beings and sucks their blood.
flea (flē) □*noun, plural* **fleas**

fled *verb* The past tense and past participle of **flee:** *He stole the money and fled.*
fled (fled) □*verb*

flee *verb* **1.** To run away: *tried to flee from the burning building.* **2.** To pass quickly: *The days fled by.*
flee (flē) □*verb* **fled, fleeing, flees**

fleece *noun* The wool that covers a sheep.
□*verb* To cut the fleece from.

a	bat	ī	bite	ōō	tool	*th*	feather
ā	make	î	fierce	ou	out	th	bath
â	dare	o	dot	u	nut	hw	wheat
ä	father	ō	no	û	turn	zh	measure
e	net	ô	law, for	ch	church	ə	about, open
ē	be	oi	soil	ng	ring		pencil, atom
i	dip	oo	look	sh	shade		circus

fleece (flēs) □*noun* □*verb* **fleeced, fleecing, fleeces**

fleece

fleet[1]　*noun* **1.** A group of warships. **2.** A large group of ships, cars, or other vehicles: *a fleet of buses.*
fleet (flēt) □*noun, plural* **fleets**

fleet[2]　*adjective* Fast; swift: *a fleet runner.*
fleet (flēt) □*adjective* **fleeter, fleetest**

flesh　*noun* **1.** The soft part of the body that covers the bones and is under the skin. **2.** The soft part of a fruit or vegetable.
flesh (flesh) □*noun*

fleshy　*adjective* Like flesh; plump.
flesh·y (flesh′ē) □*adjective* **fleshier, fleshiest**

flew　*verb* The past tense of **fly**[1]: *The plane flew north.*
flew (flōō) □*verb*

flex　*verb* To bend: *She flexed her toes.*
flex (fleks) □*verb* **flexed, flexing, flexes**

flexible　*adjective* Capable of being bent or twisted without breaking: *Gymnastics will help to make your body more flexible.*
flex·i·ble (flek′sə bəl) □*adjective*

flexible

flick　*noun* A light, quick motion: *With a flick of her finger she turned on the light.*
□*verb* **1.** To hit or remove quickly and lightly: *She flicked the crumbs from her lap.* **2.** To move with a flick: *The snake flicked its tongue.*
flick (flik) □*noun, plural* **flicks** □*verb* **flicked, flicking, flicks**

flicker　*verb* **1.** To give off a wavering, unsteady light: *The candle flickered in the wind.* **2.** To move back and forth quickly; flutter: *Shadows flickered on the wall.*
□*noun* **1.** A wavering, unsteady light: *the flicker of candlelight.* **2.** A quick back-and-forth movement; flutter: *the flicker of an eyelash.*
flick·er (flik′ər) □*verb* **flickered, flickering, flickers** □*noun, plural* **flickers**

flied　*verb* A past tense and past participle of **fly**[1]: *She flied to right field.*
flied (flīd) □*verb*

flier　*noun* Someone or something that flies, as an airplane pilot or a bird.
fli·er (flī′ər) □*noun, plural* **fliers**

flight[1]　*noun* **1.** The act or process of flying through the air by means of wings: *the flight of a bee.* **2.** An airplane trip: *I had a four o'clock flight to New York.* **3.** A group, especially of birds or aircraft, flying together: *a flight of geese.* **4.** A series of stairs between landings or floors of a building.
flight (flīt) □*noun, plural* **flights**

flight[2]　*noun* The act of running away; escape.
flight (flīt) □*noun, plural* **flights**

flimsy　*adjective* Light, thin, or weak; without strength: *a flimsy dress; a flimsy excuse.*
flim·sy (flim′zē) □*adjective* **flimsier, flimsiest**

flinch　*verb* To pull back quickly in pain or fear: *I flinched when I burned my hand.*
flinch (flinch) □*verb* **flinched, flinching, flinches**

fling　*verb* To throw hard; hurl: *She flung her books on the table.*
□*noun* **1.** A hard throw. **2.** A short time of doing what one wants: *He is having a last fling before school begins.*
fling (fling) □*verb* **flung, flinging, flings** □*noun, plural* **flings**

flint　*noun* A very hard stone that makes sparks when it strikes against steel. Flint is a kind of quartz and is usually gray.
flint (flint) □*noun, plural* **flints**

flip　*verb* **1.** To throw with a quick motion, so as to cause to turn over in the air: *They flipped*

a coin to decide who would take the first turn.
2. To move with a snap or jerk: *She flipped through the pages of the book.*
□*noun* An act of flipping; toss: *I gave the pancake a flip.*
flip (flip) □*verb* **flipped, flipping, flips**
□*noun, plural* **flips**

flipper *noun* **1.** A wide, flat limb, as on a seal or walrus, that is used for swimming. **2.** One of a pair of wide, flat rubber shoes shaped like a fin and worn by swimmers and skin divers.
flip·per (flip′ər) □*noun, plural* **flippers**

flirt *verb* To act romantic in a playful manner: *He flirts with all the girls.*
flirt (flûrt) □*verb* **flirted, flirting, flirts**

flit *verb* To move quickly and lightly: *The bird flitted from branch to branch.*
flit (flit) □*verb* **flitted, flitting, flits**

float *verb* **1.** To be held up by liquid or air: *The bottle floated in the pond.* **2.** To move on a current of air or water: *They floated the logs down the river.*
□*noun* **1.** Something, such as a raft used by swimmers, that floats in or on the water. **2.** A large platform on wheels that carries an exhibit in a parade.
float (flōt) □*verb* **floated, floating, floats**
□*noun, plural* **floats**

flock *noun* **1.** A group of animals, such as geese or sheep, that live, move, or feed together. **2.** A large group of people, especially the members of a church.
□*verb* To gather or travel in a crowd: *People flocked to the museum to see the paintings.*
flock (flok) □*noun, plural* **flocks** □*verb* **flocked, flocking, flocks**

floe *noun* A large, flat mass of floating ice.
floe (flō) □*noun, plural* **floes**

flood *noun* **1.** A great flow of water onto land that is usually dry: *The river overflowed and caused a flood.* **2.** A large flow or quantity: *a flood of tears; a flood of applications.*
□*verb* **1.** To cover or fill with water: *The river floods the valley every spring.* **2.** To fill as if with a flood: *Shoppers flooded into the store.*
flood (flud) □*noun, plural* **floods** □*verb* **flooded, flooding, floods**

floor *noun* **1.** The part of a room on which a person stands or walks: *The bathroom has a tile floor.* **2.** The ground surface: *The explorer found a sunken ship on the ocean floor.* **3.** A story or level of a building.
□*verb* **1.** To put a floor on: *We floored the hall*

with oak. **2.** To knock to the floor: *The boxer floored his opponent in the first round.*
floor (flôr) □*noun, plural* **floors** □*verb* **floored, flooring, floors**

flop *verb* **1.** To fall in a noisy and heavy way: *She flopped down into her chair.* **2.** To move back and forth or up and down; flap: *She flopped her handkerchief in farewell.* **3.** To fail completely: *Even though the critics liked it, the show flopped.*
□*noun* **1.** The noise or motion of flopping. **2.** A complete failure: *The interview was a flop.*
flop (flop) □*verb* **flopped, flopping, flops**
□*noun, plural* **flops**

floppy *adjective* Flopping or tending to flop: *a dog with floppy ears.*
flop·py (flop′ē) □*adjective* **floppier, floppiest**

floppy disk *noun* A portable computer disk on which information and computer programs can be stored; diskette.

floral *adjective* Of flowers: *floral decorations.*
flo·ral (flôr′əl) □*adjective*

florist *noun* Someone whose work is raising or selling flowers and plants.
flo·rist (flôr′ist) □*noun, plural* **florists**

flounder[1] *verb* To move with difficulty or in a clumsy way: *We floundered through the mud to get to the shore.*
floun·der (floun′dər) □*verb* **floundered, floundering, flounders**

flounder

a bat	ī bite	oo tool	*th* feather
ā make	î fierce	ou out	th bath
â dare	o dot	u nut	hw wheat
ä father	ō no	û turn	zh measure
e net	ô law, for	ch church	ə about, open
ē be	oi soil	ng ring	pencil, atom
i dip	oo look	sh shade	circus

flounder² *noun* A flatfish often used as food.
floun·der (floun′dər) □*noun, plural* **flounder**
or **flounders**

flour *noun* A fine powder made by grinding
grain, especially wheat. It is used to make
bread, cake, and many other foods.
flour (flour) □*noun, plural* **flours**

> ### WORD HISTORY: flour
>
> Until about 200 years ago there was no fixed way of
> spelling many English words. *Flour* and *flower* were
> once two different ways of spelling the same word.
> Finely ground meal that has had all the bran sifted
> out was considered the best part, or "flower," of the
> grain. The spelling *flour* has now developed into a
> separate word meaning "a fine powder made by
> grinding grain."

flourish *verb* **1.** To grow or develop well;
thrive: *Our tulips were flourishing. The town
flourished after the discovery of oil.* **2.** To wave
in a bold or showy way: *The pirate flourished
his sword.*
□*noun* A bold or showy movement or action:
He took off his hat with a flourish.
flour·ish (flûr′ish) □*verb* **flourished,
flourishing, flourishes** □*noun, plural*
flourishes

flow *verb* **1.** To move freely in a steady
stream: *A brook flowed behind the house. Cars
flowed over the bridge.* **2.** To hang or fall
loosely: *The cape flowed from her shoulders.*
□*noun* **1.** The act of flowing: *The bandage
stopped the flow of blood.* **2.** A flowing mass;
stream: *A steady flow of ideas came to him.*
flow (flō) □*verb* **flowed, flowing, flows**
□*noun, plural* **flows**

flower *noun* **1.** The part of a plant that produces seeds. **2.** The best or finest part or time:
the flower of knighthood.
□*verb* To produce flowers; blossom.
flow·er (flou′ər) □*noun, plural* **flowers**
□*verb* **flowered, flowering, flowers**

flown *verb* A past participle of **fly¹**: *I have
never flown in an airplane.*
flown (flōn) □*verb*

flu *noun* A disease resembling a cold that is
caused by viruses; influenza.
flu (flōō) □*noun, plural* **flus**

flue *noun* A pipe, tube, or passage through
which smoke or hot air can escape.
flue (flōō) □*noun, plural* **flues**

fluff *noun* Soft, light material like down: *The
baby chicks looked like little balls of fluff.*
□*verb* To make or become fluffy: *fluff up a
pillow.*
fluff (fluf) □*noun* □*verb* **fluffed, fluffing,
fluffs**

fluffy *adjective* **1.** Having, covered with, or
like fluff: *a fluffy kitten.* **2.** Light, soft, and
airy: *fluffy pastry.*
fluff·y (fluf′ē) □*adjective* **fluffier, fluffiest**

fluid *noun* A substance, such as a liquid or
gas, that flows easily and takes the shape of its
container.
□*adjective* Capable of flowing like a liquid or
gas: *Water is fluid.*
flu·id (flōō′id) □*noun, plural* **fluids**
□*adjective*

flung *verb* The past tense and past participle
of **fling**: *The little girl flung her doll on the bed.*
flung (flung) □*verb*

flurry *noun* **1.** A light fall of snow or rain.
2. A sudden outburst: *a flurry of excitement.*
flur·ry (flûr′ē) □*noun, plural* **flurries**

flush *verb* **1.** To turn red; blush: *She flushed
with anger.* **2.** To wash or empty out with a
flow of water: *She flushed out the barrel with a
hose.* **3.** To flow suddenly: *Water flushed
through the channel.*
□*noun* **1.** A blush or rosy glow: *A slight flush
rose to her cheeks.* **2.** The act of flushing with
water.
□*adjective* On the same level; even: *The door
was flush with the wall.*
flush (flush) □*verb* **flushed, flushing,
flushes** □*noun, plural* **flushes** □*adjective*

flush

fluster *verb* To make nervous or excited: *Seeing so many strange faces flustered her.*
□*noun* A nervous or excited condition.
flus·ter (flus′tər) □*verb* **flustered,
flustering, flusters** □*noun, plural* **flusters**

flute *noun* A long, slender musical instrument that is played by blowing across the mouthpiece and covering different holes with the fingers or with keys.
flute (flo͞ot) □*noun, plural* **flutes**

flutter *verb* **1.** To flap the wings lightly in flying: *A moth fluttered around the room.* **2.** To wave or flap in a rapid, uneven way: *curtains fluttering in the breeze.*
□*noun* **1.** An act of fluttering: *With a flutter of her fan she left the room.* **2.** A stir, as of excitement: *a flutter of anger.*
flut·ter (flŭt′ər) □*verb* **fluttered, fluttering, flutters** □*noun, plural* **flutters**

fly[1] *verb* **1.** To move through the air with wings: *A bird flew over our garden.* **2.** To travel in or pilot an aircraft or spacecraft. **3.** To move through the air: *leaves flying in the wind.* **4.** To wave or float in air: *The flag flew from the pole. She flew her new kite.* **5.** To hit a baseball high into the air. **6.** To pass or move quickly; rush: *He flew to the window to get a glimpse of the parade.*
□*noun* **1.** A cloth flap that covers a fastening, as a zipper or a set of buttons, in clothing. **2.** A baseball that is hit high in the air.
fly (flī) □*verb* **flew** (**flied** *for verb sense 5*), **flown** (**flied** *for verb sense 5*), **flying, flies** □*noun, plural* **flies**

fly[2] *noun* One of a large group of insects, including the common housefly, that have one pair of thin, clear wings.
fly (flī) □*noun, plural* **flies**

flyer *noun* Another spelling for **flier.**
fly·er (flī′ər) □*noun, plural* **flyers**

flying fish *noun* An ocean fish with large fins that it uses like wings as it leaps out of the water and glides through the air.

flying saucer *noun* An unidentified flying object shaped like a saucer that many people believe comes from outer space.

foal *noun* A young horse, zebra, or donkey.
foal (fōl) □*noun, plural* **foals**

foam *noun* A mass of tiny bubbles; froth: *white foam on the crest of the wave.*
□*verb* To form foam: *The soda foamed and overflowed the glass.*
foam (fōm) □*noun, plural* **foams** □*verb* **foamed, foaming, foams**

foam rubber *noun* A light, spongy rubber used for pillows, mattresses, and cushions.

focus *noun* **1.** A point at which rays of light meet after being bent by a lens. **2.** The distance from the surface of a lens to the point at which rays of light meet. **3.** The adjustment at which a lens gives its sharpest image: *Now the microscope is in focus.* **4.** A center of activity or interest: *The baby was the focus of attention.*
□*verb* **1.** To bring or come to a focus: *The lens focused the light on the leaf.* **2.** To adjust to produce a clear image: *He focused the telescope on the moon.*
fo·cus (fō′kəs) □*noun, plural* **focuses** □*verb* **focused, focusing, focuses**

fodder *noun* Dry food such as chopped corn stalks and hay for farm animals; feed.
fod·der (fŏd′ər) □*noun, plural* **fodders**

foe *noun* An enemy.
foe (fō) □*noun, plural* **foes**

fog *noun* **1.** A mass of tiny drops of water that looks like a cloud and is on or near the ground. **2.** A confused condition of mind: *I got no sleep and went around in a fog the next day.*
□*verb* To cover or be covered with a fog or with something like a fog: *My glasses fogged up in the steamy room.*
fog (fôg) □*noun, plural* **fogs** □*verb* **fogged, fogging, fogs**

foggy *adjective* **1.** Full of or covered with fog: *a foggy mountain top.* **2.** Confused; vague: *She had only a foggy idea of what had gone wrong.*
fog·gy (fô′gē) □*adjective* **foggier, foggiest**

foil[1] *verb* To prevent from being successful: *Our unexpected return foiled the thief.*
foil (foil) □*verb* **foiled, foiling, foils**

foil

a	bat	ī	bite	o͞o	tool	*th*	feather
ā	make	î	fierce	ou	out	th	bath
â	dare	o	dot	u	nut	hw	wheat
ä	father	ō	no	û	turn	zh	measure
e	net	ô	law, for	ch	church	ə	about, open
ē	be	oi	soil	ng	ring		pencil, atom
i	dip	oo	look	sh	shade		circus

foil² *noun* A very thin, flexible sheet of metal: *aluminum foil.*
foil (foil) □*noun, plural* **foils**

foil³ *noun* A long, light, thin fencing sword with a button on the tip to prevent injuries.
foil (foil) □*noun, plural* **foils**

fold¹ *verb* **1.** To bend over so that one part lies on another: *He folded the paper in thirds.* **2.** To clasp together: *She folded her hands.* **3.** To embrace: *She folded the baby in her arms.*
□*noun* A crease, line, pleat, or hollow made by folding: *The curtains hung in loose folds.*
fold (fōld) □*verb* **folded, folding, folds**
□*noun, plural* **folds**

fold² *noun* A pen for sheep.
fold (fōld) □*noun, plural* **folds**

folder *noun* **1.** A folded sheet of heavy paper or cardboard used to hold loose papers. **2.** A booklet or pamphlet made of folded sheets of paper: *a travel folder.*
fold·er (fōl′ dər) □*noun, plural* **folders**

foliage *noun* The leaves of plants or trees.
fo·li·age (fō′ lē ij) □*noun*

folk *noun* **1.** People of a particular kind: *Young folk have a great deal of energy.* **2. folks** People in general: *Folks say the mayor is honest.* **3. folks** The members of one's family; relatives: *He sent his love to my folks.*
□*adjective* Of, created by, or coming from the common people: *folk music; a folk dance.*
folk (fōk) □*noun, plural* **folk** or **folks**
□*adjective*

folklore *noun* Traditional beliefs, legends, and customs of a people passed on from generation to generation.
folk·lore (fōk′ lôr′) □*noun*

follow *verb* **1.** To go or come after: *Night follows day.* **2.** To proceed or walk along: *We followed a path beside the sea.* **3.** To act in agreement with; obey: *You must follow directions.* **4.** To listen or watch closely: *I followed the baseball game on the radio.* **5.** To understand; grasp: *I don't follow your argument.*
fol·low (fol′ ō) □*verb* **followed, following, follows**

follower *noun* **1.** Somone or something that follows. **2.** Someone who follows the beliefs, teachings, or theories of another: *a follower of Buddha.*
fol·low·er (fol′ ō ər) □*noun, plural* **followers**

following *adjective* Coming just after; next: *We left for the country the following day.*
fol·low·ing (fol′ ō ing) □*adjective*

folly *noun* Lack of good sense; foolishness: *It was folly to waste money gambling.*
fol·ly (fol′ ē) □*noun*

fond *adjective* Having or expressing feelings of love; affectionate: *She's fond of her sister.*
fond (fond) □*adjective* **fonder, fondest**

fondle *verb* To touch or pat in a loving way; caress: *She fondled the rabbit.*
fon·dle (fon′ dəl) □*verb* **fondled, fondling, fondles**

fondle

font *noun* A basin that holds water for baptism.
font (font) □*noun, plural* **fonts**

food *noun* Something that plants, animals, or people eat or take in to keep them alive and help them grow; nourishment.
food (fōōd) □*noun, plural* **foods**

fool *noun* **1.** A person without good sense: *Only a fool would walk in that street at night.* **2.** A person formerly kept to entertain at the court of a king or nobleman.
□*verb* **1.** To trick; mislead: *Your disguise didn't fool anybody.* **2.** To joke, pretend, or tease: *Don't be angry; I'm just fooling.* **3.** To waste time; play: *He fooled around outdoors.*
fool (fōōl) □*noun, plural* **fools** □*verb* **fooled, fooling, fools**

foolish *adjective* Lacking or showing a lack of good sense: *a foolish idea.*
fool·ish (fōō′ lish) □*adjective*

foolish

foot   *noun* **1.** The part of the leg of a person or animal that touches the ground in standing or walking. **2.** The lowest part of something high or long; bottom: *the foot of a mountain.* **3.** The part that is opposite the head: *the foot of the bed.* **4.** A unit of length that equals 12 inches, or 30.4 centimeters.
▢*verb* To pay: *She footed the bill for the trip.*
foot (foot) ▢*noun, plural* **feet** ▢*verb* **footed, footing, foots**

football   *noun* **1.** A game in which two teams of 11 players each try to carry or kick a ball over the other team's goal. **2.** The oval ball used in football.
foot·ball (foŏt′bôl′) ▢*noun, plural* **footballs**

footing   *noun* **1.** A firm placing of the feet: *He lost his footing on the icy street.* **2.** A safe place on which to walk or stand: *The steep hill offered no footing.* **3.** A position with respect to others; standing: *The two rivals were on an equal footing.*
foot·ing (foŏt′ing) ▢*noun, plural* **footings**

footnote   *noun* A note at the bottom of a page about something on the page.
foot·note (foŏt′nōt′) ▢*noun, plural* **footnotes**

footprint   *noun* A mark left by a foot or shoe.
foot·print (foŏt′print′) ▢*noun, plural* **footprints**

footstep   *noun* **1.** A step of the foot. **2.** The sound of a foot stepping: *I heard footsteps in the next room.*
foot·step (foŏt′step′) ▢*noun, plural* **footsteps**

footstool   *noun* A low stool on which to rest the feet.
foot·stool (foŏt′stool′) ▢*noun, plural* **footstools**

for   *preposition* **1.** Throughout the time of; during: *He ran for an hour.* **2.** Over the distance or extent of: *I drove for 50 miles in the snow.* **3.** In the amount of: *a bill for $50.* **4.** As being equal to, especially in an exchange: *bought a ticket for $6.* **5.** Used to indicate the person or thing that receives or benefits from an action: *Will you run an errand for me? They gave a party for everyone on the block.* **6.** In favor or support of: *We all voted for her.* **7.** Used to indicate the purpose, goal, or aim of an action: *ran for president; was hunting for a pair of gloves; went shopping for new clothes.* **8.** In order to go to or reach: *They left for town an hour ago.* **9.** Meant to be sent or given to: *That package is for you.* **10.** Because of: *He was punished for lying.* **11.** As being: *She is*

often mistaken for her sister.
▢*conjunction* Because; since: *He could not see for he was blind.*
for (fôr *or* fər) ▢*preposition* ▢*conjunction*

forage   *noun* Food, such as grass or pasture, for domestic animals, such as horses and cattle, that graze.
▢*verb* To search for forage.
for·age (fôr′ij) ▢*noun* ▢*verb* **foraged, foraging, forages**

forbade   *verb* The past tense of **forbid**: *He forbade me to stay out after dark.*
for·bade (fər **bad′** *or* fər **bād′**) ▢*verb*

forbid   *verb* To order not to do; prohibit: *The hospital rule forbids smoking.*
for·bid (fər **bid′**) ▢*verb* **forbade, forbidden, forbidding**

SYNONYMS: **forbid, outlaw, prohibit**

These verbs mean to refuse to allow: *My parents forbid me to play football. Many people want the government to outlaw the hunting of whales. This restaurant prohibits smoking.*

---

forbidden   *verb* The past participle of **forbid**: *The mayor has forbidden the police to strike.*
for·bid·den (fər **bid′**ən) ▢*verb*

force   *noun* **1.** Strength; power: *the force of the wind; a personality of great force.* **2.** Physical strength used on someone or something: *We used force to open the window.* **3.** Something that can start, change, or stop the motion of a body: *the force of gravity.* **4.** A group of people who are organized for action or are available for service: *a work force; a police force.*
▢*verb* **1.** To make someone do something: *I forced him to apologize.* **2.** To move, make, or get by pressure: *I forced my way to the front of the crowd.* **3.** To break open with force: *He forced the lock on the window.*
force (fôrs) ▢*noun, plural* **forces** ▢*verb* **forced, forcing, forces**

ford   *noun* A place in a body of water that is shallow enough to walk or ride across.

a	bat	ī	bite	oo	tool	*th*	feather
ā	make	î	fierce	ou	out	th	bath
â	dare	o	dot	u	nut	hw	wheat
ä	father	ō	no	û	turn	zh	measure
e	net	ô	law, for	ch	church	ə	about, open
ē	be	oi	soil	ng	ring		pencil, atom
i	dip	oo	look	sh	shade		circus

□*verb* To cross at a ford: *They forded the stream on horseback.*
ford (fôrd) □*noun, plural* **fords** □*verb* **forded, fording, fords**

ford

forearm *noun* The part of the arm between the wrist and the elbow.
fore·arm (fôr′ärm′) □*noun, plural* **forearms**

forecast *verb* To say what will happen ahead of time; predict: *The radio forecasts rain.*
□*noun* A prediction of things to come: *I listened to the 10 o'clock weather forecast.*
fore·cast (fôr′kast′) □*verb* **forecast** or **forecasted, forecasting, forecasts** □*noun, plural* **forecasts**

forefather *noun* An ancestor. —See Synonyms at **ancestor.**
fore·fath·er (fôr′fä′thər) □*noun, plural* **forefathers**

forefinger *noun* The finger next to the thumb.
fore·fin·ger (fôr′fing′gər) □*noun, plural* **forefingers**

forefoot *noun* One of the front feet of an animal.
fore·foot (fôr′foot′) □*noun, plural* **forefeet**

forefoot

foregone *adjective* Already decided or done: *The team's victory was a foregone conclusion.*
fore·gone (fôr′gôn′) □*adjective*

foreground *noun* The part of a scene or picture that is or seems to be closest to the person looking at it.
fore·ground (fôr′ground′) □*noun, plural* **foregrounds**

foreground
A basket in the foreground

forehead *noun* The part of the face above the eyes.
fore·head (fôr′id *or* fôr′hed′) □*noun, plural* **foreheads**

foreign *adjective* **1.** Being outside or different from one's own country: *foreign lands.* **2.** Of, from, or for a different country: *a foreign language; our government's foreign policy.*
for·eign (fôr′in) □*adjective*

foreigner *noun* Someone from a foreign country.
for·eign·er (fôr′ə nər) □*noun, plural* **foreigners**

foreleg *noun* One of the front legs of an animal.
fore·leg (fôr′leg′) □*noun, plural* **forelegs**

foreman *noun* **1.** Someone in charge of a group of workers. **2.** The chairman of a jury.
fore·man (fôr′mən) □*noun, plural* **foremen**

foremost *adjective* First in time, place, rank, or position; most important: *She is the foremost expert on the subject.*
fore·most (fôr′mōst′) □*adjective*

forerunner *noun* Someone or something that comes before another in time: *I have the headache that is the forerunner of a cold.*
fore·run·ner (fôr′run′ər) □*noun, plural* **forerunners**

foresaw *verb* The past tense of **foresee:** *I foresaw what was going to happen.*
fore·saw (fôr sô´) □*verb*

foresee *verb* To see or realize in advance: *I did not foresee how cold it would get.*
fore·see (fôr sē´) □*verb* **foresaw, foreseen, forseeing, foresees**

foreseen *verb* The past participle of **foresee:** *She had foreseen the problem.*
fore·seen (fôr sēn´) □*verb*

foresight *noun* The ability to foresee and especially to plan for the future: *We didn't have the foresight to bring enough money on our trip.*
fore·sight (fôr´ sīt´) □*noun*

forest *noun* A thick growth of trees and plants that covers a large area.
for·est (fôr´ ist) □*noun, plural* **forests**

foretell *verb* To tell beforehand; predict: *Who could foretell what would happen?*
fore·tell (fôr tel´) □*verb* **foretold, foretelling, foretells**

foretold *verb* The past tense and past participle of **foretell:** *The fortuneteller foretold the future. The wizard had foretold the great war.*
fore·told (fôr tōld´) □*verb*

forever *adverb* **1.** For all time; always: *a cathedral that will stand forever.* **2.** At all times; constantly: *He is forever complaining.*
for·ev·er (fər ev´ ər) □*adverb*

forfeit *verb* To lose or give up through a failure, error, or offense: *We forfeited the golf match because we didn't show up for the game.* □*noun* Something forfeited.
for·feit (fôr´ fit) □*verb* **forfeited, forfeiting, forfeits** □*noun, plural* **forfeits**

forgave *verb* The past tense of **forgive:** *The teacher forgave them for being late.*
for·gave (fər gāv´) □*verb*

forge[1] *noun* A furnace or hearth where metal is heated so that it can be hammered or bent into shape.
□*verb* **1.** To work and shape by heating and hammering: *The blacksmith forged iron into horseshoes.* **2.** To make or form: *The governor forged an agreement with the state workers.* **3.** To copy or imitate in order to deceive; counterfeit: *forge a signature.*
forge (fôrj) □*noun, plural* **forges** □*verb* **forged, forging, forges**

forge[2] *verb* To move forward in a slow but steady way or with a final burst of speed: *We forged on through the deep snow.*

forge (fôrj) □*verb* **forged, forging, forges**

forget *verb* **1.** To be unable to remember or think of: *I forgot the telephone number.* **2.** To fail to do or think of; overlook: *I forgot to make an appointment with the dentist.*
for·get (fər get´) □*verb* **forgot, forgotten** or **forgot, forgetting, forgets**

forgetful *adjective* Likely to forget: *The forgetful man left his wallet at home.*
for·get·ful (fər get´ fəl) □*adjective*

forget-me-not *noun* A plant with clusters of small blue flowers.
for·get-me-not (fər get´ mē not´) □*noun, plural* **forget-me-nots**

forget-me-not

forgive *verb* To stop being angry at; pardon: *He forgave her for being rude.* —See Synonyms at **pardon.**
for·give (fər giv´) □*verb* **forgave, forgiven, forgiving, forgives**

forgiven *verb* The past participle of **forgive:** *I have forgiven him for forgetting my name.*
for·giv·en (fər giv´ ən) □*verb*

forgot *verb* The past tense and a past participle of **forget:** *I forgot where I left the book.*
for·got (fər got´) □*verb*

forgotten *verb* A past participle of **forget:** *She had forgotten to tell him she would be out.*
for·got·ten (fər got´ ən) □*verb*

a	bat	ī	bite	oo	tool	*th*	feather
ā	make	i	fierce	ou	out	th	bath
â	dare	o	dot	u	nut	hw	wheat
ä	father	ō	no	û	turn	zh	measure
e	net	ô	law, for	ch	church	ə	about, open
ē	be	oi	soil	ng	ring		pencil, atom
i	dip	oo	look	sh	shade		circus

fork *noun* **1.** A tool with two or more sharp points at one end and a handle at the other, used to take up food or pitch hay. **2.** A place where something separates into parts or branches: *We came to a fork in the road.* □*verb* **1.** To take up or pitch with a fork: *The farmers forked hay into the barn.* **2.** To divide into parts or branches: *The road forks on the other side of the mountain.*
fork (fôrk) □*noun, plural* **forks** □*verb* **forked, forking, forks**

fork

form *noun* **1.** The shape, structure, or outline of something: *cookies in the form of stars and hearts.* **2.** Kind; variety: *Democracy is a form of government.* **3.** A way of doing something; manner: *She can play tennis, but her form is weak.* **4.** A document with blanks to be filled in: *a tax form.* **5.** Any of the ways in which a word may be spelled or pronounced: *"Flyer" is a form of the word "flier."*
□*verb* **1.** To give shape or form to: *The sculptor formed the marble into a beautiful statue.* **2.** To come into being: *Rust formed on the iron pipe.* **3.** To make up; constitute: *The six girls formed a committee to choose a speaker.*
form (fôrm) □*noun, plural* **forms** □*verb* **formed, forming, forms**

formal *adjective* **1.** Following strict rules, customs, and forms: *a formal wedding.* **2.** Stiff and cold: *a formal greeting.* **3.** Of or for occasions where elegant clothes are worn and fine manners are expected: *a formal dinner.* □*noun* **1.** An occasion, especially a dance, requiring formal clothing. **2.** An evening gown.
for·mal (fôr′məl) □*adjective* □*noun, plural* **formals**

formation *noun* **1.** The act or process of forming; development: *the formation of buds on a tree.* **2.** Something that has been formed: *a cloud formation.* **3.** A particular arrangement: *The geese flew in a V formation.*
for·ma·tion (fôr mā′shən) □*noun, plural* **formations**

formation
A V formation

former *adjective* **1.** Happening, having been, or coming earlier in time: *a former member of Congress; former ages.* **2.** Being the first of two: *He tried law and medicine but enjoyed only the former study.*
for·mer (fôr′mər) □*adjective*

formula *noun* **1.** A fixed way of doing something; method: *There is no formula for writing good stories.* **2.** A set of symbols that tells what is in a chemical compound: *The formula for table salt is NaCl.* **3.** A rule in mathematics, often written in symbols.
for·mu·la (fôr′myə lə) □*noun, plural* **formulas**

forsake *verb* To give up or leave; abandon: *He forsook teaching to become a musician.*
for·sake (fôr sāk′) □*verb* **forsook, forsaken, forsaking, forsakes**

forsaken *verb* The past participle of **forsake**: *She has forsaken all her friends.*
for·sak·en (fôr sā′kən) □*verb*

forsook *verb* The past tense of **forsake**: *He forsook his studies and joined the army.*
for·sook (fôr sook′) □*verb*

forsythia *noun* A garden shrub with yellow flowers that bloom early in spring.
for·syth·i·a (fôr sith′ē ə) □*noun, plural* **forsythias**

fort *noun* An area or building that has been fortified against possible attacks by enemies.
fort (fôrt) ◻*noun, plural* **forts**

fort

forth *adverb* **1.** Out into view: *Water gushed forth from the fountain.* **2.** Forward or onward: *From this moment forth I will try harder.*
forth (fôrth) ◻*adverb*

fortieth *noun* **1.** In a group of people or things that are in numbered order, the one that matches the number forty. **2.** One of forty equal parts, written ¹/₄₀.
◻*adjective* Coming after the thirty-ninth.
for·ti·eth (fôr′tē ith) ◻*noun, plural* **fortieths**

fortify *verb* **1.** To make stronger or more secure: *They fortified the castle with a stone wall.* **2.** To add to in order to improve or strengthen: *The cereal was fortified with vitamins.*
for·ti·fy (fôr′tə fī′) ◻*verb* **fortified, fortifying, fortifies**

fortress *noun* A fort or other strong place built to resist attacks.
for·tress (fôr′tris) ◻*noun, plural* **fortresses**

fortunate *adjective* Having or bringing good fortune; lucky: *How fortunate she is to have so many friends.*
for·tu·nate (fôr′chə nit) ◻*adjective*

fortune *noun* **1.** Luck; chance: *It was my good fortune to be there when he sang.* **2.** What will happen in the future: *It may be his fortune to fail.* **3.** A large amount of money or property; wealth: *They made a fortune in the steel business.*
for·tune (fôr′chən) ◻*noun, plural* **fortunes**

fortuneteller *noun* Someone who claims to be able to foretell the future.
for·tune·tell·er (fôr′chən tel′ər) ◻*noun, plural* **fortunetellers**

forty *noun* A number equal to the product of 4 × 10; 40.
◻*adjective* Being ten more than thirty.
for·ty (fôr′tē) ◻*noun, plural* **forties**
◻*adjective*

forum *noun* **1.** The main public square of an ancient Roman city, serving as a market and a place for public assemblies. **2.** A meeting at which matters of public interest are discussed: *We held a forum to discuss air pollution.*
fo·rum (fôr′əm) ◻*noun, plural* **forums**

forward *adjective* **1.** At, near, or belonging to the front of something: *I had a seat in the forward car of the train.* **2.** Going or moving toward the front: *took a forward step.*
◻*adverb* To or toward what is ahead or in front: *He moved forward. I look forward to my vacation.*
◻*verb* To send on to another destination: *I forwarded the package to your new address.*
◻*noun* A player in certain games whose position is toward the front line: *She's a forward on the basketball team.*
for·ward (fôr′wərd) ◻*adjective* ◻*adverb*
◻*verb* **forwarded, forwarding, forwards**
◻*noun, plural* **forwards**

forwards *adverb* Another spelling for the adverb **forward.**
for·wards (fôr′wərdz) ◻*adverb*

fossil *noun* The remains or traces of a plant or animal that lived long ago, embedded in rocks and the earth's crust.
fos·sil (fos′əl) ◻*noun, plural* **fossils**

fossil

foster *verb* To help grow or develop: *My teacher fostered my love of reading.*
◻*adjective* Receiving or giving care in a family that is not related by blood or adoption: *her*

a	bat	ī	bite	o͞o	tool	*th*	feather
ā	make	î	fierce	ou	out	th	bath
â	dare	o	dot	u	nut	hw	wheat
ä	father	ō	no	û	turn	zh	measure
e	net	ô	law, for	ch	church	ə	about, open
ē	be	oi	soil	ng	ring		pencil, atom
i	dip	o͝o	look	sh	shade		circus

foster daughter; a foster father.
fos·ter (fô′stər) ☐*verb* **fostered, fostering, fosters** ☐*adjective*

fought *verb* The past tense and past participle of **fight:** *The army fought for freedom. The two boxers have fought each other often.*
fought (fôt) ☐*verb*

foul *adjective* **1.** Disgusting to smell, see, or taste: *the foul odor of rotten meat.* **2.** Full of dirt; filthy: *His clothes were foul rags.* **3.** Evil; wicked: *Murder is a foul crime.* **4.** Very unpleasant; nasty: *foul weather.* **5.** Not according to the rules of a game or sport: *The boxer received a foul blow below the belt.* **6.** Outside the foul lines in a baseball game: *a foul ball.* ☐*noun* **1.** A move or play that is against the rules of a game or sport: *The hockey player committed a foul by tripping his opponent.* **2.** A ball hit outside the foul lines in baseball. ☐*verb* **1.** To make foul: *Exhaust from the car's engine fouled the air.* **2.** To entangle or become entangled: *The anchor fouled on a rock.* **3.** To hit a baseball outside the foul lines.
foul (foul) ☐*adjective* **fouler, foulest** ☐*noun,* *plural* **fouls** ☐*verb* **fouled, fouling, fouls**

foul line *noun* Either of the two straight lines that run from home plate through first or third base to the end of a baseball field.

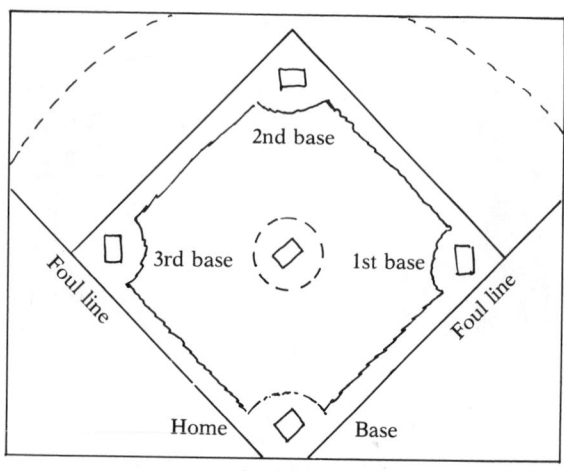

foul line

found¹ *verb* The past tense and past participle of **find:** *I found my glasses. They have never found their lost puppy.*
found (found) ☐*verb*

found² *verb* To bring into being; establish: *She founded a company.*
found (found) ☐*verb* **founded, founding, founds**

foundation *noun* **1.** The base on which a structure stands: *The house has a concrete foundation.* **2.** Supporting facts or reasons; basis: *There is no foundation for that accusation.*
foun·da·tion (foun dā′shən) ☐*noun, plural* **foundations**

foundry *noun* A place where metal is melted and cast.
foun·dry (foun′drē) ☐*noun, plural* **foundries**

fountain *noun* **1.** A stream or jet of water, as for drinking or decoration. **2.** A point of origin; source: *a fountain of wisdom.*
foun·tain (foun′tən) ☐*noun, plural* **fountains**

fountain pen *noun* A pen with a tube of ink inside that feeds the writing point.

four *noun* A number equal to the sum of 3 + 1; 4.
☐*adjective* Being one more than three.
four (fôr) ☐*noun, plural* **fours** ☐*adjective*

fourteen *noun* A number equal to the sum of 13 + 1; 14.
☐*adjective* Being one more than thirteen.
four·teen (fôr′tēn′) ☐*noun, plural* **fourteens** ☐*adjective*

fourteenth *noun* **1.** In a group of people or things that are in numbered order, the one that matches the number fourteen. **2.** One of fourteen equal parts, written $\frac{1}{14}$.
☐*adjective:* Coming after the thirteenth.
four·teenth (fôr′tēnth′) ☐*noun, plural* **fourteenths** ☐*adjective*

fourth *noun* **1.** In a group of people or things that are in numbered order, the one that matches the number four. **2.** One of four equal parts, written $\frac{1}{4}$.
☐*adjective* Coming after the third.
fourth (fôrth) ☐*noun, plural* **fourths** ☐*adjective*

fowl *noun* A bird such as a chicken, duck, or turkey that is raised or hunted for food.
fowl (foul) ☐*noun, plural* **fowl** or **fowls**

fox *noun* **1.** An animal that is related to dogs and wolves and has a pointed snout and a long, bushy tail. **2.** A clever or sly person.
fox (foks) ☐*noun, plural* **foxes**

fraction *noun* **1.** A small part: *I moved a fraction of a step.* **2.** A number that expresses one or more equal parts of a whole. The fraction $\frac{7}{10}$ means the whole is divided into 10 equal parts and that 7 of them make up the quantity expressed by the fraction.
frac·tion (frak′shən) ☐*noun, plural* **fractions**

fracture *noun* A break or crack, as in a bone. □*verb* To break or crack: *fracture a rib.*
frac·ture (frak′chər) □*noun, plural* **fractures** □*verb* **fractured, fracturing, fractures**

fragile *adjective* Easily broken or damaged: *a fragile crystal vase.*
frag·ile (fraj′əl) □*adjective*

fragment *noun* A piece broken off: *a fragment of pottery.*
frag·ment (frag′mənt) □*noun, plural* **fragments**

fragrance *noun* 1. A sweet or pleasant smell: *the fragrance of lilacs.* 2. Perfume.
fra·grance (frā′grəns) □*noun, plural* **fragrances**

fragrant *adjective* Having a sweet or pleasant smell: *air fragrant with flowers.*
fra·grant (frā′grənt) □*adjective*

frail *adjective* 1. Thin and not very strong; weak: *a frail child.* 2. Easily broken; fragile: *a frail thread.*
frail (frāl) □*adjective* **frailer, frailest**

frame *noun* 1. A structure that shapes, supports, or borders something: *a door frame; a picture frame.* 2. The structure of a human body: *an athlete with a big frame.*
□*verb* 1. To put in a frame; border: *We framed the oil painting.* 2. To put together; build or design: *The commission framed a trade treaty.*
frame (frām) □*noun, plural* **frames** □*verb* **framed, framing, frames**

frame

framework *noun* A structure that shapes or supports something: *The ship has a framework of steel.*
frame·work (frām′wûrk′) □*noun, plural* **frameworks**

frank *adjective* Open and sincere in expressing one's thoughts and feelings: *The coach was frank with me about his reasons for not selecting me for the team.*
frank (frangk) □*adjective* **franker, frankest**

frankfurter *noun* A smoked sausage made of beef or of beef and pork.
frank·furt·er (frangk′fər tər) □*noun, plural* **frankfurters**

frantic *adjective* Very much excited with fear or nervousness: *She was frantic when the child didn't come home.*
fran·tic (fran′tik) □*adjective*

fraternity *noun* An organization of boys or men, as at a college.
fra·ter·ni·ty (frə tûr′ni tē) □*noun, plural* **fraternities**

fraud *noun* 1. A dishonest act that is intended to cheat or deceive: *He didn't own the house he sold and was arrested for fraud.* 2. Someone who pretends to be something he is not: *That fraud claims he's a scientist.*
fraud (frôd) □*noun, plural* **frauds**

fray *verb* To wear away so that loose threads show: *The sleeves of his new jacket frayed.*
fray (frā) □*verb* **frayed, fraying, frays**

freak *noun* A person, event, or thing that is abnormal, unusual, or strange: *The snowstorm in June was a freak.*
freak (frēk) □*noun, plural* **freaks**

freckle *noun* A small brown spot on the skin.
freck·le (frek′əl) □*noun, plural* **freckles**

freckle

a bat	ī bite	o͞o tool	*th* feather
ā make	î fierce	ou out	th bath
â dare	o dot	u nut	hw wheat
ä father	ō no	û turn	zh measure
e net	ô law, for	ch church	ə about, open
ē be	oi soil	ng ring	pencil, atom
i dip	oo look	sh shade	circus

free *adjective* **1.** Not controlled by another: *a free nation.* **2.** Not affected by a particular condition; clear: *free of infection; free from fear.* **3.** Not filled or busy; available: *Do you have a free moment?* **4.** Costing nothing: *a free ticket to the movies.*
□*adverb* Without charge: *Children can go to the zoo free.*
□*verb* To make or set free: *The sheriff freed the prisoner.*
free (frē) □*adjective* **freer, freest** □*adverb*
□*verb* **freed, freeing, frees**

freedom *noun* **1.** The condition of being free: *The rebels fought for freedom.* **2.** Ease of action or movement: *His broken arm has healed, and he can now use it with total freedom.* —See Synonyms at **liberty.**
free·dom (frē′dəm) □*noun, plural* **freedoms**

freeway *noun* A highway on which no tolls are charged.
free·way (frē′wā′) □*noun, plural* **freeways**

freeze *verb* **1.** To change from a liquid to a solid by loss of heat; harden with cold: *The lake freezes in winter. I froze the meat for later use.* **2.** To block or become blocked with ice: *The radiator of our car froze.* **3.** To become motionless or fixed: *She froze when she saw the audience.* **4.** To be or become painfully cold: *The furnace broke down and we froze.*
freeze (frēz) □*verb* **froze, frozen, freezing, freezes**

freezer *noun* A refrigerator or part of a refrigerator used to freeze food and store frozen foods.
freez·er (frē′zər) □*noun, plural* **freezers**

freight *noun* **1.** Goods carried in a vehicle such as a train or truck; cargo. **2.** The act or business of transporting goods.
freight (frāt) □*noun, plural* **freights**

freighter *noun* A ship that carries goods.
freight·er (frā′tər) □*noun, plural* **freighters**

freighter

French *noun* **1.** The Romance language of France. **2.** The people of France.
□*adjective* Of France, the French, or their language.
French (french) □*noun* □*adjective*

French fries *plural noun* Potatoes that are sliced into strips and fried in deep fat.

French horn *noun* A brass musical instrument with a long coiled tube that flares from a narrow mouthpiece to a wide bell at the end.

frenzy *noun* Wild excitement: *She was in a frenzy of delight when she won the prize.*
fren·zy (fren′zē) □*noun, plural* **frenzies**

WORD HISTORY: **frenzy**

Frenzy comes from a Greek word that means "a mental disturbance." This word was derived from a Greek word for "mind." *Frenzy* is related to the word *frantic,* which also comes from the same Greek word for "mind."

frequency *noun* **1.** The number of times something happens within a given period of time: *a magazine that appears with a frequency of four times a year.* **2.** The condition of happening often: *The frequency of the robberies has frightened the citizens.*
fre·quen·cy (frē′kwən sē) □*noun, plural* **frequencies**

frequent *adjective* Happening often: *He made frequent visits to the museum.*
fre·quent (frē′kwənt) □*adjective*

fresh *adjective* **1.** Just made, grown, or gathered: *fresh cake; fresh fruit.* **2.** Not salty: *fresh water.* **3.** New or different: *I began a fresh paragraph. He put on a fresh shirt.* **4.** Refreshing; brisk: *a fresh spring breeze.* **5.** Rude; impolite: *Don't be fresh with your teacher.*
fresh (fresh) □*adjective* **fresher, freshest**

freshman *noun* A student in the first year of high school or college.
fresh·man (fresh′mən) □*noun, plural* **freshmen**

freshwater *adjective* Of or living in water that is not salty: *a freshwater fish.*
fresh·wa·ter (fresh′wô′tər) □*adjective*

fret¹ To be or cause to be troubled, worried, or annoyed: *She fretted about the exam all day.*
fret (fret) □*verb* **fretted, fretting, frets**

fret² *noun* One of the ridges placed across the neck of a stringed musical instrument.
fret (fret) □*noun, plural* **frets**

friar *noun* A member of a religious order for men in the Roman Catholic Church.
fri·ar (frī′ ər) □*noun, plural* **friars**

friction *noun* **1.** The rubbing of one object against another: *The friction between the ropes caused them both to fray.* **2.** A force that slows or stops the motion of two objects touching each other: *He waxed his skis to lessen the friction.* **3.** Conflict, as among people with different ideas; disagreement: *There was no friction in the family.*
fric·tion (frik′ shən) □*noun*

Friday *noun* The sixth day of the week.
Fri·day (frī′ dē *or* frī′ dā′) □*noun, plural* **Fridays**

WORD HISTORY: **Friday**

Friday is named after Frigg, the queen of the gods in Germanic mythology.

---

fried *verb* The past tense and past participle of **fry**: *I fried potatoes. He had fried the fish.*
fried (frīd) □*verb*

friend *noun* Someone one knows and likes.
friend (frend) □*noun, plural* **friends**

friendly *adjective* **1.** Showing friendship; warm and kind: *friendly neighbors; a friendly smile.* **2.** Not hostile or fighting: *The natives on the island were friendly.*
friend·ly (frend′ lē) □*adjective* **friendlier, friendliest**

friendship *noun* The close feeling or relationship between friends: *He showed his friendship by visiting me when I was sick.*
friend·ship (frend′ ship′) □*noun, plural* **friendships**

friendship

fright *noun* Sudden, intense fear: *I jumped with fright at the sound of thunder.*
fright (frīt) □*noun, plural* **frights**

frighten *verb* **1.** To make or become afraid; alarm: *The ghost story frightened the child.* **2.** To force or drive by frightening: *The alarm frightened the burglar away.*
fright·en (frīt′ ən) □*verb* **frightened, frightening, frightens**

frigid *adjective* **1.** Very cold: *a frigid day; frigid water.* **2.** Cold in manner; unfriendly: *She stopped me with a frigid stare.*
frig·id (frij′ id) □*adjective*

frill *noun* **1.** A ruffle. **2.** An extra feature, especially one just for show: *a new car with a lot of frills.*
fill (fril) □*noun, plural* **frills**

fringe *noun* **1.** A border made of hanging cords or strips. **2.** Something like a fringe: *The clown had a fringe of hair on his head.*
fringe (frinj) □*noun, plural* **fringes**

fringe

frog *noun* A small animal that has smooth skin, webbed feet, and long hind legs used for leaping. Frogs live in or near water.
frog (frôg *or* frog) □*noun, plural* **frogs**

frogman *noun* A swimmer who is equipped and trained to work under water.
frog·man (frôg′ man′ *or* frog′ man′) □*noun, plural* **frogmen**

frolic *verb* To behave playfully; romp: *The children frolicked happily on the lawn.*

a	bat	ī	bite	o͞o	tool	*th*	feather
ā	make	î	fierce	ou	out	th	bath
â	dare	o	dot	u	nut	hw	wheat
ä	father	ō	no	û	turn	zh	measure
e	net	ô	law, for	ch	church	ə	about, open
ē	be	oi	soil	ng	ring		pencil, atom
i	dip	oo	look	sh	shade		circus

frol·ic (frol′ik) □*verb* **frolicked, frolicking, frolics**

from *preposition* **1.** Starting at; beginning with: *We live 12 miles from the airport. The party is from eight to twelve o'clock.* **2.** Used to indicate an origin or cause: *a birthday card from a friend; tired from all the excitement.* **3.** Used to indicate separation or removal: *took some papers from the file; freedom from worry.* **4.** As being unlike or different: *She doesn't know one flower from another.*
from (frum *or* from *or* frəm) □*preposition*

frond *noun* The leaf of a fern or palm tree.
frond (frond) □*noun, plural* **fronds**

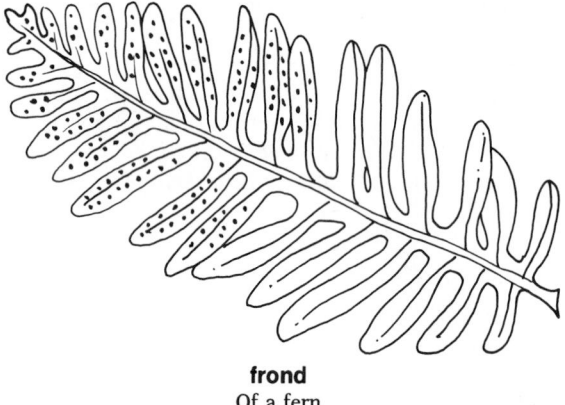

frond
Of a fern

front *noun* **1.** The forward part or surface of something: *a blackboard at the front of the room; a coat with buttons down the front.* **2.** Land that faces or borders a body of water or a street: *a lake front.* **3.** An area where fighting is taking place during a war: *The soldier was sent to the front.* **4.** The boundary between masses of air at different temperatures: *a warm front.*
□*adjective* In or facing the front: *the front seat of the car.*
□*verb* To face or look toward: *The building fronts on the river.*
front (frunt) □*noun, plural* **fronts**
□*adjective* □*verb* **fronted, fronting, fronts**

frontier *noun* **1.** A border between two countries. **2.** An area that marks the point of farthest settlement: *Life was hard on the western frontier.* **3.** An area or field not yet developed: *exploring new frontiers in medicine.*
fron·tier (frun tîr′) □*noun, plural* **frontiers**

frost *noun* **1.** A covering of tiny ice crystals formed by the freezing of water vapor in the air. **2.** Cold weather with temperatures below

freezing: *Frost damaged the orange crop.*
□*verb* **1.** To cover or become covered with or as if with frost: *The windows of the car frosted over.* **2.** To cover with frosting: *Mother frosted the cake.*
frost (frôst) □*noun, plural* **frosts** □*verb* **frosted, frosting, frosts**

frostbite *noun* Damage to tissue of the body caused by freezing.
frost·bite (frôst′bīt′) □*noun*

frosting *noun* A sweet glaze used to decorate cakes and cookies; icing.
frost·ing (frô′sting) □*noun, plural* **frostings**

frosty *adjective* Cold enough for frost; freezing: *a frosty winter night.*
frost·y (frô′stē) □*adjective* **frostier, frostiest**

froth *noun* Bubbles in or on a liquid; foam: *He beat the egg whites into a froth.*
□*verb* To form froth: *The soda frothed in the glass.*
froth (frôth) □*noun, plural* **froths** □*verb* **frothed, frothing, froths**

frown *verb* **1.** To wrinkle the forehead, as in thought: *She frowned over the puzzle.* **2.** To look with disapproval: *She frowns on smoking.*
□*noun* The act of wrinkling the forehead.
frown (froun) □*verb* **frowned, frowning, frowns** □*noun, plural* **frowns**

frown

froze *verb* The past tense of **freeze**: *The water froze in the pipe.*
froze (frōz) □*verb*

frozen *verb* The past participle of **freeze**: *The fruit had frozen on the trees and was spoiled.*
fro·zen (frō′zən) □*verb*

frugal *adjective* Careful not to waste money: *frugal housekeeper.* —See Synonyms at **eco-**

nomical.

fru·gal (froo′gəl) □*adjective*

fruit *noun* The part of a flowering plant that contains the seeds and is often sweet and used as food. Apples, bananas, and nuts are fruits.
fruit (froot) □*noun, plural* **fruit** or **fruits**

frustrate *verb* **1.** To prevent from achieving a goal: *She was frustrated from going to college by lack of money.* **2.** To discourage: *Her failure to be promoted frustrated her.*
frus·trate (frus′trāt′) □*verb* **frustrated, frustrating, frustrates**

fry *verb* To cook in hot oil or fat: *He fried the trout he had caught.*
fry (frī) □*verb* **fried, frying, fries**

ft. An abbreviation for **foot.**

fudge *noun* A soft rich candy, often flavored with chocolate.
fudge (fuj) □*noun*

fuel *noun* Something, such as coal or oil, that can be burned to give off heat or energy.
fu·el (fyoo′əl) □*noun, plural* **fuels**

fugitive *noun* Someone who runs away: *The fugitive was caught and put in jail.*
fu·gi·tive (fyoo′ji tiv) □*noun, plural* **fugitives**

–ful A suffix that means: **1.** Full of or having: *useful.* **2.** An amount that will fill: *armful.*

fulcrum *noun* The support on which a lever turns.
ful·crum (fool′krəm) □*noun, plural* **fulcrums**

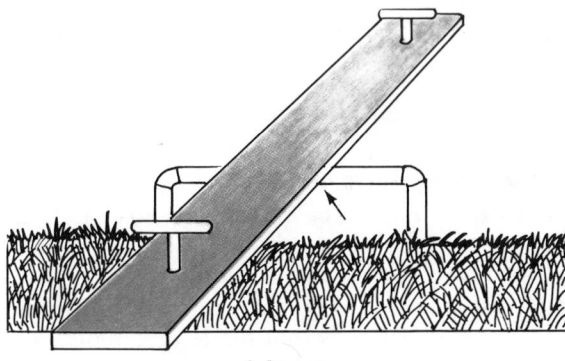

fulcrum

fulfill *verb* **1.** To carry out: *She fulfilled all her responsibilities.* **2.** To measure up to; satisfy: *He fulfilled all the requirements of the job.*
ful·fill (fool fil′) □*verb* **fulfilled, fulfilling, fulfills**

full *adjective* **1.** Holding all that is normal or possible: *a full pail; a full bus.* **2.** Complete in

every way; entire: *a full meal.* **3.** Rounded in shape or outline; plump: *a full face.* **4.** Made with a generous amount of fabric: *a full skirt.* □*adverb* Entirely; completely: *I know full well what you mean.*
full (fool) □*adjective* **fuller, fullest** □*adverb*

fully *adverb* **1.** Totally; completely: *He is fully aware of his problems.* **2.** No less than; at least: *She arrived fully an hour early.*
full·y (fool′ē) □*adverb*

fumble *verb* **1.** To grope or feel about clumsily: *She fumbled in the dark for the light switch.* **2.** To lose one's grasp on; drop: *The quarterback fumbled the ball.*
□*noun* An act of fumbling.
fum·ble (fum′bəl) □*verb* **fumbled, fumbling, fumbles** □*noun, plural* **fumbles**

fumble

fume *noun* A disagreeable or harmful smoke, gas, or vapor: *cigar fumes.*
□*verb* **1.** To produce or give off fumes. **2.** To be angry: *The woman fumed over the delay.*
fume (fyoom) □*noun, plural* **fumes** □*verb* **fumed, fuming, fumes**

fun *noun* Enjoyment; amusement: *We had fun at the party.*
make fun of To laugh at; ridicule.
fun (fun) □*noun*

a	bat	ī	bite	oo	tool	th	feather
ā	make	î	fierce	ou	out	th	bath
â	dare	o	dot	u	nut	hw	wheat
ä	father	ō	no	û	turn	zh	measure
e	net	ô	law, for	ch	church	ə	about, open
ē	be	oi	soil	ng	ring		pencil, atom
i	dip	oo	look	sh	shade		circus

function *noun* **1.** The normal or proper activity of a person or thing; purpose: *It is the lawyer's function to serve his client.* **2.** A formal ceremony or social gathering: *The opening of the exhibit was a big social function.*
□*verb* To have or perform a function: *The class president functions as our representative on the student council.*
func·tion (fungk′shən) □*noun, plural* **functions** □*verb* **functioned, functioning, functions**

fund *noun* **1.** A sum of money for a certain purpose: *a campaign fund.* **2. funds** Available money: *We lacked the funds to buy a new car.* **3.** A supply; stock: *a fund of knowledge.*
fund (fund) □*noun, plural* **funds**

fundamental *adjective* Forming or being a foundation; basic: *a fundamental belief.*
□*noun* A basic principle, fact, or part: *Reading is one of the fundamentals of education.*
fun·da·men·tal (fun′də men′təl) □*adjective* □*noun, plural* **fundamentals**

funeral *noun* The ceremonies held at the time of the burial of a dead person.
fu·ner·al (fyōō′nər əl) □*noun, plural* **funerals**

fungi *noun* A plural of **fungus.**
fun·gi (fun′jī′) □*noun*

fungus *noun* One of a group of plants, such as mushrooms, molds, and yeast, that have no flowers and leaves and no green coloring.
fun·gus (fung′gəs) □*noun, plural* **fungi** or **funguses**

fungus
Mushrooms

funnel *noun* **1.** A utensil shaped like a cone that narrows to a small, open tube and is used to direct a substance, such as a liquid, into a container. **2.** A pipe, such as the stack of a steamship, for the passage of smoke.
fun·nel (fun′əl) □*noun, plural* **funnels**

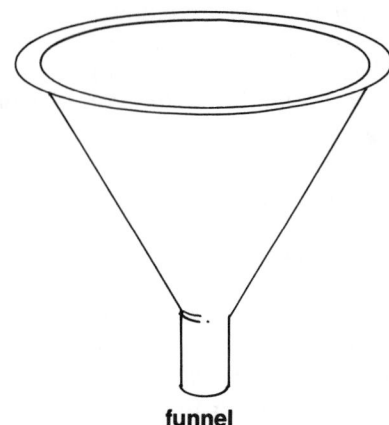

funnel

funny *adjective* **1.** Causing laughter or amusement: *I thought the joke was funny.* **2.** Strange; odd: *I heard a funny noise.*
fun·ny (fun′ē) □*adjective* **funnier, funniest**

fur *noun* **1.** The thick, soft hair that covers the body of certain animals, such as cats and foxes. **2.** The skin of an animal with fur on it.
fur (fûr) □*noun, plural* **furs**

furious *adjective* **1.** Extremely angry: *She was furious when I broke the vase.* **2.** Violent; intense: *a furious storm.* —See Synonyms at **intense.**
fu·ri·ous (fyoor′ē əs) □*adjective*

furnace *noun* An enclosed chamber in which fuel is burned to produce heat.
fur·nace (fûr′nis) □*noun, plural* **furnaces**

furnish *verb* **1.** To equip with furniture: *We furnished our new office.* **2.** To supply with what is wanted or needed: *They furnished the visitors with refreshments.*
fur·nish (fûr′nish) □*verb* **furnished, furnishing, furnishes**

furniture *noun* The movable items, such as chairs and tables, in a home or office.
fur·ni·ture (fûr′nə chər) □*noun*

furrow *noun* A long, narrow cut or groove in the ground, such as that made by a plow.
fur·row (fûr′ō) □*noun, plural* **furrows**

furry *adjective* Covered with or resembling fur: *a furry animal; thick, furry velvet.*
fur·ry (fûr′ē) □*adjective* **furrier, furriest**

further *adjective* **1.** More distant: *the further side of the street.* **2.** Additional: *He gave me further instructions.*
□*adverb* **1.** To a greater extent; more: *She was going to study further.* **2.** In addition; also:

I further feel that you should be there. **3.** At or to a more distant point: *Drive further south.*
□*verb* To help the progress of; advance: *He furthered his cause by being honest.*
fur·ther (fûr′ thər) □*adjective* □*adverb*
□*verb* **furthered, furthering, furthers**

furthermore *adverb* In addition; moreover: *I don't want to go, and furthermore, I can't.*
fur·ther·more (fûr′ thər môr′) □*adverb*

furthest *adjective* Most distant: *the furthest car in the line.*
□*adverb* **1.** To the greatest extent or degree: *She went furthest in her efforts.* **2.** At or to the most distant point: *Of all the family she had traveled furthest from home.*
fur·thest (fûr′ thist) □*adjective* □*adverb*

fury *noun* **1.** Violent anger; rage. **2.** Violent action; turbulence: *the fury of the tornado.*
fu·ry (fyoor′ ē) □*noun, plural* **furies**

fuse[1] *noun* A length of cord that is lighted at one end to carry a flame that ignites a charge at the other.
fuse (fyooz) □*noun, plural* **fuses**

fuse[2] *verb* **1.** To soften or reduce to a liquid by heating; melt: *The current fused the wires.* **2.** To unite by or as if by melting; blend: *The writer fused the two stories into one novel.*
□*noun* A device with a wire that melts and breaks an electrical circuit when the current becomes too strong.
fuse (fyooz) □*verb* **fused, fusing, fuses**
□*noun, plural* **fuses**

fuselage *noun* The central body of an airplane to which the wings and tail are attached.
fu·se·lage (fyoo′ sə läzh′ *or* fyoo′ sə lij)
□*noun, plural* **fuselages**

fuss *noun* Unnecessary excitement or useless activity about something unimportant: *They made a big fuss about having to walk three blocks to the store.*
□*verb* To become excited needlessly; make a fuss: *He fussed when the guests were late.*
fuss (fus) □*noun, plural* **fusses** □*verb*
fussed, fussing, fusses

fussy *adjective* Hard to please: *He is very fussy about what he eats.*
fuss·y (fus′ ē) □*adjective* **fussier, fussiest**

future *noun* Time that is yet to come: *I'll try harder in the future.*
□*adjective* Coming in the future: *a future occasion.*
fu·ture (fyoo′ chər) □*noun, plural* **futures**

future tense *noun* A verb tense used to express future time and formed in English with *shall* and *will.*

fuzz *noun* Soft, light fibers or hairs: *the fuzz on a caterpillar.*
fuzz (fuz) □*noun*

fuzzy *adjective* **1.** Covered with or like fuzz: *a fuzzy rug.* **2.** Not clear; blurred: *a fuzzy photograph.*
fuzz·y (fuz′ ē) □*adjective* **fuzzier, fuzziest**

a	bat	ī	bite	oo	tool	*th*	feather
ā	make	î	fierce	ou	out	th	bath
â	dare	o	dot	u	nut	hw	wheat
ä	father	ō	no	û	turn	zh	measure
e	net	ô	law, for	ch	church	ə	about, open
ē	be	oi	soil	ng	ring		pencil, atom
i	dip	oo	look	sh	shade		circus

ANCIENT GREEK

The letter **G** has evolved from many forms of ancient writing. One of the earliest known examples is the Greek character shown above, which dates from almost 3,000 years ago. Over the years, artists and designers have created their own versions of the English letter **G**. Some of the more common examples seen today are shown below.

Gg Gg	Gg Gg	Gg Gg	Gg Gg	Gg Gg
HANDWRITING	CALLIGRAPHY	MODERN SANS SERIF	MODERN SERIF	SCRIPT

g or **G** *noun* The seventh letter of the English alphabet.
g or **G** (jē) □*noun, plural* **g's** or **G's**

gab *verb* To talk in an idle way about unimportant things.
gab (gab) □*verb* **gabbed, gabbing, gabs**

gable *noun* The triangular section of wall between the two sloping sides of a roof.
ga·ble (gā′bəl) □*noun, plural* **gables**

gadget *noun* An often small tool or device: *We bought a gadget for removing the pits from cherries.*
gadg·et (gaj′it) □*noun, plural* **gadgets**

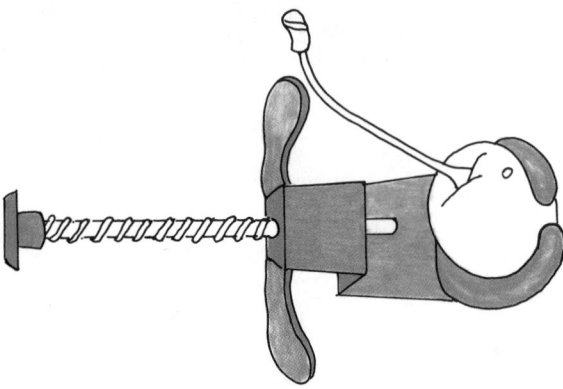

gadget
A cherry pitter

gag *noun* **1.** Something put into the mouth to keep a person from talking or crying out. **2.** A joke.
□*verb* **1.** To stop up the mouth of with a gag:

The thieves gagged him and locked him in a closet. **2.** To have a choking feeling: *He gagged at the sight of the medicine.*
gag (gag) □*noun, plural* **gags** □*verb* **gagged, gagging, gags**

gaiety *noun* The quality or condition of being gay; cheer: *The gaiety of the children at play made the parents nod and smile.*
gai·e·ty (gā′i tē) □*noun*

gaily *adverb* In a cheerful manner; merrily: *Colorful flags fluttered gaily in the wind.*
gai·ly (gā′lē) □*adverb*

gain *verb* **1.** To get possession of; obtain or win: *She gained experience working in the library.* **2.** To increase in: *The airplane gained altitude.*
□*noun* Something gained: *a gain of five points; a gain in speed.*
gain (gān) □*verb* **gained, gaining, gains** □*noun, plural* **gains**

gait *noun* A way of walking or running: *a fast gait; an awkward gait.*
gait (gāt) □*noun, plural* **gaits**

galaxy *noun* One of the very large groups of stars that are found in the universe.
gal·ax·y (gal′ək sē) □*noun, plural* **galaxies**

WORD HISTORY: **galaxy**

The word *galaxy* comes from a Greek word meaning "milky." Galaxies look like milky white blobs or streaks in the sky. "Milky Way" is an English translation of the Greek word.

gale *noun* **1.** A very strong wind. **2.** A sudden outburst: *gales of laughter.*
gale (gāl) □*noun, plural* **gales**

gall *verb* **1.** To make the skin sore by rubbing. **2.** To annoy: *I was galled by his insulting remarks.*
gall (gôl) □*verb* **galled, galling, galls**

gallant *adjective* Showing courage and determination; brave: *a gallant soldier.* —See Synonyms at **brave.**
gal·lant (gal′ənt) □*adjective*

gallbladder *noun* A small sac that is attached to the liver and in which bile is stored.
gall·blad·der (gôl′blad′ər) □*noun, plural* **gallbladders**

galleon *noun* A large sailing ship with three masts that was used mainly in the sixteenth century.
gal·le·on (gal′ē ən) □*noun, plural* **galleons**

gallery *noun* **1.** A room or building where works of art are shown or sold. **2.** The highest balcony of a theater, hall, or church.
gal·ler·y (gal′ə rē) □*noun, plural* **galleries**

galley *noun* **1.** A low, long ship of former times having sails and oars. **2.** The kitchen of a ship or airplane.
gal·ley (gal′ē) □*noun, plural* **galleys**

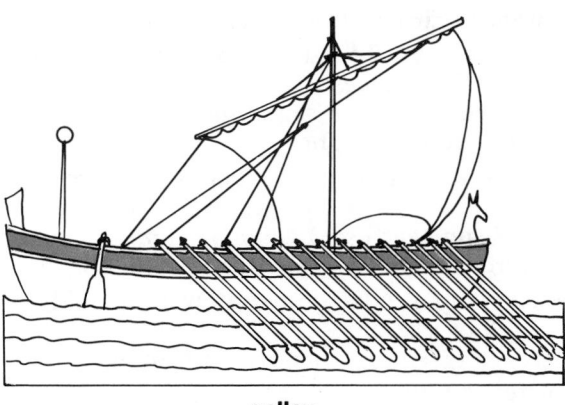

galley

gallivant *verb* To roam about in search of amusement.
gal·li·vant (gal′ə vant′) □*verb* **gallivanted, gallivanting, gallivants**

gallon *noun* A unit of measure for liquids that is equal to four quarts, or 3.785 liters.
gal·lon (gal′ən) □*noun, plural* **gallons**

gallop *noun* The fastest gait of an animal with four feet, especially a horse.

□*verb* To run or ride at a gallop: *The horses galloped over the fields.*
gal·lop (gal′əp) □*noun, plural* **gallops** □*verb* **galloped, galloping, gallops**

gallows *noun* A frame from which criminals are hanged.
gal·lows (gal′ōz) □*noun, plural* **gallows**

galoshes *plural noun* Waterproof overshoes that are worn in rain or snow.
ga·losh·es (gə losh′iz) □*plural noun*

gamble *verb* **1.** To play a game for money or something of value; bet: *She gambled on the football game.* **2.** To take a chance: *I gambled on losing his friendship.*
□*noun* A risk: *I was afraid to take the gamble.*
gam·ble (gam′bəl) □*verb* **gambled, gambling, gambles** □*noun, plural* **gambles**

game *noun* **1.** A way of amusing oneself; play: *The children were busy at their games.* **2.** A contest played according to rules with the players or teams competing against each other: *a baseball game; a game of chess.* **3.** Wild animals, birds, or fish that are hunted for food or sport.
□*adjective* Full of spirit and resolution; courageous: *I'm game to try.*
game (gām) □*noun, plural* **games** □*adjective* **gamer, gamest**

gander *noun* A male goose.
gan·der (gan′dər) □*noun, plural* **ganders**

gang *noun* A group of people who do things together regularly: *a gang of workmen; a gang of criminals.*
gang (gang) □*noun, plural* **gangs**

gangplank *noun* A movable bridge for getting on and off a ship.
gang·plank (gang′plangk′) □*noun, plural* **gangplanks**

gangster *noun* A member of a gang of criminals.
gang·ster (gang′stər) □*noun, plural* **gangsters**

gangway *noun* **1.** A gangplank. **2.** A passageway along either side of the upper deck of a ship.

a bat	ī bite	ōō tool	*th* feather
ā make	î fierce	ou out	th bath
â dare	o dot	u nut	hw wheat
ä father	ō no	û turn	zh measure
e net	ô law, for	ch church	ə about, open
ē be	oi soil	ng ring	pencil, atom
i dip	oo look	sh shade	circus

gang·way (gang′wā′) □*noun, plural* **gangways**

gap *noun* An opening, crack, or break: *He saw the garden through a gap in the wall.*
gap (gap) □*noun, plural* **gaps**

gape *verb* **1.** To open the mouth wide; yawn. **2.** To stare with the mouth open. **3.** To be or become widely open or separated: *The canyon gaped beneath the narrow bridge.*
gape (gāp) □*verb* **gaped, gaping, gapes**

garage *noun* A building where cars and trucks are repaired or parked.
ga·rage (gə **räzh′**) □*noun, plural* **garages**

garbage *noun* Waste food and trash from a kitchen.
gar·bage (gär′ bij) □*noun, plural* **garbages**

garble *verb* To distort and make difficult to understand: *The reporter garbled the news story.*
gar·ble (gär′ bəl) □*verb* **garbled, garbling, garbles**

garden *noun* A piece of land where flowers, fruits, or vegetables are grown.
□*verb* To take care of or work in a garden: *I garden on weekends.*
gar·den (gär′ dən) □*noun, plural* **gardens**
□*verb* **gardened, gardening, gardens**

gardener *noun* Someone who works in or takes care of a garden.
gar·den·er (gär′ dən ər) □*noun, plural* **gardeners**

gardenia *noun* A flower with whitish petals and a very sweet fragrance.
gar·de·nia (gär dēn′ yə) □*noun, plural* **gardenias**

gargle *verb* To exhale air through a liquid held in the mouth or throat, especially to rinse or cleanse.
gar·gle (gär′ gəl) □*verb* **gargled, gargling, gargles**

gargoyle *noun* **1.** A spout in the shape of a grotesque human or animal figure that carries rain water off the roof of a building. **2.** A grotesque figure.
gar·goyle (gär′ goil′) □*noun, plural* **gargoyles**

WORD HISTORY: **gargoyle**

The word *gargoyle* comes from an old French word that probably meant "throat." The word *gargle* comes from the same French word.

gargoyle

garish *adjective* Gaudy: *a garish costume of purple and red.*
gar·ish (gâr′ ish) □*adjective*

garlic *noun* A plant related to the onion that is used to flavor foods.
gar·lic (gär′ lik) □*noun*

garment *noun* An article of clothing.
gar·ment (gär′ mənt) □*noun, plural* **garments**

garnet *noun* A stone having a deep red color that is used as a gem.
gar·net (gär′ nit) □*noun, plural* **garnets**

garnish *verb* To add decoration to: *I garnished the potatoes with parsley.*
gar·nish (gär′ nish) □*verb* **garnished, garnishing, garnishes**

garrison *noun* A place where troops are stationed.
gar·ri·son (gar′ i sən) □*noun, plural* **garrisons**

garter *noun* A band or strap worn to hold up a sock or stocking.
gar·ter (gär′ tər) □*noun, plural* **garters**

garter snake *noun* A nonpoisonous North American snake with lengthwise stripes.

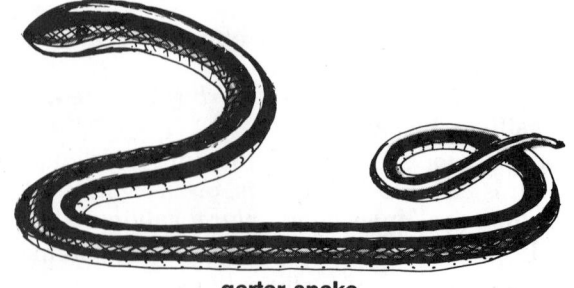

garter snake

gas *noun* **1.** A substance, such as air, that is neither a solid nor a liquid and does not have a definite volume or shape. **2.** Gasoline.
gas (gas) □*noun, plural* **gases**

WORD HISTORY: **gas**

The word *gas* was coined by J.B. Van Helmont, a Dutch chemist. *Gas* is a Dutch spelling of the same Greek word that appears in English as *chaos*. The Greek word means "empty space" and "formless matter."

---

gaseous *adjective* Of or being a gas: *Steam is the gaseous form of water.*
gas·e·ous (gas'ē əs) □*adjective*

gash *noun* A long, deep cut or wound: *Vandals made gashes in the seats of the bus.*
□*verb* To make a gash in.
gash (gash) □*noun, plural* **gashes** □*verb* **gashed, gashing, gashes**

gas mask *noun* A mask that protects the face and lungs from a poisonous gas or other harmful substance.

gasoline *noun* A liquid that is made mostly from petroleum, burns easily, and is used as a fuel for cars, trucks, and airplanes.
gas·o·line (gas'ə **lēn'** *or* gas'ə lēn') □*noun, plural* **gasolines**

gasp *verb* To breathe in suddenly or with difficulty: *He gasped for breath when he reached the top of the stairs.*
□*noun* The act or sound of gasping: *With a gasp of surprise she opened the box of flowers.*
gasp (gasp) □*verb* **gasped, gasping, gasps** □*noun, plural* **gasps**

gas station *noun* A place where cars, trucks, and other vehicles are serviced with gasoline and oil. Vehicles can also be repaired at some gas stations.

gate *noun* **1.** An opening in a wall or fence. **2.** A structure like a door that opens and closes a gate.
gate (gāt) □*noun, plural* **gates**

gateway *noun* An opening for a gate.
gate·way (gāt'wā') □*noun, plural* **gateways**

gather *verb* **1.** To bring or come together: *We gathered a supply of canned food for our camping trip. A group gathered to listen to the music.* **2.** To form an opinion; conclude: *I gather he didn't enjoy himself.* **3.** To bring together into folds or pleats: *a blouse that was gathered at the neck.*

gath·er (gath'ər) □*verb* **gathered, gathering, gathers**

SYNONYMS: **gather, assemble, collect**

These verbs mean to bring or come together: *Dad gathered the whole family in the living room. The students assembled at the station for the class trip. Collect the old newspapers and pile them in the garage.*

---

gaucho *noun* A South American cowboy.
gau·cho (gou'chō) □*noun, plural* **gauchos**

gaudy *adjective* Too showy or bright: *a gaudy, cheap necklace.*
gaud·y (gô'dē) □*adjective* **gaudier, gaudiest**

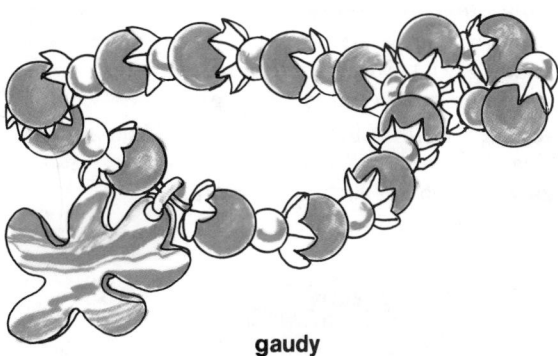

gaudy

gauge *noun* **1.** A standard of measurement. **2.** An instrument for measuring: *a wind gauge.*
□*verb* To measure precisely: *We gauged the speed of the wind during every storm last fall.*
gauge (gāj) □*noun, plural* **gauges** □*verb* **gauged, gauging, gauges**

gaunt *adjective* Thin and bony: *The hungry woman looked gaunt.*
gaunt (gônt) □*adjective* **gaunter, gauntest**

gauze *noun* A thin, loosely woven cloth that is often used for bandages.
gauze (gôz) □*noun*

gave *verb* The past tense of **give**: *He gave her a present.*
gave (gāv) □*verb*

a bat	ī bite	o͞o tool	*th* feather
ā make	î fierce	ou out	th bath
â dare	o dot	u nut	hw wheat
ä father	ō no	û turn	zh measure
e net	ô law, for	ch church	ə about, open
ē be	oi soil	ng ring	pencil, atom
i dip	oo look	sh shade	circus

gavel   *noun* A small wooden hammer used by a person in charge of an assembly to signal for order or attention.
gav·el (**gav′**əl) □*noun, plural*
gavels

gawk   *verb* To stare or gape in a stupid way.
gawk (gôk) □*verb* **gawked, gawking, gawks**

gawky   *adjective* Awkward; clumsy: *the gawky movements of someone just learning to dance.*
gawk·y (**gô′**kē) □*adjective* **gawkier, gawkiest**

gay   *adjective* **1.** Cheerful and lively: *We had a gay time at their party.* **2.** Bright in color: *gay decorations.*
gay (gā) □*adjective* **gayer, gayest**

gaze   *verb* To look steadily; stare: *We gazed at each other in surprise.*
□*noun* A long, steady look; stare.
gaze (gāz) □*verb* **gazed, gazing, gazes**
□*noun, plural* **gazes**

gazelle   *noun* A horned animal of Asia and Africa that can run very fast.
ga·zelle (gə **zel′**) □*noun, plural*
gazelles

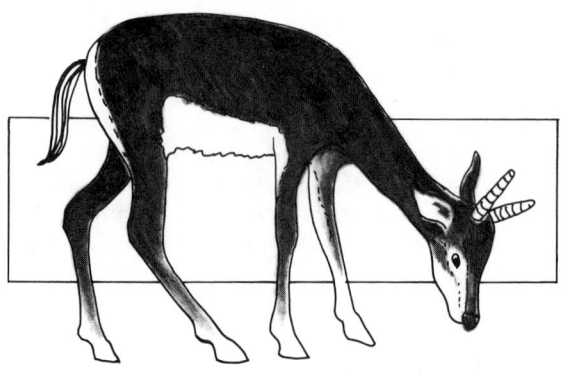

gazelle

gear   *noun* **1.** A wheel with teeth around the edge that fit into the teeth of another wheel so as to cause it to move or turn. **2.** Equipment for a special purpose: *fishing gear; the landing gear of an airplane.*
□*verb* To adjust or adapt: *The school is geared to the needs of the deaf.*
gear (gîr) □*noun, plural* **gears** □*verb* **geared, gearing, gears**

gearshift   *noun* A device that connects a motor, as in a car, to a set of gears.
gear·shift (**gîr′**shift′) □*noun, plural*
gearshifts

geese   *noun* The plural of **goose.**
geese (gēs) □*noun*

Geiger counter   *noun* A device used to detect and measure radioactivity.
Gei·ger counter (**gī′**gər) □*noun*

gelatin   *noun* A substance like jelly made from the skin, bones, and tissue of animals and used to make glues, jellies, and desserts.
gel·a·tin (**jel′**ə tən) □*noun*

gem   *noun* A precious stone, especially one that has been cut and polished.
gem (jem) □*noun, plural* **gems**

gene   *noun* A tiny unit of a plant or animal cell that determines a characteristic that will be passed on to the offspring of the parent.
gene (jēn) □*noun, plural* **genes**

general   *adjective* **1.** Of or having to do with all: *general unhappiness; a general meeting.* **2.** Of or concerned with the main parts of something rather than details: *I have only a general idea of their plan.*
□*noun* A high-ranking commissioned officer in the army, marine corps, or air force.
gen·er·al (**jen′**ər əl) □*adjective* □*noun, plural* **generals**

generally   *adverb* **1.** As a rule; usually: *He generally drives to work.* **2.** In a general way: *Generally speaking, we enjoyed ourselves.*
gen·er·al·ly (**jen′**ər ə lē) □*adverb*

generate   *verb* To bring about; produce: *Water power can be used to generate electricity.*
gen·er·ate (**jen′**ə rāt′) □*verb* **generated, generating, generates**

generation   *noun* **1.** A group of people born and living at about the same time: *My father's grandfather belonged to the generation that settled our frontier.* **2.** A stage or step in the line of descent from an ancestor: *My grandparents, my parents, and I make up three generations.*
gen·er·a·tion (jen′ə **rā′**shən) □*noun, plural* **generations**

generator   *noun* A machine that produces electricity.
gen·er·a·tor (**jen′**ə rā′tər) □*noun, plural* **generators**

generosity   *noun* **1.** Willingness to give or share; unselfishness: *He was noted for his generosity to many charities.* **2.** A generous act.
gen·er·os·i·ty (jen′ə **ros′**i tē) □*noun, plural* **generosities**

generous   *adjective* **1.** Willing to give or share; unselfish: *Her generous father treated*

her friends to the movies. **2.** Abundant; ample: *She gave me a generous helping of potatoes.*
gen·er·ous (jen′ər əs) ▫*adjective*

genial *adjective* Cheerful and friendly: *her genial personality.*
gen·ial (jēn′yəl) ▫*adjective*

genie *noun* A magic spirit in Arab folklore.
ge·nie (jē′nē) ▫*noun, plural* **genies**

genie

genius *noun* **1.** Very great natural ability to think and create: *A great artist possesses genius.* **2.** Someone who has genius: *Only a genius could solve that problem.*
gen·ius (jēn′yəs) ▫*noun, plural* **geniuses**

gentle *adjective* **1.** Not violent, harsh, or severe; mild: *a gentle tap on the window.* **2.** Of a kindly and considerate nature: *a gentle person.* **3.** Not steep or sudden; gradual: *a gentle slope.*
gen·tle (jen′təl) ▫*adjective* **gentler, gentlest**

gentleman *noun* **1.** A man who is polite, considerate, honorable, and kind. **2.** A man of high birth or social standing. **3.** A man.
gen·tle·man (jen′təl mən) ▫*noun, plural* **gentlemen**

genuine *adjective* Not false; real or true: *a genuine interest in science.*
gen·u·ine (jen′yo͞o in) ▫*adjective*

geographic *adjective* Another spelling for **geographical.**
ge·o·graph·ic (jē′ə **graf′**ik) ▫*adjective*

geographical *adjective* Of or having to do with geography.
ge·o·graph·i·cal (jē′ə **graf′**i kəl) ▫*adjective*

geography *noun* The study of the earth and its plant and animal life, including the earth's countries, peoples, products, climates, and natural features and resources.
ge·og·ra·phy (jē og′rə fē) ▫*noun*

WORD HISTORY: geography

The word *geography* comes from two Greek words that mean "earth" and "writing." *Geography* literally means "the description of the earth."

geological *adjective* Of or having to do with geology.
ge·o·log·i·cal (jē′ə **loj′**i kəl) ▫*adjective*

geology *noun* The study of the origin, structure, and history of the earth especially of the layers of soil, rock, and minerals that make up the earth's crust.
ge·ol·o·gy (jē ol′ə jē) ▫*noun*

geometric *adjective* Of or having to do with geometry.
ge·o·met·ric (jē′ə **met′**rik) ▫*adjective*

geometry *noun* A part of mathematics that deals with the measurement and comparison of lines, angles, points, planes, surfaces, and solids.
ge·om·e·try (jē om′i trē) ▫*noun*

geranium *noun* A plant with rounded clusters of red, pink, or white flowers.
ge·ra·ni·um (jə rā′nē əm) ▫*noun, plural* **geraniums**

geranium

gerbil *noun* A small rodent with long hind legs and a long tail that is often kept as a pet.

a bat	ī bite	o͞o tool	*th* feather
ā make	î fierce	ou out	th bath
â dare	o dot	u nut	hw wheat
ä father	ō no	û turn	zh measure
e net	ô law, for	ch church	ə about, open
ē be	oi soil	ng ring	pencil, atom
i dip	oo look	sh shade	circus

ger·bil (**jûr′**bil) ☐*noun, plural*
gerbils

gerbil

germ *noun* An animal or plant so small that it can be seen only through a microscope. Some germs cause disease.
germ (jûrm) ☐*noun, plural* **germs**

German *noun* **1.** Someone who was born in or is a citizen of Germany. **2.** The language of Germany, Austria, and parts of Switzerland.
☐*adjective* Of Germany, the Germans, or their language.
Ger·man (**jûr′**mən) ☐*noun, plural* **Germans**
☐*adjective*

Germanic *noun* A prehistoric language that is the ancestor of English, German, and the Scandinavian languages.
☐*adjective* Of a people who spoke Germanic or a language descended from it.
Ger·man·ic (jər **man′**ik) ☐*noun* ☐*adjective*

germinate *verb* To begin to grow; sprout: *Seeds need water and warmth to germinate.*
ger·mi·nate (**jûr′**mə nāt′) ☐*verb*
germinated, germinating, germinates

gesture *noun* **1.** A movement of a body part that expresses a feeling or idea: *He clapped his hand on his head in a gesture of surprise.* **2.** An act that expresses one's feelings or intentions: *It was a kind gesture to visit her at the hospital.*
☐*verb* To make a gesture.
ges·ture (**jes′**chər) ☐*noun, plural* **gestures**
☐*verb* **gestured, gesturing, gestures**

gesture

get *verb* **1.** To come into possession of, as by receiving, winning, or earning: *got a lot of presents; get permission.* **2.** To cause to be or become: *get mad; get sick; get ready.* **3.** To cause; make happen: *I got Father to raise my allowance.* **4.** To have: *I've only got a quarter.*
   get along To be on friendly terms.
   get away with To do something wrong and escape blame or punishment.
   get by To manage somehow.
   get up To arise from bed.
get (get) ☐*verb* **got, got** or **gotten, getting, gets**

geyser *noun* A natural hot spring that shoots steam and hot water in the air.
gey·ser (**gī′**zər) ☐*noun, plural* **geysers**

ghastly *adjective* Terrible; horrible: *a ghastly murder.*
ghast·ly (**gast′**lē) ☐*adjective* **ghastlier, ghastliest**

ghetto *noun* A section of a city, often a slum, in which members of a minority group live.
ghet·to (**get′**ō) ☐*noun, plural* **ghettos** or **ghettoes**

ghost *noun* Something believed to be the spirit of a dead person.
ghost (gōst) ☐*noun, plural* **ghosts**

ghostly *adjective* Of or like a ghost: *He saw the ghostly form of a ship in the fog.*
ghost·ly (**gōst′**lē) ☐*adjective* **ghostlier, ghostliest**

giant *noun* **1.** Someone or something that is very large, powerful, or important: *He was a giant among poets.* **2.** An imaginary creature with a human form of great size.
☐*adjective* Of very large size.
gi·ant (**jī′**ənt) ☐*noun, plural* **giants**
☐*adjective*

SYNONYMS: **giant, enormous, gigantic, huge, mammoth**

These adjectives mean of very large size: *a giant sunflower; an enormous company; a gigantic football player; a huge piece of cake; a mammoth crowd.*

---

gibberish *noun* Rapid, meaningless talk: *The announcement sounded like gibberish to me because the loudspeaker wasn't working right.*
gib·ber·ish (**jib′**ər ish) ☐*noun*

gibbon *noun* An Asian ape with a slender body and long arms.
gib·bon (**gib′**ən) ☐*noun, plural* **gibbons**

giblet *noun* An edible organ of a fowl, such as the liver or heart.
gib·let (**jib′**lit) □*noun, plural* **giblets**

giddy *adjective* **1.** Having a feeling of whirling or spinning; dizzy: *He felt giddy when he looked down from the top of the skyscraper.* **2.** Not serious; silly: *a giddy mood.*
gid·dy (**gid′**ē) □*adjective* **giddier, giddiest**

gift *noun* **1.** Something given; a present. **2.** Talent or ability: *He has a gift for drawing.*
gift (gift) □*noun, plural* **gifts**

gifted *adjective* Having a special talent or ability: *a gifted pianist; a gifted athlete.*
gift·ed (**gif′**tid) □*adjective*

gigantic *adjective* Great in size or power; huge: *a gigantic tree.* —See Synonyms at **giant.**
gi·gan·tic (jī **gan′**tik) □*adjective*

giggle *verb* To laugh in a silly way.
□*noun* A silly laugh.
gig·gle (**gig′**əl) □*verb* **giggled, giggling, giggles** □*noun, plural* **giggles**

Gila monster *noun* A poisonous lizard of the southwestern United States that has a thick body marked with black and pink.
Gi·la monster (**hē′**lə) □*noun*

gild *verb* To cover with a thin layer of gold: *They gilded the dome of the state capitol.*
gild (gild) □*verb* **gilded, gilding, gilds**

gill *noun* A body part with which fish and many other water animals breathe.
gill (gil) □*noun, plural* **gills**

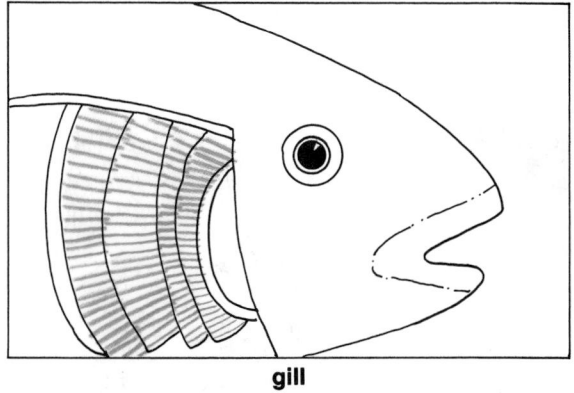

gill

gin¹ *noun* A strong, clear alcoholic beverage flavored with juniper berries.
gin (jin) □*noun, plural* **gins**

gin² *noun* A machine that separates the seeds from the fibers of cotton.
gin (jin) □*noun, plural* **gins**

ginger *noun* A hot spice from the root of a tropical plant, used in medicine and as a flavoring in food.
gin·ger (**jin′**jər) □*noun*

ginger ale *noun* A soft drink flavored with ginger.

gingerbread *noun* A cake flavored with ginger and molasses.
gin·ger·bread (**jin′**jər bred′) □*noun*

gingerly *adverb* With great care; cautiously: *I handled the delicate china gingerly.*
gin·ger·ly (**jin′**jər lē) □*adverb*

gingersnap *noun* A flat, crisp cookie made with molasses and ginger.
gin·ger·snap (**jin′**jər snap′) □*noun, plural* **gingersnaps**

gingham *noun* A cotton fabric that often has a pattern of stripes, checks, or plaids.
ging·ham (**ging′**əm) □*noun*

giraffe *noun* A tall African animal with spotted fur, short horns, and a very long neck and legs.
gi·raffe (jə **raf′**) □*noun, plural* **giraffes**

girder *noun* A large beam that supports the frameworks of buildings and bridges.
gird·er (**gûr′**dər) □*noun, plural* **girders**

girl *noun* A female child who has not yet become a woman.
girl (gûrl) □*noun, plural* **girls**

girlfriend *noun* A special female companion or sweetheart.
girl·friend (**gûrl′**frend) □*noun, plural* **girlfriends**

girlhood *noun* The time of being a girl: *She spent her girlhood on a farm.*
girl·hood (**gûrl′**hood′) □*noun, plural* **girlhoods**

girlish *adjective* Of, like, or suitable for a girl: *a girlish giggle; a girlish expression.*
girl·ish (**gûrl′**ish) □*adjective*

girl scout *noun* A member of the Girl Scouts.

a	bat	ī	bite	ōō	tool	*th*	feather
ā	make	î	fierce	ou	out	th	bath
â	dare	o	dot	u	nut	hw	wheat
ä	father	ō	no	û	turn	zh	measure
e	net	ô	law, for	ch	church	ə	about, open
ē	be	oi	soil	ng	ring		pencil, atom
i	dip	oo	look	sh	shade		circus

Girl Scouts *noun* An organization for girls that tries to help them develop good citizenship, good character, and outdoor skills.

give *verb* **1.** To make a present of: *We gave her a bracelet for her birthday.* **2.** To grant or turn over to another: *She gave five dollars to the baby-sitter.* **3.** To be a source of; provide: *Furnaces give heat.* **4.** To cause to have or receive: *a book that gave me pleasure.* **5.** To yield, as to pressure: *The board gave under my weight.*
give (giv) □*verb* **gave, given, giving, gives**

given *verb* The past participle of **give**: *She has given most of her money away.*
□*adjective* **1.** Specified; stated: *on a given day.* **2.** Having a tendency: *He is a friendly person, but somewhat given to boasting.*
giv·en (giv′ən) □*verb* □*adjective*

glacier *noun* A large mass of ice moving very slowly down a valley or a mountain.
gla·cier (glā′shər) □*noun, plural* **glaciers**

glad *adjective* Pleased; happy: *I was glad to help.*
glad (glad) □*adjective* **gladder, gladdest**

glade *noun* An open space in the woods or a forest.
glade (glād) □*noun, plural* **glades**

gladiator *noun* In ancient Rome, a person who fought to the death as an entertainment for the public.
glad·i·a·tor (glad′ē ā′tər) □*noun, plural* **gladiators**

gladiolus *noun* A plant with large, colorful flowers that grow in a long cluster.
glad·i·o·lus (glad′ē ō′ləs) □*noun, plural* **glad·i·o·li** (glad′ē ō′lī′) or **gladioluses**

glamorous *adjective* Having or showing glamour: *a glamorous movie star.*
glam·or·ous (glam′ər əs) □*adjective*

glamour *noun* Attractiveness and charm, especially when it is deceptive and misleading: *the glamour of a celebrity's life.*
glam·our (glam′ər) □*noun*

glance *verb* To look quickly: *She glanced at the picture.* **2.** To strike a surface and fly off to one side: *The pebble he threw glanced off the water.*
□*noun* A quick look.
glance (glans) □*verb* **glanced, glancing, glances** □*noun, plural* **glances**

gland *noun* An organ in the body that makes and releases a substance, as a hormone, that the body gives off or uses.
gland (gland) □*noun, plural* **glands**

glare *verb* **1.** To stare angrily: *She glared at the bully.* **2.** To shine brightly and harshly: *The sun glared down on the desert.*
□*noun* **1.** An angry stare. **2.** A bright, harsh light.
glare (glâr) □*verb* **glared, glaring, glares** □*noun, plural* **glares**

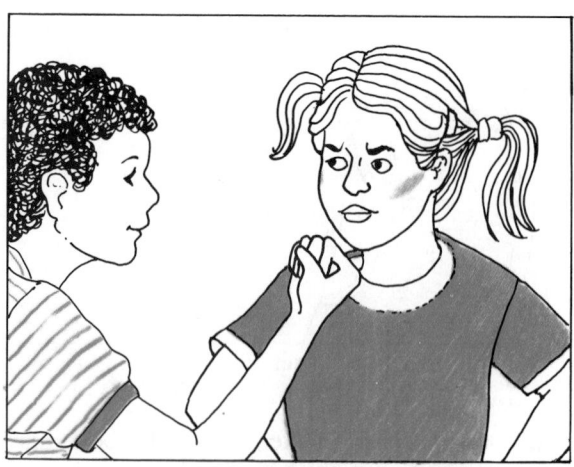

glare

glass *noun* **1.** A hard, brittle, usually transparent substance used for making window panes and containers. **2.** A container made of glass, used for drinking: *He set the glass on the table.* **3. glasses** A pair of lenses used to aid vision; eyeglasses.
glass (glas) □*noun, plural* **glasses**

glaze *noun* A coating or surface that resembles glass, as in smoothness or hardness: *a glaze of ice on the road.*
□*verb* **1.** To put glass into: *glaze a window.* **2.** To apply a glaze to: *glazing pottery.*
glaze (glāz) □*noun, plural* **glazes** □*verb* **glazed, glazing, glazes**

gleam *noun* A beam or flash of light: *We saw gleams of sunlight through the cracks.*
□*verb* To give off a gleam: *A light gleamed in the dark.* —See Synonyms at **blaze.**
gleam (glēm) □*noun, plural* **gleams** □*verb* **gleamed, gleaming, gleams**

glee *noun* Merriment; delight: *She was filled with glee by her success.*
glee (glē) □*noun*

glen *noun* A small valley.
glen (glen) □*noun, plural* **glens**

glib *adjective* **1.** Speaking or writing easily but often with a lack of sincerity or thought: *a glib salesman.* **2.** Flowing easily but shallow or insincere in meaning: *a glib explanation.*
glib (glib) □*adjective*

glide *verb* To move smoothly and easily: *The submarine glided through the icy water.*
glide (glīd) □*verb* **glided, gliding, glides**

glider *noun* An aircraft that has no engine and glides on air currents.
glid·er (glī′dər) □*noun, plural* **gliders**

glider

glimmer *noun* **1.** A dim, flickering light: *the glimmer of moonlight.* **2.** A faint indication;

trace: *a glimmer of hope.*
□*verb* To give off a dim, flickering light: *The fire glimmered on the hearth.*
glim·mer (glim′ər) □*noun, plural* **glimmers** □*verb* **glimmered, glimmering, glimmers**

glimpse *noun* A quick view or look: *I caught a glimpse of her face behind the curtain.*
□*verb* To get a glimpse of: *She glimpsed the mailman as he passed her house.*
glimpse (glimps) □*noun, plural* **glimpses** □*verb* **glimpsed, glimpsing, glimpses**

glisten *verb* To shine with reflected light: *The dew glistened in the morning sun.*
glis·ten (glis′ən) □*verb* **glistened, glistening, glistens**

glitch *noun* A failure to operate or function properly or normally.
glitch (glich) □*noun, plural* **glitches**

glitter *noun* Sparkling light: *the glitter of diamonds.*
□*verb* To sparkle brightly.
glit·ter (glit′ər) □*noun* □*verb* **glittered, glittering, glitters**

gloat *verb* To feel or show great satisfaction: *The miser gloated over his gold.*
gloat (glōt) □*verb* **gloated, gloating, gloats**

globe *noun* **1.** A round object; ball. **2.** A globe with a map of the world on it. **3.** The earth: *When he was a reporter, he traveled to all parts of the globe.*
globe (glōb) □*noun, plural* **globes**

globe

a	bat	ī	bite	o͞o	tool	*th*	feather
ā	make	î	fierce	ou	out	th	bath
â	dare	o	dot	u	nut	hw	wheat
ä	father	ō	no	û	turn	zh	measure
e	net	ô	law, for	ch	church	ə	about, open
ē	be	oi	soil	ng	ring		pencil, atom
i	dip	oo	look	sh	shade		circus

gloom *noun* **1.** Partial or total darkness: *the gloom of night.* **2.** Low spirits; sadness: *Losing the game filled him with gloom.*
gloom (glōōm) □*noun*

gloomy *adjective* **1.** Dark, dismal, or dreary: *a gloomy day.* **2.** In low spirits; sad: *She felt gloomy without her friends.*
gloom·y (glōō′mē) □*adjective* **gloomier, gloomiest**

glorify *verb* **1.** To give glory, honor, or high praise to: *glorify heroes.* **2.** To give glory through worship: *glorify God.*
glo·ri·fy (glôr′ə fī′) □*verb* **glorified, glorifying, glorifies**

glorious *adjective* Having or deserving glory; magnificent: *glorious achievements; a glorious day.*
glo·ri·ous (glôr′ē əs) □*adjective*

glory *noun* **1.** Great honor or praise: *a career that brought glory and wealth.* **2.** Great beauty; splendor: *the glory of a sunrise over the mountains.*
glo·ry (glôr′ē) □*noun, plural* **glories**

gloss *noun* A bright, smooth shine on a surface; luster: *the gloss of old silver.*
gloss (glôs) □*noun, plural* **glosses**

glossary *noun* A list of hard words with their meanings, often found at the end of a book.
glos·sa·ry (glô′sə rē) □*noun, plural* **glossaries**

glossy *adjective* Having a bright, smooth, shiny surface: *glossy satin.*
gloss·y (glô′sē) □*adjective* **glossier, glossiest**

glove *noun* A covering for the hand with a separate section for each finger and the thumb.
glove (gluv) □*noun, plural* **gloves**

glow *verb* **1.** To give off a steady light; shine: *The lights glowed through the windows.* **2.** To have rosy, healthy color: *Her face glowed from the cold.*
□*noun* **1.** A steady light; shine: *the glow of embers in the fireplace.* **2.** A rosy, healthy color: *the glow in his cheeks.*
glow (glō) □*verb* **glowed, glowing, glows** □*noun, plural* **glows**

glower *verb* To look or stare angrily: *He glowered at me when I contradicted him.*
glow·er (glou′ər) □*verb* **glowered, glowering, glowers**

glue *noun* A thick substance used to stick things together.
□*verb* **1.** To stick with glue: *He glued the chair*

together. **2.** To fix or hold tightly: *She kept her eyes glued to the road.*
glue (glōō) □*noun, plural* **glues** □*verb* **glued, gluing, glues**

glum *adjective* **1.** In low spirits; gloomy. **2.** Not hopeful; pessimistic: *a glum view of our chances of winning the game.*
glum (glum) □*adjective* **glummer, glummest**

glut *verb* **1.** To fill, feed, or eat too much: *They glutted themselves with chocolate cake.* **2.** To provide with so many goods that the supply is much greater than the demand.
□*noun* Too great an amount of something.
glut (glut) □*verb* **glutted, glutting, gluts** □*noun, plural* **gluts**

glutton *noun* A person who eats too much.
glut·ton (glut′ən) □*noun, plural* **gluttons**

gnat *noun* A very small biting insect with wings.
gnat (nat) □*noun, plural* **gnats**

gnaw *verb* To bite or chew on so as to wear away: *The puppy gnawed the bone.*
gnaw (nô) □*verb* **gnawed, gnawing, gnaws**

gnome *noun* In legends and fables, a being resembling a dwarf that lives underground and guards treasure.
gnome (nōm) □*noun, plural* **gnomes**

gnu *noun* A large African antelope with a mane and curved horns.
gnu (nōō *or* nyōō) □*noun, plural* **gnus**

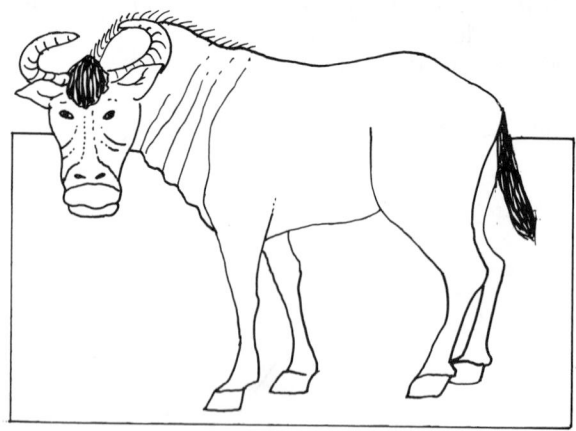

gnu

go *verb* **1.** To pass from one place to another; proceed: *Let's go to my house.* **2.** To move away; leave: *We must go now or we'll miss the*

plane. **3.** To lead to; reach: *This path goes to the pool.* **4.** To run, work, or operate: *I couldn't get the car to go.* **4.** To have a place; belong: *Your clothes go in the closet.* **6.** To be suited; fit: *These shoes go with your dress.* **7.** To be about to; intend: *We are going to leave soon.* **8.** To be or come to be in a certain state: *go to sleep; go crazy.*
go (gō) ▢*verb* **went, gone, going, goes**

goal *noun* **1.** Something wanted and worked for: *His goal is to become a lawyer.* **2.** An area in certain games into or over which a player must get a ball or puck in order to score.
goal (gōl) ▢*noun, plural* **goals**

goat *noun* An animal that has hoofs, horns, and a beard and is raised in many parts of the world for its milk, meat, and wool.
goat (gōt) ▢*noun, plural* **goats**

goatee *noun* A small beard that comes to a point just below the chin.
goat·ee (gō tē′) ▢*noun, plural* **goatees**

goatee

gobble¹ *verb* To eat quickly in large gulps.
gob·ble (gob′əl) ▢*verb* **gobbled, gobbling, gobbles**

gobble² *noun* The sound made by a male turkey.
▢*verb* To make a gobble.
gob·ble (gob′əl) ▢*noun, plural* **gobbles**
▢*verb* **gobbled, gobbling, gobbles**

goblet *noun* A drinking glass with a stem and a base.
gob·let (gob′lit) ▢*noun, plural* **goblets**

goblin *noun* In legends and fables, a grotesque being that does mischief or evil.
gob·lin (gob′lin) ▢*noun, plural* **goblins**

god *noun* **1.** **God** A being worshipped as the creator and ruler of the universe. **2.** A being

believed to have supernatural powers: *the Roman god of war.*
god (god) ▢*noun, plural* **gods**

godchild *noun* A person for whom another person acts as a sponsor at baptism.
god·child (god′chīld′) ▢*noun, plural* **godchildren**

goddess *noun* A female being supposed to have supernatural powers.
god·dess (god′is) ▢*noun, plural* **goddesses**

godfather *noun* A man or boy who is a godparent.
god·fath·er (god′fä′thər) ▢*noun, plural* **godfathers**

godmother *noun* A woman or girl who is a godparent.
god·moth·er (god′muth′ər) ▢*noun, plural* **godmothers**

godparent *noun* A person who acts as a sponsor at a baptism.
god·par·ent (god′pâr′ənt) ▢*noun, plural* **godparents**

goes *verb* The third person singular present tense of **go**: *The earth goes around the sun in a little over 365 days.*
goes (gōz) ▢*verb*

goggles *plural noun* Large eyeglasses with protective side pieces that are worn to shield the eyes from dust, sun, water, or wind.
gog·gles (gog′əlz) ▢*plural noun*

gold *noun* **1.** A soft, yellow precious metal that is a chemical element and is used especially to make jewelry and coins. **2.** A bright yellow.
▢*adjective* Bright yellow.
gold (gōld) ▢*noun, plural* **golds** ▢*adjective*

golden *adjective* **1.** Made of gold: *a golden necklace.* **2.** Of the color of gold: *golden hair.* **3.** Very favorable or valuable: *a golden opportunity.*
gold·en (gōl′dən) ▢*adjective*

goldenrod *noun* A plant with branching clusters of small yellow flowers that bloom in the late summer and fall.
gold·en·rod (gōl′dən rod′) ▢*noun*

a	bat	ī	bite	o͞o	tool	*th*	feather
ā	make	î	fierce	ou	**out**	th	bath
â	dare	o	dot	u	**nut**	hw	**wheat**
ä	father	ō	no	û	turn	zh	measure
e	net	ô	law, for	ch	**church**	ə	about, open
ē	be	oi	soil	ng	**ring**		pencil, atom
i	dip	oo	look	sh	**shade**		circus

goldfinch *noun* A small North American bird that has yellow feathers and a black tail, wings, and head patch.
gold·finch (gōld′finch′) □*noun, plural* **goldfinches**

goldfinch

goldfish *noun* A small usually golden-orange fish often kept in home aquariums.
gold·fish (gōld′fish′) □*noun, plural* **goldfish** or **goldfishes**

golf *noun* A game played by hitting a small, hard ball with one of a set of clubs around an outdoor course into a series of holes in as few strokes as possible.
□*verb* To play golf.
golf (golf) □*noun* □*verb* **golfed, golfing, golfs**

gone *verb* The past participle of **go**: *We had already gone when they arrived.*
gone (gôn) □*verb*

gong *noun* A metal disk that makes a deep, ringing sound when struck.
gong (gông) □*noun, plural* **gongs**

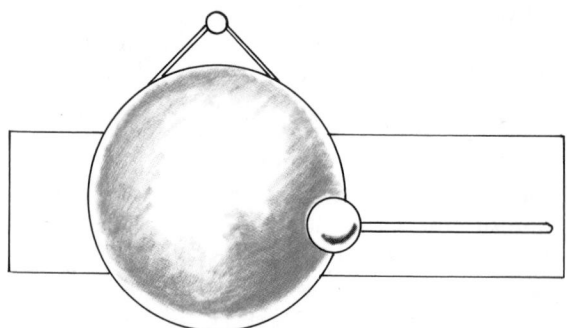

gong
Gong and hammer

good *adjective* **1.** Having desirable qualities; not bad or poor: *a good book; good health.* **2.** Suitable to a need: *good to eat.* **3.** Helpful and friendly: *a good neighbor.* **4.** Honorable and moral: *a good person.* **5.** Well-behaved: *Be a good girl.* **6.** Not less than; full: *I slept a good hour.*
□*noun* **1.** Something that is good: *You have to take the good along with the bad.* **2.** Benefit; advantage: *He did it for your own good.* **3. goods** Things that can be bought and sold: *All the goods in the store are on sale.* **4. goods** Personal property; belongings: *household goods.*
good (good) □*adjective* **better, best** □*noun, plural* **goods**

good-by or **good-bye** *interjection* A word used to express farewell.
□*noun* An expression of farewell.
good-by or **good-bye** (good bī′) □*interjection* □*noun, plural* **good-bys** or **good-byes**

WORD HISTORY: **good-by**
Good-by is short for the phrase "God be with you."

Good Friday *noun* The Friday before Easter, observed in memory of the Crucifixion of Jesus.

good-natured *adjective* Cheerful and pleasant: *a good-natured baby.*
good-na·tured (good′nā′chərd) □*adjective*

goodness *noun* The quality or condition of being good; kindness or excellence.
□*interjection* A word used to express surprise: *Goodness, I didn't know that!*
good·ness (good′nis) □*noun* □*interjection*

goof *verb* To make a silly or careless mistake.
□*noun* **1.** A silly or careless mistake. **2.** A silly or stupid person.
goof off To waste time.
goof (goof) □*verb* **goofed, goofing, goofs** □*noun, plural* **goofs**

goose *noun* **1.** A large water bird that has webbed feet and resembles a duck. **2.** A female goose. **3.** A silly person.
goose (goos) □*noun, plural* **geese**

goose flesh *noun* Goose pimples.

goose pimples *plural noun* Tiny bumps that appear on the skin, caused by a sensation such as cold or fear.

gopher *noun* A small, burrowing North American animal that has pouches like pockets in its cheeks.
go·pher (gō′fər) □*noun, plural* **gophers**

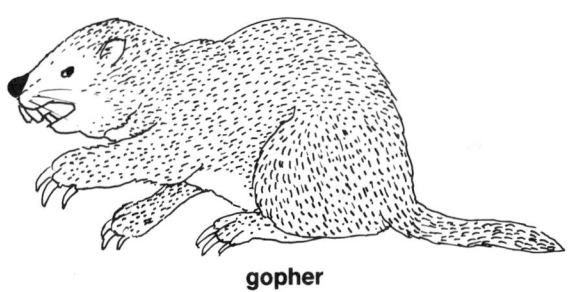

gopher

gore[1] *noun* Blood, especially dried blood from a wound.
gore (gôr) □*noun*

gore[2] *verb* To stab or pierce with a horn or tusk.
gore (gôr) □*verb* **gored, goring, gores**

gorge *noun* A deep, narrow valley with high, rocky sides.
□*verb* To stuff with food: *He gorged himself at dinner.*
gorge (gôrj) □*noun, plural* **gorges** □*verb* **gorged, gorging, gorges**

gorge

gorgeous *adjective* Extremely beautiful: *a gorgeous costume.*
gor·geous (gôr′ jəs) □*adjective*

gorilla *noun* An African ape that has a broad, heavy body and dark hair and is the largest and most powerful of the apes.
go·ril·la (gə ril′ə) □*noun, plural* **gorillas**

gory *adjective* Covered with blood; bloody.
gor·y (gôr′ē) □*adjective* **gorier, goriest**

gosling *noun* A young goose.
gos·ling (goz′ling) □*noun, plural* **goslings**

gospel *noun* **1.** The teachings of Christ and his Apostles. **2.** Gospel Any of the four accounts of the life of Christ in the New Testament. **3.** Something accepted as absolutely true: *He took the newspaper article as gospel.*
gos·pel (gos′pəl) □*noun, plural* **gospels**

> **WORD HISTORY: gospel**
>
> The word *gospel* comes from an Old English word that was a compound of the words for "good" and "news." *Gospel* therefore literally means "good news."

gossip *noun* **1.** Idle talk or rumors that are often not true. **2.** Someone who likes to tell and hear gossip.
□*verb* To engage in or spread gossip.
gos·sip (gos′əp) □*noun, plural* **gossips** □*verb* **gossiped, gossiping, gossips**

got *verb* The past tense and a past participle of **get**: *She got no answer.*
got (got) □*verb*

gotten *verb* A past participle of **get**.
got·ten (got′ən) □*verb*

gouge *noun* **1.** A metal tool with a rounded blade for cutting grooves in wood. **2.** A hole or groove cut with or as if with a gouge.
□*verb* To cut or dig out with a gouge.
gouge (gouj) □*noun, plural* **gouges** □*verb* **gouged, gouging, gouges**

gouge

a bat	ī bite	ōō tool	*th* feather
ā make	î fierce	ou out	th bath
â dare	o dot	u nut	hw wheat
ä father	ō no	û turn	zh measure
e net	ô law, for	ch church	ə about, open
ē be	oi soil	ng ring	pencil, atom
i dip	oo look	sh shade	circus

goulash   *noun* A stew of beef or veal and vegetables that is seasoned with paprika.
goul·ash (gōō′läsh′) ▢*noun*

gourd   *noun* A fruit related to the pumpkin and squash and having a hard rind.
gourd (gôrd *or* goord) ▢*noun, plural* **gourds**

govern   *verb* To direct or manage; rule: *Congress and the President govern the nation. His decision was governed by his feelings.*
gov·ern (guv′ərn) ▢*verb* **governed, governing, governs**

government   *noun* **1.** A system of governing: *We have a democratic government.* **2.** A group of people who govern: *The Secretary of State is a member of the government.*
gov·ern·ment (guv′ərn mənt) ▢*noun, plural* **governments**

governor   *noun* Someone elected to govern a state in the United States.
gov·er·nor (guv′ər nər) ▢*noun, plural* **governors**

govt. An abbreviation for **government.**

gown   *noun* **1.** A woman's dress. **2.** A loose outer robe, such as that worn by a judge.
gown (goun) ▢*noun, plural* **gowns**

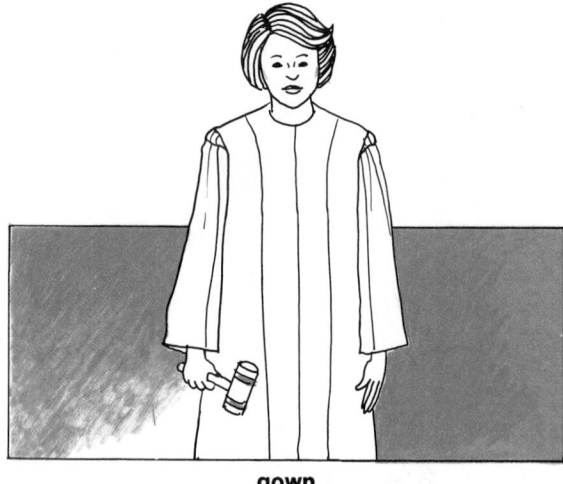

gown

grab   *verb* To take suddenly; snatch: *She grabbed her books and ran.*
▢*noun* An act of grabbing: *The greedy child made a grab for the candy.*
grab (grab) ▢*verb* **grabbed, grabbing, grabs** ▢*noun, plural* **grabs**

grace   *noun* **1.** Ease and beauty of movement or form: *a skater with natural grace.* **2.** A pleasing quality: *She had all the social graces.* **3.** A short prayer of blessing or thanks at the beginning of a meal.
▢*verb* To add beauty or honor to: *Flowers graced the banquet table.*
grace (grās) ▢*noun, plural* **graces** ▢*verb* **graced, gracing, graces**

graceful   *adjective* Showing grace of movement, form, or action: *She was the most graceful dancer of her time.*
grace·ful (grās′fəl) ▢*adjective*

gracious   *adjective* Courteous and kind: *a gracious hostess.*
gra·cious (grā′shəs) ▢*adjective*

grackle   *noun* An American blackbird with glossy feathers and a long tail.
grack·le (grak′əl) ▢*noun, plural* **grackles**

grade   *noun* **1.** A step in a scale of quality or rank; level: *fabric of a very low grade.* **2.** A class or level in a school: *the sixth grade.* **3.** A mark showing how well a student has done: *a grade of 75 in English.* **4.** The degree of slope, as in a road.
▢*verb* **1.** To arrange in grades; sort: *grade lumber by size.* **2.** To give a grade to: *The teacher graded the papers.*
grade (grād) ▢*noun, plural* **grades** ▢*verb* **graded, grading, grades**

grade school   *noun* An elementary school.

gradual   *adjective* Happening or moving little by little: *a gradual improvement in his health.*
grad·u·al (graj′ōō əl) ▢*adjective*

graduate   *verb* **1.** To finish a course of study and receive a diploma: *She graduated from college.* **2.** To mark with evenly spaced lines for measuring: *a ruler that is graduated in inches and feet.*
▢*noun* Someone who has graduated from a school or college.
grad·u·ate (graj′ōō āt′) ▢*verb* **graduated, graduating, graduates** ▢*noun* (graj′ōō it), *plural* **graduates**

graduation   *noun* **1.** The act of graduating. **2.** A ceremony at which graduating students receive diplomas.
grad·u·a·tion (graj′ōō ā′shən) ▢*noun, plural* **graduations**

graft   *verb* **1.** To insert a plant shoot or bud into another living plant so that the two grow together as a single plant. **2.** To transfer body tissue to a different place in the body or to another person's body.
▢*noun* Something that has been grafted.

graft (graft) □*verb* **grafted, grafting, grafts**
□*noun, plural* **grafts**

graft
Grafted trees

grain   *noun* **1.** The seed of a cereal plant such as wheat, corn, or rice. **2.** A tiny hard particle: *a grain of sugar.* **3.** The pattern or arrangement of fibers in wood.
grain (grān) □*noun, plural* **grains**

gram   *noun* A unit of weight in the metric system equal to .035 of an ounce.
gram (gram) □*noun, plural* **grams**

grammar   *noun* **1.** The study of word forms and their use in sentences. **2.** A set of rules for making sentences in a language. **3.** The use of words and word forms in a way that is considered to be according to the rules of grammar.
gram·mar (gram′ər) □*noun, plural* **grammars**

grammar school   *noun* An elementary school.

grammatical   *adjective* Of or following the rules of grammar.
gram·mat·i·cal (grə mat′i kəl) □*adjective*

grand   *adjective* **1.** Very fine; wonderful: *He felt grand.* **2.** Very large, beautiful, and impressive: *a grand cathedral.* **3.** Higher in rank or importance than others; main: *the grand staircase.* **4.** Including everything: *a grand total.*
grand (grand) □*adjective* **grander, grandest**

SYNONYMS: **grand, magnificent, majestic**
These adjectives mean very large and impressive: *The princess greeted her guests at the top of the grand staircase of the castle. The view of the city from the top of the skyscraper is magnificent. We looked up at the majestic, snow-covered mountains.*

---

grandaunt   *noun* A great-aunt.
grand·aunt (grand′ant′ *or* grand′änt′)
□*noun, plural* **grandaunts**

grandchild   *noun* A child of one's son or daughter.
grand·child (grand′chīld′ *or* gran′chīld′)
□*noun, plural* **grandchildren**

granddaughter   *noun* The daughter of one's son or daughter.
grand·daugh·ter (gran′dô′tər) □*noun, plural* **granddaughters**

grandfather   *noun* The father of one's mother or father.
grand·fa·ther (grand′fä′thər *or* gran′fä′thər)
□*noun, plural* **grandfathers**

grandfather clock   *noun* A clock whose tall, narrow cabinet stands on the floor.

grandmother   *noun* The mother of one's father or mother.
grand·moth·er (grand′muth′ər *or* gran′muth′ər) □*noun, plural* **grandmothers**

grandnephew   *noun* The son of one's nephew or niece.
grand·neph·ew (grand′nef′yōō) □*noun, plural* **grandnephews**

grandniece   *noun* The daughter of one's nephew or niece.
grand·niece (grand′nēs′) □*noun, plural* **grandnieces**

grandparent   *noun* The mother or father of one's mother or father.
grand·par·ent (grand′pâr′ənt) □*noun, plural* **grandparents**

grandson   *noun* The son of one's son or daughter.
grand·son (grand′sun′ *or* gran′sun′) □*noun, plural* **grandsons**

grandstand   *noun* The main seating area for spectators, as at a stadium.
grand·stand (grand′stand′) □*noun, plural* **grandstands**

granduncle   *noun* A great-uncle.
grand·un·cle (grand′ung′kəl) □*noun, plural* **granduncles**

granite   *noun* A hard rock used in buildings and monuments.
gran·ite (gran′it) □*noun, plural* **granites**

---

a bat	ī bite	ōō tool	*th* feather
ā make	î fierce	ou out	th bath
â dare	o dot	u nut	hw wheat
ä father	ō no	û turn	zh measure
e net	ô law, for	ch church	ə about, open
ē be	oi soil	ng ring	pencil, atom
i dip	oo look	sh shade	circus

granny knot *noun* A knot that resembles a square knot but does not hold as firmly.
gran·ny knot (grăn′ē) □*noun, plural* **granny knots**

grant *verb* **1.** To permit or allow to have: *I will grant your wish.* **2.** To admit; acknowledge: *I grant you were right.*
□*noun* Something granted: *She received a grant of money for her studies.*
grant (grănt) □*verb* **granted, granting, grants** □*noun, plural* **grants**

grape *noun* A small, juicy fruit that grows in clusters on a vine and is used to make wine and raisins.
grape (grāp) □*noun, plural* **grapes**

grapefruit *noun* A large, round fruit that is related to the orange and the lemon, having a yellow skin and a rather sour taste.
grape·fruit (grāp′fro͞ot′) □*noun, plural* **grapefruit** or **grapefruits**

grapevine *noun* **1.** A vine on which grapes grow. **2.** An informal way of spreading gossip or news: *I heard through the grapevine that you had moved.*
grape·vine (grāp′vīn′) □*noun, plural* **grapevines**

graph *noun* A diagram that shows the relationship between two or more things: *This graph shows the town's decrease in population over the past 10 years.*
graph (grăf) □*noun, plural* **graphs**

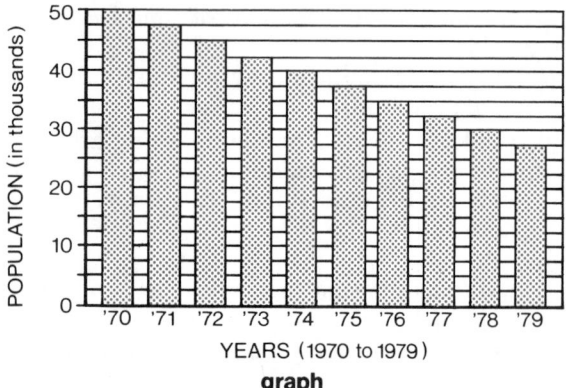

graph

graphics *noun* **1.** A picture, diagram, or chart, especially when created or displayed on a computer. **2.** The making of drawings.
graph·ics (grăf′iks) □*noun*

graphite *noun* A soft, black substance that is a form of the element carbon and is used as the writing lead in pencils.
graph·ite (grăf′īt′) □*noun*

grapple *verb* **1.** To grasp with an instrument such as a hook. **2.** To struggle with; wrestle: *The policemen grappled with the thief when he tried to escape. I wasn't prepared to grapple with such difficult problems.*
grap·ple (grăp′əl) □*verb* **grappled, grappling, grapples**

grasp *verb* **1.** To seize and hold firmly with the hand: *She grasped the dog's leash.* **2.** To understand: *He couldn't grasp what I said.*
□*noun* **1.** A firm hold; grip: *She had a grasp on the horse's bridle.* **2.** Understanding; comprehension: *She has a good grasp of English.*
grasp (grăsp) □*verb* **grasped, grasping, grasps** □*noun, plural* **grasps**

grasping *adjective* Desiring material gain; greedy: *a stingy, grasping person.*
grasp·ing (grăs′ping) □*adjective*

grass *noun* One of a large group of plants with narrow leaves. Corn, wheat, rice, bamboo, and sugar cane are grasses.
grass (grăs) □*noun, plural* **grasses**

grasshopper *noun* A large insect with two pairs of wings and long hind legs used for jumping.
grass·hop·per (grăs′hop′ər) □*noun, plural* **grasshoppers**

grate¹ *verb* **1.** To break into small pieces or shreds by rubbing or scraping against a rough surface: *grate an onion.* **2.** To make a harsh, scraping sound by rubbing: *The elevator grated as it went up the shaft.* **3.** To be irritating; annoy: *His constant complaints grate on my nerves.*
grate (grāt) □*verb* **grated, grating, grates**

grate

grate² *noun* **1.** A frame of parallel or crossed bars over an opening, as a window. **2.** A framework of metal bars used to hold burning fuel in a furnace or fireplace.
grate (grāt) ☐*noun, plural* **grates**

grateful *adjective* Feeling or showing gratitude; thankful: *I am grateful for your help.*
grate·ful (grāt′fəl) ☐*adjective*

gratify *verb* To be a source of pleasure or satisfaction to: *I was gratified by his compliments.*
grat·i·fy (grat′ə fī′) ☐*verb* **gratified, gratifying, gratifies**

grating *noun* A set of parallel or crossed bars across an opening; grate.
gra·ting (grā′ting) ☐*noun, plural* **gratings**

gratitude *noun* A feeling of being thankful, as for a gift, favor, or kindness; appreciation.
grat·i·tude (grat′i tōōd′ *or* grat′i tyōōd′) ☐*noun*

grave¹ *noun* A hole in the ground in which a corpse is buried.
grave (grāv) ☐*noun, plural* **graves**

grave² *adjective* **1.** Very important: *Our President has grave responsibilities.* **2.** Solemn in character, appearance, or behavior: *a grave expression.*
grave (grāv) ☐*adjective* **graver, gravest**

WORD HISTORY: **grave²**

The adjective *grave* comes from a Latin word that means "heavy" in a physical sense as well as "weighty, serious, solemn." The word *gravity* also comes from the same Latin word.

---

gravel *noun* A mixture of pebbles or small pieces of rock used to cover roads and paths.
grav·el (grav′əl) ☐*noun*

gravestone *noun* A stone placed over a grave as a monument or marker.
grave·stone (grāv′stōn′) ☐*noun, plural* **gravestones**

graveyard *noun* A cemetery.
grave·yard (grāv′yärd) ☐*noun, plural* **graveyards**

gravitation *noun* The force that makes all objects in the universe tend to move toward one another.
grav·i·ta·tion (grav′i tā′shən) ☐*noun*

gravity *noun* **1.** The force of gravitation exerted by the earth, the moon, a star, or a planet, that pulls smaller objects near the surface toward the center. **2.** Serious nature; importance: *We had not realized the gravity of the problem.*
grav·i·ty (grav′i tē) ☐*noun, plural* **gravities**

gravy *noun* A sauce made from the juices that drip from cooking meat.
gra·vy (grā′vē) ☐*noun, plural* **gravies**

gravy

gray *noun* A color that is made by mixing black and white.
☐*adjective* Of the color gray.
gray (grā) ☐*noun, plural* **grays** ☐*adjective* **grayer, grayest**

grayish *adjective* Somewhat gray.
gray·ish (grā′ish) ☐*adjective*

graze¹ *verb* To feed on growing grass: *Cattle and sheep grazed in the field.*
graze (grāz) ☐*verb* **grazed, grazing, grazes**

graze

a bat	ī bite	ōō tool	*th* feather
ā make	î fierce	ou out	th bath
â dare	o dot	u nut	hw wheat
ä father	ō no	û turn	zh measure
e net	ô law, for	ch church	ə about, open
ē be	oi soil	ng ring	pencil, atom
i dip	oo look	sh shade	circus

graze² *verb* To touch lightly in passing: *She grazed her knee on the desk.*
graze (grāz) □*verb* **grazed, grazing, grazes**

grease *noun* **1.** Soft or melted animal fat, used in cooking. **2.** Thick oil or a similar substance that is put on the moving parts of machines to make them run more smoothly.
□*verb* To put grease or a greasy substance on: *grease a cake pan.*
grease (grēs) □*noun, plural* **greases** □*verb* **greased, greasing, greases**

greasy *adjective* **1.** Covered with grease: *a greasy pot.* **2.** Containing or resembling grease: *greasy food.*
greas·y (grē′sē) □*adjective* **greasier, greasiest**

great *adjective* **1.** Very large; big: *A great crowd attended the parade.* **2.** More than usual; exceptional: *a great surprise.* **3.** Important; outstanding; famous: *a great scientific discovery.* —See Synonyms at **big.**
great (grāt) □*adjective* **greater, greatest**

great-aunt *noun* The sister of one's grandmother or grandfather.
great-aunt (grāt′ant′ *or* grāt′änt′) □*noun, plural* **great-aunts**

Great Dane *noun* A large, strong dog with a short coat.

Great Dane

great-grandchild *noun* The child of one's grandson or granddaughter.
great-grand·child (grāt′ grand′chīld′) □*noun, plural* **great-grandchildren**

great-grandparent *noun* The mother or father of one's grandparent.
great-grand·par·ent (grāt′ grand′ pâr′ənt) □*noun, plural* **great-grandparents**

greatly *adverb* To a large degree; very much: *I greatly appreciated her help.*
great·ly (grāt′lē) □*adverb*

great-uncle *noun* The brother of one's grandmother or grandfather.
great-uncle (grāt′ung′kəl) □*noun, plural* **great-uncles**

greed *noun* A selfish desire to get more and more of something.
greed (grēd) □*noun*

greedy *adjective* Wanting all one can get: *The dictator was greedy for power.*
greed·y (grē′dē) □*adjective* **greedier, greediest**

Greek *noun* **1.** Someone who was born in or is a citizen of Greece. **2.** The language of the Greeks.
□*adjective* Of Greece, its people, or their language.
Greek (grēk) □*noun, plural* **Greeks** □*adjective*

green *noun* **1.** The color of most plant leaves and growing grass. **2. greens** Green leaves and stems of plants eaten as vegetables. **3.** A grassy area or park: *the village green in the center of town.* **4.** The area of smooth, short grass around a hole on a golf course.
□*adjective* **1.** Of the color green: *a green blouse.* **2.** Covered with grass, trees, or other plant growth: *green pastures.* **3.** Not ripe: *a green banana.* **4.** Without training or experience: *a green ballplayer playing her first game.*
green (grēn) □*noun, plural* **greens** □*adjective* **greener, greenest**

greenhouse *noun* A building made of glass in which plants are grown.
green·house (grēn′hous′) □*noun, plural* **greenhouses**

greenhouse

greenish *adjective* Somewhat green.
green·ish (grē′nish) □*adjective*

greet *verb* **1.** To welcome in a friendly or polite way: *She greeted us at the entrance.* **2.** To receive in a certain way: *We greeted the team with cheers.*
greet (grēt) □*verb* **greeted, greeting, greets**

greeting *noun* **1.** An act or expression of welcome: *She welcomed us with a cheerful greeting.* **2. greetings** A message of friendly wishes: *He sent his greetings to you in the letter.*
greet·ing (grēt′ing) □*noun, plural* **greetings**

grenade *noun* A small bomb usually thrown by hand.
gre·nade (grə nād′) □*noun, plural* **grenades**

WORD HISTORY: **grenade**

The word *grenade* was borrowed from French. In French the word means "pomegranate" as well as "grenade." The bomb was thought to resemble a pomegranate in shape.

---

grew *verb* The past tense of **grow**: *We grew tomatoes and carrots in the garden.*
grew (grōō) □*verb*

grey *noun* Another spelling for **gray**.
grey (grā) □*noun, plural* **greys**

greyhound *noun* A slender dog with long legs, a smooth coat, and a narrow head. Greyhounds can run very fast.
grey·hound (grā′hound′) □*noun, plural* **greyhounds**

greyish *adjective* Another spelling for **grayish.**
grey·ish (grā′ish) □*adjective*

griddle *noun* A flat surface or pan for frying foods such as pancakes.
grid·dle (grid′əl) □*noun, plural* **griddles**

grief *noun* Great sadness over a loss or misfortune: *Everyone felt grief over the death of the President.* —See Synonyms at **sorrow.**
grief (grēf) □*noun, plural* **griefs**

grieve *verb* To feel or cause to feel grief: *He grieved for his lost friend. The news of her death grieved him deeply.*
grieve (grēv) □*verb* **grieved, grieving, grieves**

grill *noun* A cooking utensil with parallel metal bars on which to broil food.
□*verb* To cook on a grill: *grill hot dogs.*
grill (gril) □*noun, plural* **grills** □*verb* **grilled, grilling, grills**

grim *adjective* **1.** Harsh; forbidding; stern: *men with grim faces.* **2.** Not giving up; firm: *a grim determination to take first place.*
grim (grim) □*adjective* **grimmer, grimmest**

grimace *noun* A tightening and twisting of the face muscles.
□*verb* To make a grimace: *grimaced with pain.*
grim·ace (grim′əs *or* gri **mās′**) □*noun, plural* **grimaces** □*verb* **grimaced, grimacing, grimaces**

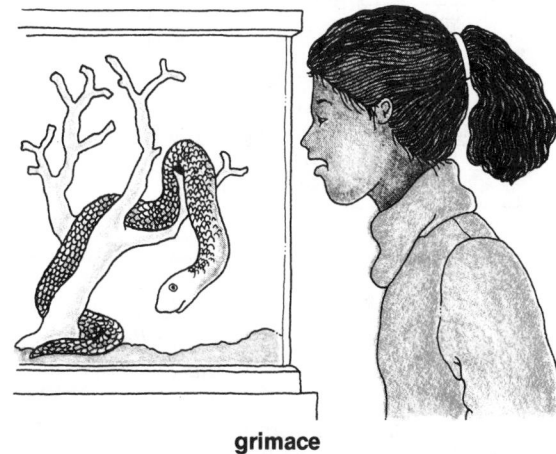

grimace

grime *noun* Heavy dirt covering or rubbed into a surface: *The windows were thick with grime.*
grime (grīm) □*noun*

grin *verb* To smile broadly: *She grinned at the good news.*
□*noun* A very broad, happy smile.
grin (grin) □*verb* **grinned, grinning, grins** □*noun, plural* **grins**

grind *verb* **1.** To turn into very small pieces or powder by crushing, pounding, or rubbing: *grind wheat into flour.* **2.** To shape, sharpen, or make smooth by rubbing: *grind an ax.* **3.** To rub together noisily: *He grinds his teeth in his sleep.*
grind (grīnd) □*verb* **ground, grinding, grinds**

grindstone *noun* A flat, circular stone that revolves in a frame and is used to grind, polish, and sharpen tools.

a bat	ī bite	ōō tool	*th* feather
ā make	î fierce	ou out	th bath
â dare	o dot	u nut	hw wheat
ä father	ō no	û turn	zh measure
e net	ô law, for	ch church	ə about, open
ē be	oi soil	ng ring	pencil, atom
i dip	oo look	sh shade	circus

grind·stone (**grīnd′** stōn′) □*noun, plural*
grindstones

grindstone

grip   *noun* **1.** A firm hold or grasp: *He got a good grip on the handle and pulled the gate open.* **2.** Power; control: *The city was in the grip of a blizzard.*
□*verb* To seize and hold on to firmly: *She gripped the dog's leash.* —See Synonyms at **hold.**
grip (grip) □*noun, plural* **grips** □*verb* **gripped, gripping, grips**

gristle   *noun* Strands of tough white tissue in meat.
gris·tle (**gris′** əl) □*noun*

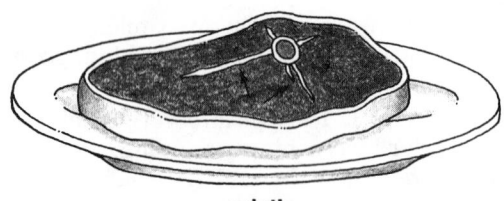

gristle

grit   *noun* **1.** Tiny, rough bits of sand or stone. **2.** Great spirit; courage: *It took a lot of grit to go for help through the blizzard.*
□*verb* To clamp or grind together: *He gritted his teeth against the pain.*
grit (grit) □*noun* □*verb* **gritted, gritting, grits**

grits   *plural noun* Coarsely ground grain, especially corn.
grits (grits) □*plural noun*

grizzled   *adjective* Streaked or marked with gray: *grizzled hair.*
griz·zled (**griz′** əld) □*adjective*

grizzled

grizzly bear   *noun* A large gray or brown bear of western North America.
griz·zly bear (**griz′** lē) □*noun*

groan   *verb* To make a deep sound low in the throat showing pain, grief, or annoyance: *She groaned when he stepped on her toe.*
□*noun* The deep, sad sound made in groaning; moan.
groan (grōn) □*verb* **groaned, groaning, groans** □*noun, plural* **groans**

grocer   *noun* Someone who sells fresh food, canned goods, and household supplies.
gro·cer (**grō′** sər) □*noun, plural* **grocers**

grocery   *noun* **1.** A store that sells fresh food, canned goods, and household supplies. **2. groceries** Things sold by a grocer.
gro·cer·y (**grō′** sə rē) □*noun, plural* **groceries**

groggy   *adjective* Dizzy, weak, and unsteady, as from illness, an injury, or lack of sleep.
grog·gy (**grog′** ē) □*adjective* **groggier, groggiest**

groom   *noun* **1.** Someone who takes care of horses. **2.** A bridegroom.
□*verb* **1.** To clean and brush horses. **2.** To make neat: *The cat groomed her kittens.*
groom (grōōm) □*noun, plural* **grooms** □*verb* **groomed, grooming, grooms**

groom

groove   *noun* A long, narrow cut or channel: *the grooves of a phonograph record.*
□*verb* To cut a groove in: *The carpenter grooved the board.*
groove (grōōv) □*noun, plural* **grooves** □*verb* **grooved, grooving, grooves**

grope   *verb* **1.** To feel about blindly or uncertainly: *She groped in her purse for her keys.* **2.** To find one's way without seeing clearly: *He groped his way up the dark stairs.*
grope (grōp) □*verb* **groped, groping, gropes**

gross   *adjective* **1.** Without anything taken out; total: *a gross income of $20,000.* **2.** Extreme; obvious: *a gross mistake.* **3.** Vulgar; coarse: *a gross action.*
□*noun* **1.** A total amount received: *The gross for that movie was a million dollars.* **2.** A group of 144; twelve dozen.
gross (grōs) □*adjective* **grosser, grossest**
□*noun, plural* **grosses** (**gross** for noun sense 2)

grotesque   *adjective* Very ugly or strange: *a grotesque monster.*
gro·tesque (grō tesk′) □*adjective*

grotto   *noun* **1.** A cave or cavern. **2.** A man-made structure resembling a cave.
grot·to (grot′ō) □*noun, plural* **grottoes**

grouch   *noun* Someone who is always cross and complaining.
grouch (grouch) □*noun, plural* **grouches**

ground¹   *noun* **1.** The solid part of the earth's surface. **2.** Often **grounds** An area or plot of land set aside and used for a special purpose: *parade grounds.* **3.** Often **grounds** The land around and belonging to a house or other building: *the grounds of the university.* **4.** Often **grounds** The reason for a belief, action, or thought; basis: *What grounds do you have for your claim?* **5. grounds** The small pieces of solid material at the bottom of a liquid, especially coffee; sediment. —See Synonyms at **land.**
□*verb* **1.** To touch or cause to touch the bottom of a river, lake, or other body of water: *The sailboat grounded on the sandbar.* **2.** To make come down to or stay on the ground: *They grounded all the planes because of the storm.* **3.** To establish or base: *rights grounded on the Constitution.* **4.** To connect an electric wire to the ground. **5.** To hit a baseball so that it bounces on the ground.
ground (ground) □*noun, plural* **grounds**
□*verb* **grounded, grounding, grounds**

ground

ground²   *verb* The past tense and past participle of **grind:** *He ground the corn into meal.*
ground (ground) □*verb*

ground hog   *noun* The woodchuck.

groundless   *adjective* Unsupported by facts or reason: *a groundless fear; a groundless accusation.*
ground·less (ground′lis) □*adjective*

group   *noun* **1.** A number of persons or things together: *a group of students.* **2.** A number of persons or things belonging together.
□*verb* To gather in a group.
group (grōōp) □*noun, plural* **groups** □*verb* **grouped, grouping, groups**

group

a bat	ī bite	ōō tool	*th* feather
ā make	î fierce	ou out	th bath
â dare	o dot	u nut	hw wheat
ä father	ō no	û turn	zh measure
e net	ô law, for	ch church	ə about, open
ē be	oi soil	ng ring	pencil, atom
i dip	oo look	sh shade	circus

grouse *noun* A game bird that has a plump body with brown or gray feathers.
grouse (grous) □*noun, plural* **grouse**

grouse

grove *noun* A group of trees with open ground between them.
grove (grōv) □*noun, plural* **groves**

grow *verb* **1.** To become larger in size: *My hair grew four inches last year.* **2.** To come into being and develop: *Orchids grow wild in the tropics.* **3.** To plant and raise; produce: *We grow roses in our garden.* **4.** To become: *It grows dark when the sun goes down. He grew impatient.*
     grow up To become an adult: *When I grow up I would like to be a doctor.*
grow (grō) □*verb* **grew, grown, growing, grows**

grow up

growl *noun* A low, deep sound such as the one made by an angry dog.

□*verb* To utter a growl.
growl (groul) □*noun, plural* **growls** □*verb* **growled, growling, growls**

grown *verb* The past participle of **grow**: *The corn had grown to six feet.*
grown (grōn) □*verb*

grownup or **grown-up** *noun* A fully grown person; adult.
grown·up or **grown-up** (grōn′up′) □*noun, plural* **grownups** or **grown-ups**

grown-up *adjective* Adult; mature: *a grown-up woman.*
grown-up (grōn′up′) □*adjective*

growth *noun* **1.** The process of growing: *the growth of the city's population.* **2.** Complete development: *He reached his full growth when he was sixteen.* **3.** Something that has grown: *a thick growth of grass.*
growth (grōth) □*noun, plural* **growths**

grub *noun* A beetle after it has hatched from an egg and before it is fully grown. It looks like a small, thick worm.
□*verb* To dig in the ground: *The pigs grubbed for food.*
grub (grub) □*noun, plural* **grubs** □*verb* **grubbed, grubbing, grubs**

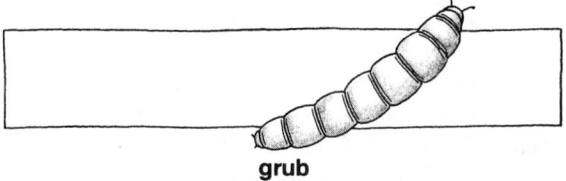

grub
Of a beetle

grubby *adjective* Dirty and untidy: *I wore my grubbiest clothes when I fixed my bicycle.*
grub·by (grub′ē) □*adjective* **grubbier, grubbiest**

grudge *noun* Anger or resentment felt for a long time: *She has held a grudge against her cousin ever since he broke her bicycle.*
□*verb* To give or allow with resentment: *She grudged him even his few pleasures.*
grudge (gruj) □*noun, plural* **grudges** □*verb* **grudged, grudging, grudges**

gruel *noun* A thin watery porridge.
gru·el (grōō′əl) □*noun*

grueling *adjective* Exhausting or difficult: *a grueling climb.*
gru·el·ing (grōō′ə ling) □*adjective*

gruesome *adjective* Causing shock or horror; awful: *a gruesome accident.*
grue·some (grōō′səm) □*adjective*

gruff *adjective* **1.** Having a harsh and deep sound: *a gruff voice.* **2.** Not friendly; impolite: *a gruff manner.*
gruff (gruf) □*adjective* **gruffer, gruffest**

grumble *verb* To complain in a low, discontented voice: *She grumbled about having to wash the dishes without any help.*
grum·ble (grum′bəl) □*verb* **grumbled, grumbling, grumbles**

grumpy *adjective* In a bad mood; irritable: *a tired, grumpy baby.*
grump·y (grum′pē) □*adjective* **grumpier, grumpiest**

grunt *noun* A short, deep, harsh sound. □*verb* To utter a grunt: *The man grunted as he tried to move the piano.*
grunt (grunt) □*noun, plural* **grunts** □*verb* **grunted, grunting, grunts**

guarantee *noun* A promise to repair or replace a product that breaks before a certain time: *a machine with a two-year guarantee.* □*verb* **1.** To make certain: *Her talent guaranteed her a part in the play.* **2.** To promise: *I guarantee that I will be home on time.* **3.** To give a guarantee for: *The company guarantees its cars for 25,000 miles.*
guar·an·tee (gar′ən tē) □*noun, plural* **guarantees** □*verb* **guaranteed, guaranteeing, guarantees**

guard *verb* **1.** To protect from harm: *Two dogs guard the property at night.* **2.** To watch over. **3.** To try to prevent an opponent from scoring. □*noun* **1.** A person or group that guards: *a bank guard.* **2.** Control: *The prisoner is under guard.* **3.** A device that protects or shields the user: *a shin guard.* **4.** Either of the two players on a football team's line next to the center. **5.** Either of the two basketball players stationed farthest from the opponents′ basket.
guard (gärd) □*verb* **guarded, guarding, guards** □*noun, plural* **guards**

guard
A shin guard

guardian *noun* **1.** Someone or something that guards or protects. **2.** Someone who is appointed by a court of law to look after a person who is too young, too old, or too sick to take care of himself or herself.
guard·i·an (gär′dē ən) □*noun, plural* **guardians**

guerrilla *noun* A member of a small group of soldiers fighting to overthrow a government. Guerrillas move and attack quickly.
guer·ril·la (gə ril′ə) □*noun, plural* **guerrillas**

guess *verb* **1.** To form an opinion without enough information to be sure: *I can only guess who will win the election.* **2.** To form such an opinion and be right; choose correctly: *I guessed the answer to the riddle and won the prize.* **3.** To suppose; assume: *I guess he agrees because he nodded his head.* □*noun* An opinion formed without enough information to be sure: *My guess is that it will snow all night.*
guess (ges) □*verb* **guessed, guessing, guesses** □*noun, plural* **guesses**

guesswork *noun* **1.** An answer or result gotten by guessing. **2.** The act of making guesses.
guess·work (ges′wûrk′) □*noun*

guest *noun* **1.** Someone who is at another person's home for a visit or a meal. **2.** Someone who is a customer at a hotel, club, or restaurant.
guest (gest) □*noun, plural* **guests**

guffaw *noun* A burst of hearty laughter. □*verb* To laugh in a hearty and loud way.
guf·faw (gə fô′) □*noun, plural* **guffaws** □*verb* **guffawed, guffawing, guffaws**

guidance *noun* **1.** The act of guiding or being guided. **2.** Help or advice: *We went to our pastor for guidance about our problems.*
guid·ance (gīd′əns) □*noun*

guide *noun* Someone or something that directs or shows the way: *We need two guides for our fishing trip.* □*verb* To show the way to; direct: *The usher guided me down the aisle with a flashlight.*

a	bat	ī	bite	ōō	tool	th	feather
ā	make	î	fierce	ou	out	th	bath
â	dare	o	dot	u	nut	hw	wheat
ä	father	ō	no	û	turn	zh	measure
e	net	ô	law, for	ch	church	ə	about, open
ē	be	oi	soil	ng	ring		pencil, atom
i	dip	oo	look	sh	shade		circus

guide (gīd) □*noun, plural* **guides** □*verb*
guided, guiding, guides

guide

guided missile   *noun* A missile whose course can be controlled throughout flight.

guideword   *noun* A word that appears at the top of a page in a dictionary and certain other books. It tells you what the first or last word is on that page.
guide·word (gīd′wûrd′) □*noun, plural* **guidewords**

guild   *noun* **1.** A union of merchants or craftsmen in the Middle Ages that set standards of workmanship for their trade or craft and looked after the welfare of the members. **2.** An association of people who share a trade, interest, or cause.
guild (gild) □*noun, plural* **guilds**

guile   *noun* Slyness and deceit: *an innocent, trusting person who was without guile.*
guile (gīl) □*noun*

guillotine   *noun* A machine for executing people by cutting off their heads. A guillotine is made of a heavy blade that slides up and down between two posts.
guil·lo·tine (gil′ə tēn′) □*noun, plural* **guillotines**

guilt   *noun* **1.** The fact of having done wrong: *We believed that he was a thief, but we couldn't prove his guilt.* **2.** Painful awareness of having done something wrong; shame: *I felt guilt for my selfishness.*
guilt (gilt) □*noun*

guilty   *adjective* **1.** Having committed a crime or offense: *The guilty man was sent to prison.* **2.** Feeling shame: *I felt guilty after breaking my promise.*
guilt·y (gil′tē) □*adjective* **guiltier, guiltiest**

guinea pig   *noun* An animal with short ears, short legs, and a stout body. Guinea pigs are often kept as pets or used in scientific experiments.
guin·ea pig (gin′ē) □*noun*

guitar   *noun* A musical instrument with a long neck and usually having six strings that are plucked with the fingers or a pick.
gui·tar (gi tär′) □*noun, plural* **guitars**

guitar

gulch   *noun* A small, shallow canyon or ravine.
gulch (gulch) □*noun, plural* **gulches**

gulf   *noun* A large area of ocean or sea that is partly enclosed by land.
gulf (gulf) □*noun, plural* **gulfs**

gull   *noun* A bird with webbed feet, gray and white feathers, and long wings. Gulls live on or near bodies of water.
gull (gul) □*noun, plural* **gulls**

gullible   *adjective* Easily tricked or fooled.
gul·li·ble (gul′ə bəl) □*adjective*

gully   *noun* A ditch cut in the earth by flowing water.
gul·ly (gul′ē) □*noun, plural* **gullies**

gully

gulp *verb* **1.** To swallow quickly or greedily: *He gulped down his breakfast and ran to school.* **2.** To gasp, especially from fear: *I gulped when I saw the snake.*
□*noun* A large, quick swallow: *a gulp of cold milk.*
gulp (gulp) □*verb* **gulped, gulping, gulps** □*noun, plural* **gulps**

gum¹ *noun* **1.** A thick, sticky juice produced by different trees and plants. Gums are used to make candies and chemicals and on the backs of stamps. **2.** Chewing gum.
gum (gum) □*noun, plural* **gums**

gum² *noun* The firm flesh in the mouth that holds the teeth in place.
gum (gum) □*noun, plural* **gums**

gumbo *noun* **1.** Okra. **2.** A soup or stew thickened with okra pods: *chicken gumbo.*
gum·bo (gum′bō) □*noun, plural* **gumbos**

gumdrop *noun* A small jellied candy covered with sugar.
gum·drop (gum′drop′) □*noun, plural* **gumdrops**

gumption *noun* A daring and bold spirit; courage: *He didn't have the gumption to ask a stranger for directions when he got lost.*
gump·tion (gump′shən) □*noun*

gun *noun* **1.** A weapon that shoots bullets or other missiles through a metal tube. Pistols, rifles, and cannons are guns. **2.** A device that shoots something out: *a staple gun.*
□*verb* To shoot with a gun.
gun (gun) □*noun, plural* **guns** □*verb* **gunned, gunning, guns**

gunner *noun* A member of the armed forces who fires cannons or other large guns.
gun·ner (gun′ər) □*noun, plural* **gunners**

gunpowder *noun* An explosive powder used to shoot bullets out of guns.
gun·pow·der (gun′pou′dər) □*noun, plural* **gunpowders**

gunwale *noun* The upper edge of the side of a boat or ship.
gun·wale (gun′əl) □*noun, plural* **gunwales**

guppy *noun* A small, brightly colored tropical fish that is often kept in home aquariums.
gup·py (gup′ē) □*noun, plural* **guppies**

gurgle *verb* **1.** To flow with a low, bubbling sound: *The brook gurgled through the woods.* **2.** To make low, bubbling sounds: *The baby gurgled happily.*
□*noun* A low, bubbling sound.

gur·gle (gûr′gəl) □*verb* **gurgled, gurgling, gurgles** □*noun, plural* **gurgles**

gush *verb* **1.** To flow out suddenly and in great quantity: *Water gushed from the hydrant.* **2.** To show too much feeling or enthusiasm: *Everyone gushed over the new baby.*
□*noun* A sudden or large flow: *a gush of tears.*
gush (gush) □*verb* **gushed, gushing, gushes** □*noun, plural* **gushes**

gush

gust *noun* **1.** A sudden, strong breeze. **2.** A sudden outburst of feeling: *a gust of anger.*
gust (gust) □*noun, plural* **gusts**

gut *noun* **1.** The alimentary canal or any part of it, especially the stomach or intestines. **2. guts** The internal organs of the abdomen; entrails. **3. guts** Courage.
gut (gut) □*noun, plural* **guts**

gutter *noun* **1.** A channel along the side of a street for carrying off water. **2.** A pipe or trough along the edge of a roof for carrying off rain water.
gut·ter (gut′ər) □*noun, plural* **gutters**

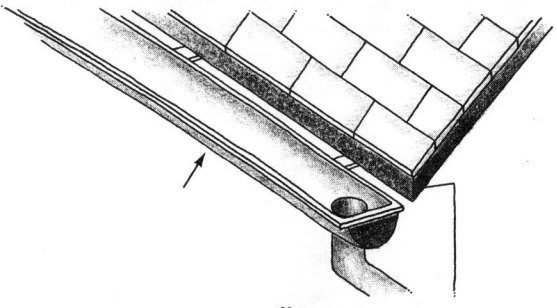

gutter

a bat	ī bite	o͞o tool	*th* feather
ā make	î fierce	ou out	th bath
â dare	o dot	u nut	hw wheat
ä father	ō no	û turn	zh measure
e net	ô law, for	ch church	ə about, open
ē be	oi soil	ng ring	pencil, atom
i dip	oo look	sh shade	circus

guy¹ *noun* A rope or wire used to hold, steady, or guide something.
guy (gī) □*noun, plural* **guys**

guy² *noun* A man or boy.
guy (gī) □*noun, plural* **guys**

> *WORD HISTORY:* **guy²**
>
> Almost 400 years ago an Englishman named Guy Fawkes was involved in a plot to blow up Parliament. The plot was foiled; Guy Fawkes and other plotters were hanged. Since that time the day of the plot, November 5, has been celebrated in England by burning stuffed figures of Guy Fawkes. These figures are called "guys." In England the word *guy* means "a grotesque person," but in the United States it simply means "a man" or "a boy."

gym *noun* **1.** A gymnasium. **2.** A class in gymnastics and sports.
gym (jim) □*noun, plural* **gyms**

gymnasium *noun* A room or building for gymnastics and indoor sports.
gym·na·si·um (jim **nā′**zē əm) □*noun, plural* **gymnasiums**

> *WORD HISTORY:* **gymnasium**
>
> The word *gymnasium* comes from a Greek word that means "a gymnastic school." The Greek word is derived from another word that means "naked." In ancient Greece it was usual for men and boys to exercise naked.

gymnast *noun* Someone who is trained in gymnastics.
gym·nast (**jim′**nast′) □*noun, plural* **gymnasts**

gymnastics *noun* Exercises and physical feats done with the use of the bars, mats, and other equipment in a gymnasium.
gym·nas·tics (jim **nas′**tiks) □*noun*

gymnastics
On the parallel bars

Gypsy *noun* A member of a wandering group of people who came to Europe from India in the 14th and 15th centuries.
Gyp·sy (**jip′**sē) □*noun, plural* **Gypsies**

> *WORD HISTORY:* **Gypsy**
>
> We now know that Gypsies originally came from India, but in earlier times Gypsies were thought to come from Egypt. The word *Gypsy* is an alteration of the word *Egyptian*.

gypsy moth *noun* A small brownish moth that develops from a hairy caterpillar that feeds on leaves and does great damage to trees.

gypsy moth
In the adult stage

gyroscope *noun* A wheel mounted on a vertical axis that can tilt at various angles to its base. When the base is tilted, the gyroscope's axis tends to tilt the opposite way. Gyroscopes are used to keep ships and airplanes steady.
gy·ro·scope (**jī′**rə skōp′) □*noun, plural* **gyroscopes**

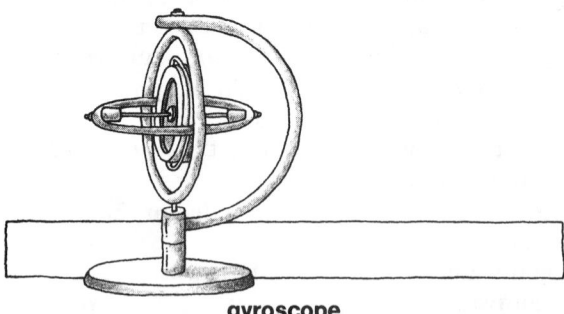

gyroscope

a	bat	ī	bite	ōō	tool	*th*	feather
ā	make	î	fierce	ou	out	th	bath
â	dare	o	dot	u	nut	hw	wheat
ä	father	ō	no	û	turn	zh	measure
e	net	ô	law, for	ch	church	ə	about, open
ē	be	oi	soil	ng	ring		pencil, atom
i	dip	oo	look	sh	shade		circus

ANCIENT GREEK

The letter **H** has evolved from many forms of ancient writing. One of the earliest known examples is the Greek character shown above, which dates from almost 3,000 years ago. Over the years, artists and designers have created their own versions of the English letter **H**. Some of the more common examples seen today are shown below.

Hh Hh	Hh Hh	Hh Hh	Hh Hh	Hh Hh
HANDWRITING	CALLIGRAPHY	MODERN SANS SERIF	MODERN SERIF	SCRIPT

h or **H** *noun* The eighth letter of the English alphabet.
h or **H** (āch) ▢*noun, plural* **h's** or **H's**

ha *interjection* **1.** A word used to express surprise, wonder, or triumph: *Ha! I've caught you.* **2.** A word used to imitate laughter: *Ha, ha, that's very funny.*
ha (hä) ▢*interjection*

habit *noun* **1.** An action done so often that one does it without thinking: *The baby had the bad habit of sucking his thumb.* **2.** A person's usual practice or custom: *It is my habit to read the newspaper every morning.* **3.** Clothing worn for a special activity or by a particular profession: *a riding habit; a nun's habit.*
hab·it (hăb′ĭt) ▢*noun, plural* **habits**

habit
A riding habit

habitat *noun* The place or kind of place where an animal or plant usually lives or grows: *The ocean is the habitat of sharks.*
hab·i·tat (hăb′ĭ tăt′) ▢*noun, plural* **habitats**

habitual *adjective* **1.** Having the nature of a habit: *habitual bad temper.* **2.** Doing or being because of habit: *He is a habitual liar.* **3.** Usual; customary: *their habitual time for eating dinner.*
ha·bit·u·al (hə bĭch′ōō əl) ▢*adjective*

hack *verb* **1.** To cut with heavy repeated blows: *She hacked the branch off the tree.* **2.** To cough harshly.
hack (hăk) ▢*verb* **hacked, hacking, hacks**

hack

hackneyed *adjective* Not fresh or original: *His essay was full of hackneyed expressions that we had heard too many times.*
hack·neyed (hăk′nēd) ▢*adjective*

hacksaw *noun* A saw having a tough blade with fine teeth and used for cutting metal.
hack·saw (**hak′**sô′) □*noun, plural* **hacksaws**

had *verb* The past tense and past participle of **have:** *He had a beautiful new car. She has had a headache all day.*
had (had) □*verb*

haddock *noun* A food fish related to the cod that lives in the northern regions of the Atlantic Ocean.
had·dock (**had′**ək) □*noun, plural* **haddock** or **haddocks**

hadn't Contraction of "had not."
had·n't (**had′**ənt)

hag *noun* **1.** An ugly old woman. **2.** A witch.
hag (hag) □*noun, plural* **hags**

haggard *adjective* Looking very tired and worn: *He was haggard from lack of sleep.*
hag·gard (**hag′**ərd) □*adjective*

haggle *verb* To argue in trying to agree on something, such as a price: *I could have bought this coat for a much lower price if I had haggled with the salesperson.*
hag·gle (**hag′**əl) □*verb* **haggled, haggling, haggles**

hail[1] *noun* **1.** Small, rounded pieces of ice that fall to earth like rain. **2.** Something like hail in force or quantity: *A hail of arrows hit the target.*
□*verb* **1.** To fall as hail: *It hailed and thundered all night.* **2.** To pour down like hail: *Fans hailed insults at the opposing team.*
hail (hāl) □*noun* □*verb* **hailed, hailing, hails**

hail[2] *verb* **1.** To call to in greeting or welcome: *She hailed her friend and shook his hand.* **2.** To attract the attention of by calling: *I hailed a passing bus.*
hail from To come or originate from: *We hail from the country.*
hail (hāl) □*verb* **hailed, hailing, hails**

hailstone *noun* A pellet of snow or ice.
hail·stone (**hāl′**stōn′) □*noun, plural* **hailstones**

hailstorm *noun* A storm in which hail falls.
hail·storm (**hāl′**stôrm′) □*noun, plural* **hailstorms**

hair *noun* **1.** One of the thin, fine strands that grow from the skin of animals and human beings. **2.** A mass or covering of hair: *The boy had black hair.* **3.** A growth like a hair on a plant or insect.
hair (hâr) □*noun, plural* **hairs**

hairbrush *noun* A brush for grooming the hair.
hair·brush (**hâr′**brush′) □*noun, plural* **hairbrushes**

haircut *noun* The act or style of cutting the hair.
hair·cut (**hâr′**kut′) □*noun, plural* **haircuts**

haircut

hairdo *noun* A style of arranging the hair.
hair·do (**hâr′**dōō′) □*noun, plural* **hairdos**

hair-raising *adjective* Causing horror, fear, or excitement: *a hair-raising adventure; a hair-raising ghost story.*
hair-rais·ing (**hâr′**rā′zing) □*adjective*

hairy *adjective* Covered with hair: *hairy arms.*
hair·y (**hâr′**ē) □*adjective* **hairier, hairiest**

hale *adjective* In good health: *a hale and hearty old man.*
hale (hāl) □*adjective*

half *noun* **1.** Either of two equal parts into which something can be divided: *Would you like half my apple?* **2.** Either of two playing periods into which certain games are divided.
□*adjective* Being a half: *a half piece of bread.*
□*adverb* Not completely; partly: *He was half awake.*
half (haf) □*noun, plural* **halves** □*adjective* □*adverb*

half brother *noun* A brother related through only one parent.

halfhearted *adjective* Done with or having little interest or enthusiasm: *She made a halfhearted effort to read the book but gave up because it was too long.*
half·heart·ed (**haf′hâr′**tid) □*adjective*

half knot *noun* A knot in which the ends of two ropes or cords are wrapped once around each other. A half knot is used as the first step in tying many other knots.

half-mast *noun* The position of a flag when it is halfway up the pole. It is a symbol of mourning for a person who has died or a signal of distress.
half-mast (haf′mast′) □*noun*

half-mast

half sister *noun* A sister related through only one parent.

halfway *adjective* **1.** In the middle between two points: *Her house is halfway between the library and the post office.* **2.** Incomplete; partial: *You can't solve the problem with halfway measures.*
□*adverb* **1.** To or at half the distance: *I'll meet you halfway between your house and mine.* **2.** Very nearly; almost: *She halfway agreed.*
half·way (haf′wā′) □*adjective* □*adverb*

half-wit *noun* A stupid or foolish person.
half-wit (haf′wit′) □*noun, plural* **half-wits**

halibut *noun* A very large ocean flatfish used as food.
hal·i·but (hal′ə bət) □*noun, plural* **halibut** or **halibuts**

hall *noun* **1.** A passageway in a building onto which rooms open: *His apartment is on the left at the end of the hall.* **2.** An entrance room in a building; lobby. **3.** A large building or room for public gatherings: *a lecture hall.*
hall (hôl) □*noun, plural* **halls**

hallelujah *interjection* Used to express praise or joy.
hal·le·lu·jah (hal′ə lōō′yə) □*interjection*

hallow *verb* To make, set apart as, or treat as holy: *The place was hallowed by the saint's tomb, and many people visited it every year.*
hal·low (hal′ō) □*verb* **hallowed, hallowing, hallows**

Halloween *noun* October 31, on which children often dress in costumes and go out in the evening to play tricks or ask for treats.
Hal·low·een (hal′ə wēn′) □*noun, plural* **Halloweens**

Halloween

hallucination *noun* An illusion of seeing, hearing, or otherwise sensing something that does not exist. Hallucinations may be caused by mental disorders or the effects of a drug.
hal·lu·ci·na·tion (hə lōō′sə nā′shən) □*noun, plural* **hallucinations**

hallway *noun* A hall or corridor in a building.
hall·way (hôl′wā′) □*noun, plural* **hallways**

halo *noun* **1.** A ring of light or bright haze around a heavenly body such as the sun or moon. **2.** A ring of light drawn around the head of a saint or angel in a religious painting.
ha·lo (hā′lō) □*noun, plural* **halos**

halt *noun* A temporary stop; pause: *Work came to a halt during the lunch hour.*
□*verb* To bring or come to a halt: *The engineer halted the train. The soldiers halted.*

a bat	ī bite	ōō tool	*th* feather
ā make	î fierce	ou out	th bath
â dare	o dot	u nut	hw wheat
ä father	ō no	û turn	zh measure
e net	ô law, for	ch church	ə about, open
ē be	oi soil	ng ring	pencil, atom
i dip	oo look	sh shade	circus

halt (hôlt) ☐*noun, plural* **halts** ☐*verb*
halted, halting, halts

halter *noun* A rope or strap for leading or tying an animal.
hal·ter (hôl′tər) ☐*noun, plural* **halters**

halve *verb* **1.** To divide into two parts: *We halved the pear.* **2.** To reduce by half: *We tried to halve our expenses.*
halve (hav) ☐*verb* **halved, halving, halves**

halves *noun* The plural of **half.**
halves (havz) ☐*noun*

ham *noun* **1.** The meat from the thigh of a hog. **2.** Someone who operates an amateur radio station.
ham (ham) ☐*noun, plural* **hams**

hamburger *noun* **1.** Ground beef. **2.** A round, flat portion of ground beef, usually fried or broiled and served in a roll or bun.
ham·burg·er (ham′bûr′gər) ☐*noun, plural* **hamburgers**

hamlet *noun* A small village.
ham·let (ham′lit) ☐*noun, plural* **hamlets**

hammer *noun* **1.** A hand tool made of a heavy, solid head attached to a handle and used chiefly for driving in nails and for shaping metals. **2.** The part of a gun that strikes the firing pin and causes the gun to go off. ☐*verb* **1.** To drive in or shape with a hammer: *hammer a nail; hammer a bowl out of silver.* **2.** To strike with or as if with a hammer: *She hammered on the car door with her fists.*
ham·mer (ham′ər) ☐*noun, plural* **hammers** ☐*verb* **hammered, hammering, hammers**

hammock *noun* A swinging bed made of rope or strong fabric that is hung between two supports.
ham·mock (ham′ək) ☐*noun, plural* **hammocks**

hammock

hamper[1] *verb* To prevent the movement, actions, or progress of: *Heavy rain hampered our efforts to put up the tent.*
ham·per (ham′pər) ☐*verb* **hampered, hampering, hampers**

hamper[2] *noun* A large basket, usually with a cover: *a laundry hamper.*
ham·per (ham′pər) ☐*noun, plural* **hampers**

hamster *noun* A small rodent with soft fur, large cheek pouches, and a short tail.
ham·ster (ham′stər) ☐*noun, plural* **hamsters**

hand *noun* **1.** The part of the arm below the wrist, consisting of the palm, four fingers, and a thumb, used for grasping and holding. **2.** Something like a hand, as the pointer on a clock or gauge. **3.** Assistance; help: *I gave her a hand with her luggage.* **4.** Often **hands** Possession or control: *She kept her property in her own hands.* **5.** Someone who does manual labor: *a ranch hand.* **6.** A round of applause: *He got a good hand for his performance.* **7.** An active part in something; role or share: *She had a hand in planning the party.* **8.** The cards dealt to a player in a card game. **9.** A unit of length equal to four inches used especially for the height of a horse. ☐*verb* To give or pass with the hand: *I handed the salt to him.*
   hand down To pass along; transmit: *a bracelet that has been handed down from generation to generation.*
   on hand Ready when needed; available: *I always keep stamps on hand.*
hand (hand) ☐*noun, plural* **hands** ☐*verb* **handed, handing, hands**

handbag *noun* A woman's bag for carrying personal items; purse.
hand·bag (hand′bag′) ☐*noun, plural* **handbags**

handball *noun* **1.** A game for two or four players in which a ball is hit against a wall with the hand. **2.** The small, hard rubber ball used in handball.
hand·ball (hand′bôl′) ☐*noun, plural* **handballs**

handbill *noun* A printed sheet or leaflet given out by hand.
hand·bill (hand′bil′) ☐*noun, plural* **handbills**

handbook *noun* A book of instructions or information on a particular subject: *a handbook of botany.*
hand·book (hand′book′) ☐*noun, plural* **handbooks**

handcart *noun* A small cart pushed or pulled by hand.
hand·cart (**hand′**kärt′) □*noun, plural* **handcarts**

handcuff *noun* One of a pair of sturdy metal rings connected by a chain and locked around a prisoner's wrists.
□*verb* To put handcuffs on.
hand·cuff (**hand′**kuf′) □*noun, plural* **handcuffs** □*verb* **handcuffed, handcuffing, handcuffs**

handful *noun* **1.** The amount that can be held in the hand: *a handful of pennies.* **2.** A small amount or number: *Only a handful of children saw the movie.*
hand·ful (**hand′**fool′) □*noun, plural* **handfuls**

handicap *noun* A disadvantage that makes achievement or success difficult.
□*verb* To put at a disadvantage: *Lack of experience handicapped him in his search for a job.*
hand·i·cap (**han′**dē kap′) □*noun, plural* **handicaps** □*verb* **handicapped, handicapping, handicaps**

handicapped *adjective* Having a handicap.
hand·i·capped (**han′**dē kapt′) □*adjective*

handicraft *noun* A craft or occupation, such as weaving, requiring skilled use of the hands.
hand·i·craft (**han′**dē kraft′) □*noun, plural* **handicrafts**

handicraft

handily *adverb* In a handy or easy manner: *We won the game handily and by a large margin.*
hand·i·ly (**han′**di lē) □*adverb*

handiwork *noun* Work done by hand: *These quilts are fine examples of American women's handiwork.*
hand·i·work (**han′**dē wûrk′) □*noun*

handkerchief *noun* A small square of cloth used to wipe the nose or face.
hand·ker·chief (**hang′**kər chif) □*noun, plural* **handkerchiefs**

handle *noun* A part of an object that is designed to be held or operated by the hand.
□*verb* **1.** To touch or hold with the hand: *Please handle the eggs with care.* **2.** To deal with: *He knew how to handle the problem.*
—See Synonyms at **touch.**
han·dle (**han′**dəl) □*noun, plural* **handles** □*verb* **handled, handling, handles**

handlebars *plural noun* A curved metal bar for steering a bicycle or motorcycle.
han·dle·bars (**han′**dəl bärz′) □*plural noun*

handmade *adjective* Made by hand rather than by machine: *handmade lace.*
hand·made (**hand′**mād′) □*adjective*

hand-me-down *noun* Something handed on to one person after being used and discarded by another: *Most of the baby's clothes are hand-me-downs from her sisters and cousins.*
hand-me-down (**hand′**mē doun′) □*noun, plural* **hand-me-downs**

handout *noun* **1.** Something, such as money, given to a beggar. **2.** Something, such as a leaflet, given out by hand.
hand·out (**hand′**out′) □*noun, plural* **handouts**

handrail *noun* A narrow rail to be grasped by the hand for support.
hand·rail (**hand′**rāl′) □*noun, plural* **handrails**

handshake *noun* The act of grasping a person's hand, as in greeting.
hand·shake (**hand′**shāk′) □*noun, plural* **handshakes**

handsome *adjective* **1.** Of pleasing appearance: *a handsome woman; a handsome house.* **2.** Generous; liberal: *a handsome tip.* —See Synonyms at **beautiful.**
hand·some (**han′**səm) □*adjective* **handsomer, handsomest**

handspring *noun* The act of flipping the body completely over from a standing posi-

a bat	ī bite	ōō tool	*th* feather
ā make	î fierce	ou out	th bath
â dare	o dot	u nut	hw wheat
ä father	ō no	û turn	zh measure
e net	ô law, for	ch church	ə about, open
ē be	oi soil	ng ring	pencil, atom
i dip	oo look	sh shade	circus

tion, landing first on the hands and then on the feet.

hand·spring (hand′spring′) □*noun, plural* **handsprings**

handstand *noun* The act of balancing on the hands with the feet in the air.

hand·stand (hand′stand′) □*noun, plural* **handstands**

handwriting *noun* Writing done with the hand.

hand·writ·ing (hand′rī′ting) □*noun*

handy *adjective* **1.** Skilled in the use of one's hands: *She is handy with a hammer and nails.* **2.** Within easy reach: *a market that is handy to the house.* **3.** Easy to use or handle; convenient: *A vacuum cleaner is a handy household tool.* —See Synonyms at **convenient.**

hand·y (han′dē) □*adjective* **handier, handiest**

hang *verb* **1.** To fasten or be fastened at the upper end only with no support from below: *I hung the cup on a hook. A painting hung on the wall.* **2.** To fasten something in a way that allows free motion back and forth: *hang a door.* **3.** *Past tense and past participle* **hanged** To put to death by suspending from a rope tied around the neck. **4.** To hold or bend downward; let droop: *The man hung his head in embarrassment.*
□*noun* **1.** The way in which something hangs: *the hang of a skirt.* **2.** The proper way of doing something; knack: *I can't get the hang of driving a car.*

hang (hang) □*verb* **hung** (**hanged** *for verb sense 3*), **hanging, hangs** □*noun*

hangar *noun* A building used for sheltering and repairing aircraft.

han·gar (hang′ər) □*noun, plural* **hangars**

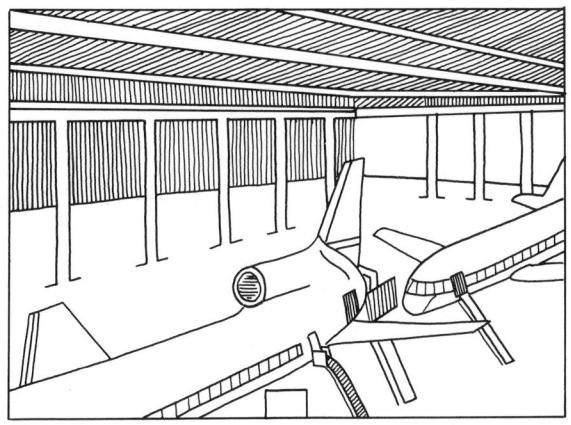

hangar

hanger *noun* A device on which a garment is hung.

hang·er (hang′ər) □*noun, plural* **hangers**

hangman *noun* Someone whose job is to execute convicted criminals by hanging.

hang·man (hang′mən) □*noun, plural* **hangmen**

hangnail *noun* A small flap of dead skin that hangs from the side of a fingernail.

hang·nail (hāng′nāl′) □*noun, plural* **hangnails**

hangout *noun* A place visited regularly by a person or group, especially to waste time.

hang·out (hang′out′) □*noun, plural* **hangouts**

hanker *verb* To long or yearn for; crave: *I was hankering for one of the cupcakes that mother made for the cake sale, but she wouldn't let me have one.*

han·ker (hang′kər) □*verb* **hankered, hankering, hankers**

hansom *noun* A carriage with two wheels that is drawn by a horse and has the driver's seat high up at the rear.

han·som (han′səm) □*noun, plural* **hansoms**

Hanukkah *noun* Another spelling for **Chanukah.**

Ha·nuk·kah (hä′noo kä′) □*noun*

haphazard *adjective* Not having any plan or order; random: *His selection of books to read over the vacation was quite haphazard.*

hap·haz·ard (hap haz′ərd) □*adjective*

hapless *adjective* Unlucky: *No sooner had the hapless boy picked himself up out of the puddle than he fell into the mud.*

hap·less (hap′lis) □*adjective*

happen *verb* **1.** To take place; occur: *What happened at the office yesterday?* **2.** To come about by chance: *I just happened to be at home when he rang the doorbell.* **3.** To be the fate or experience of: *Good things happened to her.*

hap·pen (hap′ən) □*verb* **happened, happening, happens**

happening *noun* Something that happens; event: *the important happenings of the day.*

hap·pen·ing (hap′ə ning) □*noun, plural* **happenings**

happily *adverb* **1.** In a cheerful or happy manner: *The children happily played with their new toys.* **2.** By good luck or chance: *Happily I found someone to help me.*

hap·pi·ly (hap′ə lē) □*adverb*

happiness *noun* The condition of being happy: *He finds happiness in being with his family.*
hap·pi·ness (hap′i nis) ☐*noun*

happy *adjective* Showing or feeling joy or pleasure: *a happy child; a happy smile.* —See Synonyms at **cheerful.**
hap·py (hap′ē) ☐*adjective* **happier, happiest**

happy-go-lucky *adjective* Free from care and trouble; lighthearted: *a happy-go-lucky person who is never in a bad mood.*
hap·py-go-luck·y (hap′ē gō luk′ē) ☐*adjective*

harass *verb* To bother again and again: *The crowd harassed the candidate by interrupting his speech with questions.*
har·ass (har′əs *or* hə ras′) ☐*verb* **harassed, harassing, harasses**

WORD HISTORY: **harass**

Harass comes from an old French word that means "to set a dog on."

---

harbor *noun* A sheltered place along a coast that serves as a port for ships.
☐*verb* **1.** To give shelter to; take in: *They harbored the lost child.* **2.** To have and keep in the mind: *He harbored a grudge against her because she insulted him.*
har·bor (här′bər) ☐*noun, plural* **harbors**
☐*verb* **harbored, harboring, harbors**

harbor

hard *adjective* **1.** Not easily penetrated, pierced, or cut; firm or rigid: *Granite is a hard stone.* **2.** Requiring or using great effort: *Shoveling snow is hard work. That was a hard problem to solve.* **3.** Difficult to endure: *The first*
winter was a hard time for the Pilgrims. **4.** Having great strength or force: *She hit me with a hard punch.* —See Synonyms at **difficult.**
☐*adverb* **1.** With great energy or effort: *You work too hard.* **2.** With great force; heavily: *It snowed hard all night.* **3.** With difficulty or distress: *She took the news very hard.*
hard (härd) ☐*adjective* **harder, hardest** ☐*adverb* **harder, hardest**

SYNONYMS: **hard, solid**

These adjectives mean not easily penetrated, pierced, or cut: *The cement will be hard when it dries. The ice was a solid mass that was difficult to chip.*

---

hard-boiled *adjective* Cooked by boiling until hard: *hard-boiled eggs.*
hard-boiled (härd′boild′) ☐*adjective*

harden *verb* To make or become hard or harder: *Cold will harden butter. The mixture hardened as it dried.*
hard·en (här′dən) ☐*verb* **hardened, hardening, hardens**

hardheaded *adjective* Practical and realistic: *a hardheaded but painful decision.*
hard·head·ed (härd′hed′id) ☐*adjective*

hardhearted *adjective* Having no sympathy or pity: *The hardhearted man was unkind even to his own children.*
hard·heart·ed (härd′här′tid) ☐*adjective*

hardly *adverb* **1.** Only just; barely: *I hardly knew what to do.* **2.** Surely not: *You can hardly expect me to say yes.*
hard·ly (härd′lē) ☐*adverb*

hardship *noun* Something causing suffering or difficulty: *It is a hardship to be in a strange city without money or friends.*
hard·ship (härd′ship′) ☐*noun, plural* **hardships**

hardware *noun* **1.** Metal goods and articles such as tools, nails, locks, and keys. **2.** A computer and all the physical parts that go with it

a	bat	ī	bite	ōō	tool	th	feather
ā	make	î	fierce	ou	out	th	bath
â	dare	o	dot	u	nut	hw	wheat
ä	father	ō	no	û	turn	zh	measure
e	net	ô	law, for	ch	church	ə	about, open
ē	be	oi	soil	ng	ring		pencil, atom
i	dip	oo	look	sh	shade		circus

to form a computer system.
hard·ware (härd′ wâr′) ☐*noun*

hardwood *noun* The wood of a tree that has leaves and flowers rather than needles and cones. Maple and oak are hardwoods.
hard·wood (härd′ wood′) ☐*noun, plural* **hardwoods**

hardy *adjective* Strong and healthy; robust: *hardy campers; a hardy plant.*
har·dy (här′ dē) ☐*adjective* **hardier, hardiest**

hare *noun* An animal that looks like a rabbit but is larger and has longer ears.
hare (hâr) ☐*noun, plural* **hares**

hare

harm *noun* An act of hurting or condition of being hurt.
☐*verb* To cause harm to; injure: *Smoking harms your health.*
harm (härm) ☐*noun* ☐*verb* **harmed, harming, harms**

SYNONYMS: **harm, damage, injury**

These nouns mean an act of hurting or the condition of being hurt: *The seat belts in an automobile are designed to protect us from harm. The fire caused great damage to the house. I fell and hurt my arm, but the injury was not serious.*

---

harmful *adjective* Causing harm: *a harmful drug.*
harm·ful (härm′ fəl) ☐*adjective*

harmless *adjective* Causing no harm: *a harmless snake.*
harm·less (härm′ lis) ☐*adjective*

harmonica *noun* A small musical instrument with metal reeds that is played by blowing in and out through a set of holes.
har·mon·i·ca (här mon′ i kə) ☐*noun, plural* **harmonicas**

harmonious *adjective* Showing or feeling harmony: *harmonious music; a harmonious*

friendship.
har·mo·ni·ous (här mō′ nē əs) ☐*adjective*

harmonize *verb* **1.** To sing or play in harmony. **2.** To be in harmony; blend: *The rug harmonized with the sofa.*
har·mo·nize (här′ mə nīz′) ☐*verb* **harmonized, harmonizing, harmonizes**

harmony *noun* **1.** The playing of musical tones together in chords. **2.** A pleasing combination of parts: *color harmony.* **3.** Agreement in opinion or feeling; accord: *We live in harmony with our neighbors.*
har·mo·ny (här′ mə nē) ☐*noun, plural* **harmonies**

harness *noun* A set of leather straps and metal pieces by which an animal, such as a horse, is attached to a vehicle or plow.
☐*verb* **1.** To put a harness on. **2.** To control and direct the force of: *Scientists are trying to harness the atom for peaceful use.*
har·ness (här′ nis) ☐*noun, plural* **harnesses**
☐*verb* **harnessed, harnessing, harnesses**

harness

harp *noun* A musical instrument consisting of a triangular frame with strings that are plucked with the fingers.
harp (härp) ☐*noun, plural* **harps**

harpoon *noun* A spear with an attached rope, used in hunting whales and other large sea animals.
☐*verb* To strike or kill with a harpoon.
har·poon (här poon′) ☐*noun, plural* **harpoons** ☐*verb* **harpooned, harpooning, harpoons**

harpsichord *noun* A keyboard instrument similar to the piano with strings that are plucked by quills or picks.
harp·si·chord (härp′ si kôrd′) ☐*noun, plural* **harpsichords**

harrow *noun* A heavy frame with metal teeth or disks used to break up and level plowed ground.

har·row (har′ō) □*noun, plural* **harrows**

harry *verb* **1.** To make a raid on, as in war. **2.** To disturb by constant attacks: *The neighbors harried the young mother with advice about caring for babies.*
har·ry (har′ē) □*verb* **harried, harrying, harries**

harsh *adjective* **1.** Rough and unpleasant to the senses: *a harsh voice.* **2.** Cruel; severe: *harsh punishment.*
harsh (härsh) □*adjective* **harsher, harshest**

harvest *noun* **1.** The act of gathering a crop: *corn that is ready for harvest.* **2.** The crop that is gathered: *the wheat harvest.*
□*verb* To gather: *The farmer harvested a crop of peaches.*
har·vest (här′vist) □*noun, plural* **harvests**
□*verb* **harvested, harvesting, harvests**

has *verb* The third person singular present tense of **have:** *He has many friends.*
has (haz) □*verb*

hash *noun* **1.** Chopped meat and potatoes cooked together. **2.** A mess; jumble: *He made a hash of the job.*
hash (hash) □*noun, plural* **hashes**

hasn't Contraction of "has not."
has·n't (haz′ənt)

hasp *noun* A hinged fastener for a door that fits over a staple and is locked with a pin, bolt, or padlock.
hasp (hasp) □*noun, plural* **hasps**

hassle *noun* **1.** An argument. **2.** Bother; annoyance: *It's such a hassle trying to get across town during rush hour.*
has·sle (has′əl) □*noun, plural* **hassles**

hassock *noun* A thick, firm cushion used as a footstool.
has·sock (has′ək) □*noun, plural* **hassocks**

haste *noun* Speed of motion or action; hurry: *We left the house in haste.*
haste (hāst) □*noun*

hasten *verb* To move or act swiftly; hurry: *The rain hastened our departure.*
has·ten (hā′sən) □*verb* **hastened, hastening, hastens**

hasty *adjective* **1.** Marked by speed; rapid: *The enemy made a hasty retreat.* **2.** Done too quickly to be accurate or wise: *a hasty decision.*
hast·y (hā′stē) □*adjective* **hastier, hastiest**

hat *noun* A covering for the head, often having a crown and a brim.
hat (hat) □*noun, plural* **hats**

hatch¹ *verb* **1.** To cause to come out of an egg: *The hen hatched a brood of chickens.* **2.** To come out of an egg: *We watched the ducklings hatch.*
hatch (hach) □*verb* **hatched, hatching, hatches**

hatch

hatch² *noun* **1.** A small door, as in an airplane: *an escape hatch.* **2.** An opening in the deck of a ship that leads to a lower deck.
hatch (hach) □*noun, plural* **hatches**

hatchery *noun* A place for hatching eggs: *a fish hatchery.*
hatch·er·y (hach′ə rē) □*noun, plural* **hatcheries**

hatchet *noun* A small ax with a short handle.
hatch·et (hach′it) □*noun, plural* **hatchets**

hate *verb* To dislike very much: *She hates washing dishes.*
□*noun* Strong dislike; hatred.
hate (hāt) □*verb* **hated, hating, hates**
□*noun, plural* **hates**

hateful *adjective* Arousing or deserving hatred: *Murder is a hateful crime.*
hate·ful (hāt′fəl) □*adjective*

hatred *noun* Extremely strong dislike.
ha·tred (hā′trid) □*noun*

a	bat	ī	bite	o͞o	tool	*th*	feather
ā	make	î	fierce	ou	out	th	bath
â	dare	o	dot	u	nut	hw	wheat
ä	father	ō	no	û	turn	zh	measure
e	net	ô	law, for	ch	church	ə	about, open
ē	be	oi	soil	ng	ring		pencil, atom
i	dip	o͝o	look	sh	shade		circus

hatter *noun* Someone who makes, sells, or repairs hats.
hat·ter (hăt′ər) □*noun, plural* **hatters**

haughty *adjective* Too proud of oneself: *She's too haughty to speak to us.*
haugh·ty (hô′tē) □*adjective* **haughtier, haughtiest**

haul *verb* **1.** To pull or drag with force: *We hauled the beams to the truck.* **2.** To transport; carry: *Huge tankers haul oil.*
□*noun* **1.** The act of hauling. **2.** The distance over which something is transported: *It's a short haul from Boston to New York.* **3.** An amount won, caught, or taken in: *She came home with a big haul of fish.*
haul (hôl) □*verb* **hauled, hauling, hauls**
□*noun, plural* **hauls**

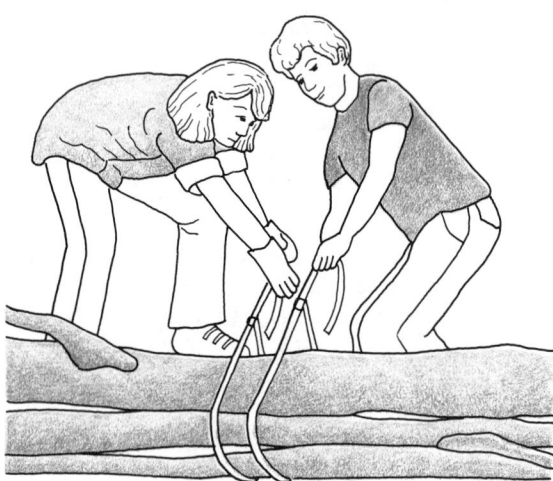

haul

haunch *noun* **1.** The hip, buttock, and upper thigh of a human being or animal. **2.** The loin and leg of an animal as used for food.
haunch (hônch) □*noun, plural* **haunches**

haunt *verb* To visit or return to regularly, especially as a spirit or a ghost: *They say a ghost haunts the old house.*
haunt (hônt) □*verb* **haunted, haunting, haunts**

have *verb* **1.** To be in possession of: *I have only a few dollars. He has a great idea.* **2.** To get; obtain: *There was no water to be had.* **3.** To cause to do or be done: *I'll have him call you.* **4.** To keep or harbor in the mind: *He has a good idea.* **5.** To suffer from: *She has a cold.* **6.** To be obliged or forced: *I have to go.* **7.** To give birth to: *Our cat had three kittens yesterday.* **8.** Used with the past participle of another verb to show completed action: *They have just left. We had already finished dinner when they arrived.*
have (hăv) □*verb* **had, having, has**

haven *noun* A place of safety or shelter: *She found a haven in her friend's home.*
ha·ven (hā′vən) □*noun, plural* **havens**

haven't Contraction of "have not."
have·n't (hăv′ənt)

havoc *noun* **1.** Great destruction: *The hurricane wreaked havoc along the coast.* **2.** A condition of confusion and disorder: *The children created havoc in the house.*
hav·oc (hăv′ək) □*noun*

Hawaiian *noun* **1.** Someone who was born or lives in Hawaii. **2.** The language of the Hawaiians.
□*adjective* Of Hawaii, the Hawaiians, or their language.
Ha·wai·ian (hə wä′yən) □*noun, plural* **Hawaiians** □*adjective*

hawk¹ *noun* A bird with a short, hooked bill and strong claws with which it catches small animals for food.
hawk (hôk) □*noun, plural* **hawks**

hawk

hawk² *verb* To offer for sale by calling out; peddle: *He hawked frankfurters at the circus.*
hawk (hôk) □*verb* **hawked, hawking, hawks**

hawthorn *noun* A thorny shrub with white or pinkish flowers and red berries.
haw·thorn (hô′thôrn′) □*noun, plural* **hawthorns**

hay *noun* Plants such as grass and clover that have been cut and dried for use as fodder.
hay (hā) □*noun*

hay fever *noun* An allergy with symptoms like a cold that is caused especially by the pollen of certain plants.

hayloft *noun* A loft in a barn or stable for storing hay.
hay·loft (hā′lôft′) □*noun, plural* **haylofts**

haystack *noun* A large stack of hay stored outdoors.
hay·stack (hā′stak′) □*noun, plural* **haystacks**

haywire *adjective* **1.** Not in proper working order; out of control: *The alarm clock went haywire and rang every fifteen minutes.* **2.** Mentally or emotionally excited or upset: *The town went haywire after hearing the news.*
hay·wire (hā′wīr′) □*adjective*

hazard *noun* Something that can cause harm: *a fire hazard.* —See Synonyms at **danger.**
haz·ard (haz′ərd) □*noun, plural* **hazards**

haze *noun* Smoke, dust, or mist in the air: *A haze over the town hid the buildings.*
haze (hāz) □*noun, plural* **hazes**

hazel *noun* **1.** A small tree or shrub bearing an edible nut with a smooth brown shell. **2.** A light or yellowish brown.
□*adjective* Light or yellowish brown: *hazel eyes.*
ha·zel (hā′zəl) □*noun, plural* **hazels** □*adjective*

hazelnut *noun* The nut of the hazel tree.
ha·zel·nut (hā′zəl nut′) □*noun, plural* **hazelnuts**

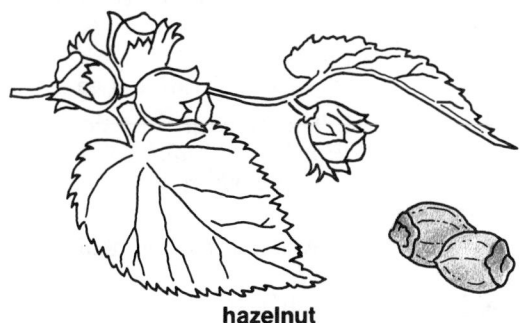
hazelnut

hazy *adjective* **1.** Cloudy or dim with haze: *a hazy day; a hazy sky.* **2.** Not clear; vague: *I have only a hazy idea of what I want to do.*
haz·y (hā′zē) □*adjective* **hazier, haziest**

he *pronoun* **1.** The male referred to or mentioned earlier: *My father is a pilot and he travels a great deal.* **2.** Anyone: *He who laughs last laughs best.*
he (hē) □*pronoun*

head *noun* **1.** The part of the body containing the brain, eyes, ears, nose, and mouth. **2.** Someone who is in charge; leader: *a head of state.* **3.** The leading position; front: *She went to the head of the line.* **4.** The upper part; top: *the head of the bed.* **5.** A rounded part that looks like a head: *a head of cabbage; the head of a nail.* **6.** *plural* **head** A single animal: *100 head of cattle.* **7.** Often **heads** The side of a coin having the main design and the date.
□*adjective* Principal; chief: *the head cook.*
□*verb* **1.** To move or cause to move in a certain direction: *They headed for the pool. He headed the bus eastward.* **2.** To be in the first or foremost position of: *She heads the list of candidates.* **3.** To be in charge of: *He headed the science project.*
head (hed) □*noun, plural* **heads** □*adjective* □*verb* **headed, heading, heads**

headache *noun* A pain in the head.
head·ache (hed′āk′) □*noun, plural* **headaches**

headband *noun* A band worn on the head.
head·band (hed′band′) □*noun, plural* **headbands**

headdress *noun* A covering or ornament worn on the head.
head·dress (hed′dres′) □*noun, plural* **headdresses**

headdress

headfirst *adverb* With the head leading: *He fell headfirst into the puddle.*
head·first (hed′fûrst′) □*adverb*

a	bat	ī	bite	ōō	tool	*th*	feather
ā	make	î	fierce	ou	out	th	bath
â	dare	o	dot	u	nut	hw	wheat
ä	father	ō	no	û	turn	zh	measure
e	net	ô	law, for	ch	church	ə	about, open
ē	be	oi	soil	ng	ring		pencil, atom
i	dip	oo	look	sh	shade		circus

headgear   *noun* Something worn on the head, such as a hat or helmet.
head·gear (hed′gîr′) □*noun*

heading   *noun* A title at the top of a page, chapter, or letter.
head·ing (hed′ing) □*noun, plural* **headings**

headland   *noun* A point of high land extending out into a body of water.
head·land (hed′land′) □*noun, plural* **headlands**

headlight   *noun* A light mounted on the front of a vehicle such as an automobile.
head·light (hed′līt′) □*noun, plural* **headlights**

headline   *noun* A line usually printed in large type at the top of a newspaper article.
head·line (hed′līn′) □*noun, plural* **headlines**

headline

headlong   *adverb* **1.** With the head leading; headfirst. **2.** Without thinking; recklessly: *He rushed headlong into the project without a plan.*
□*adjective* **1.** Done with the head leading: *a headlong fall.* **2.** Reckless; rash: *a headlong decision.*
head·long (hed′lông′) □*adverb* □*adjective*

headmaster   *noun* A man who is the principal of a private school.
head·mas·ter (hed′mas′tər) □*noun, plural* **headmasters**

headmistress   *noun* A woman who is the principal of a private school.
head·mis·tress (hed′mis′tris) □*noun, plural* **headmistresses**

head-on   *adjective* and *adverb* With the front end first: *two trains in a head-on crash. The car crashed head-on into the tree.*

head-on (hed′on′ *or* hed′ôn′) □*adjective* and *adverb*

headphone   *noun* An earphone kept in place by a headband.
head·phone (hed′fōn′) □*noun, plural* **headphones**

headquarters   *plural noun* A center of operations: *Our company's headquarters are in Washington.*
head·quar·ters (hed′kwôr′tərz) □*plural noun*

headstand   *noun* The act of balancing on the head and hands with the feet in the air.
head·stand (hed′stand′) □*noun, plural* **headstands**

head start   *noun* An advantage given at the beginning of an activity or competition.

headstone   *noun* A memorial stone set at the head of a grave.
head·stone (hed′stōn′) □*noun, plural* **headstones**

headstrong   *adjective* Wanting to have one's own way; willful: *The headstrong girl would not listen to advice and was always getting into trouble.*
head·strong (hed′strông′) □*adjective*

headway   *noun* Forward movement; progress: *The boat couldn't make any headway against the flood waters.*
head·way (hed′wā′) □*noun*

heal   *verb* To make or become healthy and sound: *She worked to heal the sick. My cut healed quickly.*
heal (hēl) □*verb* **healed, healing, heals**

health   *noun* **1.** The general condition of the body or mind: *How is his health?* **2.** Freedom from sickness: *She quickly returned to health.*
health (helth) □*noun*

healthful   *adjective* Good for the health: *I eat good healthful food.*
health·ful (helth′fəl) □*adjective*

healthy   *adjective* Having, promoting, or showing good health: *a healthy diet.*
health·y (hel′thē) □*adjective* **healthier, healthiest**

SYNONYMS: **healthy, fit, sound, well**

These adjectives mean having or showing good health: *She is a happy, healthy baby. She exercises every day to keep herself fit. The stray dog we picked up is skinny but sound. I was sick with a cold but now I'm well.*

heap   *noun* A group of things piled together: *a heap of dirty clothes.*
□*verb* **1.** To make into a heap: *I heaped the books on the floor.* **2.** To fill to overflowing: *We heaped the wagon with straw.*
heap (hēp) □*noun, plural* **heaps** □*verb* **heaped, heaping, heaps**

heap

hear   *verb* **1.** To take in sound by the ear: *He heard distant thunder. She doesn't hear well.* **2.** To get information by hearing; learn: *I heard that you were going away.* **3.** To listen to with attention: *She wouldn't even hear my side of the argument.*
hear (hîr) □*verb* **heard, hearing, hears**

hearing   *noun* **1.** The ability to hear: *He has excellent hearing.* **2.** The range within which sound can be heard: *They talked within my hearing.* **3.** An opportunity to be heard: *The principal gave her a fair hearing.*
hear·ing (hîr′ ing) □*noun, plural* **hearings**

hearing aid   *noun* A small electronic device worn in the ear in order to make sounds louder so a partially deaf person can hear them.

hearken   *verb* To listen with attention: *The people hearkened to the message of the prophet.*
heark·en (här′ kən) □*verb* **hearkened, hearkening, hearkens**

hearsay   *noun* Information or news heard from another person.
hear·say (hîr′ sā′) □*noun*

hearse   *noun* A vehicle for carrying the dead in funeral ceremonies.
hearse (hûrs) □*noun, plural* **hearses**

heart   *noun* **1.** The organ that pumps blood throughout the body. **2.** Something shaped like a heart. **3.** The central or main part: *the heart of the business district; the heart of the*

problem. **4.** Courage: *Don't lose heart.* **5.** Feelings; emotions: *He has no heart.* **6.** A playing card marked with a red figure that looks like a heart.
  by heart By memory: *learn a poem by heart.*
heart (härt) □*noun, plural* **hearts**

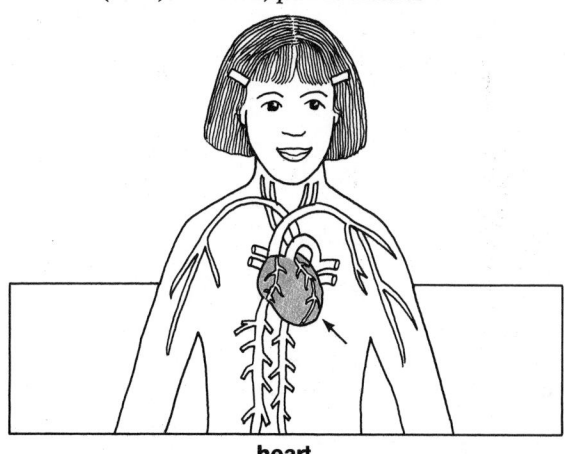

heart

heartache   *noun* A sorrowful feeling or experience: *His life contained more heartache than joy.*
heart·ache (härt′ āk′) □*noun, plural* **heartaches**

heartbeat   *noun* A single cycle of contraction and relaxation of the heart.
heart·beat (härt′ bēt′) □*noun, plural* **heartbeats**

heartbroken   *adjective* Suffering great sorrow or grief.
heart·bro·ken (härt′ brō′kən) □*adjective*

hearten   *verb* To give strength or hope to; encourage.
heart·en (här′ tən) □*verb* **heartened, heartening, heartens**

hearth   *noun* The floor of a fireplace.
hearth (härth) □*noun, plural* **hearths**

heartless   *adjective* Having no sympathy or pity; hardhearted.
heart·less (härt′ lis) □*adjective*

hearty   *adjective* **1.** Showing warm, friendly feeling: *a hearty greeting.* **2.** Giving or needing

a bat	ī bite	ōō tool	*th* feather
ā make	î fierce	ou out	th bath
â dare	o dot	u nut	hw wheat
ä father	ō no	û turn	zh measure
e net	ô law, for	ch church	ə about, open
ē be	oi soil	ng ring	pencil, atom
i dip	oo look	sh shade	circus

much nourishment: *a hearty appetite.*
heart·y (här′tē) □*adjective* **heartier, heartiest**

heat *noun* **1.** The condition of being hot; warmth: *the heat of an oven.* **2.** Intensity, as of emotion: *He shouted at her in the heat of excitement.*
□*verb* To make or become warm or hot: *The sun heated the pavement.*
heat (hēt) □*noun* □*verb* **heated, heating, heats**

heated *adjective* Angry: *a heated discussion.*
heat·ed (hē′tid) □*adjective*

heater *noun* A device for supplying heat: *a heater in a car.*
heat·er (hē′tər) □*noun, plural* **heaters**

heath *noun* **1.** An open, level area of land covered with small, usually evergreen plants and shrubs. **2.** A plant that grows naturally on a heath.
heath (hēth) □*noun, plural* **heaths**

heathen *noun* Someone who does not believe in the God of the Bible; pagan.
hea·then (hē′thən) □*noun, plural* **heathens** or **heathen**

heather *noun* A low shrub with many small purplish flowers.
heath·er (heth′ər) □*noun*

heave *verb* **1.** To raise, lift, or throw with effort or force; hoist: *He heaved the trunk onto the truck.* **2.** To utter with effort: *She heaved a sigh of relief.* **3.** To rise up or swell; bulge: *Frost made the pavement heave.*
heave (hēv) □*verb* **heaved, heaving, heaves**

heave

heaven *noun* **1.** Often **heavens** The sky as seen from the earth. **2.** The dwelling place of God and the angels.
heav·en (hev′ən) □*noun, plural* **heavens**

heavenly *adjective* **1.** Of or having to do with the heavens: *heavenly bodies such as planets.* **2.** Of or like heaven: *a heavenly blessing.* **3.** Pleasing in every way; delightful: *a heavenly party.*
heav·en·ly (hev′ən lē) □*adjective*

heavily *adverb* In a heavy manner.
heav·i·ly (hev′əl ē) □*adverb*

heavy *adjective* **1.** Having great weight: *a heavy chair.* **2.** Great in amount or force: *a heavy fog; heavy seas.* **3.** Greater in weight or thickness than usual: *a heavy winter coat.*
heav·y (hev′ē) □*adjective* **heavier, heaviest**

Hebrew *noun* **1.** A member or descendant of one of a group of peoples including the ancient Jews. **2.** The language of the Hebrews.
□*adjective* Of the Hebrews or their language.
He·brew (hē′brōō) □*noun, plural* **Hebrews** □*adjective*

hectare *noun* A metric unit of area equal to about 2.5 acres.
hec·tare (hek′târ′) □*noun, plural* **hectares**

hectic *adjective* Full of confusion, excitement, or activity: *a hectic day at the office.*
hec·tic (hek′tik) □*adjective*

hectic

hecto- A prefix that means "hundred": *hectometer.*

hectometer *noun* A metric unit of length equal to 100 meters.
hec·to·me·ter (hek′tə mē′tər) □*noun, plural* **hectometers**

he'd Contraction of "he had" or "he would."
he'd (hēd)

hedge   *noun* A fence formed by a row of closely planted shrubs or small trees.
□*verb* **1.** To enclose with a hedge. **2.** To avoid giving a direct answer: *I tried to hedge because I really didn't know the answer to the question.*
hedge (hej) □*noun, plural* **hedges** □*verb* **hedged, hedging, hedges**

hedgehog   *noun* A small animal with short, stiff spines covering its back. It rolls itself into a ball to protect itself.
hedge·hog (hej′hôg′) □*noun, plural* **hedgehogs**

heed   *verb* To pay careful attention to: *Heed his advice.*
heed (hēd) □*verb* **heeded, heeding, heeds**

heel¹   *noun* **1.** The rounded back part of the human foot under the ankle. **2.** The part of a shoe or boot that supports the heel.
□*verb* **1.** To put a heel on. **2.** To follow closely behind: *She trained the dog to heel.*
heel (hēl) □*noun, plural* **heels** □*verb* **heeled, heeling, heels**

heel²   *verb* To tilt to one side: *The boat heeled to the right.*
heel (hēl) □*verb* **heeled, heeling, heels**

hefty   *adjective* Having great weight; heavy: *That dictionary is a pretty hefty book.*
heft·y (hef′tē) □*adjective* **heftier, heftiest**

heifer   *noun* A young cow.
heif·er (hef′ər) □*noun, plural* **heifers**

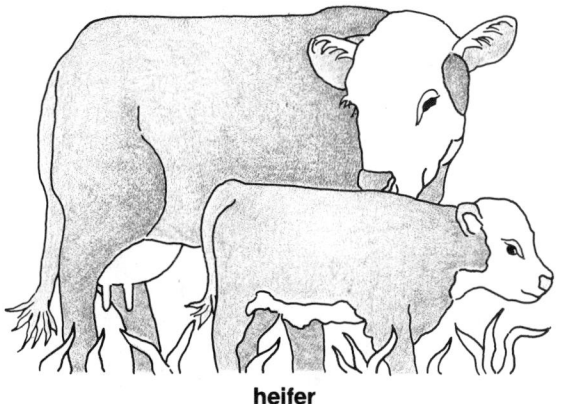

heifer

height   *noun* **1.** The distance from the bottom to the top of something: *The height of the table is three feet.* **2.** A high place: *She is afraid of heights.* **3.** The highest point; peak: *the height of excitement.*
height (hīt) □*noun, plural* **heights**

heighten   *verb* To make or become greater: *Our fear heightened as the hours passed.*
height·en (hī′tən) □*verb* **heightened, heightening, heightens**

heir   *noun* Someone who inherits or has the right to inherit the money or property of another person.
heir (âr) □*noun, plural* **heirs**

heiress   *noun* A woman or girl who inherits or has the right to inherit the money or property of another person.
heir·ess (âr′is) □*noun, plural* **heiresses**

heirloom   *noun* An object of special value passed down from generation to generation.
heir·loom (âr′lōōm′) □*noun, plural* **heirlooms**

held   *verb* The past tense and past participle of **hold**: *She held the baby in her arms. He has held the job for ten years.*
held (held) □*verb*

helicopter   *noun* An aircraft supported in the air by rotating blades mounted above.
hel·i·cop·ter (hel′i kop′tər) □*noun, plural* **helicopters**

WORD HISTORY: helicopter
Helicopter comes from two Greek words, one meaning ''spiral'' and the other meaning ''wing.''

helium   *noun* A very light gaseous chemical element used to fill balloons and dirigibles.
he·li·um (hē′lē əm) □*noun*

hell   *noun* A place of punishment where the souls of wicked people go after death.
hell (hel) □*noun, plural* **hells**

he'll Contraction of ''he will'' or ''he shall.''
he'll (hēl)

a bat	ī bite	ōō tool	*th* feather
ā make	î fierce	ou out	th bath
â dare	o dot	u nut	hw wheat
ä father	ō no	û turn	zh measure
e net	ô law, for	ch church	ə about, open
ē be	oi soil	ng ring	pencil, atom
i dip	oo look	sh shade	circus

hello *interjection* A word used to greet someone or to attract attention.
□*noun* A call or greeting of "hello."
hel·lo (he lō′ *or* hə lō′) □*interjection*
  □*noun, plural* **hellos**

helm *noun* The steering wheel or tiller of a ship.
helm (helm) □*noun, plural* **helms**

helmet *noun* A covering of hard material worn especially by workers, soldiers, and football players as a protection for the head.
hel·met (hel′mit) □*noun, plural*
  helmets

helmet
Three kinds of helmets

help *verb* **1.** To provide with what is needed or useful; assist: *She helped him move the boxes.* **2.** To give relief to; ease: *She took aspirin to help her headache.* **3.** To prevent: *Don't be angry; I couldn't help it.* **4.** To refrain from; avoid: *She couldn't help noticing.*
□*noun* **1.** The act or an example of helping: *I need your help.* **2.** Someone or something that helps: *He is a great help to his mother.*
help (help) □*verb* **helped, helping, helps**
  □*noun*

helpful *adjective* Providing help; useful.
help·ful (help′fəl) □*adjective*

helping *noun* A portion of food: *She took a helping of salad.*
help·ing (hel′ping) □*noun, plural*
  helpings

helpless *adjective* Not capable of taking care of oneself: *He is sick in bed and helpless.*
help·less (help′lis) □*adjective*

helter-skelter *adverb* In disorder or in a haphazard manner: *When the alarm sounded we ran helter-skelter from the building.*
hel·ter-skel·ter (hel′tər skel′tər) □*adverb*

hem *noun* A border of a garment or piece of cloth made by folding under the edge and sewing it down.
□*verb* To fold under and sew down the edge of: *She hemmed the sheet.*
hem (hem) □*noun, plural* **hems** □*verb*
  hemmed, hemming, hems

hemisphere *noun* **1.** One half of a sphere. **2.** One of the halves of the earth as divided either by the equator or the zero meridian, which passes through Greenwich, England.
hem·i·sphere (hem′i sfîr′) □*noun, plural*
  hemispheres

hemlock *noun* **1.** An evergreen tree with short, flat needles and small cones. **2.** A poisonous plant with feathery leaves and clusters of small whitish flowers.
hem·lock (hem′lok′) □*noun, plural*
  hemlocks

hemoglobin *noun* A protein that gives red blood cells their red color. Hemoglobin contains iron and carries oxygen from the lungs to other parts of the body.
he·mo·glo·bin (hē′mə glō′bin) □*noun*

hemp *noun* A tall plant with stems that yield a tough, strong fiber used to make rope.
hemp (hemp) □*noun, plural* **hemps**

hen *noun* **1.** An adult female chicken. **2.** The female of a bird, as the peacock or turkey.
hen (hen) □*noun, plural* **hens**

hence *adverb* **1.** For this reason; therefore: *a rare jewel and hence expensive.* **2.** From this time: *ten years hence.*
hence (hens) □*adverb*

heptagon *noun* A plane geometric figure with seven sides.
hep·ta·gon (hep′tə gon′) □*noun, plural*
  heptagons

her *pronoun* The objective case of **she**: *I met her on the stairs. I have a letter for her.*
□*adjective* Belonging or relating to her: *Her typewriter needs cleaning. I accepted her invitation to the party.*
her (hûr) □*pronoun* □*adjective*

herald *noun* **1.** An official messenger, as for a king. **2.** Someone or something that announces or gives a sign of something: *The robin is the herald of spring.*
□*verb* To give a sign or news of; announce: *The cheers of the crowd heralded the hero's arrival.*
her·ald (her′əld) □*noun, plural* **heralds**
  □*verb* **heralded, heralding, heralds**

herb *noun* **1.** A plant used as medicine or to flavor food. **2.** A plant that has soft stems that die back at the end of each growing season.
herb (ûrb *or* hûrb) □*noun, plural* **herbs**

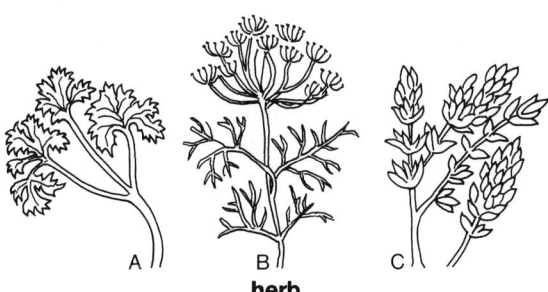

herb
(A) parsley, *(B)* dill, *(C)* thyme

herbivorous *adjective* Feeding on plants or plant parts: *The deer is a herbivorous animal.*
her·biv·o·rous (hər **biv′**ər əs) ▢*adjective*

herd *noun* A group of animals that live or are kept together.
▢*verb* To gather, keep, or drive in a herd: *They herded the sheep to the pasture.*
herd (hûrd) ▢*noun, plural* **herds** ▢*verb*
herded, herding, herds

herdsman *noun* A person who tends, drives, or owns a flock or herd, as of sheep or cattle.
herds·man (**hûrdz′**mən) ▢*noun, plural*
herdsmen

here *adverb* At, in, or to this place: *Make a left turn here. Put the chair here.*
▢*noun* This place: *a house a mile from here.*
here (hîr) ▢*adverb* ▢*noun*

hereafter *adverb* From now on; after this: *I hurt your feelings, hereafter I will be kinder to you.*
▢*noun* Life after death: *He was sure his good deeds would be rewarded in the hereafter.*
here·af·ter (hîr **af′**tər) ▢*adverb* ▢*noun*

hereditary *adjective* Passing or capable of passing from parent to offspring: *a hereditary disease.*
he·red·i·tar·y (hə **red′**i ter′ē) ▢*adjective*

heredity *noun* The passing of physical characteristics from parent to offspring.
he·red·i·ty (hə **red′**i tē) ▢*noun*

here's Contraction of "here is."
here's (hîrz)

heritage *noun* Something that is passed down from earlier generations: *our heritage of folk music.*
her·i·tage (**her′**i tij) ▢*noun*

hermit *noun* Someone who lives alone and away from other people.
her·mit (**hûr′**mit) ▢*noun, plural* **hermits**

hero *noun* **1.** Someone who is admired for bravery or outstanding accomplishment.

2. The main male character in a story, poem, play, or movie.
he·ro (**hîr′**ō) ▢*noun, plural* **heroes**

heroic *adjective* **1.** Of, like, or having to do with heroes: *heroic legends.* **2.** Very brave and daring: *a heroic deed.*
he·ro·ic (hi **rō′**ik) ▢*adjective*

heroin *noun* A dangerous, habit-forming drug.
her·o·in (**her′**ō in) ▢*noun*

heroine *noun* **1.** A woman or girl who is admired for bravery or outstanding accomplishment. **2.** The main female character in a story, poem, play, or movie.
her·o·ine (**her′**ō in) ▢*noun, plural* **heroines**

heroism *noun* Great bravery; courage.
her·o·ism (**her′**ō iz′əm) ▢*noun*

heron *noun* A wading bird with a long neck, long legs, and a long, pointed bill.
her·on (**her′**ən) ▢*noun, plural* **herons**

heron

herring *noun* A fish of the North Atlantic Ocean that is caught for food.
her·ring (**her′**ing) ▢*noun, plural* **herring** or **herrings**

herring

a bat	î bite	ōō tool	*th* feather
ā make	î fierce	ou out	th bath
â dare	o dot	u nut	hw wheat
ä father	ō no	û turn	zh measure
e net	ô law, for	ch church	ə about, open
ē be	oi soil	ng ring	pencil, atom
i dip	oo look	sh shade	circus

hers *pronoun* The one or ones belonging to her: *I lost my pen so she lent me hers.*
hers (hûrz) ☐*pronoun*

herself *pronoun* Her own self: *She found it hard to keep herself busy. The teacher herself could not answer the question.*
her·self (hər **self′**) ☐*pronoun*

he's Contraction of "he is" or "he has."
he's (hēz)

hesitant *adjective* Tending to hesitate, as from fear or doubt: *She was hesitant about applying for the job.*
hes·i·tant (**hez′**i tənt) ☐*adjective*

hesitate *verb* To pause, especially from doubt: *The boy hesitated before jumping into the icy lake.*
hes·i·tate (**hez′**i tāt′) ☐*verb* **hesitated, hesitating, hesitates**

hesitation *noun* The act of hesitating.
hes·i·ta·tion (hez′i **tā′**shən) ☐*noun, plural* **hesitations**

hew *verb* **1.** To make or shape with an ax: *The beams of the house were hewn by hand out of oak logs.* **2.** To cut down with an ax: *The settlers hewed many trees for firewood.*
hew (hyōō) ☐*verb* **hewed, hewn** or **hewed, hewing, hews**

hex *noun* **1.** An evil spell: *The witch put a hex on the prince so that everything he said sounded like gibberish.* **2.** Someone or something that brings bad luck.
☐*verb* **1.** To put a hex on. **2.** To wish or bring bad luck to.
hex (heks) ☐*noun, plural* **hexes** ☐*verb* **hexed, hexing, hexes**

hexagon *noun* A plane geometric figure with six sides.
hex·a·gon (**hek′**sə gon′) ☐*noun, plural* **hexagons**

hey *interjection* A word used to express surprise or attract attention: *Hey, be careful!*
hey (hā) ☐*interjection*

heyday *noun* The period of greatest power, popularity, or success: *He made his fortune during the heyday of silent movies.*
hey·day (**hā′**dā′) ☐*noun, plural* **heydays**

hi *interjection* A word used as a greeting.
hi (hī) ☐*interjection*

hibernate *verb* To spend the winter in a state resembling deep sleep, as some bears do.
hi·ber·nate (**hī′**bər nāt′) ☐*verb* **hibernated, hibernating, hibernates**

hiccup *noun* **1.** A sudden catching of the breath in the throat. **2. hiccups** An attack in which a person has one hiccup after another. ☐*verb* To have the hiccups.
hic·cup (**hik′**up) ☐*noun, plural* **hiccups** ☐*verb* **hiccupped, hiccupping, hiccups**

hickory *noun* A North American tree that has hard wood and edible nuts with a hard shell.
hick·o·ry (**hik′**ə rē) ☐*noun, plural* **hickories**

hid *verb* The past tense and a past participle of **hide¹**: *She hid her face in her hands.*
hid (hid) ☐*verb*

hidden *verb* A past participle of **hide¹**: *Where have you hidden my glasses?*
hid·den (**hid′**ən) ☐*verb*

hide¹ *verb* **1.** To put or keep out of sight: *I hid the keys in a cookie jar.* **2.** To keep secret: *She tried to hide her anger.*
hide (hīd) ☐*verb* **hid, hidden** or **hid, hiding, hides**

SYNONYMS: **hide, conceal**

These verbs mean to put or keep out of sight: *I hid the money in my closet. The children concealed themselves in the bushes.*

---

hide² *noun* The skin of an animal.
hide (hīd) ☐*noun, plural* **hides**

hide-and-seek *noun* A children's game in which one player tries to find and catch others who are hiding.
hide-and-seek (**hīd′**ən sēk′) ☐*noun*

hide-and-seek

hideous *adjective* Very ugly; horrible: *a hideous scar.* —See Synonyms at **ugly.**
hid·e·ous (**hid′**ē əs) ☐*adjective*

hide-out *noun* A place for hiding: *The bandits' hide-out was an old mine.*
hide-out (hīd'out') □*noun, plural* **hide-outs**

hieroglyphic *noun* A symbol in the writing system of ancient Egypt, in which pictures represent words or sounds.
hi·er·o·glyph·ic (hī'ər ə glif'ik) □*noun, plural* **hieroglyphics**

hi-fi *noun* Equipment, such as a phonograph, that reproduces sound very accurately.
hi-fi (hī'fī') □*noun, plural* **hi-fis**

higgledy-piggledy *adverb* In disorder or confusion: *She threw her clothes higgledy-piggledy into a suitcase and dashed out the door.*
hig·gle·dy-pig·gle·dy (hig'əl dē pig'əl dē) □*adverb*

high *adjective* **1.** Having great height: *high buildings on every side.* **2.** Having a particular height: *a tower 600 feet high.* **3.** At a great distance above the ground: *The kite was high in the air.* **4.** Above others in rank or importance: *a high government official.* **5.** Greater than usual in size or amount: *a high speed; the high cost of food.* **6.** Above another sound in pitch: *the high tones of a flute.* —See Synonyms at **tall.**
□*adverb* At, in, or to a high position or level: *The airplane climbed high in the sky.*
□*noun* A high level, point, or position: *The temperature reached a high of 105 degrees.*
high (hī) □*adjective* **higher, highest** □*adverb* □*noun, plural* **highs**

high jump *noun* A contest in which a person tries to jump over a bar that is set between two posts.

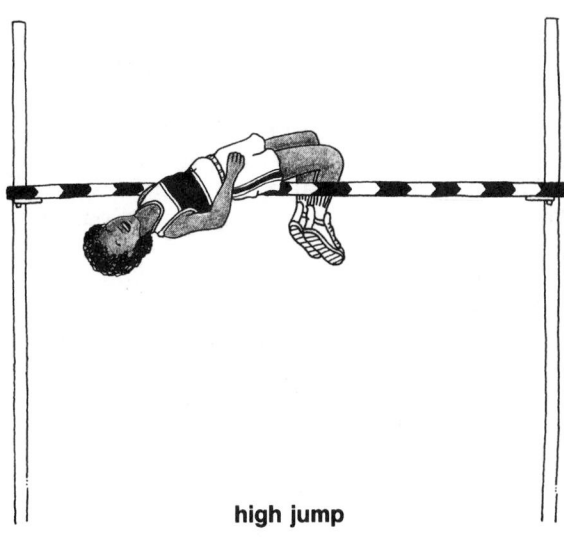

high jump

highland *noun* A high or hilly region.
high·land (hī'lənd) □*noun, plural* **highlands**

highlight *noun* **1.** A light or brightly lighted area, as in a painting or photograph. **2.** An outstanding event or part: *The fireworks display was the highlight of the celebration.*
□*verb* To cause to stand out; emphasize.
high·light (hī'līt') □*noun, plural* **highlights** □*verb* **highlighted, highlighting, highlights**

highly *adverb* **1.** To a great degree or amount: *a highly interesting movie.* **2.** With favor or approval: *I don't think highly of the book.*
high·ly (hī'lē) □*adverb*

Highness *noun* A title of honor for a member of a royal family: *Her Royal Highness.*
High·ness (hī'nis) □*noun, plural* **Highnesses**

high school *noun* A school that usually includes grades nine through twelve.

high-strung *adjective* Very sensitive and nervous: *My cousin is very high-strung and jumps at every noise.*
high-strung (hī'strung') □*adjective*

high tide *noun* The tide when the water reaches its highest level.

highway *noun* A main public road.
high·way (hī'wā') □*noun, plural* **highways**

hijack *verb* To take over by force: *The fugitive hijacked an airplane.*
hi·jack (hī'jak') □*verb* **hijacked, hijacking, hijacks**

hike *verb* To go on a long walk: *We hiked through the woods yesterday.*
□*noun* A long walk.
hike (hīk) □*verb* **hiked, hiking, hikes** □*noun, plural* **hikes**

hiker *noun* Someone who hikes.
hik·er (hī'kər) □*noun, plural* **hikers**

hilarious *adjective* Noisily funny or merry: *a hilarious joke; a hilarious party.*
hi·lar·i·ous (hi lâr'ē əs) □*adjective*

hill *noun* **1.** An often rounded elevation of earth that is not as high as a mountain. **2.** A small mound of earth, as that made by ants.
hill (hil) □*noun, plural* **hills**

a	bat	ī	bite	o͞o	tool	*th*	feather
ā	make	î	fierce	ou	out	th	bath
â	dare	o	dot	u	nut	hw	wheat
ä	father	ō	no	û	turn	zh	measure
e	net	ô	law, for	ch	church	ə	about, open
ē	be	oi	soil	ng	ring		pencil, atom
i	dip	oo	look	sh	shade		circus

hilly *adjective* Having many hills.
hill·y (hĭl′ē) □*adjective* **hillier, hilliest**

hilt *noun* The handle of a sword or dagger.
hilt (hĭlt) □*noun, plural* **hilts**

him *pronoun* The objective case of **he:** *Have you seen him recently? We know very little about him.*
him (hĭm) □*pronoun*

himself *pronoun* His own self: *He blamed himself for the accident. I want to speak to the principal himself.*
him·self (hĭm **sĕlf′**) □*pronoun*

hind *adjective* Located at or forming the back; rear: *the hind legs of a cat.*
hind (hīnd) □*adjective*

hinder *verb* To make difficult or slow: *Thick mud underfoot hindered our progress.*
hind·er (hĭn′dər) □*verb* **hindered, hindering, hinders**

hindrance *noun* Someone or something that hinders; obstacle.
hin·drance (hĭn′drəns) □*noun, plural* **hindrances**

hinge *noun* A jointed device on which a door, gate, or cover turns or swings back and forth. □*verb* **1.** To attach by means of a hinge. **2.** To depend: *Success often hinges on hard work.*
hinge (hĭnj) □*noun, plural* **hinges** □*verb* **hinged, hinging, hinges**

hinge

hint *noun* A slight indication or indirect suggestion: *His smile gave no hint that he was angry.* □*verb* To give a hint: *She hinted that he would be getting a new typewriter for Christmas.* —See Synonyms at **suggest.**
hint (hĭnt) □*noun, plural* **hints** □*verb*

hinted, hinting, hints

hip *noun* The bony part that projects outward on each side of the body between the waist and the thigh.
hip (hĭp) □*noun, plural* **hips**

hippo *noun* A hippopotamus.
hip·po (hĭp′ō) □*noun, plural* **hippos**

hippopotamus *noun* A large African animal that lives in or near water and has short legs, a broad snout, and a wide mouth.
hip·po·pot·a·mus (hĭp′ə **pŏt′**ə məs) □*noun, plural* **hippopotamuses**

hippopotamus

hire *verb* **1.** To pay for working or performing a service; employ: *I hired two men to paint the house.* **2.** To pay for the use of for a limited time: *hire a hall for a wedding.* □*noun* The condition of being hired; employment: *He is in the hire of a large corporation.*
hire (hīr) □*verb* **hired, hiring, hires** □*noun* **hires**

his *adjective* Belonging or relating to him: *The guard asked the boy to show his pass. His criticism annoyed me.* □*pronoun* The one or ones belonging to him: *I know her parents but I don't know his.*
his (hĭz) □*adjective* □*pronoun*

Hispanic *noun* An American who has Spanish or Latin-American ancestors. □*adjective* Of or relating to Hispanics or to the people, language, or culture of Spain or Latin America.
His·pan·ic (hĭ **spăn′**ĭk) □*noun, plural* **Hispanics** □*adjective*

hiss *noun* A sound like a long *s: the hiss of a snake.* □*verb* **1.** To make a hiss: *The cat hissed.* **2.** To show dislike for by making a hiss: *The audience hissed the speaker.*
hiss (hĭs) □*noun, plural* **hisses** □*verb* **hissed, hissing, hisses**

historian *noun* Someone who writes about or studies history.
his·to·ri·an (hi **stôr′** ē ən) □*noun, plural* **historians**

historic *adjective* Important or famous in history: *a historic building; a historic decision.*
his·tor·ic (hi **stôr′** ik) □*adjective*

historical *adjective* Of, having to do with, or based on history: *a historical event.*
his·tor·i·cal (hi **stôr′** i kəl) □*adjective*

history *noun* A record or story of past events: *the history of the United States.*
his·to·ry (**his′** tə rē) □*noun, plural* **histories**

hit *verb* **1.** To give a blow to; strike: *The tennis player hit the ball. She fell and hit her arm.* **2.** To get to; reach: *The car hit 55 miles an hour. He hit upon the right answer by chance.* **3.** To affect as if by a blow: *His father's death hit him hard.*
□*noun* **1.** A blow: *a direct hit on the target; a hit on the elbow.* **2.** A great success: *The book was a real hit.* **3.** A baseball that is hit so that the batter can reach base safely.
hit (hit) □*verb* **hit, hitting, hits** □*noun, plural* **hits**

hitch *verb* **1.** To tie or fasten with or as if with a rope: *She hitched a mule to the wagon.* **2.** To move or raise with a jerk: *He hitched his chair closer to the desk.*
□*noun* **1.** A short pull or jerk: *She gave her skirt a hitch.* **2.** A delay or difficulty: *The rain put a hitch in our plans.* **3.** A knot used to fasten things together temporarily.
hitch (hich) □*verb* **hitched, hitching, hitches** □*noun, plural* **hitches**

hitchhike *verb* To travel by getting free rides from passing cars or trucks: *We hitchhiked to the next town.*
hitch·hike (**hich′** hīk′) □*verb* **hitchhiked, hitchhiking, hitchhikes**

hither *adverb* To or toward this place.
□*adjective* Located on the near side: *the hither shore.*
hith·er (**hith′** ər) □*adverb* □*adjective*

hive *noun* **1.** A structure for housing a swarm of bees. **2.** A swarm of bees living in a hive.
hive (hīv) □*noun, plural* **hives**

hives *plural noun* An itching skin rash.
hives (hīvz) □*plural noun*

ho *interjection* Used to express surprise or triumph.
ho (hō) □*interjection*

hoard *noun* A supply of something that is stored away or kept hidden: *She had a hoard of money in her dresser.*
□*verb* To save and store away: *I hoarded sugar in case of a shortage.*
hoard (hôrd) □*noun, plural* **hoards** □*verb* **hoarded, hoarding, hoards**

hoarfrost *noun* Frozen dew that forms a white coating on a surface.
hoar·frost (**hôr′** frôst′) □*noun*

hoarse *adjective* **1.** Low and harsh in sound: *the hoarse cry of a crow.* **2.** Having a low, rough voice: *The cough made me hoarse.*
hoarse (hôrs) □*adjective* **hoarser, hoarsest**

hoary *adjective* **1.** White or grayish, as if covered with hoarfrost. **2.** Very old: *a hoary joke.*
hoar·y (**hôr′** ē) □*adjective* **hoarier, hoariest**

hoax *noun* Something intended to trick or deceive: *His story about catching a flying pig was a hoax.*
hoax (hōks) □*noun, plural* **hoaxes**

hobble *verb* **1.** To walk or move with difficulty; limp: *She hobbled around with a cane.* **2.** To tie the legs of an animal to prevent free movement.
□*noun* **1.** An awkward or clumsy walk; limp. **2.** Something used to hobble an animal.
hob·ble (**hob′** əl) □*verb* **hobbled, hobbling, hobbles** □*noun, plural* **hobbles**

hobby *noun* An activity, such as collecting stamps, that a person engages in for pleasure.
hob·by (**hob′** ē) □*noun, plural* **hobbies**

hobbyhorse *noun* **1.** A stick with a horse's head for children to ride on. **2.** A rocking horse.
hob·by·horse (**hob′** ē hôrs′) □*noun, plural* **hobbyhorses**

hobgoblin *noun* **1.** An elf who causes trouble. **2.** An imaginary source of fear or horror.
hob·gob·lin (**hob′** gob′lin) □*noun, plural* **hobgoblins**

hobo *noun* Someone who wanders from place to place doing odd jobs and begging for a living.
ho·bo (**hō′** bō) □*noun, plural* **hoboes**

a	bat	ī	bite	ŏŏ	tool	th	feather
ā	make	î	fierce	ou	out	th	bath
â	dare	o	dot	u	nut	hw	wheat
ä	father	ō	no	û	turn	zh	measure
e	net	ô	law, for	ch	church	ə	about, open
ē	be	oi	soil	ng	ring		pencil, atom
i	dip	oo	look	sh	shade		circus

hockey *noun* A game played on ice or a field by two teams who try to hit a puck or ball into the other team's goal.
hock·ey (hŏk′ē) □*noun*

hodgepodge *noun* A mixture of different ingredients; jumble: *Dinner was a hodgepodge of everything we could find in the refrigerator.*
hodge·podge (hŏj′pŏj′) □*noun, plural* **hodgepodges**

hoe *noun* A tool with a long handle and a flat blade used to loosen soil and dig up weeds. □*verb* To loosen, cut, or dig with a hoe.
hoe (hō) □*noun, plural* **hoes** □*verb* **hoed, hoeing, hoes**

hoe

hog *noun* **1.** A pig, especially a fully grown pig raised for meat. **2.** A very greedy person. □*verb* To take more than a fair share of: *Don't hog the pancakes; I want some too.*
hog (hôg) □*noun, plural* **hogs** □*verb* **hogged, hogging, hogs**

hoist *verb* To raise up or lift, often with the help of a machine: *The men hoisted the crates onto a truck.* —See Synonyms at **raise.**
□*noun* **1.** A device used to lift heavy objects. **2.** The act of hoisting; lift: *He needed a hoist to get on the train.*
hoist (hoist) □*verb* **hoisted, hoisting, hoists** □*noun, plural* **hoists**

hold¹ *verb* **1.** To have or keep in the hands: *I held her hand.* **2.** To take or have in one's control or possession: *soldiers holding a village. Hold your temper.* **3.** To keep in a certain place or position: *Hold the tray steady.* **4.** To contain: *The elevator only holds four people.* **5.** To keep up; support: *legs too thin to hold the table.* **6.** To have, be in, or occupy: *held the position of chairman of the board.* **7.** To cause to take place; conduct: *hold an election.* **8.** To think; judge: *Why does he hold that opinion?*

□*noun* **1.** An act or way of holding; grip: *a loose hold.* **2.** Something used for support: *climbed the tree, using branches as a hold.* **3.** Control; possession.
hold (hōld) □*verb* **held, holding, holds** □*noun, plural* **holds**

SYNONYMS: **hold, clasp, grip**
These verbs mean to have and keep in the hands: *Hold the rail when you go down the stairs. She clasped my hand and said she was glad to see me. Grip the rope and pull.*

hold² *noun* The part of a ship or airplane where cargo is carried.
hold (hōld) □*noun, plural* **holds**

holdup *noun* **1.** A robbery, especially by someone having a weapon. **2.** A delay.
hold·up (hōld′ŭp′) □*noun, plural* **holdups**

hole *noun* **1.** An opening through or in something: *There was a hole in his shirt.* **2.** A cavity in something solid: *They dug a hole for the foundation.* **3.** A small hollow on a golf course into which the ball must be hit.
hole (hōl) □*noun, plural* **holes**

holiday *noun* A day on which people do not work, often in celebration of an important event.
hol·i·day (hŏl′ĭ dā′) □*noun, plural* **holidays**

holler *verb* To call out; shout: *They hollered for help.*
hol·ler (hŏl′ər) □*verb* **hollered, hollering, hollers**

hollow *adjective* **1.** Having an empty space inside; not solid: *a hollow pipe.* **2.** Curved in; sunken: *hollow cheeks.* **3.** Like a sound made in a large, empty space: *a hollow rumble.* □*noun* **1.** A sunken area; depression: *a hollow in a road.* **2.** A small valley. □*verb* To make or become hollow.
hol·low (hŏl′ō) □*adjective* **hollower, hollowest** □*noun, plural* **hollows** □*verb* **hollowed, hollowing, hollows**

holly *noun* A shrub or tree that has evergreen leaves with prickly edges and red berries.
hol·ly (hŏl′ē) □*noun, plural* **hollies**

hollyhock *noun* A tall garden plant with a long cluster of large, colorful flowers.
hol·ly·hock (hŏl′ē hŏk′) □*noun, plural* **hollyhocks**

holster *noun* A leather case for holding a pistol, usually worn on a belt.
hol·ster (hōl′stər) □*noun, plural* **holsters**

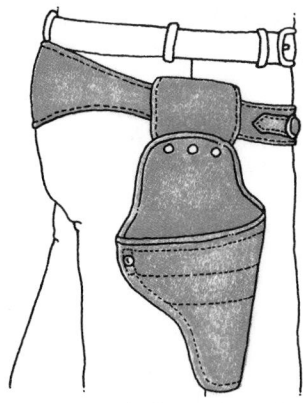

holster

home plate *noun* The base that a baseball runner must touch in order to score.

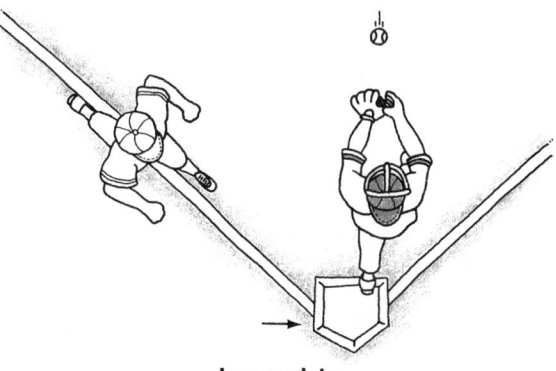

home plate

holy *adjective* **1.** Of, having to do with, or dedicated to God; sacred: *holy altar.* **2.** Deeply religious; saintly: *Charity is a holy virtue.*
ho·ly (hō′lē) □*adjective* **holier, holiest**

homage *noun* A display of esteem and regard: *The king received the homage of his subjects in silence.*
hom·age (hom′ij) □*noun*

home *noun* **1.** The place where a person lives: *Her home is in the country.* **2.** The place where one was born or raised: *I went home to visit my family.* **3.** A place for the care of those who cannot care for themselves. **4.** The goal in some games and sports.
□*adverb* **1.** To or at home: *She stayed home and cooked.* **2.** To the place aimed at: *The arrow struck home.*
home (hōm) □*noun, plural* **homes** □*adverb*

homecoming *noun* A return home: *His homecoming was a joyful event.*
home·com·ing (hōm′kum′ing) □*noun, plural* **homecomings**

homeland *noun* The country where a person was born.
home·land (hōm′land′) □*noun, plural* **homelands**

homely *adjective* **1.** Not good-looking; plain: *a homely little boy.* **2.** Typical of home life; simple: *a comfortable, homely room.*
home·ly (hōm′lē) □*adjective* **homelier, homeliest**

homemade *adjective* Made at home: *a homemade dress.*
home·made (hom′mād′) □*adjective*

homemaker *noun* Someone who manages a household.
home·mak·er (hōm′mā′ker) □*noun, plural* **homemakers**

homer *noun* A home run.
hom·er (hō′mər) □*noun, plural* **homers**

homeroom *noun* A classroom to which all the pupils in a class report in the morning.
home·room (hōm′rōōm′ *or* hōm′rŏŏm′) □*noun, plural* **homerooms**

home run *noun* A hit in baseball that allows the batter to touch all bases and score a run.

homesick *adjective* Sad and lonely because of being away from home.
home·sick (hōm′sik′) □*adjective*

homespun *noun* A plain coarse cloth made of yarn that is spun at home.
home·spun (hōm′spun′) □*noun*

homestead *noun* **1.** A house with the land and buildings around it. **2.** A piece of land that was granted by the United States government to a settler for farming.
home·stead (hōm′sted′) □*noun, plural* **homesteads**

homeward *adverb* and *adjective* Toward home: *She walked homeward from the office. We began our homeward journey.*
home·ward (hōm′wərd) □*adverb* and *adjective*

homework *noun* School lessons, to be done at home.
home·work (hōm′wûrk′) □*noun*

a bat	ī bite	ōō tool	*th* feather
ā make	î fierce	ou out	th bath
â dare	o dot	u nut	hw wheat
ä father	ō no	û turn	zh measure
e net	ô law, for	ch church	ə about, open
ē be	oi soil	ng ring	pencil, atom
i dip	oo look	sh shade	circus

homey *adjective* Cheerful and cozy like a home: *The kitten sleeping on a chair and the green plants gave the room a homey atmosphere.*
hom·ey (hō′mē) □*adjective* **homier, homiest**

homicide *noun* The killing of one person by another: *Homicide is a crime.*
hom·i·cide (hom′i sīd′) □*noun, plural* **homicides**

hominy *noun* Kernels of corn hulled and boiled as a food.
hom·i·ny (hom′ə nē) □*noun*

homogenize *verb* To make milk uniform in consistency by breaking up the fat content into very small particles.
ho·mog·e·nize (hō moj′ə nīz′) □*verb* **homogenized, homogenizing, homogenizes**

homograph *noun* One of two or more words that have the same spelling but differ in origin, meaning, and sometimes pronunciation. *Bat,* meaning "a wooden stick," and *bat,* meaning "a flying animal," are homographs.
hom·o·graph (hom′ə graf′) □*noun, plural* **homographs**

homonym *noun* One of two or more words that have the same pronunciation and often the same spelling but differ in origin and meaning. *Loaf,* meaning "an oblong mass of bread," and *loaf,* meaning "to spend time in a lazy way," are homonyms.
hom·o·nym (hom′ə nim′) □*noun, plural* **homonyms**

homophone *noun* One of two or more words that have the same pronunciation but differ in spelling, origin, and meaning. *Reel* and *real* are homophones.
hom·o·phone (hom′ə fōn′) □*noun, plural* **homophones**

hone *noun* A special stone used to sharpen a cutting tool, such as a knife.
□*verb* To sharpen with or as if with a hone.
hone (hōn) □*noun, plural* **hones** □*verb* **honed, honing, hones**

honest *adjective* **1.** Not lying, stealing, or cheating; upright: *an honest man.* **2.** Frank; sincere: *an honest answer.*
hon·est (on′ist) □*adjective*

honesty *noun* The quality of being honest.
hon·es·ty (on′i stē) □*noun*

honey *noun* **1.** A thick, sweet, yellowish substance made by bees from the nectar of flowers. **2.** A person who is loved; darling.
hon·ey (hun′ē) □*noun, plural* **honeys**

honeybee *noun* A bee that makes honey.
hon·ey·bee (hun′ē bē′) □*noun, plural* **honeybees**

honeycomb *noun* A wax structure with many small cells built by honeybees to hold honey.
□*verb* To fill with spaces like those of a honeycomb: *a mine honeycombed with tunnels.*
hon·ey·comb (hun′ē kōm′) □*noun, plural* **honeycombs** □*verb* **honeycombed, honeycombing, honeycombs**

honeydew melon *noun* A melon with a smooth, whitish rind and green flesh.
hon·ey·dew melon (hun′ē dōō′ *or* hun′ē dyōō′) □*noun*

honeymoon *noun* A trip or vacation taken by two people who have just been married.
□*verb* To go or be on a honeymoon.
hon·ey·moon (hun′ē mōōn′) □*noun, plural* **honeymoons** □*verb* **honeymooned, honeymooning, honeymoons**

WORD HISTORY: **honeymoon**

The word *honeymoon* is a combination of the word *honey* and the word *moon* meaning "month." The first month of marriage was supposed to be the sweetest.

---

honeysuckle *noun* A vine or shrub with fragrant yellow, white, or pink flowers.
hon·ey·suck·le (hun′ē suk′əl) □*noun*

honeysuckle

honk *noun* **1.** The sound made by a wild goose. **2.** A sound similar to a goose's honk: *the honk of an automobile horn.*
□*verb* To make or cause to make a honk: *He honked his horn as he passed us.*
honk (hôngk) □*noun, plural* **honks** □*verb* **honked, honking, honks**

honor *noun* **1.** Special respect; esteem: *gave a luncheon in honor of the senator.* **2.** Something that is a sign of respect or esteem: *Winning first prize is a great honor.* **3.** Good name; reputation: *He had to defend his honor.* **4.** A sense of what is right: *He lived by a code of honor.* **5. Honor** A title of address for important officials, such as mayors and judges. —See Synonyms at **prestige.**
□*verb* **1.** To give an honor to: *The mayor honored the foreign minister by giving him the keys to the city.* **2.** To respect: *She was honored by everyone for her achievements.*
hon·or (on′ər) □*noun, plural* **honors** □*verb* **honored, honoring, honors**

honorable *adjective* **1.** Deserving or winning honor or respect: *an honorable occupation.* **2.** Doing what is right; upright: *An honorable person always keeps a promise.*
hon·or·a·ble (on′ər ə bəl) □*adjective*

hood *noun* **1.** A soft, loose covering for the head and neck. **2.** Something that is like a hood in shape or use. **3.** A hinged metal lid over an automobile engine.
hood (hood) □*noun, plural* **hoods**

hood

hoodlum *noun* A tough, destructive young person.
hood·lum (hood′ləm) □*noun, plural* **hoodlums**

hoodwink *verb* To deceive; trick: *He was hoodwinked into buying land that turned out to be worthless.*
hood·wink (hood′wingk′) □*verb* **hoodwinked, hoodwinking, hoodwinks**

hoof *noun* A tough, horny covering on the foot of some animals, as horses and pigs.
hoof (hoof *or* hoof) □*noun, plural* **hoofs** or **hooves**

hook *noun* **1.** A curved or bent object or part that is used to hold or fasten something: *a*
hook for keeping the screen door closed. **2.** Something shaped like a hook.
□*verb* To fasten or catch with a hook: *She hooked a trout.*
hook (hook) □*noun, plural* **hooks** □*verb* **hooked, hooking, hooks**

hoop *noun* A circular band or strip used to hold together the staves of a barrel. **2.** A circular object; ring: *a basketball hoop.*
hoop (hoop *or* hoop) □*noun, plural* **hoops**

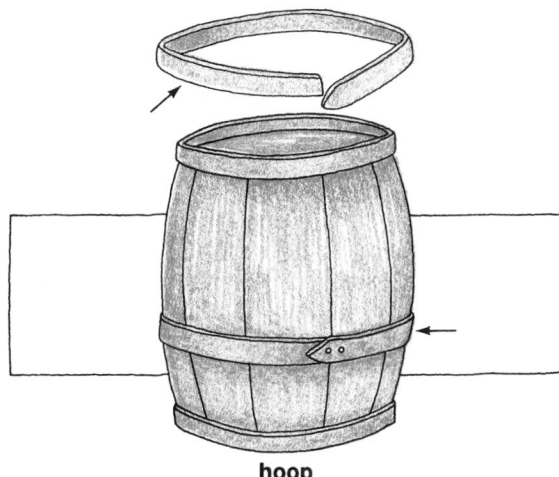
hoop

hooray *interjection* A word used to express praise or joy: *She shouted "Hooray!" when she realized that she had won the prize.*
hoo·ray (hoo rā′) □*interjection*

hoot *noun* **1.** The cry of an owl. **2.** A similar sound indicating ridicule or lack of approval.
□*verb* To make a hoot: *The crowd hooted when the actor forgot his lines.*
hoot (hoot) □*noun, plural* **hoots** □*verb* **hooted, hooting, hoots**

hooves *noun* A plural of **hoof.**
hooves (hoovz *or* hoovz) □*noun*

hop[1] *verb* **1.** To move with short, light jumps: *The robin hopped around the lawn.* **2.** To jump on one foot. **3.** To jump over: *hop a fence.*
□*noun* A short, light jump.
hop (hop) □*verb* **hopped, hopping, hops** □*noun, plural* **hops**

a bat	ī bite	oo tool	*th* feather
ā make	î fierce	ou out	th bath
â dare	o dot	u nut	hw wheat
ä father	ō no	û turn	zh measure
e net	ô law, for	ch church	ə about, open
ē be	oi soil	ng ring	pencil, atom
i dip	oo look	sh shade	circus

hop²   *noun* A vine with green flowers that look like small pine cones.
hop (hop) □*noun, plural* **hops**

hope   *verb* To wish for something very much: *I hope she answers my letter.*
□*noun* **1.** A wish for something, especially with the belief that the wish will be granted. **2.** Something hoped for: *It is my hope that you will feel better soon.*
hope (hōp) □*verb* **hoped, hoping, hopes** □*noun, plural* **hopes**

hopeful   *adjective* **1.** Having or showing hope: *He was hopeful that he would win.* **2.** Giving hope: *a hopeful beginning.*
hope·ful (hōp′fəl) □*adjective*

hopeless   *adjective* Having or offering no hope: *a hopeless problem.*
hope·less (hōp′lis) □*adjective*

hopper   *noun* A container that is usually shaped like a funnel and is used to give out or deliver material such as grain.
hop·per (hop′ər) □*noun, plural* **hoppers**

hopscotch   *noun* A children's game in which players toss a stone into numbered squares drawn on the ground and then hop through the squares and back to pick up the stone.
hop·scotch (hop′skoch′) □*noun*

hopscotch

horde   *noun* A large group or crowd: *a horde of insects; hordes of tourists.*
horde (hôrd) □*noun, plural* **hordes**

horizon   *noun* **1.** The line where the sky and the land or water seem to meet. **2.** The limit of a person's experience, knowledge, and interests: *Reading widened her horizons.*
ho·ri·zon (hə rī′zən) □*noun, plural* **horizons**

horizontal   *adjective* Parallel to or level with the horizon: *a horizontal line.*
hor·i·zon·tal (hôr′i **zon**′təl) □*adjective*

hormone   *noun* A substance that is produced by an organ of the body and released into the bloodstream. Hormones control growth and have an effect on such body functions as growth and digestion.
hor·mone (hôr′mōn′) □*noun, plural* **hormones**

horn   *noun* **1.** One of the hard, pointed growths on the head of some animals, as cattle, sheep, and goats. **2.** A brass musical instrument, such as a French horn or tuba. **3.** A device on a vehicle that makes a loud warning noise: *The driver honked his horn.*
horn (hôrn) □*noun, plural* **horns**

horn
Three kinds of horns

horned toad   *noun* A lizard of southwestern North America that has a short tail, a broad, spiny body, and sharp spines on its head.
horned toad (hôrnd) □*noun*

horned toad

hornet   *noun* A large wasp that can give a painful sting.
hor·net (hôr′nit) □*noun, plural* **hornets**

horny   *adjective* Like or made of horn: *horny skin.*
horn·y (hôr′nē) □*adjective* **hornier, horniest**

horrible   *adjective* Causing horror; terrible: *a horrible crime; a horrible accident.*
hor·ri·ble (hôr′ə bəl) □*adjective*

horrid *adjective* **1.** Causing disgust; nasty: *a horrid smell.* **2.** Horrible.
hor·rid (**hôr′**id) ▫*adjective*

horrify *verb* To cause to feel horror: *The automobile accident horrified the bystanders.*
hor·ri·fy (**hôr′**ə fī′) ▫*verb* **horrified, horrifying, horrifies**

horror *noun* **1.** A strong feeling of dread, shock, or fear: *She watched with horror as her house burned.* **2.** Someone or something that causes horror: *Death and destruction are among the horrors of war.* **3.** A strong feeling of dislike; hatred: *He had a horror of lying.*
hor·ror (**hôr′**ər) ▫*noun, plural* **horrors**

horse *noun* **1.** A large animal that has hoofs and a long mane and tail and is used for riding and for pulling heavy loads. **2.** A supporting frame with legs. **3.** A padded frame on four legs used for gymnastic exercises.
horse (hôrs) ▫*noun, plural* **horses**

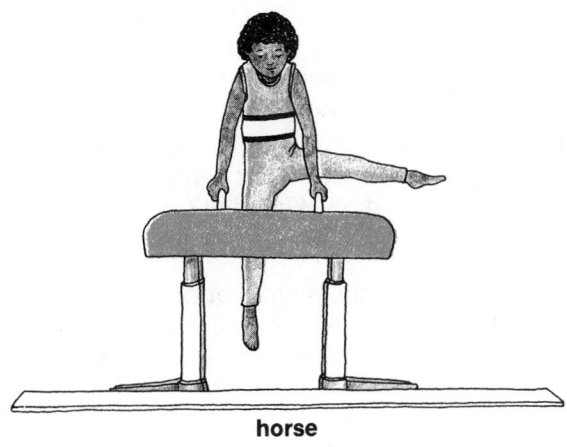

horse

horseback *adverb* On the back of a horse: *ride horseback.*
horse·back (**hôrs′**bak′) ▫*adverb*

horsecar *noun* **1.** A streetcar that is drawn by horses. **2.** A car for carrying a horse from place to place.
horse·car (**hôrs′**kär′) ▫*noun, plural* **horsecars**

horse chestnut *noun* **1.** A tree that bears upright clusters of white flowers and shiny, brown nuts in prickly burs. **2.** The nut growing on this tree.

horsefly *noun* A large fly that bites and sucks blood from animals.
horse·fly (**hôrs′**flī′) ▫*noun, plural* **horseflies**

horseman *noun* **1.** Someone who rides a horse. **2.** Someone who is skilled in handling horses.
horse·man (**hôrs′**mən) ▫*noun, plural* **horsemen**

horseplay *noun* Rough, noisy play: *When will you stop the horseplay and get to work?*
horse·play (**hôrs′**plā′) ▫*noun*

horsepower *noun* A unit used for measuring the power of an engine.
horse·pow·er (**hôrs′**pou′ər) ▫*noun*

horseradish *noun* **1.** A tall, coarse plant related to the mustard. **2.** The grated root of the horseradish that has a sharp taste and is often used as a relish.
horse·rad·ish (**hôrs′**rad′ish) ▫*noun*

horseshoe *noun* **1.** A U-shaped piece of iron fitted and nailed to a horse's hoof. **2. horseshoes** A game in which players try to throw horseshoes so that they land around a post.
horse·shoe (**hôrs′**shoō′) ▫*noun, plural* **horseshoes**

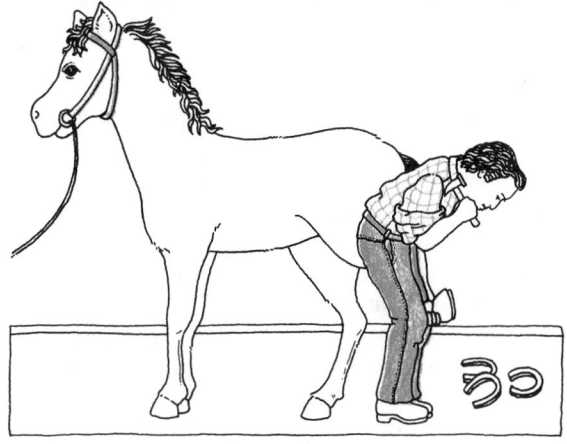

horseshoe

horsewoman *noun* **1.** A woman who rides a horse. **2.** A woman who is skilled in handling horses.
horse·wom·an (**hôrs′**woom′ən) ▫*noun, plural* **horsewomen**

hosanna *interjection* Used as an expression of praise or worship.
ho·san·na (hō **zan′**ə) ▫*interjection*

a	bat	ī	bite	oō	tool	*th*	feather
ā	make	î	fierce	ou	out	th	bath
â	dare	o	dot	u	nut	hw	wheat
ä	father	ō	no	û	turn	zh	measure
e	net	ô	law, for	ch	church	ə	about, open
ē	be	oi	soil	ng	ring		pencil, atom
i	dip	oo	look	sh	shade		circus

hose *noun* **1.** *plural* **hoses** A flexible tube, as of rubber, used to carry liquids or air. **2.** *plural* **hose** Stockings.
□*verb* To wash or spray with a hose.
hose (hōz) □*noun, plural* **hoses** or **hose**
□*verb* **hosed, hosing, hoses**

hospitable *adjective* Generous and friendly to guests: *The hospitable hostess offered the unexpected visitors dinner.*
hos·pi·ta·ble (hos′pi tə bəl *or* ho **spit′**ə bəl)
□*adjective*

hospital *noun* A place where people who are sick or hurt are cared for.
hos·pi·tal (hos′pi təl) □*noun, plural* **hospitals**

hospitality *noun* Generous and friendly treatment of guests.
hos·pi·tal·i·ty (hos′pi tal′i tē) □*noun*

hospitalize *verb* To put in a hospital for medical treatment.
hos·pi·tal·ize (hos′pi tə līz′) □*verb*
hospitalized, hospitalizing, hospitalizes

host¹ *noun* Someone who invites and entertains guests.
host (hōst) □*noun, plural* **hosts**

host² *noun* A large number; multitude: *A host of bees swarmed around the flowers.*
host (hōst) □*noun, plural* **hosts**

hostage *noun* Someone who is held prisoner until certain conditions are met: *The government refused to pay a ransom for the ambassador who was held as a hostage.*
hos·tage (hos′tij) □*noun, plural* **hostages**

hostel *noun* An inexpensive lodging that is managed especially for young people.
hos·tel (hos′təl) □*noun, plural* **hostels**

hostess *noun* **1.** A woman who acts as host. **2.** A woman who welcomes or serves people as on an airplane or in a restaurant.
host·ess (hō′stis) □*noun, plural* **hostesses**

hostile *adjective* Feeling or showing hostility; unfriendly: *a hostile tone of voice.*
hos·tile (hos′təl) □*adjective*

hostility *noun* Antagonism; ill will: *The hostility between the two countries resulted in war.*
hos·til·i·ty (ho **stil′**i tē) □*noun, plural*
hostilities

hot *adjective* **1.** Having a high temperature; very warm: *The hot coffee burned his tongue. I was so hot that I turned on the fan.* **2.** Spicy and sharp to the taste: *hot pepper.* **3.** Easily aroused: *a hot temper.* **4.** Close: *The police were in hot pursuit of the thief.*
hot (hot) □*adjective* **hotter, hottest**

hot dog *noun* A long, thin sausage, usually served on a long roll; frankfurter.

hotel *noun* A business establishment that provides rooms and often meals.
ho·tel (hō tel′) □*noun, plural* **hotels**

hothead *noun* Someone who is hotheaded: *He is a real hothead and can't take any criticism.*
hot·head (hot′hed′) □*noun, plural* **hotheads**

hotheaded *adjective* Easily excited or angered.
hot·head·ed (hot′hed′ed) □*adjective*

hothouse *noun* A heated house, usually with a glass roof and sides, for growing plants.
hot·house (hot′hous′) □*noun, plural*
hothouses

hot rod *noun* An automobile that has been altered to increase its power and speed.

hound *noun* A dog originally bred and trained for hunting.
□*verb* To urge over and over; nag: *She hounded him until he repaid the loan.*
hound (hound) □*noun, plural* **hounds**
□*verb* **hounded, hounding, hounds**

hour *noun* **1.** A unit of time that is equal to sixty minutes. A day has twenty-four hours. **2.** The time of day: *Why aren't you in bed at this hour?* **3.** A fixed or customary time: *the dinner hour.*
hour (our) □*noun, plural* **hours**

hourglass *noun* An instrument for measuring time in which a quantity of sand takes one hour to pass through a narrow neck from the upper to the lower part of a glass.
hour·glass (our′glas′) □*noun, plural*
hourglasses

hourglass

hourly *adjective* **1.** Done or happening every hour: *hourly news broadcasts.* **2.** By the hour:

an hourly wage.
□*adverb* Every hour: *The bus departs hourly.*
hour·ly (**our′**lē) □*adjective* □*adverb*

house *noun* **1.** A building in which people live. **2.** A building used for a particular purpose: *a movie house.* **3.** A business firm: *a printing house.* **4.** The people who live in a house; household: *The doorbell rang and woke the whole house.* **5.** An audience: *The actors played to a full house.* **6.** A group of people who make laws; legislature. The House of Representatives and the Senate are the two houses of the United States Congress.
□*verb* To provide living quarters for: *The campers were housed in tents.*
house (hous) □*noun, plural* **houses** (**hou′**ziz) □*verb* (houz) **housed, housing, houses**

houseboat *noun* A large flat-bottomed boat on which people can live.
house·boat (**hous′**bōt′) □*noun, plural* **houseboats**

houseboat

housefly *noun* A common fly that is found in or near houses and often carries and spreads disease germs.
house·fly (**hous′**flī′) □*noun, plural* **houseflies**

household *noun* All the people who live in a house.
house·hold (**hous′**hōld′) □*noun, plural* **households**

housekeeper *noun* Someone who is hired to take care of a house.
house·keeper (**hous′**kē′pər) □*noun, plural* **housekeepers**

House of Commons *noun* The lower house of the British or Canadian Parliaments.

House of Lords *noun* The upper house of the British Parliament.

House of Representatives *noun* The lower branch of the United States Congress whose members are elected every two years.

housewarming *noun* A party given to celebrate moving into a new house: *They invited all their neighbors to the housewarming.*
house·warm·ing (**hous′**wôr′ming) □*noun, plural* **housewarmings**

housewife *noun* A married woman who takes care of her family's household.
house·wife (**hous′**wīf′) □*noun, plural* **housewives**

housework *noun* Tasks, such as cooking, cleaning, and washing, that are involved in taking care of a house.
house·work (**hous′**wûrk′) □*noun*

housing *noun* **1.** Buildings in which a number of people live: *There is a shortage of housing in the city.* **2.** Something that covers, contains, or protects a machine or part of a machine: *the housing on an electric drill.*
hous·ing (**hou′**zing) □*noun, plural* **housings**

hovel *noun* A house that is small, miserable, and usually filthy.
hov·el (**huv′**əl) □*noun, plural* **hovels**

hover *verb* To stay up in the air over one spot: *The hummingbird hovered over the flower.*
hov·er (**huv′**ər) □*verb* **hovered, hovering, hovers**

hover

how *adverb* **1.** In what way; by what means: *How can you tell when meat is cooked? How*

a bat	ī bite	o͞o tool	*th* feather
ā make	î fierce	ou out	th bath
â dare	o dot	u nut	hw wheat
ä father	ō no	û turn	zh measure
e net	ô law, for	ch church	ə about, open
ē be	oi soil	ng ring	pencil, atom
i dip	oo look	sh shade	circus

can I earn more money? **2.** In what condition: *How is your mother?* **3.** To what degree or amount: *How happy are they?*
□*conjunction* In what way or manner: *Show her how it is done.*
how (hou) □*adverb* □*conjunction*

however *adverb* **1.** By whatever manner or means: *However you do it, do it well.* **2.** To whatever degree or amount: *However small the gift is, she will be grateful for it.*
□*conjunction* Nevertheless; yet: *He is very busy; however, he will get the job done.*
how·ev·er (hou ev′ər) □*adverb*
□*conjunction*

howl *noun* A long, wailing cry: *the howl of a dog in pain.*
□*verb* To make a howl or a sound similar to a howl: *His jokes made us howl with laughter. The wind howled through the branches of the trees.*
howl (houl) □*noun, plural* **howls** □*verb*
howled, howling, howls

hr An abbreviation for **hour.**

ht An abbreviation for **height.**

hub *noun* **1.** The center part of a wheel, fan, or propeller. **2.** A center of activity: *a town that is the hub of a mining region.*
hub (hub) □*noun, plural* **hubs**

hub

hubbub *noun* A confused mixture of sounds and noise: *The hubbub of the crowd made it hard to hear the music played by the band.*
hub·bub (hub′ub′) □*noun*

huckleberry *noun* A shiny, blackish, edible berry that looks like a blueberry.
huck·le·ber·ry (huk′əl ber′ē) □*noun, plural* **huckleberries**

huddle *noun* A closely packed group or crowd: *The football players formed a huddle.*
□*verb* To crowd together: *We huddled under the umbrella.*
hud·dle (hud′əl) □*noun, plural* **huddles**
□*verb* **huddled, huddling, huddles**

hue *noun* A color; shade: *all the hues of the rainbow.*
hue (hyōō) □*noun, plural* **hues**

huff *noun* A fit of anger: *She went off in a huff when I refused to lend her my skates.*
□*verb* **1.** To let out the breath in sharp bursts or gusts: *huffed and puffed and blew the house down.* **2.** To get angry; take offense.
huff (huf) □*noun, plural* **huffs** □*verb*
huffed, huffing, huffs

huffy *adjective* **1.** Angry or annoyed: *He got huffy because we criticized his work.* **2.** Easily offended.
huff·y (huf′ē) □*adjective* **huffier, huffiest**

hug *verb* **1.** To put the arms around and hold tightly; embrace: *She hugged her aunt and said good-by.* **2.** To be or keep close to: *a road that hugs the mountain.*
□*noun* An embrace: *She gave me a hug when I arrived.*
hug (hug) □*verb* **hugged, hugging, hugs**
□*noun, plural* **hugs**

huge *adjective* Of very great size; enormous: *a huge stadium.* —See Synonyms at **giant.**
huge (hyōōj) □*adjective* **huger, hugest**

hulk *noun* **1.** Someone or something that is very large and awkward. **2.** The hull of an old or wrecked ship.
hulk (hulk) □*noun, plural* **hulks**

hull *noun* **1.** The sides and bottom of a ship. **2.** The cluster of small leaves near the stem of a fruit such as a strawberry. **3.** The dry outer covering of a fruit, seed, or nut.
□*verb* To remove the hulls from.
hull (hul) □*noun, plural* **hulls** □*verb* **hulled, hullings, hulls**

hull
Of a strawberry

hullabaloo *noun* A confused noise or uproar: *The hullabaloo woke everyone in the neighborhood.*
hul·la·ba·loo (hul′ə bə lōō′) □*noun*

hum *verb* **1.** To make a sound like a long *m*: *He always hums when he is working.* **2.** To make the droning sound of an insect: *Through the open window we could hear the bees humming.* **3.** To sing without opening the lips: *hum a tune.*
□*noun* The act or sound of humming.
hum (hum) □*verb* **hummed, humming, hums** □*noun, plural* **hums**

human *adjective* Of or characteristic of people: *the human voice; human nature.*
□*noun* A person.
hu·man (hyōō′mən) □*adjective* □*noun, plural* **humans**

humane *adjective* Not cruel; kind: *the humane treatment of animals.*
hu·mane (hyōō mān′) □*adjective*

humanity *noun* **1.** Human beings as a group; people: *working to serve humanity.* **2.** The quality of being humane; kindness: *They showed their humanity by being generous to the flood victims.*
hu·man·i·ty (hyōō man′i tē) □*noun*

humble *adjective* **1.** Not proud; modest: *He had a humble manner even though he was famous.* **2.** Not important: *a humble family.*
□*verb* To make humble: *She felt humbled by her lack of knowledge.*
hum·ble (hum′bəl) □*adjective* **humbler, humblest** □*verb* **humbled, humbling, humbles**

humbug *noun* **1.** Nonsense; rubbish: *Her speech was nothing but humbug.* **2.** Something that is designed to trick or deceive. **3.** Someone who deceives or plays a part: *He told us he was a prince but we found out that he's a humbug.*
hum·bug (hum′bug′) □*noun, plural* **humbugs**

humdinger *noun* Someone or something that is superior or very unusual: *I've had good meals before, but the lunch he made us was a humdinger.*
hum·ding·er (hum′ding′ər) □*noun, plural* **humdingers**

humdrum *adjective* Lacking in excitement or variety; boring: *They lead a humdrum life and never have any fun.*
hum·drum (hum′drum′) □*adjective*

humid *adjective* Damp; moist: *a humid day.*
hu·mid (hyōō′mid) □*adjective*

humidity *noun* Moisture, especially of the air.
hu·mid·i·ty (hyōō mid′i tē) □*noun*

humiliate *verb* To lower the self-respect or pride of: *Her father humiliated her by scolding her in front of her friends.*
hu·mil·i·ate (hyōō mil′ē āt′) □*verb* **humiliated, humiliating, humiliates**

humility *noun* The quality or state of being modest or humble.
hu·mil·i·ty (hyōō mil′i tē) □*noun*

hummingbird *noun* A very small, brightly colored bird with a long, slender bill and wings that beat so fast that they make a humming sound.
hum·ming·bird (hum′ing bûrd′) □*noun, plural* **hummingbirds**

humor *noun* **1.** The quality of being amusing or funny: *His idea of humor is throwing a custard pie in someone's face.* **2.** The ability to see or express what is funny: *a good sense of humor.* **3.** A mood: *She's in a fine humor today.*
□*verb* To go along with the wishes of: *He's sick, so try to humor him.*
hu·mor (hyōō′mər) □*noun* □*verb* **humored, humoring, humors**

humorous *adjective* Funny; amusing: *a humorous cartoon.*
hu·mor·ous (hyōō′mər əs) □*adjective*

hump *noun* A rounded lump, as on the back of a camel.
hump (hump) □*noun, plural* **humps**

hump
On a camel

humpback *noun* **1.** A large whale with a rounded back and very long flippers. **2.** A hunchback.

a	bat	ī	bite	ōō	tool	*th*	feather
ā	make	î	fierce	ou	out	th	bath
â	dare	o	dot	u	nut	hw	wheat
ä	father	ō	no	û	turn	zh	measure
e	net	ô	law, for	ch	church	ə	about, open
ē	be	oi	soil	ng	ring		pencil, atom
i	dip	oo	look	sh	shade		circus

hump·back (hump′bak′) □*noun, plural* **humpbacks**

humus *noun* Dark, rich soil that is formed from decayed plant material, such as dead leaves.
hu·mus (hyōō′məs) □*noun*

hunch *noun* A feeling about what is going to happen: *I had a hunch they would drop in, so I prepared lunch.*
□*verb* To bend or draw up into a hump: *We hunched up our shoulders.*
hunch (hunch) □*noun, plural* **hunches**
□*verb* **hunched, hunching, hunches**

hunchback *noun* **1.** A crooked or abnormally curved back. **2.** A person with a hunchback.
hunch·back (hunch′bak′) □*noun, plural* **hunchbacks**

hundred *noun* A number equal to the product of 10 × 10; 100.
□*adjective* Being ten more than ninety.
hun·dred (hun′drid) □*noun, plural* **hundreds** □*adjective*

hundredth *noun* **1.** In a group of people or things that are in numbered order, the one that matches the number 100. **2.** One of a hundred equal parts, written 1/100.
□*adjective* Coming after the ninety-ninth.
hun·dredth (hun′dridth) □*noun, plural* **hundredths** □*adjective*

hung *verb* A past tense and a past participle of **hang:** *We hung a mirror on the wall. She had hung the clothes out to dry.*
hung (hung) □*verb*

hunger *noun* **1.** A strong desire or need for food. **2.** A strong desire: *a hunger for power.*
□*verb* To have a strong desire or craving: *She was lonely and hungered for news of her friends.*
hun·ger (hung′gər) □*noun, plural* **hungers**
□*verb* **hungered, hungering, hungers**

hungry *adjective* **1.** Wanting or needing food: *The hungry child asked for a cookie.* **2.** Having a strong desire; eager: *hungry for affection.*
hun·gry (hung′grē) □*adjective* **hungrier, hungriest**

hunk *noun* A large piece; chunk: *a hunk of cheese.*
hunk (hungk) □*noun, plural* **hunks**

hunt *verb* **1.** To look for so as to capture or kill: *They are hunting deer.* **2.** To make a careful search; look: *I hunted for her address.*
□*noun* **1.** The act or activity of hunting. **2.** A careful search.
hunt (hunt) □*verb* **hunted, hunting, hunts**
□*noun, plural* **hunts**

hunter *noun* A person or animal who hunts.
hunt·er (hun′tər) □*noun, plural* **hunters**

hurdle *noun* **1.** A barrier that must be jumped over in a race. **2. hurdles** A race in which runners must jump over hurdles. **3.** A problem that must be overcome; obstacle.
□*verb* To jump over while running: *We hurdled the stone wall.*
hur·dle (hûr′dəl) □*noun, plural* **hurdles**
□*verb* **hurdled, hurdling, hurdles**

hurdle

hurdy-gurdy *noun* A musical instrument that is played by turning a crank or handle: *A quaint figure leading a trained bear strolled through the streets playing opera tunes on a hurdy-gurdy.*
hur·dy-gur·dy (hûr′dē **gûr′**dē) □*noun, plural* **hurdy-gurdies**

hurl *verb* To throw with force: *He hurled the book at the wall.* —See Synonyms at **throw.**
hurl (hûrl) □*verb* **hurled, hurling, hurls**

hurrah *interjection* A word used to express joy or praise: *"Hurrah!" shouted the crowd as the winner crossed the finish line.*
hur·rah (hoo rä′) □*interjection*

hurricane *noun* A powerful storm with very strong winds and heavy rains.
hur·ri·cane (hûr′i kān′) □*noun, plural* **hurricanes**

hurried *adjective* Done or made in a hurry: *a hurried dinner; gave hurried instructions.*
hur·ried (hûr′ēd) □*adjective*

hurry *verb* To move or cause to move quickly: *If we don't hurry, we'll miss the con-*

cert. Don't hurry me when I am eating. —See Synonyms at **rush.**

□*noun* The need or wish to hurry; haste: *We were in a hurry to get to the movies.*
hur·ry (**hur′** ē)   □*verb* **hurried, hurrying, hurries** □*noun*

hurt   *verb* **1.** To cause pain or injury to: *I hurt my leg when I fell.* **2.** To have a feeling of pain: *His stomach hurts.* **3.** To upset; offend: *It hurts my feelings when you ignore me.* **4.** To have a bad effect on; harm: *The scandal hurt his chances of winning the election.*
□*noun* Something that hurts; injury.
hurt (hûrt)   □*verb* **hurt, hurting, hurts** □*noun, plural* **hurts**

hurtle   *verb* **1.** To move with great speed and with or as if with a rushing noise: *The rocket hurtled into space.* **2.** To throw with great force; hurl: *hurtle a spear through the air.*
hur·tle (**hûr′** təl)   □*verb* **hurtled, hurtling, hurtles**

husband   *noun* A married man.
hus·band (**huz′** bənd)   □*noun, plural* **husbands**

WORD HISTORY: husband

Husband comes from an old Norse word meaning "master of a house."

---

hush   *verb* To make quiet: *She hushed the crying child.*
□*noun* A stillness; quiet: *There was a sudden hush and then she spoke.*
hush (hush)   □*verb* **hushed, hushing, hushes** □*noun, plural* **hushes**

husk   *noun* The dry outer covering of certain fruits and seeds, as an ear of corn.
□*verb* To remove the husk from: *husk corn.*
husk (husk)   □*noun, plural* **husks** □*verb* **husked, husking, husks**

husk

husky¹   *adjective* **1.** Big and strong: *a husky truck driver.* **2.** Rough; hoarse: *a husky voice.*
husk·y (**hus′** kē)   □*adjective* **huskier, huskiest**

husky²   *noun* A dog with a thick, furry coat. Huskies are used to pull sleds in the far north.
husk·y (**hus′** kē)   □*noun, plural* **huskies**

hustle   *verb* To hurry; rush: *We will have to hustle to make the train.*
hus·tle (**hus′** əl)   □*verb* **hustled, hustling, hustles**

hut   *noun* A small, simple house or shed.
hut (hut)   □*noun, plural* **huts**

hut

hutch   *noun* **1.** A pen for small animals, especially rabbits. **2.** A cupboard having drawers for storage and usually having open shelves above.
hutch (huch)   □*noun, plural* **hutches**

hyacinth   *noun* A plant that grows from a bulb and has a cluster of fragrant flowers.
hy·a·cinth (**hī′** ə sinth)   □*noun, plural* **hyacinths**

hybrid   *noun* A plant or animal that has parents of different varieties or species. A mule is a hybrid whose parents are a female horse and a male donkey.
□*adjective* Being a hybrid: *a hybrid tulip.*
hy·brid (**hī′** brid)   □*noun, plural* **hybrids** □*adjective*

hydrangea   *noun* A shrub bearing large, rounded clusters of pink, blue, or white flowers.

a	bat	ī	bite	o͞o	tool	*th*	feather
ā	make	î	fierce	ou	out	th	bath
â	dare	o	dot	u	nut	hw	wheat
ä	father	ō	no	û	turn	zh	measure
e	net	ô	law, for	ch	church	ə	about, open
ē	be	oi	soil	ng	ring		pencil, atom
i	dip	oo	look	sh	shade		circus

hy·dran·gea (hī **drān′** jə) ☐*noun, plural* **hydrangeas**

hydrant *noun* A large pipe that sticks up out of the ground and from which water can be drawn for putting out fires.
hy·drant (**hī′** drənt) ☐*noun, plural* **hydrants**

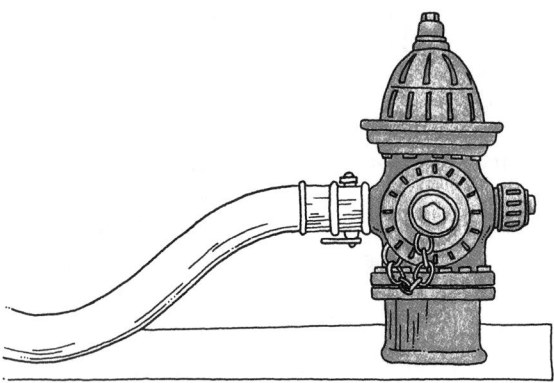

hydrant

hydrofoil *noun* A motorboat having fins designed to lift the hull clear of the water as the speed of the boat increases.
hy·dro·foil (**hī′** drə foil) ☐*noun, plural* **hydrofoils**

hydrogen *noun* A gas that is very light, burns easily, and is one of the chemical elements.
hy·dro·gen (**hī′** drə jən) ☐*noun*

hydrogen bomb *noun* A very powerful bomb in which hydrogen atoms combine to form helium atoms and energy is released in a tremendous explosion.

hydroplane *noun* **1.** A plane designed to land on and take off from a body of water. **2.** A hydrofoil.
hy·dro·plane (**hī′** drə plān′) ☐*noun, plural* **hydroplanes**

hyena *noun* An Asian or African animal that looks rather like a large dog, and has thick, coarse hair and powerful jaws. Hyenas often feed on the flesh of dead animals.
hy·e·na (hī **ē′** nə) ☐*noun, plural* **hyenas**

hygiene *noun* The rules of cleanliness leading to good health.
hy·giene (**hī′** jēn′) ☐*noun*

hygrometer *noun* An instrument for measuring the humidity of the atmosphere.
hy·grom·e·ter (hī **grom′** i tər) ☐*noun, plural* **hygrometers**

hymn *noun* A song of joy, praise, or thanksgiving, especially to God.
hymn (him) ☐*noun, plural* **hymns**

hyphen *noun* A mark (-) used to connect words, parts of a compound word, or parts of a word divided at the end of a line.
hy·phen (**hī′** fən) ☐*noun, plural* **hyphens**

hyphenate *verb* To connect or divide with a hyphen.
hy·phen·ate (**hī′** fə nāt′) ☐*verb* **hyphenated, hyphenating, hyphenates**

hypnotize *verb* To put someone into a state resembling sleep. Someone who has been hypnotized will usually obey the commands of the person who has hypnotized him.
hyp·no·tize (**hip′** nə tīz′) ☐*verb* **hypnotized, hypnotizing, hypnotizes**

hypocrite *noun* Someone who pretends to have virtues or moral principals and qualities he does not have: *A hypocrite will praise honesty and steal an apple when you're not looking.*
hyp·o·crite (**hip′** ə krit′) ☐*noun, plural* **hypocrites**

hysterical *adjective* Showing a loss of emotional control: *The child was hysterical with fear.*
hys·ter·i·cal (hi **ster′** i kəl) ☐*adjective*

a bat	ī bite	o͞o tool	*th* feather
ā make	î fierce	ou **out**	th bath
â dare	o dot	u nut	hw **wheat**
ä father	ō no	û turn	zh measure
e net	ô law, for	ch **church**	ə about, open
ē be	oi soil	ng ring	pencil, atom
i dip	oo **look**	sh **shade**	circus

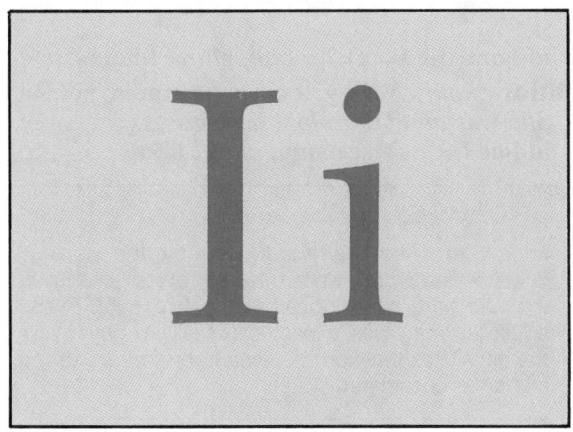

ANCIENT GREEK

The letter **I** has evolved from many forms of ancient writing. One of the earliest known examples is the Greek character shown above, which dates from almost 3,000 years ago. Over the years, artists and designers have created their own versions of the English letter **I**. Some of the more common examples seen today are shown below.

Ii Ii	**Ii Ii**	**Ii Ii**	**Ii Ii**	*Ii Ii*
HANDWRITING	CALLIGRAPHY	MODERN SANS SERIF	MODERN SERIF	SCRIPT

i or **I** *noun* The ninth letter of the English alphabet.
i or **I** (ī) ▢*noun, plural* **i's** or **I's**

I *pronoun* The person who is speaking or writing: *I was glad to see them.*
I (ī) ▢*pronoun*

ice *noun* **1.** Water that has frozen solid. **2.** A frozen dessert made of sugar, water, and flavoring.
▢*verb* **1.** To chill with ice: *She iced the orange juice.* **2.** To cover with icing: *ice a cake.* **3.** To cover or become covered with ice: *The lake iced over last winter.*
ice (īs) ▢*noun, plural* **ices** ▢*verb* **iced, icing, ices**

iceberg *noun* A very large mass of floating ice that has broken off from a glacier.
ice·berg (īs′bûrg′) ▢*noun, plural* **icebergs**

icebox *noun* **1.** A heavy box for storing food that is cooled with ice. **2.** A refrigerator.
ice·box (īs′boks′) ▢*noun, plural* **iceboxes**

ice cap *noun* A sheet of ice and snow that covers an area of land all year round.

ice cream *noun* A smooth, sweet frozen dessert made of milk or cream.

ice skate *noun* A boot or shoe with a metal blade on the sole, worn for skating on ice.

ice-skate *verb* To skate on ice.
ice-skate (īs′skāt′) ▢*verb* **ice-skated, ice-skating, ice-skates**

icicle *noun* A thin, pointed, hanging mass of ice formed from water that freezes as it drips.
i·ci·cle (ī′si kəl) ▢*noun, plural* **icicles**

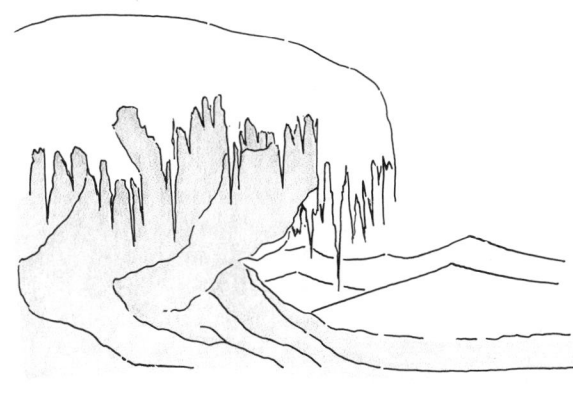

icicle

icing *noun* A smooth, sweet mixture of sugar, butter, and sometimes eggs that is used to cover baked goods such as cakes and cookies.
ic·ing (ī′sing) ▢*noun, plural* **icings**

icy *adjective* **1.** Covered with ice: *an icy street.* **2.** Very cold: *icy water.* **3.** Cold and unfriendly: *an icy greeting.*
ic·y (ī′sē) ▢*adjective* **icier, iciest**

I'd Contraction of "I had," "I would," or "I should."
I'd (īd)

idea *noun* **1.** Something, such as a thought, that exists in the mind: *He had no clear idea of what to do.* **2.** A plan of action: *He had the idea that he might become a teacher.*
i·de·a (ī dē′ə) □*noun, plural* **ideas**

ideal *noun* Someone or something that is thought of as being perfect: *Her mother was her ideal.*
□*adjective* Perfect or best possible: *an ideal day for a picnic.*
i·de·al (ī dē′əl) □*noun, plural* **ideals**
□*adjective*

identical *adjective* **1.** Exactly alike: *They wore identical dresses.* **2.** The very same: *the identical place we visited last week.* —See Synonyms at **same.**
i·den·ti·cal (ī den′ti kəl) □*adjective*

identical

identification *noun* **1.** The act of identifying. **2.** Something used to prove who a person is: *She used her license as identification.*
i·den·ti·fi·ca·tion (ī den′tə fi kā′shən)
□*noun, plural* **identifications**

identify *verb* **1.** To establish the identity of: *She identified the child from his picture.* **2.** To think of as being the same: *She identifies success with wealth.*
i·den·ti·fy (ī den′tə fī′) □*verb* **identified, identifying, identifies**

identity *noun* The condition of being the same as the person or thing that is described: *He proved his identity by showing his driver's license.*
i·den·ti·ty (ī den′ti tē) □*noun, plural* **identities**

idiom *noun* A phrase or expression that has a special meaning that cannot be understood from the meanings of the separate words in it. For example, *up in the air* is an idiom that means "not settled or decided."

id·i·om (id′ē əm) □*noun, plural* **idioms**

idiot *noun* A very foolish or stupid person: *She was an idiot to lose her glasses.*
id·i·ot (id′ē ət) □*noun, plural* **idiots**

> **WORD HISTORY: idiot**
>
> *Idiot* comes from a word used by the ancient Greeks. The Greek word referred to someone who took no part in the government of his city. Every educated man was expected to help in governing the city. Thus the word became a term of abuse for someone considered stupid.

idle *adjective* **1.** Not working or in use: *an idle employee; idle machines.* **2.** Avoiding work; lazy: *idle boys playing ball.* **3.** Worthless or useless: *idle gossip.*
□*verb* **1.** To spend time without working: *She idled away the afternoon reading comic books.* **2.** To run at low speed or while not in gear: *The car engine idled smoothly.*
i·dle (īd′əl) □*adjective* **idler, idlest** □*verb* **idled, idling, idles**

idol *noun* **1.** Something, such as a statue, that is worshiped as a god. **2.** Someone who is admired or loved very much: *The actor is an idol to millions.*
i·dol (īd′əl) □*noun, plural* **idols**

if *conjunction* **1.** On condition that: *She will go only if you pay her fare.* **2.** Supposing that; in case that: *If what he says is true, what should we do about it?* **3.** Whether: *Ask her if she is going away.*
if (if) □*conjunction*

igloo *noun* A dome-shaped Eskimo house, often made from blocks of hard snow.
ig·loo (ig′loo) □*noun, plural* **igloos**

> **WORD HISTORY: igloo**
>
> *Igloo* comes from an Eskimo word that means "house."

igloo

igneous   *adjective* Formed from molten mineral material: *igneous rocks.*
ig·ne·ous (ig′ nē əs) □*adjective*

ignite   *verb* To set on fire or catch fire: *We ignited the charcoal.*
ig·nite (ig nīt′) □*verb* **ignited, igniting, ignites**

ignition   *noun* **1.** The act or process of igniting. **2.** An electrical system that provides a hot spark to ignite the fuel in a gasoline engine.
ig·ni·tion (ig nish′ən) □*noun, plural* **ignitions**

ignorance   *noun* The condition of being ignorant; lack of knowledge.
ig·no·rance (ig′ nər əns) □*noun*

ignorant   *adjective* Lacking or showing a lack of education or knowledge: *an ignorant mistake.*
ig·no·rant (ig′ nər ənt) □*adjective*

ignore   *verb* To pay no attention to; disregard: *I ignored his bad manners.*
ig·nore (ig nôr′) □*verb* **ignored, ignoring, ignores**

iguana   *noun* A large tropical American lizard with a ridge of spines along the back.
i·gua·na (i gwä′ nə) □*noun, plural* **iguanas**

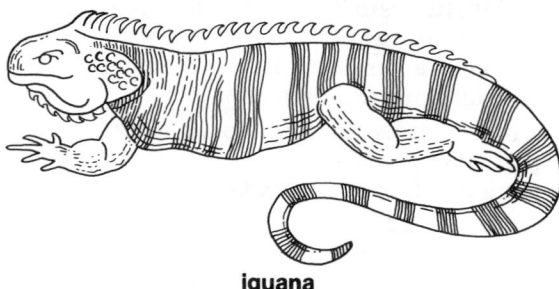

iguana

ill   *adjective* **1.** Not healthy; sick: *He is ill with the flu.* **2.** Not favorable; bad: *ill luck.*
□*adverb* Not kindly; badly or cruelly: *You shouldn't speak ill of someone who is absent.*
□*noun* **1.** Evil; sin: *for good or for ill.* **2.** Sickness: *the ills of childhood.* **3.** Harm; trouble: *the ills of life.*
ill (il) □*adjective* **worse, worst** □*adverb* **worse, worst** □*noun, plural* **ills**

I'll   Contraction of "I shall" or "I will."
I'll (īl)

illegal   *adjective* Against the law: *Speeding is illegal.* —See Synonyms at **criminal.**
il·le·gal (i lē′ gəl) □*adjective*

illiterate   *adjective* Not able to read and write.
il·lit·er·ate (i lit′ ər it) □*adjective*

illness   *noun* Sickness; disease: *Cancer is a serious illness.*
ill·ness (il′ nis) □*noun, plural* **illnesses**

illuminate   *verb* To provide with light; light up: *Only one lamp illuminated the study.*
il·lu·mi·nate (i lōō′ mə nāt′) □*verb* **illuminated, illuminating, illuminates**

illusion   *noun* **1.** A false or misleading image: *an optical illusion.* **2.** A false or mistaken idea or belief: *She had the illusion that she would be happy if she were rich.*
il·lu·sion (i lōō′ zhən) □*noun, plural* **illusions**

illustrate   *verb* **1.** To explain by using examples, stories, or comparisons: *Snowflakes illustrate the great variety that can be found in nature.* **2.** To provide with pictures or diagrams that explain or decorate: *illustrated the history book with photographs.*
il·lus·trate (il′ ə strāt′ *or* i lus′ trāt′) □*verb* **illustrated, illustrating, illustrates**

illustration   *noun* **1.** A picture or diagram that explains or decorates: *an illustration of the solar system.* **2.** Something serving as an example or explanation: *A town meeting is an illustration of democracy in action.*
il·lus·tra·tion (il′ ə strā′ shən) □*noun, plural* **illustrations**

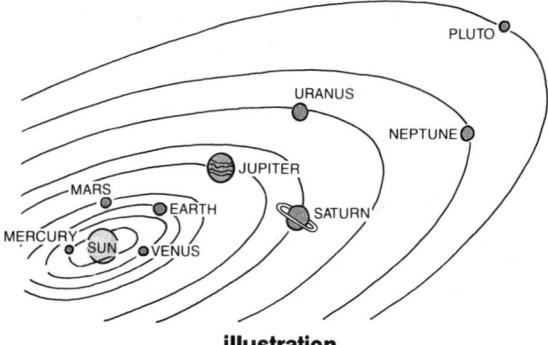

illustration

ill will   *noun* Unfriendly feeling: *He felt no ill will toward the person who won the race.*

I'm   Contraction of "I am."
I'm (īm)

a	bat	ī	bite	ōō	tool	*th*	feather
ā	make	î	fierce	ou	out	th	bath
â	dare	o	dot	u	nut	hw	wheat
ä	father	ō	no	û	turn	zh	measure
e	net	ô	law, for	ch	church	ə	about, open
ē	be	oi	soil	ng	ring		pencil, atom
i	dip	oo	look	sh	shade		circus

image *noun* **1.** A picture of something in the mind: *A year later she still had an image of the car accident.* **2.** A reproduction of a person or thing, especially a statue: *an image of a bear.* **3.** Something or someone that looks very much like another: *He is the image of his uncle.* —See Synonyms at **double.**
im·age (**im′**ij) ▢*noun, plural* **images**

imaginary *adjective* Existing only in the imagination; not real: *Dragons are imaginary creatures.*
i·mag·i·nar·y (i **maj′**ə ner′ē) ▢*adjective*

imagination *noun* **1.** The ability to form pictures or images in the mind: *In her imagination she traveled all over the world.* **2.** The ability to create: *the lively imagination of a painter.*
i·mag·i·na·tion (i maj′ə **nā′**shən) ▢*noun, plural* **imaginations**

imaginative *adjective* **1.** Having a strong imagination: *an imaginative writer.* **2.** Of or showing imagination: *an imaginative story.*
i·mag·i·na·tive (i **maj′**ə nə tiv) ▢*adjective*

imagine *verb* **1.** To form a picture in the mind: *Can you imagine what it's like to fly in a spaceship?* **2.** To make a guess: *I imagine that it will be hot tomorrow.*
i·mag·ine (i **maj′**in) ▢*verb* **imagined, imagining, imagines**

imitate *verb* **1.** To copy the actions or appearance of another: *She always imitates her sister.* **2.** To look like; resemble: *a kind of stone that imitates marble.*
im·i·tate (**im′**i tāt′) ▢*verb* **imitated, imitating, imitates**

imitation *noun* **1.** The act of imitating: *Her imitation of the circus clown made everyone laugh.* **2.** A copy of something else: *an imitation of a diamond.* ▢*adjective* Being a copy of something else: *imitation fur.*
im·i·ta·tion (im′i **tā′**shən) ▢*noun, plural* **imitations** ▢*adjective*

immature *adjective* Not fully grown, developed, or ripe: *immature fruit.*
im·ma·ture (im′ə **choor′** *or* im′ə **tyoor′** *or* im′ə **toor′**) ▢*adjective*

immediate *adjective* **1.** Taking place or done at once; without delay: *I need immediate care.* **2.** Coming next or very soon: *my immediate plans.* **3.** Close; nearby: *There are several stores in the immediate neighborhood.*
im·me·di·ate (i **mē′**dē it) ▢*adjective*

immediately *adverb* Right away; at once: *Come home immediately.*
im·me·di·ate·ly (i **mē′**dē it lē) ▢*adverb*

immense *adjective* Of great size, extent, or degree: *an immense watermelon.*
im·mense (i **mens′**) ▢*adjective*

immense

immigrant *noun* Someone who comes to live in a country in which he or she was not born.
im·mi·grant (**im′**i grənt) ▢*noun, plural* **immigrants**

immigrate *verb* To come to live in a country in which one was not born.
im·mi·grate (**im′**i grāt′) ▢*verb* **immigrated, immigrating, immigrates**

immoral *adjective* Not moral; evil: *Cheating is an immoral act.*
im·mor·al (i **môr′**əl) ▢*adjective*

immortal *adjective* Living or lasting forever: *Do you think that a great poem is immortal?*
im·mor·tal (i **môr′**tl) ▢*adjective*

immune *adjective* Protected from disease: *This vaccine will make you immune to polio.*
im·mune (i **myoon′**) ▢*adjective*

immunity *noun* **1.** The ability to resist disease: *The body can develop an immunity against certain viruses.* **2.** Protection against a punishment or penalty.
im·mu·ni·ty (i **myoo′**ni tē) ▢*noun, plural* **immunities**

impact *noun* The striking of one object against another; collision: *We felt the enormous impact of the crash.*
im·pact (**im′**pakt′) ▢*noun, plural* **impacts**

impair *verb* To lower the strength or quality of: *A poor diet can impair a person's health.*
im·pair (im **pâr′**) ▢*verb* **impaired, impairing, impairs**

impala *noun* An African antelope that has curved, spreading horns and can leap a great distance.
im·pa·la (im pal′ə) □*noun, plural* **impalas**

impartial *adjective* Not favoring one more than another: *an impartial judge.* —See Synonyms at **fair¹**.
im·par·tial (im **pär′**shəl) □*adjective*

impatience *noun* The condition of being impatient.
im·pa·tience (im **pā′**shəns) □*noun*

impatient *adjective* Not able or willing to wait calmly or put up with opposition or annoyance: *impatient at the delay.*
im·pa·tient (im **pā′**shənt) □*adjective*

impeach *verb* To accuse a public official with wrong or illegal behavior in office.
im·peach (im **pēch′**) □*verb* **impeached, impeaching, impeaches**

imperfect *adjective* Having a deficiency, fault, or error: *imperfect eyesight.*
im·per·fect (im **pûr′**fikt) □*adjective*

SYNONYMS: **imperfect, defective**

These adjectives mean having a fault or error: *She had only an imperfect memory of the accident. The new phonograph record is defective because it has a scratch.*

---

imperial *adjective* Of or having to do with an empire, an empress, or an emperor.
im·pe·ri·al (im **pîr′**ē əl) □*adjective*

implement *noun* A tool or piece of equipment used to do a particular job or task: *A pen is a writing implement.*
im·ple·ment (**im′**plə mənt) □*noun, plural* **implements**

imply *verb* To suggest without saying directly; hint: *She didn't say she agreed, but she implied that she did.* —See Synonyms at **suggest**.
im·ply (im **plī′**) □*verb* **implied, implying, implies**

impolite *adjective* Not polite; rude. —See Synonyms at **rude**.
im·po·lite (im′pə **līt′**) □*adjective*

import *verb* To bring in goods or products from a foreign country for sale or use: *a country that imports much of its food.* □*noun* Something imported: *One of our main imports is oil.*
im·port (im **pôrt′**) □*verb* **imported,**

importing, imports □*noun* (**im′**pôrt′), *plural* **imports**

importance *noun* The condition of being important: *the importance of a good diet.*
im·por·tance (im **pôrt′**əns) □*noun*

important *adjective* Having great value, meaning, or influence: *an important occasion; an important decision.*
im·por·tant (im **pôrt′**ənt) □*adjective*

SYNONYMS: **important, momentous, significant**

These adjectives mean having great value, meaning, or influence: *Do you believe that scientists are more important than artists? The landing of astronauts on the moon was a momentous event. July 4, 1776, is a significant date in the history of the United States.*

---

impose *verb* To establish or assign something that is a burden: *The legislature imposed a tax on clothing.*
im·pose (im **pōz′**) □*verb* **imposed, imposing, imposes**

impossible *adjective* **1.** Not capable of happening, being done, or existing: *It is impossible to be in two places at the same time.* **2.** Difficult to deal with: *an impossible situation.*
im·pos·si·ble (im **pos′**ə bəl) □*adjective*

impress *verb* **1.** To have a strong effect on the feelings or mind of: *The beauty of the mountain impressed us.* **2.** To fix firmly in the mind: *They impressed the importance of being fair on their children.*
im·press (im **pres′**) □*verb* **impressed, impressing, impresses**

impression *noun* **1.** An effect or feeling that stays in the mind: *The new teacher made a good impression on the students.* **2.** An idea or belief: *I have the impression that I've seen this movie before.* **3.** A mark or design produced on a surface by pressing: *The robber left an impression of his feet in the mud.*
im·pres·sion (im **presh′**ən) □*noun, plural* **impressions**

a	bat	ī	bite	o͞o	tool	*th*	feather
ā	make	î	fierce	ou	out	th	bath
â	dare	o	dot	u	nut	hw	wheat
ä	father	ō	no	û	turn	zh	measure
e	net	ô	law, for	ch	church	ə	about, open
ē	be	oi	soil	ng	ring		pencil, atom
i	dip	o͝o	look	sh	shade		circus

impressive *adjective* Making a strong impression: *an impressive accomplishment.*
im·pres·sive (im **pres'** iv) □*adjective*

imprint *noun* A mark or design made by stamping or pressing something on a surface: *the imprint of a boot in the snow.*
□*verb* To mark by pressing; stamp: *He imprinted his name on the note paper.*
im·print (im' print') □*noun, plural* **imprints**
□*verb* (im **print'**) **imprinted, imprinting, imprints**

imprison *verb* To put in prison.
im·pris·on (im **priz'** ən) □*verb* **imprisoned, imprisoning, imprisons**

improper *adjective* **1.** Not proper; incorrect: *an improper tool for the job.* **2.** Showing or having bad manners or bad taste: *It is improper for a man to keep his hat on in the presence of the king.*
im·prop·er (im **prop'** ər) □*adjective*

improper fraction *noun* A fraction, as $^3/_3$ and $^4/_3$, that is equal to or greater than 1.

improve *verb* To make or become better: *He improved his piano playing by practicing. Her health is improving.*
im·prove (im **prōōv'**) □*verb* **improved, improving, improves**

improvement *noun* **1.** A change or addition that improves: *The new kitchen was an improvement to the old house.* **2.** The act or result of improving: *I see a real improvement in your handwriting.*
im·prove·ment (im **prōōv'** mənt) □*noun, plural* **improvements**

improvise *verb* **1.** To make up and present without preparing beforehand: *improvise a speech.* **2.** To make from whatever materials are nearby: *They improvised chairs from orange crates.*
im·pro·vise (im' prə vīz') □*verb* **improvised, improvising, improvises**

improvise

impudent *adjective* Bold and disrespectful: *The impudent clerk insulted all the customers.*
im·pu·dent (im' pyə dənt) □*adjective*

impulse *noun* **1.** A sudden urge or desire; whim: *I had an impulse to take a long trip.* **2.** A sudden driving force; thrust: *The impulse of the wind knocked the fence down.*
im·pulse (im' puls') □*noun, plural* **impulses**

impure *adjective* Not pure; dirty: *impure drinking water.*
im·pure (im pyoor') □*adjective*

in *preposition* **1.** Within the area or limits of; inside: *Put your clothes in the closet. He lives in an apartment.* **2.** To or at a condition or situation of: *in debt; in love.* **3.** From the outside to a point within; into: *I could not get in the room.* **4.** During: *I go away in the summer.* **5.** By means of; with: *a letter written in ink.* **6.** With the purpose of: *said nothing in reply.*
□*adverb* **1.** To or toward the inside: *I called him and he came in.* **2.** Inside a usual place, as of business: *The doctor's not in today.*
in (in) □*preposition* □*adverb*

in– A prefix that means "without, not": *informal; insane.*

in. An abbreviation for **inch.**

inaugurate *verb* **1.** To place in office with a formal ceremony: *inaugurate a governor.* **2.** To open for public use with a formal ceremony: *The mayor will inaugurate the new park.*
in·au·gu·rate (i nô' gyə rāt') □*verb* **inaugurated, inaugurating, inaugurates**

inauguration *noun* **1.** The formal ceremony of placing a person in office. **2.** A formal beginning or opening.
in·au·gu·ra·tion (i nô' gyə rā' shən) □*noun, plural* **inaugurations**

inborn *adjective* Present in a person or animal from birth: *an inborn talent for writing.*
in·born (in' bôrn') □*adjective*

incense¹ *verb* To make very angry; infuriate: *His rudeness incenses me.*
in·cense (in sens') □*verb* **incensed, incensing, incenses**

incense² *noun* A substance that gives off a sweet smell when it is burned.
in·cense (in' sens') □*noun, plural* **incenses**

incentive *noun* Something that encourages a person to make an effort: *The promise of new ice skates was his incentive to pass the test.*
in·cen·tive (in sen' tiv) □*noun, plural* **incentives**

inch *noun* A unit of length equal to ¹/₁₂ of a foot, or 2.54 centimeters.
□*verb* To move very slowly or by small degrees: *He inched down the icy road.*
inch (inch) □*noun, plural* **inches** □*verb* **inched, inching, inches**

WORD HISTORY: **inch**

The word *inch* comes from a Latin word meaning "a one-twelfth part." The word *ounce* comes from the same Latin word.

---

inchworm *noun* A caterpillar that moves by pulling up its body and then stretching it out.
inch·worm (inch′ wûrm′) □*noun, plural* **inchworms**

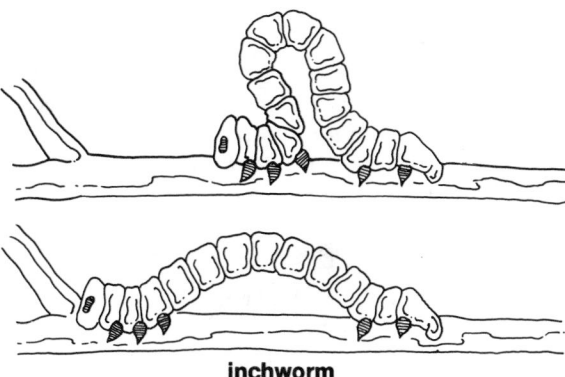

inchworm

incident *noun* Something that happens; event: *She described an interesting incident from her childhood.*
in·ci·dent (in′ si dənt) □*noun, plural* **incidents**

incidentally *adverb* By the way: *Incidentally, where are you going?*
in·ci·den·tal·ly (in′si **den′**tl ē) □*adverb*

incinerator *noun* A furnace for burning trash or garbage.
in·cin·er·a·tor (in **sin′**ə rā′tər) □*noun, plural* **incinerators**

inclination *noun* **1.** A tendency: *He has an inclination to eat too much.* **2.** A liking: *She has an inclination for music.* **3.** A slant; slope: *a steep inclination.*
in·cli·na·tion (in′klə **nā′**shən) □*noun, plural* **inclinations**

incline *verb* To lean, slant, or slope: *The path inclines sharply upward.*
□*noun* A slant or slope.
in·cline (in **klīn′**) □*verb* **inclined, inclining, inclines** □*noun* (in′ klīn′), *plural* **inclines**

include *verb* To take in as part of a whole; contain: *Does the price include the tax? Please include my friend on your list of guests.*
in·clude (in **klood′**) □*verb* **included, including, includes**

income *noun* The amount of money received from work, goods, services, or property.
in·come (in′kum′) □*noun, plural* **incomes**

income tax *noun* A tax on a person's income.

incomplete *adjective* Not complete; not finished: *I couldn't hand in my essay because it was incomplete.*
in·com·plete (in′kəm **plēt′**) □*adjective*

incorporate *verb* To combine into a whole: *The teacher incorporated our suggestions into her report.*
in·cor·po·rate (in **kôr′**pə rāt′) □*verb* **incorporated, incorporating, incorporates**

incorrect *adjective* Not correct; wrong: *an incorrect answer.* —See Synonyms at **false.**
in·cor·rect (in′kə **rekt′**) □*adjective*

increase *verb* To make or become greater or larger: *He increased his knowledge by reading. Sales increased rapidly.*
□*noun* **1.** Growth: *an increase in income.* **2.** The amount or rate by which something is increased: *a 10% increase in taxes.*
in·crease (in **krēs′**) □*verb* **increased, increasing, increases** □*noun* (in′ krēs′), *plural* **increases**

increasingly *adverb* More and more: *The problem became increasingly clear.*
in·creas·ing·ly (in **krē′**sing lē) □*adverb*

incredible *adjective* Hard to believe: *an incredible story.*
in·cred·i·ble (in **kred′**ə bəl) □*adjective*

incubate *verb* To keep eggs warm in order to hatch them.
in·cu·bate (in′kyə bāt′ *or* ing′kyə bāt′) □*verb* **incubated, incubating, incubates**

incubator *noun* A device that provides heat. One kind of incubator is used to hatch eggs. Another kind is used for a baby that has been born too soon.

a bat	ī bite	oo tool	*th* feather
ā make	î fierce	ou out	th bath
â dare	o dot	u nut	hw wheat
ä father	ō no	û turn	zh measure
e net	ô law, for	ch church	ə about, open
ē be	oi soil	ng ring	pencil, atom
i dip	oo look	sh shade	circus

in·cu·ba·tor (**in'**kyə bā'tər *or* **ing'**kyə bā'tər) □*noun, plural* **incubators**

indeed *adverb* In fact; really: *We were indeed glad to see him.*
in·deed (in **dēd'**) □*adverb*

indefinite *adjective* **1.** Not fixed or clear; vague: *Our vacation plans are still indefinite.* **2.** Lacking precise limits: *an indefinite period of time.*
in·def·i·nite (in **def'**ə nit) □*adjective*

indefinite article *noun* Either of the articles *a* or *an*, used to indicate that the noun that follows refers to no particular person or thing.

indent *verb* To begin a line of writing farther in than the other lines.
in·dent (in **dent'**) □*verb* **indented, indenting, indents**

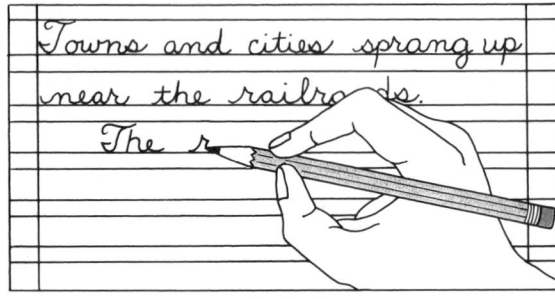

indent

independence *noun* The condition or quality of being independent. —See Synonyms at **liberty.**
in·de·pen·dence (in'di **pen'**dəns) □*noun*

independent *adjective* **1.** Not under the control of a foreign government: *an independent nation.* **2.** Not guided by others: *an independent life.* **3.** Not depending on others for food and shelter: *He has a job and is independent of his family.*
in·de·pen·dent (in'di **pen'**dənt) □*adjective*

index *noun* An alphabetical list of the names and subjects in a printed work. It tells the page on which each can be found. □*verb* To make or write an index for.
in·dex (**in'**deks') □*noun, plural* **indexes** □*verb* **indexed, indexing, indexes**

WORD HISTORY: **index**
The word *index* comes from a Latin word that means "the index finger." Just as the index finger can be used for pointing, an index, or alphabetical list, can be used to point to further information.

index finger *noun* The finger next to the thumb.

Indian *noun* **1.** Someone who was born in or is a citizen of India. **2.** A Native American. □*adjective* **1.** Of India or its people. **2.** Of Native Americans or their languages.
In·di·an (**in'**dē ən) □*noun, plural* **Indians** □*adjective*

WORD HISTORY: **Indian**
Columbus sailed west from Europe hoping to find a route to Asia. At that time the name *India* was used as a general term for all the lands in eastern Asia. So when Columbus reached the islands that are now called the West Indies, he thought that he had come to "India." As a result of Columbus's mistake, the native peoples of the American continents came to be called *Indians.*

indicate *verb* **1.** To point out: *The map indicates the location of the town.* **2.** To serve as a sign of: *Her smile indicated her pleasure.*
in·di·cate (**in'**di kāt') □*verb* **indicated, indicating, indicates**

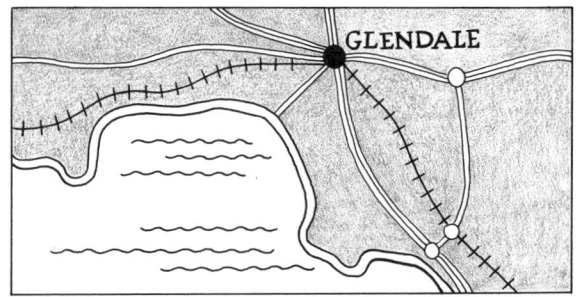

indicate

indication *noun* Something that indicates; sign: *His face gave no indication of his mood.*
in·di·ca·tion (in'di **kā'**shən) □*noun, plural* **indications**

indict *verb* To accuse of a crime; charge.
in·dict (in **dīt'**) □*verb* **indicted, indicting, indicts**

indifference *noun* Lack of concern or interest: *His indifference to our complaints made us angry.*
in·dif·fer·ence (in **dif'**ər əns) □*noun*

indifferent *adjective* Having or showing no concern or interest: *Her warm coat made her indifferent to the cold.*
in·dif·fer·ent (in **dif'**ər ənt) □*adjective*

indigestion *noun* Difficulty or discomfort in digesting food.

in·di·ges·tion (in′di **jes′** chən *or* in′dī **jes′** chən) □*noun*

indignant *adjective* Feeling or showing anger about something that is unfair or cruel: *I became indignant when he broke his promise.*
in·dig·nant (in **dig′**nənt) □*adjective*

indigo *noun* **1.** A plant from which a blue dye is made. **2.** A dark-blue dye that can be made from the indigo plant or man-made. □*adjective* Dark blue.
in·di·go (**in′**di gō′) □*noun, plural* **indigos** or **indigoes** □*adjective*

> **WORD HISTORY:**   **indigo**
>
> The word *indigo* comes from a Greek phrase that means "Indian dye." The Greeks called the dye by this name because the indigo plant grew in India.

indigo

indirect *adjective* **1.** Not direct; roundabout: *We took an indirect route across town.* **2.** Not straight to the point: *an indirect answer.* **3.** Not directly connected: *an indirect result.*
in·di·rect (in′də **rekt′**) □*adjective*

individual *adjective* **1.** Single; separate: *Cut the pie into individual portions.* **2.** Having a special quality; unique: *He has an individual style of singing.*
□*noun* A single person, plant, or animal: *the rights of the individual.*
in·di·vid·u·al (in′də **vij′**o͞o əl) □*adjective*
□*noun, plural* **individuals**

individuality *noun* The qualities that make a person or thing different from others: *She expressed her individuality through her paintings.*
in·di·vid·u·al·i·ty (in′də vij′o͞o **al′**i tē) □*noun, plural* **individualities**

individually *adverb* One by one: *She spoke to each student individually.*
in·di·vid·u·al·ly (in′də **vij′**o͞o ə lē) □*adverb*

indoor *adjective* Of, in, or taking place within a building: *an indoor pool; indoor sports.*
in·door (**in′** dôr′) □*adjective*

indoors *adverb* In or into a building: *I stayed indoors all day.*
in·doors (in **dôrz′**) □*adverb*

industrial *adjective* **1.** Of or having to do with industry: *industrial products.* **2.** Having highly developed industries: *an industrial country.*
in·dus·tri·al (in **dus′**trē əl) □*adjective*

industrialize *verb* To make or become industrial: *The new government wanted to industrialize the country.*
in·dus·tri·al·ize (in **dus′**trē ə līz′) □*verb* **industrialized, industrializing, industrializes**

industrious *adjective* Working hard; diligent: *an industrious student.*
in·dus·tri·ous (in **dus′**trē əs) □*adjective*

industry *noun* **1.** The manufacture of goods: *a town that is a center of industry.* **2.** A specific branch of industry: *the automobile industry.* **3.** Hard work; steady effort: *He studied for the test with industry.*
in·dus·try (**in′**də strē) □*noun, plural* **industries**

inedible *adjective* Not suitable for food; not edible: *an inedible mushroom.*
in·ed·i·ble (in **ed′**ə bəl) □*adjective*

inequality *noun* The condition of being unequal: *There is an inequality between his income and mine.*
in·e·qual·i·ty (in′i **kwol′**i tē) □*noun, plural* **inequalities**

inert *adjective* Unable to move or act: *A rock is an inert object.*
in·ert (i **nûrt′**) □*adjective*

inevitable *adjective* Not capable of being avoided or prevented: *It was inevitable that the tired child would soon fall asleep.*
in·ev·i·ta·ble (in **ev′**i tə bəl) □*adjective*

inexpensive *adjective* Not expensive; cheap: *an inexpensive dress.*
in·ex·pen·sive (in′ik **spen′**siv) □*adjective*

a	bat	ī	bite	o͞o	tool	*th*	feather
ā	make	î	fierce	ou	out	th	bath
â	dare	o	dot	u	nut	hw	wheat
ä	father	ō	no	û	turn	zh	measure
e	net	ô	law, for	ch	church	ə	about, open
ē	be	oi	soil	ng	ring		pencil, atom
i	dip	oo	look	sh	shade		circus

infant *noun* A child from birth to about two years of age; baby.
in·fant (**in′**fənt) □*noun, plural* **infants**

WORD HISTORY: **infant**

Infant comes from a Latin word that means "unable to speak."

---

infantile paralysis *noun* Poliomyelitis.
in·fan·tile paralysis (**in′**fən tīl′) □*noun*

infantry *noun* The part of an army that fights on foot.
in·fan·try (**in′**fən trē) □*noun, plural* **infantries**

infect *verb* To give or transfer a disease to: *One person with flu infected the whole class.*
in·fect (**in fekt′**) □*verb* **infected, infecting, infects**

infection *noun* A disease caused by viruses or germs: *He had an ear infection.*
in·fec·tion (**in fek′**shən) □*noun, plural* **infections**

infectious *adjective* Caused or spread by infection: *Chicken pox is an infectious disease.*
in·fec·tious (**in fek′**shəs) □*adjective*

inferior *adjective* **1.** Of poor quality; below average: *an inferior movie.* **2.** Low or lower in quality or value: *This movie is inferior to the one I saw last week. My athletic ability is inferior to hers.* **3.** Lower in rank or position: *A lieutenant is inferior to a general.*
in·fe·ri·or (**in fîr′**ē ər) □*adjective*

infield *noun* **1.** The playing area of a baseball field enclosed by the three bases and home plate. **2.** The shortstop and the three players who cover the bases.
in·field (**in′**fēld′) □*noun, plural* **infields**

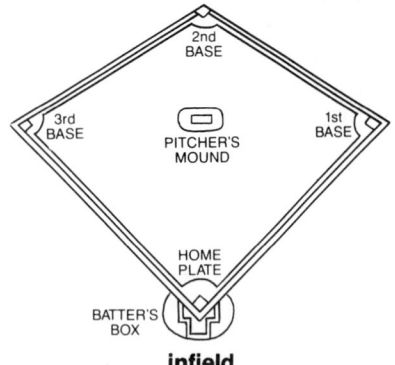

infield

infinite *adjective* **1.** Having no limits; endless: *galaxies in infinite space.* **2.** Seeming to have no limits; very great: *He has infinite patience with students.*
in·fi·nite (**in′**fə nit) □*adjective*

infinitive *noun* A verb form that in English does not indicate person, number, or tense and is often preceded by the word *to.* In the sentence *They want to walk, to walk* is an infinitive.
in·fin·i·tive (**in fin′**i tiv) □*noun, plural* **infinitives**

inflame *verb* **1.** To make sore, red, swollen, or hot: *My eyes were inflamed by the chemicals in the pool.* **2.** To make very upset or angry: *Her speech inflamed the audience.*
in·flame (**in flām′**) □*verb* **inflamed, inflaming, inflames**

inflammable *adjective* Easily set on fire: *Alcohol and gasoline are inflammable liquids.*
in·flam·ma·ble (**in flam′**ə bəl) □*adjective*

inflammation *noun* A condition in which a part of the body is sore, red, or swollen.
in·flam·ma·tion (**in′**flə **mā′**shən) □*noun, plural* **inflammations**

inflate *verb* **1.** To expand by filling with a gas: *inflate a tire.* **2.** To become greater or larger: *Clothing has inflated in price.*
in·flate (**in flāt′**) □*verb* **inflated, inflating, inflates**

inflate

inflation *noun* **1.** The act of inflating. **2.** A continuing rise in the cost of goods and services.
in·fla·tion (**in flā′**shən) □*noun, plural* **inflations**

influence *noun* **1.** The power to change or have an effect on others: *He had great influence with his students.* **2.** Someone or something that can cause a change or have an effect: *Her aunt was a good influence on her.* □*verb* To have an influence on: *What influenced you to change your mind?*
in·flu·ence (**in′**floo əns) □*noun, plural*

influences □*verb* **influenced, influencing, influences**

influenza *noun* A disease caused by a virus and marked by fever, coughing, and pains in the muscles and chest; flu.
in·flu·en·za (in'floo en'zə) □*noun*

WORD HISTORY: **influenza**

In the days before people understood the medical reasons for illness it was thought that disease could be caused by the evil influence of the stars. The word *influenza* comes from an Italian word that originally meant "influence."

---

inform *verb* To give information to; advise: *The coach informed me that I had made the baseball team.*
in·form (in fôrm') □*verb* **informed, informing, informs**

informal *adjective* Not following strict rules or customs: *an informal dinner; informal clothes.*
in·for·mal (in fôr'məl) □*adjective*

information *noun* Facts or knowledge about a particular event or subject: *We got the latest information on the election results.*
in·for·ma·tion (in'fər mā'shən) □*noun*

infuriate *verb* To make furious; enrage: *His carelessness infuriated his father.*
in·fu·ri·ate (in fyoor'ē āt') □*verb* **infuriated, infuriating, infuriates**

-ing A suffix that forms the present participle of verbs: *leading, seeing, frying.*

ingenuity *noun* Skill in inventing or planning; imagination: *a house that is designed with great ingenuity.*
in·ge·nu·i·ty (in'jə noo'i tē) □*noun*

ingredient *noun* A substance that is part of a mixture or compound: *Flour, butter, and salt are among the ingredients of a pie crust.*
in·gre·di·ent (in grē'dē ənt) □*noun, plural* **ingredients**

ingredient
Some ingredients of a pie crust

inhabit *verb* To live in or have as a home: *The family inhabits a large apartment.*
in·hab·it (in hab'it) □*verb* **inhabited, inhabiting, inhabits**

inhabitant *noun* A person or animal that lives in a particular place.
in·hab·i·tant (in hab'i tənt) □*noun, plural* **inhabitants**

inhale *verb* To draw into the lungs; breathe in.
in·hale (in hāl') □*verb* **inhaled, inhaling, inhales**

inherent *adjective* Of or being a basic quality or characteristic of a person or thing: *His inherent kindness won him many friends.*
in·her·ent (in hîr'ənt *or* in her'ənt) □*adjective*

inherit *verb* **1.** To receive from someone after he or she has died: *He inherited a watch from his uncle.* **2.** To receive from one's parents or ancestors: *She inherited her father's good temper.*
in·her·it (in her'it) □*verb* **inherited, inheriting, inherits**

inheritance *noun* Something that is inherited: *He received a large inheritance from his aunt.*
in·her·i·tance (in her'i təns) □*noun, plural* **inheritances**

inhuman *adjective* Lacking in kindness or pity; cruel: *He was a tyrant who gave out inhuman punishments.*
in·hu·man (in hyoo'mən) □*adjective*

initial *adjective* Of or happening at the beginning: *My initial reaction is to say yes.* —See Synonyms at **first.**
□*noun* The first letter of a word or name: *Abraham Lincoln's initials are A.L.*
□*verb* To mark or sign with one's initials: *He initialed the contract.*
in·i·tial (i nish'əl) □*adjective* □*noun, plural* **initials** □*verb* **initialed, initialing, initials**

initiate *verb* **1.** To begin; start: *They initiated a campaign to raise money.* **2.** To bring into a club or other organization as a new member,

a bat	ī bite	oo tool	*th* feather
ā make	î fierce	ou out	th bath
â dare	o dot	u nut	hw wheat
ä father	ō no	û turn	zh measure
e net	ô law, for	ch church	ə about, open
ē be	oi soil	ng ring	pencil, atom
i dip	oo look	sh shade	circus

often with a special ceremony.
in·i·ti·ate (i **nish'**ē āt') □*verb* **initiated, initiating, initiates**

initiative   *noun* **1.** The ability and energy to begin or carry out a plan or task: *showed his initiative by starting his own business.* **2.** The first step or action: *She took the initiative by asking a question.*
in·i·tia·tive (i **nish'**ə tiv) □*noun*

injection   *noun* The act of forcing a liquid medicine into the body with a needle.
in·jec·tion (in **jek'**shən) □*noun, plural* **injections**

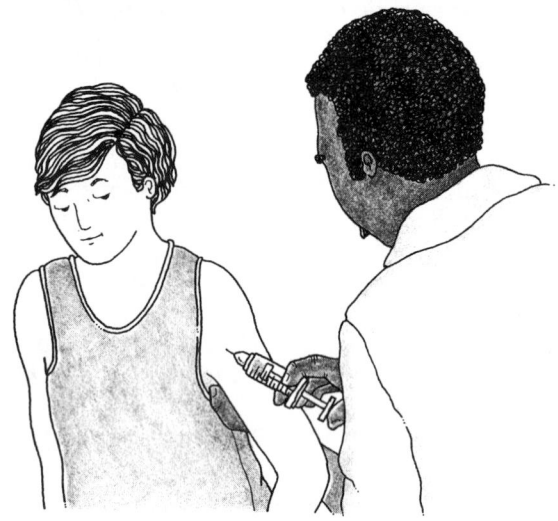

injection

injure   *verb* To harm or damage; hurt: *He injured his leg in a baseball game. Her lie injured my reputation.*
in·jure (**in'**jər) □*verb* **injured, injuring, injures**

injury   *noun* Harm or damage to someone or something: *an eye injury; an injury to her pride.* —See Synonyms at **harm.**
in·ju·ry (**in'**jə rē) □*noun, plural* **injuries**

injustice   *noun* **1.** Lack of justice: *We protested the injustice of the punishment.* **2.** An unjust act: *You did him an injustice when you called him a thief.*
in·jus·tice (in **jus'**tis) □*noun, plural* **injustices**

ink   *noun* A colored liquid used for writing, drawing, or printing.
ink (ingk) □*noun, plural* **inks**

inkwell   *noun* A small container for ink.
ink·well (**ingk'**wel') □*noun, plural* **inkwells**

inland   *adjective* Of or located in the part of a country away from the coast: *an inland lake.* □*adverb* To or toward the inland part of a country: *The hurricane moved inland.*
in·land (**in'**lənd) □*adjective* □*adverb*

inlet   *noun* A recess, such as a bay, along a shore.
in·let (**in'**let') □*noun, plural* **inlets**

inn   *noun* A small hotel.
inn (in) □*noun, plural* **inns**

inner   *adjective* **1.** Located farther in: *an inner room.* **2.** Of the spirit or mind: *inner feelings.*
in·ner (**in'**ər) □*adjective*

inner ear   *noun* The innermost part of the ear. It has nerves that go to the brain so that sounds can be perceived.

innermost   *adjective* Located farthest in: *the innermost part of the city.*
in·ner·most (**in'**ər mōst') □*adjective*

inning   *noun* A division of a baseball game during which each team comes to bat.
in·ning (**in'**ing) □*noun, plural* **innings**

innkeeper   *noun* Someone who owns or manages an inn.
inn·keep·er (**in'**kē'pər) □*noun, plural* **innkeepers**

innocence   *noun* The condition or quality of being innocent.
in·no·cence (**in'**ə səns) □*noun*

innocent   *adjective* **1.** Not guilty of a crime or fault: *He said he was innocent.* **2.** Not intended to cause harm; harmless: *innocent fun.*
in·no·cent (**in'**ə sənt) □*adjective*

innovation   *noun* Something new: *The computer was an important innovation.*
in·no·va·tion (in'ə **vā'**shən) □*noun, plural* **innovations**

inoculate   *verb* To give an injection of something, such as a vaccine, in order to protect against a disease.
in·oc·u·late (i **nok'**yə lāt') □*verb* **inoculated, inoculating, inoculates**

input   *noun* **1.** Power, energy, or work used to drive a device or system. **2.** Information or data fed into a computer for processing. **3.** Comments; advice: *He asked all of us to give him input on his plan.*
in·put (**in'**poot) □*noun, plural* **inputs**

inquire   *verb* To try to find out by asking questions: *I inquired about the way to the library.*
in·quire (in **kwīr'**) □*verb* **inquired, inquiring, inquires**

inquiry *noun* **1.** A request for information; question: *The store received many inquiries about the jobs that were advertised.* **2.** A detailed examination; investigation: *an inquiry into the cause of the crash.*
in·quir·y (in **kwīr'** ē *or* **in'** kwə rē) □*noun, plural* **inquiries**

inquisitive *adjective* Eager to learn or know; curious: *an inquisitive mind.*
in·quis·i·tive (in **kwiz'** i tiv) □*adjective*

insane *adjective* **1.** Of, showing, or affected by mental illness; mad. **2.** Of or for insane people: *an insane asylum.* **3.** Very foolish; wild: *insane talk.*
in·sane (in **sān'**) □*adjective*

inscribe *verb* To write, print, carve, or engrave something in or on: *The author inscribed his name in the book.*
in·scribe (in **skrīb'**) □*verb* **inscribed, inscribing, inscribes**

inscribe

insect *noun* **1.** A small animal with six legs, a body divided into three main parts, and often wings. Ants, bees, and flies are insects. **2.** An animal that is similar to an insect.
in·sect (**in'** sekt') □*noun, plural* **insects**

WORD HISTORY: **insect**

The word *insect* comes from a Latin word that literally means "something that has been cut into." The body of most insects is divided into three sections and looks as if someone might have cut into it.

---

insecticide *noun* A poison or other substance used to kill insects.
in·sec·ti·cide (in **sek'** ti sīd') □*noun, plural* **insecticides**

insecure *adjective* Not safe or secure.
in·se·cure (in' si **kyoor'**) □*adjective*

insert *verb* To put or set in: *He inserted the letter into the slot.*
□*noun* Something that is inserted: *an advertising insert in a magazine.*
in·sert (in **sûrt'**) □*verb* **inserted, inserting, inserts** □*noun* (**in'** sûrt'), *plural* **inserts**

insert

inside *noun* The inner part, side, or surface: *the inside of a basket.*
□*adjective* **1.** Inner; interior: *an inside door.* **2.** Of or coming from someone who has special knowledge: *inside information.*
□*adverb* Into, toward, on, or in the inside; within: *I went inside.*
□*preposition* On or to the inside of: *We went inside the museum.*
in·side (**in'** sīd' *or* in **sīd'**) □*noun, plural* **insides** □*adjective* □*adverb* (in **sīd'**) □*preposition* (in **sīd'**)

insignia *noun* A medal, mark, or badge of office, rank, or honor; emblem: *A metal star is the insignia of a sheriff.*
in·sig·ni·a (in **sig'** nē ə) □*noun, plural* **insignias**

insignificant *adjective* Having little or no importance, meaning, or value: *an insignificant mistake.*
in·sig·nif·i·cant (in'sig **nif'** i kənt) □*adjective*

a bat	ī bite	ōō tool	th feather
ā make	î fierce	ou out	th bath
â dare	o dot	u nut	hw wheat
ä father	ō no	û turn	zh measure
e net	ô law, for	ch church	ə about, open
ē be	oi soil	ng ring	pencil, atom
i dip	oo look	sh shade	circus

insincere *adjective* Not sincere; dishonest: *I could tell her compliment was insincere.*
in·sin·cere (in′sin sîr′) □*adjective*

insist *verb* To be firm in making a demand or statement: *I insisted that he return my book immediately.*
in·sist (in sist′) □*verb* **insisted, insisting, insists**

inspect *verb* **1.** To look at carefully: *He inspected the car before buying it.* **2.** To examine officially or formally: *The general inspected the troops.*
in·spect (in spekt′) □*verb* **inspected, inspecting, inspects**

inspect

inspection *noun* The act of inspecting.
in·spec·tion (in spek′shən) □*noun, plural* **inspections**

inspiration *noun* **1.** Someone or something that inspires: *His courage was an inspiration to us all.* **2.** A sudden, original idea: *Painting this dark room bright yellow was an inspiration.*
in·spi·ra·tion (in′spə rā′shən) □*noun, plural* **inspirations**

inspire *verb* **1.** To have an exciting influence on the emotions or mind of: *a symphony that inspired the audience.* **2.** To cause a person to act, think, or feel in a certain way: *He inspired us to work harder. She inspired everyone with confidence.*
in·spire (in spīr′) □*verb* **inspired, inspiring, inspires**

install *verb* **1.** To put in place for use: *We installed a sink in the basement.* **2.** To place in office with ceremony: *The new mayor was installed today.*
in·stall (in stôl′) □*verb* **installed, installing, installs**

installment *noun* **1.** One of a series of payments for repaying a debt: *The second install-*

ment on the car is due next week. **2.** A portion or part of something, such as a story in a magazine, issued at intervals.
in·stall·ment (in stôl′mənt) □*noun, plural* **installments**

instance *noun* A case; example: *His failure to thank us was an instance of his rudeness.*
  for instance For example.
in·stance (in′stəns) □*noun, plural* **instances**

instant *noun* **1.** A very short period of time: *We were an instant too late.* **2.** A particular moment: *He called the instant I returned.*
—See Synonyms at **moment.**
□*adjective* **1.** Immediate: *an instant success.* **2.** Processed to be prepared quickly: *instant coffee.*
in·stant (in′stənt) □*noun, plural* **instants** □*adjective*

instantly *adverb* At once; immediately: *I'll be there instantly.*
in·stant·ly (in′stənt lē) □*adverb*

instead *adverb* As a substitute: *They had no fish, so I ordered chicken instead.*
in·stead (in sted′) □*adverb*

instead of *preposition* In place of; rather than: *I telephoned instead of going.*

instep *noun* The middle part of the top of the human foot, between the toes and the ankle.
in·step (in′step′) □*noun, plural* **insteps**

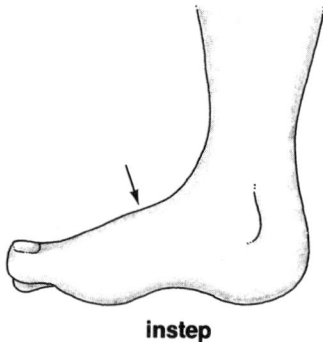

instep

instinct *noun* An ability or way of behaving that a person or animal possesses from birth and does not need to learn: *Birds can find their way by instinct.*
in·stinct (in′stingkt′) □*noun, plural* **instincts**

institute *noun* An organization set up for a particular purpose: *an art institute.*
in·sti·tute (in′sti tōōt′ *or* in′sti tyōōt′) □*noun, plural* **institutes**

institution *noun* **1.** An important custom or practice of a group of people: *the institution of*

the family. **2.** An organization, especially one that has been set up for public service: *an institution of higher learning.*
in·sti·tu·tion (in′sti too′shən *or* in′sti-tyoo′shən) ◻*noun, plural* **institutions**

instruct *verb* **1.** To give knowledge or skill to: *The professor instructed the students in English.* **2.** To give orders to; direct: *My father instructed me to be home early.* —See Synonyms at **teach.**
in·struct (in strukt′) ◻*verb* **instructed, instructing, instructs**

instruction *noun* **1.** The act or process of teaching; education: *a new method of instruction.* **2. instructions** Directions; orders: *I read the instructions before assembling the table.* **3.** A specific operation to be performed by a computer.
in·struc·tion (in struk′shən) ◻*noun, plural* **instructions**

instructor *noun* Someone who instructs; teacher.
in·struc·tor (in struk′tər) ◻*noun, plural* **instructors**

instrument *noun* **1.** A device used for a particular kind of work: *dental instruments.* **2.** A device, as a piano or violin, for producing music.
in·stru·ment (in′strə mənt) ◻*noun, plural* **instruments**

SYNONYMS: **instrument, tool, utensil**

These nouns mean a device used for a particular kind of work: *The dentist has some strange-looking instruments. The carpenter keeps all his tools in a metal box. Pans and mixing spoons are cooking utensils.*

---

insulate *verb* To cover, surround, or line with a material that slows or stops the passage of electricity, sound, or heat.
in·su·late (in′sə lāt′) ◻*verb* **insulated, insulating, insulates**

insult *verb* To speak to or treat in a way that hurts or is rude; offend: *You insulted him by refusing to believe him.*
◻*noun* An action or remark that insults.
in·sult (in sult′) ◻*verb* **insulted, insulting, insults** ◻*noun* (in′sult′), *plural* **insults**

insurance *noun* Protection against loss. Insurance is a guarantee that a specified sum of money will be paid for loss or damage resulting from an event such as a fire or flood. A

customer buys insurance from a company organized to give this service.
in·sur·ance (in shoor′əns) ◻*noun, plural* **insurances**

insure *verb* To protect with insurance.
in·sure (in shoor′) ◻*verb* **insured, insuring, insures**

intake *noun* **1.** An opening in a container or pipe through which liquid or gas enters. **2.** An amount of something taken in: *I cut down on my intake of food.*
in·take (in′tāk′) ◻*noun, plural* **intakes**

integrate *verb* **1.** To make into a whole: *We integrated all of your ideas into a complete program.* **2.** To open to people of all races, classes, or ethnic groups.
in·te·grate (in′ti grāt′) ◻*verb* **integrated, integrating, integrates**

integration *noun* The act or process of making something open to people of all ethnic groups: *the integration of schools and colleges.*
in·te·gra·tion (in′ti grā′shən) ◻*noun*

integrity *noun* Complete personal honesty: *The President must be a person of integrity.*
in·teg·ri·ty (in teg′ri tē) ◻*noun*

intellect *noun* The ability to think, reason, and learn; intelligence.
in·tel·lect (int′əl ekt′) ◻*noun, plural* **intellects**

intellectual *adjective* Of or requiring use of the intellect: *Chess is an intellectual game.*
◻*noun* Someone of superior intelligence.
in·tel·lec·tu·al (in′təl ek′choo əl) ◻*adjective* ◻*noun, plural* **intellectuals**

intelligence *noun* **1.** The ability to learn, think, and understand. **2.** Information, especially secret information: *We received the latest intelligence on the enemy's activities.*
in·tel·li·gence (in tel′ə jəns) ◻*noun*

intelligent *adjective* Having or showing intelligence: *an intelligent decision.*
in·tel·li·gent (in tel′ə jənt) ◻*adjective*

intend *verb* To have in mind as a goal, plan, or purpose: *I intend to put a stop to that. This letter was intended for you.*

a bat	ī bite	oo tool	th feather
ā make	î fierce	ou out	th bath
â dare	o dot	u nut	hw wheat
ä father	ō no	û turn	zh measure
e net	ô law, for	ch church	ə about, open
ē be	oi soil	ng ring	pencil, atom
i dip	oo look	sh shade	circus

in·tend (in **tend'**) ☐*verb* **intended, intending, intends**

intense *adjective* **1.** Very deep, strong, or concentrated: *intense sunlight.* **2.** Having or showing strong feelings: *He is an intense person who takes everything seriously.*
in·tense (in **tens'**) ☐*adjective*

SYNONYMS: **intense, fierce, furious**

These adjectives mean very deep, strong, or concentrated: *The intense heat of the tropical sun made her sleepy. The lion gave a fierce growl. Last winter we had a furious blizzard that lasted for three days.*

---

intensity *noun* **1.** The condition or quality of being intense; great strength: *intensity of interest.* **2.** Degree or amount of strength or force: *The light increased in intensity.*
in·ten·si·ty (in **ten'**si tē) ☐*noun, plural* **intensities**

intent *adjective* **1.** Showing concentration; intense: *Her face was intent as she read.* **2.** Having the mind fixed on a purpose; determined: *I am intent on succeeding.*
☐*noun* **1.** Purpose: *What is your intent in coming here?* **2.** Meaning: *What was the intent of the letter?*
in·tent (in **tent'**) ☐*adjective* ☐*noun, plural* **intents**

intention *noun* Something intended; plan or purpose: *It is my intention to go to college.*
in·ten·tion (in **ten'**shən) ☐*noun, plural* **intentions**

intentional *adjective* Done on purpose; intended: *an intentional lie.*
in·ten·tion·al (in **ten'**shə nəl) ☐*adjective*

intercept *verb* To meet, stop, or interrupt on the way to a destination: *We intercepted the letter and read it.*
in·ter·cept (in'tər **sept'**) ☐*verb* **intercepted, intercepting, intercepts**

intercom *noun* A device used for talking between one location and another.
in·ter·com (in'tər kom') ☐*noun, plural* **intercoms**

interest *noun* **1.** A feeling of special concern or curiosity about something: *I have an interest in music.* **2.** The quality of attracting interest: *a book that lacked interest.* **3.** Something in which one has interest: *Art is his chief interest.* **4.** Advantage; benefit: *I acted in my own best interest.* **5.** A right or legal share in some-

thing: *He owns an interest in a computer company.* **6.** Money paid or charged for the use of someone else's money.
☐*verb* To arouse or hold the interest of: *He has interested many people in his project. He bought a record that interested him.*
in·ter·est (in'trist *or* in'tər ist) ☐*noun, plural* **interests** ☐*verb* **interested, interesting, interests**

interesting *adjective* Arousing or holding interest or attention: *an interesting book.*
in·ter·est·ing (in'tri sting *or* in'tər i sting) ☐*adjective*

interfere *verb* **1.** To come in between so as to hinder: *Interruptions interfere with my work.* **2.** To meddle in the business of others: *She interfered in her daughter's life.*
in·ter·fere (in'tər **fîr'**) ☐*verb* **interfered, interfering, interferes**

interior *noun* **1.** The inner part of something; inside: *the interior of the garage.* **2.** An inland part, as of a country: *He has made expeditions to the interior of Brazil.*
☐*adjective* Of or located on the inside; inner: *the interior walls of the room.*
in·te·ri·or (in **tîr'**ē ər) ☐*noun, plural* **interiors** ☐*adjective*

interjection *noun* A word or phrase, such as *ouch* or *ha*, that expresses a strong or sudden emotion or feeling.
in·ter·jec·tion (in'tər **jek'**shən) ☐*noun, plural* **interjections**

intermediate *adjective* In between; in the middle: *an intermediate stage of growth.*
in·ter·me·di·ate (in'tər **mē'**dē it) ☐*adjective*

intermission *noun* A break or recess in an activity: *an intermission between the acts of a play.*
in·ter·mis·sion (in'tər **mish'**ən) ☐*noun, plural* **intermissions**

intern *noun* Someone who has recently graduated from medical school and is receiving further training under the supervision of other doctors.
in·tern (in'**tûrn'**) ☐*noun, plural* **interns**

internal *adjective* **1.** Of or located on the inside; interior: *The liver is an internal organ of the body.* **2.** Of or relating to matters within a country or state: *internal trade.*
in·ter·nal (in **tûr'**nəl) ☐*adjective*

international *adjective* Of or between two or more nations: *an international conference.*
in·ter·na·tion·al (in'tər **nash'**ə nəl) ☐*adjective*

international

interpret *verb* **1.** To make clear or explain the meaning of: *Can you interpret this poem?* **2.** To understand or see in a certain way: *He interpreted her smile as agreement.* **3.** To make an oral translation from one language to another.
in·ter·pret (in **tûr′**prit) □*verb* **interpreted, interpreting, interprets**

interpretation *noun* The act or result of interpreting: *an interpretation of a law.*
in·ter·pre·ta·tion (in tûr′pri **tā′**shən) □*noun, plural* **interpretations**

interrogative *adjective* Having the form of a question: *an interrogative sentence.*
□*noun* A word, as *who* or *what*, used in asking a question.
in·ter·rog·a·tive (in′tə **rog′**ə tiv) □*adjective* □*noun, plural* **interrogatives**

interrupt *verb* **1.** To stop by breaking in on: *He interrupted the teacher with a question.* **2.** To keep from being continuous: *The war interrupted her education.*
in·ter·rupt (in′tə **rupt′**) □*verb* **interrupted, interrupting, interrupts**

interruption *noun* **1.** The act of interrupting: *His constant interruptions were annoying.* **2.** The condition of being interrupted: *The interruption in the bus service was caused by a storm.*
in·ter·rup·tion (in′tə **rup′**shən) □*noun, plural* **interruptions**

intersect *verb* To cut across or through; cross: *The two highways intersect east of town.*
in·ter·sect (in′tər **sekt′**) □*verb* **intersected, intersecting, intersects**

intersection *noun* A point where two or more things intersect.

in·ter·sec·tion (in′tər **sek′**shən) □*noun, plural* **intersections**

interval *noun* **1.** A period of time between two events: *After a short interval he began to speak.* **2.** A space between two things: *trees planted at regular intervals along the street.*
in·ter·val (in′tər vəl) □*noun, plural* **intervals**

interview *noun* A meeting to give or obtain information: *People who applied for the job were called in for interviews.*
□*verb* To have an interview with: *The reporter interviewed the senator on television.*
in·ter·view (in′tər vyōō′) □*noun, plural* **interviews** □*verb* **interviewed, interviewing, interviews**

intestine *noun* The part of the digestive system below the stomach in which food is digested. The intestine is divided into the large intestine and the small intestine.
in·tes·tine (in **tes′**tin) □*noun, plural* **intestines**

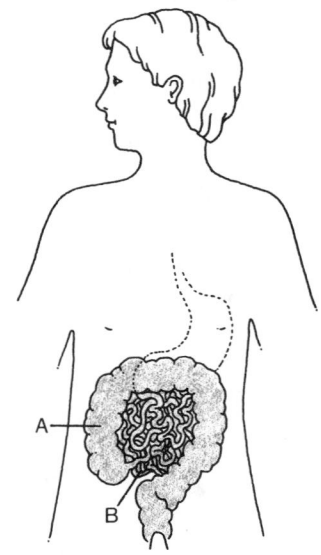

intestine
(A) large intestine, *(B)* small intestine

intimate *adjective* **1.** Showing deep understanding: *an intimate knowledge of the subject.* **2.** Private and personal in nature: *his intimate*

a bat	ī bite	ōō tool	*th* feather
ā make	î fierce	ou out	th bath
â dare	o dot	u nut	hw wheat
ä father	ō no	û turn	zh measure
e net	ô law, for	ch church	ə about, open
ē be	oi soil	ng ring	pencil, atom
i dip	oo look	sh shade	circus

feelings. **3.** Very close: *an intimate friend.*
in·ti·mate (**in′**tə mit) ☐*adjective*

into *preposition* **1.** To the inside of: *went into the store.* **2.** So as to come in contact with; against: *The bicycle crashed into a fence.* **3.** To the form, state, or condition of: *The caterpillar changed into a butterfly. He got into trouble.*
in·to (**in′**to͞o) ☐*preposition*

intolerant *adjective* Not willing to put up with opinions and beliefs that are different from one's own.
in·tol·er·ant (in **tol′**ər ənt) ☐*adjective*

intoxicate *verb* To make drunk.
in·tox·i·cate (in **tok′**si kāt′) ☐*verb*
intoxicated, intoxicating, intoxicates

WORD HISTORY: **intoxicate**

Intoxicate comes from the Latin word for "poison." The original meaning of *intoxicate* was "to poison."

---

intricate *adjective* Difficult to understand, do, or follow; complicated: *an intricate diagram.*
in·tri·cate (**in′**tri kit) ☐*adjective*

intrigue *verb* To catch the interest or curiosity of; fascinate: *The child's drawings intrigued me.*
in·trigue (in **trēg′**) ☐*verb* **intrigued, intriguing, intrigues**

introduce *verb* **1.** To present by name to another; make known: *She introduced me to her father.* **2.** To bring into use or notice: *The company introduced a new car.*
in·tro·duce (in′trə **do͞os′** *or* in′trə **dyo͞os′**)
☐*verb* **introduced, introducing, introduces**

introduce

introduction *noun* **1.** The act of introducing or the process of being introduced: *After our*

introduction we became good friends. **2.** Something that introduces: *a book that is an introduction to social studies.*
in·tro·duc·tion (in′trə **duk′**shən) ☐*noun, plural* **introductions**

invade *verb* **1.** To enter with force; attack: *The enemy invaded the country.* **2.** To intrude on; interfere with: *He invaded her privacy by listening in on her phone calls.*
in·vade (in **vād′**) ☐*verb* **invaded, invading, invades**

invalid *noun* A sick or disabled person.
in·va·lid (**in′**və lid) ☐*noun, plural* **invalids**

invent *verb* **1.** To create or make for the first time: *Who invented the light bulb?* **2.** To make up: *He invented a reason for not going.*
in·vent (in **vent′**) ☐*verb* **invented, inventing, invents**

WORD HISTORY: **invent**

The word *invent* at first had the meaning "to discover something that already exists" rather than "to think up or create something new."

---

invention *noun* **1.** Something invented: *The machine was his own invention.* **2.** The act of inventing: *No one person can take credit for the invention of writing.* **3.** An untrue statement: *Her excuse is an obvious invention.*
in·ven·tion (in **ven′**shən) ☐*noun, plural* **inventions**

inventor *noun* Someone who invents.
in·ven·tor (in **ven′**tər) ☐*noun, plural* **inventors**

inventory *noun* **1.** A detailed list of items, as goods or supplies. **2.** The supply of goods on hand: *Our inventory of canned food is low.*
in·ven·to·ry (**in′**vən tôr′ē) ☐*noun, plural* **inventories**

invert *verb* **1.** To turn upside down: *She inverted her purse, and the money spilled out.* **2.** To reverse the order or position of: *A countdown inverts the usual order of the numbers.*
in·vert (in **vûrt′**) ☐*verb* **inverted, inverting, inverts**

invertebrate *noun* An animal that has no backbone.
☐*adjective* Having no backbone: *A jellyfish is an invertebrate animal.*
in·ver·te·brate (in **vûr′**tə brit *or* in **vûr′**tə brāt′) ☐*noun, plural* **invertebrates**
☐*adjective*

invest *verb* **1.** To put money into something that will earn interest or make a profit: *She invested her savings in real estate.* **2.** To spend or use for future gain: *He invested a great deal in his education.*
in·vest (in **vest′**) □*verb* **invested, investing, invests**

investigate *verb* To examine carefully in a search for facts, knowledge, or information: *Officials investigated the cause of the fire.*
in·ves·ti·gate (in **ves′**ti gāt′) □*verb* **investigated, investigating, investigates**

investigation *noun* The act of investigating: *made an investigation into the cause of the crime.*
in·ves·ti·ga·tion (in ves′ti **gā′**shən) □*noun, plural* **investigations**

investment *noun* **1.** The act of investing: *made a wise investment in real estate.* **2.** An amount of money invested: *He made a large investment in his brother's business.* **3.** Something in which money, time, or effort is invested: *a plan requiring an investment of hard work.*
in·vest·ment (in **vest′**mənt) □*noun, plural* **investments**

invisible *adjective* Not capable of being seen; not visible: *Air is invisible.*
in·vis·i·ble (in **viz′**ə bəl) □*adjective*

invitation *noun* A spoken or written request to come somewhere or do something: *I accepted an invitation to the party.*
in·vi·ta·tion (in′vi **tā′**shən) □*noun, plural* **invitations**

invite *verb* **1.** To ask to come somewhere or do something: *I invited guests for lunch.* **2.** To ask for; welcome: *She invited our comments.* **3.** To tempt; attract: *The forest invites campers.*
in·vite (in **vīt′**) □*verb* **invited, inviting, invites**

involuntary *adjective* Not done by choice: *She gave an involuntary gasp.*
in·vol·un·tar·y (in **vol′**ən ter′ē) □*adjective*

involve *verb* **1.** To call for; require: *Education involves study.* **2.** To have as a part; include: *Opera involves music and drama.* **3.** To draw in; engage: *He involved himself in his work.*
in·volve (in **volv′**) □*verb* **involved, involving, involves**

inward *adverb* Toward the inside or center: *The window opened inward.*
□*adjective* Directed toward or located on the inside or interior.
in·ward (**in′**wərd) □*adverb* □*adjective*

inward

iodine *noun* **1.** A poisonous gray solid that is one of the chemical elements. **2.** A liquid mixture that contains iodine and is used to treat skin wounds.
i·o·dine (**ī′**ə dīn′ *or* **ī′**ə dēn′) □*noun*

iris *noun* **1.** The colored part around the pupil of the eye. It controls the amount of light that gets through the lens. **2.** A plant that has large flowers in various colors and long, pointed leaves.
i·ris (**ī′**ris) □*noun, plural* **irises**

WORD HISTORY: **iris**

The word *iris* comes from Greek. Iris was the ancient Greek goddess of the rainbow, and the Greeks used her name to mean "rainbow." They also used the same word for the iris of the eye and for the iris plant because both were colorful like a rainbow.

Irish *noun* **1.** People who were born in or are citizens of Ireland. **2.** People whose ancestors were from Ireland. **3.** A language of Ireland.
□*adjective* Of Ireland, the Irish, or their language.
I·rish (**ī′**rish) □*noun* □*adjective*

a	bat	ī	bite	ōō	tool	*th*	feather
ā	make	î	fierce	ou	out	th	bath
â	dare	o	dot	u	nut	hw	wheat
ä	father	ō	no	û	turn	zh	measure
e	net	ô	law, for	ch	church	ə	about, open
ē	be	oi	soil	ng	ring		pencil, atom
i	dip	oo	look	sh	shade		circus

Irish setter   *noun* A rather large dog with a silky reddish coat.

Irish setter

iron   *noun* **1.** A hard, gray metal that is one of the chemical elements used to make steel. **2.** Something made of iron: *a branding iron.* **3.** A metal appliance that is heated and used for pressing wrinkles out of cloth. ☐*adjective* **1.** Made of iron: *an iron gate.* **2.** Like iron; strong and hard: *an iron will.* ☐*verb* To press with a heated iron.
i·ron (ī′ərn) ☐*noun, plural* **irons** ☐*adjective* ☐*verb* **ironed, ironing, irons**

irony   *noun* The use of words that mean the opposite of what is really intended. For example, saying "That was brilliant!" to someone who has made a mistake is making use of irony.
i·ro·ny (ī′rə nē) ☐*noun, plural* **ironies**

irregular   *adjective* **1.** Not even or regular: *irregular teeth.* **2.** Not following a usual or regular schedule: *irregular hours.*
ir·reg·u·lar (i reg′yə lər) ☐*adjective*

irresistible   *adjective* Impossible to resist: *an irresistible urge to laugh.*
ir·re·sist·i·ble (ir′i **zis**′tə bəl) ☐*adjective*

irresponsible   *adjective* Not responsible; not reliable: *irresponsible behavior.*
ir·re·spon·si·ble (ir′i **spon**′sə bəl) ☐*adjective*

irrigate   *verb* To supply land with water by using streams, ditches, or pipes.
ir·ri·gate (ir′i gāt′) ☐*verb* **irrigated, irrigating, irrigates**

irrigation   *noun* The act of supplying water to land or crops.
ir·ri·ga·tion (ir′i gā′shən) ☐*noun*

irritable   *adjective* Easily irritated: *The loud music made her irritable.*
ir·ri·ta·ble (ir′i tə bəl) ☐*adjective*

irritate   *verb* **1.** To make angry or impatient: *Rudeness irritates me.* **2.** To cause to become sore: *The gas fumes irritated his eyes.*
ir·ri·tate (ir′i tāt′) ☐*verb* **irritated, irritating, irritates**

is   *verb* The third person singular present tense of **be.**
is (iz) ☐*verb*

Is. or **is.** An abbreviation for **island.**

–ish   A suffix that forms adjectives and means "looking like; somewhat; very much like": *greenish; childish.*

Islam   *noun* A religion based on the teachings of the prophet Mohammed.
Is·lam (is′läm *or* iz′läm) ☐*noun*

island   *noun* **1.** An area of land that is surrounded by water. **2.** Something that resembles an island: *an island of ice in the punch bowl.*
is·land (ī′lənd) ☐*noun, plural* **islands**

isle   *noun* An island, especially a small one.
isle (īl) ☐*noun, plural* **isles**

islet   *noun* A very small island.
is·let (ī′lit) ☐*noun, plural* **islets**

isn't   Contraction of "is not."
is·n't (iz′ənt)

isolate   *verb* To keep or set apart from others: *The doctor isolated the patients with contagious diseases.*
i·so·late (ī′sə lāt′) ☐*verb* **isolated, isolating, isolates**

issue   *noun* **1.** The act of sending out, giving out, or releasing: *the school's issue of new football uniforms.* **2.** Something that is put into circulation: *the most recent issue of the newspaper.* **3.** A subject of discussion or argument; problem: *Job equality is an important issue.* ☐*verb* **1.** To send or give out: *The publisher issued a new novel. The state issues fishing licenses.*
is·sue (ish′ōō) ☐*noun, plural* **issues** ☐*verb* **issued, issuing, issues**

–ist   A suffix that forms nouns and means: **1.** Someone who makes or has to do with a certain thing: *pianist; cartoonist.* **2.** Someone who has a certain set of beliefs or principles: *socialist.* **3.** Someone who performs a certain action: *specialist.* **4.** One who practices or is knowledgeable in a certain skill, art, or science: *economist, biologist.*

isthmus   *noun* A narrow strip of land connecting two larger masses of land.
isth·mus (is′məs) ☐*noun, plural* **isthmuses**

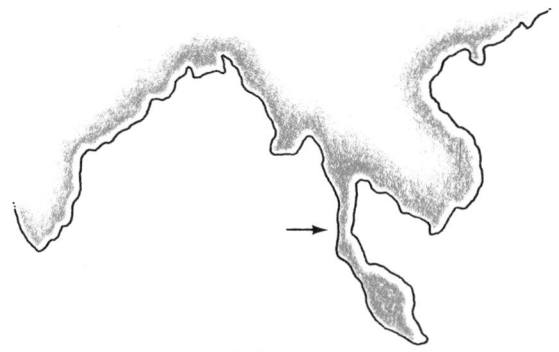

isthmus
Isthmus of Kra in southeast Asia

it   *pronoun* **1.** The animal, plant, or object referred to or mentioned earlier: *Please put the book back where it belongs.* **2.** The whole state of affairs: *He left because he couldn't stand it anymore.* **3.** Used as the subject of a certain kind of verb: *It is raining. It has been very hot lately.*
it (it) ▢*pronoun*

Italian   *noun* **1.** Someone who was born in or is a citizen of Italy. **2.** The language of Italy.
▢*adjective* Of Italy, the Italians, or their language.
I·tal·ian (i **tal′**yən) ▢*noun, plural* **Italians**
▢*adjective*

italic   *adjective* Of or in a style of type in which the letters slant to the right: *This sentence is printed in italic type.*
▢*noun* Italic type or an italic letter.
i·tal·ic (i **tal′**ik) ▢*adjective* ▢*noun, plural*
italics

itch   *noun* **1.** A tickling feeling of the skin that causes one to want to scratch. **2.** A strong, restless desire: *an itch for adventure.*
▢*verb* **1.** To feel, have, or cause an itch: *I itch all over when I wear wool.* **2.** To have a strong, restless desire: *She was just itching to go to the beach.*
itch (ich) ▢*noun, plural* **itches** ▢*verb*
itched, itching, itches

item   *noun* **1.** A single article of a group: *an item from my files.* **2.** A piece of news: *a funny item in the newspaper.*
i·tem (**ī′**təm) ▢*noun, plural* **items**

it'll   Contraction for "it will" or "it shall."
it'll (**it′**əl)

its   *pronoun* Belonging or relating to it: *The cat licked its fur. The table was in its usual place.*
its (its) ▢*pronoun*

it's   Contraction for "it is" or "it has."
it's (its)

itself   *pronoun* Its own self: *The team outdid itself. The Constitution itself defines treason very clearly.*
it·self (it **self′**) ▢*pronoun*

–ity   A suffix that forms nouns and means "a quality or condition": *ability; equality.*

I've   Contraction for "I have."
I've (īv)

–ive   A suffix that forms adjectives and means: **1.** Tending to perform or achieve something: *attractive.* **2.** Of or having to do with: *instinctive.*

ivory   *noun* **1.** The smooth, hard, yellowish-white material forming the tusks of elephants and certain other animals. It is used for making ornaments and piano keys. **2.** A yellowish white.
▢*adjective* **1.** Made of ivory: *an ivory necklace.* **2.** Yellowish white: *an ivory dress.*
i·vo·ry (**ī′**və rē) ▢*noun, plural* **ivories**
▢*adjective*

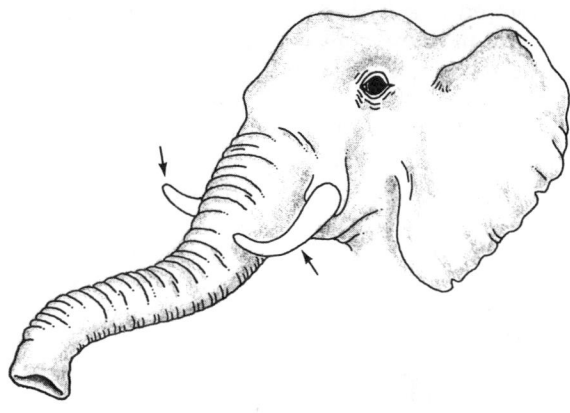

ivory
Elephant tusks

ivy   *noun* **1.** A plant with evergreen leaves and long stems that can climb up walls. **2.** A plant, such as poison ivy, that is similar to ivy.
i·vy (**ī′**vē) ▢*noun, plural* **ivies**

a bat	ī bite	o͞o tool	*th* feather
ā make	î fierce	ou out	th bath
â dare	o dot	u nut	hw wheat
ä father	ō no	û turn	zh measure
e net	ô law, for	ch church	ə about, open
ē be	oi soil	ng ring	pencil, atom
i dip	oo look	sh shade	circus

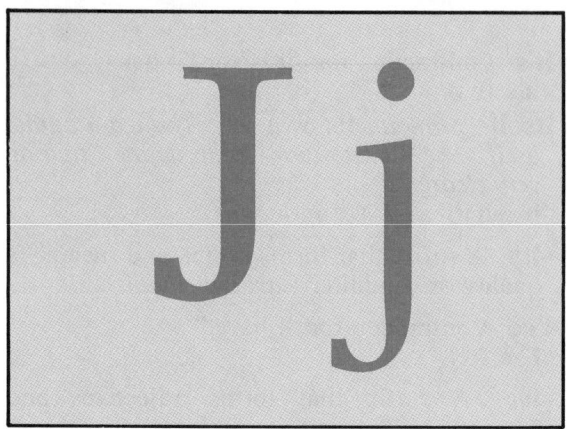

J j

ANCIENT GREEK

The letter **J** has evolved from many forms of ancient writing. One of the earliest known examples is the Greek character shown above, which dates from almost 3,000 years ago. Over the years, artists and designers have created their own versions of the English letter **J**. Some of the more common examples seen today are shown below.

Jj *Jj*	Jj Jj	Jj Jj	Jj Jj	*Jj Jj*
HANDWRITING	CALLIGRAPHY	MODERN SANS SERIF	MODERN SERIF	SCRIPT

j or **J** *noun* The tenth letter of the English alphabet.
j or **J** (jā) ▢*noun, plural* **j's** or **J's**

jab *verb* To poke or hit with something pointed: *He jabbed his finger in my stomach.* ▢*noun, plural* **jabs** A poke or hit with something pointed: *a jab in the ribs.*
jab (jab) ▢*verb* **jabbed, jabbing, jabs** ▢*noun, plural* **jabs**

jack *noun* **1.** A tool or device that is used to lift something heavy a short distance: *He used a jack to raise one end of the car in order to change the flat tire.* **2.** A playing card that has the picture of a young man on it. **3. jacks** A game that is played with a set of small, six-pointed metal pieces and a small ball. The object of the game is to pick up the metal pieces as the ball bounces.
▢*verb* To lift with a jack: *jack up a car.*
jack (jak) ▢*noun, plural* **jacks** ▢*verb* **jacked, jacking, jacks**

jack

jackal *noun* A wild dog of Africa and Asia that often feeds on what is left of the prey of lions or leopards.
jack·al (jak′əl) ▢*noun, plural* **jackals**

jackal

jacket *noun* **1.** A short coat: *a warm winter jacket.* **2.** A protective outer cover for a book or record album.
jack·et (jak′it) ▢*noun, plural* **jackets**

jack-in-the-box *noun* A toy that consists of a box with a doll or puppet inside that pops out when the box lid is opened.
jack-in-the-box (jak′in *thə* boks′) ▢*noun, plural* **jack-in-the-boxes**

jackknife *noun* A large pocketknife with blades that can be folded into the handle.
jack·knife (jak′nīf′) ▢*noun, plural* **jackknives**

jack-o'-lantern *noun* A pumpkin hollowed out and cut to look like a face. Jack-o'-lanterns are made for Halloween.

jack-o'-lan·tern (jak′ə lan′tərn) □*noun,*
plural **jack-o'-lanterns**

jackpot *noun* The largest prize in a game or
contest.
jack·pot (jak′pot′) □*noun, plural* **jackpots**

jack rabbit *noun* A hare of western North
America with strong legs and long ears.

jade *noun* A hard green or white stone. Jade
is used for jewelry and ornaments.
jade (jād) □*noun, plural* **jades**

jagged *adjective* Having notches or sharp
points: *He scraped his knee on a jagged rock.*
jag·ged (jag′id) □*adjective*

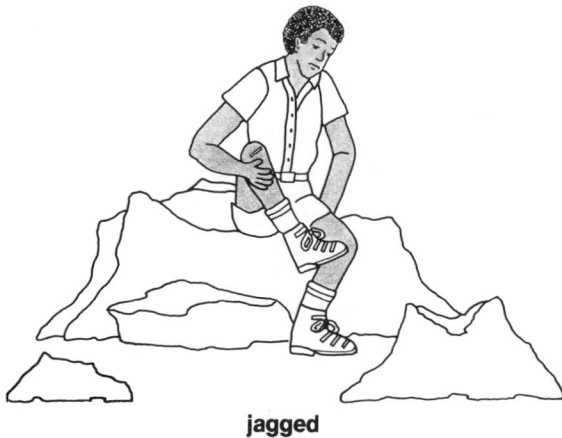

jagged

jaguar *noun* A large, spotted wild cat of
tropical America that looks like a leopard.
jag·uar (jag′wär′) □*noun, plural* **jaguars**

jail *noun* A place where persons who are
waiting for a trial or serving a prison sentence
are locked up; prison.
□*verb* To put into jail: *jail an outlaw.*
jail (jāl) □*noun, plural* **jails** □*verb* **jailed,**
jailing, jails

jam¹ *verb* **1.** To squeeze or become squeezed
into a tight space: *She jammed all her clothes
into the drawer. People jammed into the movie
theater.* **2.** To become or cause to become
stuck so as not to be able to work: *The typewriter jams all the time.* **3.** To thrust or push
hard: *She jammed on the brakes.* **4.** To bruise
or crush by squeezing: *I jammed my finger in
the door.*
□*noun* **1.** A mass of people or things crowded
together so that it is hard to move: *a traffic
jam.* **2.** A difficult situation: *He got into a jam
when he lost his keys.*
jam (jam) □*verb* **jammed, jamming, jams**
□*noun, plural* **jams**

jam

jam² *noun* A sweet food made by boiling fruit
and sugar until the mixture is thick.
jam (jam) □*noun, plural* **jams**

janitor *noun* Someone whose job it is to
clean and take care of a building.
jan·i·tor (jan′i tər) □*noun, plural* **janitors**

January *noun* The first month of the year.
January has 31 days.
Jan·u·ar·y (jan′yoō er′ē) □*noun, plural*
Januarys

WORD HISTORY: **January**

The name *January* comes from the Latin name for
the first month of the year. The Romans named the
month after Janus, the god of doors and beginnings.
Janus was depicted with two faces, one looking forward and the other looking backward.

Japanese *adjective* Of Japan, its people, or
their language.
□*noun* **1.** Someone who was born in or is a
citizen of Japan. **2.** The language of these
people.
Jap·a·nese (jap′ə **nēz′**) □*adjective* □*noun,*
plural **Japanese**

jar¹ *noun* A container with a wide mouth.
Jars are usually made of glass or pottery.
jar (jär) □*noun, plural* **jars**

jar² *verb* To cause to shake violently: *The explosion jarred houses all over town.* **2.** To have
an upsetting effect on: *The noisy students*

a	bat	ī	bite	ōō	tool	*th*	feather
ā	make	i	fierce	ou	out	th	bath
â	dare	o	dot	u	nut	hw	wheat
ä	father	ō	no	û	turn	zh	measure
e	net	ô	law, for	ch	church	ə	about, open
ē	be	oi	soil	ng	ring		pencil, atom
i	dip	oo	look	sh	shade		circus

jarred the teacher's nerves.
□*noun* A violent shaking movement; jolt.
jar (jär) □*verb* **jarred, jarring, jars** □*noun,* *plural* **jars**

javelin *noun* A light spear that is thrown for distance in an athletic contest.
jave·lin (jav′lin) □*noun, plural* **javelins**

jaw *noun* **1.** Either of a pair of bony structures of the mouth. The jaws give shape to the mouth and hold the teeth. **2.** One of two parts of a tool that can be closed and are used to grasp or hold something. A pair of pliers has jaws.
jaw (jô) □*noun, plural* **jaws**

jay *noun* A bird with a loud, harsh voice and feathers that are often brightly colored.
jay (jā) □*noun, plural* **jays**

jaywalk *verb* To cross a street without paying attention to traffic laws.
jay·walk (jā′wôk′) □*verb* **jaywalked, jaywalking, jaywalks**

jazz *noun* A kind of American music that was first played by Blacks in the southern United States. Jazz has strong rhythms and accented notes or beats that come at unusual places.
jazz (jaz) □*noun*

jealous *adjective* **1.** Fearful of losing someone's exclusive affection: *The child was jealous when his parents played with his baby sister.* **2.** Resenting what another person has or can do: *He's jealous of my new sled.*
jeal·ous (jel′əs) □*adjective*

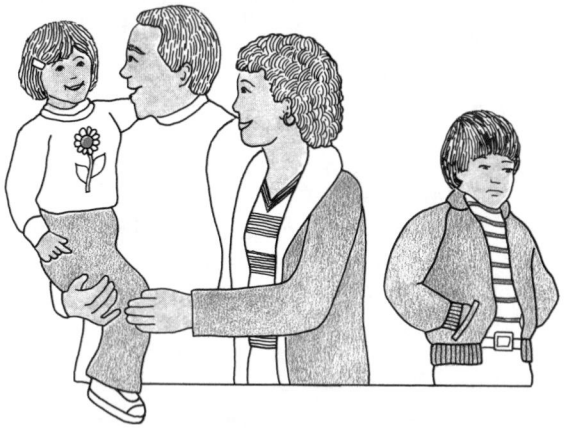
jealous

jealousy *noun* A jealous feeling; envy: *The coach said he hoped there wouldn't be jealousy among the players on the team.*
jeal·ous·y (jel′ə sē) □*noun, plural* **jealousies**

jeans *plural noun* Pants made of heavy cotton cloth, such as denim.
jeans (jēnz) □*plural noun*

jeep *noun* A small, powerful, rugged automobile, usually used for driving in places where there are no good roads.
jeep (jēp) □*noun, plural* **jeeps**

jelly *noun* A food that is soft but also firm and springy. Jelly is usually made by boiling fruit juice with sugar.
jel·ly (jel′ē) □*noun, plural* **jellies**

jellyfish *noun* A sea animal with a soft, rounded body that looks and feels like jelly. Jellyfish have tentacles that can sting.
jel·ly·fish (jel′ē fish′) □*noun, plural* **jellyfish** or **jellyfishes**

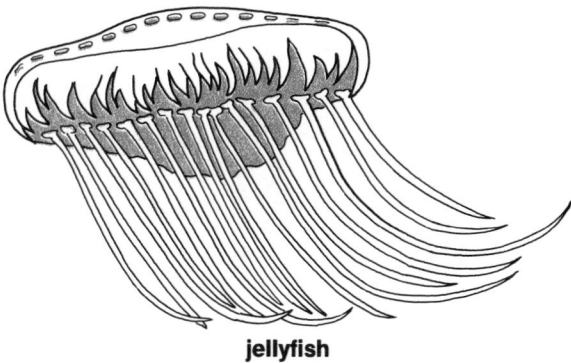
jellyfish

jerk *verb* **1.** To give something a quick pull, push, or twist: *We had to jerk the door open because it was stuck.* **2.** To move with or make a sudden, sharp movement: *I jerked my head around when I heard the crash.*
□*noun* A sudden, sharp movement.
jerk (jûrk) □*verb* **jerked, jerking, jerks** □*noun, plural* **jerks**

SYNONYMS: **jerk, wrench, yank**

These verbs mean to give something a quick pull, push, or twist: *I jerked the window open. We had to wrench the nails out of the board. She yanked the book out of my hands.*

---

jerkin *noun* A short jacket that does not have sleeves.
jer·kin (jûr′kən) □*noun, plural* **jerkins**

jerky *adjective* Making sudden stops and starts: *The ride in the wagon was very jerky.*
jerk·y (jûr′kē) □*adjective* **jerkier, jerkiest**

jersey *noun* **1.** A soft, knitted cloth made of wool, cotton, or other materials. **2.** A shirt or sweater made of this material. It is pulled down over the head.

jer·sey (jûr′zē) ▢*noun, plural* **jerseys**

WORD HISTORY: **jersey**

Jersey takes its name from the island of Jersey between England and France, where such cloth was originally made.

jest *noun* Something said or done for fun; joke or prank.
jest (jest) ▢*noun, plural* **jests**

jester *noun* In the Middle Ages, a person whose job was to entertain and amuse a ruler or lord.
jes·ter (jes′tər) ▢*noun, plural* **jesters**

jester

Jesus *noun* The founder of Christianity.
Je·sus (jē′zəs) ▢*noun*

jet *noun* **1.** A very fast stream of liquid or gas that is forced out of a small hole by great pressure: *The fountain shoots out a jet of water.* **2.** A jet-propelled aircraft.
▢*verb* To gush forth: *Water jetted from the garden hose.*
jet (jet) ▢*noun, plural* **jets** ▢*verb* **jetted, jetting, jets**

jet engine *noun* An engine that causes motion by discharging a jet of hot gasses from a small hole in the back.

jet-pro·pelled *adjective* Powered or propelled by a jet engine: *a jet-propelled airplane.*
jet-pro·pelled (jet′prə peld′) ▢*adjective*

jetty *noun* A wall that is built out into a body of water, usually made of rocks and wood. It protects the coast from strong waves.
jet·ty (jet′ē) ▢*noun, plural* **jetties**

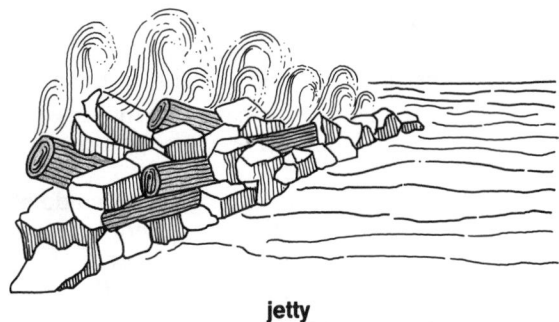
jetty

Jew *noun* **1.** Someone whose religion is Judaism. **2.** Someone who is descended from the Hebrew people described in the Bible or Old Testament.
Jew (jo͞o) ▢*noun, plural* **Jews**

jewel *noun* **1.** A precious stone; gem. **2.** A valuable piece of jewelry made with precious stones, such as a ring or necklace.
jew·el (jo͞o′əl) ▢*noun, plural* **jewels**

jeweler *noun* Someone who makes, repairs, or sells jewelry.
jew·el·er (jo͞o′ə lər) ▢*noun, plural* **jewelers**

jewelry *noun* Ornaments that are made to be worn, such as a bracelet, necklace, or ring.
jew·el·ry (joo′əl rē) ▢*noun*

Jewish *adjective* Of the Jews or Judaism.
Jew·ish (jo͞o′ish) ▢*adjective*

jigsaw *noun* A saw with a narrow blade that is placed in a frame. It is used for cutting curved or wavy lines.
jig·saw (jig′sô′) ▢*noun, plural* **jigsaws**

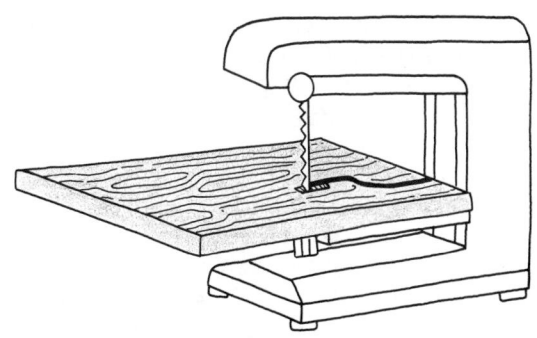
jigsaw

a	bat	ī	bite	o͞o	tool	*th*	feather
ā	make	î	fierce	ou	out	th	bath
â	dare	o	dot	u	nut	hw	wheat
ä	father	ō	no	û	turn	zh	measure
e	net	ô	law, for	ch	church	ə	about, open
ē	be	oi	soil	ng	ring		pencil, atom
i	dip	oo	look	sh	shade		circus

jigsaw puzzle *noun* A puzzle made of differently shaped pieces of wood or cardboard that make a picture when they are fitted together.

jingle *verb* To make or cause to make a tinkling or ringing sound: *He jingled the coins in his pocket.*
□*noun* **1.** A tinkling or ringing sound made by small metal objects striking one another. **2.** A simple tune that is easy to remember.
jin·gle (jĭng′ gəl) □*verb* **jingled, jingling, jingles** □*noun, plural* **jingles**

job *noun* **1.** A piece of work that needs to be done; task: *His job is to wash the dishes.* **2.** A position of employment: *His mother got a job at the bank.* —See Synonyms at **work.**
job (jŏb) □*noun, plural* **jobs**

jockey *noun* Someone who rides horses in races.
jock·ey (jŏk′ ē) □*noun, plural* **jockeys**

jockey

jog *verb* To run at a slow, steady pace: *We saw him jogging down the street.*
□*noun* A slow, steady pace.
jog (jŏg) □*verb* **jogged, jogging, jogs** □*noun, plural* **jogs**

join *verb* **1.** To come or put together so as to become one: *The stream joins the river a mile downstream.* **2.** To connect with; link: *We joined the puzzle pieces together.* **3.** To become a member of: *When did he join the army?* **4.** To enter into the company of: *She will join us later for dinner.*
join (join) □*verb* **joined, joining, joins**

SYNONYMS: **join, connect, link**

These verbs mean to meet and unite with: *This stream joins the river just past the town. The lamp cord connects with the extension cord near the desk. The two railroad lines link up at the depot.*

---

joint *noun* **1.** The place where two or more bones meet or come together. The elbow and knee are joints. **2.** A place where two or more things come together: *a pipe joint.*
□*adjective* Done or shared by two or more people: *a joint bank account.*
joint (joint) □*noun, plural* **joints** □*adjective*

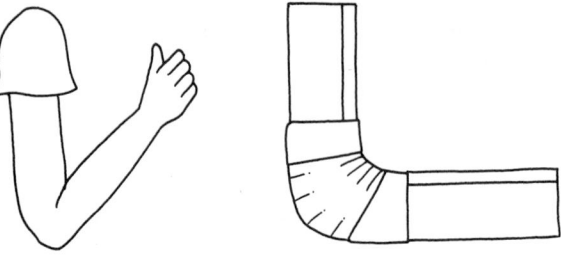

joint
Two types of joints

joke *noun* Something that is said or done to make people laugh.
□*verb* To say or do something as a joke.
joke (jōk) □*noun, plural* **jokes** □*verb* **joked, joking, jokes**

joker *noun* **1.** Someone who tells or plays jokes. **2.** An extra playing card in a deck of cards that has a figure of a jester on it.
jok·er (jō′ kər) □*noun, plural* **jokers**

jolly *adjective* Full of fun; cheerful: *a jolly holiday.*
jol·ly (jŏl′ ē) □*adjective* **jollier, jolliest**

jolt *verb* To move or cause to move with a sudden jerk: *The car jolted along the rocky road. The horse jolted me when he jumped.*
□*noun* **1.** A sudden bump or jerk: *The bus stopped with a jolt.* **2.** A sudden shock or surprise: *The bad news gave us a jolt.*
jolt (jōlt) □*verb* **jolted, jolting, jolts** □*noun, plural* **jolts**

jonquil *noun* A plant with yellow flowers that look like daffodils.
jon·quil (jŏng′ kwĭl) □*noun, plural* **jonquils**

jostle *verb* To push or bump: *People were jostling each other to get into the stadium.*
jos·tle (jŏs′ əl) □*verb* **jostled, jostling, jostles**

jot *verb* To write down quickly or briefly: *He jotted down my telephone number.*
jot (jŏt) □*verb* **jotted, jotting, jots**

journal *noun* **1.** A daily record of events: *I kept a journal during my visit to Florida.* **2.** A magazine or newspaper.
jour·nal (jûr′ nəl) □*noun, plural* **journals**

journalism *noun* The gathering of news for presentation or publication in media such as newspapers and television.
jour·nal·ism (jûr′ nə liz′əm) □*noun, plural* **journalisms**

journalist *noun* Someone who writes for a newspaper or magazine.
jour·nal·ist (jûr′ nə list) □*noun, plural* **journalists**

journey *noun* A trip over a great distance: *We took a journey across the United States.* □*verb* To make a long trip; travel: *We journeyed around the world.*
jour·ney (jûr′ nē) □*noun, plural* **journeys** □*verb* **journeyed, journeying, journeys**

joust *noun* A combat between two mounted knights wearing armor and armed with lances. □*verb* To take part in a joust.
joust (joust) □*noun, plural* **jousts** □*verb* **jousted, jousting, jousts**

jovial *adjective* Full of fun; jolly: *a jovial person.*
jo·vi·al (jō′ vē əl) □*adjective*

WORD HISTORY: **jovial**

The original meaning of *jovial* was "born under the influence of the planet Jupiter." The word *jovial* comes from a Latin name for the god Jupiter. It was once believed that the position of the stars and planets at a person's birth determined certain qualities in that person's character, and anyone born under the influence of Jupiter was supposed to have a cheerful disposition.

---

jowl *noun* The flesh under the lower jaw, especially when hanging loosely.
jowl (joul) □*noun, plural* **jowls**

jowl

joy *noun* **1.** A feeling of great happiness or delight: *She jumped for joy when she saw the new doll.* **2.** Someone or something that causes great happiness: *She is a joy to her parents.*
joy (joi) □*noun, plural* **joys**

joyful *adjective* Full of, causing, or showing joy: *a joyful celebration; a joyful smile.*
joy·ful (joi′ fəl) □*adjective*

joyous *adjective* Full of joy; joyful: *a joyous event.*
joy·ous (joi′ əs) □*adjective*

jr. or **Jr.** An abbreviation for **junior** or **Junior.**

Judaism *noun* A religion that originated among the ancient Hebrews that is based on the belief in one God and obedience to the moral laws recorded in the Old Testament.
Ju·da·ism (jōō′ dē iz′əm) □*noun*

judge *noun* **1.** A public official who hears and decides cases in a court of law. **2.** Someone who decides the winner of a contest or race: *She was the judge at the school science fair.* **3.** Someone who gives an opinion about the value or quality of something: *a good judge of cars.* □*verb* **1.** To hear and pass judgment on, especially in a court of law: *The jury judged him innocent.* **2.** To decide the winner of: *judge a contest.* **3.** To form an opinion of: *Judge the book by reading it yourself.*
judge (juj) □*noun, plural* **judges** □*verb* **judged, judging, judges**

SYNONYMS: **judge, decide, rule**

These verbs mean to hear and pass judgment on: *The jury judged her innocent of the charge. You can tell your stories to the principal and she will decide which of you is at fault. The Supreme Court ruled the new law unconstitutional.*

---

judgment *noun* **1.** A decision reached after hearing all sides of a question or complaint in a court of law: *It was the judgment of the court that the men were innocent.* **2.** The ability to choose or decide wisely; good sense: *He always shows good judgment.* **3.** An opinion formed after careful thought: *In my judgment, she's the smartest person I know.*

a bat	ī bite	ōō tool	*th* feather
ā make	î fierce	ou out	th bath
â dare	o dot	u nut	hw wheat
ä father	ō no	û turn	zh measure
e net	ô law, for	ch church	ə about, open
ē be	oi soil	ng ring	pencil, atom
i dip	oo look	sh shade	circus

judg·ment (juj′mənt) ☐*noun, plural* **judgments**

judicial *adjective* Of or ordered by judges or courts of law: *the judicial branch of the government.*
ju·di·cial (jōō dish′əl) ☐*adjective*

judo *noun* A way of fighting and defending oneself by making one's opponents use their weight and strength against themselves.
ju·do (jōō′dō) ☐*noun*

> **WORD HISTORY:** **judo**
>
> The word *judo* comes from a Japanese word that literally means "soft way."

jug *noun* A large container for holding liquids. A jug usually has a narrow mouth and a small handle.
jug (jug) ☐*noun, plural* **jugs**

juggle *verb* To keep two or more objects in the air at one time by skillful tossing and catching: *We watched him juggle the hoops.*
jug·gle (jug′əl) ☐*verb* **juggled, juggling, juggles**

juggle

juggler *noun* Someone who juggles.
jug·gler (jug′lər) ☐*noun, plural* **jugglers**

juice *noun* A liquid contained in meats or in the fruit, stem, or roots of plants: *orange juice.*
juice (jōōs) ☐*noun, plural* **juices**

juicy *adjective* Full of juice: *a juicy tomato.*
juic·y (jōō′sē) ☐*adjective* **juicier, juiciest**

July *noun* The seventh month of the year. July has 31 days.
Ju·ly (jōō lī′) ☐*noun, plural* **Julys**

> **WORD HISTORY:** **July**
>
> The name *July* comes from the Latin word for this month. The Romans named the month in honor of the dictator Julius Caesar.

jumble *verb* To mix or throw together without order: *Papers were jumbled on the desk.* ☐*noun* A confused, crowded grouping: *He left a jumble of clothes on the bed.*
jum·ble (jum′bəl) ☐*verb* **jumbled, jumbling, jumbles** ☐*noun, plural* **jumbles**

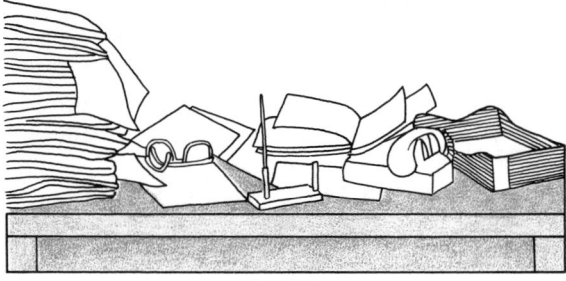

jumble

jump *verb* **1.** To rise up off the ground by using the legs: *She jumped and touched the ceiling.* **2.** To move suddenly and in one motion: *He jumped when he heard the doorbell.* **3.** To leap over: *He jumped the fence.* ☐*noun* **1.** A leap off the ground. **2.** A sudden movement: *She gave a jump when I shouted.* **3.** A sudden rise: *a jump in temperature.*
jump (jump) ☐*verb* **jumped, jumping, jumps** ☐*noun, plural* **jumps**

jumper¹ *noun* Someone or something that jumps: *Cats are good jumpers.*
jum·per (jum′pər) ☐*noun, plural* **jumpers**

jumper² *noun* A dress without sleeves, worn over a blouse or sweater.
jum·per (jum′pər) ☐*noun, plural* **jumpers**

junction *noun* The place at which two things join, meet, or cross: *The gas station is at the junction of two highways.*
junc·tion (jungk′shən) ☐*noun, plural* **junctions**

June *noun* The sixth month of the year. June has 30 days.
June (jōōn) ☐*noun, plural* **Junes**

> **WORD HISTORY:** **June**
>
> The name *June* comes from the Latin name for this month. The Roman month was named after the goddess Juno, the queen of the gods.

jungle *noun* Land that is covered with a thick growth of tropical trees and plants.
jun·gle (jŭng′gəl) ▢*noun, plural* **jungles**

junior *adjective* **1.** Of or for younger or smaller persons: *She played in the junior basketball championship.* **2. Junior** A term used with the name of a son who has the same name as his father: *William Smith, Junior.* **3.** Of lower rank or shorter length of service: *a junior vice president.* **4.** Of the third year of high school or college.
▢*noun* **1.** Someone who is younger than another. **2.** A student in the third year of a four-year high school or college.
jun·ior (jōōn′yər) ▢*adjective* ▢*noun, plural* **juniors**

juniper *noun* An evergreen tree or shrub with very small prickly needles and blue berries with a strong, spicy smell.
ju·ni·per (jōō′nə pər) ▢*noun, plural* **junipers**

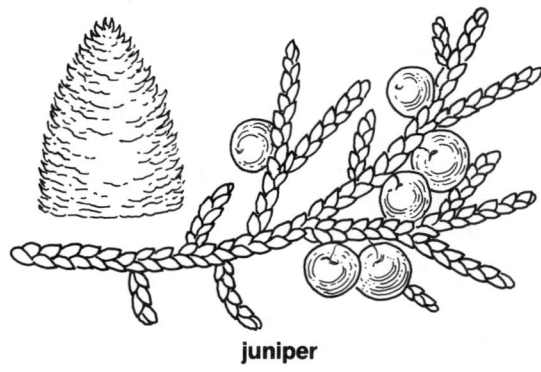

juniper

junk¹ *noun* Something that is ready to be thrown away; trash.
junk (jŭngk) ▢*noun*

junk² *noun* A Chinese sailing ship.
junk (jŭngk) ▢*noun, plural* **junks**

junk

Jupiter *noun* The largest planet of our solar system, fifth in order from the sun.
Ju·pi·ter (jōō′pi tər) ▢*noun*

juror *noun* A member of a jury.
ju·ror (jōōr′ər) ▢*noun, plural* **jurors**

jury *noun* A group of people selected to hear the facts and evidence on cases presented in a court of law. The jury makes decisions based on the evidence presented.
ju·ry (jōōr′ē) ▢*noun, plural* **juries**

just *adjective* Honest and fair: *A just ruler will earn the respect of the people. Do you think that the court made a just decision?* —See Synonyms at **fair.**
▢*adverb* **1.** Exactly: *That is just what we need to do the job.* **2.** Quite recently: *I just finished my homework.* **3.** Barely: *You can just see their house from the window.* **4.** Simply; merely: *He tried once and then just gave up.* **5.** Very; quite: *That's just great news!*
just (jŭst) ▢*adjective* ▢*adverb*

justice *noun* **1.** The quality of being just or fair. **2.** Fair treatment according to law or honor: *They appealed to the king for justice.* **3.** A judge: *The Chief Justice is the head of the Supreme Court.*
jus·tice (jŭs′tis) ▢*noun, plural* **justices**

justify *verb* To show or prove to be fair, right, or reasonable: *He justified buying a new coat by showing that his old one was torn so that it could not be mended.*
jus·ti·fy (jŭs′tə fī′) ▢*verb* **justified, justifying, justifies**

jut *verb* To stick out; project: *The church steeple juts into the sky.*
jut (jŭt) ▢*verb* **jutted, jutting, juts**

jute *noun* A strong fiber used to make rope, cord, and coarse cloth. Jute comes from a plant that grows in tropical Asia.
jute (jōōt) ▢*noun*

juvenile *adjective* Of or for young people: *juvenile clothes; a section of the library for juvenile books.*
▢*noun* A young person.
ju·ve·nile (jōō′və nəl *or* jōō′və nīl′) ▢*adjective* ▢*noun, plural* **juveniles**

a	bat	ī	bite	ōō	tool	*th*	feather
ā	make	î	fierce	ou	out	th	bath
â	dare	o	dot	u	nut	hw	wheat
ä	father	ō	no	û	turn	zh	measure
e	net	ô	law, for	ch	church	ə	about, open
ē	be	oi	soil	ng	ring		pencil, atom
i	dip	oo	look	sh	shade		circus

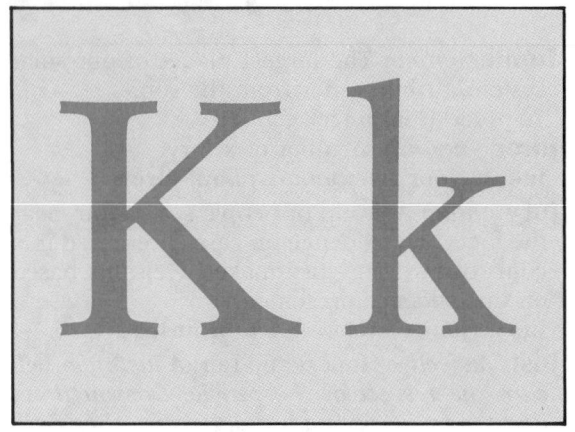

ANCIENT GREEK

The letter **K** has evolved from many forms of ancient writing. One of the earliest known examples is the Greek character shown above, which dates from almost 3,000 years ago. Over the years, artists and designers have created their own versions of the English letter **K.** Some of the more common examples seen today are shown below.

Kk *Kk*	**Kk Kk**	Kk Kk	**Kk** Kk	*Kk Kk*
HANDWRITING	CALLIGRAPHY	MODERN SANS SERIF	MODERN SERIF	SCRIPT

k or **K** *noun* The eleventh letter of the English alphabet.
k or **K** (kā) □*noun, plural* **k's** or **K's**

k An abbreviation for kilo.

kaleidoscope *noun* A tube containing mirrors that reflect patterns made by small pieces of colored glass. The patterns, which change as the tube is rotated, can be seen by looking through a hole at the end opposite the one that contains the pieces of glass.
ka·lei·do·scope (kə lī′ də skōp′) □*noun, plural* **kaleidoscopes**

WORD HISTORY: kaleidoscope

The word *kaleidoscope* was created from three Greek words meaning ''beautiful,'' ''shape,'' and ''to look at.''

kaleidoscope

kangaroo *noun* An Australian animal with a long tail and strong back legs used for leaping. The female kangaroo carries her newborn young in a pouch on the outside of the body.
kan·ga·roo (kang′gə **rōo**′) □*noun, plural* **kangaroos**

karate *noun* A kind of fighting in which the fighters do not use weapons but strike blows with the hands or feet.
ka·ra·te (kə **rä**′tē) □*noun*

katydid *noun* An insect that looks like a large green grasshopper. The male rubs his wings together to make a noise that sounds like its name.
ka·ty·did (kā′tē did) □*noun, plural* **katydids**

kayak *noun* An Eskimo canoe made of animal skins stretched over a light wooden frame. The top is closed except for a hole in the middle in which one person can sit.
kay·ak (kī′ak′) □*noun, plural* **kayaks**

kayak

keel *noun* A piece of wood or metal that runs down the center of the bottom of a ship or boat that supports the whole frame.
□*verb* **keel over 1.** To turn upside-down; capsize: *The sailboat keeled over in the strong wind.* **2.** To fall down: *He was so dizzy from the blow on the head that he keeled over.*
keel (kēl) □*noun, plural* **keels** □*verb* **keeled, keeling, keels**

keen *adjective* **1.** Having a sharp edge or point: *a keen knife.* **2.** Able to think or understand quickly and well: *a good student with a keen mind.* **3.** Very sensitive in seeing, hearing, tasting, or smelling: *a keen sense of smell.* **4.** Full of enthusiasm; eager: *She is keen about swimming.* —See Synonyms at **sharp.**
keen (kēn) □*adjective* **keener, keenest**

keep *verb* **1.** To have and not give up: *She let me keep the scarf I borrowed.* **2.** To continue or cause to continue in a particular condition or place: *Please keep quiet. The ice cream won't keep frozen long.* **3.** To store or put away: *I keep an extra set of car keys in the desk.* **4.** To take care of; tend: *keep house.* **5.** To carry out or fulfill: *keep your promise.* **6.** To prevent; stop: *She couldn't keep him from leaving.*
□*noun* **1.** Food, clothing, and a place to live: *He earns his keep by helping around the farm.* **2.** The safest and strongest part of a castle.
keep (kēp) □*verb* **kept, keeping, keeps** □*noun, plural* **keeps**

keeper *noun* Someone who watches over or cares for people, animals, or things: *a lighthouse keeper.*
keep·er (kē′pər) □*noun, plural* **keepers**

keeping *noun* **1.** Care or custody; charge: *We left the pets in our aunt's keeping.* **2.** The condition of agreeing with; harmony: *What he says is not always in keeping with how he acts.*
keep·ing (kē′ping) □*noun*

keg *noun* A small barrel.
keg (keg) □*noun, plural* **kegs**

kelp *noun* Brown seaweed that is used to make fertilizer.
kelp (kelp) □*noun*

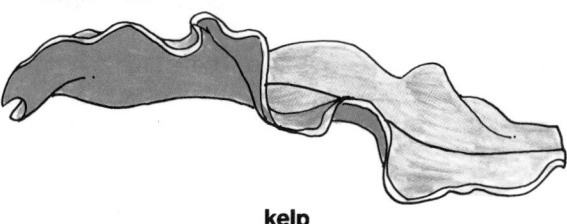

kelp

kennel *noun* **1.** A small shelter or house for a dog. **2.** A place in which dogs are raised, trained, or cared for.
ken·nel (ken′əl) □*noun, plural* **kennels**

kept *verb* The past tense and past participle of **keep:** *She kept the stray dog she found. Why have you kept these old magazines?*
kept (kept) □*verb*

kerchief *noun* A square scarf or piece of cloth worn over the head or around the neck.
ker·chief (kûr′chif) □*noun, plural* **kerchiefs**

kerchief

kernel *noun* **1.** A grain or seed of corn, wheat, or rice. **2.** The part inside the shell of a nut or the hard pit of some fruit.
ker·nel (kûr′nəl) □*noun, plural* **kernels**

kerosene *noun* A thin, light-colored oil that is made from petroleum. It is used as a fuel in such things as lamps and jet engines.
ker·o·sene (ker′ə sēn′) □*noun*

ketchup *noun* A thick, spicy red sauce made with tomatoes.
ketch·up (kech′əp) □*noun, plural* **ketchups**

kettle *noun* A metal pot for boiling liquids or cooking food.
ket·tle (ket′əl) □*noun, plural* **kettles**

kettledrum A large drum with a bowl-shaped body. It is made of copper or brass and has a top made of parchment.
ket·tle·drum (ket′əl drum′) □*noun, plural* **kettledrums**

a	bat	ī	bite	ōō	tool	*th*	feather
ā	make	î	fierce	ou	out	th	bath
â	dare	o	dot	u	nut	hw	wheat
ä	father	ō	no	û	turn	zh	measure
e	net	ô	law, for	ch	church	ə	about, open
ē	be	oi	soil	ng	ring		pencil, atom
i	dip	oo	look	sh	shade		circus

key¹ *noun* **1.** A small piece of shaped metal that is used to open or close a lock. **2.** Something shaped or used like a key, as to wind the spring in a clock or a toy. **3.** Something that solves a problem or puzzle: *This clue is the key to the mystery.* **4.** The most important element or part: *Hard work is the key to success.* **5.** A list or chart that explains the symbols, colors, or abbreviations used in such things as a map or dictionary. **6.** One of a set of buttons or levers that is pressed down to operate a machine or certain musical instruments: *a typewriter key; piano keys.* **7.** A group or scale of musical tones all related to a basic tone: *the key of D.*
key (kē) □*noun, plural* **keys**

key² *noun* A low island or reef along a coast. There are many keys off the coast of Florida.
key (kē) □*noun, plural* **keys**

keyboard *noun* A set of keys, as on a piano, organ, typewriter, or computer.
key·board (kē′bôrd′) □*noun, plural* **keyboards**

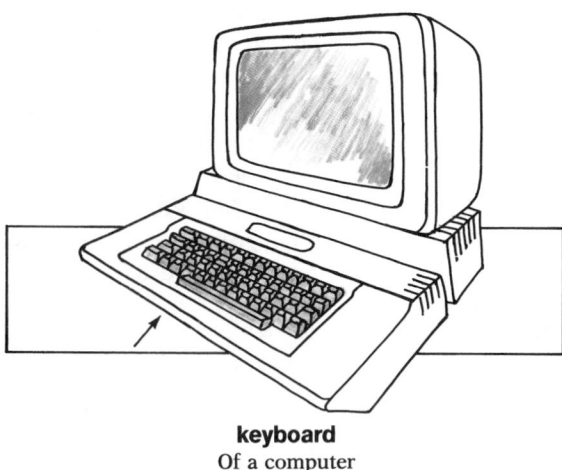

keyboard
Of a computer

keyhole *noun* The hole in a lock into which a key is put.
key·hole (kē′hōl′) □*noun, plural* **keyholes**

keystone *noun* The middle stone at the top of an arch. It holds the other stones of the arch in place.
key·stone (kē′stōn′) □*noun, plural* **keystones**

kg An abbreviation for **kilogram.**

khaki *noun* **1.** A dull, yellowish-brown color. **2.** A strong, khaki-colored cloth, used especially for army uniforms.
□*adjective* Yellowish brown.
khak·i (kak′ē *or* kä′kē) □*noun* □*adjective*

kick *verb* **1.** To hit or strike out with the foot: *She kicked me in the leg. The mule kicks if you come too close.* **2.** To make repeated motions with the feet or legs, as in swimming. **3.** To move by striking with the foot: *kick up dust; kick a ball.* **4.** To spring back suddenly when fired.
□*noun* **1.** A blow with the foot. **2.** The act of kicking a ball, as in soccer or football. **3.** The backward spring of a gun when it is fired. **4.** A feeling of excitement; thrill: *They got a kick out of going to the zoo.*
kick (kik) □*verb* **kicked, kicking, kicks**
□*noun, plural* **kicks**

kickoff *noun* A kick in football or soccer that puts the ball into play, as at the beginning of a game.
kick·off (kik′ôf′) □*noun, plural* **kickoffs**

kickstand *noun* A bar or rod for holding up a vehicle with two wheels, such as a bicycle, when parked or not being used.
kick·stand (kik′stand′) □*noun, plural* **kickstands**

kid *noun* **1.** A young goat. **2.** Soft leather made from the skin of a young goat. **3.** A child.
□*verb* **1.** To make fun of playfully; tease: *His friends were kidding him about his red sneakers.* **2.** To trick or deceive in fun: *He's not kidding you.* **3.** To take part in playful fooling: *Stop kidding around and be serious!*
kid (kid) □*noun, plural* **kids** □*verb* **kidded, kidding, kids**

kidnap *verb* To carry off and hold someone by force: *They kidnaped the politician and demanded a large sum of money before they would free him.*
kid·nap (kid′nap′) □*verb* **kidnaped** or **kidnapped, kidnaping** or **kidnapping, kidnaps**

kidney *noun* One of two body organs that separate waste from the blood and pass it out from the body in the form of urine. The kidneys are located in the abdomen.
kid·ney (kid′nē) □*noun, plural* **kidneys**

kidney bean *noun* A plant bearing an edible, large, dark-red bean.

kidskin *noun* **1.** The skin of a goat. **2.** A soft leather made from the skin of a goat.
kid·skin (kid′skin′) □*noun*

kid stuff *noun* **1.** Something that is appropriate only for children. **2.** Something that is very easy or simple: *That job was kid stuff.*

kill *verb* **1.** To cause the death of: *The forest fire killed many animals.* **2.** To put an end to; eliminate: *Nothing could kill the taste of the cough medicine.* **3.** To use up time: *We killed two hours waiting for the movie to start.* □*noun* **1.** An act of killing: *The hunter wounded the bear and then moved in for the kill.* **2.** Something that has just been killed: *The tiger stood over its kill.*
kill (kil) □*verb* **killed, killing, kills** □*noun, plural* **kills**

SYNONYMS: **kill, murder, slay**

These verbs mean to cause the death of: *Most animals will kill for food or to protect their young. The cruel tyrant murdered many people. The princess slew the dragon.*

---

killer *noun* Someone or something that kills.
kill·er (kil′ ər) □*noun, plural* **killers**

kiln *noun* An oven or furnace used for hardening, drying, or burning something. Pottery and bricks are baked in a kiln.
kiln (kiln *or* kil) □*noun, plural* **kilns**

kiln

kilo *noun* **1.** A kilogram. **2.** A kilometer.
ki·lo (kē′lō *or* kil′ō) □*noun, plural* **kilos**

kilo- A prefix that means "one thousand": *kilogram.*

kilogram *noun* The basic unit of mass in the metric system equal to 1,000 grams or about 2.2 pounds.
kil·o·gram (kil′ ə gram′) □*noun, plural* **kilograms**

kilometer *noun* A unit of length in the metric system equal to 1,000 meters or 0.6214 mile.
kil·o·me·ter (kil′ ə mē′tər *or* ki lom′ i tər) □*noun, plural* **kilometers**

kilowatt *noun* A unit of electric power equal to 1,000 watts.
kil·o·watt (kil′ ə wot′) □*noun, plural* **kilowatts**

kilt *noun* A pleated plaid skirt that reaches down to the knees. Kilts are worn by men in Scotland.
kilt (kilt) □*noun, plural* **kilts**

kimono *noun* A loose robe that is tied with a wide sash. Kimonos are worn by both women and men in Japan.
ki·mo·no (ki mō′nə) □*noun, plural* **kimonos**

kimono

kin *noun* A person's relatives; family: *All of our kin came to my sister's wedding.*
kin (kin) □*noun*

kind¹ *adjective* **1.** Helpful and considerate: *a kind person who is always helping others.* **2.** Thoughtful; courteous: *It was kind of them to visit me when I was sick.*
kind (kīnd) □*adjective* **kinder, kindest**

kind² *noun* A group of the same or similar things: *We planted a few different kinds of flowers. A tiger is a kind of cat.*
kind (kīnd) □*noun, plural* **kinds**

SYNONYMS: **kind², sort, type**

These nouns mean a group of the same or similar things: *I saw all kinds of animals on the farm. What sort of dog is that? How many different types of insects can you name?*

---

a	bat	ī	bite	ōō	tool	*th* feather
ā	make	î	fierce	ou	out	th bath
â	dare	o	dot	u	nut	hw wheat
ä	father	ō	no	û	turn	zh measure
e	net	ô	law, for	ch church	ə about, open
ē	be	oi	soil	ng ring	pencil, atom
i	dip	oo	look	sh shade	circus

kindergarten *noun* A school class for children from the ages of four to six. Kindergarten prepares children for elementary school.
kin·der·gar·ten (kin′ dər gär′tən) □*noun*, plural **kindergartens**

WORD HISTORY: **kindergarten**

Kindergarten is borrowed from a German word that literally means "children's garden."

---

kindle *verb* **1.** To start a fire: *She used matches to kindle the camp fire.* **2.** To catch fire: *The newspaper kindled quickly.* **2.** To stir up or excite: *His nasty remarks kindled my anger.*
kin·dle (kin′ dəl) □*verb* **kindled, kindling, kindles**

kindly *adjective* Considerate and friendly; kind: *He has a kindly face.*
□*adverb* In a kind way: *Everyone treated the new student kindly. He kindly took the time to help me.*
kind·ly (kīnd′ lē) □*adjective* **kindlier, kindliest** □*adverb*

kindness *noun* **1.** The quality of being kind: *She was known all over town for her kindness.* **2.** A kind act; favor: *I thanked them for the many kindnesses they showed me.*
kind·ness (kīnd′ nis) □*noun*, plural **kindnesses**

king *noun* **1.** A man who rules a country. **2.** A person or thing that is the best, the most important, or the most powerful of its type: *He became known as the king of rock and roll.* **3.** The most important piece in chess. **4.** A playing card having the picture of a king. **5.** In checkers, a piece that has reached the opponent's back row.
king (king) □*noun*, plural **kings**

kingdom *noun* **1.** A country that is ruled by a king or queen. **2.** One of the three groups into which all living things and natural substances are divided. These groups are the animal kingdom, the plant kingdom, and the mineral kingdom.
king·dom (king′ dəm) □*noun*, plural **kingdoms**

kingfisher *noun* A bird with a large bill and a crest on its head.
king·fish·er (king′ fish′ ər) □*noun*, plural **kingfishers**

kink *noun* **1.** A tight curl or twist of hair, wire, or rope. **2.** A pain or stiff feeling in a muscle; cramp: *a kink in the shoulder.*
□*verb* To form a kink: *Be careful not to kink the rope.*
kink (kingk) □*noun*, plural **kinks** □*verb* **kinked, kinking, kinks**

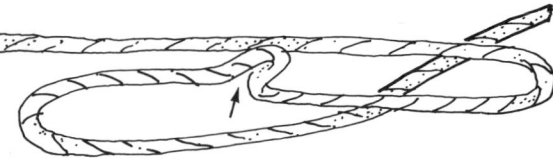

kink

kiss *verb* To touch and press with the lips as a sign of love, friendship, or greeting.
□*noun* **1.** A touch with the lips: *She gave him a kiss.* **2.** A small piece of candy.
kiss (kis) □*verb* **kissed, kissing, kisses** □*noun*, plural **kisses**

kit *noun* **1.** A set of parts or pieces to be put together: *a model airplane kit.* **2.** A small set of tools or equipment for a special purpose: *a first-aid kit.*
kit (kit) □*noun*, plural **kits**

kitchen *noun* A room where food is cooked or prepared.
kitch·en (kich′ ən) □*noun*, plural **kitchens**

kitchenette *noun* A small kitchen.
kitch·en·ette (kich′ə **net′**) □*noun*, plural **kitchenettes**

kite *noun* **1.** A bird with a hooked bill and a long, often forked tail. **2.** A light wooden frame covered with cloth, paper, or plastic, flown in the wind at the end of a long string.
kite (kīt) □*noun*, plural **kites**

kitten *noun* A young cat.
kit·ten (kit′ ən) □*noun*, plural **kittens**

kitten

km An abbreviation for **kilometer.**

knack *noun* A special talent or skill: *She has a knack for fixing cars.*
knack (nak) □*noun*, plural **knacks**

knapsack *noun* A fabric or leather bag made to be worn on the back and used to carry equipment on a hike or march.
knap·sack (**nap′**sak′) □*noun, plural* **knapsacks**

knapsack

knead *verb* To mix and work a substance by folding, pressing, or stretching with the hands: *knead bread dough.*
knead (nēd) □*verb* **kneaded, kneading, kneads**

knee *noun* The joint at which the thigh and the lower leg come together.
knee (nē) □*noun, plural* **knees**

kneecap *noun* A small, movable bone at the front of the knee.
knee·cap (nē′kap′) □*noun, plural* **kneecaps**

kneel *verb* To go down on a bent knee or knees: *I had to kneel to reach under the bed.*
kneel (nēl) □*verb* **knelt** or **kneeled, kneeling, kneels**

knelt *verb* A past tense and a past participle of **kneel**: *I knelt down to pick up the rock.*
knelt (nelt) □*verb*

knew *verb* The past tense of **know**: *We knew they were coming to visit.*
knew (nōo *or* nyōo) □*verb*

knife *noun* A tool or device used for cutting that consists of a sharp blade attached to a handle.
□*verb* To cut or stab with a knife.
knife (nīf) □*noun, plural* **knives** □*verb* **knifed, knifing, knifes**

knight *noun* **1.** A mounted soldier in the Middle Ages who gave military service to a king or lord in return for the right to hold land. **2.** In Great Britain, a man who is given the title "knight" for service to his country or for his personal achievements. A knight uses "Sir" before his name. **3.** A piece in the game of chess.
□*verb* To make someone a knight.
knight (nīt) □*noun, plural* **knights** □*verb* **knighted, knighting, knights**

knit *verb* **1.** To make by looping together yarn or thread, either by hand with special needles or by machine: *I knitted a sweater for her. Can you knit?* **2.** To join or grow closely together: *It took a few months for his broken arm to knit.*
knit (nit) □*verb* **knit** or **knitted, knitting, knits**

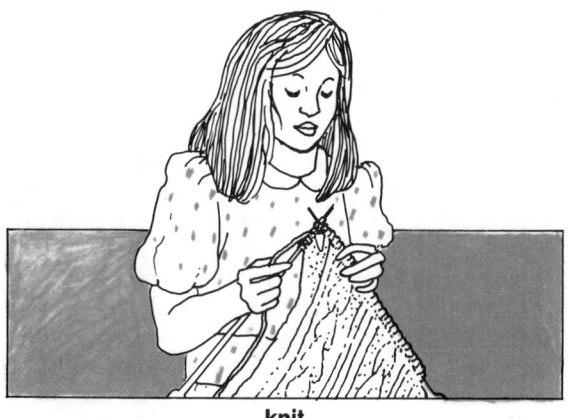
knit

knives *noun* The plural of **knife.**
knives (nīvz) □*noun*

knob *noun* **1.** A rounded handle for opening such things as a door or drawer or for operating such things as a radio or television. **2.** A rounded lump, as on the trunk of a tree.
knob (nob) □*noun, plural* **knobs**

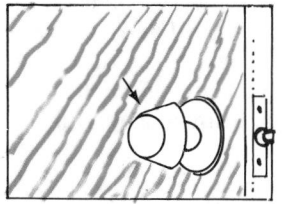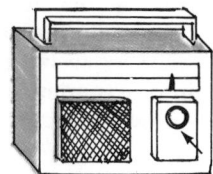
knob

a	bat	ī	bite	ōō	tool	*th*	feather
ã	make	î	fierce	ou	out	th	bath
â	dare	o	dot	u	nut	hw	wheat
ä	father	ō	no	û	turn	zh	measure
e	net	ô	law, for	ch	church	ə	about, open
ē	be	oi	soil	ng	ring		pencil, atom
i	dip	oo	look	sh	shade		circus

knock *verb* **1.** To strike with a hard blow or blows; hit: *She knocked me on the head.* **2.** To make a pounding or clanking noise: *He knocked on the door. The automobile engine was knocking.*
□*noun* **1.** A hard or sharp blow: *a knock on the head; a knock at the door.* **2.** A pounding or clanking noise, as of an engine that needs to be fixed.
  knock out To hit so hard as to make unconscious.
knock (nok) □*verb* **knocked, knocking, knocks** □*noun, plural* **knocks**

knocker *noun* A small metal ring or knob that is attached to a door by a hinge. It is used for knocking on a door to attract the attention of someone inside.
knock·er (nok′ər) □*noun, plural* **knockers**

knoll *noun* A small, rounded hill.
knoll (nōl) □*noun, plural* **knolls**

knot *noun* **1.** A fastening made by tying together one or more flexible lengths of material, as string, rope, or twine: *He tied the cord around his waist with a knot.* **2.** A tightly twisted roll or clump of hair: *The dog's fur is full of knots.* **3.** A tight group or cluster of persons or things: *A knot of people were waiting for the store to open.* **4.** A hard, dark spot in wood or in a board. **5.** A unit of measurement of speed, used by ships and aircraft. A knot is equal to one nautical mile, or about 6,076 feet, per hour.
□*verb* To tie or fasten in or with a knot: *She knotted the sash in the back.*
knot (not) □*noun, plural* **knots** □*verb* **knotted, knotting, knots**

know *verb* **1.** To be certain of the facts or truth of; understand clearly: *Nobody knows how the fire started. She knows I'm right.* **2.** To be acquainted or familiar with: *I've known her since we were in kindergarten.* **3.** To have skill in or experience with: *He knows French.*
know (nō) □*verb* **knew, known, knowing, knows**

knowledge *noun* **1.** What can be learned from study or experience; information: *a knowledge of geometry.* **2.** The fact of knowing or being aware: *The knowledge that the river might flood the town made them leave the house.*
knowl·edge (nol′ij) □*noun*

known *verb* The past participle of **know**: *How long have you two known each other?*
known (nōn) □*verb*

knuckle *noun* A joint of a finger.
knuck·le (nuk′əl) □*noun, plural* **knuckles**

koala *noun* An animal of Australia that looks something like a small, furry bear. It lives in eucalyptus trees and feeds on their leaves.
ko·a·la (kō ä′lə) □*noun, plural* **koalas**

koala

Koran *noun* The sacred book of Islam.
Ko·ran (kə ran′ *or* kô rän′) □*noun*

a	bat	ī	bite	o͞o	tool	th	feather
ā	make	î	fierce	ou	out	th	bath
â	dare	o	dot	u	nut	hw	wheat
ä	father	ō	no	û	turn	zh	measure
e	net	ô	law, for	ch	church	ə	about, open
ē	be	oi	soil	ng	ring		pencil, atom
i	dip	oo	look	sh	shade		circus

ANCIENT GREEK

The letter **L** has evolved from many forms of ancient writing. One of the earliest known examples is the Greek character shown above, which dates from almost 3,000 years ago. Over the years, artists and designers have created their own versions of the English letter **L**. Some of the more common examples seen today are shown below.

Ll Ll	Ll ll	Ll Ll	Ll Ll	Ll Ll
HANDWRITING	CALLIGRAPHY	MODERN SANS SERIF	MODERN SERIF	SCRIPT

l or **L** *noun* The twelfth letter of the English alphabet.
l or **L** (el) ▫*noun, plural* **l's** or **L's**
l An abbreviation for **length** and **liter**.

lab *noun* A laboratory.
lab (lab) ▫*noun, plural* **labs**

label *noun* A tag or sticker attached to something to give useful information: *The price of the dress is on the label.*
▫*verb* To put a label on: *She labeled the box to show what was in it.*
la·bel (lā′bəl) ▫*noun, plural* **labels** ▫*verb* **labeled, labeling, labels**

labor *noun* **1.** Physical or mental exertion: *With great labor they built a rough shelter of logs.* **2.** Workers as a group: *The candidate wanted the votes of labor.*
▫*verb* **1.** To work; toil: *workers laboring in the factory.* **2.** To move slowly and with effort: *The car labored up the hill.*
la·bor (lā′bər) ▫*noun, plural* **labors** ▫*verb* **labored, laboring, labors**

SYNONYMS: **labor, work**

These nouns mean physical exertion that is usually difficult and tiring: *It takes a great deal of hard labor to run a farm. Building the new porch was hard work.*

---

laboratory *noun* A room or building with special tools and machines for doing scientific research, experiments, and testing.

lab·o·ra·to·ry (lab′rə tôr′ē) ▫*noun, plural* **laboratories**

laborer *noun* A worker, especially one who does hard physical labor.
la·bor·er (lā′bər ər) ▫*noun, plural* **laborers**

lace *noun* **1.** A delicate fabric of fine threads woven in an open pattern. **2.** A cord or string drawn through holes or around hooks to pull and tie opposite edges together.
▫*verb* To fasten or tie with a lace: *Lace up your shoes.*
lace (lās) ▫*noun, plural* **laces** ▫*verb* **laced, lacing, laces**

lack *noun* An absence of something; want: *Lack of rain harmed the wheat crop.*
▫*verb* To be without; to be in need of: *He lacked the money to go to college. The movie lacked interest.*
lack (lak) ▫*noun, plural* **lacks** ▫*verb* **lacked, lacking, lacks**

lacquer *noun* A liquid coating that is put on metal or wood to give it a glossy finish.
lac·quer (lak′ər) ▫*noun, plural* **lacquers**

lacrosse *noun* A ball game that is played on a field with a stick having a net on the end to

a	bat	ī	bite	ōō	tool	*th*	feather
ā	make	î	fierce	ou	out	th	bath
â	dare	o	dot	u	nut	hw	wheat
ä	father	ō	no	û	turn	zh	measure
e	net	ô	law, for	ch	church	ə	about, open
ē	be	oi	soil	ng	ring		pencil, atom
i	dip	oo	look	sh	shade		circus

catch, carry, and throw the ball.
la·crosse (lə krôs′) □*noun*

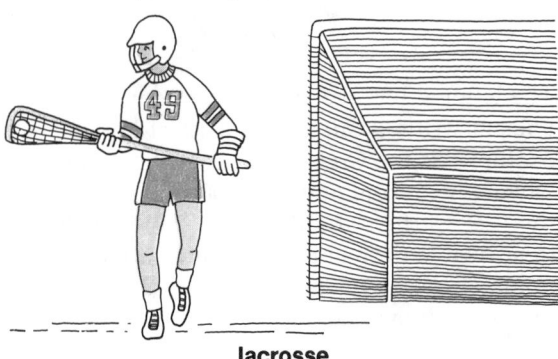

lacrosse

lad *noun* A boy or young man.
lad (lad) □*noun, plural* **lads**

ladder *noun* A piece of equipment that is used for climbing and has two side pieces connected by evenly spaced rungs.
lad·der (lad′ər) □*noun, plural* **ladders**

laden *adjective* Loaded or filled: *a basket laden with fruit.*
lad·en (lā′dən) □*adjective*

ladle *noun* A spoon with a long handle and a bowl shaped like a cup, used for dipping.
la·dle (lā′dəl) □*noun, plural* **ladles**

lady *noun* **1.** A woman of high social position or wealth. **2.** A woman or young girl who has good manners. **3.** A woman: *the lady who sells flowers.* **4.** **Lady** A woman of noble rank in Great Britain.
la·dy (lā′dē) □*noun, plural* **ladies**

WORD HISTORY: lady

Lady comes from an old English word that literally means "one who kneads the bread."

---

ladybug *noun* A small, round, reddish or yellowish beetle with black spots that eats and destroys insects that are harmful to plants.
la·dy·bug (lā′dē bug′) □*noun, plural* **ladybugs**

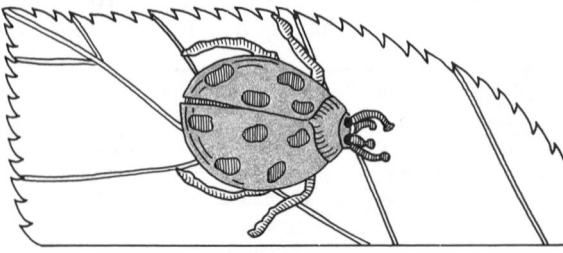

ladybug

lag *verb* To move slowly and fail to keep up: *The little boy lagged behind his mother.*
□*noun* The act of lagging: *There was a lag of only a second between the time I heard the phone and the time I answered it.*
lag (lag) □*verb* **lagged, lagging, lags** □*noun, plural* **lags**

lagoon *noun* A shallow body of water that is usually connected to a larger body of water.
la·goon (lə gōon′) □*noun, plural* **lagoons**

laid *verb* The past tense and past participle of **lay¹**: *She laid the pen on the desk. The hen has laid two eggs today.*
laid (lād) □*verb*

lain *verb* The past participle of **lie¹**: *She had lain down on the couch.*
lain (lān) □*verb*

lair *noun* The den or home of a wild animal.
lair (lâr) □*noun, plural* **lairs**

lake *noun* A large inland body of fresh or salt water.
lake (lāk) □*noun, plural* **lakes**

lamb *noun* **1.** A young sheep. **2.** Meat from a lamb.
lamb (lam) □*noun, plural* **lambs**

lame *adjective* **1.** Not able to walk well; crippled: *The lame woman walked with a limp.* **2.** Sore and stiff: *a lame shoulder.* **3.** Weak; not satisfactory: *a lame excuse for being late.*
□*verb* To make lame; cripple: *The injury lamed him.*
lame (lām) □*adjective* **lamer, lamest** □*verb* **lamed, laming, lames**

lamp *noun* A device that produces light: *an electric lamp; a kerosene lamp.*
lamp (lamp) □*noun, plural* **lamps**

lance *noun* A weapon made of a long spear with a sharp metal head.
□*verb* To cut into with a surgeon's knife: *lance a boil.*
lance (lans) □*noun, plural* **lances** □*verb* **lanced, lancing, lances**

land *noun* **1.** The part of the earth's surface not covered by water. **2.** A region or area: *a land of many lakes.* **3.** A country; nation: *people of foreign lands.*
□*verb* **1.** To come or bring to shore: *The ship landed before dawn. Boats landed the soldiers on the beach.* **2.** To come or cause to come down and stop: *The balloon landed in a field. She landed the airplane smoothly.* **3.** To arrive or cause to arrive in a place or condition: *He landed in trouble after running away.*

land (land) □*noun, plural* **lands** □*verb*
landed, landing, lands

SYNONYMS: **land, ground, soil**

These nouns mean the part of the earth's surface not covered by water: *After three months at sea, the sailors were happy to be on land again. Leaves drifted slowly to the ground. Wheat and corn flourish in the fertile soil of the plains.*

---

landing *noun* **1.** The act of coming to a stop and settling after a voyage or flight: *a helicopter landing.* **2.** A place where boats can stop and unload; wharf or pier. **3.** A level area at the top or bottom of a set of stairs.
land·ing (lan′ding) □*noun, plural* **landings**

landlady *noun* **1.** A woman who owns a house or apartments that she rents to others. **2.** A woman who runs a rooming house or inn.
land·la·dy (land′lā′dē) □*noun, plural* **landladies**

landlord *noun* **1.** A man who owns a house or apartments that he rents to others. **2.** A man who runs a rooming house or inn.
land·lord (land′lôrd′) □*noun, plural* **landlords**

landmark *noun* **1.** A familiar or easily seen object or feature of the landscape that can be used as a guide: *A skyscraper is one of the city's landmarks.* **2.** A very important event or work: *The revolution was a landmark in the country's history.*
land·mark (land′märk′) □*noun, plural* **landmarks**

landscape *noun* **1.** A view or scene of land: *a desert landscape.* **2.** A painting or photograph showing a landscape.
□*verb* To make a piece of ground pretty by planting trees, bushes, or flowers.
land·scape (land′skāp′) □*noun, plural* **landscapes** □*verb* **landscaped, landscaping, landscapes**

landslide *noun* **1.** The sliding of a large amount of earth and rock down the side of a mountain. **2.** A victory in an election won by a very large number of votes.
land·slide (land′slīd′) □*noun, plural* **landslides**

lane *noun* **1.** A narrow path or road, often having grass, trees, hedges, or fences along its sides. **2.** A division along the length of a road for a single line of vehicles.
lane (lān) □*noun, plural* **lanes**

language *noun* **1.** Human speech. **2.** A particular system of human speech that is shared by a group of people: *the French language.* **3.** A system of symbols used for giving information or expressing ideas: *sign language; a computer language.*
lan·guage (lang′gwij) □*noun, plural* **languages**

WORD HISTORY: **language**

Language comes from a Latin word meaning ''tongue.''

---

lantern *noun* A covering for a light, with sides or an opening through which the light can shine.
lan·tern (lan′tərn) □*noun, plural* **lanterns**

lap[1] *noun* The front part of the body of a seated person from the knees to the waist.
lap (lap) □*noun, plural* **laps**

lap[2] *verb* To place or be placed so that one part is over or partly over another; overlap: *The upper row of shingles lapped over the lower row.*
□*noun* One complete time over or around the entire length of something: *The girl swam two laps of the pool.*
lap (lap) □*verb* **lapped, lapping, laps** □*noun, plural* **laps**

lap[3] *verb* **1.** To drink by taking up with the tongue: *The puppy lapped up the water.* **2.** To splash with a light, slapping sound: *Waves lapped against the dock.*
lap (lap) □*verb* **lapped, lapping, laps**

lapel *noun* A flap of a collar that folds back against the chest.
la·pel (lə pel′) □*noun, plural* **lapels**

lard *noun* A white, greasy substance made from the melted-down fat of pigs or hogs.
lard (lärd) □*noun*

large *adjective* Great in size, amount, or number: *a large animal; a large sum of money.*
—See Synonyms at **big**.
large (lärj) □*adjective* **larger, largest**

---

a bat	ī bite	o͞o tool	*th* feather
ā make	î fierce	ou out	th bath
â dare	o dot	u nut	hw wheat
ä father	ō no	û turn	zh measure
e net	ô law, for	ch church	ə about, open
ē be	oi soil	ng ring	pencil, atom
i dip	oo look	sh shade	circus

large intestine *noun* The lower part of the intestine in which water is absorbed from the waste matter left after food is digested.

largely *adverb* For the most part; mainly: *He is largely at fault for the mistake.*
large·ly (**lärj′**lē) ▢*adverb*

lariat *noun* A long rope with a sliding noose at one end, used to catch horses or cattle.
lar·i·at (**lar′**ē ət) ▢*noun, plural* **lariats**

WORD HISTORY: **lariat**

The word *lariat* comes from two Spanish words that mean "the rope."

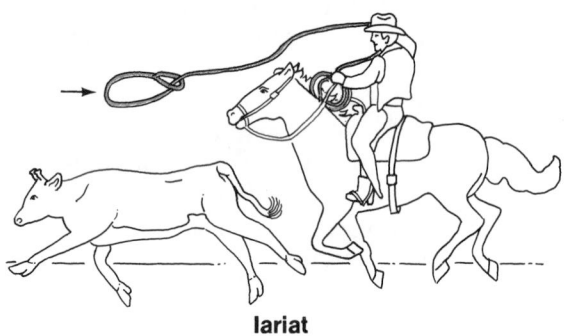

lariat

lark¹ *noun* A small gray-brown songbird that sings as it flies high in the air.
lark (lärk) ▢*noun, plural* **larks**

lark² *noun* A merry adventure; frolic.
lark (lärk) ▢*noun, plural* **larks**

larkspur *noun* A plant with a long cluster of blue, white, or pink flowers.
lark·spur (**lärk′**spûr′) ▢*noun, plural* **larkspurs**

larva *noun* The early form of an insect, such as a caterpillar or grub, when it has just hatched from an egg. A larva looks like a worm.
lar·va (**lär′**və) ▢*noun, plural* **larv·ae** (**lär′**vē)

WORD HISTORY: **larva**

The word *larva* is borrowed from Latin, where it means "mask." This early form of an insect looks completely different from its final shape. For this reason the early stage was thought to "mask" the true form of the insect.

---

larynx *noun* The upper part of the passage between the nose and mouth and the lungs in which vocal cords are located.
lar·ynx (**lar′**ingks) ▢*noun, plural* **larynxes**

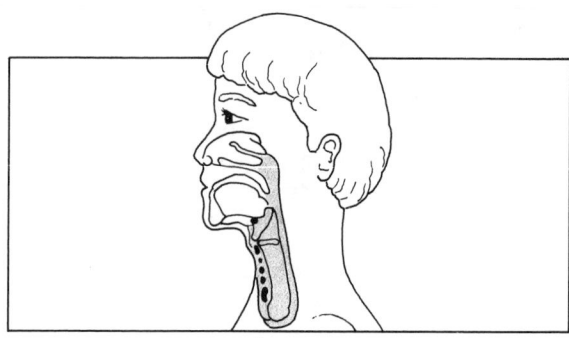

larynx

laser *noun* A device that uses atoms or molecules to make a very strong beam of light.
la·ser (**lā′**zər) ▢*noun, plural* **lasers**

lash¹ *noun* **1.** A whip. **2.** A blow with a whip. **3.** An eyelash.
▢*verb* **1.** To hit with or as if with a whip: *High waves lashed against the shore during the storm.* **2.** To move back and forth with a motion like that of a whip: *The tiger lashed its tail.*
lash (lash) ▢*noun, plural* **lashes** ▢*verb* **lashed, lashing, lashes**

lash² *verb* To tie in place with ropes, chains, or straps: *We lashed the bicycles to the roof of the car.*
lash (lash) ▢*verb* **lashed, lashing, lashes**

lasso *noun* A long rope with a sliding noose at one end, used for catching animals such as horses and cattle.
▢*verb* To catch with a lasso.
las·so (**las′**ō *or* la **soo′**) ▢*noun, plural* **lassos** or **lassoes** ▢*verb* **lassoed, lassoing, lassoes**

last¹ *adjective* **1.** Coming after all others: *The last one to leave should turn off the lights.* **2.** Just past: *last week.* **3.** Least likely: *Telling a lie was the last thing we expected him to do.*
▢*adverb* **1.** At the end; finally: *The horses came last in the parade.* **2.** Most recently: *I last spoke with him yesterday.*
▢*noun* Someone or something that is last: *She was the last to arrive.*
last (last) ▢*adjective* ▢*adverb* ▢*noun*

SYNONYMS: **last¹, final**

These adjectives mean coming after all others: *The last person to leave should turn off the lights. Tomorrow I take my final exam in geography.*

---

last² *verb* **1.** To continue for a period of time: *The storm lasted all day.* **2.** To remain in good condition: *a cheap toy that won't last.*

last (last) □*verb* **lasted, lasting, lasts**

lasting *adjective* Continuing for a long time: *a book of lasting importance.*
last·ing (lăs′ting) □*adjective*

lat. An abbreviation for **latitude.**

latch *noun* A movable bar that fits into a notch or slot and fastens a door or gate. □*verb* To fasten with a latch.
latch (lăch) □*noun, plural* **latches** □*verb* **latched, latching, latches**

late *adjective* **1.** Coming after the usual or expected time: *I ate a late breakfast.* **2.** Near or toward the end: *We took our vacation in late summer.* **3.** Of a time just past; recent: *This television set is a late model.* **4.** Having died recently: *Her late sister was a doctor.* □*adverb* After or beyond the usual or expected time: *Try not to come late.*
late (lāt) □*adjective* **later, latest** □*adverb* **later, latest**

lately *adverb* Not long ago; recently: *He hasn't been to the dentist lately.*
late·ly (lāt′lē) □*adverb*

lateral *adjective* On, of, toward, or from the side: *a lateral view of the house.*
lat·er·al (lăt′ər əl) □*adjective*

lathe *noun* A machine for holding a piece of material, such as metal, while turning and shaping it against a cutting tool.
lathe (lāth) □*noun, plural* **lathes**

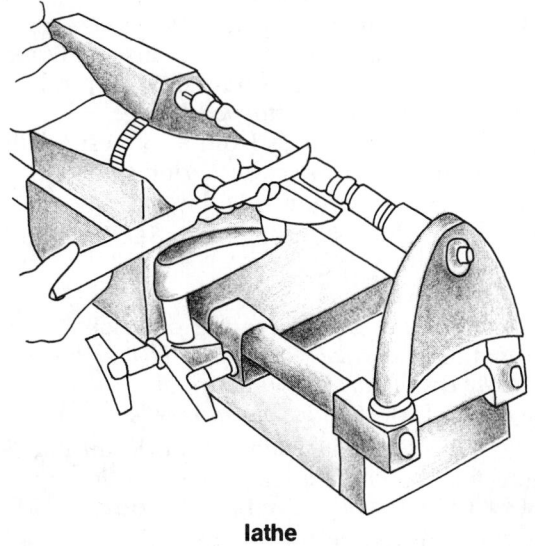

lathe

lather *noun* **1.** A foam formed by mixing soap with water. **2.** Froth formed by sweating, especially on a horse.

□*verb* **1.** To cover with lather: *He lathered his face with shaving cream.* **2.** To form lather: *The shampoo doesn't lather well in cold water.*
lath·er (lăth′ər) □*noun, plural* **lathers** □*verb* **lathered, lathering, lathers**

Latin *adjective* **1.** Of or having to do with the language of the ancient Romans. **2.** Of or having to do with those peoples or countries that use Romance languages, especially the countries of Latin America. □*noun* **1.** The language of the ancient Romans. **2.** A member of a people who speak a Romance language.
Lat·in (lăt′ən) □*adjective* □*noun, plural* **Latins**

Latin-American *adjective* Of or having to do with Latin America or its people.
Lat·in-A·mer·i·can (lăt′ən ə mĕr′i kən) □*adjective*

latitude *noun* Distance north or south of the equator measured in degrees.
lat·i·tude (lăt′i tōōd′ *or* lăt′i tyōōd) □*noun, plural* **latitudes**

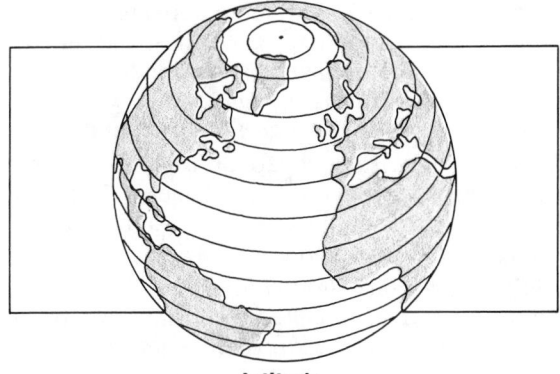

latitude

latter *adjective* **1.** Of or being the second or second mentioned of two: *Of the two stories only the latter story is true.* **2.** Closer to the end: *the latter part of the book.*
lat·ter (lăt′ər) □*adjective*

lattice *noun* A framework made of strips of wood or metal that cross each other.
lat·tice (lăt′is) □*noun, plural* **lattices**

a	bat	ī	bite	ōō	tool	*th*	feather
ā	make	î	fierce	ou	out	th	bath
â	dare	o	dot	u	nut	hw	wheat
ä	father	ō	no	û	turn	zh	measure
e	net	ô	law, for	ch	church	ə	about, open
ē	be	oi	soil	ng	ring		pencil, atom
i	dip	oo	look	sh	shade		circus

laugh *verb* To smile and make sounds that express happiness, amusement, or scorn: *He laughed at the joke.*
□*noun* The act or sound of laughing.
laugh (laf) □*verb* **laughed, laughing, laughs** □*noun, plural* **laughs**

laughter *noun* The act or sound of laughing.
laugh·ter (laf′tər) □*noun*

launch¹ *verb* **1.** To set in motion, especially with force; send off: *launch a torpedo.* **2.** To put or lower into the water: *launched a battleship.* **3.** To start or begin something: *The two friends launched a new business.*
launch (lônch) □*verb* **launched, launching, launches**

launch² *noun* A partly open motorboat.
launch (lônch) □*noun, plural* **launches**

launch pad or **launching pad** *noun* The platform or base from which a spacecraft is launched.

launder *verb* To wash clothes and linens.
laun·der (lôn′dər) □*verb* **laundered, laundering, launders**

laundry *noun* **1.** A place or business where things are laundered. **2.** Clothes and linens that need to be or have been washed: *A service picks up and delivers the laundry.*
laun·dry (lôn′drē) □*noun, plural* **laundries**

laurel *noun* **1.** A shrub or tree with shiny evergreen leaves used in ancient times to make crowns of victory or achievement. **2.** The mountain laurel.
lau·rel (lôr′əl) □*noun, plural* **laurels**

lava *noun* **1.** Hot melted rock that flows from a volcano. **2.** The rock formed when lava cools and hardens.
la·va (lä′və *or* lav′ə) □*noun*

lavender *noun* **1.** A plant with small, fragrant purplish flowers that yield an oil used to make perfume. **2.** A pale or light purple.
□*adjective* Pale or light purple.
lav·en·der (lav′ən dər) □*noun* □*adjective*

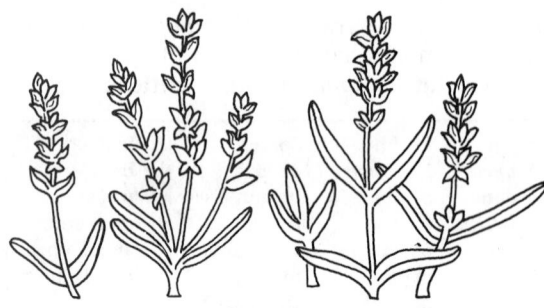

lavender

law *noun* **1.** A rule made by a country, state, city, or town for the people living there: *The legislature makes laws.* **2.** A set of laws: *obey the law.* **3.** The profession of a lawyer: *practice law.* **4.** A rule, principle, or practice: *the laws of grammar.*
law (lô) □*noun, plural* **laws**

lawful *adjective* **1.** Allowed by law: *a lawful act.* **2.** Recognized by law: *the lawful owner.*
law·ful (lô′fəl) □*adjective*

lawless *adjective* Not obeying the law: *a lawless mob.*
law·less (lô′lis) □*adjective*

lawmaker *noun* Someone who helps write or pass laws; legislator.
law·mak·er (lô′mā′kər) □*noun, plural* **lawmakers**

lawn *noun* An area of ground planted with grass that is usually mowed regularly.
lawn (lôn) □*noun, plural* **lawns**

lawnmower *noun* A machine for cutting grass.
lawn·mow·er (lôn′mō′ər) □*noun, plural* **lawnmowers**

lawsuit *noun* A complaint brought before a court of law for settlement.
law·suit (lô′sōot′) □*noun, plural* **lawsuits**

lawyer *noun* Someone who is trained and qualified to give legal advice to people and to represent them in a court of law.
law·yer (lô′yər) □*noun, plural* **lawyers**

lay¹ *verb* **1.** To put or place: *He laid the book on the table.* **2.** To put in place; install: *Workers will lay new railroad tracks.* **3.** To produce an egg: *That hen has stopped laying.*
  lay off 1. To dismiss from a job, especially temporarily. **2.** To stop bothering someone.
lay (lā) □*verb* **laid, laying, lays**

lay² *verb* The past tense of **lie¹**: *She lay on the bed and rested.*
lay (lā) □*verb*

layer *noun* A single coating or thickness of something: *a cake with three layers. We put two layers of varnish on the floor.*
lay·er (lā′ər) □*noun, plural* **layers**

lazy *adjective* Not willing to work: *an intelligent but lazy student.*
la·zy (lā′zē) □*adjective* **lazier, laziest**

lb. An abbreviation for **pound.**

lead¹ *verb* **1.** To show or guide along the way: *She led me to the kitchen.* **2.** To be first or ahead of others in: *He leads the team in home runs.* **3.** To be or form a way, route, or pas-

sage: *A narrow path led to the lake.* **4.** To direct; conduct: *The conductor led the orchestra in a symphony.* **5.** To live; experience: *She led a good life.*
□*noun* **1.** The front or most important position: *She took the lead in the race.* **2.** A clue or hint: *The police had a lead on the missing child.*
lead (lēd) □*verb* **led, leading, leads** □*noun, plural* **leads**

lead²   *noun* **1.** A soft, heavy, dull-gray metallic chemical element that is used to make pipes, fuses, and solder. **2.** A material used in pencils as the writing substance.
lead (led) □*noun, plural* **leads**

leader   *noun* Someone who leads: *a political leader; the leader in a race.*
lead·er (lē′dər) □*noun, plural* **leaders**

leaf   *noun* **1.** A thin, flat green part that grows from the stem of a plant. **2.** One of the sheets of paper forming the pages of a book, magazine, or notebook.
□*verb* **1.** To produce or put forth leaves. **2.** To turn over or glance at pages: *He leafed through a pile of letters.*
leaf (lēf) □*noun, plural* **leaves** □*verb* **leafed, leafing, leafs**

leaflet   *noun* **1.** A small leaf. **2.** A small pamphlet or booklet.
leaf·let (lēf′lit) □*noun, plural* **leaflets**

league¹   *noun* **1.** A group of nations, people, or organizations working together for a common purpose. **2.** An association of sports teams that compete mainly among themselves: *a basketball league.*
league (lēg) □*noun, plural* **leagues**

league²   *noun* An old unit of distance equal to three miles.
league (lēg) □*noun, plural* **leagues**

leak   *noun* A hole or crack that lets something pass in or out: *There is a leak in the canoe.*
□*verb* **1.** To pass or cause to pass in or out through a hole or crack: *Fumes leaked from the oil burner. The pail leaked water.* **2.** To become or allow to become known by accident or deliberately: *He leaked information about the scandal to the newspapers.*
leak (lēk) □*noun, plural* **leaks** □*verb* **leaked, leaking, leaks**

lean¹   *verb* **1.** To bend or slant away from the vertical: *She leaned her skis against the door.* **2.** To rest on for support: *He leaned on his cane as he walked.* **3.** To rely, as for help; depend: *He leans on his mother for advice.*
lean (lēn) □*verb* **leaned, leaning, leans**

lean

lean²   *adjective* **1.** Having little or no fat: *a lean body; lean meat.* **2.** Not productive or plentiful: *a lean harvest.*
lean (lēn) □*adjective* **leaner, leanest**

leap   *verb* To move with a sudden springing motion: *The cowboy leaped on his horse.*
□*noun* The act of leaping; jump.
leap (lēp) □*verb* **leaped** or **leapt, leaping, leaps** □*noun, plural* **leaps**

leapfrog   *noun* A game in which one player crouches down and the one behind leaps over him.
leap·frog (lēp′frôg′ *or* lēp′frog′) □*noun*

leapfrog

a bat	ī bite	o͞o tool	*th* feather
ā make	î fierce	ou out	th bath
â dare	o dot	u nut	hw wheat
ä father	ō no	û turn	zh measure
e net	ô law, for	ch church	ə about, open
ē be	oi soil	ng ring	pencil, atom
i dip	oo look	sh shade	circus

leapt   *verb* A past tense and past participle of **leap:** *He leapt up and ran out of the room.*
leapt (lept *or* lēpt) ▢*verb*

leap year   *noun* A year that has 366 days and occurs every fourth year. The extra day is February 29.

learn   *verb* **1.** To gain knowledge or skill through study, practice, or experience: *He learned algebra. She is learning how to dance.* **2.** To find out; discover: *Have you learned when he will arrive?* **3.** To memorize: *The actor learned the lines for the play.*
learn (lûrn) ▢*verb* **learned, learning, learns**

learned   *adjective* Having or showing knowledge: *a learned man.*
learn·ed (lûr′nid) ▢*adjective*

learning   *noun* Knowledge gained by study: *She is a woman of great learning.*
learn·ing (lûr′ning) ▢*noun*

lease   *noun* An agreement between the owner of a piece of property and the person who rents it. The lease states how much rent is to be paid and the length of time the agreement is to be in effect.
▢*verb* To rent: *He leased his land to a farmer.*
lease (lēs) ▢*noun, plural* **leases** ▢*verb* **leased, leasing, leases**

leash   *noun* A chain or strap used to hold or lead an animal: *We saw a cat on a leash.*
▢*verb* To hold or lead with a leash: *He leashed his dog.*
leash (lēsh) ▢*noun, plural* **leashes** ▢*verb* **leashed, leashing, leashes**

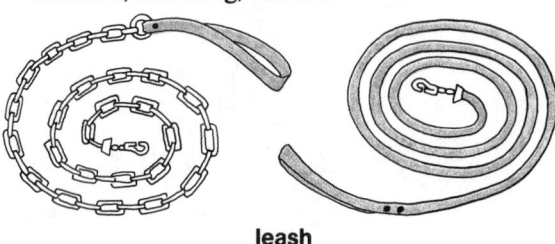

leash

least   *adjective* Smallest in amount, degree, or importance: *The least noise frightened her. What he thinks is my least worry.*
▢*adverb* To or in the smallest degree: *Of the three books, that was the least enjoyable.*
▢*noun* Something that is least, as in importance: *The least you can do is thank him.*
least (lēst) ▢*adjective* ▢*adverb* ▢*noun*

leather   *noun* A material made from animal skin or hide that has been cleaned and tanned.
leath·er (le*th*′ər) ▢*noun* **leathers**

leave¹   *verb* **1.** To go away from; depart: *He left the house without saying good-by. I leave for my vacation on Friday.* **2.** To go without taking; forget: *She left her glasses at home.* **3.** To allow to be or remain in a certain condition or place: *She left the window open.* **4.** To withdraw from; quit: *He left his job.* **5.** To give to another to do or use: *Leave the arrangements to me.* **6.** To give in a will: *He left everything he had to his son.* **7.** To have as a result: *The ink left an ugly stain on the cloth.* **8.** To remain: *Ten minus two leaves eight.*
leave (lēv) ▢*verb* **left, leaving, leaves**

leave²   *noun* **1.** Permission: *She asked for leave to be late.* **2.** Permission to be absent from duty: *The army canceled all leaves.*
leave (lēv) ▢*noun, plural* **leaves**

leaves   *noun* The plural of **leaf.**
leaves (lēvz) ▢*noun*

lecture   *noun* **1.** A speech or talk given to an audience: *The composer gave a lecture on his music.* **2.** A warning or scolding: *My mother gave me a lecture for my part in the prank.*
▢*verb* **1.** To give a lecture: *He lectured on literature at the college.* **2.** To warn or scold at length: *She lectured me about my manners.*
lec·ture (lek′chər) ▢*noun, plural* **lectures** ▢*verb* **lectured, lecturing, lectures**

led   *verb* The past tense and past participle of **lead¹:** *He led the child to safety. She has led the chorus for two years.*
led (led) ▢*verb*

ledge   *noun* **1.** A flat space like a shelf in the side of a cliff or rock wall. **2.** A narrow shelf that juts out from a wall: *a window ledge.*
ledge (lej) ▢*noun, plural* **ledges**

leech   *noun* A worm that lives in water and sucks blood from other animals.
leech (lēch) ▢*noun, plural* **leeches**

leek   *noun* A vegetable that is related to the onion and has long, dark-green leaves and a narrow white bulb.
leek (lēk) ▢*noun, plural* **leeks**

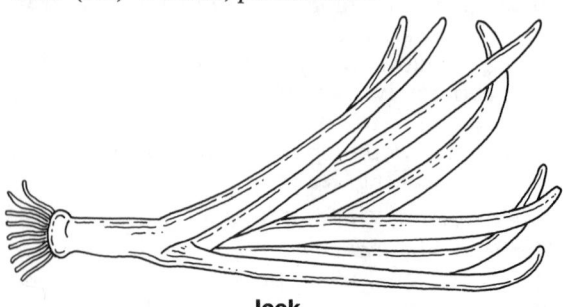

leek

left¹ *noun* The side from which one begins to read a line of English: *You will see a house on the left.*
□*adjective* **1.** Located on the left: *his left eye.* **2.** Directed to the left: *a left turn.*
□*adverb* On or to the left: *The bus turned left.*
left (left) □*noun, plural* **lefts** □*adjective* □*adverb*

left² *verb* The past tense and past participle of **leave¹**: *We left the city early. She had left the lights on.*
left (left) □*verb*

left-hand *adjective* **1.** Located on the left. **2.** Of or for the left hand; left-handed.
left-hand (**left′**hand′) □*adjective*

left-handed *adjective* **1.** Using the left hand more easily and naturally than the right hand. **2.** Done with the left hand: *a left-handed pitch of the ball.*
left-hand·ed (**left′**han′did) □*adjective*

leftover *noun* Something that has not been used or eaten and is left: *I made lunch from yesterday's leftovers.*
left·o·ver (**left′**ō′vər) □*noun, plural* **leftovers**

leg *noun* **1.** One of the parts of the body that a human being or animal uses in standing or moving about. **2.** A part that resembles a leg: *the leg of a chair.*
leg (leg) □*noun, plural* **legs**

legal *adjective* **1.** Of law or lawyers: *legal problems.* **2.** Permitted by law: *legal rights.*
le·gal (**lē′**gəl) □*adjective*

legend *noun* A story that has been handed down from earlier times and is believed by many people, but that may not be true.
leg·end (**lej′**ənd) □*noun, plural* **legends**

WORD HISTORY: legend

Legend comes from a Latin word meaning "something to be read." In the Middle Ages the word *legend* was used of the story of a saint's life or of a collection of such stories.

---

legendary *adjective* Of, based on, or like a legend: *legendary heroes.*
leg·en·dar·y (**lej′**ən der′ē) □*adjective*

leggings *plural noun* Leg coverings usually made of cloth or leather.
leg·gings (**leg′**ingz) □*plural noun*

legible *adjective* Capable of being read: *Her messy handwriting is not legible.*
leg·i·ble (**lej′**ə bəl) □*adjective*

legion *noun* **1.** A unit of the ancient Roman army consisting of at least 3,000 foot soldiers. **2.** A large group of soldiers; army.
le·gion (**lē′**jən) □*noun, plural* **legions**

legislate *verb* To make or pass laws.
leg·is·late (**lej′**i slāt′) □*verb* **legislated, legislating, legislates**

legislation *noun* **1.** The act of making or passing laws: *Legislation is the main concern of Congress.* **2.** The laws that are made: *new legislation to lower taxes.*
leg·is·la·tion (lej′i **slā′**shən) □*noun*

legislative *adjective* **1.** Of or having to do with making or passing laws: *a legislative committee.* **2.** Having power to make or pass laws: *Congress is a legislative body.*
leg·is·la·tive (**lej′**i slā′tiv) □*adjective*

legislator *noun* A member of a legislature.
leg·is·la·tor (**lej′**i slā′tər) □*noun, plural* **legislators**

legislature *noun* A group of persons with power to make and pass laws.
leg·is·la·ture (**lej′**i slā′chər) □*noun, plural* **legislatures**

legitimate *adjective* **1.** Being or acting in agreement with the law: *the legitimate owner of the business.* **2.** Reasonable; fair: *She didn't have a legitimate reason for being late.*
le·git·i·mate (lə **jit′**ə mit) □*adjective*

lei *noun* A wreath of flowers worn around the neck, especially in Hawaii.
lei (lā) □*noun, plural* **leis**

lei

a	bat	ī	bite	o͞o	tool	*th*	feather
ā	make	î	fierce	ou	out	th	bath
â	dare	o	dot	u	nut	hw	wheat
ä	father	ō	no	û	turn	zh	measure
e	net	ô	law, for	ch	church	ə	about, open
ē	be	oi	soil	ng	ring		pencil, atom
i	dip	o͝o	look	sh	shade		circus

leisure *noun* Free time in which to do what one wants or likes: *He spends his leisure listening to music.*
lei·sure (lē′zhər) ☐*noun*

lemon *noun* **1.** A juicy yellow fruit that has a sour taste. **2.** A bright, clear yellow. ☐*adjective* Bright, clear yellow.
lem·on (lem′ən) ☐*noun, plural* **lemons** ☐*adjective*

lemonade *noun* A drink made of lemon juice, water, and sugar.
lem·on·ade (lem′ə nād′) ☐*noun, plural* **lemonades**

lend *verb* **1.** To let someone use something for a period of time: *The teacher lent me a book.* **2.** To give someone money that is to be returned after an agreed period of time, usually with interest. **3.** To give; add: *Flowers lent beauty to the room.*
lend (lend) ☐*verb* **lent, lending, lends**

length *noun* **1.** Distance from one end to the other: *the length of the car.* **2.** A piece cut from a larger piece: *a length of cloth.* **3.** The amount of time something lasts: *the length of the meeting.*
length (lengkth *or* length) ☐*noun, plural* **lengths**

lengthen *verb* To make or become longer: *She lengthened her skirt. The shadows lengthened at sunset.*
length·en (lengk′thən *or* leng′thən) ☐*verb* **lengthened, lengthening, lengthens**

lengthwise *adverb* and *adjective* Along the direction of the length: *Cut the paper lengthwise. The curtains have lengthwise stripes.*
length·wise (lengkth′wīz′ *or* length′wīz′) ☐*adverb* and *adjective*

lengthy *adjective* Long: *a lengthy book.*
length·y (lengk′thē *or* leng′thē) ☐*adjective* **lengthier, lengthiest**

lens *noun* **1.** A piece of glass or other clear material that has been shaped to cause light rays that pass through it to meet or to spread out. **2.** A clear part of the eye behind the iris that focuses light onto the retina.
lens (lenz) ☐*noun, plural* **lenses**

lent *verb* The past tense and past participle of **lend:** *She lent him some money. He had lent the car to his sister.*
lent (lent) ☐*verb*

Lent *noun* A period of 40 weekdays before Easter marked by fasting and sorrow for sins.
Lent (lent) ☐*noun*

leopard *noun* A large wild cat of Africa and Asia with a yellowish coat with black spots.
leop·ard (lep′ərd) ☐*noun, plural* **leopards**

> **WORD HISTORY: leopard**
>
> The word *leopard* comes from two Greek words, one meaning "lion" and the other meaning "panther." In ancient times the leopard was thought to be a cross between a lion and a panther.

leopard

leotard *noun* Often **leotards** A one-piece garment that fits tightly on the body. Dancers and gymnasts wear leotards.
le·o·tard (lē′ə tärd′) ☐*noun, plural* **leotards**

less *adjective* **1.** Not as great in amount: *She has less time than ever.* **2.** Fewer: *Less than five years had passed.* ☐*adverb* To a smaller extent or degree: *She was less angry.* ☐*preposition* Minus; subtracting: *Ten less 1 is 9.* ☐*noun* A smaller amount or part: *She ate less than I did.*
less (les) ☐*adjective* ☐*adverb* ☐*preposition* ☐*noun*

–less A suffix that forms adjectives and means "without; free of": *motherless; nameless; childless.*

lessen *verb* To make or become less: *He took aspirin to lessen the pain. His hunger lessened as he ate.*
less·en (les′ən) ☐*verb* **lessened, lessening, lessens**

lesser *adjective* Smaller in size or importance: *a lesser writer.*
less·er (les′ər) ☐*adjective*

lesson *noun* **1.** Something learned or to be learned: *She did her geography lesson.* **2.** A period of time for teaching or learning; class: *He has a dancing lesson every week.*
les·son (les′ən) ☐*noun, plural* **lessons**

lest *conjunction* For fear that: *Drive carefully lest you have an accident.*
lest (lest) □*conjunction*

let *verb* **1.** To permit or allow to: *She wouldn't let him go.* **2.** To cause to; make: *Let me know what your plans are.* **3.** To permit to enter, pass, or go: *Let me through. He let the air out of the tire.* **4.** To rent or lease: *She lets rooms to students.* —See Synonyms at **permit.**
   let down 1. To slow down; ease up: *She worked without ever letting down.* **2.** To disappoint: *His friend let him down by forgetting their appointment.*
   let up To become slower or less strong: *By morning the snow had let up a little.*
let (let) □*verb* **let, letting, lets**

let's Contraction of "let us."
let's (lets)

letter *noun* **1.** A written or printed mark that stands for a speech sound and is one of the signs of the alphabet. **2.** A written message that is usually sent by mail in an envelope: *He wrote a letter to his family.*
let·ter (let′ər) □*noun, plural* **letters**

lettuce *noun* Any of several plants with light-green leaves that are eaten as salad.
let·tuce (let′is) □*noun*

WORD HISTORY: **lettuce**

The word *lettuce* comes from Latin. The Latin word for the plant comes from the word for "milk" because many kinds of lettuce have a milky juice.

---

level *adjective* **1.** Having a smooth, even surface: *a level road.* **2.** Being at the same height or position; even: *The top of her head is level with his chin.*
□*noun* **1.** A particular height: *We arranged the books at eye level.* **2.** A level surface. **3.** A device or tool used to show whether or not a surface is level.
□*verb* To make or become flat: *They leveled the field and built a swimming pool.*
lev·el (lev′əl) □*adjective* □*noun, plural* **levels** □*verb* **leveled, leveling, levels**

SYNONYMS: **level, flat**

These adjectives mean having a smooth, even surface: *Not one floor in the old house is perfectly level. The house stood in the flat landscape of the river valley.*

---

lever *noun* **1.** A strong, stiff bar that rests on a fulcrum and is used to lift heavy things. **2.** A handle that juts out and is used to control or operate a machine.
lev·er (lev′ər *or* lē′vər) □*noun, plural* **levers**

levy *verb* To impose or collect by authority: *The government levied a tax on cigarettes.*
lev·y (lev′ē) □*verb* **levied, levying, levies**

lg. or **lge.** An abbreviation for **large.**

liable *adjective* **1.** Responsible under the law: *He is liable for any damage he does.* **2.** Likely: *She is liable to fall if she's not careful.*
li·a·ble (lī′ə bəl) □*adjective*

liar *noun* Someone who tells lies.
li·ar (lī′ər) □*noun, plural* **liars**

liberal *adjective* **1.** Giving freely; generous: *a man who is liberal with his money.* **2.** Generous in amount; ample: *a liberal reward.* **3.** Having respect for different people and different ideas; tolerant. **4.** Wanting or supporting political reform and social progress.
□*noun* Someone who has liberal political or social opinions.
lib·er·al (lib′ər əl) □*adjective* □*noun, plural* **liberals**

liberate *verb* To set free: *Abraham Lincoln liberated the slaves.*
lib·er·ate (lib′ə rāt′) □*verb* **liberated, liberating, liberates**

liberty *noun* Freedom from the control or rule of another: *The American colonies fought Great Britain for their liberty.*
lib·er·ty (lib′ər tē) □*noun*

SYNONYMS: **liberty, freedom, independence**

These nouns mean the condition of not being under the control or rule of another: *The dog broke its leash and wandered around the neighborhood at liberty. Abraham Lincoln gave the slaves their freedom. She moved out of her parents' house after college because she wanted her independence.*

---

librarian *noun* Someone who works in or is in charge of a library.

a	bat	ī	bite	oo	tool	*th*	feather
ā	make	î	fierce	ou	out	th	bath
â	dare	o	dot	u	nut	hw	wheat
ä	father	ō	no	û	turn	zh	measure
e	net	ô	law, for	ch	church	ə	about, open
ē	be	oi	soil	ng	ring		pencil, atom
i	dip	oo	look	sh	shade		circus

li·brar·i·an (lī brâr′ē ən) □*noun, plural* **librarians**

library *noun* **1.** A large, permanent collection of books, magazines, films, or records. **2.** A room or building where a library is kept.
li·brar·y (lī′brer′ē) □*noun, plural* **libraries**

lice *noun* The plural of **louse**.
lice (līs) □*noun*

license *noun* **1.** Legal permission to do something: *He has a license to teach.* **2.** A document showing that legal permission has been given: *a driver's license.*
□*verb* To grant a license to or for: *Is he licensed to practice medicine?*
li·cense (lī′səns) □*noun, plural* **licenses**
□*verb* **licensed, licensing, licenses**

lichen *noun* A small plant that has no flowers and often forms a covering on rocks and tree trunks.
li·chen (lī′kən) □*noun, plural* **lichens**

lichen

lick *verb* **1.** To pass the tongue over: *He licked his lips.* **2.** To move or flicker like a tongue: *The flames licked around the logs.* **3.** To defeat; overcome: *He licked his problem.*
□*noun* **1.** A movement of the tongue over something: *She gave the envelope a lick and sealed it.* **2.** A natural deposit of salt that is licked by animals.
lick (lik) □*verb* **licked, licking, licks**
□*noun, plural* **licks**

licorice *noun* **1.** A flavoring with a blackish color and a sweet, strong taste. It is made from the root of a plant related to peas and clover. **2.** Candy flavored with licorice.
lic·o·rice (lik′ə ris *or* lik′ər ish) □*noun*

lid *noun* **1.** A cover for a container; top: *the lid of a pot; the lid on a box.* **2.** An eyelid.
lid (lid) □*noun, plural* **lids**

lie[1] *verb* **1.** To be in or take a flat or resting position: *She likes to lie in front of the fire.* **2.** To rest or be on a horizontal surface: *The magazine is lying on the table.* **3.** To be located: *Vast prairies lie west of the river.* **4.** To remain in a certain condition or position: *She let her hair lie loose.* **5.** To be; exist: *The solution to the mystery lies in these clues.*
lie (lī) □*verb* **lay, lain, lying, lies**

lie[2] *noun* An untrue statement made by someone who knows that it is untrue.
□*verb* To tell a lie.
lie (lī) □*noun, plural* **lies** □*verb* **lied, lying, lies**

lieutenant *noun* **1.** An officer in the Army, Air Force, or Marine Corps ranking below a captain. A **first lieutenant** ranks above a **second lieutenant**. **2.** An officer in the Navy ranking above an ensign and below a lieutenant commander. **3.** An officer in a police or fire department ranking below a captain.
lieu·ten·ant (loo ten′ənt) □*noun, plural* **lieutenants**

WORD HISTORY: **lieutenant**

Lieutenant comes from two French words that mean "holding the place." A lieutenant was originally a person who took the place of another. The word was used especially for a military officer who was acting for his superior.

---

life *noun* **1.** The property or quality that distinguishes people, plants, and animals from rocks, metals, and other objects that cannot grow and reproduce. **2.** The period of time between birth and death; lifetime: *He stayed there all of his life.* **3.** The period during which something is useful, working, or in existence: *the life of a washing machine.* **4.** Living things in general: *plant life; marine life.* **5.** A living being: *Hundreds of lives were lost in the battle.* **6.** A way of living: *an exciting life; a sailor's life.* **7.** The story of someone's life; biography: *a life of George Washington.*
life (līf) □*noun, plural* **lives**

lifeboat An open boat carried on a large ship for use if the ship must be abandoned.
life·boat (līf′bōt′) □*noun, plural* **lifeboats**

lifeguard *noun* Someone whose job it is to look out for the safety of swimmers.
life·guard (līf′gärd′) □*noun, plural* **lifeguards**

lifeless *adjective* **1.** No longer alive; dead. **2.** Without living things: *a lifeless desert.*
life·less (līf′lis) □*adjective*

lifelike *adjective* Resembling a living person or thing; closely imitating life: *a lifelike statue.*
life·like (līf′līk′) □*adjective*

lifelong *adjective* Lasting over a lifetime: *a lifelong friend; a lifelong ambition.*
life·long (līf′lông′) □*adjective*

life preserver *noun* A ring, jacket, belt, or other device that keeps a person from sinking in water. It is filled with air or made of cork or other material that floats.

life preserver
Two kinds of life preservers

lifetime *noun* The period of time during which someone or something remains alive, exists, or functions: *He spent most of his lifetime working on the farm. What is the lifetime of an automobile?*
life·time (līf′tīm′) □*noun, plural* **lifetimes**

lift *verb* **1.** To raise into the air from a resting position: *She lifted the fork to her mouth.* **2.** To move or direct upward: *She lifted her eyes to the sky.* **3.** To rise and disappear: *The fog lifted at noon.* —See Synonyms at **raise.**
    lift off To begin flight, as a rocket.
□*noun* **1.** The act of lifting or being lifted: *I need a lift to get up into the truck.* **2.** A short ride in a car or other vehicle: *She gave me a lift home from the school.* **3.** A rise in spirits.
lift (lift) □*verb* **lifted, lifting, lifts** □*noun, plural* **lifts**

liftoff *noun* The takeoff of a rocket or spacecraft from the launching pad.
lift·off (lift′ôf′) □*noun, plural* **liftoffs**

light¹ *noun* **1.** A form of energy that makes it possible for human beings to see: *the light of the full moon.* **2.** Something that gives off light, as an electric lamp, a candle, or a star. **3.** A means of setting something on fire: *a light for the bonfire.* **4.** A way of thinking about something: *Those facts put the situation in a different light.* **5.** Open knowledge: *New facts about the robbery have come to light.*
□*adjective* **1.** Bright; not dark: *a light basement. It gets light early in the morning in summer.* **2.** Pale in color: *light blue; light skin.*
□*verb* **1.** To begin or cause to burn: *The candle won't light. He lighted the bonfire.* **2.** To cause to give off light: *She lit the lamp.* **3.** To provide with light: *The dining room was lit only with candles.* **4.** To guide or show with a light: *Take a flashlight to light your way.* **5.** To make lively: *A smile lighted his face.*
light (līt) □*noun, plural* **lights** □*adjective* **lighter, lightest** □*verb* **lighted** or **lit, lighting, lights**

light² *adjective* **1.** Having little weight; not heavy: *a light handbag.* **2.** Small in amount, force, or intensity: *a light meal; a light wind; a light tap.* **3.** Not serious; entertaining: *a light opera.* **4.** Moving easily and gracefully: *light on one's feet.* **5.** Easy to do or to deal with: *light chores.*
□*verb* **1.** To come to rest; land: *The bird lit on its perch.* **2.** To get down; alight: *Six soldiers lighted from the truck.*
light (līt) □*adjective* **lighter, lightest** □*verb* **lighted** or **lit, lighting, lights**

lighten¹ *verb* To make or become brighter or less dark: *Adding bleach to laundry lightens it.*
light·en (līt′ən) □*verb* **lightened, lightening, lightens**

lighten² *verb* **1.** To reduce the weight or burden of: *He lightened the load of furniture by leaving the piano behind. A vacuum cleaner lightens housework.* **2.** To make happier; to cheer: *The fine day lightened our spirits.*
light·en (līt′ən) □*verb* **lightened, lightening, lightens**

lighthearted *adjective* Carefree and gay: *a lighthearted melody.*
light·heart·ed (līt′här′tid) □*adjective*

lighthouse *noun* A tower with a powerful light at the top for guiding ships.
light·house (līt′hous′) □*noun, plural* **lighthouses**

lightning *noun* A flash of light that appears in the sky from natural causes and is a form of

a bat	ī bite	ōō tool	*th* feather
ā make	î fierce	ou out	th bath
â dare	o dot	u nut	hw wheat
ä father	ō no	û turn	zh measure
e net	ô law, for	ch church	ə about, open
ē be	oi soil	ng ring	pencil, atom
i dip	oo look	sh shade	circus

electricity.

light·ning (līt′ning) ▢*noun*

like[1]   *verb* To be fond of: *She likes her teacher a lot. I like music.*

▢*noun* Something a person enjoys or favors: *I know his likes and dislikes.*

like (līk) ▢*verb* **liked, liking, likes** ▢*noun, plural* **likes**

like[2]   *preposition* **1.** Similar to. **2.** In character with; typical of: *It's not like her to tell a lie.* **3.** In the same manner as: *He acts like a clown.* **4.** Such as: *sports like football, baseball, and basketball.* **5.** In the mood for: *I feel like going for a walk.* **6.** As if something is happening or will happen: *It looks like snow.*

▢*adjective* Exactly or nearly the same: *She gave a dollar to me and a like sum to my brother.*

▢*noun* The equal of a person, animal, or thing: *I have never seen his like before!*

like (līk) ▢*preposition* ▢*adjective* ▢*noun*

–like   *noun* A suffix that forms adjectives and means "similar to; having the nature of": *birdlike; lifelike.*

likelihood   *noun* The chance of something happening: *a likelihood of rain tomorrow.*

like·li·hood (līk′lē hood′) ▢*noun, plural* **likelihoods**

likely   *adjective* **1.** Having or showing a good chance of happening: *I think it's likely to snow.* **2.** Seeming to be true: *a likely explanation.* **3.** Suitable: *a likely day for the race.* —See Synonyms at **possible.**

▢*adverb* Probably: *He will most likely come back tonight.*

like·ly (līk′lē) ▢*adjective* **likelier, likeliest** ▢*adverb*

likeness   *adverb* **1.** Similarity or resemblance: *the likeness between the boy and his father.* **2.** A copy or picture: *The artist painted a perfect likeness of my grandfather.*

like·ness (līk′nis) ▢*noun, plural* **likenesses**

likewise   *adverb* In the same way; similarly: *He jumped into the lake and I did likewise.*

like·wise (līk′wīz′) ▢*adverb*

liking   *noun* Preference or a special feeling: *I have a liking for adventure stories.*

lik·ing (lī′king) ▢*noun, plural* **likings**

lilac   *noun* **1.** A garden shrub with clusters of fragrant purple or white flowers. **2.** A pale purple color.

▢*adjective* Pale purple.

li·lac (lī′lək) ▢*noun, plural* **lilacs** ▢*adjective*

lily   *noun* A plant with white or brightly colored flowers shaped like trumpets.

lil·y (lil′ē) ▢*noun, plural* **lilies**

lily of the valley   *noun* A plant with small, fragrant white flowers shaped like bells. The flowers grow in a row along a stalk.

lily of the valley ▢*noun, plural* **lilies of the valley**

lily of the valley

lima bean   *noun* A large light-green bean that is eaten as a vegetable.

li·ma bean (lī′mə) ▢*noun*

limb   *noun* **1.** A leg, arm, wing, or flipper. **2.** One of the larger branches of a tree.

limb (lim) ▢*noun, plural* **limbs**

limber   *adjective* Bending or moving easily: *limber muscles; a limber runner.*

▢*verb* To make or become limber: *You should do exercises to limber up before jogging.*

lim·ber (lim′bər) ▢*adjective* ▢*verb* **limbered, limbering, limbers**

lime[1]   *noun* A juicy green fruit with a sour taste, related to lemons and oranges.

lime (līm) ▢*noun, plural* **limes**

lime[2]   *noun* A white powder made up of calcium and oxygen and used in making steel, glass, and cement.

lime (līm) ▢*noun*

limerick   *noun* A humorous poem having five lines. The first and second lines rhyme with the last line. The third and fourth lines are shorter and rhyme with each other.

lim·er·ick (lim′ər ik) ▢*noun, plural* **limericks**

limestone   *noun* A rock used for building and in making lime and cement.

lime·stone (līm′stōn′) ▢*noun*

limit   *noun* **1.** A point or line beyond which one cannot go: *the limit of the view from the*

tower; a limit to my ability. **2.** Often **limits** The boundary around a certain area: *within the city limits.* **3.** The greatest amount or number allowed or possible: *a limit of one to a customer.*
▢*verb* To place a limit on; confine: *I'm limiting myself to one comic book a week.*
lim·it (**lim′**it) ▢*noun, plural* **limits** ▢*verb* **limited, limiting, limits**

limp¹ *verb* To walk with an uneven or awkward movement by placing the body's weight mostly on one leg.
▢*noun* An uneven or awkward way of walking: *My dog has a limp.*
limp (limp) ▢*verb* **limped, limping, limps**

limp² *adjective* Not firm or stiff; drooping: *a dog with limp, floppy ears.*
limp (limp) ▢*adjective* **limper, limpest**

limp

line¹ *noun* **1.** A long, thin mark that can be made by a writing instrument or a tool. **2.** A border or boundary: *the line between the neighbor's lawn and ours.* **3.** A group of people or things in a row: *a line at the ticket window; a line of old bottles on a shelf.* **4.** A row of words on a page or in a column. **5. lines** The words said by an actor in a play. **6.** A wrinkle or crease on the skin. **7.** A rope, string, cord, or wire with a special use: *a fishing line; a telephone line.* **8.** A route in a system of transportation: *a subway line.* **9.** A kind of goods having several styles and sizes: *a new line of blue jeans.* **10.** A person's job or ability: *Banking is his line of work.* **11.** A short letter: *I received a line from my sister.*
▢*verb* **1.** To mark with lines. **2.** To form a line along: *People lined the parade route.*
   line up To arrange in or form a line: *line up the books on the shelf; line up to get on the bus.*
line (līn) ▢*noun, plural* **lines** ▢*verb* **lined, lining, lines**

line² *verb* **1.** To cover the inside of something: *lined the crate with newspaper.* **2.** To

serve as a lining of: *Books lined the walls.*
line (līn) ▢*verb* **lined, lining, lines**

linear *adjective* **1.** Of or using a line: *a linear diagram.* **2.** Of length: *An inch is a linear measurement.*
lin·e·ar (**lin′**ē ər) ▢*adjective*

linen *noun* **1.** A strong cloth made from flax fibers. **2.** Often **linens** Items such as tablecloths, sheets, and napkins make of linen or other cloth.
lin·en (**lin′**ən) ▢*noun, plural* **linens**

liner *noun* A ship or airplane that carries passengers on a regular route.
lin·er (**lī′**nər) ▢*noun, plural* **liners**

linger *verb* To stay on as if not willing to leave: *lingering in the playground after school.*
lin·ger (**ling′**gər) ▢*verb* **lingered, lingering, lingers**

lining *noun* A layer of material used on the inside surface of something: *the lining of a wool skirt.*
lin·ing (**lī′**ning) ▢*noun, plural* **linings**

link *noun* **1.** A ring or loop that is part of a chain. **2.** Something that joins or connects: *The bridge is a link between the islands.*
▢*verb* To join or connect: *link railroad cars.*
—See Synonyms at **join.**
link (lingk) ▢*noun, plural* **links** ▢*verb* **linked, linking, links**

linking verb *noun* A verb that does not express an action but functions only to connect the subject of a sentence and a word or phrase that tells something about the subject. In the sentences "She was very happy," "He became angry," and "I feel sleepy," the verbs "was," "became," and "feel" are linking verbs.
link·ing verb (**ling′**king) ▢*noun*

linoleum *noun* A covering for floors that is made by pressing a mixture of ground cork and hot linseed oil onto a cloth backing.
li·no·le·um (li **nō′**lē əm) ▢*noun, plural* **linoleums**

linseed oil *noun* A yellowish oil from the seeds of the flax plant. Linseed oil is used in paints and varnishes.
lin·seed oil (**lin′**sēd′) ▢*noun*

a	bat	ī	bite	o͞o	tool	*th*	feather
ā	make	î	fierce	ou	out	th	bath
â	dare	o	dot	u	nut	hw	wheat
ä	father	ō	no	û	turn	zh	measure
e	net	ô	law, for	ch	church	ə	about, open
ē	be	oi	soil	ng	ring		pencil, atom
i	dip	oo	look	sh	shade		circus

lint　*noun* Bits of fiber and fluff from yarn or cloth.
lint (lint) □*noun*

lintel　*noun* A beam across the top of a door or window to hold up the structure above it.
lin·tel (lĭn′təl) □*noun, plural* **lintels**

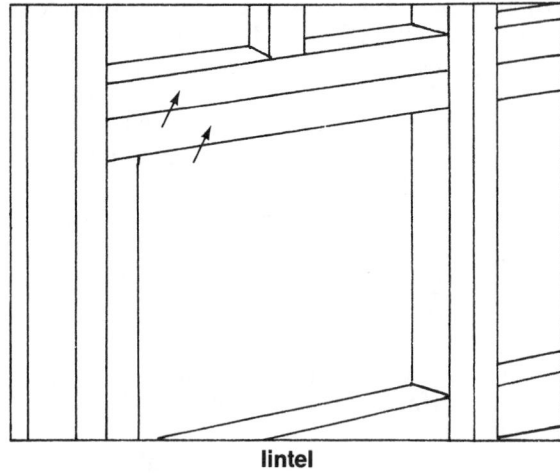

lintel

lion　*noun* A large, powerful animal of the cat family of Africa and India. Lions have a smooth, light-brown coat. Males have a shaggy mane.
li·on (lī′ən) □*noun, plural* **lions**

lioness　*noun* A female lion.
li·on·ess (lī′ə nĭs) □*noun, plural* **lionesses**

lip　*noun* **1.** One of the two muscular folds of tissue that form the outside edge of the mouth. **2.** The rim or edge of a container: *the lip of a cup.*
lip (lĭp) □*noun, plural* **lips**

lipstick　*noun* A stick of waxlike material that is used to color the lips.
lip·stick (lĭp′stĭk′) □*noun, plural* **lipsticks**

liquid　*noun* A form of matter that is not a gas or a solid. A liquid flows readily and takes the shape of its container, but will not necessarily fill it. Water and milk are liquids.
□*adjective* In the state of a liquid: *liquid fuel.*
liq·uid (lĭk′wĭd) □*noun, plural* **liquids**
□*adjective*

liquor　*noun* An alcoholic beverage such as whiskey.
liq·uor (lĭk′ər) □*noun, plural* **liquors**

lisp　*noun* A speech problem in which the sounds *s* and *z* are pronounced *th.*
□*verb* To speak with a lisp.
lisp (lĭsp) □*noun, plural* **lisps** □*verb* **lisped, lisping, lisps**

list¹　*noun* A series of names of people or things: *a list of members; a shopping list.*
□*verb* **1.** To make a list of: *She listed the groceries she needed.* **2.** To include in a list: *He is not listed in the phone book.*
list (lĭst) □*noun, plural* **lists** □*verb* **listed, listing, lists**

list²　*noun* A tilt to one side.
□*verb* To tilt to one side: *The ship listed dangerously.*
list (lĭst) □*noun, plural* **lists** □*verb* **listed, listing, lists**

listen　*verb* To pay attention in order to hear something: *They listened closely. I love to listen to music.*
lis·ten (lĭs′ən) □*verb* **listened, listening, listens**

lit¹　*verb* A past tense and a past participle of **light¹**: *The bonfire lit easily.*
lit (lĭt) □*verb*

lit²　*verb* A past tense and past participle of **light²**: *The bird lit on the branch.*
lit (lĭt) □*verb*

liter　*noun* A unit of liquid measure in the metric system that is equal to about 1.056 liquid quarts.
li·ter (lē′tər) □*noun, plural* **liters**

literal　*adjective* **1.** Matching word for word: *a literal translation of her message from Spanish into French.* **2.** Corresponding to fact: *She gave us a literal account of the accident.*
lit·er·al (lĭt′ər əl) □*adjective*

literature　*noun* **1.** A body of writing that has lasting value. Literature includes plays, poetry, and stories. **2.** Printed material of any kind: *campaign literature.*
lit·er·a·ture (lĭt′ər ə chər) □*noun*

litmus　*noun* A paper treated with a dye that changes from blue to red in an acid solution and from red to blue in a base solution.
lit·mus (lĭt′məs) □*noun*

litter　*noun* **1.** A couch on poles on which a person is carried. **2.** A stretcher for carrying sick or wounded people. **3.** Young animals born at one time: *a litter of kittens.* **4.** Scraps of paper and other trash left lying around.
□*verb* To make a place messy by leaving litter around: *Please don't litter the streets.*
lit·ter (lĭt′ər) □*noun, plural* **litters** □*verb* **littered, littering, litters**

little　*adjective* **1.** Small in size or quantity. **2.** Young: *The little child didn't cry.* **3.** Short in time or distance; brief: *Walk down the hill a*

little way. **4.** Unimportant: *a little problem.*
□*adverb* Not much: *She exercises very little.*
□*noun* **1.** A small amount: *She gave me a little of her cake.* **2.** A short time or distance: *It's a little before noon. Move back a little.*
lit·tle (**lit′** əl) □*adjective* **littler, littlest** or **least** □*adverb* **less, least** □*noun*

live¹   *verb* **1.** To have life: *People cannot live without air.* **2.** To continue to stay alive: *He has lived for almost a century.* **3.** To support oneself: *He lives comfortably on his salary.* **4.** To dwell: *She lives in Maine.* **5.** To use as food: *Tigers live on meat.*
live (liv) □*verb* **lived, living, lives**

live²   *adjective* **1.** Having life; alive: *a live snake.* **2.** Glowing or burning: *live coals.* **3.** Carrying electric current: *live wires.* **4.** Broadcast while actually being performed: *a live program from London.*
live (līv) □*adjective*

livelihood   *noun* The means by which a person earns a living: *He fixes cars for a livelihood.*
live·li·hood (līv′lē hood′) □*noun, plural* **livelihoods**

lively   *adjective* Full of life; energetic: *a lively bear cub; a lively piece of music.*
live·ly (līv′lē) □*adjective* **livelier, liveliest**

liver   *noun* **1.** A large organ in the abdomen of people and animals that makes bile and helps the body process food. **2.** The liver of an animal used as food.
liv·er (liv′ər) □*noun, plural* **livers**

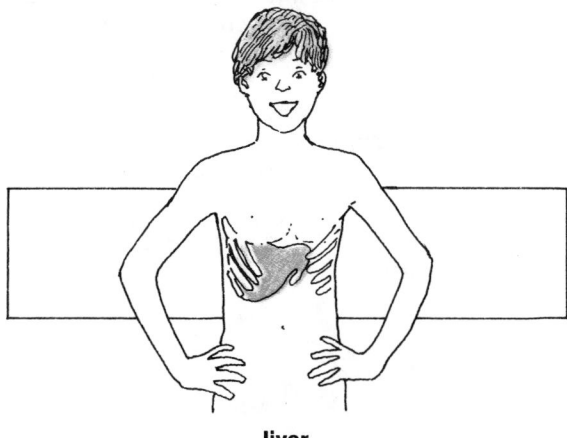
liver

livery   *noun* **1.** A uniform worn by male servants. **2.** The care and shelter of horses for money.
liv·er·y (liv′ə rē) □*noun, plural* **liveries**

livery

lives   *noun* The plural of **life**.
lives (līvz) □*noun*

livestock   *noun* Animals raised on a farm, such as cows, horses, and pigs.
live·stock (līv′stok′) □*noun*

livid   *adjective* **1.** Changed in color because of a bruise. **2.** Very pale or white, as from strong feeling: *livid with anger.*
liv·id (liv′id) □*adjective*

living   *adjective* **1.** Having life; alive: *living plants; living relatives.* **2.** In present use: *a living language.* **3.** Of or for life: *Living conditions have improved here since the war.*
□*noun* **1.** The condition of being alive. **2.** A manner or style of life: *city living.* **3.** A livelihood: *He earns his living as a jockey.*
liv·ing (liv′ing) □*adjective* □*noun, plural* **livings**

living room   *noun* A room in a home for general use.

lizard   *noun* An animal that has a scaly body, four legs, and a long tail. There are many kinds of lizards, most of which live in warm climates.
liz·ard (liz′ərd) □*noun, plural* **lizards**

llama   *noun* A South American animal with a soft coat, used for carrying loads. The llama is

a bat	ī bite	ōō tool	*th* feather
ā make	î fierce	ou out	th bath
â dare	o dot	u nut	hw wheat
ä father	ō no	û turn	zh measure
e net	ô law, for	ch church	ə about, open
ē be	oi soil	ng ring	pencil, atom
i dip	oo look	sh shade	circus

related to the camel and the alpaca.
lla·ma (lä′mə) ▢*noun, plural* **llamas** or
llama

llama

load *noun* **1.** Something that is carried: *He brought a load of firewood.* **2.** Something that troubles or weighs down: *a load of sadness.* **3.** Often **loads** A great number or amount: *loads of excitement.*
▢*verb* **1.** To put something to be carried in or on: *load cargo onto a ship.* **2.** To put needed materials into a machine: *load a pistol; load film into a camera.*
load (lōd) ▢*noun, plural* **loads** ▢*verb* **loaded, loading, loads**

loaf[1] *noun* **1.** Bread baked in one piece. **2.** Food shaped like a loaf: *a salmon loaf.*
loaf (lōf) ▢*noun, plural* **loaves**

loaf[2] *verb* To spend time in a lazy manner or without purpose: *I loafed all summer.*
loaf (lōf) ▢*verb* **loafed, loafing, loafs**

loafer *noun* Someone who loafs.
loaf·er (lō′fər) ▢*noun, plural* **loafers**

loan *noun* **1.** The act of lending: *the loan of a book.* **2.** Something borrowed: *I got a loan of a hundred dollars at the bank.*
▢*verb* To lend: *He loaned me a dollar.*
loan (lōn) ▢*noun, plural* **loans** ▢*verb* **loaned, loaning, loans**

loaves *noun* The plural of **loaf.**
loaves (lōvz) ▢*noun*

lobby *noun* **1.** A hall or waiting room in a hotel, apartment house, or theater. **2.** A group of people who try to influence lawmakers.
▢*verb* To try to influence lawmakers.
lob·by (lob′ē) ▢*noun, plural* **lobbies** ▢*verb* **lobbied, lobbying, lobbies**

lobster *noun* A sea animal that has a long body covered with a hard shell. The two front legs have large, heavy claws. Lobsters are often eaten as food.
lob·ster (lob′stər) ▢*noun, plural* **lobsters**

local *adjective* **1.** Of a certain area or place: *a local government.* **2.** Making many stops: *a local bus.*
▢*noun* A local train or bus.
lo·cal (lō′kəl) ▢*adjective* ▢*noun, plural* **locals**

locality *noun* A certain neighborhood, place, or area.
lo·cal·i·ty (lō kal′i tē) ▢*noun, plural* **localities**

locate *verb* **1.** To find and show the position of: *Locate France on the map.* **2.** To place or settle in a certain spot: *Locate your fence on the boundary line. They located the factory in a nearby town.* —See Synonyms at **find.**
lo·cate (lō′kāt′) ▢*verb* **located, locating, locates**

location *noun* **1.** A place or position where something is located: *I don't know the location of the new restaurant.* **2.** The act of locating.
lo·ca·tion (lō kā′shən) ▢*noun, plural* **locations**

lock[1] *noun* **1.** A fastener worked by a key or a combination for doors, windows, drawers, and many other things. **2.** A part of a canal, closed off with gates, in which a ship can be raised or lowered by changing the level of the water.
▢*verb* **1.** To fasten with a lock. **2.** To shut or close up in: *lock the money in the safe.* **3.** To fasten or become fastened tightly in place: *The door locks automatically when it is pulled shut.*
lock (lok) ▢*noun, plural* **locks** ▢*verb* **locked, locking, locks**

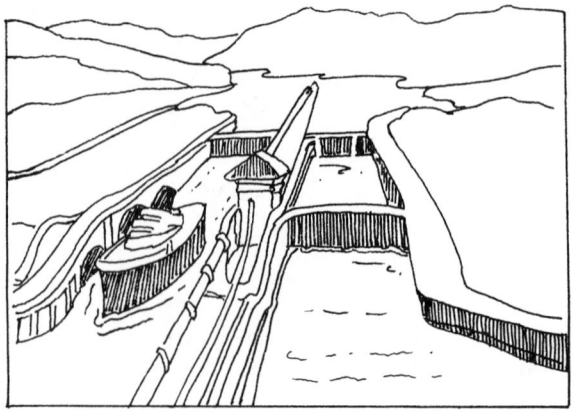
lock

lock² *noun* **1.** A curl of hair; ringlet. **2. locks** The hair of the head.
lock (lok) □*noun, plural* **locks**

locker *noun* A small closet in a gymnasium or public place in which clothes and valuables can be locked up.
lock·er (lok′ər) □*noun, plural* **lockers**

locket *noun* A small, ornamental metal case for holding a picture or other object. Lockets are usually worn on a chain around the neck.
lock·et (lok′it) □*noun, plural* **lockets**

locket

locksmith *noun* Someone who makes or repairs locks.
lock·smith (lok′smith′) □*noun, plural* **locksmiths**

locomotive *noun* An engine used to pull or push railroad cars along a track.
lo·co·mo·tive (lō′kə mō′tiv) □*noun, plural* **locomotives**

WORD HISTORY: **locomotive**

Locomotive comes from two Latin words that mean "place" and "able to move." Originally *locomotive* meant "able to move from place to place."

---

locust *noun* **1.** A kind of grasshopper that travels in huge swarms and does great damage to growing crops. **2.** A tree with feathery leaves and clusters of fragrant white flowers.
lo·cust (lō′kəst) □*noun, plural* **locusts**

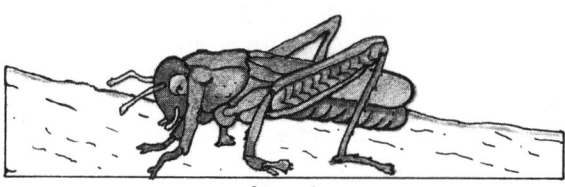

locust

lode *noun* A deposit of ore: *a lode of lead.*
lode (lōd) □*noun, plural* **lodes**

lodge *noun* **1.** A cottage or cabin, especially a small one used as a temporary shelter. **2.** A branch of a secret society.
□*verb* **1.** To provide with a temporary place to sleep: *We lodged six students in the attic last weekend.* **2.** To live in a rented room or rooms in someone else's home. **3.** To be or become stuck or caught: *A seed lodged between his teeth.* **4.** To present a charge to the proper official: *The citizens lodged a protest with the mayor about litter in the park.*
lodge (loj) □*noun, plural* **lodges** □*verb* **lodged, lodging, lodges**

lodger *noun* Someone who rents a room or rooms in another person's house.
lodg·er (loj′ər) □*noun, plural* **lodgers**

lodging *noun* **1.** A temporary place to sleep. **2. lodgings** A rented room or rooms in someone else's house.
lodg·ing (loj′ing) □*noun, plural* **lodgings**

loft *noun* **1.** A large, often open floor in a building, usually used as a storage area, work area, or artist's studio. **2.** An open space under a roof, as in a barn. **3.** A balcony in a church or large hall, usually in the back: *an organ loft.*
loft (lôft) □*noun, plural* **lofts**

loft

lofty *adjective* **1.** Of great height; very tall: *lofty towers.* **2.** On a high moral level; noble:

a	bat	ī	bite	ōō	tool	*th*	feather
ā	make	î	fierce	ou	out	th	bath
â	dare	o	dot	u	nut	hw	wheat
ä	father	ō	no	û	turn	zh	measure
e	net	ô	law, for	ch	church	ə	about, open
ē	be	oi	soil	ng	ring		pencil, atom
i	dip	oo	look	sh	shade		circus

lofty ideals. —See Synonyms at **tall.**
loft·y (lôf′tē) □*adjective* **loftier, loftiest**

log *noun* **1.** A large piece of the trunk of a tree. **2.** An official record of speed, progress, and important events, kept on a ship or aircraft. **3.** A written report or record: *a log of business meetings.*
□*verb* **1.** To cut down trees and saw them into logs. **2.** To enter something in a log or other record.
log (lôg *or* **log)** □*noun, plural* **logs** □*verb* **logged, logging, logs**

loganberry *noun* A large, dark-red berry related to the raspberry and the blackberry.
lo·gan·ber·ry (lō′gən ber′ē) □*noun, plural* **loganberries**

> **WORD HISTORY: loganberry**
> The *loganberry* is named after James H. Logan, who was a fruit grower at the turn of this century.

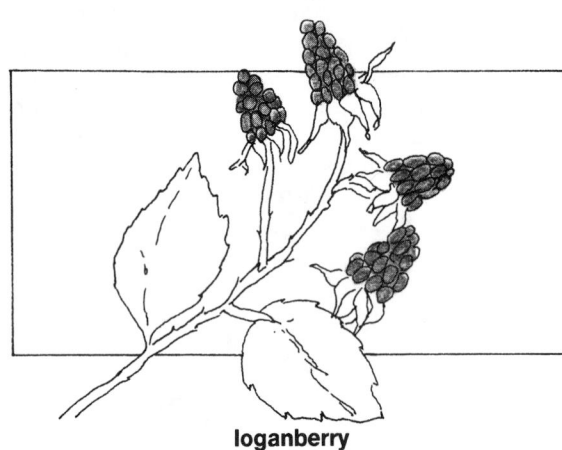
loganberry

logger *noun* Someone who cuts down trees and saws them into logs; lumberjack.
log·ger (lô′gər *or* **log′ər)** □*noun, plural* **loggers**

logic *noun* Clear thinking or reasoning: *Her argument is built on good logic.*
log·ic (loj′ik) □*noun*

logical *adjective* **1.** Having to do with clear thinking and reasoning: *a logical explanation.* **2.** Able to think clearly and sensibly: *a logical thinker.* **3.** Reasonably to be expected: *He is the logical choice for governor.*
log·i·cal (loj′i kəl) □*adjective*

loin *noun* **1.** Often **loins** The part of the sides and back of the body between the ribs and hip. **2.** A cut of meat taken from this part

of an animal.
loin (loin) □*noun, plural* **loins**

loiter *verb* **1.** To stand about in an idle manner; linger: *The girls loitered in the drugstore.* **2.** To go slowly, stopping often: *He loitered on the way to school.*
loi·ter (loi′tər) □*verb* **loitered, loitering, loiters**

lollipop *noun* A piece of hard candy on the end of a stick.
lol·li·pop (lol′ē pop′) □*noun, plural* **lollipops**

lone *adjective* **1.** Not with another person or persons: *a lone man in the car.* **2.** Being the only one: *the lone survivor of a shipwreck.*
lone (lōn) □*adjective*

lonely *adjective* **1.** Sad at being alone: *The lonely little boy cried loudly.* **2.** Not with another person or persons: *a lonely hiker.* **3.** Far away and not visited by many people; remote: *a lonely little village.*
lone·ly (lōn′lē) □*adjective* **lonelier, loneliest**

lonesome *adjective* **1.** Sad and upset at being alone. **2.** Far away and not visited by many people; remote: *a lonesome country road.*
lone·some (lōn′səm) □*adjective*

lonesome

long¹ *adjective* **1.** Having great length or duration; not short: *a long flight of stairs; a long, tiring bus ride.* **2.** Of a certain extent or duration: *The alligator was 20 feet long. The performance was two hours long.* **3.** Having a sound that is drawn out: *The "a" in "pane" is a long vowel, while the "a" in "pan" is short.*
□*adverb* **1.** During or for a great amount of time: *She visited but did not stay long.* **2.** For or throughout a certain period: *all week long.* **3.** At a very distant time: *It happened long ago.*
long (lông) □*adjective* **longer, longest** □*adverb* **longer, longest**

long² *verb* To have a strong desire; wish for very much: *I long to go to the theater.*
long (lông) □*verb* **longed, longing, longs**

long. An abbreviation for **longitude.**

longhand *noun* Ordinary handwriting, rather than typing, shorthand, or printing.
long·hand (lông′hand′) □*noun*

longhorn *noun* One of a breed of cattle with long, spreading horns.
long·horn (lông′hôrn′) □*noun, plural* **longhorns**

longhorn

longing *noun* A deep wish; a strong desire: *I have a longing to build a sailboat.*
□*adjective* Showing a deep wish or strong desire: *a longing look at the new sports car.*
long·ing (lông′ing) □*noun, plural* **longings** □*adjective*

longitude *noun* Distance east or west of the meridian line at Greenwich, England, expressed in degrees. On a map or globe, longitude lines run north and south.
lon·gi·tude (lon′ji to͞od′ *or* lon′ji tyo͞od′) □*noun, plural* **longitudes**

longitude

look *verb* **1.** To use the eyes to see: *She looked everywhere, but couldn't find her friend.* **2.** To seem or seem to be: *He does not look well.* —See Synonyms at **appear.**
□*noun* **1.** The action of looking; glance: *a quick look.* **2.** An expression or appearance: *a*

look of happiness. **3. looks** Personal appearance: *He is not aware of his good looks.*
　　look after To take care of: *Look after the chickens.*
　　look down on or **look down upon** To regard with contempt: *He looks down on liars.*
　　look forward to To wait for with pleasure: *I'm looking forward to seeing them.*
　　look over To examine: *He looked over my record collection.*
　　look up To search for: *Look up facts in the encyclopedia.*
　　look up to To admire and respect: *He looks up to his father.*
look (look) □*verb* **looked, looking, looks** □*noun, plural* **looks**

looking glass *noun* A mirror.

lookout *noun* **1.** Someone whose job it is to watch carefully. **2.** The action of watching and waiting: *He kept a lookout for the mailman.* **3.** A place from which a careful watch can be kept: *a mountain lookout.*
look·out (look′out′) □*noun, plural* **lookouts**

loom¹ *verb* To come into view as large and dangerous: *Clouds loomed over the rough sea.*
loom (lo͞om) □*verb* **loomed, looming, looms**

loom² *noun* A machine or frame for weaving threads to make cloth and rugs.
loom (lo͞om) □*noun, plural* **looms**

loom

a	bat	ī	bite	o͞o	tool	*th*	feather
ā	make	î	fierce	ou	out	th	bath
â	dare	o	dot	u	nut	hw	wheat
ä	father	ō	no	û	turn	zh	measure
e	net	ô	law, for	ch	church	ə	about, open
ē	be	oi	soil	ng	ring		pencil, atom
i	dip	oo	look	sh	shade		circus

loon *noun* A diving bird that has a back with small whitish spots, a pointed bill, and a cry that sounds like a wild laugh.
loon (lo͞on) □*noun, plural* **loons**

loop *noun* **1.** A circular or oval piece of rope, wire, or other material folded over or joined at the ends. **2.** Something that looks like a loop: *The railroad tracks make a loop around the city.*
□*verb* **1.** To form into a loop or loops. **2.** To fasten or join with a loop or loops: *looped the rope around the box.*
loop (lo͞op) □*noun, plural* **loops** □*verb* **looped, looping, loops**

loose *adjective* **1.** Not attached or fastened tightly: *a loose belt.* **2.** Not confined; free: *The hens are loose in the vegetable garden.* **3.** Not fitting tightly: *a loose robe.* **4.** Not bound, tied, or joined together. **5.** Not tightly packed: *Loose sand covered the paths.*
□*verb* **1.** To set free; release: *I loosed the canary from its cage.* **2.** To make less tight; loosen: *He loosed his belt.*
loose (lo͞os) □*adjective* **looser, loosest** □*verb* **loosed, loosing, looses**

loosen *verb* To make or become loose or looser: *He loosened his hold on my arm.*
loos·en (lo͞o′sən) □*verb* **loosened, loosening, loosens**

loot *noun* Valuable things that have been stolen: *The robbers hid the loot in a basement.*
□*verb* To rob of valuable things; steal: *The thief looted the jewelry store.*
loot (lo͞ot) □*noun* □*verb* **looted, looting, loots**

lord *noun* **1.** Someone, such as a king or an owner of an estate, who has great authority or power. **2.** **Lord** A man of noble rank in Great Britain. **3.** **Lord** God. **4.** **Lord** Christ.
lord (lôrd) □*noun, plural* **lords**

WORD HISTORY: **lord**

Lord comes from an old English word that is a compound of the words for "bread" and "guardian." *Lord*, therefore, literally means "guardian of the bread."

---

lose *verb* **1.** To be unable to find: *I lost my umbrella.* **2.** To be unable to keep or maintain: *lose one's self-respect; lose control of a car.* **3.** To fail to win: *They lost the game.* **4.** To waste: *We'll lose time if we don't go by the turnpike.* **5.** To be deprived of: *I lost my job.*
lose (lo͞oz) □*verb* **lost, losing, loses**

loss *noun* **1.** The act of losing something: *a loss of money; the loss of a bet.* **2.** Someone or something that is lost.
loss (lôs) □*noun, plural* **losses**

lost *verb* The past tense and past participle of **lose.**
□*adjective* **1.** Misplaced or missing: *a lost watch; a lost cat.* **2.** Not won: *a lost game.* **3.** Gone or passed away: *a lost art.* **4.** Uncertain; strange: *He felt lost in his new neighborhood.* **5.** Thrown away or wasted: *lost time; lost opportunities.*
lost (lôst) □*verb* □*adjective*

lot *noun* **1.** A large amount or number: *A lot of work lies ahead. There were a lot of people at the concert.* **2.** A number of people or things of a kind: *the ripest apple of the lot.* **3.** A kind, type, or sort: *Those people are a bad lot.* **4.** A piece of land: *a vacant lot; a lot on which to build a cabin.* **5.** **lots** Straws, slips of paper, coins, or other objects used to decide or choose something by chance: *We drew lots to see who would run first.* **6.** The use of such objects to decide or choose something: *We selected the class president by lot.* **7.** One's fortune; fate: *It was my lot to be tall and thin.*
lot (lot) □*noun, plural* **lots**

lotion *noun* A liquid used on the skin as a medicine or cosmetic.
lo·tion (lō′shən) □*noun, plural* **lotions**

lottery *noun* A contest in which the winner is chosen by drawing lots.
lot·ter·y (lot′ə rē) □*noun, plural* **lotteries**

lotus *noun* A water plant with large, colorful flowers and broad leaves.
lo·tus (lō′təs) □*noun, plural* **lotuses**

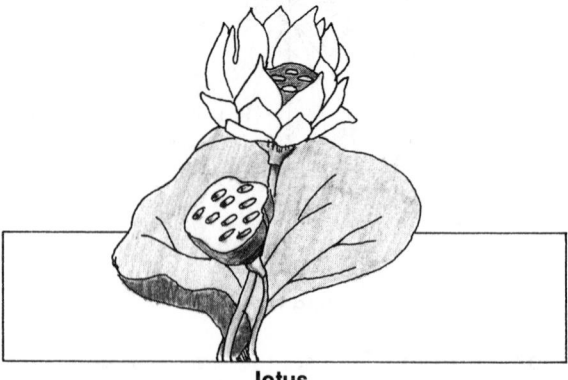

lotus

loud *adjective* Having or making sounds of great volume: *loud singing; a loud explosion.*
loud (loud) □*adjective* **louder, loudest**

loudspeaker *noun* A device that converts an electrical signal into sound.
loud·speak·er (loud′ spē′kər) □*noun, plural* **loudspeakers**

lounge *verb* To stand, sit, or lie in a lazy or relaxed way: *She lounged in the hammock.*
□*noun* A room where a person may relax, rest, or wait: *a hotel lounge filled with chairs.*
lounge (lounj) □*verb* **lounged, lounging, lounges** □*noun, plural* **lounges**

louse *noun* A small insect without wings. Lice bite and suck blood from the skin of animals and human beings.
louse (lous) □*noun, plural* **lice**

lovable *adjective* Having qualities that attract affection: *a lovable baby; a lovable puppy.*
lov·a·ble (luv′ə bəl) □*adjective*

love *noun* **1.** Strong affection and warm feeling for another. **2.** A strong liking for something: *a love of books.*
□*verb* **1.** To feel love or strong affection for: *love one's family and close friends.* **2.** To have a strong liking for: *I love museums.*
love (luv) □*noun, plural* **loves** □*verb* **loved, loving, loves**

lovely *adjective* **1.** Having pleasing and attractive qualities; beautiful: *a lovely child; a lovely flower garden.* **2.** Giving pleasure; delightful: *I had a lovely time at the party.* —See Synonyms at **beautiful.**
love·ly (luv′ lē) □*adjective* **lovelier, loveliest**

lover *noun* Someone who is in love with someone or something.
lov·er (luv′ ər) □*noun, plural* **lovers**

low *adjective* **1.** Not high or tall: *a low building.* **2.** Of less than usual depth: *We gathered shells at low tide.* **3.** At or near the horizon: *The star was low in the sky.* **4.** Below average: *a low mark on a test.* **5.** Not loud: *She spoke in a quiet, low voice.* **6.** Not adequate in amount; not sufficient: *Our supplies of groceries are low.* **7.** Not favorable; bad: *a low opinion of other people.* **8.** Having deep tones: *A bassoon can play very low notes.*
□*adverb* **1.** At or to a low position or level: *wild geese flying low.* **2.** Not loudly; softly: *speaking low.*
□*noun* **1.** A low level, position, or degree: *The stock market dropped to a new low.* **2.** An arrangement of gears in a car, truck, or bus that produces the greatest power but at the lowest speed.
low (lō) □*adjective* **lower, lowest** □*adverb* **lower, lowest** □*noun, plural* **lows**

lower *verb* **1.** To let, bring, or move something down to a lower level: *Lower the line so that I can reach it.* **2.** To make or become less: *Lower your voice when in church.*
low·er (lō′ ər) □*verb* **lowered, lowering, lowers**

low tide *noun* The tide at its lowest point.

loyal *adjective* Faithful to a person, country, idea, or thing: *a loyal friend; loyal soldiers.*
loy·al (loi′ əl) □*adjective*

loyalty *noun* The condition of being loyal; faithful and loyal behavior.
loy·al·ty (loi′ əl tē) □*noun, plural* **loyalties**

lubricate *verb* To apply oil or grease to the moving parts of a machine or apparatus so they will move easily.
lu·bri·cate (lōō′ bri kāt′) □*verb* **lubricated, lubricating, lubricates**

luck *noun* **1.** The chance happening of good or bad events. **2.** Good fortune; success.
luck (luk) □*noun*

luckily *adverb* By good luck; fortunately.
luck·i·ly (luk′ə lē) □*adverb*

lucky *adjective* **1.** Having good luck: *He was very lucky to win the lottery.* **2.** Bringing good luck: *a lucky charm.*
luck·y (luk′ ē) □*adjective* **luckier, luckiest**

lug *verb* To drag or carry with difficulty: *I lugged the heavy bags home from the store.*
lug (lug) □*verb* **lugged, lugging, lugs**

luggage *noun* The bags, suitcases, boxes, and trunks taken on a trip; baggage.
lug·gage (lug′ ij) □*noun*

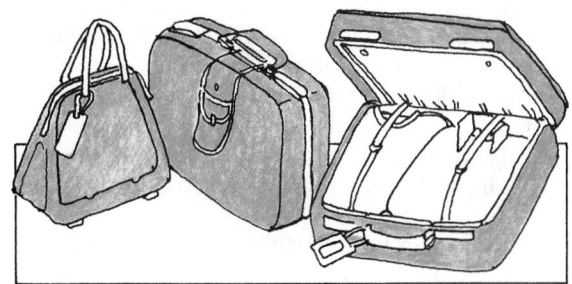

luggage

a bat	ī bite	ōō tool	th feather
ā make	i fierce	ou out	th bath
â dare	o dot	u nut	hw wheat
ä father	ō no	û turn	zh measure
e net	ô law, for	ch church	ə about, open
ē be	oi soil	ng ring	pencil, atom
i dip	oo look	sh shade	circus

lukewarm *adjective* Slightly or mildly warm: *lukewarm milk.*
luke·warm (lōōk′wôrm′) ☐*adjective*

lull *verb* To make or become quiet; calm: *lull a baby to sleep.*
☐*noun* A brief period of quiet or calm: *a lull in the storm.*
lull (lul) ☐*verb* **lulled, lulling, lulls** ☐*noun,* **plural lulls**

lullaby *noun* A soothing song used to help put a child to sleep.
lull·a·by (lul′ə bī′) ☐*noun, plural* **lullabies**

lumber¹ *noun* Timber that has been sawed into boards and planks.
lum·ber (lum′bər) ☐*noun*

lumber² *verb* To move or walk in a clumsy, noisy manner: *The big bus lumbered up the hill. The elephant lumbered into the water.*
lum·ber (lum′bər) ☐*verb* **lumbered, lumbering, lumbers**

lumberjack *noun* Someone whose work is to chop down trees and get the logs to a sawmill.
lum·ber·jack (lum′bər jak′) ☐*noun, plural* **lumberjacks**

luminous *adjective* Giving off light; shining: *The moon is a luminous object.*
lu·mi·nous (lōō′mə nəs) ☐*adjective*

lump *noun* **1.** An irregularly shaped piece of something; hunk: *a lump of clay.* **2.** A swelling or bump: *a lump on his head.*
☐*verb* **1.** To become full of lumps. **2.** To put or consider together in one group or pile.
lump (lump) ☐*noun, plural* **lumps** ☐*verb* **lumped, lumping, lumps**

lunar *adjective* Of, like, or having to do with the moon: *He drew a map of the lunar landscape. I've never seen a lunar eclipse.*
lu·nar (lōō′nər) ☐*adjective*

lunatic *noun* An insane person.
☐*adjective* **1.** Of or for the insane: *a lunatic asylum.* **2.** Wildly or recklessly foolish: *a lunatic idea.*
lu·na·tic (loo′nə tik) ☐*noun, plural* **lunatics** ☐*adjective*

WORD HISTORY: **lunatic**

Lunatic comes from the Latin word for "the moon." In the past people thought that insanity was caused by the moon.

---

lunch *noun* A meal eaten at midday.
lunch (lunch) ☐*noun, plural* **lunches**

luncheon *noun* A midday meal; lunch.
lunch·eon (lun′chən) ☐*noun, plural* **luncheons**

lung *noun* One of two organs for breathing found in the chest of man and many animals. The lungs take in oxygen from the atmosphere and give out carbon dioxide.
lung (lung) ☐*noun, plural* **lungs**

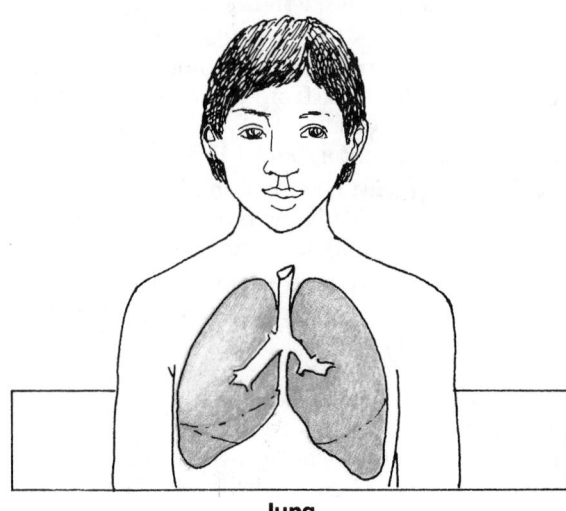

lung

lunge *noun* A forceful movement forward: *a sudden lunge.*
☐*verb* To make a forceful movement forward: *A powerful figure lunged from the crowd and ran to the rescue.*
lunge (lunj) ☐*noun, plural* **lunges** ☐*verb* **lunged, lunging, lunges**

lure *noun* **1.** Something that attracts: *The lure of riches and adventure made him eager to explore the unknown territory.* **2.** Something used as bait, especially an artificial device used to catch fish.
☐*verb* To attract; tempt: *The beautiful weather lured us all outside.*
lure (loor) ☐*noun, plural* **lures** ☐*verb* **lured, luring, lures**

lush *adjective* Thick and abundant: *lush vegetation.*
lush (lush) ☐*adjective* **lusher, lushest**

luster *noun* A bright shine or gloss: *the luster of polished leather.*
lus·ter (lus′tər) ☐*noun, plural* **lusters**

lute *noun* A musical instrument with a body shaped like half a pear, a long, bent neck, and strings played by plucking.
lute (lōōt) ☐*noun, plural* **lutes**

lute

lynx

lynx *noun* A wild cat with thick, soft fur, a short tail, and tufts of hair on its ears.
lynx (lingks) □*noun, plural* **lynx** or **lynxes**

lyre *noun* An ancient stringed instrument like a small harp.
lyre (līr) □*noun, plural* **lyres**

lyre

luxurious *adjective* Very rich, comfortable, or costly: *a luxurious car; a luxurious home.*
lux·u·ri·ous (lug **zhoor′**ē əs *or* luk **shoor′**ē əs) □*adjective*

luxury *noun* **1.** Something expensive or hard to find that is not necessary but gives great pleasure or comfort: *A second car was more a luxury than a necessity.* **2.** A very rich, costly, or comfortable way of living: *He grew up in luxury.*
lux·u·ry (**lug′**zhə rē *or* **luk′**shə rē) □*noun, plural* **luxuries**

–ly¹ A suffix that forms adjectives and means: **1.** Having the nature of; characteristic of: *fatherly advice; a friendly hug.* **2.** Appearing or happening at certain intervals: *a yearly celebration; a monthly magazine.*

–ly² A suffix that forms adverbs and means: **1.** In a given manner: *strongly; softly.* **2.** At certain intervals: *The local paper comes out weekly.*

lye *noun* A dangerously strong solution used in making soaps, detergents, and cleaning fluids. Lye is produced by allowing water to wash through wood ashes.
lye (lī) □*noun*

lying¹ *verb* The present participle of **lie¹**: *She is lying across her bed.*
ly·ing (**lī′**ing) □*verb*

lying² *verb* The present participle of **lie²**: *He is lying when he says he did not eat the cookies.*
ly·ing (**lī′**ing) □*verb*

lymph *noun* A clear liquid in the tissues of the body. It brings nourishment to the tissues and returns waste to the bloodstream.
lymph (limf) □*noun*

lyric *adjective* Expressing deep feelings; very emotional: *lyric music; a lyric love poem.*
□*noun* **1.** A short poem expressing personal feelings and thoughts. **2. lyrics** The words of a song.
lyr·ic (**lir′**ik) □*adjective* □*noun, plural* **lyrics**

lyrical *adjective* Lyric.
lyr·i·cal (**lir′**i kəl) □*adjective*

a	bat	ī	bite	ōō	tool	*th*	feather
ā	make	i	fierce	ou	out	th	bath
â	dare	o	dot	u	nut	hw	wheat
ä	father	ō	no	û	turn	zh	measure
e	net	ô	law, for	ch	church	ə	about, open
ē	be	oi	soil	ng	ring		pencil, atom
i	dip	oo	look	sh	shade		circus

The letter **M** has evolved from many forms of ancient writing. One of the earliest known examples is the Greek character shown above, which dates from almost 3,000 years ago. Over the years, artists and designers have created their own versions of the English letter **M**. Some of the more common examples seen today are shown below.

Mm *Mm* **Mm Mm** Mm Mm **Mm Mm** *Mm Mm*

HANDWRITING   CALLIGRAPHY   MODERN SANS SERIF   MODERN SERIF   SCRIPT

---

m or **M** *noun* The thirteenth letter of the English alphabet.
m or **M** (em) □*noun, plural* **m's** or **M's**

m An abbreviation for **meter**.

m. An abbreviation for **mile**.

Ma'am *noun* Madam: *Good morning, Ma'am.*
Ma'am (mam) □*noun, plural* **Ma'ams**

macaroni *noun* Thin tubes of dried flour paste, boiled and eaten as a food.
mac·a·ro·ni (mak′ə rō′nē) □*noun*

macaroon *noun* A cookie made with sugar and egg whites and flavored with almond or coconut.
mac·a·roon (mak′ə rōōn′) □*noun, plural* **macaroons**

WORD HISTORY: **macaroon**

Both *macaroon* and *macaroni* come from the same Italian word. The Italian word means "dumpling" and "macaroni."

---

macaw *noun* A large parrot of tropical America that has a long tail. Many macaws have brightly colored feathers.
ma·caw (mə kô′) □*noun, plural* **macaws**

mace[1] *noun* **1.** A heavy club with a spiked head that was used as a weapon in the Middle Ages. **2.** A club often carried or displayed in a ceremony as a symbol of authority.
mace (mās) □*noun, plural* **maces**

mace[2] *noun* A spice made from the bright red covering of the nutmeg.
mace (mās) □*noun*

machete *noun* A large, heavy knife with a broad blade. Machetes are used as weapons and also for cutting sugar cane.
ma·chet·e (mə shet′ē) □*noun, plural* **machetes**

machine *noun* **1.** A device that uses energy to do a particular job or make work easier: *an adding machine.* **2.** A device that dispenses goods when coins are inserted: *There was a vending machine in the bus station.*
□*verb* To shape, cut, or finish off by machine.
ma·chine (mə shēn′) □*noun, plural* **machines** □*verb* **machined, machining, machines**

machine gun *noun* A rifle that keeps firing as long as the trigger is pressed.

machinery *noun* Machines or machine parts: *a clock's machinery.*
ma·chin·er·y (mə shē′nə rē) □*noun*

machine shop *noun* A workshop where machine tools are used.

machine tool *noun* A tool driven by steam or electric power that is used in machining.

machinist *noun* Someone who is skilled in the use of machine tools.
ma·chin·ist (mə shē′nist) □*noun, plural* **machinists**

mackerel *noun* An ocean fish with a silvery body that is often used as food.
mack·er·el (mak′ər əl) □*noun, plural* **mackerel** or **mackerels**

macron *noun* A mark (ˉ) placed over a vowel in a pronunciation to show that the vowel is long.

ma·cron (**mā′**kron′) ☐*noun, plural* **macrons**

mad   *adjective* **1.** Crazy; insane. **2.** Very annoyed; angry: *He gets mad when people disagree with him.* **3.** Not sensible; foolish: *a mad plan.* **4.** Very interested and enthusiastic: *He's mad about ice hockey.* **5.** Very confused and excited: *a mad rush.* **6.** Having rabies: *a mad dog.*
mad (mad) ☐*adjective* **madder, maddest**

Madam   *noun* A word used as a polite way of addressing a woman.
Mad·am (**mad′**əm) ☐*noun, plural* **Madams**

madcap   *adjective* Not sensible; rash: *a madcap idea.*
mad·cap (**mad′**kap′) ☐*adjective*

madden   *verb* To make mad: *My brother's habit of wiggling his foot simply maddens me.*
mad·den (**mad′**ən) ☐*verb* **maddened, maddening, maddens**

made   *verb* The past tense and past participle of **make**: *She made spaghetti for dinner.*
made (mād) ☐*verb*

made-up   *adjective* Not real; imaginary: *a made-up story.*
made-up (**mād′up′**) ☐*adjective*

madhouse   *noun* **1.** An asylum for insane people. **2.** A place of great noise and confusion: *The crowd of people trying to mail Christmas presents at the last minute turned the post office into a madhouse.*
mad·house (**mad′**hous′) ☐*noun, plural* **madhouses**

maelstrom   *noun* A large, violent whirlpool.
mael·strom (**māl′**strəm) ☐*noun, plural* **maelstroms**

magazine   *noun* A printed collection of articles, stories, and pictures. Magazines usually have paper covers and come out weekly or monthly.
mag·a·zine (mag′ə **zēn′** *or* **mag′**ə zēn′) ☐*noun, plural* **magazines**

WORD HISTORY: **magazine**

Magazine comes from an Arabic word that means "storehouse." This was also the original meaning of the English word. The modern meaning developed because a magazine is a "storehouse" of written articles.

---

maggot   *noun* The larva of a fly, similar to a small worm in appearance.
mag·got (**mag′**ət) ☐*noun, plural* **maggots**

magic   *noun* **1.** A power that is supposed to make someone, such as a witch, able to do things that are not usually possible: *a wicked wizard whose magic turned the prince into a frog.* **2.** The art of entertaining people with tricks.
☐*adjective* Of, for, or done by magic.
mag·ic (**maj′**ik) ☐*noun* ☐*adjective*

magical   *adjective* Of or made by magic: *a magical spell.*
mag·i·cal (**maj′**i kəl) ☐*adjective*

magician   *noun* **1.** An entertainer who does magic tricks. **2.** Someone who is supposed to have magic powers.
ma·gi·cian (mə **jish′**ən) ☐*noun, plural* **magicians**

magician

magistrate   *noun* **1.** A government official who administers the laws. **2.** An official of a local government.
mag·is·trate (**maj′**i strāt′) ☐*noun, plural* **magistrates**

magma   *noun* Hot molten material under the earth's crust that forms rocks when it cools and hardens. Granite is formed from magma.
mag·ma (**mag′**mə) ☐*noun*

magnanimity   *noun* The quality of being magnanimous.
mag·na·nim·i·ty (mag′nə **nim′**i tē) ☐*noun*

a bat	ī bite	o͞o tool	*th* feather
ā make	i fierce	ou out	th bath
â dare	o dot	u nut	hw wheat
ä father	ō no	û turn	zh measure
e net	ô law, for	ch church	ə about, open
ē be	oi soil	ng ring	pencil, atom
i dip	oo look	sh shade	circus

magnanimous *adjective* Having or showing noble qualites of mind and spirit, especially generosity and forgiveness: *He made a magnanimous attempt to forgive his father, who had unjustly punished him.*
mag·nan·i·mous (mag **nan′** ə məs) □*adjective*

WORD HISTORY: **magnanimous**

The word *magnanimous* comes from a Latin word literally meaning "having a large soul."

---

magnesium *noun* A chemical element that is a light, silver-white metal used in many alloys.
mag·ne·si·um (mag **nē′** zē əm) □*noun*

magnet *noun* A piece of metal or rock that attracts iron, steel, and some other substances. Magnets are used in machines and compasses.
mag·net (**mag′** nit) □*noun, plural* **magnets**

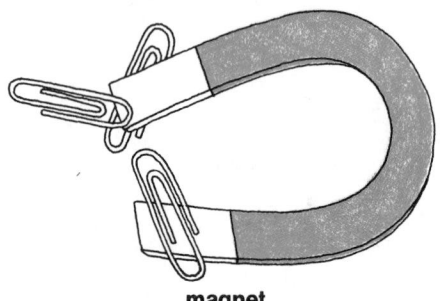

magnet

magnetic *adjective* **1.** Having the power to attract iron and steel: *a magnetic rock.* **2.** Having the ability to attract: *He was a magnetic leader who gained followers wherever he went.*
mag·net·ic (mag **net′** ik) □*adjective*

magnetic field *noun* An area of space around a body that exerts a magnetic force in which the force can be felt.

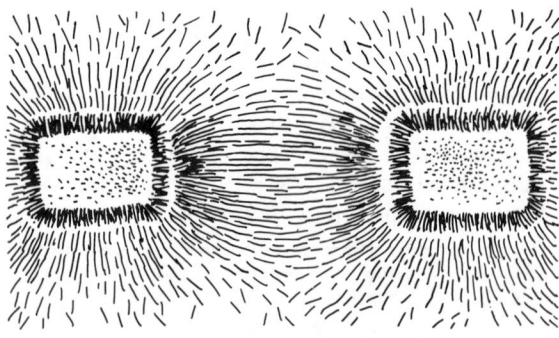

magnetic field

magnetic pole *noun* **1.** Either of the two points or areas at the ends of a magnet where

the magnetic field is strongest. **2.** Either of two points on the earth toward which a compass needle points. The magnetic poles are near the North and South Poles.

magnetic tape *noun* A special tape used to record something, such as music or a television program.

magnetism *noun* **1.** The power to attract iron, steel, and some other substances. An electric current has magnetism. **2.** The ability to attract: *She possessed a great deal of charm and magnetism.*
mag·net·ism (**mag′** ni tiz′əm) □*noun*

magnetize *verb* To make something into a magnet.
mag·net·ize (**mag′** ni tīz′) □*verb* **magnetized, magnetizing, magnetizes**

magnificence *noun* Great beauty or splendor.
mag·nif·i·cence (mag **nif′** i səns) □*noun*

magnificent *adjective* **1.** Very grand and fine; splendid: *a magnificent palace.* **2.** Outstanding; excellent: *a magnificent voice.* —See Synonyms at **grand.**
mag·nif·i·cent (mag **nif′** i sənt) □*adjective*

magnify *verb* **1.** To make an object appear larger than it really is: *The microscope magnified the fly's wing 80 times.* **2.** To exaggerate: *She likes to magnify her achievements.*
mag·ni·fy (**mag′** nə fī′) □*verb* **magnified, magnifying, magnifies**

magnifying glass *noun* A lens that makes things look bigger.
mag·ni·fy·ing glass (**mag′** nə fī′ing) □*noun*

magnifying glass

magnitude *noun* **1.** The condition of being great in size or extent: *measuring the magnitude of an earthquake.* **2.** Importance; significance.

mag·ni·tude (**mag′**ni tōōd′ *or* **mag′**ni tyōōd′) ▢*noun, plural* **magnitudes**

magnolia *noun* A tree with long leaves and large, white or pink flowers.
mag·no·lia (mag **nōl′**yə) ▢*noun, plural* **magnolias**

magpie *noun* **1.** A noisy bird with black and white feathers and a long tail. **2.** Someone who chatters or talks a great deal.
mag·pie (**mag′**pī′) ▢*noun, plural* **magpies**

magpie

mahogany *noun* **1.** A tropical American tree that has hard, reddish-brown wood used to make furniture. **2.** A dark reddish-brown color.
▢*adjective* Reddish brown.
ma·hog·a·ny (mə **hog′**ə nē) ▢*noun* ▢*adjective*

maid *noun* **1.** A girl or woman who has not married. **2.** A female servant.
maid (mād) ▢*noun, plural* **maids**

maid of honor *noun* An unmarried woman who is the chief witness for the bride at a wedding.
maid of honor▢*noun, plural* **maids of honor**

maiden *noun* A girl or woman who has not married.
▢*adjective* **1.** Never having married: *a maiden aunt.* **2.** First; earliest: *a ship's maiden voyage.*
maid·en (**mād′**ən) ▢*noun, plural* **maidens** ▢*adjective*

maiden name *noun* A woman's last name before she was married.

mail¹ *noun* **1.** Letters and packages sent and received through a postal system. **2.** The sys-

tem by which letters and packages are sent, usually run by a country's government.
▢*verb* To send by mail: *mail a letter.*
mail (māl) ▢*noun, plural* **mails** ▢*verb* **mailed, mailing, mails**

WORD HISTORY: **mail**

Mail¹ originally meant "a bag." In the days before the postal system, letters were carried by horsemen in their traveling bags. The word *mail* came to be used for the contents of these bags.

---

mail² *noun* Armor made of connected metal rings or loops or of overlapping scales. Mail will bend so the body can move easily.
mail (māl) ▢*noun*

mailbox *noun* **1.** A public box in which letters are put for collection by a mailman. **2.** A private box for mail delivered to a home or business.
mail·box (**māl′**boks′) ▢*noun, plural* **mailboxes**

mailman *noun* Someone who delivers mail.
mail·man (**māl′**man′) ▢*noun, plural* **mailmen**

maim *verb* To disable; cripple.
maim (mām) ▢*verb* **maimed, maiming, maims**

main *adjective* Most important; principal: *the main street of a town; the main course of a meal.*
▢*noun* A large pipe or cable: *a water main.*
main (mān) ▢*adjective* ▢*noun, plural* **mains**

mainland *noun* A continent or the main part of a continent that does not include islands: *Hawaii is far from the mainland of the United States.*
main·land (**mān′**land′) ▢*noun, plural* **mainlands**

mainly *adverb* For the most part; chiefly.
main·ly (**mān′**lē) ▢*adverb*

mainmast *noun* The most important mast of a sailing ship.
main·mast (**mān′**məst) ▢*noun, plural* **mainmasts**

a	bat	ī	bite	ōō	tool	*th*	feather
ā	make	î	fierce	ou	out	th	bath
â	dare	o	dot	u	nut	hw	wheat
ä	father	ō	no	û	turn	zh	measure
e	net	ô	law, for	ch	church	ə	about, open
ē	be	oi	soil	ng	ring		pencil, atom
i	dip	oo	look	sh	shade		circus

mainsail *noun* The largest sail on the main-mast of a sailing ship.
main·sail (mān′ səl) □*noun, plural* **mainsails**

mainspring *noun* The spring that drives a mechanical device, such as a watch or clock, by uncoiling.
main·spring (mān′ spring′) □*noun, plural* **mainsprings**

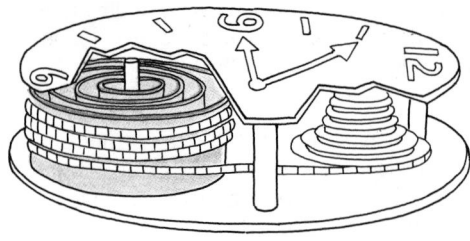

mainspring

mainstay *noun* **1.** A strong rope or cable that holds a mainmast in place. **2.** A main support of someone or something: *Her income is the mainstay of a large family.*
main·stay (mān′ stā′) □*noun, plural* **mainstays**

maintain *verb* **1.** To continue doing or having: *The plane maintained an altitude of 20,000 feet.* **2.** To keep in good condition: *The state maintains the roads for all the cities and towns.* **3.** To take care of; support: *maintain a family.* **4.** To say firmly; declare: *He maintains that he once saw a ghost.*
main·tain (mān tān′) □*verb* **maintained, maintaining, maintains**

maintenance *noun* **1.** The act of maintaining: *This machinery needs proper maintenance.* **2.** A means of support: *She worked hard to earn money for the maintenance of her family.*
main·te·nance (mān′ tə nəns) □*noun*

maize *noun* The corn plant or its kernels.
maize (māz) □*noun*

maize

majestic *adjective* Dignified and noble: *a majestic temple of white marble.* —See Synonyms at **grand.**
ma·jes·tic (mə **jes′** tik) □*adjective*

majesty *noun* **1.** A stately, grand appearance; splendor: *the majesty of the earth seen from space.* **2.** Great power or authority: *the majesty of the law.* **3. Majesty** A title of honor used when speaking to or about a king or queen.
maj·es·ty (maj′ i stē) □*noun, plural* **majesties**

major *adjective* Greater in number, amount, or importance: *A major part of the forest has been cut down.*
□*noun* A military officer who ranks above a captain.
ma·jor (mā′ jər) □*adjective* □*noun, plural* **majors**

majority *noun* **1.** A number that is more than half of a total: *A majority of the senators voted for the new law.* **2.** The difference between a larger and a smaller number: *The governor got 200,000 votes and her opponent got 180,000, so the governor won with a majority of 20,000 votes.*
ma·jor·i·ty (mə **jôr′** i tē) □*noun, plural* **majorities**

make *verb* **1.** To bring into being; create: *make a new dress.* **2.** To cause to be, become, or occur: *The warm room made her sleepy. Please don't make any noise.* **3.** To force; compel: *I made him stay in his room until dinner.* **4.** To perform; carry out: *make war.* **5.** To add up to; produce: *7 and 6 make 13.* **6.** To get for oneself; earn: *make ten dollars a day; make many friends.* **7.** To win or gain a place on: *make the tennis team.* **8.** To get to; reach: *make a train on time.* **9.** To think: *What do you make of that painting?*
□*noun* A style or type of something made: *What make of automobile does he drive?*

make believe To pretend; imagine: *Let's make believe we're pirates.*

made do To manage; get along: *I had to make do with a boiled egg and an apple for dinner.*

make fun of To laugh at in an insulting way; mock: *They used to make fun of her because her voice squeaked when she got excited.*

make out **1.** To manage to see or hear: *make out a sail on the horizon.* **2.** To figure out; understand. **3.** To get along: *We'll make out all right.*

make up **1.** To invent: *make up an excuse.* **2.** To settle a quarrel. **3.** To decide: *Make up your mind.* **4.** To put make-up on.

make way To give room or space for: *The traffic made way for the fire engine to get through.*
make (māk) □*verb* **made, making, makes** □*noun, plural* **makes**

SYNONYMS: **make, construct, manufacture**

These verbs mean to bring into being: *She makes her own clothes. I watched the workers construct the building. That factory manufactures refrigerators.*

---

make-believe *noun* A pretending or imagining that something false is true: *Ghosts and goblins belong to the world of make-believe.* □*adjective* Not real; imaginary: *a make-believe playmate.*
make·be·lieve (māk′bi lēv′) □*noun* □*adjective*

makeshift *adjective* Used as a temporary substitute: *She held a newspaper over her head as a makeshift umbrella.*
make·shift (māk′shift′) □*adjective*

make-up *noun* **1.** The way something is put together or arranged. **2.** Lipstick, rouge, and other cosmetics.
make·up (māk′up′) □*noun, plural* **make-ups**

malady *noun* An ailment of the mind or body; disease.
mal·a·dy (mal′ə dē) □*noun, plural* **maladies**

malaria *noun* An infectious disease that causes chills and fever. Malaria is carried from person to person by a particular kind of mosquito.
ma·lar·i·a (mə lâr′ē ə) □*noun*

male *adjective* **1.** Of or belonging to the sex that can become fathers: *A stallion is a male horse.* **2.** Of or being a man or boy. □*noun* A male person or animal.
male (māl) □*adjective* □*noun, plural* **males**

malformation *noun* **1.** The condition of being wrongly or badly formed. **2.** A structure, such as a part of the body, that does not have a normal form.
mal·for·ma·tion (mal′fôr mā′shən) □*noun, plural* **malformations**

malice *noun* The desire to hurt others or see them unhappy; ill will: *She felt no malice toward her rivals.*
mal·ice (mal′is) □*noun*

malicious *adjective* **1.** Wanting to see others unhappy or in trouble. **2.** Done in a spirit of ill will: *a malicious attack.*
ma·li·cious (mə lish′əs) □*adjective*

malign *verb* To speak evil of: *His enemies maligned him by spreading vicious gossip.* □*adjective* **1.** Showing or having malice: *Her sudden friendliness is prompted by malign intentions.* **2.** Evil in nature; causing injury: *They thought their problems were the result of the malign influence of the stars and planets.*
ma·lign (mə līn′) □*verb* **maligned, maligning, maligns** □*adjective* **malign**

malignant *adjective* **1.** Having or showing ill will: *a malignant smile.* **2.** Threatening life or health: *a malignant disease.*
ma·lig·nant (mə lig′nənt) □*adjective*

mallard *noun* A wild duck. The male has a shiny green head and neck.
mal·lard (mal′ərd) □*noun, plural* **mallards**

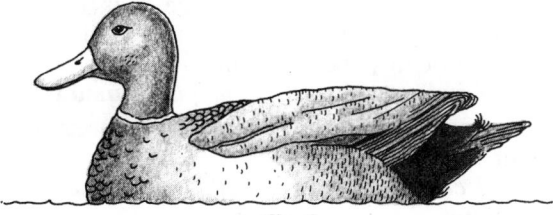
mallard

malleable *adjective* Able to be shaped or formed, as by hammering: *Copper is a malleable metal.*
mal·le·a·ble (mal′ē ə bəl) □*adjective*

mallet *noun* A hammer with a head that is shaped like a barrel.
mal·let (mal′it) □*noun, plural* **mallets**

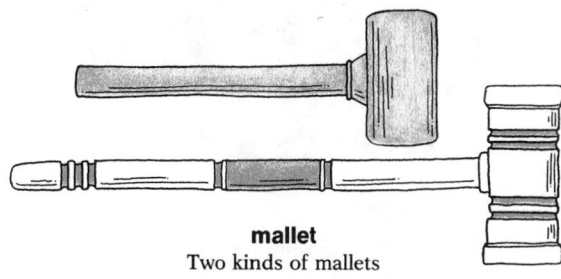
mallet
Two kinds of mallets

a bat	ī bite	o͞o tool	*th* feather
ā make	î fierce	ou out	th bath
â dare	o dot	u nut	hw wheat
ä father	ō no	û turn	zh measure
e net	ô law, for	ch church	ə about, open
ē be	oi soil	ng ring	pencil, atom
i dip	oo look	sh shade	circus

malnutrition   *noun* A condition that comes from not having enough nourishment.
mal·nu·tri·tion (mal′nōō **trish′** ən *or* mal′nyōō **trish′**ən)   ▢*noun*

malt   *noun* Barley or other grain that has been soaked until it sprouts and then dried. Malt is used in making beer.
malt (môlt)   ▢*noun, plural* **malts**

malted milk   *noun* A drink made of milk and a powder containing malt.
malt·ed milk (môl′tid)   ▢*noun, plural* **malted milks**

maltreat   *verb* To treat in a rough or bad way.
mal·treat (mal trēt′)   ▢*verb* **maltreated, maltreating, maltreats**

mama *or* **mamma**   *noun* Mother.
ma·ma *or* **mam·ma** (mä′mə)   ▢*noun, plural* **mamas** *or* **mammas**

mammal   *noun* Any of a group of animals that have hair on their bodies. Female mammals have glands that produce milk to feed their young. Cats, elephants, mice, whales, and human beings are all mammals.
mam·mal (mam′əl)   ▢*noun, plural* **mammals**

mammoth   *noun* An elephant with shaggy hair that lived thousands of years ago. ▢*adjective* Very large; huge. —See Synonyms at **giant.**
mam·moth (mam′əth)   ▢*noun, plural* **mammoths** ▢*adjective*

mammoth

man   *noun* **1.** A fully grown male human being. **2.** A human being: *A man must eat.* **3.** The human race: *Man may have first appeared in Africa.* **4.** A piece used in chess or other board games. ▢*verb* To supply with people to do work: *man a ship.*

man (man)   ▢*noun, plural* **men** ▢*verb* **manned, manning, mans**

manage   *verb* **1.** To run; direct: *manage an office.* **2.** To succeed in doing: *We managed to push the car up the hill.*
man·age (man′ij)   ▢*verb* **managed, managing, manages**

management   *noun* **1.** The act of managing; control: *We admired his management of the wild elephant.* **2.** The people in charge; managers: *This business is under new management.*
man·age·ment (man′ij mənt)   ▢*noun, plural* **managements**

manager   *noun* Someone who manages something: *a store manager.*
man·a·ger (man′i jər)   ▢*noun, plural* **managers**

mandarin   *noun* An important public official in the Chinese empire.
man·da·rin (man′də rin)   ▢*noun, plural* **mandarins**

mandible   *noun* **1.** The lower jaw in animals that have backbones. **2.** A part that forms the mouth of an insect or crustacean.
man·di·ble (man′də bəl)   ▢*noun, plural* **mandibles**

mandolin   *noun* A musical instrument similar to a guitar that has a pear-shaped body and metal strings.
man·do·lin (man′də **lin′**)   ▢*noun, plural* **mandolins**

mandolin

mane   *noun* The long hair that grows on the neck of certain animals such as horses and male lions.
mane (mān)   ▢*noun, plural* **manes**

maneuver   *noun* **1.** A planned movement of soldiers, ships, or aircraft: *Surrounding the* enemy was a successful maneuver. **2.** A clever move.

□*verb* To move or guide in a planned way: *The captain maneuvered the boat out of the harbor.*
ma·neu·ver (mə noo′ vər) □*noun, plural* **maneuvers** □*verb* **maneuvered, maneuvering, maneuvers**

manganese *noun* A chemical element that is a gray metal used in making steel.
man·ga·nese (mang′ gə nēz′) □*noun*

mange *noun* A skin disease of dogs and other animals that causes itching and loss of hair.
mange (mānj) □*noun*

manger *noun* An open box to hold food for horses or cattle.
man·ger (mān′ jər) □*noun, plural* **mangers**

manger

mango *noun* A tropical fruit with sweet, yellow-orange flesh.
man·go (mang′ gō) □*noun, plural* **mangoes** or **mangos**

mangrove *noun* A tree or shrub of tropical areas that has many roots resembling stilts growing above the ground. Mangroves form thickets in marshes and along the shore.
man·grove (man′ grōv′) □*noun, plural* **mangroves**

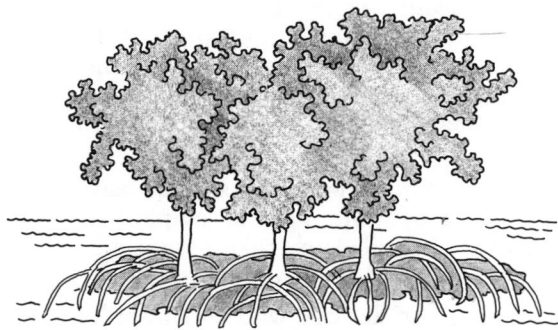

mangrove

mangy *adjective* Having or appearing to have mange: *a mangy dog.*
man·gy (mān′ jē) □*adjective* **mangier, mangiest**

manhole *noun* A large, covered hole through which workers can go to repair sewers, pipes, and electrical lines.
man·hole (man′ hōl′) □*noun, plural* **manholes**

manhood *noun* **1.** The time or condition of being a grown man. **2.** Grown men considered as a group: *The speech appealed to the entire manhood of the country.* **3.** The qualities thought proper to being a grown man, such as courage: *He went on dangerous adventures to prove his manhood.*
man·hood (man′ hood′) □*noun*

mania *noun* **1.** A state of great excitement that causes too much physical or mental activity. **2.** A great enthusiasm: *a mania for collecting stamps.*
ma·ni·a (mā′ nē ə) □*noun, plural* **manias**

maniac *noun* A person suffering from mental illness, especially one who acts in a violent way.
ma·ni·ac (mā′ nē ak′) □*noun, plural* **maniacs**

manicure *noun* A cleaning and shaping of the fingernails.
□*verb* To clean and shape the fingernails.
man·i·cure (man′ i kyoor′) □*noun, plural* **manicures** □*verb* **manicured, manicuring, manicures**

manifest *verb* To show plainly; reveal: *He manifested a desire to become a doctor.*
□*adjective* Plainly seen; obvious: *Their scheme for getting rich was a manifest hoax.*
man·i·fest (man′ ə fest′) □*verb* **manifested, manifesting, manifests** □*adjective*

manifestation *noun* **1.** The act of manifesting. **2.** Something that reveals something else; sign: *The doctor noticed the first manifestations of disease in the apparently healthy patient.*
man·i·fes·ta·tion (man′ə fe stā′ shən) □*noun, plural* **manifestations**

manifold *adjective* Of many kinds; various: *She was often overwhelmed by her manifold*

a	bat	ī	bite	oo	tool	*th*	feather
ā	make	i	fierce	ou	out	th	bath
â	dare	o	dot	u	nut	hw	wheat
ä	father	ō	no	û	turn	zh	measure
e	net	ô	law, for	ch	church	ə	about, open
ē	be	oi	soil	ng	ring		pencil, atom
i	dip	oo	look	sh	shade		circus

duties.

man·i·fold (man′ə fōld′) □*adjective*

manipulate   *verb* **1.** To work or control with the hands: *manipulate the dials of the instrument.* **2.** To influence or control with skill and often intending to deceive: *He manipulated his parents into letting him do whatever he wanted.*
ma·nip·u·late (mə **nip′**yə lāt′) □*verb* **manipulated, manipulating, manipulates**

mankind   *noun* All human beings; the human race.
man·kind (man′kīnd′) □*noun*

manly   *adjective* Having or showing the qualities thought proper to a man: *manly courage; a manly voice*
man·ly (man′lē) □*adjective* **manlier, manliest**

manmade   *adjective* Created by people, not by nature: *Plastic is a manmade material.*
man·made (man′mād′) □*adjective*

manner   *noun* **1.** A way of doing things: *He spoke in a quiet manner.* **2.** A way of behaving: *her pleasant manner.* **3. manners** Behavior: *He has bad manners.* **4. manners** Good behavior: *It isn't manners to play with your food.*
man·ner (man′ər) □*noun, plural* **manners**

mannerly   *adjective* Having or showing good manners; polite: *mannerly children who said "please" and "thank you."*
man·ner·ly (man′ər lē) □*adjective*

manor   *noun* **1.** The land and buildings belonging to a lord in the Middle Ages. Peasants also lived and worked on the manor. **2.** A mansion or large house.
man·or (man′ər) □*noun, plural* **manors**

mansion   *noun* A large, fine house.
man·sion (man′shən) □*noun, plural* **mansions**

manslaughter   *noun* The unlawful killing of a person, especially when it is accidental.
man·slaugh·ter (man′slô′tər) □*noun*

mantel   *noun* The shelf above a fireplace.
man·tel (man′təl) □*noun, plural* **mantels**

mantel

mantelpiece   *noun* A mantel.
man·tel·piece (man′təl pēs′) □*noun, plural* **mantelpieces**

mantle   *noun* **1.** A loose, sleeveless cloak worn over outer clothing. **2.** Something that covers or conceals like a mantle: *A mantle of snow covered the earth.*
man·tle (man′təl) □*noun, plural* **mantles**

manual   *adjective* Of or using the hands: *manual controls; manual labor.*
□*noun* A small book of instructions: *The washing machine comes with a repair manual.*
man·u·al (man′yo̅o̅ əl) □*adjective* □*noun, plural* **manuals**

manufacture   *verb* **1.** To make a product especially through the use of machinery: *That factory manufactures tires.* **2.** To make up: *He manufactured an excuse for being late.* —See Synonyms at **make.**
□*noun* The act or process of manufacturing.
man·u·fac·ture (man′yə **fak′**chər) □*verb* **manufactured, manufacturing, manufactures** □*noun*

manure   *noun* Animal waste used to fertilize soil.
ma·nure (mə **noor′** *or* mə **nyoor′**) □*noun*

manuscript   *noun* Something written by hand or on a typewriter: *The writer sent his manuscript to be printed.*
man·u·script (man′yə skript′) □*noun, plural* **manuscripts**

many   *adjective* Consisting of a large number: *There are many trees in a forest.*
□*noun* A large number: *A great many of us have summer jobs.*
□*pronoun* A large number of people or things: *Many tried to make the school team.*
man·y (men′ē) □*adjective* **more, most**
□*noun* □*pronoun*

map   *noun* A drawing of all or part of the earth's surface: *The map showed countries, cities, oceans, and other features.*
□*verb* **1.** To make a map of: *The explorers mapped the strange island.* **2.** To plan in detail: *He mapped out his program carefully.*
map (map) □*noun, plural* **maps** □*verb* **mapped, mapping, maps**

maple   *noun* A tree that has broad leaves with deep notches. One kind of maple has sweet sap that is boiled to make syrup and sugar.
ma·ple (mā′pəl) □*noun, plural* **maples**

mar   *verb* To damage with a mark or blemish: *She marred the table by putting a hot dish on it.*

2. To spoil the quality of: *A family argument marred the holiday.*
mar (mär) ▢*verb* **marred, marring, mars**

maraca *noun* A musical instrument made of a hollow gourd containing seeds or pebbles. Maracas are played by shaking.
ma·ra·ca (mə **rä′**kə) ▢*noun, plural* **maracas**

marathon *noun* **1.** A race for runners over a distance of 26 miles and 385 yards or about 42 kilometers. **2.** A very long contest or show.
mar·a·thon (**mar′**ə thon′) ▢*noun, plural* **marathons**

marble *noun* **1.** A kind of hard stone that is used for statues, buildings, and table tops. **2.** A little glass ball, often brightly colored, used in games.
mar·ble (**mär′**bəl) ▢*noun, plural* **marbles**

march *verb* **1.** To move forward with a regular rhythm and in step with others: *The soldiers marched in an orderly formation.* **2.** To advance or move along in a steady way: *He marched past me without a word.*
▢*noun* **1.** The act of marching. **2.** Forward movement: *the march of progress.* **3.** A piece of music having a rhythm that is suitable for marching.
march (märch) ▢*verb* **marched, marching, marches** ▢*noun, plural* **marches**

march

March *noun* The third month of the year. March has 31 days.
March (märch) ▢*noun, plural* **Marches**

WORD HISTORY: March

The name *March* comes from Latin. The Romans named the month after Mars, the god of war.

---

mare *noun* A female horse or a female animal of the horse family.
mare (mâr) ▢*noun, plural* **mares**

margarine *noun* A food made of vegetable oils and coloring, used as a butter substitute.
mar·ga·rine (**mär′**jər in) ▢*noun, plural* **margarines**

margin *noun* **1.** The blank space around the printing or writing on a page. **2.** An extra amount: *We allowed a margin of twenty minutes in case the bus was late.*
mar·gin (**mär′**jin) ▢*noun, plural* **margins**

marigold *noun* A garden plant that has orange, yellow, or reddish flowers.
mar·i·gold (**mar′**i gōld′) ▢*noun, plural* **marigolds**

marigold

marine *adjective* **1.** Of or living in the sea: *marine animals.* **2.** Of ships and shipping: *marine supplies.*
▢*noun* Often **Marine** A member of the U.S. Marine Corps.
ma·rine (mə **rēn′**) ▢*adjective* ▢*noun, plural* **marines**

Marine Corps *noun* A branch of the U.S. armed forces whose troops are trained to be sent into battle by ship or aircraft.

mariner *noun* A sailor.
mar·i·ner (**mar′**ə nər) ▢*noun, plural* **mariners**

marionette *noun* A puppet or doll moved by strings from above.

a bat	ī bite	oo tool	th feather
ā make	i fierce	ou out	th bath
â dare	o dot	u nut	hw wheat
ä father	ō no	û turn	zh measure
e net	ô law, for	ch church	ə about, open
ē be	oi soil	ng ring	pencil, atom
i dip	oo look	sh shade	circus

mar·i·o·nette (mar′ē ə **net**′) ☐*noun, plural*
marionettes

marionette

marital *adjective* Of or having to do with
marriage: *marital vows.*
mar·i·tal (**mar**′i təl) ☐*adjective*

maritime *adjective* **1.** Located on or near the
sea: *maritime provinces.* **2.** Having to do with
trading or navigating across the ocean: *maritime laws.*
mar·i·time (**mar**′i tīm′) ☐*adjective*

mark *noun* **1.** A scratch, stain, or other spot
made on something: *The burn left a mark on
the table.* **2.** A line or other symbol made to
show something: *an identification mark.* **3.** A
sign; indication: *His nervousness seemed to be
a mark of guilt.* **4.** Something that is aimed at;
target. **5.** A letter or number that shows how
well a student has done: *Her mark in English
was a B.* —See Synonyms at **sign.**
☐*verb* **1.** To make a mark on: *mark up a floor.*
2. To show plainly; indicate: *mark a path with
signs.* **3.** To put grades on: *mark tests.* **4.** To
set apart as different or special: *The red dots
on the map mark the higher mountains.*
mark (märk) ☐*noun, plural* **marks** ☐*verb*
marked, marking, marks

marked *adjective* **1.** Having a mark or
marks: *The desk was marked with scratches.*
2. Noticeable; distinct: *He walks with a
marked limp.*
marked (märkt) ☐*adjective*

marker *noun* Someone or something that
marks: *a boundary marker; brightly colored
markers for drawing posters.*
mark·er (**mär**′kər) ☐*noun, plural* **markers**

market *noun* **1.** A meeting of people for the
purpose of buying and selling goods, usually
held at a special place or time. **2.** A public
place where such a meeting is held. **3.** A particular area for selling goods: *the overseas
market.* **4.** A store for buying and selling
goods: *a fish market.*
☐*verb* **1.** To sell or offer for sale: *marketing
farm products.* **2.** To go shopping for food.
mar·ket (**mär**′kit) ☐*noun, plural* **markets**
☐*verb* **marketed, marketing, markets**

marking *noun* A mark or pattern of marks: *a
bird's colorful markings.*
mark·ing (**mär**′king) ☐*noun, plural*
markings

marksman *noun* A person who can shoot a
gun or other weapon with skill.
marks·man (**märks**′mən) ☐*noun, plural*
marksmen

marmalade *noun* A jam made from the pulp
and rind of fruit.
mar·ma·lade (**mär**′mə lād′) ☐*noun, plural*
marmalades

marmoset *noun* A small monkey of tropical
America that has soft, thick fur and a long tail.
mar·mo·set (**mär**′mə set′) ☐*noun, plural*
marmosets

maroon¹ *verb* To leave a person helpless on a
deserted shore: *The shipwreck marooned him
on an island.*
ma·roon (mə **roon**′) ☐*verb* **marooned,
marooning, maroons**

maroon

maroon² *noun* A dark purplish red.
☐*adjective* Dark purplish red.
ma·roon (mə **roon**′) ☐*noun, plural* **maroons**
☐*adjective*

marquis　*noun* A nobleman above the rank of earl or count and below the rank of duke.
mar·quis (**mär′**kwis *or* mär **kē′**) □*noun, plural* **marquis** *or* **marquises**

marriage　*noun* **1.** The condition of being married. **2.** The act of marrying. **3.** The wedding ceremony and the celebration connected with it.
mar·riage (**mar′**ij) □*noun, plural* **marriages**

married　*adjective* **1.** Having a husband or wife: *a married woman.* **2.** United by marriage: *a married couple.*
mar·ried (**mar′**ēd) □*adjective*

marrow　*noun* The soft material that is inside the hollow part of most bones.
mar·row (**mar′**ō) □*noun, plural* **marrows**

marry　*verb* **1.** To take as a husband or wife: *They will marry in June.* **2.** To perform the wedding ceremony for someone: *The rabbi married them two weeks ago.*
mar·ry (**mar′**ē) □*verb* **married, marrying, marries**

Mars　*noun* A planet of our solar system, fourth in order from the sun.
Mars (märz) □*noun*

marsh　*noun* An area of low, wet land.
marsh (märsh) □*noun, plural* **marshes**

marshal　*noun* **1.** An officer of the federal government. **2.** The head of a police or fire department. **3.** Someone in charge of a ceremony: *a parade marshal.*
□*verb* **1.** To place in the proper position or rank: *He marshaled the troops for the Memorial Day parade.* **2.** To place in good order: *She marshaled her facts before writing her report.*
mar·shal (**mär′**shəl) □*noun, plural* **marshals** □*verb* **marshaled, marshaling, marshals**

marshmallow　*noun* A soft, white candy.
marsh·mal·low (**märsh′**mel′ō *or* **märsh′**mal′ō) □*noun, plural* **marshmallows**

marshy　*adjective* Being or resembling a marsh: *This marshy land is too wet to build on.*
marsh·y (**mär′**shē) □*adjective* **marshier, marshiest**

marsupial　*noun* A kind of animal, the female of which has a pouch for carrying her young. Kangaroos and opossums are marsupials.
mar·su·pi·al (mär **sōō′**pē əl) □*noun, plural* **marsupials**

marsupial
Kangaroo and offspring

mart　*noun* A place for trading; market.
mart (märt) □*noun, plural* **marts**

marten　*noun* An animal related to the weasel and the mink that is valued for its thick, soft brown fur.
mar·ten (**mär′**tən) □*noun, plural* **martens**

martial　*adjective* Of or for war: *martial music.*
mar·tial (**mär′**shəl) □*adjective*

> *WORD HISTORY:* **martial**
> *Martial* comes from a Latin word meaning "of Mars." Mars was the Roman god of war.

Martian　*adjective* Of or having to do with the planet Mars.
□*noun* A being that is believed to live on Mars.
Mar·tian (**mär′**shən) □*noun, plural* **Martians**

martin　*noun* A bird that is like a swallow and has dark feathers and a forked tail.
mar·tin (**mär′**tən) □*noun, plural* **martins**

martyr　*noun* Someone who chooses to suffer or die rather than give up a belief.
mar·tyr (**mär′**tər) □*noun, plural* **martyrs**

marvel　*noun* Someone or something that is wonderful or astonishing: *The artificial heart is a marvel of medical science.*

a	bat	ī	bite	ōō	tool	*th*	feather
ā	make	î	fierce	ou	out	th	bath
â	dare	o	dot	u	nut	hw	wheat
ä	father	ō	no	û	turn	zh	measure
e	net	ô	law, for	ch	church	ə	about, open
ē	be	oi	soil	ŋ	ring		pencil, atom
i	dip	oo	look	sh	shade		circus

□*verb* To be filled with wonder: *We marveled at her quickness in solving the problem.*
mar·vel (**mär′** vəl) □*noun, plural* **marvels**
□*verb* **marveled, marveling, marvels**

marvelous *adjective* **1.** Causing wonder or admiration; amazing: *a marvelous adventure.* **2.** Very good; excellent: *That's a marvelous idea!*
mar·vel·ous (**mär′** və ləs) □*adjective*

mascot *noun* An animal or person believed to bring good luck: *The team's mascot is a goat.*
mas·cot (**mas′** kot) □*noun, plural* **mascots**

mascot

masculine *adjective* Having to do with men rather than women: *George and William are masculine names.*
mas·cu·line (**mas′** kyə lin) □*adjective*

mash *verb* To crush or grind into a soft mixture: *You can cook the steak while I mash the potatoes.*
□*noun* A soft mixture of grain and water, fed to horses and other animals.
mash (mash) □*verb* **mashed, mashing, mashes** □*noun, plural* **mashes**

mask *noun* **1.** Something that covers and hides the face: *a Halloween mask.* **2.** Something that disguises: *He hid his jealousy behind the mask of friendship.* **3.** A covering to protect the face: *a catcher's mask.*
□*verb* **1.** To put a mask on. **2.** To hide or disguise: *mask one's true feelings.*
mask (mask) □*noun, plural* **masks** □*verb* **masked, masking, masks**

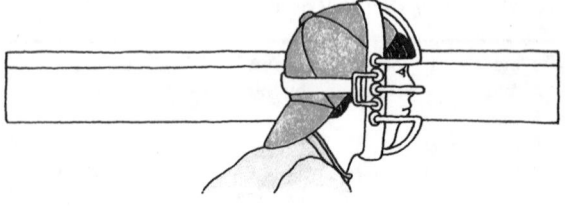
mask
A catcher's mask

mason *noun* Someone who builds things of stone or brick.
ma·son (**mā′** sən) □*noun, plural* **masons**

mason

masonry *noun* **1.** The trade or occupation of a mason. **2.** Work done by a mason. **3.** Something made of stones, bricks, or concrete.
ma·son·ry (**mā′** sən rē) □*noun*

masquerade *noun* A party where people wear masks and costumes.
mas·que·rade (mas′kə **rād′**) □*noun, plural* **masquerades**

mass *noun* **1.** A thing or body of things with no particular shape: *a mass of clay.* **2.** A large amount or quantity: *a mass of people.* **3.** The largest part of something: *The great mass of citizens obey the law.* **4.** Bulk; size: *the enormous mass of a whale.* **5.** The amount of matter in a body.
□*verb* To gather into a mass or group: *The crowd massed at the entrance to the stadium.*
□*adjective* **1.** Of or including many people: *a mass meeting.* **2.** On a large scale: *mass production.*
mass (mas) □*noun, plural* **masses** □*verb* **massed, massing, masses** □*adjective*

Mass *noun* The main religious service in the Roman Catholic and some other churches.
Mass (mas) □*noun, plural* **Masses**

massacre *noun* A brutal killing of many people or animals.
□*verb* To kill many people or animals in a bloody or cruel way.
mas·sa·cre (**mas′** ə kər) □*noun, plural* **massacres** □*verb* **massacred, massacring, massacres**

massage *noun* A rubbing of the body to relax the muscles and improve the flow of blood.
□*verb* To give a massage to.
mas·sage (mə **säzh′**) □*noun, plural*

massages ◻*verb* **massaged, massaging, massages**

massive *adjective* Very large and heavy; huge: *A massive boulder blocked the entrance of the cave.*
mas·sive (**mas′**iv) ◻*adjective*

mast *noun* A tall pole for the sails and rigging of a ship or boat.
mast (mast) ◻*noun, plural* **masts**

master *noun* **1.** Someone who has power to rule or control: *the master of a ship; a dog's master.* **2.** A man who teaches. **3.** Someone who is very good at something: *a master at painting.* **4. Master** A word used in speaking of or to a young boy. —See Synonyms at **expert.**
◻*adjective* **1.** Very skilled: *a master plumber.* **2.** Chief; main: *the master bedroom.*
◻*verb* **1.** To bring under control: *She mastered her fear of flying.* **2.** To become very skilled in: *master a foreign language.*
mas·ter (**mas′**tər) ◻*noun, plural* **masters** ◻*adjective* ◻*verb* **mastered, mastering, masters**

masterful *adjective* **1.** Tending to take charge: *It was hard to resist his masterful personality.* **2.** Having or showing mastery; skillful: *a masterful sculpture.*
mas·ter·ful (**mas′**tər fəl) *adjective*

masterly *adjective* Having or showing the skill of a master; masterful: *a masterly work by a great poet.*
mas·ter·ly (**mas′**tər lē) ◻*adjective*

masterpiece *noun* An outstanding work: *That painting is a masterpiece.*
mas·ter·piece (**mas′**tər pēs′) ◻*noun, plural* **masterpieces**

mastery *noun* **1.** Complete control or rule over: *mastery over his emotions.* **2.** The possession of great skill or knowledge: *a mastery of Spanish; a mastery of horsemanship.*
mas·ter·y (**mas′**tə rē) ◻*noun*

masthead *noun* The top of a ship's mast.
mast·head (**mast′**hed′) ◻*noun, plural* **mastheads**

mastiff *noun* A large dog with a short coat and short, square jaws.
mas·tiff (**mas′**tif) ◻*noun, plural* **mastiffs**

mastodon *noun* An animal related to and resembling the elephant. Mastodons once lived in North America but they are now extinct.
mas·to·don (**mas′**tə don′) ◻*noun, plural* **mastodons**

mat *noun* **1.** A small rug: *a bath mat; a welcome mat.* **2.** A small piece of material that can be put under dishes, vases, and other things: *We put each dish on a place mat.* **3.** A thick pad used on the floor for activities like wrestling and gymnastics. **4.** A thick, tangled mass: *a mat of hair.*
◻*verb* To tangle into a thick mass.
mat (mat) ◻*noun, plural* **mats** ◻*verb* **matted, matting, mats**

matador *noun* Someone who fights and kills bulls in a bullfight.
mat·a·dor (**mat′**ə dôr′) ◻*noun, plural* **matadors**

> **WORD HISTORY:** **matador**
> The word *matador* comes from Spanish. The Spanish word comes from a Latin word meaning "to kill."

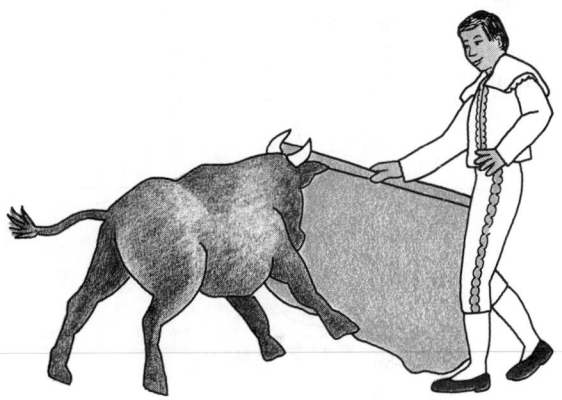

matador

match¹ *noun* **1.** Someone or something that is very much like another or goes well with it: *That sweater is a good match for my slacks.* **2.** A game or contest: *a boxing match.*
◻*verb* **1.** To be or look alike: *The two fingerprints match exactly.* **2.** To do as well as; equal: *Can you match that joke?* **3.** To go well with: *Her blouse does not match her skirt.* **4.** To put two similar things together: *match up socks.*
match (mach) ◻*noun, plural* **matches** ◻*verb* **matched, matching, matches**

a	bat	ī	bite	o͞o	tool	*th*	feather
ā	make	î	fierce	ou	out	th	bath
â	dare	o	dot	u	nut	hw	wheat
ä	father	ō	no	û	turn	zh	measure
e	net	ô	law, for	ch	church	ə	about, open
ē	be	oi	soil	ng	ring		pencil, atom
i	dip	oo	look	sh	shade		circus

match²   *noun* A small stick coated at one end with a chemical substance that catches fire when it is rubbed on a rough surface.
match (mach) ◻*noun, plural* **matches**

matchbook   *noun* A small piece of folded cardboard containing paper matches.
match·book (**mach′**book′) ◻*noun, plural* **matchbooks**

matchless   *adjective* Having no match or equal: *a diamond of matchless beauty.*
match·less (**mach′**lis) ◻*adjective*

matchlock   *noun* A musket with a powder charge ignited by a cord or wick.
match·lock (**mach′**lok′) ◻*noun, plural* **matchlocks**

mate   *noun* **1.** One of a pair: *a sock without a mate.* **2.** A husband or wife. **3.** The male or female of a pair of animals. **4.** An officer on a ship.
◻*verb* To join together for breeding.
mate (māt) ◻*noun, plural* **mates** ◻*verb* **mated, mating, mates**

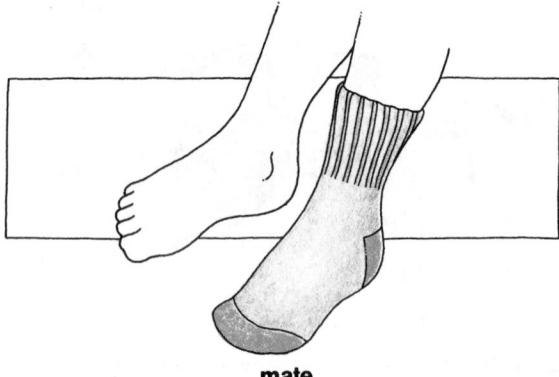

mate

material   *noun* Something that can be used to make something else: *material for a dress; good material for a novel.*
◻*adjective* Of or in the form of matter; physical: *Water and rocks are material things.*
ma·te·ri·al (mə **tîr′**ē əl) ◻*noun, plural* **materials** ◻*adjective*

materialize   *verb* To become real: *Her dreams of going to college never materialized.*
ma·te·ri·al·ize (mə **tîr′**ē ə līz′) ◻*verb* **materialized, materializing, materializes**

maternal   *adjective* **1.** Of or like a mother: *maternal love.* **2.** Related through one's mother: *my maternal grandfather.*
ma·ter·nal (mə **tûr′**nəl) ◻*adjective*

maternity   *noun* The state of being a mother.
ma·ter·ni·ty (mə **tûr′**ni tē) ◻*noun*

math   *noun* Mathematics.
math (math) ◻*noun*

mathematical   *adjective* Of or using mathematics: *mathematical problems.*
math·e·mat·i·cal (math′ə **mat′**i kəl) ◻*adjective*

mathematician   *noun* An expert or specialist in mathematics.
math·e·ma·ti·cian (math′ə mə **tish′**ən) ◻*noun, plural* **mathematicians**

mathematics   *noun* The study of numbers, quantities, shapes, and measurements and their relations. Mathematics includes arithmetic, algebra, and geometry.
math·e·mat·ics (math′ə **mat′**iks) ◻*noun*

matinee   *noun* An afternoon performance in a theater.
mat·i·nee (mat′ən **ā′**) ◻*noun, plural* **matinees**

matrimony   *noun* The condition of being married; marriage.
mat·ri·mo·ny (**mat′**rə mō′nē) ◻*noun*

matron   *noun* **1.** A married woman. **2.** A woman official in a public institution, such as a prison.
ma·tron (**mā′**trən) ◻*noun, plural* **matrons**

matter   *noun* **1.** Something that takes up space and has weight. All things are made of matter, including solids, liquids, and gases. **2.** Material; substance: *matter for thought.* **3.** A subject of interest: *business matters.* **4.** Trouble; problem: *What's the matter with you?*
◻*verb* To be important: *It doesn't matter to me what game we play.*
mat·ter (**mat′**ər) ◻*noun, plural* **matters** ◻*verb* **mattered, mattering, matters**

matter-of-fact   *adjective* **1.** Concerned only with the facts; not imaginative: *a matter-of-fact account of the game.* **2.** Not showing emotion: *a matter-of-fact tone of voice.*
mat·ter-of-fact (**mat′**ər əv **fakt′**) ◻*adjective*

matting   *noun* Material used for making mats.
mat·ting (**mat′**ing) ◻*noun*

mattress   *noun* A large pad stuffed with soft material, used as a bed or on a bed.
mat·tress (**mat′**ris) ◻*noun, plural* **mattresses**

mature   *adjective* Fully grown or developed: *mature grain.*
◻*verb* To reach full growth or development: *The kitten matured into a cat.*

ma·ture (mə **toor′** or mə **tyoor′** or mə **choor′**) □adjective □verb **matured, maturing, matures**

SYNONYMS: **mature, adult**

These adjectives mean fully grown or developed: *a mature person; a mature tree; an adult horse; an adult plant.*

---

maturity *noun* The time or condition of being mature.
ma·tur·i·ty (mə **toor′** i tē) □noun

maul *noun* A heavy hammer with a long handle that is used to drive stakes, piles, or wedges.
□*verb* To injure or damage by beating or rough handling.
maul (môl) □*noun, plural* **mauls** □*verb* **mauled, mauling, mauls**

maxim *noun* A short phrase or sentence expressing a basic truth or rule of behavior; saying. For example, *Waste not, want not* is a maxim.
max·im (**mak′** sim) □*noun, plural* **maxims**

maximum *noun* The highest possible number or degree: *The bus holds a maximum of 40 people.*
□*adjective* Highest or greatest possible: *maximum speed.*
max·i·mum (**mak′** sə məm) □*noun, plural* **maximums** □*adjective*

may *verb* **1.** To be possible or likely: *It may snow tonight.* **2.** To be permitted: *May I have more?* **3.** It is wished that: *May all your wishes come true.*
may (mā) □*verb*

May *noun* The fifth month of the year. May has 31 days.
May (mā) □*noun, plural* **Mays**

WORD HISTORY: **May**

May comes from the Latin name for this month. The Romans named May after a goddess called *Maia.*

---

maybe *adverb* Possibly; perhaps.
may·be (**mā′** bē) □*adverb*

May Day *noun* May 1 celebrated as a spring festival.

mayonnaise *noun* A thick dressing made of egg yolks, oil, and lemon juice or vinegar.
may·on·naise (mā′ə **nāz′**) □*noun*

mayor *noun* The highest official of a city or town.
may·or (**mā′** ər) □*noun, plural* **mayors**

maypole *noun* A tall pole decorated with flowers that is a center for dances and games on May Day.
may·pole (**mā′** pōl′) □*noun, plural* **maypoles**

maypole

maze *noun* A complicated, winding series of paths through which it is hard to find one's way: *We got lost in a maze of hallways.*
maze (māz) □*noun, plural* **mazes**

maze

M.D. An abbreviation for **doctor of medicine.**

me *pronoun* The objective case of **I:** *They didn't see me. She wrote me a letter. He kicked*

a	bat	ī	bite	o͞o	tool	*th* feather
ā	make	î	fierce	ou	out	th bath
â	dare	o	dot	u	nut	hw wheat
ä	father	ō	no	û	turn	zh measure
e	net	ô	law, for	ch church		ə about, open
ē	be	oi	soil	ng ring		pencil, atom
i	dip	oo	look	sh shade		circus

the ball to me.
me (mē) □*pronoun*

meadow *noun* An area of grassy ground.
mead·ow (med′ō) □*noun, plural* **meadows**

meadowlark *noun* A songbird that has a yellow breast marked with a black V.
mead·ow·lark (med′ō lärk′) □*noun, plural* **meadowlarks**

meadowlark

meager *adjective* Barely enough; very small or poor: *We were still hungry after the meager meal.*
mea·ger (mē′gər) □*adjective*

meal¹ *noun* Coarsely ground grain.
meal (mēl) □*noun, plural* **meals**

meal² *noun* The food served and eaten in one sitting: *Supper is my main meal of the day.*
meal (mēl) □*noun, plural* **meals**

mealy *adjective* **1.** Containing or covered with meal. **2.** Resembling meal in texture or consistency: *mealy potatoes.*
meal·y (mē′lē) □*adjective* **mealier, mealiest**

mean¹ *verb* **1.** To have as a sense or meaning; signify: *"Profound" means "deep" or "wise." What does that poem mean?* **2.** To have in mind; intend: *He meant to call the next day.*
mean (mēn) □*verb* **meant, meaning, means**

mean² *adjective* **1.** Not kind or good; cruel: *It was mean to tease the new girl.* **2.** Selfish; stingy. **3.** Having a low rank or value: *a mean, shabby part of town.*
mean (mēn) □*adjective* **meaner, meanest**

mean³ *noun* **1.** Something that is between two extremes: *Find a happy mean between being lazy and being too active.* **2. means** Something used to help reach a goal; method: *A knapsack is a practical means of carrying supplies on a hike.* **3. means** Money; wealth.
□*adjective* In the middle; average: *Yesterday the mean temperature was 65 degrees.*
mean (mēn) □*noun, plural* **means**
□*adjective*

meander *verb* **1.** To follow a winding course: *The path meandered through the woods.* **2.** To wander without a purpose or direction: *I meandered through the store while my mother shopped.*
me·an·der (mē an′dər) □*verb* **meandered, meandering, meanders**

> *WORD HISTORY:* **meander**
> The word *meander* comes from the ancient Greek name for a river in Turkey that has a winding course.

meaning *noun* **1.** What something means: *A dictionary explains the meaning of words.* **2.** Something that is intended; intention or purpose: *What was the meaning of that remark?*
mean·ing (mē′ning) □*noun, plural* **meanings**

meaningful *adjective* Full of meaning; significant: *a meaningful discussion.*
mean·ing·ful (mē′ning fəl) □*adjective*

meaningless *adjective* Having no meaning.
mean·ing·less (mē′ning lis) □*adjective*

meant *verb* The past tense and past participle of **mean**: *She meant no harm.*
meant (ment) □*verb*

meantime *noun* The time between: *The bus leaves in an hour; in the meantime, I'll read.*
mean·time (mēn′tīm′) □*noun*

meanwhile *adverb* **1.** During the time in between: *I'll leave tonight; meanwhile I'll pack my bags.* **2.** At the same time: *I'll wash the pots; meanwhile you clear the table.*
mean·while (mēn′hwīl′ *or* mēn′wīl′) □*adverb*

measles *plural noun* A contagious disease that gives people a fever and makes them break out in red spots. Measles is caused by a virus.
mea·sles (mē′zəlz) □*plural noun*

measly *adjective* Of such small size or value as to deserve scorn: *I spent two hours shoveling snow and all I got was a measly quarter.*
meas·ly (mē′zlē) □*adjective* **measlier, measliest**

measurable *adjective* Able to be measured: *a measurable amount of rainfall.*
meas·ur·a·ble (mezh′ər ə bəl) □*adjective*

measure *noun* **1.** The size, amount, weight, or volume of something: *I took the measure of the board with a ruler.* **2.** A unit for figuring out size, amount, or volume: *Feet and meters*

are measures of length. **3.** An instrument for figuring out size, amount, weight, or volume. **4.** Amount or extent: *Use a large measure of caution when handling a knife.* **5.** An action taken for a purpose: *What measures have been taken to prevent accidents?* **6.** A bill or law: *a measure to lower taxes.* **7.** The music between two bars on a staff.
□*verb* **1.** To find or show the size, amount, weight, or volume of: *measured the height of a wall.* **2.** To have as size, amount, weight, or volume: *The board measures 2 by 8 feet.*
meas·ure (**mezh′**ər) □*noun, plural* **measures** □*verb* **measured, measuring, measures**

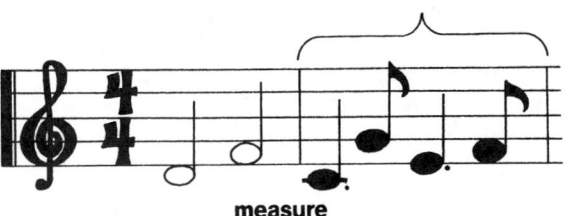

measure

measurement *noun* **1.** The act of measuring. **2.** A system of measuring: *metric measurement.* **3.** A dimension or number found by measuring: *What are the measurements of your living room?*
meas·ure·ment (**mezh′**ər mənt) □*noun,* *plural* **measurements**

meat *noun* **1.** The parts of an animal that can be eaten as food. Beef and pork are kinds of meat. **2.** The part of a nut or fruit that can be eaten. **3.** The main part: *Definitions are the meat of this dictionary.*
meat (mēt) □*noun, plural* **meats**

WORD HISTORY: **meat**

Meat comes from an old English word that referred to solid food of any kind in contrast to liquids.

---

mechanic *noun* Someone who is skilled in using or repairing machines.
me·chan·ic (mə **kan′**ik) □*noun, plural* **mechanics**

mechanical *adjective* **1.** Of or relating to machines: *mechanical skill.* **2.** Made or run by a machine. **3.** Lacking warmth or feeling as if done or produced by a machine: *played the piano in a dull, mechanical fashion.*
me·chan·i·cal (mə **kan′**i kəl) □*adjective*

mechanics *noun* **1.** The scientific study of the action of forces on bodies: *Mechanics is a branch of physics.* **2.** How something works or

is done: *The mechanics of football are learned with practice.*
me·chan·ics (mə **kan′**iks) □*noun*

mechanism *noun* The working parts of a machine: *The mechanism of the electric fan broke.*
mech·a·nism (**mek′**ə niz′əm) □*noun, plural* **mechanisms**

medal *noun* A flat, round piece of metal with a design or writing on it: *The soldier was given a medal for bravery.*
med·al (**med′**əl) □*noun, plural* **medals**

WORD HISTORY: **medal**

Medal comes from the Latin word that means "middle" or "half." A medal was at one time a coin that was half the value of another coin.

---

medallion *noun* **1.** A large medal. **2.** Something shaped like a medallion.
me·dal·lion (mə **dal′**yən) □*noun, plural* **medallions**

meddle *verb* To take part in other people's business without being asked; interfere.
med·dle (**med′**əl) □*verb* **meddled, meddling, meddles**

meddlesome *adjective* Tending to meddle: *a meddlesome person who is always giving advice.*
med·dle·some (**med′**əl səm) □*adjective*

media *noun* A plural of **medium**: *magazines, television, and other media.*
me·di·a (**mē′**dē ə) □*noun*

medical *adjective* Of doctors or medicine: *Injured people need medical help.*
med·i·cal (**med′**i kəl) □*adjective*

medicate *verb* **1.** To treat with medicine. **2.** To add medicine to: *a medicated lotion.*
med·i·cate (**med′**i kāt′) □*verb* **medicated, medicating, medicates**

medication *noun* **1.** The act of medicating. **2.** Medicine.
med·i·ca·tion (med′i **ka′**shən) □*noun, plural* **medications**

a	bat	ī	bite	o͞o	tool	*th*	feather
ā	make	î	fierce	ou	out	th	bath
â	dare	o	dot	u	nut	hw	wheat
ä	father	ō	no	û	turn	zh	measure
e	net	ô	law, for	ch	church	ə	about, open
ē	be	oi	soil	ng	ring		pencil, atom
i	dip	oo	look	sh	shade		circus

medicinal *adjective* Of, having to do with, or resembling medicine: *a liquid with a medicinal taste.*
me·dic·i·nal (mə **dis′**ə nəl) □*adjective*

medicine *noun* **1.** A substance used to treat or prevent disease or to relieve pain. **2.** The study and treatment of diseases and injuries.
med·i·cine (**med′**i sin) □*noun, plural* **medicines**

medicine man *noun* Someone in certain Native American tribes who was believed to have magic powers for healing the sick and dealing with spirits.
medicine man □*noun, plural* **medicine men**

medieval *adjective* Of, from, or like the Middle Ages.
me·di·e·val (mē′dē **ē′**vəl *or* med′ē **ē′**vəl) □*adjective*

mediocre *adjective* Neither very good nor very bad; of average quality: *a mediocre student; a mediocre performance.*
me·di·o·cre (mē′dē **ō′**kər) □*adjective*

> **WORD HISTORY: mediocre**
>
> The word *mediocre* comes from French. The French word is derived from a Latin word meaning "middle."

meditate *verb* To think deeply and at length; reflect: *Many wise people have meditated on how to live a good life.*
med·i·tate (**med′**i tāt′) □*verb* **meditated, meditating, meditates.**

medium *noun* **1.** Something in the middle: *finding a happy medium between too hot and too cold.* **2.** A substance in which something lives, moves, or is done: *Pond water is a good medium for floating weeds.* **3.** Any of the means used to transfer information: *Television is an important medium.*
□*adjective* In the middle between two extremes: *a medium speed.*
me·di·um (**mē′**dē əm) □*noun, plural* **mediums** or **media** (*for senses 2 and 3*)
□*adjective*

medley *noun* **1.** A piece of music made up of a series of tunes or parts of other musical compositions. **2.** A mixture: *a medley of voices.*
med·ley (**med′**lē) □*noun, plural* **medleys**

meek *adjective* **1.** Patient when attacked or injured. **2.** Lacking in spirit or courage.
meek (mēk) □*adjective* **meeker, meekest**

meet *verb* **1.** To join; touch: *Parallel lines never meet.* **2.** To come face to face with: *I met an old friend on the street.* **3.** To come together with by appointment: *I'll meet you in front of the gym after school.* **4.** To be introduced to. **5.** To pay or provide for: *meet one's expenses.* **6.** To hold a meeting: *The committee met on the last day of the month.*
□*noun* A gathering for a sports competition.
meet (mēt) □*verb* **met, meeting, meets** □*noun, plural* **meets**

meeting *noun* **1.** The act of coming together: *a chance meeting of two friends.* **2.** A gathering of people: *a club meeting.*
meet·ing (**mē′**ting) □*noun, plural* **meetings**

megaphone *noun* A device shaped like a funnel for making the voice sound louder.
meg·a·phone (**meg′**ə fōn′) □*noun, plural* **megaphones**

megaphone

melancholy *noun* A sad, gloomy feeling.
□*adjective* **1.** Sad; gloomy: *a melancholy look.* **2.** Making one feel sad: *a melancholy tale.*
mel·an·chol·y (**mel′**ən kol′ē) □*noun* □*adjective*

mellow *adjective* **1.** Soft and sweet: *mellow sounds.* **2.** Grown gentler with age.
mel·low (**mel′**ō) □*adjective* **mellower, mellowest**

melodious *adjective* Pleasant to listen to because resembling or containing a melody: *a bird's melodious song.*
me·lo·di·ous (mə **lō′**dē əs) □*adjective*

melody *noun* A pleasing series of musical tones; tune.
mel·o·dy (**mel′**ə dē) □*noun, plural* **melodies**

melon *noun* A large fruit with a hard rind and juicy flesh. A cantaloupe is a melon.
mel·on (**mel′**ən) □*noun, plural* **melons**

melt *verb* **1.** To change from a solid into a liquid by heating: *The ice melted in the sun.* **2.** To dissolve: *Sugar melts in hot water.* **3.** To fade or disappear: *The clouds melted away.* **4.** To make or become gentler: *The child's tears* *melted my heart.*

melt (melt) □*verb* **melted, melting, melts**

member *noun* **1.** Someone or something that belongs to a group: *a member of the student council; a member of the cat family.* **2.** A body part, as an arm or leg.
mem·ber (mem′bər) □*noun, plural* **members**

membership *noun* **1.** The condition of being a member. **2.** The total number of people who are members.
mem·ber·ship (mem′bər ship′) □*noun, plural* **memberships**

membrane *noun* A thin layer of tissue in the body of an animal or plant.
mem·brane (mem′brān′) □*noun, plural* **membranes**

memento *noun* A reminder of someone or something in the past: *a memento of a summer spent with my cousins at the seashore.*
me·men·to (mə men′tō) □*noun, plural* **mementos**

WORD HISTORY: memento

The noun *memento* comes from a form of the Latin verb meaning "to remember." In Latin *memento* means "Remember!"

---

memorable *adjective* Worth being remembered: *a memorable experience.*
mem·o·ra·ble (mem′ər ə bəl) □*adjective*

memorial *noun* Something built or done in memory of a person or event: *The statue is a memorial to those who died in the war.*
me·mo·ri·al (mə môr′ē əl) □*noun, plural* **memorials**

We will not forget...

memorial

Memorial Day *noun* A holiday falling on the last Monday in May and celebrated in memory of the servicemen who died in American wars.

memorize *verb* To learn by heart: *memorize the words of a song.*
mem·o·rize (mem′ə_rīz′) □*verb* **memorized, memorizing, memorizes**

memory *noun* **1.** The ability to remember: *She has a good memory for names.* **2.** Everything that is remembered: *He can recite the poem from memory.* **3.** Something that is remembered: *Her earliest memory is of kindergarten.* **4.** The unit of a computer in which information is stored.
mem·o·ry (mem′ə rē) □*noun, plural* **memories**

men *noun* The plural of **man.**
men (men) □*noun*

menace *noun* A threat; danger: *Ice on roads is a menace to cars.*
□*verb* To threaten with harm.
men·ace (men′is) □*noun, plural* **menaces**
□*verb* **menaced, menacing, menaces**

menagerie *noun* **1.** A collection of wild animals kept in pens or cages. **2.** A place where a menagerie is kept.
me·nag·er·ie (mə naj′ə rē) □*noun, plural* **menageries**

mend *verb* **1.** To repair; fix: *mend a torn shirt.* **2.** To get better; heal: *Her broken finger mended quickly.* **3.** To improve: *You must mend your ways.*
mend (mend) □*verb* **mended, mending, mends**

SYNONYMS: mend, fix, repair

These verbs mean to put back into proper or useful condition: *He mended the rip in my pants. Can you fix the clock so that it will run again? It was impossible to repair the broken stereo.*

---

menial *noun* A household servant.
□*adjective* **1.** Of or having to do with a household servant. **2.** Needing little skill or responsibility: *a menial job.*
me·ni·al (mē′nē əl) □*noun, plural* **menials**
□*adjective*

–ment A suffix that means: **1.** An act or process: *management.* **2.** A condition: *excitement.* **3.** The result of an action: *improvement.*

a bat	ī bite	ōō tool	*th* feather
ā make	î fierce	ou out	th bath
â dare	o dot	u nut	hw **wh**eat
ä father	ō no	û turn	zh mea**s**ure
e net	ô law, for	ch **ch**urch	ə about, open
ē be	oi soil	ng ri**ng**	pencil, atom
i dip	oo look	sh **sh**ade	circus

mental *adjective* **1.** Of or done by the mind: *a mental image.* **2.** Of, relating to, or suffering from a disease of the mind: *a mental patient; a mental hospital.*
men·tal (**men′** təl) □*adjective*

mentality *noun* **1.** Mental capacity or ability; intelligence. **2.** A habitual frame of mind: *a cautious mentality.*
men·tal·i·ty (men **tal′** i tē) □*noun, plural* **mentalities**

mention *verb* To speak about in a brief way; refer to: *He mentioned that he would phone tonight.*
□*noun* An example of mentioning or calling attention to: *He made no mention of the fact that his assistant had done most of the work.*
men·tion (**men′** shən) □*verb* **mentioned, mentioning, mentions** □*noun, plural* **mentions**

menu *noun* A list of the food available in a restaurant or other eating place: *We asked the waiter to bring us a menu.*
men·u (**men′** yo͞o) □*noun, plural* **menus**

meow *noun* The sound a cat makes.
□*verb* To make the sound typical of a cat.
me·ow (mē **ou′**) □*noun, plural* **meows** □*verb* **meowed, meowing, meows**

merchandise *noun* Goods bought and sold.
mer·chan·dise (**mûr′** chən dīz′ *or* **mûr′** chən dīs′) □*noun*

merchant *noun* **1.** Someone whose work is buying and selling goods. **2.** Someone who runs a store.
mer·chant (**mûr′** chənt) □*noun, plural* **merchants**

mercenary *adjective* **1.** Working only for pay or reward. **2.** Greedy for money.
□*noun* A soldier wo fights in a foreign army for pay.
mer·ce·nar·y (**mûr′** sə ner′ē) □*adjective* □*noun, plural* **mercenaries**

merciful *adjective* Having or showing mercy.
mer·ci·ful (**mûr′** si fəl) □*adjective*

merciless *adjective* Having or showing no mercy; cruel.
mer·ci·less (**mûr′** si lis) □*adjective*

mercury *noun* A chemical element that is a metal having a silver color, is liquid at normal temperatures, and used especially in thermometers.
mer·cu·ry (**mûr′** kyə rē) □*noun*

Mercury *noun* The planet of our solar system

that is closest to the sun.
Mer·cu·ry (**mûr′** kyə rē) □*noun*

mercy *noun* **1.** Kind treatment of a person in one's power: *The thief asked the judge for mercy.* **2.** Something due to good luck: *It's a mercy no one was hurt in the accident.*
mer·cy (**mûr′** sē) □*noun, plural* **mercies**

mere *adjective* Being just that and no more; only: *The job took a mere two minutes.*
mere (mîr) □*adjective*

merely *adverb* Simply; only: *He merely smiled in reply.*
mere·ly (**mîr′** lē) □*adverb*

merge *verb* To come together; combine: *The two streams merged to form a great river.*
merge (mûrj) □*verb* **merged, merging, merges**

meridian *noun* A line of longitude.
me·rid·i·an (mə **rid′** ē ən) □*noun, plural* **meridians**

meringue *noun* A mixture of beaten egg whites and sugar. Meringue is used as a topping for cakes and pies or baked into shells to be filled with fruit or ice cream.
me·ringue (mə **rang′**) □*noun*

merino *noun* **1.** A sheep of a breed having fine, soft wool. **2.** Cloth or yarn made from the wool of a merino.
me·ri·no (mə **rē′** nō) □*noun, plural* **merinos**

merit *noun* **1.** A quality that deserves praise: *a book of great merit.* **2. merits** The actual facts: *I judge a case on its merits.*
□*verb* To deserve: *Her criticism merits our attention.*
mer·it (**mer′** it) □*noun, plural* **merits** □*verb* **merited, meriting, merits**

SYNONYMS: **merit, deserve, earn**

These verbs mean to be entitled to: *All the work he's done around the house merits a reward. She deserved a good mark because her book report was outstanding. He earned great praise for his discovery.*

---

mermaid *noun* An imaginary sea creature with the head and body of a woman and the tail of a fish.
mer·maid (**mûr′** mād′) □*noun, plural* **mermaids**

merman *noun* An imaginary sea creature with the head and body of a man and the tail of a fish.

mer·man (**mûr′**man′) □*noun, plural*
mermen

merman

merriment *noun* Lighthearted gaiety; mirth.
mer·ri·ment (**mer′**i mənt) □*noun*

merry *adjective* Full of fun and gaiety; jolly.
mer·ry (**mer′**ē) □*adjective* **merrier, merriest**

merry-go-round *noun* A round, turning platform with seats shaped like horses and other
animals on which people ride.
mer·ry-go-round (**mer′**ē gō round′) □*noun,*
plural **merry-go-rounds**

merry-go-round

merrymaking *noun* **1.** Merry fun. **2.** A joyful party or celebration.
mer·ry·mak·ing (**mer′**ē mā′king) □*noun*

mesa *noun* A hill with a flat top or a small
plateau with steep sides. Mesas are common
in the southwestern United States.
me·sa (**mā′**sə) □*noun, plural* **mesas**

WORD HISTORY: **mesa**

The word *mesa* comes from Spanish. In Spanish the
word literally means ''table.''

---

mesh *noun* **1.** A network of threads or wires
that cross: *A window screen is made of metal*
or plastic mesh. **2.** One of the spaces enclosed
by the threads or wires of such a network.
mesh (mesh) □*noun, plural* **meshes**

mess *noun* **1.** A disorderly or untidy condition: *This room is a mess.* **2.** A confused, difficult situation: *He made a mess of his life.* **3.** A
group of people, especially in military service,
who regularly eat together.
□*verb* **1.** To make dirty or untidy: *She cer-*
tainly messed up the kitchen when she made
lunch. **2.** To spoil; ruin: *Coming down with the*
flu messed up my plans.
mess (mes) □*noun, plural* **messes** □*verb*
messed, messing, messes

message *noun* Words sent from one person
or group to another: *There's a phone message*
for you.
mes·sage (**mes′**ij) □*noun, plural* **messages**

messenger *noun* Someone who carries a
message or goes on an errand.
mes·sen·ger (**mes′**ən jər) □*noun, plural*
messengers

messy *adjective* Sloppy or cluttered.
mess·y (**mes′**ē) □*adjective* **messier, messiest**

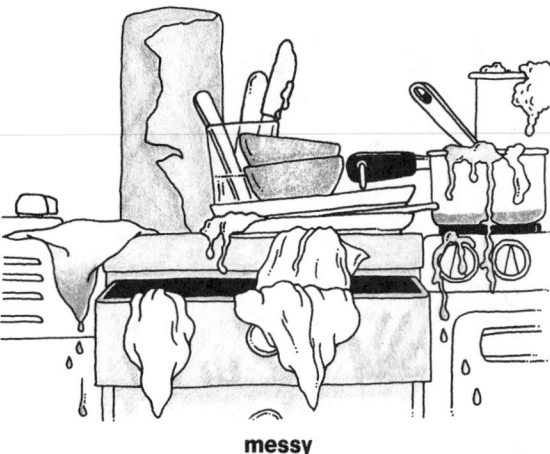

messy

met *verb* The past tense and past participle of
meet: *They met at the street corner.*
met (met) □*verb*

a bat	ī bite	ōō tool	*th* feather
ā make	î fierce	ou out	th bath
â dare	o dot	u nut	hw wheat
ä father	ō no	û turn	zh measure
e net	ô law, for	ch church	ə about, open
ē be	oi soil	ng ring	pencil, atom
i dip	oo look	sh shade	circus

metabolism *noun* The biological processes by which a living being carries out the activities necessary for life. Metabolism includes the changing of food into forms that a living being can use.
me·tab·o·lism (mə **tab′**ə liz′əm) □*noun*

metal *noun* A substance that is shiny and conducts heat and electricity. Iron, steel, tin, and gold are metals.
□*adjective* Made of metal: *a metal fence*.
met·al (**met′**əl) □*noun, plural* **metals**
  □*adjective*

metallic *adjective* **1.** Of, relating to, or like metal: *a metallic gleam*. **2.** Made of or containing metal.
me·tal·lic (mə **tal′**ik) □*adjective*

metallurgy *noun* The science of extracting metals from ores and making them ready for use.
met·al·lur·gy (**met′**əl ûr′jē) □*noun*

metamorphosis *noun* Change in form that some animals go through during their natural development. A caterpillar becomes a butterfly by metamorphosis.
met·a·mor·pho·sis (met′ə **môr′**fə sis) □*noun, plural* **metamorphoses** (met′ə **môr′**fə sēz′)

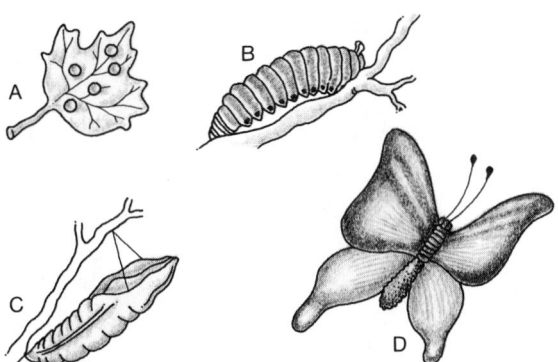

metamorphosis
Of a butterfly: *(A)* eggs, *(B)* larva, *(C)* pupa, *(D)* adult

metaphor *noun* A figure of speech in which two things are compared without using "like" or "as." For example, *Her heart was stone* is a metaphor.
met·a·phor (**met′**ə fôr′) □*noun, plural* **metaphors**

WORD HISTORY: **metaphor**

The word *metaphor* comes from a Greek word meaning "to transfer." A metaphor is a figure of speech that transfers the name of one thing to something that is similar in some way.

---

meteor *noun* A streak of light in the sky. A meteor appears when a mass of matter from outer space burns as it enters the earth's atmosphere.
me·te·or (**mē′**tē ər) □*noun, plural* **meteors**

meteorite *noun* A chunk of matter from outer space that lands on earth.
me·te·or·ite (**mē′**tē ə rīt′) □*noun, plural* **meteorites**

meteorology *noun* The scientific study of the atmosphere and weather.
me·te·or·ol·o·gy (mē′tē ə **rol′**ə jē) □*noun*

meter¹ *noun* The basic unit of length in the metric system, equal to about 39.37 inches.
me·ter (**mē′**tər) □*noun, plural* **meters**

meter² *noun* An instrument that measures something: *a water meter*.
me·ter (**mē′**tər) □*noun, plural* **meters**

meter³ *noun* A pattern of rhythm in music or poetry.
me·ter (**mē′**tər) □*noun, plural* **meters**

method *noun* **1.** A way of doing something: *Boiling and frying are two methods of cooking an egg.* **2.** Definite order or purpose: *The clothing was piled into drawers without method.*
meth·od (**meth′**əd) □*noun, plural* **methods**

methodical *adjective* **1.** Arranged or done according to a clear plan or method: *a methodical inspection.* **2.** Orderly and systematic: *methodical habits; a methodical worker.*
me·thod·i·cal (mə **thod′**i kəl) □*adjective*

metric *adjective* Of or using the metric system.
met·ric (**met′**rik) □*adjective*

metric system *noun* A system of weights and measures based on the number 10. In the metric system, the meter is the basic unit of length, the kilogram is the basic unit of weight, and the liter is the basic unit of volume.

metronome *noun* A device that makes a series of regular clicks to give a steady beat for practicing music.
met·ro·nome (**met′**rə nōm′) □*noun, plural* **metronomes**

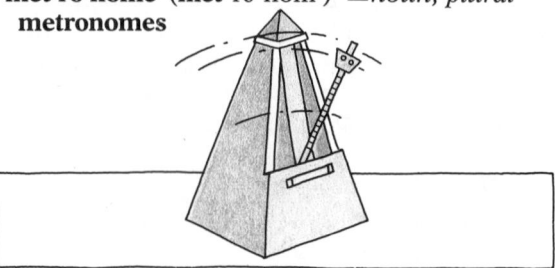

metronome

metropolis *noun* A large or important city.
me·trop·o·lis (mə **trop′**ə lis) □*noun, plural* **metropolises**

metropolitan *adjective* Of or having to do with a metropolis: *a metropolitan transportation system.*
met·ro·pol·i·tan (met′rə **pol′**i tən) □*adjective*

mettle *noun* Strength of character or spirit; courage: *He volunteered for many dangerous missions to prove his mettle as a soldier.*
met·tle (**met′**əl) □*noun*

mew *noun* The cry of a cat; meow.
□*verb* To make a sound like the cry of a cat.
mew (myōō) □*noun, plural* **mews** □*verb* **mewed, mewing, mews**

Mexican *noun* Someone who was born in or lives in Mexico.
□*adjective* Of Mexico, the Mexicans, or their language.
Mex·i·can (**mek′**si kən) □*noun, plural* **Mexicans** □*adjective*

mice *noun* The plural of **mouse.**
mice (mīs) □*noun*

microbe *noun* A tiny plant or animal: *a disease caused by microbes.*
mi·crobe (**mī′**krōb′) □*noun, plural* **microbes**

microchip *noun* A small electronic device that contains many different switches on a single electronic circuit. All computers made today contain microchips.
mi·cro·chip (**mī′**krō chip′) □*noun, plural* **microchips**

microorganism *noun* An organism that can only be seen through a microscope.
mi·cro·or·gan·ism (mī′krō **ôr′**gə niz′əm) □*noun, plural* **microorganisms**

microphone *noun* An electrical instrument used to send sound over a distance or to make it louder.
mi·cro·phone (**mī′**krə fōn′) □*noun, plural* **microphones**

microphone

microscope *noun* An instrument that uses lenses to make an enlarged image of something that is too small to see with the naked eye.
mi·cro·scope (**mī′**krə skōp′) □*noun, plural* **microscopes**

microscope

microscopic *adjective* Too small to be seen except through a microscope: *Yeast is a microscopic plant used in the making of bread and wine.*
mi·cro·scop·ic (mī′krə **skop′**ik) □*adjective*

mid *adjective* Middle: *mid afternoon.*
mid (mid) □*adjective*

midair *noun* A point or region in the air: *The kite string caught on a wire and the kite was left hanging in midair.*
mid·air (mid âr′) □*noun*

midday *noun* The middle of the day; noon.
mid·day (**mid′**dā′) □*noun, plural* **middays**

middle *noun* **1.** A point about halfway between two things: *a town in the middle of the state; in the middle of the night.* **2.** A person's waist.
□*adjective* At or in the middle: *She sat in the middle seat between the two brothers.*
mid·dle (**mid′**əl) □*noun, plural* **middles** □*adjective*

middle age *noun* The time of human life between youth and old age.

a	bat	ī	bite	ōō	tool	*th*	feather
ā	make	î	fierce	ou	out	th	bath
â	dare	o	dot	u	nut	hw	wheat
ä	father	ō	no	û	turn	zh	measure
e	net	ô	law, for	ch	church	ə	about, open
ē	be	oi	soil	ng	ring		pencil, atom
i	dip	oo	look	sh	shade		circus

middle-aged *adjective* Between youth and old age: *a middle-aged person.*
mid·dle-aged (mid′əl ājd′) □*adjective*

Middle Ages *plural noun* The period in European history from about A.D. 500 to about 1400.

middle class *noun* A social class between the rich and the poor.

middle ear *noun* The part of the ear between the eardrum and the inner ear.

Middle East *noun* A region including the countries of southwestern Asia and northeastern Africa.

Middle West *noun* A region of the United States from Minnesota and Missouri on the west to Ohio on the east.

midge *noun* A very small gnat or fly.
midge (mij) □*noun, plural* **midges**

midget *noun* An unusually small person whose body has normal proportions.
mid·get (mij′it) □*noun, plural* **midgets**

midnight *noun* Twelve o'clock at night.
mid·night (mid′nīt′) □*noun, plural* **midnights**

midriff *noun* The part of the human body that extends from the middle of the chest to the waist.
mid·riff (mid′rif′) □*noun, plural* **midriffs**

midst *noun* **1.** The middle part: *a cabin in the midst of the forest.* **2.** A position close to a group of people: *a spy in our midst.*
midst (midst) □*noun*

midst

midstream *noun* The middle of a stream.
mid·stream (mid′strēm′) □*noun, plural* **midstreams**

midsummer *noun* The middle of the summer.

mid·sum·mer (mid′sum′ər) □*noun, plural* **midsummers**

midway *adverb* In the middle: *Our car broke down midway across the desert.*
□*adjective* Occurring in the middle: *the midway point of the school year.*
mid·way (mid′wā′) □*adverb* □*adjective*

Midwest *noun* The Middle West.
Mid·west (mid′west′) □*noun*

midwinter *noun* The middle of the winter.
mid·win·ter (mid′win′tər) □*noun, plural* **midwinters**

midyear *noun* The middle of a year: *We always have exams at midyear.*
mid·year (mid′yîr′) □*noun, plural* **midyears**

might[1] *noun* Great power or strength: *the might of a hundred men.*
might (mīt) □*noun*

might[2] *verb* Used to show that it is possible that something can happen, but not likely: *We might take a trip next summer. If he hurries, he might be on time.*
might (mīt) □*verb*

mighty *adjective* Having or showing great strength or size: *a mighty warrior.*
□*adverb* Very; extremely: *That was a mighty fine dinner!*
might·y (mī′tē) □*adjective* **mightier, mightiest** □*adverb*

migrate *verb* To move from one living place to another: *Birds migrate every spring and fall.*
mi·grate (mī′grāt′) □*verb* **migrated, migrating, migrates**

migration *noun* Movement to another place to live or stay.
mi·gra·tion (mī grā′shən) □*noun, plural* **migrations**

mike *noun* A microphone.
mike (mīk) □*noun, plural* **mikes**

mild *adjective* **1.** Gentle: *a mild, sweet person.* **2.** Not rough or harsh: *a mild climate.*
mild (mīld) □*adjective* **milder, mildest**

mildew *noun* A fungus that grows as a white or grayish coating on living plants or decaying matter.
□*verb* To become covered or spotted with mildew.
mil·dew (mil′dōō′ *or* mil′ dyōō′) □*noun, plural* **mildews** □*verb* **mildewed, mildewing, mildews**

mile *noun* A unit of length equal to 5,280 feet or 1,609.34 meters.
mile (mīl) □*noun, plural* **miles**

mileage   *noun* **1.** The number of miles measured or traveled in a period of time. **2.** The number of miles a car can travel on one gallon of gasoline.
mile·age (**mī′**lij) ◻*noun*

milestone   *noun* **1.** A stone marker that tells the distance in miles to another point. **2.** An important event in the history or development of someone or something: *Learning to talk is a great milestone in the life of a child.*
mile·stone (**mīl′**stōn′) ◻*noun, plural* **milestones**

military   *adjective* Of or having to do with soldiers or war: *military supplies.*
◻*noun* The armed forces.
mil·i·tar·y (**mil′**i ter′ē) ◻*adjective* ◻*noun*

militia   *noun* A group of citizens who are trained to fight in a national emergency.
mi·li·tia (mi **lish′**ə) ◻*noun, plural* **militias**

milk   *noun* **1.** A white liquid produced by glands of female mammals for feeding their young. **2.** The milk of cows as used as food by human beings.
◻*verb* To draw milk from a cow or other animal.
milk (milk) ◻*noun* ◻*verb* **milked, milking, milks**

milk

milkmaid   *noun* A girl or woman who milks cows and works in a dairy.
milk·maid (**milk′**mād′) ◻*noun, plural* **milkmaids**

milkman   *noun* A man who sells or delivers milk.

milk·man (**milk′**man′) ◻*noun, plural* **milkmen**

milk shake   *noun* A drink made by blending milk, flavoring, and sometimes ice cream.

milk tooth   *noun* A temporary tooth that grows in the mouth of a young mammal before the permanent teeth appear.

milkweed   *noun* A plant that has stems containing milky juice and pods containing fluffy white seeds.
milk·weed (**milk′**wēd′) ◻*noun*

milkweed

milky   *adjective* **1.** Resembling milk: *a milky liquid.* **2.** Containing milk: *a milky sauce.*
milk·y (**mil′**kē) ◻*adjective* **milkier, milkiest**

Milky Way   *noun* A band of hazy light stretching across the sky caused by a large group of stars.

mill   *noun* **1.** A machine that grinds or crushes something: *a pepper mill.* **2.** A building with machines for grinding grains into meal or flour. **3.** A building with machines for making things: *a steel mill.*
◻*verb* **1.** To grind: *mill wheat into flour.* **2.** To move around in a confused way: *The children milled around in the playground.*
mill (mil) ◻*noun, plural* **mills** ◻*verb* **milled, milling, mills**

miller   *noun* A person who works in or runs a mill for grinding grain.
mill·er (**mil′**ər) ◻*noun, plural* **millers**

a	bat	ī	bite	o͞o	tool	*th*	feather
ā	make	î	fierce	ou	out	th	bath
â	dare	o	dot	u	nut	hw	wheat
ä	father	ō	no	û	turn	zh	measure
e	net	ô	law, for	ch	church	ə	about, open
ē	be	oi	soil	ng	ring		pencil, atom
i	dip	oo	look	sh	shade		circus

seeds and for use as hay.
mil·let (mil′it) ☐*noun*

milligram *noun* A unit of mass or weight in the metric system equal to ¹/₁₀₀₀ gram.
mil·li·gram (mil′i gram′) ☐*noun, plural* **milligrams**

milliliter *noun* A unit of fluid volume or capacity in the metric system equal to ¹/₁₀₀₀ liter.
mil·li·li·ter (mil′ə lē′tər) ☐*noun, plural* **milliliters**

millimeter *noun* A metric unit of length equal to ¹/₁₀₀₀ meter.
mil·li·me·ter (mil′ə mē′tər) ☐*noun, plural* **millimeters**

milliner *noun* Someone who makes or sells women's hats.
mil·li·ner (mil′ə nər) ☐*noun, plural* **milliners**

> **WORD HISTORY: milliner**
> The word *milliner* was once spelled *millaner,* and meant "someone who lives in Milan, Italy." The word came to mean "someone who makes or sells women's hats" because many fancy and stylish hats came from the city of Milan.

million *noun* A number equal to the product of 1,000 × 1,000; 1,000,000.
☐*adjective* Being equal to one thousand thousands.
mil·lion (mil′yən) ☐*noun, plural* **million** or **millions** ☐*adjective*

millionaire *noun* Someone who has at least a million dollars.
mil·lion·aire (mil′yə nâr′) ☐*noun, plural* **millionaires**

millionth *noun* **1.** In a group of people or things in numbered order, the one that matches the number 1,000,000. **2.** One of a million equal parts, written ¹/₁,₀₀₀,₀₀₀.
☐*adjective* Coming after the 999,999th.
mil·lionth (mil′yənth) ☐*noun, plural* **millionths** ☐*adjective*

millstone *noun* One of a pair of circular stones used for grinding grain.
mill·stone (mil′stōn′) ☐*noun, plural* **millstones**

mill wheel *noun* A large water wheel used to turn a millstone.

mimeograph *noun* A machine that makes copies of written or typed pages.
☐*verb* To copy with a mimeograph.

mim·e·o·graph (mim′ē ə graf′) ☐*noun, plural* **mimeographs** ☐*verb* **mimeographed, mimeographing, mimeographs**

mimic *verb* To imitate, especially in order to make fun of: *Some birds can mimic the sounds of other birds.*
☐*noun* A person or animal that mimics.
mim·ic (mim′ik) ☐*verb* **mimicked, mimicking, mimics** ☐*noun, plural* **mimics**

min. An abbreviation for **minute.**

minaret *noun* A tall, slender tower on a mosque from which people are called to prayer.
min·a·ret (min′ə ret′) ☐*noun, plural* **minarets**

minaret

mince *verb* To chop into very small pieces: *mince an onion.*
mince (mins) ☐*verb* **minced, mincing, minces**

mince

mincemeat *noun* A pie filling made of finely chopped fruit, spices, and sometimes meat.
mince·meat (mins′mēt′) ☐*noun*

mind *noun* **1.** The part of a human being that thinks, feels, learns and imagines. **2.** Attention: *Keep your mind on your work.* **3.** Opinion; view: *He's always changing his mind.*
□*verb* **1.** To dislike; object to: *He really minds hot weather.* **2.** To obey: *A dog should mind its master.* **3.** To take care of: *Please mind the children until I get back.* **4.** To be careful about: *Mind your manners.* —See Synonyms at **obey.**
mind (mīnd) □*noun, plural* **minds** □*verb* **minded, minding, minds**

mindful *adjective* Having in mind; aware: *mindful of the feelings of other people.*
mind·ful (mīnd′fəl) □*adjective*

mine¹ *noun* **1.** A hole dug in the earth to take out minerals: *a coal mine.* **2.** A source of something valuable: *a mine of information.* **3.** A bomb placed underwater or just under the ground.
□*verb* **1.** To take minerals from the earth: *mine coal.* **2.** To put bombs in or under: *mine a battlefield.*
mine (mīn) □*noun, plural* **mines** □*verb* **mined, mining, mines**

mine² *pronoun* The one or ones belonging to me: *That basketball is mine.*
mine (mīn) □*pronoun*

miner *noun* Someone who works in a mine.
min·er (mī′nər) □*noun, plural* **miners**

miner

mineral *noun* A natural substance that is not an animal or plant. Gold, coal, and salt are minerals.
min·er·al (min′ər əl) □*noun, plural* **minerals**

mingle *verb* To mix or be mixed; combine: *Their voices mingled in song. We mingled with the crowd.*
min·gle (ming′gəl) □*verb* **mingled, mingling, mingles**

miniature *adjective* Much smaller than usual: *miniature cars.*
□*noun* **1.** A small model or copy: *She has a miniature of the Washington Monument on her desk.* **2.** A very small portrait or painting.
min·i·a·ture (min′ē ə chər) □*adjective* □*noun, plural* **miniatures**

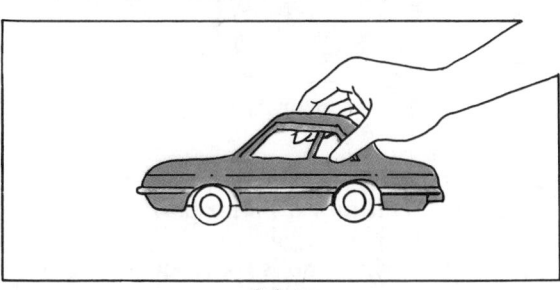
miniature

minimize *verb* To make as small as possible: *We are trying to minimize the amount of fuel we burn in the winter.*
min·i·mize (min′ə mīz′) □*verb* **minimized, minimizing, minimizes**

minimum *noun* The lowest or smallest amount: *Theater seats cost a minimum of eight dollars.*
□*adjective* Lowest or smallest possible: *the minimum age.*
min·i·mum (min′ə məm) □*noun, plural* **minimums** □*adjective*

minister *noun* **1.** Someone who conducts religious services in a church. **2.** Someone in charge of a government department.
min·is·ter (min′i stər) □*noun, plural* **ministers**

> *WORD HISTORY:* **minister**
> *Minister* comes from a Latin word meaning "servant."

a bat	ī bite	ōō tool	*th* feather
ā make	î fierce	ou out	th bath
â dare	o dot	u nut	hw wheat
ä father	ō no	û turn	zh measure
e net	ô law, for	ch church	ə about, open
ē be	oi soil	ng ring	pencil, atom
i dip	oo look	sh shade	circus

mink *noun* An animal whose thick, soft fur is used to make or trim clothing.
mink (mingk) □*noun, plural* **mink** *or* **minks**

minnow *noun* A very small fish.
min·now (min′ō) □*noun, plural* **minnows**

minnow

minor *adjective* **1.** Small in size or importance: *She had only a minor part in the play.* **2.** Being under the legal age.
□*noun* Someone who is too young to vote or who is not legally an adult.
mi·nor (mī′nər) □*adjective* □*noun, plural* **minors**

minority *noun* **1.** The smaller of two groups forming a whole: *Only a small minority voted for him.* **2.** A group of people of a different race, religion, or nationality from the rest of society.
mi·nor·i·ty (mi **nôr′**i tē *or* mī **nôr′**i tē) □*noun, plural* **minorities**

minstrel *noun* A musician of the Middle Ages who recited poetry and played the harp.
min·strel (min′strəl) □*noun, plural* **minstrels**

mint¹ *noun* **1.** A plant with leaves that are used to flavor candy, chewing gum, and other things. **2.** A candy flavored with mint.
mint (mint) □*noun, plural* **mints**

mint

mint² *noun* **1.** A place where coins are made by the government. **2.** A large amount: *That tennis racket must have cost a mint.*
□*verb* To make by stamping metal: *Each country mints its own coins.*
mint (mint) □*noun, plural* **mints** □*verb* **minted, minting, mints**

minuend *noun* A number from which another number is subtracted. In $7 - 4 = 3$, 7 is the minuend.
min·u·end (min′yoo end′) □*noun, plural* **minuends**

minus *preposition* Made less by: *Five minus three equals two.*
□*adjective* **1.** Less than zero; negative: *The temperature was minus two degrees this morning.* **2.** A little lower than: *a mark of A minus.*
□*noun* The sign ($-$), used to show that the number following is to be subtracted or has a negative value.
mi·nus (mī′nəs) □*preposition* □*adjective* □*noun, plural* **minuses**

minute¹ *noun* **1.** A unit of time equal to $\frac{1}{60}$ of an hour or sixty seconds. **2.** A short time; moment. **3. minutes** A record of what happened at a meeting.
min·ute (min′it) □*noun, plural* **minutes**

minute² *adjective* **1.** Very small; tiny: *a minute speck of dust.* **2.** Careful and detailed: *a minute examination.*
mi·nute (mī noot′ *or* mī nyoot′) □*adjective*

minuteman *noun* An armed man during the time of the American Revolution who promised to fight on the side of the colonists at a minute's notice.
min·ute·man (min′it man′) □*noun, plural* **minutemen**

miracle *noun* **1.** An event that seems impossible because it is impossible to explain by the laws of nature: *It would be a miracle if a person walked on water.* **2.** Something that is amazing and unusual: *It was a miracle that they escaped alive.*
mir·a·cle (mir′ə kəl) □*noun, plural* **miracles**

miraculous *adjective* Being or resembling a miracle: *a miraculous escape.*
mi·rac·u·lous (mi **rak′**yə ləs) □*adjective*

mirage *noun* An illusion of pools of water or reflections of distant objects. Mirages occur when light passes between layers of air that are at different temperatures.
mi·rage (mi **räzh′**) □*noun, plural* **mirages**

mire *noun* Deep, thick mud.
mire (mīr) □*noun*

mirror *noun* 1. A smooth surface that shows the image of an object placed in front of it. Most mirrors are made of glass that has been coated on the back with silver or aluminum. 2. Something that reflects a true picture. □*verb* To reflect in or as if in a mirror: *The pond mirrored the trees and sky.*
mir·ror (**mir′**ər) □*noun, plural* **mirrors** □*verb* **mirrored, mirroring, mirrors**

mirth *noun* Gladness or happiness, especially as expressed by laughter.
mirth (mîrth) □*noun*

WORD HISTORY: mirth

The word *mirth* is related to the word *merry* in exactly the same way *warmth* is related to *warm*. In very ancient Germanic times, the suffix *-th* was added to adjectives to make nouns.

---

mirthful *adjective* Having or showing mirth.
mirth·ful (**mîrth′**fəl) □*adjective*

mis– A prefix that means: 1. Wrong or wrongly: *misplace.* 2. Bad or badly: *misbehave.*

misadventure *noun* An unlucky or unfortunate event; misfortune: *After many misadventures, the hero returned to his own country and lived happily ever after.*
mis·ad·ven·ture (mis′əd **ven′**chər) □*noun, plural* **misadventures**

misbehave *verb* To behave badly: *Don't misbehave at the dinner table.*
mis·be·have (mis′bi **hāv′**) □*verb* **misbehaved, misbehaving, misbehaves**

misbehavior *noun* Bad behavior.
mis·be·hav·ior (mis′bi **hāv′**yər) □*noun*

miscellaneous *adjective* Made up of different kinds of things; various: *The attic was filled with miscellaneous items.*
mis·cel·la·ne·ous (mis′ə **lā′**nē əs) □*adjective*

mischance *noun* Something bad that happens by chance or luck: *By some mischance I lost my way and didn't return home until long after dark.*
mis·chance (mis **chans′**) □*noun*

mischief *noun* 1. Playful but annoying behavior. 2. Harm; damage. 3. The state of being mischievous.
mis·chief (**mis′**chif) □*noun*

mischievous *adjective* 1. Full of mischief; naughty: *The mischievous girl put a frog in her brother's bed.* 2. Causing harm or injury.
mis·chie·vous (**mis′**chə vəs) □*adjective*

misconduct *noun* Bad conduct; misbehavior.
mis·con·duct (mis kon′dukt′) □*noun*

miscount *verb* To make a mistake in counting. □*noun* A wrong count.
mis·count (mis **kount′**) □*verb* **miscounted, miscounting, miscounts** □*noun* (**mis′**kount′), *plural* **miscounts**

misdeed A bad act or deed: *He was sorry for his misdeeds.*
mis·deed (mis **dēd′**) □*noun, plural* **misdeeds**

miser *noun* A stingy, selfish person who loves to hoard money and spends as little as possible.
mi·ser (**mī′**zər) □*noun, plural* **misers**

miserable *adjective* 1. Very unhappy: *She was miserable because she was lonely.* 2. Very uncomfortable: *A cold makes you feel miserable.* 3. Very bad; awful: *a miserable, rainy day.*
mis·er·a·ble (**miz′**ər ə bəl) □*adjective*

miserly *adjective* Of, having to do with, or resembling a miser: *a miserly attitude towards money.*
mi·ser·ly (**mī′**zər lē) □*adjective*

misery *noun* Great suffering or unhappiness: *War causes great misery.*
mis·er·y (**miz′**ə rē) □*noun*

misfit *noun* Someone or something that does not fit in or belong: *The shabby chair was a misfit among the new furniture.*
mis·fit (**mis′**fit′) □*noun, plural* **misfits**

misfortune *noun* 1. Bad luck. 2. An unlucky happening: *The injury to their best player was a great misfortune to the team.*
mis·for·tune (mis **fôr′**chən) □*noun, plural* **misfortunes**

misgiving *noun* A feeling of doubt or concern about something that one is about to do or that is about to happen: *I had misgivings about riding on the roller coaster.*

a	bat	ī	bite	o͞o	tool	th	feather
ā	make	î	fierce	ou	out	th	bath
â	dare	o	dot	u	nut	hw	wheat
ä	father	ō	no	û	turn	zh	measure
e	net	ô	law, for	ch	church	ə	about, open
ē	be	oi	soil	ng	ring		pencil, atom
i	dip	o͝o	look	sh	shade		circus

mis·giv·ing (mis **giv'**ing) □*noun, plural* **misgivings**

mishap *noun* **1.** An unlucky accident. **2.** Bad luck; misfortune.
mis·hap (**mis'**hap') □*noun, plural* **mishaps**

misjudge *verb* To judge, estimate, or value in an incorrect way: *I misjudged the distance between the trees. I misjudged his character and trusted him too much.*
mis·judge (mis **juj'**) □*verb* **misjudged, misjudging, misjudges**

mislaid *verb* The past tense and past participle of **mislay:** *I mislaid my keys and was locked out of the house.*
mis·laid (mis **lād'**) □*verb*

mislay *verb* To put in a place and then forget where: *If I were more careful I wouldn't mislay my homework so often.*
mis·lay (mis **lā'**) □*verb* **mislaid, mislaying, mislays**

mislead *verb* **1.** To cause to go in the wrong direction: *The confusing signs completely misled us.* **2.** To cause to make a mistake: *False rumors misled us into accusing the wrong person.*
mis·lead (mis **lēd'**) □*verb* **misled, misleading, misleads**

misleading *adjective* Causing a mistake: *misleading information.*
mis·lead·ing (mis **lē'**ding) □*adjective*

misled *verb* The past tense and past participle of **mislead:** *The title of the book misled me.*
mis·led (mis **led'**) □*verb*

misplace *verb* To put in a place and forget where; lose: *He misplaced his wallet.*
mis·place (mis **plās'**) □*verb* **misplaced, misplacing, misplaces**

misprint *noun* A mistake in printing.
mis·print (**mis'**print') □*noun, plural* **misprints**

mispronounce *verb* To pronounce incorrectly.
mis·pro·nounce (mis'prə **nouns'**) □*verb* **mispronounced, mispronouncing, mispronounces**

miss¹ *verb* **1.** To fail to touch, hit, or reach: *miss a target; miss a bus.* **2.** To fail to notice or understand: *miss the point of the story.* **3.** To fail to attend: *miss a day of school.* **4.** To get away from; escape: *just missed being hurt.* **5.** To feel the loss of: *I miss my old friends.* □*noun* A failure to hit, reach, or touch something.

miss (mis) □*verb* **missed, missing, misses** □*noun, plural* **misses**

miss² *noun* **1.** A woman or girl who is not married. **2. Miss** A title used before the name of a woman or girl who is not married.
miss (mis) □*noun, plural* **misses**

misshapen *adjective* Badly shaped; deformed.
mis·shap·en (mis **shā'**pən) □*adjective*

missile *noun* Something that is thrown or fired at a target. Arrows, stones, and rockets are missiles.
mis·sile (**mis'**əl) □*noun, plural* **missiles**

missing *adjective* Lost; absent: *Six cards are missing from the deck.*
miss·ing (**mis'**ing) □*adjective*

mission *noun* **1.** A special job for someone; task: *a rescue mission.* **2.** A place where missionaries do their work. **3.** A group of persons sent to represent their government in a foreign country. **4.** A purpose; goal.
mis·sion (**mish'**ən) □*noun, plural* **missions**

missionary *noun* Someone sent to teach a religion in a foreign country. Missionaries often help to set up schools and hospitals.
mis·sion·ar·y (**mish'**ə ner'ē) □*noun, plural* **missionaries**

misspell *verb* To spell incorrectly.
mis·spell (mis **spel'**) □*verb* **misspelled, misspelling, misspells**

misspend *verb* To spend unwisely or in a wasteful way: *They misspent the summer just loafing around.*
mis·spend (mis **spend'**) □*verb* **misspent, misspending, misspends**

misstep *noun* **1.** A misplaced or awkward step. **2.** A mistake in action or conduct: *She discovered that the one misstep of her childhood would be held against her all her life.*
mis·step (mis **step'**) □*noun, plural* **missteps**

mist *noun* **1.** A mass of tiny drops of liquid suspended in the air. **2.** Something that dims the sight.
□*verb* **1.** To cover with mist. **2.** To become or make dim.
mist (mist) □*noun, plural* **mists** □*verb* **misted, misting, mists**

mistake *noun* **1.** Something that is done in an incorrect way; error: *a mistake in adding.* **2.** A misunderstanding. —See Synonyms at **error.**
□*verb* **1.** To understand wrongly. **2.** To make a mistake in recognizing: *I mistook your sister*

for you.

mis·take (mi stāk') □*noun, plural* **mistakes**
□*verb* **mistook, mistaken, mistaking,
mistakes**

mistaken *verb* The past participle of **mistake:** *She has mistaken me for my sister.*
□*adjective* Wrong: *mistaken ideas.*
mis·tak·en (mi stā'kən) □*verb* □*adjective*

mister *noun* **1.** A word used in speaking to a
man: *You dropped your scarf, mister.* **2. Mister**
A title used before the name of a man.
mis·ter (mis'tər) □*noun, plural* **misters**

mistletoe *noun* A plant with light-green
leaves and white berries, often used as a
Christmas decoration.
mis·tle·toe (mis'əl tō') □*noun, plural*
mistletoes

mistletoe

mistook *verb* The past tense of **mistake:** *He
mistook her for her sister.*
mis·took (mi stook') □*verb*

mistreat *verb* To treat in a bad way: *There
are laws against mistreating animals.*
mis·treat (mis trēt') □*verb* **mistreated,
mistreating, mistreats**

mistress *noun* A woman who owns or is in
charge of something: *the mistress of the house.*
mis·tress (mis'tris) □*noun, plural*
mistresses

mistrust *noun* Lack of trust.
□*verb* To have no trust in; doubt: *I mistrust
his intentions and suspect that he is trying to
cheat us.*
mis·trust (mis trust') □*noun* □*verb*
mistrusted, mistrusting, mistrusts

misty *adjective* Clouded with or as if with
mist: *a misty morning; misty memories.*
mist·y (mis'tē) □*adjective* **mistier, mistiest**

misunderstand *verb* To understand incorrectly.

mis·un·der·stand (mis un' dər **stand'**) □*verb*
**misunderstood, misunderstanding,
misunderstands**

misunderstanding *noun* **1.** A failure to understand or agree: *Because of a misunderstanding, I waited on the wrong corner.* **2.** A
quarrel.
mis·un·der·stand·ing (mis un' dər **stan'** ding)
□*noun, plural* **misunderstandings**

misunderstood *verb* The past tense of **misunderstand:** *She misunderstood the teacher's
instructions.*
mis·un·der·stood (mis un' dər **stood'**) □*verb*

misuse *verb* To use incorrectly: *misuse a tool.*
□*noun* Wrong or improper use: *the misuse of
a word.*
mis·use (mis yōōz') □*verb* **misused,
misusing, misuses** □*noun* (mis yōōs'),
□*plural* **misuses**

misuse

mite *noun* A tiny animal that looks like a spider and often lives on plants or other animals.
mite (mīt) □*noun, plural* **mites**

mitt *noun* **1.** A baseball glove. **2.** A mitten.
mitt (mit) □*noun, plural* **mitts**

mitten *noun* A warm covering for the hand
that has one section for the four fingers and
another for the thumb.
mit·ten (mit'ən) □*noun, plural* **mittens**

a bat	ī bite	ōō tool	*th* feather
ā make	i fierce	ou out	th bath
â dare	o dot	u nut	hw wheat
ä father	ō no	û turn	zh measure
e net	ô law, for	ch church	ə about, open
ē be	oi soil	ng ring	pencil, atom
i dip	oo look	sh shade	circus

mix   *verb* **1.** To put together and combine: *I mixed milk and chocolate syrup to make a milk shake.* **2.** To get along in a friendly way: *The party guests mixed well.*
□*noun* Something made by mixing: *a cake mix.*

mix up To confuse: *I mixed up the dates and went to the dentist's office on Tuesday instead of Friday.*
mix (miks) □*verb* **mixed, mixing, mixes** □*noun, plural* **mixes**

mixed   *adjective* **1.** Containing more than one kind or ingredient: *a mixed salad; mixed nuts.* **2.** Containing members of both sexes: *a mixed audience.*
mixed (mikst) □*adjective*

mixed number   *noun* A number made up of a whole number and a fraction. The number 4¹/₅ is a mixed number.

mixer   *noun* A machine that mixes things together: *a food mixer.*
mix·er (mik′sər) □*noun, plural* **mixers**

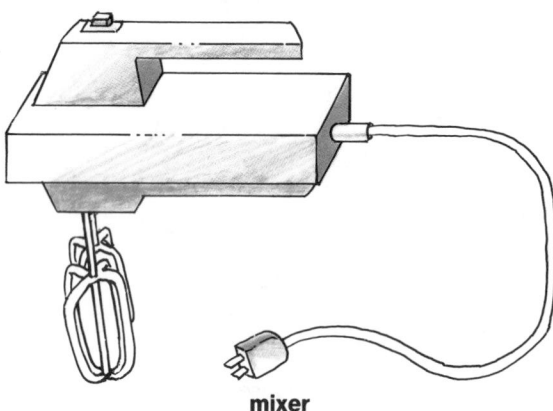

mixer

mixture   *noun* Something made up of different things; combination: *Paste is a mixture of starch and water.*
mix·ture (miks′chər) □*noun, plural* **mixtures**

mix-up   *noun* Confusion caused by misunderstanding: *a mix-up about when the bus would leave for the class trip to the museum.*
mix-up (miks′up′) □*noun, plural* **mix-ups**

mm An abbreviation for **millimeter.**

mo. An abbreviation for **month.**

moan   *noun* A long, low sound of pain or sadness: *The injured man let out a moan when he tried to move.*
□*verb* **1.** To make a moan. **2.** To complain: *He is always moaning about how tired he is.*

moan (mōn) □*noun, plural* **moans** □*verb* **moaned, moaning, moans**

moat   *noun* A wide, deep ditch usually filled with water. Moats around castles and towns formerly served as a protection against attack.
moat (mōt) □*noun, plural* **moats**

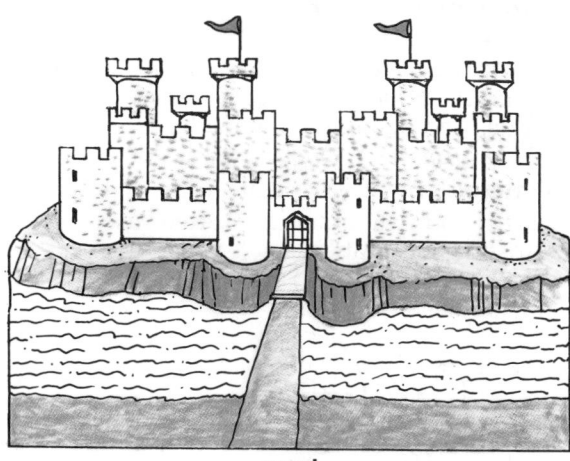

moat

mob   *noun* A large crowd, especially one that acts in a dangerous or lawless way.
□*verb* To crowd around in excitement: *The singer was mobbed by her admirers.*
mob (mob) □*noun, plural* **mobs** □*verb* **mobbed, mobbing, mobs**

> *WORD HISTORY:* **mob**
>
> *Mob* comes from a Latin word meaning "movable" or "easily swayed." People were thought to be easily excited when they were together in a crowd.

mobile   *adjective* Able to move or to be moved from place to place: *a mobile hospital.*
□*noun* A sculpture whose parts can be moved by currents of air.
mo·bile (mō′bəl) □*adjective* □*noun* (mō′bēl′), *plural* **mobiles**

moccasin   *noun* **1.** A soft, leather shoe without a heel. Moccasins were first worn by North American Indians. **2.** A poisonous snake, the water moccasin.
moc·ca·sin (mok′ə sin) □*noun, plural* **moccasins**

mock   *verb* **1.** To make fun of in a cruel way: *She mocked him for running away.* **2.** To mimic or copy as a cruel joke: *He mocked the old woman's limp.*
□*adjective* Not real; imitation: *a mock battle.*

mock (mok) □*verb* **mocked, mocking, mocks** □*adjective*

mockery *noun* **1.** The act of mocking. **2.** A ridiculous or false appearance: *Their disrespect made a mockery of the holy ceremony.*
mock·er·y (mok′ə rē) □*noun, plural* **mockeries**

mockingbird *noun* A gray and white American songbird that imitates the songs of other birds.
mock·ing·bird (mok′ing bûrd′) □*noun, plural* **mockingbirds**

mockingbird

mock orange *noun* A shrub that has fragrant white flowers and loses it leaves in the fall.

mode *noun* **1.** A way of doing or acting: *new modes of expression.* **2.** A popular style of dressing or acting: *Short skirts are the mode in her school.*
mode (mōd) □*noun, plural* **modes**

model *noun* **1.** A small copy of something: *a model of the solar system.* **2.** A style or kind of thing: *This car is the latest model.* **3.** A good example to be copied: *Lincoln was a model of a great president.* **4.** A pattern for making something. **5.** Someone whose job is to display clothes for sale by wearing them. **6.** Someone who poses for an artist or photographer.
□*verb* **1.** To make out of clay or other material: *model animals in wax.* **2.** To follow an example or pattern by copying: *He wants to model himself after his uncle.* **3.** To work or serve as a model.
□*adjective* **1.** Worthy of being copied: *He was a model child.* **2.** Being a very small copy: *model trains.*
mo·del (mod′əl) □*noun, plural* **models** □*verb* **modeled, modeling, models** □*adjective*

moderate *adjective* **1.** Not too much or too little; avoiding the extreme: *a moderate cli-*mate. **2.** Reasonable: *a moderate price.*
□*verb* To make or become less intense or extreme: *A cool breeze moderated the heat of the sun.*
mod·er·ate (mod′ər it) □*adjective* □*verb* (mod′ə rāt′) **moderated, moderating, moderates**

moderation *noun* **1.** The act of moderating: *a moderation in the cold weather.* **2.** The state of being moderate.
mod·er·a·tion (mod′ə rā′shən) □*noun*

modern *adjective* Of the present time or the recent past: *The computer is a modern invention.*
mod·ern (mod′ərn) □*adjective*

modernize *verb* To make or become modern: *The businessman modernized his office and replaced the adding machine with a computer.*
mo·dern·ize (mod′ər nīz′) □*verb* **modernized, modernizing, modernizes**

modest *adjective* **1.** Not thinking too well of oneself; not boastful: *He was so modest that we thought he was shy.* **2.** Not extreme; moderate: *a modest salary.* **3.** Proper in speech, dress, or conduct.
mod·est (mod′ist) □*adjective*

modesty *noun* The state of being modest.
mod·es·ty (mod′i stē) □*noun*

modifier *noun* A word, such as an adjective, that is used to limit the meaning of another word.
mod·i·fi·er (mod′ə fī′ər) □*noun, plural* **modifiers**

modify *verb* **1.** To change; alter: *My father's illness forced us to modify our vacation plans.* **2.** To limit the meaning of a word. In the phrase "a red book," "red" modifies "book."
mod·i·fy (mod′ə fī′) □*verb* **modified, modifying, modifies**

module *noun* A separate part of a spacecraft, used for a special purpose: *a lunar module.*
mod·ule (moj′ōol) □*noun, plural* **modules**

mohair *noun* **1.** The soft, silky hair of an Asian goat. **2.** Yarn or cloth made of mohair.
mo·hair (mō′hâr′) □*noun*

a bat	ī bite	ōō tool	*th* feather
ā make	î fierce	ou out	th bath
â dare	o dot	u nut	hw wheat
ä father	ō no	û turn	zh measure
e net	ô law, for	ch church	ə about, open
ē be	oi soil	ng ring	pencil, atom
i dip	oo look	sh shade	circus

Mohammed *noun* The founder of Islam, the Moslem religion.
Mo·ham·med (mō **ham′** id) □*noun*

moist *adjective* Slightly wet; damp: *a moist sponge; moist air.*
moist (moist) □*adjective*

moisten *verb* To make slightly wet or damp.
mois·ten (**moi′** sən) □*verb* **moistened, moistening, moistens**

moisture *noun* Water or other liquid in the form of tiny drops: *Humidity is moisture in the air.*
mois·ture (**mois′** chər) □*noun*

molar *noun* Any one of the teeth at the back of the jaw. Molars have broad surfaces for grinding food. Human beings have 12 molars.
mo·lar (**mō′** lər) □*noun, plural* **molars**

molasses *noun* A thick, sweet syrup made from sugar cane.
mo·las·ses (mə **las′** iz) □*noun*

mold¹ *noun* A hollow form into which a soft material is put. When the material hardens, it takes the shape of the mold.
□*verb* **1.** To make or form into a shape: *mold wax into candles.* **2.** To influence; shape: *Good books can mold and develop the mind.*
mold (mōld) □*noun, plural* **molds** □*verb* **molded, molding, molds**

mold

mold² *noun* A tiny plant that forms a furry coating on food and damp surfaces.
mold (mōld) □*noun, plural* **molds**

molding *noun* **1.** The act of shaping something in a mold. **2.** A shaped piece of material used to decorate something, such as a wall or a door.
mold·ing (**mōl′** ding) □*noun, plural* **moldings**

moldy *adjective* Covered with mold: *moldy bread.*
mold·y (**mōl′** dē) □*adjective* **moldier, moldiest**

mole¹ *noun* A small brown spot on the skin.
mole (mōl) □*noun, plural* **moles**

mole² *noun* A small animal that digs burrows under the ground.
mole (mōl) □*noun, plural* **moles**

mole

molecule *noun* The smallest particle into which a substance can be divided and still remain the same substance: *A water molecule is made up of two atoms of hydrogen and one atom of oxygen.*
mol·e·cule (**mol′** i kyool′) □*noun, plural* **molecules**

mollusk *noun* An animal with a soft body that usually lives in water. Some mollusks, such as clams, have hard outer shells.
mol·lusk (**mol′** əsk) □*noun, plural* **mollusks**

mollusk
Left: snail, *Right:* scallop

molt *verb* To shed an outer covering such as skin or hair. Birds, insects, and snakes molt.
molt (mōlt) □*verb* **molted, molting, molts**

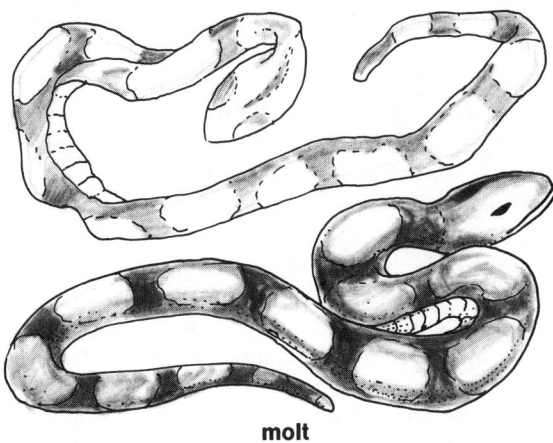

molt

molten *adjective* Melted by heat: *molten iron.*
molt·en (mōl′tən) ▢*adjective*

mom *noun* Mother.
mom (mom) ▢*noun, plural* **moms**

moment *noun* **1.** A very short period of time: *I'll be back in a moment.* **2.** The present time: *At the moment she is very busy.* **3.** Importance: *This is a matter of some moment for all of us.*
mo·ment (mō′mənt) ▢*noun, plural* **moments**

momentary *adjective* Lasting only for a short time: *a momentary doubt.*
mo·men·tar·y (mō′mən ter′ē) ▢*adjective*

momentous *adjective* Very important or significant: *The discovery of the New World was a momentous event.* —See Synonyms at **important.**
mo·men·tous (mō men′təs) ▢*adjective*

momentum *noun* The force or speed of a moving object: *The sled gained momentum as it came down the hill.*
mo·men·tum (mō men′təm) ▢*noun, plural* **momentums**

monarch *noun* **1.** A king, queen, or emperor. **2.** A large orange and black butterfly.
mon·arch (mon′ərk) ▢*noun, plural* **monarchs**

monarchy *noun* **1.** Government by a monarch. **2.** A country governed by a monarch.
mon·ar·chy (mon′ər kē) ▢*noun, plural* **monarchies**

monastery *noun* A place where monks live and work.
mon·as·ter·y (mon′ə ster′ē) ▢*noun, plural* **monasteries**

Monday *noun* The second day of the week.
Mon·day (mun′ dē *or* mun′dā′) ▢*noun, plural* **Mondays**

money *noun* The coins and paper bills of a country, used to pay for goods and services.
mon·ey (mun′ē) ▢*noun, plural* **moneys**

mongoose *noun* An animal with a long, narrow body and a long tail, noted for its ability to kill poisonous snakes.
mon·goose (mong′gōōs′) ▢*noun, plural* **mongooses**

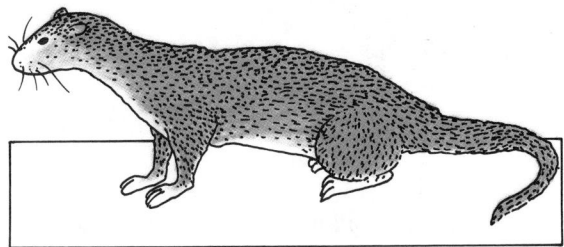

mongoose

mongrel *noun* A dog of a mixed breed.
mon·grel (mung′grəl *or* mong′grəl) ▢*noun, plural* **mongrels**

monitor *noun* **1.** A student who is given a special job: *an attendance monitor.* **2.** A device used to check or record a process or condition: *a heart monitor.* **3.** The part of a computer that contains the video screen.
▢*verb* To keep watch over: *The nurse carefully monitored the patient's condition.*
mon·i·tor (mon′i tər) ▢*noun, plural* **monitors** ▢*verb* **monitored, monitoring, monitors**

monk *noun* A man who lives in a monastery and observes the rules of a religious order.
monk (mungk) ▢*noun, plural* **monks**

a bat	ī bite	ōō tool	*th* feather
ā make	î fierce	ou out	th bath
â dare	o dot	u nut	hw wheat
ä father	ō no	û turn	zh measure
e net	ô law, for	ch church	ə about, open
ē be	oi soil	ng ring	pencil, atom
i dip	oo look	sh shade	circus

monkey *noun* A furry, active animal with long arms and legs that are used for climbing. □*verb* **1.** To play or tamper with: *He likes to monkey with old clocks and engines.* **2.** To take part in mischievous play.
mon·key (**mung′**kē) □*noun, plural* **monkeys** □*verb* **monkeyed, monkeying, monkeys**

monkey

monkeyshines *plural noun* Playful mischief; pranks.
mon·key·shines (**mung′**kē shīnz′) □*plural noun*

monkey wrench *noun* A wrench with a jaw that can be made larger and smaller.

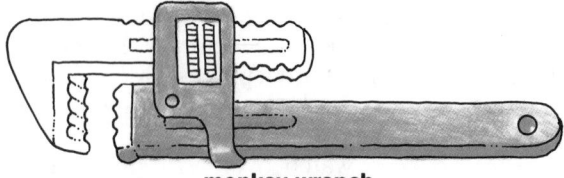
monkey wrench

monogram *noun* A design made up of the initials of someone's name. □*verb* To mark with a monogram.
mon·o·gram (**mon′**ə gram′) □*noun, plural* **monograms** □*verb* **monogrammed, monogramming, monograms**

monopoly *noun* Complete control over selling or making something: *That company has a monopoly on supplying electricity to this area.*
mo·nop·o·ly (mə **nop′**ə lē) □*noun, plural* **monopolies**

monosyllable *noun* A word having only one syllable: *The word "let" is a monosyllable.*
mon·o·syl·la·ble (**mon′**ə **sil′**ə bəl) □*noun, plural* **monosyllables**

monotonous *adjective* Always the same; never changing: *Peeling potatoes is a monotonous job.*
mo·not·o·nous (mə **not′**ən əs) □*adjective*

monotony *noun* The condition of being monotonous.
mo·not·o·ny (mə **not′**ən ē) □*noun*

monsoon *noun* A wind in southern Asia that changes with the seasons. Monsoons bring heavy rains during the wet season.
mon·soon (mon **soon′**) □*noun, plural* **monsoons**

monster *noun* **1.** A huge, frightening, imaginary creature. **2.** An animal or plant that is not normal: *A dog with two heads would be a monster.* **3.** A very cruel person. **4.** Something that is very large.
mon·ster (**mon′**stər) □*noun, plural* **monsters**

monstrosity *noun* **1.** The condition of being monstrous. **2.** Someone or something that is monstrous.
mon·stros·i·ty (mon **stros′**i tē) □*noun, plural* **monstrosities**

monstrous *adjective* **1.** Huge and frightening. **2.** Evil or cruel: *a monstrous crime.*
mon·strous (**mon′**strəs) □*adjective*

month *noun* One of the twelve divisions of the year.
month (munth) □*noun, plural* **months**

monthly *adjective* **1.** Happening or coming once every month: *monthly meetings.* **2.** For one month: *the monthly rainfall for August.* □*adverb* Every month: *She visits us monthly.* □*noun* A magazine that comes out once a month.
month·ly (**munth′**lē) □*adjective* □*adverb* □*noun, plural* **monthlies**

monument *noun* A structure or other object made in memory of a person, group, or event: *That chapel is a monument to those who died for their country.*
mon·u·ment (**mon′**yə mənt) □*noun, plural* **monuments**

moo *noun* The deep sound that a cow makes. □*verb* To make this sound.
moo (moo) □*noun, plural* **moos** □*verb* **mooed, mooing, moos**

mood *noun* The way someone feels at a certain time: *a cheerful mood; a sad mood.*
mood (mood) □*noun, plural* **moods**

moody *adjective* **1.** Changing moods often. **2.** Gloomy: *a moody silence.*
mood·y (**moo′**dē) □*adjective* **moodier, moodiest**

moon *noun* **1.** A heavenly body that orbits the earth and reflects the sun's light. **2.** The natural satellite of any other planet: *Jupiter*

has four large moons and many small ones.
moon (moon) ▢*noun, plural* **moons**

moonbeam *noun* A ray of moonlight.
moon·beam (moon′bēm′) ▢*noun, plural* **moonbeams**

moonlight *noun* The light that comes from the moon.
moon·light (moon′līt′) ▢*noun*

moonlit *adjective* Lighted by the moon: *The trees cast black shadows on the moonlit snow.*
moon·lit (moon′lit′) ▢*adjective*

moor¹ *verb* To fasten a boat in place.
moor (moor) ▢*verb* **moored, mooring, moors**

moor

moor² *noun* A stretch of open land usually covered with heather, weeds, and grasses.
moor (moor) ▢*noun, plural* **moors**

mooring *noun* **1.** A place where a boat can be moored. **2.** An object to which a boat can be moored. **3.** A chain or rope with which a boat can be moored.
moor·ing (moor′ing) ▢*noun, plural* **moorings**

moose *noun* A large animal of northern regions related to the deer. The male has large antlers.
moose (moos) ▢*noun, plural* **moose**

WORD HISTORY: moose

Moose probably comes from an Indian word that means "he trims." The reason for this name is the moose's habit of stripping off and eating the bark and lower branches of trees.

moose

mop *noun* A long stick with a sponge or strands of yarn at the end for washing floors. ▢*verb* To wash or soak up with a mop or other material: *mop up spilled milk.*
mop (mop) ▢*noun, plural* **mops** ▢*verb* **mopped, mopping, mops**

mope *verb* To be in a gloomy and dull state of mind: *After he lost the game, he sat around moping and feeling sorry for himself.*
mope (mōp) ▢*verb* **moped, moping, mopes**

moped *noun* A bicycle that is powered by a small motor. It can also be pedaled.
mo·ped (mō′ped′) ▢*noun, plural* **mopeds**

moraine *noun* A mass of earth and rocks left behind by a glacier.
mo·raine (mə rān′) ▢*noun, plural* **moraines**

moral *adjective* **1.** Good and just. **2.** Having to do with what is right and wrong: *The story of George Washington and the cherry tree teaches us the moral lesson that it is always best to tell the truth.* ▢*noun* **1.** The lesson taught by a story or event. **2. morals** Beliefs about what is right and wrong.
mor·al (môr′əl) ▢*adjective* ▢*noun, plural* **morals**

morale *noun* The spirit or enthusiasm shown by a person or group: *Doing well on the test improved her morale.*
mo·rale (mə ral′) ▢*noun*

a bat	ī bite	oo tool	*th* feather
ā make	î fierce	ou out	th bath
â dare	o dot	u nut	hw wheat
ä father	ō no	û turn	zh measure
e net	ô law, for	ch church	ə about, open
ē be	oi soil	ng ring	pencil, atom
i dip	oo look	sh shade	circus

morality *noun* **1.** A set of ideas about what is right and wrong in human behavior. **2.** The quality of being moral. **3.** Moral behavior.
mo·ral·i·ty (mə **ral′** i tē) □*noun, plural* **moralities**

more *adjective* **1.** Greater in number, amount, or degree: *She has more brains than he has.* **2.** Additional; extra: *Could I have more gravy, please?*
□*adverb* **1.** To a greater extent or degree: *Which dress is more becoming? The climb was more difficult than I expected.* **2.** Again: *I'll repeat the riddle once more.*
□*noun* A greater or extra amount: *The more he got, the more he wanted. More of these books are being ordered.*
more (môr) □*adjective* □*adverb* □*noun*

moreover *adverb* Beyond what has been said; besides: *I don't own a suit, and moreover I don't want one.*
more·o·ver (môr ō′ vər) □*adverb*

morn *noun* The morning.
morn (môrn) □*noun, plural* **morns**

morning *noun* The early part of the day, from midnight or sunrise to noon.
morn·ing (môr′ ning) □*noun, plural* **mornings**

morning glory *noun* A twining vine related to the sweet potato that has large flowers shaped like trumpets.

morning glory

morning star *noun* A planet, especially Venus, that can be seen in the eastern sky before sunrise.

moron *noun* A very foolish or stupid person.
mo·ron (môr′on′) □*noun, plural* **morons**

morrow *noun* The following day; tomorrow: *He lived a carefree life with no thought for the morrow.*
mor·row (môr′ō) □*noun, plural* **morrows**

morsel *noun* A small piece of food.
mor·sel (môr′səl) □*noun, plural* **morsels**

mortal *adjective* **1.** Certain to die someday: *All human beings are mortal.* **2.** Causing death: *a mortal injury.*
□*noun* A human being.
mor·tal (môr′təl) □*adjective* □*noun, plural* **mortals**

mortar *noun* **1.** A bowl in which things are crushed or ground with a pestle. **2.** A material made of sand, water, and lime, used to hold bricks or stones together.
mor·tar (môr′tər) □*noun, plural* **mortars**

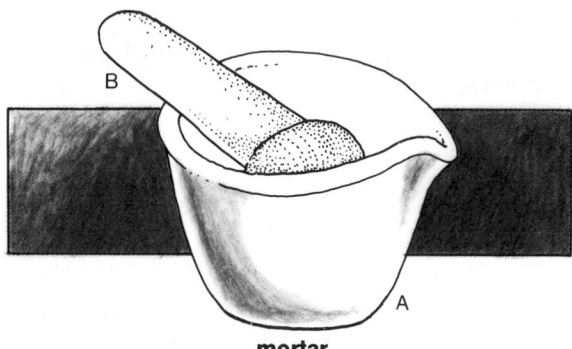

mortar
(A) mortar, *(B)* pestle

mosaic *noun* A design made by fitting together and cementing small pieces of colored tile, glass, or stone.
mo·sa·ic (mō zā′ik) □*noun, plural* **mosaics**

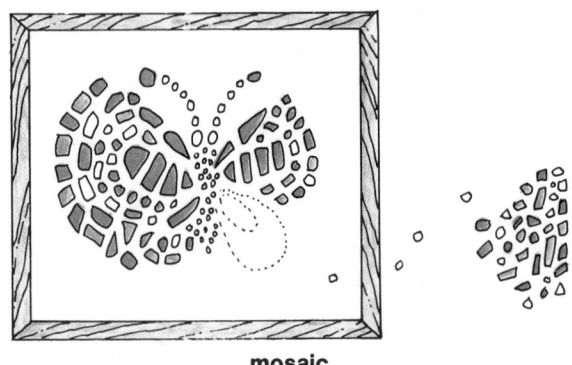

mosaic

Moslem *noun* Someone who believes in the religion of Islam.
□*adjective* Of Islam: *a Moslem prayer.*
Mos·lem (moz′ləm) □*noun, plural* **Moslems** □*adjective*

mosque *noun* A Moslem place of worship.
mosque (mosk) □*noun, plural* **mosques**

mosquito *noun* A small flying insect. The female bites and sucks blood from animals and human beings.

mos·qui·to (mə **skē′**tō) ☐*noun, plural* **mosquitoes** or **mosquitos**

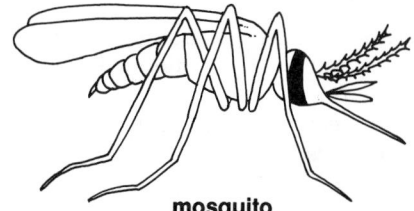

mosquito

moss   *noun* A small green plant that forms a thick covering on damp ground, rocks, or tree trunks.
moss (môs) ☐*noun, plural* **mosses**

mossy   *adjective* Resembling or covered with moss: *a mossy stone.*
moss·y (**mô′**sē) ☐*adjective* **mossier, mossiest**

most   *adjective* **1.** Greatest in number, amount, or degree: *I picked many apples, but she picked the most apples.* **2.** Almost all: *Most people like ice cream.*
☐*adverb* **1.** To the greater extent or degree: *the most powerful of all magicians.* **2.** Very: *We had a most pleasant evening.*
☐*noun* The greatest amount or largest number: *Is that the most you can do to help us?*
most (mōst) ☐*adjective* ☐*adverb* ☐*noun*

mostly   *adverb* Mainly; chiefly: *Air consists mostly of nitrogen and oxygen.*
most·ly (**mōst′**lē) ☐*adverb*

motel   *noun* A hotel located on or near a main road for guests with cars.
mo·tel (mō **tel′**) ☐*noun, plural* **motels**

moth   *noun* An insect that is similar to a butterfly but usually flies at night.
moth (môth) ☐*noun, plural* **moths** (môthz or môths)

mother   *noun* A female parent.
moth·er (**muth′**ər) ☐*noun, plural* **mothers**

mother-in-law   *noun* The mother of someone's wife or husband.
moth·er-in-law (**muth′**ər in lô′) ☐*noun, plural* **mothers-in-law**

motherly   *adjective* Of, having to do with, or resembling a mother: *She showed a motherly concern for the neglected child.*
moth·er·ly (**muth′**ər lē) ☐*adjective*

mother-of-pearl   *noun* The hard, smooth lining of the shells of some mollusks, such as the oyster. Mother-of-pearl is used to make objects such as buttons.
moth·er-of-pearl (muth′ər əv **pûrl′**) ☐*noun*

Mother's Day   *noun* The second Sunday in May, set aside to honor mothers.

motion   *noun* **1.** The act of moving; movement: *The motion of the train made us sleepy. She called us over with a motion of her hand.* **2.** A formal request or proposal made at a meeting.
☐*verb* To signal with a motion: *The waiter motioned us to follow him.*
mo·tion (**mō′**shən) ☐*noun, plural* **motions** ☐*verb* **motioned, motioning, motions**

motion picture   *noun* A series of pictures projected so quickly on a screen that the people and objects in the pictures seem to be moving.

motivate   *verb* To give a motive to: *A desire to learn motivated him to study hard.*
mo·ti·vate (**mō′**tə vāt′) ☐*verb* **motivated, motivating, motivates**

motive   *noun* A reason for doing something: *the motive for a crime.*
mo·tive (**mō′**tiv) ☐*noun, plural* **motives**

motley   *noun* A costume of many colors worn by a clown or jester.
☐*adjective* **1.** Having many different colors. **2.** Made up of an odd assortment of different types: *a motley group of workers.*
mot·ley (**mot′**lē) ☐*noun* ☐*adjective*

motor   *noun* A device that provides the power to make something go: *a car motor.*
☐*adjective* **1.** Of or having to do with a motor or a vehicle driven by a motor: *a motor scooter; a motor accident.* **2.** Controlling or bringing about body movements: *motor nerves.*
☐*verb* To drive in a car.
mo·tor (**mō′**tər) ☐*noun, plural* **motors** ☐*adjective* ☐*verb* **motored, motoring, motors**

motorbike   *noun* A light motorcycle.
mo·tor·bike (**mō′**tər bīk′) ☐*noun, plural* **motorbikes**

motorboat   *noun* A boat run by a motor.
mo·tor·boat (**mō′**tər bōt′) ☐*noun, plural* **motorboats**

a bat	ī bite	ōō tool	th feather
ā make	î fierce	ou out	th bath
â dare	o dot	u nut	hw wheat
ä father	ō no	û turn	zh measure
e net	ô law, for	ch church	ə about, open
ē be	oi soil	ng ring	pencil, atom
i dip	oo look	sh shade	circus

motorcycle *noun* A vehicle with two wheels and a motor to drive it.
mo·tor·cy·cle (mō′tər sī′kəl) □*noun, plural* **motorcycles**

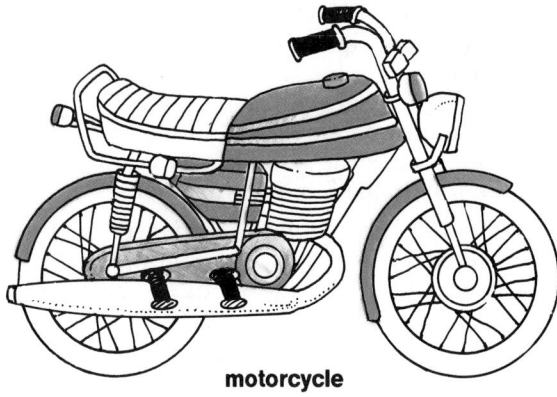
motorcycle

motorist *noun* A person who drives or rides in an automobile.
mo·tor·ist (mō′tər ist) □*noun, plural* **motorists**

motor vehicle *noun* A vehicle, such as an automobile, that is driven by a motor and does not run on rails.

mottled *adjective* Marked with spots or streaks of different colors: *a bird with mottled feathers.*
mot·tled (mot′əld) □*adjective*

motto *noun* A saying that expresses what is important to a person or group: *The motto of the Boy Scouts is "Be prepared."*
mot·to (mot′ō) □*noun, plural* **mottoes** or **mottos**

mound *noun* **1.** A small rounded hill. **2.** A heap or pile: *a mound of stones.* **3.** The raised area where a baseball pitcher stands.
mound (mound) □*noun, plural* **mounds**

mount¹ *verb* **1.** To go up; climb: *mount a ladder.* **2.** To get up on: *mount a stage.* **3.** To take one's seat on a horse: *He mounted and rode away.* **4.** To put in place; set: *mount a pearl in a ring.* **5.** To increase: *The temperature mounted as the day went on.*
□*noun* **1.** A horse or other animal for riding. **2.** A frame or structure for holding something.
mount (mount) □*verb* **mounted, mounting, mounts** □*noun, plural* **mounts**

mount² *noun* A mountain.
mount (mount) □*noun, plural* **mounts**

mountain *noun* **1.** An area of land that rises high above the land around it. **2.** A large quantity or amount: *mountains of papers and books.*
moun·tain (moun′tən) □*noun, plural* **mountains**

mountaineer *noun* **1.** Someone who lives in the mountains. **2.** Someone who climbs mountains for sport.
moun·tain·eer (moun′tə nîr′) □*noun, plural* **mountaineers**

mountain goat *noun* An antelope resembling a goat that lives in the mountains of northwestern North America.

mountain laurel *noun* A North American shrub with shiny leaves and rounded clusters of pink and white flowers.

mountain lion *noun* A large wild cat of western North America and South America.

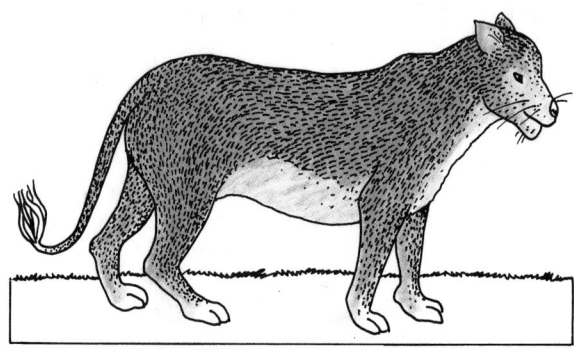
mountain lion

mountainous *adjective* **1.** Having many mountains. **2.** Very large: *a mountainous drift of snow.*
moun·tain·ous (moun′tə nəs) □*adjective*

mountain range *noun* A series of mountains.

mountainside *noun* The side of a mountain.
moun·tain·side (moun′tən sīd′) □*noun, plural* **mountainsides**

mourn *verb* To feel or show grief: *She still mourns for her child who died.*
mourn (môrn) □*verb* **mourned, mourning, mourns**

mournful *adjective* **1.** Feeling or expressing sorrow: *a mournful look on her face.* **2.** Causing sorrow or grief: *a mournful event.*
mourn·ful (môrn′fəl) □*adjective*

mourning *noun* **1.** The act of showing sorrow or grief. **2.** Black clothing worn as a sign of grief for a death.
mourn·ing (môr′ning) □*noun*

mouse *noun* **1.** A small, furry animal with a pointed snout and a long, hairless tail. **2.** A small device on some computers that is moved with the hand in order to move and activate the cursor on the video screen.

mouse (mous) □*noun, plural* **mice**

mousetrap *noun* A trap for catching mice.
mouse·trap (**mous'**trap') □*noun, plural* **mousetraps**

mousetrap

moustache *noun* Another spelling for **mustache.**
mous·tache (**mus'**tash' *or* mə **stash'**) □*noun, plural* **moustaches**

mouth *noun* **1.** The opening in a human or animal body through which food is taken in. **2.** An opening like a mouth: *A river empties into the sea at its mouth.*
mouth (mouth) □*noun, plural* **mouths** (mou*th*z)

mouthful *noun* An amount put or that can be put into the mouth at one time.
mouth·ful (**mouth'**fool') □*noun, plural* **mouthfuls**

mouth organ *noun* A harmonica.

mouthpiece *noun* The part of a device that goes in or near the mouth: *the mouthpiece of a telephone.*
mouth·piece (**mouth'**pēs') □*noun, plural* **mouthpieces**

movable *adjective* Capable of being moved: *a movable table.*
mov·a·ble (**mōō'**və bəl) □*adjective*

move *verb* **1.** To change the position of something: *Move that lamp closer.* **2.** To go ahead; advance: *This story moves slowly.* **3.** To make someone feel pity or some other strong emotion: *His sad story moved me to tears* **4.** To cause to act: *Fear moved him to run away.* **5.** To propose in a formal way: *The council member moved to end the meeting.* **6.** To change one's residence: *We're moving next week.*
□*noun* **1.** The act of moving: *He made a move to dodge the ball.* **2.** A turn to move a piece in a game: *It's your move!*
move (mōōv) □*verb* **moved, moving, moves**
□*noun, plural* **moves**

moveable *adjective* Another spelling for **movable.**
move·a·ble (**mōō'**və bəl) □*adjective*

movement *noun* **1.** The act of moving: *the movement of curtains in the breeze.* **2.** The moving parts of a device: *the movement of a clock.* **3.** Actions of a group of people taken to reach a particular goal.
move·ment (**mōōv'**mənt) □*noun, plural* **movements**

mover *noun* A person or company that moves people's furniture and other belongings from one place to another.
mov·er (**mōō'**vər) □*noun, plural* **movers**

movie *noun* **1.** A motion picture. **2. movies** The making or showing of motion pictures.
mov·ie (**mōō'**vē) □*noun, plural* **movies**

moving *adjective* **1.** Changing position: *a moving object in the sky.* **2.** Able to arouse the feelings and especially the sympathies: *a moving story of devotion.*
mov·ing (**mōō'**ving) □*adjective*

moving picture A motion picture.

mow *verb* To cut grass or grain: *mow the lawn.*
mow (mō) □*verb* **mowed, mowed** or **mown, mowing, mows**

mow

mown *verb* A past participle of **mow:** *The lawn was mown last week.*
mown (mōn) □*verb*

a bat	ī bite	ōō tool	*th* feather
ā make	î fierce	ou out	th bath
â dare	o dot	u nut	hw wheat
ä father	ō no	û turn	zh measure
e net	ô law, for	ch church	ə about, open
ē be	oi soil	ng ring	pencil, atom
i dip	oo look	sh shade	circus

Mr. An abbreviation used as a title before a man's name: *Mr. Hays.*
Mr. (**mis'** tər)

Mrs. An abbreviation used as a title before a married woman's name: *Mrs. Saxby.*
Mrs. (**mis'** iz)

Ms. or **Ms** An abbreviation used instead of Miss or Mrs. as a title before a woman's name.
Ms. or **Ms** (miz)

mt. or **Mt.** An abbreviation for **mountain.**

much *adjective* Great in amount, degree, or extent: *Is there much glue left? How much money does it cost?*
□*noun* A large amount: *Did you eat much?*
□*adverb* **1.** To a large extent; greatly: *She was sick, but she's much better now.* **2.** Just about: *I think much as you do.*
much (much) □*adjective* **more, most** □*noun* □*adverb*

mucilage *noun* A sticky substance used especially for gluing things together.
mu·ci·lage (myōō' sə lij) □*noun*

muck *noun* **1.** Wet dirt; mud. **2.** Animal waste; manure. **3.** Filthy or disgusting material.
muck (muk) □*noun*

mucous *adjective* **1.** Of, relating to, or similar to mucus. **2.** Producing or containing mucus: *the mucous membrane.*
mu·cous (myōō' kəs) □*adjective*

mucus *noun* The slippery fluid that lines and protects the insides of the mouth, throat, and other body parts.
mu·cus (myōō' kəs) □*noun*

mud *noun* Wet, soft dirt.
mud (mud) □*noun*

muddle *verb* **1.** To mix up in a confused way: *He muddled up the papers so that I couldn't find anything I needed.* **2.** To manage badly; make a mess of.
□*noun* A mess; jumble: *She tried to straighten out the muddle, but it seemed like a hopeless task.*
mud·dle (mud' əl) □*verb* **muddled, muddling, muddles** □*noun, plural* **muddles**

muddy *adjective* **1.** Full of or covered with mud. **2.** Not clear or bright; dull like mud: *a muddy color.* **3.** Confused; mixed up: *a muddy thinker.*
□*verb* **1.** To make dirty with or as if with mud: *His shoes muddied the clean floor.* **2.** To make dull.
mud·dy (mud' ē) □*adjective* **muddier, muddiest** □*verb* **muddied, muddying, muddies**

muff *noun* A tube of fur or cloth for keeping the hands warm.
muff (muf) □*noun, plural* **muffs**

muff

muffin *noun* A small cup-shaped bread that is often sweetened.
muf·fin (muf' in) □*noun, plural* **muffins**

muffle *verb* **1.** To wrap up especially in order to hide or protect. **2.** To soften the sound of: *The deep snow muffled our footsteps.*
muf·fle (muf' əl) □*verb* **muffled, muffling, muffles**

muffler *noun* **1.** A long scarf wrapped around the neck. **2.** A device to lessen the noise of an automobile engine.
muf·fler (muf' lər) □*noun, plural* **mufflers**

muffler

mug *noun* A large, heavy cup with a handle.
mug (mug) □*noun, plural* **mugs**

muggy *adjective* Very warm and humid.
mug·gy (mug' ē) □*adjective* **muggier, muggiest**

mulberry *noun* A tree with sweet, purplish or white edible berries.
mul·ber·ry (**mul′**ber′ē) ☐*noun, plural*
mulberries

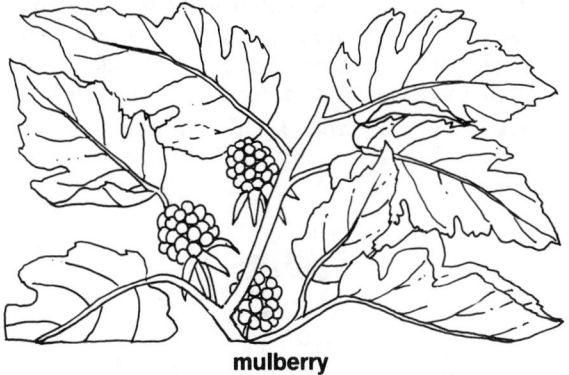
mulberry

mulch *noun* A material, such as hay, that is spread on the ground to protect the roots of plants from heat, cold, or loss of moisture.
mulch (mulch) ☐*noun, plural* **mulches**

mule *noun* An animal that is part horse and part donkey, used to pull and carry loads.
mule (myo͞ol) ☐*noun, plural* **mules**

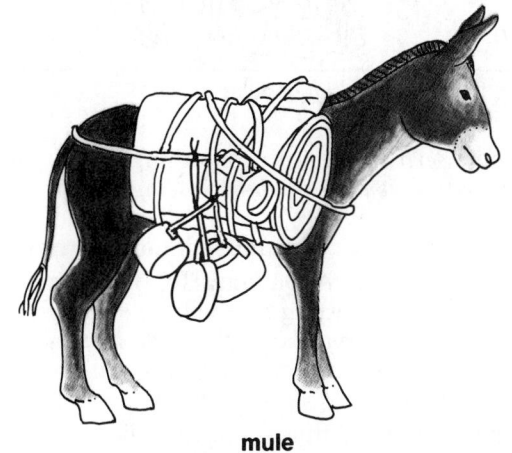
mule

muleskinner *noun* One who drives mules.
mule·skin·ner (**myo͞ol′**skin′ər) ☐*noun,*
plural **muleskinners**

mulish *adjective* Stubborn like a mule.
mul·ish (**myo͞o′**lish) ☐*adjective*

multimedia *adjective* Of or being a computer program that combines words, graphics, video, and sound.
mul·ti·me·di·a (mul′tē **mē′**dē ə) ☐*adjective*

multiple *noun* A number that is the product of one number multiplied by another number:
9 and 15 are multiples of 3.
☐*adjective* More than one; many: *multiple injuries.*
mul·ti·ple (**mul′**tə pəl) ☐*noun, plural*
multiples ☐*adjective*

multiplicand *noun* A number that is multiplied by another number. In 7 × 5, the multiplicand is 7.
mul·ti·pli·cand (mul′tə pli **kand′**) ☐*noun,*
plural **multiplicands**

multiplication *noun* A mathematical operation that is like adding a number to itself a specified number of times. For example, both 5 × 3 and 5+5+5 = 15.
mul·ti·pli·ca·tion (mul′tə pli **kā′**shən)
☐*noun, plural* **multiplications**

multiplier *noun* A number by which another number is to be multiplied. In 7 × 5, the multiplier is 5.
mul·ti·pli·er (**mul′**tə plī′ər) ☐*noun, plural*
multipliers

multiply *verb* **1.** To increase fast: *The bacteria multiplied.* **2.** To perform multiplication on a pair of numbers.
mul·ti·ply (**mul′**tə plī′) ☐*verb* **multiplied,**
multiplying, multiplies

multitude *noun* A very large number: *A great multitude of people assembled in the square.*
mul·ti·tude (**mul′**ti to͞od′ *or* **mul′**ti tyo͞od′)
☐*noun, plural* **multitudes**

mum *adjective* Silent: *He told me to keep mum about what I had seen.*
mum (mum) ☐*adjective*

mumble *verb* To say in a low voice that is hard to understand: *She mumbled an answer and ran from the room.*
☐*noun* Speech that is not loud or clear enough to understand.
mum·ble (**mum′**bəl) ☐*verb* **mumbled,**
mumbling, mumbles ☐*noun, plural*
mumbles

mummy *noun* A dead body that has been preserved and kept from decaying.
mum·my (**mum′**ē) ☐*noun, plural*
mummies

a bat	ī bite	o͞o tool	*th* feather
ā make	î fierce	ou out	th bath
â dare	o dot	u nut	hw wheat
ä father	ō no	û turn	zh measure
e net	ô law, for	ch church	ə about, open
ē be	oi soil	ng ring	pencil, atom
i dip	oo look	sh shade	circus

mumps *plural noun* A contagious disease. Mumps causes swelling of the glands around the lower cheeks.
mumps (mumps) □*plural noun*

munch *verb* To chew in a noisy way: *munching celery.*
munch (munch) □*verb* **munched, munching, munches**

municipal *adjective* Of or having to do with a city government: *a municipal election.*
mu·nic·i·pal (myoō **nis′**ə pəl) □*adjective*

municipality *noun* A city or town that has its own local government.
mu·nic·i·pal·i·ty (myoō nis′ə **pal′**i tē) □*noun, plural* **municipalities**

munitions *plural noun* The military supplies and equipment for war, especially weapons and ammunition.
mu·ni·tions (myoō **nish′**ənz) □*plural noun*

mural *noun* A large painting on a wall or ceiling.
mu·ral (myoor′əl) □*noun, plural* **murals**

murder *noun* The unlawful and deliberate killing of a person.
□*verb* To kill on purpose. —See Synonyms at **kill.**
mur·der (mûr′dər) □*noun, plural* **murders** □*verb* **murdered, murdering, murders**

murderer *noun* Someone who commits murder.
mur·der·er (mûr′dər ər) □*noun, plural* **murderers**

murderous *adjective* **1.** Intending, capable of, or causing murder or bloodshed: *a murderous attack.* **2.** Very difficult to put up with: *murderous tension.*
mur·der·ous (mûr′dər əs) □*adjective*

murk *noun* Darkness; gloom.
murk (mûrk) □*noun*

murky *adjective* **1.** Dark and gloomy: *a murky, underground passage.* **2.** Hard to see through especially because of smoke or fog: *murky air.*
murk·y (mûr′kē) □*adjective* **murkier, murkiest**

murmur *noun* A low, soft sound: *the murmur of voices from the next room.*
□*verb* To make or say with a low, soft sound: *A gentle wind murmured through the forest.*
mur·mur (mûr′mər) □*noun, plural* **murmurs** □*verb* **murmured, murmuring, murmurs**

muscadine *noun* A vine of the southeastern United States that bears grapes in small clusters.
mus·ca·dine (mus′kə dīn′) □*noun*

muscle *noun* A tissue in the body that can be tightened or relaxed to make body parts move: *Runners have strong leg muscles.*
mus·cle (mus′əl) □*noun, plural* **muscles**

muscular *adjective* **1.** Of or in muscles: *muscular pains.* **2.** Having strong muscles: *a muscular lifeguard.*
mus·cu·lar (mus′kyə lər) □*adjective*

muscular

muse *verb* To think something over: *She spent a great deal of time musing about their plans.*
muse (myoōz) □*verb* **mused, musing, muses**

museum *noun* A building for keeping and displaying interesting and valuable things: *an art museum; a museum of natural history.*
mu·se·um (myoō **zē′**əm) □*noun, plural* **museums**

mush¹ *noun* Cornmeal boiled in liquid.
mush (mush) □*noun*

mush² *noun* To travel by means of a sled drawn across the snow by dogs.
mush (mush) □*verb* **mushed, mushing, mushes**

mushroom *noun* A white or brown plant shaped like a little umbrella. Mushrooms are a kind of fungus and some are good to eat.
□*verb* To grow or spread quickly: *New houses mushroomed all over town.*
mush·room (mush′roōm′ *or* mush′room′) □*noun, plural* **mushrooms** □*verb* **mushroomed, mushrooming, mushrooms**

mushroom

mushy *adjective* Soft like mush.
mush·y (mush′ē) □*adjective* **mushier, mushiest**

music *noun* **1.** The art of creating pleasing combinations of sounds. **2.** A pleasing or delightful sound. **3.** The symbols or signs that stand for the sounds of a musical composition: *Can you read music?* **4.** A printed or written musical composition: *I can't find my music.*
mu·sic (myōō′zik) □*noun*

musical *adjective* **1.** Of or for music: *a musical instrument.* **2.** Resembling music: *a musical voice.* **3.** Having a great liking or talent for music: *He is very musical.* **4.** Set to or accompanied by music: *a musical play.*
□*noun* A play that has songs and dances.
mu·si·cal (myōō′zi kəl) □*adjective* □*noun, plural* **musicals**

music box *noun* A box containing a mechanical device that plays music.

musician *noun* Someone who is skilled in composing or performing music.
mu·si·cian (myōō zish′ən) □*noun, plural* **musicians**

musk *noun* A greasy, strong-smelling substance produced by a gland of the musk deer and used in making perfume.
musk (musk) □*noun*

musk deer *noun* A small Asian deer, the male of which produces musk.

musket *noun* An old kind of gun with a long barrel like a rifle.
mus·ket (mus′kit) □*noun, plural* **muskets**

musketeer *noun* A soldier armed with a musket.
mus·ket·eer (mus′ki tîr′) □*noun, plural* **musketeers**

muskmelon *noun* A small melon with sweet orange or green flesh.

musk·mel·on (musk′mel′ən) □*noun, plural* **muskmelons**

musk ox *noun* A large animal of northern North America with shaggy hair and curved horns.

muskrat *noun* A small North American animal that lives near water and has webbed feet and thick brown fur.
musk·rat (mus′krat′) □*noun, plural* **muskrats**

musky *adjective* Having a smell that resembles or suggests musk.
musk·y (mus′kē) □*adjective* **muskier, muskiest**

Muslim *noun* Another spelling for **Moslem.**
Mus·lim (muz′ləm *or* moos′ləm) □*noun, plural* **Muslims**

muslin *noun* A cotton cloth used for sheets, curtains, and clothing.
mus·lin (muz′lin) □*noun, plural* **muslins**

muss *verb* To make untidy or messy: *The wind mussed her hair.*
□*noun* A state of disorder; mess.
muss (mus) □*verb* **mussed, mussing, musses** □*noun*

mussel *noun* A water animal with a blue-black shell. Mussels are sometimes gathered and used as food.
mus·sel (mus′əl) □*noun, plural* **mussels**

must *verb* **1.** Be required or obliged to: *Citizens must be 18 to vote.* **2.** Ought to; should: *You must try harder.* **3.** Be likely to: *This button must be the one that turns on the motor.*
must (must) □*verb*

mustache *noun* The hair on a man's upper lip.
mus·tache (mus′tash′ *or* mə stash′) □*noun, plural* **mustaches**

mustang *noun* A small, wild horse of western North America.
mus·tang (mus′tang′) □*noun, plural* **mustangs**

mustard *noun* A sharp-tasting yellow paste or powder made from the ground seeds of a plant and used to flavor food.
mus·tard (mus′tərd) □*noun*

a bat	ī bite	ōō tool	*th* feather
ā make	î fierce	ou out	th bath
â dare	o dot	u nut	hw wheat
ä father	ō no	û turn	zh measure
e net	ô law, for	ch church	ə about, open
ē be	oi soil	ng ring	pencil, atom
i dip	oo look	sh shade	circus

muster *verb* **1.** To gather together; assemble: *muster troops for an inspection.* **2.** To call forth: *muster up courage for a daring feat.* □*noun* **1.** An act of gathering or assembling. **2.** A military inspection. **3.** A gathering; collection.
mus·ter (mus′tər) □*verb* **mustered, mustering, musters** □*noun, plural* **musters**

mustn't Contraction of "must not."
must·n't (mus′ənt)

musty *adjective* Having a stale, moldy smell or taste because of mildew or dampness.
must·y (mus′tē) □*adjective* **mustier, mustiest**

mutant *noun* An individual that differs from its parent as the result of mutation. □*adjective* Of, relating to, or produced by mutation.
mu·tant (myōō′tənt) □*noun, plural* **mutants** □*adjective*

mutate *verb* **1.** To undergo great change. **2.** To undergo change through the mutation of a gene.
mu·tate (myōō′tāt′) □*verb* **mutated, mutating, mutates**

mutation *noun* **1.** A change in the nature or form of something. **2.** A change in a gene. **3.** Something that is the result of such a change in a gene.
mu·ta·tion (myōō tā′shən) □*noun, plural* **mutations**

mute *adjective* **1.** Not able or willing to speak or make sounds; silent: *She remained mute.* **2.** Not pronounced: *The "k" in "knight" is mute.* □*noun* **1.** Someone who cannot speak. **2.** A device used to soften or muffle the tone of a musical instrument.
mute (myōōt) □*adjective* □*noun, plural* **mutes**

mute

mutilate *verb* **1.** To cut off or destroy an essential part, such as an arm or leg. **2.** To make imperfect by changing or cutting: *mutilate a composition.*
mu·ti·late (myōō′tə lāt′) □*verb* **mutilated, mutilating, mutilates**

mutineer *noun* Someone who takes part in a mutiny: *The mutineers seized control of the ship.*
mu·ti·neer (myōō′tə **nîr′**) □*noun, plural* **mutineers**

mutinous *adjective* Tending to or being in a state of mutiny: *The mutinous sailors left their captain on a deserted island.*
mu·ti·nous (myōō′tə nəs) □*adjective*

mutiny *noun* Open rebellion against people in charge: *a mutiny of sailors on ship.* □*verb* To rebel against one's leaders: *The soldiers mutinied.*
mu·ti·ny (myōōt′ən ē) □*noun, plural* **mutinies** □*verb* **mutinied, mutinying, mutinies**

mutt *noun* A dog that is a mixture of different breeds.
mutt (mut) □*noun, plural* **mutts**

mutter *verb* **1.** To speak in a low voice that is hard to hear: *She should speak clearly instead of muttering.* **2.** To complain; grumble. □*noun* Something said in a low voice that others can barely hear.
mut·ter (mut′ər) □*verb* **muttered, muttering, mutters** □*noun, plural* **mutters**

mutton *noun* The meat of a fully grown sheep.
mut·ton (mut′ən) □*noun*

mutual *adjective* **1.** Shared in common: *We found that we had a mutual friend.* **2.** Given equally to each other: *mutual respect.*
mu·tu·al (myōō′chōō əl) □*adjective*

muzzle *noun* **1.** An animal's projecting nose and jaws. **2.** A set of straps or wires that fits over an animal's snout to keep it from biting. **3.** The open front end of a gun. □*verb* To put a muzzle on: *muzzle a dog.*
muz·zle (muz′əl) □*noun, plural* **muzzles** □*verb* **muzzled, muzzling, muzzles**

my *adjective* Belonging or relating to me: *my coat; my job.*
my (mī) □*adjective*

myna or **mynah** *noun* An Asian bird related to the starling and sometimes able to mimic human speech.

my·na or **my·nah** (mī′nə) □*noun, plural* **mynas** or **mynahs**

myna

myriad *noun* A very large number that is not specified: *the myriads of grains of sand on the beach.*
□*adjective* Very numerous.
myr·i·ad (mîr′ē əd) □*noun, plural* **myriads** □*adjective*

myrrh *noun* A fragrant substance obtained from certain Asian and African trees and used especially in perfumes.
myrrh (mûr) □*noun*

myrtle *noun* **1.** An evergreen plant that grows close to the ground and has shiny, dark-green leaves and blue or white flowers. **2.** An evergreen shrub found in southern Europe and western Asia.
myr·tle (mûr′təl) □*noun*

myself *pronoun* My own self: *I fell and hurt myself. I myself can't read my writing.*
my·self (mī self′) □*pronoun*

mysterious *adjective* Hard to explain or understand; filled with mystery: *A mysterious light appeared in the sky.*
mys·te·ri·ous (mi stîr′ē əs) □*adjective*

mystery *noun* **1.** Something that is not known or understood: *Where he got the money is a mystery to me.* **2.** A story, play, or motion picture about a puzzling crime.
mys·te·ry (mis′tə rē) □*noun, plural* **mysteries**

mystify *verb* To puzzle; confuse: *I was completely mystified by his instructions.*
mys·ti·fy (mis′tə fī′) □*verb* **mystified, mystifying, mystifies**

myth *noun* **1.** A story that expresses the beliefs and values of a people. Myths often deal with heroes or gods and try to explain how things came into being. **2.** A story or idea that is not true: *It is a myth that getting the feet wet will cause a cold.*
myth (mith) □*noun, plural* **myths**

mythical *adjective* **1.** Of or told about in myths: *Unicorns and dragons are mythical beasts.* **2.** Not real; imaginary.
myth·i·cal (mith′i kəl) □*adjective*

mythology *noun* A collection of myths: *Roman mythology.*
my·thol·o·gy (mi thol′ə jē) □*noun, plural* **mythologies**

a	bat	ī	bite	ōō	tool	*th*	feather
ā	make	î	fierce	ou	out	th	bath
â	dare	o	dot	u	nut	hw	wheat
ä	father	ō	no	û	turn	zh	measure
e	net	ô	law, for	ch	church	ə	about, open
ē	be	oi	soil	ng	ring		pencil, atom
i	dip	oo	look	sh	shade		circus

ANCIENT GREEK

The letter **N** has evolved from many forms of ancient writing. One of the earliest known examples is the Greek character shown above, which dates from almost 3,000 years ago. Over the years, artists and designers have created their own versions of the English letter **N**. Some of the more common examples seen today are shown below.

| HANDWRITING | CALLIGRAPHY | MODERN SANS SERIF | MODERN SERIF | SCRIPT |

---

n or **N** *noun* The fourteenth letter of the English alphabet.
n or **N** (en) □*noun, plural* **n's** or **N's**

N.A. An abbreviation for **North America.**

nag *verb* To annoy by complaining, scolding, or finding fault all the time: *His sister nags him about doing his homework.*
nag (nag) □*verb* **nagged, nagging, nags**

nail *noun* **1.** A slim, pointed piece of metal with a flat or round head. Nails are hammered into pieces of wood or other material to hold them together. **2.** The thin, hard covering at the end of a finger or toe.
□*verb* To join or attach with a nail: *nail the old chair together.*
nail (nāl) □*noun, plural* **nails** □*verb* **nailed, nailing, nails**

naked *adjective* **1.** Not wearing clothing or covering: *a naked child; naked arms.* **2.** Without the help of a device: *I saw the planet with the naked eye.* —See Synonyms at **bare.**
na·ked (nā′kid) □*adjective*

name *noun* **1.** A word or words by which a person, place, animal, or thing is called or known. **2.** Reputation or fame: *He made a name for himself in politics.* **3.** A cruel or insulting word: *He called the children names.*
□*verb* **1.** To give a name to: *We named the baby after her aunt.* **2.** To call or mention by name; identify: *He could not name the capital of Montana.* **3.** To appoint or nominate: *He was named captain of the team.*

name (nām) □*noun, plural* **names** □*verb* **named, naming, names**

nameless *adjective* Having no name: *a nameless kitten.*
name·less (nām′lis) □*adjective*

namely *adverb* That is to say: *The policeman questioned the victim's closest relatives, namely his brothers.*
name·ly (nām′lē) □*adverb*

nap¹ *noun* A short sleep, usually at a time other than one's regular sleeping hours.
□*verb* To sleep for a short time; doze: *The old man napped on the porch.*
nap (nap) □*noun, plural* **naps** □*verb* **napped, napping, naps**

nap² *noun* A soft or fuzzy surface on certain kinds of cloth or leather.
nap (nap) □*noun, plural* **naps**

napkin *noun* A piece of cloth or paper used while eating to protect the clothes or to wipe the mouth and fingers.
nap·kin (nap′kin) □*noun, plural* **napkins**

narcissus *noun* A garden plant related to the daffodil and having yellow or white flowers with a central part that is shaped like a cup.

nar·cis·sus (när **sis′** əs) □*noun, plural*
narcissuses or **narcissus**

narcissus

narcotic *noun* A drug that dulls the senses,
causes sleep, and stops pain. A narcotic taken
often and in large doses may make the user
dependent on it.
nar·cot·ic (när **kot′** ik) □*noun, plural*
narcotics

narrate *verb* To tell the story of in speech or
writing; relate: *She narrated her experiences at
the Olympic games.*
nar·rate (**nar′** āt′ *or* na **rāt′**) □*verb* **narrated,
narrating, narrates**

narrow *adjective* **1.** Small in width: *a narrow
hallway.* **2.** Small or limited: *a narrow margin
of favorable votes.*
□*verb* To make or become narrow or narrower: *The valley narrows down there.*
□*noun* **narrows** A narrow body of water connecting two wider ones.
nar·row (**nar′** ō) □*adjective* **narrower,
narrowest** □*verb* **narrowed, narrowing,
narrows** □*noun, plural* **narrows**

narrow

nasal *adjective* Of or in the nose: *a nasal passage; a nasal voice.*
na·sal (**nā′** zəl) □*adjective*

nasturtium *noun* A garden plant with
rounded, edible leaves and orange, yellow, or
red flowers.
na·stur·tium (nə **stûr′** shəm) □*noun, plural*
nasturtiums

nasty *adjective* **1.** Mean; malicious: *a nasty
man with a quick temper.* **2.** Very unpleasant:
nasty weather; a nasty disposition. **3.** Very
harmful or dangerous: *a nasty injury.*
nas·ty (**nas′** tē) □*adjective* **nastier, nastiest**

nasty

nation *noun* **1.** A group of people organized
under a single government; country. **2.** The
territory occupied by a country.
na·tion (**nā′** shən) □*noun, plural* **nations**

national *adjective* Of or involving a nation as
a whole: *a national election; national pride.*
na·tion·al (**nash′** ə nəl) □*adjective*

nationalism *noun* Devotion and loyalty to
one's country.
na·tion·al·ism (**nash′** ə nə liz′əm) □*noun*

nationality *noun* **1.** The condition of belonging to a particular nation: *Their nationality is
Italian.* **2.** A group of people sharing the same
origins, traditions, or language: *Many nationalities have migrated to America.*

a bat	ī bite	ōō tool	*th* feather
ā make	î fierce	ou out	th bath
â dare	o dot	u nut	hw wheat
ä father	ō no	û turn	zh measure
e net	ô law, for	ch church	ə about, open
ē be	oi soil	ng ring	pencil, atom
i dip	oo look	sh shade	circus

na·tion·al·i·ty (nash′ə **nal**′i tē) ☐*noun, plural* **nationalities**

native *adjective* **1.** Belonging to a person by nature or birth: *a native talent for music; one's native language.* **2.** Born in a particular country or place: *a native Mexican.* **3.** Originally living, growing, or produced in a particular place: *a plant native to South America.*
☐*noun* **1.** Someone born in a particular country or place: *a native of Ireland.* **2.** One of the original inhabitants of a region or place: *Alaskan natives are Eskimos. The giraffe is a native of Africa.*
na·tive (**nā**′tiv) ☐*adjective* ☐*noun, plural* **natives**

Native American *noun* **1.** A member of any of the groups of peoples, except the Eskimos, who had been living in North America, South America, or the West Indies before the European explorers first arrived. **2.** A descendant of these peoples.

natural *adjective* **1.** Present in or produced by nature; not artificial: *a natural lake; the natural odor of a skunk.* **2.** Of or having to do with nature: *a museum of natural history.* **3.** Expected or occurring in the normal course of things: *a natural loyalty to one's family.* **4.** Present from birth: *a natural talent for science; a natural singing voice.*
☐*noun* Someone who is very good at some activity because of inborn qualities or talents.
nat·u·ral (**nach**′ər əl) ☐*adjective* ☐*noun, plural* **naturals**

naturalist *noun* Someone who is an expert in the study of plants and animals.
nat·u·ral·ist (**nach**′ər ə list) ☐*noun, plural* **naturalists**

naturally *adverb* **1.** In a natural manner: *Don't be nervous; just behave naturally.* **2.** By nature: *naturally blond hair.* **3.** Without a doubt: *Naturally, if you don't water the plants, they will die.*
nat·u·ral·ly (**nach**′ər ə lē) ☐*adverb*

natural resource *noun* Something, such as a forest, mineral deposit, animal, or water, that grows or exists in nature and is the source of something necessary or useful to human beings.

nature *noun* **1.** The physical world, all living things, and events in it, except for things produced by people. **2.** The basic characteristics of a person, animal, or thing: *a man with a warm, friendly nature.* **3.** Kind; type: *an event*

of a mysterious nature.
na·ture (**nā**′chər) ☐*noun, plural* **natures**

naught *noun* **1.** Nothing: *His hard work came to naught.* **2.** Zero; the digit 0.
naught (nôt) ☐*noun*

naughty *adjective* Disobedient; mischievous: *The naughty boys grabbed her hat.*
naugh·ty (**nô**′tē) ☐*adjective* **naughtier, naughtiest**

naughty

nausea *noun* A feeling of sickness in the stomach and often of a need to vomit.
nau·se·a (**nô**′zē ə *or* **nô**′shə) ☐*noun*

WORD HISTORY: **nausea**

The word *nausea* comes from the Greek word for "seasickness."

---

nautical *adjective* Of ships, sailors, or navigation: *a nautical map.*
nau·ti·cal (**nô**′ti kəl) ☐*adjective*

nautical mile *noun* A unit of distance used in air and sea navigation, equal to 1,852 meters or about 6,076 feet.

naval *adjective* Of or having to do with a navy or ships: *naval battles; a great naval power.*
na·val (**nā**′vəl) ☐*adjective*

navel *noun* A hollow in the abdomen of humans and other mammals left by the cord that connects an unborn infant to its mother.
na·vel (**nā**′vəl) ☐*noun, plural* **navels**

navigate *verb* **1.** To guide and control the course of a ship or aircraft. **2.** To sail over, on, or across: *The large ship could not navigate the river.*

nav·i·gate (năv′ ĭ gāt′) □*verb* **navigated, navigating, navigates**

navigation *noun* **1.** The act of navigating: *Heavy winds made navigation of the ship difficult.* **2.** The science of locating the position or planning the course of a ship or aircraft.
nav·i·ga·tion (năv′ĭ gā′shən) □*noun*

navigator *noun* **1.** A crew member who plans and directs the course of a ship or aircraft. **2.** Someone who leads voyages of exploration.
nav·i·ga·tor (năv′ ĭ gā′tər) □*noun, plural* **navigators**

navigator

navy *noun* **1.** All of a nation's warships. **2.** Often **Navy** A nation's whole organization for war at sea, including ships, men and officers, and shore bases. **3.** A very dark blue.
□*adjective* Of the color navy.
na·vy (nā′vē) □*noun, plural* **navies**
□*adjective*

navy blue *noun* A very dark blue.

nay *adverb* No: *Four senators voted nay to the proposal.*
□*noun* **1.** A vote of "no." **2.** Those who vote no.
nay (nā) □*adverb* □*noun, plural* **nays**

near *adverb* To, at, or within a short distance in space or time: *The squirrel overcame his fear of us and crept near. As fall draws near, leaves begin to change color.*
□*adjective* **1.** Close in space, time, position, or degree: *a near neighbor.* **2.** Closely related or connected: *a near relative.* **3.** Achieved or avoided by a small margin: *a near catastrophe.*
□*preposition* Close to: *a bicycle rack near the baseball field.*
□*verb* To draw near or nearer: *As the big truck neared the corner it slowed down.*
near (nîr) □*adverb* **nearer, nearest**
□*adjective* **nearer, nearest** □*preposition*
□*verb* **neared, nearing, nears**

nearby *adverb* Not far away; close by: *The train tracks were built nearby.*
□*adjective* Located a short distance away: *a nearby grocery store.* —See Synonyms at **convenient.**
near·by (nîr′bī′) □*adverb* □*adjective*

nearly *adverb* Almost but not quite: *That meat cost nearly six dollars a pound.*
near·ly (nîr′lē) □*adverb*

nearsighted *adjective* Unable to see objects that are far away as clearly as objects that are close by.
near·sight·ed (nîr′sī′tĭd) □*adjective*

neat *adjective* **1.** In clean condition; tidy: *a neat desk; a neat child.* **2.** Performed with precision and skill: *a neat dive into the pool.* **3.** Very fine; wonderful: *a neat new bike.*
neat (nēt) □*adjective* **neater, neatest**

SYNONYMS: **neat, orderly, tidy**

These adjectives mean in good order or clean condition: *He is responsible for keeping his bedroom neat at all times. She arranged all the cans and jars in the cupboard in an orderly way. Wash up and make yourself tidy before dinner.*

---

necessarily *adverb* As a sure result: *Hard work does not necessarily lead to success.*
nec·es·sar·i·ly (nĕs′ĭ sĕr′ə lē) □*adverb*

necessary *adjective* **1.** Impossible to do without; essential: *Water is necessary for plants.* **2.** Happening as a certain result: *A headache was the necessary consequence of reading in a poor light.*
nec·es·sar·y (nĕs′ĭ sĕr′ē) □*adjective*

SYNONYMS: **necessary, essential, vital**

These adjectives mean impossible to do without: *It's necessary to study hard if you want to do well on the test. Vegetables are essential for good nutrition. Water and sunshine are vital for plants.*

---

necessity *noun* **1.** Something impossible to get along without: *A good night's sleep is a ne-*

a	bat	ī	bite	o͞o	tool	*th*	feather
ā	make	î	fierce	ou	out	th	bath
â	dare	o	dot	u	nut	hw	wheat
ä	father	ō	no	û	turn	zh	measure
e	net	ô	law, for	ch	church	ə	about, open
ē	be	oi	soil	ng	ring		pencil, atom
i	dip	oo	look	sh	shade		circus

cessity for someone who works hard. **2.** The fact of being necessary: *She felt the necessity of being on time.*
ne·ces·si·ty (nə ses′i tē) □*noun, plural* **necessities**

neck *noun* **1.** The part of the body that joins the head to the shoulders. **2.** The part of a garment that fits around the neck. **3.** A narrow or connecting part: *the neck of a guitar; a narrow neck of land.*
neck (nek) □*noun, plural* **necks**

neckerchief *noun* A scarf or cloth worn around the neck.
neck·er·chief (nek′ər chif) □*noun, plural* **neckerchiefs**

necklace *noun* An ornament worn around the neck: *She wore a pearl necklace.*
neck·lace (nek′ləs) □*noun, plural* **necklaces**

necktie *noun* A narrow band of cloth worn around the neck under the shirt collar. It is tied in front in a knot.
neck·tie (nek′tī′) □*noun, plural* **neckties**

nectar *noun* A sweet liquid produced by many flowers. Bees make honey from nectar.
nec·tar (nek′tər) □*noun*

need *noun* **1.** Something required or wanted: *The house is in need of a new coat of paint; a need for affection.* **2.** Necessity or obligation: *There is no need for you to hurry.* **3.** Extreme poverty: *a family in great need.*
□*verb* **1.** To require or have need of: *Our car needs gas. I need a new winter coat.* **2.** To be obliged to; have to: *You don't need to bring anything to the party.*
need (nēd) □*noun, plural* **needs** □*verb* **needed, needing, needs**

needle *noun* **1.** A small, thin tool for sewing, usually made of polished steel. A needle has a sharp point at one end and a hole at the other through which thread is passed and held. **2.** A slender, pointed rod used in knitting. **3.** The pointer or indicator of a compass or gauge. **4.** A thin tube with a sharp point used to pierce the skin and take material from or put material into the body. **5.** A sharp, pointed instrument like a needle. **6.** A narrow, stiff leaf, such as that found on a pine tree or fir tree.
□*verb* To tease, annoy, or provoke: *The children needled him for running too slowly.*
nee·dle (nēd′əl) □*noun, plural* **needles** □*verb* **needled, needling, needles**

needless *adjective* Not needed or wanted; not necessary: *needless noise; needless work.*
need·less (nēd′lis) □*adjective*

needn't Contraction of "need not."
need·n't (nēd′ənt)

needy *adjective* Being in need; very poor: *needy children.*
need·y (nē′dē) □*adjective* **needier, neediest**

negative *adjective* **1.** Expressing a refusal or denial; saying "no": *a negative reply.* **2.** Not positive or helpful: *negative attitudes toward school.* **3.** Showing that a particular disease or germ is not present: *The results of the allergy test were negative.* **4.** Less than zero: *Subtracting 29 from 19 gives −10, a negative number.* **5.** Having one of two opposite electrical charges. One end of a magnet has a negative charge, the opposite end a positive charge.
□*noun* **1.** In grammar, a word or part of a word that expresses denial or refusal. *No, not, and un-* are negatives. **2.** An image on photographic film in which the areas that are normally light and those that are normally dark are reversed.
neg·a·tive (neg′ə tiv) □*adjective* □*noun, plural* **negatives**

neglect *verb* **1.** To fail to give proper care or attention to: *He never neglects his dog.* **2.** To fail to do: *She neglected to tell us that she would be late for dinner.*
□*noun* **1.** The act of neglecting: *My neglect of household chores annoyed my mother.* **2.** The condition of being neglected: *Our once well-kept neighborhood is falling into neglect.*
ne·glect (ni glekt′) □*verb* **neglected, neglecting, neglects** □*noun*

neglect

negotiate *verb* To discuss or talk over in order to reach a settlement or understanding: *The two nations negotiated a treaty.*

ne·go·ti·ate (ni gō′shē āt′) □*verb* **negotiated, negotiating, negotiates**

negotiation *noun* The act of negotiating: *the negotiation of an armistice.*
ne·go·ti·a·tion (ni gō′shē ā′shən) □*noun,* *plural* **negotiations**

neigh *noun* The long, high-pitched sound made by a horse.
□*verb* To make such a sound.
neigh (nā) □*noun, plural* **neighs** □*verb* **neighed, neighing, neighs**

neighbor *noun* **1.** Someone who lives next door to or near another. **2.** Something or someone located next to or near another: *New Zealand is a neighbor of Australia.*
neigh·bor (nā′bər) □*noun, plural* **neighbors**

neighborhood *noun* **1.** A district or area, especially of a city or town: *Older neighborhoods in our town are being improved.* **2.** The people who live in the same area or district: *The whole neighborhood came out to watch the Thanksgiving Day parade.*
neigh·bor·hood (nā′bər hood′) □*noun,* *plural* **neighborhoods**

neighboring *adjective* Located close by; bordering: *Mexico and Canada are both neighboring countries to the United States.*
neigh·bor·ing (nā′bər ing) □*adjective*

neighborly *adjective* Of or like a friendly neighbor.
neigh·bor·ly (nā′bər lē) □*adjective*

neither *adjective* Not one nor the other; not either: *Neither shirt fits comfortably.*
□*pronoun* Not the one nor the other: *Neither of them passed the math test.*
□*conjunction* **1.** The conjunction **neither** is used with **nor** to present two negative alternatives: *The boys had neither seen nor heard us. I have brought neither warm clothes nor boots.* **2.** Also not: *You don't really want to get a hamburger and neither do I.*
nei·ther (nē′thər *or* nī′thər) □*adjective* □*pronoun* □*conjunction*

neon *noun* A gaseous chemical element that has no color and no odor and is found in very small amounts in the earth's atmosphere. Neon is used in certain electric signs.
ne·on (nē′on′) □*noun*

WORD HISTORY: neon

Neon comes from a Greek word that means "new." The gas was given this name when it was newly discovered about 100 years ago.

---

nephew *noun* **1.** A son of a person's brother or sister. **2.** A son of the brother or sister of a person's husband or wife.
neph·ew (nef′yōō) □*noun, plural* **nephews**

Neptune *noun* A planet of our solar system, eighth in order from the sun.
Nep·tune (nep′tōōn′ *or* nep′tyōōn′) □*noun*

nerve *noun* **1.** Any of the bundles of fibers that link the brain and spinal cord with the other parts of the body and carry messages that make the muscles and organs work. **2.** Strong will; courage: *It took nerve to climb that tree.*
nerve (nûrv) □*noun, plural* **nerves**

nervous *adjective* **1.** Easily excited or upset: *A race horse is a nervous animal.* **2.** Uneasy; anxious: *I'm nervous about the test.*
nerv·ous (nûr′vəs) □*adjective*

nervous system *noun* The system including the brain, spinal cord, and nerves that controls all the actions of the body.

–ness A suffix that forms nouns and means "a state, condition, or quality": *promptness; sadness; redness.*

nest *noun* **1.** A container or shelter made by birds for holding their eggs and young. It may be made of grass, mud, twigs, hair, or other materials. **2.** A similar shelter made by insects, fish, mice, or other animals. **3.** A number of birds, insects, or other animals living as a group in a nest: *a nest of baby sparrows.* **4.** A snug, cozy place.
□*verb* To build or stay in a nest: *Pigeons nested under the eaves.*
nest (nest) □*noun, plural* **nests** □*verb* **nested, nesting, nests**

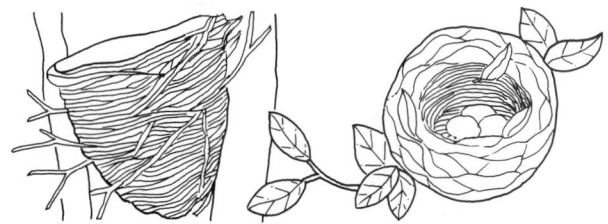

nest
Two kinds of birds' nests

a	bat	ī	bite	ōō	tool	*th*	feather
ā	make	î	fierce	ou	out	th	bath
â	dare	o	dot	u	nut	hw	wheat
ä	father	ō	no	û	turn	zh	measure
e	net	ô	law, for	ch	church	ə	about, open
ē	be	oi	soil	ng	ring		pencil, atom
i	dip	oo	look	sh	shade		circus

net¹ *noun* An open fabric made of threads, cords, or ropes woven or knotted together so as to leave holes at regular intervals: *a hairnet; a heavy fish net; the net on a tennis court.*
□*verb* To catch in or as if in a net: *I netted three trout today.*
net (net) □*noun, plural* **nets** □*verb* **netted, netting, nets**

net

net² *adjective* Remaining after all necessary additions, subtractions, or adjustments have been made: *a worker's net income.*
□*verb* To bring in or gain as profit.
net (net) □*adjective* □*verb* **netted, netting, nets**

network *noun* **1.** A system or pattern of lines, routes, passages, or parts that cross: *a network of highways; a network of fine wrinkles.* **2.** A group of radio or television stations that are linked together and that present many of the same programs at the same time. **3.** A system of computers or computer terminals that are connected together.
net·work (net′wûrk′) □*noun, plural* **networks**

neutral *adjective* **1.** Not supporting either side in a war, dispute, or fight: *a neutral country not involved in the war.* **2.** Lacking color or tint: *Beige is a neutral color.* **3.** In chemistry, being neither an acid nor a base.
□*noun* The arrangement of gears in an engine in which no motion can be transmitted.
neu·tral (noo′trəl *or* nyoo′trəl) □*adjective* □*noun*

neutron *noun* A small particle found in the nucleus of an atom. A neutron has no electrical charge and is slightly larger than a proton.
neu·tron (noo′tron′ *or* nyoo′tron′) □*noun, plural* **neutrons**

never *adverb* **1.** At no time; not ever: *I have never met him.* **2.** Absolutely not; not at all: *She would never lie to the teacher.*
nev·er (nev′ər) □*adverb*

nevertheless *adverb* All the same: *The work is not easy, but you must try nevertheless.*
□*conjunction* However: *He earns a lot of money; nevertheless, he wants more.*
nev·er·the·less (nev′ər thə les′) □*adverb* □*conjunction*

new *adjective* **1.** Recently made or grown; not old: *a new school building; a new flower.* **2.** Just found, discovered, learned about, or obtained: *new facts about the common cold; a new neighbor.* **3.** Modern; up-to-date: *a new type of computer; a new style of hat.* **4.** Not trained or experienced: *He is new at coaching basketball.*
□*adverb* Freshly; recently: *new-mown hay.*
new (noo *or* nyoo) □*adjective* **newer, newest** □*adverb*

newborn *adjective* Just born: *A newborn calf can stand up the first day.*
new·born (noo′bôrn′ *or* nyoo′bôrn′) □*adjective*

newcomer *noun* Someone who has only recently arrived or appeared: *a newcomer to our church.*
new·com·er (noo′kum′ər *or* nyoo′kum′ər) □*noun, plural* **newcomers**

New England *noun* The northeastern part of the United States consisting of the states of Maine, New Hampshire, Vermont, Massachusetts, Connecticut, and Rhode Island.
New Eng·land (ing′glənd) □*noun*

newly *adverb* Recently; just: *a newly painted porch.*
new·ly (noo′lē *or* nyoo′lē) □*adverb*

news *plural noun* Information about one or more events that have recently happened. News is passed on from person to person or reported by newspapers, news magazines, radio, or television.
news (nooz *or* nyooz) □*plural noun*

newscast *noun* A radio or television program that gives news reports.
news·cast (nooz′kast′ *or* nyooz′kast′) □*noun, plural* **newscasts**

newspaper *noun* A publication printed daily or weekly and containing news, articles, pictures, and advertisements.
news·pa·per (nooz′pā′pər *or* nyooz′pā′pər) □*noun, plural* **newspapers**

newspaper

newt *noun* A small salamander with soft, smooth skin, short legs, and a long tail. A newt lives both on land and in the water.
newt (nōot *or* nyōot) □*noun, plural* **newts**

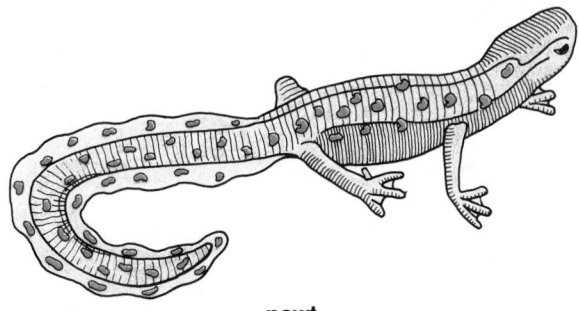

newt

New Testament *noun* The second part of the Christian Bible, containing the life and teachings of Christ and his disciples.

New World *noun* North America and South America.

next *adjective* **1.** Coming right after the present or previous one: *Next year we plan to buy a new piano. The next person to speak was my uncle.* **2.** Closest: *the next house down the block.*
□*adverb* **1.** Following right after the present or previous one: *What happens next?* **2.** On the first occasion after this: *When will you go hiking next?*
□*preposition* Close to; near: *I keep my books next to my desk.*
next (nekst) □*adjective* □*adverb*
□*preposition*

next-door *adjective* In, to, or at the nearest house, building, apartment, or office: *His best friend at school is his next-door neighbor.*
next-door (nekst′dôr′) □*adjective*

next door *adverb* In or to the nearest house, building, apartment, or office: *She went next door to borrow some flour.*

nibble *verb* To eat by taking small bites: *nibble on a carrot.* **2.** To bite or nip lightly: *I felt a fish nibbling on my line.*
□*noun* A small, gentle bite.
nib·ble (nib′əl) □*verb* **nibbled, nibbling, nibbles** □*noun, plural* **nibbles**

nice *adjective* **1.** Very pleasing; good: *a nice birthday party; a nice dress.* **2.** Of good quality: *a home full of nice things.* **3.** Kind and good; thoughtful: *That teacher was always nice to me.* **4.** Showing skill; very fine: *a nice piece of weaving.*
nice (nīs) □*adjective* **nicer, nicest**

nick *noun* A small cut or chip in a surface or edge: *I found a nick on the antique table.*
□*verb* To make a small cut or chip in: *nick a finger while slicing tomatoes.*
　in the nick of time Just at the last moment: *I braked in the nick of time and avoided hitting the pole.*
nick (nik) □*noun, plural* **nicks** □*verb* **nicked, nicking, nicks**

nickel *noun* **1.** A hard, silvery metal that is one of the chemical elements. **2.** A United States or Canadian coin worth five cents.
nick·el (nik′əl) □*noun, plural* **nickels**

WORD HISTORY: **nickel**

Nickel comes from the German name for the ore in which the metal nickel is found. The German name literally means "copper demon." The Germans called the ore by this name because it has a color like copper but has no copper in it.

nickel
United States nickel

a	bat	ī	bite	ōō	tool	*th*	feather
ā	make	î	fierce	ou	out	th	bath
â	dare	o	dot	u	nut	hw	wheat
ä	father	ō	no	û	turn	zh	measure
e	net	ô	law, for	ch	church	ə	about, open
ē	be	oi	soil	ng	ring		pencil, atom
i	dip	oo	look	sh	shade		circus

nickname *noun* A name used instead of or along with a real name: *One nickname for Boston is "Beantown."*
☐*verb* To call by a nickname.
nick·name (nĭk′nām′) ☐*noun, plural* **nicknames** ☐*verb* **nicknamed, nicknaming, nicknames**

nicotine *noun* A poisonous substance that is found in tobacco leaves.
nic·o·tine (nĭk′ə tēn′) ☐*noun*

> *WORD HISTORY:* **nicotine**
> *Nicotine* is named after Jacques Nicot, a French diplomat who lived about 400 years ago. He introduced tobacco into France.

niece *noun* **1.** A daughter of a person's brother or sister. **2.** A daughter of the brother or sister of a person's husband or wife.
niece (nēs) ☐*noun, plural* **nieces**

night *noun* The time between sunset and sunrise, especially the hours of darkness: *The owl hunts at night.*
night (nīt) ☐*noun, plural* **nights**

nightfall *noun* The coming of darkness at the end of the day.
night·fall (nīt′fôl) ☐*noun*

nightgown *noun* A loose gown for sleeping.
night·gown (nīt′goun′) ☐*noun, plural* **nightgowns**

nightingale *noun* A brownish bird of Europe and Asia. The nightingale has a sweet song and often sings at night.
night·in·gale (nīt′ən gāl′ *or* nī′ting gāl′) ☐*noun, plural* **nightingales**

nightingale

nightly *adjective* Taking place at night or every night: *a nightly newscast; a nightly shower.*
☐*adverb* Every night: *My father reads a story to us nightly.*
night·ly (nīt′lē) ☐*adjective* ☐*adverb*

nightmare *noun* **1.** A bad dream that is very frightening. **2.** A frightening experience.
night·mare (nīt′mâr′) ☐*noun, plural* **nightmares**

> *WORD HISTORY:* **nightmare**
> Early in the history of English *mare* was a word for an evil spirit. A *nightmare* was thought to be an evil spirit that bothered people at night by sitting on them and causing a feeling of suffocation. The word came to be used also for the bad dream that produced such a feeling.

nighttime *noun* The time between sunset and sunrise; night.
night·time (nīt′tīm′) ☐*noun*

nimble *adjective* Moving or able to move quickly, lightly, and easily: *a nimble dancer.*
nim·ble (nĭm′bəl) ☐*adjective* **nimbler, nimblest**

nine *noun* A number equal to the sum of 8 + 1; 9.
☐*adjective* Being one more than eight.
nine (nīn) ☐*noun, plural* **nines** ☐*adjective*

nineteen *noun* A number equal to the sum of 10 + 9; 19.
☐*adjective* Being one more than eighteen.
nine·teen (nīn′tēn′) ☐*noun, plural* **nineteens** ☐*adjective*

nineteenth *noun* **1.** In a group of people or things that are in numbered order, the one that matches the number nineteen. **2.** One of nineteen equal parts, written 1/19.
☐*adjective* Coming after the eighteenth.
nine·teenth (nīn′tēnth′) ☐*noun, plural* **nineteenths** ☐*adjective*

ninetieth *noun* **1.** In a group of people or things that are in numbered order, the one that matches the number ninety. **2.** One of ninety equal parts, written 1/90.
☐*adjective* Coming after the eighty-ninth.
nine·ti·eth (nīn′tē ith) ☐*noun, plural* **ninetieths** ☐*adjective*

ninety *noun* A number equal to the product of 9 × 10; 90.
☐*adjective* Being ten more than eighty.
nine·ty (nīn′tē) ☐*noun, plural* **nineties** ☐*adjective*

ninth *noun* **1.** In a group of people or things that are in numbered order, the one that matches the number nine. **2.** One of nine equal parts, written 1/9.
☐*adjective* Coming after the eighth.

ninth (nīnth) □*noun, plural* **ninths**
□*adjective*

nip *verb* **1.** To give a small, sharp bite or pinch to: *The kitten nipped my finger with its teeth.* **2.** To remove by biting or pinching: *I nipped the dead flowers off the plant.* **3.** To sting or chill: *The icy wind nipped our faces.*
□*noun* **1.** A small, sharp bite or pinch. **2.** Sharp, biting cold: *a nip in the air.*
nip (nip) □*verb* **nipped, nipping, nips**
□*noun, plural* **nips**

nipple *noun* **1.** The small tip at the center of a breast or udder through which an infant or a baby animal can suck milk from its mother. **2.** A soft rubber cap on a baby's bottle from which the baby drinks.
nip·ple (nip′əl) □*noun, plural* **nipples**

nitrogen *noun* A gaseous chemical element that has no color or smell and makes up about fourth fifths of the earth's atmosphere.
ni·tro·gen (nī′trə jən) □*noun*

no *adverb* The adverb **no** is used: **1.** To express refusal, denial, or disagreement: *Let's eat! No, I'm not hungry.* **2.** With the comparative of adjectives or adverbs: *They are no faster than they were yesterday. She is no more afraid of snakes than her brothers are.*
□*adjective* **1.** Not any: *no eggs in the refrigerator.* **2.** Not a: *She is no coward.*
□*noun* **1.** A denial or refusal: *The answer is a firm "no."* **2.** A negative vote or voter: *The noes kept the amendment from being passed.*
no (nō) □*adverb* □*adjective* □*noun, plural* **noes**

no. or **No.** An abbreviation for **number.**

nobility *noun* **1.** A social class having titles of rank and often wealth and power. **2.** Noble qualities of character: *He showed great nobility toward his enemies.*
no·bil·i·ty (nō bil′i tē) □*noun, plural* **nobilities**

noble *adjective* **1.** Of or belonging to the nobility. **2.** Having or showing qualities of high character, as courage or generosity.
□*noun* A person of noble birth, position, or title: *A count is a noble.*
no·ble (nō′bəl) □*adjective* **nobler, noblest**
□*noun, plural* **nobles**

nobleman *noun* A man of noble birth, position, or title.
no·ble·man (nō′bəl mən) □*noun, plural* **noblemen**

noblewoman *noun* A woman of noble birth, position, or title.
no·ble·wom·an (nō′bəl woom′ən) □*noun, plural* **noblewomen**

nobody *pronoun* No person; no one: *Nobody in the store came to wait on us.*
no·bod·y (nō′bod′ē) □*pronoun*

nocturnal *adjective* **1.** Of the night or happening at night: *the nightingale's nocturnal song.* **2.** Active at night rather than during the day: *The sounds of nocturnal animals kept us awake.*
noc·tur·nal (nok tûr′nəl) □*adjective*

nod *verb* **1.** To move the head down and then up in a quick motion to show agreement or approval or to greet someone. **2.** To show agreement, approval, or a greeting by moving the head in this way: *She nodded her consent to my suggestion.* **3.** To let the head droop and fall forward: *The sleepy old man nodded by the fire.*
□*noun* A nodding motion of the head.
nod (nod) □*verb* **nodded, nodding, nods**
□*noun, plural* **nods**

noise *noun* **1.** Sound that is loud, unpleasant, or unexpected: *A peacock makes a screeching noise. Don't make noise as you go upstairs.* **2.** Sound of any kind: *There was no noise except the hoot of an owl.*
noise (noiz) □*noun, plural* **noises**

SYNONYMS: **noise, racket**

These nouns mean sound that is loud, unpleasant, or unexpected: *We covered our ears to block out the noise of the jet plane. The children were making a racket that could be heard a block away.*

---

noisy *adjective* **1.** Making a lot of noise: *If the children are too noisy, they will be sent home.* **2.** Full of noise: *The town has a noisy main street.*
nois·y (noi′zē) □*adjective* **noisier, noisiest**

nomad *noun* A member of a group or tribe of people who move about from place to place looking for food, water, and grazing land for

a bat	ī bite	ōō tool	*th* feather
ā make	î fierce	ou out	th bath
â dare	o dot	u nut	hw wheat
ä father	ō no	û turn	zh measure
e net	ô law, for	ch church	ə about, open
ē be	oi soil	ng ring	pencil, atom
i dip	oo look	sh shade	circus

their livestock.

no·mad (nō′mad′) ▢*noun, plural* **nomads**

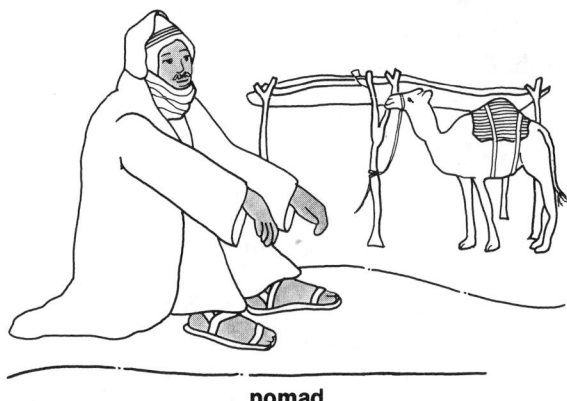

nomad

nomadic *adjective* Of, having to do with, or like a nomad.
no·mad·ic (nō **mad′**ik) ▢*adjective*

nominate *verb* **1.** To choose as a candidate in an election: *nominate a woman for mayor.* **2.** To appoint to a position or office: *The President nominates members of the cabinet.*
nom·i·nate (nom′ə nāt′) ▢*verb* **nominated, nominating, nominates**

nomination *noun* **1.** The act of choosing a candidate for election. **2.** Appointment to a position, office, or honor.
nom·i·na·tion (nom′ə nā′shən) ▢*noun, plural* **nominations**

nominee *noun* Someone chosen as a candidate for an office or position: *His father is a nominee for governor.*
nom·i·nee (nom′ə nē′) ▢*noun, plural* **nominees**

non– A prefix that means "not; absence of": *noninterference.* When "non–" is followed by a capital letter, it appears with a hyphen: *non-Asiatic.*

none *pronoun* **1.** Not any: *I looked through the books, but none belonged to him.* **2.** No part or quantity: *You have done none of your chores.* **3.** Not one: *Many people were invited, but none came.*
▢*adverb* Not at all.
none (nun) ▢*pronoun* ▢*adverb*

nonsense *noun* Foolish or silly talk or behavior: *His tale of the flying saucer was nonsense.*
non·sense (non′sens′) ▢*noun*

noodle *noun* A long, thin strip of dried dough, made of eggs, flour, and water.
noo·dle (nōod′əl) ▢*noun, plural* **noodles**

noon *noun* Twelve o'clock in the daytime.
noon (nōon) ▢*noun, plural* **noons**

no one *noun* No person; nobody: *No one had to stay after school today.*

noose *noun* A loop formed in a rope with a knot that lets the loop tighten as the rope is pulled.
noose (nōos) ▢*noun, plural* **nooses**

noose

nor *conjunction* And not: *He had neither brushed his teeth nor bathed. I have no pets, nor do I want any.*
nor (nôr) ▢*conjunction*

normal *adjective* **1.** Usual or ordinary: *Heavy traffic is normal on weekends. Hot weather is normal in July.* **2.** Happening in a natural, healthy way: *normal hearing and eyesight.* —See Synonyms at **ordinary.**
▢*noun* The normal condition or measure: *His intelligence is above normal. There was more snow than normal last winter.*
nor·mal (nôr′məl) ▢*adjective* ▢*noun*

Norse *adjective* Of ancient Scandinavia, its people, or their language.
▢*noun* The people of ancient Scandinavia.
Norse (nôrs) ▢*adjective* ▢*noun*

north *noun* **1.** The direction to the right of someone who faces the sunset. **2.** Often **North** A region in this direction. **3. North** The Arctic region. **4. North** The northern part of the United States, especially the states north of Maryland, West Virginia, Kentucky, and Missouri.
▢*adjective* **1.** Of, in, or toward the north: *the north bank of the river.* **2.** Coming from the north: *the north wind.*
▢*adverb* Toward the north: *birds flying north.*
north (nôrth) ▢*noun* ▢*adjective* ▢*adverb*

North American *noun* Someone born in or living in North America.
▢*adjective* Of North America.

northeast *noun* **1.** The direction that is halfway between north and east. **2.** Often **North-**

east A region in this direction. **3. Northeast** The part of the United States that includes New England and usually New York, Pennsylvania, and New Jersey.
□*adjective* **1.** Of, in, or toward the northeast: *the northeast part of the county.* **2.** Coming from the northeast: *a northeast storm.*
□*adverb* Toward the northeast: *We walked northeast along the ridge of the mountains.*
north·east (nôrth **ēst′**) □*noun* □*adjective* □*adverb*

northern *adjective* **1.** Of, in, or toward the north: *the northern edge of the forest.* **2.** Coming from or lying toward the north: *a northern breeze.* **3.** Like what is found in the north: *cold northern winters.*
north·ern (nôr′ thərn) □*adjective*

northern lights *plural noun* A brilliant display of flashing and moving lights seen in the night sky, especially in polar regions.

North Pole *noun* The northern end of the axis around which the earth rotates and the point on the surface of the earth that is farthest north.

North Star *noun* A bright star in the sky almost directly over the North Pole.

northward *adverb* To or toward the north: *He headed northward.*
□*adjective* Moving to or toward the north.
north·ward (nôrth′wərd) □*adverb* □*adjective*

northwest *noun* **1.** The direction that is halfway between north and west. **2. Northwest** The northwestern part of the United States, especially the region that includes the states of Washington, Oregon, Idaho, and Montana.
□*adjective* **1.** Of, in, or toward the northwest: *the northwest part of town.* **2.** Coming from the northwest.
□*adverb* Toward the northwest: *I hiked northwest through the woods.*
north·west (nôrth **west′**) □*noun* □*adjective* □*adverb*

nose *noun* **1.** The part of the face or head of humans and animals for breathing and smelling. **2.** The sense of smell: *A hunting dog has a good nose.* **3.** The narrow front end of an airplane, rocket, submarine, or other structure.
□*verb* **1.** To search for by smell; sniff out: *The dogs nosed out the fox's den.* **2.** To touch, push, or examine with the nose: *The rats nosed through the dump.*
   under one's nose In plain view: *The ruler is right under your nose.*

nose (nōz) □*noun, plural* **noses** □*verb* **nosed, nosing, noses**

nose cone *noun* The front end of a rocket or missile. A nose cone is narrower at the front than at the back. Many nose cones are made to separate from the rocket or missile at some time in the flight.

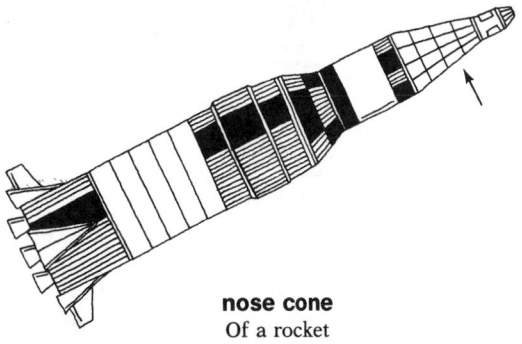

nose cone
Of a rocket

nostril *noun* Either of the two outer openings of the nose.
nos·tril (nos′trəl) □*noun, plural* **nostrils**

nosy *adjective* Overly curious about other people's business: *a nosy neighbor.*
nos·y (nō′zē) □*adjective* **nosier, nosiest**

not *adverb* In no way; to no degree: *I called but he's not there. It is not too late to change your mind.*
not (not) □*adverb*

notable *adjective* Worth noticing; remarkable: *The first computer was a notable achievement.*
□*noun* A well-known or important figure: *Many of the country's notables have dined at the White House.*
no·ta·ble (nō′tə bəl) □*adjective* □*noun, plural* **notables**

notation *noun* **1.** A short note: *I made a notation of her phone number.* **2.** A system of figures or symbols used to stand for numbers, words, or other things: *musical notation.*
no·ta·tion (nō tā′shən) □*noun, plural* **notations**

notch *noun* A V-shaped cut.
□*verb* To cut a notch or notches in.

a	bat	ī	bite	o͞o	tool	*th*	feather
ā	make	î	fierce	ou	out	th	bath
â	dare	o	dot	u	nut	hw	wheat
ä	father	ō	no	û	turn	zh	measure
e	net	ô	law, for	ch	church	ə	about, open
ē	be	oi	soil	ng	ring		pencil, atom
i	dip	oo	look	sh	shade		circus

notch (noch) □*noun, plural* **notches** □*verb*
notched, notching, notches

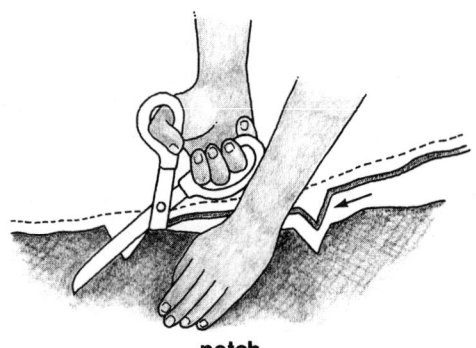

notch

note *noun* **1.** A short letter or message: *She sent a note thanking us for the gift.* **2.** A short written record; reminder: *She took notes on the candidate's speech.* **3.** An explanation for a word, paragraph, or section of a book. **4.** Importance: *Many artists of note came to the exhibition.* **5.** Notice; attention: *Take note of how she sings this difficult passage.* **6.** A symbol that represents a musical tone. **7.** A musical tone. **8.** A piano key. **9.** A sign; hint: *There was a note of anger in her voice.*
□*verb* **1.** To observe; notice: *Note how she fixes her hair.* **2.** To write down: *He noted down the address on a desk calendar.*
note (nōt) □*noun, plural* **notes** □*verb* **noted, noting, notes**

note

notebook *noun* A book with blank pages to write on.
note·book (nōt′book′) □*noun, plural* **notebooks**

noted *adjective* Well known; famous: *a noted athlete.*
not·ed (nō′tid) □*adjective*

nothing *pronoun* **1.** Not anything: *I have nothing new to tell you.* **2.** Zero: *They won, seven to nothing.* **3.** Someone or something that is not important.
□*adverb* Not at all: *The hotel looked nothing like the one on the postcard.*
noth·ing (nuth′ing) □*pronoun* □*adverb*

notice *verb* To become aware of; perceive: *He noticed a police car driving slowly by.*
□*noun* **1.** A condition of being observed: *Her tardiness escaped notice.* **2.** An announcement in a public place or publication. **3.** An announcement or warning: *The telephone company cut off our service without notice.*
no·tice (nō′tis) □*verb* **noticed, noticing, notices** □*noun, plural* **notices**

notify *verb* To let know; inform: *Please notify the post office when you move.*
no·ti·fy (nō′tə fī′) □*verb* **notified, notifying, notifies**

notion *noun* **1.** A picture in the mind; a general idea: *Do you have any notion of how to play chess?* **2.** A sudden idea or whim: *She had a notion to bake a batch of cookies.* **3. notions** Small, useful items, such as needles, thread, ribbons, and pins sold in a store.
no·tion (nō′shən) □*noun, plural* **notions**

notorious *adjective* Well known for something bad or unpleasant: *a notorious criminal.*
no·to·ri·ous (nō tôr′ē əs) □*adjective*

nought *pronoun* Another spelling for **naught.**
nought (nôt) □*pronoun*

noun *noun* A word used to name a person, place, thing, quality, or action. For example, in the sentence "My two friends and I played hopscotch on the sidewalk all morning," *friends, hopscotch, sidewalk,* and *morning* are nouns. Nouns can be singular (*hopscotch, sidewalk*) or plural (*friends*).
noun (noun) □*noun, plural* **nouns**

nourish *verb* To provide with what is needed to grow and develop.
nour·ish (nûr′ish) □*verb* **nourished, nourishing, nourishes**

nourishment *noun* Something needed to maintain life and growth.
nour·ish·ment (nûr′ish mənt) □*noun*

novel[1] *noun* A long story about fictitious people and events.
nov·el (nov′əl) □*noun, plural* **novels**

novel[2] *adjective* Very new or different: *a novel design.*
nov·el (nov′əl) □*adjective*

novelist *noun* Someone who writes novels.
nov·el·ist (nov′ə list) □*noun, plural* **novelists**

novelty *noun* **1.** The condition of being new or different: *the novelty of riding in a car with the top down.* **2.** A thing that is new and unusual: *At first the computer was a fascinating novelty.* **3. novelties** Small, cheap items for sale, such as toys and decorations.

nov·el·ty (nov′əl tē) ☐*noun, plural* **novelties**

November *noun* The eleventh month of the year. November has 30 days.

No·vem·ber (nō vem′bər) ☐*noun, plural* **Novembers**

WORD HISTORY: **November**

November comes from a Latin name meaning "the ninth month." In an early Roman calendar March was the first month and November the ninth.

---

novice *noun* **1.** Someone new to a field or activity; beginner: *a novice at painting pictures.* **2.** Someone who is training to become a nun or monk but has not yet taken final vows.

nov·ice (nov′is) ☐*noun, plural* **novices**

now *adverb* **1.** At the present time: *The baby is sleeping now.* **2.** At once; immediately: *You had better write that letter now.*
☐*conjunction* Since; seeing that: *Now that we've seen all the sights let's go home.*
☐*noun* The present: *He should be awake by now.*

now (nou) ☐*adverb* ☐*conjunction* ☐*noun*

nowadays *adverb* In the present times; in these days: *Very few farmers use horses for plowing nowadays.*

now·a·days (nou′ə dāz′) ☐*adverb*

nowhere *adverb* In or to no place: *My purse was nowhere to be seen.*
☐*noun* A place that is not known: *Our car broke down in the middle of nowhere.*

no·where (nō′hwâr′ *or* nō′wâr′) ☐*adverb* ☐*noun*

nozzle *noun* A metal spout at the end of a hose or pipe through which a liquid or a gas is forced out.

noz·zle (noz′əl) ☐*noun, plural* **nozzles**

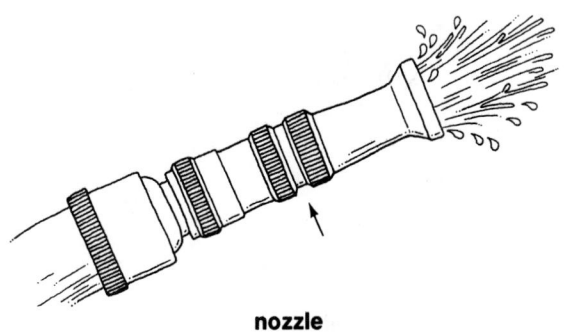

nozzle

nuclear *adjective* **1.** Of or forming a nucleus: *the nuclear material in a cell.* **2.** Of or using

energy from the nuclei of atoms: *a nuclear bomb.*

nu·cle·ar (nōō′klē ər *or* nyōō′klē ər) ☐*adjective*

nuclear energy *noun* Atomic energy.

nuclei *noun* The plural of **nucleus**.

nu·cle·i (nōō′klē ī′ *or* nyōō′klē ī′) ☐*noun*

nucleus *noun* **1.** A structure in a living cell that controls its important activities, such as growth, development, and reproduction. **2.** The central part of an atom. Protons and neutrons make up the nucleus.

nu·cle·us (nōō′klē əs *or* nyōō′klē əs) ☐*noun, plural* **nuclei**

nudge *verb* To poke or push in a gentle way. ☐*noun* A gentle poke or push.

nudge (nuj) ☐*verb* **nudged, nudging, nudges** ☐*noun, plural* **nudges**

nugget *noun* A hard lump of gold before it is refined.

nug·get (nug′it) ☐*noun, plural* **nuggets**

nuisance *noun* Someone or something that annoys or tires: *Cleaning muddy boots is a nuisance. A badly trained dog is a nuisance.*

nui·sance (nōō′səns *or* nyōō′səns) ☐*noun, plural* **nuisances**

numb *adjective* Having no feeling or no ability to move: *numb fingers; numb with fear.*
☐*verb* To lose or cause to lose the ability to feel or move: *The doctor numbed her arm before treating the boil.*

numb (num) ☐*adjective* **number, numbest** ☐*verb* **numbed, numbing, numbs**

number *noun* **1.** A unit of counting; numeral: *The figures 5, 14, and 900 are numbers.* **2.** A numeral or series of numerals assigned to a person or thing: *He lost her telephone number.* **3.** An amount or quantity that is the sum of the units; total: *the number of students in a class.* **4.** Quantity; amount. **5. numbers** Arithmetic.
☐*verb* **1.** To add up to: *The flock of sheep numbered more than four hundred.* **2.** To give a number or numbers to: *The pages of the pamphlet were not numbered.* **3.** To include in

a bat	ī bite	ōō tool	*th* feather
ā make	i fierce	ou out	th bath
â dare	o dot	u nut	hw wheat
ä father	ō no	û turn	zh measure
e net	ô law, for	ch church	ə about, open
ē be	oi soil	ng ring	pencil, atom
i dip	oo look	sh shade	circus

a certain group: *I number her among my closest friends.* **4.** To count; estimate: *The theater owner numbered the people in the audience at 500.*
num·ber (**num′**bər) □*noun, plural* **numbers** □*verb* **numbered, numbering, numbers**

numeral *noun* A symbol or group of symbols that represents a number: *4 and IV are both numerals for four.*
nu·mer·al (**noo′**mər əl *or* **nyoo′**mər əl) □*noun, plural* **numerals**

numerator *noun* The number above or to the left of the line in a fraction. For example, in the fraction ²/₇ the numerator is 2.
nu·mer·a·tor (**noo′**mə rā′tər *or* **nyoo′**mə rā′tər) □*noun, plural* **numerators**

numerical *adjective* Of a number or series of numbers.
nu·mer·i·cal (noo **mer′**i kəl *or* nyoo **mer′**i kəl) □*adjective*

numerous *adjective* Large in number; many: *At the fair the judges awarded numerous prizes.*
nu·mer·ous (**noo′**mər əs *or* **nyoo′**mər əs) □*adjective*

nun *noun* A woman who becomes a member of a church order.
nun (nun) □*noun, plural* **nuns**

nurse *noun* **1.** Someone trained to take care of people who are sick. Nurses usually work in hospitals and carry out the instructions of doctors. **2.** A woman who is hired to take care of someone else's children.
□*verb* **1.** To take care of: *When I was very sick my mother nursed me back to health.* **2.** To feed or be fed at the breast or a milk gland: *The lioness nursed her cubs.*
nurse (nûrs) □*noun, plural* **nurses** □*verb* **nursed, nursing, nurses**

nurse

nursery *noun* **1.** A room for babies or young children. **2.** A place in which babies and young children are cared for away from home. **3.** A place where young plants are raised to be sold.
nurs·er·y (**nûr′**sə rē) □*noun, plural* **nurseries**

nursery

nursery school *noun* A school for children who are too young to go to kindergarten.

nut *noun* **1.** A seed or dry fruit with a hard outer shell. Many kinds of nuts are good to eat. **2.** A metal, wood, or plastic block having a hole with spiral threads in the center. A nut screws onto a bolt or rod and holds it in place.
nut (nut) □*noun, plural* **nuts**

nutcracker *noun* **1.** A tool for cracking nuts. **2.** A gray and white bird with a sharp bill.
nut·crack·er (**nut′**krak′ər) □*noun, plural* **nutcrackers**

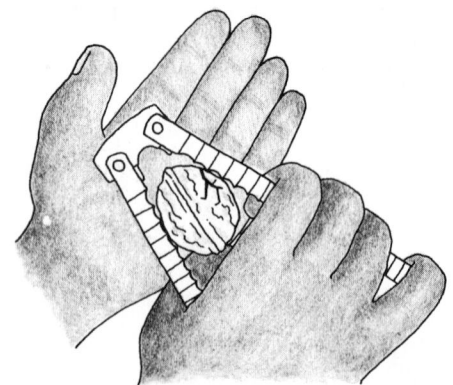
nutcracker

nutmeg *noun* The hard seed of a tropical tree. The seed is shaped like an egg, has a pleasant smell, and is used as a spice when ground or grated.

nut·meg (**nut′**meg′) □*noun, plural* **nutmegs**

nutrient *noun* Something that nourishes people, plants, and animals and keeps them healthy and growing.

nu·tri·ent (**noo′**trē ənt *or* **nyoo′**trē ənt) □*noun, plural* **nutrients**

nutrition *noun* **1.** The act or process of nourishing or being nourished: *Good nutrition is the basis of good health.* **2.** The processes by which a living organism takes in and uses food: *Her project was to study plant nutrition.*

nu·tri·tion (noo **trish′**ən *or* nyoo **trish′**ən) □*noun*

nutritious *adjective* Giving nourishment; beneficial as food: *I prepared a nutritious lunch for the family.*

nu·tri·tious (noo **trish′**əs *or* nyoo **trish′**əs) □*adjective*

nuzzle *verb* **1.** To rub or push in a gentle way with the nose or snout: *My cat nuzzles my ankles when it is hungry.* **2.** To snuggle up to: *The puppies nuzzled against each other to keep warm.*

nuz·zle (**nuz′**əl) □*verb* **nuzzled, nuzzling, nuzzles**

nylon *noun* A strong, elastic synthetic material that can be produced in the form of cloth, thread, yarn, bristles, or plastic. It is used for making clothing, parachutes, rugs, brushes, and rope.

ny·lon (**nī′**lon′) □*noun, plural* **nylons**

nymph *noun* **1.** In myths and legends, a graceful female spirit thought to have lived in woods and water. **2.** A young insect that has not yet developed into its adult state.

nymph (nimf) □*noun, plural* **nymphs**

a	bat	ī	bite	oo	tool	*th*	feather
ā	make	î	fierce	ou	out	th	bath
â	dare	o	dot	u	nut	hw	wheat
ä	father	ō	no	û	turn	zh	measure
e	net	ô	law, for	ch	church	ə	about, open
ē	be	oi	soil	ng	ring		pencil, atom
i	dip	oo	look	sh	shade		circus

ANCIENT GREEK

The letter **O** has evolved from many forms of ancient writing. One of the earliest known examples is the Greek character shown above, which dates from almost 3,000 years ago. Over the years, artists and designers have created their own versions of the English letter **O**. Some of the more common examples seen today are shown below.

| HANDWRITING | CALLIGRAPHY | MODERN SANS SERIF | MODERN SERIF | SCRIPT |

---

o or **O**   *noun* The fifteenth letter of the English alphabet.
o or **O** (ō)   □*noun, plural* **o's** or **O's**

oak   *noun* **1.** Any of several trees that bear acorns and leaves that often have uneven notches along the edges. **2.** The hard, strong wood of an oak tree.
oak (ōk)   □*noun, plural* **oaks**

oar   *noun* A long, thin pole with a flat blade at one end, used in pairs to row boats.
oar (ôr)   □*noun, plural* **oars**

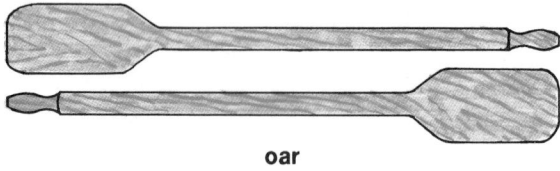

oar

oasis   *noun* An area in a desert where there is water and where plants are able to grow.
o·a·sis (ō ā′sis)   □*noun, plural* **oases**

oasis

oat   *noun* The seed of a grain plant. Oats are eaten by people and used as feed for horses and cattle.
oat (ōt)   □*noun, plural* **oats**

oath   *noun* **1.** A promise to tell the truth or act in a particular way: *take an oath in court by placing one's hand on the Bible.* **2.** A word or phrase used in cursing and swearing.
oath (ōth)   □*noun, plural* **oaths**

oatmeal   *noun* **1.** Oats that have been ground or pressed flat. **2.** A cooked cereal made from this.
oat·meal (ōt′mēl′)   □*noun*

obedience   *noun* The practice of obeying rules, laws, or requests: *Obedience to traffic laws is necessary for everyone's safety.*
o·be·di·ence (ō bē′dē əns)   □*noun*

obedient   *adjective* Doing what is asked, ordered, or required: *an obedient child.*
o·be·di·ent (ō bē′dē ənt)   □*adjective*

obey   *verb* **1.** To carry out or follow a law, order, or request: *obey the rules of the game.* **2.** To follow the wishes or orders of: *He seldom obeyed his father.*
o·bey (ō bā′)   □*verb* **obeyed, obeying, obeys**

SYNONYMS: **obey, mind**

These verbs mean to carry out or follow a law, order, or request: *Always obey the traffic laws. Be sure to mind the directions on the package.*

obi   *noun* A wide sash worn with a kimono.
o·bi (ō′bē)   □*noun, plural* **obis**

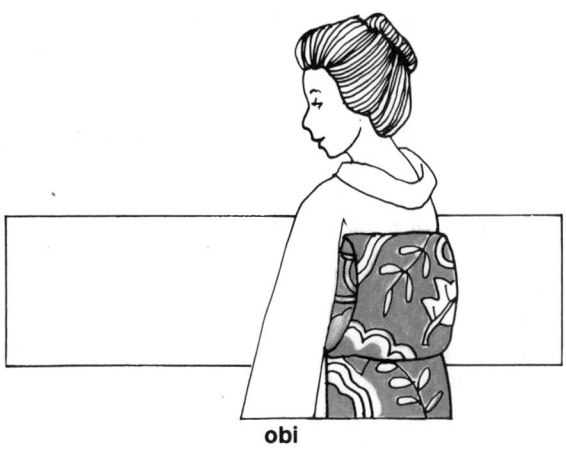

obi

object *noun* **1.** Something that has shape and can be seen or felt; thing: *The parcel contained an oddly shaped object.* **2.** Someone or something toward which a feeling or attitude is directed: *She is the object of everyone's admiration.* **3.** A purpose; goal: *The object of our discussion is to find out the true facts.* **4.** In grammar, a word that receives the action of a verb or follows a preposition. For example, in the sentence "He rode the horse," "horse" is the object of "rode." In the phrase "up the hill," "the hill" is the object of "up."
☐*verb* **1.** To give or state as an objection: *They objected to the silliness of the TV show.* **2.** To say in protest: *"I will not change my plans," she objected.*
ob·ject ☐*noun* (**ob**′jikt), *plural* **objects**
  ☐*verb* (əb **jekt**′) **objected, objecting, objects**

objection *noun* A reason for or cause of being against something: *His objection to buying the car is that it is too expensive.*
ob·jec·tion (əb **jek**′shən) ☐*noun, plural* **objections**

objective *adjective* Not influenced by one's own feelings or prejudices: *A judge must give an objective opinion.*
☐*noun* Something that one tries to achieve or reach: *A college education is my objective.*
ob·jec·tive (əb **jek**′tiv) ☐*adjective* ☐*noun, plural* **objectives**

obligate *verb* To bind by a sense of duty or law: *She felt obligated to ask them to the party.*
ob·li·gate (**ob**′li gāt′) ☐*verb* **obligated, obligating, obligates**

obligation *noun* A duty one must carry out: *He felt an obligation to return the money he borrowed.*

ob·li·ga·tion (ob′li **gā**′shən) ☐*noun, plural* **obligations**

oblige *verb* **1.** To force someone to do something by a law or a sense of responsibility: *He is obliged to pay the family's bills.* **2.** To make grateful or thankful: *I am obliged to them for helping me repair the car.*
o·blige (ə **blīj**′) ☐*verb* **obliged, obliging, obliges**

oblique angle *noun* An acute or obtuse angle.
o·blique angle (ə **blēk**′) ☐*noun*

oblong *adjective* Greater in length than in width: *an oblong piece of paper.*
ob·long (**ob**′lông′) ☐*adjective*

Dear Mom,

oblong

oboe *noun* A musical instrument of the woodwind family with a high, piercing sound. The oboe is played by blowing into a mouthpiece.
o·boe (**ō**′bō) ☐*noun, plural* **oboes**

obscure *adjective* **1.** Difficult to understand: *an obscure riddle.* **2.** Not easy to see or figure out; not distinct: *obscure handwriting.* **3.** Not well known: *an obscure young artist.*
☐*verb* To make hard to see or understand: *The trees obscure our view.*
ob·scure (əb **skyoor**′) ☐*adjective* ☐*verb* **obscured, obscuring, obscures**

observation *noun* **1.** The act or power of watching or noticing: *The doctor put the patient in the hospital for observation.* **2.** The fact

a bat	ī bite	ōō tool	*th* feather
ā make	î fierce	ou out	th bath
â dare	o dot	u nut	hw wheat
ä father	ō no	û turn	zh measure
e net	ô law, for	ch church	ə about, open
ē be	oi soil	ng ring	pencil, atom
i dip	oo look	sh shade	circus

of being noticed: *The heavy snowfall helped the soldier avoid observation.* **3.** A comment or note on something.
ob·ser·va·tion (ob′zər **vā**′shən) ☐*noun, plural* **observations**

observatory *noun* A place with telescopes and other instruments for studying the stars, planets, and the heavens.
ob·ser·va·to·ry (əb **zûr**′və tôr′ē) ☐*noun, plural* **observatories**

observatory

observe *verb* **1.** To watch in a close and careful way: *She was observing a spider spinning its web.* **2.** To make a remark: *"It's time to pack up and go home," she observed.* **3.** To abide by a law, duty, or custom: *observe the speed limit.*
ob·serve (əb **zûrv**′) ☐*verb* **observed, observing, observes**

obsolete *adjective* No longer used or done: *As military equipment, suits of armor have been obsolete for centuries.*
ob·so·lete (ob′sə **lēt**′ *or* ob′sə lēt′) ☐*adjective*

obstacle *noun* Something that blocks the way or progress of: *The fallen tree was an obstacle in our path.*
ob·sta·cle (**ob**′stə kəl) ☐*noun, plural* **obstacles**

obstacle

obstruct *verb* **1.** To block with an obstacle: *A bad cold obstructed his breathing.* **2.** To get in the way of: *Their car is obstructing the driveway and we can't get out.*
ob·struct (əb **strukt**′) ☐*verb* **obstructed, obstructing, obstructs**

obtain *verb* To get by means of planning or effort: *tried to obtain tickets for tonight's concert.*
ob·tain (əb **tān**′) ☐*verb* **obtained, obtaining, obtains**

obtuse angle *noun* An angle that measures between 90 and 180 degrees.
ob·tuse angle (əb **tōos**′ *or* əb **tyōos**′) ☐*noun*

obvious *adjective* Easy to notice or understand; very clear: *It is obvious that he is ill. The pianist made obvious mistakes.*
ob·vi·ous (**ob**′vē əs) ☐*adjective*

occasion *noun* **1.** The time when something takes place. **2.** An important event: *The parade was a grand occasion.* **3.** A chance: *He never missed an occasion to play tennis.* —See Synonyms at **opportunity.**
oc·ca·sion (ə **kā**′ zhən) ☐*noun, plural* **occasions**

occasional *adjective* Happening from time to time: *an occasional trip to the zoo.*
oc·ca·sion·al (ə **kā**′zhə nəl) ☐*adjective*

occasionally *adverb* From time to time; now and then: *We visit them occasionally.*
oc·ca·sion·al·ly (ə **kā**′zhə nə lē) ☐*adverb*

Occident *noun* The countries of Europe, Africa, and the Americas.
Oc·ci·dent (**ok**′si dent) ☐*noun*

Occidental *adjective* Of the Occident or its people.
☐*noun* Someone born in or having ancestors from the Occident.
Oc·ci·den·tal (ok′si **den**′təl) ☐*adjective* ☐*noun, plural* **Occidentals**

occupant *noun* Someone who occupies a place or position: *Who is the occupant of the apartment next door?*
oc·cu·pant (**ok**′yə pənt) ☐*noun, plural* **occupants**

occupation *noun* **1.** The work a person does to earn a living: *His occupation is designing buildings.* **2.** The act of taking possession of and using: *the occupation of the castle by enemy soldiers.* —See Synonyms at **work.**
oc·cu·pa·tion (ok′yə **pā**′shən) ☐*noun, plural* **occupations**

occupy *verb* **1.** To live in; inhabit: *My aunt is now occupying our spare bedroom.* **2.** To fill; take up: *Fixing up the house occupies his weekends.* **3.** To keep busy: *I occupied myself with cleaning out my closet.* **4.** To take and control by force: *Soldiers seized and occupied the enemy fort.* **5.** To have or hold: *He occupies the post of college president.*
oc·cu·py (ok′yə pī′) □*verb* **occupied, occupying, occupies**

occur *verb* **1.** To take place; happen: *Many storms occurred last winter.* **2.** To appear or exist: *Spelling errors occur frequently in his book report.* **3.** To come to the mind of: *It never occurred to me that I had hurt his feelings.*
oc·cur (ə kûr′) □*verb* **occurred, occurring, occurs**

occurrence *noun* **1.** The act of taking place: *There were many occurrences of flu this winter.* **2.** Something that takes place; event: *An eclipse is an unusual occurrence.*
oc·cur·rence (ə kûr′əns) □*noun, plural* **occurrences**

ocean *noun* **1.** The great mass of salt water that covers almost three quarters of the earth's surface. **2.** Any of the four main divisions of this mass of salt water; the Atlantic, Pacific, Indian, or Arctic Ocean.
o·cean (ō′shən) □*noun, plural* **oceans**

ocelot *noun* A wild cat of Mexico, Central America, and South America, having a yellowish coat spotted with black.
oc·e·lot (os′ə lot′ *or* ō′sə lot′) □*noun, plural* **ocelots**

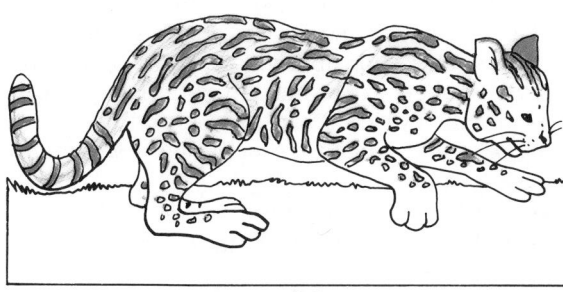

ocelot

o'clock *adverb* Of or according to the clock: *Please come about eight o'clock.*
o'clock (ə klok′) □*adverb*

octagon *noun* A geometric figure with eight sides and eight angles.
oc·ta·gon (ok′tə gon′) □*noun, plural* **octagons**

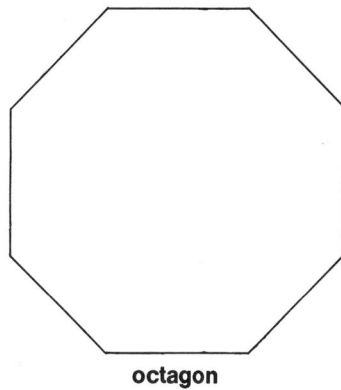

octagon

octave *noun* **1.** An interval of eight steps between two musical tones. **2.** A series of tones that are included in this interval: *the highest octave of a violin.*
oc·tave (ok′tiv) □*noun, plural* **octaves**

October *noun* The tenth month of the year. October has 31 days.
Oc·to·ber (ok tō′bər) □*noun, plural* **Octobers**

WORD HISTORY: **October**

October comes from a Latin name meaning "the eighth month." In an early Roman calendar March was the first month and October the eighth.

---

octopus *noun* A sea animal that has a soft body with eight parts that look like arms. The undersides of the arms have suckers that help the octopus cling to surfaces, move about, and seize food.
oc·to·pus (ok′tə pəs) □*noun, plural* **octopuses**

WORD HISTORY: **octopus**

Octopus comes from a Greek word meaning "having eight feet."

---

odd *adjective* **1.** Not ordinary or usual: *an odd creaking sound; odd behavior.* **2.** Leaving a remainder of 1 when divided by two; not

a	bat	ī	bite	o͞o	tool	*th*	feather
ā	make	î	fierce	ou	out	th	bath
â	dare	o	dot	u	nut	hw	wheat
ä	father	ō	no	û	turn	zh	measure
e	net	ô	law, for	ch	church	ə	about, open
ē	be	oi	soil	ng	ring		pencil, atom
i	dip	oo	look	sh	shade		circus

even: *7, 13, and 19 are odd numbers.* **3.** Forming one of a pair or set: *an odd earring.* **4.** Available or happening now and then: *She does odd sewing jobs for us.* —See Synonyms at **strange.**

odd (od) □*adjective* **odder, oddest**

odds *plural noun* The chance that a particular thing will happen; probability: *The odds are that our team will win. The odds are 3 to 1 that they'll beat the other team.*

odds (odz) □*plural noun*

odor *noun* A smell; scent: *The odor of freshly baked bread filled the house.*

o·dor (ō′dər) □*noun, plural* **odors**

of *preposition* **1.** Made with or from: *a stairway of marble.* **2.** Containing: *a crate of strawberries.* **3.** Belonging or connected to: *the bells of the church; the top of the hill.* **4.** From: *voters of the South; west of the Rockies.* **5.** Named or called: *the state of Maine.* **6.** Before; until: *five minutes of eight.* **7.** Among: *A few of our neighbors came to see us.* **8.** Having; with: *Someone of high ideals.*

of (uv *or* ov *or* əv) □*preposition*

off *adverb* **1.** Away from the present place or time: *about a hundred miles off.* **2.** So as to be no longer on or connected: *Turn off the water.* **3.** Away from work or duty: *She took a week off to go abroad.* □*adjective* **1.** Not on: *Her coat and hat were off.* **2.** Not in use or operation: *The car engine is off.* **3.** Canceled: *The sailing trip is off.* **4.** Less or smaller; below the usual standard: *Sales are off this week.* **5.** Away from work or duty: *Because of the holiday I'm off.* □*preposition* **1.** So as to be removed or away from: *I took the books off the shelf.* **2.** Away or relieved from: *off duty for the whole week.* **3.** Extending from: *We live in the second house off the avenue.* **4.** Less than or below the usual level: *The store was selling coffee cakes at 30 per cent off the regular price.*

off (ôf) □*adverb* □*adjective* □*preposition*

offend *verb* To cause hurt feelings, pain, or anger: *Her insulting comments offended us.*

of·fend (ə fend′) □*verb* **offended, offending, offends**

offense *noun* **1.** Something that offends: *His rude remarks were an offense to all of us.* **2.** A crime or sin: *Robbery is a legal offense.* **3.** The person or team who is leading an attack against the other side.

of·fense (ə fens′ for senses 1 and 2, ô′fens for sense 3) □*noun, plural* **offenses**

offensive *adjective* **1.** Unpleasant to the senses: *the offensive sight of littered streets.* **2.** Causing hurt feelings or anger. **3.** Making an attack: *an offensive player.* □*noun* An act or position of attack: *the enemy's worst offensive during the war; take the offensive in an argument.*

of·fen·sive (ə fen′siv) □*adjective* □*noun, plural* **offensives**

offer *verb* **1.** To put forward to be accepted or refused: *She offered the guests refreshments. He offered to help us.* **2.** To suggest; propose: *offer a suggestion.* **3.** To put up; attempt: *The robbers offered no resistance to the police.* □*noun* **1.** The act of offering: *an offer to visit a sick friend.* **2.** Something put forward to be accepted or refused: *He made an offer of twenty dollars for the boots.*

of·fer (ô′fər) □*verb* **offered, offering, offers** □*noun, plural* **offers**

SYNONYMS: **offer, present**

These verbs mean to put forward to be accepted or refused: *He offered us a cold drink. The mayor presented his budget to the city council.*

---

office *noun* **1.** A place for people who do business or professional work: *a dentist's office; the main office of a large company.* **2.** All the people who work in such a place: *The office bought her a wedding present.* **3.** A position of trust or responsibility: *She was appointed to the office of superintendent.*

of·fice (ô′fis) □*noun, plural* **offices**

officer *noun* **1.** Someone who has a position of trust or responsibility: *an officer of a bank.* **2.** Someone in a position to command others, as in military service or on a ship: *A colonel, a major, and a captain are all officers.* **3.** A member of a police force.

of·fi·cer (ô′fi sər) □*noun, plural* **officers**

official *noun* Someone who is in a position of command or authority: *a government official.* □*adjective* **1.** Of or connected with a position of trust or command: *the mayor's official duties.* **2.** Coming from the proper authority: *I received official permission to go home early.*

of·fi·cial (ə fish′əl) □*noun, plural* **officials** □*adjective*

offset *verb* To balance against something else; make up for: *The high pay offsets the long hours I must work at my job.*

off·set (ôf′set′) □*verb* **offset, offsetting, offsets**

offshoot *noun* **1.** A shoot that branches out from the main stem of a plant. **2.** Something that comes from a main source: *The new TV show is an offshoot of an old one.*
off·shoot (ôf′shōōt′) □*noun, plural* **offshoots**

offshoot

offshore *adjective* Moving or located away from the shore: *offshore islands; an offshore lighthouse.*
□*adverb* In a direction away from shore: *A boat whistle blasted offshore.*
off·shore (ôf′shôr′) □*adjective* □*adverb*

offspring *noun* The young of humans, animals, or plants: *My aunt and uncle had no offspring.* —See Synonyms at **descendant.**
off·spring (ôf′spring′) □*noun, plural* **offspring** or **offsprings**

often *adverb* Many times; again and again: *We often go skiing in the winter.*
of·ten (ô′fən) □*adverb*

oh *interjection* A word used to express sudden strong feelings: *"Oh! What a beautiful ship!" Oh! How terrible for her!*
oh (ō) □*interjection*

oil *noun* **1.** A thick, slippery, greasy liquid, or a fat that easily becomes liquid when heated. Oils may be made of mineral, vegetable, or animal substances. Oils do not mix with water, and they burn easily. **2.** Petroleum.
□*verb* To cover or polish with oil or put oil in or on: *He oiled the squeaking wheels.*
oil (oil) □*noun, plural* **oils** □*verb* **oiled, oiling, oils**

oil paint *noun* A paint made by mixing coloring material with oil, especially linseed oil.

oil well *noun* A deep hole drilled in the earth or the ocean floor to locate petroleum.

oily *adjective* **1.** Of or like oil: *an oily skin cream.* **2.** Covered with or containing much oil: *an oily brush; oily hair.*
oil·y (oi′lē) □*adjective* **oilier, oiliest**

ointment *noun* A thick substance made to be rubbed on to heal or soothe the skin.
oint·ment (oint′mənt) □*noun, plural* **ointments**

O.K. or **OK** *adverb* Well; fine: *I'm doing O.K. thanks.*
□*adjective* All right; fine: *Your idea to climb the mountain is O.K. with me.*
□*interjection* All right; very well: *O.K., let's play ball.*
□*noun* An approval: *I'll have to get the teacher's O.K. to go to the library.*
□*verb* To approve; agree to: *The coach O.K.'d the game schedule.*
O.K. or **OK** (ō′kā′ *or* ō kā′) □*adverb* □*adjective* □*interjection* □*noun, plural* **O.K.'s** or **OK's** □*verb* **O.K.'d** or **OK'd, O.K.'ing** or **OK'ing, O.K.'s** or **OK's**

okra *noun* A tall plant whose narrow, sticky seed pods are used in soups or as a vegetable.
ok·ra (ō′krə) □*noun*

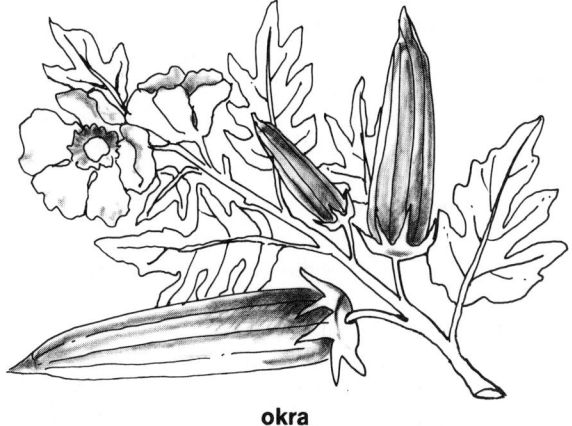

okra

old *adjective* **1.** Having lived or existed for many years: *an old man; an old fort from the Civil War.* **2.** Of a specific age: *Our dog is nine years old.* **3.** Showing signs of age and use; not new: *old shoes.* **4.** Belonging to an earlier

a	bat	ī	bite	ōō	tool	*th*	feather
ā	make	î	fierce	ou	out	th	bath
â	dare	o	dot	u	nut	hw	wheat
ä	father	ō	no	û	turn	zh	measure
e	net	ô	law, for	ch	church	ə	about, open
ē	be	oi	soil	ng	ring		pencil, atom
i	dip	oo	look	sh	shade		circus

time: *old tales of heroic deeds.* **5.** Known and familiar for a long time: *The two men were old buddies.* **6.** Former: *Yesterday I met my old piano teacher. Do you know who's living in your old house?*
□*noun* Times of the past: *Were there giants in days of old?*
> **old** (ōld) □*adjective* **older** or **elder, oldest** or **eldest** □*noun*

olden *adjective* Of an earlier time: *knights and kings of olden days.*
> **old·en** (ōl′dən) □*adjective*

old-fashioned *adjective* **1.** Of the style of an earlier time; out-of-date: *old-fashioned furniture.* **2.** Preferring the ways, customs, or ideas of an earlier time: *Older people sometimes seem old-fashioned to me.*
> **old-fash·ioned** (ōld′fash′ənd) □*adjective*

Old Testament *noun* The collection of sacred writings that make up the whole of the Jewish Bible and the first division of the Christian Bible.

Old World *noun* The portion of the world that consists of Europe, Africa, and Asia.

oleomargarine *noun* Margarine.
> **o·le·o·mar·ga·rine** (ō′lē ō mär′jər in) □*noun, plural* **oleomargarines**

olive *noun* **1.** The small, oval greenish or blackish fruit of a tree that grows in warm regions. Olives are used to produce olive oil and are often eaten as a relish. **2.** A dull yellowish-green color.
□*adjective* Dull yellowish green.
> **ol·ive** (ol′iv) □*noun, plural* **olives** □*adjective*

olive oil *noun* A yellowish oil pressed from olives and used for cooking, in salad dressings, and for making soap.

Olympic games *plural noun* **1.** An ancient Greek series of competitions and contests in athletics, poetry, and dancing held in honor of the Greeks' chief god. **2.** A modern series of international competitions in athletics, held every four years in different parts of the world.
> **O·lym·pic games** (ō lim′pik) □*plural noun*

Olympics *plural noun* The modern Olympic games.
> **O·lym·pics** (ō lim′piks) □*plural noun*

omelet *noun* A dish of eggs that have been beaten, cooked quickly in a pan, and often folded around a filling of cheese, jelly, mushrooms, or meat.
> **om·e·let** (om′ə lit *or* om′lit) □*noun, plural* **omelets**

omen *noun* Something thought to be a sign of good or bad luck to come: *Walking under a ladder is thought to be a bad omen.*
> **o·men** (ō′mən) □*noun, plural* **omens**

ominous *adjective* Seeming to be a sign of trouble; threatening: *an ominous silence.*
> **om·i·nous** (om′ə nəs) □*adjective*

omit *verb* To leave out; not include: *Her name was accidentally omitted from the class roll.*
> **o·mit** (ō mit′) □*verb* **omitted, omitting, omits**

on *preposition* **1.** Supported by and touching; upon. **2.** Located upon or near: *a house on the river.* **3.** Against: *bump one's knee on a chair.* **4.** In the direction of: *I live in the house on the right.* **5.** Concerning; about: *a book on kangaroos.* **6.** In the course of; during: *We will buy groceries on Saturday.* **7.** Taking part in: *She is on the entertainment committee.* **8.** In the condition or process of: *on sale; on fire.*
□*adverb* **1.** In or into a position of covering or being attached to something: *She put a sweater on.* **2.** Forward; ahead: *Move on to the next page.* **3.** In or into action or operation: *Please leave the porch lights on.*
□*adjective* **1.** In use or operation: *The radiator is on.* **2.** In progress or taking place: *The movie was already on when we arrived.*
> **on** (on *or* ôn) □*preposition* □*adverb* □*adjective*

once *adverb* **1.** One time only: *I visit my grandparents once a month.* **2.** At some time in the past: *I was once very good at baseball.*
□*noun* One single time: *I wish you'd lend me your ball, just this once.*
□*conjunction* As soon as; when: *Once you learn to swim, you will never forget how.*
> **once** (wuns) □*adverb* □*noun* □*conjunction*

one *noun* **1.** A number, written 1, which, when multiplied with a number, leaves that number unchanged: $1 \times 8 = 8$. **2.** A single person or thing.
□*pronoun* **1.** A particular person or thing: *one of my sisters; one of my crayons.* **2.** A person: *One should try to get enough sleep.*
□*adjective* **1.** Being a single person or thing: *We have one dog and six cats.* **2.** Some: *One day he'll be glad he studied hard.*
> **one** (wun) □*noun, plural* **ones**

oneself *pronoun* One's very own self: *It is easy for one to cut oneself while peeling apples.*
> **one·self** (wun self′) □*pronoun*

one-sided *adjective* **1.** Favoring one side or group; biased: *a one-sided view of a problem.* **2.** Not equal: *When one boxer is much heavier than the other, the fight is one-sided.*
one·sid·ed (**wun′ sī′** did) □*adjective*

one-way *adjective* Moving or allowing movement in one direction only: *a one-way street.*
one-way (**wun′ wā′**) □*adjective*

onion *noun* The rounded bulb of a plant widely grown as a vegetable. Onions have a strong smell and a sharp taste.
on·ion (**un′** yən) □*noun, plural* **onions**

onion

only *adjective* **1.** One and no more; sole: *His only pet is a turtle. This is her only chance to succeed.* **2.** The best and most suitable: *The only way to learn a skill is by doing it.*
□*adverb* **1.** Without anyone or anything else: *Only one person escaped injury in the accident.* **2.** Just; merely: *I only heard about it later.*
□*conjunction* But: *Go ahead and buy the skates, only don't complain later that they are too big.*
on·ly (**ōn′ lē**) □*adjective* □*adverb*
□*conjunction*

onto *preposition* To a position on or upon: *Climb onto the bus. The room opens onto a hall.*
on·to (**on′** to͞o′ *or* **ôn′** to͞o′) □*preposition*

onward *adverb* In a direction or toward a position that is ahead; forward: *The hikers walked onward through the bushes.*
□*adjective* Moving to or toward a position ahead in space or time: *The onward passage of time.*
on·ward (**on′** wərd *or* **ôn′** wərd) □*adverb*
□*adjective*

ooze *verb* To leak or flow slowly out or through; seep: *Water oozed from the leaky pipe.*
ooze (o͞oz) □*verb* **oozed, oozing, oozes**

opal *noun* A mineral used as a gemstone. Opals may be white, black, blue, or yellow, but flash rainbow colors when moved in the light.
o·pal (**ō′** pəl) □*noun, plural* **opals**

opaque *adjective* Not letting light through: *Wood is opaque.*
o·paque (ō **pāk′**) □*adjective*

open *adjective* **1.** Providing entrance and exit; not closed: *an open gate; an open desk drawer.* **2.** Allowing free passage or view: *an open book; an open road; an open freight car.* **3.** Having no cover or protection: *an open box; an open bottle.* **4.** Not filled or engaged: *The position at the bank is still open.* **5.** Ready for business. **6.** Frank; honest: *an open, trustworthy manner.* **7.** Able to take in new ideas; not prejudiced: *open to new ways of thinking.*
□*verb* **1.** To make or become no longer shut, fastened, sealed, or closed: *His eyes opened suddenly. They opened all the windows.* **2.** To spread out or apart: *open the blades of the scissors; watch new leaves open.* **3.** To begin: *The story opens in 1776.* **4.** To start operation: *They opened a restaurant. The theater opens at noon.*
□*noun* An area that is not covered or hidden: *The bears lumbered out of the woods into the open.*
o·pen (**ō′** pən) □*adjective* □*verb* **opened, opening, opens** □*noun*

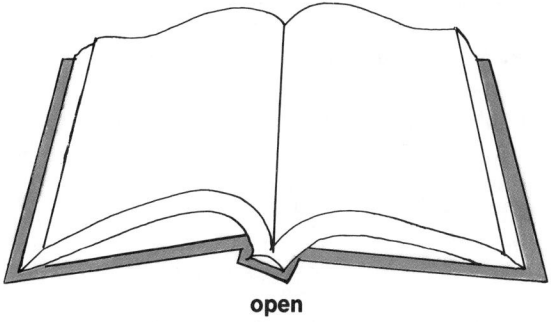

open

opener *noun* **1.** Something that is used to open closed or sealed containers: *a bottle opener.* **2.** The first in a series: *We went to the opener of the basketball season.*
o·pen·er (**ō′** pə nər) □*noun, plural* **openers**

a	bat	ī	bite	o͞o	tool	*th*	feather
ā	make	î	fierce	ou	out	th	bath
â	dare	o	dot	u	nut	hw	wheat
ä	father	ō	no	û	turn	zh	measure
e	net	ô	law, for	ch	church	ə	about, open
ē	be	oi	soil	ng	ring		pencil, atom
i	dip	oo	look	sh	shade		circus

opening *noun* **1.** An open space or clearing: *an opening in the garden wall; a sunny opening in a forest.* **2.** The first period or stage of something: *The opening of the movie is set on a ship.* **3.** The act of becoming open: *The opening of the fair is next week.* **4.** A job or position that is not filled: *two openings on the football team.*
o·pen·ing (ō′pə ning) □*noun, plural* **openings**

opera *noun* A play whose words are set to music that is accompanied by an orchestra.
op·er·a (op′ər ə) □*noun, plural* **operas**

> *WORD HISTORY:* **opera**
>
> *Opera* comes from a Latin word meaning ''work'' or ''effort.''

operate *verb* **1.** To work: *The boat engine operates poorly.* **2.** To control the running of something: *He operates complicated machinery.* **3.** To perform surgery: *The surgeon operated on my father yesterday.*
op·er·ate (op′ə rāt′) □*verb* **operated, operating, operates**

operation *noun* **1.** The act of operating: *the operation of an elevator.* **2.** The condition of being able to operate or function: *a factory now in full operation.* **3.** A process of treatment for diseases and disorders by using surgery: *an operation to remove tonsils.*
op·er·a·tion (op′ə rā′shən) □*noun, plural* **operations**

operator *noun* Someone who operates a machine or device: *the operator of a printing press.*
op·er·a·tor (op′ə rā′tər) □*noun, plural* **operators**

operetta *noun* A short comic opera that has some spoken parts.
op·er·et·ta (op′ə ret′ə) □*noun, plural* **operettas**

opinion *noun* **1.** A belief based on what one thinks or feels rather than on actual facts: *It is his opinion that his brother will win the match.* **2.** A judgment based on special knowledge and given by an expert: *I wanted my doctor's opinion before taking up jogging.*
o·pin·ion (ə pin′yən) □*noun, plural* **opinions**

opium *noun* A bitter, powerful narcotic drug prepared from a poppy plant.
o·pi·um (ō′pē əm) □*noun*

opossum *noun* A marsupial of eastern North America that lives in trees and feeds at night. The female opossum carries her young in a pouch.
o·pos·sum (ə pos′əm) □*noun, plural* **opossums**

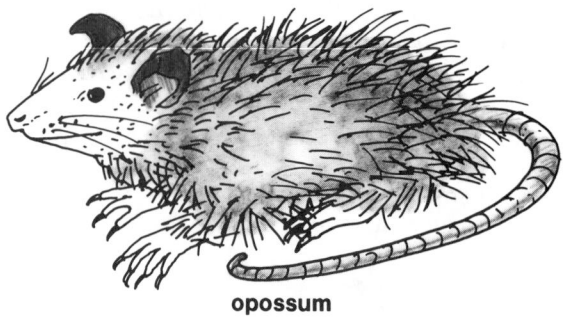

opossum

opponent *noun* Someone who is against another person in a fight or contest: *Her opponent in the debate was very clever.*
op·po·nent (ə pō′nənt) □*noun, plural* **opponents**

opportunity *noun* A time or situation that is good for a purpose: *an opportunity to learn how to swim.*
op·por·tu·ni·ty (op′ər tōō′ni tē *or* op′ər-tyōō′ni tē) □*noun, plural* **opportunities**

> *SYNONYMS:* **opportunity, chance, occasion**
>
> These nouns mean a time or situation that is good for a purpose: *I'm going to take the first opportunity to ask my parents for a raise in my allowance. Today is our last chance to buy tickets for the play. If the weather is nice, this weekend will be a good occasion to go on a picnic.*

oppose *verb* **1.** To be against: *One team opposes the other. I oppose the idea of having a picnic this weekend.* **2.** To contrast: *beauty opposed to ugliness.*
op·pose (ə pōz′) □*verb* **opposed, opposing, opposes**

opposite *adjective* **1.** Placed or located directly across from someone or something: *They sat on opposite sides of the theater.* **2.** Moving away from each other: *Two deer ran off in opposite directions.* **3.** Completely different; unlike: *We gave opposite answers to the same question.*
□*noun* Someone or something that is completely different from another: *Kindness and cruelty are opposites.*
op·po·site (op′ə zit) □*adjective* □*noun, plural* **opposites**

opposite

opposition *noun* **1.** The act or condition of opposing; resistance: *We all expected his opposition to the plan. The team met with strong opposition in the finals.* **2.** A political party opposed to the party of the government in power.
op·po·si·tion (op′ə **zish′** ən) ☐*noun, plural* **oppositions**

oppress *verb* **1.** To control or rule in an unjust or harsh way: *The people rebelled because their government was oppressing them.* **2.** To weigh heavily on; depress: *She was oppressed by many troubles.*
op·press (ə **pres′**) ☐*verb* **oppressed, oppressing, oppresses**

optical *adjective* **1.** Of or having to do with sight: *an optical illusion.* **2.** Helping to see: *Glasses are optical instruments.*
op·ti·cal (**op′** ti kəl) ☐*adjective*

optimistic *adjective* Tending to see the bright side of things: *Optimistic people think that things will always turn out for the best.*
op·ti·mis·tic (op′tə **mis′** tik) ☐*adjective*

optional *adjective* Left to choice; not required: *Taking that course is optional.*
op·tion·al (**op′** shə nəl) ☐*adjective*

or *conjunction* **1.** Used to connect words or groups of words that are alternatives: *milk or orange juice.* **2.** Used to connect to terms that have the same meaning: *The Netherlands, or Holland, is a country on the North Sea.* **3.** Used between numbers or quantities to indicate an approximate amount: *I wrote her three or four letters.*
or (ôr *or* ər) ☐*conjunction*

–or A suffix that forms nouns from verbs and means "someone or something that does a particular thing": *legislator.*

oral *adjective* **1.** Not written; spoken: *an oral report.* **2.** Of or for the mouth: *an oral thermometer.*
o·ral (**ôr′** əl) ☐*adjective*

orange *noun* **1.** A round fruit with a reddish-yellow skin and juicy pulp. Orange trees grow in warm climates. **2.** The reddish-yellow color of an orange.
☐*adjective* Reddish yellow.
or·ange (**ôr′** inj *or* **or′** inj) ☐*noun, plural* **oranges** ☐*adjective*

orangutan *noun* A large Asian ape that has long arms and shaggy reddish-brown hair.
o·rang·u·tan (ô **rang′** ə tan′) ☐*noun, plural* **orangutans**

WORD HISTORY: **orangutan**

The name *orangutan* was given to this animal by the people of the islands where the orangutan lives. The name means "man of the woods."

orangutan

orbit *noun* **1.** The path that a heavenly body takes as it moves around another heavenly body. **2.** The path a manmade satellite or spacecraft takes around a heavenly body.
☐*verb* To move in an orbit around: *The earth orbits the sun.*
or·bit (**ôr′** bit) ☐*noun, plural* **orbits** ☐*verb* **orbited, orbiting, orbits**

a bat	ī bite	o͞o tool	*th* feather
ā make	î fierce	ou **out**	th bath
â dare	o dot	u nut	hw **wheat**
ä father	ō no	û turn	zh measure
e net	ô law, for	ch **church**	ə about, open
ē be	oi soil	ng ring	pencil, atom
i dip	oo look	sh **shade**	circus

orchard *noun* **1.** A piece of land where fruit trees are grown. **2.** The trees growing on such a piece of land.
or·chard (ôr′ chərd) □*noun, plural* **orchards**

orchestra *noun* **1.** A group of musicians who play together on various instruments. **2.** The instruments played by such a group of musicians. **3.** The main floor of a theater.
or·ches·tra (ôr′ ki strə) □*noun, plural* **orchestras**

orchid *noun* A plant with large flowers that often have bright colors and unusual shapes.
or·chid (ôr′ kid) □*noun, plural* **orchids**

ordain *verb* **1.** To order or decide by law: *The king ordained a holiday.* **2.** To make someone a minister, priest, or rabbi in a formal ceremony.
or·dain (ôr dān′) □*verb* **ordained, ordaining, ordains**

ordeal *noun* A very difficult or painful experience.
or·deal (ôr dēl′) □*noun, plural* **ordeals**

order *noun* **1.** A condition in which everything is in its correct place: *Put your locker in order.* **2.** The placing of things one after another: *The words in a dictionary are listed in alphabetical order.* **3.** A condition in which rules or customs are obeyed: *law and order.* **4.** A command. **5.** Something requested or supplied: *We mailed our order for clothes to the store.* **6.** A group of people who belong to the same organization or live under the same rules: *an order of monks.*
□*verb* **1.** To give an order to: *The general ordered his men to halt.* **2.** To place a request for: *order a pizza.* **3.** To arrange in proper order. —See Synonyms at **command.**
   in order to For the purpose of: *He exercises in order to keep healthy.*
   out of order Not working.
or·der (ôr′ dər) □*noun, plural* **orders** □*verb* **ordered, ordering, orders**

orderly *adjective* **1.** Arranged in good order. **2.** Without making trouble or noise: *an orderly crowd.* —See Synonyms at **neat.**
or·der·ly (ôr′ dər lē) □*adjective*

ordinal number *noun* A number that shows position in a series: *First, fourth, and tenth are ordinal numbers.*
or·di·nal number (ôr′ dən əl) □*noun*

ordinarily *adverb* As a general rule; usually.
or·di·nar·i·ly (ôr′ dən er′ ə lē) □*adverb*

ordinary *adjective* **1.** Usual; normal: *Are you going to wear a costume or ordinary clothes?*

2. Of no special quality: *just an ordinary meal.*
or·di·nar·y (ôr′ dən er′ē) □*adjective*

SYNONYMS: **ordinary, normal, usual**
These adjectives mean of a kind that is to be expected: *My ordinary routine includes an hour of practice on the piano. We ate dinner at the normal time. The usual charge for admission is two dollars.*

---

ore *noun* A mineral or rock that contains a valuable substance worth mining: *iron ore.*
ore (ôr) □*noun, plural* **ores**

organ *noun* **1.** A musical instrument that has pipes through which air is blown to produce different tones. An organ has one or more keyboards. **2.** A part of a living thing that does a particular job: *The eyes and lungs are human organs.*
or·gan (ôr′ gən) □*noun, plural* **organs**

organ

organic *adjective* **1.** Of or coming from living things: *Leaves, grass, and animal manure are organic matter.* **2.** Not using or grown with added chemicals: *organic farming.*
or·gan·ic (ôr gan′ ik) □*adjective*

organism *noun* A living thing; plant or animal.
or·gan·ism (ôr′ gə niz′ əm) □*noun, plural* **organisms**

organization *noun* **1.** The act of organizing: *the organization of a class picnic.* **2.** A way of being organized; arrangement. **3.** A group of people joined together: *Political parties, clubs, and business companies are organizations.*
or·gan·i·za·tion (ôr′gə ni zā′ shən) □*noun, plural* **organizations**

organize *verb* **1.** To plan or put together in an orderly way: *organize a fishing expedition.* **2.** To form a group in order to work together: *organize a club.* **3.** To persuade employees to

join a labor union: *organize factory workers.*
or·gan·ize (ôr′gə nīz′) ▢*verb* **organized, organizing, organizes**

Orient *noun* The countries of Asia.
O·ri·ent (ôr′ē ənt) ▢*noun*

> **WORD HISTORY: Orient**
>
> *Orient* comes from a Latin word meaning "the place of the rising sun." The sun rises in the east.

Oriental *adjective* Of the Orient or its peoples.
▢*noun* Someone born in or having ancestors from the Orient.
O·ri·en·tal (ôr′ē **en′**təl) ▢*adjective* ▢*noun*, *plural* **Orientals**

origin *noun* **1.** The cause, source, or beginning of something: *the origin of an argument.* **2.** Line of descent; parents: *He is of Chinese origin.*
or·i·gin (ôr′ə jin) ▢*noun, plural* **origins**

original *adjective* **1.** Existing from the beginning; first: *the original owner of a house.* **2.** Not done before, or copied from something else; new: *an original idea.*
▢*noun* Something not done before or copied from something else. —See Synonyms at **first.**
o·rig·i·nal (ə **rij′**ə nəl) ▢*adjective* ▢*noun*, *plural* **originals**

originally *adverb* In the beginning; from the start: *The song originally came from England.*
o·rig·i·nal·ly (ə **rij′**ə nə lē) ▢*adverb*

originate *verb* To bring or come into being: *Tobacco and potatoes originated in America.*
o·rig·i·nate (ə **rij′**ə nāt′) ▢*verb* **originated, originating, originates**

oriole *noun* A songbird with feathers that are usually black and orange.
o·ri·ole (ôr′ē ōl′) ▢*noun, plural* **orioles**

ornament *noun* An object added to make something more attractive: *Christmas tree ornaments.*
▢*verb* To supply with ornaments: *The building was ornamented with arches and statues.*
or·na·ment (ôr′nə mənt) ▢*noun, plural* **ornaments** ▢*verb* **ornamented, ornamenting, ornaments**

orphan *noun* A child whose parents are dead.
or·phan (ôr′fən) ▢*noun, plural* **orphans**

orphanage *noun* A home for orphans.
or·phan·age (ôr′fə nij) ▢*noun, plural* **orphanages**

orthodontist *noun* A dentist who specializes in straightening teeth.
or·tho·don·tist (ôr′thə **don′**tist) ▢*noun, plural* **orthodontists**

orthodox *adjective* **1.** Accepted as true or right by most people; conventional: *the orthodox way of holding a tennis racket.* **2.** Holding accepted beliefs: *orthodox Muslims.*
or·tho·dox (ôr′thə doks′) ▢*adjective*

ostrich *noun* A very large African bird with long legs and a long neck. Ostriches cannot fly, but can run very fast.
os·trich (os′trich *or* ô′strich) ▢*noun, plural* **ostriches**

ostrich

other *adjective* **1.** Besides that one or those ones; being the one or ones remaining: *Our other two cats are outside.* **2.** Different: *some other time.* **3.** Just recent: *the other day.* **4.** Alternate; second: *every other day.*
▢*pronoun* A different or additional one: *He is always worrying about something or other.*
▢*adverb* Otherwise: *We couldn't see other than by flashlight.*
▢*noun* **1.** The remaining one: *One girl sang while the other danced.* **2.** A different or additional person or thing: *Let's not wait for the others.*
oth·er (u*th*′ər) ▢*adjective* ▢*pronoun* ▢*adverb* ▢*noun, plural* **others**

a	bat	ī	bite	o͞o	tool	*th*	feather
ā	make	î	fierce	ou	out	th	bath
â	dare	o	dot	u	nut	hw	wheat
ä	father	ō	no	û	turn	zh	measure
e	net	ô	law, for	ch	church	ə	about, open
ē	be	oi	soil	ng	ring		pencil, atom
i	dip	oo	look	sh	shade		circus

otherwise *adverb* **1.** In a different way: *He could not act otherwise.* **2.** In other ways: *I was in a hurry, but otherwise careful.*
□*adjective* Different: *The facts were otherwise.*
□*conjunction* Or else: *I already have a partner, otherwise I'd ask you.*
oth·er·wise (*uth'* ər wīz') □*adverb* □*adjective* □*conjunction*

otter *noun* A playful animal that has a long body and tail, dark-brown fur, and webbed feet for swimming.
ot·ter (ot' ər) □*noun, plural* **otters**

ouch *interjection* A word used to express sudden pain: *Ouch! I cut my finger!*
ouch (ouch) □*interjection*

ought *verb* Used to show: **1.** A duty or obligation: *You ought to obey your parents.* **2.** What is almost certain or expected: *The piano ought to sound better when it's tuned. You ought to be able to do those math problems.* **3.** What is necessary or wise: *She ought to leave now if she is not going to be late. The doctor said he ought to get plenty of rest.*
ought (ôt) □*verb*

ounce *noun* A unit of weight equal to ¹/₁₆ of a pound, or 28.350 grams.
ounce (ouns) □*noun, plural* **ounces**

> *WORD HISTORY:* **ounce**
>
> The word *ounce* comes from a Latin word meaning "a one-twelfth part." There were twelve ounces in the Roman pound.

our *pronoun* Belonging or relating to us: *our books; our task.*
our (our) □*pronoun*

ours *pronoun* The one or ones belonging to us: *These books are ours. If your car is not working, use ours.*
ours (ourz) □*pronoun*

ourselves *pronoun* Our own selves: *We injured ourselves when the car hit the tree. We ourselves are going to the party.*
our·selves (our **selvz'**) □*pronoun*

out *adverb* **1.** Away from the inside or middle: *walk out of a room.* **2.** To an end: *Time ran out.* **3.** Into being or view: *The flowers have come out.* **4.** In a loud or bold way: *Speak out.* **5.** In baseball, so as to be no longer batting or on base: *The runner was thrown out.*
□*adjective* **1.** Not in use, operation, or consideration: *The lights are out.* **2.** In baseball, no longer at bat or on base.

□*preposition* Toward the outside of: *out the window.*
□*noun* **1.** A way to escape. **2.** A baseball play in which a batter or base runner is put out.
out (out) □*adverb* □*adjective* □*preposition* □*noun, plural* **outs**

outboard motor *noun* A small motor attached to the stern of a boat.
out·board motor (**out'** bôrd') □*noun*

outboard motor

outbreak *noun* A sudden breaking out: *an outbreak of measles.*
out·break (**out'** brāk') □*noun, plural* **outbreaks**

outburst *noun* A bursting forth: *an outburst of laughter.*
out·burst (**out'** bûrst') □*noun, plural* **outbursts**

outcome *noun* A final result: *the outcome of a tournament.*
out·come (**out'** kum') □*noun, plural* **outcomes**

outcry *noun* **1.** A loud cry or scream. **2.** A strong protest: *an outcry against high taxes.*
out·cry (**out'** krī') □*noun, plural* **outcries**

outdid *verb* The past tense of **outdo.**
out·did (out **did'**) □*verb*

outdo *verb* To do better than: *He outdid the rest of the class on the reading test.*
out·do (out dōō') □*verb* **outdid, outdone, outdoing, outdoes**

outdone *verb* The past participle of **outdo.**
out·done (out **dun'**) □*verb*

outdoor *adjective* Placed, used, or done in the open air: *outdoor games.*
out·door (**out'** dôr') □*adjective*

outdoors *adverb* In or into the open air; outside: *play outdoors.*
□*noun* The world outside buildings; the open air: *The outdoors is the best place to exercise.*
out·doors (out **dôrz'**) □*adverb* □*noun*

outer *adjective* On the outside: *Her outer clothing got muddy.*
out·er (out′ər) □*adjective*

outer space *noun* The space beyond the earth's atmosphere.

outfield *noun* **1.** The grassy area of a baseball field beyond the infield. **2.** The players in the outfield.
out·field (out′fēld′) □*noun, plural* **outfields**

outfit *noun* **1.** A set of equipment needed for something: *a camping outfit.* **2.** A set of clothes: *That skirt and sweater make a nice outfit.* **3.** A group working, fighting, or playing together.
□*verb* To supply with the necessary equipment or clothing.
out·fit (out′fit′) □*noun, plural* **outfits** □*verb* **outfitted, outfitting, outfits**

outgoing *adjective* Making friends easily; friendly.
out·go·ing (out′gō′ing) □*adjective*

outgrow *verb* **1.** To grow too large for: *She outgrew her shoes.* **2.** To leave behind in the course of growing up: *He outgrew his stuffed animals.*
out·grow (out grō′) □*verb* **outgrew, outgrowing, outgrows**

outing *noun* A trip or walk outdoors for fun: *We went on an outing to the zoo.*
out·ing (ou′ting) □*noun, plural* **outings**

outlaw *noun* Someone who breaks the law. □*verb* To make illegal: *outlaw firecrackers.* —See Synonyms at **forbid.**
out·law (out′lô′) □*noun, plural* **outlaws** □*verb* **outlawed, outlawing, outlaws**

outlet *noun* **1.** A way to get out; exit. **2.** A way of releasing something: *Sports are a good outlet for one's energy.* **3.** A place in the wall for plugging in electrical devices.
out·let (out′let′) □*noun, plural* **outlets**

outline *noun* **1.** A line along the edge or boundary of something: *the jagged outline of buildings far away.* **2.** A summary that gives the main points of a subject in an organized way.
□*verb* To give the main points of: *outline your plans.*
out·line (out′līn′) □*noun, plural* **outlines** □*verb* **outlined, outlining, outlines**

outlook *noun* **1.** A way of looking at something: *a happy outlook on life.* **2.** A look into the future; prediction.
out·look (out′look′) □*noun, plural* **outlooks**

outlying *adjective* Far from the center: *outlying suburbs.*
out·ly·ing (out′lī′ing) □*adjective*

outnumber *verb* To be more in number than: *Girls outnumber boys in our school.*
out·num·ber (out **num′**bər) □*verb* **outnumbered, outnumbering, outnumbers**

out-of-date *adjective* No longer in use; old-fashioned.
out-of-date (out′əv dāt′) □*adjective*

outpost *noun* **1.** A small group of soldiers placed to guard an area and stop attacks against a main army camp. **2.** A settlement in a distant place.
out·post (out′pōst′) □*noun, plural* **outposts**

output *noun* **1.** The amount of something produced: *the output of a factory.* **2.** The information generated by a computer.
out·put (out′poot′) □*noun, plural* **outputs**

outrage *noun* **1.** A violent or shocking act. **2.** Great anger over something terrible or shocking.
□*verb* To make very angry; shock: *The student's cheating outraged his classmates.*
out·rage (out′rāj′) □*noun, plural* **outrages** □*verb* **outraged, outraging, outrages**

outrageous *adjective* Far from what is right, just, or proper: *outrageous prices.*
out·ra·geous (out rā′jəs) □*adjective*

outrigger *noun* A long float attached by a frame to the outside of a canoe to keep it from turning over.
out·rig·ger (out′rig′ər) □*noun, plural* **outriggers**

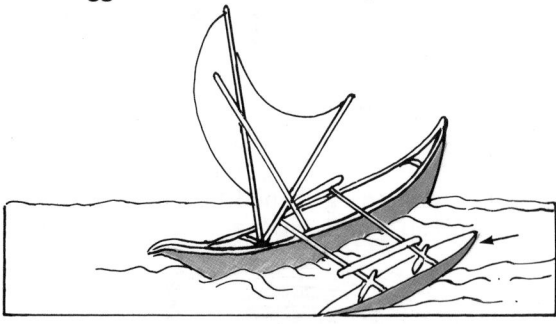

outrigger

a	bat	ī	bite	ōō	tool	*th*	feather
ā	make	î	fierce	ou	out	ͻth	bath
â	dare	o	dot	u	nut	hw	wheat
ä	father	ō	no	û	turn	zh	measure
e	net	ô	law, for	ch	church	ə	about, open
ē	be	oi	soil	ng	ring		pencil, atom
i	dip	oo	look	sh	shade		circus

outright *adjective* Complete; absolute: *an outright lie.*
□*adverb* **1.** Completely; altogether: *I paid for the boat outright.* **2.** Without delay; immediately: *We told him the news outright.*
out·right (out′ rīt′) □*adjective* □*adverb*

outside *noun* The outer side or surface.
□*adjective* **1.** Coming from another place: *outside help.* **2.** Very small: *an outside chance.*
□*adverb* On or to the outside: *going outside.*
□*preposition* Beyond the limits of: *outside the neighborhood.*
out·side (out sīd′ *or* out′ sīd′) □*noun, plural* **outsides** □*adjective* □*adverb* □*preposition*

outskirts *plural noun* The areas at the edge of a place: *the outskirts of town.*
out·skirts (out′ skûrts′) □*plural noun*

outsmart *verb* To get the better of by cunning; outwit: *The robber outsmarted the police by not falling into their trap.*
out·smart (out smärt′) □*verb* **outsmarted, outsmarting, outsmarts**

outspoken *adjective* Bold in speaking out: *an outspoken opponent.*
out·spo·ken (out spō′ kən) □*adjective*

outstanding *adjective* **1.** Standing out from others because of excellence: *an outstanding writer.* **2.** Not settled: *outstanding problems.*
out·stand·ing (out stan′ ding) □*adjective*

outward *adverb* Away from the center.
□*adjective* **1.** Toward the outside: *an outward direction.* **2.** Seen on the surface: *an outward calm.*
out·ward (out′ wərd) □*adverb* □*adjective*

outwit *verb* To outsmart: *The fox outwitted the hunters and escaped.*
out·wit (out wit′) □*verb* **outwitted, outwitting, outwits**

oval *adjective* Shaped like an egg or a flattened circle: *an oval running track.*
□*noun* Something shaped like an oval.
o·val (ō′ vəl) □*adjective* □*noun, plural* **ovals**

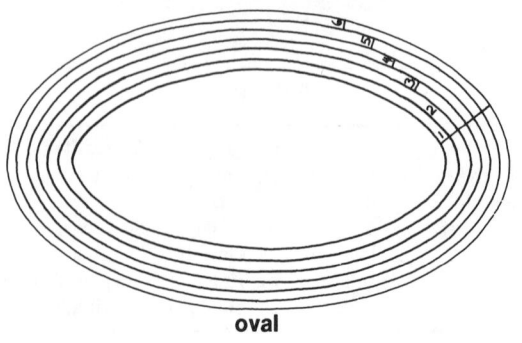

oval

ovary *noun* **1.** A part of a female animal that produces egg cells. **2.** A plant part in which seeds are formed.
o·va·ry (ō′ və rē) □*noun, plural* **ovaries**

oven *noun* An enclosed space for baking or heating food.
ov·en (uv′ ən) □*noun, plural* **ovens**

over *preposition* **1.** In a place or position that is above or higher than: *There is a sign over the door. He envied those over him.* **2.** From one side to the other side of; across: *The horse jumped over the fence.* **3.** On the other side of: *They live in a town over the border.* **4.** Across or along the surface of; upon: *He spilled milk all over the floor. We drove over a new road.* **5.** On top of; upon: *Apply a second coat of varnish over the first.* **6.** Through the period of; during: *The stores will be closed over the weekend.* **7.** In excess of; more than: *I spent over fifteen dollars for the tickets.* **8.** Here and there in; throughout: *She has traveled over most of Europe.* **9.** Because of: *She cried over her lost money.*
□*adverb* **1.** Across to another or an opposite side: *She ran over to the window.* **2.** Across the edge or brim: *The coffee in the pot boiled over.* **3.** So as to pass or move from one place, side, or person to another: *I'll be over shortly. He handed over all his property to his daughter.* **4.** From an upright position: *The fence toppled over during the last storm.* **5.** So that the underside will be up: *Turn over to the next page.* **6.** Completely: *The river froze over.* **7.** From beginning to end; through: *Let's talk that matter over.* **8.** Again: *She had to do her homework over.* **9.** In addition; beyond what was planned: *I have a dollar left over.*
□*adjective* At an end; finished: *When will the movie be over?*
o·ver (ō′ vər) □*preposition* □*adverb* □*adjective*

over– A prefix that means: **1.** Too much: *overdo.* **2.** Extra: *overtime.* **3.** Above or across: *overseas.* **4.** From an upright position: *overturn.*

overalls *plural noun* Loose-fitting trousers with straps and a top part that covers the chest.
o·ver·alls (ō′ vər ôlz′) □*plural noun*

overboard *adverb* Over the side of a boat.
o·ver·board (ō′ vər bôrd′) □*adverb*

overcame *verb* The past tense of **overcome:** *She overcame many obstacles.*
o·ver·came (ō′ vər kām′) □*verb*

overcast *adjective* Covered over with clouds: *an overcast sky.*
o·ver·cast (ō′vər kast′) □*adjective*

overcoat *noun* A long, heavy coat worn over other clothing.
o·ver·coat (ō′vər kōt′) □*noun, plural* **overcoats**

overcome *verb* To get the better of; conquer: *He wants to overcome his fear of heights.*
o·ver·come (ō′vər **kum′**) □*verb* **overcame, overcome, overcoming, overcomes**

overdid *verb* The past tense of **overdo.**
o·ver·did (ō′vər **did′**) □*verb*

overdo *verb* **1.** To do or use too much: *Add some sugar, but don't overdo it.* **2.** To cook too long: *an overdone roast.*
o·ver·do (ō′vər **doo′**) □*verb* **overdid, overdone, overdoing, overdoes**

overdone *verb* The past participle of **overdo.**
o·ver·done (ō′vər **dun′**) □*verb*

overdue *adjective* **1.** Not paid on time: *The rent is overdue.* **2.** Later than usual: *an overdue bus.*
o·ver·due (ō′vər **doo** or ō′vər **dyoo′**) □*adjective*

overflow *verb* **1.** To flow over: *The stream overflowed its banks.* **2.** To fill and spread out beyond: *The audience overflowed the hall.*
□*noun* Something that flows over.
o·ver·flow □*verb* (ō′vər **flō′**) **overflowed, overflowing, overflows** □*noun* (ō′vər flō′), *plural* **overflows**

overhand *adjective* With the hand moving above the shoulder: *an overhand throw.*
□*adverb* With the hand above the shoulder: *She tossed the ball overhand.*
o·ver·hand (o′vər hand′) □*adjective* □*adverb*

overhand

overhaul *verb* **1.** To look over carefully and make needed changes and repairs: *overhaul an old car.* **2.** To overtake: *The motorboat quickly overhauled the canoe.*
□*noun* The act of overhauling.
o·ver·haul □*verb* (ō′vər **hôl′**) **overhauled, overhauling, overhauls** □*noun* (ō′vər hôl′), *plural* **overhauls**

overhead *adverb* Above the head: *An airplane passed overhead.*
□*adjective* Placed above the head: *an overhead light.*
□*noun* Money spent by a business for rent, lighting, and other expenses.
o·ver·head (ō′vər **hed′**) □*adverb* □*adjective* □*noun*

overhear *verb* To hear something not meant to be heard: *I overheard two teachers talking in the hallway.*
o·ver·hear (ō′vər **hîr′**) □*verb* **overheard, overhearing, overhears**

overheard *verb* The past tense and past participle of **overhear.**
o·ver·heard (ō′vər **hûrd′**) □*verb*

overjoyed *adjective* Very happy or delighted.
o·ver·joyed (ō′vər **joid′**) □*adjective*

overlap *verb* To rest over and extend beyond: *The roof tiles overlapped.*
o·ver·lap (ō′vər **lap′**) □*verb* **overlapped, overlapping, overlaps**

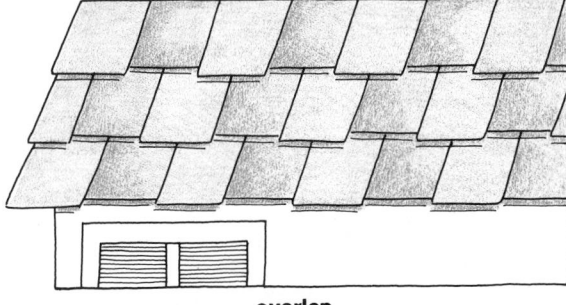

overlap

overlook *verb* **1.** To look over from a higher place: *The mountain overlooks a plain.* **2.** To fail to see or do: *When you wash the windows,*

a bat	ī bite	oo tool	*th* feather
ā make	î fierce	ou out	th bath
â dare	o dot	u nut	hw wheat
ä father	ō no	û turn	zh measure
e net	ô law, for	ch church	ə about, open
ē be	oi soil	ng ring	pencil, atom
i dip	oo look	sh shade	circus

don't overlook the corners. **3.** To ignore: *He overlooked my faults.*
o·ver·look (ō′vər **look**′) ☐*verb* **overlooked, overlooking, overlooks**

overnight *adjective* **1.** Happening or lasting for a night: *an overnight flight.* **2.** Used for short trips: *an overnight bag.*
☐*adverb* **1.** During or through the night: *staying overnight.* **2.** Very quickly; suddenly: *He seemed to grow up overnight.*
o·ver·night ☐*adjective* (ō′vər nīt′) ☐*adverb* (ō′vər **nīt**′)

overpass *noun* A place where one road crosses above another road.
o·ver·pass (ō′vər pas′) ☐*noun, plural* **overpasses**

overpower *verb* **1.** To get the better of by greater strength: *The big wrestler overpowered the smaller man.* **2.** To affect strongly; overcome: *The smell was overpowering.*
o·ver·pow·er (ō′vər pou′ər) ☐*verb* **overpowered, overpowering, overpowers**

overseas *adverb* Across the sea: *The army sent him overseas.*
☐*adjective* Of, from, or across the sea: *an overseas business office.*
o·ver·seas (ō′vər **sēz**′) ☐*adverb* ☐*adjective*

overshoe *noun* A shoe or boot worn over another shoe.
o·ver·shoe (ō′vər shoo′) ☐*noun, plural* **overshoes**

overshoes

oversight *noun* A careless mistake: *By an oversight, that actor's name is not listed on the program.*
o·ver·sight (ō′vər sīt′) ☐*noun, plural* **oversights**

overtake *verb* To catch up with: *I gave her a head start but soon overtook her.*

o·ver·take (ō′vər **tāk**′) ☐*verb* **overtook, overtaken, overtaking, overtakes**

overtaken *verb* The past participle of **overtake.**
o·ver·tak·en (ō′vər **tā**′kən) ☐*verb*

overtime *noun* Time beyond the regular limit: *We won the basketball game in overtime.*
☐*adverb* Beyond the regular hours: *She worked overtime all week.*
☐*adjective* Of or for overtime: *overtime pay.*
o·ver·time (ō′vər tīm′) ☐*noun, plural* **overtimes** ☐*adverb* ☐*adjective*

overtook *verb* The past tense of **overtake.**
o·ver·took (ō′vər **took**′) ☐*verb*

overture *noun* **1.** A musical introduction to a larger work. **2.** An offer to begin something: *overtures of friendship.*
o·ver·ture (ō′vər chər) ☐*noun, plural* **overtures**

overturn *verb* To turn over; upset: *overturn a rowboat.*
o·ver·turn (ō′vər **tûrn**′) ☐*verb* **overturned, overturning, overturns**

overweight *adjective* Weighing more than usual, necessary, or desirable.
o·ver·weight (ō′vər **wāt**′) ☐*adjective*

overwhelm *verb* To overcome completely; overpower: *The soldiers overwhelmed the small band defending the camp.*
o·ver·whelm (ō′vər **hwelm**′ *or* ō′vər **welm**′) ☐*verb* **overwhelmed, overwhelming, overwhelms**

overwork *verb* To work or make someone work too hard.
☐*noun* Too much work: *His fatigue was caused by overwork.*
o·ver·work ☐*verb* (ō′vər **wûrk**′) **overworked, overworking, overworks** ☐*noun* (ō′vər-wûrk′)

owe *verb* **1.** To have to pay: *He owes me a dollar.* **2.** To have to give: *I owe you an apology.* **3.** To be obligated for: *He owes a lot to his parents for their help.*
owe (ō) ☐*verb* **owed, owing, owes**

owl *noun* A bird with a large head, large eyes, and a short, hooked bill. It hunts for small animals at night.
owl (oul) ☐*noun, plural* **owls**

own *adjective* Belonging to oneself or itself: *my own comb; her own achievement.*
☐*verb* **1.** To have or possess: *We own our house and the land behind it.* **2.** To confess or admit: *I own up to my mistakes.*

own (ōn) □*adjective* □*verb* **owned, owning, owns**

owner *noun* Someone who owns something: *Who is the owner of that motorcycle?*
own·er (ō′nər) □*noun, plural* **owners**

ox *noun* **1.** A fully grown male of cattle, used for pulling plows and wagons. **2.** Any of several related animals, such as the musk ox.
ox (oks) □*noun, plural* **oxen**

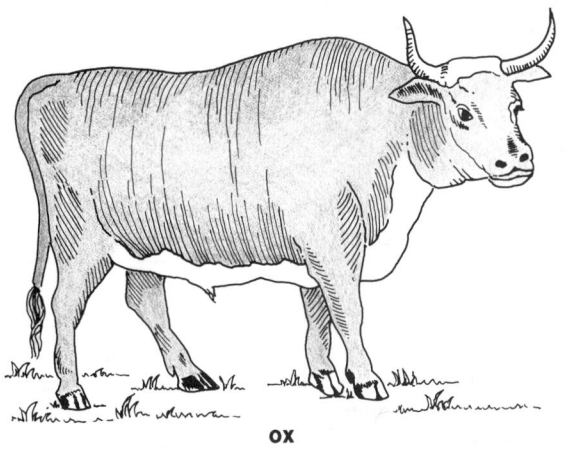

ox

oxide *noun* A compound of oxygen and another chemical element.
ox·ide (ok′sīd′) □*noun, plural* **oxides**

oxidize *verb* To combine with oxygen: *Iron rusts when it oxidizes.*

ox·i·dize (ok′si dīz′) □*verb* **oxidized, oxidizing, oxidizes**

oxygen *noun* A chemical element that is a gas in the air. Living things need oxygen to live.
ox·y·gen (ok′si jən) □*noun*

oyster *noun* A sea animal that has a soft body and a rough shell with two parts. Some kinds are used as food, and others produce pearls inside their shells.
oy·ster (oi′stər) □*noun, plural* **oysters**

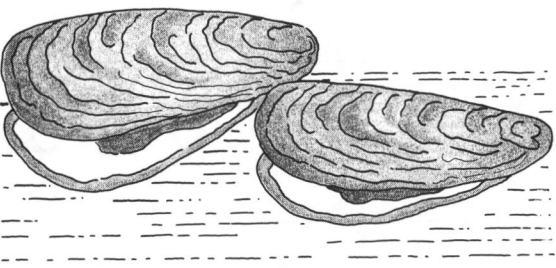

oyster

oz. An abbreviation for **ounce.**

a bat	ī bite	ōō tool	*th* feather
ā make	î fierce	ou out	th bath
â dare	o dot	u nut	hw wheat
ä father	ō no	û turn	zh measure
e net	ô law, for	ch church	ə about, open
ē be	oi soil	ng ring	pencil, atom
i dip	oo look	sh shade	circus

P p

The letter **P** has evolved from many forms of ancient writing. One of the earliest known examples is the Greek character shown above, which dates from almost 3,000 years ago. Over the years, artists and designers have created their own versions of the English letter **P**. Some of the more common examples seen today are shown below.

Pp *Pp*	**Pp Pp**	Pp Pp	**Pp** Pp	*Pp Pp*
HANDWRITING	CALLIGRAPHY	MODERN SANS SERIF	MODERN SERIF	SCRIPT

p or **P** *noun* The sixteenth letter of the English alphabet.
p or **P** (pē) □*noun, plural* **p's** or **P's**

pace *noun* **1.** A step made in walking. **2.** The length of a step in walking. **3.** The speed at which something moves or happens: *He types at a very fast pace.* **4.** A step of a horse in walking or running.
□*verb* **1.** To walk back and forth: *She paced outside the doctor's office nervously.* **2.** To measure length or distance by counting paces.
pace (pās) □*noun, plural* **paces** □*verb*
paced, pacing, paces

pacifist *noun* Someone who is opposed to war. A pacifist believes that disputes between nations should be settled by peaceful means.
pac·i·fist (pas′ə fist) □*noun, plural* **pacifists**

pack *noun* **1.** A group of things tied or wrapped together; bundle. **2.** A group of similar things: *a pack of dogs.* **3.** A large amount: *a pack of lies.*
□*verb* **1.** To put in a container: *pack books for storage.* **2.** To fill with things: *pack a trunk.* **3.** To press closely together: *The recipe says to pack the brown sugar firmly in the cup.* **4.** To fill up tight: *Tourists packed the bus.*
pack (pak) □*noun, plural* **packs** □*verb*
packed, packing, packs

package *noun* **1.** A wrapped or boxed parcel holding one or more things: *a package of tissues.* **2.** A container used to store or send something.
□*verb* To put or make into a package: *I'll package the toys and mail them to you.*
pack·age (pak′ij) □*noun, plural* **packages**
□*verb* **packaged, packaging, packages**

packet *noun* A small package or bundle.
pack·et (pak′it) □*noun, plural* **packets**

pact *noun* An agreement made between countries, groups, or persons to act a certain way or do certain things; treaty.
pact (pakt) □*noun, plural* **pacts**

pad *noun* **1.** A piece of soft, firmly packed material used for comfort, stuffing, or protection: *a mattress pad; football shoulder pads.* **2.** An ink-soaked cushion in a container used with a marking stamp. **3.** A number of sheets of paper glued together at one end. **4.** The part that is like a small cushion on the bottom of the feet of dogs, cats, and other animals.
□*verb* To line, stuff, or cover with soft, firmly packed material: *He padded the seat of the chair.*
pad (pad) □*noun, plural* **pads** □*verb*
padded, padding, pads

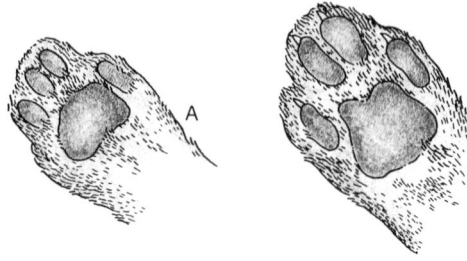

pad
Of a cat:*(A)*front, *(B)*rear

padding *noun* Material used to pad something.
pad·ding (pad′ing) ▢*noun*

paddle *noun* **1.** A short oar with a flat blade used to move and steer a canoe or other boat through water. **2.** A tool with a flat blade used for stirring, mixing, or beating. **3.** A small, flat board with a short handle used in some games. **4.** One of the broad boards on a paddle wheel.
▢*verb* **1.** To move and steer a boat through the water with a paddle. **2.** To beat with or as if with a paddle; spank. **3.** To stir or shape something with a paddle.
pad·dle (pad′əl) ▢*noun, plural* **paddles**
▢*verb* **paddled, paddling, paddles**

paddle boat A boat that is driven through the water by a paddle wheel.

paddle wheel *noun* A large wheel with boards around its edge. It is powered by steam and used to move a ship.

paddle wheel

paddock *noun* A fenced field or area where horses exercise and graze.
pad·dock (pad′ək) ▢*noun, plural* **paddocks**

paddy *noun* A wet field where rice is grown.
pad·dy (pad′ē) ▢*noun, plural* **paddies**

padlock *noun* A lock that can be put on and taken off. A padlock has a bar on the top shaped like the letter U that locks into a catch.
▢*verb* To lock with a padlock.
pad·lock (pad′lok′) ▢*noun, plural* **padlocks**
▢*verb* **padlocked, padlocking, padlocks**

pagan *noun* Someone who is not a Christian, Moslem, or Jew and may worship many gods or no god.
pa·gan (pā′gən) ▢*noun, plural* **pagans**

WORD HISTORY: pagan

The word *pagan* comes from a Latin word meaning "a person who lives in the country." When Christianity first began to spread, it was adopted more quickly in the towns of the Roman Empire than in the countryside, where people continued to worship the Roman gods. The Latin word for someone who lived in the country, therefore, came also to be used of someone who was neither a Christian nor a Jew.

page¹ *noun* One side of a sheet of paper in a book, newspaper, letter, or magazine.
page (pāj) ▢*noun, plural* **pages**

page² *noun* **1.** A boy in the Middle Ages who served a knight as the first step in training to become a knight. **2.** Someone who runs errands, carries messages, or acts as a guide.
▢*verb* To call or summon someone by name in a public place.
page (pāj) ▢*noun, plural* **pages** ▢*verb*
paged, paging, pages

pageant *noun* **1.** A play or dramatic program usually about an event in history: *a Christmas pageant*. **2.** A parade, procession, or celebration for a special event: *a funeral pageant for the slain warrior*.
pag·eant (paj′ənt) ▢*noun, plural* **pageants**

pagoda *noun* A tower with many stories, usually built as a shrine or memorial in countries of eastern Asia.
pa·go·da (pə gō′də) ▢*noun, plural* **pagodas**

pagoda

a	bat	ī	bite	o͞o	tool	*th*	feather
ā	make	î	fierce	ou	out	th	bath
â	dare	o	dot	u	nut	hw	wheat
ä	father	ō	no	û	turn	zh	measure
e	net	ô	law, for	ch	church	ə	about, open
ē	be	oi	soil	ng	ring		pencil, atom
i	dip	oo	look	sh	shade		circus

paid *verb* The past tense and past participle of **pay:** *She paid her rent last month.*
paid (pād) □*verb*

pail *noun* A round, open container with a handle, used for carrying things; bucket.
pail (pāl) □*noun, plural* **pails**

pain *noun* **1.** A sharp ache or sore place in the body that is caused by an injury or sickness. **2.** Mental or emotional suffering: *Her son's misfortune caused her great pain.* **3. pains** Trouble, care, or effort: *They took pains to do their job right.*
□*verb* To cause to suffer: *Her back pained her greatly. The insult pained the gentle boy.*
pain (pān) □*noun, plural* **pains** □*verb* **pained, paining, pains**

painful *adjective* **1.** Causing pain: *a painful insect bite.* **2.** Causing worry or suffering: *a painful experience.*
pain·ful (pān′fəl) □*adjective*

painstaking *adjective* Needing or showing great care: *Repairing the broken plate was painstaking work.*
pains·tak·ing (pānz′ta′king) □*adjective*

paint *noun* A mixture of coloring matter and a liquid that is put on surfaces to protect or decorate them.
□*verb* **1.** To cover with paint: *paint a house.* **2.** To draw a picture using paint. **3.** To describe clearly with words: *Your story paints an exciting picture of the race.*
paint (pānt) □*noun, plural* **paints** □*verb* **painted, painting, paints**

painter *noun* Someone who paints.
paint·er (pān′tər) □*noun, plural* **painters**

painting *noun* **1.** The art, process, or work of one who paints. **2.** A picture or design done with paint: *She does paintings of animals.*
paint·ing (pān′ting) □*noun, plural* **paintings**

pair *noun* **1.** A set of two like things that are usually used together: *a pair of mittens.* **2.** One thing that is made of two parts joined together: *a pair of eyeglasses.* **3.** Two persons or animals that are alike or go together: *a pair of wrestlers; a pair of robins.*
□*verb* **1.** To form into sets of two: *We paired off and stood in line.* **2.** To provide a partner for: *At camp they paired each beginner with an expert swimmer.*
pair (pâr) □*noun, plural* **pairs** *or* **pair** □*verb* **paired, pairing, pairs**

pajamas *plural noun* A jacket and matching trousers that are worn for sleeping.

pa·ja·mas (pə jä′məz *or* pə jam′əz) □*plural noun*

pal *noun* A close friend; chum: *The two boys have been pals for years.*
pal (pal) □*noun, plural* **pals**

palace *noun* The official residence of a king, queen, or other ruler.
pal·ace (pal′is) □*noun, plural* **palaces**

WORD HISTORY: **palace**

The word *palace* comes from the Latin name for the Palatine Hill in Rome. The Palatine was one of the most fashionable areas to live. Because the emperors built their palaces on the Palatine, the name of the hill came to be used also for the palaces themselves.

palace

palatable *adjective* Pleasing to the taste: *This dish is more than palatable; it's delicious!*
pal·at·a·ble (pal′ə tə bəl) □*adjective*

palate *noun* The roof of the mouth in humans and other animals.
pal·ate (pal′it) □*noun, plural* **palates**

pale *adjective* **1.** Having less color than usual or no color at all: *Pale skin may be a sign of illness.* **2.** Light in color: *a pale pink.*
□*verb* To turn or become pale: *He paled when she told him he had lost the contest.*
pale (pāl) □*adjective* **paler, palest** □*verb* **paled, paling, pales**

palette *noun* A thin board upon which an artist mixes colors. It is held with the hand and often has a hole for the thumb.
pal·ette (pal′it) □*noun, plural* **palettes**

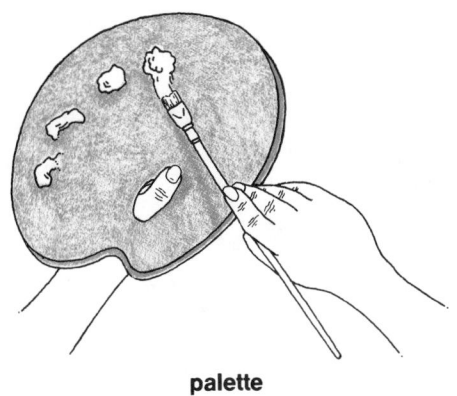

palette

palisades *plural noun* A line of high cliffs, usually along a river.
pal·i·sades (pal'i **sādz'**) □*plural noun*

pall *noun* **1.** A cloth for covering a coffin or tomb. **2.** A covering that darkens or makes something gloomy: *a pall of smoke.* **3.** A gloomy atmosphere: *In past times, rumors of the plague would cast a pall of fear over the crowded cities of Europe.*
□*verb* To become dull and uninteresting: *After a whole day at the fair, we found that the amusements had begun to pall.*
pall (pôl) □*noun, plural* **palls** □*verb* **palled, palling, palls**

palm¹ *noun* The inside of a person's hand from the wrist to the fingers.
□*verb* To hide something in the palm of the hand: *The thief palmed the watch.*
palm (päm) □*noun, plural* **palms** □*verb* **palmed, palming, palms**

palm² *noun* One of many related trees found in warm parts of the world, with leaves that look like feathers or fans and often grow at the top of a tall trunk with no branches.
palm (päm) □*noun, plural* **palms**

WORD HISTORY: palm²

Palm² comes from the Latin word for "palm of the hand." The Romans used this word for the palm tree because the leaves of the tree look like the fingers of an outspread palm.

---

palmetto *noun* A palm tree of the southeastern United States with leaves shaped like fans.
pal·met·to (pal met'ō) □*noun, plural* **palmettos** or **palmettoes**

palomino *noun* A horse with a light tan coat and a whitish mane and tail.

pal·o·mi·no (pal'ə **mē'**nō) □*noun, plural* **palominos**
pamper *verb* To give too much attention and care to: *She pampered the child because he was ill.*
pam·per (pam'pər) □*verb* **pampered, pampering, pampers**
pamphlet *noun* A short book with a paper cover; booklet.
pam·phlet (pam'flit) □*noun, plural* **pamphlets**
pan *noun* A wide, shallow, open metal container used for cooking or other purposes.
□*verb* To wash dirt or gravel in a pan in search of gold.
pan (pan) □*noun, plural* **pans** □*verb* **panned, panning, pans**
pancake *noun* A thin, flat cake of batter, cooked on a griddle or in a skillet.
pan·cake (pan'kāk') □*noun, plural* **pancakes**
pancreas *noun* A gland behind the stomach that helps to digest food.
pan·cre·as (pan'krē əs) □*noun, plural* **pancreases**

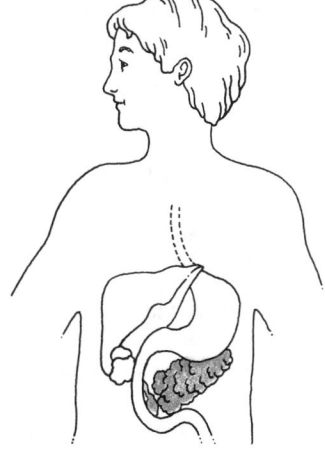

pancreas

panda *noun* An animal that looks like a bear and lives in the mountains of China. The giant panda has long, thick fur with black and white markings.
pan·da (pan'də) □*noun, plural* **pandas**

a	bat	ī	bite	o͞o	tool	*th*	feather
ā	make	î	fierce	ou	out	th	bath
â	dare	o	dot	u	nut	hw	wheat
ä	father	ō	no	û	turn	zh	measure
e	net	ô	law, for	ch	church	ə	about, open
ē	be	oi	soil	ng	ring		pencil, atom
i	dip	o͝o	look	sh	shade		circus

pane *noun* A sheet of glass in a window or door.
pane (pān) □*noun, plural* **panes**

panel *noun* **1.** A flat part or section of a wall, ceiling, or door that is framed by a border or by the surrounding parts. **2.** A board with instruments or controls for a vehicle or machine. **3.** A group of persons brought together to discuss or decide something: *A panel of doctors studied the case.*
□*verb* To cover or decorate with panels: *The den was paneled in oak.*
pan·el (pan′əl) □*noun, plural* **panels** □*verb* **paneled, paneling, panels**

panel truck *noun* A small delivery truck with a closed top and back.

pang *noun* A short, sharp pain or feeling: *She felt a pang of regret.*
pang (pang) □*noun, plural* **pangs**

panic *noun* A sudden feeling of great fear: *She felt panic when she heard the police siren.*
□*verb* **1.** To feel panic: *The cat panicked and ran upstairs.* **2.** To cause panic in: *The smell of smoke panicked the shoppers in the store.*
pan·ic (pan′ik) □*noun, plural* **panics** □*verb* **panicked, panicking, panics**

WORD HISTORY: panic

Panic comes from a Greek word that means "of Pan." The Greeks thought that the nature god Pan caused the feeling of terror that can overtake people in the woods or on the mountains.

---

panorama *noun* A view or picture of everything that can be seen over a wide area: *From the church tower we saw a panorama of the whole town.*
pan·o·ram·a (pan′ə **ram**′ə) □*noun, plural* **panoramas**

pansy *noun* A garden plant bearing flowers with rounded, velvety petals.
pan·sy (pan′zē) □*noun, plural* **pansies**

WORD HISTORY: pansy

The word *pansy* comes from an old French word that means "thought."

---

pant *verb* To breathe in short, quick gasps: *The runner panted after the race.*
pant (pant) □*verb* **panted, panting, pants**

panther *noun* **1.** A leopard, especially a black leopard. **2.** A mountain lion or other wild cat.
pan·ther (pan′thər) □*noun, plural* **panthers**

panther

pantomime *noun* **1.** Acting out a story by body movements and gestures without speaking. **2.** A play or other entertainment acted in this way.
□*verb* To perform or show by pantomime.
pan·to·mime (pan′tə mīm′) □*noun, plural* **pantomimes** □*verb* **pantomimed, pantomiming, pantomimes**

pantry *noun* A small room or closet where food, dishes, and utensils are kept.
pan·try (pan′trē) □*noun, plural* **pantries**

pants *plural noun* Trousers or slacks.
pants (pants) □*plural noun*

papal *adjective* Of or by the pope: *a papal blessing.*
pa·pal (pā′pəl) □*adjective*

papaya *noun* The large, sweet yellow fruit of a tropical American tree.
pa·pa·ya (pə **pä**′yə) □*noun, plural* **papayas**

paper *noun* **1.** A material made from wood pulp, rags, and other things and usually produced in thin sheets. Paper is used for writing, printing, drawing, wrapping, and for covering walls. **2.** A single sheet of this material. **3.** A sheet of this material with writing or printing on it; document: *The doctor took several papers out of her file.* **4.** A report or essay assigned in school: *Write a paper on George Washington.* **5.** A newspaper.
□*verb* To cover with wallpaper: *Mother wants to paper the dining room next week.*
pa·per (pā′pər) □*noun, plural* **papers** □*verb* **papered, papering, papers**

WORD HISTORY: paper

Paper comes from the Greek word for "papyrus." In ancient times a paperlike material was made from this plant.

paperback *noun* A book with a soft paper cover.
pa·per·back (pā′pər bak′) □*noun, plural* **paperbacks**

paper clip *noun* A bent piece of wire that is used to hold loose papers together.

papoose *noun* A North American Indian baby.
pa·poose (pa **poos′**) □*noun, plural* **papooses**

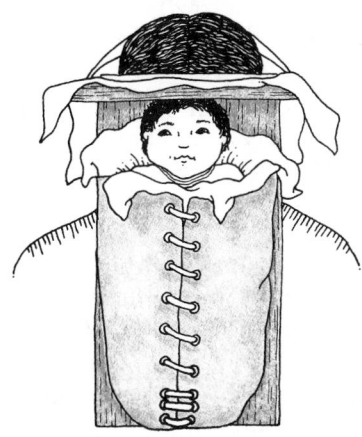

papoose

paprika *noun* A spice made from powdered sweet red peppers.
pap·ri·ka (pa **prē′**kə *or* **pap′**ri kə) □*noun*

papyrus *noun* A tall water plant of northern Africa.
pa·py·rus (pə **pī′**rəs) □*noun*

parachute *noun* A large cloth device shaped like an umbrella that opens in midair and slows the fall of a person or object from great heights.
□*verb* To come or drop down by parachute: *The soldiers parachuted into enemy territory.*
par·a·chute (**par′**ə shoot′) □*noun, plural* **parachutes** □*verb* **parachuted, parachuting, parachutes**

parachute

parade *noun* A public event in which bands, people, and vehicles pass before crowds of spectators: *the Thanksgiving Day parade.*
□*verb* **1.** To take part in a parade: *The circus clowns paraded in their funny costumes.* **2.** To show oneself or one's things too proudly.
pa·rade (pə **rād′**) □*noun, plural* **parades** □*verb* **paraded, parading, parades**

paradise *noun* **1.** Heaven. **2.** A place or condition of perfect happiness or beauty.
par·a·dise (**par′**ə dīs′) □*noun*

paraffin *noun* A substance like wax that is used in making candles and wax paper and in sealing jars of jelly.
par·af·fin (**par′**ə fin) □*noun*

paragraph *noun* A division of a piece of writing that consists of one or more sentences on a single subject or idea: *Start each paragraph on a new line and indent it.*
par·a·graph (**par′**ə graf′) □*noun, plural* **paragraphs**

WORD HISTORY: **paragraph**

Paragraph comes from a Greek word used for a sign made in the margin of a piece of writing to indicate the end of a sentence. The Greek word literally means ''written by the side.''

---

parakeet *noun* A small parrot with a long, pointed tail and brightly colored feathers.
par·a·keet (**par′**ə kēt′) □*noun, plural* **parakeets**

parakeet

a bat	ī bite	oo tool	*th* feather
ā make	î fierce	ou out	th bath
â dare	o dot	u nut	hw wheat
ä father	ō no	û turn	zh measure
e net	ô law, for	ch church	ə about, open
ē be	oi soil	ng ring	pencil, atom
i dip	oo look	sh shade	circus

parallel *adjective* **1.** Lying in the same plane but not touching at any point: *The farmer planted the corn in parallel rows.* **2.** Matching feature for feature; alike or corresponding: *She and her friend have parallel likes and dislikes.*
□*adverb* In a parallel course or direction: *The road runs parallel to the river.*
□*noun* **1.** Any of a set of parallel geometric lines or other figures. **2.** Something that closely resembles something else: *The parallel between your adventure at the airport and mine at the train station is remarkable.* **3.** Any of the imaginary lines circling the earth parallel to the equator, used to mark latitude.
□*verb* **1.** To be or extend in a parallel way to: *The fence parallels the highway.* **2.** To be like; resemble: *Her ambitions parallel her sister's.*
par·al·lel (par′ə lel′) □*adjective* □*adverb* □*noun, plural* **parallels** □*verb* **paralleled, paralleling, parallels**

parallelogram *noun* A plane geometric figure with four sides whose opposite sides are equal and parallel. Rhombuses and rectangles are parallelograms.
par·al·lel·o·gram (par′ə lel′ə gram′) □*noun, plural* **parallelograms**

paralysis *noun* Complete or partial loss of the ability to feel anything in a part of the body or to move a part of the body.
par·a·ly·sis (pə ral′i sis) □*noun, plural* **paralyses** (pə ral′i sēz′)

paralyze *verb* **1.** To cause a person to have paralysis: *The injury paralyzed his arm.* **2.** To make unable to move or do anything: *The collision paralyzed traffic for miles.*
par·a·lyze (par′ə līz′) □*verb* **paralyzed, paralyzing, paralyzes**

paramecium *noun* A very small, slipper-shaped water animal that has only one cell. It can be seen only with a microscope.
par·a·me·ci·um (par′ə mē′shē əm) □*noun, plural* **par·a·me·ci·a** (par′ə mē′shē ə)

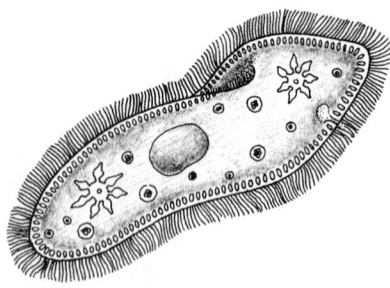

paramecium

parapet *noun* A low wall or railing along the edge of a roof or balcony.
par·a·pet (par′ə pet′) □*noun, plural* **parapets**

paraphrase *noun* A restatement of something in different words: *His book report was just a paraphrase of a review he had read in a magazine.*
□*verb* To restate something in different words.
par·a·phrase (par′ə frāz′) □*noun, plural* **paraphrases** □*verb* **paraphrased, paraphrasing, paraphrases**

parasite *noun* A plant or animal that lives in or on another plant or animal. The parasite gets its food from the other plant or animal and is often harmful.
par·a·site (par′ə sīt′) □*noun, plural* **parasites**

parasol *noun* A small, light umbrella used to protect a person from the sun.
par·a·sol (par′ə sôl′) □*noun, plural* **parasols**

paratrooper *noun* A soldier who is trained to parachute from airplanes and then engage in battle on the ground.
par·a·troop·er (par′ə trōo′pər) □*noun, plural* **paratroopers**

parcel *noun* **1.** Something wrapped up in a bundle; package: *This parcel came in the mail today.* **2.** A section or piece of land; plot: *We bought two parcels of our neighbor's farm.*
□*verb* To divide into parts and distribute: *The guard parceled out clothes to the prisoners.*
par·cel (pär′səl) □*noun, plural* **parcels** □*verb* **parceled, parceling, parcels**

parch *verb* **1.** To make or become very dry: *The sun parched the fields.* **2.** To make or become very thirsty: *I was parched after running to the top of the hill.*
parch (pärch) □*verb* **parched, parching, parches**

parchment *noun* The skin of a sheep or goat prepared as a material to write on.
parch·ment (pärch′mənt) □*noun, plural* **parchments**

pardon *verb* **1.** To free or release a person from punishment: *The President pardoned the prisoner.* **2.** To excuse or overlook a mistake or fault: *Will you pardon my clumsiness?*
□*noun* **1.** Forgiveness of a mistake or fault: *I beg your pardon.* **2.** The act of releasing from punishment by an official.
par·don (pär′dən) □*verb* **pardoned, pardoning, pardons** □*noun, plural* **pardons**

pare *verb* To remove the skin or rind of something with a knife or other device: *She pared the apples for the pie.*
pare (pâr) □*verb* **pared, paring, pares**

parent *noun* A plant or animal that has produced offspring.
par·ent (pâr′ənt) □*noun, plural* **parents**

parental *adjective* **1.** Of a parent: *parental love.* **2.** Like a parent: *a teacher who takes a parental interest in his pupils.*
pa·ren·tal (pə ren′təl) □*adjective*

parenthesis *noun* Either of two upright curved lines ( ), used in writing or printing to set off a phrase or explanation.
pa·ren·the·sis (pə ren′thi sis) □*noun, plural* **pa·ren·the·ses** (pə ren′thi sēz′)

parish *noun* **1.** A district with its own church and pastor. **2.** The people who belong to such a district and attend this church.
par·ish (par′ish) □*noun, plural* **parishes**

park *noun* **1.** An area of public land used for amusement and recreation by the people of a town or city. **2.** An area of land set apart by the government to be kept in its natural state. □*verb* To leave a vehicle in a certain place when it is not in use: *Park your car in front of the house.*
park (pärk) □*noun, plural* **parks** □*verb* **parked, parking, parks**

parka *noun* A warm jacket with a hood and often a fur lining.
par·ka (pär′kə) □*noun, plural* **parkas**

parka

parkway *noun* A wide road or highway with grass, bushes, and trees along the sides.
park·way (pärk′wā′) □*noun, plural* **parkways**

parliament *noun* The highest legislative body in certain countries, such as Canada and the United Kingdom.
par·lia·ment (pär′lə mənt) □*noun, plural* **parliaments**

parlor *noun* **1.** A room for entertaining visitors. **2.** A room or building designed for some special use or business: *a game parlor; a funeral parlor.*
par·lor (pär′lər) □*noun, plural* **parlors**

parochial *adjective* Of a church parish: *a parochial high school.*
pa·ro·chi·al (pə rō′kē əl) □*adjective*

parole *noun* The release of someone from prison before the end of his or her full sentence. People are usually given parole for good behavior and then must follow certain rules. □*verb* To release someone on parole.
pa·role (pə rōl) □*noun, plural* **paroles** □*verb* **paroled, paroling, paroles**

parrot *noun* Any of several brightly colored tropical birds with a short, hooked bill. Some kinds of parrots can imitate human speech. □*verb* To repeat or imitate another person's words or actions without understanding their meaning: *At first the pupils parroted what the Spanish teacher was saying.*
par·rot (par′ət) □*noun, plural* **parrots** □*verb* **parroted, parroting, parrots**

parrot

a	bat	ī	bite	o͞o	tool	*th*	feather
ā	make	î	fierce	ou	out	th	bath
â	dare	o	dot	u	nut	hw	wheat
ä	father	ō	no	û	turn	zh	measure
e	net	ô	law, for	ch	church	ə	about, open
ē	be	oi	soil	ng	ring		pencil, atom
i	dip	oo	look	sh	shade		circus

parsley *noun* A plant with feathery or curly leaves that are used to flavor or decorate food.
pars·ley (pär′ slē) □*noun*

parsnip *noun* The tapering whitish root of a plant that is eaten as a vegetable.
pars·nip (pär′ snip) □*noun, plural* **parsnips**

parson *noun* A minister who is in charge of a parish; pastor.
par·son (pär′ sən) □*noun, plural* **parsons**

part *noun* **1.** Something that along with other things makes a whole: *I only ate part of my dessert.* **2.** One of the equal portions of a whole: *I mixed one part of white paint with three parts of red paint.* **3.** Something or someone thought of as an equal or necessary feature or element: *Our dog has always been regarded as part of the family.* **4.** A piece in a machine or mechanism that can be taken out and replaced: *a new part for the television.* **5.** A role or character in a play or movie: *What part did you get in the school play?* **6.** A side in an argument or dispute: *No one took my part in the disagreement.* **7.** A dividing line formed across the scalp when the hair is combed to one side or the other.
□*verb* **1.** To leave or go away; separate: *They parted at the bus station.* **2.** To put or keep apart; separate: *The war parted them for several years.* **3.** To comb hair so that it falls along a dividing line.
□*adjective* Not full; partial: *His parents are part owners of a grocery store.*
□*adverb* In part; partially: *Her mood was part anger, part sadness.*
for the most part In most cases; chiefly: *I read novels for the most part.*
part with To give up; let go of: *The little boy wouldn't part with his pillow.*
take part To be active; join: *take part in an activity.* —See Synonyms at **separate**.
part (pärt) □*noun, plural* **parts** □*verb* **parted, parting, parts** □*adjective* □*adverb*

partake *verb* **1.** To take part; participate: *All the children stayed up late so they could partake in the celebration.* **2.** To take a share or portion: *The rich man invited the beggar to partake of the feast.*
par·take (pär tāk′) □*verb* **partook, partaken, partaking, partakes**

partial *adjective* **1.** Not total or complete: *partial deafness.* **2.** Favoring one side; prejudiced: *A teacher should not be partial.*
par·tial (pär′ shəl) □*adjective*

participant *noun* Someone who participates: *All the participants in the contest won a prize.*
par·tic·i·pant (pär tis′ ə pənt) □*noun, plural* **participants**

participate *verb* To join with others in being active; take part: *She participated in a scientific experiment.*
par·tic·i·pate (pär tis′ ə pāt′) □*verb* **participated, participating, participates**

participle *noun* A word formed from a verb that can act as an adjective. Participles have tenses and can take objects.
par·ti·ci·ple (pär′ ti sip′əl) □*noun, plural* **participles**

particle *noun* A very small piece or amount of something solid; speck: *Particles of dirt settled on the tablecloth.*
par·ti·cle (pär′ ti kəl) □*noun, plural* **particles**

particular *adjective* **1.** Of or for a single person, group, or thing: *Clam chowder is the particular specialty of this restaurant.* **2.** Distinct from any other; specific: *This particular bowl is an antique.* **3.** Special or exceptional; unusual: *Pay particular attention to the spelling of their names.* **4.** Showing or demanding close attention to details; fussy: *He's very particular about his clothes.*
□ *noun* A single item or fact; detail: *The directions are clear in every particular.*
par·tic·u·lar (pər tik′ yə lər) □*adjective* □*noun, plural* **particulars**

partition *noun* A wall, panel, or screen that divides up a room or space.
□*verb* **1.** To divide into separate spaces or sections: *They partitioned the large room into five offices.* **2.** To make into a separate space by means of a partition: *We used a curtain to partition the hall from the living room.*
par·ti·tion (pär tish′ ən) □*noun, plural* **partitions** □*verb* **partitioned, partitioning, partitions**

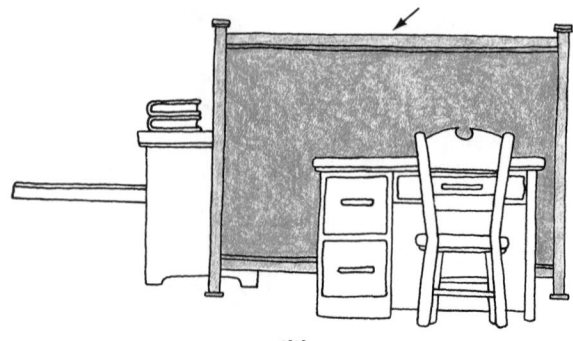

partition

partly *adverb* To some extent or degree; in part: *The garden is partly hidden by a fence.*
part·ly (pärt′lē) ▢*adverb*

partner *noun* **1.** One of two or more persons joined in an activity, especially a business: *The shoe store has three partners.* **2.** Someone with whom one dances: *I had no partner for the waltz.* **3.** Either of two persons playing together in a game: *a golf partner.*
part·ner (pärt′nər) ▢*noun, plural* **partners**

partnership *noun* The condition of being partners: *Their partnership started right after they graduated from college.*
part·ner·ship (pärt′nər ship′) ▢*noun, plural* **partnerships**

part of speech *noun* A class of words defined according to the way they are used in a phrase or sentence.

partook *verb* The past tense of **partake.**
par·took (pär took′) ▢*verb*

partridge *noun* A plump bird with brownish feathers that is often hunted as game.
par·tridge (pär′trij) ▢*noun, plural* **partridges** or **partridge**

partridge

part-time *adjective* For or during only part of the usual working time: *a part-time job.*
part-time (pärt′tīm′) ▢*adjective*

party *noun* **1.** A group of persons who join together in some activity: *A search party is looking for the missing child.* **2.** A gathering of people for pleasure: *a birthday party.* **3.** A group of people who are organized for political activity: *the Democratic Party.* **4.** A person or group who takes part in some action: *I won't be a party to your practical joke.*
par·ty (pär′tē) ▢*noun, plural* **parties**

pass *verb* **1.** To go from one place to another: *The truck passed through the tunnel.* **2.** To go by without stopping: *She always waves when* she passes my house. **3.** To catch up with and go by: *The bus passed all the cars on the highway.* **4.** To go by in time; spend time: *We passed the afternoon watching a movie.* **5.** To come to an end: *The storm passed last night.* **6.** To hand or throw from one person to another: *Pass these pencils to the pupils in the back row.* **7.** To move: *She passed her fingers over the piano keys.* **8.** To complete with satisfactory results: *The whole class passed the history test.* **9.** To make into a law; become a law: *The legislature passed the tax bill.*
▢*noun* **1.** A motion with the hand or something held in the hand: *The magician made a few passes with the wand over the table.* **2.** A way or opening that is hard to get through: *a narrow pass through the mountains.* **3.** Written or printed permission: *You cannot walk the halls without a pass.* **4.** A ticket that gives free admission: *two passes to the concert.* **5.** In sports, the act of passing a ball or puck to someone on the same team.
   pass away To die.
   pass out 1. To hand out: *The club passed out pamphlets about its work.* **2.** To faint: *The man passed out from hunger.*
pass (pas) ▢*verb* **passed, passing, passes** ▢*noun, plural* **passes**

passable *adjective* **1.** Able to be traveled on or crossed: *This mountain track is not passable during the winter.* **2.** Only just good enough; adequate: *The young actor gave a passable performance in a very difficult role.*
pass·a·ble (pas′ə bəl) ▢*adjective*

passage *noun* **1.** The act of passing; movement: *The open windows allowed the passage of air into the room.* **2.** A means of passing between two places or points: *a hidden passage from the cellar to the attic.* **3.** A trip or journey, especially on a ship: *Our passage across the bay took an hour.* **4.** A channel or tube in the body through which something may pass: *nasal passages.* **5.** The act of making a law by a legislative body: *The passage of the bill is doubtful.* **6.** A part of a written work or a piece of music: *She read a passage from the*

a	bat	ī	bite	oo	tool	*th*	feather
ā	make	î	fierce	ou	out	th	bath
â	dare	o	dot	u	nut	hw	wheat
ä	father	ō	no	û	turn	zh	measure
e	net	ô	law, for	ch	church	ə	about, open
ē	be	oi	soil	ng	ring		pencil, atom
i	dip	oo	look	sh	shade		circus

Bible aloud.
pas·sage (**pas′**ij) ▢*noun, plural* **passages**

passageway *noun* A way or route along which someone or something can pass.
pas·sage·way (**pas′**ij wā′) ▢*noun, plural* **passageways**

passenger *noun* Someone riding in a train, airplane, bus, ship, car, or other vehicle: *How many passengers can the ferry hold?*
pas·sen·ger (**pas′**ən jər) ▢*noun, plural* **passengers**

passenger pigeon *noun* A pigeon that was once common in North America but has been extinct since the late nineteenth century.

passenger pigeon

passer-by *noun* Someone who happens to be passing by at a certain time: *The reporter stood on a busy street corner and asked passers-by questions about the election.*
pass·er·by (**pas′**ər **bī′**) ▢*noun, plural* **passers-by**

passing *adjective* **1.** Going by; moving by: *A passing stranger helped us find our way.* **2.** Not lasting long; brief: *My sister had only a passing interest in chess.* **3.** Said or done quickly; casual: *A passing glance at the store window showed that the clothes on display were very expensive.* **4.** Showing that one has passed a test; satisfactory: *You have to work very hard to get a passing grade in that class.*
▢*noun* The act of going by: *She's too busy to notice the passing of time.*
pass·ing (**pas′**ing) ▢*adjective* ▢*noun*

passion *noun* **1.** A powerful or very strong feeling, such as love, joy, anger, or hatred. **2.** A strong liking: *The whole family has a passion for sports.*
pas·sion (**pash′**ən) ▢*noun, plural* **passions**

passionflower *noun* The large, brightly colored flower of a vine that grows in warm regions.

pas·sion·flow·er (**pash′**ən flou′ər) ▢*noun, plural* **passionflowers**

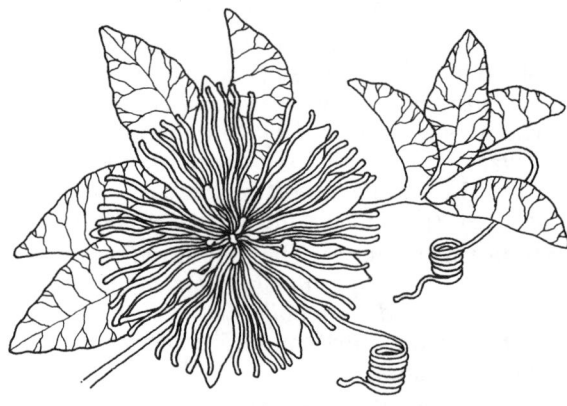

passionflower

passive *adjective* **1.** Not joining in or taking part; not acting: *passive spectators.* **2.** Giving no resistance: *passive acceptance of his fate.* **3.** Indicating that the subject of the sentence is the receiver of the action of the verb. In the sentence *The money was stolen,* the verb form *was stolen* is passive.
pas·sive (**pas′**iv) ▢*adjective*

Passover *noun* A Jewish festival that comes in the spring and lasts eight days. It celebrates the escape of the Jews from ancient Egypt.
Pass·o·ver (**pas′**ō′vər) ▢*noun, plural* **Passovers**

WORD HISTORY: **Passover**

The name *Passover* comes from the account in the Bible of events leading up to the escape of the Jews from Egypt. According to the account, God "passed over" the houses of the Jews, which were marked with the blood of a lamb, and entered the houses of the Egyptians, killing their first-born.

---

passport *noun* A document that identifies a person as a citizen and gives official permission to travel in foreign countries.
pass·port (**pas′**pôrt′) ▢*noun, plural* **passports**

password *noun* A secret word or phrase spoken to a guard that identifies the speaker and allows him or her to enter a special place.
pass·word (**pas′**wûrd′) ▢*noun, plural* **passwords**

past *adjective* **1.** Just ended; just over: *We ate at the diner only twice in the past month.* **2.** Having existed or taken place at an earlier time; former: *a past winner of the award.*

□*noun* **1.** All the time gone by before the present: *In the past people traveled by horse and buggy.* **2.** A person's history and background: *He keeps his past a secret.*
□*preposition* **1.** Alongside and beyond: *The road goes past his house.* **2.** Beyond in time or age: *It is ten past four. She is one year past retirement age.* **3.** Beyond in position: *How did they get past the dogs?*
□*adverb* To and beyond a point near at hand; by: *The children threw confetti as the President's car went past.*
past (past) □*adjective* □*noun, plural* **pasts** □*preposition* □*adverb*

paste *noun* **1.** A smooth, sticky substance that is used to fasten things together. Paste is often made of a mixture of flour and water. **2.** A food that has been made soft by pounding or grinding: *tomato paste.*
□*verb* To fasten or stick together with paste: *She tried to paste the label onto the package.*
paste (pāst) □*noun, plural* **pastes** □*verb* **pasted, pasting, pastes**

pasteboard *noun* A thin, stiff board made of many sheets of paper pasted together or of wood pulp that is wet, formed into a special shape, and then dried until it is hard.
paste·board (pāst′bôrd′) □*noun*

pastel *noun* **1.** A crayon with a texture like chalk that is used in drawing or marking. **2.** A drawing made with pastels. **3.** A soft, delicate color.
pas·tel (pa stel′) □*noun, plural* **pastels**

pasteurize *verb* To heat milk or other foods hot enough so that certain germs are killed.
pas·teur·ize (pas′chə rīz′) □*verb* **pasteurized, pasteurizing, pasteurizes**

WORD HISTORY: pasteurize

The word *pasteurize* comes from the name of Louis Pasteur, a French scientist who discovered this method of killing germs in milk.

---

pastime *noun* A hobby or other activity that helps make time pass in a pleasant way: *Photography is my sister's favorite pastime.*
pas·time (pas′tīm′) □*noun, plural* **pastimes**

pastor *noun* A minister in charge of a church.
pas·tor (pas′tər) □*noun, plural* **pastors**

pastoral *adjective* **1.** Of or having to do with shepherds or simple country life: *A pastoral way of life.* **2.** Of or having to do with the pastor of a church: *The minister needed help with his pastoral duties.*
pas·tor·al (pas′tər əl) □*adjective*

past participle *noun* A form of a verb that shows a completed action, condition, or state. For example, in the sentence *She had known the candidate for many years and so she was asked to introduce him, known* is the past participle of *know* and *asked* is the past participle of *ask.*

pastry *noun* **1.** Baked foods, such as pies and tarts. **2.** Dough used to make pastry crusts.
pas·try (pā′strē) □*noun, plural* **pastries**

past tense *noun* A verb tense that shows an action that happened or a condition that existed in or during the past. In the sentence *She patted the dog,* the verb *patted* is in the past tense.

pasture *noun* **1.** A piece of land covered with grass and other plants that are eaten by animals that graze. **2.** The grass and other plants eaten by animals that graze.
□*verb* To put animals in a pasture to graze: *The farmer pastures the cows every morning.*
pas·ture (pas′chər) □*noun, plural* **pastures** □*verb* **pastured, pasturing, pastures**

pat *verb* **1.** To touch or stroke gently with the open hand: *He seemed afraid to pat the horse.* **2.** To flatten or shape by patting: *She patted the chopped meat into a hamburger.*
□*noun* **1.** A gentle stroke or tap: *a pat on the cheek.* **2.** A small piece or lump: *Put a pat of butter into the pan.*
pat (pat) □*verb* **patted, patting, pats** □*noun, plural* **pats**

patch *noun* **1.** A piece of material used to cover a hole, a tear, or a worn place: *Can you put a patch on my tire?* **2.** A bandage or pad worn over a sore or injured place to protect it: *an eye patch.* **3.** A small piece of land with plants growing on it: *an onion patch.* **4.** A small area that is different from what is around it: *a patch of blue in the cloudy sky.*
□*verb* **1.** To put a patch on: *I patched the hole in your slacks.* **2.** To mend quickly or carelessly: *We patched up the broken chair, but it won't hold much weight.*

a bat	ī bite	ōō tool	*th* feather
ā make	î fierce	ou out	th bath
â dare	o dot	u nut	hw wheat
ä father	ō no	û turn	zh measure
e net	ô law, for	ch church	ə about, open
ē be	oi soil	ng ring	pencil, atom
i dip	oo look	sh shade	circus

patch (pach) □*noun, plural* **patches** □*verb*
patched, patching, patches

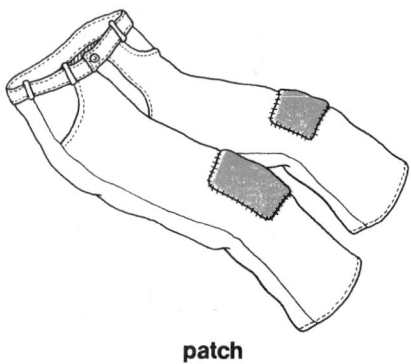

patch

patchwork *noun* Pieces of cloth of different colors, shapes, and sizes that are sewn together.
patch·work (pach′wûrk′) □*noun*

patent *noun* A document given by the government to an inventor or company that gives the person or company the right to be the only one to make, use, or sell an invention for a certain number of years.
□*verb* To get a patent for: *The scientist patented her invention.*
pat·ent (pat′ənt) □*noun, plural* **patents**
□*verb* **patented, patenting, patents**

patent leather *noun* Leather with a smooth, hard, shiny surface, used to make shoes, belts, and pocketbooks.

paternal *adjective* **1.** Of or like a father: *He has paternal feelings for his cousins.* **2.** Related to through one's father: *My paternal grandparents live in Maine.*
pa·ter·nal (pə tûr′nəl) □*adjective*

path *noun* **1.** A trail or way made for walking: *A brick path encircles the garden.* **2.** The line or route along which something or someone moves: *the path of a tornado.*
path (path) □*noun, plural* **paths** (pa*th*z or paths)

pathetic *adjective* Causing or making one feel pity or sorrow; sad: *She told the pathetic story of her life during the war.*
pa·thet·ic (pə thet′ik) □*adjective*

patience *noun* The condition or quality of being patient: *He has a lot of patience with very small children.*
pa·tience (pā′shəns) □*noun*

patient *adjective* Putting up with trouble, hardship, delay, and pain without complaining or getting angry: *If you'll be patient for a few minutes the waiter will take your order.*
□*noun* Someone who is under the treatment or care of a doctor.
pa·tient (pā′shənt) □*adjective* □*noun, plural* **patients**

patio *noun* **1.** An inside yard or court that has no roof but is open to the sky. **2.** A space or part of a yard next to a house or apartment that is usually paved with stones or tiles.
pat·i·o (pat′ē ō′) □*noun, plural* **patios**

patriot *noun* Someone who loves, supports, and defends his or her country.
pa·tri·ot (pā′trē ət) □*noun, plural* **patriots**

patriotic *adjective* Feeling or showing love and support for one's country: *a patriotic speech; a patriotic organization.*
pa·tri·ot·ic (pā′trē ot′ik) □*adjective*

patriotism *noun* Love of and loyalty to one's country.
pa·tri·ot·ism (pā′trē ə tiz′əm) □*noun*

patrol *verb* To go or walk through an area to guard it and make sure that there is no trouble: *police patrolling the neighborhood.*
□*noun* **1.** The act of patrolling: *The police are out on patrol.* **2.** A person or group of persons who do such a job: *the highway patrol.*
pa·trol (pə trōl′) □*verb* **patrolled, patrolling, patrols** □*noun, plural* **patrols**

patron *noun* **1.** Someone who helps or supports a person, group, or institution by giving money: *a patron of the opera company.* **2.** A regular customer of a store or restaurant: *One of our patrons has been buying our pies for twenty years.*
pa·tron (pā′trən) □*noun, plural* **patrons**

patter *verb* **1.** To make a series of quick, light taps: *Rain pattered against the window.* **2.** To walk or move softly or quickly.
pat·ter (pat′ər) □*verb* **pattered, pattering, patters**

pattern *noun* **1.** The way in which shapes and colors are arranged; design: *Her skirt has a pattern of blue and white squares.* **2.** A guide or model for something to be made: *a dress pattern.* **3.** A combination of actions or qualities that always happen the same way or in the same order: *the pattern of events.*
□*verb* To make or follow according to a special pattern or model: *That ballet is patterned after an English country dance.*
pat·tern (pat′ərn) □*noun, plural* **patterns**
□*verb* **patterned, patterning, patterns**

pause *verb* To stop for a short time in the middle of something: *The band paused for a few minutes between marches.*
□*noun* A short stop or rest.
pause (pôz) □*verb* **paused, pausing, pauses** □*noun, plural* **pauses**

pave *verb* To cover a road, sidewalk, driveway, or other area with pavement.
pave (pāv) □*verb* **paved, paving, paves**

pavement *noun* A hard covering or surface used on roads, streets, sidewalks, and driveways. Pavement may be made from concrete, tar, asphalt, or crushed rocks.
pave·ment (pāv′mənt) □*noun, plural* **pavements**

pavilion *noun* **1.** A fancy or elaborate tent. **2.** An open structure with a roof and often a raised wooden floor that is used at parks and fairs for amusement or shelter. **3.** A small building that is connected to a larger building.
pa·vil·ion (pə vil′yən) □*noun, plural* **pavilions**

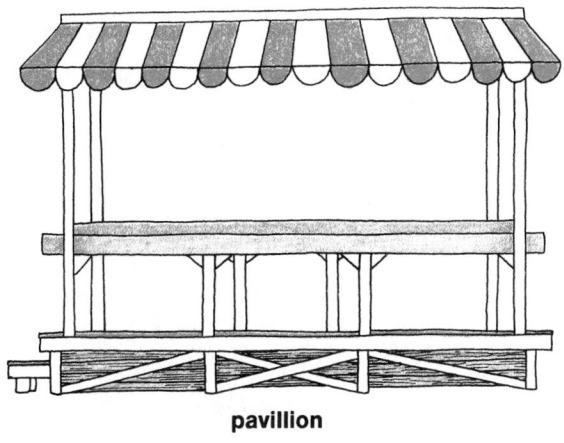
pavillion

paw *noun* The foot of an animal that has four feet and claws or nails.
□*verb* **1.** To touch, strike, or scrape with a paw or front foot: *The horse pawed the ground and neighed.* **2.** To handle in a clumsy or rude way: *Too many customers have pawed this merchandise.*
paw (pô) □*noun, plural* **paws** □*verb* **pawed, pawing, paws**

pawn¹ *verb* To give or leave something valuable with someone temporarily in exchange for a loan: *He pawned his bicycle in June, but he got it back in July by repaying the money.*
pawn (pôn) □*verb* **pawned, pawning, pawns**

pawn² *noun* **1.** The least valuable piece in the game of chess. **2.** Someone who is used or controlled by another who seeks to get something: *He used people as pawns in his schemes to get ahead.*
pawn (pôn) □*noun, plural* **pawns**

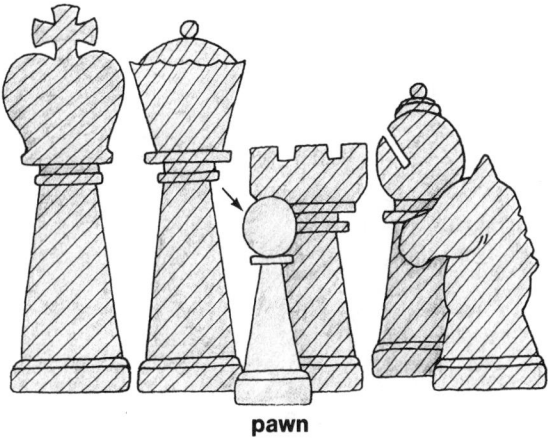
pawn

pay *verb* **1.** To give money to someone in exchange for goods or for work done: *How much will you pay me to clean the yard? She paid a hundred dollars for her new suit.* **2.** To give a particular amount of money that is owed or due: *We pay our taxes once a year.* **3.** To be worthwhile or helpful: *It doesn't pay to be mean to people.* **4.** To give or make: *Pay us another visit soon. She paid him a compliment on his singing voice.*
□*noun* Money given in return for work done; salary: *He wants a raise in pay.*
pay back To get even with; revenge: *He'll pay her back for that remark.*
pay for To suffer because of something: *Someday she will have to pay for all the trouble she caused.*
pay (pā) □*verb* **paid, paying, pays** □*noun*

payment *noun* **1.** The act of paying: *Full payment must be made before we can get the new car.* **2.** Something that is paid: *We made our last car payment today.*
pay·ment (pā′mənt) □*noun, plural* **payments**

a	bat	ī	bite	o͞o	tool	*th*	feather
ā	make	î	fierce	ou	out	th	bath
â	dare	o	dot	u	nut	hw	wheat
ä	father	ō	no	û	turn	zh	measure
e	net	ô	law, for	ch	church	ə	about, open
ē	be	oi	soil	ng	ring		pencil, atom
i	dip	oo	look	sh	shade		circus

payroll   *noun* **1.** A list of all employees and their salaries: *a company with fifty workers on the payroll.* **2.** The total amount of money or salaries paid to employees at one time.
pay·roll (pā′rōl′) ☐*noun, plural* **payrolls**

PC An abbreviation for **personal computer.**

pea   *noun* One of the round green seeds of a plant that has long green pods. Peas are eaten as a vegetable.
pea (pē) ☐*noun, plural* **peas**

WORD HISTORY: **pea**

About 400 years ago the word *pea* had the same form in the singular and the plural. That form was *pease.* Because *pease* ended in an *s*-sound, it sounded like a plural. People began to drop the *s*-sound when they were using the word in the singular, and the modern form *pea* developed.

---

peace   *noun* **1.** Freedom from war or fighting. **2.** A condition of calm and order; tranquillity: *I need peace and quiet to do my homework.*
peace (pēs) ☐*noun*

peaceful   *adjective* **1.** Against war or fighting; liking to live in peace: *a peaceful country.* **2.** Calm and quiet; serene: *It's so peaceful in this church.*
peace·ful (pēs′fəl) ☐*adjective*

peace pipe   *noun* A pipe that North American Indians smoked in certain Native American ceremonies as a sign of friendship.

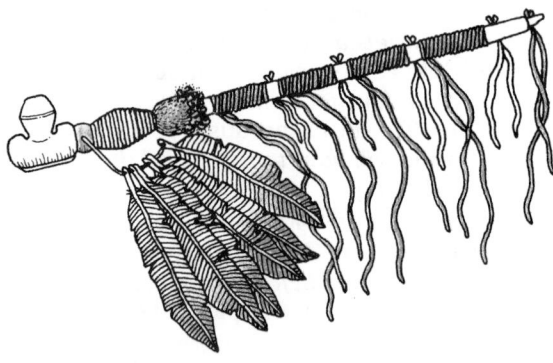

peace pipe

peach   *noun* **1.** A sweet, round, juicy fruit with fuzzy yellow or reddish skin and a pit with a hard shell. **2.** A light yellowish-pink color.
☐*adjective* Light yellowish pink.
peach (pēch) ☐*noun, plural* **peaches**
☐*adjective*

WORD HISTORY: **peach**

Peach comes from a Latin word meaning "Persian." The Romans called this fruit "the Persian fruit" because it was native to the ancient land of Persia.

---

peacock   *noun* The male peafowl. It has long, brilliant blue or green tail feathers with spots that look like eyes. These feathers can be spread out like a large fan.
pea·cock (pē′kok′) ☐*noun, plural* **peacocks**

peacock

peafowl   *noun* A large bird related to the pheasants; peacock or peahen.
pea·fowl (pē′foul′) ☐*noun, plural* **peafowls** or **peafowl**

peahen   *noun* The female peafowl. It does not have the bright colors of the peacock.
pea·hen (pē′hen′) ☐*noun, plural* **peahens**

peak   *noun* **1.** The pointed or narrow top of a mountain. **2.** A mountain. **3.** A pointed top or end: *The monument came to a peak.* **4.** The highest point of development or value: *She was at the peak of her career.* **5.** The round brim of a cap that sticks out in front.
peak (pēk) ☐*noun, plural* **peaks**

peal   *noun* **1.** A loud ringing of bells. **2.** A long, loud noise or series of noises: *a peal of laughter.*
☐*verb* To ring out in a peal or shout loudly: *The bells in the tower peal every hour.*
peal (pēl) ☐*noun, plural* **peals** ☐*verb*
  pealed, pealing, peals

peanut   *noun* A plant seed that resembles a nut. Peanuts grow in pods that ripen underground.
pea·nut (pē′nut′) ☐*noun, plural* **peanuts**

peanut butter   *noun* A soft food made by grinding roasted peanuts, used as a spread.

pear   *noun* A sweet, juicy, bell-shaped fruit with smooth yellowish or brown skin.
pear (pâr) ☐*noun, plural* **pears**

pearl *noun* **1.** A smooth whitish or grayish beadlike object with a soft shine that is formed inside the shells of oysters and is used as a gem. **2.** Something that looks like a pearl: *pearls of dew.* **3.** Something that is very good or valuable: *His words were pearls of wisdom.*
pearl (pûrl) □*noun, plural* **pearls**

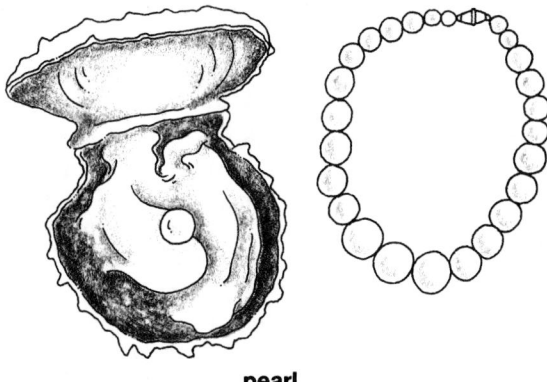

pearl

peasant *noun* Someone who belongs to the group or class of small farmers and farm workers in Europe.
peas·ant (pez′ ənt) □*noun, plural* **peasants**

peat *noun* A kind of rich soil found in bogs and marshes that is made up of decaying plants and used to improve soil and for fuel.
peat (pēt) □*noun*

pebble *noun* A small stone that has been made smooth and round by wind and water.
peb·ble (peb′ əl) □*noun, plural* **pebbles**

pecan *noun* An edible nut that grows on a tall tree and has a smooth, oval shell.
pe·can (pi **kän′** *or* pi **kan′**) □*noun, plural* **pecans**

peccary *noun* A tropical American animal that resembles a pig and has long, dark bristles.
pec·ca·ry (pek′ ə rē) □*noun, plural* **peccaries**

peccary

peck[1] *verb* **1.** To strike something with a beak or a pointed instrument: *The chickens pecked at the ground.* **2.** To pick up grain or other food with the beak: *The sparrows pecked up the grass seed on the lawn.*
□*noun* **1.** A short blow with the beak: *The angry bird gave the dog a peck on the nose.* **2.** A light, quick kiss: *a peck on the cheek.*
peck (pek) □*verb* **pecked, pecking, pecks** □*noun, plural* **pecks**

peck[2] *noun* **1.** A unit of measure for grain, vegetables, fruit, and other dry things, equal to one quarter of a bushel. **2.** A great deal: *She caused a peck of trouble.*
peck (pek) □*noun, plural* **pecks**

peculiar *adjective* **1.** Unusual or odd: *We were distressed by his peculiar behavior.* **2.** Belonging to a special or particular person, group, place, or thing: *Penguins are peculiar to the Southern Hemisphere.* —See Synonyms at **strange.**
pe·cu·liar (pi **kyōōl′** yər) □*adjective*

peculiarity *noun* **1.** Something that is peculiar or odd: *One of her peculiarities is that she will never sit in the front seat of a car.* **2.** The condition or quality of being peculiar: *the peculiarity of his spelling.*
pe·cu·li·ar·i·ty (pi kyōō′lē **ar′** i tē) □*noun, plural* **peculiarities**

pedal *noun* A lever that is worked by the foot, used to control a machine or instrument. □*verb* To use or operate the pedals of something: *pedal a bicycle.*
ped·al (ped′ əl) □*noun, plural* **pedals** □*verb* **pedaled, pedaling, pedals**

peddle *verb* To travel from place to place selling goods: *The salesman peddled books from town to town.*
ped·dle (ped′ əl) □*verb* **peddled, peddling, peddles**

peddler *noun* A person who travels from place to place selling goods.
ped·dler (ped′lər) □*noun, plural* **peddlers**

pedestal *noun* A base on which something stands: *The statue was placed on a marble pedestal.*

a bat	ī bite	ōō tool	*th* feather
ā make	î fierce	ou out	th bath
â dare	o dot	u nut	hw wheat
ä father	ō no	û turn	zh measure
e net	ô law, for	ch church	ə about, open
ē be	oi soil	ng ring	pencil, atom
i dip	oo look	sh shade	circus

ped·es·tal (ped′i stəl) □*noun, plural* **pedestals**

pedestrian *noun* Someone who travels on foot: *Only pedestrians are allowed in this park.* **pe·des·tri·an** (pə des′trē ən) □*noun, plural* **pedestrians**

pediatrician *noun* A doctor who treats children and babies. **pe·di·a·tri·cian** (pē′dē ə trish′ən) □*noun, plural* **pediatricians**

pedigree *noun* The line of ancestors of a person or animal. **ped·i·gree** (ped′i grē′) □*noun, plural* **pedigrees**

peek *verb* To look or glance quickly or secretly: *I peeked into the oven to see what we were going to have for dinner.*
□*noun* A quick or secret look or glance: *I'll take a peek and see if the baby is asleep.* **peek** (pēk) □*verb* **peeked, peeking, peeks** □*noun, plural* **peeks**

peel *noun* The skin or rind of certain fruits, such as an orange or banana.
□*verb* **1.** To remove the skin or outer covering from: *peel an apple.* **2.** To strip away; pull off: *He peeled the wrapper off the box.* **3.** To come off in thin strips or layers: *plaster peeling from the ceiling.* **4.** To lose or shed skin or other covering: *My sunburn is starting to peel.* **peel** (pēl) □*noun, plural* **peels** □*verb* **peeled, peeling, peels**

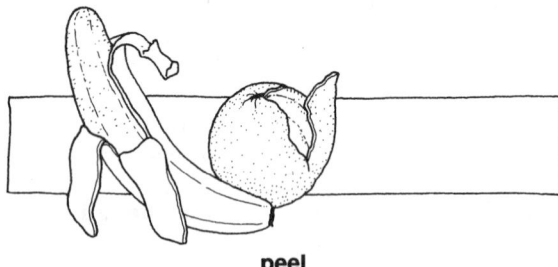

peel

peep¹ *noun* A weak, high sound, like that made by a young bird; chirp.
□*verb* To make a peep: *The little chicks began to peep because they were hungry.* **peep** (pēp) □*noun, plural* **peeps** □*verb* **peeped, peeping, peeps**

peep² *verb* **1.** To look quickly or secretly, especially through a small hole or from a hiding place; peek: *We peeped through the fence to watch the game.* **2.** To be able to be seen; become visible: *The sun peeped out from behind the clouds.*
□*noun* A quick look; peek. **peep** (pēp) □*verb* **peeped, peeping, peeps** □*noun, plural* **peeps**

peeper *noun* A small tree frog with a high, chirping call that is heard in the early spring. **peep·er** (pē′pər) □*noun, plural* **peepers**

peer¹ *verb* **1.** To look closely in order to see something clearly: *He peered at me through the curtains.* **2.** To come into view; appear: *The headlights of the car peered over the hill.* **peer** (pîr) □*verb* **peered, peering, peers**

peer² *noun* **1.** Someone who is equal to another in age, ability, or rank: *A person who is accused of a crime has a right to a trial by a jury of his peers.* **2.** Someone who belongs to one of the five highest ranks of the British nobility. **peer** (pîr) □*noun, plural* **peers**

peevish *adjective* Given to complaining a great deal or as a habit: *Our peevish neighbor always thought we were causing trouble and chased us away whenever we played near his house.* **pee·vish** (pē′vish) □*adjective*

peg *noun* A piece of wood or metal that is used to fasten things together, to plug a hole, or to hang things on.
□*verb* To fasten or plug with pegs. **peg** (peg) □*noun, plural* **pegs** □*verb* **pegged, pegging, pegs**

Pekingese *noun* A small dog with short legs, long hair, and a flat nose. The Pekingese was originally from China. **Pe·king·ese** (pē′ki nēz′) □*noun, plural* **Pekingese**

pelican *noun* A large bird with a long bill, webbed feet, and a large pouch under its lower bill for holding the fish it has caught. **pel·i·can** (pel′i kən) □*noun, plural* **pelicans**

pellet *noun* A very small, hard ball as of medicine, food, or paper. **pel·let** (pel′it) □*noun, plural* **pellets**

pell-mell *adverb* In hasty confusion: *The dogs escaped from the yard and ran pell-mell after every car that went by.* **pell-mell** (pel′mel′) □*adverb*

pelt¹ *noun* An animal skin with the hair or fur still on it. **pelt** (pelt) □*noun, plural* **pelts**

pelt² *verb* **1.** To hit or strike with something over and over: *The girls were laughing as they pelted each other with pillows.* **2.** To beat against over and over: *Sleet pelted the win-*

dows with a steady sound.
pelt (pelt) □*verb* **pelted, pelting, pelts**

pelt

pelvic *adjective* Of or having to do with the pelvis.
pel·vic (pel′vik) □*adjective*

pelvis *noun* The part of the skeleton made up of the bones that form the hips and contain the organs of the lower abdomen. The pelvis rests on the legs and supports the spine.
pel·vis (pel′vis) □*noun, plural* **pelvises**

pen¹ *noun* An instrument for writing with ink.
pen (pen) □*noun, plural* **pens**

WORD HISTORY: pen¹

The word *pen¹* comes from a Latin word that originally meant ''feather.'' By the Middle Ages the Latin word also meant ''a pen made from a feather.''

---

pen² *noun* A small, fenced area in which animals are kept.
□*verb* To put or keep in or as if in a pen: *The farmer pens the goats at night.*
pen (pen) □*noun, plural* **pens** □*verb* **penned, penning, pens**

penalize *verb* To give a punishment to: *The coach penalizes any player who breaks training.*
pe·nal·ize (pē′nə līz′) □*verb* **penalized, penalizing, penalizes**

penalty *noun* **1.** A punishment set by law for a crime: *The criminal got a penalty of twenty years in jail.* **2.** Something that must be given up for an offense: *I had to pay a fine as the penalty for losing the library book.* **3.** A loss or disadvantage placed on a team or player in various sports for breaking the rules.
pen·al·ty (pen′əl tē) □*noun, plural* **penalties**

pence *noun* A plural of **penny.**
pence (pens) □*noun*

pencil *noun* A thin stick of a hard material inside a covering of wood, used for writing or drawing.
□*verb* To write or draw with a pencil: *She penciled in the answer at the bottom of the page.*
pen·cil (pen′səl) □*noun, plural* **pencils**
□*verb* **penciled, penciling, pencils**

pendant *noun* Something hanging from something else, such as a piece of jewelry hanging from a necklace or bracelet.
pen·dant (pen′dənt) □*noun, plural* **pendants**

pendulum *noun* A weight hung by a cord, chain, or bar so that it can freely swing back and forth.
pen·du·lum (pen′jə ləm) □*noun, plural* **pendulums**

penetrate *verb* **1.** To go into or through: *The arrow penetrated the target. Dampness penetrated the house.* **2.** To study and understand: *Many scholars have tried to penetrate the mystery of these ancient ruins.*
pen·e·trate (pen′i trāt′) □*verb* **penetrated, penetrating, penetrates**

penguin *noun* A sea bird with webbed feet and narrow wings that look like flippers. Penguins cannot fly, but use their wings for swimming. Many penguins live in or near Antarctica.
pen·guin (peng′gwin) □*noun, plural* **penguins**

penicillin *noun* An antibiotic drug made from a mold and used to kill bacteria that cause certain diseases and infections.
pen·i·cil·lin (pen′i sil′ən) □*noun*

peninsula *noun* A piece of land that is almost surrounded by water and connected to a larger body of land. Most of Florida is a peninsula.
pen·in·su·la (pə nin′sə lə *or* pə nins′yə lə)
□*noun, plural* **peninsulas**

WORD HISTORY: peninsula

Peninsula comes from a Latin word that literally means ''almost an island.''

---

a	bat	ī	bite	ōō	tool	*th*	feather
ā	make	î	fierce	ou	out	th	bath
â	dare	ō	dot	u	nut	hw	wheat
ä	father	ō	no	û	turn	zh	measure
e	net	ô	law, for	ch	church	ə	about, open
ē	be	oi	soil	ng	ring		pencil, atom
i	dip	oo	look	sh	shade		circus

penitentiary *noun* A prison for people who are found guilty of serious crimes.
pen·i·ten·tia·ry (pen′i **ten′**shə rē) ☐*noun, plural* **penitentiaries**

penknife *noun* A small pocketknife.
pen·knife (pen′nīf′) ☐*noun, plural* **penknives**

penmanship *noun* The art, skill, style, or manner of handwriting.
pen·man·ship (pen′mən ship′) ☐*noun*

pennant *noun* A long, narrow flag shaped like a triangle, used for giving signals or as an emblem.
pen·nant (pen′ənt) ☐*noun, plural* **pennants**

penniless *adjective* **1.** Having no money at all. **2.** Very poor: *a story about how a penniless young man became rich and famous.*
pen·ni·less (pen′ē lis) ☐*adjective*

penny *noun* **1.** A United States or Canadian coin worth ¹/₁₀₀ of a dollar; cent. **2.** A British coin worth ¹/₁₀₀ of a pound.
pen·ny (pen′ē) ☐*noun, plural* **pennies** or **pence** *(for sense 2).*

penny pincher *noun* A person who is very stingy with money.
pen·ny pinch·er (pen′ē pin′chər) ☐*noun, plural* **penny pinchers**

pen pal *noun* A friend made and known through the exchange of letters.

pension *noun* A sum of money paid regularly to someone who has retired from work.
pen·sion (pen′shən) ☐*noun, plural* **pensions**

pentagon *noun* A geometric figure that has five sides and five angles.
pen·ta·gon (pen′tə gon′) ☐*noun, plural* **pentagons**

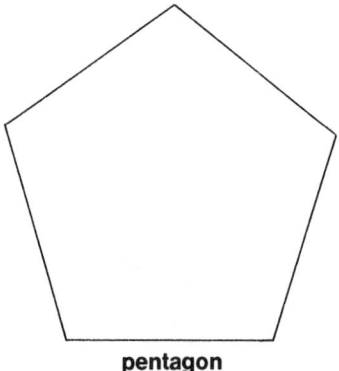

pentagon

penthouse *noun* An apartment located on the roof of a building.

pent·house (pent′hous′) ☐*noun, plural* **penthouses**

pent-up *adjective* Not given expression or release: *the pent-up excitement of the children waiting for the party to begin.*
pent-up (pent′up′) ☐*adjective*

penultimate *adjective* Next to last: *The penultimate letter in the word "penultimate" is "t."* ☐*noun* The next to the last one.
pe·nul·ti·mate (pi **nul′**tə mit), ☐*adjective* ☐*noun, plural* **penultimates**

peony *noun* A garden plant with large pink, red, or white flowers.
pe·o·ny (pē′ə nē) ☐*noun, plural* **peonies**

people *noun* **1.** Human beings. **2.** A group of people sharing the same religion, culture, and language and often united under one national government: *primitive peoples; the Chinese people.* **3.** Ordinary people as distinguished from an upper class: *the voice of the people.* ☐*verb* To give a population to: *Thousands of immigrants peopled the new territory.*
peo·ple (pē′pəl) ☐*noun, plural* **peoples** *(only for noun sense 2)* ☐*verb* **peopled, peopling, peoples**

pep *noun* High spirits or energy.
pep (pep) ☐*noun*

pepper *noun* **1.** A seasoning that is made from the dried, blackish berries of a vine and has a very sharp taste. **2.** The hollow green or red fruit of a bushy plant, eaten as a vegetable or used as a spice. Some kinds have a mild taste, and some have a very sharp taste. ☐*verb* **1.** To season with pepper. **2.** To sprinkle or hit with many small things: *We peppered the ground with acorns to attract the squirrels.*
pep·per (pep′ər) ☐*noun, plural* **peppers** ☐*verb* **peppered, peppering, peppers**

peppercorn *noun* The dried, blackish berry of the pepper vine.
pep·per·corn (pep′ər kôrn′) ☐*noun, plural* **peppercorns**

peppermint *noun* **1.** A plant with a strong, pleasant taste and smell. **2.** Oil from this plant, used to flavor candy, chewing gum, and other things. **3.** A candy flavored with peppermint.
pep·per·mint (pep′ər mint′) ☐*noun, plural* **peppermints**

pepperoni *noun* A spicy beef and pork sausage.
pep·per·o·ni (pep′ə **rō′**nē) ☐*noun, plural* **pepperonis**

pep talk *noun* A speech given by a leader to fill a group with enthusiasm and encouragement: *The team played much better after the coach's pep talk.*

per *preposition* For every: *a hundred dollars per week.*
> **per** (pûr) □*preposition*

perceive *verb* **1.** To become aware of by seeing, hearing, tasting, smelling, or touching: *The nurse perceived a swelling in the patient's knee when she touched it.* **2.** To get an understanding of: *I don't perceive the point of your remarks.*
> **per·ceive** (pər **sēv′**) □*verb* **perceived, perceiving, perceives**

percent or **per cent** *noun* One part in a hundred: *Eighty percent of the students passed the test.* The symbol for percent (%) is used with a number: *This fruit punch is 90% water.*
> **per·cent** or **per cent** (pər **sent′**) □*noun*

percentage *noun* **1.** A fraction that is understood to have 100 as its denominator. **2.** A part of a whole: *He saves a certain percentage of his income every month.*
> **per·cent·age** (pər **sen′** tij) □*noun, plural* **percentages**

perch¹ *noun* **1.** A branch or rod that a bird holds with its claws while resting. **2.** Any resting place, especially one that is up high: *We watched the parade from our perch on top of the roof.*
> □*verb* **1.** To land or rest on or as if on a perch: *The owl perched on the roof.* **2.** To be in a high position: *The helicopter was perched on the rim of the canyon.*
> **perch** (pûrch) □*noun, plural* **perches** □*verb* **perched, perching, perches**

perch

perch² *noun* A fish that is used for food. Some kinds of perch live in fresh water, and others live in salt water.
> **perch** (pûrch) □*noun, plural* **perch** or **perches**

percolate *verb* To pass or cause something, such as a liquid, to pass through a porous substance or filter: *water percolated through the sand.*
> **per·co·late** (pûr′ kə lāt′) □*verb* **percolated, percolating, percolates**

percussion instrument *noun* A musical instrument, such as a drum, xylophone, or piano, in which sound is made by striking one thing against another.
> **per·cus·sion instrument** (pər **kush′** ən) □*noun*

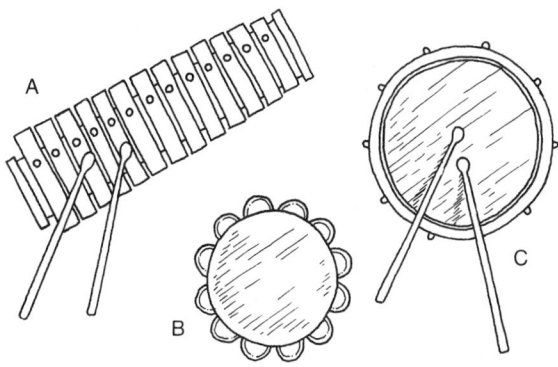
percussion instrument
*(A)*xylophone, *(B)*tambourine, *(C)*drum

peregrine falcon *noun* A gray and white falcon that is used for hunting.
> **per·e·grine falcon** (per′ ə grin) □*noun*

perennial *adjective* **1.** Lasting a long time: *a perennial problem.* **2.** Having a life span of more than two years: *perennial plants.*
> □*noun* A plant with a life span of more than two years.
> **per·en·ni·al** (pə **ren′** ē əl) □*adjective* □*noun, plural* **perennials**

perfect *adjective* **1.** Completely free from mistakes, omissions, or defects: *a perfect piece of silk.* **2.** Completely right or suitable: *She's*

a bat	ī bite	oͦo tool	*th* feather
ā make	î fierce	ou out	th bath
â dare	o dot	u nut	hw wheat
ä father	ō no	û turn	zh measure
e net	ô law, for	ch church	ə about, open
ē be	oi soil	ng ring	pencil, atom
i dip	oo look	sh shade	circus

the perfect person for the job. **3.** Excellent in every way: *a perfect traveling companion.*
□*verb* To make perfect or complete: *It took them months to perfect the experiment.*
per·fect□*adjective* (**pûr′**fikt) □*verb* (pər**fekt′**) **perfected, perfecting, perfects**

perfection *noun* **1.** The act of perfecting: *The perfection of the model airplane occupied all his time.* **2.** The condition of being perfect: *It took many years to bring the design to perfection.*
per·fec·tion (pər **fek′**shən) □*noun*

perfectly *adverb* **1.** In a perfect manner: *The shoes fit perfectly.* **2.** To a perfect degree: *This circle is perfectly round.* **3.** Completely; totally: *We had a perfectly wonderful time in Europe.*
per·fect·ly (**pûr′**fikt lē) □*adverb*

perforate *verb* **1.** To punch a hole or holes in: *The paper was perforated to fit the binder.* **2.** To punch rows of holes in something to make it easy to pull apart: *These labels are perforated so that they can be removed one at a time.*
per·fo·rate (**pûr′**fə rāt′) □*verb* **perforated, perforating, perforates**

perform *verb* **1.** To begin and carry through to the end; do: *The science pupils performed a new experiment.* **2.** To sing, dance, act, play a musical instrument, or do tricks in front of people: *The pianists performed a duet for their guests.*
per·form (pər **fôrm′**) □*verb* **performed, performing, performs**

performance *noun* **1.** The act of performing: *Your performance in the debate was outstanding.* **2.** The way in which something or someone works: *Engineers will test the performance of these tires.* **3.** A public entertainment, such as a play or concert.
per·form·ance (pər **fôr′**məns) □*noun, plural* **performances**

performer *noun* Someone who acts, sings, dances, plays a musical instrument, or entertains an audience in some way.
per·form·er (pər **fôr′**mər) □*noun, plural* **performers**

perfume *noun* **1.** A pleasant-smelling liquid made from flowers. **2.** A pleasant smell.
□*verb* To put on or fill with perfume: *The scent of lilacs perfumed the garden.*
per·fume□*noun* (**pûr′**fyo͞om), *plural* **perfumes** □*verb* (pər **fyo͞om′**) **perfumed, perfuming, perfumes**

perhaps *adverb* Maybe; possibly: *Perhaps she'll change her mind.*
per·haps (pər **haps′**) □*adverb*

peril *noun* **1.** The chance of harm or loss: *He was in peril of drowning.* **2.** Something dangerous: *He was such a bad driver that he was a peril to others on the road.*
per·il (**per′**əl) □*noun, plural* **perils**

perimeter *noun* **1.** The outer boundary enclosing a figure or an area. **2.** The length of the boundary enclosing a figure or an area.
pe·rim·e·ter (pə **rim′**i tər) □*noun, plural* **perimeters**

period *noun* **1.** A portion of time: *a study period. The medieval period in Europe lasted about a thousand years.* **2.** The punctuation mark (.) used at the end of certain sentences and after many abbreviations.
pe·ri·od (**pîr′**ē əd) □*noun, plural* **periods**

periodic *adjective* Happening at regular periods of time: *a periodic visit to the barber.*
pe·ri·od·ic (pîr′ē **od′**ik) □*adjective*

periodical *noun* A publication that is printed at regular intervals.
pe·ri·od·i·cal (pîr′ē **od′**i kəl) □*noun, plural* **periodicals**

periscope *noun* An instrument with mirrors or prisms that allows a view of something that a person cannot see directly. Periscopes are used in submarines.
per·i·scope (**per′**i skōp′) □*noun, plural* **periscopes**

periscope

perish *verb* To pass from existence; die: *Fossils show that many forms of life have perished from the earth.*
per·ish (**per′**ish) □*verb* **perished, perishing, perishes**

perishable *adjective* Likely to decay or spoil easily: *Milk and butter are perishable foods.*
per·ish·a·ble (**per′**i shə bəl) □*adjective*

periwinkle[1] *noun* A small sea snail that is sometimes eaten as food.
per·i·win·kle (per′i wing′kəl) ◻*noun, plural* **periwinkles**

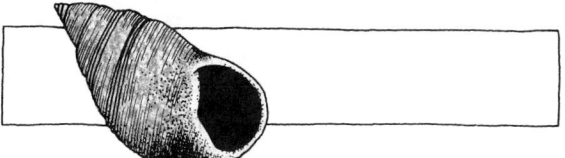
periwinkle

periwinkle[2] *noun* A trailing vine with shiny evergreen leaves and blue flowers.
per·i·win·kle (per′i wing′kəl) ◻*noun, plural* **periwinkles**

perjury *noun* Lying when one has sworn to tell the truth.
per·ju·ry (pûr′jə rē) ◻*noun, plural* **perjuries**

perk *verb* To raise in a brisk or alert way: *The dog perked his ears and growled.*
  perk up 1. To become or cause to become lively or bright again: *A chat with my best friend always perks me up.* **2.** To make more attractive: *The new curtains perked up the kitchen.*
perk (pûrk) ◻*verb* **perked, perking, perks**

permanent *adjective* Likely or meant to last for a long time: *The injury left a permanent scar on her thumb.*
per·ma·nent (pûr′mə nənt) ◻*adjective*

permission *noun* Agreement to let someone do or have something: *The boy got permission to leave class early.*
per·mis·sion (pər mish′ən) ◻*noun*

permit *verb* **1.** To give permission to; allow: *Did you permit her to drive the car?* **2.** To provide an opportunity: *If time permits, we'll stop by to see you.*
  ◻*noun* A written order or license that allows a person to do something: *a permit to dig for clams on this beach.*
per·mit (pər mit′) ◻*verb* **permitted, permitting, permits** ◻*noun* (pûr′mit *or* pər mit′), *plural* **permits**

SYNONYMS: permit, let

These verbs mean to give permission to: *The teacher does not permit us to talk in class. My parents said they'll let me have a dog.*

---

pernicious *adjective* **1.** Causing death or serious injury: *a pernicious disease.* **2.** Causing great harm; destructive: *Gambling is a pernicious habit.*
per·ni·cious (pər nish′əs) ◻*adjective*

perpendicular *adjective* **1.** Crossing at or making a right angle or angles: *perpendicular lines.* **2.** At right angles to the horizon; vertical: *The flag pole is perpendicular to the ground.*
per·pen·dic·u·lar (pûr′pen dik′yə lər) ◻*adjective*

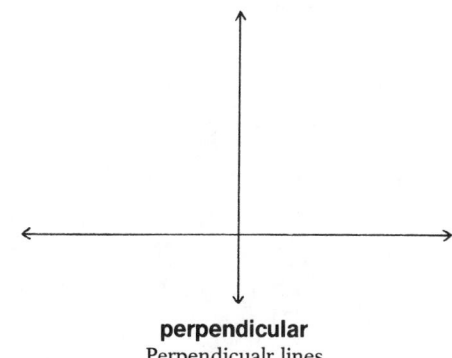
perpendicular
Perpendicualr lines

perpetrate *verb* To carry out; commit: *We tried to find out who perpetrated those practical jokes.*
per·pe·trate (pûr′pi trāt′) ◻*verb* **perpetrated, perpetrating, perpetrates**

perpetual *adjective* **1.** Lasting forever: *the perpetual gloom of the deep forest.* **2.** Repeated again and again or going on without stopping: *the perpetual pounding of the waves.*
per·pet·u·al (pər pech′ ⌒oo əl) ◻*adjective*

perplex *verb* To confuse or puzzle: *The strange ending of the movie perplexed me.*
per·plex (pər pleks′) ◻*verb* **perplexed, perplexing, perplexes**

persecute *verb* To treat continually in a cruel way, especially because of political or religious beliefs.
per·se·cute (pûr′si kyo̅o̅t′) ◻*verb* **persecuted, persecuting, persecutes**

persecution *noun* The act of persecuting or the condition of being persecuted: *the persecution of the early Christians by the Romans.*

a	bat	ī	bite	o̅o̅	tool	*th*	feather
ā	make	î	fierce	ou	out	th	bath
â	dare	o	dot	u	nut	hw	wheat
ä	father	ō	no	û	turn	zh	measure
e	net	ô	law, for	ch	church	ə	about, open
ē	be	oi	soil	ng	ring		pencil, atom
i	dip	oo	look	sh	shade		circus

per·se·cu·tion (pûr'si **kyoō'** shən) □*noun,* *plural* **persecutions**

persevere *verb* To continue doing something or trying to do something in spite of opposition or discouragement: *I persevered in my attempt to learn Latin.*
per·se·vere (pûr'sə **vîr'**) □*verb* **persevered, persevering, perseveres**

Persian cat *noun* A cat with long silky fur that is often kept as a pet.
Per·sian cat (pûr'zhən) □*noun*

persian cat

persimmon *noun* An edible, orange-red fruit with juicy pulp that becomes sweet only when it is fully ripe.
per·sim·mon (pər **sim'**ən) □*noun, plural* **persimmons**

persist *verb* **1.** To keep on doing something no matter what happens: *Although he fell many times, the baby persisted in trying to walk across the room.* **2.** To continue to happen or exist; last: *The storm persisted for a week.*
per·sist (pər **sist'**) □*verb* **persisted, persisting, persists**

persistent *adjective* **1.** Refusing to give up or let go: *The persistent detective solved the case.* **2.** Lasting for a long time: *a persistent fever.*
per·sist·ent (pər **sis'**tənt) □*adjective*

person *noun* **1.** A living human being. **2.** The body of a living human being: *He had no money on his person.*
　in person In one's own physical presence: *She applied for the job in person.*
per·son (pûr'sən) □*noun, plural* **persons**

personal *adjective* **1.** Of a certain person; private: *I keep my personal papers in a locked drawer.* **2.** Done or made in person: *She granted a personal interview to the reporter.* **3.** Of the body: *personal hygiene.*
per·son·al (pûr'sə nəl) □*adjective*

personal computer *noun* A small computer for use by a person at home, at school, or in an office.

personality *noun* **1.** The characteristics of behavior and feelings that make one person different from everyone else: *He has a warm, friendly personality.* **2.** A famous or important person: *Many sports personalities came to the opening game of the season.*
per·son·al·i·ty (pûr'sə **nal'**i tē) □*noun, plural* **personalities**

personally *adverb* **1.** Without the help of others; by oneself: *I will do the job personally.* **2.** As far as oneself is concerned: *Personally, I think you're right.*
per·son·al·ly (pûr'sə nə lē) □*adverb*

personify *verb* **1.** To think of an inanimate object or idea as having the qualities of a living being. **2.** To represent or embody an abstract quality or idea: *In some fables the lion personifies pride and majesty.*
per·son·i·fy (pər **son'**ə fī') □*verb* **personified, personifying, personifies**

personnel *noun* The people who work for a company or organization: *This cafeteria is only for personnel of the company.*
per·son·nel (pûr'sə **nel'**) □*noun*

perspective *noun* **1.** The way of drawing objects on a flat surface so that they appear to be the same, as in distance and depth, as when seen by the eye. **2.** A point of view: *From my perspective the problem is not very serious.*
per·spec·tive (pər **spek'**tiv) □*noun, plural* **perspectives**

perspiration *noun* **1.** The salty moisture given off through the skin by the sweat glands; sweat: *She wiped the perspiration from her face.* **2.** The act of perspiring: *Perspiration is an important bodily function.*
per·spi·ra·tion (pûr'spə **rā'**shən) □*noun*

perspire *verb* To give off perspiration; sweat.
per·spire (pər **spīr'**) □*verb* **perspired, perspiring, perspires**

persuade *verb* To cause someone to do or believe something by arguing or reasoning; convince: *She persuaded her father to let her go to the dance.*
per·suade (pər **swād'**) □*verb* **persuaded, persuading, persuades**

persuasion *noun* **1.** The act of persuading. **2.** The ability to persuade.
per·sua·sion (pər **swā'**zhən) □*noun*

pertain *verb* To belong to or have to do with; be related to: *all the data pertaining to the experiment.*
per·tain (pər tān′) □*verb* **pertained, pertaining, pertains**

pervade *verb* To be present throughout: *The scent of lilacs pervaded the air.*
per·vade (pər vād′) □*verb* **pervaded, pervading, pervades**

perverse *adjective* **1.** Inclined away from what is right or good: *perverse opinions.* **2.** Continuing in an error or fault in a stubborn, willful way: *perverse people who still believe the earth is flat.*
per·verse (pər vûrs′) □*adjective*

pesky *adjective* Troublesome and annoying: *a pesky fly buzzing around the picnic table.*
pes·ky (pes′kē) □*adjective* **peskier, peskiest**

peso *noun* A coin used in Mexico and certain other Latin-American countries.
pe·so (pā′sō) □*noun, plural* **pesos**

pessimistic *adjective* Believing that one's situation or things in general will not improve; gloomy: *We musn't be pessimistic about our chances of winning the game.*
pes·si·mis·tic (pes′ə mis′tik) □*adjective*

pest *noun* Someone or something that is irritating or troublesome: *That yapping dog is a pest.*
pest (pest) □*noun, plural* **pests**

pester *verb* To annoy or bother: *Stop pestering me with your complaints.* —See Synonyms at **annoy.**
pes·ter (pes′tər) □*verb* **pestered, pestering, pesters**

pesticide *noun* A chemical used to kill pests such as insects or rodents.
pes·ti·cide (pes′ti sīd′) □*noun, plural* **pesticides**

pestle *noun* A tool with a rounded end used for crushing or mashing things in a mortar.
pes·tle (pes′əl *or* pes′təl) □*noun, plural* **pestles**

pet *noun* **1.** An animal that a person keeps for pleasure and companionship. **2.** Someone who is a favorite: *He is his grandmother's pet.* □*adjective* **1.** Kept as a pet: *my pet turtle.* **2.** Favorite: *the scientist's pet project.* □*verb* To stroke or pat gently: *pet a horse.*
pet (pet) □*noun, plural* **pets** □*adjective* □*verb* **petted, petting, pets**

petal *noun* One of the usually brightly colored leaflike parts of a flower.
pet·al (pet′əl) □*noun, plural* **petals**

petition *noun* A special or formal request, usually in writing, to someone in charge: *The neighbors submitted a petition asking the town to put up traffic lights near the school.* □*verb* To make a formal request: *The citizens petitioned the legislature for a change in the law.*
pe·ti·tion (pə tish′ən) □*noun, plural* **petitions** □*verb* **petitioned, petitioning, petitions**

petrel *noun* A small sea bird that flies over the open ocean far from land.
pet·rel (pet′rəl) □*noun, plural* **petrels**

petrify *verb* **1.** To turn plant or animal material into stone. Water petrifies wood when it seeps into the wood of a dead tree. Over a long period of time, the water leaves minerals that replace the dead wood cells. **2.** To daze with fear or surprise: *The ghost story she told petrified me.*
pet·ri·fy (pet′rə fī′) □*verb* **petrified, petrifying, petrifies**

petroleum *noun* A kind of dark yellowish-black oil that is found below the ground. Gasoline, fuel oil, and kerosene are made from petroleum.
pe·tro·le·um (pə trō′lē əm) □*noun*

petticoat *noun* A skirt or slip worn by girls and women as an undergarment.
pet·ti·coat (pet′ē kōt′) □*noun, plural* **petticoats**

petty *adjective* **1.** Having no importance or significance; trivial: *petty problems that can ruin your day.* **2.** Having limited interests or views: *petty people who care only for their own well-being and do not think about the good of people in general.*
pet·ty (pet′ē) □*adjective* **pettier, pettiest**

petunia *noun* A garden plant with white, reddish, or purple flowers shaped like funnels.
pe·tu·nia (pə too′nyə *or* pə tyoo′nyə) □*noun, plural* **petunias**

a	bat	ī	bite	oo	tool	*th*	feather
ā	make	î	fierce	ou	out	th	bath
â	dare	o	dot	u	nut	hw	wheat
ä	father	ō	no	û	turn	zh	measure
e	net	ô	law, for	ch	church	ə	about, open
ē	be	oi	soil	ng	ring		pencil, atom
i	dip	oo	look	sh	shade		circus

pew *noun* A bench for people to sit on in a church.
pew (pyōō) ▢*noun, plural* **pews**

pewee *noun* A small, brownish North American bird that makes a sound resembling its name.
pe·wee (pē′ wē) ▢*noun, plural* **pewees**

pewee

pewter *noun* A metal made from tin mixed with copper or lead, used to make dishes, candlesticks, and other utensils.
pew·ter (pyōō′tər) ▢*noun*

phantom *noun* An unreal image that can be sensed in some way, such as by hearing: *The bells he heard were just a phantom of his imagination.*
phan·tom (fan′təm) ▢*noun, plural* **phantoms**

pharaoh *noun* The title of the rulers of ancient Egypt.
phar·aoh (fâr′ō) ▢*noun, plural* **pharaohs**

pharmacist *noun* Someone who is trained to prepare drugs and medicines; druggist.
phar·ma·cist (fär′mə sist) ▢*noun, plural* **pharmacists**

pharmacy *noun* A place where drugs are prepared and sold; drugstore.
phar·ma·cy (fär′mə sē) ▢*noun, plural* **pharmacies**

phase *noun* **1.** A clear or distinct stage of development: *The first phase of building the house is to dig the foundation.* **2.** A part, side, or aspect: *Every phase of your training program seems well prepared.* **3.** Any of the forms in which the moon or the planets appear at any given time.
phase (fāz) ▢*noun, plural* **phases**

pheasant *noun* A large, brightly colored bird with a long tail, often hunted as game.
pheas·ant (fez′ənt) ▢*noun, plural* **pheasants**

phenomenon *noun* **1.** A fact or event that can be seen, heard, or otherwise known: *A comet is a natural phenomenon.* **2.** Someone or something that is unusual or extraordinary: *As a dancer she is a phenomenon.*
phe·nom·e·non (fi nom′ə non′) ▢*noun, plural* **phe·nom·e·na** (fi nom′ə nə) or **phenomenons**

phew *interjection* Used to express relief, fatigue, surprise, or disgust.
phew (fyōō) ▢*interjection*

philanthropy *noun* **1.** The desire or effort to help other people. **2.** An organization that gives or receives charity.
phil·an·thro·py (fi lan′thrə pē) ▢*noun, plural* **philanthropies**

philodendron *noun* A plant with glossy leaves, often grown as a house plant.
phil·o·den·dron (fil′ə den′drən) ▢*noun, plural* **philodendrons**

philodendron

philosopher *noun* Someone who studies philosophy.
phi·los·o·pher (fi los′ə fər) ▢*noun, plural* **philosophers**

philosophy *noun* **1.** The study of the truths and ideas about right and wrong, about knowledge, and about values. **2.** A system of ideas based on this kind of study. **3.** A person's own beliefs and opinions about life and the world.
phi·los·o·phy (fi los′ə fē) ▢*noun, plural* **philosophies**

phlegm *noun* Thick mucus found in the respiratory organs.
phlegm (flem) ▢*noun*

phlox *noun* A plant with clusters of reddish, purple, or white flowers.
phlox (floks) ▢*noun, plural* **phlox** or **phloxes**

phobia *noun* A strong fear or dislike of something, especially one that has no reasonable cause: *He has a phobia about crossing bridges.*
pho·bi·a (fō′ bē ə) □*noun, plural* **phobias**

phoebe *noun* A small, grayish North American bird whose call sounds like its name.
phoe·be (fē′ bē) □*noun, plural* **phoebes**

phoebe

phone *noun* A telephone.
□*verb* To call by telephone.
phone (fōn) □*noun, plural* **phones** □*verb* **phoned, phoning, phones**

phonetic *adjective* Of, having to do with, or standing for spoken language or speech sounds.
pho·net·ic (fə net′ik) □*adjective*

phonograph *noun* A machine that picks up sounds from grooves cut into a record and plays these sounds through loudspeakers.
pho·no·graph (fō′ nə graf′) □*noun, plural* **phonographs**

phony *adjective* Not genuine or real; fake: *a phony one-dollar bill.*
□*noun* **1.** Something that is not genuine: *These pearls are phonies.* **2.** Someone who is not what he or she seems to be; impostor: *He says he's a spy but he's a phony.*
pho·ny (fō′ nē) □*noun, plural* **phonies**

phooey *interjection* Used to express disgust or scorn.
phoo·ey (foo′ ē) □*interjection*

phosphorus *noun* A poisonous chemical element that is found in white, yellow, red, and black forms and shines in the dark. Phosphorus is used to make matches, fireworks, and smoke bombs and is also widely used for detergents and fertilizers.
phos·pho·rus (fos′ fər əs) □*noun*

photo *noun* A photograph.
pho·to (fō′ tō) □*noun, plural* **photos**

photograph *noun* A picture formed by means of a camera on a surface that is sensitive to light.
□*verb* To take a photograph of: *A friend of ours photographed the wedding.*
pho·to·graph (fō′ tə graf′) □*noun, plural* **photographs** □*verb* **photographed, photographing, photographs**

photographer *noun* Someone who takes photographs, especially as a job.
pho·tog·ra·pher (fə tog′ rə fər) □*noun, plural* **photographers**

photographic *adjective* Of, resembling, or used in photography or a photograph: *a photographic lens; a photographic memory.*
pho·to·graph·ic (fō′tə graf′ ik) □*adjective*

photography *noun* The art or job of taking and making photographs.
pho·tog·ra·phy (fə tog′ rə fē) □*noun*

phrase *noun* **1.** A group of words that has meaning but is not a complete sentence. For example, *in the yard* is a phrase. **2.** A short saying.
□*verb* To express something in words.
phrase (frāz) □*noun, plural* **phrases** □*verb* **phrased, phrasing, phrases**

physical *adjective* **1.** Of the body rather than the mind or feelings: *physical health.* **2.** Solid or material: *physical objects.* **3.** Of or having to do with the natural features of the earth's surface: *He drew a physical map of the town showing just the valley, the creek, and the hills.*
phys·i·cal (fiz′ i kəl) □*adjective*

physical science *noun* Any of the sciences, such as physics, chemistry, and geology, that analyze the nature and properties of energy and matter that is not alive.

physician *noun* Someone who has a license to treat and care for people who are sick or hurt; medical doctor.
phy·si·cian (fi zish′ ən) □*noun, plural* **physicians**

physics *noun* The science of matter and energy and the laws that rule them, dealing with light, motion, sound, heat, electricity, and

a bat	ī bite	ōō tool	*th* feather
ā make	î fierce	ou out	th bath
â dare	o dot	u nut	hw wheat
ä father	ō no	û turn	zh measure
e net	ô law, for	ch church	ə about, open
ē be	oi soil	ng ring	pencil, atom
i dip	oo look	sh shade	circus

force.

phy·sics (**fiz'**iks) ▢*noun*

pi   *noun* A number that equals the quotient of the circumference of a circle divided by its diameter. Pi is equal to about 3.1416. Its symbol is π.

pi (pī) ▢*noun, plural* **pis**

pianist   *noun* Someone who plays the piano.

pi·an·ist (pē **an'**ist *or* pē'ə nist) ▢*noun, plural* **pianists**

piano   *noun* A large musical instrument with a keyboard and wire strings. When a key on the keyboard is struck, the movement makes a hammer hit a metal string to produce a tone.

pi·an·o (pē **an'**ō) ▢*noun, plural* **pianos**

WORD HISTORY: **piano**

The *piano* was originally called the "fortepiano." The word *fortepiano* was borrowed from an Italian name for the instrument that meant "loud and soft."

---

piccolo   *noun* A small flute that produces sounds in a range that is an octave higher than an ordinary flute.

pic·co·lo (**pik'**ə lō') ▢*noun, plural* **piccolos**

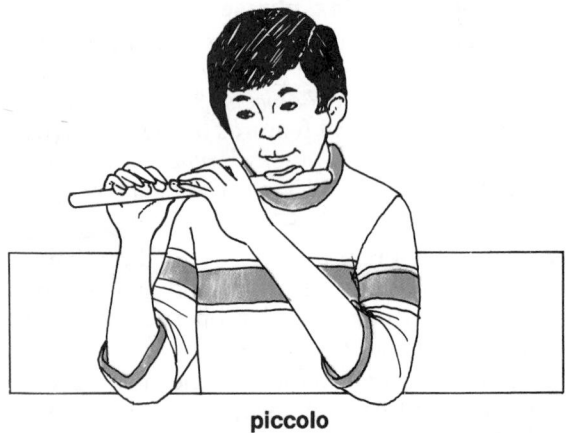

piccolo

pick¹   *verb* **1.** To choose or select: *I picked the winner in every race.* **2.** To gather with the fingers; pluck: *She went to the orchard to pick apples.* **3.** To dig at with something pointed: *She used a fork to pick the meat off the bones.* **4.** To cause on purpose; provoke: *Did he try to pick a fight with you?* **5.** To open without using a key: *He used a piece of wire to pick the lock.* **6.** To steal the contents of: *A thief picked her purse on the bus.* **7.** To pluck the strings of a musical instrument in order to play a tune: *We heard the cowboy picking out a song on his guitar.* —See Synonyms at **choose.**

▢*noun* **1.** A choice: *Take your pick of the desserts.* **2.** The best one: *These oranges are from the pick of the crop.*

  pick on 1. To tease or bully: *Stop picking on your sister.* **2.** To criticize someone for small, unimportant things.

  pick up 1. To lift up or take on: *She picked up her books and left the room.* **2.** To take on board a vehicle: *The bus will not pick up passengers between regular stops.* **3.** To receive: *The ship picked up a radio message from the lost plane.* **4.** To put things in order; clean up: *If you don't pick up the mess in your room, you can't go out.* **5.** To get by luck or chance: *He picked up a rare coin at a junk shop.* **6.** To get by study or experience; learn: *He picked up a knowledge of Spanish during his travels.*

pick (pik) ▢*verb* **picked, picking, picks** ▢*noun, plural* **picks**

pick²   *noun* **1.** A tool with a slightly curved bar pointed at both ends and fitted onto a long wooden handle. It is used for loosening or breaking up soil or other hard material. **2.** A pointed tool for breaking, piercing, or picking. **3.** A small, flat piece of plastic, metal, or bone for plucking the strings of a guitar or other instrument.

pick (pik) ▢*noun, plural* **picks**

pickerel   *noun* A freshwater fish that looks like the pike but is smaller.

pick·er·el (**pik'**ər əl) ▢*noun, plural* **pickerel** or **pickerels**

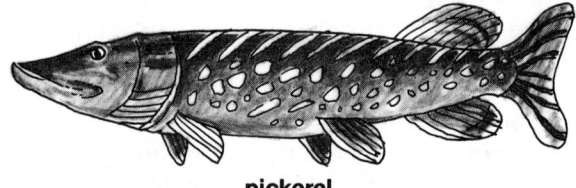

pickerel

picket   *noun* **1.** A pointed stake or spike that is driven into the ground to hold up a fence or keep something in place. **2.** Someone who walks in front of a place of work to protest something, usually during a strike.

▢*verb* To protest against something by walking as a picket: *We picketed the store because two workers had been fired unfairly.*

pick·et (**pik'**it) ▢*noun, plural* **pickets** ▢*verb* **picketed, picketing, pickets**

pickle   *noun* A food that has been preserved and flavored in vinegar or salt water: *cucumber pickles.*

▢*verb* To preserve in or flavor with vinegar or

salt water.

pick·le (pik′əl) □*noun, plural* **pickles** □*verb*
pickled, pickling, pickles

pickpocket *noun* Someone who steals from
a person's pocket or purse.
pick·pock·et (pik′pok′it) □*noun, plural*
pickpockets

pickup *noun* **1.** The act of picking up packages, mail, freight, or passengers for delivery
to another place: *an early mail pickup.* **2.** The
ability to increase speed quickly: *Does your
car have good pickup?* **3.** A pickup truck.
pick·up (pik′up′) □*noun, plural* **pickups**

pickup truck *noun* A small, light truck with
an open body and low sides, used for carrying
small loads.

picky *adjective* Very fussy or choosy: *a picky
eater.*
pick·y (pik′ē) □*adjective* **pickier, pickiest**

picnic *noun* A meal eaten outdoors.
□*verb* To have a picnic: *We're going to picnic
at the beach.*
pic·nic (pik′nik) □*noun, plural* **picnics**
□*verb* **picnicked, picnicking, picnics**

picture *noun* **1.** A painting, drawing, or photograph that represents someone or something: *an album filled with pictures of horses.*
2. The image on a television or movie screen.
3. A clear description in words: *His letters give
a good picture of life on a farm.* **4.** A good likeness or example: *The boy is the picture of his
father.* **5.** A motion picture; movie.
□*verb* **1.** To make a picture of: *The painter
pictured dancers rehearsing on a stage.* **2.** To
imagine: *I can't picture him riding a horse.*
3. To describe clearly: *She pictured the circus
to us very vividly.*
pic·ture (pik′chər) □*noun, plural* **pictures**
□*verb* **pictured, picturing, pictures**

picturesque *adjective* Charming; quaint: *a
picturesque fishing village.*
pic·tur·esque (pik′chə resk′) □*adjective*

pie *noun* A food made of a pastry shell filled
with fruit, meat, or custard and baked.
pie (pī) □*noun, plural* **pies**

piece *noun* **1.** A part that has been cut or
separated from a whole: *a piece of cheese.*
2. One part of a set or larger group: *a chess
piece; a rock 'n' roll band with five pieces.*
3. An artistic, musical, or literary work: *Did
you learn your piece for the piano recital?* **4.** An
example; instance: *That table is an excellent*

piece of work. **5.** A coin: *a gold piece.*
□*verb* To join the parts of: *We pieced the
statue together after it fell and broke.*
piece (pēs) □*noun, plural* **pieces** □*verb*
pieced, piecing, pieces

piecemeal *adverb* **1.** Piece by piece: *She acquired her set of china teacups piecemeal.* **2.** In
pieces; apart.
piece·meal (pēs′mēl′) □*adverb*

piece of eight *noun* An old Spanish silver
coin.

pier *noun* **1.** A platform built over water
from a shore, used as a landing place or protection for boats or ships. **2.** A pillar or other
supporting structure that holds up a bridge.
pier (pîr) □*noun, plural* **piers**

pier

pierce *verb* To run through or into; penetrate: *The pin pierced my finger. A ray of sunlight pierced the clouds.*
pierce (pîrs) □*verb* **pierced, piercing,
pierces**

piety *noun* **1.** The state of being faithful to
religious duties. **2.** The state of being faithful
to family duties.
pi·e·ty (pī′i tē) □*noun*

pig *noun* A hoofed animal with short legs, a
curly tail, bristles, and a blunt snout. Pigs are
raised for food.
pig (pig) □*noun, plural* **pigs**

pigeon *noun* A bird with short legs, a plump
body, and a small head.
pi·geon (pij′in) □*noun, plural* **pigeons**

a	bat	ī	bite	ōō	tool	*th*	feather
ā	make	î	fierce	ou	out	th	bath
â	dare	o	dot	u	nut	hw	wheat
ä	father	ō	no	û	turn	zh	measure
e	net	ô	law, for	ch	church	ə	about, open
ē	be	oi	soil	ng	ring		pencil, atom
i	dip	oo	look	sh	shade		circus

pigeon-toed *adjective* Having the toes turned inward.
pi·geon-toed (pij′ən tōd′) ☐*adjective*

piggyback *adverb* On the shoulders or back of another: *She carried the baby piggyback up the hill.*
pig·gy·back (pig′ē bak′) ☐*adverb*

piggyback

piglet *noun* A young pig.
pig·let (pig′lit) ☐*noun, plural* **piglets**

pigment *noun* A material or substance used to give color to something: *This paint color is a mixture of three different pigments.*
pig·ment (pig′mənt) ☐*noun, plural* **pigments**

pigpen *noun* **1.** A fenced area where pigs are kept. **2.** A very messy or disorderly place.
pig·pen (pig′pen′) ☐*noun, plural* **pigpens**

pigtail *noun* A braid of hair that hangs from the back of the head.
pig·tail (pig′tāl′) ☐*noun, plural* **pigtails**

pike *noun* A large freshwater fish with a narrow body and long jaws.
pike (pīk) ☐*noun, plural* **pike** or **pikes**

pile¹ *noun* **1.** A group of things heaped or stacked together, one on top of another; heap: *a pile of wood; a pile of laundry.* **2.** A large amount: *I did a pile of homework last night.* ☐*verb* **1.** To place or stack in a heap: *They piled the newspapers near the door.* **2.** To cover with a pile: *She piled her desk with books.*
pile (pīl) ☐*noun, plural* **piles** ☐*verb* **piled, piling, piles**

WORD HISTORY: **pile¹**

Pile¹ comes from a Latin word that means "pillar."

---

pile² *noun* A heavy beam of wood, concrete, or steel that is driven into the ground as a support or foundation for a structure: *The bridge is supported by concrete piles.*
pile (pīl) ☐*noun, plural* **piles**

pile³ *noun* The soft, thick fibers of yarn that form the surface of a carpet or of fabrics like velvet.
pile (pīl) ☐*noun, plural* **piles**

pilfer *verb* To steal a small amount or item.
pil·fer (pil′fər) ☐*verb* **pilfered, pilfering, pilfers**

pilgrim *noun* **1.** Someone who travels to a religious shrine or other sacred place. **2. Pilgrim** One of the English settlers who founded Plymouth, Massachusetts, in 1620.
pil·grim (pil′grim) ☐*noun, plural* **pilgrims**

WORD HISTORY: **pilgrim**

The word *pilgrim* comes from a Latin word that means "foreigner." Pilgrims traveling to visit a religious shrine would often journey through foreign lands.

Pilgrim

pill *noun* A small ball or tablet of medicine to be taken by mouth.
pill (pil) ☐*noun, plural* **pills**

pillar *noun* A column that is used to hold up or decorate a building, or that stands alone: *The roof of the temple was supported by eight pillars.*
pil·lar (pil′ər) ☐*noun, plural* **pillars**

pillory *noun* A wooden frame with holes for the head and hands. People who had done something wrong used to be locked into pillo-

ries in public as a punishment.
pil·lo·ry (**pil′ə** rē) □*noun, plural* **pillories**

pillory

pillow *noun* A cloth case stuffed with a soft material, used to support the head while resting or sleeping.
pil·low (**pil′ō**) □*noun, plural* **pillows**

pillowcase *noun* A cloth cover with an open end, used to fit over a pillow.
pil·low·case (**pil′ō** kās′) □*noun, plural* **pillowcases**

pilot *noun* **1.** Someone who operates an aircraft or spacecraft. **2.** Someone specially trained to steer large ships in and out of a harbor or through dangerous waters.
□*verb* To operate and set the course of a plane, ship, or other vehicle.
pi·lot (**pī′lət**) □*noun, plural* **pilots** □*verb* **piloted, piloting, pilots**

pilot light *noun* A small jet of gas that is kept burning in order to ignite a gas burner. Many furnaces and kitchen stoves have pilot lights.

pimiento or **pimento** *noun* A red pepper with a mild taste, often used to stuff olives or to give color and flavor to foods.
pi·mien·to or **pi·men·to** (pi **men′tō**) □*noun, plural* **pimientos** or **pimentos**

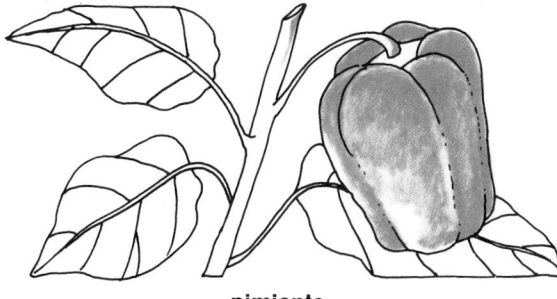

pimiento

pimple *noun* A small swelling on the skin, sometimes red and sore.
pim·ple (**pim′pəl**) □*noun, plural* **pimples**

pin *noun* **1.** A short, straight piece of wire with a round head at one end and a point at the other, used to fasten one thing to another. **2.** Something like a pin in shape or use: *hair pins.* **3.** An ornament fastened to clothing by a pin or clasp: *She has a diamond pin to wear on her dress.* **4.** One of the ten wooden clubs at which a ball is rolled in bowling.
□*verb* **1.** To fasten or attach with a pin: *The general pinned a medal on the corporal.* **2.** To cause to be unable to move.
　　on pins and needles Anxious or nervous: *I was on pins and needles before the test.*
pin (pin) □*noun, plural* **pins** □*verb* **pinned, pinning, pins**

pinafore *noun* A girl's garment without sleeves that looks like an apron.
pin·a·fore (**pin′ə** fôr′) □*noun, plural* **pinafores**

piñata *noun* A colorfully decorated container filled with candy and toys that is hung from the ceiling. In some countries it is a Christmas tradition for a blindfolded child to try to break the piñata open with a stick.
pi·ña·ta (pin **yä′tə**) □*noun, plural* **piñatas**

piñata

pinch *verb* **1.** To squeeze between the thumb and fingers or between edges: *My aunt*

a	bat	ī	bite	o͞o	tool	*th*	feather
ā	make	î	fierce	ou	out	th	bath
â	dare	o	dot	u	nut	hw	wheat
ä	father	ō	no	û	turn	zh	measure
e	net	ô	law, for	ch	church	ə	about, open
ē	be	oi	soil	ng	ring		pencil, atom
i	dip	oo	look	sh	shade		circus

pinched me on the cheek. **2.** To squeeze so hard as to cause pain: *These boots are pinching my toes.* **3.** To make thin or shriveled: *Hunger and cold had pinched their faces.*
□*noun* **1.** A squeeze or other pressure caused by pressing between the thumb and a finger or between edges. **2.** The amount that can be held between the thumb and a finger: *a pinch of sugar.* **3.** A time of trouble; emergency: *His parents will always help him in a pinch.*
pinch (pinch) □*verb* **pinched, pinching, pinches** □*noun, plural* **pinches**

pinch-hit *verb* In baseball, to bat for another player.
pinch-hit (pinch′hit′) □*verb* **pinch-hit, pinch-hitting, pinch-hits**

pincushion *noun* A small, firm cushion in which pins and needles are stuck when they are not being used.
pin·cush·ion (pin′koosh′ən) □*noun, plural* **pincushions**

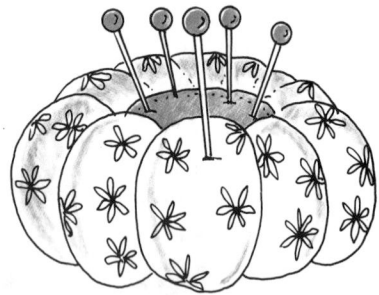

pincushion

pine *noun* **1.** An evergreen tree that has cones and clusters of leaves shaped like needles. **2.** The wood of a pine tree.
pine (pīn) □*noun, plural* **pines**

pineapple *noun* A large, juicy tropical fruit with rough, thorny skin and a tuft of narrow, prickly leaves at the top.
pine·ap·ple (pīn′ap′əl) □*noun, plural* **pineapples**

WORD HISTORY: pineapple

The word *pineapple* was originally used of the cone of a pine tree. The name came to be used for the tropical fruit because of its similarity to a pine cone.

Ping-Pong A trademark for table tennis and the equipment used in the game.
Ping-Pong (ping′pong′)

pink *noun* **1.** A light or pale red. **2.** A garden plant that has white or reddish flowers with a pleasant, spicy smell.
□*adjective* Light red or pale red.
pink (pingk) □*noun, plural* **pinks** □*adjective* **pinker, pinkest**

pinkie or **pinky** *noun* The fifth and smallest finger.
pink·ie or **pink·y** (ping′kē) □*noun, plural* **pinkies**

pinkish *adjective* Somewhat pink.
pink·ish (ping′kish) □*adjective*

pint *noun* A unit of measurement equal to sixteen fluid ounces, or one-half of a quart. A pint equals 0.47 liters.
pint (pīnt) □*noun, plural* **pints**

pinto *noun* A horse with spots or other markings that are not regular.
pin·to (pin′tō) □*noun, plural* **pintos**

pioneer *noun* **1.** Someone who is the first to enter and settle a region. **2.** Someone who leads the way in an area of thought or study: *Louis Pasteur was a pioneer in medical research.*
□*verb* To be the first to explore a region or develop something new.
pi·o·neer (pī′ə nîr′) □*noun, plural* **pioneers** □*verb* **pioneered, pioneering, pioneers**

WORD HISTORY: pioneer

The word *pioneer* comes from a French word meaning ''foot soldier,'' which in turn comes from the Latin for ''foot.'' A pioneer was originally a soldier who prepared the way for the rest of the troops marching to a new area. Later the word came to be used of anyone who opens up an unknown region.

---

pious *adjective* Having or showing piety.
pi·ous (pī′əs) □*adjective*

pipe *noun* **1.** A tube through which a liquid or gas flows. **2.** A tube with a small bowl at one end for smoking tobacco. **3.** A musical instrument shaped like a tube, played by blowing air into one end.
□*verb* **1.** To carry through a pipe: *piping water from a reservoir.* **2.** To play music on a pipe: *pipe a cheerful tune.*
pipe (pīp) □*noun, plural* **pipes** □*verb* **piped, piping, pipes**

pirate *noun* Someone who robs ships at sea.
pi·rate (pī′rit) □*noun, plural* **pirates**

pistachio *noun* A tree of the Mediterranean region that bears a small nut with a hard shell and an edible green kernel.
pis·ta·chio (pi stash′ē ō′) □*noun, plural* **pistachios**

pistil   *noun* The part of a flower that receives pollen and produces seeds.
  pis·til (pis′təl) ▢*noun, plural* **pistils**

pistol   *noun* A small gun held in the hand.
  pis·tol (pis′təl) ▢*noun, plural* **pistols**

piston   *noun* A part in an engine consisting of a disk that fits snugly into a hollow cylinder and moves back and forth.
  pis·ton (pis′tən) ▢*noun, plural* **pistons**

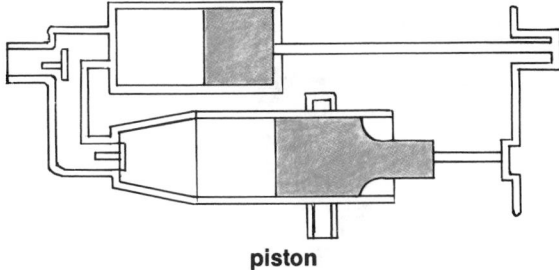

piston

pit¹   *noun* **1.** A hole in the ground: *The campers dug a pit to hold the campfire.* **2.** A hollow place on a surface.
  ▢*verb* **1.** To make small holes or marks in: *Hail pitted the picnic table.* **2.** To set in competition; match: *The race pitted the two fastest runners against each other.*
  pit (pit) ▢*noun, plural* **pits** ▢*verb* **pitted, pitting, pits**

pit²   *noun* The single hard seed of some fruits: *a peach pit.*
  pit (pit) ▢*noun, plural* **pits**

pitch¹   *noun* A sticky, dark substance used to cover roofs and pave streets.
  pitch (pich) ▢*noun*

pitch²   *verb* **1.** To throw; hurl: *pitch a baseball.* **2.** To put up: *pitch a tent.* **3.** To fall suddenly: *The man tripped and pitched over.*
  ▢*noun* **1.** An act of pitching; throw or toss. **2.** A degree or level: *a high pitch of excitement.* **3.** A slant: *the steep pitch of the roof.* **4.** The high or low quality of a musical sound.
  pitch (pich) ▢*verb* **pitched, pitching, pitches** ▢*noun, plural* **pitches**

pitcher¹   *noun* The baseball player who pitches the ball to the batter.
  pitch·er (pich′ər) ▢*noun, plural* **pitchers**

pitcher²   *noun* A container with a handle and a spout or lip, used to pour out liquids.
  pitch·er (pich′ər) ▢*noun, plural* **pitchers**

pitchfork   *noun* A very large fork with sharp prongs, used to move hay or straw.
  pitch·fork (pich′fôrk′) ▢*noun, plural* **pitchforks**

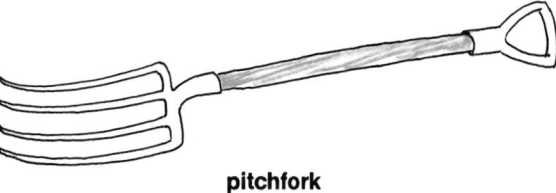

pitchfork

pith   *noun* The soft substance in the center of plant stems.
  pith (pith) ▢*noun*

pitiful   *adjective* Arousing pity and sympathy: *The lost, frightened child was a pitiful sight.*
  pit·i·ful (pit′i fəl) ▢*adjective*

pity   *noun* **1.** Sorrow or sympathy for someone else's pain or trouble: *We felt pity for the starving children.* **2.** A cause for regret: *It's a pity that you can't come with us.*
  ▢*verb* To feel pity for: *We pitied the homeless cat and took it in.*
  pi·ty (pit′ē) ▢*noun, plural* **pities** ▢*verb* **pitied, pitying, pities**

pivot   *noun* A short rod or shaft that something turns on: *The gun was mounted on a pivot.*
  ▢*verb* To swing or turn on or as if on a pivot: *She pivoted around when I called her name.*
  piv·ot (piv′ət) ▢*noun, plural* **pivots** ▢*verb* **pivoted, pivoting, pivots**

pixy or **pixie**   *noun* An imaginary being resembling a fairy or an elf.
  pix·y or **pix·ie** (pik′sē) ▢*noun, plural* **pixies**

pizza   *noun* A baked food made of a flat crust covered with tomatoes, cheese, sausage, and other foods.
  piz·za (pēt′sə) ▢*noun, plural* **pizzas**

place   *noun* **1.** A particular area; location: *the place where I was born.* **2.** A house; residence: *Let's meet at my place.* **3.** A duty or right: *It's not my place to complain.* **4.** Position or rank: *She won second place in the chess tournament.* **5.** A seat that is empty or available.
  ▢*verb* **1.** To put in a particular spot or position: *Place the cups on the table.* **2.** To identify by connecting with the right location or time: *He looks familiar, but I can't quite place him.*

a	bat	ī	bite	ōō	tool	*th*	feather
ā	make	î	fierce	ou	out	th	bath
â	dare	o	dot	u	nut	hw	wheat
ä	father	ō	no	û	turn	zh	measure
e	net	ô	law, for	ch	church	ə	about, open
ē	be	oi	soil	ng	ring		pencil, atom
i	dip	oo	look	sh	shade		circus

3. To finish a contest in a certain position: *I placed third in the race.*
in place of Instead of.
take place To happen: *The action of the play takes place in a garden.*
place (plās) □*noun, plural* **places** □*verb* **placed, placing, places**

placid *adjective* Calm or peaceful: *He has a placid personality.*
plac·id (plas′id) □*adjective*

plague *noun* **1.** A very serious disease that spreads rapidly among people. **2.** Something that causes great trouble: *a plague of ants.* □*verb* To bother: *He's always plaguing me with foolish questions.*
plague (plāg) □*noun, plural* **plagues** □*verb* **plagued, plaguing, plagues**

plaid *noun* A pattern formed by stripes of different widths and colors that cross one another.
plaid (plad) □*noun, plural* **plaids**

plain *adjective* **1.** Easy to see or understand: *in plain words.* **2.** Not fancy or decorated; simple: *plain food.* **3.** Ordinary or average. **4.** Not beautiful or handsome: *a plain face.* **5.** Frank; direct: *The plain truth is I don't want to go.* □*noun* A large area of flat land without trees.
plain (plān) □*adjective* **plainer, plainest** □*noun, plural* **plains**

SYNONYMS: **plain, simple**

These adjectives mean not fancy or decorated: *They prepared a plain but delicious dinner. She wore a simple blue dress.*

---

plaintive *adjective* Expressing sorrow; mournful: *The call of the dove has a plaintive sound.*
plain·tive (plān′tiv) □*adjective*

plait *noun* **1.** A braid of hair. **2.** A pleat. □*verb* **1.** To braid. **2.** To pleat.
plait (plāt) □*noun, plural* **plaits** □*verb* **plaited, plaiting, plaits**

plan *noun* **1.** An idea of what to do that is thought out ahead of time: *What are your plans for the summer?* **2.** A drawing that shows how to make something: *a plan for a new park.* □*verb* **1.** To think out what to do: *plan a way of escaping.* **2.** To have as a purpose; intend: *I plan to visit them next week.*
plan (plan) □*noun, plural* **plans** □*verb* **planned, planning, plans**

plane¹ *noun* **1.** A level flat surface. **2.** A stage or level: *a high plane of success.* **3.** An airplane. □*adjective* Level; flat: *a plane figure.*
plane (plān) □*noun, plural* **planes** □*adjective*

plane² *noun* A hand tool with a blade for smoothing wood. □*verb* To smooth with a plane.
plane (plān) □*noun, plural* **planes** □*verb* **planed, planing, planes**

plane

planet *noun* A large heavenly body that moves around the sun. There are nine known planets that orbit our sun, including Earth.
plan·et (plan′it) □*noun, plural* **planets**

WORD HISTORY: **planet**

Planet comes from a Greek word that means "wanderer." The planets appeared to be wandering because their positions changed from night to night with respect to the fixed stars.

---

planetarium *noun* A building that shows the movements of the sun, moon, planets, and stars by projecting lights on the inside of a rounded ceiling.
plan·e·tar·i·um (plan′i târ′ē əm) □*noun, plural* **planetariums**

plank *noun* A long, thick piece of sawed wood: *a floor made of oak planks.*
plank (plangk) □*noun, plural* **planks**

plankton *noun* Tiny plants and animals that float in water, used as food by many fish and sea animals.
plank·ton (plangk′tən) □*noun*

plant *noun* **1.** A living thing that is not an animal. Plants cannot move from place to

place, and most make their own food. Flowers, trees, grasses, and mushrooms are plants. **2.** A factory: *an automobile plant.*
□*verb* **1.** To put in the ground to grow: *plant vegetables.* **2.** To fix firmly: *plant a flag on a mountain top.*
plant (plant) □*noun, plural* **plants** □*verb* **planted, planting, plants**

plantation *noun* A large farm or estate on which crops such as cotton, sugar, or rubber are grown.
plan·ta·tion (plan **tā'** shən) □*noun, plural* **plantations**

planter *noun* **1.** Someone or something that plants. **2.** The owner of a plantation. **3.** A container for growing plants.
plant·er (**plan'** tər) □*noun, plural* **planters**

plaque *noun* **1.** A flat plate or disk that is ornamented or engraved for mounting. **2.** A thin film of mucus and germs that forms on the surface of a tooth.
plaque (plak) □*noun, plural* **plaques**

plasma *noun* The clear, yellowish liquid part of blood.
plas·ma (**plaz'** mə) □*noun*

plaster *noun* A mixture of sand, lime, and water that hardens when dry: *a wall covered with plaster.*
□*verb* **1.** To cover with plaster: *plaster a crack in the ceiling.* **2.** To cover all over: *He plastered his room with posters.*
plas·ter (**plas'** tər) □*noun* □*verb* **plastered, plastering, plasters**

plastic *noun* A material made from chemicals that can be molded or drawn into almost any shape when hot.
□*adjective* **1.** Able to be shaped easily: *Clay is a plastic material.* **2.** Made of plastic: *a plastic bowl.*
plas·tic (**plas'** tik) □*noun, plural* **plastics** □*adjective*

plate *noun* **1.** A flat, round dish. **2.** The food on such a dish: *Finish your plate.* **3.** A thin, flat piece of metal: *The treasure was buried in a chest covered with steel plates.* **4.** A piece of flat metal on which letters or numbers are written: *a name plate.* **5.** Home plate on a baseball field.
□*verb* To cover with a layer of metal: *plate the pot with copper.*
plate (plāt) □*noun, plural* **plates** □*verb* **plated, plating, plates**

plateau *noun* A flat area higher than the land around it.
pla·teau (pla **tō'**) □*noun, plural* **plateaus**

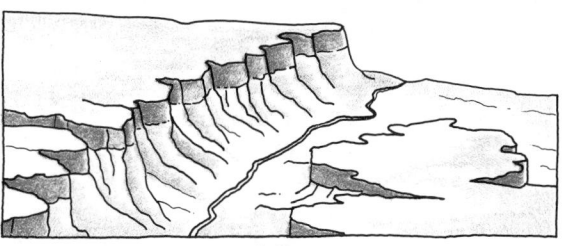
plateau

platform *noun* **1.** A raised floor or flat surface: *a platform for speakers.* **2.** A statement of beliefs: *The candidate's platform was in favor of lower taxes.*
plat·form (**plat'** fôrm') □*noun, plural* **platforms**

platinum *noun* A chemical element that is a valuable, silver-white metal.
plat·i·num (**plat'** ən əm) □*noun*

platter *noun* A large, shallow dish for serving food.
plat·ter (**plat'** ər) □*noun, plural* **platters**

platypus *noun* A furry water animal of Australia. It has webbed feet and a bill like that of a duck.
plat·y·pus (**plat'** ə pəs) □*noun, plural* **platypuses**

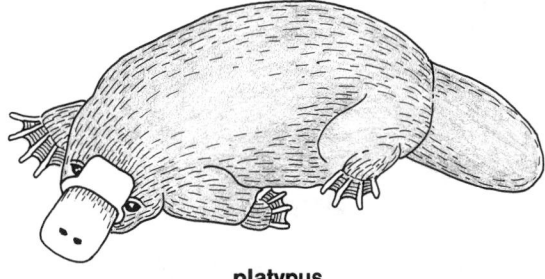
platypus

play *verb* **1.** To amuse oneself: *Can the children play outdoors today?* **2.** To take part in as a game: *play cards.* **3.** To act the part of: *He played the father in the movie we made.* **4.** To

a	bat	ī	bite	ōō	tool	*th*	feather
ā	make	î	fierce	ou	out	th	bath
â	dare	o	dot	u	nut	hw	wheat
ä	father	ō	no	û	turn	zh	measure
e	net	ô	law, for	ch	church	ə	about, open
ē	be	oi	soil	ng	ring		pencil, atom
i	dip	oo	look	sh	shade		circus

behave; act: *She doesn't play fair.* **5.** To make or produce music: *play a guitar; play the radio.* **6.** To handle in an idle or careless manner: *He played with a piece of string as he talked.*
□*noun* **1.** A story meant to be acted on the stage: *a play by Shakespeare.* **2.** An activity done for fun or relaxation. **3.** A move, turn, or act in a game: *That fast throw was a good play.*
play (plā) □*verb* **played, playing, plays** □*noun, plural* **plays**

player *noun* **1.** Someone who takes part in a game. **2.** An actor. **3.** A person or machine that plays music: *a piano player; a record player.*
play·er (plā′ər) □*noun, plural* **players**

playful *adjective* **1.** Liking to play and have fun. **2.** Not serious; joking: *a playful punch.*
play·ful (plā′fəl) □*adjective*

playground *noun* An outdoor area for playing.
play·ground (plā′ground′) □*noun, plural* **playgrounds**

playground

playmate *noun* A person who plays with another.
play·mate (plā′māt′) □*noun, plural* **playmates**

playpen *noun* A small pen for a baby to play in.
play·pen (plā′pen′) □*noun, plural* **playpens**

playwright *noun* Someone who writes plays.
play·wright (plā′rīt′) □*noun, plural* **playwrights**

plaza *noun* A public square in a town or city.
pla·za (plaz′ə) □*noun, plural* **plazas**

plea *noun* **1.** A request for something wanted very badly: *a plea for help.* **2.** The answer of

an accused person to a charge: *a plea of guilty.*
plea (plē) □*noun, plural* **pleas**

plead *verb* **1.** To make an earnest request: *She pleaded for another chance.* **2.** To give an answer to charges in a court: *plead not guilty.* **3.** To speak for; defend: *plead a case in court.* **4.** To give as an excuse: *You know the rules so you can't plead ignorance.*
plead (plēd) □*verb* **pleaded** or **pled, pleading, pleads**

pleasant *adjective* **1.** Giving pleasure or comfort; pleasing: *pleasant weather.* **2.** Pleasing in manner; friendly: *a pleasant person.*
pleas·ant (plez′ənt) □*adjective* **pleasanter, pleasantest**

SYNONYMS: **pleasant, enjoyable**

These adjectives mean giving pleasure or comfort: *We had a pleasant afternoon at the beach. Was the movie enjoyable?*

---

please *verb* **1.** To give pleasure or satisfaction to: *The magic tricks pleased the children.* **2.** To wish: *Eat what you please.*
□*adverb* Used in making a polite request: *Please open the door.*
please (plēz) □*verb* **pleased, pleasing, pleases** □*adverb*

pleasure *noun* **1.** A pleasant, happy feeling: *The movie gave pleasure to all of us.* **2.** Something that gives enjoyment or happiness: *Stamp collecting is his main pleasure.*
pleas·ure (plezh′ər) □*noun, plural* **pleasures**

pleat *noun* A flat fold made by doubling cloth on itself and pressing or sewing it in place.
□*verb* To make pleats in: *pleat a skirt.*
pleat (plēt) □*noun, plural* **pleats** □*verb* **pleated, pleating, pleats**

pled *verb* A past tense and past participle of **plead:** *I pled with him to lend me the money.*
pled (pled) □*verb*

pledge *noun* **1.** A solemn promise: *They made a pledge to help one another.* **2.** Something given until a loan is paid back.
□*verb* **1.** To promise: *pledge one's support.* **2.** To give something valuable until a loan is paid back: *She pledged her ring to get the loan.*
pledge (plej) □*noun, plural* **pledges** □*verb* **pledged, pledging, pledges**

plentiful *adjective* In a great amount; abundant: *a plentiful supply of food.*
plen·ti·ful (plen′ti fəl) □*adjective*

plenty *noun* A full amount or supply: *We had plenty of time to catch the train.*
plen·ty (**plen′**tē) □*noun*

pliers *plural noun* A tool with jaws that close when the handle is squeezed. Pliers are used for holding and bending things.
pli·ers (**plī′**ərz) □*plural noun*

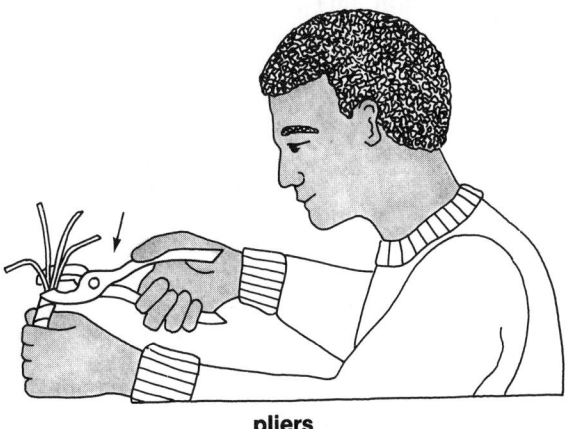

pliers

plod *verb* To go or move slowly and with effort: *plod through the woods; plod through a boring book.*
plod (plod) □*verb* **plodded, plodding, plods**

plop *noun* A sound like that of something falling into water.
□*verb* **1.** To make a noise like a plop. **2.** To fall or drop heavily: *I was in a hurry so I just plopped the books on the table.*
plop (plop) □*noun, plural* **plops** □*verb* **plopped, plopping, plops**

plot *noun* **1.** A small piece of ground: *a plot for growing vegetables.* **2.** The events in a story or play. **3.** A secret plan: *a plot to overthrow the government.*
□*verb* **1.** To mark on a map or chart: *plot a course across the ocean.* **2.** To plan in a secret way: *They plotted to take over the ship.*
plot (plot) □*noun, plural* **plots** □*verb* **plotted, plotting, plots**

SYNONYMS: plot, scheme

These nouns mean a secret plan: *a plot to overthrow the king; a scheme to rob a bank.*

---

plover *noun* A bird with a short bill and a short tail.
plov·er (**pluv′**ər *or* **plō′**vər) □*noun, plural* **plovers**

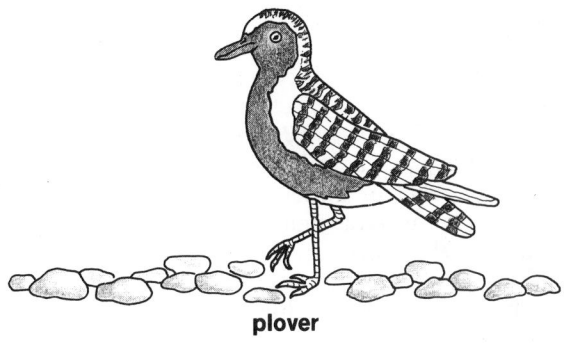

plover

plow *noun* **1.** A farm tool used for breaking up soil and cutting rows for seeds. **2.** A machine like a plow: *a plow for clearing snow from roads.*
□*verb* **1.** To break soil with a plow: *plow a field.* **2.** To move ahead at a steady rate.
plow (plou) □*noun, plural* **plows** □*verb* **plowed, plowing, plows**

ploy *noun* A trick for getting an advantage over an opponent.
ploy (ploi) □*noun, plural* **ploys**

pluck *verb* **1.** To pull off: *pluck the petals off a flower.* **2.** To pull out the feathers or hair of: *pluck a turkey.* **3.** To pull or tug.
□*noun* **1.** A sharp tug or pull. **2.** Courage; daring.
pluck (pluk) □*verb* **plucked, plucking, plucks** □*noun, plural* **plucks**

pluck

a bat	ī bite	o͞o tool	*th* feather
ā make	î fierce	ou out	th bath
â dare	o dot	u nut	hw wheat
ä father	ō no	û turn	zh measure
e net	ô law, for	ch church	ə about, open
ē be	oi soil	ng ring	pencil, atom
i dip	oo look	sh shade	circus

plug *noun* **1.** A piece of material used to stop a hole or leak: *a plug in a sink.* **2.** A device at the end of an electrical cord that fits into a socket to make an electrical connection.
□*verb* **1.** To stop up: *He plugged the leak with rags.* **2.** To put the plug of an electrical device into a socket or outlet: *plug in a lamp.* **3.** To keep working in a steady manner: *He plugged away at the lesson until he understood it.*
plug (plug) □*noun, plural* **plugs** □*verb* **plugged, plugging, plugs**

plum *noun* A juicy fruit with smooth, purple skin and a hard pit.
plum (plum) □*noun, plural* **plums**

plumage *noun* The feathers of a bird.
plum·age (plo͞o′mij) □*noun*

plumb *noun* A weight at the end of a cord, used to measure how deep something is or how straight up and down.
□*verb* To test with a plumb.
□*adjective* Exactly vertical: *If the walls are not plumb, the stripes on the wallpaper will not look straight.*
plumb (plum) □*noun, plural* **plumbs** □*verb* **plumbed, plumbing, plumbs** □*adjective*

plumber *noun* Someone whose work is putting in water pipes and repairing them.
plumb·er (plum′ər) □*noun, plural* **plumbers**

plumbing *noun* The water pipes, fixtures, and similar equipment in a building.
plumb·ing (plum′ing) □*noun*

plume *noun* **1.** A large, fluffy feather. **2.** Something that looks like a plume: *a plume of smoke.*
plume (plo͞om) □*noun, plural* **plumes**

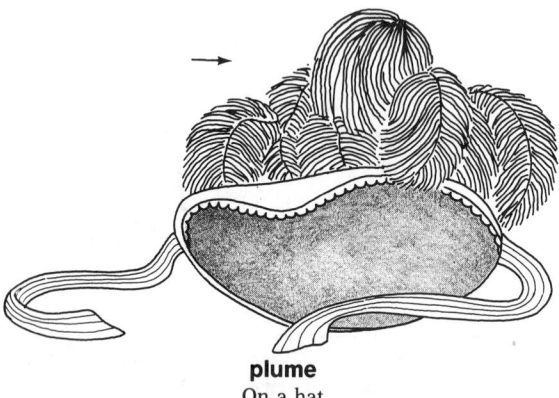

plume
On a hat

plummet *verb* To drop straight down: *The gull plummeted into the sea after a fish.*
plum·met (plum′it) □*verb* **plummeted, plummeting, plummets**

plump *adjective* Rounded and full: *a plump figure.*
plump (plump) □*adjective* **plumper, plumpest**

plunder *verb* To take from by force; rob: *Pirates plundered the coast.*
□*noun* Stolen things.
plun·der (plun′dər) □*verb* **plundered, plundering, plunders** □*noun*

plunge *verb* To throw oneself suddenly down or in: *We plunged into the lake.*
□*noun* An act of plunging: *We took a plunge into the pool.*
plunge (plunj) □*verb* **plunged, plunging, plunges** □*noun, plural* **plunges**

plural *adjective* Meaning more than one.
□*noun* The form of a word that means more than one person or thing. For example, *chairs* is the plural of *chair*, and *mice* of *mouse*.
plu·ral (ploor′əl) □*adjective* □*noun, plural* **plurals**

plus *preposition* Added to: *Two plus five equals seven.*
□*adjective* **1.** Of addition: *a plus sign.* **2.** Somewhat more than: *a grade of B plus.*
□*noun* The sign (+), used to show addition.
plus (plus) □*preposition* □*adjective* □*noun, plural* **pluses**

Pluto *noun* The planet of our solar system that is farthest from the sun.
Plu·to (plo͞o′tō) □*noun*

plutonium *noun* A man-made chemical element that is a radioactive metal used to produce atomic energy.
plu·to·ni·um (plo͞o tō′nē əm) □*noun*

plywood *noun* A building material made of thin layers of wood glued together.
ply·wood (plī′wood′) □*noun*

p.m. or **P.M.** Between noon and midnight: *We have dinner at 6:00 p.m.*

pneumonia *noun* A serious disease in which the lungs become inflamed.
pneu·mo·nia (noo mōn′yə *or* nyoo mōn′yə) □*noun*

poach *verb* To cook in gently boiling water.
poach (pōch) □*verb* **poached, poaching, poaches**

pocket *noun* A small bag that is sewn into or onto clothing to hold things.
□*adjective* Small enough to be carried in a pocket: *a pocket watch.*
□*verb* To put in a pocket.
pock·et (pok′it) □*noun, plural* **pockets**

□*adjective* □*verb* **pocketed, pocketing, pockets**

pocketbook   *noun* A bag for carrying money, papers, and other small things.
pock·et·book (**pok′**it book′) □*noun, plural* **pocketbooks**

pocketknife   *noun* A small knife with blades that fold into the handle.
pock·et·knife (**pok′**it nīf′) □*noun, plural* **pocketknives**

pod   *noun* A plant part in which seeds grow: *The pea pods split open.*
pod (pod) □*noun, plural* **pods**

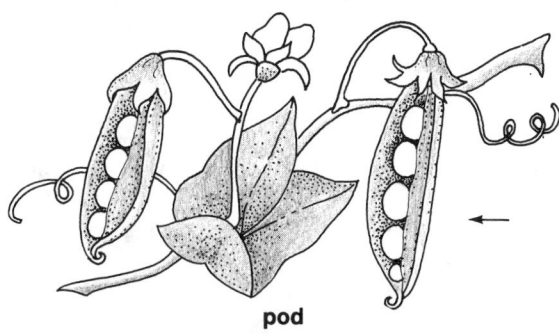

pod

poem   *noun* A composition that makes use of rhythm and sometimes rhyme to describe strong feelings or tell a story.
po·em (**pō′**əm) □*noun, plural* **poems**

poet   *noun* A writer of poems.
po·et (**pō′**it) □*noun, plural* **poets**

poetic   *adjective* Of, having to do with, or like poetry or poets: *He has no poetic talent.*
po·et·ic (pō **et′**ik) □*adjective*

poetry   *noun* **1.** The writings produced by a poet; poems. **2.** A piece of writing with a certain pattern of rhythm; verse.
po·et·ry (**pō′**i trē) □*noun*

poinsettia   *noun* A plant with showy, bright-red leaves that look like petals. They are often used for decoration at Christmas.
poin·set·ti·a (poin **set′**ē ə) □*noun, plural* **poinsettias**

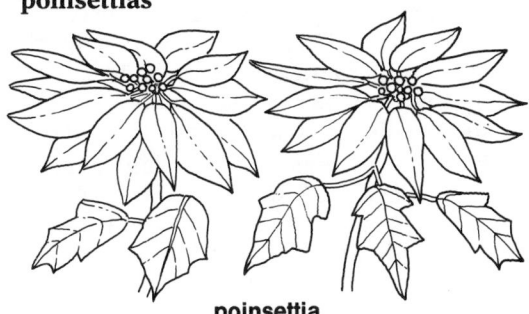

poinsettia

point   *noun* **1.** A sharp end: *the point of a knife.* **2.** A thin piece of land that extends into water. **3.** A written or printed dot: *2.8 is read two point eight.* **4.** A place or position: *attacking the fort at a weak point.* **5.** A degree or level: *the boiling point.* **6.** A moment in time: *At that point he decided to leave.* **7.** A main idea, purpose, or reason: *What was the point of his question?* **8.** A special quality: *good points.* **9.** A score of 1 in a game. **10.** A direction shown on a compass.
□*verb* **1.** To direct; aim: *point a gun.* **2.** To show with or as if with the finger: *He pointed at the shirt he wanted. She pointed out a mistake.*
point (point) □*noun, plural* **points** □*verb* **pointed, pointing, points**

pointer   *noun* **1.** Something that points or is used to point, such as a long stick. **2.** A piece of advice: *She gave me some pointers on sailing.* **3.** A dog with a short coat, often used to help hunters find game.
point·er (**poin′**tər) □*noun, plural* **pointers**

pointless   *adjective* Not having a purpose: *Arriving early for my piano lesson was pointless because the teacher was always ten minutes late.*
point·less (**point′**lis) □*adjective*

point of view   *noun* A way of thinking about or looking at something: *From the point of view of a baby, adults seem like giants.*
point of view □*noun, plural* **points of view**

poise   *noun* **1.** Calm assurance: *She spoke before the class with perfect poise.* **2.** Balance.
□*verb* To balance or be balanced: *The dancer poised on one leg.*
poise (poiz) □*noun* □*verb* **poised, poising, poises**

poison   *noun* A substance that can hurt or kill a living being: *Some insect sprays contain powerful poisons.*
□*verb* **1.** To kill or harm with poison. **2.** To put poison in or on: *poison the air with smoke and fumes.* **3.** To have a bad effect on; harm: *jealousy can poison the mind.*
poi·son (**poi′**zən) □*noun, plural* **poisons** □*verb* **poisoned, poisoning, poisons**

a bat	ī bite	ōō tool	*th* feather
ā make	î fierce	ou out	th bath
â dare	o dot	u nut	hw wheat
ä father	ō no	û turn	zh measure
e net	ô law, for	ch church	ə about, open
ē be	oi soil	ng ring	pencil, atom
i dip	oo look	sh shade	circus

poison ivy *noun* A climbing plant having leaves with three leaflets and capable of causing an itching skin rash.

poison ivy

poisonous *adjective* Containing, producing, or able to cause harm with poison: *a poisonous spider.*
poi·son·ous (poi′zə nəs) □*adjective*

poke *verb* **1.** To give a sharp jab: *He poked me in the ribs with his elbow.* **2.** To push forward; thrust: *The woodchuck poked its head out of the ground.* **3.** To move slowly: *poking along on a tricycle.*
□*noun* A sharp jab.
poke (pōk) □*verb* **poked, poking, pokes**
□*noun, plural* **pokes**

poker¹ *noun* A metal rod used to stir fires.
pok·er (pō′kər) □*noun, plural* **pokers**

poker² *noun* A card game in which the players bet on the value of the cards they have.
poker (pō′kər) □*noun*

polar *adjective* Of or near the North Pole or South Pole.
po·lar (pō′lər) □*adjective*

polar bear *noun* A large white bear living in arctic regions.

pole¹ *noun* **1.** Either end of the earth's axis. The two poles are called the North Pole and the South Pole. **2.** Either end of a battery or magnet where the force is strongest.
pole (pōl) □*noun, plural* **poles**

pole² *noun* A long, thin, rounded piece of wood or other material: *a telephone pole.*
pole (pōl) □*noun, plural* **poles**

polecat *noun* **1.** A small European animal that is related to the weasel. **2.** A skunk.
pole·cat (pōl′kat′) □*noun, plural* **polecats**

pole vault *noun* A sport in which a person tries to jump over a high bar with the help of a long pole.

pole vault

police *noun* The government department that keeps order and makes sure that laws are obeyed.
□*verb* To guard or keep order in: *police the streets.*
po·lice (pə lēs′) □*noun* □*verb* **policed, policing, polices**

policeman *noun* A man who is a member of the police.
po·lice·man (pə lēs′mən) □*noun, plural* **policemen**

policewoman *noun* A woman who is a member of the police.
po·lice·wom·an (pə lēs′woom′ən) □*noun, plural* **policewomen**

policy¹ *noun* A method or plan for action: *What is the school's policy on skipping grades?*
pol·i·cy (pol′i sē) □*noun, plural* **policies**

policy² *noun* A written agreement between an insurance company and a person who is insured.
pol·i·cy (pol′i sē) □*noun, plural* **policies**

polio *noun* Poliomyelitis.
po·li·o (pō′lē ō′) □*noun*

poliomyelitis *noun* A virus disease that causes paralysis by affecting the nerves and the spinal cord. There is now a vaccine that prevents people and especially children from getting this disease.
po·li·o·my·e·li·tis (pō′lē ō mī′ə lī′tis) □*noun*

polish *verb* To make smooth and shiny by rubbing: *polish one's shoes.*
□*noun* **1.** A substance used to make something smooth and shiny: *silver polish.* **2.** A smooth and shiny surface: *a table with a bright polish.*

pol·ish (pŏl′ish) □*verb* **polished, polishing, polishes** □*noun, plural* **polishes**

polite *adjective* Showing good manners: *It is polite to thank someone who gives you a present.* —See Synonyms at **courteous.**
po·lite (pə līt′) □*adjective* **politer, politest**

political *adjective* Of government, politics, or politicians: *a political party.*
po·lit·i·cal (pə lĭt′i kəl) □*adjective*

politician *noun* Someone who runs for or holds a position in government.
pol·i·ti·cian (pŏl′i tĭsh′ən) □*noun, plural* **politicians**

politics *noun* **1.** The management or activities of government: *Politics is her greatest interest.* **2.** A person's opinions about government: *His politics are very conservative.*
pol·i·tics (pŏl′i tĭks) □*noun*

polka *noun* A lively dance.
pol·ka (pōl′kə *or* pō′kə) □*noun, plural* **polkas**

polka dot *noun* A round dot in a pattern of dots on fabric.

polka dot

poll *noun* **1.** The casting and counting of votes or opinions: *They conducted a poll to find out what the students thought.* **2. polls** The place where votes are cast.
□*verb* **1.** To get votes in an election: *Who polled the most votes?* **2.** To question people about their opinions: *We polled the class to find out which trip to take.*
poll (pōl) □*noun, plural* **polls** □*verb* **polled, polling, polls**

pollen *noun* A fine powder that is produced by the anthers of a flower and fertilizes seeds.
pol·len (pŏl′ən) □*noun*

polliwog *noun* A tadpole.
pol·li·wog (pŏl′ē wŏg′) □*noun, plural* **polliwogs**

pollute *verb* To make impure: *We should not pollute our rivers with waste from sewers.*
pol·lute (pə lōōt′) □*verb* **polluted, polluting, pollutes**

polo *noun* A game played by two teams of horseback riders who use mallets with long handles to hit a wooden ball.
po·lo (pō′lō) □*noun*

poly– A prefix that means "many": *polytheism.*

polygamy *noun* The practice or condition of having more than one wife or husband at the same time.
po·lyg·a·my (pə lĭg′ə mē) □*noun*

polygon *noun* A closed plane figure with three or more sides.
pol·y·gon (pŏl′ē gŏn′) □*noun, plural* **polygons**

polyhedron *noun* A solid figure whose faces are polygons.
pol·y·he·dron (pŏl′ē hē′drən) □*noun, plural* **polyhedrons** *or* **pol·y·he·dra** (pŏl′ē hē′drə)

polyp *noun* A small water animal with a body shaped like a tube and a mouth surrounded by tentacles. Coral is made of polyps.
pol·yp (pŏl′ĭp) □*noun, plural* **polyps**

polysyllable *noun* A word having three or more syllables: *The word "polysyllable" is a polysyllable.*
pol·y·syl·la·ble (pŏl′ē sĭl′ə bəl) □*noun, plural* **polysyllables**

polytheism *noun* The belief in or worship of more than one god.
pol·y·the·ism (pŏl′ē thē ĭz′əm) □*noun*

pomegranate *noun* A fruit with a tough, reddish skin, tasty red flesh, and many seeds.
pome·gran·ate (pŏm′grăn′ĭt) □*noun, plural* **pomegranates**

pommel *noun* **1.** A knob on the hilt of a sword. **2.** The curved upper front part of a saddle.
pom·mel (pŭm′əl *or* pŏm′əl) □*noun, plural* **pommels**

pomp *noun* A dignified and splendid display, especially of a ceremonial kind: *the pomp of a royal coronation.*
pomp (pŏmp) □*noun*

a bat	ī bite	ōō tool	*th* feather
ā make	î fierce	ou out	th bath
â dare	o dot	u nut	hw wheat
ä father	ō no	û turn	zh measure
e net	ô law, for	ch church	ə about, open
ē be	oi soil	ng ring	pencil, atom
i dip	oo look	sh shade	circus

pompom *noun* **1.** A tuft of fibers, feathers, or other material worn as a decoration: *a knitted hat with a pompom on top.* **2.** The small flower of some plants, such as zinnias and chrysanthemums.
pom·pom (**pom′**pom′) ◻*noun, plural* **pompoms**

poncho *noun* A garment like a blanket with a hole in the center for the head. Waterproof ponchos are worn as raincoats.
pon·cho (**pon′**chō) ◻*noun, plural* **ponchos**

poncho

pond *noun* A body of water that is smaller than a lake.
pond (pond) ◻*noun, plural* **ponds**

ponder *verb* To think slowly and carefully: *ponder over a decision.*
pon·der (**pon′**dər) ◻*verb* **pondered, pondering, ponders**

pony *noun* A small horse.
po·ny (**pō′**nē) ◻*noun, plural* **ponies**

poodle *noun* A dog with thick, curly hair.
poo·dle (**pōō′**dəl) ◻*noun, plural* **poodles**

> **WORD HISTORY: poodle**
> *Poodle* comes from a German word made up of two parts. The first part of the German word means "to splash in water," and the second part means "dog." This breed was so called because it likes water.

poodle

pool¹ *noun* **1.** A small, deep body of water. **2.** A tank of water for swimming. **3.** A small amount of a liquid: *a pool of melted butter.*
pool (pōōl) ◻*noun, plural* **pools**

pool² *noun* **1.** A game played on a table that has pockets at the corners and sides. Players take turns trying to knock hard balls into the pockets with a long stick called a cue. **2.** People or things put or brought together for a particular purpose: *A car pool can help save gas.* ◻*verb* To put together for common use: *We pooled our money to buy her present.*
pool (pōōl) ◻*noun, plural* **pools** ◻*verb* **pooled, pooling, pools**

> **WORD HISTORY: pool²**
> *Pool²* comes from the French word for "hen." It seems that there was once a game in which the prize was a hen.

poor *adjective* **1.** Having little money: *too poor to buy new clothes.* **2.** Low in quality; not good: *poor health.* **3.** Less than is needed; not enough: *a poor harvest.* **4.** Pitiful; unfortunate: *The poor thing is frightened!*
poor (poor) ◻*adjective* **poorer, poorest**

pop *noun* **1.** A sudden sharp sound: *The balloon broke with a pop.* **2.** A soft drink with bubbles in it; soda.
◻*verb* **1.** To make or cause to make a sound like a pop: *I like to hear corn pop.* **2.** To come, appear, or move suddenly: *He popped in to say hello.*
pop (pop) ◻*noun, plural* **pops** ◻*verb* **popped, popping, pops**

popcorn *noun* Edible corn kernels that burst open into a white, fluffy mass when heated.
pop·corn (**pop′**kôrn′) ◻*noun*

popcorn

pope *noun* Often **Pope** The head of the Roman Catholic Church.
pope (pōp) ◻*noun, plural* **popes**

> **WORD HISTORY: pope**
> The word *pope* comes from the ancient Greek equivalent of "dad."

poplar *noun* A slender tree with soft wood, rough bark, and flower clusters in long stalks.
pop·lar (pop′lər) □*noun, plural* **poplars**

poppy *noun* A plant with showy red, white, or yellow flowers and a hairy stem.
pop·py (pop′ē) □*noun, plural* **poppies**

popular *adjective* **1.** Enjoyed, accepted, or liked by many people: *a popular form of entertainment; a popular student.* **2.** Of, for, or by the people: *popular government.*
pop·u·lar (pop′yə lər) □*adjective*

popularity *noun* The condition of being liked by many people.
pop·u·lar·i·ty (pop′yə lar′i tē) □*noun*

population *noun* **1.** The people or things that exist or live in a particular place: *the population of the town.* **2.** The number of people who live in a place: *What is the population of Canada?*
pop·u·la·tion (pop′yə lā′shən) □*noun, plural* **populations**

populous *adjective* Having many inhabitants: *a populous city.*
pop·u·lous (pop′yə ləs) □*adjective*

porcelain *noun* A hard, fine pottery made from clay; china.
por·ce·lain (pôr′sə lin) □*noun*

porch *noun* A platform with a roof, attached to the outside of a house.
porch (pôrch) □*noun, plural* **porches**

porcupine *noun* An animal covered with long, sharp quills.
por·cu·pine (pôr′kyə pīn′) □*noun, plural* **porcupines**

> **WORD HISTORY: porcupine**
> *Porcupine* comes from two Latin words meaning "pig" and "thorn."

porcupine

pore¹ *noun* A tiny opening in the skin or another surface.
pore (pôr) □*noun, plural* **pores**

> **WORD HISTORY: pore¹**
> *Pore¹* comes from a Greek word meaning "passage."

pore² *verb* To look at or study with great care: *She pored over the science book.*
pore (pôr) □*verb* **pored, poring, pores**

pork *noun* The meat of a pig used as food.
pork (pôrk) □*noun*

porous *adjective* **1.** Having pores. **2.** Allowing a liquid or gas to pass through pores or small holes or openings: *Clay flower pots are porous.*
po·rous (pôr′əs) □*adjective*

porpoise *noun* A sea animal similar to a whale and having a short, blunt snout.
por·poise (pôr′pəs) □*noun, plural* **porpoises**

> **WORD HISTORY: porpoise**
> The word *porpoise* comes from a medieval Latin word that literally means "pig fish."

porpoise

porridge *noun* A food made by boiling oatmeal or another grain in water or milk.
por·ridge (pôr′ij) □*noun, plural* **porridges**

port¹ *noun* **1.** A place where ships can be safe from storms. **2.** A city or town with a harbor.
port (pôrt) □*noun, plural* **ports**

a bat	ī bite	ŏŏ tool	*th* feather
ā make	î fierce	ou out	th bath
â dare	o dot	u nut	hw wheat
ä father	ō no	û turn	zh measure
e net	ô law, for	ch church	ə about, open
ē be	oi soil	ng ring	pencil, atom
i dip	oo look	sh shade	circus

port² *noun* The side of a ship or aircraft that is on the left when one is facing forward.
port (pôrt) ☐*noun*

portable *adjective* Easy to carry: *a portable typewriter.*
port·a·ble (pôr′tə bəl) ☐*adjective*

porter *noun* **1.** Someone hired to carry luggage: *a hotel porter.* **2.** Someone who waits on train passengers.
por·ter (pôr′tər) ☐*noun, plural* **porters**

porthole *noun* A small, round window in the side of a ship.
port·hole (pôrt′hōl′) ☐*noun, plural* **portholes**

portico *noun* A porch or walk with a roof held up by columns.
por·ti·co (pôr′ti kō′) ☐*noun, plural* **porticos**

portion *noun* A part or share of something. ☐*verb* To give out in parts or helpings.
por·tion (pôr′shən) ☐*noun, plural* **portions** ☐*verb* **portioned, portioning, portions**

portrait *noun* A picture of a person.
por·trait (pôr′trit *or* pôr′trāt′) ☐*noun, plural* **portraits**

portray *verb* **1.** To make a picture of: *The artist portrayed the President at his desk.* **2.** To describe in vivid words: *a book that portrays frontier life.* **3.** To play the part of: *The actress portrayed a young factory worker.*
por·tray (pôr trā′) ☐*verb* **portrayed, portraying, portrays**

pose *verb* **1.** To take a position for a picture: *The family posed outside the house.* **2.** To pretend to be someone or something: *He posed as a reporter to get into the meeting.* ☐*noun* **1.** A way of holding the body: *"Hold that pose," said the photographer.* **2.** A false way of acting: *His surprise was just a pose.*
pose (pōz) ☐*verb* **posed, posing, poses** ☐*noun, plural* **poses**

position *noun* **1.** The place where someone or something is. **2.** The way a person or thing is placed: *a relaxed position.* **3.** Rank or standing: *a high position in society.* **4.** A way of thinking; opinion. **5.** A job.
po·si·tion (pə zish′ən) ☐*noun, plural* **positions**

positive *adjective* **1.** Certain; sure: *He is positive that he locked the door.* **2.** Expressing consent or approval: *a positive answer.* **3.** Helpful; constructive: *positive criticism.* **4.** Greater than zero: *One, three, and seven are positive numbers.* **5.** Having one of two opposite electrical charges: *This end of the magnet is positive.* —See Synonyms at **certain.**
pos·i·tive (poz′i tiv) ☐*adjective*

posse *noun* A group of people called together by a sheriff to help capture an outlaw.
pos·se (pos′ē) ☐*noun, plural* **posses**

WORD HISTORY: **posse**

The word *posse* is short for the phrase *posse comitatus,* which was borrowed from medieval Latin. The Latin phrase means "force of the county." A sheriff had the right when necessary to summon all the able-bodied men in the county to help him in enforcing the law.

---

possess *verb* **1.** To have or own: *possess land; possess talent.* **2.** To influence strongly: *What possessed him to act so foolishly?*
pos·sess (pə zes′) ☐*verb* **possessed, possessing, possesses**

possession *noun* **1.** The condition of owning something. **2.** Something that is owned: *Her possessions could fit in one suitcase.* **3.** A land ruled by a foreign country: *Some Caribbean islands are still French possessions.*
pos·ses·sion (pə zesh′ən) ☐*noun, plural* **possessions**

possessive *adjective* **1.** Showing ownership: *"Their" is the possessive form of the pronoun "they."* **2.** Having a strong desire to own or control things: *He's too possessive to let anyone borrow his bicycle.* ☐*noun* A word that shows ownership: *"Ann's" and "my" are possessives.*
pos·ses·sive (pə zes′iv) ☐*adjective* ☐*noun, plural* **possessives**

possibility *noun* **1.** The fact of being possible: *There is a good possibility of rain tonight.* **2.** Something that may happen or exist: *Life on other planets is a possibility.*
pos·si·bil·i·ty (pos′ə bil′i tē) ☐*noun, plural* **possibilities**

possible *adjective* **1.** Capable of happening or existing: *Come as soon as possible.* **2.** Capable of being considered or used: *This is a possible site for the picnic.*
pos·si·ble (pos′ə bəl) ☐*adjective*

SYNONYMS: **possible, likely**

These adjectives mean capable of happening or existing: *It's possible that she will become a famous artist. I think it's likely to snow tomorrow.*

---

possibly *adverb* **1.** Perhaps; maybe: *Possibly you're right.* **2.** Under any circumstances: *I couldn't possibly do that.*
pos·si·bly (pos′ə blē) □*adverb*

possum *noun* An opossum.
pos·sum (pos′əm) □*noun, plural* **possums**

post¹ *noun* A straight piece of wood or metal set up in the ground to mark or support something.
□*verb* To put up for everyone to see: *She posted a notice on the bulletin board.*
post (pōst) □*noun, plural* **posts** □*verb* **posted, posting, posts**

post² *noun* **1.** A place where a group of soldiers is stationed. **2.** A place where a soldier, guard, or police officer is told to stay. **3.** A job or position: *a high post in government.*
□*verb* To assign to a post: *post guards at all the exits.*
post (pōst) □*noun, plural* **posts** □*verb* **posted, posting, posts**

post³ *noun* **1.** A system for carrying and delivering mail. **2.** The mail that is delivered.
□*verb* **1.** To send by mail: *post a letter.* **2.** To inform of the latest news: *Keep me posted.*
post (pōst) □*noun, plural* **posts** □*verb* **posted, posting, posts**

post– A prefix that means "after": *postpone.*

postage *noun* The money charged for sending something by mail.
post·age (pō′stij) □*noun*

postage stamp *noun* A small piece of printed paper bought from the government, attached to mail to pay for mailing.

postal *adjective* Of the mail service: *postal rates; a postal worker.*
post·al (pō′stəl) □*adjective*

postcard *noun* A card, often with a picture on one side, that can be mailed without an envelope.
post·card (pōst′kärd′) □*noun, plural* **postcards**

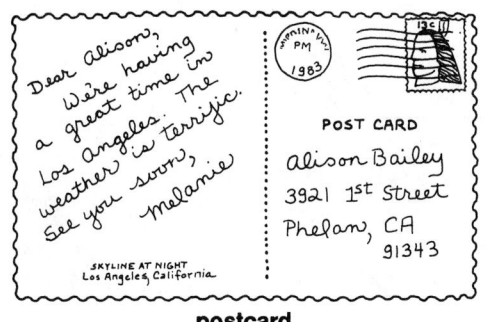

postcard

poster *noun* A large printed sign: *an advertising poster.*
post·er (pō′stər) □*noun, plural* **posters**

postman *noun* Someone who delivers mail.
post·man (pōst′mən) □*noun, plural* **postmen**

postman

postmark *noun* An official mark stamped on mail to cancel the stamp and to show the date and place of mailing.
post·mark (pōst′märk′) □*noun, plural* **postmarks**

postmaster *noun* Someone in charge of a post office.
post·mas·ter (pōst′mas′tər) □*noun, plural* **postmasters**

post office *noun* A place for receiving and delivering mail and for selling stamps.

postpone *verb* To put off until later: *We postponed the picnic because of rain.*
post·pone (pōst pōn′) □*verb* **postponed, postponing, postpones**

postscript *noun* A message added at the end of a letter.
post·script (pōst′skript′) □*noun, plural* **postscripts**

posture *noun* The way a person holds the body: *Good posture is essential for a dancer.*
pos·ture (pos′chər) □*noun, plural* **postures**

a bat	ī bite	oo tool	th feather
ā make	î fierce	ou out	th bath
â dare	o dot	u nut	hw wheat
ä father	ō no	û turn	zh measure
e net	ô law, for	ch church	ə about, open
ē be	oi soil	ng ring	pencil, atom
i dip	oo look	sh shade	circus

pot *noun* A deep, round container: *a coffee pot; a flower pot.*
pot (pot) □*noun, plural* **pots**

potash *noun* A chemical compound that contains potassium. Potash can be gotten from wood ashes and is used in fertilizer.
pot·ash (pot′ash′) □*noun*

potassium *noun* A chemical element that is a soft, silver-white metal, used in compounds to make soaps, fertilizers, and explosives.
po·tas·si·um (pə tas′ē əm) □*noun*

potato *noun* A vegetable that grows underground and has a rounded shape and white flesh.
po·ta·to (pə tā′tō) □*noun, plural* **potatoes**

potato chip *noun* A thin slice of potato fried in deep fat until crisp.

potential *adjective* Not yet real, but possible in the future: *She is a potential track star.*
po·ten·tial (pə ten′shəl) □*adjective*

pothole *noun* A deep hole in the surface of a road.
pot·hole (pot′hōl′) □*noun, plural* **potholes**

potion *noun* A drink having a medicinal, magical, or poisonous effect.
po·tion (pō′shən) □*noun, plural* **potions**

potter *noun* Someone who makes pottery.
pot·ter (pot′ər) □*noun, plural* **potters**

pottery *noun* Pots and other objects made from clay and hardened by baking.
pot·ter·y (pot′ə rē) □*noun*

pouch *noun* **1.** A bag or sack: *a letter carrier's pouch.* **2.** A hollow, rounded part like a bag: *a kangaroo's pouch.*
pouch (pouch) □*noun, plural* **pouches**

pouch

poultry *noun* Chickens, turkeys, and other birds raised for their meat or eggs.
poul·try (pōl′trē) □*noun*

poultry

pounce *verb* To leap on suddenly in order to catch something: *The cat pounced on the mouse.*
□*noun* A sudden leap to catch something.
pounce (pouns) □*verb* **pounced, pouncing, pounces** □*noun, plural* **pounces**

pound¹ *noun* **1.** A unit of weight that equals 16 ounces. **2.** A unit of money in Great Britain and some other countries.
pound (pound) □*noun, plural* **pounds** or **pound**

pound² *verb* **1.** To hit hard and often: *pounded a nail into the board.* **2.** To beat heavily: *Her heart pounded.*
pound (pound) □*verb* **pounded, pounding, pounds**

pound³ *noun* A place for keeping stray dogs, cats, or other animals.
pound (pound) □*noun, plural* **pounds**

pour *verb* **1.** To flow or cause to flow in a stream: *pour milk into a glass.* **2.** To rain hard.
pour (pôr) □*verb* **poured, pouring, pours**

pout *verb* To push out the lips to show that one is displeased.
pout (pout) □*verb* **pouted, pouting, pouts**

pout

poverty   *noun* **1.** The condition of being poor: *They lived in poverty.* **2.** Poor quality: *Nothing would grow in our garden because of the poverty of the rocky soil.*
pov·er·ty (**pov′** ər tē)   ▢*noun*

powder   *noun* **1.** Fine particles of solid material: *baby powder; dry earth that crumbled to powder.* **2.** Gunpowder.
▢*verb* **1.** To turn into powder. **2.** To cover with a powder: *She powdered the frosted cake with crushed nuts.*
pow·der (**pou′** dər)   ▢*noun, plural* **powders**
▢*verb* **powdered, powdering, powders**

power   *noun* **1.** The ability to do something: *the power of speech.* **2.** Strength: *the power of a giant.* **3.** The right to do something; authority: *the power to pass laws.* **4.** A person, group, or nation that has strength or influence: *Our country is a world power.* **5.** Energy that can be used to do work: *Electric power can be made from sunlight.* **6.** The number of times a number is multiplied by itself to obtain a product: *The third power of 2 is 8.*
▢*verb* To supply with power: *A small motor powers the boat.*
pow·er (**pou′** ər)   ▢*noun, plural* **powers**
▢*verb* **powered, powering, powers**

powerful   *adjective* Having great power: *a powerful leader; a powerful engine.*
pow·er·ful (**pou′** ər fəl)   ▢*adjective*

practical   *adjective* **1.** Good for actual use or wear; sensible: *practical walking shoes.* **2.** Having to do with experience or practice instead of study or thought: *practical training as a nurse.* **3.** Concerned with getting things done, not just with thinking or dreaming: *A practical person learns how to make a living.*
prac·ti·cal (**prak′** ti kəl)   ▢*adjective*

practical joke   *noun* A mischievous trick or prank played on someone.

practically   *adverb* **1.** Almost, but not quite: *The theater is practically full.* **2.** In a practical way: *They dressed practically for the cold.*
prac·ti·cal·ly (**prak′** tik lē)   ▢*adverb*

practice   *verb* **1.** To do something over and over again in order to learn it well: *practice the piano.* **2.** To do or carry out in a regular way: *practice the principles of a religion.* **3.** To work at a profession: *She practices law.*
▢*noun* **1.** The doing of something over and over to learn it well: *Playing the flute takes lots of practice.* **2.** A usual way of doing things; habit: *I avoid the practice of eating between meals.* **3.** The work of a profession: *the prac-*

tice of medicine.
prac·tice (**prak′** tis)   ▢*verb* **practiced, practicing, practices**   ▢*noun, plural* **practices**

prairie   *noun* A wide area of flat country with tall grass.
prai·rie (**prâr′** ē)   ▢*noun, plural* **prairies**

prairie dog   *noun* A brown, furry animal related to the woodchuck. Prairie dogs dig tunnels and live in large colonies.

prairie schooner   *noun* A wagon with a canvas cover used by pioneers to cross the North American prairies.
prairie schoon·er (**skōō′** nər)   ▢*noun, plural* **prairie schooners**

praise   *noun* Words of admiration or approval: *The movie received great praise.*
▢*verb* To express approval or admiration for: *The teacher praised her science project.*
praise (prāz)   ▢*noun, plural* **praises** ▢*verb* **praised, praising, praises**

prance   *verb* **1.** To run, leap, or move in a lively, proud way: *She pranced into the room to show us her prize.* **2.** To spring or move forward on the back legs: *The horses in the circus parade pranced in time to a march.*
prance (prans)   ▢*verb* **pranced, prancing, prances**

prance

prank   *noun* A playful trick or joke.
prank (prangk)   ▢*noun, plural* **pranks**

a bat	ī bite	ōō tool	th feather
ā make	î fierce	ou out	th bath
â dare	o dot	u nut	hw wheat
ä father	ō no	û turn	zh measure
e net	ô law, for	ch church	ə about, open
ē be	oi soil	ng ring	pencil, atom
i dip	oo look	sh shade	circus

prattle   *noun* Childish or meaningless sounds; babble: *The baby's prattle was very amusing.* □*verb* To utter a great deal of silly or childish speech: *My aunt prattled on about her grandchildren and we could not get her to stop.* **prat·tle** (prat′əl) □*noun* □*verb* **prattled, prattling, prattles**

pray   *verb* **1.** To speak to God, giving thanks or asking for something. **2.** To request in an earnest way; beg: *I pray your forgiveness.* **pray** (prā) □*verb* **prayed, praying, prays**

prayer   *noun* **1.** Words spoken to God. **2.** The act of praying: *His head was bowed in prayer.* **3.** A humble request; plea: *His prayer for mercy was granted by the judge.* **prayer** (prâr) □*noun, plural* **prayers**

pre– A prefix that means "before": *preview.*

preach   *verb* **1.** To give a talk on a religious or moral subject. **2.** To teach or urge: *preach honesty and thrift.* **preach** (prēch) □*verb* **preached, preaching, preaches**

preacher   *noun* Someone who preaches. **preach·er** (prē′chər) □*noun, plural* **preachers**

precaution   *noun* Something done to avoid possible danger or harm: *I always lock my bike as a precaution against theft.* **pre·cau·tion** (pri kô′shən) □*noun, plural* **precautions**

precede   *verb* To come before: *Thursday precedes Friday.* **pre·cede** (pri sēd′) □*verb* **preceded, preceding, precedes**

preceding   *adjective* Coming just before: *We bought all the food on the day preceding the party.* **pre·ced·ing** (pri sē′ding) □*adjective*

precinct   *noun* A district: *The city is divided into fifty police precincts.* **pre·cinct** (prē′singkt′) □*noun, plural* **precincts**

precious   *adjective* **1.** Having great value: *Silver and gold are precious metals.* **2.** Dear; beloved: *Their baby was precious to them.* **pre·cious** (presh′əs) □*adjective*

precipice   *noun* A steep or overhanging mass of rock, such as the face of a cliff. **prec·i·pice** (pres′ə pis) □*noun, plural* **precipices**

precipitate   *verb* To change from vapor into water and fall as rain, snow, sleet, or hail. **pre·cip·i·tate** (pri sip′i tāt′) □*verb* **precipitated, precipitating, precipitates**

precipitation   *noun* Rain, snow, sleet, or hail. **pre·cip·i·ta·tion** (pri sip′i tā′shən) □*noun*

precise   *adjective* **1.** Clearly expressed: *precise instructions.* **2.** Exact; accurate: *precise measurements.* **3.** Clear and careful: *a precise way of speaking.* **pre·cise** (pri sīs′) □*adjective*

precision   *noun* The quality of being precise or exact. **pre·cis·ion** (pri sizh′ən) □*noun*

predator   *noun* An animal that catches and eats other animals. **pred·a·tor** (pred′ə tər) □*noun, plural* **predators**

predecessor   *noun* Someone who held a position before another: *George Washington was our first president and the predecessor of John Adams.* **pred·e·ces·sor** (pred′i ses′ər) □*noun, plural* **predecessors**

predicament   *noun* A difficult or embarrassing situation. **pre·dic·a·ment** (pri dik′ə mənt) □*noun, plural* **predicaments**

predicate   *noun* The part of a sentence that tells what the subject does or is. In the sentences *He felt tired* and *The cat curled up and slept,* the predicates are *felt tired* and *curled up and slept.* **pred·i·cate** (pred′i kit) □*noun, plural* **predicates**

predict   *verb* To tell what will happen; foretell: *I can't predict who will win the game tomorrow.* **pre·dict** (pri dikt′) □*verb* **predicted, predicting, predicts**

prediction   *noun* **1.** Something that is predicted. **2.** The act of predicting. **pre·dic·tion** (pri dik′shən) □*noun, plural* **predictions**

preen   *verb* **1.** To smooth or clean with the beak: *The parakeet preened its feathers several times a day.* **2.** To dress or groom oneself with great care. **preen** (prēn) □*verb* **preened, preening, preens**

preface   *noun* An introduction to a book or speech. **pre·face** (pref′is) □*noun, plural* **prefaces**

prefer *verb* To like better: *Do you prefer funny stories or sad ones?*
pre·fer (pri fûr') □*verb* **preferred, preferring, prefers**

preference *noun* Something liked better than another: *Chocolate ice cream is my preference.*
pref·er·ence (**pref'** ər əns) □*noun, plural* **preferences**

prefix *noun* A syllable or group of syllables with its own meaning that appears at the beginning of a word and often changes its meaning. For example, *un-* in *unpack* is a prefix.
pre·fix (**prē'** fiks') □*noun, plural* **prefixes**

pregnant *adjective* Having offspring developing inside the body.
preg·nant (**preg'** nənt) □*adjective*

prehistoric *adjective* Of a time before events were written down: *prehistoric animals.*
pre·his·tor·ic (prē'hi **stôr'** ik) □*adjective*

prejudice *noun* A strong feeling or opinion held without good reason: *a prejudice against foreigners.*
□*verb* To fill with prejudice: *His stories prejudiced everyone against our new neighbor.*
prej·u·dice (**prej'** ə dis) □*noun, plural* **prejudices** □*verb* **prejudiced, prejudicing, prejudices**

preliminary *adjective* Happening or coming before the main part: *a preliminary outline for a speech.*
pre·lim·i·nar·y (pri **lim'** ə ner'ē) □*adjective*

premature *adjective* Appearing, happening, or done before the usual, expected, or correct time: *a premature birth; a premature decision.*
pre·ma·ture (prē'mə **toor'** or prē'mə **tyoor'** or prē'mə **choor'**) □*adjective*

premier *noun* A prime minister.
pre·mier (pri **mîr'**) □*noun, plural* **premiers**

premise *noun* 1. A statement that is taken as true used as the basis for an argument; assumption. 2. **premises** Land along with the buildings on it: *They don't allow dogs on the premises.*
prem·ise (**prem'** is) □*noun, plural* **premises**

preoccupied *adjective* So absorbed in what one is doing or thinking that one does not notice anything else: *I was so preoccupied with learning my lines for the play that I didn't hear the bell.*
pre·oc·cu·pied (prē **ok'** yə pīd') □*adjective*

preparation *noun* 1. The act of getting ready: *the preparation of food.* 2. An action

done in getting ready for something: *We made preparations for the trip.* 3. A mixture prepared for a certain use: *a preparation to soothe a burn.*
prep·a·ra·tion (prep'ə **rā'** shən) □*noun, plural* **preparations**

prepare *verb* 1. To get ready: *The soldiers prepared for an attack.* 2. To put together and make: *prepare a meal.*
pre·pare (pri **pâr'**) □*verb* **prepared, preparing, prepares**

preposition *noun* A word or group of words that shows the relation between a noun or pronoun and another word or words. *To, from,* and *with* are prepositions. In the sentence *I want mustard on my sandwich,* the word *on* is a preposition.
prep·o·si·tion (prep'ə **zish'** ən) □*noun, plural* **prepositions**

preposterous *adjective* Making no sense; absurd: *He has the preposterous idea that he can become rich by raising kangaroos.*
pre·pos·ter·ous (pri **pos'** tər əs) □*adjective*

prescribe *verb* To advise the use of: *The doctor prescribed a medicine and lots of rest.*
pre·scribe (pri **skrīb'**) □*verb* **prescribed, prescribing, prescribes**

prescription *noun* 1. A written order from a doctor for medicine. 2. The medicine that is ordered.
pre·scrip·tion (pri **skrip'** shən) □*noun, plural* **prescriptions**

presence *noun* 1. The fact of being present. 2. The place or area where someone is: *Please be quiet in his presence.*
pres·ence (**prez'** əns) □*noun*

present¹ *noun* The period of time happening now: *My sister is away at present.*
□*adjective* 1. Happening now: *the present government.* 2. In a place; attending: *Six club members were present and one was absent.*
pres·ent (**prez'** ənt) □*noun* □*adjective*

present² *verb* 1. To make a gift of: *present an award to the winner.* 2. To give to: *I presented him with a book.* 3. To introduce: *I presented*

a	bat	ī	bite	oo	tool	th	feather
ā	make	î	fierce	ou	out	th	bath
â	dare	o	dot	u	nut	hw	wheat
ä	father	ō	no	û	turn	zh	measure
e	net	ô	law, for	ch	church	ə	about, open
ē	be	oi	soil	ng	ring		pencil, atom
i	dip	oo	look	sh	shade		circus

my friend to my parents. **4.** To put on for an audience: *present a show.* —See Synonyms at **offer.**
□*noun* A gift.
pre·sent□*verb* (pri **zent′**) **presented, presenting, presents** □*noun* **present** (**prez′**ənt), *plural* **presents**

presentation *noun* The act of presenting.
pres·en·ta·tion (prez′ən **tā′**shən *or* prē′zen-**tā′**shən) □*noun, plural* **presentations**

presently *adverb* **1.** In a short time; soon: *The teacher will arrive presently.* **2.** Now: *I am presently reading a very good book.*
pres·ent·ly (**prez′**ənt lē) □*adverb*

present participle *noun* A verb form that shows an action or condition happening at the same time as the main verb. In the sentence *Even while resting, our bodies burn up energy,* the word *resting* is a present participle.

present tense *noun* A verb tense that expresses an action or condition that is customary or is always true. In the sentence *We go to school every day,* the verb *go* is in the present tense.

preservative *noun* Something used to preserve: *Salt is a food preservative.*
pre·serv·a·tive (pri **zûr′**və tiv) □*noun, plural* **preservatives**

preserve *verb* **1.** To keep safe; protect: *preserve one's health; preserve an old photograph by covering it with glass.* **2.** To protect food from spoiling: *Smoking meat is a way of preserving it.*
□*noun* **1.** Often **preserves** Fruit cooked with sugar and stored in jars. **2.** A place where wild animals and plants can live or grow safely.
pre·serve (pri **zûrv′**) □*verb* **preserved, preserving, preserves** □*noun, plural* **preserves**

president *noun* **1. President** The chief executive of the United States. **2.** The person in charge of an organization; leader: *the president of a corporation.*
pres·i·dent (**prez′**i dənt) □*noun, plural* **presidents**

press *verb* **1.** To put pressure against; push on: *Press the button.* **2.** To squeeze: *press juice from lemons.* **3.** To smooth by heat and pressure; iron: *press a pair of pants.* **4.** To push one's way: *We pressed forward through the crowd.*
□*noun* **1.** An act of pushing or squeezing. **2.** A device for pressing. **3.** A printing press.

4. Newspapers and magazines and the people who write for them.
press (pres) □*verb* **pressed, pressing, presses** □*noun, plural* **presses**

pressing *adjective* Requiring attention right away: *a pressing need; a pressing problem.*
press·ing (**pres′**ing) □*adjective*

pressure *noun* **1.** The force of one thing pressing directly on another: *Don't lean on that old table because it can't take the pressure.* **2.** A physical or mental burden; strain: *She is under great pressure on her job.* **3.** A strong influence or force: *We put pressure on him to repay the loan.*
pres·sure (**presh′**ər) □*noun, plural* **pressures**

prestige *noun* Great respect in the eyes of others: *His new job helped him gain prestige.*
pres·tige (pre **stēzh′**) □*noun*

SYNONYMS: **prestige, honor**

These nouns mean great respect in the eyes of others: *The award brought great prestige to the scientist. He fought the duel to defend his honor.*

---

pretend *verb* **1.** To put on a false show: *He pretended to be reading.* **2.** To make believe: *Let's pretend that we are on a space voyage.* **3.** To make a false claim.
pre·tend (pri **tend′**) □*verb* **pretended, pretending, pretends**

pretty *adjective* Attractive and pleasing: *a pretty cottage set in the middle of a garden.*
□*adverb* Somewhat: *I'm pretty tired.* —See Synonyms at **beautiful.**
pret·ty (**prit′**ē) □*adjective* **prettier, prettiest** □*adverb*

pretzel *noun* A crisp, salted cracker often baked in the shape of a knot.
pret·zel (**pret′**səl) □*noun, plural* **pretzels**

pretzel

prevail *verb* **1.** To be stronger or more successful: *Her natural good sense prevailed over the temptation to go along with the latest fad.* **2.** To be most common or frequent: *Cold weather prevailed throughout the entire country.*
pre·vail (pri **vāl'**) □*verb* **prevailed, prevailing, prevails**

prevent *verb* **1.** To keep from happening: *prevent an accident.* **2.** To keep someone from doing something: *A bad cold prevented me from sleeping.*
pre·vent (pri **vent'**) □*verb* **prevented, preventing, prevents**

prevention *noun* The act of preventing: *The prevention of forest fires is everyone's responsibility.*
pre·ven·tion (pri **ven'**shən) □*noun*

preview *noun* A showing of something before it is shown to everyone: *We saw a preview of the new movie.*
pre·view (prē'vyōō') □*noun, plural* **previews**

previous *adjective* Coming before; earlier: *the previous chapter.*
pre·vi·ous (prē'vē əs) □*adjective*

prey *noun* **1.** An animal hunted by another animal for food: *Mice are the prey of cats.* **2.** A victim: *Small children are often a prey to bullies.*
□*verb* **1.** To hunt for food: *Foxes prey on rabbits.* **2.** To trouble; bother: *His anxiety about his father preyed on his mind.*
prey (prā) □*noun* □*verb* **preyed, preying, preys**

price *noun* **1.** The amount of money asked or given for something. **2.** Something that must be given up to gain something: *Hard work is the price of success.*
□*verb* **1.** To put a price on. **2.** To find out the price of: *Let's price those shoes in the window.*
price (prīs) □*noun, plural* **prices** □*verb* **priced, pricing, prices**

priceless *adjective* Very valuable. —See Synonyms at **valuable.**
price·less (prīs'lis) □*adjective*

prick *noun* A small hole left by a sharp point.
□*verb* To make a small hole or mark: *She pricked her finger with a needle.*
prick (prik) □*noun, plural* **pricks** □*verb* **pricked, pricking, pricks**

prickly *adjective* **1.** Having small, sharp thorns: *a prickly plant.* **2.** Tingling: *This rough material gives me a prickly feeling.*

prick·ly (prik'lē) □*adjective* **pricklier, prickliest**

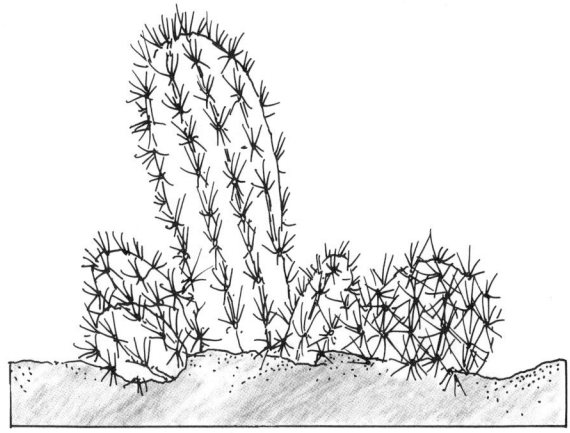

prickly

pride *noun* **1.** A feeling of one's own worth; self-respect. **2.** Pleasure in what one has done or in the things one owns: *She takes pride in her record collection.* **3.** A too high opinion of oneself: *His pride would not let him admit he was wrong.*
pride (prīd) □*noun*

priest *noun* A clergyman in the Roman Catholic Church and certain other churches.
priest (prēst) □*noun, plural* **priests**

WORD HISTORY: **priest**

Priest comes from a Greek word for an official of the early Christian church. The Greek word originally meant "elder," and it came from a word meaning "old man."

---

prim *adjective* Very formal or precise in appearance or manner.
prim (prim) □*adjective* **primmer, primmest**

primary *adjective* **1.** First in time or in order: *primary school.* **2.** First in importance; chief: *Food is a primary need for human beings.*
□*noun* An election to choose a political party's candidate for office in the regular election.
pri·mar·y (prī'mer'ē) □*adjective* □*noun, plural* **primaries**

a bat	ī bite	ōō tool	*th* feather
ā make	î fierce	ou out	th bath
â dare	o dot	u nut	hw wheat
ä father	ō no	û turn	zh measure
e net	ô law, for	ch church	ə about, open
ē be	oi soil	ng ring	pencil, atom
i dip	oo look	sh shade	circus

primary color *noun* Any of the three colors, red, yellow, or blue, from which all other colors can be made.

primate *noun* A member of the order of mammals that includes human beings, monkeys, and apes.
pri·mate (**prī′**māt′) ☐*noun, plural* **primates**

prime *adjective* **1.** Most important; greatest: *Her prime concern was to earn money for college.* **2.** Of the highest quality: *prime beef.*
☐*noun* The highest or best stage: *That actor is in his prime.*
prime (prīm) ☐*adjective* ☐*noun*

prime minister *noun* The chief executive of a country governed by a parliament, such as Great Britain or Canada.

prime number *noun* A whole number that can be divided only by itself and 1 without leaving a remainder.

primer *noun* A beginning book on a subject.
prim·er (**prim′**ər) ☐*noun, plural* **primers**

primitive *adjective* Of or in an early stage of development: *a primitive form of life.*
prim·i·tive (**prim′**i tiv) ☐*adjective*

primrose *noun* A plant with clusters of colorful flowers.
prim·rose (**prim′**rōz′) ☐*noun, plural* **primroses**

WORD HISTORY: **primrose**
The name *primrose* comes from a French phrase that means "first rose." The primrose is one of the first flowers to bloom in the spring.

primrose

prince *noun* **1.** The son of a king or queen. **2.** A nobleman of high rank.
prince (prins) ☐*noun, plural* **princes**

princess *noun* **1.** The daughter of a king or queen. **2.** A prince's wife.
prin·cess (**prin′**sis *or* **prin′**ses′) ☐*noun, plural* **princesses**

principal *adjective* Most important; chief: *Corn, wheat, and soybeans are the principal crops of the Middle West.*
☐*noun* **1.** The head of a school. **2.** An important or leading member of a group.
prin·ci·pal (**prin′**sə pəl) ☐*adjective* ☐*noun, plural* **principals**

principle *noun* **1.** A basic truth or belief: *Our government is based on the principles of democracy.* **2.** A rule of conduct or behavior: *It is against my principles to lie.*
prin·ci·ple (**prin′**sə pəl) ☐*noun, plural* **principles**

print *verb* **1.** To write in individual letters such as those that appear in the usual type of a book: *Please print your name clearly at the top of the page.* **2.** To put words or designs on paper or another surface: *We printed his article in our school magazine.*
☐*noun* **1.** Letters made by printing: *Small print is hard to read.* **2.** A mark made in a surface by pressure. **3.** Cloth with a design on it. **4.** A photograph made from a negative.
print (print) ☐*verb* **printed, printing, prints** ☐*noun, plural* **prints**

printer *noun* A person or company that prints books or other material.
print·er (**prin′**tər) ☐*noun, plural* **printers**

printing *noun* **1.** The process or business of making printed material. **2.** Letters like those used in print.
print·ing (**prin′**ting) ☐*noun*

printing press *noun* A machine that prints letters or designs on paper.

print-out *noun* The printed output of a computer.
print-out (**print′**out′) ☐*noun, plural* **print-outs**

prism *noun* A transparent solid object that breaks up light passing through it into the colors of the rainbow.
prism (**priz′**əm) ☐*noun, plural* **prisms**

prison *noun* A place where persons convicted or accused of crimes are kept.
pris·on (**priz′**ən) ☐*noun, plural* **prisons**

prisoner *noun* **1.** Someone kept in a prison. **2.** Someone who is captured or held by another.

pris·on·er (priz′ə nər) □*noun, plural* **prisoners**

privacy *noun* The condition of being alone or away from others: *He is a person who needs privacy in order to work well.*
pri·va·cy (prī′və sē) □*noun, plural* **privacies**

private *adjective* **1.** Owned by one person or group: *The public is not allowed on a private beach.* **2.** Not meant to be shared; personal: *a private letter.* **3.** Not holding public office: *a private citizen.*
□*noun* A soldier of the lowest rank.
pri·vate (prī′vit) □*adjective* □*noun, plural* **privates**

privilege *noun* A special right or permission: *I was given the privilege of using their tennis court on weekends.*
priv·i·lege (priv′ə lij) □*noun, plural* **privileges**

prize *noun* Something to be won in a game or contest: *The top prize at the fair was a car.*
□*adjective* Worthy of a prize: *a prize song.*
□*verb* To value highly: *She prizes honesty more than any other virtue.* —See Synonyms at **appreciate.**
prize (prīz) □*noun, plural* **prizes** □*adjective* □*verb* **prized, prizing, prizes**

pro *noun* Someone who is a professional, especially in sports.
pro (prō) □*noun, plural* **pros**

probability *noun* **1.** The condition of being likely to happen: *The probability of making a mistake increases when you are tired.* **2.** Something that is likely to happen: *A surprise test is a strong probability.*
prob·a·bil·i·ty (prob′ə bil′i tē) □*noun, plural* **probabilities**

probable *adjective* Likely to happen or be true: *We don't think it's probable that we will finish before noon.*
prob·a·ble (prob′ə bəl) □*adjective*

probation *noun* A period of time for testing a person's ability or behavior: *She is on probation until next month.*
pro·ba·tion (prō bā′shən) □*noun, plural* **probations**

probe *noun* **1.** A thorough investigation into something. **2.** A tool used to explore something. **3.** A vehicle sent into space to collect information.
□*verb* To investigate or explore.
probe (prōb) □*noun, plural* **probes** □*verb* **probed, probing, probes**

probe

problem *noun* A question or situation that needs an answer or has to be solved or dealt with: *a math problem; the problem of pollution.*
prob·lem (prob′ləm) □*noun, plural* **problems**

procedure *noun* A way of doing something in a correct and orderly fashion: *What's the procedure for getting a driver's license?*
pro·ce·dure (prə sē′jər) □*noun, plural* **procedures**

proceed *verb* **1.** To move on: *The car proceeded on its way after stopping at the light.* **2.** To do or carry on an action: *She proceeded to tell me the whole story.* —See Synonyms at **advance.**
pro·ceed (prə sēd′) □*verb* **proceeded, proceeding, proceeds**

proceeds *plural noun* The amount of money made or raised: *The proceeds from the sale were donated to the church.*
pro·ceeds (prō′sēdz′) □*plural noun*

process *noun* An action that has steps or stages: *the process of growing up; the process of building a sailboat.*
□*verb* To prepare or treat by a process: *Hides are processed to make leather.*
proc·ess (pros′es′) □*noun, plural* **processes** □*verb* **processed, processing, processes**

a	bat	ī	bite	oo	tool	*th*	feather
ā	make	î	fierce	ou	out	th	bath
â	dare	o	dot	u	nut	hw	wheat
ä	father	ō	no	û	turn	zh	measure
e	net	ô	law, for	ch	church	ə	about, open
ē	be	oi	soil	ng	ring		pencil, atom
i	dip	oo	look	sh	shade		circus

procession *noun* A group moving in an orderly line: *a wedding procession.*
pro·ces·sion (prə **sesh′** ən) □*noun, plural* **processions**

proclaim *verb* To announce publicly: *The President proclaimed a day of mourning.*
pro·claim (prə **klām′**) □*verb* **proclaimed, proclaiming, proclaims**

proclamation *noun* An official public announcement.
proc·la·ma·tion (prok′lə **mā′**shən) □*noun, plural* **proclamations**

procrastinate *verb* To put off doing something until a future time, especially for no good reason: *I procrastinated so long about doing my homework that I did not have time to finish it.*
pro·cras·ti·nate (prə **kras′**tə nāt′) □*verb* **procrastinated, procrastinating, procrastinates**

prod *verb* **1.** To push with something pointed; jab: *The farmer prodded the mule with a stick.* **2.** To urge by or as if by pushing: *She prodded him into applying for a new job.*
prod (prod) □*verb* **prodded, prodding, prods**

prodigy *noun* **1.** A person with unusual talents or abilities: *Mozart was a child prodigy.* **2.** An extraordinary or marvelous act or event: *a terrible storm that was a prodigy of nature.*
prod·i·gy (**prod′**ə jē) □*noun, plural* **prodigies**

produce *verb* **1.** To make or build: *This factory produces tires.* **2.** To bring forth; yield: *The tree will produce apples in September.* **3.** To bring forward for viewing; show: *Who produced the play we saw?* □*noun* Products from a farm or garden: *fruits, vegetables, and other produce.*
pro·duce□*verb* (prə **dōōs′** *or* prə **dyōōs′**) **produced, producing, produces** □*noun* (**prod′** ōōs *or* **prō′** dōōs)

producer *noun* A person, company, or thing that produces something: *a movie producer.*
pro·duc·er (prə **dōō′** sər *or* prə **dyōō′** sər) □*noun, plural* **producers**

product *noun* **1.** Something that is made: *factory products.* **2.** A number that is the result of multiplying two or more numbers: *The product of 9 times 7 is 63.*
prod·uct (**prod′**əkt) □*noun, plural* **products**

production *noun* **1.** The act of making or producing something. **2.** Something that is produced: *The show was a popular production.*

pro·duc·tion (prə **duk′**shən) □*noun, plural* **productions**

productive *adjective* Producing large amounts: *a productive farm.*
pro·duc·tive (prə **duk′**tiv) □*adjective*

profane *adjective* **1.** Not having to do with religion or sacred things; secular: *an artist who painted both sacred and profane subjects.* **2.** Showing contempt for sacred things; irreverent: *profane remarks.* **3.** Using or containing language that expresses disrespect, scorn, or abuse.
pro·fane (prə **fān′**) □*adjective*

profession *noun* A job that calls for special study or training: *the profession of law.*
pro·fes·sion (prə **fesh′**ən) □*noun, plural* **professions**

professional *adjective* **1.** Of or working in a profession: *Teachers are professional people.* **2.** Getting paid for doing something that other people do for pleasure: *a professional athlete.* □*noun* **1.** Someone who works at a profession: *Architects are professionals.* **2.** Someone who gets paid for doing something that other people do for pleasure.
pro·fes·sion·al (prə **fesh′**ə nəl) □*adjective* □*noun, plural* **professionals**

professor *noun* A teacher in a college or university.
pro·fes·sor (prə **fes′**ər) □*noun, plural* **professors**

profile *noun* **1.** A side view of something, especially of a person's head. **2.** A short description: *Write a profile of your best friend.*
pro·file (**prō′**fīl′) □*noun, plural* **profiles**

profile

profit *noun* **1.** Money made from a business after paying all its expenses: *We made lemonade for ten cents a glass and sold it for a quarter*

a glass; this gave us a profit of fifteen cents for each glass. **2.** A gain; benefit: *It would be to your profit to read this book.*
□*verb* To gain an advantage; benefit: *We profited from his advice.*
prof·it (prŏf′ĭt) □*noun, plural* **profits** □*verb* **profited, profiting, profits**

profitable *adjective* Yielding a profit or benefit: *a profitable business.*
prof·it·a·ble (prŏf′ĭ tə bəl) □*adjective*

profound *adjective* **1.** Showing great knowledge or understanding; wise: *a profound truth.* **2.** Very deep or great: *profound interest.*
pro·found (prə found′) □*adjective*

program *noun* **1.** A list of the order of events and the people performing at a show, concert, or meeting. **2.** A show or performance: *a television program.* **3.** A plan of things to be done: *a program to reduce poverty.* **4.** The set of instructions that a computer must carry out in solving a problem, answering a question, storing information, or getting stored information back again.
□*verb* To provide a computer with a program: *My computer is programmed to run multimedia software.*
pro·gram (prō′grăm′) □*noun, plural* **programs** □*verb* **programmed, programming, programs**

programmer *noun* A person who prepares programs for computers.
pro·gram·mer (prō′grăm′ər) □*noun, plural* **programmers**

progress *noun* Forward movement: *He made rapid progress to a high position.*
□*verb* To move forward: *The explorers progressed deep into the jungle.* —See Synonyms at **advance.**
prog·ress (prŏg′rĕs′) □*noun* □*verb*
pro·gress (prə grĕs′) **progressed, progressing, progresses**

progressive *adjective* **1.** Moving forward step by step: *progressive development.* **2.** Favoring or promoting improvement or reform: *We need progressive programs that will help the poor.*
□*noun* Someone who favors or works for improvement or reform.
pro·gres·sive (prə grĕs′ĭv) □*adjective*
□*noun, plural* **progressives**

prohibit *verb* To forbid or prevent; not allow: *Smoking is prohibited in the theater.* —See Synonyms at **forbid.**
pro·hib·it (prō hĭb′ĭt) □*verb* **prohibited,**

prohibiting, prohibits

prohibition *noun* **1.** The act of prohibiting something: *Our principal is very strict and believes that the prohibition of many harmless activities builds discipline and character.* **2.** A law or an order that prohibits something: *The prohibition against firecrackers was widely ignored on the Fourth of July.*
pro·hi·bi·tion (prō′ə bĭsh′ən) □*noun, plural* **prohibitions**

project *noun* **1.** A plan for doing something: *Repairing that door is one of my vacation projects.* **2.** A special study, task, or activity: *a student's science project.* **3.** A group of houses or apartment buildings built as a unit.
□*verb* **1.** To stick out: *A rusty nail projected from the fence post.* **2.** To cast on a surface: *project slides on a wall.*
proj·ect □*noun* (prŏj′ĕkt′), *plural* **projects**
□*verb* **pro·ject** (prə jĕkt′), **projected, projecting, projects**

projectile *noun* An object that can be thrown or shot forward through the air or through space. Arrows, bullets, and rockets are projectiles.
pro·jec·tile (prə jĕk′təl) □*noun, plural* **projectiles**

projector *noun* A machine that projects movies or slides on a surface.
pro·jec·tor (prə jĕk′tər) □*noun, plural* **projectors**

prolong *verb* To lengthen in extent or time: *We tried to prolong their visit by inviting them to stay to dinner.*
pro·long (prə lông′) □*verb* **prolonged, prolonging, prolongs**

prom *noun* A formal school dance.
prom (prŏm) □*noun, plural* **proms**

prominent *adjective* **1.** Standing or sticking out: *She has a prominent nose.* **2.** Important or well-known: *a prominent musician.*
prom·i·nent (prŏm′ə nənt) □*adjective*

promise *noun* **1.** A statement in which a person says something will or will not be done. **2.** A reason to hope for success: *That young*

a	bat	ī	bite	o͞o	tool	*th*	feather
ā	make	î	fierce	ou	out	th	bath
â	dare	o	dot	u	nut	hw	wheat
ä	father	ō	no	û	turn	zh	measure
e	net	ô	law, for	ch	church	ə	about, open
ē	be	oi	soil	ng	ring		pencil, atom
i	dip	o͝o	look	sh	shade		circus

athlete shows promise.

□*verb* **1.** To make a promise; swear: *I promised to help her.* **2.** To give a reason to expect something: *His bad mood promised trouble.*
prom·ise (prŏm′is) □*noun, plural* **promises** □*verb* **promised, promising, promises**

promontory *noun* A high piece of land that extends out into a body of water.
pro·mon·to·ry (prŏm′ən tôr′ē) □*noun, plural* **promontories**

promote *verb* **1.** To raise to a higher rank: *He was promoted to chief of police.* **2.** To encourage or support: *A balanced diet promotes growth.*
pro·mote (prə mōt′) □*verb* **promoted, promoting, promotes**

promotion *noun* **1.** An advance in rank: *She received a promotion.* **2.** The act of promoting.
pro·mo·tion (prə mō′shən) □*noun, plural* **promotions**

prompt *adjective* Acting or done right away: *I received a prompt answer to my letter.*
□*verb* **1.** To cause someone to act: *The cold wind prompted him to button his coat.* **2.** To remind someone what to do or say: *I'll prompt you if you forget your speech.*
prompt (prompt) □*adjective* **prompter, promptest** □*verb* **prompted, prompting, prompts**

promptly *adverb* Without delay; at once.
prompt·ly (prompt′lē) □*adverb*

prone *adjective* **1.** Lying with the front or face downward. **2.** Having a certain tendency; liable: *He is prone to be careless.*
prone (prōn) □*adjective*

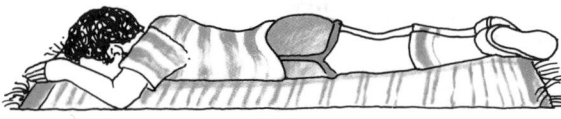

prone

prong *noun* One of the pointed ends of a fork or other tool.
prong (prông) □*noun, plural* **prongs**

pronghorn *noun* An animal that has short, forked horns and can run very fast. Pronghorns live in North America.
prong·horn (prông′hôrn′) □*noun, plural* **pronghorns**

pronoun *noun* A word used in place of a noun to refer to a person or thing already named or understood. *I, she, them, who,* and *which* are pronouns.

pro·noun (prō′noun′) □*noun, plural* **pronouns**

pronounce *verb* **1.** To make the sound of a letter or word: *He pronounced his words with great care.* **2.** To declare that something is so: *The judge pronounced the man guilty.*
pro·nounce (prə nouns′) □*verb* **pronounced, pronouncing, pronounces**

pronounced *adjective* Easy to notice: *He walks with a pronounced limp.*
pro·nounced (prə nounst′) □*adjective*

pronto *adverb* Right away; immediately. *I want this room cleaned pronto!*
pron·to (prŏn′tō) □*adverb*

pronunciation *noun* The way a letter or word is or should be spoken: *Sometimes there is more than one correct pronunciation for a word.*
pro·nun·ci·a·tion (prə nun′sē ā′shən) □*noun, plural* **pronunciations**

proof *noun* Evidence or facts that show that something is true: *He brought a birth certificate along as proof of his age.*
proof (prōof) □*noun, plural* **proofs**

proofread *verb* To read over printed or written material and correct mistakes: *Proofread your essay before handing it in.*
proof·read (prōof′rēd′) □*verb* **proofread, proofreading, proofreads**

prop *verb* To hold up by putting a support under or against: *prop up a sagging roof.*
□*noun* Something used to hold up another thing.
prop (prop) □*verb* **propped, propping, props** □*noun, plural* **props**

propaganda *noun* Information and ideas deliberately spread to influence the way people think. Propaganda may not be completely true or fair.
prop·a·gan·da (prop′ə gan′də) □*noun*

propel *verb* To make something move forward: *The sailboat was propelled by the wind.*
pro·pel (prə pel′) □*verb* **propelled, propelling, propels**

propeller *noun* A device made up of blades that stick out from a hub. When the blades spin around, they move air or water and propel an aircraft or boat.
pro·pel·ler (prə pel′ər) □*noun, plural* **propellers**

proper *adjective* **1.** Right for a certain purpose or occasion; appropriate: *He doesn't have the proper training for the job.* **2.** Belonging to

a certain person, place, or thing: *London is a proper name.* **3.** Limited to the strict meaning of a word: *The suburbs are not part of the city proper.*
prop·er (**prop′**ər) ☐*adjective*

properly *adverb* In a proper or correct way: *Hold the racket properly.*
prop·er·ly (**prop′**ər lē) ☐*adverb*

property *noun* **1.** Something owned by a person: *That wagon is my property.* **2.** Land owned by someone. **3.** A characteristic; quality: *Being invisible and without odor are two properties of fresh air.*
prop·er·ty (**prop′**ər tē) ☐*noun, plural* **properties**

prophecy *noun* Something said that tells about what will happen in the future: *He made a prophecy that the war would end soon.*
proph·e·cy (**prof′**i sē) ☐*noun, plural* **prophecies**

prophet *noun* **1.** A religious leader whose messages are believed to come from God. **2.** Someone who can foresee the future.
proph·et (**prof′**it) ☐*noun, plural* **prophets**

proportion *noun* **1.** A part of a whole; fraction: *What is the proportion of copper in a penny?* **2.** The size or amount of one thing when compared to the size or amount of another thing: *The proportion of girls to boys in the school is about even.* **3. proportions** Size or extent: *a meal of huge proportions.*
pro·por·tion (prə **pôr′**shən) ☐*noun*

proposal *noun* **1.** The act of proposing. **2.** A suggestion or plan. **3.** An offer of marriage.
pro·pos·al (prə **pō′**zəl) ☐*noun, plural* **proposals**

propose *verb* **1.** To bring up for consideration: *propose a new law.* **2.** To intend to do something: *Columbus proposed to sail west to reach the Orient.* **3.** To make an offer of marriage.
pro·pose (prə **pōz′**) ☐*verb* **proposed, proposing, proposes**

proprietor *noun* Someone who owns a business or property: *The proprietor of a shoe store.*
pro·pri·e·tor (prə **prī′**i tər) ☐*noun, plural* **proprietors**

propulsion *noun* **1.** The act of making something go forward. **2.** A force that propels: *Jet propulsion is used to launch a satellite into orbit.*
pro·pul·sion (prə **pul′**shən) ☐*noun*

prose *noun* Ordinary, everyday writing or speech that is not poetry.
prose (prōz) ☐*noun*

prosecute *verb* To bring before a court of law for a trial: *They will prosecute any official who takes bribes.*
pros·e·cute (**pros′**i kyōōt′) ☐*verb* **prosecuted, prosecuting, prosecutes**

prospect *noun* **1.** Something that is expected: *The pioneers faced the prospect of a cold winter.* **2.** A possible customer or candidate: *That new player is a good prospect for the first team.*
☐*verb* To search or explore: *prospect for gold.*
pros·pect (**pros′**pekt′) ☐*noun, plural* **prospects** ☐*verb* **prospected, prospecting, prospects**

prospector *noun* Someone who searches for gold or other valuable minerals.
pros·pec·tor (**pros′**pek′tər) ☐*noun, plural* **prospectors**

prospector

prosper *verb* To do well; be successful: *The pioneers prospered because they worked hard.*
pros·per (**pros′**pər) ☐*verb* **prospered, prospering, prospers**

prosperity *noun* Success or good fortune: *Years of prosperity made up for the hardships they had suffered.*

a	bat	ī	bite	ōō	tool	*th*	feather
ā	make	î	fierce	ou	out	th	bath
â	dare	o	dot	u	nut	hw	wheat
ä	father	ō	no	û	turn	zh	measure
e	net	ô	law, for	ch	church	ə	about, open
ē	be	oi	soil	ng	ring		pencil, atom
i	dip	oo	look	sh	shade		circus

pros·per·i·ty (pro **sper′**i tē) □*noun, plural*
prosperities

prosperous *adjective* Having wealth, success,
or good fortune: *a prosperous farmer.*
pros·per·ous (pros′pər əs) □*adjective*

protect *verb* To guard or keep from harm:
*Baseball catchers wear masks to protect their
faces.* —See Synonyms at **defend.**
pro·tect (prə **tekt′**) □*verb* **protected,
protecting, protects**

protection *noun* **1.** The condition of being
kept from harm: *The construction workers
wore metal helmets for protection.* **2.** Someone
or something that protects: *A thin jacket is a
poor protection against cold.*
pro·tec·tion (prə **tek′**shən) □*noun, plural*
protections

protective *adjective* Helping to protect: *a
protective coat of paint.*
pro·tec·tive (prə **tek′**tiv) □*adjective*

protector *noun* Someone or something that
protects.
pro·tec·tor (prə **tek′**tər) □*noun, plural*
protectors

protein *noun* A substance necessary to life
that animals use in their bodies to grow and
replace living tissue. Meat, milk, and beans
contain a great deal of protein.
pro·tein (prō′tēn′) □*noun, plural* **proteins**

protest *noun* An objection or complaint
made against something: *The workers refused
to work for a day as a protest against low
wages.*
□*verb* To make strong objections: *The students protested against the new rules.*
pro·test □*noun* (prō′test′), *plural* **protests**
　□*verb* (prə **test′**) **protested, protesting,
protests**

Protestant *noun* A Christian belonging to a
church that broke away from the Roman
Catholic Church in the 16th century.
Prot·es·tant (prot′i stənt) □*noun, plural*
Protestants

proton *noun* A tiny particle of an atom that
has a positive electric charge.
pro·ton (prō′ton′) □*noun, plural* **protons**

protoplasm *noun* The material that is similar
to a jelly and found in all living cells.
pro·to·plasm (prō′tə plaz′əm) □*noun, plural*
protoplasms

protozoan *noun* One of a large group of tiny
animals made up of only one cell. Amebas are
protozoans.

pro·to·zo·an (prō′tə **zō′**ən) □*noun, plural*
protozoans

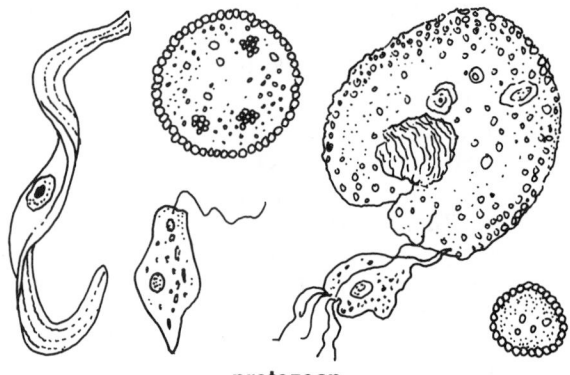

protozoan
Several kinds of protozoans

protrude *verb* To stick out: *A loaf of bread
protruded from her shopping bag.*
pro·trude (prō **trōōd′**) □*verb* **protruded,
protruding, protrudes**

protrude

proud *adjective* **1.** Feeling pleased or satisfied about something: *He was proud of his
heritage.* **2.** Full of self-respect: *She is too
proud to ask for a loan.*
proud (proud) □*adjective* **prouder, proudest**

prove *verb* **1.** To show something is true: *He
proved that he could juggle three oranges.* **2.** To
turn out: *The experiment proved to be a failure.*
prove (prōōv) □*verb* **proved** or **proven,
proving, proves**

> *SYNONYMS:* **prove, demonstrate**
>
> These verbs mean to show that something is true:
> *Her success proves that hard work will be rewarded.
> His letter clearly demonstrates that he cannot spell.*

proven *verb* A past participle of **prove:** *He
has proven his innocence.*
prov·en (prōō′vən) □*verb*

proverb *noun* A saying that expresses some-thing many people believe to be true. *A rolling stone gathers no moss* is a proverb.
prov·erb (prov′ərb) □*noun, plural* **proverbs**

provide *verb* **1.** To give what is needed or useful: *The teacher provided paper for the test.* **2.** To make ready; prepare: *She was saving money to provide for her retirement.* **3.** To set down a condition or requirement: *The Constitution provides for freedom of speech.*
pro·vide (prə vīd′) □*verb* **provided, providing, provides**

provided *conjunction* On the condition: *You may leave provided you have finished your work.*
pro·vid·ed (prə vī′did) □*conjunction*

province *noun* **1.** A division or district of a country: *Ontario and Manitoba are Canadian provinces.* **2.** The range of someone's knowl-edge or authority: *She teaches science, and so history is outside her province.*
prov·ince (prov′ins) □*noun, plural* **provinces**

provision *noun* **1.** The act of giving what is needed or useful: *the provision of supplies for a camping trip.* **2.** **provisions** Food and other necessary things. **3.** A plan or preparation: *He is making provisions for a long trip.* **4.** A condi-tion or requirement: *the provisions of a contract.*
pro·vi·sion (prə vizh′ən) □*noun, plural* **provisions**

provoke *verb* **1.** To bring on; arouse: *The joke provoked much laughter.* **2.** To cause to act: *The government's action provoked her to protest.* **3.** To make angry: *Her foolish prank provoked me.*
pro·voke (prə vōk′) □*verb* **provoked, provoking, provokes**

prow *noun* The pointed front part of a ship or boat.
prow (prou) □*noun, plural* **prows**

prow

prowl *verb* To move about slowly and qui-etly: *A cat prowls at night.*
prowl (proul) □*verb* **prowled, prowling, prowls**

prudence *noun* Caution in practical matters; careful judgment: *She has too much prudence to gamble.*
pru·dence (prōō′dəns) □*noun*

prune¹ *noun* A dried plum.
prune (prōōn) □*noun, plural* **prunes**

prune² *verb* To cut or trim branches from: *prune a rose bush to improve its growth.*
prune (prōōn) □*verb* **pruned, pruning, prunes**

pry¹ *verb* **1.** To raise or move by force: *I had to pry the rock loose with a stick.* **2.** To find out with much effort: *He pried the secret from me.*
pry (prī) □*verb* **pried, prying, pries**

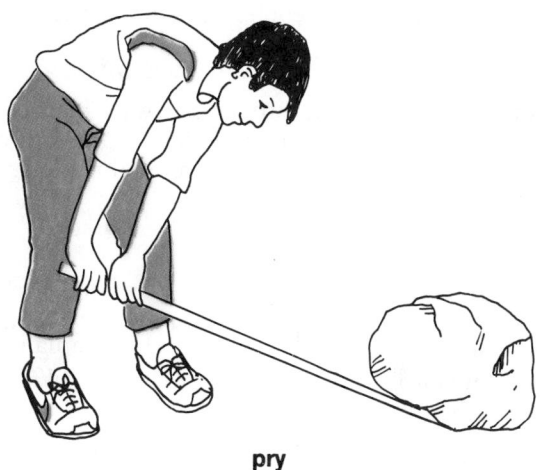

pry

pry² *verb* To look with curiosity; be nosy: *Stop prying into my affairs.*
pry (prī) □*verb* **pried, prying, pries**

P.S. An abbreviation for **postscript.**

psalm *noun* A sacred song or poem.
psalm (säm) □*noun, plural* **psalms**

psychiatrist *noun* A doctor who treats men-tal illness.
psy·chi·a·trist (sī kī′ə trist) □*noun, plural* **psychiatrists**

a bat	ī bite	ōō tool	*th* feather
ā make	î fierce	ou out	th bath
â dare	o dot	u nut	hw wheat
ä father	ō no	û turn	zh measure
e net	ô law, for	ch church	ə about, open
ē be	oi soil	ng ring	pencil, atom
i dip	oo look	sh shade	circus

psychologist *noun* Someone who is an expert in psychology. A psychologist often counsels people with emotional problems.
psy·chol·o·gist (sī kol′ə jist) □*noun, plural* **psychologists**

psychology *noun* The science of the mind and of human behavior.
psy·chol·o·gy (sī kol′ə jē) □*noun, plural* **psychologies**

pt. An abbreviation for **pint.**

pterodactyl *noun* An extinct flying reptile that lived millions of years ago during the age of the dinosaurs.
pter·o·dac·tyl (ter′ə dak′təl) □*noun, plural* **pterodactyls**

public *adjective* **1.** Of or for all the people: *public health; a public library.* **2.** Working for the people or community: *public officials.* □*noun* All of the people: *The new skating rink will be open to the public.*
pub·lic (pub′lik) □*adjective* □*noun*

public-address system *noun* An electronic system that uses loudspeakers and other equipment to send sound throughout a large area, as an arena or a school.
pub·lic-ad·dress system (pub′lik ə dres′) □*noun*

publication *noun* Something printed and published: *books, magazines, and other publications.*
pub·li·ca·tion (pub′li kā′shən) □*noun, plural* **publications**

publicity *noun* Information given out to get public attention: *Publicity for the school play included posters and a full-page ad in the local newspaper.*
pub·lic·i·ty (pu blis′i tē) □*noun*

publicize *verb* To give publicity to; make known: *The concert was publicized several weeks in advance in hopes of getting a big crowd to attend.*
pub·li·cize (pub′li sīz′) □*verb* **publicized, publicizing, publicizes**

public school *noun* A free school supported by the government.

publish *verb* To print and offer for sale: *His book was published last year. The magazine is published six times a year.*
pub·lish (pub′lish) □*verb* **published, publishing, publishes**

publisher *noun* A person or company that publishes books or other printed material.

pub·lish·er (pub′li shər) □*noun, plural* **publishers**

puck *noun* A hard rubber disk used in ice hockey.
puck (puk) □*noun, plural* **pucks**

pucker *verb* To gather or be gathered into small folds or wrinkles: *She puckered her lips. The seams puckered after the dress was washed.*
puck·er (puk′ər) □*verb* **puckered, puckering, puckers**

pudding *noun* A sweet, soft dessert usually made of flour, milk, sugar, and flavoring: *chocolate pudding.*
pud·ding (pood′ing) □*noun, plural* **puddings**

puddle *noun* A small, shallow pool of liquid: *The rain left puddles in the yard.*
pud·dle (pud′əl) □*noun, plural* **puddles**

pudgy *adjective* Short and chubby: *pudgy fingers; a pudgy little dog.*
pud·gy (puj′ē) □*adjective* **pudgier, pudgiest**

pueblo *noun* An American Indian village of the southwest made up of stone and adobe buildings built close together, often around a central plaza.
pueb·lo (pweb′lō) □*noun, plural* **pueblos**

WORD HISTORY: **pueblo**
The word *pueblo* is borrowed from Spanish, where it means "people" and "village."

Puerto Rican *noun* Someone who was born in Puerto Rico. Puerto Ricans are United States citizens. □*adjective* Of Puerto Rico and its people.
Puer·to Ri·can (pwer′tō rē′kən) □*noun, plural* **Puerto Ricans** □*adjective*

puff *noun* **1.** A short, sudden gust: *Puffs of steam and smoke came from the engine.* **2.** Something that looks light and fluffy: *a powder puff; a pastry puff.* □*verb* **1.** To blow or breathe in puffs: *The wind puffed. We were puffing after climbing the hill.* **2.** To swell up: *His sore thumb puffed up.*
puff (puf) □*noun, plural* **puffs** □*verb* **puffed, puffing, puffs**

pull *verb* **1.** To grasp something and make it move forward or toward oneself: *pull a wagon.* **2.** To draw out of a firm position: *pull a tooth.* **3.** To move: *The train pulled away from the station.* □*noun* **1.** The act of pulling. **2.** The force or effort used in pulling: *the pull of a magnet.*

  pull through To get through a hard situation: *The sick child managed to pull through.*
pull (pool) □*verb* **pulled, pulling, pulls**
  □*noun, plural* **pulls**

pulley *noun* A wheel with a rope or chain moving around it in a groove, used to lift heavy weights.
pul·ley (pool′ē) □*noun, plural* **pulleys**

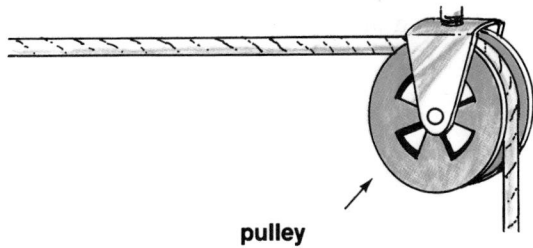

pulley

pulp *noun* **1.** The soft, juicy part of fruits and certain vegetables. **2.** Ground-up wood or rags mixed with water, used for making paper.
pulp (pulp) □*noun, plural* **pulps**

pulpit *noun* A platform in a church from which a minister speaks.
pul·pit (pool′pit) □*noun, plural* **pulpits**

pulse *noun* **1.** The rhythmic movement of the arteries as the heart pumps blood through them. **2.** A regular beat: *the pulse of drums.*
pulse (puls) □*noun, plural* **pulses**

puma *noun* The mountain lion.
pu·ma (pyoo′mə) □*noun, plural* **pumas**

pump *noun* A device used to move a liquid or gas from one place to another: *an air pump.*
□*verb* **1.** To move with a pump: *pump water from a boat.* **2.** To fill with air or another gas by using a pump: *pump up a flat tire.* **3.** To question presistently: *We pumped her for news.*
pump (pump) □*noun, plural* **pumps** □*verb*
pumped, pumping, pumps

pump

pumpkin *noun* A large, round fruit with a thick, orange rind, used for making pies and jack-o'-lanterns.
pump·kin (pump′kin *or* pung′kin) □*noun, plural* **pumpkins**

pun *noun* A funny use of a word that has more than one meaning or of a word that sounds like another word. For example, "I'll join you in a cup of tea, if you think there's room" is a pun on the two ways of understanding "join you in."
pun (pun) □*noun, plural* **puns**

punch[1] *verb* To make a hole, mark, or design in: *punch a new hole in a belt.*
□*noun* A tool for making holes: *a paper punch.*
punch (punch) □*verb* **punched, punching, punches** □*noun, plural* **punches**

punch[2] *verb* **1.** To hit with the fist. **2.** To herd cattle: *They punch cows for a living.*
□*noun* A blow with the fist.
punch (punch) □*verb* **punched, punching, punches** □*noun, plural* **punches**

punch[3] *noun* A drink made by mixing fruit juices, soda, or other ingredients.
punch (punch) □*noun, plural* **punches**

WORD HISTORY: **punch**[3]

Punch[3] probably comes from a Hindi word that means "five." The drink may originally have had five ingredients.

---

punctual *adjective* On time; prompt: *Please be punctual for our appointment.*
punc·tu·al (pungk′choo əl) □*adjective*

punctuate *verb* To mark written material with periods, commas, and other signs to make the meaning clear.
punc·tu·ate (pungk′choo āt′) □*verb*
punctuated, punctuating, punctuates

punctuation *noun* The use of periods, commas, and other marks to make the meaning of writing clear.
punc·tu·a·tion (pungk′choo ā′shən) □*noun*

a	bat	ī	bite	ōō	tool	*th*	feather
ā	make	î	fierce	ou	out	th	bath
â	dare	o	dot	u	nut	hw	wheat
ä	father	ō	no	û	turn	zh	measure
e	net	ô	law, for	ch	church	ə	about, open
ē	be	oi	soil	ng	ring		pencil, atom
i	dip	oo	look	sh	shade		circus

punctuation mark *noun* Any of the marks used to make the meaning of written material clear. Commas, semicolons, and periods are punctuation marks.

puncture *verb* To make a hole in with something sharp: *A piece of glass punctured the bicycle tire.*
□*noun* A hole made by something sharp.
punc·ture (**pungk′**chər) □*verb* **punctured, puncturing, punctures** □*noun, plural* **punctures**

punish *verb* To make someone suffer for a crime or wrong: *She punished him for his rudeness by sending him to his room.*
pun·ish (**pun′**ish) □*verb* **punished, punishing, punishes**

punishment *noun* **1.** The act of punishing: *The state is responsible for the punishment of criminals.* **2.** A penalty for a crime or wrong: *The loss of his allowance was a heavy punishment for his foolish behavior.*
pun·ish·ment (**pun′**ish mənt) □*noun, plural* **punishments**

punt *noun* To drop a football and kick it before it hits the ground.
□*verb* To make a punt.
punt (punt) □*noun, plural* **punts** □*verb* **punted, punting, punts**

pup *noun* A young dog, seal, wolf, or fox.
pup (pup) □*noun, plural* **pups**

pupa *noun* An insect during a stage when it is changing from a larva into an adult.
pu·pa (**pyoo′**pə) □*noun, plural* **pupas**

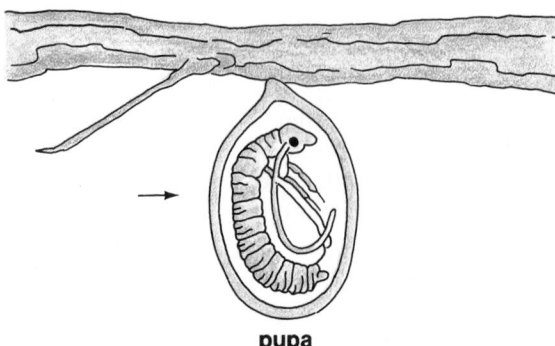
pupa

pupil¹ *noun* Someone studying in school or with a private teacher; student.
pu·pil (**pyoo′**pəl) □*noun, plural* **pupils**

pupil² *noun* The black dot in the center of the iris through which light enters the eye.
pu·pil (**pyoo′**pəl) □*noun, plural* **pupils**

WORD HISTORY: pupil²
Pupil² comes from a Latin word for ''pupil of the eye.'' The Latin word literally means ''little girl.'' The pupil of the eye is so called because it is possible to see a tiny reflection of oneself by looking into the pupil of another person's eye.

puppet *noun* A small figure of a person or animal that fits over the hand or is moved by strings from above.
pup·pet (**pup′**it) □*noun, plural* **puppets**

puppet

puppy *noun* A young dog.
pup·py (**pup′**ē) □*noun, plural* **puppies**

purchase *verb* To get by paying money; buy: *We want to purchase a new house.*
□*noun* Something that is bought.
pur·chase (**pûr′**chis) □*verb* **purchased, purchasing, purchases** □*noun, plural* **purchases**

pure *adjective* Not mixed with anything: *pure water; pure luck.*
pure (pyoor) □*adjective* **purer, purest**

purify *verb* To make pure or clean: *Boiling will purify water.*
pu·ri·fy (**pyoor′**ə fī′) □*verb* **purified, purifying, purifies**

Puritan *noun* A member of a group of Protestants in England and the American Colonies in the 16th and 17th centuries. The Puritans favored very simple forms of worship and strict moral behavior.
Pu·ri·tan (**pyoor′**i tən) □*noun, plural* **Puritans**

purity *noun* The condition of being pure or clean: *The town tested the purity of its water.*
pu·ri·ty (**pyoor′**i tē) □*noun*

purple *noun* A color that is a mixture of red and blue.
□*adjective* Of the color purple.
pur·ple (**pûr′**pəl) □*noun, plural* **purples** □*adjective*

purplish *adjective* Somewhat purple.
pur·plish (**pûr′**plish) □*adjective*

purpose *noun* The reason for which something exists or is done; aim: *The purpose of the fan is to cool off the room.*
pur·pose (**pûr′**pəs) □*noun, plural* **purposes**

purposely *adverb* Done deliberately: *She purposely gave me the wrong number.*
pur·pose·ly (**pûr′**pəs lē) □*adverb*

purr *noun* A low, murmuring sound made by a contented cat.
□*verb* To make a purr.
purr (**pûr**) □*noun, plural* **purrs** □*verb* **purred, purring, purrs**

purse *noun* **1.** A woman's handbag. **2.** A small bag for holding money.
□*verb* To draw together: *She pursed her lips in annoyance.*
purse (**pûrs**) □*noun, plural* **purses** □*verb* **pursed, pursing, purses**

pursue *verb* **1.** To chase in order to capture: *The guard pursued the bank robber.* **2.** To carry on: *pursue a career in business.*
pur·sue (pər **sōō′**) □*verb* **pursued, pursuing, pursues**

pursuit *noun* **1.** The act of pursuing: *The prisoner escaped, and the police followed in pursuit.* **2.** A hobby or activity: *Reading is his favorite pursuit.*
pur·suit (pər **sōōt′**) □*noun, plural* **pursuits**

pus *noun* A yellowish-white liquid that forms in an infection.
pus (**pus**) □*noun*

push *verb* **1.** To press against something in order to move it: *He pushed the door but it wouldn't open.* **2.** To move forward by using force: *We had to push our way through the crowd.* **3.** To try to promote: *The citizens pushed for better schools.*
□*noun* **1.** The act of pushing. **2.** A strong effort: *a big push to get finished on time.*
push (**poosh**) □*verb* **pushed, pushing, pushes** □*noun, plural* **pushes**

pushcart *noun* A light cart that is pushed by hand: *She sold hot pretzels from a pushcart.*
push·cart (**poosh′**kärt′) □*noun, plural* **pushcarts**

pushcart

pushup *noun* An exercise in which a person lies face down and raises and lowers the body by straightening and bending the arms while keeping the back straight.
push·up (**poosh′**up′) □*noun, plural* **pushups**

pussy willow *noun* A shrub that has small, silky gray flower clusters.
puss·y willow (**poos′**ē) □*noun*

put *verb* **1.** To cause to be in a certain place or condition; place: *I put the books on my desk. Put on your coat. She put the room in order.* **2.** To cause to undergo something: *I hate to put you to any trouble.* **3.** To express: *He put his fear into words.*
put down To criticize: *She's always putting her little brother down.*
put off To postpone: *put off a decision.*
put on To present; perform: *put on a play.*
put out To cause trouble for: *We're sorry to put you out.*
put up **1.** To build. **2.** To provide with a place to stay or sleep.
put up with To tolerate; endure.
put (**poot**) □*verb* **put, putting, puts**

putt *verb* To hit a golf ball gently when it is near the hole.
□*noun* Such a hit.
putt (**put**) □*verb* **putted, putting, putts** □*noun, plural* **putts**

putty *noun* A soft cement used to fill cracks and hold panes of glass in place.
put·ty (**put′**ē) □*noun, plural* **putties**

a bat	ī bite	ōō tool	*th* feather
ā make	î fierce	ou out	th bath
â dare	o dot	u nut	hw wheat
ä father	ō no	û turn	zh measure
e net	ô law, for	ch church	ə about, open
ē be	oi soil	ng ring	pencil, atom
i dip	oo look	sh shade	circus

puzzle *noun* Something that is hard to solve or understand: *She likes to do math puzzles. Her strange behavior was a puzzle to us.*
◻*verb* **1.** To be hard to understand: *A moving light in the deserted house puzzled us.* **2.** To work hard trying to find a solution: *We were puzzling over the problem when she called.* —See Synonyms at **confuse.**
puz·zle (**puz′**əl) ◻*noun, plural* **puzzles**
◻*verb* **puzzled, puzzling, puzzles**

pygmy *noun* An unusually small person or thing.
pyg·my (**pig′**mē) ◻*noun, plural* **pygmies**

pyramid *noun* A solid object with a flat base and four triangular sides that meet in a point at the top. The pyramids of Egypt are huge stone structures that were built as tombs in ancient times.
pyr·a·mid (**pir′**ə mid) ◻*noun, plural* **pyramids**

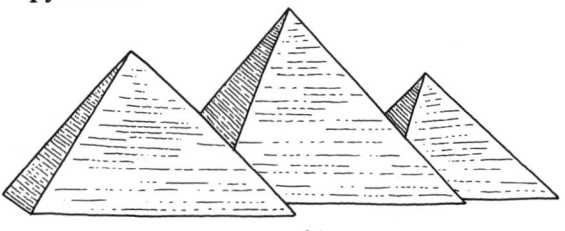

pyramid

python *noun* A large, nonpoisonous snake that coils around and crushes its prey.
py·thon (**pī′**thon′) ◻*noun, plural* **pythons**

ANCIENT GREEK

The letter **Q** has evolved from many forms of ancient writing. One of the earliest known examples is the Greek character shown above, which dates from almost 3,000 years ago. Over the years, artists and designers have created their own versions of the English letter **Q**. Some of the more common examples seen today are shown below.

Qq 2q	**Qq Qq**	Qq Qq	**Qq Qq**	*2q 2q*
HANDWRITING	CALLIGRAPHY	MODERN SANS SERIF	MODERN SERIF	SCRIPT

q or **Q** *noun* The seventeenth letter of the English alphabet.
q or **Q** (kyōō) ▢*noun, plural* **q's** or **Q's**

qt. An abbreviation for **quart.**

quack *noun* The sound made by a duck. ▢*verb* To make a quack.
quack (kwak) ▢*noun, plural* **quacks** ▢*verb* **quacked, quacking, quacks**

quadrilateral *noun* A geometric figure, such as a square or rectangle, that has four sides.
quad·ri·lat·er·al (kwod'ri **lat'**ər əl) ▢*noun, plural* **quadrilaterals**

quadruped *noun* An animal that has four feet. Dogs and horses are quadrupeds.
quad·ru·ped (**kwod'**rə ped') ▢*noun, plural* **quadrupeds**

quail *noun* A small plump bird with a short tail and brownish feathers.
quail (kwāl) ▢*noun, plural* **quail** or **quails**

quaint *adjective* Old-fashioned in a pleasing way: *a quaint old house.*
quaint (kwānt) ▢*adjective* **quainter, quaintest**

quake *verb* To shake, tremble, or shiver: *The girl quaked with fear. The building quaked when the train passed.*
▢*noun* An earthquake.
quake (kwāk) ▢*verb* **quaked, quaking, quakes** ▢*noun, plural* **quakes**

qualification *noun* **1.** Something that makes a person fit for a certain kind of work: *He has the qualifications to be a teacher.* **2.** Something that limits or restricts: *They accepted her proposal without qualification.*
qual·i·fi·ca·tion (kwol'ə fi **kā'**shən) ▢*noun, plural* **qualifications**

qualify *verb* **1.** To make or become fit for a certain kind of work or position: *His experience and education qualified him for the job.* **2.** To limit or restrict: *Adverbs qualify adjectives and verbs.*
qual·i·fy (**kwol'**ə fī') ▢*verb* **qualified, qualifying, qualifies**

quail

a bat	ī bite	ōō tool	*th* feather
ā make	î fierce	ou **out**	th bath
â dare	o dot	u nut	hw **wheat**
ä father	ō no	û turn	zh measure
e net	ô law, for	ch church	ə about, open
ē be	oi soil	ng ring	pencil, atom
i dip	oo look	sh shade	circus

quality *noun* **1.** The nature or character of something that makes it what it is: *The chief quality of sugar is its sweetness.* **2.** A special trait; characteristic: *She has many excellent qualities.* **3.** The degree of how good or bad something is: *That company manufactures woolen cloth of very high quality.*
qual·i·ty (**kwol′**i tē) □*noun, plural* **qualities**

SYNONYMS: **quality, characteristic, feature**

These nouns mean a special element or trait: *Honesty is her finest quality. An important characteristic of the new, small cars is that they use less gas. A large nose is his most prominent feature.*

---

qualm *noun* **1.** A sudden feeling of doubt or fear: *I had qualms about diving from the high board.* **2.** A pang of conscience: *He had no qualms about cheating.*
qualm (kwäm) □*noun, plural* **qualms**

quantity *noun* **1.** An amount or number: *I used a small quantity of butter.* **2.** A large amount or number: *The store buys dresses in quantity.*
quan·ti·ty (**kwon′**ti tē) □*noun, plural* **quantities**

quarantine *noun* The act of keeping a person, animal, or plant apart from others to stop the spread of disease.
□*verb* To keep or place in quarantine.
quar·an·tine (**kwôr′**ən tēn′) □*noun, plural* **quarantines** □*verb* **quarantined, quarantining, quarantines**

WORD HISTORY: **quarantine**

Quarantine comes from the Latin word for "forty." In the past the period of quarantine for infectious diseases was generally 40 days.

---

quarrel *noun* An angry argument or dispute: *They had a quarrel over who would have the first turn.*
□*verb* **1.** To have a quarrel: *The family quarreled about money.* **2.** To find fault: *I can't quarrel with your decision.*
quar·rel (**kwôr′**əl) □*noun, plural* **quarrels** □*verb* **quarreled, quarreling, quarrels**

quarry *noun* An open pit from which stone is obtained by cutting or blasting.
quar·ry (**kwôr′**ē) □*noun, plural* **quarries**

quart *noun* A unit of liquid measure equal to two pints, or 0.946 liter.
quart (kwôrt) □*noun, plural* **quarts**

quarter *noun* **1.** One of four equal parts: *Cut the cake into quarters.* **2.** One of two phases of the moon: *first quarter; last quarter.* **3.** A United States or Canadian coin worth twenty-five cents. **4.** One of the four time periods that make up a game in some sports, such as football and basketball. **5.** A district or section, as of a city: *the French quarter.* **6. quarters** A place to sleep or live: *She is looking for temporary quarters for her family.*
□*verb* To cut or divide into four equal parts: *She quartered the peach.*
quar·ter (**kwôr′**tər) □*noun, plural* **quarters** □*verb* **quartered, quartering, quarters**

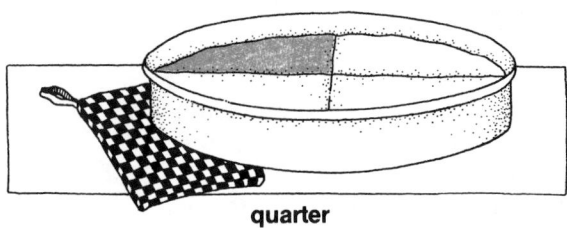
quarter

quarterly *adjective* Happening or done every three months: *a quarterly payment.*
□*adverb* Every three months: *We receive tax bills quarterly.*
quar·ter·ly (**kwôr′**tər lē) □*adjective* □*adverb*

quartet *noun* **1.** A group of four persons or things, especially a group of four musicians who perform together. **2.** A musical composition for four performers.
quar·tet (kwôr **tet′**) □*noun, plural* **quartets**

quartz *noun* A clear, hard rock that is often seen as tiny, sparkling bits in rock such as granite.
quartz (kwôrts) □*noun*

quasar *noun* A heavenly body that is like a star. Quasars give off radio waves or very bright light and are at great distances from the earth.
qua·sar (**kwā′**zär′) □*noun, plural* **quasars**

quaver *verb* **1.** To shake, especially because of fear; tremble: *I was quavering at the thought of meeting a lot of strangers.* **2.** To say or speak in a shaking or trembling tone.
□*noun* A shaking or trembling sound: *There was a quaver in his voice as if he were trying hard not to cry.*
qua·ver (**kwā′**vər) □*verb* **quavered, quavering, quavers** □*noun, plural* **quavers**

quay *noun* A stone wharf or bank where ships are loaded or unloaded.
quay (kē) ◻*noun, plural* **quays**

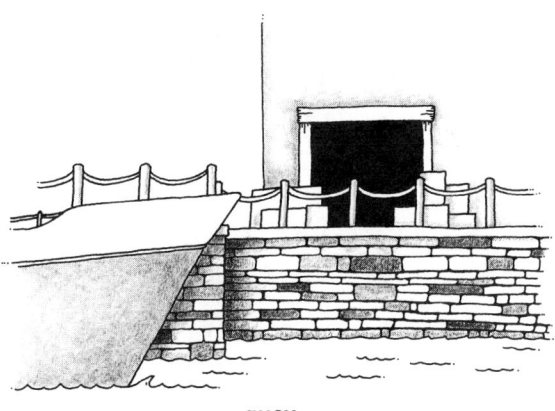

quay

queen *noun* **1.** A woman who is the ruler of a kingdom. **2.** The wife of a king. **3.** A woman or girl who is outstanding in some way: *a movie queen.* **4.** A playing card bearing the figure of a queen. **5.** The most powerful piece in the game of chess. **6.** A large female bee, ant, or termite that lays eggs.
queen (kwēn) ◻*noun, plural* **queens**

queer *adjective* Unusual and odd; strange: *He gave a queer laugh.*
queer (kwîr) ◻*adjective* **queerer, queerest**

quench *verb* **1.** To put out: *She quenched the fire with water.* **2.** To put an end to by satisfying: *He drank lemonade to quench his thirst.*
quench (kwench) ◻*verb* **quenched, quenching, quenches**

query *noun* A question: *Please answer this query.*
◻*verb* **1.** To ask questions of: *The doctor queried her about her health.* **2.** To express doubt about; question: *We queried the instructions.*
que·ry (kwîr′ē) ◻*noun, plural* **queries**
◻*verb* **queried, querying, queries**

quest *noun* A search: *people drilling wells in a quest for oil.*
quest (kwest) ◻*noun, plural* **quests**

question *noun* **1.** Something that is asked: *Please put your question in writing.* **2.** A subject that is being argued about or discussed: *The question was how to raise the money.* **3.** A point that is not certain; doubt: *There is no question about his ability to do the job.*
◻*verb* **1.** To ask questions of: *My father questioned me about my plans.* **2.** To have or show doubt about: *No one questions her orders.*

out of the question Not to be considered or thought about; impossible: *A vacation in September is out of the question.*
ques·tion (kwes′chən) ◻*noun, plural* **questions** ◻*verb* **questioned, questioning, questions**

question mark *noun* A punctuation mark (?) written at the end of a sentence to show that a question is being asked.

quetzal *noun* A bird of Central America with bright green and red feathers.
quet·zal (ket säl′) ◻*noun, plural* **quetzals**

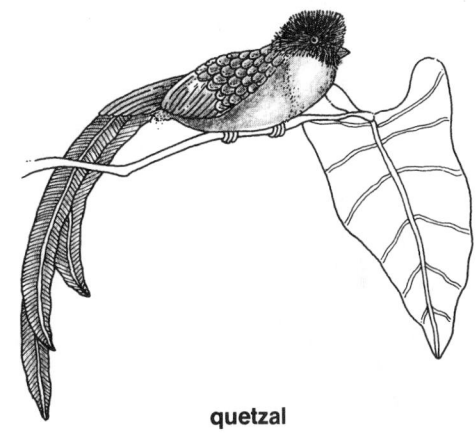

quetzal

quick *adjective* **1.** Moving, acting, or done with speed: *a quick look; a quick trip.* **2.** Fast to understand, think, or learn: *a student with a quick mind.* —See Synonyms at **fast.**
◻*adverb* Rapidly; fast: *Come quick!*
◻*noun* A sensitive, tender area of skin, such as that under the fingernails.
quick (kwik) ◻*adjective* **quicker, quickest** ◻*adverb* ◻*noun*

quicken *verb* To make or become more rapid: *He quickened his pace. Her pulse quickened.*
quick·en (kwik′ən) ◻*verb* **quickened, quickening, quickens**

quicksand *noun* A naturally occurring mixture of sand and water into which anything resting on its surface sinks.
quick·sand (kwik′sand′) ◻*noun*

a	bat	ī	bite	ōō	tool	*th*	feather
ā	make	î	fierce	ou	out	th	bath
â	dare	o	dot	u	nut	hw	wheat
ä	father	ō	no	û	turn	zh	measure
e	net	ô	law, for	ch	church	ə	about, open
ē	be	oi	soil	ng	ring		pencil, atom
i	dip	oo	look	sh	shade		circus

quiet *adjective* **1.** Free or almost free from noise: *a quiet room.* **2.** Free from motion or activity; calm: *a quiet Sunday at home.*
□*noun* The quality or condition of being quiet: *My father enjoys the quiet of the den after work.*
□*verb* To make or become quiet: *The teacher had trouble quieting the class. The crowd soon quieted down.*
qui·et (**kwī′**it) □*adjective* **quieter, quietest** □*noun* □*verb* **quieted, quieting, quiets**

quill *noun* **1.** A long, stiff feather. **2.** The hollow, hard central part of a feather. **3.** A pen made from a long, stiff feather. **4.** One of the sharp, hollow spines of a porcupine.
quill (kwil) □*noun, plural* **quills**

quill

quilt *noun* A bed covering made of two layers of cloth sewn together with a padding of cotton, feathers, or other material in between.
□*verb* To make a quilt.
quilt (kwilt) □*noun, plural* **quilts** □*verb* **quilted, quilting, quilts**

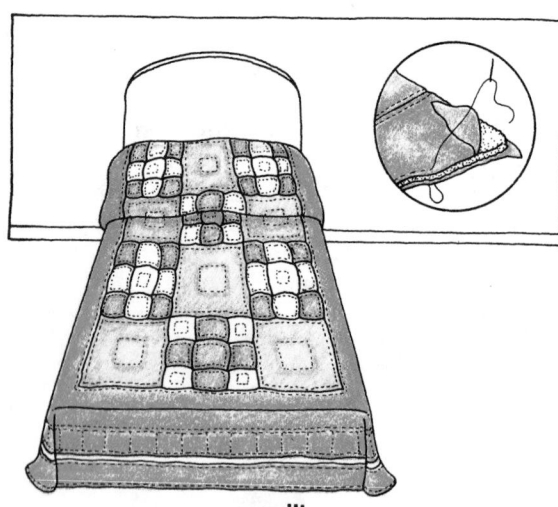

quilt

quince *noun* A hard fruit that looks like an apple, has a pleasant smell, and is used mostly for making jelly.
quince (kwins) □*noun, plural* **quinces**

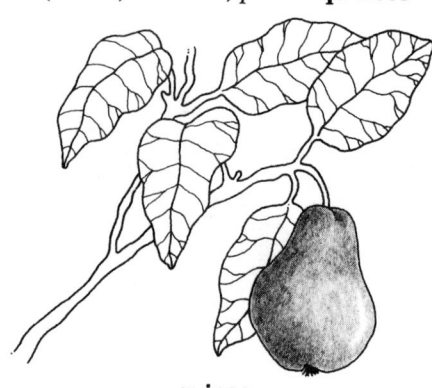

quince

quinine *noun* A bitter, colorless drug used to treat malaria.
qui·nine (**kwī′**nīn′) □*noun*

quintet *noun* **1.** A group of five persons or things, especially a group of five musicians who perform together. **2.** A musical composition for five performers.
quin·tet (kwin **tet′**) □*noun, plural* **quintets**

quit *verb* **1.** To stop: *He quit biting his nails.* **2.** To give up; resign: *I quit my job in order to finish writing my book.* **3.** To depart from; leave: *She quit school.*
quit (kwit) □*verb* **quit, quitting, quits**

quite *adverb* **1.** Completely; altogether: *I'm quite sure my facts are correct.* **2.** Somewhat; rather: *He's quite sick.*
quite (kwīt) □*adverb*

quiver¹ *verb* To shake with a slight vibrating motion; tremble: *The dog's tail quivered with excitement.*
quiv·er (**kwiv′**ər) □*verb* **quivered, quivering, quivers**

quiver² *noun* A case for holding arrows.
quiv·er (**kwiv′**ər) □*noun, plural* **quivers**

quiz *noun* A short test: *We have an arithmetic quiz every day.*
□*verb* To question closely: *The police quizzed the suspect about his activities on the night that the crime took place.*
quiz (kwiz) □*noun, plural* **quizzes** □*verb* **quizzed, quizzing, quizzes**

quota *noun* A share of something given to or expected from each member of a group; portion: *I did my quota of work.*
quo·ta (**kwō′**tə) □*noun, plural* **quotas**

quotation *noun* The words of one person repeated exactly by another: *a quotation from a book of poems.*
quo·ta·tion (kwō tā′shən) □*noun, plural* **quotations**

quotation mark *noun* Either of a pair of punctuation marks (" ") used to mark the beginning (") and the end (") of a quotation.

quote *verb* To repeat the words of exactly: *She quoted the President. He quoted his favorite poem.* □*noun* **1.** A quotation. **2.** A quotation mark.
quote (kwōt) □*verb* **quoted, quoting, quotes** □*noun, plural* **quotes**

quotient *noun* The number obtained by dividing one number by another.
quo·tient (kwō′shənt) □*noun, plural* **quotients**

a	bat	ī	bite	ōō	tool	*th*	feather
ā	make	î	fierce	ou	out	th	bath
â	dare	o	dot	u	nut	hw	wheat
ä	father	ō	no	û	turn	zh	measure
e	net	ô	law, for	ch	church	ə	about, open
ē	be	oi	soil	ng	ring		pencil, atom
i	dip	oo	look	sh	shade		circus

ANCIENT GREEK

The letter **R** has evolved from many forms of ancient writing. One of the earliest known examples is the Greek character shown above, which dates from almost 3,000 years ago. Over the years, artists and designers have created their own versions of the English letter **R**. Some of the more common examples seen today are shown below.

| HANDWRITING | CALLIGRAPHY | MODERN SANS SERIF | MODERN SERIF | SCRIPT |

---

r or **R**   *noun* The eighteenth letter of the English alphabet.
r or **R** (är) □*noun, plural* **r's** or **R's**

rabbi   *noun* **1.** The leader of a Jewish congregation. **2.** A teacher of Jewish laws and customs.
rab·bi (rab′ī) □*noun, plural* **rabbis**

rabbit   *noun* A burrowing animal with long ears, soft fur, and a short, furry tail.
rab·bit (rab′it) □*noun, plural* **rabbits**

rabies   *noun* A disease of warm-blooded animals such as dogs that is caused by a virus, can be transmitted to a person by the bite of an infected animal, and almost always causes death unless it is treated quickly.
ra·bies (rā′bēz) □*noun*

raccoon   *noun* A small animal with black face markings that look like a mask, grayish-brown fur, and a bushy tail with black rings.
rac·coon (ra ko͞on′) □*noun, plural* **raccoons**

raccoon

race[1]   *noun* A contest of speed, as in running, riding, or swimming: *a canoe race.*

□*verb* **1.** To take part in a race: *Twenty cars raced for the championship.* **2.** To move or go very fast: *We raced for the bus.*
race (rās) □*noun, plural* **races** □*verb* **raced, racing, races**

race[2]   *noun* A large group of people that share certain inherited physical characteristics that can be easily distinguished.
race (rās) □*noun, plural* **races**

racetrack   *noun* A course or route laid out for racing. Racetracks are usually oval or round.
race·track (rās′trak′) □*noun, plural* **racetracks**

racial   *adjective* Of or having to do with race: *racial characteristics; racial prejudice.*
ra·cial (rā′shəl) □*adjective*

rack   *noun* **1.** A framework or stand used for storing, hanging, or displaying things: *a hat rack; a cake rack.* **2.** An instrument of torture on which a person's body was stretched.
□*verb* To cause great suffering: *She was racked with pain from her broken arm.*
rack (rak) □*noun, plural* **racks** □*verb* **racked, racking, racks**

racket[1]   *noun* A wooden or metal frame with tightly laced strings and a handle, used in games like tennis and badminton.
rack·et (rak′it) □*noun, plural* **rackets**

racket[2]   *noun* **1.** A loud, continuous, unpleasant noise: *The alarm clock made an awful racket.* **2.** A dishonest way of making money or earning a living. —See Synonyms at **noise.**
rack·et (rak′it) □*noun, plural* **rackets**

radar *noun* A device that uses radio waves to detect the location and speed of distant or unseen objects, such as airplanes.
ra·dar (rā′ där′) □*noun*

WORD HISTORY: **radar**

The word *radar* comes from the phrase "*ra*dio *de*tecting *a*nd *r*anging." As you can probably see, it is made up of the first two letters of *radio* and the first letter of the other three words.

---

radiant *adjective* **1.** Sending forth light or heat: *the radiant tropical sun.* **2.** Filled with happiness; glowing: *a radiant smile.* **3.** Made up of or given off as radiation: *radiant heat.* —See Synonyms at **brilliant.**
ra·di·ant (rā′ dē ənt) □*adjective*

radiant energy *noun* Energy, such as heat and light, that is sent or given off as rays or waves.

radiate *verb* **1.** To give off as rays or waves: *The sun radiates heat.* **2.** To be given off as rays or waves: *Light radiated from the star.* **3.** To spread out from a center: *Streets radiate from the monument in all directions.*
ra·di·ate (rā′ dē āt′) □*verb* **radiated, radiating, radiates**

radiation *noun* The process of sending out rays of energy, such as heat or light, that travel through the air.
ra·di·a·tion (rā′ dē ā′ shən) □*noun*

radiator *noun* **1.** A device for heating a room. **2.** A device for cooling something, such as an automobile engine.
ra·di·a·tor (rā′ dē ā′tər) □*noun, plural* **radiators**

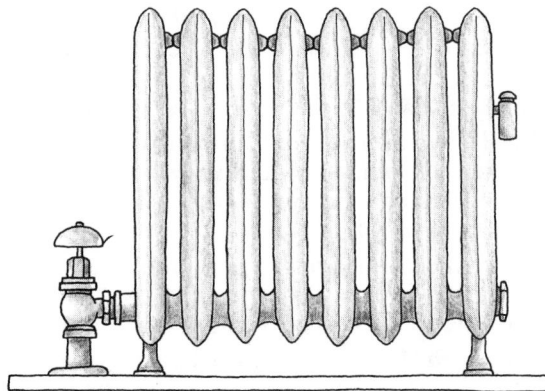
radiator

radical *adjective* **1.** Of, having to do with, or affecting the most important or basic part of something; fundamental: *a radical change.* **2.** Wanting or favoring extreme changes or reforms, especially in politics or government.
□*noun* Someone who favors extreme changes or reforms.
rad·i·cal (rad′i kəl) □*adjective* □*noun, plural* **radicals**

radii *noun* A plural of **radius.**
ra·di·i (rā′ dē ī′) □*noun*

radio *noun* **1.** A way of sending sounds through the air by means of waves that have both an electric and magnetic effect. **2.** The equipment used to send or receive sounds by electric waves.
□*verb* To signal or send a message by radio.
ra·di·o (rā′ dē ō′) □*noun, plural* **radios**
□*verb* **radioed, radioing, radios**

radioactive *adjective* Of, having, or caused by radioactivity: *Radium is a radioactive element.*
ra·di·o·ac·tive (rā′dē ō ak′tiv) □*adjective*

radioactivity *noun* The property or capability of certain metals, such as uranium, to give off energy in the form of rays.
ra·di·o·ac·tiv·i·ty (rā′dē ō ak **tiv′**i tē) □*noun*

radish *noun* A plant with a white root that has a strong, sharp taste.
rad·ish (rad′ish) □*noun, plural* **radishes**

radish

radium *noun* A white, highly radioactive metallic chemical element that is used in treating cancer.
ra·di·um (rā′ dē əm) □*noun*

a	bat	ī	bite	ōō	tool	*th*	feather
ā	make	î	fierce	ou	out	th	bath
â	dare	o	dot	u	nut	hw	wheat
ä	father	ō	no	û	turn	zh	measure
e	net	ô	law, for	ch	church	ə	about, open
ē	be	oi	soil	ng	ring		pencil, atom
i	dip	oo	look	sh	shade		circus

radius   *noun* **1.** A straight line that goes from the center to the circumference of a circle or the surface of a sphere. **2.** A circular area or region measured by its radius: *There are no gas stations within a radius of two miles.*
ra·di·us (rā′dē əs) □*noun, plural* **radii** or **radiuses**

raft   *noun* A platform that floats on water and is used for transportation or support.
raft (raft) □*noun, plural* **rafts**

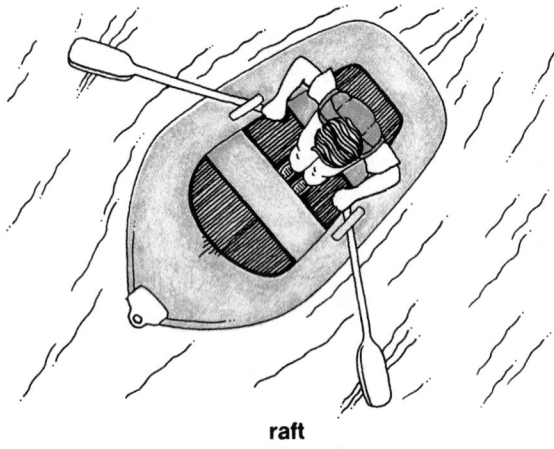

raft
A rubber raft

rag   *noun* **1.** A piece or scrap of old, torn, or leftover cloth. **2. rags** Shabby, torn, or worn-out clothing.
rag (rag) □*noun, plural* **rags**

ragamuffin   *noun* A ragged child.
rag·a·muf·fin (rag′ə muf′ in) □*noun, plural* **ragamuffins**

rage   *noun* Very great or violent anger.
□*verb* **1.** To show rage: *He raged at her for losing her passport.* **2.** To continue with violence or intensity: *The storm raged for a week.*
rage (rāj) □*noun, plural* **rages** □*verb* **raged, raging, rages**

ragged   *adjective* **1.** Tattered and worn-out: *a ragged coat.* **2.** Dressed in torn or shabby clothes: *a ragged tramp.* **3.** Rough or jagged; uneven: *a board with a ragged edge.*
rag·ged (rag′id) □*adjective*

raid   *noun* A sudden attack: *an air raid.*
□*verb* To carry out or make a raid on.
raid (rād) □*noun, plural* **raids** □*verb* **raided, raiding, raids**

rail   *noun* **1.** A bar, as of wood, that is placed lengthwise and held by upright supports, as in a fence. **2.** A steel bar used to form a track for railroad cars. **3.** Railroad: *travel by rail.*
rail (rāl) □*noun, plural* **rails**

railing   *noun* **1.** A fence made of rails. **2.** A rail or banister.
rail·ing (rā′ling) □*noun, plural* **railings**

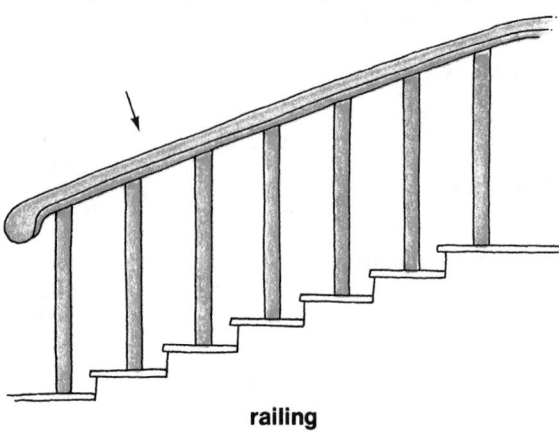

railing

railroad   *noun* **1.** A road that has a pair of parallel metal rails on which a train rides. **2.** A system of transportation consisting of a railroad and all the trains, tracks, stations, land, and other equipment needed to operate it.
rail·road (rāl′rōd′) □*noun, plural* **railroads**

rain   *noun* **1.** Water that falls from the clouds to the earth in drops. **2.** A fall of rain: *The rains flooded the fields.*
□*verb* **1.** To fall in drops of water from the clouds: *It's raining.* **2.** To fall or cause to fall like rain: *Confetti rained on the newly married couple.*
rain (rān) □*noun, plural* **rains** □*verb* **rained, raining, rains**

rainbow   *noun* An arc of colors that is seen in the sky opposite the sun caused by sunlight shining through small drops of water.
rain·bow (rān′bō′) □*noun, plural* **rainbows**

raincoat   *noun* A waterproof coat that keeps a person dry when it is raining.
rain·coat (rān′kōt′) □*noun, plural* **raincoats**

rainfall   *noun* The total amount of water in the form of rain, sleet, and snow that falls on an area during a certain length of time.
rain·fall (rān′fôl′) □*noun*

rainy   *adjective* Having much rain: *a rainy region.*
rain·y (rā′nē) □*adjective* **rainier, rainiest**

raise   *verb* **1.** To move to a higher position; lift: *She raised the window. I raised my hand.* **2.** To increase in amount, size, or value: *I hope they won't raise the price.* **3.** To build; erect: *The farmers raised a new barn.* **4.** To bring up and take care of: *She raised her sister's child.*

5. To gather together; collect: *They raised funds for the hospital.* **6.** To bring up for consideration; ask: *I have to raise a question.*
□*noun* An increase in pay.
raise (rāz) □*verb* **raised, raising, raises** □*noun, plural* **raises**

SYNONYMS: **raise, hoist, lift**

These verbs mean to move something to higher position: *Raise your hand if you know the answer. Workers hoisted the steel beams with a crane. The box is so heavy I can't lift it.*

---

raisin *noun* A sweet dried grape.
rai·sin (rā′zən) □*noun, plural* **raisins**

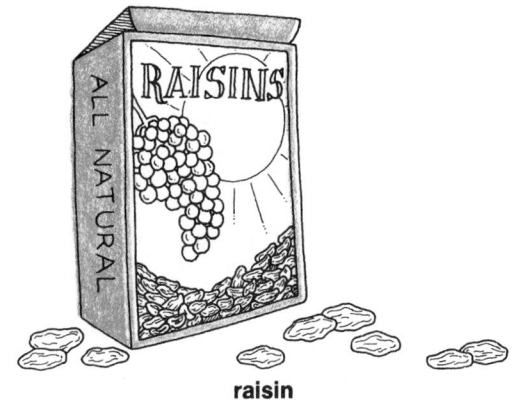

raisin

rake *noun* A garden tool with a long handle and teeth or prongs at one end, used to gather leaves and grass or to loosen or smooth dirt.
□*verb* To gather or smooth with a rake.
rake (rāk) □*noun, plural* **rakes** □*verb* **raked, raking, rakes**

rake

rally *verb* **1.** To bring or come to order again: *The general rallied his men.* **2.** To come or

bring together in a common cause: *His friends rallied behind him when he was in trouble.* **3.** To improve suddenly in strength and health: *The patient rallied during the night.*
□*noun* A meeting of many people for a particular purpose: *a peace rally.*
ral·ly (ral′ē) □*verb* **rallied, rallying, rallies** □*noun, plural* **rallies**

ram *noun* **1.** A male sheep. **2.** A heavy pole or special device used to batter or force something, especially to knock down walls or gates.
□*verb* **1.** To drive or force down or in: *He rammed the cork into the bottle.* **2.** To crash or smash into: *Her car rammed into the wall.*
ram (ram) □*noun, plural* **rams** □*verb* **rammed, ramming, rams**

ram

ramp *noun* A sloping passage or roadway that leads from one level to another.
ramp (ramp) □*noun, plural* **ramps**

ramrod *noun* A metal rod used to ram ammunition into the barrel of a gun that is loaded from the muzzle.
ram·rod (ram′rod′) □*noun, plural* **ramrods**

ran *verb* The past tense of **run.**
ran (ran) □*verb*

ranch *noun* A large farm on which cattle, sheep, or horses are raised.
ranch (ranch) □*noun, plural* **ranches**

random *adjective* Without plan, pattern, or purpose: *He made a random choice among the many delicious desserts.*
ran·dom (ran′dəm) □*adjective*

a bat	ī bite	ōō tool	*th* feather
ā make	î fierce	ou out	th bath
â dare	o dot	u nut	hw wheat
ä father	ō no	û turn	zh measure
e net	ô law, for	ch church	ə about, open
ē be	oi soil	ng ring	pencil, atom
i dip	oo look	sh shade	circus

rang *verb* The past tense of **ring.**
rang (rang) □*verb*

range *noun* **1.** A region or extent within which something can vary: *a wide range of colors.* **2.** The maximum distance within which something can work or travel: *a gun with a range of 100 feet.* **3.** A place for shooting at targets. **4.** A large area of open land on which livestock graze freely. **5.** A stove with an oven, broiler, and burners. **6.** A group or series of mountains.
□*verb* **1.** To move or vary within certain limits: *sizes ranging from large to small.* **2.** To roam or wander: *Buffaloes ranged over the plains.*
range (rānj) □*noun, plural* **ranges** □*verb* **ranged, ranging, ranges**

ranger *noun* **1.** Someone whose job is to patrol and guard a forest or park. **2.** A member of a group of armed men who maintain order in a particular region.
rang·er (**rān'** jər) □*noun, plural* **rangers**

ranger

rank¹ *noun* **1.** A position or grade within a group or class: *a composer of the first rank; the rank of captain in the navy.* **2.** A row or line of people or things side by side: *ranks of trees on both sides of the road.* **3. ranks** Soldiers who are not officers.
□*verb* **1.** To have a rank: *He ranked high in his class.* **2.** To assign a rank to; evaluate: *We ranked the gymnasts according to their skill.* **3.** To arrange in rows or lines.
rank (rangk) □*noun, plural* **ranks** □*verb* **ranked, ranking, ranks**

rank² *adjective* **1.** Strong or unpleasant in odor or taste: *The air was rank with the smell of garbage.* **2.** Complete; total: *a rank amateur.*
rank (rangk) □*adjective* **ranker, rankest**

ransom *noun* A price demanded or paid for the release of a prisoner: *The ambassador was kidnapped and held for ransom.*
□*verb* To obtain the release of by paying a demanded price.
ran·som (**ran'** səm) □*noun, plural* **ransoms** □*verb* **ransomed, ransoming, ransoms**

rant *verb* To talk in a wild and loud way.
rant (rant) □*verb* **ranted, ranting, rants**

rap *verb* To hit or knock sharply; strike: *I rapped on the door.*
□*noun* A quick, sharp knock or blow.
rap (rap) □*verb* **rapped, rapping, raps** □*noun, plural* **raps**

rapid *adjective* Very fast or quick: *a rapid train; a rapid trip.* —See Synonyms at **fast.**
□*plural noun* **rapids** A place in a river where the water flows very quickly.
rap·id (**rap'** id) □*adjective* □*plural noun* **rapids**

rare¹ *adjective* **1.** Not found, seen, or happening very often: *Indoor plumbing was rare in that part of the world.* **2.** Unusually valuable or good; special: *rare coins.* —See Synonyms at **uncommon.**
rare (râr) □*adjective* **rarer, rarest**

rare² *adjective* Cooked for a short time: *rare steak.*
rare (râr) □*adjective* **rarer, rarest**

> **WORD HISTORY:** **rare²**
>
> The word *rare²* meaning "lightly cooked" was used originally only of eggs. It was not applied to meat until modern times.

rash¹ *adjective* Too hasty; reckless: *Don't make a rash decision you'll regret later.*
rash (rash) □*adjective* **rasher, rashest**

rash² *noun* An outbreak of red spots on the skin.
rash (rash) □*noun, plural* **rashes**

rasp *noun* A harsh, grating sound: *He spoke with a rasp in his throat.*
□*verb* To make a rasp.
rasp (rasp) □*noun, plural* **rasps** □*verb* **rasped, rasping, rasps**

raspberry *noun* A sweet red or black berry that grows on a prickly bush.
rasp·ber·ry (**raz'** ber'ē) □*noun, plural* **raspberries**

raspberry

rat *noun* An animal with a long tail that is related to the mouse.
rat (rat) □*noun, plural* **rats**

rate *noun* **1.** An amount of something measured in terms of something else: *a rate of 55 miles an hour.* **2.** A charge or price according to a scale: *postal rates.*
□*verb* **1.** To regard; consider: *I rate her an excellent tennis player.* **2.** To have a certain rank or level: *Our city rates high in culture.*
rate (rāt) □*noun, plural* **rates** □*verb* **rated, rating, rates**

rather *adverb* **1.** To a certain extent; somewhat: *He's feeling rather sick.* **2.** More willingly: *I'd rather not go.* **3.** More exactly: *The cost is ten dollars or, rather, nine dollars and sixty cents.* **4.** Instead: *was not his friend but rather his enemy.*
rath·er (ra*th*′ ər) □*adverb*

ratio *noun* The relationship in number, quantity, or size between two different things: *the ratio of men to women here is two to one.*
ra·tio (rā′ shē ō′) □*noun, plural* **ratios**

ration *noun* A fixed amount or portion, as of food: *gave the cattle their daily ration of hay.*
□*verb* **1.** To give out as rations. **2.** To limit the amount each person can use or have: *The government rationed gas during the war.*
ra·tion (rash′ən *or* rā′ shən) □*noun, plural* **rations** □*verb* **rationed, rationing, rations**

rational *adjective* **1.** Able to reason: *Humans are rational beings.* **2.** Based on reason: *rational behavior; a rational decision.*
ra·tion·al (rash′ə nəl) □*adjective*

rattle *verb* **1.** To make or cause to make a quick series of short, sharp sounds: *The wind rattled the window shade.* **2.** To talk or say quickly and without stopping: *She rattled on about her camping trip.* **3.** To confuse or upset: *The audience rattled her, and she forgot her lines.*

□*noun* **1.** A quick series of short, sharp sounds: *the rattle of hail on the roof.* **2.** A device, such as a baby's toy, that rattles when shaken.
rat·tle (rat′ əl) □*verb* **rattled, rattling, rattles** □*noun, plural* **rattles**

rattlesnake *noun* A poisonous American snake with dry, hard rings at the end of its tail that rattle when the snake shakes them.
rat·tle·snake (rat′ əl snāk′) □*noun, plural* **rattlesnakes**

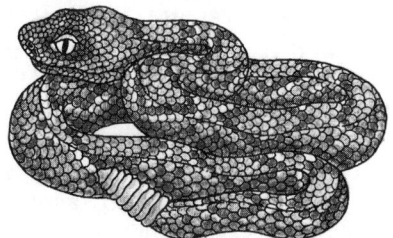

rattlesnake

rave *verb* **1.** To speak wildly or without making sense: *The angry customer raved at the cashier.* **2.** To speak with very great enthusiasm: *He raved about the new play.*
rave (rāv) □*verb* **raved, raving, raves**

ravel *verb* To separate into single loose threads: *The sleeve of the sweater began to ravel.*
rav·el (rav′ əl) □*verb* **raveled, raveling, ravels**

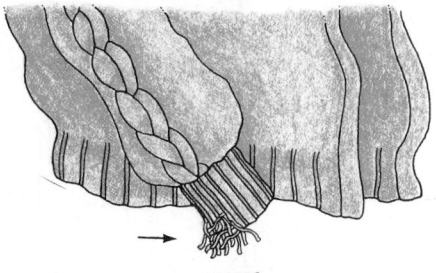

ravel

raven *noun* A large black bird that resembles the crow and has a croaking cry.
ra·ven (rā′ vən) □*noun, plural* **ravens**

a	bat	ī	bite	o͞o	tool	*th*	feather
ā	make	î	fierce	ou	out	th	bath
â	dare	o	dot	u	nut	hw	wheat
ä	father	ō	no	û	turn	zh	measure
e	net	ô	law, for	ch	church	ə	about, open
ē	be	oi	soil	ng	ring		pencil, atom
i	dip	oo	look	sh	shade		circus

ravine *noun* A deep, narrow valley similar to a gorge.
ra·vine (rə **vēn′**) ☐*noun, plural*
ravines

raw *adjective* **1.** Not cooked: *raw fish.* **2.** In the natural state; not treated or processed: *raw wood; raw materials.* **3.** Not trained; without experience: *raw recruits in the army.* **4.** Having the skin scraped off: *a raw elbow.* **5.** Cold and damp: *a raw winter day.*
raw (rô) ☐*adjective* **rawer, rawest**

rawhide *noun* **1.** The hide of cattle before it has been tanned. **2.** A whip or rope made of rawhide.
raw·hide (rô′hīd′) ☐*noun*

ray *noun* **1.** A thin line or narrow beam of light or other radiation: *sound rays; a ray of sunlight.* **2.** A small amount; trace: *a ray of hope.* **3.** One of several lines or parts extending from a center, such as the spokes of a wheel.
ray (rā) ☐*noun, plural* **rays**

rayon *noun* A cloth or fiber made from cellulose.
ray·on (rā′on′) ☐*noun*

razor *noun* An instrument with a sharp blade that is used to shave hair.
ra·zor (rā′zər) ☐*noun, plural* **razors**

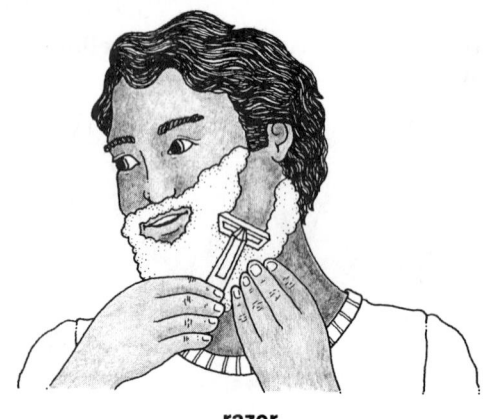

razor

rd. An abbreviation for **road.**

re– A prefix that means: **1.** Again: *refill.* **2.** Back: *recall.*

reach *verb* **1.** To go as far as: *I reached home before dark. What speed can you reach on your bike?* **2.** To stretch out; extend: *Her skirt reaches almost to the floor.* **3.** To stretch or hold out a part of the body, as an arm or hand: *I reached up for the dish on the top shelf.*
4. To touch or grasp by stretching out a part of the body: *I couldn't reach the telephone from where I was sitting.* **5.** To get in touch with; communicate with: *If he has any questions, he can reach me at my office.*
☐*noun* **1.** An act of reaching: *grabbed the book with a reach of his arm.* **2.** The distance to which a person can stretch an arm: *The top drawer is within your reach.*
reach (rēch) ☐*verb* **reached, reaching, reaches** ☐*noun, plural* **reaches**

react *verb* To act in a particular way in response to: *He reacted to her criticism by getting angry. The sick man reacted well to the treatment.*
re·act (rē akt′) ☐*verb* **reacted, reacting, reacts**

reaction *noun* An action or effect in response to something: *The rebellion was a reaction to the harsh rule of a tyrant.*
re·ac·tion (rē ak′shən) ☐*noun, plural* **reactions**

reactor *noun* A device in which atoms are split under controlled conditions, resulting in the production of heat.
re·ac·tor (rē ak′tər) ☐*noun, plural* **reactors**

read *verb* **1.** To look at and understand the meaning of something that is printed or written: *He read the letter. Do you like to read?* **2.** To speak out loud something that is printed or written: *She read a chapter of the book to the children every night before they went to bed.* **3.** To learn or find out by reading: *Last week I read about the discovery of a chest full of gold coins and jewels in a deserted house.* **4.** To discover the meaning of: *Dad says he can read my mind.* **5.** To indicate or show: *The thermometer reads 90°.* **6.** To tell what is going to happen; predict: *He says that he can read the future.*
read (rēd) ☐*verb* **read** (red), **reading, reads**

reader *noun* **1.** Someone who reads. **2.** A book for learning and practicing reading.
read·er (rē′dər) ☐*noun, plural* **readers**

readily *adverb* **1.** Willingly and promptly: *She readily agreed to my plan.* **2.** Without difficulty; easily: *a problem that is readily solved.* **3.** Without delay; quickly: *Help is readily available if it is needed.*
read·i·ly (red′ə lē) ☐*adverb*

reading *noun* **1.** The act of looking at and understanding something that is printed or written. **2.** Something, such as a book, to be read. **3.** The act of speaking out loud something that is printed or written: *a poetry reading.*
read·ing (rē′ding) □*noun, plural* **readings**

ready *adjective* **1.** Prepared for action or use: *She is ready to leave.* **2.** Willing: *I'm ready to help.* **3.** Likely to do something: *She seemed ready to give up.* **4.** Prompt; quick: *He has a ready smile.* **5.** Easy to get at; available: *I keep a flashlight ready.*
□*verb* To make ready; prepare: *She readied the turkey for roasting.*
read·y (red′ē) □*adjective* **readier, readiest** □*verb* **readied, readying, readies**

real *adjective* **1.** Not imaginary; actual or true: *What was the real reason?* **2.** Not artificial; genuine or authentic: *real gold.*
re·al (rē′əl *or* rēl) □*adjective*

real estate *noun* Land with the buildings and natural resources on it.

realistic *adjective* **1.** Resembling real people or things: *a realistic novel; a realistic painting.* **2.** Practical and reasonable: *She is realistic about money.*
re·al·is·tic (rē′ə lis′tik) □*adjective*

reality *noun* **1.** The condition or quality of being real; actual existence: *the reality of poverty in a wealthy country.* **2.** Someone or something that is real: *He made his dream of success into a reality.*
re·al·i·ty (rē al′i tē) □*noun, plural* **realities**

realize *verb* **1.** To be aware of; understand: *I didn't realize how unhappy he was.* **2.** To make real; achieve: *She worked hard to realize her ambition of becoming a lawyer.*
re·al·ize (rē′ə līz′) □*verb* **realized, realizing, realizes**

really *adverb* **1.** In fact; actually: *Did he really say that?* **2.** Truly: *She wore a really beautiful dress.*
re·al·ly (rē′ə lē *or* rē′lē) □*adverb*

realm *noun* **1.** A kingdom. **2.** A field of interest or activity: *the realm of art.*
realm (relm) □*noun, plural* **realms**

reap *verb* **1.** To cut down and gather; harvest: *reap grain.* **2.** To gather a crop from: *reap a field.* **3.** To gain as a benefit or reward: *He reaped fame from his talent and hard work.*
reap (rēp) □*verb* **reaped, reaping, reaps**

reap

rear[1] *noun* The back part of something: *the rear of the truck.*
□*adjective* Of or at the rear: *a rear door.*
rear (rîr) □*noun, plural* **rears** □*adjective*

rear[2] *verb* **1.** To bring up; raise: *Her parents reared two children.* **2.** To rise on the hind legs: *The horse reared at the sight of the car.*
rear (rîr) □*verb* **reared, rearing, rears**

reason *noun* **1.** A cause: *You have no reason to be angry.* **2.** An explanation: *She gave me no reason for her behavior.* **3.** The ability to think clearly: *She used reason to solve the problem.*
□*verb* **1.** To use the faculty of reason: *He reasoned that there was only one possible solution to the problem.* **2.** To argue with another in a sensible way so as to change his or her mind: *She was so angry we could not reason with her.*
rea·son (rē′zən) □*noun, plural* **reasons**

reasonable *adjective* **1.** Using or capable of using the faculty of reason: *a reasonable man.* **2.** Fair or logical: *a reasonable idea.* **3.** Not excessive; moderate: *a reasonable amount of time.* —See Synonyms at **sensible.**
rea·son·a·ble (rē′zə nə bəl) □*adjective*

reasoning *noun* **1.** The process of reaching an answer or coming to a conclusion through the use of reason. **2.** An argument or reason: *I don't follow your reasoning.*
rea·son·ing (rē′zə ning) □*noun*

rebel *verb* **1.** To resist or oppose authority: *The people rebelled against the king's harsh*

a	bat	ī	bite	ōō	tool	*th*	feather
ā	make	î	fierce	ou	out	th	bath
â	dare	o	dot	u	nut	hw	wheat
ä	father	ō	no	û	turn	zh	measure
e	net	ô	law, for	ch	church	ə	about, open
ē	be	oi	soil	ng	ring		pencil, atom
i	dip	oo	look	sh	shade		circus

rule. **2.** To show strong dislike or resentment: *I rebelled at the unfairness of the punishment.* ▢*noun* Someone who resists or opposes authority.
re·bel ▢*verb* (ri **bel′**) **rebelled, rebelling, rebels** ▢*noun* **reb·el** (**reb′**əl), *plural* **rebels**

rebellion *noun* **1.** An armed action intended to overthrow one's government by force. **2.** Open defiance of authority: *rebellion against high taxes.*
re·bel·lion (ri **bel′**yən) ▢*noun, plural* **rebellions**

recall *verb* **1.** To ask or order to return: *The audience recalled the actor for another bow.* **2.** To bring back to memory: *I couldn't recall his name.* —See Synonyms at **remember.**
re·call (ri **kôl′**) ▢*verb* **recalled, recalling, recalls**

receipt *noun* **1.** A written acknowledgment that money or merchandise has been received: *I signed a receipt for a package.* **2. receipts** The quantity or amount of something received: *receipts from the sale of tickets.*
re·ceipt (ri **sēt′**) ▢*noun, plural* **receipts**

receive *verb* **1.** To get or acquire something given, offered, paid, or sent: *I received your letter.* **2.** To greet or welcome: *She received her guests at the door.*
re·ceive (ri **sēv′**) ▢*verb* **received, receiving, receives**

receiver *noun* **1.** Someone or something that receives. **2.** A device, as in a telephone or radio, that receives electrical signals and converts them into sound or pictures.
re·ceiv·er (ri **sē′**vər) ▢*noun, plural* **receivers**

recent *adjective* Of or having to do with a time just before the present: *a recent book; recent news.*
re·cent (**rē′**sənt) ▢*adjective*

reception *noun* **1.** The act or manner of receiving: *We got a friendly reception from her sister.* **2.** A social gathering in honor of someone: *a wedding reception.* **3.** The quality of electrical signals received by a radio or television set: *An outdoor antenna can improve TV reception.*
re·cep·tion (ri **sep′**shən) ▢*noun, plural* **receptions**

recess *noun* **1.** A temporary halt in an activity: *We ate a snack during recess.* **2.** A small hollow place: *a recess in the wall.* ▢*verb* To take a recess; adjourn: *We recessed for lunch.*

re·cess (ri **ses′** *or* **rē′**ses′) ▢*noun, plural* **recesses** ▢*verb* **recessed, recessing, recesses**

recipe *noun* A set of directions for preparing something to eat or drink.
rec·i·pe (**res′**ə pē) ▢*noun, plural* **recipes**

recital *noun* **1.** A detailed account or report: *her recital of her experiences.* **2.** A public performance, especially one given by one person: *a violin recital.*
re·cit·al (ri **sī′**təl) ▢*noun, plural* **recitals**

recite *verb* **1.** To repeat something memorized: *He recited a poem to us.* **2.** To tell about in detail: *She recited her problems.*
re·cite (ri **sīt′**) ▢*verb* **recited, reciting, recites**

reckless *adjective* Without care or caution; careless: *reckless driving.*
reck·less (**rek′**lis) ▢*adjective*

reckon *verb* **1.** To count; compute: *The waiter reckoned the bill.* **2.** To think or assume; suppose: *I reckon he'll come tomorrow.*
reck·on (**rek′**ən) ▢*verb* **reckoned, reckoning, reckons**

recognition *noun* **1.** The act of recognizing or the condition of being recognized. **2.** Favorable notice; attention: *The musician received recognition for his work.*
rec·og·ni·tion (rek′əg **nish′**ən) ▢*noun*

recognize *verb* **1.** To know or identify from past experience: *I recognized her face.* **2.** To acknowledge; accept: *We recognize his right to his own opinion.*
rec·og·nize (**rek′**əg nīz′) ▢*verb* **recognized, recognizing, recognizes**

recommend *verb* **1.** To speak highly of to another: *I recommend the movie.* **2.** To advise; suggest: *The doctor recommended that I stay in bed for a few days.*
rec·om·mend (rek′ə **mend′**) ▢*verb* **recommended, recommending, recommends**

record *noun* **1.** A written account, as of facts: *The doctor kept a record of each patient's illnesses.* **2.** The history of a person's performance or achievements: *He has a fine record as mayor.* **3.** The best performance or achievement known: *He holds the record for the marathon.* **4.** A disk designed to reproduce sound when it is played on a phonograph.
▢*verb* **1.** To set down in writing: *She recorded her reactions in her diary.* **2.** To register or indicate: *A thermometer records the temperature.*

3. To register on a disk or magnetic tape.
rec·ord □*noun* (**rek′** ərd), *plural* **records**
□*verb* **re·cord** (ri **kôrd′**) **recorded,
recording, records**

recorder *noun* **1.** Someone or something
that records: *a tape recorder.* **2.** A wooden
flute with eight finger holes and a mouthpiece
resembling a whistle.
re·cord·er (ri **kôr′** dər) □*noun, plural*
recorders

recorder

recording *noun* A phonograph record or
magnetic tape.
re·cord·ing (ri **kôr′** ding) □*noun, plural*
recordings

recover *verb* **1.** To get back; regain: *They recovered the stolen car.* **2.** To return to a normal
condition: *He recovered from pneumonia.*
re·cov·er (ri **kuv′** ər) □*verb* **recovered,
recovering, recovers**

recovery *noun* The act of recovering: *made a
quick recovery from his illness; the recovery of
the lost purse.*
re·cov·er·y (ri **kuv′** ə rē) □*noun, plural*
recoveries

recreation *noun* Something done for amusement or relaxation: *My favorite recreation is
playing chess.*
rec·re·a·tion (rek′rē **ā′** shən) □*noun, plural*
recreations

recruit *verb* To secure the services of: *recruit
men for the army.*
□*noun* A newly enlisted member, as of the
armed forces.
re·cruit (ri **krōot′**) □*verb* **recruited,
recruiting, recruits** □*noun, plural* **recruits**

rectangle *noun* A geometric figure that has
four sides and four right angles.

rec·tan·gle (**rek′** tang′gəl) □*noun, plural*
rectangles

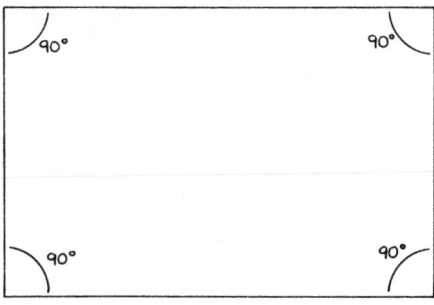

rectangle

red *noun* The color of blood or of a ripe
strawberry.
□*adjective* Of the color red: *a red dress.*
red (red) □*noun, plural* **reds**
□*adjective* **redder, reddest**

red blood cell *noun* Any of the cells in the
blood that carry oxygen to other cells and tissues of the body.

reddish *adjective* Somewhat red.
red·dish (**red′**ish) □*adjective*

reduce *verb* **1.** To make or become smaller or
less: *The store reduced prices during the sale.*
2. To lose body weight by diet or exercise.
re·duce (ri **dōos′** *or* ri **dyōos′**) □*verb*
reduced, reducing, reduces

reduction *noun* **1.** The act of reducing.
2. The amount by which something is reduced: *a price reduction of $10.*
re·duc·tion (ri **duk′**shən) □*noun, plural*
reductions

redwood *noun* A very tall evergreen tree of
northwestern California that has strong reddish-brown wood.
red·wood (**red′**wood′) □*noun, plural*
redwoods

reed *noun* **1.** Any of several tall grasses that
have hollow stems and grow in wet places.
2. A thin strip of cane, metal, or plastic used in
the mouthpiece of certain wind instruments. It
vibrates when air passes over it and produces
a musical tone. **3.** A woodwind instrument,

a bat	ī bite	ōo tool	*th* feather
ā make	î fierce	ou out	th bath
â dare	o dot	u nut	hw wheat
ä father	ō no	û turn	zh measure
e net	ô law, for	ch church	ə about, open
ē be	oi soil	ng ring	pencil, atom
i dip	oo look	sh shade	circus

such as the clarinet, that is fitted with a reed.
reed (rēd) □*noun, plural* **reeds**

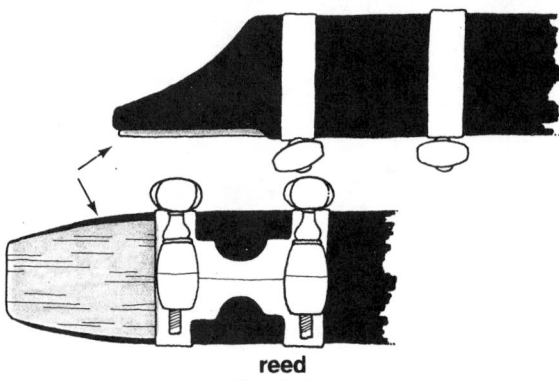

reed
Of a clarinet

reef *noun* A strip or ridge of rock, sand, or coral at or near the surface of a body of water.
reef (rēf) □*noun, plural* **reefs**

reel[1] *noun* A device similar to a large spool on which something flexible, such as a hose or wire, can be wound.
□*verb* **1.** To wind on a reel. **2.** To pull in by winding on a reel: *She reeled in a trout.*
reel (rēl) □*noun, plural* **reels**
□*verb* **reeled, reeling, reels**

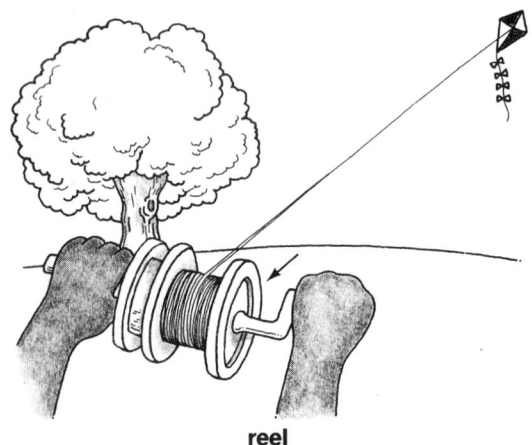

reel

reel[2] *verb* **1.** To move unsteadily; stagger: *He reeled as he stepped off the roller coaster.* **2.** To go or seem to go round and round; whirl: *The exciting news made my head reel.*
reel (rēl) □*verb* **reeled, reeling, reels**

re-elect *verb* To elect again.
re·e·lect (rē′i lekt′) □*verb* **re-elected, re-electing, re-elects**

re-entry *noun* **1.** The act of entering again. **2.** The return of a missile or spacecraft to the earth's atmosphere.
re·en·try (rē en′trē) □*noun, plural* **re-entries**

refer *verb* **1.** To direct or turn to for help, information, or authority: *The doctor referred his patient to a surgeon. The speaker referred to his notes.* **2.** To call or direct attention: *He referred to the work of others who had tried to solve similar problems.*
re·fer (ri fûr′) □*verb* **referred, referring, refers**

referee *noun* An official in certain sports who enforces the rules during play.
ref·e·ree (ref′ə rē′) □*noun, plural* **referees**

referee
A football referee

reference *noun* **1.** Relation, regard, or respect: *in reference to what you just said.* **2.** A printed work, such as a dictionary, that contains information. **3.** A statement about a person's character or qualifications: *He gave her a good reference.* **4.** A mention: *He made frequent references to his promotion.*
ref·er·ence (ref′ər əns) □*noun, plural* **references**

refill *verb* To fill again: *refill the gas tank.*
□*noun* A replacement for something used up: *She bought a refill for her notebook.*
re·fill □*verb* (rē fil′) **refilled, refilling, refills** □*noun* (rē′fil′), *plural* **refills**

refine *verb* To make pure: *refine sugar.*
re·fine (ri fīn′) □*verb* **refined, refining, refines**

refinery *noun* A factory where raw materials are purified and processed: *an oil refinery.*
re·fin·er·y (ri fī′nə rē) □*noun, plural* **refineries**

reflect *verb* **1.** To throw back or bend light rays, heat, or sounds: *The surface of the desk*

reflected the light. **2.** To give back an image of: *The lake reflected the trees along its banks.* **3.** To give back as a result: *His behavior reflects credit on his parents.* **4.** To give serious thought: *She reflected on her bad study habits and tried to think of how to improve them.*
re·flect (ri **flekt′**) □*verb* **reflected, reflecting, reflects**

reflection *noun* **1.** The process of reflecting. **2.** Something, such as sound or light, that is reflected. **3.** An image formed by or as if by a mirror: *She saw her own reflection in the pool.* **4.** Serious thought: *After much reflection he decided to refuse the offer.*
re·flec·tion (ri **flek′**shən) □*noun, plural* **reflections**

reform *verb* **1.** To improve by correcting errors or abuses: *trying to reform the city's political system.* **2.** To give up or cause to give up evil ways: *an institution to reform criminals.* □*noun* A change for the better; improvement.
re·form (ri **fôrm′**) □*verb* **reformed, reforming, reforms** □*noun, plural* **reforms**

reformatory *noun* An institution for reforming and educating young people who have broken the law.
re·form·a·to·ry (ri **fôr′**mə tôr′ē) □*noun, plural* **reformatories**

refrain *noun* A phrase repeated several times in a poem or song.
re·frain (ri **frān′**) □*noun, plural* **refrains**

refresh *verb* To make or become fresh again: *He refreshed himself with a quick dip in the lake.*
re·fresh (ri **fresh′**) □*verb* **refreshed, refreshing, refreshes**

refreshment *noun* Something, such as food or drink, that refreshes.
re·fresh·ment (ri **fresh′**mənt) □*noun, plural* **refreshments**

refrigerate *verb* To make or keep cool or cold: *refrigerate milk to keep it from spoiling.*
re·frig·er·ate (ri **frij′**ə rāt′) □*verb* **refrigerated, refrigerating, refrigerates**

refrigerator *noun* A device or room used to store food and other articles at low temperatures.
re·frig·er·a·tor (ri **frij′**ə rā′tər) □*noun, plural* **refrigerators**

refuge *noun* Protection or shelter from danger: *sought refuge from the storm in a cave.*
ref·uge (**ref′**yo͞oj) □*noun*

refugee *noun* Someone who flees from his or her own country to find protection or safety.
ref·u·gee (ref′yo͞o **jē′**) □*noun, plural* **refugees**

refund *verb* To give back; repay: *The store refunded my money because the camera I bought didn't work.* □*noun* The return of money paid.
re·fund □*verb* (ri **fund′**) **refunded, refunding, refunds** □*noun* (**rē′**fund′), *plural* **refunds**

refusal *noun* The act of refusing: *I was shocked by her refusal to answer my question.*
re·fus·al (ri **fyo͞o′**zəl) □*noun, plural* **refusals**

refuse¹ *verb* To say one will not do, accept, give, or allow: *He refused to help us.* —See Synonyms at **reject.**
re·fuse (ri **fyo͞oz′**) □*verb* **refused, refusing, refuses**

refuse² *noun* Something useless or worthless; trash: *The stadium was littered with refuse after the game.*
ref·use (**ref′**yo͞os) □*noun*

regain *verb* **1.** To get back; recover: *He regained his good humor.* **2.** To reach again: *The sailors regained the shore.*
re·gain (ri **gān′**) □*verb* **regained, regaining, regains**

regard *verb* **1.** To look at; observe: *She regarded the people around her with interest.* **2.** To consider in a particular way; judge: *She didn't regard any work as beneath her.* **3.** To value: *I regard my friends highly.* □*noun* **1.** Affection or esteem: *She holds her teacher in high regard.* **2. regards** Best wishes; greetings: *Please give your parents my regards.*
re·gard (ri **gärd′**) □*verb* **regarded, regarding, regards** □*noun, plural* **regards**

regardless *adverb* In spite of everything: *We tried to discourage him from going out in the storm, but he went regardless.*
re·gard·less (ri **gärd′**lis) □*adverb*

regardless of *preposition* With no thought or consideration for: *I'll take the job regardless of the pay.*

a	bat	ī	bite	o͞o	tool	*th*	feather
ā	make	î	fierce	ou	out	th	bath
â	dare	o	dot	u	nut	hw	wheat
ä	father	ō	no	û	turn	zh	measure
e	net	ô	law, for	ch	church	ə	about, open
ē	be	oi	soil	ng	ring		pencil, atom
i	dip	oo	look	sh	shade		circus

regime *noun* A system of government: *a democratic regime.*
re·gime (ri **zhēm′** *or* rā **zhēm′**) □*noun,* *plural* **regimes**

regiment *noun* A unit of soldiers made up of two or more battalions.
reg·i·ment (rej′ə mənt) □*noun, plural* **regiments**

region *noun* A large area of the earth's surface: *tropical regions.*
re·gion (rē′jən) □*noun, plural* **regions**

register *noun* **1.** A written list or record: *The town keeps a register of marriages.* **2.** A machine that records and counts automatically: *a cash register.* **3.** A device that can be adjusted to control a flow of air.
□*verb* **1.** To enter in a written list or record: *They registered their car. The student registered for college.* **2.** To indicate or be indicated, as on a scale: *The thermometer registered 90°.* **3.** To reveal or show: *Her face registered fear.*
reg·is·ter (rej′i stər) □*noun, plural* **registers** □*verb* **registered, registering, registers**

regret *verb* To feel sorry about: *I regret my mistake.*
□*noun* A feeling of distress or sadness: *I felt regret for having told a lie.*
re·gret (ri **gret′**) □*verb* **regretted, regretting, regrets** □*noun, plural* **regrets**

regular *adjective* **1.** Usual; normal: *Nine o'clock is his regular bedtime.* **2.** Steady: *a regular customer.* **3.** Happening, arriving, or returning at fixed times: *a regular salary.*
reg·u·lar (reg′yə lər) □*adjective*

regulate *verb* **1.** To control or direct according to rule or authority: *The government regulates the price of certain farm products.* **2.** To adjust to function accurately and properly: *regulate a clock.*
reg·u·late (reg′yə lāt′) □*verb* **regulated, regulating, regulates**

regulation *noun* **1.** The act of regulating or the condition of being regulated. **2.** A law or set of rules by which something is regulated: *new tax regulations.*
reg·u·la·tion (reg′yə lā′shən) □*noun, plural* **regulations**

rehearsal *noun* A session devoted to practicing in order to prepare for a performance.
re·hears·al (ri **hûr′**səl) □*noun, plural* **rehearsals**

rehearse *verb* To practice in order to prepare for a performance: *We rehearsed the play.*

re·hearse (ri **hûrs′**) □*verb* **rehearsed, rehearsing, rehearses**

reign *noun* **1.** The period of time during which a monarch rules. **2.** The rule or authority of a monarch.
□*verb* **1.** To rule as a monarch: *a queen who reigned for 25 years.* **2.** To be widespread; prevail: *Confusion reigned in the house.*
reign (rān) □*noun, plural* **reigns** □*verb* **reigned, reigning, reigns**

rein *noun* **1.** Often **reins** A long leather strap attached to the bit in a horse's mouth and held by the rider or driver to control the horse. **2.** A means of control or guidance: *The newly elected President took over the reins of government.*
□*verb* To stop or control with or as if with reins: *She reined in her temper with difficulty.*
rein (rān) □*noun, plural* **reins** □*verb* **reined, reining, reins**

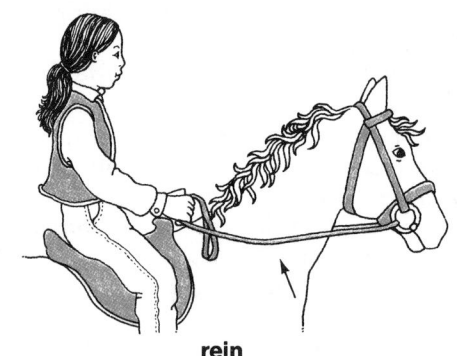

rein

reindeer *noun* A deer that is found in Arctic regions and has large, spreading antlers.
rein·deer (rān′ dîr′) □*noun, plural* **reindeer**

reindeer

reinforce *verb* To make stronger by adding extra support: *reinforced the wall with steel girders; troops that reinforced the brigade.*
re·in·force (rē'in fôrs') ▢*verb* **reinforced, reinforcing, reinforces**

reject *verb* To refuse to accept, use, consider, or receive: *He rejected my offer of help.*
re·ject (ri jekt') ▢*verb* **rejected, rejecting, rejects**

SYNONYMS: **reject, decline, refuse**

These verbs mean to be unwilling to accept, use, consider, or receive: *She rejected all my suggestions. I had to decline her invitation to stay for dinner because I had other plans. He refused all our offers to help.*

---

rejoice *verb* To feel or show joy: *The couple rejoiced when their daughter was born.*
re·joice (ri jois') ▢*verb* **rejoiced, rejoicing, rejoices**

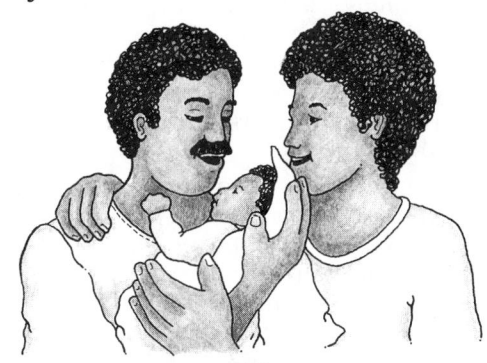

rejoice

relapse *noun* The act or condition of falling back into a previous condition: *The patient suffered a relapse.*
re·lapse (ri laps') ▢*noun, plural* **relapses**

relate *verb* To tell; narrate: *related the story of his trip.*
re·late (ri lāt') ▢*verb* **related, relating, relates**

related *adjective* **1.** Having a connection or relationship: *English is closely related to German.* **2.** Connected by blood or marriage.
re·lat·ed (ri lā'tid) ▢*adjective*

relation *noun* **1.** A connection between two or more things: *an idea that has no relation to fact.* **2.** Someone who belongs to the same family as another; relative. **3. relations** Connections or dealings with other nations, persons, or groups: *two countries that have friendly relations.*

re·la·tion (ri lā'shən) ▢*noun, plural* **relations**

relationship *noun* The condition of being related; connection: *the relationship between rain and the growth of crops.*
re·la·tion·ship (ri lā'shən ship') ▢*noun, plural* **relationships**

relative *adjective* Considered or existing in comparison with something else: *We moved from the city because we like the relative quiet of the suburbs.*
▢*noun* Someone related to another by blood or marriage.
rel·a·tive (rel'ə tiv) ▢*adjective* ▢*noun, plural* **relatives**

relax *verb* **1.** To make or become less tight or tense: *He relaxed his hold on my arm.* **2.** To make or become less severe or strict: *The judge relaxed the rules.*
re·lax (ri laks') ▢*verb* **relaxed, relaxing, relaxes**

relay *noun* **1.** A crew, group, or team that relieves another: *They worked in relays all night long.* **2.** A race between two groups of runners or swimmers in which each member goes only part of the total distance.
▢*verb* To pass or send along by or as if by relay: *He relayed the news to his mother.*
re·lay ▢*noun* (rē'lā'), *plural* **relays** ▢*verb* (rē'lā' *or* ri lā') **relayed, relaying, relays**

relay
Relay race

a bat	ī bite	o͞o tool	*th* feather
ā make	î fierce	ou out	th bath
â dare	o dot	u nut	hw wheat
ä father	ō no	û turn	zh measure
e net	ô law, for	ch church	ə about, open
ē be	oi soil	ng ring	pencil, atom
i dip	oo look	sh shade	circus

release *verb* To set free from confinement or obligation: *She released the bird from the cage. The lieutenant released the soldier from duty.* □*noun* The act of releasing or the condition of being released: *the release of a prisoner from jail.*
re·lease (ri **lēs′**) □*verb* **released, releasing, releases** □*noun, plural* **releases**

release

relevant *adjective* Having some connection with the matter at hand; related.
rel·e·vant (rel′ə vənt) □*adjective*

reliable *adjective* Capable of being relied on; dependable: *a reliable friend; a reliable car.*
re·li·a·ble (ri lī′ə bəl) □*adjective*

relic *noun* Something that survives from the past: *This wall is a relic of an ancient town.*
rel·ic (rel′ik) □*noun, plural* **relics**

relief *noun* **1.** A lessening or removal of pain or anxiety: *It was a relief to be finished with my exams.* **2.** Help or assistance given to the needy: *The governor sent relief to the fire victims.* **3.** Release from a job or duty: *The policeman had to wait an hour longer for his relief.* **4.** Elevation of figures and forms from a flat background, as in sculpture.
re·lief (ri **lēf′**) □*noun, plural* **reliefs**

relieve *verb* **1.** To lessen or reduce the pain or anxiety of; ease: *This medicine only relieves the symptoms of a cold; it does not cure the disease.* **2.** To free from worry or distress: *I was relieved to hear that she arrived safely.* **3.** To release from a duty or position: *The officer was relieved of his command.*
re·lieve (ri **lēv′**) □*verb* **relieved, relieving, relieves**

religion *noun* **1.** Belief in and worship of God or gods. **2.** A particular system of religion: *the Hindu religion.*
re·lig·ion (ri **lij′** ən) □*noun, plural* **religions**

religious *adjective* **1.** Of or having to do with religion: *a religious service.* **2.** Following the beliefs of a religion: *a religious family.*
re·lig·ious (ri **lij′** əs) □*adjective*

relish *noun* A spicy mixture, as of chopped vegetables, that is used as a side dish or to flavor foods.
rel·ish (rel′ish) □*noun, plural* **relishes**

reluctant *adjective* Lacking inclination; not willing: *He was reluctant to try out for the team.*
re·luc·tant (ri **luk′** tənt) □*adjective*

rely *verb* To have confidence or trust; depend: *You have to rely on your own judgment.*
re·ly (ri **lī′**) □*verb* **relied, relying, relies**

remain *verb* **1.** To continue to be: *We remained friendly.* **2.** To stay in the same place: *She remained in the house all afternoon.* **3.** To be left: *Only one day remains before school starts.*
re·main (ri **mān′**) □*verb* **remained, remaining, remains**

remainder *noun* **1.** The remaining part; rest: *I saved the remainder of the pie for another meal.* **2.** The number left over when one number is subtracted from another: *When 17 is subtracted from 19, the remainder is 2.* **3.** The number left over when one number is divided by another: *5 divided by 2 gives 2 and a remainder of 1.*
re·main·der (ri **mān′** dər) □*noun, plural* **remainders**

remains *plural noun* **1.** What is left over: *the remains of a sandwich.* **2.** A dead body; corpse.
re·mains (ri **mānz′**) □*plural noun*

remark *noun* A brief comment: *She made a nasty remark about my dress.*
□*verb* To make a remark; mention: *He remarked that he was going away the next day.*
re·mark (ri **märk′**) □*noun, plural* **remarks** □*verb* **remarked, remarking, remarks**

remarkable *adjective* Worthy of notice; unusual: *a remarkable performance.*
re·mark·a·ble (ri **mär′** kə bəl) □*adjective*

remedy *noun* Something that cures, relieves, or corrects a bad condition: *a remedy for a cold.*
□*verb* To be or provide a remedy for.

rem·e·dy (rĕm′ĭ dē) □*noun, plural* **remedies**
□*verb* **remedied, remedying, remedies**

remember *verb* **1.** To bring back to mind: *I can't remember your telephone number.* **2.** To keep carefully in mind: *Remember your appointment.*
re·mem·ber (rĭ mĕm′bər) □*verb*
remembered, remembering, remembers

SYNONYMS: **remember, recall**

These verbs mean to bring back to mind: *I can't remember where I left the book. She looks familiar, but I don't recall her name.*

---

remind *verb* To cause to remember: *Please remind him to pick up a newspaper for me.*
re·mind (rĭ mīnd′) □*verb* **reminded, reminding, reminds**

remote *adjective* **1.** Far away in time or place: *the remote past; a remote town.* **2.** Very small; slight: *The danger of fire is remote.*
re·mote (rĭ mōt′) □*adjective* **remoter, remotest**

remote control *noun* The controlling of an activity or machine from a distance: *The rocket was steered by remote control.*

removal *noun* The act of removing or condition of being removed: *the removal of snow from the sidewalk.*
re·mov·al (rĭ mōō′vəl) □*noun*

remove *verb* **1.** To move by taking off or away: *He removed his coat.* **2.** To do away with: *Her concert removed all my doubts about her ability.*
re·move (rĭ mōōv′) □*verb* **removed, removing, removes**

render *verb* **1.** To cause to become; make: *The news rendered her speechless.* **2.** To give or make available: *The store renders bills monthly.* **3.** To perform: *render a song.*
ren·der (rĕn′dər) □*verb* **rendered, rendering, renders**

renew *verb* **1.** To make or become new or as if new again; restore. **2.** To begin or take up again; revive: *She renewed her efforts.* **3.** To extend the term of: *renewed their membership in the club.*
re·new (rĭ nōō′ *or* rĭ nyōō′) □*verb* **renewed, renewing, renews**

rent *noun* A payment made at regular intervals for the use of the property of another.
□*verb* **1.** To occupy or use in return for rent: *rent a car.* **2.** To grant the use of for rent: *She rented her farm to friends.* **3.** To be for rent: *The apartment rents for $500 a month.*
rent (rĕnt) □*noun, plural* **rents** □*verb* **rented, renting, rents**

repaid *verb* The past tense and past participle of **repay:** *I repaid the loan.*
re·paid (rĭ pād′) □*verb*

repair *verb* To put back into proper or useful condition: *She repaired the chair.* —See Synonyms at **mend.**
□*noun* **1.** The act of repairing: *a house in need of repair.* **2.** Operating condition; working order: *He keeps his tractor in good repair.*
re·pair (rĭ pâr′) □*verb* **repaired, repairing, repairs** □*noun, plural* **repairs**

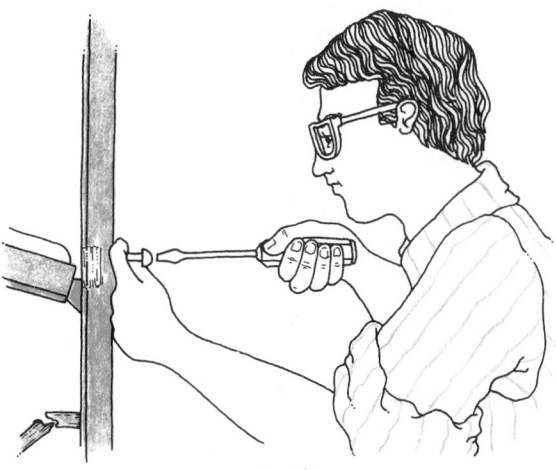

repair

repay *verb* **1.** To pay back: *repay a loan.* **2.** To give, make, or do in return for: *She repaid his friendship with kindness.*
re·pay (rĭ pā′) □*verb* **repaid, repaying, repays**

repeal *verb* To do away with officially: *Congress repealed the law.*
re·peal (rĭ pēl′) □*verb* **repealed, repealing, repeals**

repeat *verb* To say or do again: *Repeat the instructions she gave you. Try not to repeat your mistakes.*

a bat	ī bite	ōō tool	*th* feather
ā make	î fierce	ou out	th bath
â dare	o dot	u nut	hw wheat
ä father	ō no	û turn	zh measure
e net	ô law, for	ch church	ə about, open
ē be	oi soil	ng ring	pencil, atom
i dip	oo look	sh shade	circus

re·peat (ri pēt´) ☐*verb* **repeated, repeating, repeats**

repel *verb* **1.** To drive off, back, or away: *The army repelled the invasion.* **2.** To disgust: *Snakes repel me.* **3.** To keep off or out; resist: *a fabric that repels water.*
re·pel (ri pel´) ☐*verb* **repelled, repelling, repels**

repetition *noun* The act of repeating: *The constant repetition of the tune got on our nerves.*
rep·e·ti·tion (rep´i tish´ən) ☐*noun, plural* **repetitions**

replace *verb* **1.** To take or fill the place of: *Electric lights have replaced candles.* **2.** To put back in place: *He replaced the books neatly.* **3.** To provide a new one in the place of: *I had to replace the record I broke.*
re·place (ri plās´) ☐*verb* **replaced, replacing, replaces**

replacement *noun* **1.** The act of replacing. **2.** Someone or something that replaces another; substitute: *The coach had to find a replacement for the injured player.*
re·place·ment (ri plās´mənt) ☐*noun, plural* **replacements**

reply *verb* To do or say in answer: *He never replied to my letter.* —See Synonyms at **answer.**
☐*noun* An answer or response.
re·ply (ri plī´) ☐*verb* **replied, replying, replies** ☐*noun, plural* **replies**

report *noun* A spoken or written account or description: *a news report; a book report.*
☐*verb* **1.** To make or present a report: *The scientist reported the result of his experiment.* **2.** To write or provide an account of for publication or broadcast: *She reports the morning news on television.* **3.** To present oneself: *They reported for work on time.*
re·port (ri pôrt´) ☐*noun, plural* **reports** ☐*verb* **reported, reporting, reports**

report card *noun* A report of a student's grades and behavior.

reporter *noun* Someone who gathers and reports news, as for a newspaper.
re·port·er (ri pôr´tər) ☐*noun, plural* **reporters**

represent *verb* **1.** To be a sign or symbol of; stand for: *The dove represents peace.* **2.** To act for: *Lawyers represent clients.*
rep·re·sent (rep´ri zent´) ☐*verb* **represented, representing, represents**

representative *noun* Someone who represents another: *He was elected to be our representative in Congress.*
☐*adjective* **1.** Of, formed of, or carried on by elected members: *a representative government.* **2.** Being a characteristic example: *a book that is representative of the writer's style.*
rep·re·sen·ta·tive (rep´ri zen´tə tiv) ☐*noun, plural* **representatives** ☐*adjective*

reproduce *verb* **1.** To make a copy, image, or counterpart of: *a machine that reproduces sound.* **2.** To produce offspring.
re·pro·duce (rē´prə dōos´ *or* rē´prə dyōos´) ☐*verb* **reproduced, reproducing, reproduces**

reproduction *noun* **1.** The act of reproducing. **2.** Something that is reproduced; copy: *a reproduction of a famous sculpture.*
re·pro·duc·tion (rē´prə duk´shən) ☐*noun, plural* **reproductions**

reptile *noun* Any of a group of cold-blooded animals, such as snakes and turtles, that creep or crawl on the ground, have a backbone, and are covered with scales or bony plates.
rep·tile (rep´tīl´) ☐*noun, plural* **reptiles**

WORD HISTORY: **reptile**
Reptile comes from a Latin word that means "creeping."

reptile
Above: turtle
Below: snake

republic *noun* **1.** A form of government in which the voters elect their representatives and in which the head of state is usually a president and not a monarch. **2.** A country, as the United States, that has a republican form of government.
re·pub·lic (ri pub´lik) ☐*noun, plural* **republics**

republican *adjective* **1.** Of, like, or for a republic: *a republican government.* **2. Republican** Of the Republican Party.
□*noun* **1.** Someone who believes in or supports a republican form of government. **2. Republican** A member or supporter of the Republican Party.
re·pub·li·can (ri **pub′**li kən) □*adjective* □*noun, plural* **republicans**

Republican Party *noun* One of the two main political parties of the United States.

reputation *noun* The general worth or quality of someone or something as judged by others: *She has the reputation of being a good doctor.*
rep·u·ta·tion (rep′yə **tā′**shən) □*noun, plural* **reputations**

request *verb* To ask or ask for: *I requested him to answer. She requested information.*
□*noun* **1.** The act of asking for something: *I repeated my request for help.* **2.** Something that is asked for: *We have had many requests for tickets.*
re·quest (ri **kwest′**) □*verb* **requested, requesting, requests** □*noun, plural* **requests**

require *verb* **1.** To have need of: *Plants require water.* **2.** To impose an obligation or duty upon: *The law requires all workers to pay income tax.*
re·quire (ri **kwīr′**) □*verb* **required, requiring, requires**

requirement *noun* Something required or necessary: *What are the requirements for the job?*
re·quire·ment (ri **kwīr′**mənt) □*noun, plural* **requirements**

rescue *verb* To save from danger: *Neighbors rescued the family from the burning house.*
□*noun* The act of rescuing.
res·cue (res′kyōō) □*verb* **rescued, rescuing, rescues** □*noun, plural* **rescues**

research *noun* Close and careful study of a subject or problem; investigation.
re·search (ri **sûrch′** *or* rē′sûrch′) □*noun, plural* **researches**

resemblance *noun* Similarity in appearance; likeness: *I see a resemblance between the sisters.*
re·sem·blance (ri **zem′**bləns) □*noun, plural* **resemblances**

resemble *verb* To be like or similar to: *His handwriting resembles mine.*
re·sem·ble (ri **zem′**bəl) □*verb* **resembled, resembling, resembles**

resent *verb* To feel angry or bitter about: *I resented his rudeness.*
re·sent (ri **zent′**) □*verb* **resented, resenting, resents**

resentment *noun* Anger or bitterness about something thought to be insulting or unfair: *She felt resentment at being criticized.*
re·sent·ment (ri **zent′**mənt) □*noun*

reservation *noun* **1.** An arrangement by which something, such as a hotel room, is held for one's use. **2.** Something that limits or restricts: *I have reservations about trusting him.* **3.** An area set aside by the government for a particular purpose.
res·er·va·tion (rez′ər **vā′**shən) □*noun, plural* **reservations**

reserve *verb* **1.** To set aside for a particular purpose or later use. **2.** To arrange for the use of in advance: *We reserved a hotel room for the weekend.* **3.** To keep for oneself: *I reserve the right to change my mind.*
□*noun* **1.** Something set aside for later use: *reserves of petroleum.* **2.** A tendency to keep one's feelings and thoughts to oneself. **3. reserves** Armed forces not on active duty but ready to be called up in an emergency.
re·serve (ri **zûrv′**) □*verb* **reserved, reserving, reserves** □*noun, plural* **reserves**

reservoir *noun* A body of water that has been collected and stored for use.
res·er·voir (rez′ər vwär′) □*noun, plural* **reservoirs**

reside *verb* To make one's home; live: *She resides in New York.*
re·side (ri **zīd′**) □*verb* **resided, residing, resides**

residence *noun* **1.** The house or building in which a person lives. **2.** The act or fact of living somewhere: *We met them during their residence in our neighborhood.*
res·i·dence (rez′i dəns) □*noun, plural* **residences**

resident *noun* Someone who lives in a place: *residents of the city.*
res·i·dent (rez′i dənt) □*noun, plural* **residents**

a bat	ī bite	ōō tool	*th* feather
ā make	i fierce	ou out	th bath
â dare	o dot	u nut	hw wheat
ä father	ō no	û turn	zh measure
e net	ô law, for	ch church	ə about, open
ē be	oi soil	ng ring	pencil, atom
i dip	oo look	sh shade	circus

residential *adjective* Suitable for or containing residences: *a residential neighborhood.*
res·i·den·tial (rez′i **den′**shəl) □*adjective*

resign *verb* To give up officially or formally: *He resigned from the committee.*
re·sign (ri **zīn′**) □*verb* **resigned, resigning, resigns**

resignation *noun* The act of resigning: *The prime minister announced his resignation.*
res·ig·na·tion (rez′ig **nā′**shən) □*noun, plural* **resignations**

resin *noun* A yellowish or brownish sticky substance that oozes from certain trees, such as the pine, and is used in making varnishes, lacquers, and plastics.
res·in (rez′in) □*noun, plural* **resins**

resist *verb* 1. To work or fight against; oppose: *resist an attack; couldn't resist temptation.* 2. To withstand the effect or force of: *a fabric that resists wrinkling.*
re·sist (ri **zist′**) □*verb* **resisted, resisting, resists**

resistance *noun* 1. The act of resisting: *There was little resistance to the new law.* 2. The ability to resist: *He got sick because his resistance is low.* 3. A force that tends to hinder motion: *The airplane is designed to lessen wind resistance.*
re·sis·tance (ri **zis′**təns) □*noun*

resolution *noun* 1. The quality of having strong will and determination: *They faced their problem with resolution.* 2. A vow; promise: *He made a resolution to practice every day.*
res·o·lu·tion (rez′ə **lōō′**shən) □*noun, plural* **resolutions**

resolve *verb* 1. To make a firm decision: *She resolved to study harder.* 2. To find a solution to; solve: *How can we resolve this problem?*
re·solve (ri **zolv′**) □*verb* **resolved, resolving, resolves**

resonant *adjective* Having a full, pleasing sound: *a deep, resonant voice.*
res·o·nant (rez′ə nənt) □*adjective*

resort *verb* To go or turn for help: *He resorted to his brother for a loan.*
□*noun* 1. A place where people go for rest or recreation: *a summer resort.* 2. Someone or something to which one turns for help: *Going to a lawyer was her last resort.*
re·sort (ri **zôrt′**) □*verb* **resorted, resorting, resorts** □*noun, plural* **resorts**

resound *verb* 1. To be filled with sound: *The auditorium resounded with applause.* 2. To make a loud sound: *The trumpets resounded throughout the theater.*
re·sound (ri **zound′**) □*verb* **resounded, resounding, resounds**

resource *noun* 1. Something that can be turned to for support or help: *His courage is his greatest resource.* 2. **resources** A supply or stock that is available: *natural resources.* 3. The ability to deal with situations effectively: *a person of resource.*
re·source (ri **sôrs′** *or* rē′sôrs′) □*noun, plural* **resources**

respect *noun* 1. Admiration or regard; esteem: *I have great respect for your opinion.* 2. Relation to something: *With respect to this question, there are two possible answers.* 3. **respects** Expressions of respect: *I sent my respects to his grandmother.* 4. A particular feature or detail: *In certain respects my brother and I are very similar.*
□*verb* To have or show respect for.
re·spect (ri **spekt′**) □*noun, plural* **respects** □*verb* **respected, respecting, respects**

respectable *adjective* Proper in behavior, character, or appearance: *a respectable family; respectable clothes.*
re·spect·a·ble (ri **spek′**tə bəl) □*adjective*

respectful *adjective* Having or showing respect: *He is always respectful to older people.*
re·spect·ful (ri **spekt′**fəl) □*adjective*

respective *adjective* Of or belonging to each: *They are experts in their respective fields.*
re·spec·tive (ri **spek′**tiv) □*adjective*

respectively *adverb* Each in the order given: *An apple and a carrot are a fruit and a vegetable respectively.*
re·spec·tive·ly (ri **spek′**tiv lē) □*adverb*

respiration *noun* The act of inhaling and exhaling; breathing.
res·pi·ra·tion (res′pə **rā′**shən) □*noun*

respiratory *adjective* Of or having to do with respiration: *The lungs are part of the respiratory system.*
res·pi·ra·to·ry (res′pər ə tôr′ē) □*adjective*

respond *verb* 1. To make a reply: *Did he respond to your letter?* 2. To act in return; react: *The patient is responding well to treatment.*
—See Synonyms at **answer.**
re·spond (ri **spond′**) □*verb* **responded, responding, responds**

response *noun* An answer or reply: *What was his response to your question?*
re·sponse (ri **spons′**) □*noun, plural* **responses**

responsibility *noun* **1.** The quality or condition of being responsible: *He has no sense of responsibility.* **2.** Something for which one is responsible: *It's my responsibility to mow the lawn.*
re·spon·si·bil·i·ty (ri spon′sə **bil′**i tē) ◻*noun, plural* **responsibilities**

responsible *adjective* **1.** Being in a position to receive praise or blame for something: *You are responsible for the accident.* **2.** Being the cause of something: *Haste is responsible for a lot of mistakes.* **3.** Being dependable or reliable; trustworthy: *a responsible parent.* **4.** Involving important duties or obligations: *a responsible job.*
re·spon·si·ble (ri **spon′**sə bəl) ◻*adjective*

rest¹ *noun* **1.** A period when one is relaxed, asleep, or not active: *I took a short rest.* **2.** Sleep, ease, or relaxation: *I don't need much rest.* **3.** An absence or ending of motion: *The bird came to rest on a tree.* **4.** Something used as a support: *a foot rest.* **5.** A period of silence in music.
◻*verb* **1.** To stop work or activity: *I stopped swimming and rested.* **2.** To lie down, especially to sleep: *She rested after lunch.* **3.** To give rest to: *Take off your shoes and rest your feet.* **4.** To place or lean for support: *She rested her hand on his shoulder.* **5.** To be fixed or directed: *His eyes rested on his book.*
rest (rest) ◻*noun, plural* **rests** ◻*verb* **rested, resting, rests**

rest² *noun* Something that is left over; remainder: *I ate the rest of the stew.*
rest (rest) ◻*noun*

restaurant *noun* A place where meals are served to the public.
res·tau·rant (**res′**tər ənt) ◻*noun, plural* **restaurants**

restless *adjective* **1.** Without quiet or rest: *a restless night.* **2.** Unable to rest or be still: *a restless child.*
rest·less (**rest′**lis) ◻*adjective*

restore *verb* **1.** To bring back: *The verdict restored my confidence in justice.* **2.** To bring back to an original condition: *restore an old building.* **3.** To give back: *We restored the lost dog to its owner.*
re·store (ri **stôr′**) ◻*verb* **restored, restoring, restores**

restrain *verb* **1.** To hold back by physical force: *The policemen restrained the prisoner.* **2.** To keep or hold back; check: *I couldn't restrain my laughter.*

re·strain (ri **strān′**) ◻*verb* **restrained, restraining, restrains**

restrict *verb* To keep within limits; confine: *The doctor restricted the patient to bed.*
re·strict (ri **strikt′**) ◻*verb* **restricted, restricting, restricts**

restriction *noun* **1.** The act of restricting or condition of being restricted. **2.** Something that restricts: *There are no restrictions on the number of members allowed.*
re·stric·tion (ri **strik′**shən) ◻*noun, plural* **restrictions**

result *noun* Something that comes about or follows from a cause: *The fire was the result of carelessness.*
◻*verb* **1.** To be the result of: *A broken leg resulted from his fall.* **2.** To have a particular result: *Her interview resulted in a job.*
re·sult (ri **zult′**) ◻*noun, plural* **results** ◻*verb* **resulted, resulting, results**

resume *verb* **1.** To begin again: *classes resumed after the vacation.* **2.** To take again: *He resumed his place in the line.*
re·sume (ri **zoom′**) ◻*verb* **resumed, resuming, resumes**

retail *noun* The sale of goods to the general public.
◻*adjective* Of or having to do with the selling of goods at retail: *a retail merchant.*
re·tail (**rē′**tāl′) ◻*noun* ◻*adjective*

retain *verb* **1.** To continue to have; keep: *She retained her job as a teacher.* **2.** To hold in the mind or the memory: *She retained only a vague impression of his appearance.* **3.** To keep or hold in a particular place or condition: *The oven retains heat for long periods.*
re·tain (ri **tān′**) ◻*verb* **retained, retaining, retains**

retina *noun* A membrane on the inside of the eyeball that is sensitive to light and receives images of things seen.
ret·i·na (**ret′**ən ə) ◻*noun, plural* **retinas**

retire *verb* **1.** To give up one's work permanently: *He retired from the army after 20 years.* **2.** To go to bed: *We retired late.*
re·tire (ri **tīr′**) ◻*verb* **retired, retiring, retires**

a bat	ī bite	ōō tool	*th* feather
ā make	î fierce	ou out	th bath
â dare	o dot	u nut	hw wheat
ä father	ō no	û turn	zh measure
e net	ô law, for	ch church	ə about, open
ē be	oi soil	ng ring	pencil, atom
i dip	oo look	sh shade	circus

retirement *noun* The act of retiring or condition of being retired: *She began painting after her retirement.*
re·tire·ment (ri **tīr′**mənt) □*noun*

retiring *adjective* Shy and reserved: *a quiet and retiring woman.*
re·tir·ing (ri **tī′**ring) □*adjective*

retreat *verb* To fall or move back, as before an attack; withdraw: *The enemy retreated.*
□*noun* **1.** The act of retreating: *The troops made a hasty retreat.* **2.** The signal for a military retreat: *The trumpet sounded retreat.* **3.** A quiet and private place: *a country retreat.*
re·treat (ri **trēt′**) □*verb* **retreated, retreating, retreats** □*noun, plural* **retreats**

retrieve *verb* **1.** To get back; recover: *She retrieved the letter from the wastebasket.* **2.** To find and bring back game that has been shot.
re·trieve (ri **trēv′**) □*verb* **retrieved, retrieving, retrieves**

retriever *noun* A dog that has been trained to retrieve game that has been shot.
re·triev·er (ri **trē′**vər) □*noun, plural* **retrievers**

retriever

return *verb* **1.** To go or come back: *When will you return to the city? Spring returns each year.* **2.** To bring, send, carry, put, or give back: *She returned the sweater she had borrowed.* **3.** To give back in response to something: *She returned his call.* **4.** To report officially: *The jury returned a verdict of guilty.*
□*noun* **1.** The act of returning: *a return to good humor; the return of fall.* **2.** A profit: *an investment that yields a good return.*
return (ri **tûrn′**) □*verb* **returned, returning, returns** □*noun, plural* **returns**

reunion *noun* A gathering of people after a separation: *a college reunion.*
re·un·ion (rē **yōon′**yən) □*noun, plural* **reunions**

reveal *verb* **1.** To make known; disclose: *He revealed his plans.* **2.** To show; display: *The fog lifted and revealed the skyline.*
re·veal (ri **vēl′**) □*verb* **revealed, revealing, reveals**

reveille *noun* A bugle call played in the morning to awaken soldiers or other persons in a camp.
rev·eil·le (rev′ə lē) □*noun*

revenge *verb* To do injury or harm in return for: *The brothers vowed to revenge the insult.*
□*noun* The act or an example of revenging: *She wanted revenge for her wrongs.*
re·venge (ri **venj′**) □*verb* **revenged, revenging, revenges** □*noun*

revenue *noun* **1.** The money that a government collects, as from taxes. **2.** Income from property or investments: *Rent is one form of revenue.*
rev·e·nue (rev′ə nōo′ or rev′ə nyōo′) □*noun, plural* **revenues**

reverence *noun* A feeling of awe and deep respect.
rev·er·ence (rev′ər əns) □*noun*

reverent *adjective* Feeling or showing reverence: *reverent behavior in church.*
rev·er·ent (rev′ər ənt) □*adjective*

reverse *adjective* Backward in position, direction, or order: *the reverse side of the fabric; a reverse gear.*
□*noun* **1.** The opposite or contrary of something: *They did the reverse of what the teacher told them to do.* **2.** The back or rear of something: *The reverse of the coin was stamped with an eagle.* **3.** A gear in an automobile that allows it to move backward. **4.** A change for the worse: *His career met with many reverses.*
□*verb* **1.** To move or turn in the opposite direction: *I reversed my opinion.* **2.** To turn inside out or upside-down: *She reversed the shirt to iron it.* **3.** To bring to an end; overturn: *The court reversed its decision.*
re·verse (ri **vûrs′**) □*adjective* □*noun, plural* **reverses** □*verb* **reversed, reversing, reverses**

review *verb* **1.** To look over again; examine again: *Review your lessons before the exam.* **2.** To write or give a critical report about: *He reviews movies for the newspaper.* **3.** To look back on: *He reviewed all the moves in the game he had won.*
□*noun* **1.** The act of looking over or examining something again: *made a review of his notes.* **2.** A report on something that attempts

to determine its worth: *a book review.* **3.** A general view or survey: *a review of the events of her life.*
re·view (ri **vyoo′**) □*verb* **reviewed, reviewing, reviews** □*noun, plural* **reviews**

revise *verb* **1.** To look over in order to improve or correct: *He revised the manuscript.* **2.** To change; modify: *We revised our plans.*
re·vise (ri **vīz′**) □*verb* **revised, revising, revises**

revive *verb* **1.** To bring or come back to life, consciousness, or strength: *The news revived my hopes.* **2.** To bring back into use of performance: *revive an old custom.*
re·vive (ri **vīv′**) □*verb* **revived, reviving, revives**

revoke *verb* To cancel or repeal: *The authorities revoked his passport.*
re·voke (ri **vōk′**) □*verb* **revoked, revoking, revokes**

revolt *verb* **1.** To rebel against a government or other authority: *The slaves revolted and won their freedom.* **2.** To fill or be filled with disgust; repel: *His cruelty revolted me.*
□*noun* A rebellion; uprising: *He was the leader of the revolt.*
re·volt (ri **vōlt′**) □*verb* **revolted, revolting, revolts** □*noun, plural* **revolts**

revolution *noun* **1.** An uprising or rebellion against a government. **2.** A sudden or extensive change: *The computer has caused a revolution in education.* **3.** Movement around an object: *the revolution of the moon around the earth.* **4.** A rotation about a center or axis.
rev·o·lu·tion (rev′ə **loo′**shən) □*noun, plural* **revolutions**

revolutionary *adjective* Of, having to do with, or bringing about a revolution: *a revolutionary leader; a revolutionary discovery.*
rev·o·lu·tion·ar·y (rev′ə **loo′**shə ner′ē) □*adjective*

revolve *verb* **1.** To move in an orbit: *The earth revolves around the sun.* **2.** To turn or cause to turn on an axis: *The spinning wheel revolved as she pressed the pedal.* —See Synonyms at **turn.**
re·volve (ri **volv′**) □*verb* **revolved, revolving, revolves**

revolver *noun* A pistol with a revolving cylinder holding a supply of bullets that can be fired without loading again.
re·volv·er (ri **vol′**vər) □*noun, plural* **revolvers**

reward *noun* **1.** Something given or received in return for an act or accomplishment: *The soldier received a medal as a reward for bravery.* **2.** Money offered for the capture of a criminal or the return of something lost.
□*verb* To give a reward to or for.
re·ward (ri **wôrd′**) □*noun, plural* **rewards** □*verb* **rewarded, rewarding, rewards**

rheumatism *noun* A disease in which muscles and joints are swollen, stiff, and painful.
rheu·ma·tism (**roo′**mə tiz′əm) □*noun*

rhinoceros *noun* A large African or Asian animal with short legs, thick skin, and one or two upright horns on the snout.
rhi·noc·er·os (rī **nos′**ər əs) □*noun, plural* **rhinoceros** or **rhinoceroses**

> **WORD HISTORY: rhinoceros**
>
> *Rhinoceros* comes from the Greek name for this animal. The Greek name was formed from the word for "nose" and the word for "horn."

rhinoceros

rhododendron *noun* An evergreen shrub with clusters of white, pink, or purple flowers.
rho·do·den·dron (rō′də **den′**drən) □*noun, plural* **rhododendrons**

> **WORD HISTORY: rhododendron**
>
> *Rhododendron* comes from two Greek words meaning "rose tree."

a	bat	ī	bite	oo	tool	*th*	feather
ā	make	î	fierce	ou	out	th	bath
â	dare	o	dot	u	nut	hw	wheat
ä	father	ō	no	û	turn	zh	measure
e	net	ô	law, for	ch	church	ə	about, open
ē	be	oi	soil	ng	ring		pencil, atom
i	dip	oo	look	sh	shade		circus

rhubarb *noun* A plant with large leaves and long, fleshy reddish or green stalks that are used for food.
rhu·barb (rōō′ bärb′) □*noun*

rhyme *noun* **1.** Similarity of the last sounds of two or more words or lines of verse. **2.** One of two or more words having such a likeness or similarity in their final sounds: *"May" is a rhyme for "day."* **3.** Poetry.
□*verb* To form a rhyme.
rhyme (rīm) □*noun, plural* **rhymes** □*verb* **rhymed, rhyming, rhymes**

rhythm *noun* Regular repetition of a beat, movement, action, or sound: *the rhythm of clapping hands.*
rhythm (ri*th*′ əm) □*noun, plural* **rhythms**

rib *noun* **1.** Any of the long, curved bones that extend from the backbone and enclose the chest cavity. **2.** Something resembling a rib: *the rib of a feather.*
rib (rib) □*noun, plural* **ribs**

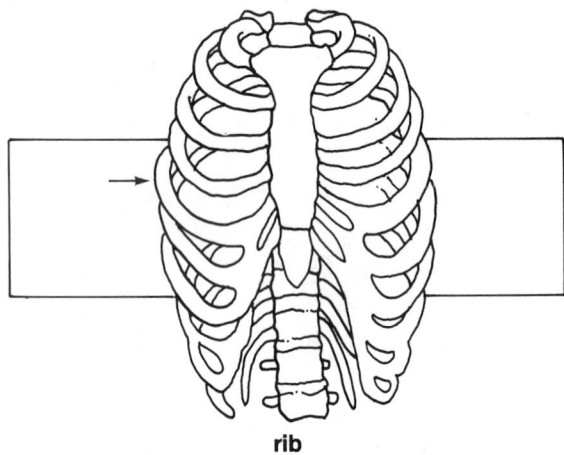

rib

ribbon *noun* **1.** A narrow strip of fabric used for decorating or tying things. **2.** A strip of material that is like a ribbon: *a typewriter ribbon.*
rib·bon (rib′ ən) □*noun, plural* **ribbons**

rice *noun* A grass that grows in warm regions and bears grains that are a staple food in many parts of the world.
rice (rīs) □*noun*

rich *adjective* **1.** Having great wealth: *a rich family.* **2.** Having an abundant supply of something: *a food that is rich in vitamins.* **3.** Fertile; productive: *rich soil.* **4.** Containing a large amount of fat or sugar: *a rich cake.* **5.** Full and deep: *a rich baritone voice.*
rich (rich) □*adjective* **richer, richest**

riches *plural noun* Great wealth.
rich·es (rich′ iz) □*plural noun*

ricksha *noun* A small, two-wheeled carriage used in the Orient. It is pulled by one or two persons.
rick·sha (rik′ shô′) □*noun, plural* **rickshas**

rid *verb* To free from something: *We are trying to rid the barn of mice.*
rid (rid) □*verb* **rid** or **ridded, ridding, rids**

ridden *verb* The past participle of **ride:** *She hasn't yet ridden her new bicycle.*
rid·den (rid′ ən) □*verb*

riddle *noun* A question or problem that is hard to answer or solve.
rid·dle (rid′ əl) □*noun, plural* **riddles**

ride *verb* **1.** To sit and travel on while controlling or driving: *ride a tricycle; ride a horse.* **2.** To be carried in a vehicle: *We rode in a donkey cart.* **3.** To be supported or carried along on: *The swimmer rode the surf.*
□*noun* **1.** A trip on an animal or in a vehicle. **2.** A device, as a roller coaster, on which one rides for pleasure at an amusement park.
ride (rīd) □*verb* **rode, ridden, riding, rides** □*noun, plural* **rides**

rider *noun* Someone who rides.
rid·er (rī′ dər) □*noun, plural* **riders**

ridge *noun* **1.** A long, narrow peak or crest: *the ridge of a roof.* **2.** A long, narrow chain of hills or mountains. **3.** A narrow raised strip: *the ridges in a plowed field.*
ridge (rij) □*noun, plural* **ridges**

ridicule *noun* Words or actions that make fun of something or someone: *The child ran away to escape his friends' ridicule.*
□*verb* To make fun of; mock: *Her classmates ridiculed her floppy hat.*
rid·i·cule (rid′ i kyōōl′) □*noun* □*verb* **ridiculed, ridiculing, ridicules**

ridiculous *adjective* Very foolish; silly; absurd: *a ridiculous plan; a ridiculous costume.*
ri·dic·u·lous (ri dik′ yə ləs) □*adjective*

rifle *noun* A gun with a long barrel that has special grooves inside to give the bullet spin as it is fired.
ri·fle (rī′ fəl) □*noun, plural* **rifles**

rig *verb* **1.** To fit out; equip: *He rigged himself out in the costume of a Roman emperor.* **2.** To fit a boat with masts, sails, lines, and other equipment. **3.** To make or construct by using material at hand: *We rigged up a tent from old sheets.*
□*noun* **1.** The arrangement of masts, sails,

lines, and other equipment on a boat. **2.** Special equipment: *a rig for drilling oil.*
rig (rig) □*verb* **rigged, rigging, rigs** □*noun,* *plural* **rigs**

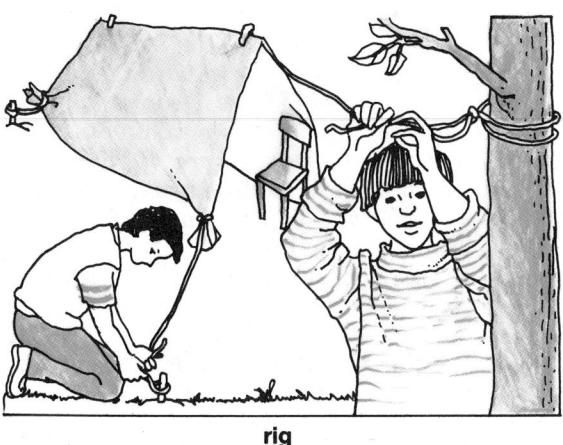

rig

right *noun* **1.** The side or direction opposite the left. **2.** Something that is correct, just, moral, or honorable: *She knew the difference between right and wrong.* **3.** A moral or legal claim: *human rights; the right to vote.*
□*adjective* **1.** Of, having to do with, located on, or toward the side opposite the left: *his right foot; the right sleeve; a right turn.* **2.** Intended to be worn facing outward: *the right side of a fabric.* **3.** Correct; accurate: *the right answer.* **4.** Morally correct; just: *the right thing to do.* **5.** Suitable; appropriate: *He is the right person for the part.*
□*adverb* **1.** On or to the right: *She looked right and left before crossing the street.* **2.** In a direct line; straight: *He went right to work.* **3.** In a correct manner; properly: *The car isn't working right.* **4.** Exactly; just: *Stay right where you are.* **5.** Immediately: *I'll see you right after lunch.*
□*verb* **1.** To put back into an upright, proper, or normal position: *They righted the overturned chair.* **2.** To set right; correct: *We must right this injustice.*
right (rīt) □*noun, plural* **rights** □*adjective* □*adverb* □*verb* **righted, righting, rights**

right angle *noun* An angle of 90 degrees, formed by two lines perpendicular to each other.

right-hand *adjective* **1.** Located on the right: *the right-hand column.* **2.** Of, with, or for the right hand: *a right-hand glove.* **3.** Most helpful or reliable: *He is the mayor's right-hand man.*
right-hand (rīt′hand′) □*adjective*

right-handed *adjective* **1.** Using the right hand more easily and naturally than the left. **2.** Done by or designed for the right hand: *a right-handed wrench; a right-handed throw.*
right-hand·ed (rīt′han′did) □*adjective*

rigid *adjective* **1.** Not changing shape or bending; stiff: *a rigid steel frame.* **2.** Severe; strict: *rigid discipline.*
rig·id (rij′id) □*adjective*

rim *noun* The border, edge, or margin of something: *the rim of a wheel.*
rim (rim) □*noun, plural* **rims**

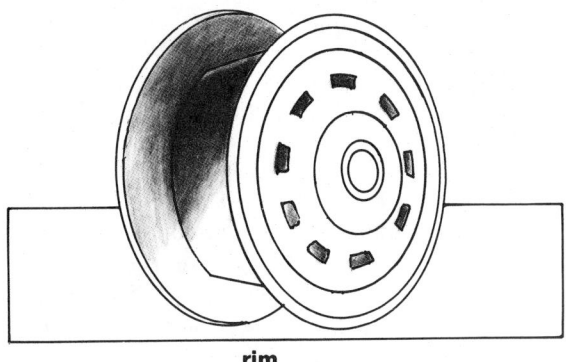

rim

rind *noun* A tough outer covering or layer, as on a lemon or melon.
rind (rīnd) □*noun, plural* **rinds**

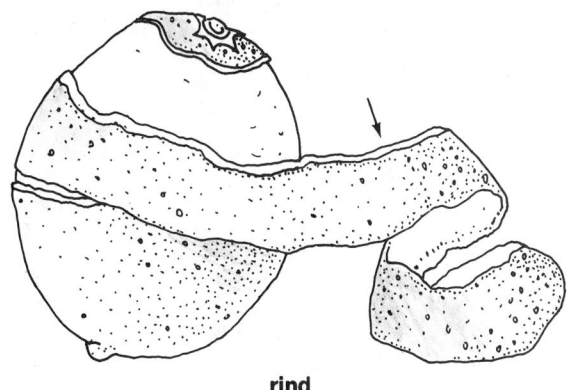

rind

ring¹ *noun* **1.** A circular line, object, form, or arrangement: *a smoke ring; a napkin ring.* **2.** A

a bat	ī bite	oo tool	*th* feather
ā make	î fierce	ou out	th bath
â dare	o dot	u nut	hw wheat
ä father	ō no	û turn	zh measure
e net	ô law, for	ch church	ə about, open
ē be	oi soil	ng ring	pencil, atom
i dip	oo look	sh shade	circus

circular band of metal, especially one worn on a finger. **3.** An enclosed area in which exhibitions or contests take place: *a boxing ring.*
□*verb* To form a ring around; encircle: *Tall trees ringed the lake.*
ring (ring) □*noun, plural* **rings** □*verb* **ringed, ringing, rings**

ring² *verb* **1.** To make or cause to make a clear piercing sound like that of a bell: *The telephone rang. Ring the doorbell.* **2.** To hear a steady buzzing or humming: *His ears rang from the explosion.* **3.** To be filled with sound: *The room rang with laughter.*
□*noun* **1.** The sound made by a bell or other metallic object when struck. **2.** A telephone call: *Give me a ring when you get home.*
ring (ring) □*verb* **rang, rung, ringing, rings** □*noun, plural* **rings**

rink *noun* An area with a smooth surface for ice-skating or roller-skating.
rink (ringk) □*noun, plural* **rinks**

rinse *verb* **1.** To wash lightly with water or a solution: *Rinse out your mouth.* **2.** To use water to remove dirt or soap from: *I rinsed the shampoo from my hair.*
□*noun* The act of rinsing.
rinse (rins) □*verb* **rinsed, rinsing, rinses** □*noun, plural* **rinses**

riot *noun* A violent disturbance created by a large number of people: *a prison riot.*
□*verb* To take part in a riot: *The students rioted as a protest against the war.*
ri·ot (rī′ət) □*noun, plural* **riots** □*verb* **rioted, rioting, riots**

rip *verb* To tear open or split apart: *She ripped her skirt on a nail. The sleeve of his jacket ripped.*
□*noun* A torn or split place; tear.
rip (rip) □*verb* **ripped, ripping, rips** □*noun, plural* **rips**

ripe *adjective* Fully developed and ready for eating: *a ripe peach.*
ripe (rīp) □*adjective* **riper, ripest**

ripen *verb* To make or become ripe: *grapes ripening on the vine.*
rip·en (rī′pən) □*verb* **ripened, ripening, ripens**

ripple *noun* **1.** A very small wave: *The pebble made a ripple on the surface of the lake.* **2.** Something like a ripple: *Her hair hung to her shoulders in soft ripples.* **3.** A sound like that of a ripple: *A ripple of laughter went through the audience.*
□*verb* To form or cause to form ripples: *A*

breeze rippled the water of the pond.
rip·ple (rip′əl) □*noun, plural* **ripples** □*verb* **rippled, rippling, ripples**

rise *verb* **1.** To move upward; ascend: *Hot air rises. The sun rises in the east.* **2.** To get up from a sitting or lying position; stand up: *We all rose when they played the national anthem.* **3.** To get out of bed: *She rose early.* **4.** To increase in size, intensity, or volume; swell: *Their voices rose with excitement.* **5.** To increase in number, amount, price, or value: *Prices rose sharply.* **6.** To gain in rank, position, or importance: *He rose to captain in a year.* **7.** To reach, slope, or extend upward: *The mountain rose thousands of feet above them.* **8.** To come into existence; originate: *Some rivers rise in the mountains.* **9.** To revolt; rebel: *The people rose against the king.*
□*noun* **1.** The act or an example of rising; ascent: *His sudden rise to fame surprised all of us.* **2.** An increase, as in amount: *a rise in temperature.* **3.** An origin; beginning: *the rise of a new nation.* **4.** A slope; incline.
rise (rīz) □*verb* **rose, risen, rising, rises** □*noun, plural* **rises**

SYNONYMS: **rise, climb, mount, soar**

These verbs mean to move upward: *Smoke rose from the chimney. The cat climbed the tree. Casualties from the battle are mounting every hour. The cost of food is soaring.*

---

risk *noun* The possibility of harm or loss; danger: *Don't take risks on your motorcycle.* —See Synonyms at **danger.**
□*verb* **1.** To take a chance of harm or loss to: *He risked his future by dropping out of school.* **2.** To leave oneself open to the chance of: *She risked an accident by speeding.*
risk (risk) □*noun, plural* **risks** □*verb* **risked, risking, risks**

ritual *noun* A body of ceremonies, as those used in a church.
rit·u·al (rich′ōō əl) □*noun, plural* **rituals**

rival *noun* Someone who tries to do as well or better than another; competitor: *They were rivals for the office of chairman.*
□*verb* **1.** To try to do as well or better than; compete with: *The two teams rival each other for the championship.* **2.** To be the equal of: *a boy who rivals his brother in intelligence.*
□*adjective* Being a rival: *rival companies.*
ri·val (rī′vəl) □*noun, plural* **rivals** □*verb* **rivaled, rivaling, rivals** □*adjective*

river   *noun* **1.** A large natural stream of water. **2.** Something like a river: *Rivers of lava poured out of the volcano.*
riv·er (**riv′**ər) ☐*noun, plural* **rivers**

rivet   *noun* A metal bolt with a head on one end used to join two pieces by passing it through a hole in each piece and hammering or compressing its plain end to form another head.
riv·et (**riv′**it) ☐*noun, plural* **rivets**

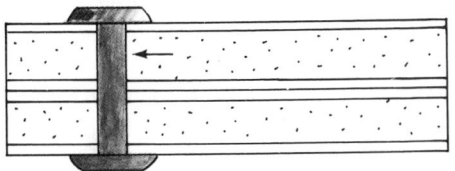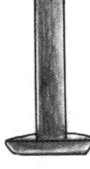

rivet

roach   *noun* A cockroach.
roach (rōch) ☐*noun, plural* **roaches**

road   *noun* **1.** An open way for the passage of vehicles, persons, and animals. **2.** A path or course: *the road to happiness.*
road (rōd) ☐*noun, plural* **roads**

roadrunner   *noun* A bird of southwestern North America that runs very fast and has a long tail, brownish, streaked feathers, and a shaggy crest.
road·run·ner (**rōd′**run′ər) ☐*noun, plural* **roadrunners**

roadrunner

roam   *verb* To go from one place to another without a goal or purpose; wander: *We spent the day roaming around in the city.*
roam (rōm) ☐*verb* **roamed, roaming, roams**

roar   *noun* A loud, deep sound or noise: *the roar of a lion; the roar of a jet engine.*
☐*verb* **1.** To make a roar: *The lion roared.* **2.** To laugh loudly: *We roared at her jokes.*
roar (rôr) ☐*noun, plural* **roars** ☐*verb* **roared, roaring, roars**

roast   *verb* **1.** To cook with dry heat, as in an oven: *He's roasting a turkey.* **2.** To dry and brown by heating: *roast coffee.* **3.** To be uncomfortably hot.
☐*noun* A cut of meat suitable for roasting.
roast (rōst) ☐*verb* **roasted, roasting, roasts** ☐*noun, plural* **roasts**

rob   *verb* To take from unlawfully and especially by force: *Two men robbed the gas station.*
rob (rob) ☐*verb* **robbed, robbing, robs**

robber   *noun* Someone who robs; thief.
rob·ber (**rob′**ər) ☐*noun, plural* **robbers**

robbery   *noun* The act or crime of robbing.
rob·ber·y (**rob′**ə rē) ☐*noun, plural* **robberies**

robe   *noun* **1.** A loose outer garment: *a beach robe.* **2.** A garment worn as a mark of office or rank: *a judge's robe.*
☐*verb* To dress in or put on a robe: *She robed herself in a gown.*
robe (rōb) ☐*noun, plural* **robes** ☐*verb* **robed, robing, robes**

robin   *noun* A North American songbird with a reddish breast and a dark gray back.
rob·in (**rob′**in) ☐*noun, plural* **robins**

robot   *noun* A machine that looks like a person and can do some of the things a person can do.
ro·bot (**rō′**bət) ☐*noun, plural* **robots**

robust   *adjective* Full of health and strength; vigorous: *a robust young athlete.*
ro·bust (rō **bust′** *or* **rō′**bust′) ☐*adjective*

rock[1]   *noun* **1.** A hard material that is formed naturally and is of mineral origin. **2.** A fragment of rock; stone: *She threw a rock into the*

a	bat	ī	bite	oo	tool	*th*	feather
ā	make	î	fierce	ou	out	th	bath
â	dare	o	dot	u	nut	hw	wheat
ä	father	ō	no	û	turn	zh	measure
e	net	ô	law, for	ch	church	ə	about, open
ē	be	oi	soil	ng	ring		pencil, atom
i	dip	oo	look	sh	shade		circus

brook. **3.** A large mass of rock: *Huge waves smashed against the rocks.* **4.** Someone or something that is very strong and dependable: *His father was a rock in times of trouble.*
rock (rok) □*noun, plural* **rocks**

rock² *verb* **1.** To move back and forth or from side to side: *Mother rocked the cradle. The boat rocked in the waves.* **2.** To shake or cause to shake violently: *The tower rocked from the explosion. The earthquake rocked the house.*
rock (rok) □*verb* **rocked, rocking, rocks**

rocker *noun* **1.** Either of the two curved pieces on which something, such as a rocking chair or a cradle, rocks. **2.** A rocking chair.
rock·er (rok′ər) □*noun, plural* **rockers**

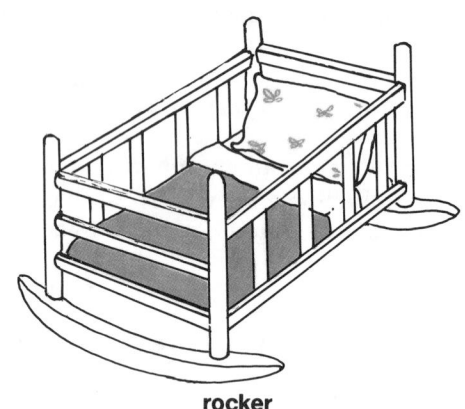
rocker

rocket *noun* **1.** A device that is driven forward or upward by a force provided by the release of gases from burning fuel. **2.** An engine whose thrust is provided by a rocket. **3.** A missile or bomb that is propelled by a rocket. **4.** A firework that is shot up into the sky.
rock·et (rok′it) □*noun, plural* **rockets**

rocking chair *noun* A chair mounted on rockers.

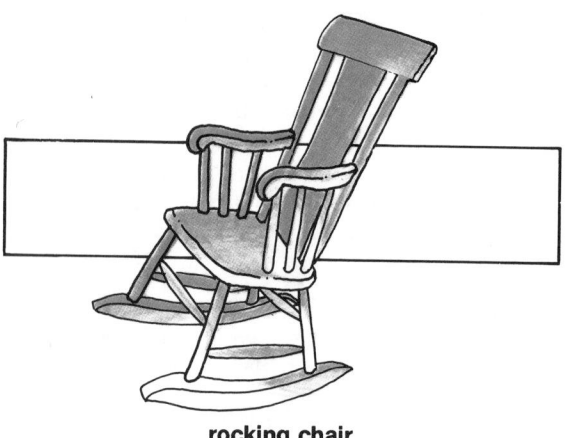
rocking chair

rock 'n' roll *noun* A kind of popular music with a very strong, steady beat and very simple words.
rock 'n' roll (rok′ən rōl′) □*noun*

rocky¹ *adjective* Full of or covered with rocks: *a rocky shore.*
rock·y (rok′ē) □*adjective* **rockier, rockiest**

rocky² *adjective* Tending to shake or wobble; unsteady: *a rocky old table.*
rock·y (rok′ē) □*adjective* **rockier, rockiest**

rod *noun* **1.** A thin, stiff, straight piece of material: *a curtain rod.* **2.** A branch or stick used to punish people by whipping or beating. **3.** A fishing rod. **4.** A unit of length equal to 16½ feet.
rod (rod) □*noun, plural* **rods**

rode *verb* The past tense of **ride.**
rode (rōd) □*verb*

rodent *noun* Any of several animals with large front teeth used for gnawing. Mice, rats, squirrels, and beavers are rodents.
ro·dent (rōd′ənt) □*noun, plural* **rodents**

rodeo *noun* A public show in which cowboys display their skills, as in horseback riding.
ro·de·o (rō′dē ō′ *or* rō dā′ō) □*noun, plural* **rodeos**

roe¹ *noun* The eggs of a fish.
roe (rō) □*noun*

roe² *noun* A small deer of Europe and Asia with short, branched antlers.
roe (rō) □*noun, plural* **roe** *or* **roes**

role *noun* **1.** A part or character played by an actor: *the leading role in a movie.* **2.** A part performed by a person or thing: *Teachers have an important role in children's lives.*
role (rōl) □*noun, plural* **roles**

roll *verb* **1.** To move along a surface while turning over and over: *The penny rolled across the sidewalk. I rolled the barrel down the ramp.* **2.** To move along on wheels or rollers: *The car rolled along the highway. He rolled the bicycle into the garage.* **3.** To turn over and over: *The dog rolled in the snow.* **4.** To wrap or wind round and round: *She rolled the string around the spool.* **5.** To make flat or even with or as if with a roller: *She rolled out the dough for a pie crust.* **6.** To move or flow in a continual stream: *Fog rolled down the mountain.* **7.** To pass steadily: *The weeks rolled by.* **8.** To move up and down or from side to side: *She rolled her eyes. The sailboat rolled in the heavy seas.* **9.** To make a deep, prolonged sound: *Thunder rolled across the sky.*

□*noun* **1.** A rolling movement: *the roll of a bowling ball down the alley; the roll of a ship.* **2.** Something rolled up in the form of a cylinder or tube: *a roll of waxed paper.* **3.** A list of the names of the members of a group: *the roll of students in the class.* **4.** A small piece of baked yeast dough: *a hamburger roll.* **5.** A deep, continuous rumble: *a roll of thunder.* **6.** A sound made by beating a drum rapidly. **roll** (rōl) □*verb* **rolled, rolling, rolls** □*noun, plural* **rolls**

roller *noun* **1.** A small wheel, as that on a roller skate. **2.** A cylinder or tube around which something, as a window shade, is wound. **3.** A cylinder for flattening, crushing, or squeezing things. **4.** A cylinder for applying paint or ink to a surface. **5.** A long, heavy wave breaking along a shore. **roll·er** (rō′lər) □*noun, plural* **rollers**

roller coaster *noun* A small elevated railroad, as in an amusement park, with sudden, steep descents and sharp turns.

roller skate *noun* A skate with four small wheels for skating on hard surfaces.

roller-skate *verb* To skate on roller skates. **rol·ler-skate** (rō′lər skāt′) □*verb* **roller-skated, roller-skating, roller-skates**

roller-skate

Roman *adjective* **1.** Of ancient or modern Rome, its people, or their culture. **2. roman** Of, having to do with, or printed in a type style with upright letters, as the letters in this sentence. □*noun* **1.** Someone born in or a citizen of Rome, especially ancient Rome. **2. roman** Roman type or letters. **Ro·man** (rō′mən) □*adjective* □*noun, plural* **Romans**

Roman Catholic *noun* A member of the Roman Catholic Church.

Roman Catholic Church *noun* The Christian church that recognizes the pope in Rome as its supreme head.

romance *noun* **1.** A story or poem about the adventures of heroes. **2.** A quality of daring, adventure, love, or mystery. **4.** A love affair. **ro·mance** (rō mans′ *or* rō′mans′) □*noun, plural* **romances**

Romance language *noun* A language, as French, Italian, Portuguese, or Spanish, that developed from Latin.

Roman numeral *noun* One of the numerals used in a numbering system based on that of the ancient Romans, in which letters stand for numbers: I = 1, V = 5, X = 10, L = 50, C = 100, D = 500, and M = 1,000.

romantic *adjective* **1.** Of or having to do with the stories of romance: *a romantic hero.* **2.** Full of adventure or heroism: *the romantic life of an explorer.* **3.** Of or having to do with love or a love affair: *soft, romantic music.* **ro·man·tic** (rō man′tik) □*adjective*

roof *noun* **1.** The outside upper covering of a building. **2.** Something that resembles a roof: *the roof of a car; the roof of the mouth.* □*verb* To cover with a roof. **roof** (ro͞of *or* roof) □*noun, plural* **roofs** □*verb* **roofed, roofing, roofs**

rook¹ *noun* One of the pieces used in the game of chess. **rook** (rook) □*noun, plural* **rooks**

rook² *noun* A European bird that resembles the crow. **rook** (rook) □*noun, plural* **rooks**

rook

a	bat	ī	bite	o͞o	tool	*th*	feather
ā	make	î	fierce	ou	out	th	bath
â	dare	o	dot	u	nut	hw	wheat
ä	father	ō	no	û	turn	zh	measure
e	net	ô	law, for	ch	church	ə	about, open
ē	be	oi	soil	ng	ring		pencil, atom
i	dip	oo	look	sh	shade		circus

rookie *noun* **1.** A first-year player in the major leagues. **2.** Someone with no experience; beginner.
rook·ie (rook′ē) □*noun, plural* **rookies**

room *noun* **1.** Space that is or can be occupied: *a chair that doesn't take up much room.* **2.** An area of a building set off by walls or partitions: *an apartment with eight rooms.* **3.** Opportunity; chance: *His decision left no room for argument.*
□*verb* To live in a room.
room (room *or* room) □*noun, plural* **rooms** □*verb* **roomed, rooming, rooms**

roommate *noun* Someone with whom one shares a room or apartment.
room·mate (room′māt′ *or* room′māt′) □*noun, plural* **roommates**

roomy *adjective* Having plenty of room: *a roomy house.*
room·y (roo′mē *or* room′ē) □*adjective* **roomier, roomiest**

roost *noun* **1.** A branch or other perch on which a bird settles for rest. **2.** A place to which birds regularly go to sleep for the night.
□*verb* To rest or sleep on or in a roost.
roost (roost) □*noun, plural* **roosts** □*verb* **roosted, roosting, roosts**

rooster *noun* A fully grown male chicken.
roost·er (roo′stər) □*noun, plural* **roosters**

root¹ *noun* **1.** The underground part of a plant that absorbs water and minerals from the soil, stores food, and keeps the plant in place. **2.** Something like a root in use or position: *the root of a hair.* **3.** A source; origin: *We tried to find the root of the difficulty.* **4.** A word or part of a word from which other words are formed by adding a prefix or suffix. *Honor is the root of honorable.*
□*verb* **1.** To develop or cause to develop roots: *Avocado seeds will root in water.* **2.** To be fixed in place by or as if by roots: *Terror rooted her to the spot.* **3.** To remove completely: *root out weeds; root out crime.*
root (root *or* root) □*noun, plural* **roots** □*verb* **rooted, rooting, roots**

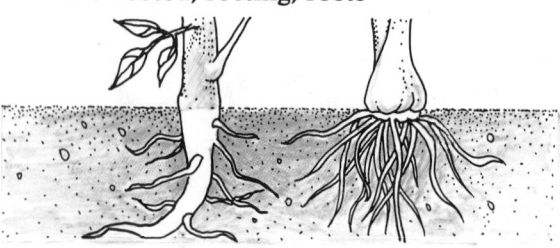
root

root² *verb* **1.** To dig in the earth with the snout: *a dog rooting for a bone.* **2.** To search for something; rummage: *She rooted through her purse for her keys.*
root (root *or* root) □*verb* **rooted, rooting, roots**

root³ *verb* To give support to a team or person in a contest.
root (root *or* root) □*verb* **rooted, rooting, roots**

rope *noun* **1.** A heavy cord made of twisted strands, as of fiber. **2.** A string of items, attached together by twisting, threading, or braiding: *a rope of pearls.*
□*verb* **1.** To tie or fasten with rope: *roped the crates to the raft.* **2.** To catch with a rope or lasso: *The cowboy roped a steer.* **3.** To enclose or divide with ropes: *The guards roped off the room to keep people from entering.*
rope (rōp) □*noun, plural* **ropes** □*verb* **roped, roping, ropes**

rose¹ *noun* **1.** A showy, fragrant red, pink, yellow, or white flower that grows as a shrub with usually prickly stems. **2.** A deep pink.
□*adjective* Deep pink.
rose (rōz) □*noun, plural* **roses** □*adjective*

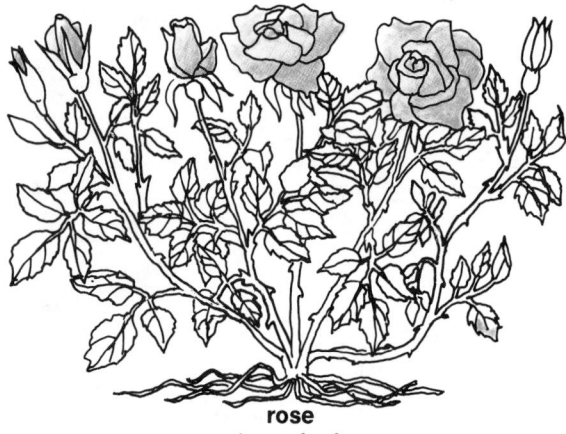
rose
A rose bush

rose² *verb* The past tense of **rise.**
rose (rōz) □*verb*

rosy *adjective* **1.** Of the color rose: *rosy cheeks.* **2.** Bright and cheerful: *a rosy future.*
ros·y (rō′zē) □*adjective* **rosier, rosiest**

rot *verb* To become or cause to become rotten; decay: *The floor in the old barn had rotted away.*
□*noun* **1.** The process of rotting or condition of being rotten; decay. **2.** A destructive disease of plants caused by fungi or bacteria.
rot (rot) □*verb* **rotted, rotting, rots** □*noun*

rotary *adjective* Of, causing, or having rotation: *rotary motion; a rotary blade.*
ro·ta·ry (rō′tə rē) □*adjective*

rotate *verb* **1.** To turn or cause to turn around a center or axis: *The planets rotate around the sun.* **2.** To pass or change in turn: *The farmer rotated his crops. Guard duty rotated among the four soldiers.* —See Synonyms at **turn.**
ro·tate (rō′tāt′) □*verb* **rotated, rotating, rotates**

rotation *noun* The act of rotating: *the rotation of a wheel.*
ro·ta·tion (rō tā′shən) □*noun, plural* **rotations**

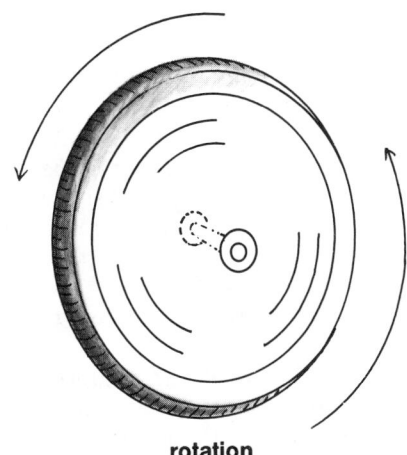

rotation

rotten *adjective* **1.** Decayed; spoiled: *a rotten apple.* **2.** Very bad: *She's in a rotten mood.*
rot·ten (rot′ən) □*adjective* **rottener, rottenest**

rough *adjective* **1.** Having a surface that is not even or smooth: *a rough woolen fabric; rough country roads.* **2.** Not gentle or smooth; harsh: *a rough push; rough seas.* **3.** Rude; impolite: *rough treatment.* **4.** Difficult or unpleasant to endure or do: *I had a rough time getting to school in the snowstorm.* **5.** In a natural state: *rough diamond.* **6.** Not perfected, completed, or fully detailed: *a rough drawing.* **7.** Not precise or exact: *a rough guess.*
□*verb* **1.** To make or sketch in a rough form: *rough out a speech.* **2.** To do physical harm to; beat up: *The boxer roughed up his opponent.*
rough (ruf) □*adjective* **rougher, roughest** □*verb* **roughed, roughing, roughs**

round *adjective* **1.** Shaped like a ball, circle, or tube: *a round balloon; a round cookie.*
2. Curved in surface or outline: *round shoulders; round cheeks.* **3.** Full; complete: *a round dozen.* **4.** Almost exact or correct: *He gave us an estimate in round numbers.*
□*noun* **1.** Something round in shape: *a round of dough.* **2.** Often **rounds** A usual course of places visited or duties performed: *The doctor made the rounds of his patients in the hospital every morning.* **3.** A series of similar events: *a round of meetings.* **4.** A single shot from a firearm: *a round of rifle fire.* **5.** Ammunition for a single shot from a firearm. **6.** A song for two or more voices in which each voice begins at a different time with the same melody at the same pitch. **7.** A complete division or unit in a game or contest: *We played a round of golf.*
□*verb* **1.** To make or become round: *She rounded the corners of the tablecloth.* **2.** To pass or go around: *The baseball player rounded the bases.*
□*adverb* Around: *The fly circled round and round the room.*
□*preposition* Around: *He tightened his belt round his waist.*
round up **1.** To herd grazing animals together. **2.** To seek out and bring together: *The police rounded up the fugitives.*
round (round) □*adjective* **rounder, roundest** □*noun, plural* **rounds** □*verb* **rounded, rounding, rounds** □*adverb* □*preposition*

roundhouse *noun* A circular building in which locomotives are repaired and kept.
round·house (round′hous′) □*noun, plural* **roundhouses**

round trip *noun* A trip from one place to another and back, usually over the same route.

roundup *noun* **1.** The act of herding grazing animals together. **2.** A gathering together, as of persons: *a roundup of suspects.*
round·up (round′up′) □*noun, plural* **roundups**

rouse *verb* **1.** To wake up from sleep; awaken: *The chirping of the birds roused him before the alarm went off.* **2.** To stir up; arouse: *The news roused her to action.*
rouse (rouz) □*verb* **roused, rousing, rouses**

a bat	ī bite	ōō tool	*th* feather
ā make	î fierce	ou out	th bath
â dare	o dot	u nut	hw wheat
ä father	ō no	û turn	zh measure
e net	ô law, for	ch church	ə about, open
ē be	oi soil	ng ring	pencil, atom
i dip	oo look	sh shade	circus

rout *noun* **1.** A complete defeat. **2.** A retreat that lacks discipline and order: *Our attack turned the enemy's withdrawal into a rout.* □*verb* **1.** To defeat completely: *The candidate routed his opponent.* **2.** To put to flight: *Our troops routed the enemy.*
rout (rout) □*noun, plural* **routs** □*verb* **routed, routing, routs**

route *noun* **1.** A road or course for traveling from one place to another. **2.** A series of places or customers visited regularly: *a delivery route.* □*verb* To send or pass on by a particular route; direct: *Express buses are routed around the city.*
route (rōot *or* rout) □*noun, plural* **routes** □*verb* **routed, routing, routes**

routine *noun* The usual or regular way of doing things: *Exercise is part of his daily routine.* □*adjective* According to routine; ordinary: *routine duties.*
rou·tine (rōo tēn′) □*noun, plural* **routines** □*adjective*

rove *verb* To wander about without a specific goal or direction: *He roved the world seeking adventure.*
rove (rōv) □*verb* **roved, roving, roves**

row¹ *noun* **1.** A series of persons or things placed next to one another in a line: *a row of houses.* **2.** A succession without a break or gap in time: *He won the contest five years in a row.*
row (rō) □*noun, plural* **rows**

row² *verb* **1.** To move a boat with oars. **2.** To carry in a rowboat: *The boy rowed his friends across the lake.* □*noun* A trip in a rowboat.
row (rō) □*verb* **rowed, rowing, rows** □*noun, plural* **rows**

row³ *noun* A noisy quarrel or fight.
row (rou) □*noun, plural* **rows**

rowboat *noun* A boat propelled by oars.
row·boat (rō′bōt′) □*noun, plural* **rowboats**

rowdy *adjective* Noisy and rough: *rowdy children; rowdy behavior.*
row·dy (rou′dē) □*adjective* **rowdier, rowdiest**

royal *adjective* **1.** Of or having to do with a king or queen: *the royal family; a royal palace.* **2.** Fit for a king or queen: *a royal banquet.*
roy·al (roi′əl) □*adjective*

royalty *noun* **1.** The members of a royal family. **2.** Royal rank or power: *The scepter is a symbol of royalty.*
roy·al·ty (roi′əl tē) □*noun*

royalty

R.R. or **RR** An abbreviation for **railroad.**

rub *verb* **1.** To press along the surface of: *I rubbed the spot with a damp cloth.* **2.** To move with a rubbing motion: *The cat rubbed against my leg.* **3.** To apply, clean, polish, or remove by rubbing: *The baby rubbed dirt into his hair. He rubbed the rust off the knife.* □*noun* The act of rubbing.
rub (rub) □*verb* **rubbed, rubbing, rubs** □*noun, plural* **rubs**

rubber *noun* **1.** An elastic, waterproof substance prepared from the milky sap of certain tropical trees. **2.** A synthetic substance that resembles rubber. **3.** A low overshoe made of rubber.
rub·ber (rub′ər) □*noun, plural* **rubbers**

WORD HISTORY: **rubber**

The word *rubber* comes from the word *rub.* One of the first discovered uses of this substance was rubbing out, or erasing, pencil marks.

---

rubbish *noun* **1.** Worthless material; trash. **2.** Silly talk or ideas; nonsense.
rub·bish (rub′ish) □*noun*

rubble *noun* Broken pieces of solid material, such as stone: *rubble from a wrecked building.*
rub·ble (rub′əl) □*noun*

ruby *noun* **1.** A hard, clear deep-red precious stone. **2.** A deep red. □*adjective* Deep red.
ru·by (rōo′bē) □*noun, plural* **rubies** □*adjective*

rudder *noun* A hinged, flat plate mounted at the rear of a ship or aircraft for steering.
rud·der (rud′ər) □*noun, plural* **rudders**

ruddy *adjective* Having a healthy pink or reddish color: *a ruddy face.*
rud·dy (rŭd′ē) □*adjective* **ruddier, ruddiest**

rude *adjective* **1.** Having or showing bad manners; impolite: *a rude answer.* **2.** Not finely made; crude: *a rude wooden chair.*
rude (rood) □*adjective* **ruder, rudest**

SYNONYMS: **rude, discourteous, impolite**

These adjectives mean having or showing bad manners: *Don't be rude to our guests. It was discourteous not to thank her for the gift. Don't you know it's impolite to interrupt people when they're talking?*

---

ruff *noun* A growth of fur or feathers around the neck of an animal or bird.
ruff (rŭf) □*noun, plural* **ruffs**

ruffle *noun* A strip of cloth, lace, or ribbon gathered or pleated on one edge.
□*verb* **1.** To disturb the smoothness or evenness of: *The canary ruffled its feathers.* **2.** To disturb or become disturbed: *ruffled tempers.* **3.** To gather into a ruffle.
ruf·fle (rŭf′əl) □*noun, plural* **ruffles** □*verb* **ruffled, ruffling, ruffles**

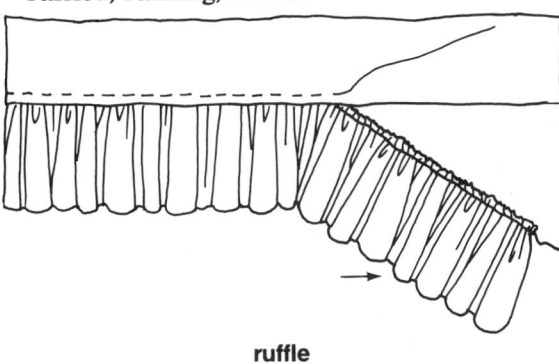

ruffle

rug *noun* A piece of thick, heavy fabric that is used to cover part or all of a floor.
rug (rŭg) □*noun, plural* **rugs**

rugged *adjective* **1.** Having a rough, uneven surface or jagged outline: *rugged mountains.* **2.** Capable of enduring a great deal; tough: *a rugged pioneer; rugged boots.* **3.** Hard to put up with; harsh or severe: *a rugged winter.*
rug·ged (rŭg′ĭd) □*adjective*

ruin *noun* **1.** Complete destruction, loss, or collapse: *He faced political ruin because of the scandal.* **2.** A cause of ruin: *Gambling was his ruin.* **3.** Often **ruins** The remains of something that has been destroyed: *the ruins of an old castle.*

□*verb* **1.** To damage completely; destroy: *moths ruined my winter clothes. The long dry spell ruined the farmer's hopes for a good harvest.*
ru·in (roo′ĭn) □*noun, plural* **ruins** □*verb* **ruined, ruining, ruins**

rule *noun* **1.** A principle of action or conduct: *He made it a rule never to cheat. Obey the rules of the game.* **2.** A usual or customary condition or course of behavior: *Short lunch hours are the rule in our office.* **3.** The act of governing or controlling; authority: *a territory under the rule of a governor.*
□*verb* To have power or authority over: *At sea a captain rules his ship.* —See Synonyms at **judge.**
rule (rool) □*noun, plural* **rules** □*verb* **ruled, ruling, rules**

ruler *noun* **1.** Someone, such as a king, who rules a country; sovereign. **2.** A strip of wood, metal, or other material with a straight edge marked off in units and used to measure and draw straight lines.
rul·er (roo′lər) □*noun, plural* **rulers**

rum *noun* An alcoholic liquor made from molasses or sugar cane.
rum (rŭm) □*noun*

rumble *verb* To make or move with a deep, long, rolling sound: *The train rumbled through the village.*
□*noun* A deep, long, rolling sound: *a rumble of thunder.*
rum·ble (rŭm′bəl) □*verb* **rumbled, rumbling, rumbles** □*noun, plural* **rumbles**

rummage *verb* To search thoroughly by moving things around: *He rummaged through his closet looking for his sneakers.*
rum·mage (rŭm′ĭj) □*verb* **rummaged, rummaging, rummages**

rumor *noun* **1.** A statement or story that is spread from one person to another but has not been proven to be true: *I heard a rumor that she's going to get married.* **2.** General talk; hearsay: *Rumor has it that the workers will strike next week.*
□*verb* To spread or report by rumor: *It was*

a	bat	ī	bite	oo	tool	th	feather
ā	make	î	fierce	ou	out	th	bath
â	dare	o	dot	u	nut	hw	wheat
ä	father	ō	no	û	turn	zh	measure
e	net	ô	law, for	ch	church	ə	about, open
ē	be	oi	soil	ng	ring		pencil, atom
i	dip	oo	look	sh	shade		circus

rumored that war was coming.
ru·mor (rōō′mər) ☐*noun, plural* **rumors**
☐*verb* **rumored, rumoring, rumors**

rump *noun* **1.** The fleshy part of an animal's body where the legs meet the back. **2.** A cut of meat from the rump.
rump (rump) ☐*noun, plural* **rumps**

rumpus *noun* A noisy quarrel.
rum·pus (rum′pəs) ☐*noun, plural* **rumpuses**

run *verb* **1.** To go on foot at a pace faster than a walk: *He ran down the street.* **2.** To go quickly; hurry: *Run and call for help.* **3.** To move about freely: *We let the horses run loose.* **4.** To leave quickly; flee: *She ran when the fight began.* **5.** To go back and forth on a regular route: *The train runs every half hour.* **6.** To pass into a certain condition: *Call me if you run into trouble.* **7.** To take part or cause to take part in a race or contest: *Who is running in the next race? He ran for mayor.* **8.** To pass through, over, or across: *I ran my fingers over the keyboard.* **9.** To cause to go; transport: *He ran me downtown in his car.* **10.** To do by or as if by moving quickly: *run errands.* **11.** To flow or cause to flow: *Water ran from the faucet.* **12.** To spread out, as a dye: *The color ran when she washed the blouse.* **13.** To emit a fluid: *His nose ran.* **14.** To suffer from; have: *She's running a high fever.* **15.** To extend; stretch: *This road runs only to the next town.* **16.** To continue in effect; last: *His term in office has two more years to run.* **17.** To operate or cause to operate: *Can you run the sewing machine?* **18.** To manage or direct; control: *She runs a dress shop.* **19.** To pass over or through: *The car ran a red light.*
☐*noun* **1.** The act of running: *I took a run around the lake.* **2.** A trip or journey: *The train makes three runs to New York a day.* **3.** Freedom to move about: *She had the run of the house.* **4.** A continuous series: *a run of sunny days.* **5.** A raveled line of stitches in a knitted fabric: *a run in a stocking.* **6.** A score in baseball made by advancing around the bases and reaching home plate safely.
run across To meet or find by chance: *Some time later I ran across the answer.*
run into To meet or find by chance: *I ran into a difficult problem.*
run (run) ☐*verb* **ran, run, running, runs**
☐*noun, plural* **runs**

rung¹ *noun* **1.** A rod or bar that forms a step on a ladder. **2.** A piece that connects and supports the legs of a chair.

rung (rung) ☐*noun, plural* **rungs**

rung² *verb* The past participle of **ring**: *The telephone hasn't rung all day.*
rung (rung) ☐*verb*

runner *noun* **1.** Someone or something that runs: *The cheetah is a fast runner.* **2.** One of the blades on which a sled, sleigh, or ice skate moves. **3.** A creeping plant stem that puts forth new roots, thus producing new plants. **4.** A long, narrow rug, as for a flight of stairs.
run·ner (run′ər) ☐*noun, plural* **runners**

runner-up *noun* A contestant who finishes a competition in second place.
run·ner-up (run′ər up′) ☐*noun, plural* **runners-up**

runt *noun* A plant, animal, or person that is smaller than the usual size.
runt (runt) ☐*noun, plural* **runts**

runway *noun* A strip of level ground on which aircraft take off and land.
run·way (run′wā′) ☐*noun, plural* **runways**

rupture *noun* The act of bursting or breaking open: *The rupture in the dam caused a flood.* ☐*verb* To burst; break.
rup·ture (rup′chər) ☐*noun, plural* **ruptures**
☐*verb* **ruptured, rupturing, ruptures**

rural *adjective* Of or having to do with the country: *a rural village.*
ru·ral (roor′əl) ☐*adjective*

rush¹ *verb* **1.** To move or act quickly; hurry: *The ambulance rushed down the street. He rushed food to the hungry family.* **2.** To act or cause to act too quickly: *He knew better than to rush into new a project. Don't rush me when I'm eating.*
☐*noun* **1.** A sudden, swift forward motion: *I felt a rush of air.* **2.** The movement of many people to or from a place: *a rush of shoppers at Christmas.* **3.** A flurry of activity; great hurry: *What's the rush?*
rush (rush) ☐*verb* **rushed, rushing, rushes**
☐*noun, plural* **rushes**

SYNONYMS: **rush, hurry**

These verbs mean to move or act quickly: *The police rushed to the scene of the crime. Hurry or you'll be late for school.*

---

rush² *noun* A tall plant that looks like grass, grows in wet places, and has hollow stems used to make baskets, chair seats, and mats.
rush (rush) ☐*noun, plural* **rushes**

Russian *noun* **1.** Someone who was born in or is a citizen of Russia. **2.** The language of Russia.
□*adjective* Of Russia, the Russians, or their language.
Rus·sian (**rush′**ən) □*noun, plural* **Russians** □*adjective*

rust *noun* **1.** A reddish-brown or orange coating that forms on iron when it is exposed to air or moisture. **2.** A plant disease that causes red or brown spots on leaves and stems. **3.** A reddish brown.
□*verb* To make or become rusty: *Rain rusted the fence. The old car rusted.*
□*adjective* Reddish brown.
rust (rust) □*noun* □*verb* **rusted, rusting, rusts** □*adjective*

rustle *verb* **1.** To make or cause to make soft fluttering or crackling sounds: *The leaves rustled in the wind. The man rustled the pages of his newspaper.* **2.** To steal cattle.
□*noun* A series of soft fluttering or crackling sounds: *I heard the rustle of her skirt.*
rus·tle (**rus′**əl) □*verb* **rustled, rustling, rustles** □*noun, plural* **rustles**

rusty *adjective* **1.** Covered or coated with rust: *a rusty nail; a rusty knife.* **2.** Working less well or done with less skill because of lack of use or practice: *I can't play the piano because my fingers are rusty.*
rust·y (**rus′**tē) □*adjective* **rustier, rustiest**

rut *noun* **1.** A track or groove made by the passage of a wheel or foot: *The tires of the car made ruts in the dirt road.* **2.** A fixed way of acting or living; routine: *She was in a rut and needed a vacation.*
□*verb* To make ruts in.
rut (rut) □*noun, plural* **ruts** □*verb* **rutted, rutting, ruts**

rut

ruthless *adjective* Having or showing no pity; cruel: *a ruthless enemy.*
ruth·less (**rōōth′**lis) □*adjective*

rye *noun* A cereal grass that bears seeds used for making flour and whiskey.
rye (rī) □*noun*

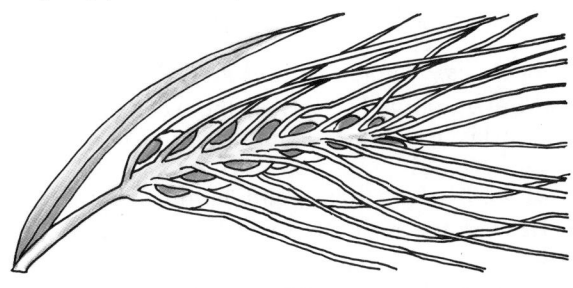

rye

a bat	ī bite	ōō tool	*th* feather
ā make	î fierce	ou out	th bath
â dare	o dot	u nut	hw wheat
ä father	ō no	û turn	zh measure
e net	ô law, for	ch church	ə about, open
ē be	oi soil	ng ring	pencil, atom
i dip	oo look	sh shade	circus

ANCIENT GREEK

The letter **S** has evolved from many forms of ancient writing. One of the earliest known examples is the Greek character shown above, which dates from almost 3,000 years ago. Over the years, artists and designers have created their own versions of the English letter **S**. Some of the more common examples seen today are shown below.

Ss *Ss*	**Ss** *Ss*	**Ss** Ss	**Ss** Ss	*Ss Ss*
HANDWRITING	CALLIGRAPHY	MODERN SANS SERIF	MODERN SERIF	SCRIPT

---

s or **S**   *noun* The nineteenth letter of the English alphabet.
s or **S** (es) ▢*noun, plural* **s's** or **S's**

Sabbath   *noun* The day of the week, such as Saturday for Jews or Sunday for Christians, that is used for rest and worship.
Sab·bath (**sab′**əth) ▢*noun, plural* **Sabbaths**

saber   *noun* A heavy sword with a curved blade.
sa·ber (**sā′**bər) ▢*noun, plural* **sabers**

sable   *noun* A small animal of northern Europe and Asia that is related to the mink and weasel and has very valuable soft, dark fur.
sa·ble (**sā′**bəl) ▢*noun, plural* **sables**

sac   *noun* An animal or plant part that is shaped like a bag and often contains liquid.
sac (sak) ▢*noun, plural* **sacs**

sack   *noun* A large bag made of strong, coarse material.
sack (sak) ▢*noun, plural* **sacks**

sacred   *adjective* **1.** Of or set aside for divine worship; holy: *a sacred temple.* **2.** Of or having to do with religion: *sacred music.*
sa·cred (**sā′**krid) ▢*adjective*

sacrifice   *noun* **1.** The act or ceremony of offering something to a god or God. **2.** Something offered as a sacrifice. **3.** The act of giving up something for the sake of something or someone else: *a sacrifice of time and effort.*
▢*verb* **1.** To offer as a sacrifice to a god or God. **2.** To give up for the sake of something or someone: *He sacrificed his free time to help his friend.*

sac·ri·fice (**sak′**rə fīs′) ▢*noun, plural* **sacrifices** ▢*verb* **sacrificed, sacrificing, sacrifices**

sad   *adjective* **1.** Filled with, showing, or expressing sorrow; unhappy: *She felt sad when her cat died.* **2.** Causing sorrow: *a sad memory.*
sad (sad) ▢*adjective* **sadder, saddest**

saddle   *noun* A seat, as for a rider on the back of a horse, padded and usually made of leather.
▢*verb* To put a saddle on: *saddle a pony.*
sad·dle (**sad′**əl) ▢*noun, plural* **saddles** ▢*verb* **saddled, saddling, saddles**

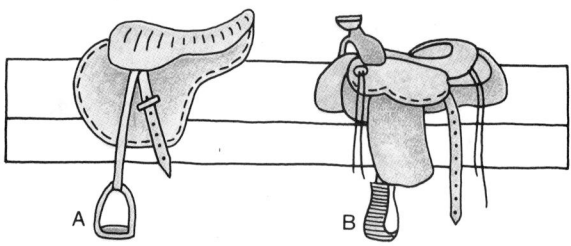

saddle
(A) English; *(B)* Western

safe   *adjective* **1.** Free from danger, harm, or risk: *Keep your money in a safe place.* **2.** Showing caution; careful: *a safe driver.* **3.** Not likely to be wrong: *a safe guess.* **4.** Having reached a base in baseball without being put out.
▢*noun* A strong metal container in which valuables are kept for protection.
safe (sāf) ▢*adjective* **safer, safest** ▢*noun, plural* **safes**

safeguard *verb* To protect, as from danger; keep safe: *The law safeguards the rights of all citizens.* —See Synonyms at **defend**.
□*noun* Something that protects or guards: *A lock is a good safeguard against theft.*
safe·guard (sāf′ gärd′) □*verb* **safeguarded, safeguarding, safeguards** □*noun, plural* **safeguards**

safety *noun* Freedom from danger or harm: *The driver is responsible for the safety of the passengers.*
safe·ty (sāf′tē) □*noun*

SYNONYMS: **safety, security**

These nouns mean freedom from danger or harm: *Police protect the safety of people and their property. We added extra locks to the house for security.*

---

safety pin *noun* A pin with a guard that covers the point of the pin.

sag *verb* To sink or slope downward below the normal level: *The mattress sagged.*
sag (sag) □*verb* **sagged, sagging, sags**

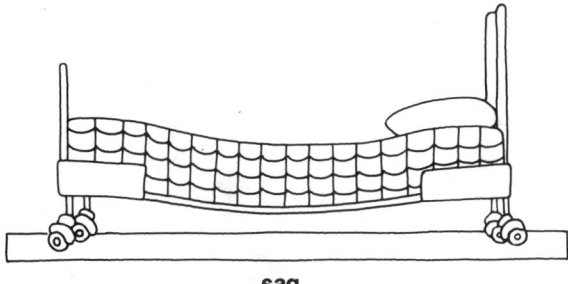
sag

sagebrush *noun* A shrub that grows in dry areas of western North America and has silver-green leaves with a sharp smell.
sage·brush (sāj′ brush′) □*noun*

said *verb* The past tense and past participle of **say**: *He said good-by.*
said (sed) □*verb*

sail *noun* **1.** A piece of strong material that is stretched out to catch the wind and cause a boat to move. **2.** Something, such as the blade of a windmill, that resembles or functions as a sail. **3.** A trip in a ship or boat, especially a sailboat: *We took a sail around the bay.*
□*verb* **1.** To travel on or across water: *The boat sailed up the river.* **2.** To operate or steer a sailboat. **3.** To start out on a trip across water: *The ship sailed for Europe yesterday.* **4.** To move smoothly, easily, or without effort: *My*

hat sailed through the air.
sail (sāl) □*noun, plural* **sails** □*verb* **sailed, sailing, sails**

sailboat *noun* A boat that has sails so that it can be moved by the wind.
sail·boat (sāl′ bōt′) □*noun, plural* **sailboats**

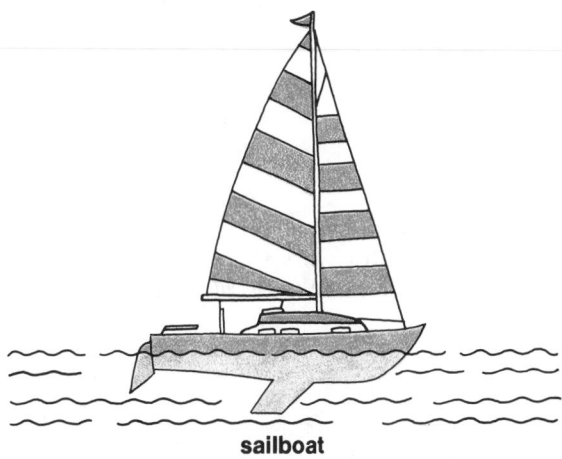
sailboat

sailor *noun* Someone who is a member of a ship's crew or who sails a ship or boat.
sail·or (sā′ lər) □*noun, plural* **sailors**

saint *noun* **1.** A very good and holy person, especially one who is officially declared to be deserving of special respect. **2.** Someone who is very good, kind, and patient.
saint (sānt) □*noun, plural* **saints**

Saint Bernard *noun* A large, strong brown and white dog with thick fur.
Saint Ber·nard (bər **närd′**) □*noun, plural* **Saint Bernards**

sake *noun* **1.** Reason or purpose: *He went only for the sake of having something to do.* **2.** Benefit; welfare: *He explained the instructions carefully for my sake.*
sake (sāk) □*noun, plural* **sakes**

salad *noun* A dish made up of raw vegetables, or meat, cheese, fish, or eggs, usually served with a dressing.
sal·ad (sal′ əd) □*noun, plural* **salads**

salamander *noun* An animal that resembles a lizard and lives in or near fresh water.

a	bat	ī	bite	o͞o	tool	*th*	feather
ā	make	î	fierce	ou	out	th	bath
â	dare	o	dot	u	nut	hw	wheat
ä	father	ō	no	û	turn	zh	measure
e	net	ô	law, for	ch	church	ə	about, open
ē	be	oi	soil	ng	ring		pencil, atom
i	dip	oo	look	sh	shade		circus

sal·a·man·der (sal′ə man′dər) □*noun, plural* **salamanders**

salamander

salary *noun* A fixed sum of money that is paid regularly for work that is done.
sal·a·ry (sal′ə rē) □*noun, plural* **salaries**

WORD HISTORY: **salary**

Salary comes from a Latin word that originally meant "money paid to soldiers for the purchase of salt." In ancient times salt was expensive but very important for preserving food.

---

sale *noun* **1.** The exchange of property or goods for money: *the sale of an office building.* **2.** The selling of goods at reduced prices: *The store is having a sale on shirts.*
sale (sāl) □*noun, plural* **sales**

salesman *noun* A man whose work is selling goods or services.
sales·man (sālz′mən) □*noun, plural* **salesmen**

salesperson *noun* A salesman or saleswoman.
sales·per·son (sālz′pûr′sən) □*noun, plural* **salespersons**

sales tax *noun* A tax on goods and services paid by the buyer.

saleswoman *noun* A woman whose work is selling goods or services.
sales·wom·an (sālz′woom′ən) □*noun, plural* **saleswomen**

saliva *noun* A watery liquid produced in the mouth by certain glands that helps keep the mouth wet and starts digestion.
sa·li·va (sə lī′və) □*noun*

salmon *noun* **1.** Any of several large fish that live in northern waters and have pinkish flesh used for food. **2.** A yellowish pink.
□*adjective* Yellowish pink.
salm·on (sam′ən) □*noun, plural* **salmon** or **salmons** □*adjective*

saloon *noun* A place where alcoholic drinks are served and drunk; bar.
sa·loon (sə loon′) □*noun, plural* **saloons**

salt *noun* **1.** A white substance found in deposits in the earth and in sea water that is used to season and preserve food. **2.** A chemical substance or compound that is formed when an acid combines with a base.
□*verb* To season or preserve with salt.
□*adjective* Of or containing salt: *a salt mine.*
salt (sôlt) □*noun, plural* **salts** □*verb* **salted, salting, salts** □*adjective*

salt-water *adjective* Of, having to do with, or living in salt water: *a salt-water fish.*
salt-wa·ter (sôlt′wô′tər) □*adjective*

salty *adjective* Of, containing, or tasting of salt: *salty crackers.*
salt·y (sôl′tē) □*adjective* **saltier, saltiest**

salute *verb* **1.** To show respect to in a formal manner, such as by raising the right hand to the forehead: *The lieutenant saluted the captain.* **2.** To greet with polite or friendly words or gestures.
□*noun* **1.** The act of saluting: *She waved in salute.* **2.** A formal gesture of respect.
sa·lute (sə loot′) □*verb* **saluted, saluting, salutes** □*noun, plural* **salutes**

WORD HISTORY: **salute**

Salute comes from a Latin word that means "to wish good health to."

salute

salvage *verb* To save from damage or destruction: *Robinson Crusoe salvaged many useful things from the shipwreck.*
□*noun* **1.** The rescue of a damaged or sunken ship or its cargo. **2.** Something salvaged.
sal·vage (sal′vij) □*verb* **salvaged, salvaging, salvages** □*noun*

salvation *noun* **1.** The act of saving or condition of being saved, as from danger, sin, or evil: *the salvation of 20 people from the fire.* **2.** Someone or something that saves or rescues: *The change I carried in my pocket was my salvation when I lost my purse.*
sal·va·tion (sal vā′shən) □*noun*

salve *noun* An ointment that is spread on wounds and sores to heal or soothe them.
salve (sav) □*noun, plural* **salves**

same *adjective* **1.** Being very much alike; similar: *The twins always wear the same clothes.* **2.** Being the very one and not another; identical: *She went to the same college as my brother.* **3.** Not changed or different: *She weighs the same as she did before going on a diet.*
□*pronoun* Someone or something identical with another: *He had a hamburger, and I ordered the same.*
same (sām) □*adjective* □*pronoun*

SYNONYMS: **same, equal, identical**

These adjectives mean being alike in value, quantity, or effect: *The two books were the same in price. One meter is equal to 39.37 inches. We were both wearing identical shirts.*

---

sample *noun* A part that shows what the whole is like: *Choose the material you like from these fabric samples.*
□*verb* To test or judge by taking a sample of: *I sampled the soup to see if it needed salt.*
sam·ple (sam′pəl) □*noun, plural* **samples**
□*verb* **sampled, sampling, samples**

sanctuary *noun* **1.** A sacred or holy place, such as a church. **2.** A place that provides protection or safety: *a bird sanctuary.* **3.** Protection or safety: *The refugee asked for sanctuary in another country.*
sanc·tu·ar·y (sangk′chōō er′ē) □*noun, plural* **sanctuaries**

sand *noun* Very small, loose grains of worn or crushed rock.
□*verb* **1.** To sprinkle or cover with sand: *We sanded the icy driveway.* **2.** To smooth by rubbing with sand or sandpaper: *He sanded the floor before he varnished it.*
sand (sand) □*noun* □*verb* **sanded, sanding, sands**

sandal *noun* A shoe that consists of a sole held to the foot by straps.
san·dal (san′dəl) □*noun, plural* **sandals**

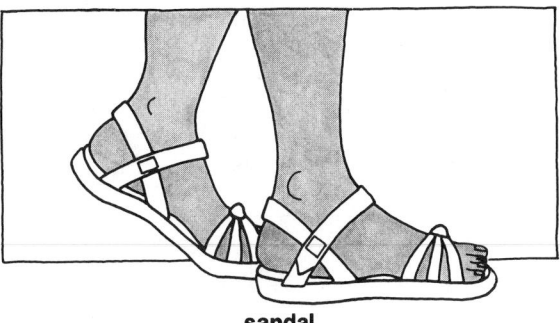
sandal

sandbox *noun* An enclosed area filled with sand for children to play in.
sand·box (sand′boks′) □*noun, plural* **sandboxes**

sandpaper *noun* Heavy paper coated on one side with rough material, such as sand, that is used for cleaning and smoothing surfaces.
□*verb* To smooth, polish, or clean by rubbing with sandpaper.
sand·pa·per (sand′pā′pər) □*noun* □*verb* **sandpapered, sandpapering, sandpapers**

sandpiper *noun* A small brown or gray shore bird with a thin, pointed bill.
sand·pi·per (sand′pī′pər) □*noun, plural* **sandpipers**

sandpiper

sandstone *noun* A kind of rock that is made of grains of sand.
sand·stone (sand′stōn′) □*noun*

sandwich *noun* Two or more slices of bread with a filling, such as meat, cheese, or peanut butter and jelly, between them.

a bat	ī bite	o͞o tool	*th* feather
ā make	i fierce	ou out	th bath
â dare	o dot	u nut	hw wheat
ä father	ō no	û turn	zh measure
e net	ô law, for	ch church	ə about, open
ē be	oi soil	ng ring	pencil, atom
i dip	oo look	sh shade	circus

□*verb* To squeeze or fit in between things: *I sandwiched my piano lesson in between soccer practice and dinner.*
sand·wich (**sand′**wich′) □*noun, plural* **sandwiches** □*verb* **sandwiched, sandwiching, sandwiches**

WORD HISTORY:　sandwich

The *sandwich* was named after the fourth Earl of Sandwich. The earl was fond of gambling at cards and is said to have invented the sandwich so that he would not have to leave the game to eat a regular meal.

---

sandy *adjective* **1.** Of, full of, or covered with sand: *a sandy beach.* **2.** Of the color of sand; yellowish red: *sandy hair.*
sand·y (**san′**dē) □*adjective* **sandier, sandiest**

sane *adjective* **1.** Having a sound and healthy mind. **2.** Having or showing good sense; sensible: *sane advice.*
sane (sān) □*adjective* **saner, sanest**

sang *verb* A past tense of **sing.**
sang (sang) □*verb*

sanitary *adjective* **1.** Of or having to do with health. **2.** Free from things, such as filth or germs, that endanger health.
san·i·tar·y (**san′**i ter′ē) □*adjective*

sanitation *noun* The act of making or keeping something sanitary.
san·i·ta·tion (san′i **tā′**shən) □*noun*

sank *verb* A past tense of **sink.**
sank (sangk) □*verb*

sans serif *noun* A letter of the alphabet written or printed without serifs.
sans ser·if (san **ser′**if) □*noun*

sap *noun* A liquid that circulates through a plant and carries food to its different parts.
sap (sap) □*noun, plural* **saps**

sapphire *noun* A hard, deep-blue stone used as a gem.
sap·phire (**saf′**īr′) □*noun, plural* **sapphires**

sarcastic *adjective* Expressing or marked by bitter remarks that show contempt for or are intended to hurt the feelings of another.
sar·cas·tic (sär **kas′**tik) □*adjective*

WORD HISTORY:　sarcastic

Sarcastic comes from a Greek word that means "to bite one's lips in rage."

---

sardine *noun* A small fish, such as a herring, that is canned in oil for use as food.
sar·dine (sär **dēn′**) □*noun, plural* **sardines**

sash¹ *noun* A wide piece of cloth worn around the waist or over the shoulder.
sash (sash) □*noun, plural* **sashes**

sash

sash² *noun* A frame for the glass in a window or door.
sash (sash) □*noun, plural* **sashes**

sat *verb* The past tense and past participle of **sit.**
sat (sat) □*verb*

Satan *noun* The devil.
Sa·tan (**sāt′**ən) □*noun*

satellite *noun* **1.** A heavenly body, such as a planet, that moves in an orbit around a larger heavenly body. **2.** A man-made object that is shot into space by a rocket and orbits the earth or another heavenly body. **3.** A nation that is controlled politically by another nation.
sat·el·lite (**sat′**əl īt′) □*noun, plural* **satellites**

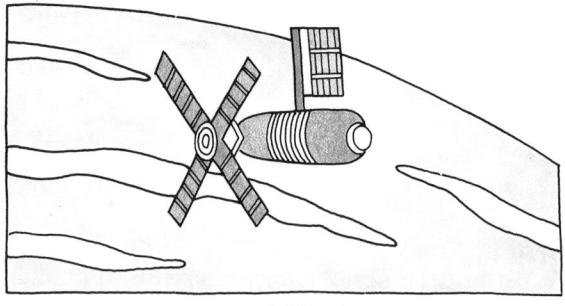

satellite

satin *noun* A smooth fabric that is shiny on one side.
sat·in (**sat′**ən) □*noun, plural* **satins**

satisfaction *noun* The condition of being satisfied: *He smiled with satisfaction after he* won the race.

sat·is·fac·tion (sat'is **fak'**shən) ☐*noun*

satisfactory *adjective* Sufficient to satisfy; adequate: *His grades were satisfactory.*
sat·is·fac·to·ry (sat'is **fak'**tə rē) ☐*adjective*

satisfy *verb* **1.** To meet the needs or desires of: *My mother was not satisfied with the way I cleaned my room.* **2.** To relieve doubt of; convince: *The jury was satisfied of his innocence.*
sat·is·fy (**sat'**is fī') ☐*verb* **satisfied, satisfying, satisfies**

saturate *verb* To soak or fill completely: *Saturate the sponge with water.*
sat·u·rate (**sach'**ə rāt') ☐*verb* **saturated, saturating, saturates**

Saturday *noun* The seventh day of the week.
Sat·ur·day (**sat'**ər dē *or* **sat'**ər dā') ☐*noun, plural* **Saturdays**

> **WORD HISTORY: Saturday**
>
> *Saturday* was named after Saturn, a Roman god of farming.

Saturn *noun* The planet of the solar system that is sixth in order from the sun and is surrounded by rings.
Sat·urn (**sat'**ərn) ☐*noun*

sauce *noun* A soft or liquid dressing that is served with food to add flavor.
sauce (sôs) ☐*noun, plural* **sauces**

saucer *noun* A small, shallow dish for holding a cup.
sau·cer (**sô'**sər) ☐*noun, plural* **saucers**

sausage *noun* Chopped meat that is spiced and stuffed into a case shaped like a tube.
sau·sage (**sô'**sij) ☐*noun, plural* **sausages**

> **WORD HISTORY: sausage**
>
> *Sausage* comes from a Latin word meaning "salted." Sausage was originally heavily seasoned with salt in order to preserve it.

savage *adjective* **1.** Not tamed; wild: *a savage animal.* **2.** Cruel and fierce; ferocious: *a savage fight.*
☐*noun* A cruel or vicious person.
sav·age (**sav'**ij) ☐*adjective* ☐*noun, plural* **savages**

> **WORD HISTORY: savage**
>
> *Savage* comes from a Latin word meaning "of the woods."

savagery *noun* **1.** A savage condition. **2.** Savage behavior.
sav·age·ry (**sav'**ij rē) ☐*noun*

save *verb* **1.** To rescue from harm or danger: *The policeman saved the boy from drowning.* **2.** To set aside for use in the future: *She saved a dollar a week to buy a new coat.* **3.** To keep from being harmed or ruined; protect: *The farmer tried to save his crops from being eaten by insects.* **4.** To keep from being wasted or spent: *She saved time by taking a taxi.*
save (sāv) ☐*verb* **saved, saving, saves**

saving *noun* **1.** Something that is saved: *a big saving of time.* **2. savings** Money that has been saved.
sav·ing (**sā'**ving) ☐*noun, plural* **savings**

saw¹ *noun* A tool or machine with a thin metal blade that has sharp teeth on one edge for cutting hard material, such as wood or metal.
☐*verb* To cut, produce, or shape with a saw: *He sawed the tree branch in half.*
saw (sô) ☐*noun, plural* **saws** ☐*verb* **sawed, sawed** or **sawn, sawing, saws**

saw² *verb* The past tense of **see.**
saw (sô) ☐*verb*

sawdust *noun* Tiny bits of wood that fall from something that is being sawed.
saw·dust (**sô'**dust') ☐*noun*

sawhorse *noun* A frame that consists of a horizontal bar with a pair of sloping legs at each end, used to support a piece of wood being sawed.
saw·horse (**sô'**hôrs') ☐*noun, plural* **sawhorses**

sawmill *noun* A place or business where lumber is cut into boards, planks, and other pieces.
saw·mill (**sô'**mil') ☐*noun, plural* **sawmills**

sawn *verb* A past participle of **saw¹**: *He had sawn the logs for the cabin.*
sawn (sôn) ☐*verb*

saxophone *noun* A musical wind instrument that has a sharply curved metal body with keys and a reed mouthpiece.

a bat	ī bite	ōō tool	*th* feather
ā make	î fierce	ou out	th bath
â dare	o dot	u nut	hw wheat
ä father	ō no	û turn	zh measure
e net	ô law, for	ch church	ə about, open
ē be	oi soil	ng ring	pencil, atom
i dip	oo look	sh shade	circus

sax·o·phone (**sak′**sə fōn′) □*noun, plural* **saxophones**

WORD HISTORY: **saxophone**

Saxophone is formed from the name of the instrument's Belgian inventor, Adolphe Sax, and a Greek word for "sound."

saxophone

say *verb* **1.** To utter aloud; speak: *She didn't say a word.* **2.** To express in words: *The sign says it is five miles to the nearest town.* □*noun* The right or chance to express an opinion: *Let me have my say.*
say (sā) □*verb* **said, saying, says** □*noun*

saying *noun* A familiar expression that contains wisdom; proverb.
say·ing (**sā′**ing) □*noun, plural* **sayings**

says *verb* The third person singular present tense of **say.**
says (sez) □*verb*

scab *noun* A crust that forms over and protects a wound or sore.
scab (skab) □*noun, plural* **scabs**

scaffold *noun* A platform used to support workers erecting or repairing a building.
scaf·fold (**skaf′**əld) □*noun, plural* **scaffolds**

scale¹ *noun* One of the small, thin parts that form the skin of fish and reptiles. □*verb* To remove the scales from: *I scaled the fish before cooking it.*
scale (skāl) □*noun, plural* **scales** □*verb* **scaled, scaling, scales**

scale² *noun* **1.** A series of marks placed at fixed distances and used for measuring: *This ruler has two scales, one in inches and the other in centimeters.* **2.** The size of a model, drawing, or map compared with the actual size of the thing it represents: *a map drawn to a scale in which every inch stands for fifty miles.* **3.** An ordered arrangement of steps, degrees, or stages: *a wage scale that goes from $100 a week to $200 a week.* **4.** Relative size or extent: *They entertain on a large scale.* **5.** A series of musical tones that goes up or down in pitch at fixed intervals.
□*verb* **1.** To climb up to the top of or over: *scale a ladder.* **2.** To adjust according to a standard or rate: *He scaled down his spending to match his salary.*
scale (skāl) □*noun, plural* **scales** □*verb* **scaled, scaling, scales**

scale³ *noun* An instrument or machine for weighing.
scale (skāl) □*noun, plural* **scales**

scallop *noun* **1.** A sea animal with a double shell shaped like a fan and a soft body used as food. **2.** One of a series of semicircles that forms a border: *a sheet trimmed with scallops.*
scal·lop (**skol′**əp *or* **skal′**əp) □*noun, plural* **scallops**

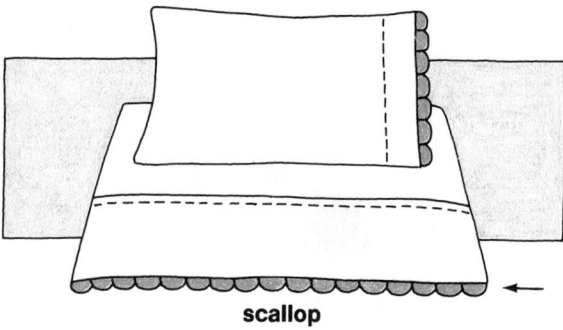

scallop

scalp *noun* The skin that covers the top of the head, and is usually covered with hair.
scalp (skalp) □*noun, plural* **scalps**

scamper *verb* To run quickly: *The squirrel scampered up the tree.*
scam·per (**skam′**pər) □*verb* **scampered, scampering, scampers**

scan *verb* **1.** To look at or examine closely: *He scanned the map to get his bearings.* **2.** To look at quickly: *I scanned the magazine while I waited.*
scan (skan) □*verb* **scanned, scanning, scans**

scandal *noun* **1.** Something that shocks people and disgraces those involved in it: *The theft of town funds was a scandal.* **2.** Talk that harms a person's reputation: *Their conversation is all gossip and scandal.*
scan·dal (**skan′**dəl) □*noun, plural* **scandals**

scant *adjective* Not enough in quantity or size: *The explorers had to turn back because of their scant food supplies.*
scant (skant) □*adjective* **scanter, scantest**

scar *noun* **1.** A mark left on the skin after a cut or wound has healed. **2.** A mark of damage: *a table with many scars.*
□*verb* To mark with or form a scar: *The injury scarred his face.*
scar (skär) □*noun, plural* **scars** □*verb* **scarred, scarring, scars**

scarce *adjective* Hard to get or find: *Raspberries are scarce this year.*
scarce (skârs) □*adjective* **scarcer, scarcest**

scarcely *adverb* Almost not; barely: *I can scarcely hear you.*
scarce·ly (skârs′lē) □*adverb*

scare *verb* To frighten or become frightened suddenly: *The sight of the snake scared me.*
□*noun* **1.** A sudden feeling of fear: *The sound of the siren gave me a scare.* **2.** A widespread condition of fear or panic: *a bomb scare.*
scare (skâr) □*verb* **scared, scaring, scares** □*noun, plural* **scares**

scarecrow *noun* A figure resembling a human being that is set up to scare birds away from crops.
scare·crow (skâr′krō′) □*noun, plural* **scarecrows**

scarecrow

scarf *noun* A piece of cloth worn around the neck or head for warmth or decoration.
scarf (skärf) □*noun, plural* **scarfs** or **scarves**

scarlet *noun* A bright red.
□*adjective* Bright red.
scar·let (skär′lit) □*noun* □*adjective*

scarves *noun* A plural of **scarf.**
scarves (skärvz) □*noun*

scatter *verb* **1.** To separate or cause to separate and go in different directions: *The wind scattered the leaves.* **2.** To spread or throw here and there: *She scattered pots and pans all over the kitchen as she worked.*
scat·ter (skat′ər) □*verb* **scattered, scattering, scatters**

scene *noun* **1.** A view; sight: *a winter scene.* **2.** The place where an action or event occurs: *the scene of the fire.* **3.** A section of an act in a play. **4.** A display of temper or misbehavior: *He made a scene when he didn't get his own way.*
scene (sēn) □*noun, plural* **scenes**

WORD HISTORY: **scene**

Scene comes from a Greek word that referred to a building on the stage that was used as a background for plays.

---

scenery *noun* **1.** The general appearance of a place; landscape: *We drove to the country to look at the autumn scenery.* **2.** The painted structures or curtains on the stage of a theater that are used as background for the action.
scen·er·y (sē′nə rē) □*noun, plural* **sceneries**

scenery

scent *noun* **1.** A particular smell; odor: *the scent of lilacs.* **2.** The odor left by an animal that has passed: *dogs picking up the scent of the fox.* **3.** The sense of smell.
scent (sent) □*noun, plural* **scents**

a bat	ī bite	͞oo tool	*th* feather
ā make	î fierce	ou out	th bath
â dare	o dot	u nut	hw wheat
ä father	ō no	û turn	zh measure
e net	ô law, for	ch church	ə about, open
ē be	oi soil	ng ring	pencil, atom
i dip	oo look	sh shade	circus

scepter *noun* A rod or staff that is carried by a queen or king as a symbol of authority.
scep·ter (sep′tər) □*noun, plural* **scepters**

sch. An abbreviation for **school.**

schedule *noun* **1.** A list of events, things to do, or times at which to do things: *an appointment schedule; a schedule of classes.* **2.** A list of the times when something arrives or departs: *a bus schedule.*
□*verb* To enter on or form into a schedule: *He scheduled a meeting for Friday.*
sched·ule (skej′ool *or* skej′əl) □*noun, plural* **schedules** □*verb* **scheduled, scheduling, schedules**

scheme *noun* **1.** A plan for doing something: *a new business scheme.* **2.** An underhanded plan: *a scheme for cheating on the exam.* **3.** An orderly arrangement or combination: *a color scheme.* —See Synonyms at **plot.**
□*verb* To make a scheme: *We were scheming to go to the movies without our parents' permission.*
scheme (skēm) □*noun, plural* **schemes** □*verb* **schemed, scheming, schemes**

scholar *noun* Someone who has a great deal of knowledge about a particular subject.
schol·ar (skol′ər) □*noun, plural* **scholars**

scholarship *noun* **1.** Money given to a student for further education. **2.** Knowledge or learning in a particular field.
schol·ar·ship (skôl′ər ship′) □*noun, plural* **scholarships**

school¹ *noun* **1.** A place for teaching and learning. **2.** A division within a university for the study of a particular field: *a law school.* **3.** The process of being educated at a school: *She began school when she was five.*
□*verb* To teach; train: *She has been well schooled in several branches of mathematics.*
school (skool) □*noun, plural* **schools** □*verb* **schooled, schooling, schools**

> **WORD HISTORY: school**
> *School* comes from a Greek word that means "leisure."

school² *noun* A large group of fish or water animals swimming together: *a school of sharks.*
school (skool) □*noun, plural* **schools**

schooner *noun* A ship with two or more masts and sails that are set across the length of the ship.

schoo·ner (skoo′nər) □*noun, plural* **schooners**

schooner

schwa *noun* A symbol (ə) used in English for vowel sounds that occur in syllables with no stress, such as the *a* in *alone.*
schwa (shwä) □*noun, plural* **schwas**

science *noun* **1.** Knowledge about nature and the universe that is based on experiments and observation and is presented in an orderly way. **2.** A branch of such knowledge, such as biology or physics.
sci·ence (sī′əns) □*noun, plural* **sciences**

scientific *adjective* Of, having to do with, or used in science: *scientific equipment; scientific research.*
sci·en·tif·ic (sī′ən tif′ik) □*adjective*

scientist *noun* Someone who is learned in a particular branch of science.
sci·en·tist (sī′ən tist) □*noun, plural* **scientists**

scissors *plural noun* A cutting tool with two sharp blades fastened in the middle so that they close against each other.
scis·sors (siz′ərz) □*plural noun*

scold *verb* To find fault with or speak angrily to: *She scolded me for being late.*
scold (skōld) □*verb* **scolded, scolding, scolds**

scoop *noun* **1.** A small tool shaped like a shovel that is used to dip into and take up a soft substance, such as sugar or ice cream. **2.** A large bucket, as of a steam shovel, used to remove material such as dirt.
□*verb* **1.** To lift up or out with or as if with a scoop: *She scooped up a handful of pennies.* **2.** To form by scooping: *scoop out a hole.*
scoop (skoop) □*noun, plural* **scoops** □*verb* **scooped, scooping, scoops**

scope *noun* The range of a person's ideas, actions, understanding, or ability: *These simple*

problems are well within his scope.
scope (skōp) ▢*noun, plural* **scopes**

scorch *verb* **1.** To burn on the surface: *She scorched the shirt with the iron.* **2.** To wither or dry out with intense heat: *The sun scorched the grass.*
▢*noun* A slight burn.
scorch (skôrch) ▢*verb* **scorched, scorching, scorches** ▢*noun, plural* **scorches**

scorch

score *noun* **1.** A record of the points made in a game, contest, or test: *Her score on the science test was 85.* **2.** A set or group of twenty: *a score of people.* **3.** The written or printed form of musical composition. **4.** A wrong or injury to be repaid: *I have a score to settle with him.*
▢*verb* **1.** To make a point in a game, contest, or test: *He scored the winning run.* **2.** To keep a record of the points made: *The professor scored the examinations.*
score (skôr) ▢*noun, plural* **scores** ▢*verb* **scored, scoring, scores**

scorn *noun* A feeling that someone or something is worthless or inferior; contempt: *He has scorn for cowards.*
▢*verb* To treat or think of with contempt; disdain: *She scorns liars.*
scorn (skôrn) ▢*noun* ▢*verb* **scorned, scorning, scorns**

scorpion *noun* An animal related to the spiders that has a narrow body and a long tail with a poisonous stinger.
scor·pi·on (skôr′pē ən) ▢*noun, plural* **scorpions**

Scottish *noun* **1.** The people of Scotland. **2.** The dialect of English spoken in Scotland.
▢*adjective* Of Scotland, its people, or their language.
Scot·tish (skot′ish) ▢*noun* ▢*adjective*

scout *noun* **1.** Someone who is sent to gather information: *The scout reported that the enemy had crossed the river.* **2.** Often **Scout** A member of the Boy Scouts or Girl Scouts.
▢*verb* To explore an area carefully in order to gather information: *We scouted around for a good place to camp.*
scout (skout) ▢*noun, plural* **scouts** ▢*verb* **scouted, scouting, scouts**

scoutmaster *noun* An adult who leads a troop of Boy Scouts.
scout·mas·ter (skout′mas′tər) ▢*noun, plural* **scoutmasters**

scowl *verb* To wrinkle the forehead in anger: *He scowled at the noisy child.*
▢*noun* An angry frown.
scowl (skoul) ▢*verb* **scowled, scowling, scowls** ▢*noun, plural* **scowls**

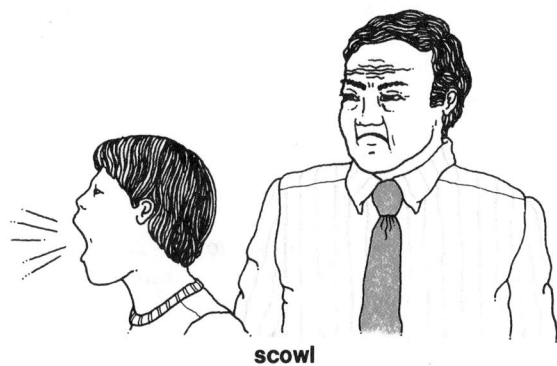
scowl

scramble *verb* **1.** To move or climb quickly, especially on the hands and knees: *She scrambled over the rocks.* **2.** To struggle or compete with others: *He had to scramble to get a seat.* **3.** To mix together in a confused way: *She scrambled the letters of the word.* **4.** To cook eggs by mixing the yolks and whites and stirring the mixture as it fries.
▢*noun* **1.** A difficult climb: *Getting to the top of the mountain was quite a scramble.* **2.** A struggle or competition: *There was a scramble for tickets to the concert.*
scram·ble (skram′bəl) ▢*verb* **scrambled, scrambling, scrambles** ▢*noun, plural* **scrambles**

a bat	ī bite	o͞o tool	*th* feather
ā make	î fierce	ou out	th bath
â dare	o dot	u nut	hw wheat
ä father	ō no	û turn	zh measure
e net	ô law, for	ch church	ə about, open
ē be	oi soil	ng ring	pencil, atom
i dip	o͞o look	sh shade	circus

scrap *noun* **1.** A small piece; bit: *a scrap of cloth.* **2. scraps** Leftover bits of food. **3.** Material, such as metal, that is left over and can be processed and used again.
□*verb* **1.** To discard as useless: *He had to scrap his plan to take a trip.* **2.** To make into scrap: *The army scrapped the tank.*
scrap (skrap) □*noun, plural* **scraps** □*verb* **scrapped, scrapping, scraps**

scrape *verb* **1.** To clean, smooth, or shape by rubbing: *He scraped the dishes before washing them.* **2.** To remove by rubbing with a sharp object: *I scraped the paint off the table.* **3.** To hurt or scratch the surface of by rubbing against something rough or sharp: *He scraped his shin on a rock.* **4.** To get with difficulty: *I scraped together a little money for a new book.*
□*noun* **1.** An injury, mark, or sound made by scraping: *a scrape on his chin; the scrape of chalk on the blackboard.* **2.** A difficult situation: *He got into a scrape at school.*
scrape (skrāp) □*verb* **scraped, scraping, scrapes** □*noun, plural* **scrapes**

scratch *verb* **1.** To dig, scrape, or injure with something sharp, such as fingernails, claws, or a tool: *The knife scratched the table. I scratched my legs on the thorns.* **2.** To rub to stop itching: *He scratched a mosquito bite.* **3.** To make a scraping sound: *The branches scratched against the window.* **4.** To cancel by or as if by drawing a line through: *Scratch his name from your list.*
□*noun* **1.** An injury or mark made by scratching: *a scratch on the arm.* **2.** A scraping sound: *the scratch of a pencil on paper.*
scratch (skrach) □*verb* **scratched, scratching, scratches** □*noun, plural* **scratches**

scream *verb* To make a loud, sharp, piercing cry or sound, as from pain or fear: *He screamed for help.*
□*noun* A loud, sharp, piercing cry or sound.
scream (skrēm) □*verb* **screamed, screaming, screams** □*noun, plural* **screams**

screech *verb* To make a shrill, harsh cry or sound: *The car screeched to a stop.*
□*noun* A shrill, harsh cry or sound: *the screech of owls.*
screech (skrēch) □*verb* **screeched, screeching, screeches** □*noun, plural* **screeches**

screen *noun* **1.** A frame covered with wire mesh that is used in windows and doors to keep out insects. **2.** A movable frame used to separate, hide, or protect: *I hid the stereo behind a screen.* **3.** Something that separates or hides like a screen: *A screen of vines covered the window.* **4.** A large, flat surface on which slides or movies are shown. **5.** The front surface of a television or of a computer monitor on which the image appears.
□*verb* To hide or protect with or as if with a screen: *I screened my eyes from the sun with my hand.*
screen (skrēn) □*noun, plural* **screens** □*verb* **screened, screening, screens**

screw *noun* A metal pin with a long ridge winding around its length and a slotted head that is used to hold things together.
□*verb* **1.** To fasten, attach, or tighten with a screw: *He screwed the knobs on the drawer.* **2.** To attach by twisting into place: *I screwed the cap onto the tube of toothpaste.*
screw (skrōō) □*noun, plural* **screws** □*verb* **screwed, screwing, screws**

screwdriver *noun* A tool used to turn screws.
screw·driv·er (skrōō′drī′vər) □*noun, plural* **screwdrivers**

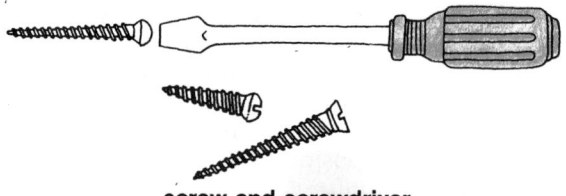

screw and screwdriver

scribble *verb* To write or draw carelessly or quickly: *I scribbled her name on the envelope.*
□*noun* Something that is scribbled.
scrib·ble (skrib′əl) □*verb* **scribbled, scribbling, scribbles** □*noun, plural* **scribbles**

scribe *noun* Someone who copied written material, such as manuscripts, before printing was invented.
scribe (skrīb) □*noun, plural* **scribes**

script *noun* **1.** Handwriting. **2.** A style of type used in printing that looks like handwriting. **3.** The written text of a play, movie, or television or radio show containing the lines of all the performers.
script (skript) □*noun, plural* **scripts**

scroll *noun* **1.** A roll of paper or parchment that has writing on it and often a rod at each end around which it is rolled. **2.** An ornament or design that looks like a scroll.
scroll (skrōl) □*noun, plural* **scrolls**

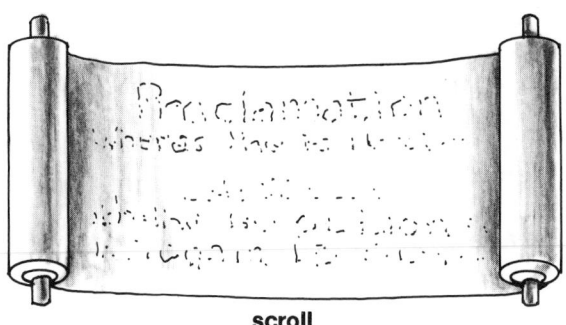

scroll

scrub *verb* To clean by rubbing hard: *I scrubbed the floor.*
□*noun* The act of scrubbing.
scrub (skrub) □*verb* **scrubbed, scrubbing, scrubs** □*noun, plural* **scrubs**

scuff *verb* **1.** To scrape or drag the feet while walking. **2.** To scrape or scratch the surface of: *He scuffed his shoes.*
scuff (skuf) □*verb* **scuffed, scuffing, scuffs**

scuffle *verb* To fight or struggle in a confused way: *The guard scuffled with the thieves.*
□*noun* A confused fight or struggle.
scuf·fle (skuf′əl) □*verb* **scuffled, scuffling, scuffles** □*noun, plural* **scuffles**

sculptor *noun* Someone who makes sculptures.
sculp·tor (skulp′tər) □*noun, plural* **sculptors**

sculpture *noun* **1.** The art of making figures or designs by shaping clay, carving or chiseling wood or stone, or casting or pouring liquid metal into a mold. **2.** A work of art created by sculpture: *We saw sculptures of ancient Roman gods.*
□*verb* To represent in sculpture.
sculp·ture (skulp′chər) □*noun, plural* **sculptures** □*verb* **sculptured, sculpturing, sculptures**

sculpture

scurry *verb* To go or move about quickly: *The rabbits scurried away.*
scur·ry (skûr′ē) □*verb* **scurried, scurrying, scurries**

scurvy *noun* A disease caused by the lack of vitamin C in the diet. Symptoms of scurvy are bleeding gums, weakness, and bleeding under the skin.
scur·vy (skûr′vē) □*noun*

scythe *noun* A tool with a long, curved blade attached to a long, bent handle, used for mowing and reaping.
scythe (sīth) □*noun, plural* **scythes**

sea *noun* **1.** The ocean. **2.** A large body of salt water completely or partly surrounded by land. **3.** The movement of the ocean's waters, especially the swell of waves: *a calm sea; heavy seas.* **4.** Something that suggests the sea, as in size: *a sea of faces.*
sea (sē) □*noun, plural* **seas**

seaboard *noun* Land near the sea; shore.
sea·board (sē′bôrd′) □*noun*

seacoast *noun* The seashore.
sea·coast (sē′kōst′) □*noun, plural* **seacoasts**

seafood *noun* Fish or shellfish that can be eaten as food.
sea·food (sē′fōōd′) □*noun*

sea gull *noun* A gull, especially one that lives along the seashore.

sea horse *noun* A small ocean fish with a head that looks like the head of a horse.

sea horse

a	bat	ī	bite	ōō	tool	*th*	feather
ā	make	î	fierce	ou	out	th	bath
â	dare	o	dot	u	nut	hw	wheat
ä	father	ō	no	û	turn	zh	measure
e	net	ô	law, for	ch	church	ə	about, open
ē	be	oi	soil	ng	ring		pencil, atom
i	dip	oo	look	sh	shade		circus

seal¹　*noun*　**1.** A device with a raised or carved design that is stamped on paper or wax. **2.** A design that is stamped on paper or wax as an official mark of identification or ownership. **3.** A piece of wax, metal, or paper with a design stamped on it. **4.** Something that is used to close tightly: *We used a rubber seal on the jar of jam.* **5.** A small paper sticker used to close or decorate an envelope.
□*verb* **1.** To put a seal on: *The town clerk sealed the document.* **2.** To close tightly with or as if with a seal: *He sealed the envelope. She wouldn't tell; her lips were sealed.*
seal (sēl) □*noun, plural* **seals** □*verb* **sealed, sealing, seals**

seal²　*noun*　A sea mammal with a streamlined body, thick fur, and large flippers.
seal (sēl) □*noun, plural* **seals** or **seal**

sea lion　*noun*　A large seal of Pacific waters that has a sleek body and brownish hair.

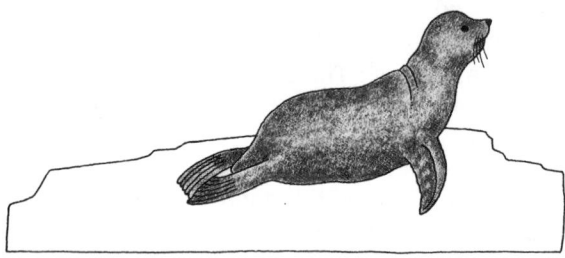

sea lion

seam　*noun*　**1.** A line formed by joining two edges of cloth or other material: *the seam in a skirt.* **2.** A line that resembles a seam: *seams in the surface of a frozen pond.*
□*verb* To join with a seam.
seam (sēm) □*noun, plural* **seams** □*verb* **seamed, seaming, seams**

seaman　*noun*　**1.** A sailor. **2.** A sailor of the lowest rank in the navy.
sea·man (sē′mən) □*noun, plural* **seamen**

seamstress　*noun*　A woman who makes her living by sewing.
seam·stress (sēm′strĭs) □*noun, plural* **seamstresses**

seaport　*noun*　**1.** A harbor or port for large ships. **2.** A city or town with a harbor or port.
sea·port (sē′pôrt′) □*noun, plural* **seaports**

search　*verb*　To look through carefully in order to find something: *I searched the house for my scarf. We searched for the lost kitten.*
□*noun* The act of searching: *I made a search for my keys.*

search (sûrch) □*verb* **searched, searching, searches** □*noun, plural* **searches**

searchlight　*noun*　A powerful light that produces a bright beam.
search·light (sûrch′līt′) □*noun, plural* **searchlights**

seashell　*noun*　The hard shell of a sea animal.
sea·shell (sē′shĕl′) □*noun, plural* **seashells**

seashore　*noun*　Land near the ocean.
sea·shore (sē′shôr′) □*noun, plural* **seashores**

seasick　*adjective*　Sick because of the side-to-side motion of a ship.
sea·sick (sē′sĭk′) □*adjective*

season　*noun*　**1.** One of the four divisions of the year: spring, summer, autumn, and winter. **2.** A period of time associated with an event or activity: *the holiday season; the dry season.*
□*verb* To give extra flavor to by adding seasoning: *Season the stew with salt and pepper.*
sea·son (sē′zən) □*noun, plural* **seasons** □*verb* **seasoned, seasoning, seasons**

seasoning　*noun*　Something, such as an herb, that is added to food to give it extra flavor.
sea·son·ing (sē′zə nĭng) □*noun, plural* **seasonings**

seat　*noun*　**1.** Something to sit on, such as a chair or bench. **2.** A place in or at which someone may sit: *She took her seat at the head of the table.* **3.** The part of something on which one sits: *a bicycle seat; the seat of his pants.* **4.** A capital or center: *a seat of learning.*
□*verb* **1.** To place in or on a seat: *Father seated the guests at the table.* **2.** To have seats for: *The theater seats 500 people.*
seat (sēt) □*noun, plural* **seats** □*verb* **seated, seating, seats**

seat belt　*noun*　A strap made to hold a person safely in a seat, as in an automobile or airplane.

seat belt

seaweed *noun* Any of the many plants that grow in the ocean, such as kelp.
sea·weed (sē′wēd) □*noun, plural* **seaweeds**

sec. An abbreviation for **second.**

second¹ *noun* One sixtieth of a minute.
sec·ond (sek′ənd) □*noun, plural* **seconds**

WORD HISTORY: second¹

Second¹ is from the same Latin word as *second².* The hour and the circle were divided into 60 parts, called in Latin "first small parts." Each of these parts was divided again into 60 parts, called in Latin "second parts." In English these smallest divisions became known as "seconds."

---

second² *adjective* **1.** Being next after the first, as in place or time: *Her apartment is on the second floor.* **2.** Another; additional: *a second term in office.* **3.** Being less than or inferior to another: *He won second prize.*
□*adverb* In second order, place, or rank: *He won the race, and I came in second.*
□*noun* **1.** In a group of people or things that are in numbered order, the one that matches the number two. **2.** An article of manufactured goods that has a defect: *Those stockings are seconds.*
□*verb* To give support to a motion or nomination so it can be voted on.
sec·ond (sek′ənd) □*adjective* □*adverb*
□*noun, plural* **seconds** □*verb* **seconded, seconding, seconds**

secondary *adjective* Being second in rank or importance: *a secondary road.*
sec·on·dar·y (sek′ən der′ē) □*adjective*

secondary accent *noun* **1.** In a word having more than one accented syllable, the accent or stress that is weaker than the primary one. **2.** The mark (′) used to indicate a secondary accent.

secondary school *adjective* A school attended between elementary school and college.

secondhand *adjective* **1.** Having had a former owner; not new: *secondhand clothes.* **2.** Obtained from another: *We heard only a secondhand account of the accident.*
sec·ond·hand (sek′ənd hand′) □*adjective*

secrecy *noun* The condition of being secret or kept secret: *The generals planned the attack in secrecy.*
se·cre·cy (sē′kri sē) □*noun*

secret *adjective* **1.** Kept hidden from the knowledge of others: *secret plans.* **2.** Working concealed from knowledge of others: *a secret agent.*
□*noun* Something kept secret.
se·cret (sē′krit) □*adjective* □*noun, plural* **secrets**

secretary *noun* **1.** Someone who writes letters and keeps records for a person, company, or organization: *He ran for secretary of the photography club.* **2.** The head of a department in a government: *the Secretary of Labor.* **3.** A writing desk with shelves on the top for books.
sec·re·tar·y (sek′ri ter′ē) □*noun, plural* **secretaries**

section *noun* **1.** A part taken from a whole: *a section of an apple.* **2.** One of the parts that makes up something; division: *the business section of the newspaper; the residential section of the city.*
□*verb* To cut or separate into sections: *She sectioned the pineapple.*
sec·tion (sek′shən) □*noun, plural* **sections** □*verb* **sectioned, sectioning, sections**

section

secular *adjective* Not related to religion or a religious organization: *The minister took an interest in the secular affairs of the community.*
sec·u·lar (sek′yə lər) □*adjective*

secure *adjective* **1.** Free from danger or risk of loss; safe: *A cookie jar is not a secure place to keep money.* **2.** Not likely to fail or give way: *Make sure the knot is secure.*
□*verb* **1.** To guard from danger or risk of loss; make safe: *We secured the fort against attack.* **2.** To fasten tightly: *I secured the windows be-*

a bat	ī bite	o͞o tool	*th* feather
ā make	î fierce	ou out	th bath
â dare	o dot	u nut	hw wheat
ä father	ō no	û turn	zh measure
e net	ô law, for	ch church	ə about, open
ē be	oi soil	ng ring	pencil, atom
i dip	oo look	sh shade	circus

fore the storm broke. **3.** To get possession of; acquire: *The workers went on strike to secure higher wages.*
se·cure (si kyoor´) □*adjective* **securer, securest** □*verb* **secured, securing, secures**

security *noun* **1.** The condition of being secure; safety. **2.** Something that provides security: *We hired a guard as security against robbers.* —See Synonyms at **safety.**
se·cu·ri·ty (si kyoor´i tē) □*noun, plural* **securities**

sedan *noun* A closed automobile with a hard top, four doors, and a front and back seat.
se·dan (si **dan´**) □*noun, plural* **sedans**

sediment *noun* Material that settles at the bottom of a liquid.
sed·i·ment (sed´ə mənt) □*noun*

see *verb* **1.** To look at with the eyes: *I saw a camel at the zoo.* **2.** To have the power of sight: *He doesn't see well without his glasses.* **3.** To understand: *I see what you mean.* **4.** To find out: *Go see if the mail has come.* **5.** To visit or accept the visit of: *She couldn't see the doctor because he was on vacation.* **6.** To go with; accompany: *I'll see you home.* **7.** To make sure; take care: *See that you behave yourself.*
see (sē) □*verb* **saw, seen, seeing, sees**

seed *noun* A structure produced by a flowering plant that can grow into a new plant of the same kind as its parent.
□*verb* **1.** To plant seeds in; sow: *The farmer seeded the field with barley.* **2.** To remove the seeds from: *I seeded the grapefruit.*
seed (sēd) □*noun, plural* **seeds** □*verb* **seeded, seeding, seeds**

seedling *noun* A young plant that has grown from a seed.
seed·ling (sēd´ling) □*noun, plural* **seedlings**

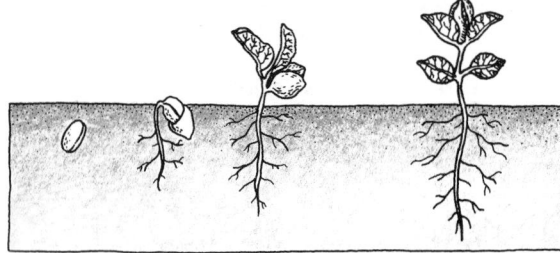
seed and seedling
Development of a seed into a seedling

seek *verb* **1.** To try to find; search for: *seeking for a book in the library.* **2.** To make an attempt; try: *He sought to make her happy.*

3. To try to get: *I sought his advice.*
seek (sēk) □*verb* **sought, seeking, seeks**

seem *verb* To give the impression of being; appear: *She certainly seems happy. You seem to agree with him.* —See Synonyms at **appear.**
seem (sēm) □*verb* **seemed, seeming, seems**

seen *verb* The past participle of **see:** *We've already seen that movie.*
seen (sēn) □*verb*

seep *verb* To pass slowly through small openings; ooze: *The water seeped slowly out of the wooden barrel.*
seep (sēp) □*verb* **seeped, seeping, seeps**

seesaw *noun* A long plank balanced on a support in the middle. When one person sits on each end, one end goes up as the other goes down.
□*verb* To ride on a seesaw.
see·saw (sē´sô´) □*noun, plural* **seesaws** □*verb* **seesawed, seesawing, seesaws**

seesaw

segment *noun* A part into which a whole is or can be divided; section: *a segment of a circle; a segment of a television series.*
seg·ment (seg´mənt) □*noun, plural* **segments**

segregate *verb* To separate or keep apart from others.
seg·re·gate (seg´ri gāt´) □*verb* **segregated, segregating, segregates**

segregation *noun* **1.** The act of segregating or condition of being segregated. **2.** The separation of one racial group from the rest of society.
seg·re·ga·tion (seg´ri gā´shən) □*noun*

seine *noun* A large fishing net with floats attached to the top edge and weights at the bottom to pull it straight down.

seine (sān) □*noun, plural* **seines**

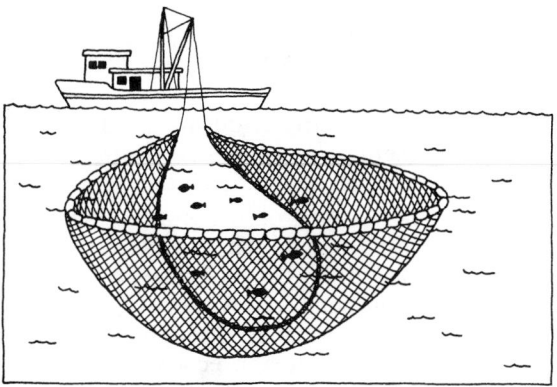

seine

seismograph *noun* An instrument that detects and records the location and intensity of an earthquake.

seis·mo·graph (**sīz′**mə graf′) □*noun, plural* **seismographs**

seize *verb* **1.** To take hold of suddenly and with force; grab: *She seized my arm.* **2.** To take possession of by force: *The rebels seized the capital.*

seize (sēz) □*verb* **seized, seizing, seizes**

seldom *adverb* Not often; rarely.

sel·dom (**sel′** dəm) □*adverb*

select *verb* To choose from among several; pick out: *I selected the magazines I wanted to read.* —See Synonyms at **choose.**

se·lect (si **lekt′**) □*verb* **selected, selecting, selects**

selection *noun* **1.** The act of selecting. **2.** Someone or something chosen; choice.

se·lec·tion (si **lek′** shən) □*noun, plural* **selections**

self *noun* **1.** A person thought of as an individual separate from all others. **2.** The character or behavior typical of a particular person: *He seems like his old friendly self again.*

self (self) □*noun, plural* **selves**

self- A prefix that forms another word and means: **1.** Oneself or itself: *self-evident.* **2.** Of, to, or by itself or oneself: *self-conscious.* **3.** In an automatic way: *self-winding.*

self-conscious *adjective* Too conscious of oneself when around other people.

self-con·scious (**self′ kon′** shəs) □*adjective*

selfish *adjective* Concerned about oneself without thinking of others.

self·ish (**sel′** fish) □*adjective*

self-respect *noun* Proper or due regard for oneself.

self-re·spect (self′ri **spekt′**) □*noun*

sell *verb* **1.** To provide in exchange for money: *He sold his car.* **2.** To deal in: *The store sells records and tapes.* **3.** To be sold: *This jam sells for $2 a jar.*

sell (sel) □*verb* **sold, selling, sells**

selves *noun* The plural of **self.**

selves (selvz) □*noun*

semaphore *noun* **1.** A signaling device with flags, lights, or moving arms, as on a railroad. **2.** A method of sending signals by means of a flag held in each hand.

sem·a·phore (**sem′** ə fôr′) □*noun, plural* **semaphores**

WORD HISTORY: **semaphore**

Semaphore comes from two Greek words, the first meaning "signal" and the second meaning "bearing" or "carrying."

semaphore

semi- A prefix that means: **1.** Half of: *semicircle.* **2.** Happening twice within a period of time: *semimonthly.*

semicircle *noun* Half of a circle.

sem·i·cir·cle (**sem′** i sûr′kəl) □*noun, plural* **semicircles**

semicolon *noun* A punctuation mark (;) that shows a greater degree of separation between

a	bat	ī	bite	ōō	tool	*th*	feather
ā	make	î	fierce	ou	out	th	bath
â	dare	o	dot	u	nut	hw	wheat
ä	father	ō	no	û	turn	zh	measure
e	net	ô	law, for	ch	church	ə	about, open
ē	be	oi	soil	ng	ring		pencil, atom
i	dip	oo	look	sh	shade		circus

parts of a sentence than a comma.

sem·i·co·lon (sem′i kō′lən) □*noun, plural* **semicolons**

seminary *noun* A school that trains people to become priests, ministers, or rabbis.

sem·i·nar·y (sem′ə ner′ē) □*noun, plural* **seminaries**

senate *noun* The upper and smaller houses of a legislative body in certain states or countries.

sen·ate (sen′it) □*noun, plural* **senates**

WORD HISTORY: **senate**

The word *senate* comes from the Latin word for "old man." The Roman senate was originally made up of a group of well-born old men.

---

senator *noun* A member of a senate.

sen·a·tor (sen′ə tər) □*noun, plural* **senators**

send *verb* **1.** To order or ask to go: *She sent me on an errand.* **2.** To cause to go: *send an arrow into the air.* **3.** To have someone pass a message on: *Please send her my greetings.* **4.** To propel with force; drive: *sent a satellite into orbit.* **5.** To put into a certain condition: *His behavior sent me into a rage.*

send (send) □*verb* **sent, sending, sends**

senior *adjective* **1.** Older: *a senior citizen.* **2. Senior** A term used with the name of a father who has the same name as his son: *James Smith, Senior.* **3.** Of higher rank or greater length of service: *a senior congressman.* **4.** Of the fourth year of high school or college: *the senior class.*

□*noun* **1.** Someone who is older or higher in rank than another: *His sister is his senior by ten years.* **2.** A student in the fourth year of high school or college.

sen·ior (sēn′yər) □*adjective* □*noun, plural* **seniors**

señor *noun* The Spanish title equivalent to "mister."

se·ñor (sān yôr′) □*noun, plural* **se·ño·res** (sān yôr′ās)

señora *noun* The Spanish title equivalent to "Mrs."

se·ño·ra (sān yôr′ə) □*noun, plural* **se·ño·ras** (sān yôr′äs)

señorita *noun* The Spanish title equivalent to "Miss."

se·ño·ri·ta (sān′yō rē′tə) □*noun, plural* **señoritas** (sān′yō rē′täs)

sensation *noun* **1.** The ability to see, hear, smell, taste, or touch. **2.** Something perceived because of stimulation of a sense or organ; feeling: *a sensation of cold.* **3.** A condition of intense interest or excitement: *The news caused a sensation.*

sen·sa·tion (sen sā′shən) □*noun, plural* **sensations**

sensational *adjective* Arousing great interest and excitement: *a sensational concert.*

sen·sa·tion·al (sen sā′shə nəl) □*adjective*

sense *noun* **1.** Any of the powers, such as sight, hearing, smell, touch, and taste, through which a living thing can be or become aware of its environment. **2.** A quality of being aware, through or as if through a sense: *a sense of fear.* **3.** An appreciation or understanding of something: *a good sense of humor.* **4.** Good judgment; practical intelligence: *He had enough sense to wear boots in the rain.* **5.** The meaning or one of the meanings of a word or phrase.

□*verb* To be or become aware of: *She sensed danger.*

sense (sens) □*noun, plural* **senses** □*verb* **sensed, sensing, senses**

sensible *adjective* Having or showing sound judgment: *a sensible decision.*

sen·si·ble (sen′sə bəl) □*adjective*

SYNONYMS: **sensible, reasonable**

These adjectives mean having or showing sound judgment and good sense: *We came up with a sensible solution to the problem. Reasonable people will cooperate in an emergency.*

---

sensitive *adjective* **1.** Capable of sensing, feeling, or responding: *Photographic film is sensitive to light.* **2.** Easily hurt, damaged, or irritated: *sensitive skin; sensitive feelings.* **3.** Easily affected by changes of condition or environment: *a sensitive barometer.*

sen·si·tive (sen′si tiv) □*adjective*

sent *verb* The past tense and past participle of **send**: *I sent him a message.*

sent (sent) □*verb*

sentence *noun* **1.** A word or group of words, such as "He left the house," that makes a statement, asks a question, or expresses a command. **2.** Punishment given by a court: *a sentence of 15 years for robbery.*

□*verb* To give a sentence to: *The judge sentenced the criminal to three years in prison.*

sen·tence (sen′təns) □*noun, plural* **sentences** □*verb* **sentenced, sentencing, sentences**

sentiment *noun* Feeling; emotion.
sen·ti·ment (**sen′**tə mənt) □*noun, plural* **sentiments**

sentimental *adjective* **1.** Of the feelings; emotional: *the sentimental value of an old family photograph.* **2.** Influenced or ruled more by emotion than by reason: *a sentimental man who cries easily.*
sen·ti·men·tal (sen′tə **men′**təl) □*adjective*

sentry *noun* Someone who is posted to keep watch; guard.
sen·try (**sen′**trē) □*noun, plural* **sentries**

sepal *noun* One of the parts forming the outer covering of a flower.
se·pal (**sē′**pəl) □*noun, plural* **sepals**

separate *verb* **1.** To keep or set apart: *A curb separates the sidewalk from the street.* **2.** To go in different directions; part: *After school they separated and did not meet again until the next day.* **3.** To see a difference between; distinguish: *separate fact from opinion.*
□*adjective* Set apart; not connected: *The gymnasium is a separate building.*
sep·a·rate □*verb* (**sep′**ə rāt′) **separated, separating, separates** □*adjective* (**sep′**ər it)

SYNONYMS: **separate, divide, part**

These verbs mean to set apart from another or others: *I separated the magazines into three piles. The argument divided the members of the team. They were such close friends that we thought that nothing would ever part them.*

---

separation *noun* The act of separating or condition of being separated: *The two brothers met after a separation of 20 years.*
sep·a·ra·tion (sep′ə **rā′**shən) □*noun, plural* **separations**

September *noun* The ninth month of the year. September has 30 days.
Sep·tem·ber (sep **tem′**bər) □*noun, plural* **Septembers**

WORD HISTORY: **September**

September comes from a Latin name meaning "seventh month." In an early Roman calendar March was the first month and September the seventh.

---

sequence *noun* **1.** The following of one thing after another; succession: *the sequence of the seasons.* **2.** A group of things in a particular order; series: *a sequence of articles on golf.*
se·quence (**sē′**kwəns) □*noun, plural* **sequences**

sequoia *noun* A very large evergreen tree of California that bears cones.
se·quoi·a (si **kwoi′**ə) □*noun, plural* **sequoias**

WORD HISTORY: **sequoia**

The *sequoia* is named after Sequoya, a Cherokee Indian who invented a way of writing his people's language.

---

serene *adjective* Peaceful and calm: *serene seas. She had a serene expression on her face.*
se·rene (sə **rēn′**) □*adjective*

serf *noun* A farm laborer of the Middle Ages who lived and worked on land owned by a lord and who was sold along with the land.
serf (sûrf) □*noun, plural* **serfs**

sergeant *noun* An officer in the U.S. Army or Marine Corps who ranks just above a corporal.
ser·geant (**sär′**jənt) □*noun, plural* **sergeants**

WORD HISTORY: **sergeant**

Sergeant comes from an old French word that originally meant "serving man."

---

serial *noun* A story that is presented one part at a time at regular intervals.
se·ri·al (**sîr′**ē əl) □*noun, plural* **serials**

series *noun* A number of similar things that occur in a row or follow one another in time: *a series of numbers; a series of lectures.*
se·ries (**sîr′**ēz) □*noun, plural* **series**

serif *noun* A fine line finishing off the main strokes of a letter of the alphabet.
ser·if (**ser′**if) □*noun, plural* **serifs**

serious *adjective* **1.** Grave or solemn in manner or appearance: *He had a serious look when he came home from the office.* **2.** Said, being, or done in earnest; not casual: *That was a serious question I asked.* **3.** Not trivial; important: *a serious problem.* **4.** Causing harm; dangerous: *a serious accident.*
se·ri·ous (**sîr′**ē əs) □*adjective*

sermon *noun* **1.** A talk on a religious subject or text usually given as part of a religious service. **2.** A serious talk about duty or behav-

a	bat	ī	bite	oo	tool	*th*	feather
ā	make	î	fierce	ou	out	th	bath
â	dare	o	dot	u	nut	hw	wheat
ä	father	ō	no	û	turn	zh	measure
e	net	ô	law, for	ch	church	ə	about, open
ē	be	oi	soil	ng	ring		pencil, atom
i	dip	oo	look	sh	shade		circus

ior: *He gave me a sermon about my rudeness.*

ser·mon (sûr′mən) ▫*noun, plural* **sermons**

serpent *noun* A snake.

ser·pent (sûr′pənt) ▫*noun, plural* **serpents**

serum *noun* The clear, yellowish liquid that remains after blood clots, contains antibodies, and can be used to cure or prevent diseases in human beings.

se·rum (sîr′əm) ▫*noun, plural* **serums**

servant *noun* **1.** Someone hired to do household work. **2.** Someone employed to perform services, as for a government: *Policemen and senators are public servants.*

ser·vant (sûr′vənt) ▫*noun, plural* **servants**

serve *verb* **1.** To be a servant: *She served as a cook in his father's family.* **2.** To work to help: *The President serves the people.* **3.** To spend time, as in fulfilling an obligation: *He served five years in the navy.* **4.** To act in a particular capacity: *She served as treasurer.* **5.** To place food or drink before; wait on: *She served me a hot breakfast.* **6.** To be sufficient for: *This cake will serve 12.* **7.** To be of use; function: *The den serves as a spare bedroom.* **8.** To put a ball or shuttlecock into play, as in tennis or badminton.

▫*noun* The act of serving in a game.

serve (sûrv) ▫*verb* **served, serving, serves** ▫*noun, plural* **serves**

serve

service *noun* **1.** The act or work of serving or being a servant: *She spent years in the service of a wealthy family.* **2.** The manner of providing food or filling customers' demands: *a restaurant with quick service.* **3.** A set of dishes or utensils: *a silver tea service.* **4.** A branch of the government and its employees: *the diplomatic service.* **5.** The armed forces of a nation. **6.** A facility that supplies the needs of the public or maintains something: *train service; mail service.* **7.** A religious ceremony: *a church service.* ▫*verb* To repair or maintain: *He drove to the gas station to have his truck serviced.*

serv·ice (sûr′vis) ▫*noun, plural* **services** ▫*verb* **serviced, servicing, services**

serviceman *noun* A member of the armed services.

ser·vice·man (sûr′vis man′) ▫*noun, plural* **ser·vice·men** (sûr′vis men′)

session *noun* **1.** A meeting: *The committee held a session to discuss the proposed bill.* **2.** A series of meetings: *The Senate was in session.* **3.** The period during which meetings or classes take place: *She attended the evening session of college.*

ses·sion (sesh′ən) ▫*noun, plural* **sessions**

set[1] *verb* **1.** To put; place: *She set the vase on the counter.* **2.** To become or cause to become hard or firm: *Allow 24 hours for the glue to set.* **3.** To put into a particular condition: *The police set him free. The book set me thinking.* **4.** To place in position or condition for use: *He set his alarm clock.* **5.** To establish; fix: *The athlete set a new world record.* **6.** To start: *Let's set to work.* **7.** To disappear below the horizon: *The sun sets early in the winter.* ▫*adjective* **1.** Not willing to change: *set in his ways.* **2.** Fixed by custom or agreement: *a set time for dinner.* **3.** Ready: *Are you set to leave?*

set (set) ▫*verb* **set, setting, sets** ▫*adjective*

set[2] *noun* **1.** A group of things of the same kind that belong and are used together: *a set of golf clubs.* **2.** The parts that make up an electronic device, such as a radio or television receiver: *a stereo set.* **3.** The scenery, furniture, and other objects on the stage for a play, show, or movie.

set (set) ▫*noun, plural* **sets**

setter *noun* A dog that has long, silky hair and is used for hunting.

set·ter (set′ər) ▫*noun, plural* **setters**

settle *verb* **1.** To fix by agreement: *Let's settle on a time for the meeting.* **2.** To come or cause to come to rest: *The bird settled on the branch. She settled herself on the couch.* **3.** To make a home: *The family settled in the city.* **4.** To come to rest at the bottom; sink: *The tea leaves settled in the pot.* **5.** To calm: *The music settled his nerves.*

set·tle (set′əl) ▫*verb* **settled, settling, settles**

settlement *noun* **1.** The act of settling or condition of being settled. **2.** A small community; village: *a farm settlement in the hills.* **3.** A colony: *a former British settlement in Asia.*
set·tle·ment (sĕt′əl mənt) □*noun, plural* **settlements**

settler *noun* Someone who settles in a new region; colonist.
set·tler (sĕt′lər) □*noun, plural* **settlers**

seven *noun* A number equal to the sum of 6 + 1; 7.
□*adjective* Being one more than six.
sev·en (sĕv′ən) □*noun, plural* **sevens** □*adjective*

seventeen *noun* A number equal to the sum of 10 + 7; 17.
□*adjective* Being one more than sixteen.
sev·en·teen (sĕv′ən tēn′) □*noun, plural* **seventeens** □*adjective*

seventeenth *noun* **1.** In a group of people or things that are in numbered order, the one that matches the number seventeen. **2.** One of seventeen equal parts, written 1/17.
□*adjective* Coming after the sixteenth.
sev·en·teenth (sĕv′ən tēnth′) □*noun, plural* **seventeenths** □*adjective*

seventh *noun* **1.** In a group of people or things that are in numbered order, the one that matches the number seven. **2.** One of seven equal parts, written 1/7.
□*adjective* Coming after the sixth.
sev·enth (sĕv′ənth) □*noun, plural* **sevenths** □*adjective*

seventieth *noun* **1.** In a group of people or things that are in numbered order, the one that matches the number seventy. **2.** One of seventy equal parts, written 1/70.
□*adjective* Coming after the sixty-ninth.
sev·en·ti·eth (sĕv′ən tē ith) □*noun, plural* **seventieths** □*adjective*

seventy *noun* A number equal to the product of 7 × 10; 70.
□*adjective* Being ten more than sixty.
sev·en·ty (sĕv′ən tē) □*noun, plural* **seventies** □*adjective*

several *adjective* More than two or three but not many: *I bought several books.*
□*noun* Several people or things: *Several of her friends came to visit.*
sev·er·al (sĕv′ər əl) □*adjective* □*noun*

severe *adjective* **1.** Strict; harsh: *a severe punishment.* **2.** Causing great pain or distress: *a severe injury.* **3.** Causing hardship: *a severe*

cold spell.
se·vere (sə vîr′) □*adjective*

sew *verb* **1.** To make, repair, or fasten with a needle and thread: *He sewed a button on his jacket.* **2.** To work with a needle and thread: *She likes to sew and knit.*
sew (sō) □*verb* **sewed, sewn** or **sewed, sewing, sews**

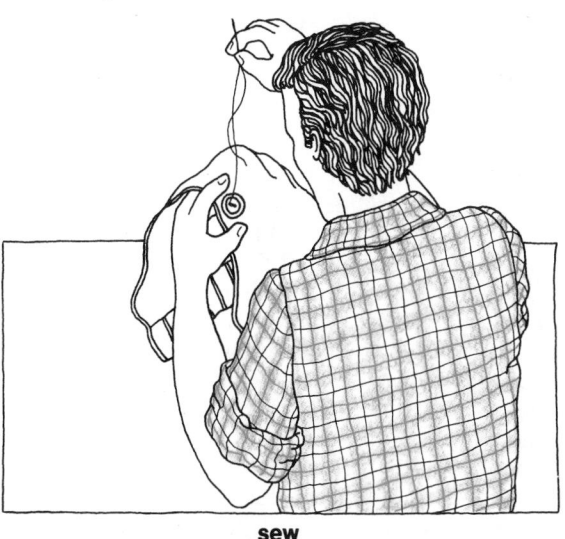
sew

sewage *noun* Waste matter that is carried off in drains or sewers.
sew·age (sōō′ij) □*noun*

sewer *noun* A pipe or channel, usually underground, for carrying off waste matter.
sew·er (sōō′ər) □*noun, plural* **sewers**

sewing machine *noun* A machine for sewing.

sewn (sōn) *noun* A past participle of **sew:** *She has sewn three dresses.*

sex *noun* **1.** Either of the two groups, male and female, into which living things are divided. **2.** The fact of being male or female.
sex (sĕks) □*noun, plural* **sexes**

shabby *adjective* Very worn and faded: *a shabby old dress.*
shab·by (shăb′ē) □*adjective* **shabbier, shabbiest**

a	bat	ī	bite	ōō	tool	*th*	feather
ā	make	î	fierce	ou	out	th	bath
â	dare	o	dot	u	nut	hw	wheat
ä	father	ō	no	û	turn	zh	measure
e	net	ô	law, for	ch	church	ə	about, open
ē	be	oi	soil	ng	ring		pencil, atom
i	dip	oo	look	sh	shade		circus

shack *noun* A small, roughly built hut or cabin.
shack (shak) □*noun, plural* **shacks**

WORD HISTORY: **shack**

Shack comes from a word in the language of an American Indian people of Mexico. The Indian word means ''adobe'' or ''clay hut.''

---

shad *noun* A food fish that swims from ocean waters up rivers and streams to lay eggs.
shad (shad) □*noun, plural* **shad** or **shads**

shade *noun* **1.** An area that is partly dark: *We sat in the shade of the elm tree.* **2.** A device that blocks off or reduces light: *a window shade.* **3.** The degree of light or dark in a color: *Lavender is a shade of purple.* **4.** A small amount; bit: *She spoke a shade too loud.*
□*verb* **1.** To keep light or heat from: *Trees shaded the house.* **2.** To mark with different degrees of dark and light: *The artist shaded the figures in the drawing.*
shade (shād) □*noun, plural* **shades** □*verb* **shaded, shading, shades**

shadow *noun* **1.** An outline or image cast by an object blocking rays of light: *I saw my shadow on the sidewalk.* **2.** An area of partial dark; shade: *The porch was already in shadow.* **3.** A small amount; trace: *He is guilty beyond the shadow of the doubt.*
□*verb* To follow after, especially in secret: *The detective shadowed the suspect.*
shad·ow (shad′ō) □*noun, plural* **shadows** □*verb* **shadowed, shadowing, shadows**

shadow

shady *adjective* **1.** Full of or providing shade: *a shady garden; a shady tree.* **2.** Not honest or upright: *a shady business deal.*
shad·y (shā′dē) □*adjective* **shadier, shadiest**

shaft *noun* **1.** The long, narrow body of a spear or arrow. **2.** The handle of a tool or instrument, such as an ax or golf club. **3.** A bar that rotates or transmits power in a machine. **4.** A ray or beam of light: *Shafts of sunlight peeked through the trees.* **5.** The main section of a structure such as a column. **6.** A vertical opening or passage: *a mine shaft.*
shaft (shaft) □*noun, plural* **shafts**

shaggy *adjective* **1.** Having long, rough hair, wool, or fibers: *a shaggy dog; a shaggy blanket.* **2.** Thick and bushy: *a shaggy mustache.*
shag·gy (shag′ē) □*adjective* **shaggier, shaggiest**

shake *verb* **1.** To move up and down or back and forth: *The trees shook in the wind. Don't shake your head.* **2.** To tremble or cause to tremble; quiver: *He was shaking with fear. The earthquake shook the building.* **3.** To remove or scatter by shaking. **4.** To upset or weaken: *The experience had shaken her self-confidence.*
□*noun* An act of shaking: *a shake of her head.*
shake (shāk) □*verb* **shook, shaken, shaking, shakes** □*noun, plural* **shakes**

shaken *verb* The past participle of **shake.**
shak·en (shā′kən) □*verb*

shaky *adjective* **1.** Trembling; shaking: *shaky legs.* **2.** Not steady or firm: *a shaky old stool.*
shak·y (shā′kē) □*adjective* **shakier, shakiest**

shale *noun* A rock composed of thin layers of hardened mud, silt, or clay.
shale (shāl) □*noun*

shall *verb* **1.** Used to express the simple future: *When shall we see you again?* **2.** Used to express determination: *They shall never enter this house.*
shall (shal) □*verb*

shallow *adjective* Not deep: *a shallow pond.*
shal·low (shal′ō) □*adjective* **shallower, shallowest**

shame *noun* **1.** A painful feeling caused by having done something wrong: *He felt no shame at being caught stealing.* **2.** Disgrace or dishonor: *His crimes brought shame to his family.* **3.** Something that causes shame or regret: *It would be a shame to miss the concert.*
□*verb* To fill with shame.
shame (shām) □*noun* □*verb* **shamed, shaming, shames**

shameful *adjective* Causing or deserving shame; disgraceful: *shameful gossip.*
shame·ful (shām′fəl) □*adjective*

shampoo   *noun* A soap or detergent used to wash the hair and scalp.
☐*verb* To wash the hair and scalp.
sham·poo (sham po͞o′) ☐*noun, plural*
shampoos ☐*verb* **shampooed, shampooing, shampoos**

shamrock   *noun* A plant that has leaves with three small leaflets.
sham·rock (sham′rok′) ☐*noun, plural*
shamrocks

shan't   Contraction of "shall not."
shan't (shant)

shape   *noun* **1.** The outward form of something; outline: *rectangles and other shapes; the shape of a watermelon.* **2.** A form in which something may exist or appear: *a cream pitcher in the shape of a cow.* **3.** Condition: *My television set is in bad shape.*
☐*verb* **1.** To give a particular form to: *She shaped the butter into little balls.* **2.** To turn out; develop: *The business is shaping up well.*
shape (shāp) ☐*noun, plural* **shapes** ☐*verb* **shaped, shaping, shapes**

share   *verb* **1.** To have, do, or use with others: *We shared an apartment.* **2.** To divide and give out in portions: *The two friends shared a sandwich.* **3.** To have or take a part: *Will you share in the work?*
☐*noun* **1.** A part or portion for one person: *I paid my share of the bill.* **2.** One of the equal parts into which the ownership of a business is divided: *500 shares of stock.*
share (shâr) ☐*verb* **shared, sharing, shares** ☐*noun, plural* **shares**

share

shark   *noun* Any of several large ocean fish with sharp teeth and tough skin.
shark (shärk) ☐*noun, plural* **sharks**

shark
Above: hammerhead
Below: great white

sharp   *adjective* **1.** Having a thin edge or a fine point: *a sharp blade; a sharp pencil.* **2.** Abrupt or sudden; not gradual: *a sharp drop in prices.* **3.** Clear; distinct: *a lens in sharp focus.* **4.** Ending in an edge or point: *a sharp nose.* **5.** Harsh and biting; severe: *sharp words; a sharp pain.* **6.** Having or showing the ability to see, hear, notice, perceive, or understand quickly: *sharp ears; a sharp mind.*
☐*adverb* **1.** Exactly: *Come at two o'clock sharp.* **2.** In an alert manner: *Look sharp!*
☐*noun* **1.** A musical tone or note that is a half step higher than the note named. **2.** A symbol (♯) that indicates that a note is a sharp.
sharp (shärp) ☐*adjective* **sharper, sharpest** ☐*adverb* ☐*noun, plural* **sharps**

SYNONYMS: **sharp, keen**

These adjectives mean having a fine edge or point: *a sharp pencil; a keen knife.* These adjectives also mean having or showing great perception: *She has a sharp mind. Dogs have a keen sense of smell.*

---

sharpen   *verb* To make or become sharp or sharper: *I sharpened the knife.*
sharp·en (shär′pən) ☐*verb* **sharpened, sharpening, sharpens**

shatter   *verb* To break into many pieces: *The headlights of the car shattered in the crash.*

a	bat	ī	bite	o͞o	tool	*th*	feather
ā	make	î	fierce	ou	out	th	bath
â	dare	o	dot	u	nut	hw	wheat
ä	father	ō	no	û	turn	zh	measure
e	net	ô	law, for	ch	church	ə	about, open
ē	be	oi	soil	ng	ring		pencil, atom
i	dip	oo	look	sh	shade		circus

shat·ter (shat′ər) □*verb* **shattered, shattering, shatters**

shave *verb* **1.** To remove the beard or hair from, especially with a razor. **2.** To cut thin slices from: *The carpenter shaved the edge of the board.*
□*noun* The act of shaving: *a smooth shave.*
shave (shāv) □*verb* **shaved, shaved** or **shaven, shaving, shaves** □*noun, plural* **shaves**

shaving *noun* A thin strip or slice that has been removed by a cutting tool: *steel shavings.*
shav·ing (shā′ving) □*noun, plural* **shavings**

shawl *noun* A piece of cloth worn around the shoulders, head, or neck.
shawl (shôl) □*noun, plural* **shawls**

shawl

she *pronoun* The female referred to or mentioned earlier: *Although my sister is older than I am, she is an inch shorter.*
she (shē) □*pronoun*

shear *verb* **1.** To remove the wool or hair from with scissors or shears: *He sheared the sheep.* **2.** To slice sharply: *The fence post was sheared off at the ground.*
shear (shîr) □*verb* **sheared, sheared** or **shorn, shearing, shears**

shears *plural noun* A tool for cutting that looks like scissors but is larger.
shears (shîrz) □*plural noun*

shed¹ *verb* **1.** To lose by a natural process; throw off: *Some trees shed their leaves. Snakes shed their skins.* **2.** To let fall: *shed tears.* **3.** To send forth: *The lamp did not shed much light.*
shed (shed) □*verb* **shed, shedding, sheds**

shed² *noun* A building for storage or shelter: *a tool shed.*
shed (shed) □*noun, plural* **sheds**

she'd Contraction of "she had" or "she would."
she'd (shēd)

sheep *noun* An animal with hoofs and a thick coat, raised for its wool and meat.
sheep (shēp) □*noun, plural* **sheep**

sheer *adjective* **1.** Thin, fine, and transparent: *a sheer silk dress.* **2.** Absolute; complete: *sheer pleasure; sheer exhaustion.* **3.** Very steep: *a sheer mountain slope.*
sheer (shîr) □*adjective* **sheerer, sheerest**

sheet *noun* **1.** A large piece of cloth, such as that used on a bed. **2.** A broad, thin piece of material: *a sheet of paper; a sheet of linoleum.* **3.** A broad surface; expanse: *a sheet of ice on the sidewalk.*
sheet (shēt) □*noun, plural* **sheets**

shelf *noun* **1.** A flat piece, as of wood, metal, or glass, attached to a wall or built into furniture for holding and storing things. **2.** Something that resembles a shelf, such as a rock ledge.
shelf (shelf) □*noun, plural* **shelves**

shell *noun* **1.** The hard outer covering of an animal, such as a scallop, turtle, or beetle. **2.** The hard outer covering of an egg or a nut. **3.** Something like a shell: *a pastry shell.* **4.** A case that contains the explosives and the shot to be fired from a gun or cannon.
□*verb* **1.** To remove the shell from: *shell walnuts.* **2.** To fire shells at; bombard: *The soldiers shelled the enemy fort.*
shell (shel) □*noun, plural* **shells** □*verb* **shelled, shelling, shells**

she'll Contraction of "she will" or "she shall."
she'll (shēl)

shellac *noun* A thin liquid varnish used to give a hard, clear finish, especially to wood.
□*verb* To apply shellac to.
shel·lac (shə lak′) □*noun* □*verb* **shellacked, shellacking, shellacs**

shellfish *noun* A water animal that has a shell or an outer covering that is like a shell. Clams and lobsters are shellfish.
shell·fish (shel′fish′) □*noun, plural* **shellfish** or **shellfishes**

shelter *noun* Something that protects or covers: *The cave was their shelter during the storm.*
□*verb* To provide shelter for: *The tree sheltered us from the rain.*
shel·ter (shel′tər) □*noun, plural* **shelters** □*verb* **sheltered, sheltering, shelters**

shelves   *noun* The plural of **shelf.**
shelves (shelvz) □*noun*

shepherd   *noun* Someone who takes care of a flock of sheep.
shep·herd (shep′ərd) □*noun, plural* **shepherds**

sherbet   *noun* A frozen dessert made of fruit juice, milk, sugar, and egg whites or gelatin.
sher·bet (shûr′bit) □*noun, plural* **sherbets**

sheriff   *noun* A county official who is in charge of enforcing the law.
sher·iff (sher′if) □*noun, plural* **sheriffs**

WORD HISTORY: **sheriff**

Sheriff comes from an old English word that means "officer of the county." A sheriff was originally the chief representative of the king in each of the English counties.

---

she's   Contraction of "she is" or "she has."
she's (shēz)

shield   *noun* **1.** A piece of armor carried on the arm to turn aside an enemy's blows. **2.** Something shaped like a shield: *a police officer's shield.* **3.** Something that protects: *She used her hand as a shield against the glare.*
□*verb* To protect with or as if with a shield: *The awning shielded us from the sun.*
shield (shēld) □*noun, plural* **shields** □*verb* **shielded, shielding, shields**

shield

shier   *adjective* A comparative of **shy.**
shi·er (shī′ər) □*adjective*

shiest   *adjective* A superlative of **shy.**
shi·est (shī′ist) □*adjective*

shift   *verb* **1.** To move from one place, position, or person to another: *He tried to shift the blame to me. She shifted around in her chair.* **2.** To change gears in an automobile.
□*noun* **1.** A change in place, position, or direction: *a shift in opinion; a shift in the wind.* **2.** A group of workers who work together during the same hours: *Four shifts keep the factory running.*
shift (shift) □*verb* **shifted, shifting, shifts** □*noun, plural* **shifts**

shilling   *noun* A former British coin worth one twentieth of a pound.
shil·ling (shil′ing) □*noun, plural* **shillings**

shimmer   *verb* To shine with a flickering light; gleam: *The pond shimmered in the evening light.*
shim·mer (shim′ər) □*verb* **shimmered, shimmering, shimmers**

shin   *noun* The front part of the leg between the knee and the ankle.
□*verb* To climb by gripping and pulling with the hands and legs: *He shinned up the pole.*
shin (shin) □*noun, plural* **shins** □*verb* **shinned, shinning, shins**

shine   *verb* **1.** To give off or reflect light: *The sun is shining.* **2.** To be bright; glisten: *Her eyes shone with pleasure.* **3.** To make glossy by polishing: *He shined his boots.* **4.** To do very well; excel: *She shines in history.* —See Synonyms at **blaze.**
□*noun* **1.** Light that is given off or reflected: *the shine of new pennies.* **2.** Polish: *She gave her shoes a quick shine.*
shine (shīn) □*verb* **shone** (or **shined** *for verb sense 3*), **shining, shines** □*noun, plural* **shines**

shingle   *noun* A thin piece of material that is laid in rows that overlap to cover the roof or sides of a building.
□*verb* To cover with shingles.
shin·gle (shing′gəl) □*noun, plural* **shingles** □*verb* **shingled, shingling, shingles**

shiny   *adjective* Reflecting light; bright: *a shiny yellow car.*
shin·y (shī′nē) □*adjective* **shinier, shiniest**

a	bat	ī	bite	ōō	tool	th	feather
ā	make	î	fierce	ou	out	th	bath
â	dare	o	dot	u	nut	hw	wheat
ä	father	ō	no	û	turn	zh	measure
e	net	ô	law, for	ch	church	ə	about, open
ē	be	oi	soil	ng	ring		pencil, atom
i	dip	oo	look	sh	shade		circus

ship *noun* **1.** A large boat. **2.** An airplane, airship, or spacecraft.
□*verb* **1.** To cause to be transported; send: *The factory ships its products by rail.* **2.** To take a job as part of a ship's crew: *He shipped as an ordinary sailor.*
ship (ship) □*noun, plural* **ships** □*verb* **shipped, shipping, ships**

-ship A suffix that forms nouns and means "the condition or quality of": *kinship; partnership; relationship.*

shipment *noun* **1.** The act of shipping: *The crates are ready for shipment.* **2.** The goods shipped at one time: *We received a new shipment of supplies.*
ship·ment (ship′mənt) □*noun, plural* **shipments**

shipping *noun* **1.** The act or business of transporting goods, as by ship or train. **2.** The ships that belong to one country, port, or industry: *enemy shipping.*
ship·ping (ship′ing) □*noun*

shipwreck *noun* **1.** The destruction or loss of a ship, such as by storm or collision. **2.** A wrecked ship.
□*verb* To cause to undergo shipwreck.
ship·wreck (ship′rek′) □*noun, plural* **shipwrecks** □*verb* **shipwrecked, shipwrecking, shipwrecks**

shipwreck

shipyard *noun* A place where ships are built or repaired.
ship·yard (ship′yärd′) □*noun, plural* **shipyards**

shirt *noun* A piece of clothing for the upper part of the body, usually having a collar, sleeves, and an opening in front.
shirt (shûrt) □*noun, plural* **shirts**

shiver *verb* To shake, as from cold; tremble.
□*noun* An act of shivering.
shiv·er (shiv′ər) □*verb* **shivered, shivering, shivers** □*noun, plural* **shivers**

shoal *noun* A shallow place in a river or other body of water.
shoal (shōl) □*noun, plural* **shoals**

shock¹ *noun* **1.** A heavy blow or impact: *The shock of the earthquake could be felt for miles.* **2.** A sudden, severe disturbance of the mind or emotions: *He couldn't get over the shock of his defeat.* **3.** The effect caused by the passage of an electric current through the body. **4.** A state in which the blood pressure falls suddenly and dangerously as a result of severe physical injury.
□*verb* To cause a feeling of surprise, horror, or disturbance in: *The murder shocked us all.*
shock (shok) □*noun, plural* **shocks** □*verb* **shocked, shocking, shocks**

shock² *noun* A pile of grain sheaves stacked on end in a field and left to dry.
shock (shok) □*noun, plural* **shocks**

shock

shocking *adjective* Causing surprise, horror, or disturbance: *a shocking accident.*
shock·ing (shok′ing) □*adjective*

shoe *noun* An outer covering for the human foot, usually having a rigid sole and heel.
shoe (shoo) □*noun, plural* **shoes**

shone *verb* A past tense and past participle of **shine:** *The stars shone overhead.*
shone (shōn) □*verb*

shook *verb* The past tense of **shake:** *He shook the rain from his coat.*
shook (shook) □*verb*

shoot *verb* **1.** To hit, wound, or kill with a missile fired from a weapon: *He thinks it is wrong to shoot animals for food.* **2.** To fire from a weapon: *shoot an arrow at a target.* **3.** To send or be sent forth with force: *We shot a satellite into space.* **4.** To move or cause to move quickly: *The ball shot through the air.* **5.** To begin to grow rapidly: *The weeds shot up overnight.* **6.** To put on film: *They shot the movie in Boston.*
□*noun* A plant or part of a plant, such as a stem, that has just begun to grow.

shoot (sho͞ot) □*verb* **shot, shooting, shoots**
□*noun, plural* **shoots**

shooting star   *noun* A meteor that is visible for a short time.

shop   *noun* **1.** A place where goods are sold; store: *a dress shop.* **2.** A place where a particular kind of work is done: *a beauty shop.*
□*verb* To go to stores to look at or buy goods: *I shop every Saturday.*
shop (shop) □*noun, plural* **shops** □*verb* **shopped, shopping, shops**

shore   *noun* The land along the edge of an ocean or other body of water.
shore (shôr) □*noun, plural* **shores**

shore

shorn   *verb* A past participle of **shear.**
shorn (shôrn) □*verb*

short   *adjective* **1.** Not long: *short hair.* **2.** Not tall: *a short man.* **3.** Covering only a small distance: *a short flight.* **4.** Brief in time: *a short vacation.* **5.** Having less than enough: *I'm short of cash this month.* **6.** Of or having the vowel sounds of the *a* in *pat,* the *e* in *pet,* the *i* in *pin,* the *o* in *pot,* or the *u* in *cut.*
□*adverb* Suddenly: *The bus stopped short.*
□*noun* **shorts 1.** Pants ending at or above the knee. **2.** Men's underpants.
short (shôrt) □*adjective* **shorter, shortest**
□*adverb* □*noun*

shortage   *noun* A lack in the amount needed; deficiency: *a shortage of oil.*
short·age (shôr′ tij) □*noun, plural* **shortages**

short circuit   *noun* An electric circuit formed by accident, as when the insulation wears off wires that touch each other.

short cut   *noun* A way that is shorter or easier.

shorten   *verb* To make or become short or shorter: *shorten a skirt; days shortening in the winter.*
short·en (shôr′ tən) □*verb* **shortened, shortening, shortens**

shortening   *noun* A fat, such as butter or lard, used in cooking.
short·en·ing (shôr′ tən ing) □*noun*

shorthand   *noun* A method of rapid writing that uses symbols for letters and words.
short·hand (shôrt′ hand′) □*noun*

shortly   *adverb* In a short time; soon: *I'll be back shortly.*
short·ly (shôrt′ lē) □*adverb*

shortstop   *noun* A baseball player whose position is between second and third base.
short·stop (shôrt′ stop′) □*noun, plural* **shortstops**

shot[1]   *noun* **1.** The firing of a weapon, such as a gun or cannon: *We heard two shots.* **2.** A bullet or pellet, as for a gun. **3.** The launching of a spacecraft, such as a rocket: *a moon shot.* **4.** The distance over which something can be shot: *within rifle shot.* **5.** An attempt to reach a goal: *He took three shots at the basket before he scored.* **6.** Someone who shoots a weapon: *He's not a very good shot.* **7.** An injection of medicine: *a flu shot.*
shot (shot) □*noun, plural* **shots** or **shot** (*for noun sense 2*).

shot[2]   *verb* The past tense and past participle of **shoot.**
shot (shot) □*verb*

should   *verb* **1.** Ought to: *You should write her a note.* **2.** Used to indicate that something may or may not happen: *If she should call, tell her that I'll be right back.*
should (sho͝od) □*verb*

shoulder   *noun* **1.** The part of the human body between the neck and the upper arm. **2.** The part of a garment that covers the shoulder. **3.** An edge along a road or highway: *We stopped on the shoulder to look at our map.*
□*verb* To push with shoulders: *He shouldered me aside.*
shoul·der (shōl′ dər) □*noun, plural* **shoulders** □*verb* **shouldered, shouldering, shoulders**

shouldn't   Contraction of "should not."
should·n't (sho͝od′ ənt)

a bat	ī bite	o͞o tool	th feather
ā make	î fierce	ou out	th bath
â dare	o dot	u nut	hw wheat
ä father	ō no	û turn	zh measure
e net	ô law, for	ch church	ə about, open
ē be	oi soil	ng ring	pencil, atom
i dip	oo look	sh shade	circus

shout   *verb* To cry out in a loud voice; yell: *I had to shout to get her attention.*
□*noun* A loud cry; yell.
shout (shout) □*verb* **shouted, shouting, shouts** □*noun, plural* **shouts**

shove   *verb* To push with force: *I shoved the suitcase under the bed.*
□*noun* A strong push.
shove (shuv) □*verb* **shoved, shoving, shoves** □*noun, plural* **shoves**

shovel   *noun* A tool with a long handle and a broad scoop used for digging or lifting.
□*verb* **1.** To dig, move, or remove with a shovel: *shovel a path through the snow.* **2.** To move or throw in a hasty way: *Don't shovel food into your mouth.*
shov·el (shuv'əl) □*noun, plural* **shovels** □*verb* **shoveled, shoveling, shovels**

shovel

show   *verb* **1.** To put in sight; display: *Show me your new car.* **2.** To be visible: *The run in my stocking shows.* **3.** To reveal or become revealed: *He showed that he was a fool.* **4.** To point out to: *Will you show him where my office is?* **5.** To instruct; teach: *She showed me how to type.* **6.** To grant; give: *show pity.*
□*noun* **1.** A public exhibition or display: *a boat show.* **2.** An entertainment program, such as on television or radio. **3.** A false appearance: *put on a show of kindness.*
show (shō) □*verb* **showed, showed** or **shown, showing, shows** □*noun, plural* **shows**

SYNONYMS: **show, display**

These verbs mean to reveal or make clear: *She showed good sense by driving slowly in the rain. He displayed his great talent at an early age.*

---

shower   *noun* **1.** A short fall of rain. **2.** Something that falls like a shower: *A shower of*

leaves fell from the trees. **3.** A bath in which water is sprayed down on a person.
□*verb* **1.** To fall or cause to fall in or as if in a shower: *The guests showered confetti on the young couple.* **2.** To give in large amounts: *My friends showered me with gifts.* **3.** To take a shower bath.
show·er (shou'ər) □*noun, plural* **showers** □*verb* **showered, showering, showers**

shown   *verb* A past participle of **show.**
shown (shōn) □*verb*

shrank   *verb* A past tense of **shrink.**
shrank (shrangk) □*verb*

shred   *noun* **1.** A narrow strip or small piece torn or cut off: *She ripped the letter to shreds.* **2.** A small amount; bit: *There isn't a shred of truth to that story.*
□*verb* To cut or tear into shreds.
shred (shred) □*noun, plural* **shreds** □*verb* **shredded, shredding, shreds**

shrew   *noun* A small animal that looks like a mouse and has a narrow, pointed snout.
shrew (shrōō) □*noun, plural* **shrews**

shrew

shrewd   *adjective* Clever and practical: *a shrewd lawyer.*
shrewd (shrōōd) □*adjective* **shrewder, shrewdest**

shriek   *noun* A loud, shrill cry: *She gave a shriek of horror.*
□*verb* To make a loud, shrill cry.
shriek (shrēk) □*noun, plural* **shrieks** □*verb* **shrieked, shrieking, shrieks**

shrill   *adjective* Having a high, sharp sound: *a shrill voice.*
shrill (shril) □*adjective* **shriller, shrillest**

shrimp   *noun* A small animal with a thin shell that lives in salt water and is used for food.
shrimp (shrimp) □*noun, plural* **shrimp** or **shrimps**

shrine   *noun* A holy place for worship, such as the tomb of a saint.
shrine (shrīn) □*noun, plural* **shrines**

shrink   *verb* **1.** To make or become smaller: *Hot water shrinks some fabrics. His shirt shrank after it was washed.* **2.** To draw back, as in fear: *The child shrank into her arms for protection.*

shrink (shringk) □*verb* **shrank** or **shrunk, shrunk** or **shrunken, shrinking, shrinks**

shrub *noun* A woody plant that is smaller than a tree and usually has, several separate stems rather than a single trunk.
shrub (shrub) □*noun, plural* **shrubs**

shrug *verb* To raise the shoulders to show doubt, dislike, or lack of interest: *He just shrugged when we asked him to help.*
□*noun* The act or gesture of shrugging.
shrug (shrug) □*verb* **shrugged, shrugging, shrugs** □*noun, plural* **shrugs**

shrug

shrunk *verb* A past tense and past participle of **shrink**: *The blanket shrunk.*
shrunk (shrungk) □*verb*

shrunken *verb* A past participle of **shrink**.
shrunk·en (shrung′kən) □*verb*

shudder *verb* To shiver suddenly from fear or cold: *He shuddered at the sight of snakes.*
□*noun* The act of shuddering.
shud·der (shud′ər) □*verb* **shuddered, shuddering, shudders** □*noun, plural* **shudders**

shuffle *verb* **1.** To drag the feet along the ground in walking: *The old man shuffled down the street.* **2.** To mix playing cards to change their order. **3.** To move from one place to another: *She shuffled the papers around her desk looking for her homework.*
□*noun* The act of shuffling.
shuf·fle (shuf′əl) □*verb* **shuffled, shuffling, shuffles** □*noun, plural* **shuffles**

shut *verb* **1.** To move or cause to move to a closed position: *Her eyes shut. Shut the door.* **2.** To block passage or access to: *The heavy drifts of snow shut off the town.* **3.** To put or keep in a place by or as if by shutting: *We shut him up in his room.*
shut (shut) □*verb* **shut, shutting, shuts**

shutter *noun* **1.** A movable cover for a window or door. **2.** A cover over a camera lens that lets in light when a picture is taken.
shut·ter (shut′ər) □*noun, plural* **shutters**

shuttle *noun* **1.** A device used in weaving that carries a thread from side to side over and under the threads on the loom. **2.** A device on a sewing machine that carries the lower thread back and forth through loops in the upper thread to form a stitch. **3.** A vehicle, such as a train or an airplane, that travels back and forth between two places.
shut·tle (shut′əl) □*noun, plural* **shuttles**

shuttlecock *noun* A small feathered ball used in badminton.
shut·tle·cock (shut′əl kok′) □*noun, plural* **shuttlecocks**

shy *adjective* **1.** Feeling uncomfortable around other people; bashful: *The shy child avoided parties.* **2.** Easily frightened; timid.
□*verb* To move back suddenly in fright: *The horse shied when it heard the sound of an automobile horn.*
shy (shī) □*adjective* **shier** or **shyer, shiest** or **shyest** □*verb* **shied, shying, shies**

sick *adjective* **1.** Suffering from disease or illness; not well. **2.** Having had too much of something; tired: *I'm sick of listening to your complaints.*
sick (sik) □*adjective* **sicker, sickest**

sicken *verb* To make or become sick: *The fumes sickened her.*
sick·en (sik′ən) □*verb* **sickened, sickening, sickens**

sickle *noun* A tool with a large curved blade and a short handle, used for cutting grain or tall grass.
sick·le (sik′əl) □*noun, plural* **sickles**

sickly *adjective* Often sick; frail: *a sickly girl.*
sick·ly (sik′lē) □*adjective* **sicklier, sickliest**

sickness *noun* Poor health; illness.
sick·ness (sik′nis) □*noun, plural* **sicknesses**

side *noun* **1.** A line or surface that forms the boundary of or encloses something: *A triangle has three sides.* **2.** A surface of an object, espe-

a bat	ī bite	o͞o tool	*th* feather
ā make	î fierce	ou out	th bath
â dare	o dot	u nut	hw wheat
ä father	ō no	û turn	zh measure
e net	ô law, for	ch church	ə about, open
ē be	oi soil	ng ring	pencil, atom
i dip	oo look	sh shade	circus

cially one that connects the top and bottom: *the side of a barn.* **3.** One of the two surfaces of a flat object: *the other side of a record; the wrong side of the fabric.* **4.** The right or left half of the trunk of a human or animal body: *I slept on my side.* **5.** A place, position, or direction to the right or left of a center: *Our house is on this side of the street.* **6.** One of two or more teams, groups, or persons: *He was on our side.* **7.** An opposing view, idea, or opinion: *Tell me your side of the story.*
□*verb* To take a particular side: *He sided against his brother in the dispute.*
□*adjective* **1.** Of, having to do with, or located at the side: *a side door.* **2.** Not as important; secondary: *a side trip.*
side (sīd) □*noun, plural* **sides** □*verb* **sided, siding, sides** □*adjective*

sideshow *noun* A small show offered in addition to a main attraction: *The sideshows at the circus are always fun.*
side·show (sīd′shō′) □*noun, plural* **sideshows**

sidewalk *noun* A usually paved path along the side of a road where people can walk.
side·walk (sīd′wôk′) □*noun, plural* **sidewalks**

sideways *adverb* **1.** To or from one side: *I looked at her sideways.* **2.** With one side forward: *I stood sideways.*
□*adjective* Toward or from one side: *a sideways look.*
side·ways (sīd′wāz) □*adverb* □*adjective*

siege *noun* The surrounding of an enemy position in order to cut off its supplies and force its surrender.
siege (sēj) □*noun, plural* **sieges**

siesta *noun* An afternoon rest or nap.
si·es·ta (sē es′tə) □*noun, plural* **siestas**

WORD HISTORY: **siesta**

The word *siesta* was borrowed from Spanish. The Spanish word comes from a Latin word meaning "sixth" that was used to refer to the sixth hour after sunrise, or about noon. This is the hottest part of the day, and people living in warm climates like that of Spain would rest during that time until it was cool enough to go back to work.

---

sieve *noun* A utensil with a mesh screen for straining liquids or for separating the fine particles from the larger particles of a mixture.
sieve (siv) □*noun, plural* **sieves**

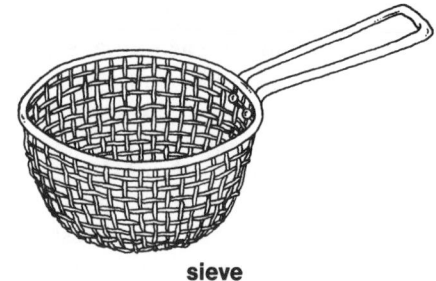
sieve

sift *verb* **1.** To pass through or as if through a sieve: *I sifted the sugar. The dust sifted in through the cracks in the window.* **2.** To separate by or as if by putting through a sieve: *She tried to sift out the important points from the article.* **3.** To examine closely: *We sifted the information carefully to find a clue that would help us.*
sift (sift) □*verb* **sifted, sifting, sifts**

sigh *verb* **1.** To let out a long, deep breath, often because one is sad or tired: *I sighed with relief.* **2.** To make a sound that is like sighing: *trees sighing in the wind.*
□*noun* The act or sound of sighing: *a sigh of regret.*
sigh (sī) □*verb* **sighed, sighing, sighs** □*noun, plural* **sighs**

sight *noun* **1.** The ability to see; eyesight: *He wore glasses to improve his sight.* **2.** The act of seeing: *I can't stand the sight of blood.* **3.** The distance that someone can see: *The enemy submarine stayed out of sight.* **4.** Something worth seeing: *I want to see the sights.* **5.** Something unpleasant, shocking, or odd to see: *My hair is a sight.* **6.** A device, as on a gun, that helps in aiming: *the sight on a telescope.*
□*verb* To see with the eye: *We sighted a plane in the distance.*
sight (sīt) □*noun, plural* **sights** □*verb* **sighted, sighting, sights**

sign *noun* **1.** Something that stands for something else: *The sign for addition is* +. **2.** A board or poster that gives information: *a stop sign.* **3.** Something that indicates what is to happen: *When birds fly south, it is a sign that winter is coming.* **4.** An action or gesture that expresses an idea, desire, command, or information: *His frown was a sign that he was angry.* **5.** Remaining evidence; trace: *She showed no sign of regret.*
□*verb* To write one's name on: *She signed the letter with her full name.*
sign (sīn) □*noun, plural* **signs** □*verb* **signed, signing, signs**

signal *noun* **1.** Something that informs, commands, or warns: *A yellow light is a signal for traffic to slow down.* **2.** A gesture, action, or word that causes an action to begin: *The referee raised his hand as a signal.*
□*verb* **1.** To make a signal to: *The conductor signaled the orchestra to begin playing.* **2.** To make known with a signal: *A bell signals the start of a school day.*
sig·nal (**sig′** nəl) □*noun, plural* **signals**
□*verb* **signaled, signaling, signals**

signal

signature *noun* **1.** The name of a person as written in his or her own handwriting. **2.** A sign at the beginning of each section of a piece of music indicating the key or the time.
sig·na·ture (**sig′** nə chər) □*noun, plural* **signatures**

significance *noun* Importance: *an invention of great significance.* **2.** Meaning: *He did not understand the significance of the word.*
sig·nif·i·cance (sig nif′ i kəns) □*noun*

significant *adjective* Having a meaning and especially a concealed meaning: *a significant glance.* **2.** Important: *a significant day in history.* —See Synonyms at **important.**
sig·nif·i·cant (sig nif′ i kənt) □*adjective*

silence *noun* The absence of sound or noise; total quiet: *There was silence in the empty house.*
□*verb* To cause to be silent: *The speaker silenced the crowd by raising his hands.*
si·lence (**sī′** ləns) □*noun, plural* **silences**
□*verb* **silenced, silencing, silences**

silent *adjective* **1.** Free from sound or noise; quiet: *an empty and silent classroom.* **2.** Saying nothing: *He remained silent while she chattered on.* **3.** Not pronounced: *The "k" in "knee" is silent.*
si·lent (**sī′** lənt) □*adjective*

silhouette *noun* **1.** A drawing or picture of the outline of something filled in with a dark color. **2.** A dark outline against a light back-

ground: *We saw the silhouette of a large ship against the night sky.*
□*verb* To show as a dark outline: *The light of the moon silhouetted the tree on the wall.*
sil·hou·ette (sil′ oo et′) □*noun, plural* **silhouettes** □*verb* **silhouetted, silhouetting, silhouettes**

silhouette

silk *noun* **1.** The fine, shiny fiber produced by a silkworm. **2.** Thread, yarn, or cloth made from silk. **3.** Something like silk, such as the strands that grow on an ear of corn.
silk (silk) □*noun, plural* **silks**

silkworm *noun* A caterpillar that spins a cocoon of strong silk.
silk·worm (**silk′** wûrm′) □*noun, plural* **silkworms**

sill *noun* A piece of wood or stone that forms the bottom of a door or window.
sill (sil) □*noun, plural* **sills**

silly *adjective* Lacking sense or reason; foolish: *a silly idea.*
sil·ly (**sil′** ē) □*adjective* **sillier, silliest**

silo *noun* A tall, round building in which food for farm animals is stored.
si·lo (**sī′** lō) □*noun, plural* **silos**

silt *noun* Very fine particles, such as of dirt or sand, that are often found at the bottom of a body of water.
silt (silt) □*noun*

silver *noun* **1.** A soft, shiny white metallic chemical element that is used to make money and jewelry. **2.** Coins made of silver: *I have a*

a	bat	ī	bite	o͞o	tool	*th*	feather
ā	make	î	fierce	ou	out	th	bath
â	dare	o	dot	u	nut	hw	wheat
ä	father	ō	no	û	turn	zh	measure
e	net	ô	law, for	ch	church	ə	about, open
ē	be	oi	soil	ng	ring		pencil, atom
i	dip	o͝o	look	sh	shade		circus

pocket full of silver. **3.** Silverware. **4.** A light, shiny, or metallic gray.
□*verb* To give a coat of silver.
□*adjective* **1.** Of the color silver: *a silver beard.* **2.** Made of or coated with silver: *a silver bowl.*
sil·ver (**sil′**vər) □*noun* □*verb* **silvered, silvering, silvers** □*adjective*

silversmith *noun* Someone who makes articles of silver.
sil·ver·smith (**sil′**vər smith′) □*noun, plural* **silversmiths**

silverware *noun* **1.** Articles, such as forks, knives, and spoons, made of or coated with silver. **2.** Metal forks, knives, and spoons.
sil·ver·ware (**sil′**vər wâr′) □*noun*

similar *adjective* Alike but not identical: *They wore similar dresses.*
sim·i·lar (**sim′**ə lər) □*adjective*

similarity *noun* The quality or condition of being similar; likeness: *There is a great similarity between bees and wasps.*
sim·i·lar·i·ty (sim′ə **lar′**i tē) □*noun, plural* **similarities**

simmer *verb* To cook below or just at the boiling point: *Simmer the chicken until it's tender.*
sim·mer (**sim′**ər) □*verb* **simmered, simmering, simmers**

simple *adjective* **1.** Easy to understand or do: *a simple problem.* **2.** Not fancy; plain: *a simple dress; simple food.* **3.** Sincere and natural: *She spoke to us in a simple and direct way.* —See Synonyms at **easy** and **plain.**
sim·ple (**sim′**pəl) □*adjective* **simpler, simplest**

simplify *verb* To make simple or simpler: *I simplified the story so that my youngest cousin could understand it.*
sim·pli·fy (**sim′**plə fī′) □*verb* **simplified, simplifying, simplifies**

simply *adverb* **1.** In a clear manner: *He gave his opinion simply and honestly.* **2.** Merely; only: *I went simply to have something to do.* **3.** In fact; really: *The meal was simply delicious.*
sim·ply (**sim′**plē) □*adverb*

simultaneously *adverb* At the same time: *The two sisters entered the room simultaneously.*
si·mul·ta·ne·ous·ly (sī′məl **tā′**nē əs lē) □*adverb*

sin *noun* **1.** The act of breaking a religious law. **2.** A wrong act: *It's a sin to lie.*
□*verb* To commit a sin.
sin (sin) □*noun, plural* **sins** □*verb* **sinned, sinning, sins**

since *adverb* **1.** From then until now: *I left and haven't gone back since.* **2.** Before now; ago: *long since forgotten.*
□*preposition* **1.** During the time after: *A lot has happened since our last meeting.* **2.** Continuously from a particular time in the past: *He has worked there since 1980.*
□*conjunction* **1.** After the time when: *It has been 20 years since he died.* **2.** Because: *Since you're not interested, we won't go.*
since (sins) □*adverb* □*preposition* □*conjunction*

sincere *adjective* Free from deceit; honest or genuine: *He made a sincere offer to help.*
sin·cere (sin **sîr′**) □*adjective* **sincerer, sincerest**

sinew *noun* A tendon.
sin·ew (**sin′**yo͞o) □*noun, plural* **sinews**

sing *verb* **1.** To make musical sounds with the voice: *The whole class sang together.* **2.** To produce musical sounds: *The birds in the forest are singing.* **3.** To make a high whine or hum: *The teakettle sang.*
sing (sing) □*verb* **sang** or **sung, sung, singing, sings**

singer *noun* A person that sings.
sing·er (**sing′**ər) □*noun, plural* **singers**

single *adjective* **1.** Not being with another; sole: *a single light in the window.* **2.** Used or intended to be used by one: *a single bed.* **3.** Not married: *a single person.*
□*noun* A hit in baseball that allows the batter to reach first base.
□*verb* **1.** To select from among others: *She singled out two workers for promotion.* **2.** To hit a single in baseball.
sin·gle (**sing′**gəl) □*adjective* □*noun, plural* **singles** □*verb* **singled, singling, singles**

SYNONYMS: **single, solitary**

These adjectives mean not being with another: *A single lamp lit the room with a soft glow. A solitary tree stood out against the sky.*

---

singular *adjective* Of, having to do with, or being a word form that indicates a single person or thing.
□*noun* A form of a word that shows or stands for a single person or thing: *"Army" is the singular of "armies."*

sin·gu·lar (sing′ gyə lər) ▢*adjective* ▢*noun,* *plural* **singulars**

sinister *adjective* **1.** Suggesting or threatening evil: *a sinister smile.* **2.** Evil: *sinister thoughts.*
sin·is·ter (sin′ i stər) ▢*adjective*

> **WORD HISTORY: sinister**
>
> *Sinister* is from a Latin word that originally meant "on the left." It came to mean unlucky because the left side was connected with bad luck and the right side with good luck.

sink *verb* **1.** To go or cause to go down beneath the surface of a liquid or soft substance: *Her feet sank into the deep snow. The ship sank during a severe storm.* **2.** To dig or drill in the ground: *They sank a well near the cabin.* **3.** To move to a lower level; fall: *She sank into her chair.* **4.** To move into a different state: *He sank into a deep sleep.* **5.** To become less or weaker: *a voice that sank to a faint whisper.* **6.** To go into; penetrate: *The melting snow sank into the ground.*
▢*noun* A basin that has a drain and faucets that supply water.
sink (singk) ▢*verb* **sank** or **sunk, sunk, sinking, sinks** ▢*noun, plural* **sinks**

sink

sip *verb* To drink little by little and in small quantities: *I sipped the lemonade through a straw.*
▢*noun* A small quantity taken by sipping: *a sip of tea.*
sip (sip) ▢*verb* **sipped, sipping, sips** ▢*noun, plural* **sips**

siphon *noun* A bent tube or pipe through which a liquid can be moved by air pressure out of a container into one at a lower level.
▢*verb* To move a liquid by means of a siphon.

si·phon (sī′ fən) ▢*noun, plural* **siphons** ▢*verb* **siphoned, siphoning, siphons**

siphon

sir *noun* **1.** A polite form of address used in place of a man's name. **2. Sir** A title of honor used before the name of a knight.
sir (sîr) ▢*noun, plural* **sirs**

siren *noun* A device that makes a loud penetrating sound as a signal or warning.
si·ren (sī′ rən) ▢*noun, plural* **sirens**

sister *noun* A girl or woman who has the same parents as another person.
sis·ter (sis′ tər) ▢*noun, plural* **sisters**

sisterhood *noun* **1.** A close feeling between sisters. **2.** A group of women who are united by a common purpose.
sis·ter·hood (sis′ tər hood′) ▢*noun*

sister-in-law *noun* **1.** The sister of one's husband or wife. **2.** The wife of one's brother.
sis·ter-in-law (sis′ tər in lô′) ▢*noun, plural* **sisters-in-law**

sit *verb* **1.** To rest with the weight of the body supported by the buttocks and not the feet: *She sat on a stool.* **2.** To cause to sit; seat: *We sat the guests at the table.* **3.** To rest on a perch, as a bird does. **4.** To cover eggs so that they will hatch, as a chicken or hen does.
sit (sit) ▢*verb* **sat, sitting, sits**

site *noun* The place where something is, was, or will be located: *a building site; a battle site.*
site (sīt) ▢*noun, plural* **sites**

situate *verb* To place in a certain position; locate: *They situated the pool next to the house.*

a bat	ī bite	ōō tool	*th* feather
ā make	î fierce	ou out	th bath
â dare	o dot	u nut	hw wheat
ä father	ō no	û turn	zh measure
e net	ô law, for	ch church	ə about, open
ē be	oi soil	ng ring	pencil, atom
i dip	oo look	sh shade	circus

sit·u·ate (sich′ōō āt′) □*verb* **situated, situating, situates**

situation *noun* A combination of circumstances at a particular time: *a difficult financial situation.*
sit·u·a·tion (sich′ōō ā′shən) □*noun, plural* **situations**

six *noun* A number equal to the sum of 5 + 1; 6.
□*adjective* Being one more than five.
six (siks) □*noun, plural* **sixes** □*adjective*

sixteen *noun* A number equal to the sum of 10 + 6; 16.
□*adjective* Being one more than fifteen.
six·teen (sik stēn′) □*noun, plural* **sixteens** □*adjective*

sixteenth *noun* **1.** In a group of people or things that are in numbered order, the one that matches the number sixteen. **2.** One of sixteen equal parts, written 1/16.
□*adjective* Coming after the fifteenth.
six·teenth (sik stēnth′) □*noun, plural* **sixteenths** □*adjective*

sixth *noun* **1.** In a group of people or things that are in numbered order, the one that matches the number six. **2.** One of six equal parts, written 1/6.
□*adjective* Coming after the fifth.
sixth (siksth) □*noun, plural* **sixths** □*adjective*

sixtieth *noun* **1.** In a group of people or things that are in numbered order, the one that matches the number sixty. **2.** One of sixty equal parts, written 1/60.
□*adjective* Coming after the fifty-ninth.
six·ti·eth (sik′stē ith) □*noun, plural* **sixtieths** □*adjective*

sixty *noun* A number equal to the product of 10 × 6; 60.
□*adjective* Being ten more than fifty.
six·ty (siks′tē) □*noun, plural* **sixties** □*adjective*

size *noun* **1.** The amount of space taken up by something; bulk: *the size of a truck.* **2.** The height, width, or length of something: *the size of a room.* **3.** One of a series of measurements according to which many articles are manufactured: *a size 14 dress.*
size (sīz) □*noun, plural* **sizes**

sizzle *verb* To make a hissing or crackling sound, such as fat does when it fries.
siz·zle (siz′əl) □*verb* **sizzled, sizzling, sizzles**

skate *noun* **1.** An ice skate. **2.** A roller skate.
□*verb* To glide or move on skates.
skate (skāt) □*noun, plural* **skates** □*verb* **skated, skating, skates**

skateboard *noun* A short, narrow board mounted on roller-skate wheels.
skate·board (skāt′bôrd′) □*noun, plural* **skateboards**

skateboard

skater *noun* Someone who skates.
skat·er (skā′tər) □*noun, plural* **skaters**

skeleton *noun* **1.** The internal framework of bones and cartilage that supports the body of all animals with backbones, such as birds, fish, and human beings. **2.** A supporting structure; framework: *the steel skeleton of a skyscraper.*
skel·e·ton (skel′i tən) □*noun, plural* **skeletons**

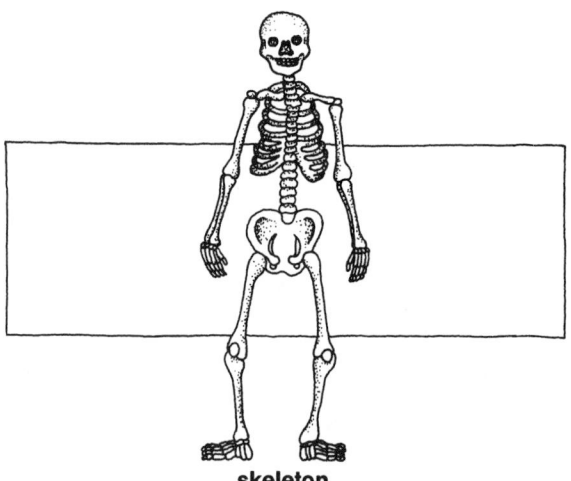

skeleton

sketch *noun* A quick, rough drawing: *We saw a sketch of the building.*

□*verb* To make a sketch of: *He sketched my portrait.*
sketch (skech) □*noun, plural* **sketches**
□*verb* **sketched, sketching, sketches**

ski *noun* One of a pair of long, narrow wood, metal, or plastic runners that is bound to a boot, shoe, or foot and used for gliding over snow or water.
□*verb* To glide on skis.
ski (skē) □*noun, plural* **skis** or **ski** □*verb* **skied, skiing, skis**

skid *noun* The act or process of sliding over a surface: *The truck went into a skid on the ice.*
□*verb* To slide sideways over a surface: *The plane skidded on the wet runway.*
skid (skid) □*noun, plural* **skids** □*verb* **skidded, skidding, skids**

skill *noun* **1.** The ability to apply what one knows effectively: *her skill as a doctor.* **2.** The ability to do something well as a result of practice, experience, or training: *skill at playing basketball.*
skill (skil) □*noun, plural* **skills**

skilled *adjective* **1.** Having skill: *a skilled carpenter.* **2.** Requiring training and skill: *a skilled job.*
skilled (skild) □*adjective*

skillet *noun* A shallow frying pan with a long handle.
skil·let (skil′it) □*noun, plural* **skillets**

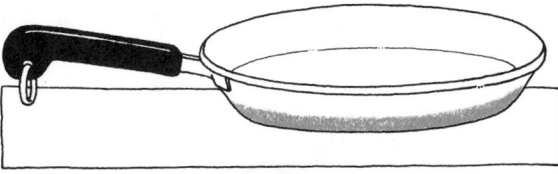

skillet

skillful *adjective* **1.** Having or showing skill: *a skillful artist.* **2.** Done with skill: *a skillful dive from the high diving board.*
skill·ful (skil′fəl) □*adjective*

skim *verb* **1.** To remove floating matter from the surface of a liquid: *I skimmed the foam from the boiling syrup.* **2.** To move or glide lightly and quickly over: *The bird skimmed the water.* **3.** To read or glance at quickly and without being thorough: *I skimmed the magazine as I ate my lunch.*
skim (skim) □*verb* **skimmed, skimming, skims**

skim milk or **skimmed milk** *noun* Milk from which the cream has been removed.

skin *noun* **1.** The tissue that forms the outer covering of the body of a person or animal. **2.** The hide of an animal, especially one with fur. **3.** An outer covering: *the skin of a grape.*
□*verb* **1.** To remove the skin from: *skin an onion.* **2.** To hurt or injure by scraping: *He skinned his knee on the sidewalk.*
skin (skin) □*noun, plural* **skins** □*verb* **skinned, skinning, skins**

skin diving *noun* The act or sport of swimming underwater with flippers, a mask, and equipment such as a snorkel or oxygen tank.

skin diving

skinny *adjective* Very thin: *a skinny man; skinny arms.* —See Synonyms at **thin.**
skin·ny (skin′ē) □*adjective* **skinnier, skinniest**

skip *verb* **1.** To move lightly by springing or hopping: *children skipping down the sidewalk.* **2.** To jump lightly over: *skip rope.* **3.** To leave out; omit: *We skipped lunch.* **4.** To be promoted in school beyond the next grade or level: *I skipped the second grade.*
□*noun* A springing or hopping step.
skip (skip) □*verb* **skipped, skipping, skips** □*noun, plural* **skips**

skirt *noun* A garment or part of a garment that hangs down from the waist.
□*verb* To form the border of; lie along or around: *Mountains skirt the town.*

a	bat	ī	bite	ōō	tool	*th*	feather
ā	make	î	fierce	ou	out	th	bath
â	dare	o	dot	u	nut	hw	wheat
ä	father	ō	no	û	turn	zh	measure
e	net	ô	law, for	ch	church	ə	about, open
ē	be	oi	soil	ng	ring		pencil, atom
i	dip	oo	look	sh	shade		circus

skirt (skûrt) ☐*noun, plural* **skirts** ☐*verb*
skirted, skirting, skirts

WORD HISTORY: **skirt**

Skirt comes from an old Norse word that means "shirt."

---

skull *noun* The hard, bony framework of the head that encloses the brain in animals with a backbone.
skull (skul) ☐*noun, plural* **skulls**

skunk *noun* An animal that has black and white fur and a bushy tail and can spray a liquid that smells very unpleasant.
skunk (skungk) ☐*noun, plural* **skunks**

sky *noun* The upper air that seems to cover the earth like a dome.
sky (skī) ☐*noun, plural* **skies**

WORD HISTORY: **sky**

Sky comes from an old Norse word meaning "cloud."

---

sky diving *noun* The act or sport of jumping from an airplane and falling to earth with the help of a parachute.

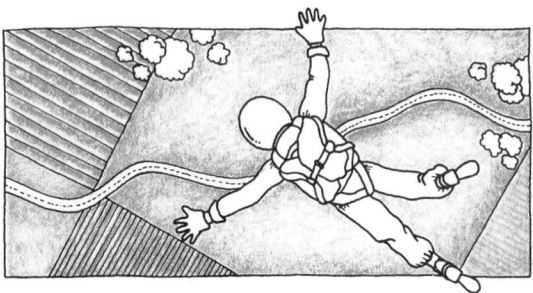

sky diving

skylight *noun* A window in a ceiling.
sky·light (skī′ līt′) ☐*noun, plural* **skylights**

skyline *noun* The outline of buildings or other large objects as seen against the sky.
sky·line (skī′ līn′) ☐*noun, plural* **skylines**

skyscraper *noun* A very tall building.
sky·scrap·er (skī′ skrā′pər) ☐*noun, plural* **skyscrapers**

slab *noun* A broad, flat, thick piece: *a slab of concrete; a slab of bread.*
slab (slab) ☐*noun, plural* **slabs**

slack *adjective* **1.** Slow: *walking at a slack pace.* **2.** Not tight; loose: *a slack rope.*
☐*noun* A loose part: *The sailor took up the slack in the line.*
slack (slak) ☐*adjective* **slacker, slackest**
☐*noun, plural* **slacks**

slacks *plural noun* Long, casual pants.
slacks (slaks) ☐*plural noun*

slain *verb* The past participle of **slay:** *Many soldiers were slain in the battle.*
slain (slān) ☐*verb*

slam *verb* **1.** To shut with force and a loud noise: *slam the door.* **2.** To throw or put with force and a loud noise: *slammed the book down.* **3.** To hit with force: *The football players slammed into each other.*
☐*noun* A hard and noisy crash or closing: *shut the door with a slam.*
slam (slam) ☐*verb* **slammed, slamming, slams** ☐*noun, plural* **slams**

slang *noun* An informal kind of language that is especially vivid or lively and is always changing. Slang occurs especially in informal speech.
slang (slang) ☐*noun*

slant *verb* To lie at an angle; slope: *Her handwriting slants to the left.*
☐*noun* A sloping line or direction: *The roof has a steep slant.*
slant (slant) ☐*verb* **slanted, slanting, slants** ☐*noun, plural* **slants**

slant

slap *verb* To strike sharply with something flat, such as the open hand.
☐*noun* A quick blow with something flat, such as the open hand.
slap (slap) ☐*verb* **slapped, slapping, slaps** ☐*noun, plural* **slaps**

slash *verb* **1.** To cut with a long stroke of a knife or other object: *He slashed the carton open with a knife.* **2.** To lower greatly: *slashing prices on every item in the store.*
☐*noun* **1.** A strong, sweeping stroke: *a slash of his sword.* **2.** A long cut; gash. **3.** A sharp

reduction: *The President made big slashes in the budget.*
slash (slash) ▢*verb* **slashed, slashing, slashes** ▢*noun, plural* **slashes**

slat *noun* A narrow strip of wood or metal: *One of the slats in the fence is broken.*
slat (slat) ▢*noun, plural* **slats**

slate *noun* A bluish-gray rock that splits easily into thin, smooth layers. It is used for blackboards and to cover floors and roofs.
slate (slāt) ▢*noun*

slaughter *noun* **1.** The killing of animals for food: *raising cattle for slaughter.* **2.** A brutal murder.
▢*verb* **1.** To kill animals for food. **2.** To kill brutally or in large numbers.
slaugh·ter (slô′tər) ▢*noun, plural* **slaughters** ▢*verb* **slaughtered, slaughtering, slaughters**

slave *noun* **1.** Someone who is owned by another person. **2.** Someone who works very hard for little or no money.
▢*verb* To work very hard: *I slaved for days on that painting job.*
slave (slāv) ▢*noun, plural* **slaves** ▢*verb* **slaved, slaving, slaves**

WORD HISTORY: slave

The word *slave* comes from the Latin word for the Slavs, a people of eastern Europe. Because a large number of Slavs were slaves in ancient times, the Latin word for "Slav" also came to mean "slave."

---

slavery *noun* **1.** The condition of being a slave: *Many Africans were sold into slavery.* **2.** The practice of owning slaves.
slav·er·y (slā′və rē) ▢*noun*

slay *verb* To kill violently: *The hero slew the dragon.* —See Synonyms at **kill.**
slay (slā) ▢*verb* **slew, slain, slaying, slays**

sled *noun* A framework mounted on runners, used for moving over ice and snow.
▢*verb* To ride on a sled.
sled (sled) ▢*noun, plural* **sleds** ▢*verb* **sledded, sledding, sleds**

sledgehammer *noun* A long, heavy hammer that is held with both hands.
sledge·ham·mer (slej′ham′ər) ▢*noun, plural* **sledgehammers**

sleek *adjective* **1.** Smooth and shiny: *sleek hair.* **2.** Neat and graceful: *a sleek new car.*
sleek (slēk) ▢*adjective* **sleeker, sleekest**

sleep *noun* The natural rest that people and animals take at regular times. During sleep, the mind is unconscious and the body refreshes itself.
▢*verb* To be in a condition of sleep: *She slept well all night.*
sleep (slēp) ▢*noun* ▢*verb* **slept, sleeping, sleeps**

sleeping bag *noun* A large, warmly lined bag for sleeping outdoors.

sleepy *adjective* **1.** Ready for sleep: *She gets sleepy when she stays up late.* **2.** Quiet or dull: *a sleepy little town.*
sleep·y (slē′pē) ▢*adjective* **sleepier, sleepiest**

sleet *noun* Frozen or partially frozen rain.
▢*verb* To rain sleet.
sleet (slēt) ▢*noun* ▢*verb* **sleeted, sleeting, sleets**

sleeve *noun* The part of a garment that covers the arm.
sleeve (slēv) ▢*noun, plural* **sleeves**

sleigh *noun* A carriage on metal runners for traveling on ice or snow.
sleigh (slā) ▢*noun, plural* **sleighs**

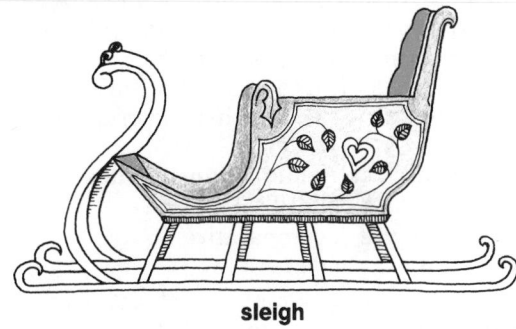

sleigh

slender *adjective* **1.** Having little width; thin: *a slender person.* **2.** Small in amount; slight: *slender hopes of winning.* —See Synonyms at **thin.**
slen·der (slen′dər) ▢*adjective* **slenderer, slenderest**

slept *verb* The past tense and past participle of **sleep:** *I slept late this morning.*
slept (slept) ▢*verb*

a bat	ī bite	ōō tool	*th* feather
ā make	î fierce	ou out	th bath
â dare	o dot	u nut	hw wheat
ä father	ō no	û turn	zh measure
e net	ô law, for	ch church	ə about, open
ē be	oi soil	ng ring	pencil, atom
i dip	oo look	sh shade	circus

slew *verb* The past tense of **slay**.
  slew (slōō) □*verb*

slice *noun* A thin, flat piece cut from something: *a slice of cheese*.
  □*verb* **1.** To cut a slice or slices of: *slice a loaf of bread*. **2.** To move through like a knife: *The canoe sliced through the water*.
  slice (slīs) □*noun, plural* **slices** □*verb* **sliced, slicing, slices**

slick *adjective* **1.** Smooth and skinny: *slick hair*. **2.** Slippery: *a slick place on a road*.
  □*noun* A smooth or slippery place or area: *oil slicks on the river*.
  slick (slik) □*adjective* **slicker, slickest** □*noun, plural* **slicks**

slid *verb* The past tense and past participle of **slide**: *Rocks slid down the mountain*.
  slid (slid) □*verb*

slide *verb* **1.** To move or push smoothly: *sliding over the snow on a sled*. **2.** To move out of position or control; slip: *His feet slid out from under him*.
  □*noun* **1.** An act of sliding. **2.** A smooth, slanted surface on which people or objects can slide: *a slide in the playground*. **3.** A kind of photograph made to be shown on a screen. **4.** A small piece of glass on which things are put to be looked at under a microscope. **5.** The fall of rocks on other material down a slope.
  slide (slīd) □*verb* **slid, sliding, slides** □*noun, plural* **slides**

slier *adjective* A comparative of **sly**.
  sli·er (slī′ər) □*adjective*

sliest *adjective* A superlative of **sly**.
  sli·est (slī′ist) □*adjective*

slight *adjective* **1.** Small in amount or importance: *a slight change; a slight pain*. **2.** Slender; thin: *a young girl with a slight figure*.
  □*verb* To treat as not important; belittle.
  slight (slīt) □*adjective* **slighter, slightest** □*verb* **slighted, slighting, slights**

slim *adjective* **1.** Thin or slender: *a slim girl*. **2.** Small in amount: *a slim margin*.
  □*verb* To make or become thinner: *I'm trying to lose weight and slim down*.
  slim (slim) □*adjective* **slimmer, slimmest** □*verb* **slimmed, slimming, slims**

sling *noun* **1.** A strong loop of material used to lift and move heavy objects. **2.** A band looped around the neck and used to support an injured arm or hand. **3.** A weapon made of a looped piece of leather in which a stone is whirled and then let go.
  □*verb* To put, carry, or hang in or with a loop of material: *slung the bag over her shoulder*.
  sling (sling) □*noun, plural* **slings** □*verb* **slung, slinging, slings**

slingshot *noun* An elastic band stretched between the prongs of a Y-shaped stick. It is used for shooting pebbles.
  sling·shot (sling′shot′) □*noun, plural* **slingshots**

slingshot

slip¹ *verb* **1.** To move smoothly; glide: *The soap slipped out of his hands*. **2.** To move or pass easily and quickly: *She slipped away from the party*. **3.** To put on or take off quickly and easily: *slip on a sweater*. **4.** To lose one's balance on a slippery surface: *slip on the ice*. **5.** To make a mistake: *I slipped up on the last question*. —See Synonyms at **error**.
  □*noun* **1.** The act of slipping. **2.** A small mistake.
  slip (slip) □*verb* **slipped, slipping, slips** □*noun, plural* **slips**

slip² *noun* **1.** A small piece of paper or other material. **2.** A part or shoot cut from a plant and used to grow a new plant.
  slip (slip) □*noun, plural* **slips**

slipper *noun* A light, low, indoor shoe that can be slipped on easily.
  slip·per (slip′ər) □*noun, plural* **slippers**

slippery *adjective* Likely to slip or to cause slipping: *a slippery sidewalk*.
  slip·per·y (slip′ə rē) □*adjective*

slit *noun* A long, narrow cut or opening: *cut slits in the paper*.
  □*verb* To cut a slit in.
  slit (slit) □*noun, plural* **slits** □*verb* **slit, slitting, slits**

sliver *noun* A thin, sharp-pointed piece; splinter: *slivers of wood*.
  sliv·er (sliv′ər) □*noun, plural* **slivers**

slogan *noun* A phrase that expresses the goal or spirit of an organization or group; motto:

The store's slogan is "The customer is always right."

slo·gan (slō′gən) ▢*noun, plural* **slogans**

slope *verb* To be or make slanted: *The hill slopes down to the valley.*
▢*noun* A line or surface that is not flat.
slope (slōp) ▢*verb* **sloped, sloping, slopes** ▢*noun, plural* **slopes**

sloppy *adjective* **1.** Full of slush or mud: *sloppy roads.* **2.** Messy or untidy: *a sloppy room.* **3.** Carelessly or poorly done: *Her teacher criticized her sloppy performance on the violin.*
slop·py (slop′ē) ▢*adjective* **sloppier, sloppiest**

slot *noun* A straight, narrow opening: *a slot for coins in a vending machine.*
slot (slot) ▢*noun, plural* **slots**

sloth *noun* A slow-moving furry animal of South America that hangs upside-down from tree branches.
sloth (slōth *or* slôth) ▢*noun, plural* **sloths**

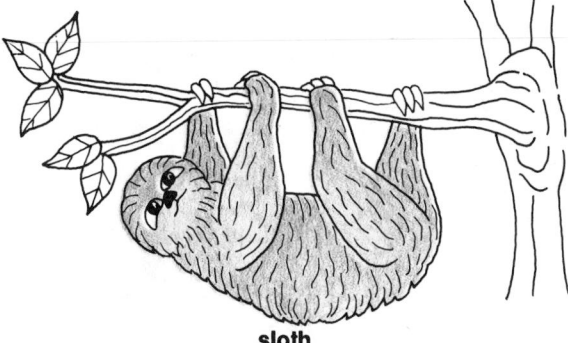

sloth

slouch *verb* To have or move with a bent posture: *Don't slouch; stand up straight.*
▢*noun* A bending down of the head and shoulders.
slouch (slouch) ▢*verb* **slouched, slouching, slouches** ▢*noun, plural* **slouches**

slow *adjective* **1.** Not moving or happening quickly: *She is a slow runner. They took the slowest bus.* **2.** Not easily moved or excited: *He is slow to laugh.* **3.** Behind the correct time: *My watch is slow.* **4.** Not quick to understand or learn: *I was a slow student and always had trouble with science and math.*
▢*adverb* In a slow manner: *Go slow on this road, please.*
▢*verb* To make or become slow: *The car slowed down.*
slow (slō) ▢*adjective* ▢*adverb* **slower, slowest** ▢*verb* **slowed, slowing, slows**

slug¹ *noun* **1.** A bullet or other piece of metal fired from a gun. **2.** A piece of metal that is used instead of a coin in some machines.
slug (slug) ▢*noun, plural* **slugs**

slug² *noun* A land animal that is like a snail but has no shell.
slug (slug) ▢*noun, plural* **slugs**

slug³ *verb* To hit hard: *She slugged the burglar and knocked him out. The batter slugged the ball into the outfield.*
▢*noun* A hard blow, especially with the fist.
slug (slug) ▢*verb* **slugged, slugging, slugs** ▢*noun, plural* **slugs**

sluice *noun* **1.** A manmade channel for water with a gate to stop and start the flow. **2.** A long, sloping water trough that is used for such things as separating ore from dirt.
sluice (slo̅o̅s) ▢*noun, plural* **sluices**

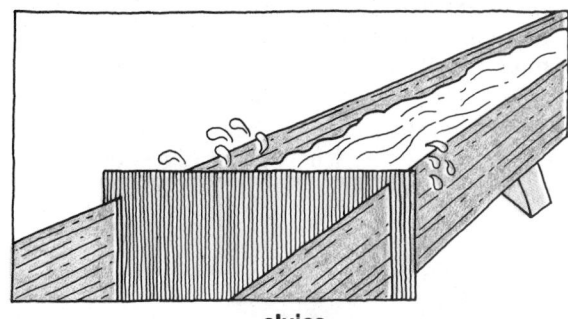

sluice

slum *noun* A poor, crowded section of a city.
slum (slum) ▢*noun, plural* **slums**

slumber *verb* To sleep.
▢*noun* Sleep.
slum·ber (slum′bər) ▢*verb* **slumbered, slumbering, slumbers** ▢*noun, plural* **slumbers**

slump *verb* To drop suddenly: *He slumped in a chair.*

a bat	ī bite	o͞o tool	*th* feather
ā make	î fierce	ou out	th bath
â dare	o dot	u nut	hw wheat
ä father	ō no	û turn	zh measure
e net	ô law, for	ch church	ə about, open
ē be	oi soil	ng ring	pencil, atom
i dip	oo look	sh shade	circus

□*noun* A sudden fall or decline: *a slump in sales after Christmas.*
slump (slump) □*verb* **slumped, slumping, slumps** □*noun, plural* **slumps**

slung *verb* The past tense and past participle of **sling.**
slung (slung) □*verb*

slush *noun* Partly melted snow or ice.
slush (slush) □*noun*

sly *adjective* **1.** Clever or tricky: *a sly plan.* **2.** Playfully mischievous: *a sly look.*
sly (slī) □*adjective* **slier** or **slyer, sliest** or **slyest**

smack *verb* **1.** To make a sharp sound by closing and opening the lips: *He smacked his lips when he saw the cake.* **2.** To kiss noisily. **3.** To strike with a loud sound: *She smacked into the door.*
□*noun* A loud kiss or slap.
□*adverb* Directly; straight: *She fell smack in the middle of the puddle.*
smack (smak) □*verb* **smacked, smacking, smacks** □*noun, plural* **smacks** □*adverb*

small *adjective* **1.** Not big; little: *a small school; a small town.* **2.** Not important: *a small problem.* **3.** Soft or low: *a small voice.*
small (smôl) □*adjective* **smaller, smallest**

small intestine *noun* The part of the digestive system that lies between the stomach and the large intestine where most digestion takes place and where digested food is absorbed by the body.

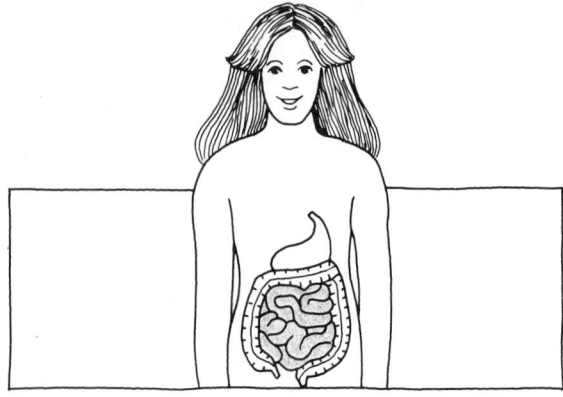

small intestine

small letter *noun* A letter that is not a capital letter. For example, *a, b,* and *c* are small letters.

smallpox *noun* A serious, very contagious disease that can leave scars on the skin.
small·pox (smôl′poks′) □*noun*

smart *adjective* **1.** Intelligent or clever: *the smartest student in the school.* **2.** Brisk; lively: *a smart pace.* **3.** Fashionable or stylish. **4.** Neat and trim: *He looked smart in his new suit.*
□*verb* To feel or cause to feel a sharp pain: *My knee smarts from the bruise.*
smart (smärt) □*adjective* **smarter, smartest** □*verb* **smarted, smarting, smarts**

smash *verb* **1.** To break into pieces: *He smashed the cup to bits.* **2.** To hurl or strike violently: *The car smashed into a pole.*
□*noun* The act or sound of smashing.
smash (smash) □*verb* **smashed, smashing, smashes** □*noun, plural* **smashes**

smear *verb* **1.** To spread, cover, or stain with something sticky or greasy: *a shirt that had been smeared with oil.* **2.** To become or cause to become messy or blurred: *Don't smear the wet paint.* **3.** To harm a person's reputation.
□*noun* A stain or smudge.
smear (smîr) □*verb* **smeared, smearing, smears** □*noun, plural* **smears**

smear

smell *verb* **1.** To become aware of by using the nose: *I smell bread baking.* **2.** To sniff: *smell a flower.* **3.** To have or give off an odor, especially a bad odor: *The garbage smells.*
□*noun* **1.** The ability to smell. **2.** An odor; scent: *the smell of cut grass.*
smell (smel) □*verb* **smelled** or **smelt, smelling, smells** □*noun, plural* **smells**

smelt¹ *verb* To melt ore in order to remove the metal in it.
smelt (smelt) □*verb* **smelted, smelting, smelts**

smelt² *verb* A past tense and past participle of **smell:** *I smelt smoke and looked for a fire.*
smelt (smelt) □*verb*

smile *noun* A happy or amused expression on the face made by turning up the corners of the mouth.

□*verb* To have or make a smile: *He smiled when I told him the joke.*
smile (smīl) □*noun, plural* **smiles** □*verb* **smiled, smiling, smiles**

smock *noun* A long, loose shirt worn over clothes to protect them.
smock (smok) □*noun, plural* **smocks**

smog *noun* Fog mixed with smoke: *A gray cloud of smog hung over the factories.*
smog (smog) □*noun*

WORD HISTORY: **smog**

The word *smog* is formed from the first two letters of *smoke* and the last two letters of *fog.*

---

smoke *noun* A gas with tiny particles in it, given off by something burning. It looks like a cloud rising in the air.
□*verb* **1.** To give off smoke: *The fire was still smoking.* **2.** To draw in and blow out smoke from tobacco. **3.** To preserve meat with wood smoke: *smoke a ham.*
smoke (smōk) □*noun, plural* **smokes** □*verb* **smoked, smoking, smokes**

smokestack *noun* A large chimney through which smoke is released.
smoke·stack (smōk′stak′) □*noun, plural* **smokestacks**

smokestack

smoky *adjective* **1.** Giving off a lot of smoke: *a smoky fire.* **2.** Filled with smoke: *smoky air.*
smok·y (smō′kē) □*adjective* **smokier, smokiest**

smooth *adjective* **1.** Having a surface that is not rough: *smooth skin.* **2.** Without jolts or bumps: *a smooth ride.* **3.** Free from difficulties or problems: *smooth progress on the journey.*

□*verb* **1.** To make level or even: *smooth out the wrinkles in a skirt.* **2.** To make easy: *His older brother helped smooth the way for him.*
smooth (smo͞oth) □*adjective* **smoother, smoothest** □*verb* **smoothed, smoothing, smooths**

smother *verb* **1.** To die or cause to die from lack of air. **2.** To go out or make a fire go out from lack of air: *Smother the fire with a wet blanket.* **3.** To cover thickly: *smother the steak with onions.* **4.** To hide or keep back: *smother a giggle.*
smoth·er (smuth′ər) □*verb* **smothered, smothering, smothers**

smudge *verb* To make or become dirty; smear: *She smudged her face with her dirty hands.*
□*noun* A dirty mark; smear.
smudge (smuj) □*verb* **smudged, smudging, smudges** □*noun, plural* **smudges**

smuggle *verb* To bring in or take out secretly and illegally: *smuggle a camera into the concert.*
smug·gle (smug′əl) □*verb* **smuggled, smuggling, smuggles**

snack *noun* A small amount of food eaten between regular meals.
snack (snak) □*noun, plural* **snacks**

snail *noun* A slow-moving land or water animal that has a soft body inside a spiral shell.
snail (snāl) □*noun, plural* **snails**

snake *noun* A crawling animal that has a long, narrow, body covered with scales and that has no legs.
snake (snāk) □*noun, plural* **snakes**

snap *verb* **1.** To make or cause to make a sharp sound: *The campfire hissed and snapped. She snapped her fingers.* **2.** To break suddenly and sharply: *snap a twig.* **3.** To grab at with a snatching motion: *The dog snapped at me.* **4.** To speak angrily: *His father snapped at him for being late.* **5.** To move or act quickly. **6.** To take a photograph.
□*noun* **1.** A sharp cracking sound. **2.** A sudden bite or grab. **3.** A fastener or clasp. **4.** A thin, crisp cooky: *ginger snaps.* **5.** A short pe-

a	bat	ī	bite	o͞o	tool	*th*	feather
ā	make	î	fierce	ou	out	th	bath
â	dare	o	dot	u	nut	hw	wheat
ä	father	ō	no	û	turn	zh	measure
e	net	ô	law, for	ch	church	ə	about, open
ē	be	oi	soil	ng	ring		pencil, atom
i	dip	oo	look	sh	shade		circus

riod of cold weather: *a cold snap.*
□*adjective* Done quickly and with little thought: *a snap judgment.*
snap (snap) □*verb* **snapped, snapping, snaps** □*noun, plural* **snaps** □*adjective*

snapdragon *noun* A plant with bunches of colorful flowers that open and close when their sides are pressed.
snap·drag·on (snap′drag′ən) □*noun, plural* **snapdragons**

snapshot *noun* An informal photograph taken with a small camera.
snap·shot (snap′shot′) □*noun, plural* **snapshots**

snare *noun* A trap in the form of a noose that grabs and holds a small animal that steps or falls into it.
□*verb* To trap in or as if in a snare.
snare (snâr) □*noun, plural* **snares** □*verb* **snare, snaring, snares**

snare

snarl¹ *noun* An angry growl that shows the teeth: *The dog attacked with a fierce snarl.*
□*verb* **1.** To growl, especially while showing teeth. **2.** To speak in an angry way.
snarl (snärl) □*noun, plural* **snarls** □*verb* **snarled, snarling, snarls**

snarl² *noun* A tangled mass: *snarls in the horse's mane.*
□*verb* **1.** To tangle or become tangled: *snarl a spool of thread.* **2.** To make or become confused: *The accident snarled up traffic for hours.*
snarl (snärl) □*noun, plural* **snarls** □*verb* **snarled, snarling, snarls**

snatch *verb* To take or try to take suddenly and quickly; grab: *It is rude to snatch things out of other people's hands.*
□*noun* **1.** The act of snatching. **2.** A small amount: *I heard snatches of what they were saying.*
snatch (snach) □*verb* **snatched, snatching, snatches** □*noun, plural* **snatches**

sneak *verb* To act, move, or take in a secret way: *sneak into a movie theater without pay-*

ing; *sneak a look at a present.*
□*noun* A sly, dishonest person.
sneak (snēk) □*verb* **sneaked, sneaking, sneaks** □*noun, plural* **sneaks**

sneakers *plural noun* Sport shoes with soft rubber soles.
sneak·ers (snē′kərz) □*plural noun*

sneer *noun* An expression or sound that shows contempt or scorn: *He raised one corner of his mouth in a sneer.*
□*verb* To make or say with a sneer.
sneer (snîr) □*noun, plural* **sneers** □*verb* **sneered, sneering, sneers**

sneer

sneeze *verb* To blow out air from the nose and mouth in a violent way. A sneeze happens because of a tickling feeling inside the nose.
□*noun* The act of sneezing.
sneeze (snēz) □*verb* **sneezed, sneezing, sneezes** □*noun, plural* **sneezes**

snicker *noun* A partly hidden laugh showing scorn or lack of respect.
□*verb* To laugh in this way: *The class snickered when the student gave the wrong answer.*
snick·er (snik′ər) □*noun, plural* **snickers** □*verb* **snickered, snickering, snickers**

sniff *verb* **1.** To breathe air into the nose in short breaths: *sniffing the fresh air.* **2.** To smell by sniffing: *sniff the roses.*
□*noun* The act of sniffing.
sniff (snif) □*verb* **sniffed, sniffing, sniffs** □*noun, plural* **sniffs**

sniffle *verb* To sniff again and again, as one does from a head cold.
□*noun* An act of sniffling.
snif·fle (snif′əl) □*verb* **sniffled, sniffling, sniffles** □*noun, plural* **sniffles**

snip *verb* To cut with quick strokes: *She snipped the ribbon and opened the package.*
□*noun* **1.** A small piece cut off. **2.** The act of snipping.
snip (snip) □*verb* **snipped, snipping, snips** □*noun, plural* **snips**

snipe *noun* A brownish marsh bird with a long bill.
snipe (snīp) □*noun, plural* **snipe** or **snipes**

snipe

snob *noun* Someone who feels that he or she is better than others or judges people by their wealth and social position.
snob (snob) □*noun, plural* **snobs**

snore *verb* To breathe in a noisy way while sleeping.
□*noun* A loud breathing noise made while sleeping.
snore (snôr) □*verb* **snored, snoring, snores** □*noun, plural* **snores**

snorkel *noun* A tube and mouthpiece used by swimmers to breathe underwater.
snor·kel (snôr′kəl) □*noun, plural* **snorkels**

snorkel

snort *noun* A rough, noisy sound made by forcing air through the nose.
□*verb* To force air through the nose in a noisy way: *The horse snorted and galloped off.*
snort (snôrt) □*noun, plural* **snorts** □*verb* **snorted, snorting, snorts**

snout *noun* The long nose, jaws, or front part of an animal's head.
snout (snout) □*noun, plural* **snouts**

snow *noun* **1.** Soft white crystals formed by water vapor that freezes high in the air and falls to the ground. **2.** A fall of snow.

□*verb* **1.** To fall to earth as snow: *It snowed last night.* **2.** To shut in because of snow: *The blizzard snowed us in.*
snow (snō) □*noun, plural* **snows** □*verb* **snowed, snowing, snows**

snowflake *noun* A single crystal of snow.
snow·flake (snō′flāk′) □*noun, plural* **snowflakes**

snowman *noun* A figure of a person made from packed and shaped snow.
snow·man (snō′man′) □*noun, plural* **snowmen**

snowmobile *noun* A vehicle like a sled with a motor for traveling on snow.
snow·mo·bile (snō′mō bēl′) □*noun, plural* **snowmobiles**

snowmobile

snowplow *noun* A machine with a wide blade in front, used to remove snow from roads.
snow·plow (snō′plou′) □*noun, plural* **snowplows**

snowshoe *noun* A light, racket-shaped frame worn under the shoe to keep from sinking into deep snow.
snow·shoe (snō′shoo′) □*noun, plural* **snowshoes**

snowstorm *noun* A storm with a heavy fall of snow.
snow·storm (snō′stôrm′) □*noun, plural* **snowstorms**

snowy *adjective* **1.** Full of or covered with snow: *snowy fields.* **2.** White like snow.
snow·y (snō′ē) □*adjective* **snowier, snowiest**

a bat	ī bite	ōō tool	*th* feather
ā make	î fierce	ou out	th bath
â dare	o dot	u nut	hw wheat
ä father	ō no	û turn	zh measure
e net	ô law, for	ch church	ə about, open
ē be	oi soil	ng ring	pencil, atom
i dip	oo look	sh shade	circus

snug *adjective* **1.** Warm and comfortable; cozy: *They have a snug little cabin that is heated by a woodstove.* **2.** Fitting closely; tight: *The sweater felt snug when he tried it on.*
snug (snug) □*adjective* **snugger, snuggest**

snuggle *verb* To press close; nestle: *The kittens snuggled next to their mother.*
snug·gle (snug′əl) □*verb* **snuggled, snuggling, snuggles**

so *adverb* **1.** In that way; thus: *How many people think so?* **2.** To such a degree: *not so fast as his brother.* **3.** To a great extent: *You're so silly.* **4.** Also; too: *She speaks Spanish and so do I.*
□*adjective* True: *If he swore to it, it must be so.*
□*conjunction* **1.** In order that: *She came early so she could get a good seat.* **2.** With the result that: *We ran out of food, so we went shopping.*
□*pronoun* The same: *She is the president and will remain so until the next election.*
so (sō) □*adverb* □*adjective* □*conjunction* □*pronoun*

soak *verb* **1.** To make very wet: *The rain soaked us.* **2.** To absorb: *A sponge soaks up water.* **3.** To let lie in liquid: *Soak the clothes before washing them.*
soak (sōk) □*verb* **soaked, soaking, soaks**

soap *noun* A substance usually made from fat and lye, used for washing.
□*verb* To rub or cover with soap.
soap (sōp) □*noun, plural* **soaps** □*verb* **soaped, soaping, soaps**

soapy *adjective* Covered or filled with soap: *soapy water.*
soap·y (sō′pē) □*adjective* **soapier, soapiest**

soar *verb* **1.** To fly high: *The eagle soared out of sight.* **2.** To go far upward: *Because of the fuel shortage, prices soared.* —See Synonyms at **rise.**
soar (sôr) □*verb* **soared, soaring, soars**

sob *verb* To cry with gasping, short breaths.
□*noun* The act or sound of sobbing.
sob (sob) □*verb* **sobbed, sobbing, sobs** □*noun, plural* **sobs**

sober *adjective* **1.** Not drunk. **2.** Serious; solemn: *a sober expression on his face.*
so·ber (sō′bər) □*adjective* **soberer, soberest**

soccer *noun* A game in which players try to knock a round ball into the opposing team's goal by kicking it or hitting it with any part of the body except the hands.
soc·cer (sok′ər) □*noun*

soccer

sociable *adjective* Liking to be with other people; friendly.
so·cia·ble (sō′shə bəl) □*adjective*

social *adjective* **1.** Dealing with human beings as a group: *Economics is a social science.* **2.** Living with others of the same kind: *Ants are social insects.* **3.** Of or for companionship: *a pleasant social gathering.* **4.** Liking company; sociable.
so·cial (sō′shəl) □*adjective*

socialism *noun* An economic system in which businesses, factories, and farms are owned by the people as a whole and run by the government.
so·cial·ism (sō′shə liz′əm) □*noun, plural* **socialisms**

socialist *noun* Someone who believes in socialism.
so·cial·ist (sō′shə list) □*noun, plural* **socialists**

society *noun* **1.** A group of human beings living and working together. **2.** The rich and fashionable people of a place. **3.** A group of people sharing goals and interests: *a society to preserve historic buildings.*
so·ci·e·ty (sə sī′i tē) □*noun, plural* **societies**

sock¹ *noun* A cloth covering for the foot reaching no higher than the knee.
sock (sok) □*noun, plural* **socks** or **sox**

sock² *verb* To hit hard; punch.
sock (sok) □*verb* **socked, socking, socks**

socket *noun* A hollow part for receiving something: *a light bulb socket; eye sockets.*
sock·et (sok′ it) □*noun, plural* **sockets**

sod *noun* Grass and soil held together by matted roots.
sod (sod) □*noun, plural* **sods**

soda *noun* **1.** Baking soda. **2.** A soft drink containing carbonated water, flavoring, and sometimes ice cream.
so·da (sō′ də) □*noun, plural* **sodas**

soda fountain *noun* A counter where sodas, sandwiches, and other snacks are served.

soda water *noun* Water mixed with carbon dioxide gas that is used in making drinks.

sodium *noun* A chemical element that is a soft, silver-white metal. Common salt is a compound of sodium.
so·di·um (sō′ dē əm) □*noun*

sofa *noun* A long seat with cushions and a back and arms.
so·fa (sō′ fə) □*noun, plural* **sofas**

soft *adjective* **1.** Easy to mold or shape; not hard: *soft clay; a soft pillow.* **2.** Out of condition; weak: *His muscles are soft from lack of exercise.* **3.** Smooth or pleasing to the touch: *a soft cloth.* **4.** Not loud: *soft voices.* **5.** Not bright or harsh: *soft colors; soft lights.*
soft (sôft) □*adjective* **softer, softest**

softball *noun* **1.** A game similar to baseball but played with a larger, softer ball. **2.** The ball used in this sport.
soft·ball (sôft′ bôl′) □*noun, plural* **softballs**

soft drink *noun* A sweet drink that contains no alcohol and is made with soda water.

soften *verb* To make or become softer: *The clay softened as I rolled it.*
soft·en (sô′ fən) □*verb* **softened, softening, softens**

software *noun* Data, such as programs and symbolic languages, needed to operate a computer.
soft·ware (sôft′ wâr′) □*noun*

soggy *adjective* Heavy with water: *soggy bread; soggy ground.*
sog·gy (sog′ ē) □*adjective* **soggier, soggiest**

soil¹ *noun* **1.** The loose top part of the ground in which plants grow. **2.** Land; country: *our native soil.* —See Synonyms at **land.**
soil (soil) □*noun, plural* **soils**

soil² *verb* To make or become dirty: *He soiled his shirt while gardening.*
soil (soil) □*verb* **soiled, soiling, soils**

solar *adjective* Of or coming from the sun: *solar energy; a solar eclipse.*
so·lar (sō′ lər) □*adjective*

solar
Solar energy panels

solar system *noun* The sun and all the planets and other heavenly bodies that orbit around the sun.

sold *verb* The past tense and past participle of **sell**: *She sold the monkey to a circus.*
sold (sōld) □*verb*

solder *noun* A metal that can be melted and used to join two metal pieces together.
□*verb* To fasten with solder.
sol·der (sod′ ər) □*noun, plural* **solders**
□*verb* **soldered, soldering, solders**

soldier *noun* Someone who is a member of an army.
sol·dier (sōl′ jər) □*noun, plural* **soldiers**

WORD HISTORY: **soldier**

The word *soldier* comes from the Latin name for a gold coin. Soldiers got their name because they served in the Roman army for pay.

---

sole¹ *noun* The bottom surface of the foot or of a shoe.
□*verb* To put a sole on a shoe.
sole (sōl) □*noun, plural* **soles** □*verb* **soled, soling, soles**

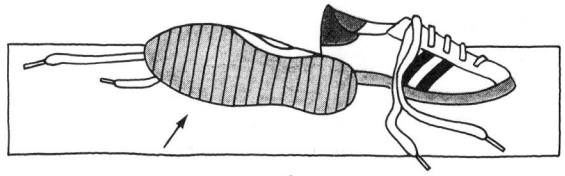
sole

a bat	ī bite	o͞o tool	*th* feather
ā make	î fierce	ou out	th bath
â dare	o dot	u nut	hw wheat
ä father	ō no	û turn	zh measure
e net	ô law, for	ch church	ə about, open
ē be	oi soil	ng ring	pencil, atom
i dip	oo look	sh shade	circus

sole² *adjective* **1.** Being the only one: *her sole reason for being there.* **2.** Belonging only to one person or group: *He took sole ownership of the store when his partner died.*
sole (sōl) □*adjective*

sole³ *noun* A flat fish that is used for food.
sole (sōl) □*noun, plural* **sole** or **soles**

solemn *adjective* Very serious and grave: *a solemn promise; a solemn ceremony.*
sol·emn (sol′əm) □*adjective*

solid *adjective* **1.** Having a definite shape; not being a liquid or gas. **2.** Not empty or hollow: *a solid brick wall.* **3.** Being the same material or color throughout: *solid silver.* **4.** Without pauses or breaks: *a solid hour.* **5.** Strong and sturdy: *a solid foundation.* —See Synonyms at **hard.**
□*noun* A substance that has a definite shape.
sol·id (sol′id) □*adjective* □*noun, plural* **solids**

solitary *adjective* **1.** Being alone: *a solitary traveler.* **2.** Happening or passed alone: *a solitary dinner.* —See Synonyms at **single.**
sol·i·tar·y (sol′i ter′ē) □*adjective*

solo *noun* Music to be played or sung by a single performer: *The jazz piece has a trumpet solo.*
□*adjective* Done alone: *a solo airplane flight.*
so·lo (sō′lō) □*noun, plural* **solos** □*adjective*

solution *noun* **1.** A mixture formed by dissolving a substance in a liquid: *a solution of salt in water.* **2.** The action or result of solving a problem.
so·lu·tion (sə lōō′shən) □*noun, plural* **solutions**

solve *verb* To find a solution to: *solve a difficult problem.*
solve (solv) □*verb* **solved, solving, solves**

somber *adjective* Dark or grim; gloomy: *a somber sky; a somber expression.*
som·ber (som′bər) □*adjective*

some *adjective* **1.** Being an amount, number, or quantity that is not specified: *some trees; some food.* **2.** Certain or particular, but not named: *Some plants catch insects.*
□*pronoun* A number or quantity not named: *Some of my friends are coming for a visit next week.*
some (sum) □*adjective* □*pronoun*

somebody *pronoun* A person who is not known or named: *Somebody phoned while you were out.*
some·bod·y (sum′bod′ē) □*pronoun*

someday *adverb* At some time in the future: *I want to go sailing someday.*
some·day (sum′dā′) □*adverb*

somehow *adverb* In a way that is not known: *We'll raise the money somehow.*
some·how (sum′hou′) □*adverb*

someone *pronoun* A person who is not known or named: *Someone is knocking at the door.*
some·one (sum′wun′) □*pronoun*

somersault *noun* The act of rolling the body heels over head.
□*verb* To perform a somersault.
som·er·sault (sum′ər sôlt′) □*noun, plural* **somersaults** □*verb* **somersaulted, somersaulting, somersaults**

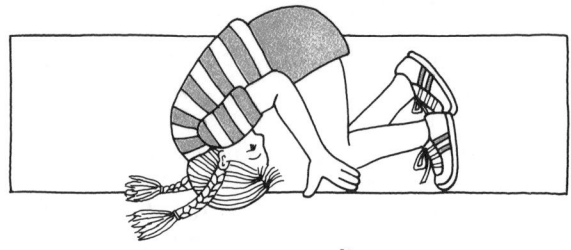

somersault

something *pronoun* A thing that is not named or known: *I want something to do.*
□*adverb* To some extent; somewhat: *A bee hive is something like a city.*
some·thing (sum′thing) □*pronoun* □*adverb*

sometime *adverb* At a time that is not known or named: *Let's get together sometime.*
some·time (sum′tīm′) □*adverb*

sometimes *adverb* Now and then: *I sometimes ride my bicycle to school.*
some·times (sum′tīmz′) □*adverb*

somewhat *adverb* To some extent; rather: *I have a jacket somewhat like yours.*
some·what (sum′hwot′ *or* sum′wot′) □*adverb*

somewhere *adverb* **1.** In, at, or to a place that is not known or named: *This rock came from somewhere in outer space.* **2.** Approximately: *somewhere around 1920.*
□*noun* A place that is not known or named: *Let's go somewhere to eat.*
some·where (sum′hwâr′ *or* sum′wâr′) □*adverb* □*noun*

son *noun* A male child.
son (sun) □*noun, plural* **sons**

sonar *noun* A system that uses sound waves to discover the location of objects under water.
so·nar (sō′när′) ▫*noun, plural* **sonars**

WORD HISTORY: **sonar**

Sonar comes from the phrase "*so*und *na*vigation *r*anging." As you can probably tell, the word is formed from the first two letters of the first and second words and the first letter of the last word.

---

sonata *noun* A piece of music that is written for one or two instruments and consists of three or four different sections.
so·na·ta (sə nä′tə) ▫*noun, plural* **sonatas**

song *noun* **1.** A musical piece that is meant to be sung. **2.** A musical call made by a bird.
song (sông) ▫*noun, plural* **songs**

songbird *noun* A bird with a musical call.
song·bird (sông′bûrd′) ▫*noun, plural* **songbirds**

son-in-law *noun* The husband of a person's daughter.
son-in-law (sun′in lô′) ▫*noun, plural* **sons-in-law**

sonnet *noun* A poem having fourteen lines that rhyme in a set pattern.
son·net (son′it) ▫*noun, plural* **sonnets**

soon *adverb* **1.** In the near future: *Soon it will be spring.* **2.** Early: *He arrived sooner than expected.* **3.** Quickly: *Get here as soon as you can.* **4.** Willingly: *Here's the bus, but I'd just as soon walk.*
soon (soon) ▫*adverb* **sooner, soonest**

soot *noun* A sticky black powder produced when wood, coal, or oil is burned.
soot (soot) ▫*noun*

soothe *verb* **1.** To make calm: *Her soft words soothed his temper.* **2.** To make less painful: *a lotion to soothe a burn.*
soothe (sooth) ▫*verb* **soothed, soothing, soothes**

sophomore *noun* A student in the second year of a four-year high school or college.
soph·o·more (sof′ə môr′) ▫*noun, plural* **sophomores**

WORD HISTORY: **sophomore**

Sophomore probably comes from two Greek words, one meaning "wise" and the other meaning "foolish."

---

soprano *noun* **1.** The highest singing voice of a woman or boy. **2.** A singer who has such a voice.
so·pran·o (sə pran′ō) ▫*noun, plural* **sopranos**

sore *adjective* **1.** Painful when touched: *a sore thumb.* **2.** Angry or annoyed.
▫*noun* A painful place on the body.
sore (sôr) ▫*adjective* **sorer, sorest** ▫*noun, plural* **sores**

sorority *noun* An organization of girls or women, as at a college.
so·ror·i·ty (sə rôr′i tē) ▫*noun, plural* **sororities**

sorrow *noun* Sadness; grief.
sor·row (sor′ō) ▫*noun, plural* **sorrows**

SYNONYMS: **sorrow, grief**

These nouns mean great sadness or anguish: *The news of his death caused great sorrow to his friends. He felt grief at the thought that he would never see his family or his native land again.*

---

sorrowful *adjective* Causing, feeling, or expressing sorrow; sad.
sor·row·ful (sor′ə fəl) ▫*adjective*

sorry *adjective* **1.** Feeling sadness, sympathy, or regret: *He was sorry for the sick child.* **2.** Not good or suitable; poor: *He was a sorry sight as he stood there in his shabby clothes.*
sor·ry (sor′ē) ▫*adjective* **sorrier, sorriest**

sort *noun* A group of similar persons or things: *That sort of jacket is very warm.* —See Synonyms at **kind²**.
▫*verb* To arrange according to kind or type: *sort the laundry.*
sort (sôrt) ▫*noun, plural* **sorts** ▫*verb* **sorted, sorting, sorts**

SOS *noun* A signal for help sent by a ship or aircraft in trouble.
SOS (es′ō es′) ▫*noun*

sought *verb* The past tense and past participle of **seek**: *She sought to make peace between the two children.*
sought (sôt) ▫*verb*

a	bat	ī	bite	oo	tool	*th*	feather
ā	make	î	fierce	ou	out	th	bath
â	dare	o	dot	u	nut	hw	wheat
ä	father	ō	no	û	turn	zh	measure
e	net	ô	law, for	ch	church	ə	about, open
ē	be	oi	soil	ng	ring		pencil, atom
i	dip	oo	look	sh	shade		circus

soul *noun* **1.** The spiritual part of a human being. **2.** A human being: *not a soul in sight.*
soul (sōl) □*noun, plural* **souls**

sound¹ *noun* **1.** A vibration that moves through the air and is heard by the ear. **2.** One of the noises that make up human speech: *the sound of "th" in "this."*
□*verb* **1.** To make or cause to make a sound: *The bell sounded. They sounded the alarm.* **2.** To be pronounced: *The words "write" and "right" sound alike.* **3.** To seem to be: *Your plan sounds good.*
sound (sound) □*noun, plural* **sounds** □*verb* **sounded, sounding, sounds**

sound² *adjective* **1.** Not damaged, injured, or weakened: *a sound mind in a sound body.* **2.** Sensible and correct: *sound advice.* **3.** Deep and not interrupted: *sound sleep.* —See Synonyms at **healthy.**
□*adverb* To the full extent; completely: *The baby is sound asleep.*
sound (sound) □*adjective* **sounder, soundest** □*adverb*

sound³ *noun* A long, narrow body of water.
sound (sound) □*noun, plural* **sounds**

sound⁴ *verb* **1.** To find out how deep water is, especially by dropping a weight tied to a line. **2.** To try to learn someone's thoughts: *We tried to sound out my mother on what she wanted for her birthday.*
sound (sound) □*verb* **sounded, sounding, sounds**

soundproof *adjective* Letting little or no sound pass in or out: *a soundproof wall.*
□*verb* To make soundproof.
sound·proof (sound′proof′) □*adjective* □*verb* **soundproofed, soundproofing, soundproofs**

soup *noun* A liquid made by boiling meat, vegetables, or fish in water.
soup (soop) □*noun, plural* **soups**

sour *adjective* **1.** Having a sharp and biting taste: *sour lemons.* **2.** Unpleasant; unfriendly: *in a sour temper.*
□*verb* To make or become sour: *If you don't put the cream back in the refrigerator it will sour.*
sour (sour) □*adjective* **sourer, sourest** □*verb* **soured, souring, sours**

source *noun* A place or thing from which something comes: *a light source; a source of information.*
source (sôrs) □*noun, plural* **sources**

south *noun* **1.** The direction to the left of a person facing the sunset. **2. South** A region in this direction, especially the southeastern part of the United States.
□*adjective* **1.** Of, in, or toward the south: *the south side of town.* **2.** Coming from the south: *a warm south wind.*
□*adverb* In, from, or toward the south: *traveling south.*
south (south) □*noun* □*adjective* □*adverb*

South African *noun* A person who was born in or lives in the Republic of South Africa.

South American *noun* Someone who was born in or lives in South America.
□*adjective* Of South America.
South American □*noun, plural* **South Americans** □*adjective*

southeast *noun* **1.** The direction halfway between south and east. **2.** Often **Southeast** A region in this direction.
□*adjective* **1.** Of, in, or toward the southeast. **2.** Coming from the southeast: *a southeast wind.*
□*adverb* Toward the southeast: *walking southeast.*
south·east (south ēst′) □*noun* □*adjective* □*adverb*

southeastern *adjective* **1.** Of, in, or toward the southeast: *a southeastern state.* **2.** Coming from or lying toward the southeast: *a southeastern wind.*
south·east·ern (south ē′stərn) □*adjective*

southern *adjective* **1.** Of, in, or toward the south: *a country's southern border.* **2.** Coming from or lying toward the south: *a southern wind.*
south·ern (suth′ərn) □*adjective*

southerner *noun* Often **Southerner** A person from a southern region.
south·ern·er (suth′ər nər) □*noun, plural* **southerners**

South Pole *noun* The southern end of the axis around which the earth rotates. The South Pole is the point on the earth that is farthest south.

southward *adverb* To or toward the south: *pointing southward.*
□*adjective* Moving to or toward the south: *a southward voyage.*
south·ward (south′wərd) □*adverb* □*adjective*

southwest *noun* **1.** The direction that is halfway between south and west. **2.** Often **Southwest** A region in this direction.

□*adjective* **1.** Of, in, or toward the southwest: *the southwest coast.* **2.** Coming from the southwest: *a southwest wind.*
□*adverb* Toward the southwest
south·west (south **west′**) □*noun* □*adjective* □*adverb*

Southwester *noun* **1.** A storm with strong winds blowing from the southwest. **2.** A waterproof hat having a broad brim in the back to protect the neck.
south·west·er (south **wes′**tər) □*noun, plural* **southwesters**

southwestern *adjective* **1.** Of, in, or toward the southwest: *a southwestern region.* **2.** From the southwest: *a southwestern breeze.*
south·west·ern (south **wes′**tərn) □*adjective*

souvenir *noun* Something kept to remember a place, person, or event: *She kept her ticket as a souvenir of the play.*
sou·ve·nir (sōō′və **nîr′**) □*noun, plural* **souvenirs**

sovereign *noun* A king or queen.
sov·er·eign (sov′rin) □*noun, plural* **sovereigns**

sow¹ *verb* **1.** To plant or scatter seeds: *We plan to sow wheat and corn in the spring.* **2.** To plant with seeds in order to produce a crop: *He plowed and sowed his fields as soon as all danger of frost had passed.*
sow (sō) □*verb* **sowed, sown** or **sowed, sowing, sows**

sow² *noun* A fully grown female pig.
sow (sou) □*noun, plural* **sows**

sown *verb* A past participle of **sow¹**: *What crops have you sown this year?*
sown (sōn) □*verb*

soybean *noun* A bean plant related to peas and beans that is widely grown for its nutritious beans, which contain oil and are used as food for humans and in animal feed.
soy·bean (soi′bēn′) □*noun, plural* **soybeans**

space *noun* **1.** The area without limits in which the entire universe exists. **2.** A separation; gap: *the space between two parked cars.* **3.** An area provided for a certain purpose: *a work space.* **4.** A period of time.
□*verb* To arrange with spaces between
space (spās) □*noun, plural* **spaces** □*verb* **spaced, spacing, spaces**

spacecraft *noun* A vehicle used for traveling in outer space.
space·craft (spās′kraft′) □*noun, plural* **spacecraft**

spacecraft

spaceship *noun* A spacecraft.
space·ship (spās′ship′) □*noun, plural* **spaceships**

spade¹ *noun* A digging tool with a long handle and a flat, pointed blade that is pressed into the ground with the foot.
spade (spād) □*noun, plural* **spades**

spade

spade² *noun* **1.** A playing card marked with a black figure that resembles the blade of a spade. **2.** **spades** The suit of cards that has this figure.
spade (spād) □*noun, plural* **spades**

WORD HISTORY: **spade²**

The word *spade²* has no connection with *spade¹*. *Spade²* comes from an Italian word meaning ''sword.'' On Italian playing cards a broad-bladed sword was used as the symbol of the suit. Because the English thought that the word *spade* referred to the digging tool, the symbol on English playing cards was changed to resemble the tool.

---

a bat	ī bite	ōō tool	*th* feather
ā make	î fierce	ou out	th bath
â dare	o dot	u nut	hw wheat
ä father	ō no	û turn	zh measure
e net	ô law, for	ch church	ə about, open
ē be	oi soil	ng ring	pencil, atom
i dip	oo look	sh shade	circus

spaghetti *noun* A food made of a mixture of flour and water and shaped into long, solid strings.
spa·ghet·ti (spə get′ē) □*noun*

span *noun* **1.** The distance between two objects, ends, or supports: *The span of a bridge.* **2.** A period of time: *the span of her life.*
□*verb* To stretch across: *The railroad spanned the continent.*
span (span) □*noun, plural* **spans** □*verb* **spanned, spanning, spans**

spaniel *noun* Any of several dogs that have drooping ears, short legs, and a silky coat.
span·iel (span′yəl) □*noun, plural* **spaniels**

> *WORD HISTORY:* **spaniel**
> *Spaniel* comes from an old French word that means ''Spanish.'' This breed of dog originally came from Spain.

Spanish *noun* **1.** The language of Spain, most of the countries of Latin America, and other countries settled by the people of Spain. **2.** The people of Spain.
□*adjective* Of Spain, the Spanish, or their language.
Span·ish (span′ish) □*noun* □*adjective*

spank *verb* To punish by slapping with the open hand or something else flat.
spank (spangk) □*verb* **spanked, spanking, spanks**

spare *verb* **1.** To be merciful or gentle with; not hurt: *spare a captive; sparing the boy's feelings.* **2.** To give away or give out: *Can you spare some time to help us?*
□*adjective* **1.** Extra: *a spare tire.* **2.** Free for other use: *spare time.* **3.** Barely enough; scant: *a spare allowance.*
□*noun* Something extra, such as a tire, to be used when needed.
spare (spâr) □*verb* **spared, sparing, spares** □*adjective* □*noun, plural* **spares**

spark *noun* **1.** A small, burning bit of material: *Sparks flew out of the bonfire.* **2.** A quick flash of light made by electricity. **3.** A hint; trace: *a spark of curiosity.*
□*verb* To give off sparks.
spark (spärk) □*noun, plural* **sparks** □*verb* **sparked, sparking, sparks**

sparkle *verb* **1.** To shine in quick flashes: *The jewels sparkled in the light.* **2.** To bubble like soda water.
□*noun* A quick flash of light; glitter.

spar·kle (spär′kəl) □*verb* **sparkled, sparkling, sparkles** □*noun, plural* **sparkles**

sparrow *noun* A small brownish or grayish bird that is common in cities.
spar·row (spar′ō) □*noun, plural* **sparrows**

sparse *adjective* Occurring here and there; scattered: *Plants are sparse in the desert.*
sparse (spärs) □*adjective* **sparser, sparsest**

spat¹ *noun* A brief quarrel.
spat (spat) □*noun, plural* **spats**

spat² *verb* A past tense and a past participle of **spit**: *The baby spat out the food.*
spat (spat) □*verb*

spatter *verb* To scatter in drops or small bits: *She spattered mud on her trousers.*
spat·ter (spat′ər) □*verb* **spattered, spattering, spatters**

spatula *noun* A tool with a wide, flat blade, used for handling or spreading soft substances: *He used a spatula to frost the cake.*
spat·u·la (spach′ə lə) □*noun, plural* **spatulas**

spatula

spawn *noun* The eggs of fish, frogs, or other water animals.
□*verb* To lay eggs and breed.
spawn (spôn) □*noun* □*verb* **spawned, spawning, spawns**

speak *verb* **1.** To say words; talk. **2.** To express in words: *speak one's mind.* —See Synonyms at **talk**.
speak (spēk) □*verb* **spoke, spoken, speaking, speaks**

speaker *noun* **1.** Someone who speaks, especially someone who gives lectures or speeches. **2.** A loudspeaker.
speak·er (spē′kər) □*noun, plural* **speakers**

spear *noun* **1.** A weapon with a sharp point attached to a long pole. **2.** A slender stalk: *an asparagus spear.*
□*verb* To stab or pierce with something sharp: *He speared the tomato with his fork.*

spear (spîr) □*noun, plural* **spears** □*verb*
speared, spearing, spears

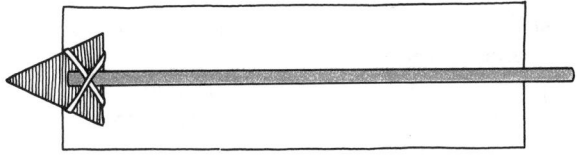

spear

spearmint *noun* A mint plant whose leaves are used for flavoring.
spear·mint (spîr′ mint′) □*noun, plural* **spearmints**

special *adjective* Different from others; exceptional: *a special day; special care.*
spe·cial (spesh′ əl) □*adjective*

specialist *noun* Someone who has skill or knowledge in a particular subject: *That doctor is a specialist in eye ailments.*
spe·cial·ist (spesh′ ə list) □*noun, plural* **specialists**

specialize *verb* To gain or use skill or knowledge in a particular subject: *a banker who specializes in loans.*
spe·cial·ize (spesh′ ə līz′) □*verb* **specialized, specializing, specializes**

specialty *noun* 1. A special area of study, work, or skill. 2. A special attraction: *The restaurant's specialty is chili.*
spe·cial·ty (spesh′ əl tē) □*noun, plural* **specialties**

species *noun* A group of animals or plants that are of the same kind and that can breed with one another.
spe·cies (spē′ shēz′) □*noun, plural* **species**

specific *adjective* Particular; definite: *He felt ill but was suffering from no specific disease.*
spe·ci·fic (spi sif′ ik) □*adjective*

specify *verb* To say in a definite and exact way: *Specify the color when you order the paint.*
spec·i·fy (spes′ ə fī′) □*verb* **specified, specifying, specifies**

specimen *noun* A thing or part that shows what a whole group is like: *We found a good specimen of swamp water to study.*
spec·i·men (spes′ ə mən) □*noun, plural* **specimens**

speck *noun* A small spot, mark, or bit.
speck (spek) □*noun, plural* **specks**

spectacle *noun* 1. An unusual sight or display: *a spectacle of fireworks.* 2. **spectacles** A pair of eyeglasses.
spec·ta·cle (spek′ tə kəl) □*noun, plural* **spectacles**

spectacular *adjective* Making an unusual sight or display: *a spectacular view.*
spec·tac·u·lar (spek tak′ yə lər) □*adjective*

spectator *noun* Someone who watches an event without taking part in it.
spec·ta·tor (spek′ tā′ tər) □*noun, plural* **spectators**

spectrum *noun* The bands of color seen when white light is broken up into parts, as when sunlight passes through a prism. Red, orange, yellow, green, blue, indigo, and violet are the colors of the spectrum.
spec·trum (spek′ trəm) □*noun, plural* **spectrums**

speculate *verb* To think or talk about something without knowing for certain: *speculating about the possibility of life on other planets.*
spec·u·late (spek′ yə lāt′) □*verb* **speculated, speculating, speculates**

sped *verb* A past tense and a past participle of **speed**: *The car sped past without stopping.*
sped (sped) □*verb*

speech *noun* 1. The act of speaking. 2. The ability to speak. 3. Something that is spoken: *The mayor stood up to give his speech.*
speech (spēch) □*noun, plural* **speeches**

speechless *adjective* Not able to speak for the time being: *She was speechless with surprise.*
speech·less (spēch′ lis) □*adjective*

speed *noun* 1. Fast movement or action. 2. A rate of moving: *She drove at a slow speed.* □*verb* 1. To move rapidly: *The missile sped toward its target.* 2. To drive faster than is lawful: *He got a ticket because he was speeding.*
speed (spēd) □*noun, plural* **speeds** □*verb* **sped** or **speeded, speeding, speeds**

speedy *adjective* Done or happening quickly: *She made a speedy recovery from surgery.* —See Synonyms at **fast.**
speed·y (spē′ dē) □*adjective*

a	bat	ī	bite	o͞o	tool	*th*	feather
ā	make	î	fierce	ou	out	th	bath
â	dare	o	dot	u	nut	hw	wheat
ä	father	ō	no	û	turn	zh	measure
e	net	ô	law, for	ch	church	ə	about, open
ē	be	oi	soil	ng	ring		pencil, atom
i	dip	o͝o	look	sh	shade		circus

spell¹   *verb* To say or be the letters of a word in the right order: *Can you spell "fascinate?"*
spell (spel) □*verb* **spelled, spelling, spells**

spell²   *noun* **1.** A word or group of words believed to have magic power: *The witch cast a spell over the boy, and he couldn't move.* **2.** Attraction; charm.
spell (spel) □*noun, plural* **spells**

spell³   *noun* A period of time: *Let's rest on this bench for a spell.*
□*verb* To work in place of for a while: *I'll spell you when you're tired.*
spell (spel) □*noun, plural* **spells** □*verb* **spelled, spelling, spells**

speller   *noun* **1.** Someone who spells words. **2.** A book used in teaching spelling.
spell·er (spel′ər) □*noun, plural* **spellers**

spelling   *noun* **1.** The act of forming words with letters in the right order. **2.** The way a word is spelled.
spell·ing (spel′ing) □*noun, plural* **spellings**

spend   *verb* **1.** To pay out money: *I spent three dollars for lunch.* **2.** To use; devote: *spent a lot of energy weeding the garden.* **3.** To pass time: *We are going to spend our vacation in the country.*
spend (spend) □*verb* **spent, spending, spends**

spent   *verb* The past tense and past participle of **spend:** *I spent an hour reading.*
spent (spent) □*verb*

sperm   *noun* A male cell of reproduction.
sperm (spûrm) □*noun, plural* **sperms**

sperm whale   *noun* A whale with a large head and a long, narrow lower jaw.

sphere   *noun* **1.** A round object like a ball. All the points on the surface of a sphere are the same distance from its center. **2.** An area of power, interest, or activity: *Geology is outside her sphere of knowledge.*
sphere (sfîr) □*noun, plural* **spheres**

sphinx   *noun* An ancient Egyptian statue with the body of a lion and the head of a hawk, ram, or man.
sphinx (sfingks) □*noun, plural* **sphinxes**

sphinx

spice   *noun* Material from a plant used to flavor food. Cinnamon and pepper are spices.
□*verb* To flavor with a spice.
spice (spīs) □*noun, plural* **spices** □*verb* **spiced, spicing, spices**

spicy   *adjective* Flavored with spice.
spic·y (spī′sē) □*adjective* **spicier, spiciest**

spider   *noun* A small animal that has eight legs and spins webs to catch insects.
spi·der (spī′dər) □*noun, plural* **spiders**

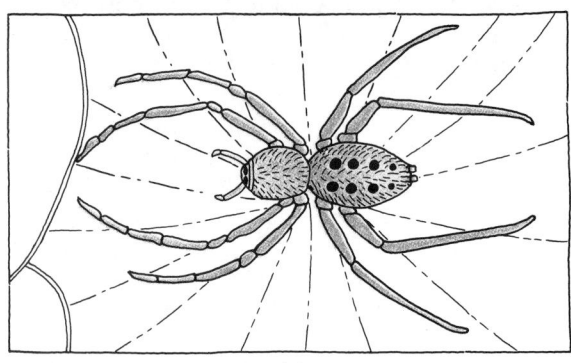
spider

spied   *verb* The past tense and past participle of **spy.**
spied (spīd) □*verb*

spike¹   *noun* **1.** A long, heavy nail. **2.** A sharp-pointed, projecting piece of wood or metal: *baseball shoes with spikes on the soles.*
spike (spīk) □*noun, plural* **spikes**

spike²   *noun* **1.** An ear of grain. **2.** A long stem with flowers growing close together along it.
spike (spīk) □*noun, plural* **spikes**

spill   *verb* **1.** To let something run or fall out of a container: *Try not to spill the soup as you carry it.* **2.** To run or fall out: *Milk spilled from the pot onto the stove.*
spill (spil) □*verb* **spilled** or **spilt, spilling, spills**

spilt   *verb* A past tense and a past participle of **spill:** *She spilt gravy on her dress.*
spilt (spilt) □*verb*

spin   *verb* **1.** To draw out and twist fibers into thread: *spin wool into yarn.* **2.** To form a web or cocoon from a liquid given off by the body: *Spiders spin webs.* **3.** To tell: *spin a tale.* **4.** To turn quickly about an axis: *spin a wheel.* **5.** To feel dizzy: *The roller coaster made my head spin.*
□*noun* **1.** A rapid turning. **2.** A short ride: *We took a spin on our bikes.*

spin (spin) □*verb* **spun, spinning, spins**
□*noun, plural* **spins**

spinach *noun* A plant with dark green leaves eaten as a vegetable.
spin·ach (spin′ich) □*noun*

spinal column *noun* The backbone.
spi·nal column (spī′nəl) □*noun*

spinal cord *noun* A band of nerve tissue extending from the brain down the back through the center of the backbone.

spindle *noun* **1.** A rod on a spinning machine that holds and winds thread. **2.** A thin rod or pin in a machine: *He put the record on the spindle of the phonograph.*
spin·dle (spin′dəl) □*noun, plural* **spindles**

spine *noun* **1.** The backbone. **2.** An animal or plant part that sticks out with a sharp point: *the spines on a cactus.*
spine (spīn) □*noun, plural* **spines**

spinning wheel *noun* A machine made up of a large wheel that turns a spindle and is operated by hand or foot. It is used to spin thread.

spinning wheel

spiral *noun* A curve that keeps getting wider or that coils around a space or structure: *The staircase formed a spiral.*
□*verb* To move in a spiral.
spi·ral (spī′rəl) □*noun, plural* **spirals** □*verb* **spiraled, spiraling, spirals**

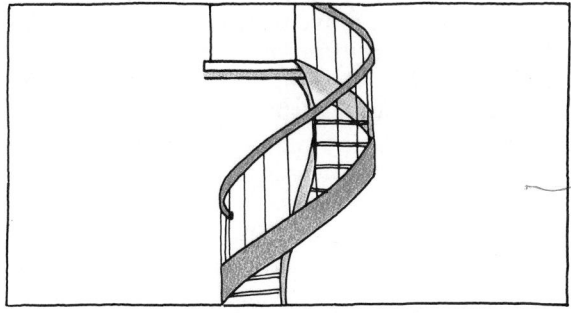

spiral
A spiral staircase

spire *noun* A tall structure that tapers upward to a point, as on a tower.
spire (spīr) □*noun, plural* **spires**

spirit *noun* **1.** The part of a human being that cannot be seen but that controls thinking and feeling and gives the person his or her identity. **2. spirits** A person's mood or state of mind: *in good spirits.* **3.** Enthusiasm: *The team showed spirit.*
spir·it (spir′it) □*noun, plural* **spirits**

spiritual *adjective* **1.** Having to do with the human spirit. **2.** Having to do with religion.
□*noun* A religious folk song.
spir·i·tu·al (spir′i cho͞o əl) □*adjective*
□*noun, plural* **spirituals**

spit *verb* To eject saliva or something else from the mouth: *We ate cherries and spat out the pits.*
spit (spit) □*verb* **spat** or **spit, spitting, spits**

spite *noun* Anger or ill will toward someone: *Spite made him tell lies about the other boy.*
□*verb* To show spite toward someone.
 in spite of Regardless of; despite: *They skated on the pond in spite of the thin ice.*
spite (spīt) □*noun* □*verb* **spited, spiting, spites**

splash *verb* To scatter liquid about: *He jumped into the pool, splashing everyone.*
□*noun* **1.** The act of splashing. **2.** A mark made by scattered liquid.
splash (splash) □*verb* **splashed, splashing, splashes** □*noun, plural* **splashes**

splash

a	bat	ī	bite	o͞o	tool	*th*	feather
ā	make	î	fierce	ou	out	th	bath
â	dare	o	dot	u	nut	hw	wheat
ä	father	ō	no	û	turn	zh	measure
e	net	ô	law, for	ch	church	ə	about, open
ē	be	oi	soil	ng	ring		pencil, atom
i	dip	oo	look	sh	shade		circus

splendid *adjective* **1.** Very beautiful or brilliant: *a splendid sunset.* **2.** Excellent: *a splendid plan.*
splen·did (**splen′**did) □*adjective*

splendor *noun* Magnificent or beautiful appearance: *the splendor of the palace.*
splen·dor (**splen′**dər) □*noun, plural* **splendors**

splint *noun* A long piece of hard material that is used to hold a broken bone in place or to support something delicate.
splint (splint) □*noun, plural* **splints**

splinter *noun* A sharp, thin piece broken off from a larger piece: *I have a splinter of wood in my foot.*
□*verb* To break into sharp, thin pieces: *The glass broke and splintered.*
splin·ter (**splin′**tər) □*noun, plural* **splinters**
□*verb* **splintered, splintering, splinters**

split *verb* To divide or become divided into parts: *He split the logs with an ax.*
□*noun* **1.** The act or result of splitting: *There's a split in the seam.* **2.** A break within a group: *a split in a political party.*
split (split) □*verb* **split, splitting, splits**
□*noun, plural* **splits**

spoil *verb* **1.** To damage or hurt; ruin: *The rain spoiled our fun.* **2.** To become rotten so as to be bad to use: *The milk spoiled.* **3.** To give in to the wishes of someone too much so as to harm his or her character: *spoil a child.*
□*noun* **spoils** Property taken by force in a war.
spoil (spoil) □*verb* **spoiled** or **spoilt, spoiling, spoils** □*noun, plural* **spoils**

spoilt *verb* A past tense and past participle of **spoil.**
spoilt (spoilt) □*verb*

spoke¹ *noun* One of the rods that connect the rim of a wheel to its hub.
spoke (spōk) □*noun, plural* **spokes**

spoke² *verb* The past tense of **speak:** *I spoke to her last week.*
spoke (spōk) □*verb*

spoken *verb* The past participle of **speak:** *English is spoken in that country.*
□*adjective* Said, not written: *spoken words.*
spo·ken (**spō′**kən) □*verb* □*adjective*

sponge *noun* **1.** A water animal that has a soft skeleton with many small holes. **2.** The dried, soft skeleton of a sponge used for bathing and cleaning. **3.** A pad made to resemble and work like a natural sponge.
□*verb* To wash or wipe with a sponge: *She sponged up the spilled water.*
sponge (spunj) □*noun, plural* **sponges**
□*verb* **sponged, sponging, sponges**

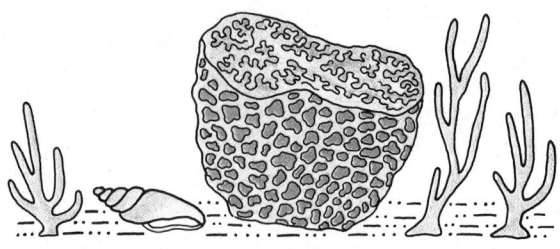

sponge
A water animal

spongy *adjective* Like a sponge; soft and elastic.
spong·y (**spun′**jē) □*adjective* **spongier, spongiest**

sponsor *noun* **1.** Someone who is responsible for or recommends a person or thing: *The minister was our sponsor when we became citizens.* **2.** Someone who presents a person for baptism or confirmation and promises to be responsible for that person's religious education. **3.** A business that pays the costs of a radio or television program.
□*verb* To act as a sponsor for.
spon·sor (**spon′**sər) □*noun, plural* **sponsors**
□*verb* **sponsored, sponsoring, sponsors**

spontaneous *adjective* Not planned or thought about in advance: *spontaneous cheers.*
spon·ta·ne·ous (spon **tā′**nē əs) □*adjective*

spooky *adjective* Mysterious and scary.
spook·y (**spoo′**kē) □*adjective* **spookier, spookiest**

spool *noun* A small cylinder with thread or wire wound around it.
spool (spool) □*noun, plural* **spools**

spoon *noun* A small, shallow bowl at the end of a handle, used in preparing and eating food.
□*verb* To lift or move with a spoon: *Spoon the batter into the muffin tins.*
spoon (spoon) □*noun, plural* **spoons** □*verb* **spooned, spooning, spoons**

spore *noun* A tiny plant part that can grow into a new plant. Mosses and ferns grow from spores instead of seeds.
spore (spôr) □*noun, plural* **spores**

sport *noun* **1.** A game or activity in which the participants are physically active. Baseball, fishing, and jogging are sports. **2.** An enjoyable activity; amusement. **3.** Someone who

behaves according to the rules and gracefully accepts either victory or defeat: *a good sport.*
sport (spôrt) □*noun, plural* **sports**

sportsmanship *noun* The qualities of a good sport; fair play.
sports·man·ship (spôrts′mən ship′) □*noun*

spot *noun* **1.** A small mark or stain: *I have red spots all over my arms.* **2.** A mark on a surface that is different from the rest: *a leopard's spots.* **3.** A place; location.
□*verb* **1.** To mark with spots: *The curtains were spotted with soot.* **2.** To locate; pick out: *I spotted him at once in the audience.* —See Synonyms at **find.**
spot (spot) □*noun, plural* **spots** □*verb* **spotted, spotting, spots**

spotlight *noun* A strong lamp used to light up a small area on a stage.
spot·light (spot′līt′) □*noun, plural* **spotlights**

spouse *noun* A wife or husband.
spouse (spous) □*noun, plural* **spouses**

spout *verb* To send or be sent out in a steady stream: *Water spouted from the hose.*
□*noun* A narrow pipe or opening through which liquid is sent out: *the spout of a teapot.*
spout (spout) □*verb* **spouted, spouting, spouts** □*noun, plural* **spouts**

spout

sprain *noun* An injury to a joint or muscle in which it is stretched or twisted.
□*verb* To cause a sprain: *sprain an ankle.*
sprain (sprān) □*noun, plural* **sprains** □*verb* **sprained, spraining, sprains**

sprang *verb* A past tense of **spring:** *We sprang from our seats when the bell rang.*
sprang (sprang) □*verb*

sprawl *verb* **1.** To sit or lie with the body and limbs spread out in a careless way. **2.** To spread out in a way that is not controlled: *The city sprawled over the surrounding country.*
sprawl (sprôl) □*verb* **sprawled, sprawling, sprawls**

spray *noun* **1.** Liquid in the form of tiny drops or mist: *the spray from a big wave.* **2.** A liquid product, such as paint, that is applied in jets of tiny drops from an aerosol can.
□*verb* To apply a liquid as a spray: *We sprayed paint on the garden furniture.*
spray (sprā) □*noun, plural* **sprays** □*verb* **sprayed, spraying, sprays**

spread *verb* **1.** To open out: *spread a blanket on the beach.* **2.** To move farther apart: *The team spread out over the field.* **3.** To cover with a thin layer: *spread bread with honey.* **4.** To make or become widely known: *spread the news.*
□*noun* **1.** The act of spreading: *the spread of a disease.* **2.** The extent to which something can be stretched out: *Some birds have a six-foot wing spread.* **3.** A cloth cover: *a quilted spread for the bed.* **4.** A soft food for spreading. Butter and peanut butter are spreads.
spread (spred) □*verb* **spread, spreading, spreads** □*noun, plural* **spreads**

spring *verb* **1.** To move upward or forward in a quick motion. **2.** To appear suddenly: *spring into view.* **3.** To make happen suddenly: *spring a surprise.*
□*noun* **1.** An elastic device that returns to its original shape after it is pushed in or pulled out: *The sofa has springs inside it to make the seats softer.* **2.** A jump; leap. **3.** A natural fountain of water. **4.** The season of the year between winter and summer.
spring (spring) □*verb* **sprang** or **sprung, sprung, springing, springs** □*noun, plural* **springs**

springboard *noun* A board used to help a person jump higher in the air: *The diver jumped off a springboard.*
spring·board (spring′bôrd′) □*noun, plural* **springboards**

a bat	ī bite	o͞o tool	*th* feather
ā make	î fierce	ou out	th bath
â dare	o dot	u nut	hw wheat
ä father	ō no	û turn	zh measure
e net	ô law, for	ch church	ə about, open
ē be	oi soil	ng ring	pencil, atom
i dip	oo look	sh shade	circus

sprinkle *verb* **1.** To scatter in drops or small pieces: *sprinkle salt on food.* **2.** To rain in small drops.
□*noun* **1.** A light fall of rain. **2. sprinkles** Tiny pieces of candy often used to cover ice cream, cookies, and other sweets.
sprin·kle (spring′kəl) □*verb* **sprinkled, sprinkling, sprinkles** □*noun, plural* **sprinkles**

sprinkler *noun* A device put on the end of a hose for watering plants.
sprin·kler (spring′klər) □*noun, plural* **sprinklers**

sprint *noun* A fast, short race.
□*verb* To run at top speed.
sprint (sprint) □*noun, plural* **sprints** □*verb* **sprinted, sprinting, sprints**

sprout *verb* To begin to grow: *After the rain, the seeds began to sprout.*
□*noun* A bud or other young plant growth.
sprout (sprout) □*verb* **sprouted, sprouting, sprouts** □*noun, plural* **sprouts**

spruce *noun* An evergreen tree with short needles.
spruce (sprōōs) □*noun, plural* **spruces**

sprung *verb* A past tense and the past participle of **spring.**
sprung (sprung) □*verb*

spun *verb* The past tense and past participle of **spin:** *The child spun the top.*
spun (spun) □*verb*

spur *noun* A sharp metal piece worn on the heel of a boot, used to make a horse go faster.
□*verb* To urge on by or as if by pricking with spurs: *spur a horse; spurred the team on with cheers.*
spur (spûr) □*noun, plural* **spurs** □*verb* **spurred, spurring, spurs**

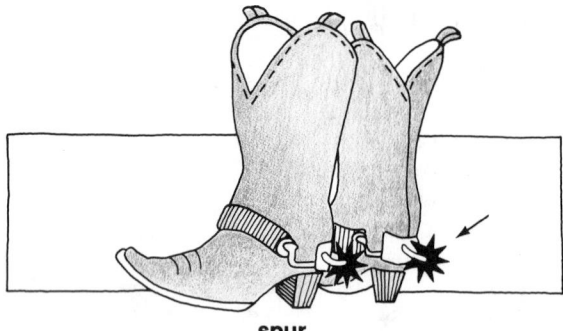

spur

spurt *noun* A sudden, strong gush or outbreak: *a spurt of blood.*

□*verb* To squirt: *Water spurted from the pipe.*
spurt (spûrt) □*noun, plural* **spurts** □*verb* **spurted, spurting, spurts**

sputter *verb* **1.** To make popping sounds: *The lawnmower engine sputtered and then stopped.* **2.** To speak in a quick or confusing manner: *The lost child sputtered his name to the policeman.*
sput·ter (sput′ər) □*verb* **sputtered, sputtering, sputters**

spy *noun* Someone who secretly watches others. Sometimes a government uses spies to get secret information about a foreign country.
□*verb* **1.** To watch others as a spy: *spying on an enemy.* **2.** To recognize; see: *spy a mistake.*
spy (spī) □*noun, plural* **spies** □*verb* **spied, spying, spies**

squad *noun* A small group of people working or playing together.
squad (skwod) □*noun, plural* **squads**

squadron *noun* A group of planes, ships, or other military units.
squad·ron (skwod′rən) □*noun, plural* **squadrons**

squander *verb* To use or spend wastefully: *Don't squander your money on cheap toys.*
—See Synonyms at **waste.**
squan·der (skwon′dər) □*verb* **squandered, squandering, squanders**

square *noun* **1.** A geometric figure having four equal sides and four right angles. **2.** A figure or object having this shape. **3.** The product of a number multiplied by itself: *Nine is the square of three.* **4.** An open area where two or more streets cross one another.
□*adjective* **1.** Having the shape of a square. **2.** Forming a right angle: *a square corner.* **3.** Being or using units that measure areas in squares that are a certain length on each side: *The rug measures 150 square feet.* **4.** Honest or fair: *a square deal.*
□*verb* **1.** To form into a square: *We had to square the board.* **2.** To multiply a number by itself. **3.** To make or be consistent; agree: *His answers square with mine.*
square (skwâr) □*noun, plural* **squares** □*adjective* **squarer, squarest** □*verb* **squared, squaring, squares**

square dance *noun* A dance in which sets of four couples form a square at the beginning of the dance.

square knot *noun* A knot that is made of two half-knots tied in opposite directions.

square root *noun* The factor of a number which, when multiplied by itself, will give the number: *The square root of 25 is 5.*

squash¹ *noun* A fruit that grows on a vine and is cooked and eaten as a vegetable.
squash (skwosh) □*noun, plural* **squashes**

squash² *verb* To press into a soft or flat mass; crush: *squash a tomato.*
□*noun* A game in which players hit a hard rubber ball with a racket on a court with walls.
squash (skwosh) □*verb* **squashed, squashing, squashes** □*noun*

squash

squat *verb* **1.** To bend down and sit on one's heels. **2.** To settle on land that one does not own.
□*adjective* Short and thick: *a squat armchair.*
squat (skwot) □*verb* **squatted** or **squat, squatting, squats** □*adjective* **squatter, squattest**

squat

squawk *noun* A loud, screeching sound: *the squawk of a chicken.*
□*verb* To make or say with a squawk.
squawk (skwôk) □*noun, plural* **squawks**
□*verb* **squawked, squawking, squawks**

squeak *noun* A thin, high-pitched sound or cry: *the squeak of a rusty door.*
□*verb* To make a thin, high-pitched sound: *The chalk squeaked as he wrote on the blackboard.*
squeak (skwēk) □*noun, plural* **squeaks**
□*verb* **squeaked, squeaking, squeaks**

squeal *noun* A shrill, loud sound: *The baby made a squeal of delight.*
□*verb* To make a shrill, loud sound.
squeal (skwēl) □*noun, plural* **squeals** □*verb* **squealed, squealing, squeals**

squeeze *verb* **1.** To press hard on: *squeeze a rubber toy.* **2.** To get by squeezing: *squeeze juice from an orange.* **3.** To force one's way by pressing: *We squeezed through the crowd.* **4.** To crowd; cram: *I squeezed all the clothes into one suitcase.*
□*noun* An act of squeezing.
squeeze (skwēz) □*verb* **squeezed, squeezing, squeezes** □*noun, plural* **squeezes**

squid *noun* A sea animal that has a soft, long body and ten arms surrounding the mouth.
squid (skwid) □*noun, plural* **squids** or **squid**

squint *verb* To look with the eyes half closed: *squinting at the bad handwriting.*
squint (skwint) □*verb* **squinted, squinting, squints**

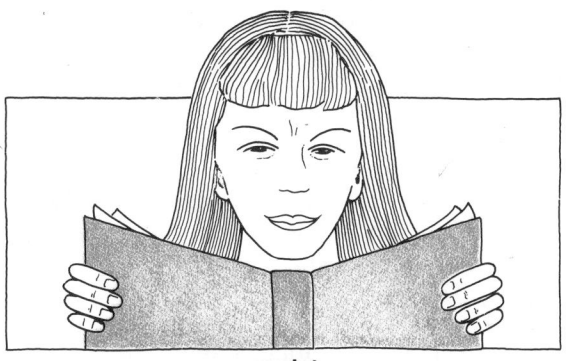

squint

squire *noun* **1.** In the Middle Ages, a young man who served as a knight's attendant. **2.** An English country gentleman.
squire (skwīr) □*noun, plural* **squires**

a bat	ī bite	ōō tool	*th* feather
ā make	î fierce	ou out	th bath
â dare	o dot	u nut	hw wheat
ä father	ō no	û turn	zh measure
e net	ô law, for	ch church	ə about, open
ē be	oi soil	ng ring	pencil, atom
i dip	oo look	sh shade	circus

squirm *verb* To twist the body about; wriggle: *The children squirmed with impatience.*
squirm (skwûrm) □*verb* **squirmed, squirming, squirms**

squirrel *noun* A small, furry animal with a bushy tail.
squir·rel (skwûr′əl) □*noun, plural* **squirrels**

> *WORD HISTORY:* **squirrel**
>
> The word *squirrel* comes from two Greek words, one meaning "shade" and the other meaning "tail." When a squirrel sits up, its long tail curves over its head, casting a shadow.

squirt *verb* **1.** To force or shoot liquid out in a thin stream: *She squirted oil on the squeaking hinge.* **2.** To be forced out in a thin stream: *Water squirted from the crack in the pipe.*
□*noun* An amount of liquid squirted.
squirt (skwûrt) □*verb* **squirted, squirting, squirts** □*noun, plural* **squirts**

st. An abbreviation for **street.**

stab *verb* **1.** To make a hole or cut in with a pointed weapon. **2.** To make a thrust or lunge: *She stabbed at the air with her arm.*
□*noun* **1.** A thrust or wound made with a pointed object. **2.** An attempt; try: *I'll take a stab at fixing the bicycle.*
stab (stab) □*verb* **stabbed, stabbing, stabs** □*noun, plural* **stabs**

stable¹ *adjective* **1.** Not likely to change position or condition suddenly; steady: *a stable desk; in stable health.* **2.** Likely to survive: *a stable partnership.*
sta·ble (stā′bəl) □*adjective* **stabler, stablest**

stable² *noun* A building where horses, cattle, and other animals are kept.
□*verb* To put or keep in a stable.
sta·ble (stā′bəl) □*noun, plural* **stables** □*verb* **stabled, stabling, stables**

stack *noun* A tall pile: *a stack of books.*
□*verb* To put in a stack: *I stacked the old magazines in the garage.*
stack (stak) □*noun, plural* **stacks** □*verb* **stacked, stacking, stacks**

stadium *noun* A large, often open-topped building with rising rows of seats built around a field. Athletic contests and other events are held in a stadium.
sta·di·um (stā′dē əm) □*noun, plural* **stadiums**

staff *noun* **1.** A long stick carried to help in walking or used as a weapon. **2.** A group of workers: *Teachers are members of a school's staff.* **3.** The five lines and the spaces between them on which musical notes are written.
staff (staf) □*noun, plural* **staffs**

stag *noun* A fully grown male deer.
stag (stag) □*noun, plural* **stags**

stage *noun* **1.** The raised platform in a theater on which people perform. **2.** The place where something happens; scene: *Congress has been the stage for many dramatic debates.* **3.** A stagecoach. **4.** A level or step in a process: *the stages of a disease.* **5.** A section of a rocket with its own engine and fuel.
□*verb* **1.** To present on a stage: *stage a play.* **2.** To plan and carry out: *stage a protest march.*
stage (stāj) □*noun, plural* **stages** □*verb* **staged, staging, stages**

stage

stagecoach *noun* A large, closed passenger coach with four wheels that is drawn by horses.
stage·coach (stāj′kōch′) □*noun, plural* **stagecoaches**

stagger *verb* **1.** To move or cause to move in an unsteady way: *The punch staggered the boxer.* **2.** To overwhelm with a severe shock: *He was staggered by the terrible news.* **3.** To arrange to be at different or overlapping times: *The work shifts at the factory are staggered.*
□*noun* An act of staggering.
stag·ger (stag′ər) □*verb* **staggered, staggering, staggers** □*noun, plural* **staggers**

stain *verb* **1.** To soil; spot: *stained the tablecloth with grape juice.* **2.** To color with a dye or tint: *We stained the bookcase a brown color.*
□*noun* **1.** A mark or spot. **2.** A mark of disgrace or dishonor: *a stain on her reputation.* **3.** A liquid put on wood to color it.
stain (stān) □*verb* **stained, staining, stains** □*noun, plural* **stains**

stair *noun* **1. stairs** A series of steps used to move from one level to another. **2.** One of a flight of steps.
stair (stâr) □*noun, plural* **stairs**

staircase *noun* A flight of steps and its supporting parts.
stair·case (stâr′ kās′) □*noun, plural* **staircases**

stairway *noun* A flight of stairs; staircase.
stair·way (stâr′ wā′) □*noun, plural* **stairways**

stake *noun* **1.** A stick or post with a sharp end for driving into the ground: *A row of stakes marked the end of his property.* **2.** Money or something of value that the winner of a bet or contest gets. **3.** A share in a business.
□*verb* **1.** To mark the boundaries of with stakes or other markers: *stake out a piece of land.* **2.** To hold up with a stake: *stake a tomato plant.* **3.** To gamble; risk: *He staked all his savings on the new business.*
stake (stāk) □*noun, plural* **stakes** □*verb* **staked, staking, stakes**

stalactite *noun* A long, pointed piece of stone hanging from the roof of a cave. It is formed by the evaporation of dripping water that contains minerals.
sta·lac·tite (stə lak′ tīt′) □*noun, plural* **stalactites**

stalagmite *noun* A long, pointed piece of stone rising from the floor of a cave. It is formed by water containing minerals dripping from above.
sta·lag·mite (stə lag′ mīt′) □*noun, plural* **stalagmites**

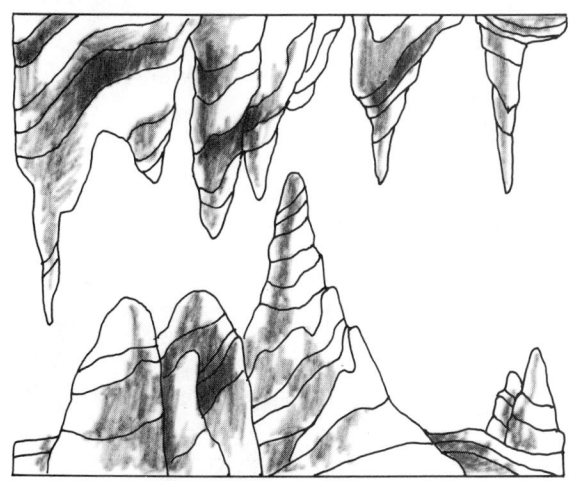

stalactite and stalagmite
Above: stalactite
Below: stalagmite

stale *adjective* **1.** Not fresh: *stale bread.* **2.** Too old or too often used: *a stale excuse.* **3.** Not in condition from lack of practice or use.
stale (stāl) □*adjective* **staler, stalest**

stalk[1] *noun* The main stem of a plant, or a stem that supports a leaf or flower.
stalk (stôk) □*noun, plural* **stalks**

stalk[2] *verb* **1.** To walk in a stiff, dignified way: *She was insulted and stalked out of the room.* **2.** To follow quietly so as to get close without being observed: *a hunter stalking game.*
stalk (stôk) □*verb* **stalked, stalking, stalks**

stall *noun* **1.** An enclosed space for an animal: *There were six stalls for horses in the stable.* **2.** A small enclosure for selling or showing goods; booth.
□*verb* To stop running: *The car stalled.*
stall (stôl) □*noun, plural* **stalls** □*verb* **stalled, stalling, stalls**

stallion *noun* A male horse.
stal·lion (stal′ yən) □*noun, plural* **stallions**

stamen *noun* A flower part made up of a thin stalk that bears organs that produce pollen.
sta·men (stā′ mən) □*noun, plural* **stamens**

stammer *verb* **1.** To speak with pauses and sometimes repeated sounds; stutter. **2.** To say in a nervous way: *He stammered a reply to the judge's question.*
□*noun* An act or habit of stammering.
stam·mer (stam′ ər) □*verb* **stammered, stammering, stammers** □*noun, plural* **stammers**

stamp *verb* **1.** To bring down one's foot heavily: *We stamped our feet to shake off the snow.* **2.** To put an end to; stop: *stamp out a fire; stamp out crime.* **3.** To mark with a tool that leaves a design or letters: *The border guard stamped our passports and let us enter.* **4.** To put a postage stamp on.
□*noun* **1.** A small piece of paper with a design on the front and a sticky back, especially one attached to a letter or package to show that a mailing charge has been paid. **2.** A tool that leaves a mark when pressed against a surface.

a	bat	ī	bite	ōō	tool	*th*	feather
ā	make	î	fierce	ou	out	th	bath
â	dare	o	dot	u	nut	hw	wheat
ä	father	ō	no	û	turn	zh	measure
e	net	ô	law, for	ch	church	ə	about, open
ē	be	oi	soil	ng	ring		pencil, atom
i	dip	oo	look	sh	shade		circus

3. An act of stamping.

stamp (stamp) □*verb* **stamped, stamping, stamps** □*noun, plural* **stamps**

stampede *noun* **1.** A sudden, violent rush of startled animals: *a cattle stampede.* **2.** A sudden rush of people.

□*verb* To rush wildly in or as if in a stampede: *The horses stampeded when the mountain lion charged them.*

stam·pede (stam pēd′) □*noun, plural* **stampedes** □*verb* **stampeded, stampeding, stampedes**

stand *verb* **1.** To be upright on the feet: *Since there were no empty chairs we stood at the back of the room.* **2.** To rest or put in an upright position: *The statue stood on its base.* **3.** To be in a certain place, condition, or situation: *The house stands on a hill.* **4.** To remain without being moved: *Let the mixture stand until it is firm.* **5.** To remain in effect: *The rule still stands.* **6.** To have a certain position or opinion: *My candidate stands for lower taxes.* **7.** To put up with; tolerate: *My parents can't stand noise.*

□*noun* **1.** An act of standing. **2.** A place for standing or stopping. **3.** A small structure for the sale of goods: *a newspaper stand.* **4.** A small rack or container for putting things in or on. **5.** A raised platform for sitting or standing: *a witness stand.* **6. stands** An outdoor seating area. **7.** A position or opinion: *a strong stand against racial prejudice.*

stand (stand) □*verb* **stood, standing, stands** □*noun, plural* **stands**

standard *noun* **1.** A measure or model against which others are compared or judged: *That craftsman has high standards of quality.* **2.** A flag or banner.

□*adjective* **1.** Widely used as a standard: *The meter is a standard measure of length.* **2.** Regularly used or done: *The standard practice in that store is to wrap all gifts at a separate counter.* **3.** Generally accepted as good and reliable: *a standard reference book.*

stand·ard (stan′ dərd) □*noun, plural* **standards** □*adjective*

stank *verb* A past tense of **stink.**

stank (stangk) □*verb*

stanza *noun* A group of lines that forms a division of a poem or song.

stan·za (stan′ zə) □*noun, plural* **stanzas**

staple¹ *noun* **1.** A major product of a region: *Beef is a staple of Argentina.* **2.** A basic food or other product that is always produced and

sold: *flour, salt, sugar and other staples.*

sta·ple (stā′ pəl) □*noun, plural* **staples**

staple² *noun* A U-shaped metal or wire fastener. Large staples are driven into surfaces to hold hooks or bolts in place. Smaller wire staples are used for fastening papers together.

□*verb* To fasten with a staple.

sta·ple (stā′ pəl) □*noun, plural* **staples** □*verb* **stapled, stapling, staples**

stapler *noun* A tool for fastening things together with staples.

sta·pler (stā′ plər) □*noun, plural* **staplers**

star *noun* **1.** A heavenly body that appears in the night sky as a fixed point of bright light. **2.** A figure with five or more points: *a scarf decorated with little silver stars.* **3.** An actor or actress who plays a leading role: *the star of a movie.* **4.** An outstanding person in a field: *a tennis star.*

□*adjective* Most outstanding: *a star runner.*

□*verb* **1.** To decorate or mark with a star. **2.** To play a leading role: *She's now starring in a television show.*

star (stär) □*noun, plural* **stars** □*adjective* □*verb* **starred, starring, stars**

starch *noun* **1.** A white substance made and stored by plants and used as food by humans and animals. Wheat, corn, rice, and potatoes contain starch. **2.** A powdered substance used to make cloth stiff.

□*verb* To make stiff with starch: *starch a shirt.*

starch (stärch) □*noun, plural* **starches** □*verb* **starched, starching, starches**

stare *verb* To look with a long, steady gaze: *We stared at the antique car driving down the street.*

□*noun* A steady gaze.

stare (stâr) □*verb* **stared, staring, stares** □*noun, plural* **stares**

starfish *noun* A sea animal with a body in the shape of a five-pointed star.

star·fish (stär′ fish′) □*noun, plural* **starfish** or **starfishes**

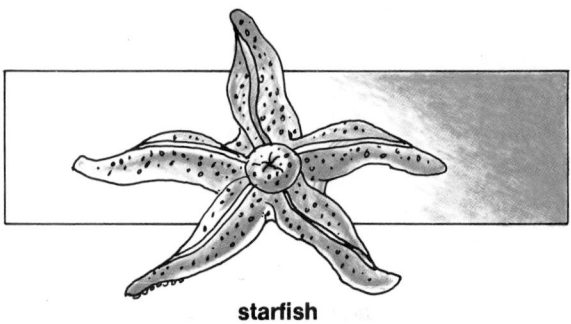

starfish

starling *noun* A bird with a short tail and dark, shiny feathers.
star·ling (stär′ling) □*noun, plural* **starlings**

starry *adjective* **1.** Shining like stars: *starry eyes.* **2.** Full of stars: *a starry night.*
star·ry (stär′ē) □*adjective* **starrier, starriest**

Stars and Stripes *plural noun* The flag of the United States.

Star-Spangled Banner *noun* The national anthem of the United States.
Star-Spangled Banner (stär′spang′gəld) □*noun*

start *verb* **1.** To begin; set out: *We started to clean the yard after breakfast.* **2.** To have a beginning: *Vacation starts in June.* **3.** To put into operation: *start an engine.* **4.** To make a sudden movement from fear or surprise: *He started when I woke him.* —See Synonyms at **begin.**
□*noun* **1.** A beginning. **2.** A startled reaction.
start (stärt) □*verb* **started, starting, starts** □*noun, plural* **starts**

starve *verb* **1.** To suffer or die because of lack of food. **2.** To be very hungry.
starve (stärv) □*verb* **starved, starving, starves**

WORD HISTORY: **starve**

Starve comes from an old English word that means ''to die.''

---

state *noun* **1.** The condition in which a person or thing exists: *a bad state of health; iron in the molten state.* **2.** A mental or emotional condition: *a state of confusion.* **3.** A nation. **4.** One of the political divisions of certain countries, such as the United States of America.
□*adjective* **1.** Of or involving a state: *a state law.* **2.** With great ceremony; formal: *a state banquet.*
□*verb* To express clearly; declare: *State your opinion.*
state (stāt) □*noun, plural* **states** □*adjective* □*verb* **stated, stating, states**

stately *adjective* Dignified or grand in manner or appearance; majestic: *a stately oak tree.*
state·ly (stāt′lē) □*adjective* **statelier, stateliest**

statement *noun* Something stated: *a statement of their beliefs.*
state·ment (stāt′mənt) □*noun, plural* **statements**

statesman *noun* Someone who is skilled in government or diplomacy.
states·man (stāts′mən) □*noun, plural* **statesmen**

static *adjective* Not changing: *The population of the city has been static for the last two years.* □*noun* Disturbance in radio or television reception, such as crackling noise, caused by electrical charges in the air.
stat·ic (stat′ik) □*adjective* □*noun*

station *noun* **1.** A place where a person or thing is supposed to stand: *We took our stations for the fire drill.* **2.** A place or special building for certain services or activities: *a police station.* **3.** A stopping place along a route: *a train station.* **4.** A place that sends radio or television signals.
□*verb* To assign to a position: *The sergeant stationed two guards at every exit.*
sta·tion (stā′shən) □*noun, plural* **stations** □*verb* **stationed, stationing, stations**

stationary *adjective* **1.** Not moving; remaining still. **2.** Not capable of being moved: *a stationary bench nailed to the floor.* **3.** Not changing; staying the same: *Prices should remain stationary this year.*
sta·tion·ar·y (stā′shə ner′ē) □*adjective*

stationery *noun* Writing paper, envelopes, and other writing materials.
sta·tion·er·y (stā′shə ner′ē) □*noun*

station wagon *noun* An automobile with rows of rear seats that can be folded down to provide cargo space, but no separate compartment for luggage.

statistics *plural noun* Facts and figures gathered together for information on a particular subject: *the latest population statistics.*
sta·tis·tics (stə tis′tiks) □*plural noun*

statue *noun* The likeness of a person or thing made by an artist out of some solid material.
stat·ue (stach′ōō) □*noun, plural* **statues**

status *noun* **1.** The condition of a person or thing: *She achieved the legal status of being an adult at the age of 18.* **2.** Position or rank compared to other people: *a higher status than*

a	bat	ĭ	bite	ōō	tool	*th*	feather
ā	make	î	fierce	ou	out	th	bath
â	dare	o	dot	u	nut	hw	wheat
ä	father	ō	no	û	turn	zh	measure
e	net	ô	law, for	ch	church	ə	about, open
ē	be	oi	soil	ng	ring		pencil, atom
i	dip	oo	look	sh	shade		circus

their neighbors.
sta·tus (**stā′**təs *or* **stat′**əs) ☐*noun*

stave *noun* One of the narrow strips of wood forming the sides of a barrel or boat.
stave (stāv) ☐*noun, plural* **staves**

stay *verb* **1.** To remain in one place: *stay home all day.* **2.** To keep on being: *stay awake.* **3.** To live or visit somewhere: *stay at a hotel.* ☐*noun* A visit: *a stay at an aunt's house.*
stay (stā) ☐*verb* **stayed, staying, stays** ☐*noun, plural* **stays**

steady *adjective* **1.** Not likely to shake or slip: *steady hands.* **2.** Not changing; constant: *a steady wind; steady progress.* **3.** Not easily excited: *steady nerves.* **4.** Regular; reliable: *a steady customer.*
☐*verb* To make or become steady.
stead·y (sted′ē) ☐*adjective* **steadier, steadiest** ☐*verb* **steadied, steadying, steadies**

steak *noun* A slice of meat or fish for broiling or frying.
steak (stāk) ☐*noun, plural* **steaks**

steal *verb* **1.** To take someone else's property without permission: *The thief was caught stealing a bicycle.* **2.** To get or enjoy secretly: *steal a few minutes for a quick telephone call.* **3.** To move or pass quietly: *He stole out of the house when no one was looking.* **4.** In baseball, to gain another base by running to it as the pitch is thrown.
steal (stēl) ☐*verb* **stole, stolen, stealing, steals**

steam *noun* Water in the state of a gas. Water turns into steam when it is boiled.
☐*verb* **1.** To give off steam. **2.** To become covered with steam: *The mirror steams up when the shower is used.* **3.** To move by steam power: *The ship steamed along the coast.* **4.** To cook or treat with steam: *steam vegetables.*
steam (stēm) ☐*noun* ☐*verb* **steamed, steaming, steams**

steamboat *noun* A boat driven by steam engines.
steam·boat (stēm′bōt′) ☐*noun, plural* **steamboats**

steam engine *noun* An engine driven by steam.

steamer *noun* A steamship.
steam·er (stē′mər) ☐*noun, plural* **steamers**

steamroller *noun* A vehicle with a large, heavy roller for pressing down and smoothing road surfaces.

steam·roll·er (stēm′rō′lər) ☐*noun, plural* **steamrollers**

steamship *noun* A large ship driven by steam engines.
steam·ship (stēm′ship′) ☐*noun, plural* **steamships**

steam shovel *noun* A large machine with a big scoop at the end of a long beam, used for digging.

steel *noun* A hard, strong metal made by mixing carbon with iron.
steel (stēl) ☐*noun, plural* **steels**

steep¹ *adjective* Having a sharp slope: *a steep hill.*
steep (stēp) ☐*adjective* **steeper, steepest**

steep² *verb* To soak in liquid: *Let the tea steep.*
steep (stēp) ☐*verb* **steeped, steeping, steeps**

steeple *noun* A tall, pointed tower on the roof of a building.
steep·le (stē′pəl) ☐*noun, plural* **steeples**

steer¹ *verb* **1.** To guide the course of a vehicle: *steer a sailboat.* **2.** To be guided or handled: *a car that steers easily.*
steer (stîr) ☐*verb* **steered, steering, steers**

steer² *noun* A young bull raised for beef.
steer (stîr) ☐*noun, plural* **steers**

stem¹ *noun* **1.** The main part of a plant that supports the branches or leaves. **2.** A connecting or supporting part that resembles such a plant part: *the stem of a glass.*
stem (stem) ☐*noun, plural* **stems**

stem² *verb* To plug up; stop: *stemming the flow of water.*
stem (stem) ☐*verb* **stemmed, stemming, stems**

step *noun* **1.** A movement made by lifting one foot and putting it down in another spot, as in walking. **2.** A short distance: *The grocery store is just a step away.* **3.** The sound of someone walking. **4.** A small platform for the foot in going up or down: *the steps of a stairway.* **5.** An act done to achieve some goal: *The mayor is taking steps to make the city cleaner.* **6.** A degree of progress: *Learning the multiplication tables is one of the first steps in arithmetic.*
☐*verb* **1.** To move by taking a step: *Step forward.* **2.** To press the foot down: *Step on that cockroach.*
step (step) ☐*noun, plural* **steps** ☐*verb* **stepped, stepping, steps**

stepfather *noun* The husband of one's mother by a later marriage.

step·fa·ther (step′fä′thər) □*noun, plural* **stepfathers**

stepladder *noun* A ladder with flat steps instead of rungs.
step·lad·der (step′lad′ər) □*noun, plural* **stepladders**

stepladder

stepmother *noun* The wife of one's father by a later marriage.
step·moth·er (step′muth′ər) □*noun, plural* **stepmothers**

stereo *noun* A record player that uses two or more speakers in such as way as to make the sound more lifelike.
ste·re·o (ster′ē ō′ *or* stîr′ē ō′) □*noun, plural* **stereos**

sterilize *verb* To make free from germs or dirt: *A dentist sterilizes his instruments.*
ster·il·ize (ster′ə līz′) □*verb* **sterilized, sterilizing, sterilizes**

stern[1] *adjective* **1.** Grave and severe: *a stern warning from the police officer.* **2.** Strict; firm: *a stern punishment.*
stern (stûrn) □*adjective* **sterner, sternest**

stern[2] *noun* The rear part of a ship or boat.
stern (stûrn) □*noun, plural* **sterns**

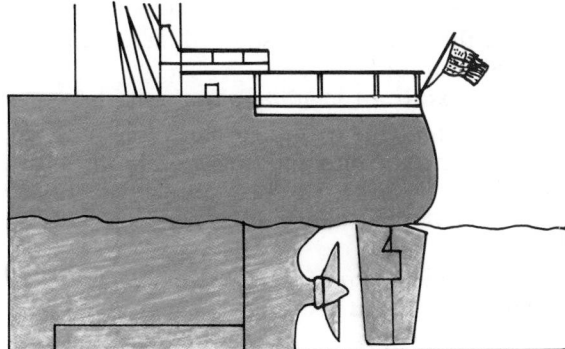

stern

stethoscope *noun* An instrument used by a doctor to listen to sounds made within the body, such as heartbeats.
steth·o·scope (steth′ə skōp) □*noun, plural* **stethoscopes**

stew *verb* To cook by simmering slowly: *We stewed the tomatoes with peppers.*
□*noun* Pieces of meat or fish and vegetables cooked slowly in a liquid.
stew (stōō *or* styōō) □*verb* **stewed, stewing, stews** □*noun, plural* **stews**

steward *noun* **1.** Someone who manages another's property, household, or finances. **2.** A male attendant on a passenger ship or airplane.
stew·ard (stōō′ərd *or* styōō′ərd) □*noun, plural* **stewards**

stewardess *noun* A woman who waits on passengers in an airplane.
stew·ard·ess (stōō′ər dis *or* styōō′ər dis) □*noun, plural* **stewardesses**

stick *noun* **1.** A long, thin piece of wood. **2.** Something having the shape of a stick: *a stick of candy.*
□*verb* **1.** To prick; pierce: *She stuck her finger with a thorn.* **2.** To push into: *She stuck a flower in her hair.* **3.** To fasten or attach: *Stick the stamp on the envelope.* **4.** To be attached and not come off easily: *The dough stuck to the cook's fingers.* **5.** To stay or keep in place: *The car got stuck in the snow.* **6.** To bring to a point where progress stops: *I got stuck on the last question.* **7.** To remain close: *Let's stick together or we'll get separated.* **8.** To keep on; continue: *Stick to the job till it's done.* **9.** To extend: *His ears stick out.*
stick (stik) □*noun, plural* **sticks** □*verb* **stuck, sticking, sticks**

sticker *noun* A small piece of paper with glue on the back, used to fasten or mark something.
stick·er (stik′ər) □*noun, plural* **stickers**

sticky *adjective* **1.** Tending to stick: *sticky candy.* **2.** Hot and humid: *sticky weather.*
stick·y (stik′ē) □*adjective* **stickier, stickiest**

a	bat	ī	bite	ōō	tool	*th*	feather
ā	make	î	fierce	ou	out	th	bath
â	dare	o	dot	u	nut	hw	wheat
ä	father	ō	no	û	turn	zh	measure
e	net	ô	law, for	ch	church	ə	about, open
ē	be	oi	soil	ng	ring		pencil, atom
i	dip	oo	look	sh	shade		circus

stiff *adjective* **1.** Not easily bent: *stiff card-board.* **2.** Not moving easily: *a stiff neck.* **3.** Formal and rigid: *stiff manners.* **4.** Strong and steady: *a stiff wind.* **5.** Harsh; severe: *a stiff punishment.*
stiff (stif) ▢*adjective* **stiffer, stiffest**

stifle *verb* **1.** To make or feel uncomfortable because of a lack of air. **2.** To hold back or check: *stifle a laugh.*
sti·fle (stī′fəl) ▢*verb* **stifled, stifling, stifles**

still *adjective* **1.** Without noise; quiet: *a still evening.* **2.** Without motion: *a still pond.*
▢*noun* Silence: *the still of the night.*
▢*adverb* **1.** Not moving: *Try to sit still.* **2.** Now as before: *She's still mad at me.* **3.** In increasing amount; even: *climbing still higher.* **4.** All the same; nevertheless: *an old but still useful pan.*
still (stil) ▢*adjective* **stiller, stillest** ▢*noun* ▢*adverb*

stilt *noun* Either of a pair of long, slender poles with a foot support. Stilts lift a person above the ground in walking.
stilt (stilt) ▢*noun, plural* **stilts**

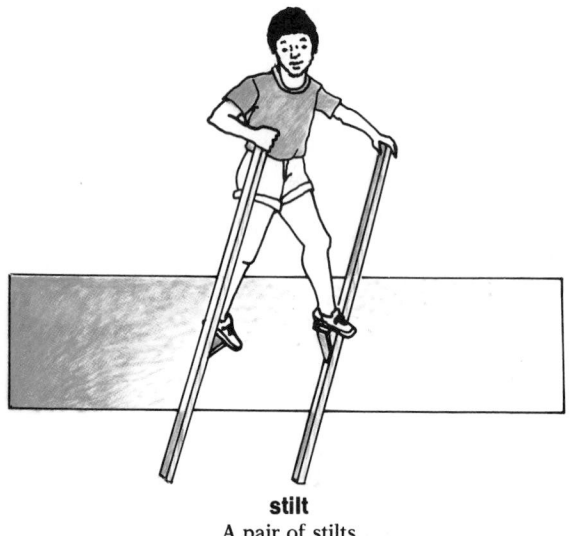

stilt
A pair of stilts

stimulate *verb* To make more active or excited: *The smell of food stimulated my appetite.*
stim·u·late (stim′yə lāt′) ▢*verb* **stimulated, stimulating, stimulates**

stimulus *noun* **1.** Something that causes a reaction in a living organism. **2.** Something that excites or stirs to action: *Her silence was a stimulus to my curiosity.*
stim·u·lus (stim′yə ləs) ▢*noun, plural* **stim·u·li** (stim′yə lī)

sting *verb* **1.** To hurt by piercing with a small, sharp point: *Have you ever been stung by a hornet?* **2.** To feel or cause to feel a sharp pain: *Soap stings if you get it in your eyes.*
▢*noun* **1.** A sharp part of an insect or animal that is used for stinging. **2.** A wound made by such a part. **3.** A sharp, painful sensation.
sting (sting) ▢*verb* **stung, stinging, stings** ▢*noun, plural* **stings**

stinger *noun* An insect or animal part that is used for stinging.
sting·er (sting′ər) ▢*noun, plural* **stingers**

stingray *noun* An ocean fish that has a flat body and a poisonous stinger on its long tail.
sting·ray (sting′rā′) ▢*noun, plural* **stingrays**

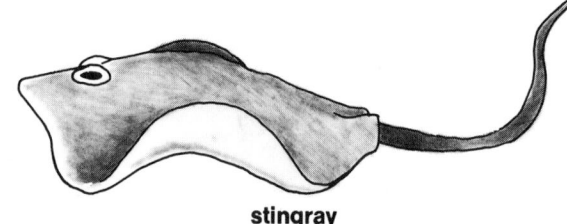

stingray

stingy *adjective* Unwilling to give, spend, or share; not generous.
stin·gy (stin′jē) ▢*adjective* **stingier, stingiest**

stink *verb* To give off a bad odor.
▢*noun* A strong, bad odor.
stink (stingk) ▢*verb* **stank** or **stunk, stunk, stinking, stinks** ▢*noun, plural* **stinks**

stir *verb* **1.** To mix something by moving it around, as with a spoon: *Stir the cocoa until the sugar dissolves.* **2.** To move slightly: *Not a leaf stirred.* **3.** To bring about; cause: *stir up trouble.* **4.** To excite the emotions of: *His speech stirred the crowd.*
▢*noun* **1.** The act of stirring. **2.** An excited reaction: *The robbery caused quite a stir.*
stir (stûr) ▢*verb* **stirred, stirring, stirs** ▢*noun, plural* **stirs**

stirrup *noun* One of a pair of rings hung from either side of a horse's saddle to support the rider's foot.
stir·rup (stûr′əp) ▢*noun, plural* **stirrups**

stitch *noun* One complete movement of a threaded needle into and out of material, as in sewing or closing up a deep cut.
▢*verb* To make, fasten, or decorate with stitches.
stitch (stich) ▢*noun, plural* **stitches** ▢*verb* **stitched, stitching, stitches**

stock *noun* **1.** A supply of things for use or sale: *a large stock of food.* **2.** Farm animals

such as cows, sheep, and pigs. **3.** A group of ancestors from which a person, animal, or plant is descended: *Her father's family comes from Hungarian stock.* **4.** Liquid in which fish, meat, or vegetables have been cooked, used in making soups and gravies. **5.** The handle of a firearm. **6. stocks** A pillory. **7.** Shares in a business.
□*verb* **1.** To provide with a stock: *We stocked the camp with food for the weekend.* **2.** To have or keep in stock: *That store stocks all kinds of fruit and vegetables.*
□*adjective* Kept regularly available: *a store's stock items.*
stock (stok) □*noun, plural* **stocks** □*verb* **stocked, stocking, stocks** □*adjective*

stockade *noun* **1.** An area surrounded and protected by a fence of strong wooden posts. **2.** A military jail.
stock·ade (sto kād′) □*noun, plural* **stockades**

stock exchange *noun* A place where stocks and bonds are bought and sold.

stocking *noun* A close-fitting covering for the foot and leg.
stock·ing (stok′ing) □*noun, plural* **stockings**

stock market *noun* **1.** A stock exchange. **2.** The business that takes place in a stock exchange.

stocky *adjective* Short and solidly built.
stock·y (stok′ē) □*adjective* **stockier, stockiest**

stockyard *noun* A large, enclosed place in which livestock is kept before being shipped elsewhere.
stock·yard (stok′yärd′) □*noun, plural* **stockyards**

stole *verb* The past tense of **steal**: *They stole down the hall on tiptoe.*
stole (stōl) □*verb*

stolen *verb* The past participle of **steal**: *When was the necklace stolen?*
sto·len (stō′lən) □*verb*

stomach *noun* **1.** An organ that receives and begins to digest swallowed food. **2.** A desire or appetite: *I have no stomach for quarreling.*
□*verb* To put up with; tolerate: *I just can't stomach that nonsense.*
stom·ach (stum′ək) □*noun, plural* **stomachs** □*verb* **stomached, stomaching, stomachs**

stomp *verb* To step or walk heavily: *He got very angry and stomped on the floor.*
stomp (stomp) □*verb* **stomped, stomping, stomps**

stone *noun* **1.** Hard material from the earth; rock. **2.** A jewel; gem. **3.** The hard seed of a fruit; pit.
□*verb* To throw stones at.
stone (stōn) □*noun, plural* **stones** □*verb* **stoned, stoning, stones**

stood *verb* The past tense and past participle of **stand**: *We stood next to our desks.*
stood (stood) □*verb*

stool *noun* **1.** A seat without arms or a back. **2.** A low support to rest the feet on.
stool (stool) □*noun, plural* **stools**

stoop¹ *verb* **1.** To bend from the waist: *She stooped to tie her shoes.* **2.** To walk or stand with the shoulders and head bent forward. **3.** To lower oneself: *wouldn't stoop to begging.*
□*noun* A forward bending of the head and shoulders: *walking with a stoop.*
stoop (stoop) □*verb* **stooped, stooping, stoops** □*noun, plural* **stoops**

stoop² *noun* A small staircase at the entrance of a building.
stoop (stoop) □*noun, plural* **stoops**

stop *verb* **1.** To cease or cause to cease moving: *The bus stopped. She stopped the car.* **2.** To plug up or block: *A large amount of hair is stopping up the drain.* **3.** To cause to change a course of action; prevent: *I tried to stop him from quitting school.* **4.** To come to an end: *It stopped raining.*
□*noun* **1.** The act or condition of stopping; halt: *The train made several stops.* **2.** A stay or visit. **3.** A place where a stop is made.
stop (stop) □*verb* **stopped, stopping, stops** □*noun, plural* **stops**

stopper *noun* A device put into an opening to close it: *The bathtub has a rubber stopper.*
stop·per (stop′ər) □*noun, plural* **stoppers**

stopwatch *noun* A watch that can be started and stopped as wished in order to measure time precisely.
stop·watch (stop′woch′) □*noun, plural* **stopwatches**

storage *noun* **1.** The act of storing or the condition of being stored. **2.** A space for storage.

a	bat	ī	bite	o͞o	tool	*th*	feather
ā	make	î	fierce	ou	out	th	bath
â	dare	o	dot	u	nut	hw	wheat
ä	father	ō	no	û	turn	zh	measure
e	net	ô	law, for	ch	church	ə	about, open
ē	be	oi	soil	ng	ring		pencil, atom
i	dip	oo	look	sh	shade		circus

3. The price charged for storing goods.
stor·age (stôr′ij) □*noun*

store   *noun* **1.** A place where things are sold; shop. **2.** A supply of goods put away for future use: *a store of wood for the winter.*
□*verb* To put away for future use: *The squirrel stored up acorns for the winter.*
store (stôr) □*noun, plural* **stores** □*verb* **stored, storing, stores**

storehouse   *noun* **1.** A place in which goods are stored. **2.** A large supply; source: *A dictionary is a storehouse of information.*
store·house (stôr′hous′) □*noun, plural* **storehouses**

stork   *noun* A large bird with long legs and a long bill.
stork (stôrk) □*noun, plural* **storks**

stork

storm   *noun* **1.** A strong wind with heavy rain or snow. **2.** A sudden, strong outburst: *a storm of protest.* **3.** A sudden, forceful attack: *The soldiers took the town by storm.*
□*verb* **1.** To blow with heavy rain or snow. **2.** To move with violent emotion: *He stormed out of the room.* **3.** To attack violently: *The knights stormed the castle.*
storm (stôrm) □*noun, plural* **storms** □*verb* **stormed, storming, storms**

stormy   *adjective* **1.** Of, having to do with, or resembling a storm: *stormy weather.* **2.** Violently emotional: *a stormy discussion about politics.*
storm·y (stôr′mē) □*adjective* **stormier, stormiest**

story¹   *noun* **1.** An account of something that happened: *a newspaper story.* **2.** An account that has been made up or told to entertain people. **3.** A lie.
sto·ry (stôr′ē) □*noun, plural* **stories**

story²   *noun* A floor of a building.
sto·ry (stôr′ē) □*noun, plural* **stories**

stout   *adjective* **1.** Having courage or determination: *stout pioneers.* **2.** Strong; sturdy: *a pair of stout shoes.* **3.** Large and fat.
stout (stout) □*adjective* **stouter, stoutest**

stove   *noun* An appliance used for cooking or heating.
stove (stōv) □*noun, plural* **stoves**

stow   *verb* **1.** To put away; store: *Stow your bag under the bed.* **2.** To load; park: *We stowed our luggage in the car.*
stow (stō) □*verb* **stowed, stowing, stows**

stowaway   *noun* Someone who hides aboard a ship or other vehicle to get a free ride.
stow·a·way (stō′ə wā′) □*noun, plural* **stowaways**

straggle   *verb* To stray or wander from a direct line: *The children straggled after their mother.*
strag·gle (strag′əl) □*verb* **straggled, straggling, straggles**

straight   *adjective* **1.** Extending in the same direction; not curved or bent: *a straight line.* **2.** Direct; honest: *a straight answer.* **3.** In good order: *He set his belongings straight.* **4.** In a row: *I won three straight games.*
□*adverb* **1.** Directly: *Come straight home.* **2.** In an upright way: *Stand up straight.*
straight (strāt) □*adjective* **straighter, straightest** □*adverb*

straighten   *verb* To make or become straight: *The path straightens out a little further on.*
straight·en (strāt′ən) □*verb* **straightened, straightening, straightens**

straightforward   *adjective* Direct and honest: *I would like a straightforward answer.*
straight·for·ward (strāt fôr′wərd) □*adjective*

strain   *verb* **1.** To stretch or pull hard: *The dogs strained at their leashes.* **2.** To try hard; strive: *She strained to understand.* **3.** To hurt by overwork: *strain one's eyes.* **4.** To pass through a strainer: *She strained the tea and discarded the leaves.*
□*noun* **1.** A heavy weight or pull: *The rope broke because the strain was too great.* **2.** An injury from too much effort: *a muscle strain.* **3.** A worry or burden.
strain (strān) □*verb* **strained, straining, strains** □*noun, plural* **strains**

strainer   *noun* A utensil with a wire network for separating solid matter from a liquid.
strain·er (strā′nər) □*noun, plural* **strainers**

strait *noun* **1.** A narrow passage that connects two bodies of water. **2. straits** Troubles; difficulties: *They were in desperate straits after he lost his job.*
strait (strāt) □*noun, plural* **straits**

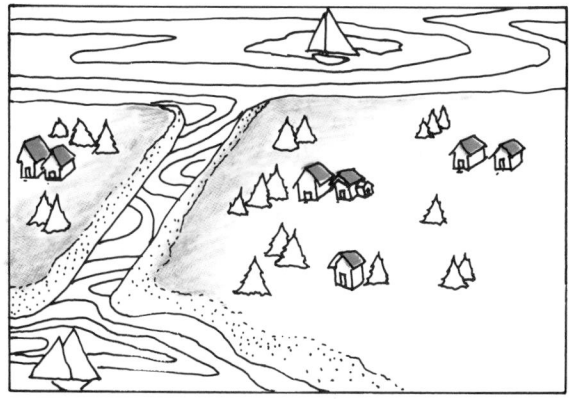

strait

strand¹ *verb* To leave in a difficult or helpless position: *They were stranded by the storm.*
strand (strand) □*verb* **stranded, stranding, strands**

strand² *noun* **1.** A wire or fiber from a cord or rope. **2.** A hair or thread.
strand (strand) □*noun, plural* **strands**

strange *adjective* **1.** Not known before: *a strange land.* **2.** Odd; unusual: *A parrot on his shoulder added to the man's strange appearance.* **3.** Out of place; uneasy: *feeling strange.*
strange (strānj) □*adjective* **stranger, strangest**

SYNONYMS: **strange, odd, peculiar**

These adjectives mean not usual or ordinary: *He told a strange story of an underwater kingdom ruled by a giant clam. It seems odd that the dog did not bark when the burglar broke into the house. She is a peculiar person who does not have any friends.*

---

stranger *noun* **1.** Someone that one does not know. **2.** Someone from another country or place.
stran·ger (strān′jər) □*noun, plural* **strangers**

strangle *verb* **1.** To kill by squeezing the throat to stop the breath. **2.** To die from having the throat squeezed to stop breath.
stran·gle (strang′gəl) □*verb* **strangled, strangling, strangles**

strap *noun* A long, thin piece of leather or other material, used to hold or fasten things.
□*verb* To fasten with a strap: *He strapped the*

knapsack to his back.
strap (strap) □*noun, plural* **straps** □*verb* **strapped, strapping, straps**

strategy *noun* **1.** The art of planning actions that lead to gaining a goal or a victory: *military strategy.* **2.** A clever plan of action.
strat·e·gy (strat′ə jē) □*noun, plural* **strategies**

straw *noun* **1.** Dry, cut stalks of grain after being threshed. **2.** A narrow tube through which a person can suck up liquids.
straw (strô) □*noun, plural* **straws**

strawberry *noun* The edible, sweet, red fruit of a plant that grows close to the ground.
straw·ber·ry (strô′ber′ē) □*noun, plural* **strawberries**

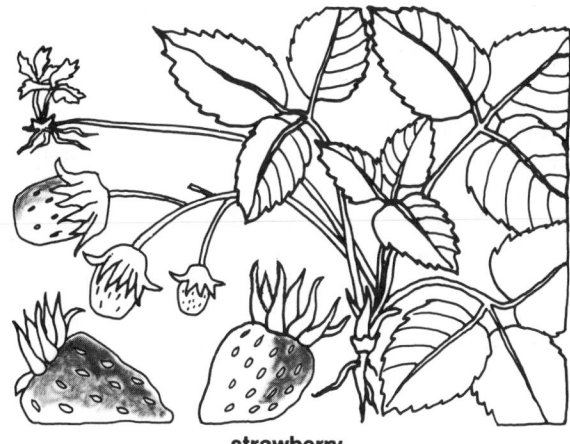

strawberry

stray *verb* To wander away from one's proper place: *The child strayed deep into the woods.*
□*noun* A lost person or animal.
□*adjective* **1.** Wandering or lost: *a stray dog.* **2.** Found here and there: *stray weeds in the vegetable garden.*
stray (strā) □*verb* **strayed, straying, strays** □*noun, plural* **strays** □*adjective*

streak *noun* **1.** A long, thin line or mark. **2.** A small amount or trace of something: *She has a selfish streak.*
□*verb* To mark with a streak: *a face streaked with tears.*

a bat	ī bite	oo tool	th feather
ā make	i fierce	ou out	th bath
â dare	o dot	u nut	hw wheat
ä father	ō no	û turn	zh measure
e net	ô law, for	ch church	ə about, open
ē be	oi soil	ng ring	pencil, atom
i dip	oo look	sh shade	circus

streak (strēk) □*noun, plural* **streaks** □*verb* **streaked, streaking, streaks**

stream *noun* **1.** A river or other body of water that flows along. **2.** A steady flow: *Streams of people filled the department store.*
□*verb* **1.** To move along as a stream does; flow: *The audience streamed out of the theater.* **2.** To float or wave: *Flags streamed in the wind.*
stream (strēm) □*noun, plural* **streams** □*verb* **streamed, streaming, streams**

streamer *noun* A long, narrow banner, flag, or strip.
stream·er (strē′mər) □*noun, plural* **streamers**

streamline *verb* **1.** To design something so that it gives the least possible resistance to water or air: *streamline a car.* **2.** To make more efficient: *He streamlined the procedures for keeping records.*
stream·line (strēm′līn′) □*verb* **streamlined, streamlining, streamlines**

street *noun* A road or public way, especially in a city or town.
street (strēt) □*noun, plural* **streets**

streetcar *noun* A vehicle that runs on rails and carries passengers mostly along city streets.
street·car (strēt′kär′) □*noun, plural* **streetcars**

streetcar

strength *noun* **1.** The quality of being strong; power: *the strength of a wrestler; strength of will.* **2.** The power to resist strain or stress: *the strength of steel.* **3.** Degree of power or force: *a motor operating at full strength.*
strength (strengkth) □*noun*

strengthen *verb* To make or become stronger: *exercise to strengthen muscles.*
strength·en (strengk′thən) □*verb* **strengthened, strengthening, strengthens**

stress *noun* **1.** Special importance placed on something: *She lay great stress on proper behavior.* **2.** The emphasis placed on the syllable pronounced loudest in a word or phrase: *In the word "lazy" the stress is on the first syllable.* **3.** A force or pressure put on something: *The stress of the heavy rains caused the dam to burst.*
□*verb* **1.** To give special importance to: *She stressed the need for careful work.* **2.** To pronounce with stress: *Stress the first syllable.*
stress (stres) □*noun, plural* **stresses** □*verb* **stressed, stressing, stresses**

stretch *verb* **1.** To make or become longer or wider: *material that stretches; stretch a rubber band.* **2.** To extend or cause to extend: *The United States stretches from ocean to ocean.* **3.** To make taut; tighten: *stretch canvas over a frame.* **4.** To reach out: *He stretched out his arm to hand me the letter.* **5.** To flex one's muscles: *I got up from bed and stretched.*
□*noun* **1.** The act of stretching: *She reached for the salt with a stretch of her arm.* **2.** A continuous length or area: *a stretch of hilly country.*
stretch (strech) □*verb* **stretched, stretching, stretches** □*noun, plural* **stretches**

stretch

stretcher *noun* A portable cot for carrying someone who is hurt or ill.
stretch·er (strech′ər) □*noun, plural* **stretchers**

stricken *adjective* **1.** Struck or wounded, as by an arrow. **2.** Affected by sickness, trouble, or sorrow: *victims stricken by the flood.*
□*verb* A past participle of **strike.**
strick·en (strik′ən) □*adjective* □*verb*

strict *adjective* **1.** Maintaining rigid discipline; stern: *She is strict but kind.* **2.** Absolute; complete: *He told me the plan in strict confi-*

dence. **3.** Carefully enforced and rigid: *strict rules.*
strict (strikt) ▫*adjective* **stricter, strictest**

stridden *verb* The past participle of **stride.**
strid·den (strĭd′ən) ▫*verb*

stride *verb* To walk with long steps: *He was striding along the shore when I saw him.*
▫*noun* **1.** A long step: *I crossed the room in six strides.* **2.** A step forward; progress: *Great strides have been made in medical research.*
stride (strīd) ▫*verb* **strode, stridden, striding, strides** ▫*noun, plural* **strides**

strike *verb* **1.** To hit: *His head struck the floor when he fell.* **2.** To indicate the time by sounding: *The clock struck five.* **3.** To make an impression on: *The idea struck her as silly.* **4.** To come upon; discover: *strike oil.* **5.** To stop work in order to get better working conditions: *The union struck for higher pay.*
▫*noun* **1.** An act of striking; hit. **2.** A stopping of work by employees in order to get better working conditions. **3.** A valuable discovery: *a gold strike.* **4.** A baseball pitch that the batter swings at and misses or that passes into the area that is over home plate and between the batter's knees and armpits.
strike out To put or be put out with three strikes in baseball.
strike (strīk) ▫*verb* **struck, struck** or **stricken, striking, strikes** ▫*noun, plural* **strikes**

string *noun* **1.** A cord thicker than thread and often made of fiber, used for fastening, tying, or binding. **2.** Something shaped like a string: *a string of cars.* **3.** A set of things with a cord running through them: *a string of beads.* **4.** A cord or wire of a musical instrument that is struck, plucked, or bowed to produce tone. **5. strings** Musical instruments, as violins, that have strings.
▫*verb* **1.** To provide with strings: *string a tennis racket.* **2.** To run a string through; thread: *string pearls.* **3.** To arrange in a series: *We strung tiny lights on the Christmas tree.* **4.** To stretch out from one place to another: *We strung the electric wire from the pole to the house.*
string (strĭng) ▫*noun, plural* **strings** ▫*verb* **strung, stringing, strings**

string bean *noun* A long, narrow green bean that grows on a bushy plant and is eaten as a vegetable.

strip¹ *verb* **1.** To remove the clothing; undress. **2.** To remove a covering: *I stripped all the old paint off the desk.*
strip (strĭp) ▫*verb* **stripped, stripping, strips**

strip² *noun* A long, narrow piece: *a strip of film; a strip of land.*
strip (strĭp) ▫*noun, plural* **strips**

stripe *noun* A long line, strip, or band that differs, as in color, from the area around it: *A skunk has a white stripe down its back.*
▫*verb* To mark with stripes.
stripe (strīp) ▫*noun, plural* **stripes** ▫*verb* **striped, striping, stripes**

stripe

strive *verb* To try hard: *It is necessary to strive in order to win.*
strive (strīv) ▫*verb* **strove, striven** or **strived, striving, strives**

striven *verb* A past participle of **strive.**
striv·en (strĭv′ən) ▫*verb*

strode *verb* The past tense of **stride**: *She strode onto the stage.*
strode (strōd) ▫*verb*

stroke *noun* **1.** An act of striking; blow: *a stroke of the sword.* **2.** A single complete movement that is repeated often, as in swimming: *the stroke of a paddle.* **3.** A mark made by a single movement of a brush, pen, or pencil: *She painted with broad strokes.* **4.** A sudden, unexpected event: *a stroke of bad luck.* **5.** A gentle rub of the hand: *gave the cat a stroke.* **6.** A sudden, severe attack or sickness caused by the blocking or breaking of a blood vessel in the brain.
▫*verb* To rub gently with the hand; caress: *He stroked the horse.*
stroke (strōk) ▫*noun, plural* **strokes** ▫*verb* **stroked, stroking, strokes**

a	bat	ī	bite	o͞o	tool	*th*	feather
ā	make	î	fierce	ou	out	th	bath
â	dare	o	dot	u	nut	hw	wheat
ä	father	ō	no	û	turn	zh	measure
e	net	ô	law, for	ch	church	ə	about, open
ē	be	oi	soil	ng	ring		pencil, atom
i	dip	oo	look	sh	shade		circus

stroll *verb* To walk in a slow and relaxed manner: *They strolled through the woods.*
□*noun* A slow, relaxed walk.
stroll (strōl) □*verb* **strolled, strolling, strolls**
□*noun, plural* **strolls**

strong *adjective* **1.** Having much power, energy, or force: *a strong lad; a strong breeze.* **2.** Capable of enduring: *a strong chair; a strong opponent.* **3.** Firmly fixed: *a strong belief.* **4.** Having intellectual force: *a strong mind.* **5.** In good health; robust: *a strong body.*
strong (strông) □*adjective* **stronger, strongest**

strove *verb* The past tense of **strive.**
strove (strōv) □*verb*

struck *verb* The past tense and a past participle of **strike:** *He struck the gong with a mallet.*
struck (struk) □*verb*

structure *noun* **1.** Something that is built, as a building or bridge. **2.** Something made up of a number of parts put together in a particular way: *The body is a complex structure.* **3.** The way in which parts are put together to form a whole: *Scientists have learned a great deal about the structure of the brain.*
struc·ture (struk′chər) □*noun, plural* **structures**

struggle *verb* **1.** To make a great effort against difficulties: *She struggled to understand the question. The horses struggled through the mud.* **2.** To battle; fight: *The two armies struggled for a day and a night.*
□*noun* **1.** A great effort: *a struggle to make a living.* **2.** Battle; fight: *the struggle against inflation.* —See Synonyms at **effort.**
strug·gle (strug′əl) □*verb* **struggled, struggling, struggles** □*noun, plural* **struggles**

strum *verb* To play by passing fingers lightly along the strings: *strum a banjo.*
strum (strum) □*verb* **strummed, strumming, strums**

strung *verb* The past tense and past participle of **string:** *She strung the beads.*
strung (strung) □*verb*

stub *noun* **1.** A short end that is left over after something has been used up or broken off: *the stub of a pencil.* **2.** The part of a check or bill kept as a record. **3.** The part of a ticket kept to show payment.
□*verb* To bump one's toe or foot against an object: *He stubbed his toe on the doorstep.*
stub (stub) □*noun, plural* **stubs** □*verb* **stubbed, stubbing, stubs**

stubble *noun* **1.** The short, stiff stalks of a grain or hay crop remaining on a field after the crop has been cut. **2.** A short, stiff growth.
stub·ble (stub′əl) □*noun*

stubborn *adjective* **1.** Not willing to change an opinion or course of action: *She's too stubborn to listen to good advice.* **2.** Hard to handle or deal with: *a stubborn cold.*
stub·born (stub′ərn) □*adjective*

stuck *verb* The past tense and past participle of **stick:** *The candy stuck to her fingers.*
stuck (stuk) □*verb*

student *noun* Someone who studies, as in a school: *a student of foreign languages.*
stu·dent (stood′ənt *or* styood′ənt) □*noun, plural* **students**

studio *noun* **1.** A room, loft, or building where an artist works. **2.** A place where motion pictures, television shows, or radio programs are made or broadcast.
stu·di·o (stoo′dē ō′ *or* styoo′dē ō′) □*noun, plural* **studios**

study *noun* **1.** The act of learning: *After four years of study, he graduated.* **2.** A branch of knowledge; subject: *the study of medicine.* **3.** A careful examination of something: *a study of the causes of crime.* **4.** A room used for studying, reading, or working.
□*verb* **1.** To use the mind to gain knowledge: *We studied mathematics.* **2.** To examine closely: *I will have to study the question carefully before answering.*
stu·dy (stud′ē) □*noun, plural* **studies** □*verb* **studied, studying, studies**

stuff *noun* **1.** The basic material of which something is made; substance: *the stuff of which heroes are made.* **2.** Something not specifically identified but understood: *Get your stuff out of here.* **3.** Things or materials to be used: *sewing stuff.*
□*verb* **1.** To pack tightly; fill up: *She stuffed her suitcase with books.* **2.** To stop up; block: *He stuffed the crack with plaster.* **3.** To fill with a stuffing: *stuff a chicken.* **4.** To fill the skin of a dead animal to make it look as it did when alive. **5.** To eat too much: *She stuffed herself with chocolates.*
stuff (stuf) □*noun* □*verb* **stuffed, stuffing, stuffs**

stuffing *noun* **1.** Material used to stuff, fill, or pad something. **2.** A mixture that is used to stuff poultry, meat, eggs, or vegetables.
stuff·ing (stuf′ing) □*noun, plural* **stuffings**

stuffy *adjective* **1.** Lacking fresh air; close: *a stuffy little room.* **2.** Having blocked breathing passages: *a stuffy nose.* **3.** Dull and boring: *a stuffy party.*
stuff·y (stuf′ē) □*adjective* **stuffier, stuffiest**

stumble *verb* **1.** To trip or fall while walking: *I stumbled on a crack in the sidewalk.* **2.** To move or speak in a clumsy way: *She stumbled through the dark living room.* **3.** To come upon by chance or accident: *I stumbled onto the solution to the problem.*
stum·ble (stum′bəl) □*verb* **stumbled, stumbling, stumbles**

stumble

stump *noun* **1.** The part of a tree trunk left in the ground after the tree has fallen or been cut down. **2.** A short or broken piece or part: *the stump of a pencil.*
□*verb* To puzzle; baffle: *a riddle that stumped us all.*
stump (stump) □*noun, plural* **stumps** □*verb* **stumped, stumping, stumps**

stun *verb* **1.** To daze, as by a blow: *The fall stunned her.* **2.** To overwhelm; shock: *The news of his defeat stunned the candidate.*
stun (stun) □*verb* **stunned, stunning, stuns**

stung *verb* The past tense and past participle of **sting:** *A wasp stung me.*
stung (stung) □*verb*

stunk *verb* A past tense and the past participle of **stink.**
stunk (stungk) □*verb*

stunt¹ *verb* To hinder the growth or development of: *Lack of rain stunted the plants.*
stunt (stunt) □*verb* **stunted, stunting, stunts**

stunt² *noun* An act or feat that shows unusual skill or courage: *an acrobatic stunt.*
stunt (stunt) □*noun, plural* **stunts**

stupid *adjective* **1.** Slow to understand; dull: *a stupid man.* **2.** Showing lack of intelligence: *stupid behavior; a stupid question.*
stu·pid (stoo′pid *or* styoo′pid) □*adjective* **stupider, stupidest**

sturdy *adjective* **1.** Strong and durable; hardy: *a sturdy oak tree.* **2.** Resolute; firm: *sturdy pioneers.*
stur·dy (stûr′dē) □*adjective* **sturdier, sturdiest**

sturgeon *noun* A large, edible fish with bony plates on its body.
stur·geon (stûr′jən) □*noun, plural* **sturgeons** or **sturgeon**

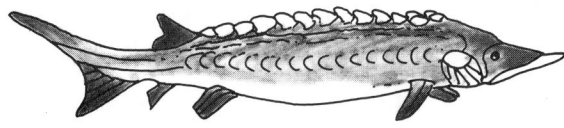

sturgeon

stutter *verb* To say or speak with involuntary pauses, repetitions, or interruptions.
□*noun* The act or habit of stuttering.
stut·ter (stut′ər) □*verb* **stuttered, stuttering, stutters** □*noun, plural* **stutters**

style *noun* **1.** A personal or particular way or manner of saying, doing, expressing, performing, or writing: *her individual style of violin playing; a modern literary style.* **2.** A way of dressing or behaving that is considered stylish; fashion: *Short dresses are in style this year.* **3.** The slender stalk of a flower pistil.
□*verb* **1.** To design or arrange according to a new or accepted style. **2.** To call; name: *He styles himself a writer.*
style (stīl) □*noun, plural* **styles** □*verb* **styled, styling, styles**

stylish *adjective* In accordance with the latest style; fashionable: *a stylish hat.*
styl·ish (stī′lish) □*adjective*

subject *noun* **1.** Someone or something that is thought about or discussed: *the subject of the conversation.* **2.** A course or area of study: *Physics was his favorite subject.* **3.** Someone or something that is the object of a study or ex-

a	bat	ī	bite	oo	tool	*th*	feather
ā	make	î	fierce	ou	out	th	bath
â	dare	o	dot	u	nut	hw	wheat
ä	father	ō	no	û	turn	zh	measure
e	net	ô	law, for	ch	church	ə	about, open
ē	be	oi	soil	ng	ring		pencil, atom
i	dip	oo	look	sh	shade		circus

periment: *Scientists gave a new drug to the subject.* **4.** Someone who is under the control or rule of another, especially one who owes allegiance to a government or ruler: *French subjects.* **5.** A word or group of words in a phrase or sentence that performs the action of a verb or about which something is stated. In the sentence *The boy threw the ball*, the subject is *boy.*
□*adjective* **1.** Under the control or authority of another: *All citizens are subject to the law.* **2.** Likely to have or get; prone: *He's subject to headaches.* **3.** Depending on: *a decision that is subject to his approval.*
□*verb* **1.** To bring under rule or control: *an empire that subjected many weak countries to its will.* **2.** To cause to undergo: *He wouldn't subject her to humiliation.*
sub·ject (sub′ jikt) □*noun, plural* **subjects** □*adjective* □*verb* (səb **jekt′**) **subjected, subjecting, subjects**

submarine   *noun* A ship that is capable of operating underwater.
□*adjective* Being, growing, or used beneath the surface of the sea: *a submarine plant.*
sub·ma·rine (sub′ mə rēn′) □*noun, plural* **submarines** □*adjective*

submarine

submerge   *verb* **1.** To cover or become covered with water: *The flood submerged the city.* **2.** To plunge or sink under the surface of water or another liquid.
sub·merge (səb **mûrj′**) □*verb* **submerged, submerging, submerges**

submit   *verb* **1.** To yield to the control, influence, or authority of another: *He submitted to his parents' decision.* **2.** To offer for the judgment or consideration of another: *She submitted her proposal to the committee.* —See Synonyms at **yield.**
sub·mit (səb **mit′**) □*verb* **submitted, submitting, submits**

subordinate   *adjective* Belonging to a lower or inferior rank or class: *The teachers are sub-*ordinate to the principal.
□*noun* Someone or something that is subordinate.
sub·or·di·nate (sə **bôr′** dən it) □*adjective* □*noun, plural* **subordinates**

subscribe   *verb* **1.** To arrange to receive and pay for a certain publication: *She subscribes to the daily newspaper.* **2.** To express agreement or approval: *I don't subscribe to that idea.*
sub·scribe (səb **skrīb′**) □*verb* **subscribed, subscribing, subscribes**

subscription   *noun* **1.** The act of subscribing. **2.** An order for a specified number of issues of a publication.
sub·scrip·tion (səb **skrip′** shən) □*noun, plural* **subscriptions**

subsequent   *adjective* Following in time or order: *Heavy rains and the subsequent floods destroyed the crops.*
sub·se·quent (sub′ si kwənt) □*adjective*

subside   *verb* **1.** To sink to a lower or more normal level: *The flood waters subsided.* **2.** To become less: *His anger subsided.*
sub·side (səb **sīd′**) □*verb* **subsided, subsiding, subsides**

substance   *noun* **1.** Something that has mass and takes up space; matter. **2.** A material of a particular kind: *a soft substance.* **3.** The fundamental part; essence: *What was the substance of the senator's speech?*
sub·stance (sub′ stəns) □*noun, plural* **substances**

substantial   *adjective* **1.** Large in amount; ample: *a substantial breakfast.* **2.** Solidly built; strong: *a substantial house.*
sub·stan·tial (səb **stan′** shəl) □*adjective*

substitute   *noun* Someone or something that takes the place of another: *I used honey as a substitute for sugar.*
□*verb* **1.** To put in the place of another: *She substituted walnuts for pecans in the recipe.* **2.** To take the place of another: *I substituted for my father's secretary when she was sick.*
sub·sti·tute (sub′ sti tōot′ *or* sub′ sti tyōot′) □*noun, plural* **substitutes** □*verb* **substituted, substituting, substitutes**

subtle   *adjective* **1.** Fine; delicate: *a subtle aroma.* **2.** Keen; acute: *a subtle mind.*
sub·tle (sut′ əl) □*adjective* **subtler, subtlest**

subtract   *verb* To take away; deduct. If you subtract 6 from 20, you get 14.
sub·tract (səb **trakt′**) □*verb* **subtracted, subtracting, subtracts**

subtraction *noun* The process of subtracting one number from another; 6 − 4 = 2 is an example of subtraction.
sub·trac·tion (səb **trak′** shən) □*noun*

subtrahend *noun* A number to be subtracted from another number. In 10 − 8 = 2, 8 is the subtrahend.
sub·tra·hend (**sub′** trə hend′) □*noun, plural* **subtrahends**

suburb *noun* A smaller community near or next to a city.
sub·urb (**sub′** ûrb′) □*noun, plural* **suburbs**

suburban *adjective* Of, having to do with, or located in a suburb: *a suburban town.*
sub·ur·ban (sə **bûr′** bən) □*adjective*

subway *noun* An electric railroad that runs underground.
sub·way (**sub′** wā′) □*noun, plural* **subways**

subway

succeed *verb* **1.** To come next after in time or order; follow: *He succeeded his father as president of the company.* **2.** To accomplish something desired or attempted: *She succeeded in learning to play golf.*
suc·ceed (sək **sēd′**) □*verb* **succeeded, succeeding, succeeds**

success *noun* **1.** The achievement of something desired or attempted: *his success as a student.* **2.** The gaining of fame, favors, or wealth: *a movie that had a great success.* **3.** Someone or something that succeeds: *She is a success as an actress.*
suc·cess (sək **ses′**) □*noun, plural* **successes**

successful *adjective* **1.** Having a desired or favorable result: *a successful experiment.* **2.** Having gained fame, favor, or wealth: *a suc-*

cessful composer.
suc·cess·ful (sək **ses′** fəl) □*adjective*

succession *noun* **1.** The process of following in order: *He was late for school three days in succession.* **2.** A group of persons or things following in order: *a succession of victories.*
suc·ces·sion (sək **sesh′** ən) □*noun, plural* **successions**

successive *adjective* Following one after another without interruption: *The exams were given on successive days.*
suc·ces·sive (sək **ses′** iv) □*adjective*

such *adjective* **1.** Of a kind to be named: *She would never do such things as lie and cheat.* **2.** Of the same or similar kind: *He gives two or three such concerts a year.* **3.** Of so great a degree or quality: *I've never heard such nonsense.*
□*pronoun* **1.** Someone or something of the kind mentioned: *Such are the joys of youth.* **2.** Someone or something similar: *cars, trucks, and such.*
such (such) □*adjective* □*pronoun*

suck *verb* **1.** To draw into the mouth by movements of the lips, cheeks, and tongue that create suction: *He sucked iced tea through a straw.* **2.** To draw liquid from by such movements: *She sucked the orange dry.* **3.** To cause to melt in the mouth by movements of the tongue and cheek: *suck on a candy.* **4.** To draw by or as if by suction: *Illness had sucked away all his energy.*
suck (suk) □*verb* **sucked, sucking, sucks**

suction *noun* The process of drawing something, such as a liquid or gas, into a space by removing part or all of the air in the space.
suc·tion (**suk′** shən) □*noun*

sudden *adjective* **1.** Happening quickly and without warning: *a sudden drop in temperature.* **2.** Hasty: *a sudden change of heart.*
sud·den (**sud′** ən) □*adjective*

suds *plural noun* **1.** Soapy water. **2.** Foam; lather.
suds (sudz) □*plural noun*

sue *verb* To bring a lawsuit against.
sue (sōō) □*verb* **sued, suing, sues**

a bat	ī bite	ōō tool	*th* feather
ā make	î fierce	ou out	th bath
â dare	o dot	u nut	hw wheat
ä father	ō no	û turn	zh measure
e net	ô law, for	ch church	ə about, open
ē be	oi soil	ng ring	pencil, atom
i dip	oo look	sh shade	circus

suede *noun* Leather that is rubbed to make it look and feel soft like velvet.
suede (swād) □*noun*

WORD HISTORY: **suede**

Suede is from the French name for Sweden. Suede leather seems to have originally come from Sweden.

---

suet *noun* The hard fat around the kidneys of cattle and sheep that is used in cooking and in making tallow.
su·et (sōō′it) □*noun*

suffer *verb* **1.** To feel pain. **2.** To experience loss, injury, or harm: *He suffered a heart attack.* **3.** To be at a disadvantage: *The book suffers from a poor plot.* **4.** To endure or bear; put up with: *Suffer the consequences.*
suf·fer (suf′ər) □*verb* **suffered, suffering, suffers**

suffering *noun* Pain or sorrow.
suf·fer·ing (suf′ər ing) □*noun*

sufficient *adjective* As much as is needed; enough: *sufficient money to pay the bills.*
suf·fi·cient (sə fish′ənt) □*adjective*

suffix *noun* An ending, such as *-er* in *hunter* or *-est* in *coldest*, that is added to a word to form a new word or show a grammatical function.
suf·fix (suf′iks) □*noun*

suffocate *verb* **1.** To kill by cutting off the breath or depriving of oxygen. **2.** To be or become smothered or choked.
suf·fo·cate (suf′ə kāt′) □*verb* **suffocated, suffocating, suffocates**

sugar *noun* A sweet substance obtained mainly from sugar cane or sugar beets.
□*verb* To coat, mix, or sprinkle with sugar.
sug·ar (shŏŏg′ər) □*noun* □*verb* **sugared, sugaring, sugars**

sugar beet *noun* A kind of beet with long whitish roots from which sugar is obtained.

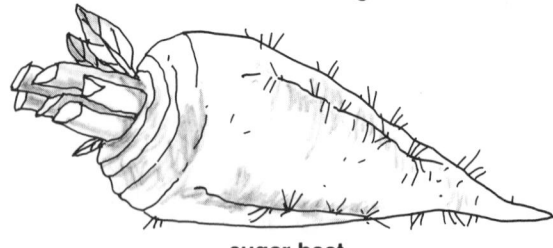

sugar beet

sugar cane *noun* A tall grass with thick, juicy stems from which sugar is obtained.

suggest *verb* **1.** To offer for consideration: *She suggested that I take a vacation.* **2.** To bring to mind through association: *His smile suggested friendliness.* **3.** To show indirectly; hint: *The number of books on his shelves suggests that he likes to read.*
sug·gest (səg jest′) □*verb* **suggested, suggesting, suggests**

SYNONYMS: **suggest, hint, imply**

These verbs mean to convey thoughts or ideas indirectly: *His remarks suggest that he's jealous of his brother. She hinted that it was time to leave by looking at her watch. Her manner implied that she did not trust me.*

---

suggestion *noun* **1.** The act of suggesting: *I ordered steak at his suggestion.* **2.** Something suggested: *I'll follow your suggestion.* **3.** A trace; hint: *a smile with a suggestion of malice.*
sug·ges·tion (səg jes′chən) □*noun, plural* **suggestions**

suicide *noun* **1.** The act of intentionally killing oneself. **2.** Someone who commits suicide.
su·i·cide (sōō′i sīd′) □*noun, plural* **suicides**

suit *noun* **1.** A set of clothes to be worn together, usually consisting of a coat or jacket with matching pants or skirt. **2.** One of the four sets of playing cards, such as clubs, that constitute a deck. **3.** An action in a court of law.
□*verb* **1.** To meet the desires or requirements of; satisfy: *The plan suited him.* **2.** To be suitable for: *Her dress suited the occasion.* **3.** To make suitable; fit: *They suited the words to the music.* **4.** To be becoming to: *The blue scarf suits you.*
suit (sōōt) □*noun, plural* **suits** □*verb* **suited, suiting, suits**

suitable *adjective* Right for a purpose or occasion: *clothes that are suitable for a wedding.*
suit·a·ble (sōō′tə bəl) □*adjective*

suitcase *noun* A flat, rectangular piece of luggage.
suit·case (sōōt′kās′) □*noun, plural* **suitcases**

suite *noun* **1.** A series of connected rooms, as in a hotel. **2.** A set of matched pieces of furniture.
suite (swēt) □*noun, plural* **suites**

suitor *noun* A man who is courting a woman.
suit·or (sōō′tər) □*noun, plural* **suitors**

sulfur *noun* A pale-yellow chemical element that is used to make gunpowder and matches.
sul·fur (sul′fər) □*noun*

sulk *verb* To be silent and moody: *He's sulking because his father wouldn't let him go to the movies.*
□*noun* A mood or display of sulking.
sulk (sulk) □*verb* **sulked, sulking, sulks**
□*noun*

sullen *adjective* **1.** Silent and angry: *a sullen mood.* **2.** Dark; gloomy: *sullen, gray skies.*
sul·len (sul′ən) □*adjective*

sultan *noun* A ruler of a Moslem country.
sul·tan (sul′tən) □*noun, plural* **sultans**

sultry *adjective* Very hot and humid: *a sultry summer night.*
sul·try (sul′trē) □*adjective* **sultrier, sultriest**

sum *noun* **1.** A number obtained as a result of addition. **2.** An amount of money: *the sum of $50.*
□*verb* To find the sum of; add.
  sum up To summarize: *He summed up the talk in a few sentences.*
sum (sum) □*noun, plural* **sums** □*verb* **summed, summing, sums**

summarize *verb* To make a summary of: *She summarized the plot of the story.*
sum·ma·rize (sum′ə rīz′) □*verb* **summarized, summarizing, summarizes**

summary *noun* A short statement of the main points of something, such as a report: *a summary of the day's news.*
sum·ma·ry (sum′ə rē) □*noun, plural* **summaries**

summer *noun* The season of the year between spring and autumn.
□*verb* To pass the summer: *Some birds summer in the Arctic.*
sum·mer (sum′ər) □*noun, plural* **summers** □*verb* **summered, summering, summers**

summit *noun* The highest point or part; top: *the summit of the hill.*
sum·mit (sum′it) □*noun, plural* **summits**

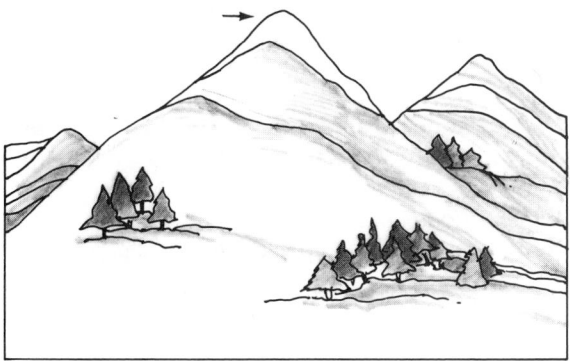

summit

summon *verb* **1.** To request to appear; send for: *She summoned him to her office.* **2.** To order to appear in a court of law. **3.** To call forth; arouse: *Summon up your courage.*
sum·mon (sum′ən) □*verb* **summoned, summoning, summons**

summons *noun* A written order for someone to appear in a court of law.
sum·mons (sum′ənz) □*noun, plural* **summonses**

sun *noun* **1.** The star around which the earth and other planets revolve and which is our source of light and heat. **2.** A star around which planets revolve. **3.** The light given off by the sun; sunlight.
□*verb* To be in or expose to the light and heat of the sun: *He sunned himself at the beach.*
sun (sun) □*noun, plural* **suns** □*verb* **sunned, sunning, suns**

sunbathe *verb* To sun.
sun·bathe (sun′bāth′) □*verb* **sunbathed, sunbathing, sunbathes**

sunburn *noun* A sore reddening of the skin from too much exposure to the sun.
sun·burn (sun′bûrn′) □*noun, plural* **sunburns**

sundae *noun* A portion of ice cream with syrup, fruit, or nuts on top.
sun·dae (sun′dē *or* sun′dā′) □*noun, plural* **sundaes**

Sunday *noun* The first day of the week.
Sun·day (sun′dē *or* sun′dā′) □*noun, plural* **Sundays**

WORD HISTORY: **Sunday**

Sunday comes from an old English word that literally means "the sun's day."

---

sundown *noun* Sunset.
sun·down (sun′doun′) □*noun, plural* **sundowns**

sunflower *noun* A tall plant that has large flowers with yellow petals and dark centers and bears seeds that are rich in oil.

a bat	ī bite	o͞o tool	*th* feather
ā make	î fierce	ou out	th bath
â dare	o dot	u nut	hw wheat
ä father	ō no	û turn	zh measure
e net	ô law, for	ch church	ə about, open
ē be	oi soil	ng ring	pencil, atom
i dip	oo look	sh shade	circus

sun·flow·er (**sun′**flou′ər) ☐*noun, plural* **sunflowers**

sunflower

sung   *verb* A past tense and the past participle of **sing.**
sung (sung) ☐*verb*

sunglasses   *plural noun* Eyeglasses with colored or tinted lenses to protect the eyes from sunlight.
sun·glass·es (**sun′**glas′iz) ☐*plural noun*

sunk   *verb* A past tense and the past participle of **sink.**
sunk (sungk) ☐*verb*

sunken   *adjective* **1.** Fallen in; hollow: *sunken cheeks.* **2.** Below the surface of the water: *sunken treasure.* **3.** Below a surrounding area: *a sunken pool.*
sunk·en (**sung′**kən) ☐*adjective*

sunlight   *noun* The light of the sun.
sun·light (**sun′**līt′) ☐*noun*

sunny   *adjective* **1.** Full of sunshine: *a sunny room.* **2.** Cheerful; happy: *a sunny mood.*
sun·ny (**sun′**ē) ☐*adjective* **sunnier, sunniest**

sunrise   *noun* The rising of the sun in the morning.
sun·rise (**sun′**rīz′) ☐*noun, plural* **sunrises**

sunset   *noun* The setting of the sun in the evening.
sun·set (**sun′**set′) ☐*noun, plural* **sunsets**

sunshine   *noun* The light of the sun; sunlight.
sun·shine (**sun′**shīn′) ☐*noun*

superb   *adjective* Of the highest quality; most excellent: *a superb performance.*
su·perb (soo **pûrb′**) ☐*adjective*

superintendent   *noun* Someone who supervises or is in charge of something: *the superin-*

tendent of schools; a building superintendent.
su·per·in·ten·dent (soo′pər in **ten′**dənt) ☐*noun, plural* **superintendents**

superior   *adjective* **1.** Higher in position, rank, quality, number, or importance: *a superior officer; a superior mind.* **2.** Considering oneself above others; arrogant: *What makes him feel so superior?*
☐*noun* Someone who is above others in position, quality, rank, or importance: *I'll have to ask my superior.*
su·pe·ri·or (sə **pîr′**ē ər) ☐*adjective* ☐*noun, plural* **superiors**

superiority   *noun* The state or quality of being superior: *He proved his superiority as a student by winning a scholarship.*
su·pe·ri·or·i·ty (sə pîr′ē **ôr′**i tē) ☐*noun*

superlative   *adjective* **1.** Of the highest order, quality, or degree; supreme: *a person of superlative abilities.* **2.** Of, having to do with, or being the form of an adjective or adverb that expresses the lowest or highest degree of comparison.
☐*noun* The superlative form of an adjective or adverb: *"Smallest" is the superlative of the adjective "small." "Best" is the superlative of the adverb "well."*
su·per·la·tive (sə **pûr′**lə tiv) ☐*adjective* ☐*noun, plural* **superlatives**

supermarket   *noun* A large store that sells food and household goods and in which customers wait on themselves.
su·per·mar·ket (**soo′**pər mär′kit) ☐*noun, plural* **supermarkets**

supernatural   *adjective* Outside of or beyond the natural world: *Ghosts and angels are supernatural beings.*
su·per·nat·u·ral (soo′pər **nach′**ər əl *or* soo′pər **nach′**rəl) ☐*adjective*

superstition   *noun* A belief or practice that is based on ignorance, faith in magic, or chance: *the superstition that a rabbit's foot brings good luck.*
su·per·sti·tion (soo′pər **stish′**ən) ☐*noun, plural* **superstitions**

superstitious   *adjective* Of, having to do with, showing, or likely to believe in superstition: *a superstitious child.*
su·per·sti·tious (soo′pər **stish′**əs) ☐*adjective*

supervise   *verb* To direct and inspect the work of: *He supervises the office staff.*
su·per·vise (**soo′**pər vīz′) ☐*verb* **supervised, supervising, supervises**

supervisor *noun* Someone who supervises.
su·per·vi·sor (soō′pər vī′zər) □*noun, plural*
supervisors

supper *noun* The evening meal; the last meal
of the day.
sup·per (sup′ər) □*noun, plural* **suppers**

supplement *noun* Something added to complete a thing or make up for a deficiency: *An
index was published as a supplement to the
book.*
□*verb* To add to; fill out: *He supplemented his
salary by working overtime.*
sup·ple·ment □*noun* (sup′lə mənt), *plural*
supplements □*verb* (sup′lə ment′)
supplemented, supplementing, supplements

supply *verb* **1.** To make available; provide:
We supplied the food for the party. **2.** To satisfy; fill: *supply a need.*
□*noun* **1.** An amount available for use; stock:
a food supply. **2.** The amount that is needed or
can be obtained: *the country's energy supply.*
sup·ply (sə plī′) □*verb* **supplied, supplying,**
supplies □*noun, plural* **supplies**

support *verb* **1.** To hold in position; keep
from falling, sinking, or slipping: *He helped to
support the ladder.* **2.** To aid the cause of; favor: *support a political candidate.* **3.** To provide for by supplying with money or care: *She
supports a large family.* **4.** To help prove; back
up: *The facts seem to support his theory.*
□*noun* **1.** The act of supporting or condition
of being supported: *I need his support.*
2. Someone or something that supports: *She
was her parents' main support.*
sup·port (sə pōrt′) □*verb* **supported,**
supporting, supports □*noun, plural*
supports

support

suppose *verb* **1.** To think; believe: *I suppose
you're right.* **2.** To assume to be true for the
sake of argument: *Suppose the earth is flat.*
3. To expect; intend: *He was supposed to call.*
sup·pose (sə pōz′) □*verb* **supposed,**
supposing, supposes

supreme *adjective* **1.** Highest in rank, power,
or authority: *the supreme commander.*
2. Highest in quality or degree: *his supreme
achievement.*
su·preme (sə prēm′) □*adjective*

Supreme Court *noun* The highest federal
court in the United States.

sure *adjective* **1.** Feeling no doubt; confident:
I'm sure you'll like him. **2.** Certain to come or
occur: *a sure success.* **3.** Steady or firm: *a sure
grip.* **4.** Dependable; reliable: *a sure cure for a
cold.* —See Synonyms at **certain.**
□*adverb* Surely: *Sure, I'm coming.*
sure (shoor) □*adjective* **surer, surest**
□*adverb*

surely *adverb* Without doubt; certainly: *She
surely seems happy.*
sure·ly (shoor′lē) □*adverb*

surf *noun* **1.** The waves of the sea as they
break upon the shore. **2.** The foam and sound
of breaking waves.
surf (sûrf) □*noun*

surface *noun* **1.** The outermost part of an
object or body: *The surface of the water sparkled.* **2.** One of the sides of an object: *a surface
of a cube.* **3.** The outward appearance: *On the
surface the idea seemed all right.*
□*verb* **1.** To come to the surface: *A huge
shark surfaced.* **2.** To cover the surface of: *We
surfaced the driveway with tar.*
sur·face (sûr′fəs) □*noun, plural* **surfaces**
□*verb* **surfaced, surfacing, surfaces**

surfboard *noun* A long, flat board with
rounded ends that is used in surfing.
surf·board (sûrf′bôrd′) □*noun, plural*
surfboards

surfing *noun* The sport of riding waves in to
shore on a surfboard.
surf·ing (sûr′fing) □*noun*

a	bat	ī	bite	ōō	tool	*th*	feather
ā	make	î	fierce	ou	out	th	bath
â	dare	o	dot	u	nut	hw	wheat
ä	father	ō	no	û	turn	zh	measure
e	net	ô	law, for	ch	church	ə	about, open
ē	be	oi	soil	ng	ring		pencil, atom
i	dip	oo	look	sh	shade		circus

surge *verb* To rise and fall in or as if in rolling waves: *The crowd surged forward.*
□*noun* **1.** A swelling motion or movement like that of a wave: *The surge of the sea rocked the boat.* **2.** A sudden rush: *a surge of interest.*
surge (sûrj) □*verb* **surged, surging, surges** □*noun, plural* **surges**

surgeon *noun* A doctor who specializes in surgery.
sur·geon (sûr′ jən) □*noun, plural* **surgeons**

surgery *noun* The medical treatment of injury, disease, or defect by means of instruments or a procedure performed by a surgeon.
sur·ger·y (sûr′ jə rē) □*noun*

surname *noun* A family name; last name.
sur·name (sûr′ nām′) □*noun, plural* **surnames**

surpass *verb* To be better, greater, or stronger than; exceed: *success that surpassed all our expectations.*
sur·pass (sər pas′) □*verb* **surpassed, surpassing, surpasses**

surplus *noun* An amount or quantity that is greater than what is needed or used: *We ate all the fruit we could and sold the surplus.*
□*adjective* Greater than what is needed or used: *surplus corn.*
sur·plus (sûr′ pləs) □*noun, plural* **surpluses** □*adjective*

surprise *verb* **1.** To come upon suddenly and without warning: *The owner of the store surprised the thieves as they were picking the lock.* **2.** To cause to feel astonishment or wonder: *His anger surprised me.*
□*noun* **1.** The act of coming upon suddenly and without warning: *The police caught them by surprise.* **2.** Something that surprises: *The gift was a complete surprise.* **3.** A feeling of astonishment or wonder: *a gasp of surprise.*
sur·prise (sər prīz′) □*verb* **surprised, surprising, surprises** □*noun, plural* **surprises**

surrender *verb* To give up to another; yield: *The enemy surrendered.* —See Synonyms at **yield.**
□*noun* The act of surrendering.
sur·ren·der (sə ren′ dər) □*verb* **surrendered, surrendering, surrenders** □*noun, plural* **surrenders**

surround *verb* To be on all sides of; encircle: *The house is surrounded by woods.*
sur·round (sə round′) □*verb* **surrounded, surrounding, surrounds**

surround

surroundings *plural noun* The things, circumstances, and conditions that surround a person: *peaceful surroundings.*
sur·round·ings (sə round′ dingz) □*plural noun*

survey *verb* **1.** To look over; examine: *The mayor surveyed the damage caused by the hurricane.* **2.** To decide and set the size, shape, or limits by measuring something such as a tract of land: *The men surveyed the boundary between the fields.*
□*noun* **1.** A view of a broad area or subject: *a survey of American history.* **2.** A detailed investigation to gather information: *a survey of unemployed workers.* **3.** The act of surveying land.
sur·vey (sər vā′) □*verb* **surveyed, surveying, surveys** □*noun* (sûr′ vā′), *plural* **surveys**

surveyor *noun* Someone whose work is surveying land.
sur·vey·or (sər vā′ ər) □*noun, plural* **surveyors**

survival *noun* **1.** The act or fact of surviving. **2.** Someone or something that survives: *a custom that is a survival from an earlier time.*
sur·viv·al (sər vī′ vəl) □*noun, plural* **survivals**

survive *verb* **1.** To remain alive or in existence: *Only one house survived from colonial times.* **2.** To live through: *None of the passengers survived the crash.* **3.** To live longer than: *Only two of the seven children survived their mother.*
sur·vive (sər vīv′) □*verb* **survived, surviving, survives**

suspect *verb* **1.** To think of as guilty without proof: *We suspect her of lying.* **2.** To have doubts about; distrust: *I suspect the salesman's motives.* **3.** To believe without being sure;

imagine: *I suspect you're right.*
□*noun* Someone who is suspected: *The police searched for the suspect.*
sus·pect (sə **spekt′**) □*verb* **suspected, suspecting, suspects** □*noun* (**sus′**pekt′), *plural* **suspects**

suspend *verb* **1.** To hang, especially so as to allow free movement: *suspend a lamp from a ceiling.* **2.** To hold or stay in place as if by hanging; to cause or seem to float: *an acrobat suspended in midair.* **3.** To stop or cause to stop for a period of time: *They suspended train service while the tracks were being repaired.* **4.** To deprive of a position or privilege for a time: *She was suspended from school.*
sus·pend (sə **spend′**) □*verb* **suspended, suspending, suspends**

suspenders *plural noun* A pair of straps worn over the shoulders to hold up trousers or a skirt.
sus·pend·ers (sə **spen′**dərz) □*plural noun*

suspense *noun* Anxiety or worry about what will happen: *We waited in suspense for the results of the test.*
sus·pense (sə **spens′**) □*noun*

suspension *noun* **1.** The act of suspending: *a suspension of the rules.* **2.** The fact or condition of being suspended: *Her parents were upset over her suspension from school.* **3.** A liquid with solid particles suspended in it.
sus·pen·sion (sə **spen′**shən) □*noun*

suspension bridge *noun* A bridge suspended from cables anchored to towers.

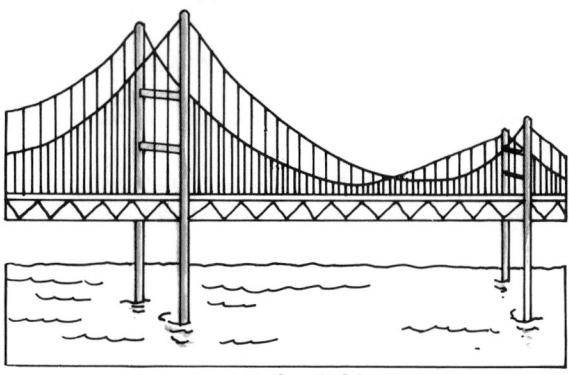

suspension bridge

suspicion *noun* **1.** A feeling or belief based on little or no evidence: *He had the suspicion he was being watched.* **2.** The condition of being suspected: *His reasons were not beyond suspicion.* **3.** Lack of trust; doubt: *She looked at the stranger with suspicion.*

sus·pi·cion (sə **spish′**ən) □*noun, plural* **suspicions**

suspicious *adjective* **1.** Causing suspicion: *suspicious behavior.* **2.** Tending to feel suspicion: *He's suspicious of strangers.* **3.** Expressing or showing suspicion: *a suspicious look.*
sus·pi·cious (sə **spish′**əs) □*adjective*

swal·low¹ *verb* **1.** To cause to pass from the mouth through the throat into the stomach. **2.** To take in completely as if by swallowing: *The little store was swallowed up by a super-market chain.* **3.** To refrain from showing or expressing; hold in: *He had to swallow his anger.*
□*noun* An act of swallowing: *I drank a glassful in one swallow.*
swal·low (swol′ō) □*verb* **swallowed, swallowing, swallows** □*noun, plural* **swallows**

swal·low² *noun* A small bird that has narrow, pointed wings and a forked tail.
swal·low (swol′ō) □*noun, plural* **swallows**

swam *verb* The past tense of **swim.**
swam (swam) □*verb*

swamp *noun* An area of soft and wet land often covered with water.
□*verb* **1.** To fill or become filled with water: *The waves swamped the boat and it sank.* **2.** To overwhelm: *We're swamped with homework.*
swamp (swomp) □*noun, plural* **swamps** □*verb* **swamped, swamping, swamps**

swan *noun* A large water bird that is usually white and has a long, slender neck and webbed feet.
swan (swon) □*noun, plural* **swans**

swan

a	bat	ī	bite	o͞o	tool	*th*	feather
ā	make	î	fierce	ou	out	th	bath
â	dare	o	dot	u	nut	hw	wheat
ä	father	ō	no	û	turn	zh	measure
e	net	ô	law, for	ch	church	ə	about, open
ē	be	oi	soil	ng	ring		pencil, atom
i	dip	oo	look	sh	shade		circus

swarm *noun* **1.** A large group of bees that moves together to find a new hive and start a new colony. **2.** A large group moving together: *a swarm of children; a swarm of flies.*
□*verb* **1.** To move in or form a swarm, as bees and other insects do. **2.** To move or gather in large numbers: *Customers swarmed into the store.* **3.** To be filled; teem: *The city is swarming with tourists.*
swarm (swôrm) □*noun, plural* **swarms** □*verb* **swarmed, swarming, swarms**

sway *verb* **1.** To move or cause to move slowly back and forth or from side to side: *The tulips swayed on their long stems. The dancers swayed their hips.* **2.** To influence: *Don't be swayed by flattery.*
□*noun* **1.** The act of swaying: *the sway of a boat riding the waves.* **2.** Power, influence, or control: *under the sway of emotions.*
sway (swā) □*verb* **swayed, swaying, sways** □*noun*

swear *verb* **1.** To make a solemn statement or promise while under oath: *Swear that you'll tell the truth.* **2.** To promise or pledge with a solemn oath; vow: *He swore his loyalty.* **3.** To use language that is bad or vulgar; curse.
swear (swâr) □*verb* **swore, sworn, swearing, swears**

sweat *noun* **1.** A salty liquid given off through the skin; perspiration. **2.** Water that forms in drops on a surface: *Sweat formed on the pitcher of iced tea.*
□*verb* **1.** To give off sweat; perspire: *I sweated as I ran.* **2.** To form water in drops on a surface: *The ice bucket was sweating.*
sweat (swet) □*noun* □*verb* **sweated, sweating, sweats**

sweater *noun* A knitted or crocheted outer garment worn on the upper part of the body.
sweat·er (swet′ər) □*noun, plural* **sweaters**

sweep *verb* **1.** To clean with a broom or brush: *sweep the floor.* **2.** To move or clear away with or as if with a broom or brush: *He swept the coins off the table.* **3.** To move or carry with a forceful sweeping motion: *The tide swept the swimmers toward shore.* **4.** To move over with violence or destruction: *The tornado swept through two states.* **5.** To move steadily through a wide curve; scan: *Her eyes swept the audience.*
□*noun* **1.** The act of sweeping. **2.** A sweeping motion: *She pushed the cat off the couch with a sweep of her arm.* **3.** A reach or extent: *a sweep of green lawn.*

sweep (swēp) □*verb* **swept, sweeping, sweeps** □*noun, plural* **sweeps**

sweep

sweet *adjective* **1.** Having a pleasant taste like that of sugar: *a sweet orange.* **2.** Not salty; fresh: *sweet butter.* **3.** Not spoiled, sour, or decaying: *sweet milk.* **4.** Having a pleasant smell; fragrant: *a sweet lilac.* **5.** Having a pleasant disposition; lovable: *a sweet child.*
□*noun* Something, such as candy, that is sweet.
sweet (swēt) □*adjective* **sweeter, sweetest** □*noun, plural* **sweets**

sweeten *verb* To make or become sweet or sweeter.
sweet·en (swēt′ən) □*verb* **sweetened, sweetening, sweetens**

sweetheart *noun* Someone who is loved by another.
sweet·heart (swēt′härt′) □*noun, plural* **sweethearts**

sweet pea *noun* A climbing plant whose colorful flowers have a pleasant smell.

sweet pea

sweet potato *noun* The thick, sweet edible yellow or orange root of a tropical vine.

swell *verb* **1.** To enlarge as a result of growth or internal pressure: *Her jaw is swelling from the infected tooth. Membership in the organization swelled.* **2.** To increase or cause to increase, as in size or volume: *Melting snow and ice swelled the river.* **3.** To fill or become filled with emotion: *swell with pride.*
□*noun* A long wave or series of waves: *the swell of the ocean.*
□*adjective* Excellent; fine: *What a swell idea!*
swell (swel) □*verb* **swelled, swelled** or **swollen, swelling, swells** □*noun, plural* **swells** □*adjective*

swelling *noun* A swollen part: *I have a swelling on my hand from the mosquito bite.*
swell·ing (swel′ing) □*noun, plural* **swellings**

swept *verb* The past tense and past participle of **sweep:** *I swept the kitchen floor.*
swept (swept) □*verb*

swerve *verb* To turn or cause to turn quickly and sharply: *The car swerved quickly to avoid the bicycle.*
□*noun* The act of swerving.
swerve (swûrv) □*verb* **swerve, swerving, swerves** □*noun, plural* **swerves**

swerve

swift *adjective* **1.** Moving with great speed: *a swift car; a swift horse.* **2.** Coming or happening quickly: *a swift response to the question.*
□*noun* A gray or blackish bird that has long, narrow wings and can fly very fast.
swift (swift) □*adjective* **swifter, swiftest** □*noun, plural* **swifts**

swim *verb* **1.** To move in or through water by moving the arms, legs, or fins. **2.** To cross by swimming: *We swam the river.* **3.** To float on or be covered with liquid: *The potatoes were swimming in gravy.* **4.** To be or feel dizzy: *The hot sun made my head swim.*
□*noun* The act or period of swimming: *We took our afternoon swim.*
swim (swim) □*verb* **swam, swum, swimming, swims** □*noun, plural* **swims**

swimmer *noun* A person or animal that swims.
swim·mer (swim′ər) □*noun, plural* **swimmers**

swindle *verb* To get money or property from by illegal or dishonest means; cheat: *The car salesman swindled the customer.*
□*noun* The act of swindling.
swin·dle (swin′dəl) □*verb* **swindled, swindling, swindles** □*noun, plural* **swindles**

swine *noun* A pig or hog.
swine (swīn) □*noun, plural* **swine**

swing *verb* **1.** To move or cause to move back and forth: *Her purse swung from her arm. He swung his keys on a chain.* **2.** To move or cause to move in a wide curve: *The car swung to the right. She swung the baseball bat.*
□*noun* **1.** The act of swinging: *He chopped down the tree with a few swings of the ax.* **2.** A seat suspended from above on which a person may swing.
swing (swing) □*verb* **swung, swinging, swings** □*noun, plural* **swings**

swing

a bat	ī bite	oo tool	*th* feather
ā make	î fierce	ou out	th bath
â dare	o dot	u nut	hw wheat
ä father	ō no	û turn	zh measure
e net	ô law, for	ch church	ə about, open
ē be	oi soil	ng ring	pencil, atom
i dip	oo look	sh shade	circus

swirl *verb* To move or cause to move around and around; spin: *The leaves swirled in the wind. She swirled the coffee in her cup.*
□*noun* **1.** A swirling motion or mass: *a swirl of smoke.* **2.** Something that is shaped like a curl or twist: *swirls of frosting.*
swirl (swûrl) □*verb* **swirled, swirling, swirls** □*noun, plural* **swirls**

swish *verb* To move or cause to move with a whistling or hissing sound: *The grass swished in the wind. The cat swished its tail.*
□*noun* A swishing sound or movement: *the swish of a silk dress.*
swish (swish) □*verb* **swished, swishing, swishes** □*noun, plural* **swishes**

switch *noun* **1.** A change: *a switch in plans.* **2.** A thin, flexible rod or stick that is used as a whip. **3.** A lashing or swinging motion: *a switch of its tail.* **4.** A device used to open or close an electric circuit: *a light switch.* **5.** A device consisting of two sections of railroad tracks and various movable parts that is used to move a streetcar or train from one track to another.
□*verb* **1.** To shift or change: *I switched rooms.* **2.** To lash or swing back and forth: *The horse switched its tail.* **3.** To open or close an electric circuit with a switch: *I switched the television off.* **4.** To move a streetcar or train from one track to another by operating a switch.
switch (swich) □*noun, plural* **switches** □*verb* **switched, switching, switches**

switchboard *noun* A panel with switches and plugs that is used for operating electric circuits: *a telephone switchboard.*
switch·board (swich′bôrd′) □*noun, plural* **switchboards**

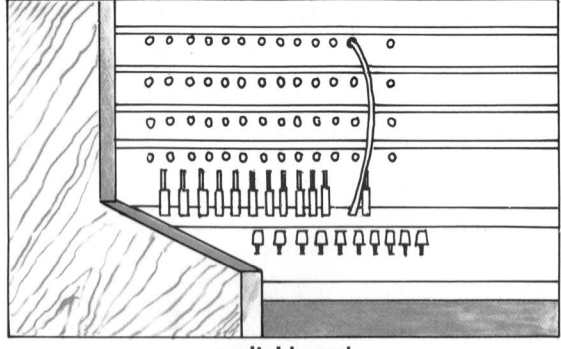
switchboard

swollen *verb* A past participle of **swell:** *Her ankles have swollen.*
swol·len (swō′lən) □*verb*

swoop *verb* **1.** To rush with a sudden sweeping motion: *The eagle swooped down and caught the mouse.* **2.** To seize with a sudden sweeping motion: *She swooped up her books and ran.*
□*noun* The act of swooping: *He picked up the packages in one swoop.*
swoop (swo͞op) □*verb* **swooped, swooping, swoops** □*noun, plural* **swoops**

swoop

sword *noun* A weapon with a long, pointed blade set in a handle or hilt.
sword (sôrd) □*noun, plural* **swords**

swordfish *noun* A large edible ocean fish whose upper jaw projects forward in a point like a sword.
sword·fish (sôrd′fish′) □*noun, plural* **swordfish** or **swordfishes**

swordfish

swore *verb* The past tense of **swear:** *He swore he wasn't lying.*
swore (swôr) □*verb*

sworn *verb* The past participle of **swear:** *You have sworn to tell the truth.*
sworn (swôrn) □*verb*

swum *verb* The past participle of **swim:** *I have never swum in the ocean.*
swum (swum) □*verb*

swung *verb* The past tense and past participle of **swing:** *He swung the bat.*
swung (swung) □*verb*

sycamore *noun* A North American tree with seed clusters that are shaped like balls and bark that peels off in flakes.
syc·a·more (**sik′**ə môr′) □*noun, plural* **sycamores**

sycamore

syllabicate *verb* To divide a word into syllables.
syl·lab·i·cate (si **lab′**i kāt′) □*verb* **syllabicated, syllabicating, syllabicates**

syllabify *verb* To syllabicate.
syl·lab·i·fy (si **lab′**ə fī′) □*verb* **syllabified, syllabifying, syllabifies**

syllable *noun* **1.** A unit of pronunciation that consists of a single sound formed by a vowel alone or a vowel together with one or more consonants: *The word "basketball" has three syllables.* **2.** A letter or group of letters used to represent a syllable.
syl·la·ble (**sil′**ə bəl) □*noun, plural* **syllables**

symbol *noun* **1.** Something that represents or stands for something else: *The lily is a symbol of purity.* **2.** A printed or written mark used to represent an operation, element, quantity, or quality, as in mathematics or music: *The mark ✕ is the symbol for multiplication.*
sym·bol (**sim′**bəl) □*noun, plural* **symbols**

symbolic *adjective* Of, having to do with, or using symbols: *a symbolic language for a computer.*
sym·bol·ic (sim **bol′**ik) □*adjective*

symbolize *verb* To be a symbol of; stand for: *The lion symbolizes courage.*
sym·bol·ize (**sim′**bə līz′) □*verb* **symbolized, symbolizing, symbolizes**

symmetry *noun* **1.** Correspondence of form and arrangement of parts on opposite sides of a line or around a center: *the symmetry of a design.* **2.** A balanced arrangement of parts.

sym·me·try (**sim′**i trē) □*noun, plural* **symmetries**

symmetry

sympathetic *adjective* **1.** Showing or feeling sympathy: *a sympathetic smile; a sympathetic friend.* **2.** In favor of: *She is sympathetic to our ideas.*
sym·pa·thet·ic (sim′pə **thet′**ik) □*adjective*

sympathize *verb* **1.** To feel or show sympathy: *I sympathize with you in your troubles.* **2.** To share or understand another's feelings or ideas: *We sympathize with her ambition to become a doctor.*
sym·pa·thize (**sim′**pə thīz′) □*verb* **sympathized, sympathizing, sympathizes**

sympathy *noun* **1.** The capacity for or act of understanding and sharing another's problems or sorrow. **2.** An expression of sympathy: *She went to her friend for sympathy.* **3.** Favor; agreement: *He is in sympathy with my plan.*
sym·pa·thy (**sim′**pə thē) □*noun, plural* **sympathies**

symphony *noun* **1.** A long musical composition with several divisions that is written to be played by an orchestra. **2.** A large orchestra that is made up of string, wind, and percussion instruments.
sym·pho·ny (**sim′**fə nē) □*noun, plural* **symphonies**

symptom *noun* An indication; sign: *A fever is a symptom of illness.*

a bat	ī bite	oo tool	th feather
ā make	î fierce	ou out	th bath
â dare	o dot	u nut	hw wheat
ä father	ō no	û turn	zh measure
e net	ô law, for	ch church	ə about, open
ē be	oi soil	ng ring	pencil, atom
i dip	oo look	sh shade	circus

symp·tom (**simp′**təm) ☐*noun, plural* **symptoms**

synagogue *noun* A building or meeting place used by Jews for worship and religious instruction.
syn·a·gogue (**sin′**ə gog′) ☐*noun, plural* **synagogues**

synonym *noun* A word that has the same or almost the same meaning as another: *"Humorous" is a synonym of "funny."*
syn·o·nym (**sin′**ə nim′) ☐*noun, plural* **synonyms**

synonymous *adjective* Having the same or almost the same meaning: *"Large" and "big" are synonymous.*
syn·on·y·mous (si **non′**ə məs) ☐*adjective*

synthetic *adjective* Produced by human beings rather than found in nature; artificial: *a synthetic diamond.*
syn·thet·ic (sin **thet′**ik) ☐*adjective*

vrup *noun* A thick, sweet liquid, such as that ⁊de by boiling the juice of a fruit or plant with sugar: *raspberry syrup; maple syrup.*
syr·up (**sir′**əp *or* **sûr′**əp) ☐*noun, plural* **syrups**

system *noun* **1.** A set of parts or elements forming a whole that functions as a unit: *a telephone system.* **2.** A group of related organs or parts of the body: *the digestive system.* **3.** An orderly method or plan of doing something: *a democratic system of government.*
sys·tem (**sis′**təm) ☐*noun, plural* **systems**

systematic *adjective* **1.** Of, having, or using a system: *a systematic worker.* **2.** Carried out according to a system: *systematic attempts.*
sys·tem·at·ic (sis′tə **mat′**ik) ☐*adjective*

a	bat	ī	bite	o͞o	tool	th	feather
ā	make	î	fierce	ou	out	th	bath
â	dare	o	dot	u	nut	hw	wheat
ä	father	ō	no	û	turn	zh	measure
e	net	ô	law, for	ch	church	ə	about, open
ē	be	oi	soil	ng	ring		pencil, atom
i	dip	oo	look	sh	shade		circus

Tt

The letter **T** has evolved from many forms of ancient writing. One of the earliest known examples is the Greek character shown above, which dates from almost 3,000 years ago. Over the years, artists and designers have created their own versions of the English letter **T**. Some of the more common examples seen today are shown below.

Tt *Tt*	**Tt** *Tt*	Tt Tt	**Tt** Tt	*Tt Tt*
HANDWRITING	CALLIGRAPHY	MODERN SANS SERIF	MODERN SERIF	SCRIPT

---

t or **T**   *noun* The twentieth letter of the English alphabet.
t or **T** (tē) □*noun, plural* **t's** or **T's**

tab   *noun* A small flap or strip that sticks out from an object.
tab (tab) □*noun, plural* **tabs**

table   *noun* **1.** A piece of furniture with a flat top that is supported by one or more vertical legs. **2.** A list of facts and information: *a table of contents.*
ta·ble (**tā′**bəl) □*noun, plural* **tables**

tablespoon   *noun* **1.** A large spoon used for serving food. **2.** A unit of measure used in cooking that is equal to three teaspoons.
ta·ble·spoon (**tā′**bəl spoon′) □*noun, plural* **tablespoons**

tablet   *noun* **1.** A flat slab of wood or stone. Ancient peoples used tablets to write on before paper was invented. **2.** A pad of writing paper in which the paper sheets are glued together at one end. **3.** A small, flat piece of medicine that is meant to be swallowed.
tab·let (**tab′**lit) □*noun, plural* **tablets**

table tennis   *noun* A game that is somewhat similar to tennis. It is played on a table with a small plastic ball and wooden paddles.

tack   *noun* **1.** A short nail with a wide, round head. **2.** A course of action.
□*verb* **1.** To fasten with a tack: *tack a poster to the wall.* **2.** To add: *I tacked a message on at the end of her letter.*
tack (tak) □*noun, plural* **tacks** □*verb* **tacked, tacking, tacks**

tackle   *noun* **1.** The equipment used in a sport or activity: *fishing tackle.* **2.** A system of ropes and pulleys used for lifting and lowering heavy objects. **3.** The act of knocking someone to the ground, especially in football.
□*verb* **1.** To take on such things as difficulties or problems: *It's time to tackle my homework.* **2.** To grab another person and throw him or her to the ground, especially in football.
tack·le (**tak′**əl) □*noun, plural* **tackles** □*verb* **tackled, tackling, tackles**

taco   *noun* A tortilla that is folded in half and stuffed with a filling such as meat or cheese.
ta·co (**tä′**kō) □*noun, plural* **tacos**

taco

tact   *noun* The ability to say or do the right thing in a difficult situation: *Her tact enabled her to settle the argument in a friendly way.*
tact (takt) □*noun*

tadpole   *noun* A stage of development of a frog or toad. A tadpole lives underwater and

has gills, a tail, and no legs.
tad·pole (tad′pōl′) ▢*noun, plural* **tadpoles**

> *WORD HISTORY:* **tadpole**
>
> *Tadpole* is formed from two early English words, the first meaning "toad" and the second meaning "head."

taffy *noun* A chewy candy made from molasses or brown sugar that is mixed with butter. It is pulled into long pieces until it hardens. **taf·fy** (taf′ē) ▢*noun, plural* **taffies**

tag¹ *noun* A small piece of paper, plastic, or other material that is attached to something: *a price tag; a name tag.*
▢*verb* **1.** To attach a tag to. **2.** To follow closely: *The dog tagged along after me.*
tag (tag) ▢*noun, plural* **tags** ▢*verb* **tagged, tagging, tags**

tag² *noun* A game in which one person chases the others until he or she touches one of them, who must then chase the others.
▢*verb* To touch another player, as in the game of tag.
tag (tag) ▢*noun, plural* **tags** ▢*verb* **tagged, tagging, tags**

tail *noun* **1.** The rear part that sticks out beyond the main part of an animal's body. **2.** Something that looks, hangs, or follows behind like an animal's tail: *the tail of a comet.* **3.** The rear or end part of anything.
▢*verb* To follow and watch: *I tailed my brother to see where he was going.*
tail (tāl) ▢*noun, plural* **tails** ▢*verb* **tailed, tailing, tails**

tailor *noun* Someone who makes, repairs, or alters clothing.
▢*verb* To make, repair, or alter clothing.
tai·lor (tā′lər) ▢*noun, plural* **tailors** ▢*verb* **tailored, tailoring, tailors**

tailor

take *verb* **1.** To capture, seize, or win: *The soldiers took the enemy fort. I hope she takes first prize.* **2.** To grasp: *Take my arm when we cross the street.* **3.** To carry to another place: *Take this book back to the library. This bus will take you to the square. They're taking her to the airport.* **4.** To move or remove: *She took the glass from the shelf.* **5.** To get for use or possession: *I took a cabin at the beach.* **6.** To eat, drink, swallow, or inhale: *She took her medicine.* **7.** To perform or do: *Let's take a walk.* **8.** To require or need: *It takes time to learn how to play the clarinet.* **9.** To choose or select; pick out: *Take any seat you want.* **10.** To subtract: *Take five away from fifteen.* **11.** To endure or put up with: *I can't take all this noise.* **12.** To accept as a guide: *Don't take his advice.* **13.** To react or respond to in a certain way: *She takes pride in her work.* **14.** To undertake as a responsibility: *When did he take office?* **15.** To use or make use of: *She took the seat near the door.* **16.** To become: *She took sick at the party.* **17.** To come upon suddenly: *Let's take them by surprise.* **18.** To study: *I'm taking French.* **19.** To find out, using a special method: *I have to take your temperature.* **20.** To please; to charm: *The whole family is taken with the new baby.* **21.** To make by photography: *Take my picture.*

take after To resemble or look like: *He takes after his mother.*

take for To think or suppose to be: *He took me for his uncle.*

take over To assume control of: *When his partner retired, my father took over the whole company.*

take (tāk) ▢*verb* **took, taken, taking**

takeoff *noun* The act of rising up in flight: *The spaceship had a smooth takeoff.*
take·off (tāk′ôf′) ▢*noun, plural* **takeoffs**

takeoff

tale *noun* **1.** A report of facts or events: *a traveler's tales about strange and wonderful places.* **2.** A made-up story; lie.
tale (tāl) ▢*noun, plural* **tales**

talent *noun* **1.** A natural ability to do something well: *musical talent.* **2.** Someone with talent: *He is the biggest talent on the football team.*
tal·ent (tal′ənt) ▢*noun, plural* **talents**

talented *adjective* Having or showing talent: *talented singer.*
tal·ent·ed (tal′ən tid) ▢*adjective*

talk *verb* **1.** To use human speech: *Can the baby talk yet?* **2.** To express ideas or feelings by using speech: *We talked about our plans for the vacation.* **3.** To discuss: *I like to talk about cars.* **4.** To influence by speech: *She talked him into staying for dinner.*
▢*noun* **1.** An informal speech or conference: *The astronaut gave a talk on flying in a spaceship.* **2.** The exchange of ideas; conversation: *I had a long talk with my mother.*
talk (tôk) ▢*verb* **talked, talking, talks** ▢*noun, plural* **talks**

SYNONYMS: talk, converse, speak
These verbs mean to express ideas or feelings using speech: *We talked about our plans for next year. They conversed quietly at dinner. He found it difficult to speak with her about his fears.*

---

tall *adjective* **1.** Having a greater than average height: *a tall man.* **2.** Having a certain height: *The fence is ten feet tall.* **3.** Hard to believe: *a tall tale.*
tall (tôl) ▢*adjective* **taller, tallest**

SYNONYMS: tall, high, lofty
These adjectives mean extending to a great height: *tall trees; a high building; lofty mountains.*

---

tallow *noun* The fat of cattle, sheep, or horses. It is used to make such things as soap and candles.
tal·low (tal′ō) ▢*noun*

Talmud *noun* The collection of ancient writings that are the basis of religious authority for traditional Judaism.
Tal·mud (täl′mood′) ▢*noun*

talon *noun* The claw of an animal or bird that seizes other animals as prey.
tal·on (tal′ən) ▢*noun, plural* **talons**

tamale *noun* Spicy ground meat steamed in husks of corn.
ta·ma·le (tə mä′lē) ▢*noun, plural* **tamales**

tambourine *noun* A small drum that has metal disks attached to the rim. The disks jingle when the tambourine is struck or shaken.
tam·bou·rine (tam′bə rēn′) ▢*noun, plural* **tambourines**

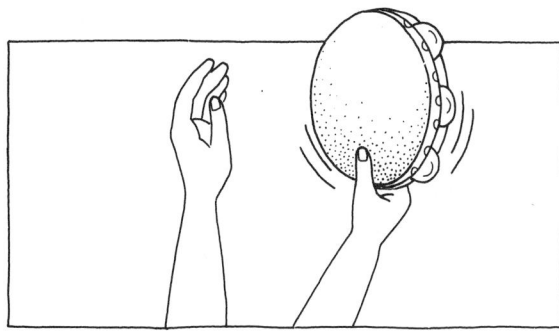

tambourine

tame *adjective* **1.** Taken from a wild state and made obedient or gentle: *I saw a tame monkey at the zoo.* **2.** Gentle and not afraid: *The deer were so tame I was able to pet them.*
▢*verb* To make or become obedient or gentle.
tame (tām) ▢*adjective* **tamer, tamest** ▢*verb* **tamed, taming, tames**

tamper *verb* To meddle in a harmful way: *He told me not to tamper with the radio.*
tam·per (tam′pər) ▢*verb* **tampered, tampering, tampers**

tan *verb* **1.** To make hide into leather by soaking in certain mixtures. **2.** To make or become brown by exposure to the sun: *skin that tans easily.*
▢*noun* **1.** A light yellowish-brown color. **2.** The brown color gotten by exposing the skin to the sun.
▢*adjective* Of the color tan.
tan (tan) ▢*verb* **tanned, tanning, tans** ▢*noun, plural* **tans** ▢*adjective* **tanner, tannest**

tangerine *noun* A fruit related to the orange with dark orange skin that peels easily.

a	bat	ī	bite	ōō	tool	*th*	feather
ā	make	î	fierce	ou	out	th	bath
â	dare	o	dot	u	nut	hw	wheat
ä	father	ō	no	û	turn	zh	measure
e	net	ô	law, for	ch	church	ə	about, open
ē	be	oi	soil	ng	ring		pencil, atom
i	dip	oo	look	sh	shade		circus

tan·ger·ine (tan′jə rēn′) ◻*noun, plural*
tangerines

WORD HISTORY: **tangerine**

Tangerine comes from the French name for Tangier,
a city in northern Africa. The fruit was originally imported to Europe from Tangier.

tangle *verb* To mix or become mixed together
in a confused mass; snarl: *Try not to tangle the
rope.*
◻*noun* A confused, snarled mass: *There's a
tangle in the lamp cord.*
tan·gle (**tang′**gəl) ◻*verb* **tangled, tangling,
tangles** ◻*noun, plural* **tangles**

tank *noun* **1.** A large container for holding
liquids: *a gas tank; a water tank.* **2.** A heavily
armored vehicle that is used in combat. It has
cannon and guns, and moves on two continuous metal belts that have treads.
tank (tangk) ◻*noun, plural* **tanks**

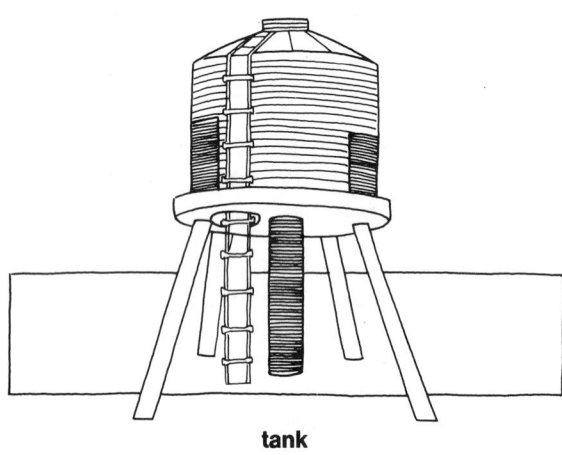

tank

tanker *noun* A ship, truck, or airplane that
carries oil or other liquids or gases.
tank·er (**tang′**kər) ◻*noun, plural* **tankers**

tanner *noun* Someone who tans hides to
make them into leather.
tan·ner (**tan′**ər) ◻*noun, plural* **tanners**

tantrum *noun* A fit or outburst of bad temper: *The boy had a tantrum when his mother
told him to go to bed.*
tan·trum (**tan′**trəm) ◻*noun, plural* **tantrums**

tap[1] *verb* **1.** To strike or hit gently: *He tapped
on the window.* **2.** To produce with light
blows: *She tapped out the rhythm of the song
with her hand.*
◻*noun* A light or gentle blow: *He gave me a
tap on the shoulder.*
tap (tap) ◻*verb* **tapped, tapping, taps**
◻*noun, plural* **taps**

tap[2] *noun* A device at the end of a pipe for
controlling the flow of water or some other liquid; faucet.
◻*verb* **1.** To put a hole in something to draw
liquid out: *Maples trees are tapped to get syrup.*
2. To cut in on and make a connection with:
The police tapped the suspect's telephone.
tap (tap) ◻*noun, plural* **taps** ◻*verb* **tapped,
tapping, taps**

tap

tape *noun* **1.** A long, narrow, flexible piece of
material, such as cloth, plastic, paper, or
metal. **2.** A long, narrow piece of specially
treated plastic on which sounds or images can
be recorded: *I have a tape of the song.*
◻*verb* **1.** To fasten with tape: *I taped a label
on the box.* **2.** To record sounds or images on
tape: *We taped the baby's first words.*
tape (tāp) ◻*noun, plural* **tapes** ◻*verb* **taped,
taping, tapes**

taper *verb* **1.** To make or become gradually
thinner toward one end: *He tapered the pole to
a point. The pencil tapers to a point.* **2.** To become slowly less: *The crowd at the beach tapered off as the evening approached.*
ta·per (**tā′**pər) ◻*verb* **tapered, tapering,
tapers**

taper

tape recorder   *noun* A machine that can record sound on specially treated plastic tape and that can also play the sound back.

tapestry   *noun* A heavy cloth with designs or pictures woven in it. It is hung on walls or used to cover furniture.
tap·es·try (**tap′** i strē) ☐*noun, plural* **tapestries**

tapeworm   *noun* A long, flat worm that looks like a ribbon. Tapeworms live as parasites in the intestines of human beings and other animals.
tape·worm (**tāp′** wûrm′) ☐*noun, plural* **tapeworms**

tapir   *noun* An animal with a heavy body and a long snout. Tapirs live in tropical America and Asia.
ta·pir (**tā′** pər) ☐*noun, plural* **tapirs**

tapir

taps   *noun* A bugle call that is played at night as a signal to put out all lights. It is also played at funerals.
taps (taps) ☐*noun*

tar¹   *noun* A dark, sticky substance that is made from wood, coal, or peat. It is used to pave roads and cover roofs.
☐*verb* To coat or cover with tar.
tar (tär) ☐*noun* ☐*verb* **tarred, tarring, tars**

tar²   *noun* A sailor.
tar (tär) ☐*noun, plural* **tars**

tarantula   *noun* A large, hairy spider whose bite is painful but not seriously poisonous. Tarantulas live in the tropics.
tar·an·tu·la (tə **ran′** chə lə) ☐*noun, plural* **tarantulas**

WORD HISTORY: **tarantula**
The *tarantula* is named after Taranto, a port in southern Italy where the spider is commonly found.

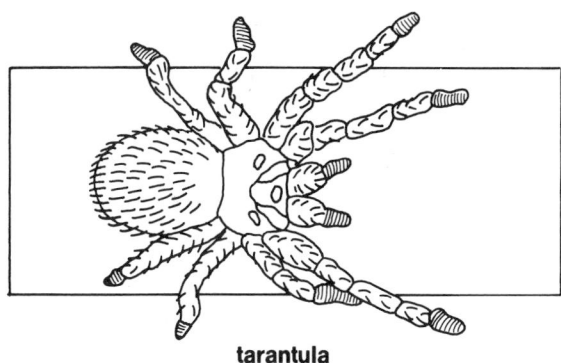
tarantula

tardy   *adjective* Delayed; late: *He's always tardy for school.* —See Synonyms at **slow.**
tar·dy (**tär′** dē) ☐*adjective* **tardier, tardiest**

target   *noun* **1.** A mark that is aimed or fired at: *We shot arrows at the target.* **2.** A person or object that is criticized or made fun of: *The little girl is always the target of her big brother's jokes.* **3.** A goal or aim.
tar·get (**tär′** git) ☐*noun, plural* **targets**

tariff   *noun* A tax or duty that a government places on imported or exported goods: *a tariff on foreign cars.*
tar·iff (**tar′** if) ☐*noun, plural* **tariffs**

tarnish   *verb* To make or become dull in color or luster: *Air and moisture tarnish silver.*
☐*noun* A dull coating on the surface of a metal. Tarnish can be removed with polish.
tar·nish (**tär′** nish) ☐*verb* **tarnished, tarnishing, tarnishes** ☐*noun*

tarpon   *noun* A large silvery fish that lives along the coast of the Atlantic Ocean.
tar·pon (**tär′** pən) ☐*noun, plural* **tarpon** or **tarpons**

tart¹   *adjective* **1.** Having a sharp taste; sour: *tart lemonade.* **2.** Sharp or harsh in tone or meaning: *a tart answer.*
tart (tärt) ☐*adjective* **tarter, tartest**

tart²   *noun* A small pie with no crust on top.
tart (tärt) ☐*noun, plural* **tarts**

tartan   *noun* A woolen fabric with a plaid pattern.
tar·tan (**tär′** tən) ☐*noun, plural* **tartans**

a	bat	ī	bite	o͞o	tool	th	feather
ā	make	î	fierce	ou	out	th	bath
â	dare	o	dot	u	nut	hw	wheat
ä	father	ō	no	û	turn	zh	measure
e	net	ô	law, for	ch	church	ə	about, open
ē	be	oi	soil	ng	ring		pencil, atom
i	dip	oo	look	sh	shade		circus

tartar *noun* A yellowish substance that forms on the teeth that becomes a hard crust if it is not removed by brushing.
tar·tar (tär′tər) □*noun*

task *noun* A piece of work assigned or done as part of one's duties.
task (task) □*noun, plural* **tasks**

tassel *noun* **1.** A bunch of loose threads or cords that are tied together at one end and hanging free at the other. **2.** Something that looks like a tassel, such as a growth of hair at the end of the tail of certain animals.
tas·sel (tas′əl) □*noun, plural* **tassels**

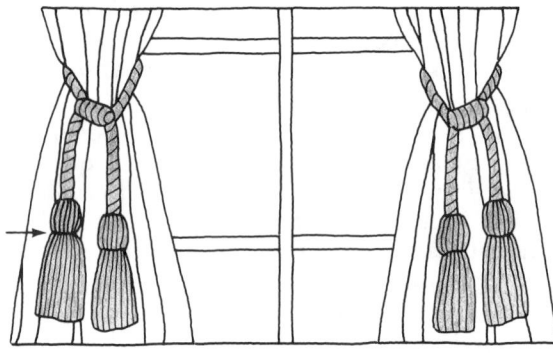

tassel

taste *noun* **1.** The sensation that is produced by food or some other substance that is placed in the mouth; flavor. The four basic tastes are sweet, sour, salty, and bitter. **2.** The sense by which one can notice the flavor of something placed in the mouth. **3.** A small amount: *She gave me a taste of her sandwich.* **4.** A liking or preference: *He has a taste for opera.* **5.** The ability to know what is good in a certain situation or to appreciate what is good, beautiful, or of high quality: *She dresses with taste.*
□*verb* **1.** To notice the flavor of by taking into the mouth: *Can you taste the onions in the soup?* **2.** To have a certain flavor: *The milk tastes sour.* **3.** To sample a small amount of: *Taste the stew.*
taste (tāst) □*noun, plural* **tastes** □*verb* **tasted, tasting, tastes**

tasty *adjective* Having a pleasing flavor: *a tasty pudding.*
tast·y (tā′stē) □*adjective* **tastier, tastiest**

SYNONYMS: tasty, delicious

These adjectives mean having a pleasing flavor: *a tasty piece of steak; a delicious dinner.*

---

tattered *adjective* Torn or worn to shreds: *The dog sleeps on a tattered blanket.*
tat·tered (tat′ərd) □*adjective*

tattered

tattle *verb* To tell secrets: *I would never tattle on my friend.*
tat·tle (tat′əl) □*verb* **tattled, tattling, tattles**

tattletale *noun* Someone who tells the secrets of another.
tat·tle·tale (tat′əl tāl′) □*noun, plural* **tattletales**

tattoo *noun* A mark or design on the skin made by pricking the skin with needles that have dye or colors on the points.
□*verb* To mark the skin with a tattoo.
tat·too (ta tōō′) □*noun, plural* **tattoos** □*verb* **tattooed, tattooing, tattoes**

taught *verb* The past tense and past participle of **teach.**
taught (tôt) □*verb*

taut *adjective* Pulled or drawn tight: *a taut rope; taut muscles.*
taut (tôt) □*adjective* **tauter, tautest**

tavern *noun* **1.** A place where alcoholic beverages are sold and drunk. **2.** A place that provides travelers with meals and a place to sleep; inn.
tav·ern (tav′ərn) □*noun, plural* **taverns**

tax *noun* **1.** Money paid to the government for public use. **2.** A heavy demand; burden: *a tax on his strength.*
□*verb* **1.** To place a tax on: *The government taxes incomes.* **2.** To make a heavy demand upon; strain: *The unruly child taxed her patience to the utmost.*
tax (taks) □*noun, plural* **taxes** □*verb* **taxed, taxing, taxes**

taxation *noun* **1.** The act of taxing. **2.** Money collected as taxes.
tax·a·tion (tak sā′shən) □*noun*

taxi *noun* A taxicab.
□*verb* **1.** To ride in a taxicab: *I taxied to the store.* **2.** To move slowly over the surface of the ground or water before taking off or landing: *The airplane taxied down the runway.*

tax·i (**tak′**sē) □*noun, plural* **taxis** or **taxies**
□*verb* **taxied, taxiing** or **taxying, taxis** or **taxies**

taxicab *noun* An automobile that can be hired to drive passengers wherever they want to go. It has a meter than registers the fare.
tax·i·cab (**tak′**sē kab′) □*noun, plural* **taxicabs**

tea *noun* **1.** The dried leaves of a shrub grown in eastern and southern Asia. **2.** A drink made by soaking tea in boiling water. **3.** A light meal or small party in the late afternoon at which tea is served.
tea (tē) □*noun, plural* **teas**

teach *verb* **1.** To make someone learn: *Who is teaching you arithmetic?* **2.** To give classes or lessons in: *teaches English in the high school.*
teach (tēch) □*verb* **taught, teaching, teaches**

SYNONYMS: teach, instruct

These verbs mean to cause someone to learn or to acquire a skill: *Who taught you to dance? Our teacher is going to instruct all the students in the use of the new computer.*

---

teacher *noun* Someone who gives instruction or classes.
teach·er (**tē′**chər) □*noun, plural* **teachers**

teaching *noun* **1.** The profession of a teacher. **2.** Something that is taught: *the teaching of religion.*
teach·ing (**tēch′**ing) □*noun, plural* **teachings**

teakettle *noun* A kettle with a handle and a spout used for boiling water.
tea·ket·tle (**tē′**ket′əl) □*noun, plural* **teakettles**

teal *noun* A small duck with brightly marked feathers.
teal (tēl) □*noun, plural* **teal** or **teals**

team *noun* **1.** Two or more animals that are harnessed together to do work: *A team of oxen pulled the plow.* **2.** A group of people who work or play together: *a team of scientists doing research; a baseball team.*
□*verb* To work together as a team; form a team: *My sisters and I teamed up to buy our parents an aniversary present.*
team (tēm) □*noun, plural* **teams** □*verb* **teamed, teaming, teams**

tear¹ *verb* **1.** To pull or become pulled apart; split: *The dog tore the newspaper to pieces. She tore up the letter.* **2.** To make an opening or

wound in: *She tore her dress on the fence.* **3.** To pull forcefully: *He tore the poster off the wall.* **4.** To move with great speed; rush: *She went tearing down the road to catch the bus.*
□*noun* A cut, hole, or opening made by tearing; rip.
    tear down To destroy or demolish: *tear down an old building.*
tear (târ) □*verb* **tore, torn, tearing, tears**
□*noun, plural* **tears**

tear² *noun* A drop of the clear, salty liquid that comes from the eye.
tear (tîr) □*noun, plural* **tears**

tease *verb* To annoy or bother by making fun of: *She teased her little brother by showing him the ball but not letting him playing with it.*
□*noun* Someone who teases.
tease (tēz) □*verb* **teased, teasing, teases**
□*noun, plural* **teases**

teaspoon *noun* **1.** A small spoon used for stirring liquids and eating soft foods. **2.** A unit of measure in cooking. A teaspoon is equal to one third of a tablespoon or half an ounce.
teaspoon (**tē′**spoon′) □*noun, plural* **teaspoons**

technical *adjective* **1.** Of or having to do with a particular subject or field, such as a science or an art: *I couldn't understand the technical language in the geology book.* **2.** Of or having to do with mechanical or industrial arts: *a technical high school; technical help.*
tech·ni·cal (**tek′**ni kəl) □*adjective*

technique *noun* A method or way of doing something difficult or complicated, as in science or art: *the technique of oil painting.*
tech·nique (tek **nēk′**) □*noun, plural* **techniques**

technology *noun* The use of scientific knowledge in industry, especially in such technical fields as engineering and the mechanical arts.
tech·nol·o·gy (tek **nol′**ə jē) □*noun, plural* **technologies**

tedious *adjective* Long and tiring; boring: *Painting the house was tedious work.*
te·di·ous (**tē′**dē əs) □*adjective*

a	bat	ī	bite	ŏŏ	tool	*th*	feather
ā	make	ī	fierce	ou	out	th	bath
â	dare	o	dot	u	nut	hw	wheat
ä	father	ō	no	û	turn	zh	measure
e	net	ô	law, for	ch	church	ə	about, open
ē	be	oi	soil	ng	ring		pencil, atom
i	dip	oo	look	sh	shade		circus

teem *verb* To be full of; swarm: *The yard was teeming with ants. The store teemed with bargain hunters.*
teem (tēm) ☐*verb* **teemed, teeming, teems**

teen·ager *noun* Someone from age thirteen to nineteen.
teen·ag·er (tēn′ā′jər) ☐*noun, plural* **teen-agers**

teens *plural noun* The years of a person's life from age thirteen to nineteen.
teens (tēnz) ☐*plural noun*

teeth *noun* The plural of **tooth.**
teeth (tēth) ☐*noun*

telegram *noun* A message that is sent by telegraph.
tel·e·gram (tel′ə gram′) ☐*noun, plural* **telegrams**

telegraph *noun* A system of sending messages over wire or radio to a special receiving station.
☐*verb* To send a message by telegraph: *We telegraphed birthday greetings to our cousin.*
tel·e·graph (tel′ə graf′) ☐*noun, plural* **telegraphs** ☐*verb* **telegraphed, telegraphing, telegraphs**

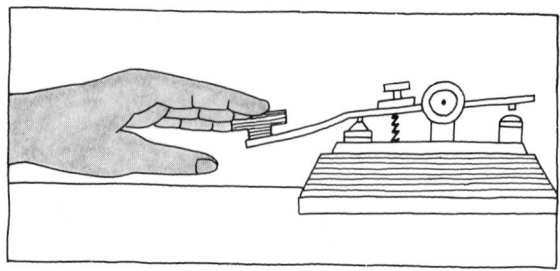

telegraph

telephone *noun* An instrument that sends and receives speech and other sounds over wires by means of electricity.
☐*verb* To talk with someone by telephone: *I'll telephone you tonight.*
tel·e·phone (tel′ə fōn′) ☐*noun, plural* **telephones** ☐*verb* **telephoned, telephoning, telephones**

WORD HISTORY: **telephone**

The word *telephone* is formed from two Greek words that mean "far off" and "voice."

---

telescope *noun* An instrument that makes distant objects appear closer and larger by using a series of lenses or mirrors arranged inside a long tube.

tel·e·scope (tel′ə skōp′) ☐*noun, plural* **telescopes**

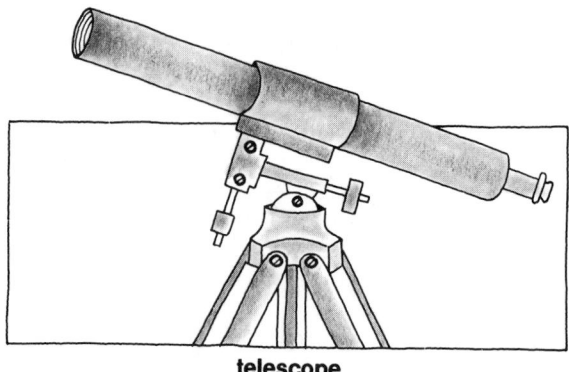

telescope

televise *verb* To broadcast by television: *All the stations televised the President's speech.*
tel·e·vise (tel′ə vīz′) ☐*verb* **televised, televising, televises**

television *noun* **1.** A system for sending and receiving pictures and sounds. **2.** A device that receives televised pictures and sounds and on which they can be seen or heard.
tel·e·vi·sion (tel′ə vizh′ən) ☐*noun, plural* **televisions**

tell *verb* **1.** To express in words; say: *Tell me what happened.* **2.** To know or recognize: *Can you tell whose voice this is?* **3.** To order or command: *He told us to be on time.*
tell (tel) ☐*verb* **told, telling, tells**

teller *noun* **1.** Someone who tells something, such as a story or tale. **2.** Someone working in a bank who receives and pays out money.
tell·er (tel′ər) ☐*noun, plural* **tellers**

temp. An abbreviation for **temperature.**

temper *noun* **1.** One's usual mood or state of mind: *She has an even temper and rarely gets angry.* **2.** The condition of being calm in the mind or emotions: *He loses his temper for no reason at all.* **3.** An angry mood: *He's in a temper.*
tem·per (tem′pər) ☐*noun, plural* **tempers**

temperate *adjective* Of or having a climate that is not too hot or too cold.
tem·per·ate (tem′pə rit) ☐*adjective*

temperature *noun* **1.** The degree of heat or cold registered on a thermometer: *The temperature tonight will drop below freezing.* **2.** A body temperature that has risen above normal because of some disease or disorder. Normal body temperature is 98.6 degrees: *She has a temperature of 102 degrees.*

tem·per·a·ture (tem′pər ə chər) □*noun,* *plural* **temperatures**

temple¹   *noun* A building used for worship.
  tem·ple (tem′pəl) □*noun, plural* **temples**

temple²   *noun* The flat part on either side of a person's head.
  tem·ple (tem′pəl) □*noun, plural* **temples**

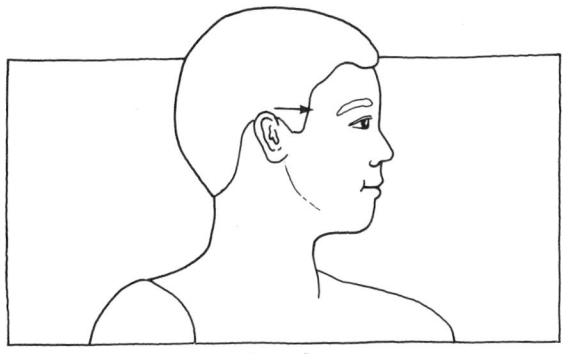

temple

temporary   *adjective* Lasting or used for a short time only: *a temporary job.*
  tem·po·rar·y (tem′pə rer′ē) □*adjective*

tempt   *verb* **1.** To persuade someone to do something foolish or wrong: *The nice weather tempted me to skip school.* **2.** To appeal strongly to; attract: *I was tempted by the fresh pie.* **3.** To take the chance of loss or injury from: *Don't tempt your luck by riding your bicycle in the dark.*
  tempt (tempt) □*verb* **tempted, tempting, tempts**

ten   *noun* A number, written 10, that is equal to the sum of 9 + 1.
  □*adjective* Being one more than nine.
  ten (ten) □*noun, plural* **tens** □*adjective*

tenant   *noun* Someone who pays rent to use land, a building, an apartment, a store, or other property owned by another person.
  ten·ant (ten′ənt) □*noun, plural* **tenants**

tend¹   *verb* **1.** To move or lead in a certain direction: *Our route tended toward the north.* **2.** To be likely: *She tends to be messy.*
  tend (tend) □*verb* **tended, tending, tends**

tend²   *verb* To take care of: *I'm tending her cat while she's away.*
  tend (tend) □*verb* **tended, tending, tends**

tendency   *noun* An inclination to think or behave in a certain way: *He has a tendency to drive too fast.*
  ten·den·cy (ten′dən sē) □*noun, plural* **tendencies**

tender   *adjective* **1.** Not hard or strong; delicate: *tender young seedlings.* **2.** Not tough; soft: *a tender steak.* **3.** Easily hurt; sensitive: *tender skin.* **4.** Painful or sore: *Her injured shoulder is very tender.* **5.** Kind and loving; gentle: *a tender hug.*
  ten·der (ten′dər) □*adjective* **tenderer, tenderest**

tendon   *noun* A strong band or cord of tissue that connects a muscle with a bone.
  ten·don (ten′dən) □*noun, plural* **tendons**

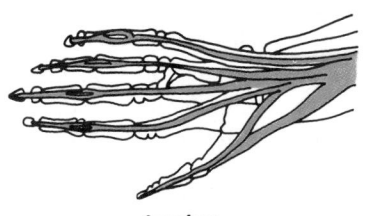

tendon

tenement   *noun* An apartment house, especially one that is badly maintained and lived in by poor people.
  ten·e·ment (ten′ə mənt) □*noun, plural* **tenements**

tennis   *noun* A game in which two or four people hit a ball back and forth over a net with a large racket. It is played on a rectangular court.
  ten·nis (ten′is) □*noun*

tennis

tenor   *noun* **1.** A man's singing voice that is higher than a baritone and lower than an alto.

a bat	ī bite	ōō tool	*th* feather
ā make	î fierce	ou out	th bath
â dare	o dot	u nut	hw wheat
ä father	ō no	û turn	zh measure
e net	ô law, for	ch church	ə about, open
ē be	oi soil	ng ring	pencil, atom
i dip	oo look	sh shade	circus

2. A singer who has such a voice.
ten·or (ten′ər) □*noun, plural* **tenors**

tense¹ *adjective* **1.** Stretched or pulled tight; strained: *tense muscles.* **2.** Causing or showing suspense, strain, or excitement: *a tense moment in the game.*
□*verb* To make or become tense.
tense (tens) □*adjective* **tenser, tensest**
□*verb* **tensed, tensing, tenses**

tense² *noun* Any of the forms of a verb that indicate the time of an action or condition.
tense (tens) □*noun, plural* **tenses**

tension *noun* The condition of being tense.
ten·sion (ten′shən) □*noun, plural* **tensions**

tent *noun* A shelter made of canvas or nylon. It is supported by poles and held to the ground by ropes and pegs.
tent (tent) □*noun, plural* **tents**

tent

tentacle *noun* One of the thin, flexible parts that extend from the body of an octopus, jellyfish, or other animal. Tentacles are used for grasping and moving.
ten·ta·cle (ten′tə kəl) □*noun, plural* **tentacles**

tentacle

tenth *noun* **1.** In a group of people or things that are in numbered order, the one that

matches the number ten. **2.** One of ten equal parts, written ¹/₁₀.
□*adjective* Coming after the ninth.
tenth (tenth) □*noun, plural* **tenths**
□*adjective*

tepee *noun* A tent in the shape of a cone that is made of animal skins or bark. Tepees were used by many tribes of Native Americans.
te·pee (tē′pē) □*noun, plural* **tepees**

tepee

term *noun* **1.** A period of time: *a school term.* **2.** A word or expression having a precise or limited meaning in a certain field: *sports terms; medical terms.* **3. terms** The conditions under which something can be done or achieved: *the terms of a peace treaty.* **4. terms** The relation between persons or groups: *She and I are not on friendly terms.*
term (tûrm) □*noun, plural* **terms**

terminal *noun* **1.** A station at the end of a transportation line. **2.** A device for communicating with a computer.
ter·mi·nal (tûr′mə nəl) □*noun, plural* **terminals**

termite *noun* An insect that looks like an ant. Termites live in large groups, feeding on and destroying wood.
ter·mite (tûr′mīt′) □*noun, plural* **termites**

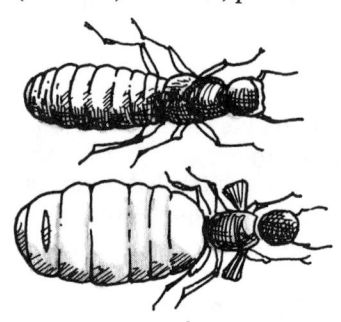

termite

terrace   *noun* **1.** A porch or balcony. **2.** An open, paved area next to a house. **3.** A raised bank of earth having straight or slanting sides and a level top.
ter·race (ter′əs) ▢*noun, plural* **terraces**

terrible   *adjective* **1.** Causing terror or extreme fear: *a terrible noise.* **2.** Very bad: *a terrible party.*
ter·ri·ble (ter′ə bəl) ▢*adjective*

terrier   *noun* Any of several dogs that are usually small and active.
ter·ri·er (ter′ē ər) ▢*noun, plural* **terriers**

> *WORD HISTORY:* **terrier**
>
> *Terrier* comes from a Latin word that means "earth." Terriers got their name because they were first used to hunt for small animals that live in burrows in the ground.

terrier

terrific   *adjective* **1.** Causing great fear or terror: *a terrific storm.* **2.** Very good: *We had a terrific time.*
ter·ri·fic (tə rif′ik) ▢*adjective*

terrify   *verb* To fill with terror; frighten greatly: *The thunder terrified the child.*
ter·ri·fy (ter′ə fī′) ▢*verb* **terrified, terrifying, terrifies**

territory   *noun* **1.** An area of land; region. **2.** The land and waters controlled by a state, nation, or government. **3.** A part of the United States not admitted as a state: *Puerto Rico is a territory.*
ter·ri·to·ry (ter′i tôr′ē) ▢*noun, plural* **territories**

terror   *noun* **1.** Great or intense fear: *The lost child was filled with terror.* **2.** A person or thing that causes such fear: *The bully was the terror of the neighborhood.*
ter·ror (ter′ər) ▢*noun, plural* **terrors**

terror

test   *noun* **1.** A way of finding out the nature or quality of something: *an allergy test.* **2.** A series of questions or tasks to determine a person's knowledge or ability: *a spelling test.*
▢*verb* To study or examine by means of a test: *The teacher tested the students in geography and history. The chemist tested the water to see if it was pure.*
test (test) ▢*noun, plural* **tests** ▢*verb* **tested, testing, tests**

Testament   *noun* Either of the two major parts of the Bible, the Old Testament and the New Testament.
Tes·ta·ment (tes′tə mənt) ▢*noun, plural* **Testaments**

testify   *verb* **1.** To state something under oath: *testify in court.* **2.** To serve as evidence or proof of: *What she did testifies to her good intentions.*
tes·ti·fy (tes′tə fī′) ▢*verb* **testified, tesifying, testifies**

testimony   *noun* **1.** A statement made under oath: *the testimony of an eyewitness.* **2.** Evidence or proof: *We gave her a gift as testimony of our appreciation.*
tes·ti·mo·ny (tes′tə mō′nē) ▢*noun, plural* **testimonies**

test tube   *noun* A long glass tube that is open at one end. Test tubes are used in laboratory experiments.

text   *noun* **1.** The actual words of a piece of writing or of a speech: *The text of the President's speech was printed in the newspaper.* **2.** The main body of writing in a book: *The text*

a	bat	ī	bite	ōō	tool	*th*	feather
ā	make	î	fierce	ou	out	th	bath
â	dare	o	dot	u	nut	hw	wheat
ä	father	ō	no	û	turn	zh	measure
e	net	ô	law, for	ch	church	ə	about, open
ē	be	oi	soil	ng	ring		pencil, atom
i	dip	oo	look	sh	shade		circus

of every chapter is followed by questions.
text (tekst) □*noun, plural* **texts**

textbook *noun* A book containing the basic information about a subject that is used in school for classroom instruction: *a geography textbook.*
text·book (**tekst′**book′) □*noun, plural* **textbooks**

textile *noun* A cloth fabric made by weaving or knitting.
tex·tile (**tek′**stəl *or* **tek′**stīl′) □*noun, plural* **textiles**

texture *noun* The look or feel of something: *a sauce with a creamy texture.*
tex·ture (**teks′**chər) □*noun, plural* **textures**

than *conjunction* Used to introduce a comparison: *Pound cake is richer than angel food cake. I would rather read than play tennis.*
than (than) □*conjunction*

thank *verb* To tell a person that one is grateful or pleased: *She thanked me for the present.*
thank (thangk) □*verb* **thanked, thanking, thanks**

thankful *adjective* Showing or feeling gratitude; grateful: *I was thankful for her help.*
thank·ful (**thangk′**fəl) □*adjective*

thanks *plural noun* An act of saying or showing that one is grateful: *I sent my thanks to her for the gift.*
□*interjection* A word used as an expression of gratitude.
thanks (thangks) □*plural noun* □*interjection*

Thanksgiving *noun* The fourth Thursday in November, observed as a legal holiday on which people give thanks for their blessings.
Thanks·giv·ing (thangks **giv′**ing) □*noun*

that *adjective* **1.** Being the person or thing at a distance: *That chair in the other office is broken again.* **2.** Indicating the person or thing already mentioned: *Give the book to that girl in the red dress.*
□*pronoun* **1.** Something already pointed out or mentioned: *The accident happened while I was away, so I couldn't tell her anything about that.* **2.** Something at a distance: *That is a bigger piece of cake than mine.* **3.** Who, whom, or which: *I got a ride from some girls that I knew. Give me a list of things that have to be done.* **4.** In, on, or for which: *She called the day that she arrived.*
□*adverb* To that extent: *Is it that difficult to do your homework?*
□*conjunction* Used to introduce another part

of a sentence: *I didn't think that you were coming.*
that (that) □*adjective, plural* **those** □*pronoun, plural* **those** □*adverb* □*conjunction*

thatch *noun* Straw, reeds, or similar material used to cover a roof.
□*verb* To cover with thatch.
thatch (thach) □*noun* □*verb* **thatched, thatching, thatches**

thatch

that's Contraction of "that is."
that's (thats)

thaw *verb* To change or cause to change from a solid to a liquid by gradual warming; melt: *The ice thawed in the sunlight.*
□*noun* Warm weather that can melt ice and snow.
thaw (thô) □*verb* **thawed, thawing, thaws** □*noun, plural* **thaws**

the¹ *definite article* **1.** Used before a noun to indicate a particular person or thing: *The man we are looking for has a scar. The pencil I need has disappeared.* **2.** Any; every: *The squirrel is a rodent.*
the (thē *or* thə) □*definite article*

the² *adverb* To that extent; by that much: *The more I see her, the more I like her.*
the (thə *or* thē) □*adverb*

theater *noun* A building or outdoor area where plays or motion pictures are presented.
the·a·ter (**thē′**ə tər) □*noun, plural* **theaters**

theft *noun* The act of stealing: *She was accused of car theft.*
theft (theft) □*noun, plural* **thefts**

their *pronoun* Belonging or relating to them: *The twins had to finish their homework.*
their (thâr) □*pronoun*

theirs *pronoun* The one or ones belonging to them: *The large package is theirs. He is no friend of theirs.*
theirs (thârz) □*pronoun*

them *pronoun* The objective case of **they:** *She asked them for directions. I gave them good advice. He gave a party for them.*
them (*th*em) □*pronoun*

theme *noun* **1.** The subject of a talk or a piece of writing: *The theme of the book was the exploration of outer space.* **2.** A melody on which a musical composition is based.
theme (thēm) □*noun, plural* **themes**

themselves *pronoun* Their own selves: *They blamed themselves for the accident. They saved all the ice cream for themselves. Her parents themselves told us the news.*
them·selves (*th*em **selvz′**) □*pronoun*

then *adverb* **1.** At that time: *Rents were lower then.* **2.** After that; next: *One more game, and then we'll go home.* **3.** In that case: *If you want to leave, then let's leave.*
□*noun* That time or moment: *From then on, I got to class on time.*
then (*th*en) □*adverb* □*noun*

theory *noun* **1.** An idea or group of ideas explaining facts or experiences: *A theory of gravity helps to explain the rise and fall of the tides.* **2.** The general rules of a science or art, especially in contrast to practice or performance: *music theory.* **3.** An idea or belief taken as the basis for an investigation.
the·o·ry (thē′ə rē) □*noun, plural* **theories**

there *adverb* **1.** At or in that place: *Put the groceries there on the table.* **2.** To or toward that place: *How long did it take to get there?*
□*pronoun* Used to introduce a sentence in which the subject follows the verb: *There is no reason to do that.*
□*noun* That place: *Her house is a long way from there.*
there (*th*âr) □*adverb* □*pronoun* □*noun*

thereabouts *adverb* **1.** Near place or time. **2.** Near that number or degree.
there·a·bouts (*th*âr′ə **bouts′**) □*adverb*

therefore *adverb* For that reason: *It snowed heavily and therefore school was canceled.*
there·fore (*th*âr′ fôr′) □*adverb*

there's Contraction of "there is" and "there has."
there's (*th*ârz)

thermometer *noun* An instrument for measuring temperature. A thermometer is usually made of a long, sealed glass tube containing liquid. The tube is marked with a scale to show degrees of temperature.
ther·mom·e·ter (*th*ər **mom′**i tər) □*noun, plural* **thermometers**

thermos *noun* A container that consists of one bottle enclosed in another bottle with a vacuum between them. A thermos keeps liquids either hot or cold.
ther·mos (thûr′məs) □*noun, plural* **thermoses**

thermostat *noun* A device that automatically controls the temperature of such things as furnaces and refrigerators.
ther·mo·stat (thûr′mə stat′) □*noun, plural* **thermostats**

these *adjective* The plural of **this:** *These shoes are too tight. Are these the right keys?*
these (thēz) □*adjective*

they *pronoun* **1.** The persons, animals, or things referred to or mentioned earlier: *I bought several books yesterday, but they have not been delivered yet.* **2.** People in general: *She's as tough as they come.*
they (*th*ā) □*pronoun*

they'd Contraction of "they had" and "they would."
they'd (*th*ād)

they'll Contraction of "they will."
they'll (*th*āl)

they're Contraction of "they are."
they're (*th*âr)

they've Contraction of "they have."
they've (*th*āv)

thick *adjective* **1.** Having much space between opposite sides or surfaces; not thin: *a thick book.* **2.** Measured in distance between opposite sides: *The shelves are one inch thick.* **3.** Not flowing easily: *thick maple syrup.* **4.** Very dense or heavy: *thick fog; thick hair.*
□*noun* The center of action or activity: *in the thick of the battle.*

a bat	ī bite	oo tool	th feather
ā make	i fierce	ou out	th bath
â dare	o dot	u nut	hw wheat
ä father	ō no	û turn	zh measure
e net	ô law, for	ch church	ə about, open
ē be	oi soil	ng ring	pencil, atom
i dip	oo look	sh shade	circus

thick (thik) □*adjective* **thicker, thickest**
□*noun*

thicken *verb* To make or become thick or thicker: *thicken gravy.*
thick·en (thik′ ən) □*verb* **thickened, thickening, thickens**

thicket *noun* A dense growth of shrubs or small trees.
thick·et (thik′ it) □*noun, plural* **thickets**

thickness *noun* **1.** The condition of being thick: *The thickness of the smoke hindered the firefighters.* **2.** The distance between opposite surfaces: *The thickness of the board is two inches.*
thick·ness (thik′ nis) □*noun, plural* **thicknesses**

thief *noun* Someone who steals.
thief (thēf) □*noun, plural* **thieves**

thieves *noun* The plural of **thief.**
thieves (thēvz) □*noun*

thigh *noun* The part of the leg between the knee and the hip.
thigh (thī) □*noun, plural* **thighs**

thimble *noun* A small metal or plastic cap worn to protect the finger that pushes the needle in sewing.
thim·ble (thim′ bəl) □*noun, plural* **thimbles**

thimble

thin *adjective* **1.** Having little space between opposite sides or surfaces; not thick: *a thin slice of bread.* **2.** Of small diameter; fine: *thin wire.* **3.** Having a lean or slender figure: *a thin girl.* **4.** Flowing easily: *thin ketchup.* **5.** Not dense or heavy: *thin hair; a thin mist.* **6.** Easy to see through; poor: *a thin excuse.*
□*verb* To make or become thin or thinner: *I thinned the stew with water.*
thin (thin) □*adjective* **thinner, thinnest**
□*verb* **thinned, thinning, thins**

> *SYNONYMS:* **thin, skinny, slender**
> These adjectives mean having little flesh or fat: *I'm thinner than both of my brothers. The witch had long, skinny fingers that looked like claws. Dancers exercise to keep slender.*

thing *noun* **1.** An object or being that is not precisely named: *Hand me that thing for removing staples.* **2.** An object that exists but is not alive: *That trunk is a heavy thing.* **3.** An animal or person: *He was a cute little thing.* **4.** An act or deed: *He did a terrible thing.* **5. things** One's personal possessions: *Pick up your things.* **6. things** Conditions in general: *Things went from bad to worse.*
thing (thing) □*noun, plural* **things**

think *verb* **1.** To have in one's mind: *Think about which movie you want to see. I keep thinking about what happened.* **2.** To have as a thought; imagine: *She thought she would like to be a nurse.* **3.** To believe or suppose: *I think he'll be late.* **4.** To invent: *thinking up ways to get rich.* **5.** To have a care for; consider: *He always thought of others' feelings.* —See Synonyms at **believe.**
think (thingk) □*verb* **thought, thinking, thinks**

third *noun* **1.** In a group of people or things that are in numbered order, the one that matches the number three. **2.** One of three equal parts, written ⅓.
□*adjective* Coming after the second.
third (thûrd) □*noun, plural* **thirds**
□*adjective*

thirst *noun* **1.** A feeling that one's mouth is very dry, caused by a desire to drink. **2.** A desire or yearning: *a thirst for adventure.*
thirst (thûrst) □*noun, plural* **thirsts**

thirsty *adjective* **1.** Feeling thirst: *I was thirsty after working in the yard.* **2.** Needing moisture: *plants thirsty for water.*
thirst·y (thûr′ stē) □*adjective* **thirstier, thirstiest**

thirteen *noun* A number, written 13, that is equal to the sum of 10 + 3.
□*adjective* Being one more than twelve.
thir·teen (thûr′ tēn′) □*noun, plural* **thirteens**
□*adjective*

thirteenth *noun* **1.** In a group of people or things that are in numbered order, the one that matches the number thirteen. **2.** One of thirteen equal parts, written 1/13.
□*adjective* Coming after the twelfth.
thir·teenth (thûr′ tēnth′) □*noun, plural* **thirteenths** □*adjective*

thirtieth *noun* **1.** In a group of people or things that are in numbered order, the one that matches the number thirty. **2.** One of thirty equal parts, written 1/30.
□*adjective* Coming after the twenty-ninth.

thir·ti·eth (thûr′tē ith) ▢*noun, plural*
thirtieths ▢*adjective*

thirty *noun* A number, written 30, that is
equal to the product of 10 × 3.
▢*adjective* Being ten more than twenty.
thir·ty (thûr′tē) ▢*noun, plural* **thirties**
▢*adjective*

this *adjective* Being the person or thing present, nearby, or just mentioned: *This book is
the one I want to buy.*
▢*pronoun* **1.** The person or thing present,
near, or just mentioned: *This is my sister. This
is my desk.* **2.** A person or thing that is nearer
than another: *Everybody agrees that this is a
better painting than that.* **4.** The present time:
Jim's been out later than this.
▢*adverb* To this extent; so: *stay out this late.*
this (*th*is) ▢*adjective, plural* **these**
▢*pronoun, plural* **these** ▢*adverb*

thistle *noun* A prickly plant with purple
flowers.
this·tle (this′əl) ▢*noun, plural* **thistles**

thistle

thong *noun* A thin strip of leather used to fasten something, such as a sandal.
thong (thông) ▢*noun, plural* **thongs**

thorax *noun* **1.** The part of the human body
between the neck and the abdomen. It is
partly surrounded by the ribs. **2.** The middle
part of the body of an insect, which is divided
into three parts.
tho·rax (thôr′aks′) ▢*noun, plural* **thoraxes**

thorn *noun* **1.** A sharp point that grows from
the stem of a plant. **2.** A shrub or tree that has
thorns.
thorn (thôrn) ▢*noun, plural* **thorns**

thorny *adjective* **1.** Full of or covered with
thorns. **2.** Causing trouble; difficult: *a thorny
problem.*

thorn·y (thôr′nē) ▢*adjective* **thornier,
thorniest**

thorough *adjective* Complete in all respects:
a thorough search.
thor·ough (thûr′ō) ▢*adjective*

those *adjective* The plural of **that:** *Those are
the girls I was telling you about.*
those (thōz) ▢*adjective*

though *adverb* However; nevertheless: *I have
a lot of work to do, but I'm tired, though, so I'm
going to take a nap.*
▢*conjunction* Even if; although: *I did poorly
on the test, though I studied very hard.*
though (thō) ▢*adverb* ▢*conjunction*

thought *verb* The past tense and past participle of **think:** *We thought about writing to her.*
▢*noun* **1.** The act of thinking: *I put a lot of
thought into my essay.* **2.** An idea: *Do you have
any thoughts about what movie to see?* **3.** Consideration or attention; concern: *They live for
the moment and have no thought for the future.*
thought (thôt) ▢*verb* ▢*noun, plural*
thoughts

thoughtful *adjective* **1.** Occupied with
thought: *He was in a thoughtful mood.*
2. Showing concern for others; considerate: *a
thoughtful thing to do.*
thought·ful (thôt′fəl) ▢*adjective*

thoughtless *adjective* Not showing concern
for others: *thoughtless behavior.*
thought·less (thôt′lis) ▢*adjective*

thousand *noun* A number, written 1,000, that
is equal to the product of 10 × 100.
▢*adjective* Being ten times more than one
hundred.
thou·sand (thou′zənd) ▢*noun, plural*
thousands ▢*adjective*

thousandth *noun* **1.** In a group of people or
things that are in numbered order, the one
that matches the number 1,000. **2.** One of a
thousand equal parts, written 1/1000.
▢*adjective* Coming after the 999th.
thou·sandth (thou′zəndth) ▢*noun, plural*
thousandths ▢*adjective*

a bat	ī bite	ōō tool	*th* feather
ā make	î fierce	ou out	th bath
â dare	o dot	u nut	hw wheat
ä father	ō no	û turn	zh measure
e net	ô law, for	ch church	ə about, open
ē be	oi soil	ng ring	pencil, atom
i dip	oo look	sh shade	circus

thrash *verb* **1.** To beat or whip: *She would never thrash her children.* **2.** To move wildly or violently: *He thrashes about when he sleeps.*
thrash (thrash) □*verb* **thrashed, thrashing, thrashes**

thread *noun* **1.** A very thin cord made of two or more strands of fiber twisted together. Thread can be woven into cloth or used to sew things together. **2.** Something that resembles a thread: *a thread of smoke.* **3.** An idea or theme that joins together: *It was difficult to follow the thread of his argument.* **4.** The winding ridge on a screw, nut, or bolt.
□*verb* **1.** To pass a thread through the eye of a needle or through the hooks and holes on a sewing machine. **2.** To make one's way through cautiously: *We threaded our way through the crowded store.*
thread (thred) □*noun, plural* **threads** □*verb* **threaded, threading, threads**

threat *noun* **1.** The saying of something that will be done to punish or hurt: *Everyone behaved because of the teacher's threat to keep troublemakers after school.* **2.** A sign of coming danger: *Dark clouds are a threat of rain.* **3.** Someone or something regarded as dangerous: *Wolves are a threat to farm animals.*
threat (thret) □*noun, plural* **threats**

threaten *verb* **1.** To say a threat against: *The old man threatened to call the police if we kept playing in his yard.* **2.** To be a threat to; endanger: *Freezing temperatures threatened the orange crop.* **3.** To give signs or warning of: *Dark skies threatened rain.*
threat·en (thret' ən) □*verb* **threatened, threatening, threatens**

three *noun* A number, written 3, that is equal to the sum of 2 + 1.
□*adjective* Being one more than two.
three (thrē) □*noun, plural* **threes** □*adjective*

thresh *verb* To separate the seeds or grain from a plant by striking or beating.
thresh (thresh) □*verb* **threshed, threshing, threshes**

threshold *noun* **1.** A piece of wood, metal, or stone placed beneath a door. **2.** The place or point of beginning: *the threshold of a new discovery.*
thresh·old (thresh' ōld) □*noun, plural* **thresholds**

threw *verb* The past tense of **throw**: *I threw the ball to her.*
threw (thrōō) □*verb*

thrift *noun* The careful management of one's money or other resources.
thrift (thrift) □*noun*

thrifty *adjective* Careful in the use of money: *a thrifty shopper who looks for bargains.* —See Synonyms at **economical**.
thrift·y (thrif' tē) □*adjective* **thriftier, thriftiest**

thrill *verb* To feel or cause to feel joy or excitement: *The sight of the circus parade thrilled the children.*
□*noun* A sudden feeling of joy or excitement: *He felt a thrill of fear at every strange noise.*
thrill (thril) □*verb* **thrilled, thrilling, thrills** □*noun, plural* **thrills**

thrive *verb* **1.** To be or stay in a healthy condition: *Many animals don't thrive in a zoo.* **2.** To be successful: *I hope his new business thrives.*
thrive (thrīv) □*verb* **throve** or **thrived, thrived** or **thriven, thriving, thrives**

throat *noun* **1.** The passage between the mouth and the esophagus and lungs. **2.** A narrow part resembling a throat: *the throat of a bottle.*
throat (thrōt) □*noun, plural* **throats**

throb *verb* To beat rapidly or heavily; pound: *I was so scared my heart throbbed.*
□*noun* A rapid or heavy beating or pounding: *a throb of pain.*
throb (throb) □*verb* **throbbed, throbbing, throbs** □*noun, plural* **throbs**

throne *noun* **1.** The chair occupied by a king, queen, or other ruler. **2.** The rank or power of a monarch: *The princess succeeded to the throne after the queen died.*
throne (thrōn) □*noun, plural* **thrones**

throng *noun* A large group of people or things: *a throng of children around the swimming pool.*
□*verb* To crowd into; fill: *People thronged the beach.*
throng (thrông) □*noun, plural* **throngs** □*verb* **thronged, thronging, throngs**

throttle *noun* A valve in an engine that controls the flow of fuel.
throt·tle (throt' əl) □*noun, plural* **throttles**

through *preposition* **1.** In one side and out the other: *We walked through the parking lot.* **2.** Among or between: *She walked through the flowers.* **3.** By means of: *We bought our house through an agent.* **4.** At or to the end of: *The baby slept through the night.* **5.** Over all of: *We*

traveled through France.
□*adverb* **1.** From one side of to the other: *The door opened and we went through.* **2.** Completely; thoroughly: *We were soaked through.* **3.** From beginning to end: *This is important, so hear me through.* **4.** At or to the conclusion: *Let's see this thing through.* **5.** All the way: *Does the bus go through to Boston?*
□*adjective* **1.** Allowing passage without stopping: *a through street.* **2.** Going all the way without stopping: *a through flight to Washington.* **3.** Finished with a task or action; done: *When you're through, I'd like a word with you.*
through (thrōō) □*preposition* □*adverb* □*adjective*

throughout *preposition* In, through, or during every part of: *We traveled throughout the country. There was smoke throughout the house.*
□*adverb* In, during, or through every part: *The book was marked throughout with ink stains.*
through·out (thrōō out′) □*preposition* □*adverb*

throve *verb* A past tense of **thrive.**
throve (thrōv) □*verb*

throw *verb* **1.** To send through the air: *Throw the ball to me.* **2.** To cause to fall: *The horse stopped suddenly and threw its rider.* **3.** To put on or take off hurriedly: *I threw on a coat and ran to the store.* **4.** To put in a particular condition or position: *The explosion threw everyone into confusion.*
□*noun* The act of throwing; toss.
  throw away To discard as useless: *She threw away the broken radio.*
throw (thrō) □*verb* **threw, thrown, throwing, throws** □*noun, plural* **throws**

SYNONYMS: **throw, toss, hurl**

These verbs mean to send through the air: *Throw the ball to me. She tossed a pillow at her brother. I hurled the rock as far as I could.*

---

thrown *verb* The past participle of **throw.**
thrown (thrōn) □*verb*

thrush *noun* Any of several birds, as a robin, known for their song.
thrush (thrush) □*noun, plural* **thrushes**

thrust *verb* **1.** To push with force; shove: *He thrust me into the snow bank.* **2.** To stab or pierce.
□*noun* A forceful push or shove.

thrust (thrust) □*verb* **thrust, thrusting, thrusts** □*noun, plural* **thrusts**

thumb *noun* **1.** The short, thick first finger of the human hand. **2.** The part of a glove or mitten that fits over the thumb.
□*verb* To turn rapidly and look at the pages of: *thumb through a book.*
thumb (thum) □*noun, plural* **thumbs** □*verb* **thumbed, thumbing, thumbs**

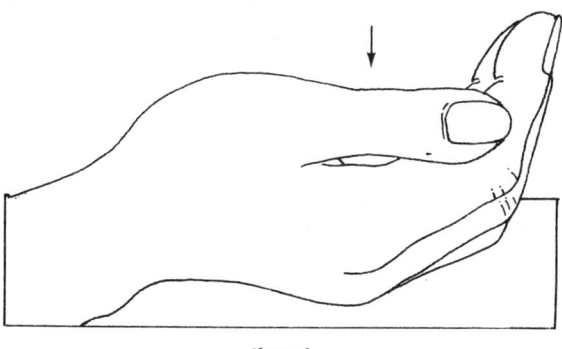

thumb

thumbtack *noun* A tack with a large, flat head that can be pressed into place with the thumb.
thumb·tack (thum′tak′) □*noun, plural* **thumbtacks**

thump *noun* **1.** A blow with a blunt object: *She gave me a thump on the shoulder.* **2.** The dull sound produced by such a blow: *The book fell with a thump.*
□*verb* **1.** To strike with a blunt object so as to produce a dull sound: *thumped the table with her fist.* **2.** To beat rapidly: *My heart thumped with excitement.*
thump (thump) □*noun, plural* **thumps** □*verb* **thumped, thumping, thumps**

thunder *noun* **1.** The rumbling or crashing noise that comes with lightning. **2.** A similar noise: *the thunder of guns.*
□*verb* **1.** To produce thunder. **2.** To produce sounds like thunder: *Trucks thundered down the highway.*
thun·der (thun′dər) □*noun* □*verb* **thundered, thundering, thunders**

a	bat	ī	bite	ōō	tool	*th*	feather
ā	make	î	fierce	ou	out	th	bath
â	dare	o	dot	u	nut	hw	wheat
ä	father	ō	no	û	turn	zh	measure
e	net	ô	law, for	ch	church	ə	about, open
ē	be	oi	soil	ng	ring		pencil, atom
i	dip	oo	look	sh	shade		circus

thunderstorm *noun* A storm accompanied by lightning and thunder.
thun·der·storm (thun′dər stôrm′) □*noun, plural* **thunderstorms**

Thursday *noun* The fifth day of the week, after Wednesday and before Friday.
Thurs·day (thûrz′dē *or* thûrz′dā′) □*noun, plural* **Thursdays**

WORD HISTORY: **Thursday**

Thursday is named after Thunor, an Old English god of thunder.

---

thus *adverb* **1.** In this way. **2.** To this degree or extent: *I haven't heard from her thus far.* **3.** As a result.
thus (thus) □*adverb*

thyme *noun* A plant that grows near the ground and has leaves used to flavor food.
thyme (tīm) □*noun*

thyroid gland *noun* A gland in the neck of human beings that regulates body growth.
thy·roid gland (thī′roid′) □*noun*

tick¹ *noun* One of a series of soft, clicking sounds, as in a clock or watch.
□*verb* To produce a series of ticks, as a clock does.
tick (tik) □*noun, plural* **ticks** □*verb* **ticked, ticking, ticks**

tick² *noun* A small animal related to spiders. Ticks attach themselves to the skin of human beings and other animals and suck their blood. Ticks often carry diseases.
tick (tik) □*noun, plural* **ticks**

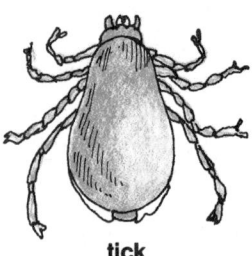

tick

ticket *noun* **1.** A paper slip or card that gives a person certain rights or services: *We have tickets to the football game.* **2.** A legal summons given to a person accused of breaking a traffic law.
□*verb* **1.** To attach a label or tag to: *The clerk ticketed the dresses with price tags.* **2.** To give a legal summons to: *Policemen were ticketing people who were speeding.*

tick·et (tik′it) □*noun, plural* **tickets** □*verb* **ticketed, ticketing, tickets**

tickle *verb* **1.** To touch the body and cause a tingling sensation or feeling. **2.** To delight or please.
tick·le (tik′əl) □*verb* **tickled, tickling, tickles**

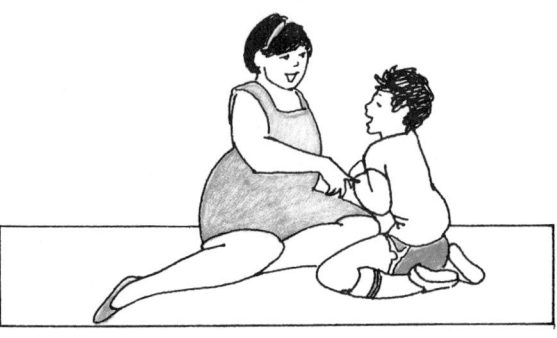

tickle

tidal wave *noun* A large, powerful ocean wave caused by hurricanes or earthquakes. A tidal wave can be very destructive.
tid·al wave (tīd′əl) □*noun*

tide *noun* The regular change in the level of the oceans, seas, and other large bodies of water of the earth. Tides usually occur twice a day and are caused by the pull of the moon and sun on the earth.
tide (tīd) □*noun, plural* **tides**

WORD HISTORY: **tide**

Tide originally meant "time." The modern sense of the word *tide* developed because the tide rises and falls at regular times of the day.

---

tidings *plural noun* News: *The messenger brought good tidings.*
tid·ings (tī′dingz) □*plural noun*

tidy *adjective* **1.** Neat and orderly: *a tidy room.* **2.** Large or fairly large; considerable: *a tidy sum of money.* —See Synonyms at **neat.**
□*verb* To put in order; make neat: *He told me to tidy my room.*
ti·dy (tī′dē) □*adjective* **tidier, tidiest** □*verb* **tidied, tidying, tidies**

tie *verb* **1.** To fasten or bind with a cord or rope: *The cowboy tied the horse to the post.* **2.** To fasten with a knot or bow: *How do you tie a necktie?* **3.** To equal the score of: *I scored a point to tie the game.*
□*noun* **1.** A cord, string, or rope with which something is tied: *The apron has a tie in back.*

2. Something that joins or holds people together: *family ties.* **3.** A necktie. **4.** An equal score or vote: *The game ended in a tie.* **5.** A heavy beam laid across a railroad bed to support the rails.

   tie up To be busy or in use: *I tried to phone, but the line was tied up.*

   tie (tī) ☐*verb* **tied, tying, ties** ☐*noun, plural* **ties**

tier *noun* One of a series of rows or layers that are placed one above another: *The stadium has ten tiers of seats.*

   tier (tîr) ☐*noun, plural* **tiers**

tiger *noun* A very large Asian wild cat that has light brown fur with black stripes.

   ti·ger (tī′gər) ☐*noun, plural* **tigers**

tiger

tight *adjective* **1.** Held or fastened firmly; secure: *a tight knot.* **2.** Made or built so that nothing can pass through: *a tight seal.* **3.** Fitting close to the body: *tight pants.* **4.** Pulled or stretched out to the fullest extent: *The ropes holding the tent were tight.* **5.** Having no room or time to spare: *a tight schedule.* **6.** Not generous or liberal; stingy: *They are very tight with their money.* **7.** Hard to deal with or get out of: *She lost the school book and is now in a tight spot.* **8.** Almost even; close: *a tight race all the way to the end.*

   ☐*adverb* **1.** Firmly; securely: *Close the door tight.* **2.** Soundly: *Sleep tight.*

   tight (tīt) ☐*adjective* **tighter, tightest** ☐*adverb*

tighten *verb* To make or become tight: *The carpenter tightened the screws.*

   tight·en (tīt′ən) ☐*verb* **tightened, tightening, tightens**

tightrope *noun* A rope or wire stretched tight high above the ground. Acrobats perform on a tightrope.

   tight·rope (tīt′rōp′) ☐*noun, plural* **tightropes**

tile *noun* A thin piece of baked clay, porcelain, or other material, used to cover floors, walls, or roofs.

   ☐*verb* To cover with tiles.

   tile (tīl) ☐*noun, plural* **tiles** ☐*verb* **tiled, tiling, tiles**

till¹ *verb* To prepare land for growing crops by plowing and fertilizing.

   till (til) ☐*verb* **tilled, tilling, tills**

till² *preposition* Until: *I won't see you till tomorrow.*

   ☐*conjunction* **1.** Before or unless: *I can't help you till you tell me what is wrong.* **2.** Until: *Wait till I call you.*

   till (til) ☐*preposition* ☐*conjunction*

till³ *noun* A drawer for keeping money.

   till (til) ☐*noun, plural* **tills**

tiller *noun* A lever or handle used to turn a rudder and steer a boat.

   til·ler (til′ər) ☐*noun, plural* **tillers**

tilt *verb* To slope or cause to slope by having one end or side raised up; tip: *tilted the table and the lamp slid off.*

   ☐*noun* A slanting position; slope: *The floor has a tilt to it.*

   tilt (tilt) ☐*verb* **tilted, tilting, tilts** ☐*noun, plural* **tilts**

timber *noun* **1.** Trees or a piece of land covered with trees; forest. **2.** Wood used for building; lumber. **3.** A long, large, heavy piece of wood shaped like a beam: *The frame of the house is built with timbers.*

   tim·ber (tim′bər) ☐*noun, plural* **timbers**

time *noun* **1.** A stretch of continued existence. **2.** A period during which an event or condition takes place or continues: *How much time did it take to drive from Texas to California?* **3.** A period in history: *the time of the Civil War.* **4.** A specific moment: *dinner time.* **5.** An instance or occasion: *I tried to call her five times.* **6.** An experience or feeling during an event: *I had a good time at the dance.*

   ☐*verb* **1.** To set the time at which something

a	bat	ī	bite	o͞o	tool	th	feather
ā	make	ĭ	fierce	ou	out	th	bath
â	dare	o	dot	u	nut	hw	wheat
ä	father	ō	no	û	turn	zh	measure
e	net	ô	law, for	ch	church	ə	about, open
ē	be	oi	soil	ng	ring		pencil, atom
i	dip	oo	look	sh	shade		circus

happens or will happen: *The alarm clock is timed to go off at eight o'clock.* **2.** To measure the speed of: *The coach timed each runner.*
time (tīm) □*noun, plural* **times** □*verb* **timed, timing, times**

times *preposition* Multiplied by: *Two times four equals eight.*
times (tīmz) □*preposition*

timid *adjective* Lacking in courage; shy: *The timid girl didn't want to meet the new children in the neighborhood.*
tim·id (tim′id) □*adjective*

tin *noun* **1.** A soft silvery metal that is one of the chemical elements. **2.** A container made of tin: *a tin of sardines.*
tin (tin) □*noun, plural* **tins**

tingle *verb* To have a prickly, stinging feeling: *Her fingers tingled from the cold.*
□*noun* A prickly or stinging feeling: *felt a tingle of excitement.*
tin·gle (ting′gəl) □*verb* **tingled, tingling, tingles** □*noun, plural* **tingles**

tinkle *verb* To make light, ringing sounds, like the sound of small bells.
□*noun* A light, ringing sound.
tin·kle (ting′kəl) □*verb* **tinkled, tinkling, tinkles** □*noun, plural* **tinkles**

tint *noun* A delicate or pale shade of color.
□*verb* To give color to: *She tinted each flower in her painting a different color.*
tint (tint) □*noun, plural* **tints** □*verb* **tinted, tinting, tints**

tiny *adjective* Very, very small.
ti·ny (tī′nē) □*adjective* **tinier, tiniest**

tip¹ *noun* **1.** The end point of something: *The tip of his nose was red.* **2.** A piece that can be fitted on the end of something: *a pen with a plastic tip.*
tip (tip) □*noun, plural* **tips**

tip² *verb* **1.** To knock over: *I tipped over a glass of milk.* **2.** To slant; tilt: *The sailboat tipped in the wind.* **3.** To touch or raise one's hat in greeting.
tip (tip) □*verb* **tipped, tipping, tips**

tip³ *noun* **1.** A sum of money given in return for service: *We left a tip for the waiter.* **2.** Useful information: *She gave me some tips to improve my tennis game.*
□*verb* To give a tip: *How much should I tip the taxi driver?*
tip (tip) □*noun, plural* **tips** □*verb* **tipped, tipping, tips**

tiptoe *verb* To walk on the tips of the toes.
tip·toe (tip′tō′) □*verb* **tiptoed, tiptoeing, tiptoes**

tire¹ *verb* To make or become weary: *The long trip tired everyone. A small child tires easily.*
tire (tīr) □*verb* **tired, tiring, tires**

tire² *noun* A covering for a wheel, usually made of rubber and filled with air.
tire (tīr) □*noun, plural* **tires**

WORD HISTORY: tire²

It is likely that *tire²* comes from the word *attire,* which means "clothing." A tire was thought of as the "attire" of a wheel.

---

tired *adjective* Weary: *I was tired after shoveling snow all day.*
tired (tīrd) □*adjective*

tissue *noun* **1.** A group of animal or plant cells that are alike in form and in what they do. Often they make up an organ or certain part of the body or plant: *muscle tissue; leaf tissue.* **2.** A light, thin paper used for wrapping or packing. **3.** A piece of soft, thin paper used as a handkerchief.
tis·sue (tish′ōō) □*noun, plural* **tissues**

title *noun* **1.** A name given to a book, painting, song, or poem. **2.** A word or name given to a person to show rank, office, or job. *Sir* and *His Majesty* are titles. **3.** The legal right to ownership or possession: *She has title to the car.* **4.** A championship.
□*verb* To give a title to. —See Synonyms at **name.**
ti·tle (tīt′əl) □*noun, plural* **titles** □*verb* **titled, titling, titles**

to *preposition* **1.** In a direction toward: *went to town; a turn to the right.* **2.** As far as the point of condition of: *starve to death.* **3.** In contact with: *back to back.* **4.** In front of: *face to face.* **5.** Until: *That shop is open from nine to six.* **6.** Into: *torn to shreds.* **7.** As compared with: *a score of four to three.* **8.** Before: *The time is ten to five.* **9.** Used for the one or ones toward whom an action is directed: *I gave the money to my sister.* **10.** Used as the mark of an infinitive: *I'd like to go.*
□*adverb* **1.** In the direction of: *walked to and fro.* **2.** Into awareness: *It was a few minutes before I came to.*
to (tōō *or* tə) □*preposition* □*adverb*

toad *noun* An animal that is very much like a frog. Toads have rougher, drier skin and live mostly on land when fully grown.
toad (tōd) □*noun, plural* **toads**

toadstool *noun* A kind of mushroom that is poisonous or not edible.
toad·stool (tōd′stool′) □*noun, plural* **toadstools**

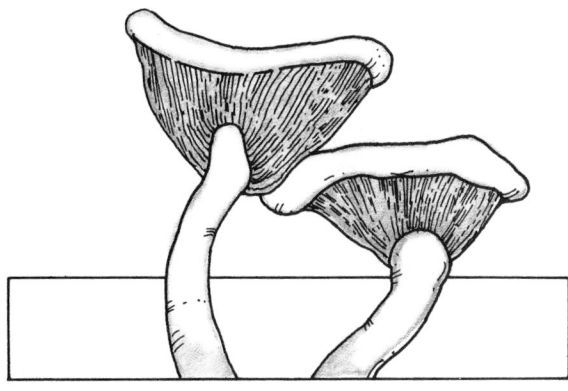

toadstool

toast¹ *verb* **1.** To heat and brown: *toast bread; toast marshmallows.* **2.** To warm all the way through: *toasted our feet by the fire.*
□*noun* Sliced bread heated and browned.
toast (tōst) □*verb* **toasted, toasting, toasts** □*noun*

toast² *noun* The act of drinking in honor of or to the health of someone or something.
□*verb* To drink in honor of or to the health of: *We toasted the bride and groom.*
toast (tōst) □*noun, plural* **toasts** □*verb* **toasted, toasting, toasts**

WORD HISTORY: toast²

It seems that *toast²* comes from *toast¹*. In the past small pieces of spiced toast were put into drinks to flavor them. It became the custom for men drinking in groups to name a woman in whose honor they would all drink. The woman's name was thought to add "flavor" to the drink as a piece of spiced toast would.

---

toaster *noun* A device used to toast bread.
toast·er (tō′stər) □*noun, plural* **toasters**

tobacco *noun* A plant whose large leaves are used for smoking and chewing. Cigarettes and cigars are made from tobacco.
to·bac·co (tə bak′ō) □*noun, plural* **tobaccos** or **tobaccoes**

toboggan *noun* A long, narrow sled without runners. It is made of thin boards curved up at the front.
□*verb* To ride on a toboggan.
to·bog·gan (tə bog′ən) □*noun, plural* **toboggans** □*verb* **tobogganed, tobogganing, toboggans**

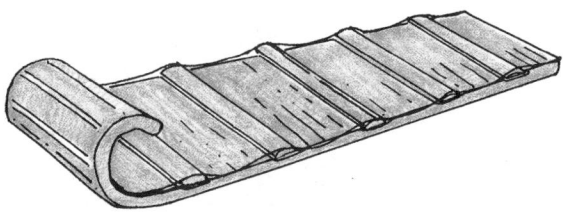

toboggan

today *noun* The present day or time: *Today is the last day of school.*
□*adverb* **1.** During or on the present day: *What are you doing today?* **2.** During or at the present time: *Today many people are interested in health and nutrition.*
to·day (tə dā′) □*noun* □*adverb*

toe *noun* **1.** One of the end parts of the foot. **2.** The part of a sock, stocking, or shoe that fits over the toes.
toe (tō) □*noun, plural* **toes**

together *adverb* **1.** In one mess, group, or place: *We all sat together at the movie.* **2.** With some other person or thing: *We cleaned the kitchen together.* **3.** Considered as a whole: *She has read more books than all of us together.* **4.** At the same time: *The clocks all sounded the hour together.*
to·geth·er (tə geth′ər *or* too geth′ər) □*adverb*

toilet *noun* A bowl with a seat and a water tank for flushing the bowl clean. A toilet is used to get rid of waste matter from the body.
toi·let (toi′lət) □*noun, plural* **toilets**

token *noun* **1.** A sign or symbol of something else: *The gift was a token of our gratitude.* **2.** A piece of metal used as a substitute for money.
to·ken (tō′kən) □*noun, plural* **tokens**

told *verb* The past tense and past participle of **tell:** *He told me the time. I have told him that*

a bat	ī bite	o͞o tool	*th* feather
ā make	î fierce	ou out	th bath
â dare	o dot	u nut	hw wheat
ä father	ō no	û turn	zh measure
e net	ô law, for	ch church	ə about, open
ē be	oi soil	ng ring	pencil, atom
i dip	oo look	sh shade	circus

he must leave.

told (tōld) □*verb*

tolerance *noun* The ability to allow other people to hold opinions that differ from one's own.

tol·er·ance (tol′ər əns) □*noun*

tolerant *adjective* Showing or having tolerance.

tol·er·ant (tol′ər ənt) □*adjective*

tolerate *verb* To put up with; endure: *Our teacher won't tolerate bad behavior.*

tol·er·ate (tol′ə rāt′) □*verb* **tolerated, tolerating, tolerates**

toll¹ *noun* A tax or fee paid for a privilege: *There is a toll for using the tunnel.*

toll (tōl) □*noun, plural* **tolls**

toll² *verb* To sound slowly and regularly: *The church bells toll every half hour.*
□*noun* The sound of a tolling bell.

toll (tōl) □*verb* **tolled, tolling, tolls** □*noun, plural* **tolls**

tomahawk *noun* A light ax used by Native Americans.

tom·a·hawk (tom′ə hôk′) □*noun, plural* **tomahawks**

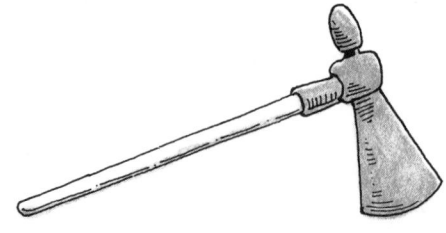

tomahawk

tomato *noun* A round, red, juicy fruit that grows on vines and is eaten as a vegetable.

to·ma·to (tə mā′tō *or* tə mä′tō) □*noun, plural* **tomatoes**

tomb *noun* A grave or building for a dead body.

tomb (to̅o̅m) □*noun, plural* **tombs**

tomboy *noun* A lively, athletic girl.

tom·boy (tom′boi) □*noun, plural* **tomboys**

tomcat *noun* A male cat.

tom·cat (tom′kat′) □*noun, plural* **tomcats**

tomorrow *noun* **1.** The day after today. **2.** The future: *I hope that the world of tomorrow will be free of hunger and poverty.*
□*adverb* On or for the day after today: *I will call you tomorrow.*

to·mor·row (tə môr′ō) □*noun, plural* **tomorrows** □*adverb*

tom-tom *noun* A small drum that is beaten with the hands.

tom-tom (tom′tom′) □*noun, plural* **tom-toms**

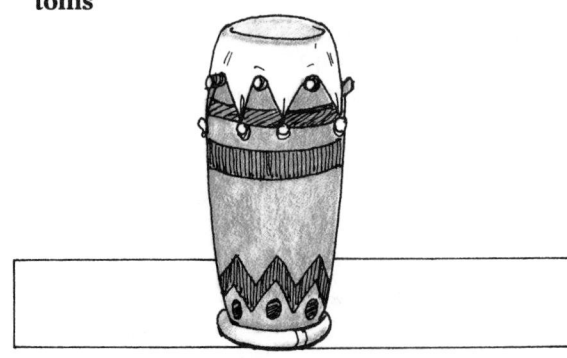

tom-tom

ton *noun* A unit of weight. A ton can be 2,000 pounds or 2,240 pounds.

ton (tun) □*noun, plural* **tons**

tone *noun* **1.** A sound with a certain pitch, length, volume, and quality: *I love the beautiful tone of a clarinet. She spoke to me in a low tone.* **2.** The difference in pitch between two musical notes. **3.** A shade of a color: *a painting in tones of pink and gray.* **4.** The general quality or mood: *There was an angry tone to our discussion.*

tone (tōn) □*noun, plural* **tones**

tongs *plural noun* A tool for lifting something, usually with two arms joined at one end.

tongs (tôngz) □*plural noun*

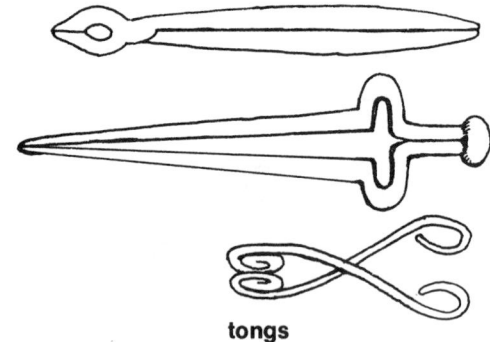

tongs
Three kinds of tongs

tongue *noun* **1.** A muscular piece of flesh in the mouth that is used in tasting and swallowing food and for speaking. **2.** An animal's tongue used for food. **3.** A flap of material under the laces or buckles of a shoe. **4.** The power to speak: *Embarrassment caused him to lose his tongue.* **5.** Language: *What is your na-*

tive tongue?
tongue (tung) ▢*noun, plural* **tongues**

tonight *adverb* On or during the night following this day: *I'll be arriving late tonight.*
▢*noun* The night of this day.
to·night (tə nīt′) ▢*adverb* ▢*noun, plural* **tonights**

tonsil *noun* Either of two small masses of tissue on the sides of the throat in the back of the mouth.
ton·sil (ton′səl) ▢*noun, plural* **tonsils**

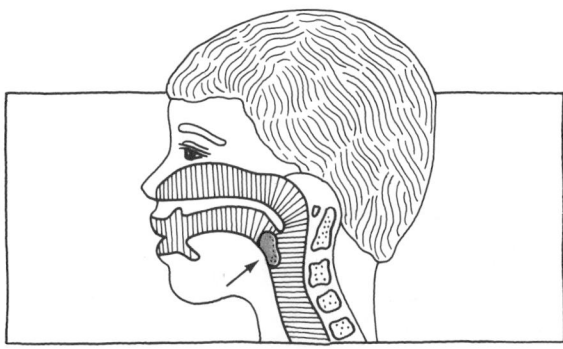

tonsil

too *adverb* **1.** Also; besides: *I can play the piano too.* **2.** More than enough: *You played too long.* **3.** Very; extremely: *I'm only too happy to help. He's not too smart.*
too (tōo) ▢*adverb*

took *verb* The past tense of **take:** *She took the magazine to the beach.*
took (took) ▢*verb*

tool *noun* **1.** An instrument used by or held in the hand. A hammer, knife, and shovel are tools. **2.** Someone or something that is used as a tool: *Books are the tools of learning.* —See Synonyms at **instrument.**
▢*verb* To form or mark with a tool: *She tooled a design on the leather purse.*
tool (tōol) ▢*noun, plural* **tools** ▢*verb* **tooled, tooling, tools**

toot *verb* To make a short, loud blast of sound, as on a whistle: *toot a horn.*
▢*noun* A short, loud blast of sound.
toot (tōot) ▢*verb* **tooted, tooting, toots** ▢*noun, plural* **toots**

tooth *noun* **1.** One of the hard, bony parts in the mouth used to chew and bite. Teeth are set in the gums around the jaws. **2.** Something that looks like or is used like a tooth: *the teeth of a comb.*
tooth (tōoth) ▢*noun, plural* **teeth**

toothbrush *noun* A small brush for cleaning the teeth.
tooth·brush (tōoth′brush′) ▢*noun, plural* **toothbrushes**

toothpaste *noun* A paste used to clean the teeth.
tooth·paste (tōoth′pāst′) ▢*noun, plural* **toothpastes**

toothpick *noun* A small, thin piece of wood or other material used to remove food from between the teeth.
tooth·pick (tōoth′pik′) ▢*noun, plural* **toothpicks**

top[1] *noun* **1.** The highest part: *We climbed to the top of the hill.* **2.** The highest rank or place: *He is at the top of his class.* **3.** The highest degree or pitch: *She shouted at the top of her voice.*
▢*adjective* The highest or greatest: *We ran at top speed. That book is on the top shelf.*
▢*verb* **1.** To be or cause to be on the top of: *Her outfit was topped by a red hat.* **2.** To do better than: *She can run fast, but she can't top me.*
top (top) ▢*noun, plural* **tops** ▢*adjective* ▢*verb* **topped, topping, tops**

top[2] *noun* A toy that spins on a point.
top (top) ▢*noun, plural* **tops**

top

topaz *noun* A light brown or yellow gem.
to·paz (tō′paz′) ▢*noun, plural* **topazes**

topic *noun* The subject, as of a book, speech, or conversation: *The speaker's topic is "How to Use the Dictionary."*
top·ic (top′ik) ▢*noun, plural* **topics**

a	bat	ī	bite	ōo	tool	*th*	feather
ā	make	î	fierce	ou	out	th	bath
â	dare	o	dot	u	nut	hw	wheat
ä	father	ō	no	û	turn	zh	measure
e	net	ô	law, for	ch	church	ə	about, open
ē	be	oi	soil	ng	ring		pencil, atom
i	dip	oo	look	sh	shade		circus

topography *noun* A detailed description or drawing of the physical features of a place or region.
to·pog·ra·phy (tə **pog′**rə fē) □*noun, plural* **topographies**

topple *verb* To fall or cause to fall: *The tree toppled over in the wind.*
top·ple (**top′**əl) □*verb* **toppled, toppling, topples**

topsoil *noun* The rich layer of soil on the surface of the ground.
top·soil (**top′**soil′) □*noun, plural* **topsoils**

Torah *noun* The first five books of the Old Testament.
To·rah (**tôr′**ə) □*noun*

torch *noun* **1.** A flaming light consisting of a long piece of wood with burning material at one end. **2.** A device for producing a flame hot enough for welding or cutting metals.
torch (tôrch) □*noun, plural* **torches**

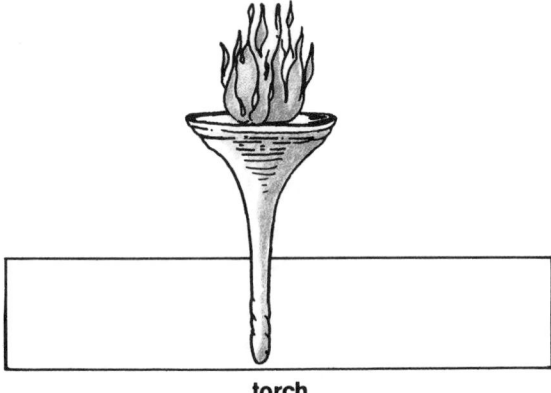

torch

tore *verb* The past tense of **tear¹**: *She tore a hole in her skirt.*
tore (tôr) □*verb*

torment *noun* Great pain or suffering: *the torment of war.*
□*verb* To cause pain or suffering: *The toothache was tormenting him all night.*
tor·ment (**tôr′**ment) □*noun* □*verb* **tormented, tormenting, torments**

torn *verb* The past participle of **tear¹**: *The page had been torn in half.*
torn (tôrn) □*verb*

tornado *noun* A violent whirlwind with an air column shaped like a funnel that spins at a high speed.
tor·na·do (tôr **nā′**dō) □*noun, plural* **tornadoes** or **tornados**

torpedo *noun* A shell shaped like a cigar that explodes when it reaches its target. A torpedo moves underwater by its own power.
□*verb* To attack or destroy with a torpedo.
tor·pe·do (tôr **pē′**dō) □*noun, plural* **torpedos** □*verb* **torpedoed, torpedoing, torpedos**

WORD HISTORY: **torpedo**
Torpedo was originally the name of a fish that produces a numbing electric shock. The word *torpedo* was borrowed from Latin, where it means "numbness." The exploding shell was named after the fish.

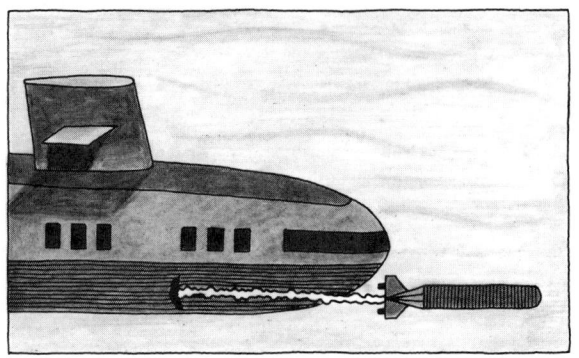

torpedo

torrent *noun* A fast, heavy stream of water or other liquid.
tor·rent (**tôr′**ənt) □*noun, plural* **torrents**

tortilla *noun* A round, flat bread made from cornmeal and water and baked on a grill.
tor·til·la (tôr **tē′**yə) □*noun, plural* **tortillas**

tortoise *noun* A turtle, especially one that lives on land.
tor·toise (**tôr′**təs) □*noun, plural* **tortoises**

tortoise

torture *noun* A cause of great physical or mental pain: *Going to dance class is torture for him.*
□*verb* To cause to feel great pain: *This tight collar is torturing me.*
tor·ture (**tôr′**chər) □*noun, plural* **tortures** □*verb* **tortured, torturing, tortures**

toss   *verb* **1.** To throw or be thrown to and fro: *Heavy seas tossed the ship.* **2.** To flip a coin to decide something: *We always toss a coin to see who will go first.* —See Synonyms at **throw.**
□*noun* A throw.
toss (tôs) □*verb* **tossed, tossing, tosses**
□*noun, plural* **tosses**

total   *noun* The whole amount: *The bill came to a total of ten dollars.*
□*adjective* **1.** Of a whole amount: *What is the total number of students in your school?* **2.** Complete; full: *a total failure.*
□*verb* **1.** To find the sum of: *Total this column of numbers.* **2.** To amount to: *The bill totals forty dollars.*
to·tal (tōt′ əl) □*noun, plural* **totals** □*adjective*
□*verb* **totaled, totaling, totals**

totally   *adverb* Completely; fully: *You are totally responsible for all mistakes.*
to·tal·ly (tōt′ əl ē) □*adverb*

totem   *noun* An animal, plant, or natural object that is the symbol for a clan or family.
to·tem (tō′ təm) □*noun, plural* **totems**

totem pole   *noun* A post carved and painted with totems and usually put up in front of the houses of Native Americans of the northwestern coast of North America.

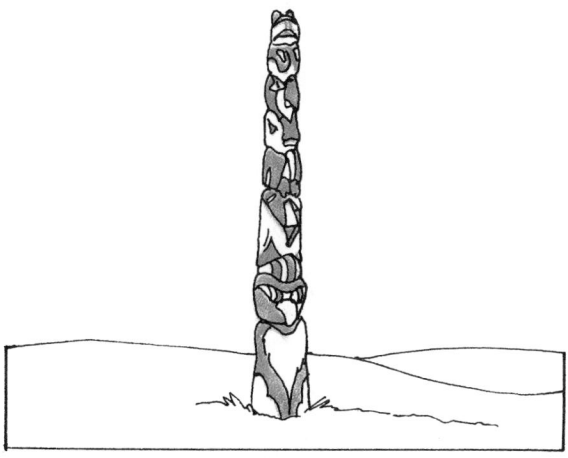

totem pole

toucan   *noun* A tropical American bird with a very large bill and brightly colored feathers.
tou·can (tōo′ kan′) □*noun, plural* **toucans**

touch   *verb* **1.** To come or bring against: *Don't let the flag touch the ground.* **2.** To feel with a part of the body, especially with the hand. **3.** To affect or move the emotions: *The sight of the sick child touched me deeply.*

□*noun* **1.** The sense by which a person can learn about an object by feeling with the hand or some other part of the body. **2.** An act of touching: *The television goes on with a touch of the button.* **3.** Contact or communication: *We haven't been in touch since she moved away.* **4.** A little bit; a trace: *a touch of salt.*
touch (tuch) □*verb* **touched, touching, touches** □*noun, plural* **touches**

SYNONYMS: **touch, feel, handle**

These verbs mean to come into contact with, especially by using the hands: *He can touch his toes without bending his knees. She felt the umbrella to see whether it was wet. Please handle those dishes carefully.*

---

touchdown   *noun* A score of six points in football made by moving the ball across the other team's goal line.
touch·down (tuch′ doun′) □*noun, plural* **touchdowns**

tough   *adjective* **1.** Not easy to tear or break; very strong: *a tough plastic that can stand lots of hard wear; a tough piece of steak.* **2.** Able to stand hardships or difficulty: *Soldiers need special training to make them tough.* **3.** Difficult; hard: *a tough problem.* **4.** Rough: *They lived in the toughest part of town.* —See Synonyms at **difficult.**
tough (tuf) □*adjective* **tougher, toughest**

tour   *noun* A trip to visit several places of interest: *a tour of Europe.*
□*verb* To go on a tour of: *We want to tour the west coast next winter.*
tour (toor) □*noun, plural* **tours** □*verb* **toured, touring, tours**

tourist   *noun* Someone who is traveling for pleasure.
tour·ist (toor′ ist) □*noun, plural* **tourists**

tournament   *noun* A contest among several persons or teams in which they compete until one is declared winner: *a tennis tournament.*
tour·na·ment (toor′ nə mənt) □*noun, plural* **tournaments**

a	bat	ī	bite	ōō	tool	*th*	feather
ā	make	î	fierce	ou	out	th	bath
â	dare	o	dot	u	nut	hw	wheat
ä	father	ō	no	û	turn	zh	measure
e	net	ô	law, for	ch	church	ə	about, open
ē	be	oi	soil	ng	ring		pencil, atom
i	dip	oo	look	sh	shade		circus

tow　*verb* To drag or pull along behind: *The truck towed my car to the garage.*
tow (tō) □*verb* **towed, towing, tows**

tow

toward　*preposition* **1.** In the direction of: *We drove toward the harbor.* **2.** Somewhat before in time; close to: *We should get home toward evening.* **3.** With or in relation to; regarding: *His attitude toward her has changed completely.*
to·ward (tôrd *or* tə **wôrd′**) □*preposition*

towards　*preposition* Another spelling for **toward.**
to·wards (tôrdz *or* tə **wôrdz′**) □*preposition*

towel　*noun* A piece of cloth or paper that is used for wiping or drying.
□*verb* To wipe or rub with a towel: *I toweled my hair dry.*
tow·el (tou′əl) □*noun, plural* **towels** □*verb* **toweled, toweling, towels**

tower　*noun* **1.** A very tall, narrow building. **2.** A very tall, narrow part of a building.
□*verb* To rise up very high: *Steep cliffs towered over the river.*
tow·er (tou′ər) □*noun, plural* **towers** □*verb* **towered, towering, towers**

towering　*adjective* **1.** Very tall: *towering skyscrapers.* **2.** Intense; very great: *a person with a towering ambition.*
tow·er·ing (tou′ər ing) □*adjective*

town　*noun* A community that is larger than a village and smaller than a city.
town (toun) □*noun, plural* **towns**

toy　*noun* Something for children to play with.
□*verb* To play with something: *She toyed with the zipper on her purse as we talked.*
toy (toi) □*noun, plural* **toys** □*verb* **toyed, toying, toys**

trace　*noun* **1.** A mark or sign left behind by someone or something: *There are traces of deer by the lake.* **2.** A very small amount: *There wasn't a trace of color in her face after she saw the snake.*
□*verb* **1.** To follow the trail or track of: *They are using dogs to trace the lost child.* **2.** To copy by following lines seen through thin paper.
trace (trās) □*noun, plural* **traces** □*verb* **traced, tracing, traces**

trachea　*noun* A tube in the throat that brings air to the lungs; windpipe.
tra·che·a (trā′kē ə) □*noun, plural* **tracheas**

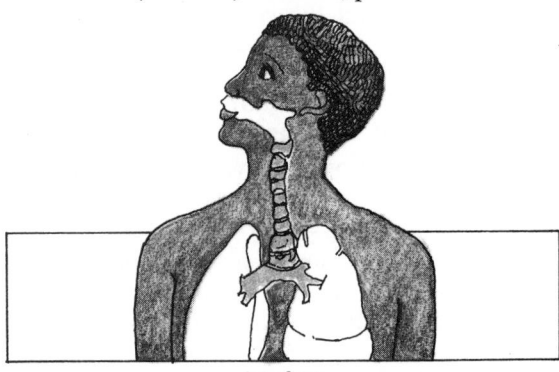

trachea

track　*noun* **1.** A mark, such as a footprint or wheel mark, showing that something has passed over a surface: *bear tracks; tire tracks.* **2.** A path: *a bicycle track.* **3.** The rail or rails on which a train or trolley moves. **4.** A racetrack. **5.** A sport that includes running, jumping, and throwing.
□*verb* **1.** To follow the footprints or trail of: *We tracked the tiger into the jungle.* **2.** To carry something on the feet and leave it as tracks: *The dog tracked dirt on the clean floor.*
track (trak) □*noun, plural* **tracks** □*verb* **tracked, tracking, tracks**

track
Train tracks

tract   *noun* **1.** An area of land: *I bought a tract of land with an ocean view.* **2.** A set of body organs and tissues that work together: *The stomach and intestines form part of the digestive tract.*
tract (trakt) □*noun, plural* **tracts**

traction   *noun* The friction that keeps a wheel from slipping or skidding: *Trucks need a lot of traction to get up that steep hill.*
trac·tion (**trak′**shən) □*noun*

tractor   *noun* A vehicle with large tires powered by an engine. Tractors are used for pulling farm machines.
trac·tor (**trak′**tər) □*noun, plural* **tractors**

tractor

trade   *noun* **1.** The business of buying and selling: *trade between North and South America.* **2.** An exchange of one thing for another: *a trade of an apple for a peach.* **3.** A kind of work, especially one that involves skill with the hands; craft: *the plumber's trade.*
□*verb* **1.** To take part in buying, selling, or bartering: *I have traded in that store for years.* **2.** To exchange or swap: *We traded tennis rackets.*
trade (trād) □*noun, plural* **trades** □*verb* **traded, trading, trades**

trademark   *noun* A name, symbol, or other sign that is put on a product to show who makes or owns it. Trademarks are registered with the government.
trade·mark (**trād′**märk′) □*noun, plural* **trademarks**

trader   *noun* A person who trades or deals.
trad·er (**trā′**dər) □*noun, plural* **traders**

trading post   *noun* A store in a frontier area. Trading posts used to give people food and supplies in exchange for local products.

tradition   *noun* Ideas, customs, and beliefs that have been passed down from one generation to the next.
tra·di·tion (trə **dish′**ən) □*noun, plural* **traditions**

traditional   *adjective* According to tradition: *a traditional song.*
tra·di·tion·al (trə **dish′**ə nəl) □*adjective*

traffic   *noun* **1.** Vehicles, people, ships, or aircraft moving along a route: *Traffic is heavy on holidays.* **2.** Trade in goods: *laws to stop the traffic in illegal drugs.*
□*verb* To carry on trade.
traf·fic (**traf′**ik) □*noun* □*verb* **trafficked, trafficking, traffics**

tragedy   *noun* **1.** A serious story that ends unhappily. **2.** A terrible event; disaster: *The loss of so many lives in the earthquake was a tragedy.*
trag·e·dy (**traj′**i dē) □*noun, plural* **tragedies**

> ### WORD HISTORY: tragedy
> *Tragedy* comes from a Greek word for a kind of play in which the main characters were gods and heroes and the action often involved sadness and suffering. The Greek word literally means "goat song." The reason for this name is not certain.

tragic   *adjective* **1.** Of or having to do with a tragedy. **2.** Very sad; unfortunate.
trag·ic (**traj′**ik) □*adjective*

trail   *verb* **1.** To drag or be dragged along behind: *The sailboat trailed a dinghy.* **2.** To follow the traces or scent of; track: *We trailed the deer over the mountain.* **3.** To lag or be behind: *He trailed the winner by three feet at the finish line.* **4.** To lie or drag along the ground or over a surface: *The bride's train trailed behind her.*
□*noun* **1.** A mark, trace, or scent left behind by a person or animal: *The hounds followed the trail of a bear.* **2.** A path or track: *The trail up the mountain is marked with signs.* **3.** Something that follows or moves along behind: *The horse raised a trail of dust as it galloped past.*
trail (trāl) □*verb* **trailed, trailing, trails** □*noun, plural* **trails**

trailer   *noun* A large vehicle pulled by a truck or car and used to carry something: *Their*

a	bat	ī	bite	ōō	tool	*th*	feather
ā	make	î	fierce	ou	out	th	bath
â	dare	o	dot	u	nut	hw	wheat
ä	father	ō	no	û	turn	zh	measure
e	net	ô	law, for	ch	church	ə	about, open
ē	be	oi	soil	ng	ring		pencil, atom
i	dip	oo	look	sh	shade		circus

truck has a trailer for hauling logs.
trail·er (trā′lər) □*noun, plural* **trailers**

trailer

train *noun* **1.** A group of connected railroad cars pulled by a locomotive or powered by electricity. Some trains carry freight and others carry passengers. **2.** A long line of moving persons, animals, or vehicles: *a circus train.* **3.** The part of a dress that trails behind the person wearing it: *the train of a ball gown.* **4.** A series of events or ideas: *The noise interrupted my train of thought.*
□*verb* **1.** To coach in a way of performing or behaving: *Mother trained us to be independent.* **2.** To teach a person or animal to perform or do something: *He trains tigers to jump through hoops.* **3.** To make or become ready by means of study, practice, or exercise: *He trained for the race by running fifteen miles a day.* **4.** To make go in a certain direction: *The roses were trained to grow around the lamp post.*
train (trān) □*noun, plural* **trains** □*verb* **trained, training, trains**

trainer *noun* A person who trains a person or animal, especially one who coaches athletes, race horses, or show animals.
train·er (trā′nər) □*noun, plural* **trainers**

training *noun* **1.** The process of being trained. **2.** The physical condition of a person or animal that has been trained: *She kept in training by swimming a mile a day.*
train·ing (trā′ning) □*noun*

trait *noun* A special feature or quality, especially of a person or animal.
trait (trāt) □*noun, plural* **traits**

traitor *noun* A person who betrays his or her country, a cause, or an idea.
trai·tor (trā′tər) □*noun, plural* **traitors**

tramp *verb* **1.** To walk with a firm, heavy step. **2.** To go on foot: *The soldiers tramped down the road.* **3.** To flatten with the feet: *tramping down snow.*

□*noun* **1.** The sound of heavy walking or marching: *the tramp of soldiers crossing the bridge.* **2.** A walking trip: *a long tramp around the ranch.* **3.** A person who wanders around and usually has no regular job or place to stay.
tramp (tramp) □*verb* **tramped, tramping, tramps** □*noun, plural* **tramps**

trample *verb* To walk heavily on something, hurting or ruining it: *The dog trampled the flowers when he chased the cat through the garden.*
tram·ple (tram′pəl) □*verb* **trampled, trampling, tramples**

trample

trampoline *noun* A sheet of canvas stretched across a metal frame and fastened with springs. A trampoline is used in gymnastics.
tram·po·line (tram′pə lēn′) □*noun, plural* **trampolines**

tranquil *adjective* Free from trouble or disturbance; peaceful: *a tranquil mind.*
tran·quil (trang′kwəl) □*adjective*

transfer *verb* **1.** To move or shift from one place, person, or thing to another: *transferred the oil by pipeline.* **2.** To change from one way of traveling to another: *We transferred from the subway to a bus.* **3.** To move or be moved from one job, school, or place of work to another: *He transferred to another college.*
□*noun* **1.** An act or example of transferring or being transferred: *the transfer of property.* **2.** A ticket for changing from one bus, plane, or train to another without paying an extra fare.
trans·fer (trans fûr′ *or* trans′fər) □*verb* **transferred, transferring, transfers** □*noun* (trans′fər), *plural* **transfers**

transform *verb* To change very much in form, nature, function, or appearance: *A steam engine transforms heat into energy.*
trans·form (trans fôrm′) □*verb* **transformed, transforming, transforms**

transformation *noun* The process of transforming or the condition of being transformed: *The transformation of ice into water.*
trans·for·ma·tion (transˈfər māˈshən) □*noun, plural* **transformations**

transfusion *noun* The putting of blood or another liquid directly into a person's or animal's veins.
trans·fu·sion (trans fyo͞oˈzhən) □*noun, plural* **transfusions**

transistor *noun* A small device that controls the flow of electricity. Transistors are used in radios, televisions, computers, calculators, and other electronic devices.
tran·sis·tor (tran zisˈtər) □*noun, plural* **transistors**

transition *noun* The process of changing or passing from one form, subject, or place to another: *the transition from tadpole to frog.*
tran·si·tion (tran zishˈən) □*noun, plural* **transitions**

translate *verb* To change into or express in another language: *He translated the Latin myths into English.* **2.** To act as a translator: *He translates at the United Nations.*
trans·late (trans lātˈ) □*verb* **translated, translating, translates**

translation *noun* **1.** The act or process of translating: *He is very quick at translation.* **2.** Something translated: *The poem is a translation from Greek.*
trans·la·tion (trans lāˈshən) □*noun, plural* **translations**

translucent *adjective* Not transparent but allowing some light to pass through: *Frosted glass is translucent.*
trans·lu·cent (trans lo͞oˈsənt) □*adjective*

transmission *noun* **1.** The act of sending something from one person or place to another: *the transmission of a disease.* **2.** The sending of radio or television waves. **3.** A series of gears in an automobile by which power is transferred from the motor to the wheels.
trans·mis·sion (trans mishˈən) □*noun, plural* **transmissions**

transmit *verb* **1.** To send from one person, place, or thing to another: *transmit an SOS; transmit malaria.* **2.** To send out signals by wire or radio: *transmit a broadcast.*
trans·mit (trans mitˈ) □*verb* **transmitted, transmitting, transmits**

transmitter *noun* **1.** Someone or something that transmits. **2.** A device that sends out electrical, radio, or television signals.
trans·mit·ter (trans mitˈər) □*noun, plural* **transmitters**

transparent *adjective* **1.** Allowing light to pass through so that objects on the other side can be clearly seen: *transparent glass; transparent plastic.* **2.** Easy to see or understand; obvious: *a transparent lie.*
trans·par·ent (trans pârˈənt *or* trans parˈənt) □*adjective*

transplant *verb* **1.** To remove a living plant from the place where it is growing and plant it in another place. **2.** To transfer tissue or an organ from one body or body part to another. □*noun* **1.** Something transplanted, especially tissue or an organ transplanted by surgery. **2.** The act or operation of transplanting: *The doctor performed a heart transplant.*
trans·plant (trans plantˈ) □*verb* **transplanted, transplanting, transplants** □*noun* (transˈplant), *plural* **transplants**

transport *verb* To carry from one place to another: *transporting cargo.* □*noun* **1.** The process of transporting: *goods lost in transport.* **2.** A ship for transporting troops or military equipment.
trans·port (trans pôrtˈ) □*verb* **transported, transporting, transports** □*noun* (transˈpôrt), *plural* **transports**

transportation *noun* **1.** The process of transporting: *the transportation of freight.* **2.** A means of transport. **3.** The business of transporting passengers and freight. **4.** A charge for transporting; fare: *Transportation is a big item in my budget.*
trans·por·ta·tion (transˈpər tāˈshən) □*noun, plural* **transportations**

trap *noun* **1.** A device for catching animals. **2.** A way of catching a person by trickery: *set a trap for the enemy.* □*verb* **1.** To catch in a trap: *trap a rabbit.* **2.** To trick someone: *She trapped me into giving the wrong answer.*
trap (trap) □*noun, plural* **traps** □*verb* **trapped, trapping, traps**

a	bat	ī	bite	o͞o	tool	th	feather
ā	make	i	fierce	ou	out	th	bath
â	dare	o	dot	u	nut	hw	wheat
ä	father	ō	no	û	turn	zh	measure
e	net	ô	law, for	ch	church	ə	about, open
ē	be	oi	soil	ng	ring		pencil, atom
i	dip	oo	look	sh	shade		circus

trap door   *noun* A hinged or sliding door in a floor or roof.

trapeze   *noun* A short bar hung between two parallel ropes, used to swing from for exercise or in gymnastics.
tra·peze (tra **pēz′**)   □*noun, plural* **trapezes**

trapeze

trapper   *noun* A person who traps wild animals for their fur.
trap·per (trap′ ər)   □*noun, plural* **trappers**

trash   *noun* Material that is thrown away; garbage.
trash (trash)   □*noun*

travel   *verb* **1.** To journey from one place to another or to a distant place: *I traveled to France last summer.* **2.** To move from one place to another: *Sound travels in waves.*
trav·el (trav′əl)   □*verb* **traveled, traveling, travels**

traveler   *noun* A person who travels.
trav·el·er (trav′ ə lər)   □*noun, plural* **travelers**

tray   *noun* A flat dish with a raised rim or edge, used to carry and display articles: *The waiter brought the food on a large tray.*
tray (trā)   □*noun, plural* **trays**

treacherous   *adjective* **1.** Betraying a trust; disloyal: *a treacherous citizen.* **2.** Not dependable: *a treacherous ladder; treacherous ice.*
treach·er·ous (trech′ər əs)   □*adjective*

tread   *verb* **1.** To walk on, over, or along: *treading a steep path up the mountain.* **2.** To step on heavily; trample: *He trod on the spider.* □*noun* **1.** The act or sound of treading: *The tread of horses; his noisy tread coming down the stairs.* **2.** The top part of a step in a staircase. **3.** The part of a wheel or shoe sole that touches the ground. **4.** The pattern of grooves in a tire that enables it to grip the road.

tread (tred)   □*verb* **trod, trodden** or **trod, treading, treads**   □*noun, plural* **treads**

tread

treason   *noun* The act of betraying one's country by helping an enemy.
trea·son (trē′zən)   □*noun, plural* **treasons**

treasure   *noun* **1.** An accumulation of valuables, such as jewels. **2.** Something that is very valuable.
□*verb* To value highly: *I treasured the souvenirs of our trip.*
treas·ure (trezh′ər)   □*noun, plural* **treasures**   □*verb* **treasured, treasuring, treasures**

treasurer   *noun* A person who has charge of money belonging to an organization.
treas·ur·er (trezh′ər ər)   □*noun, plural* **treasurers**

treasury   *noun* **1.** The place where the money of a government or organization is kept. **2.** The money in a treasury. **3. Treasury** The department of a government that collects and manages a country's money.
treas·ur·y (trezh′ə rē)   □*noun, plural* **treasuries**

treat   *verb* **1.** To handle or behave toward in a certain way: *Treat the animals with care. He treated the subject thoroughly.* **2.** To give medical attention to: *The doctor treated her for a throat infection.* **3.** To pay for the entertainment of someone else: *I'll treat you to dinner.* □*noun* **1.** The act of treating. **2.** Something considered a special pleasure: *going for a sail is always a treat for me.*
treat (trēt)   □*verb* **treated, treating, treats**   □*noun, plural* **treats**

treatment   *noun* **1.** The act or manner of treating something. **2.** The use of something to cure an illness: *heat treatments for aching muscles.*
treat·ment (trēt′mənt)   □*noun, plural* **treatments**

treaty *noun* A formal agreement between two or more states or countries: *a peace treaty.*
trea·ty (trē′tē) □*noun, plural* **treaties**

tree *noun* **1.** A woody plant that lives for many years, is usually tall, and has one main stem or trunk. **2.** Something that resembles a tree: *a clothes tree.*
tree (trē) □*noun, plural* **trees**

trellis *noun* A framework used to train climbing plants.
trel·lis (trel′is) □*noun, plural* **trellises**

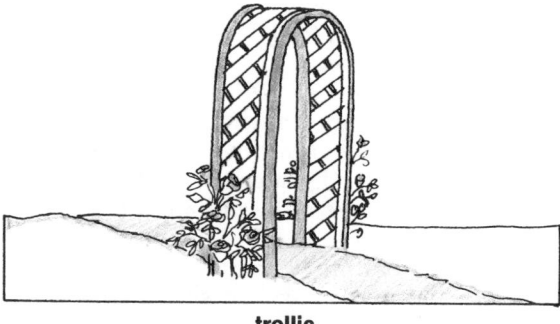
trellis

tremble *verb* To shake, such as from cold or fear; shiver: *trembling with excitement.*
trem·ble (trem′bəl) □*verb* **trembled, trembling, trembles**

tremendous *adjective* Extremely large; enormous: *the tremendous noise of a cannon firing.*
tre·men·dous (tri men′dəs) □*adjective*

tremor *noun* **1.** A shaking or trembling: *an earth tremor; a vocal tremor.* **2.** An involuntary twitching of muscles: *a facial tremor.*
tre·mor (trem′ər) □*noun, plural* **tremors**

trench *noun* A long, narrow ditch: *They dug trenches to try to keep the forest fire from spreading.*
trench (trench) □*noun, plural* **trenches**

trench

trend *noun* A direction or course that is being followed.
trend (trend) □*noun, plural* **trends**

trespass *verb* To go onto someone's property without their permission: *trespassing on the private beach.*
tres·pass (tres′pəs) □*verb* **trespassed, trespassing, trespasses**

trial *noun* **1.** The examination and deciding of a case brought before a court of law. **2.** The process of trying or testing something: *a trial of strength.*
tri·al (trī′əl) □*noun, plural* **trials**

triangle *noun* **1.** An object or a figure that has three sides and three angles. **2.** A small, triangular musical instrument that produces a clear tone like that of a bell.
tri·an·gle (trī′ang′gəl) □*noun, plural* **triangles**

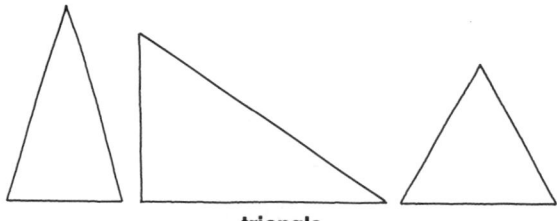
triangle
Three kinds of triangles

triangular *adjective* Shaped or looking like a triangle: *A pyramid has triangular sides.*
tri·an·gu·lar (trī ang′gyə lər) □*adjective*

tribal *adjective* Having to do with a tribe: *tribal costumes.*
trib·al (trī′bəl) □*adjective*

tribe *noun* A group of people united by social customs, language, and ancestry.
tribe (trīb) □*noun, plural* **tribes**

tribute *noun* Something done or given to show respect: *He received a medal as a tribute to his bravery.*
tri·bute (trib′yo͞ot′) □*noun, plural* **tributes**

trick *noun* **1.** A special stunt or skillful act: *juggling tricks; tricks by circus animals.* **2.** Something done to fool someone else. **3.** A

a	bat	ī	bite	o͞o	tool	*th*	feather
ā	make	î	fierce	ou	out	th	bath
â	dare	o	dot	u	nut	hw	wheat
ä	father	ō	no	û	turn	zh	measure
e	net	ô	law, for	ch	church	ə	about, open
ē	be	oi	soil	ng	ring		pencil, atom
i	dip	oo	look	sh	shade		circus

prank or practical joke: *Halloween tricks.*
□*verb* To fool, cheat, or deceive.
trick (trĭk) □*noun, plural* **tricks** □*verb*
tricked, tricking, tricks

trickery *noun* The use of tricks: *He got the money by trickery.*
trick·er·y (trĭk′ə rē) □*noun, plural* **trickeries**

trickle *verb* To flow drop by drop or in a thin stream: *Tears trickled down her face. Sand trickled through his fingers.*
□*noun* A small flow; a thin stream: *a trickle of water from the faucet.*
trick·le (trĭk′əl) □*verb* **trickled, trickling, trickles** □*noun, plural* **trickles**

tricky *adjective* **1.** Using tricks; cunning; sly: *a tricky fox.* **2.** Requiring caution or skill: *a tricky path up the mountain.*
trick·y (trĭk′ē) □*adjective* **trickier, trickiest**

tricycle *noun* A vehicle that has three wheels and is usually propelled by pedals.
tri·cy·cle (trī′sĭk′əl *or* trī′sĭ kəl) □*noun, plural* **tricycles**

tricycle

tried *verb* The past tense and past participle of *try: I tried to telephone you three times.*
tried (trīd) □*verb*

trifle *noun* **1.** Something of very little value. **2.** A small amount; a little.
□*verb* To play with something in a careless way.
tri·fle (trī′fəl) □*noun, plural* **trifles** □*verb* **trifled, trifling, trifles**

trigger *noun* A small lever that is pulled by the finger to shoot a gun.
trig·ger (trĭg′ər) □*noun, plural* **triggers**

trim *verb* **1.** To make neat and tidy by cutting or chopping: *The barber trimmed my hair. It took me a long time to trim the hedge evenly.* **2.** To decorate: *trim a hat.*
□*noun* **1.** Something that decorates or ornaments. **2.** The act of cutting or clipping: *My*

hair needs a trim.
trim (trĭm) □*verb* **trimmed, trimming, trims** □*noun, plural* **trims**

trimming *noun* Something added to decorate or complete: *lace trimming on a dress; roast turkey with all the trimmings.*
trim·ming (trĭm′ing) □*noun, plural* **trimmings**

trinket *noun* A small ornament or piece of jewelry.
trin·ket (trĭng′kĭt) □*noun, plural* **trinkets**

trio *noun* **1.** A group of three. **2.** A musical piece for three performers. **3.** The musicians who perform a trio.
tri·o (trē′ō) □*noun, plural* **trios**

trip *noun* **1.** A movement or passage from one place to another: *a trip to the store; a trip to Hawaii.* **2.** The distance traveled on a journey: *a trip of three thousand miles across the country.*
□*verb* **1.** To stumble or fall. **2.** To make a mistake. **3.** To dance or skip lightly and quickly.
trip (trĭp) □*noun, plural* **trips** □*verb* **tripped, tripping, trips**

triple *adjective* **1.** Made up of three parts. **2.** Three times as many: *She picked triple the number of strawberries that I did.*
□*verb* To make or become three times as much.
trip·le (trĭp′əl) □*adjective* □*verb* **tripled, tripling, triples**

tripod *noun* A stand with three legs, used especially to support a camera or telescope.
tri·pod (trī′pŏd′) □*noun, plural* **tripods**

triumph *verb* To be victorious or successful: *He triumphed over all the other contestants.*
—See Synonyms at **defeat.**
□*noun* **1.** The act of winning; success. **2.** Joy from winning: *a shout of triumph.* —See Synonyms at **victory.**
tri·umph (trī′əmf) □*verb* **triumphed, triumphing, triumphs** □*noun, plural* **triumphs**

triumphant *adjective* **1.** Victorious; successful: *a triumphant army.* **2.** Rejoicing over having been successful: *a triumphant parade; a triumphant shout.*
tri·um·phant (trī ŭm′fənt) □*adjective*

trivial *adjective* **1.** Of little or no importance: *a trivial problem that is easy to solve.* **2.** Ordinary; usual: *trivial household chores.*
triv·i·al (trĭv′ē əl) □*adjective*

trod *verb* The past tense and a past participle of **tread.**
trod (trod) ▢*verb*

trodden *verb* A past participle of **tread:** *She had trodden that path many times before.*
trod·den (trod′ən) ▢*verb*

trolley *noun* **1.** A streetcar. **2.** A small, grooved wheel that runs along an overhead wire and supplies current to an electrically powered vehicle.
trol·ley (trol′ē) ▢*noun, plural* **trolleys**

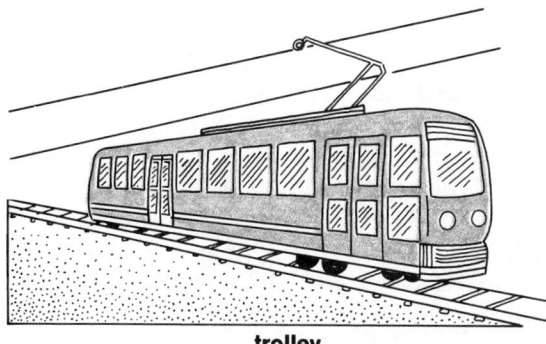
trolley

trombone *noun* A brass wind musical instrument resembling the trumpet but having two long tubes shaped like U's and a lower pitch.
trom·bone (trom bōn′ *or* trom′bōn′) ▢*noun, plural* **trombones**

troop *noun* **1.** A group of people or animals: *A troop of children toured the newspaper offices.* **2.** A group of soldiers. **3.** A unit of Boy Scouts or Girl Scouts under an adult leader. ▢*verb* To move together in a group: *The audience trooped out of the theater when the show was over.*
troop (tro͞op) ▢*noun, plural* **troops** ▢*verb* **trooped, trooping, troops**

trooper *noun* A policeman.
troop·er (tro͞o′pər) ▢*noun, plural* **troopers**

trophy *noun* A prize received as a symbol of victory.
tro·phy (trō′fē) ▢*noun, plural* **trophies**

trophy

tropical *adjective* Of, like, or having to do with the tropics: *tropical fish; tropical storms.*
trop·i·cal (trop′i kəl) ▢*adjective*

tropics *plural noun* The very hot regions of the earth that are near the equator.
trop·ics (trop′iks) ▢*plural noun*

trot *noun* A running gait of a horse that is faster than a walk and slower than a gallop. ▢*verb* **1.** To move or ride at a trot: *The horses trotted around the circus ring.* **2.** To run or walk quickly.
trot (trot) ▢*noun, plural* **trots** ▢*verb* **trotted, trotting, trots**

trouble *noun* **1.** A difficult or dangerous situation: *The sailor was in trouble when his boat sprung a leak.* **2.** A problem or difficulty: *I'm having trouble getting this door open.* **3.** Extra work or effort: *I went to a lot of trouble to find the right gift for my grandmother's birthday.* —See Synonyms at **effort.**
▢*verb* **1.** To disturb or worry; cause distress: *The fact that I hadn't done my homework troubled me.* **2.** To cause inconvenience to.
trou·ble (trub′əl) ▢*noun, plural* **troubles** ▢*verb* **troubled, troubling, troubles**

troublesome *adjective* Causing trouble; annoying: *a troublesome mosquito; a troublesome problem.*
trou·ble·some (trub′əl səm) ▢*adjective*

trough *noun* A long, narrow box or other container that is used to hold water or feed for animals.
trough (trôf) ▢*noun, plural* **troughs**

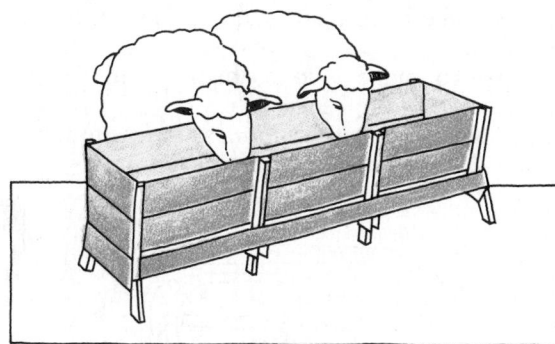
trough

a bat	ī bite	o͞o tool	*th* feather
ā make	i fierce	ou out	th bath
â dare	o dot	u nut	hw wheat
ä father	ō no	û turn	zh measure
e net	ô law, for	ch church	ə about, open
ē be	oi soil	ng ring	pencil, atom
i dip	oo look	sh shade	circus

trousers *plural noun* An outer garment covering the body from the waist to the ankles and fitting each leg separately.
trou·sers (trou′zərz) □*plural noun*

trout *noun* A fish that has a spotted body and is highly valued for sport and as food. It is related to the salmon and lives in fresh water.
trout (trout) □*noun, plural* **trout**

truce *noun* A short or temporary stop in fighting agreed to by the opposing sides.
truce (tro͞os) □*noun, plural* **truces**

truck *noun* A motor vehicle designed to carry large or heavy loads.
truck (truk) □*noun, plural* **trucks**

trudge *verb* To walk slowly with effort, as if one is tired or carrying a heavy weight: *We trudged up the hill with a load of firewood.*
trudge (truj) □*verb* **trudged, trudging, trudges**

true *adjective* **1.** In agreement with fact or reality; not false: *a true answer; a true story.* **2.** Real or genuine: *a true pearl.* **3.** Loyal to someone or something; faithful: *a true friend.*
true (tro͞o) □*adjective* **truer, truest**

truly *adverb* **1.** In a sincere, honest, or truthful manner: *He spoke truly.* **2.** In fact or indeed: *a truly magnificent view.*
tru·ly (tro͞o′lē) □*adverb*

trumpet *noun* **1.** A brass wind instrument that has a strong tone with a high pitch. It is made of a long metal tube that is coiled in a loop, with a mouthpiece at one end and a flared bell at the other. **2.** Something that sounds like a trumpet, such as the cry of an elephant.
□*verb* To make a loud, high sound like a trumpet.
trum·pet (trum′pit) □*noun, plural* **trumpets** □*verb* **trumpeted, trumpeting, trumpets**

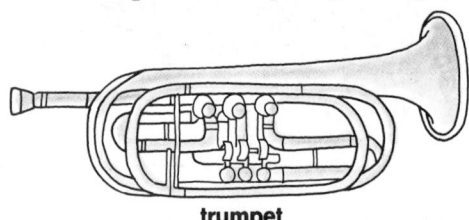

trumpet

trunk *noun* **1.** The tall main stem of a tree, from which the branches grow. **2.** A large box or case with a lid that locks or clasps shut. **3.** The covered section in the rear of an automobile that is used to hold luggage and other objects. **4.** The main part of a human or ani-

mal body, not including the arms, legs, or head. **5.** The long, flexible snout of an elephant. **6. trunks** Short pants worn for swimming and for playing certain sports.
trunk (trungk) □*noun, plural* **trunks**

trust *verb* **1.** To believe or have confidence in as being honest, fair, or dependable: *I trust him to do the right thing.* **2.** To depend or rely on; count on: *Don't trust that old car for a long trip.*
□*noun* **1.** A strong belief in someone or something; faith. **2.** The act or condition of taking care of someone or something for another person; custody. —See Synonyms at **confidence.**
trust (trust) □*verb* **trusted, trusting, trusts** □*noun*

trustworthy *adjective* Able to be relied on; dependable: *a trustworthy employee.*
trust·wor·thy (trust′wûr′thē) □*adjective*

truth *noun* **1.** Something that is true: *Neither witness told the truth.* **2.** The quality of being honest, sincere, loyal, or true: *I don't believe the truth of that story.*
truth (tro͞oth) □*noun, plural* **truths**

truthful *adjective* Telling the truth; honest: *a truthful person; a truthful account.*
truth·ful (tro͞oth′fəl) □*adjective*

try *verb* **1.** To attempt to do something; make an effort: *He tried to mend the broken plate.* **2.** To taste, sample, or test something: *She tried on the dress to see whether it would fit.* **3.** To examine or investigate a case before a court of law.
□*noun* An attempt; an effort: *After three tries he hit the target.*
try (trī) □*verb* **tried, trying, tries** □*noun, plural* **tries**

tryout *noun* A test to find out a person's skill or ability: *There will be a tryout for parts in the school play.*
try·out (trī′out′) □*noun, plural* **tryouts**

T-shirt *noun* A light shirt with short sleeves and no collar.
T-shirt (tē′shûrt′) □*noun, plural* **T-shirts**

tub *noun* **1.** A round, wide, open container used for packing, storing, or washing. **2.** A small, round container used for keeping food: *a tub of butter.* **3.** A bathtub.
tub (tub) □*noun, plural* **tubs**

tuba *noun* A large brass wind instrument that has a deep, mellow tone.
tu·ba (to͞o′bə *or* tyo͞o′bə) □*noun, plural* **tubas**

tube *noun* **1.** A long, hollow piece of metal, glass, rubber, plastic, or other material that is used to carry liquids or gas. A garden hose and a drinking straw are both tubes. **2.** Something shaped or used like a tube, such as a tunnel or pipe. **3.** A small, flexible container made of metal or plastic that is shaped like a tube and has a cap on one end. Tubes are used for holding a paste, such as toothpaste, that can be squeezed out.
tube (tōōb *or* tyōōb) ▢*noun, plural* **tubes**

tuber *noun* A swollen underground stem, such as a potato. A tuber bears buds from which new plants grow.
tu·ber (tōō′bər *or* tyōō′bər) ▢*noun, plural* **tubers**

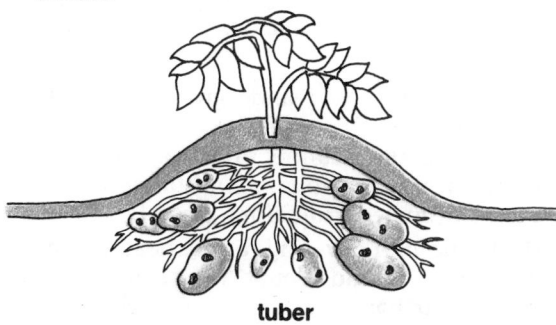

tuber

tuberculosis *noun* A disease caused by bacteria that destroys tissues of the body, especially the lungs. Tuberculosis affects both people and animals and is very contagious.
tu·ber·cu·lo·sis (too bûr′kyə lō′sis *or* tyoo bûr′kyə lō′sis) ▢*noun*

tuck *verb* **1.** To fold or push the edges or ends of a garment or piece of fabric into place: *tuck a shirt in; sheets neatly tucked in.* **2.** To cover or wrap snugly: *Tuck the baby in his crib for a nap.* **3.** To put or store in a safe or secret place: *She tucked her money away in her desk.*
▢*noun* A narrow fold sewed into a garment to decorate it or make it fit better.
tuck (tuk) ▢*verb* **tucked, tucking, tucks** ▢*noun, plural* **tucks**

Tuesday *noun* The third day of the week, after Monday and before Wednesday.
Tues·day (tōōz′dē *or* tōōz′dā′ *or* tyōōz′dē *or* tyōōz′dā′) ▢*noun, plural* **Tuesdays**

> **WORD HISTORY:** **Tuesday**
>
> *Tuesday* is named after Tiw, the god of war in Germanic mythology.

tuft *noun* A bunch of grass, feathers, hair, threads, or other flexible materials that grows or is held tightly together at one end and is loose at the other.
tuft (tuft) ▢*noun, plural* **tufts**

tug *verb* **1.** To pull hard on something: *He tugged at the door but couldn't open it.* **2.** To move something by pulling with force or effort: *She tugged the sled up the hill.*
▢*noun* A hard pull: *He gave a tug on the rope.*
tug (tug) ▢*verb* **tugged, tugging, tugs** ▢*noun, plural* **tugs**

tugboat *noun* A very powerful small boat that is designed to tow or push larger boats.
tug·boat (tug′bōt′) ▢*noun, plural* **tugboats**

tugboat

tuition *noun* Money paid for lessons or instruction, especially at a college or private school.
tu·i·tion (tōō ish′ən *or* tyōō ish′ən) ▢*noun, plural* **tuitions**

tulip *noun* A garden plant with colorful flowers. Tulips grow from bulbs.
tu·lip (tōō′lip *or* tyōō′lip) ▢*noun, plural* **tulips**

> **WORD HISTORY:** **tulip**
>
> *Tulip* comes from a Persian word meaning "turban." The plant got its name because its flower resembles a turban.

tumble *verb* **1.** To fall in a helpless way: *She tripped and tumbled down the steps.* **2.** To fall or roll end over end; toss about: *The clothes were tumbling in the dryer.* **3.** To spill or roll

a	bat	ī	bite	ōō	tool	*th*	feather
ā	make	î	fierce	ou	out	th	bath
â	dare	o	dot	u	nut	hw	wheat
ä	father	ō	no	û	turn	zh	measure
e	net	ô	law, for	ch	church	ə	about, open
ē	be	oi	soil	ng	ring		pencil, atom
i	dip	oo	look	sh	shade		circus

out in a confusing or not orderly way: *Groceries tumbled out of the torn bag.* **4.** To do somersaults, leaps, or other gymnastics.
□*noun* A fall caused by tumbling: *I took a tumble when I slipped on the icy path.*
tum·ble (tum′bəl) □*verb* **tumbled, tumbling, tumbles** □*noun, plural* **tumbles**

tumble
Groceries tumbling out of a broken bag

tumor *noun* A swelling within the body that is not normal.
tu·mor (too′mər *or* tyoo′mər) □*noun, plural* **tumors**

tuna *noun* A large ocean fish that is caught in large numbers for food.
tu·na (too′nə *or* tyoo′nə) □*noun, plural* **tuna** or **tunas**

tundra *noun* An arctic plain that remains frozen all year round except for the ground just at the surface. Mosses and small shrubs are the only kind of plant life that grows on the tundra.
tun·dra (tun′drə) □*noun, plural* **tundras**

tune *noun* **1.** A melody, especially one that is easy to remember: *I forget the words of the song, but I can hum the tune.* **2.** The correct pitch: *The piano is out of tune.* **3.** Agreement or harmony: *Her opinion is in tune with mine.*
□*verb* To put in the proper pitch; put in tune: *tune a violin.*
tune (toon *or* tyoon) □*noun, plural* **tunes** □*verb* **tuned, tuning, tunes**

tunic *noun* **1.** A garment that looks like a shirt and reaches down to the knees. Tunics were worn by men in ancient Greece and Rome and during the Middle Ages. **2.** A short, snug jacket that is usually worn as part of a

uniform by soldiers or police.
tu·nic (too′nik *or* tyoo′nik) □*noun, plural* **tunics**

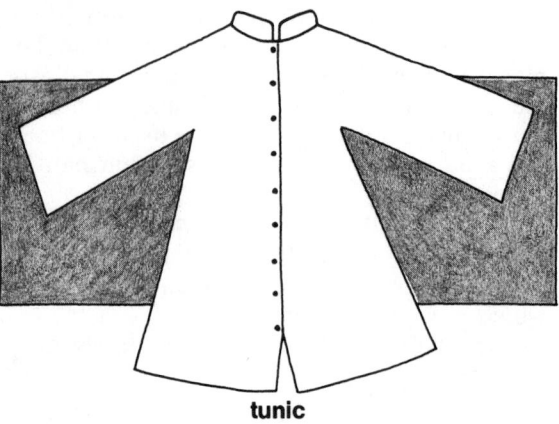

tunic

tunnel *noun* A long underground or underwater passage.
□*verb* To make a tunnel under or through.
tun·nel (tun′əl) □*noun, plural* **tunnels** □*verb* **tunneled, tunneling, tunnels**

turban *noun* A covering for the head made of a long scarf wound around the head.
tur·ban (tûr′bən) □*noun, plural* **turbans**

turbine *noun* A machine or motor in which the force of air, steam, or water is used to turn a wheel by pushing against paddles attached to the wheel.
tur·bine (tûr′bin *or* tûr′bīn′) □*noun, plural* **turbines**

turbulent *adjective* **1.** Being in a state of disturbance or unrest; stormy: *The sea was still turbulent although the storm had passed.* **2.** Causing disturbance or unrest: *turbulent emotions.*
tur·bu·lent (tûr′byə lənt) □*adjective*

tureen *noun* A deep covered dish used for serving food, such as soup, at the table.
tu·reen (too rēn′ *or* tyoo rēn′) □*noun, plural* **tureens**

turf *noun* An upper layer of earth with thick grass and roots; sod.
turf (tûrf) □*noun, plural* **turfs**

Turk *noun* Someone who lives in or was born in Turkey.
Turk (tûrk) □*noun, plural* **Turks**

turkey *noun* **1.** A large brownish American bird with a bare head and skin that hangs down in folds from its neck. Turkeys are raised for food. **2.** The meat of a turkey.
tur·key (tûr′kē) □*noun, plural* **turkeys**

Turkish *adjective* Of or having to do with Turkey, the Turks, or their language. □*noun* The language of the Turks.
Turk·ish (tûr′kish) □*adjective* □*noun*

turmoil *noun* A condition of great confusion or disorder: *There was turmoil in the city after the earthquake.*
tur·moil (tûr′moil′) □*noun, plural* **turmoils**

turn *verb* **1.** To move or cause to move around a central point; rotate. **2.** To change or cause to change direction: *She turned the car into a side street. The road turns south outside town.* **3.** To direct in a certain way; point: *He turned his face to the wall.* **4.** To change the position of so that the underside becomes the upper side: *turn pancakes.* **5.** To change: *The little boy turned into a tall, handsome man.* **6.** To pass or cause to pass from one state to another: *Leaves turn red in the fall.* **7.** To make sour: *The milk turned.* **8.** To upset: *Greasy food turns my stomach.* **9.** To get to or go beyond a certain age, time, or amount: *I have just turned 13.*
□*noun* **1.** The act of turning or the condition of being turned. **2.** A change of direction or position: *The car made a left turn.* **3.** The beginning of a new period or era: *the turn of the century.* **4.** A chance to do something: *It's my turn to use the bike.*
  turn down To reject or refuse: *I turned down her invitation to dinner.*
  turn out 1. To come out; appear: *Thousands turned out for the fireworks display.* **2.** To produce or make: *The factory turns out 100 automobiles a week.* **3.** To result; end up: *Everything turned out well.*
turn (tûrn) □*verb* **turned, turning, turns** □*noun, plural* **turns**

turnip *noun* A plant having a round yellow or white root that is eaten as a vegetable.
tur·nip (tûr′nip′) □*noun, plural* **turnips**

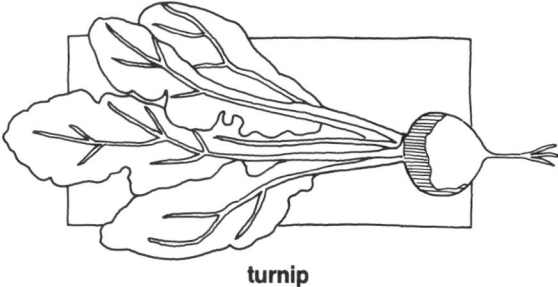

turnip

turnpike *noun* A main road or highway, especially one on which a toll is collected.
turn·pike (tûrn′pīk′) □*noun, plural* **turnpikes**

turnstile *noun* A set of horizontal bars that turn on a central vertical post. Turnstiles allow only one person at a time to walk through.
turn·stile (tûrn′stīl′) □*noun, plural* **turnstiles**

turntable *noun* **1.** A round platform with a rotating railway track that is used for turning locomotives. **2.** A round platform that turns a phonograph record.
turn·ta·ble (tûrn′tā′bəl) □*noun, plural* **turntables**

turpentine *noun* **1.** A sticky mixture of oil and resin that comes mainly from certain pine trees. **2.** An oil distilled from turpentine that is used as a paint thinner and solvent.
tur·pen·tine (tûr′pən tīn′) □*noun*

turquoise *noun* **1.** A bluish-green mineral used as a gem. **2.** A light bluish-green color. □*adjective* Light bluish green.
tur·quoise (tûr′koiz′ *or* tûr′kwoiz′) □*noun, plural* **turquoises** □*adjective*

a bat	ī bite	o͞o tool	*th* feather
ā make	î fierce	ou out	th bath
â dare	o dot	u nut	hw wheat
ä father	ō no	û turn	zh measure
e net	ô law, for	ch church	ə about, open
ē be	oi soil	ng ring	pencil, atom
i dip	oo look	sh shade	circus

turret *noun* A small tower on the side of a building.
tur·ret (tûr′it) □*noun, plural* **turrets**

turtle *noun* An animal that lives on water or land and has a body covered by a hard shell. A turtle can pull its head, legs, and tail into its shell for protection.
tur·tle (tûr′təl) □*noun, plural* **turtles**

turtledove *noun* A dove that has a soft voice and a tail with a white edge.
tur·tle·dove (tûr′təl duv′) □*noun, plural* **turtledoves**

turtleneck *noun* A high collar that fits close to the neck.
tur·tle·neck (tûr′təl nek′) □*noun, plural* **turtlenecks**

tusk *noun* A long, pointed tooth, usually one of a pair. They extend outside of the mouth of certain animals, such as the elephant, walrus, and wild boar.
tusk (tusk) □*noun, plural* **tusks**

tussle *verb* To fight in a rough way; scuffle.
□*noun* A rough fight; struggle.
tus·sle (tus′əl) □*verb* **tussled, tussling, tussles** □*noun, plural* **tussles**

tutor *noun* Someone who teaches a pupil privately.
tu·tor (tŏō′tər *or* tyŏō′tər) □*noun, plural* **tutors**

TV *noun* Television.
TV (tē′vē′) □*noun, plural* **TV's**

twang *noun* **1.** A sharp, vibrating sound, such as that of a plucked string. **2.** A nasal quality of the voice.
□*verb* **1.** To make a sound like a twang. **2.** To speak with a nasal quality of the voice.
twang (twang) □*verb* **twanged, twanging, twangs** □*noun, plural* **twangs**

'twas Contraction of "it was."
'twas (twuz)

tweak *noun* A sharp twist or pinch: *a tweak of the nose.*
□*verb* To pinch or twist in a quick, sharp way.
tweak (twēk) □*noun, plural* **tweaks** □*verb* **tweaked, tweaking, tweaks**

tweed *noun* A rough, woolen cloth, usually of several colors and used for jackets, slacks, and other clothes.
tweed (twēd) □*noun, plural* **tweeds**

tweet *noun* A high, chirping sound, such as a small bird makes.
tweet (twēt) □*noun, plural* **tweets**

tweezers *plural noun* Small pincers used for pulling or handling small objects.
tweez·ers (twē′zərz) □*plural noun*

twelfth *noun* **1.** In a group of people or things that are in numbered order, the one that matches the number twelve. **2.** One of twelve equal parts, written ¹/₁₂.
□*adjective* Coming after the eleventh.
twelfth (twelfth) □*noun, plural* **twelfths** □*adjective*

twelve *noun* A number equal to the sum of 10 + 2; 12.
□*adjective* Being one more than eleven.
twelve (twelv) □*noun, plural* **twelves** □*adjective*

twelvemonth *noun* A period of twelve months; year.
twelve·month (twelv′munth′) □*noun, plural* **twelvemonths**

twentieth *noun* **1.** In a group of people or things that are in numbered order, the one that matches the number twenty. **2.** One of twenty equal parts, written ¹/₂₀.
□*adjective* Coming after the nineteenth.
twen·ti·eth (twen′tē ith) □*noun, plural* **twentieths** □*adjective*

twenty *noun* A number that is equal to the sum of 10 + 10; 20.
□*adjective* Being one more than nineteen.
twen·ty (twen′tē) □*noun, plural* **twenties** □*adjective*

twice *adverb* **1.** Two times: *It rained twice last week.* **2.** Double the amount or degree: *twice as loud.*
twice (twīs) □*adverb*

twiddle *verb* To turn or twist in a light, quick, or idle way: *I twiddled the dial trying to tune in my favorite station.*
twid·dle (twid′əl) □*verb* **twiddled, twiddling, twiddles**

twig *noun* A small branch of a tree or shrub.
twig (twig) □*noun, plural* **twigs**

twilight *noun* The time before sunrise or after sunset when there is a little light in the sky.
twi·light (twī′līt′) □*noun*

twill *noun* **1.** A weave that makes a pattern of diagonal ribs on the surface of a fabric. **2.** Cloth with a twill weave.
twill (twill) □*noun, plural* **twills**

twin *noun* **1.** Either of two children born to the same parents at the same time. **2.** One of two persons, animals, or things that are alike.
□*adjective* **1.** Being one of two from the same birth. **2.** Being one of two persons, animals, or

things that are alike.
twin (twin) □*noun, plural* **twins** □*adjective*

twine *noun* A strong cord or string made of threads twisted together.
□*verb* **1.** To twist together. **2.** To coil about: *A vine twined about the trellis.*
twine (twīn) □*noun, plural* **twines** □*verb* **twined, twining, twines**

twinge *noun* A sudden sharp pain: *a twinge of conscience; a twinge in my neck.*
twinge (twinj) □*noun, plural* **twinges**

twinkle *verb* To shine with winking or sparkling light: *stars twinkling in the sky; eyes twinkling with excitement.*
□*noun* A winking gleam of light.
twin·kle (twing′kəl) □*verb* **twinkled, twinkling, twinkles** □*noun, plural* **twinkles**

twinkling *noun* A brief moment of time; instant.
twink·ling (twing′kling) □*noun, plural* **twinklings**

twirl *verb* To turn quickly; spin: *She twirled her baton.*
twirl (twûrl) □*verb* **twirled, twirling, twirls**

twirl

twist *verb* **1.** To wind together two or more threads to form one strand. **2.** To wind or coil around something: *She twisted her hair around her finger.* **3.** To move or go in a winding course: *The road twisted up the mountain.* **4.** To pull sharply or sprain: *I twisted my knee when I fell.* **5.** To change the shape of by turning: *He twisted the paper into a circle.*
□*noun* **1.** The act of twisting; spin: *a twist of the top.* **2.** A turn or bend: *every twist in the road.*
twist (twist) □*verb* **twisted, twisting, twists** □*noun, plural* **twists**

twister *noun* A tornado.
twist·er (twis′tər) □*noun, plural* **twisters**

twitch *verb* To move or cause to move with a quick jerk: *The horse twitched its ears.*
twitch (twich) □*verb* **twitched, twitching, twitches**

twitter *verb* To make a series of high, rapid, chirping sounds, such as a bird does.
□*noun* **1.** A series of high, rapid, chirping sounds. **2.** A condition of nervous excitement: *in a twitter about seeing the President.*
twit·ter (twit′ər) □*verb* **twittered, twittering, twitters** □*noun, plural* **twitters**

two *noun* A number that is equal to the sum of 1 + 1; 2.
□*adjective* Being one more than one.
two (tōō) □*noun, plural* **twos** □*adjective*

type *noun* **1.** A group of persons or things that are alike in certain ways that set them apart from others; class: *That type of person has no respect for the rights of others.* **2.** A small block of wood or metal with a letter on it used in printing. —See Synonyms at **kind²**.
□*verb* **1.** To put into a certain group or class: *type a person's blood.* **2.** To use a typewriter.
type (tīp) □*noun, plural* **types** □*verb* **typed, typing, types**

typewriter *noun* A machine that prints letters and numbers with keys that, when pressed by hand, strike paper through an inked ribbon.
type·writ·er (tīp′rī′tər) □*noun, plural* **typewriters**

typhoid fever *noun* A serious disease caused by bacteria that are found in dirty food and water.
ty·phoid fever (tī′foid′) □*noun*

typhoon *noun* A severe hurricane that occurs in the western Pacific Ocean.
ty·phoon (tī fōōn′) □*noun, plural* **typhoons**

WORD HISTORY: **typhoon**

Typhoon comes from two Chinese words that mean "great wind."

---

a	bat	ī	bite	ōō	tool	*th*	feather
ā	make	î	fierce	ou	out	th	bath
â	dare	o	dot	u	nut	hw	wheat
ä	father	ō	no	û	turn	zh	measure
e	net	ô	law, for	ch	church	ə	about, open
ē	be	oi	soil	ng	ring		pencil, atom
i	dip	oo	look	sh	shade		circus

typical *adjective* Showing the characteristics of a certain kind or type: *that is a typical example of his carelessness.*
typ·i·cal (**tip′**i kəl) □*adjective*

typify *verb* To be a typical example of; represent: *This song typifies the folk music of the South.*
typ·i·fy (**tip′**ə fī′) □*verb* **typified, typifying, typifies**

typist *noun* Someone who types on a typewriter.
typ·ist (**tī′**pist) □*noun, plural* **typists**

tyrannical *adjective* Of, being, or resembling a tyrant: *The tyrannical king was hated by his subjects.*
ty·ran·ni·cal (ti **ran′**i kəl) □*adjective*

tyrannosaur

tyrannosaur *noun* A very large, carnivorous dinosaur with small front legs, a large head, and sharp teeth. Tyrannosaurs once lived in North America, but they are now extinct.
ty·ran·no·saur (ti **ran′**ə sôr′) □*noun, plural* **tyrannosaurs**

tyranny *noun* **1.** A government in which one person has all the power. **2.** The use of absolute power, especially in a way that is unjust or cruel. **3.** A tyrannical act.
tyr·an·ny (**tîr′**ə nē) □*noun, plural* **tyrannies**

tyrant *noun* **1.** A ruler who has unlimited power, especially one who uses power unjustly or cruelly. **2.** A person who uses authority in an unjust and harsh way: *Her grandfather was a tyrant who insisted on absolute silence at the dinner table.*
ty·rant (**tī′**rənt) □*noun, plural* **tyrants**

a	bat	ī	bite	o͞o	tool	th	feather
ā	make	î	fierce	ou	out	th	bath
â	dare	o	dot	u	nut	hw	wheat
ä	father	ō	no	û	turn	zh	measure
e	net	ô	law, for	ch	church	ə	about, open
ē	be	oi	soil	ng	ring		pencil, atom
i	dip	oo	look	sh	shade		circus

ANCIENT GREEK

The letter **U** has evolved from many forms of ancient writing. One of the earliest known examples is the Greek character shown above, which dates from almost 3,000 years ago. Over the years, artists and designers have created their own versions of the English letter **U**. Some of the more common examples seen today are shown below.

HANDWRITING	CALLIGRAPHY	MODERN SANS SERIF	MODERN SERIF	SCRIPT
Uu Uu	Uu Uu	Uu Uu	Uu Uu	Uu Uu

u or **U** *noun* The twenty-first letter of the English alphabet.
u or **U** (yōō) ▢*noun, plural* **u's** or **U's**

ugly *adjective* **1.** Not beautiful or pleasing to look at: *The wicked witch was very ugly.* **2.** Having or showing a mean disposition: *an ugly temper.*
ug·ly (**ug′**lē) ▢*adjective* **uglier, ugliest**

SYNONYMS: **ugly, hideous**

These adjectives mean not beautiful or pleasing to look at: *an ugly face; a hideous gash.*

---

ukulele *noun* A small guitar with four strings.
u·ku·le·le (yōō′kə **lā′**lē) ▢*noun, plural* **ukuleles**

ukulele

ulcer *noun* A sore that eats away tissue and sometimes gives off pus.
ul·cer (**ul′**sər) ▢*noun, plural* **ulcers**

ultimate *adjective* **1.** Final or last: *the ulti-* *mate victory.* **2.** Most basic; fundamental: *ultimate truths.*
ul·ti·mate (**ul′**tə mit) ▢*adjective*

umbrella *noun* A folding framework covered with fabric and used for protection from rain or sun.
um·brel·la (um **brel′**ə) ▢*noun, plural* **umbrellas**

WORD HISTORY: **umbrella**

Umbrella comes from the Latin word for ''shade.''

---

umpire *noun* A person who rules on the plays in a sport such as baseball.
▢*verb* To act as an umpire.
um·pire (**um′**pīr′) ▢*noun, plural* **umpires**
▢*verb* **umpired, umpiring, umpires**

umpire

un- A prefix that means: **1.** Not; the opposite of: *unhappy.* **2.** To do the opposite of: *unlock.* **3.** Lack of: *unemployment.*

unable *adjective* Not having the skill, knowledge, or power to do something: *She was unable to solve the problem.*
un·a·ble (un ā′bəl) □*adjective*

unaccented *adjective* Not accented: *In the word "above", the first syllable is unaccented.*
un·ac·cent·ed (un ak′ sen tid) □*adjective*

unaccustomed *adjective* Not used to or accustomed to: *The unaccustomed exercise made us very sleepy.*
un·ac·cus·tomed (un′ə kus′təmd) □*adjective*

unanimous *adjective* Based on or having the agreement of all: *a unanimous decision.*
u·nan·i·mous (yōō nan′ə məs) □*adjective*

WORD HISTORY: unanimous

Unanimous comes from a Latin word that means "of one mind."

---

unbearable *adjective* Difficult or impossible to put up with: *a country of unbearable cold.*
un·bear·a·ble (un bâr′ə bəl) □*adjective*

unbecoming *adjective* Not attractive or suitable: *an unbecoming hat; unbecoming behavior.*
un·be·com·ing (un′bi kum′ing) □*adjective*

unbelievable *adjective* Too unlikely to be believed: *an unbelievable coincidence.*
un·be·liev·a·ble (un′bi lē′və bəl) □*adjective*

unbroken *adjective* **1.** Not broken or damaged. **2.** Not tamed and trained for use: *an unbroken horse.* **3.** Not interrupted; continuous: *He listened patiently to her unbroken list of complaints.*
un·bro·ken (un brō′kən) □*adjective*

unbutton *verb* To undo the buttons of: *unbutton a jacket.*
un·but·ton (un but′ən) □*verb* **unbuttoned, unbuttoning, unbuttons**

uncalled-for *adjective* Not needed or asked for: *uncalled-for criticism.*
un·called-for (un kôld′fôr′) □*adjective*

uncanny *adjective* **1.** Mysterious; strange: *There was an uncanny silence in the forest.* **2.** Not to be explained by reason: *He has an uncanny ability to tame even the wildest animals.*
un·can·ny (un kan′ē) □*adjective* **uncannier, uncanniest**

uncertain *adjective* **1.** Not certain; not knowing for sure: *He was uncertain of the answer.* **2.** Not known certainly or surely: *It's uncertain whether we can finish the work on time.* **3.** Likely to change; not dependable: *They stayed home because of the uncertain weather.*
un·cer·tain (un sûr′tən) □*adjective*

uncle *noun* **1.** The brother of one's father or mother. **2.** The husband of one's aunt.
un·cle (ung′kəl) □*noun, plural* **uncles**

uncoil *verb* To release or cause to become released from being in a coil: *The snake uncoiled itself and glided away through the grass.*
un·coil (un koil′) □*verb* **uncoiled, uncoiling, uncoils**

uncomfortable *adjective* **1.** Not comfortable; causing discomfort: *a lumpy, uncomfortable bed.* **2.** Feeling discomfort: *He was uncomfortable because his collar was too tight.* **3.** Uneasy; awkward: *He felt shy and uncomfortable with strangers.*
un·com·fort·a·ble (un kumf′tə bəl *or* un kum′fər tə bəl) □*adjective*

uncommon *adjective* Not common; rare or unusual: *An eclipse of the sun is an uncommon occurrence.*
un·com·mon (un kom′ən) □*adjective*

SYNONYMS: uncommon, rare

These adjectives mean far beyond what is usual or normal: *She is a student of uncommon intelligence. Snowstorms are rare in June.*

---

unconscious *adjective* **1.** Not conscious: *He injured his head and was unconscious for over an hour.* **2.** Not aware; not realizing: *They were so quiet that he was completely unconscious of their presence.* **3.** Not done purposely: *an unconscious error.*
un·con·scious (un kon′shəs) □*adjective*

unconstitutional *adjective* Not in keeping with the principles of the constitution of a state or country.
un·con·sti·tu·tion·al (un kon′sti tōō′shə nəl *or* un kon′sti tyōō′shə nəl) □*adjective*

uncouth *adjective* Crude and vulgar in speech or behavior: *an uncouth person.*
un·couth (un kōōth′) □*adjective*

uncover *verb* **1.** To remove the cover from: *The waiter uncovered the dish.* **2.** To make known; expose: *The investigation uncovered new information.*

un·cov·er (un **kuv′**ər) ☐*verb* **uncovered,
uncovering, uncovers**

undecided *adjective* **1.** Not yet decided upon: *The question was still undecided.* **2.** Not having reached a decision: *We are undecided about whom to invite to the party.*
un·de·cid·ed (un′di **sī′**did) ☐*adjective*

under *preposition* **1.** In or into a lower position than; beneath: *The cat is under the table. The boat will pass under the bridge.* **2.** In or into such a position as to be hidden or covered by: *She is wearing a red blouse under her sweater.* **3.** Less or lower than: *The book will cost under ten dollars.* **4.** Subject to the action or effects of: *under her influence; under treatment; under repair.* **5.** Subject to the guidance, control, or authority of: *studied under the greatest singer of the time.* **6.** Within a division or group: *under this category.*
☐*adverb* In or into a place below or beneath: *The boat tipped over and went under.*
☐*adjective* In a position below or beneath: *He checked the under part of the machine.*
un·der (un′dər) ☐*preposition* ☐*adverb*
  ☐*adjective*

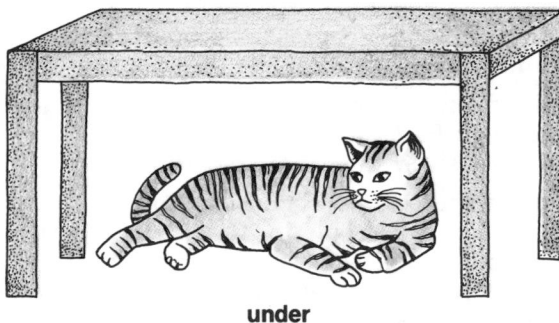

under

under- A prefix that means: **1.** Beneath; below: *underground; underwater.* **2.** Not enough: *underdeveloped.*

underbrush *noun* Small trees, shrubs, and other plants growing beneath tall trees in a forest or wooded area.
un·der·brush (un′dər brush′) ☐*noun*

underclothes *plural noun* Underwear.
un·der·clothes (un′dər klōz′) ☐*plural noun*

underdeveloped *adjective* **1.** Not developed in a full or normal way: *an underdeveloped muscles.* **2.** Having a poorly developed industry and economy: *an underdeveloped nation.*
un·der·de·vel·oped (un′dər di **vel′**əpt)
  ☐*adjective*

underdog *noun* A person or group that is ex-

pected to lose a contest or struggle: *a surprise victory by the underdog.*
un·der·dog (un′dər dôg′) ☐*noun, plural* **underdogs**

underfoot *adjective* **1.** Below or under the feet; on the ground: *The field was nothing but mud underfoot.* **2.** In the way: *The lively puppy was always underfoot.*
un·der·foot (un′dər **foot′**) ☐*adjective*

undergarment *noun* An article of underwear.
un·der·gar·ment (un′dər gär′mənt) ☐*noun, plural* **undergarments**

undergo *verb* To go through or be subjected to; experience: *The Pilgrims underwent many hardships during their first winter in Plymouth.*
un·der·go (un′dər **gō′**) ☐*verb* **underwent, undergone, undergoing, undergoes**

undergone *verb* The past participle of **undergo.**
un·der·gone (un′dər **gôn′**) ☐*verb*

underground *adjective* **1.** Below the surface of the earth: *an underground passage between the two houses.* **2.** Acting or done in secret; hidden: *an underground political organization.*
☐*noun* A secret political organization or movement.
☐*adverb* **1.** Below the surface of the earth: *Miners work underground.* **2.** In or into hiding: *He went underground to avoid capture.*
un·der·ground (un′dər ground′) ☐*adjective*
  ☐*noun* ☐*adverb*

undergrowth *noun* Small trees, plants, and shrubs that grow close to the ground in a forest or wooded area.
un·der·growth (un′dər grōth′) ☐*noun*

underhanded *adjective* Secret and dishonest: *an underhanded scheme.*
un·der·hand·ed (un′dər **han′**did) ☐*adjective*

underline *verb* To draw a line under: *We underlined all the words we didn't understand.*
un·der·line (un′dər līn′) ☐*verb* **underlined, underlining, underlines**

underneath *preposition* Beneath; below; under: *She wore a sweater underneath her rain-*

a	bat	ī	bite	ōō	tool	*th*	feather
ā	make	i	fierce	ou	out	th	bath
â	dare	o	dot	u	nut	hw	wheat
ä	father	ō	no	û	turn	zh	measure
e	net	ô	law, for	ch	church	ə	about, open
ē	be	oi	soil	ng	ring		pencil, atom
i	dip	oo	look	sh	shade		circus

coat. *The baby liked to sit underneath the table.*
□*adverb* Below: *She searched through the pile of papers and found his letter underneath.*
un·der·neath (un′dər **nēth**′) □*preposition*
□*adverb*

underpants *plural noun* Pants worn next to the skin under the outer clothing.
un·der·pants (**un**′dər pants′) □*plural noun*

underpass *noun* A passage underneath something, such as a road that passes under another road.
un·der·pass (**un**′dər pas′) □*noun, plural* **underpasses**

underprivileged *adjective* Not having the advantages or opportunities that most other people have because one is poor.
un·der·priv·i·leged (un′dər **priv**′ə lijd) □*adjective*

underrate *verb* To rate or value too low: *His work was underrated because he was so modest.*
un·der·rate (un′dər **rāt**′) □*verb* **underrated, underrating, underrates**

undersea *adjective* Existing, done, or used under the surface of the sea: *undersea plants.*
un·der·sea (**un**′dər sē′) □*adjective*

undershirt *noun* A light, close-fitting shirt worn next to the skin.
un·der·shirt (**un**′dər shûrt′) □*noun, plural* **undershirts**

underside *noun* The bottom side of something: *the underside of a rock.*
un·der·side (**un**′dər sīd′) □*noun, plural* **undersides**

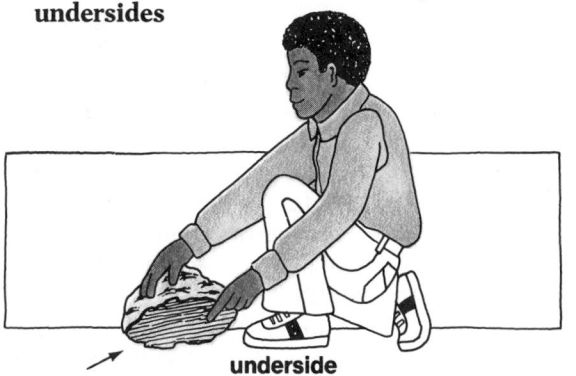

underside

understand *verb* **1.** To get or grasp the meaning of: *That explanation is too difficult [fo]r me to understand. He understands French [wel]l.* **2.** To accept as a fact: *I understood [he woul]d be back by six o'clock.* **3.** To be [___] sympathetic toward: *She really [___] young people and their problems.*

un·der·stand (un′dər **stand**′) □*verb* **understood, understanding, understands**

understandable *adjective* Easy to understand: *an understandable mistake.*
un·der·stand·a·ble (un′dər **stan**′də bəl) □*adjective*

understanding *noun* **1.** A grasp of the meaning of something; knowledge: *He has no understanding of Spanish.* **2.** The ability or capacity to understand: *a problem that was beyond his understanding.* **3.** A friendly and sympathetic relationship. **4.** An agreement, especially after a fight or argument: *We came to an understanding after our quarrel.*
□*adjective* Showing kind or sympathetic feeling: *an understanding friend.*
un·der·stand·ing (un′dər **stan**′ding) □*noun, plural* **understandings** □*adjective*

understood *verb* The past tense and past participle of **understand**: *I understood everything you said.*
un·der·stood (un′dər **stood**′) □*verb*

undertake *verb* **1.** To attempt to do: *We undertook a trip across the country.* **2.** To promise to do something: *Who will undertake the job of writing the class history?*
un·der·take (un′dər **tāk**′) □*verb* **undertook, undertaken, undertaking, undertakes**

undertaken *verb* The past participle of **undertake**: *He has undertaken a difficult job.*
un·der·tak·en (un′dər **tā**′kən) □*verb*

undertaker *noun* A person whose job is to prepare dead people for burial and to make funeral arrangements.
un·der·tak·er (**un**′dər tā′kər) □*noun, plural* **undertakers**

undertone *noun* A low tone: *She spoke in an undertone so that we could hardly hear her.*
un·der·tone (**un**′dər tōn′) □*noun*

undertook *verb* The past tense of **undertake**.
un·der·took (un′dər **took**′) □*verb*

undertow *noun* A current below the surface that pulls away from the shore while the water above moves toward the shore.
un·der·tow (**un**′dər tō′) □*noun, plural* **undertows**

underwater *adjective* Existing, done, or used under the surface of water: *equipment for underwater exploration.*
□*adverb* Under the surface of water: *Can you swim underwater?*
un·der·wa·ter (un′dər **wô**′tər) □*adjective*
□*adverb*

underwater

underwear *noun* Clothing worn next to the skin and under outer clothes.
un·der·wear (**un′**dər wâr′) □*noun*

underwent *verb* The past tense of **undergo**: *He underwent a frightening experience.*
un·der·went (un′dər **went′**) □*verb*

undid *verb* The past tense of **undo**: *He quickly undid the knot.*
un·did (un **did′**) □*verb*

undisturbed *adjective* Not bothered or annoyed; calm: *I remained undisturbed by their criticism.*
un·dis·turbed (un′di **stûrbd′**) □*adjective*

undo *verb* **1.** To do away with or reverse something that has already been done: *His carelessness will undo all our efforts.* **2.** To untie or unfasten: *undid the knot.*
un·do (un **doo′**) □*verb* **undid, undone, undoing, undoes**

undoing *noun* Destruction; ruin: *Love of gambling led to his undoing.*
un·do·ing (un **doo′**ing) □*noun*

undone *verb* The past participle of **undo**: *a mistake that can't be undone.*
un·done (un **dun′**) □*verb*

undress *verb* To take one's clothes off: *She undressed quickly and turned off the light.*
un·dress (un **dres′**) □*verb* **undressed, undressing, undresses**

undying *adjective* Lasting forever: *undying fame.*
un·dy·ing (un **dī′**ing) □*adjective*

unearth *verb* **1.** To dig up out of the ground: *The dog unearthed an old shoe in the garden.* **2.** To discover and reveal; uncover: *The investigation did not unearth any new information.*
un·earth (un **ûrth′**) □*verb* **unearthed, unearthing, unearths**

uneasy *adjective* **1.** Not feeling secure; nervous: *I was uneasy about taking a trip by my-*self. **2.** Not comfortable: *felt uneasy in front of an audience.*
un·eas·y (un **ē′**zē) □*adjective* **uneasier, uneasiest**

unemployed *adjective* Not having a job; out of work.
un·em·ployed (un′em **ploid′**) □*adjective*

unemployment *noun* The fact or condition of being unemployed.
un·em·ploy·ment (un′em **ploi′**mənt) □*noun*

unequal *adjective* **1.** Not equal; not the same: *They were unequal in size.* **2.** Not fair; not evenly matched: *an unequal competition.*
un·e·qual (un **ē′**kwəl) □*adjective*

unequal

uneven *adjective* **1.** Not straight, level, or smooth: *bumpy, uneven ground.* **2.** Not fair or equal: *an uneven contest.*
un·e·ven (un **ē′**vən) □*adjective*

unexpected *adjective* Not expected; happening without warning: *an unexpected attack.*
un·ex·pect·ed (un′ik **spek′**tid) □*adjective*

unfair *adjective* Not fair or right; unjust: *unfair treatment.*
un·fair (un **fâr′**) □*adjective*

unfairness *noun* The condition or quality of being unfair.
un·fair·ness (un **fâr′**nis) □*noun*

unfamiliar *adjective* **1.** Not well known; not easily recognized: *puzzled by the unfamiliar*

a	bat	ī	bite	oo	tool	*th*	feather
ā	make	î	fierce	ou	out	th	bath
â	dare	o	dot	u	nut	hw	wheat
ä	father	ō	no	û	turn	zh	measure
e	net	ô	law, for	ch	church	ə	about, open
ē	be	oi	soil	ng	ring		pencil, atom
i	dip	oo	look	sh	shade		circus

voice. **2.** Not acquainted: *I am unfamiliar with that subject.*
un·fa·mil·iar (un'fə **mil**'yər) □*adjective*

unfasten *verb* To open or untie: *He unfastened his seat belt.*
un·fas·ten (un **fas**'ən) □*verb* **unfastened, unfastening, unfastens**

unfit *adjective* Not fit or suitable for a certain purpose: *water that is unfit to drink.*
un·fit (un **fit**') □*adjective*

unfold *verb* **1.** To open up and spread out: *unfold a blanket.* **2.** To make known; reveal: *unfold a plan.*
un·fold (un **fold**') □*verb* **unfolded, unfolding, unfolds**

unforgettable *adjective* Difficult or impossible to forget: *The trip was an unforgettable thrill.*
un·for·get·ta·ble (un'fər **get**' ə bəl) □*adjective*

unforgivable *adjective* Not deserving to be forgiven or pardoned: *an unforgivable sin.*
un·for·giv·a·ble (un'fər **giv**'ə bəl) □*adjective*

unfortunate *adjective* Not fortunate; unlucky: *an unfortunate accident.*
un·for·tu·nate (un **fôr**'chə nit) □*adjective*

unhappy *adjective* Not happy; sad: *He's unhappy because he lost the race.*
un·hap·py (un **hap**'ē) □*adjective* **unhappier, unhappiest**

unhealthy *adjective* **1.** Showing or having poor health: *an unhealthy appearance.* **2.** Causing poor health; not wholesome: *an unhealthy climate; an unhealthy diet.*
un·health·y (un **hel**'thē) □*adjective* **unhealthier, unhealthiest**

unicorn *noun* An imaginary animal resembling a white horse with a long horn in the middle of its forehead.
u·ni·corn (yōo'ni kôrn') □*noun, plural* **unicorns**

unicorn

uniform *noun* A special suit of clothes worn by the members of a group or organization, such as an army.
□*adjective* **1.** Always the same; not changing: *a uniform rate of speed.* **2.** Having the same form as others; showing little difference: *boards of uniform length.*
u·ni·form (yōo'nə fôrm') □*noun, plural* **uniforms** □*adjective*

unimportant *adjective* Not important; having little or no value or interest: *an unimportant detail.*
un·im·por·tant (un'im **pôr**'tənt) □*adjective*

union *noun* **1.** The act of bringing or joining together two or more people or things: *The school was formed by the union of two small schools.* **2.** A group of workers who join together to protect their interests and improve working conditions. **3. Union** The states that remained loyal to and fought for the Federal government during the Civil War.
un·ion (yōon'yən) □*noun, plural* **unions**

unique *adjective* Being the only one of its kind; having no equal: *a unique manuscript of an ancient poem.*
u·nique (yōo **nēk**') □*adjective*

unison *noun* **1.** Sameness or identity of musical pitch. **2.** Complete or exact agreement.
u·ni·son (yōo'ni sən) □*noun*

unit *noun* **1.** A single thing, group, or person that is part of a larger group or whole: *The book was divided into units covering separate topics.* **2.** A defined or fixed quantity that is used for measuring: *The pound is a unit of weight.* **3.** A machine that does a certain job or a part that has a special purpose in a larger machine or device: *a heating unit.* **4.** The first whole number, represented by the numeral 1.
u·nit (yōo'nit) □*noun, plural* **units**

unite *verb* **1.** To bring together or join so as to form a whole; make one: *He worked to unite the colonies under one government.* **2.** To become joined or combined into a unit: *All the citizens united to fight the enemy.*
u·nite (yōo **nīt**') □*verb* **united, uniting, unites**

United Nations *noun* An international organization founded in 1945 that is made up of members from most of the nations of the world. Its headquarters are in New York City.

United States *noun* The United States of America.

United States of America *noun* A country chiefly in North America and made up of fifty states and the District of Columbia. The capital of the United States of America is Washington, D.C.

unity *noun* **1.** The state or quality of being one. **2.** The state or quality of agreement.
u·ni·ty (yōō′ni tē) □*noun*

universal *adjective* **1.** Affecting the whole world; being everywhere: *Poverty is a universal problem.* **2.** Of, for, or shared by everyone: *There was universal joy when the war ended.*
u·ni·ver·sal (yōō′nə vûr′səl) □*adjective*

universe *noun* All things considered as a whole; everything that exists, including the earth, the planets, and space.
u·ni·verse (yōō′nə vûrs′) □*noun, plural* **universes**

university *noun* A school of higher learning made up of different schools and colleges.
u·ni·ver·si·ty (yōō′nə vûr′si tē) □*noun, plural* **universities**

unjust *adjective* Not just or fair: *unjust criticism; an unjust ruler.*
un·just (un just′) □*adjective*

unkind *adjective* Not kind; harsh or cruel.
un·kind (un kīnd′) □*adjective*

unknown *adjective* Not known: *The author of the book is unknown.*
un·known (un nōn′) □*adjective*

unlawful *adjective* Not right or legal: *Robbery is an unlawful act.* —See Synonyms at **criminal.**
un·law·ful (un lô′fəl) □*adjective*

unless *conjunction* Except on the condition that: *I can't see unless you turn on the light.*
un·less (un les′) □*conjunction*

unlike *adjective* Not alike; different: *These paintings are so unlike that it is difficult to believe they were painted by the same artist.* □*preposition* Different from; not like: *an experience unlike any other I have ever had.*
un·like (un līk′) □*adjective* □*preposition*

unlikely *adjective* **1.** Not likely; not probable: *It's unlikely that we'll arrive on time.* **2.** Not likely to succeed; likely to fail: *He was an unlikely candidate for mayor.*
un·like·ly (un līk′lē) □*adjective* **unlikelier, unlikeliest**

unlimited *adjective* Having no limits: *We are allowed to borrow an unlimited number of books from the library.*
un·lim·it·ed (un lim′i tid) □*adjective*

unload *verb* **1.** To remove the load or cargo from: *They unloaded the truck in an hour.* **2.** To remove cargo: *We unloaded the furniture from the van.* **3.** To remove the ammunition from a firearm: *He unloaded his rifle.*
un·load (un lōd′) □*verb* **unloaded, unloading, unloads**

unlock *verb* **1.** To undo or open the lock of: *I unlocked the drawer and looked inside.* **2.** To reveal or disclose: *The telescope unlocked many of the mysteries of the universe.*
un·lock (un lok′) □*verb* **unlocked, unlocking, unlocks**

unlucky *adjective* **1.** Having bad luck: *She thinks she is an unlucky person because she's never won a prize.* **2.** Causing bad luck: *He believes that black cats are unlucky.*
un·luck·y (un luk′ē) □*adjective* **unluckier, unluckiest**

unmanned *adjective* Without a crew; built to work without a crew: *an unmanned spacecraft.*
un·manned (un mand′) □*adjective*

unmistakable *adjective* Not able to be mistaken for something else: *Her handwriting is unmistakable.*
un·mis·tak·a·ble (un′mi stā′kə bəl) □*adjective*

unnatural *adjective* Different from what normally occurs or happens in nature; not normal; unusual: *an unnatural position of the arms and legs.*
un·nat·u·ral (un nach′ər əl) □*adjective*

unnecessary *adjective* Not necessary; not needed: *It was unnecessary to turn on the heat because the room was already warm.*
un·nec·es·sar·y (un nes′i ser′ē) □*adjective*

unoccupied *adjective* Not occupied; vacant or empty: *I found an unoccupied seat on the train.*
un·oc·cu·pied (un ok′yə pīd′) □*adjective*

unpack *verb* **1.** To remove the contents of: *I unpacked my suitcase.* **2.** To remove from a container or package: *Will you help me unpack the groceries?*

a	bat	ī	bite	ōō	tool	*th*	feather
ā	make	î	fierce	ou	out	th	bath
â	dare	o	dot	u	nut	hw	wheat
ä	father	ō	no	û	turn	zh	measure
e	net	ô	law, for	ch	church	ə	about, open
ē	be	oi	soil	ng	ring		pencil, atom
i	dip	oo	look	sh	shade		circus

un·pack (un **pak′**) □*verb* **unpacked,
unpacking, unpacks**

unpleasant *adjective* Not pleasant; not pleasing: *The medicine has an unpleasant taste.*
un·pleas·ant (un **plez′**ənt) □*adjective*

unpopular *adjective* Not popular; not generally liked or accepted: *an unpopular decision.*
un·pop·u·lar (un **pop′**yə lər) □*adjective*

unprepared *adjective* Not prepared; not
ready: *He was unprepared for the test.*
un·pre·pared (un′pri **pârd′**) □*adjective*

unreasonable *adjective* **1.** Not reasonable;
not having or showing good or common sense:
She has an unreasonable fear of dogs. **2.** Excessive; too high or too great: *They asked an
unreasonable price for their house.*
un·rea·son·a·ble (un **rē′**zə nə bəl) □*adjective*

unreliable *adjective* Not reliable; not to be
depended on or trusted: *I never know what
time it is because my watch is unreliable.*
un·re·li·a·ble (un′ri **lī′**ə bəl) □*adjective*

unrest *noun* A condition of agitation; disturbance: *unrest among the students.*
un·rest (un **rest′**) □*noun*

unruly *adjective* Hard to discipline or control: *an unruly child; an unruly crowd.*
un·ru·ly (un **rōō′**lē) □*adjective* **unrulier,
unruliest**

unsettled *adjective* **1.** Not peaceful or orderly; disturbed: *unsettled conditions after the
earthquake.* **2.** Not decided: *The question is
still unsettled.* **3.** Not paid: *I have a lot of unsettled bills.* **4.** Not being lived in: *Few regions
of the country were still unsettled.*
un·set·tled (un **set′**əld) □*adjective*

unskilled *adjective* **1.** Not having skill or special training: *an unskilled worker.* **2.** Not needing or requiring special skills: *Sweeping floors
is an unskilled job.*
un·skilled (un **skild′**) □*adjective*

unsound *adjective* **1.** Not strong or solid: *The
foundation of the house is unsound.* **2.** Not
based on logic or clear thinking: *Their opinions are usually unsound.*
un·sound (un **sound′**) □*adjective*

unstable *adjective* **1.** Not steady or solid: *The
desk is unstable because one leg is a little
shorter than the others.* **2.** Having a tendency
to change: *unstable prices.*
un·sta·ble (un **stā′**bəl) □*adjective*

unsteady *adjective* **1.** Not steady; shaky or
unstable: *I wouldn't climb up the unsteady ladder.* **2.** Shaky or wavering: *an unsteady voice.*

un·stead·y (un **sted′**ē) □*adjective* **unsteadier,
unsteadiest**

untangle *verb* **1.** To free from tangles or
snarls: *I untangled the yarn.* **2.** To resolve or
clear up: *She was unable to untangle the mystery.*
un·tan·gle (un **tang′**gəl) □*verb* **untangled,
untangling, untangles**

untidy *adjective* Not tidy or neat; messy: *an
untidy room.*
un·ti·dy (un **tī′**dē) □*adjective* **untidier,
untidiest**

untie *verb* To loosen or unfasten: *She untied
the knot in his shoelace.*
un·tie (un **tī′**) □*verb* **untied, untying, unties**

until *preposition* **1.** Up to the time of: *The
party lasted until dawn.* **2.** Before: *You can't
have the bike until tomorrow.*
□*conjunction* **1.** Up to the time that: *They
slept until noon.* **2.** Before: *She couldn't rest
until she finished the task.*
un·til (un **til′**) □*preposition* □*conjunction*

untold *adjective* **1.** Not told or revealed: *an
untold secret.* **2.** Too great or too much to
count: *a person of untold wealth.*
un·told (un **tōld′**) □*adjective*

unused *adjective* **1.** Not in use or never having been used: *Put your papers in the unused
drawer of the desk.* **2.** Not accustomed; not
used to: *She was unused to hard work.*
un·used (un **yōozd′**) □*adjective*

unusual *adjective* Not usual, common, or ordinary; rare: *It's unusual to find him at home
on Saturday morning.*
un·u·su·al (un **yōō′**zhōō əl) □*adjective*

unwind *verb* To become or cause to become
uncoiled.
un·wind (un **wīnd′**) □*verb* **unwound,
unwinding, unwinds**

unwise *adjective* Not wise; foolish: *an unwise
decision.*
un·wise (un **wīz′**) □*adjective* **unwiser,
unwisest**

unwisely *adverb* In a foolish or unwise manner.
un·wise·ly (un **wīz′**lē) □*adverb*

unwound *verb* The past tense and past participle of unwind.
un·wound (un **wound′**) □*verb*

up *adverb* **1.** From a lower to a higher place:
He tossed the ball up in the air. **2.** In, at, or to a
higher position, point, or condition: *She put
the dishes up on the shelves. Prices went up yes-*

terday. **3.** In an erect position: *Please stand up.* **4.** Out of bed: *She gets up before sunrise.* **5.** Entirely; thoroughly: *Eat up everything on your plate.*
□*adjective* **1.** Moving or directed upward: *an up elevator.* **2.** In a high position; not down: *The sun is up.* **3.** Out of bed: *We've been up since seven o'clock.* **4.** Active; busy: *up and around.* **5.** Informed; having knowledge: *She is up on the latest news.* **6.** Finished; over: *Time's up.*
□*preposition* **1.** From a lower to a higher place or position in or on: *We walked slowly up the hill.* **2.** Toward the source of: *The boat sailed up the river.*
   up to 1. Busy with; engaged in: *What are you up to?* **2.** Having the authority or responsibility for: *The decision is up to him.*
up (up) □*adverb* □*adjective* □*preposition*

upholster *verb* To provide or fit chairs and other furniture with stuffing, cushions, or covering.
up·hol·ster (up hōl′stər) □*verb* **upholstered, upholstering, upholsters**

upkeep *noun* The maintenance of something in proper condition or repair: *My father works hard on the upkeep of our house.*
up·keep (up′kēp′) □*noun*

upon *preposition* On: *sat down upon a flat rock; a book lying upon the table.*
up·on (ə pon′ *or* ə pôn′) □*preposition*

upper *adjective* Higher in place or position: *This elevator serves only the upper floors of the building.*
up·per (up′ər) □*adjective*

upper hand *adjective* A position of control or advantage: *We gained the upper hand early in the game.*

upright *adjective* **1.** In a vertical position; straight up; erect: *Upright posts support the fence.* **2.** Good or honest; moral: *Upright people treat others fairly.*
up·right (up′rīt′) □*adjective*

uprising *noun* A revolt or rebellion against authority.
up·ris·ing (up′rī′zing) □*noun, plural* **uprisings**

uproar *noun* A condition of noisy excitement and confusion: *The fans were in an uproar when she won the championship.*
up·roar (up′rôr′) □*noun*

uproot *verb* **1.** To tear up by the roots; remove a plant from the ground: *Three large*

trees were uprooted by the flood. **2.** To force to leave: *The earthquake uprooted many people.*
up·root (up rŏōt′ *or* up **root**′) □*verb* **uprooted, uprooting, uproots**

upset *verb* **1.** To tip or knock over; overturn: *He upset the bowl of soup.* **2.** To disturb the order or arrangement of; interfere with: *The train strike upset our vacation plans.* **3.** To disturb or make worried: *We were upset by the bad news.* **4.** To make sick: *Onions upset my stomach.* **5.** To defeat unexpectedly in a game or contest: *Our team upset the state champions last season.*
□*noun* An unexpected result in a game or contest.
up·set (up **set**′) □*verb* **upset, upsetting, upsets** □*noun* (up′set), *plural* **upsets**

upshot *noun* The final result; outcome.
up·shot (up′shot′) □*noun*

upside down *adverb* **1.** With the top and bottom parts reversed in position: *She turned the bank upside down and shook out some coins.* **2.** In or into great disorder or confusion: *He turned his room upside down in order to find his notebook.*
up·side down (up′sīd **down**′) □*adverb*

upstairs *adverb* Up the stairs; on or to an upper floor: *ran quickly upstairs.*
□*adjective* On an upper floor: *an upstairs bedroom.*
□*noun* The upper floor of a building.
up·stairs (up′stârz′) □*adverb* □*adjective* □*noun*

upstream *adverb* In the direction toward the source of a stream or current: *They rowed a mile upstream.*
up·stream (up′strēm′) □*adverb*

up-to-date *adjective* Showing or using the latest improvements or style: *up-to-date equipment; up-to-date styles.*
up-to-date (up′tə dāt′) □*adjective*

upward *adverb* From a lower to a higher place, level, or condition: *The rocket flew upward and out of sight.*
□*adjective* Moving from a lower to a higher

a bat	ī bite	ōō tool	th feather
ā make	î fierce	ou out	th bath
â dare	o dot	u nut	hw wheat
ä father	ō no	û turn	zh measure
e net	ô law, for	ch church	ə about, open
ē be	oi soil	ng ring	pencil, atom
i dip	oo look	sh shade	circus

place, level, or condition: *the upward flight of the hawk; an upward glance.*
up·ward (up′wərd) □*adverb* □*adjective*

uranium *noun* A heavy, radioactive silver-white element that is used to produce nuclear energy.
u·ra·ni·um (yoo rā′nē əm) □*noun*

WORD HISTORY: **uranium**

Uranium is named after Uranus, one of the planets. The element was discovered a short time after the discovery of the planet.

---

urban *adjective* Of, relating to, or being a city: *urban problems; urban areas.*
ur·ban (ûr′bən) □*adjective*

urge *verb* **1.** To push or force onward: *He urged the horse on with a shout.* **2.** To try to convince; plead with: *She urged me to attend the meeting.* **3.** To recommend or argue for strongly: *We urged the mayor to run for office again.*
□*noun* A strong desire; an impulse: *I had a sudden urge to go swimming.*
urge (ûrj) □*verb* **urged, urging, urges**
□*noun, plural* **urges**

urgent *adjective* Needing immediate action or attention: *an urgent message.*
ur·gent (ûr′jənt) □*adjective*

urine *noun* A clear or yellow-colored fluid produced by the kidneys and discharged as waste from the body.
u·rine (yoor′in) □*noun*

urn *noun* **1.** A large vase set on a base and often used for decoration. **2.** A closed container, usually with a faucet, for serving hot drinks such as coffee and tea.
urn (ûrn) □*noun, plural* **urns**

urn

us *pronoun* The objective case of **we:** *She saw us at the theater. He told us the latest news. Please leave the keys with us.*
us (us) □*pronoun*

US or **U.S.** An abbreviation for **United States.**

USA or **U.S.A.** An abbreviation for **United States of America.**

usage *noun* **1.** A way of using something; treatment: *The radio was damaged from rough usage.* **2.** The way in which people actually use the words and phrases of a language.
us·age (yoo′sij *or* yoo′zij) □*noun, plural* **usages**

use *verb* **1.** To bring into action or service for a particular purpose: *Use that cloth only for dusting.* **2.** To take or consume regularly: *He uses too much sugar in his tea.* **3.** To finish completely; consume: *Did you use up the milk?*
□*noun* **1.** The act of using: *We saw the planets with the use of a telescope.* **2.** The condition of being used: *in constant use.* **3.** A method or way of using: *demonstrated the correct use of the equipment.* **4.** The right or privilege of using: *had the use of the auditorium for our rehearsal.* **5.** The power or ability of using: *lost the use of his voice.* **6.** The need to use something: *I have no use for a typewriter.*
used to (yoos′too) **1.** Accustomed to; familiar with: *It took me a while to get used to wearing braces.* **2.** Used to indicate a practice or fact in the past: *We used to go swimming there every Saturday.*
use (yooz) □*verb* **used, using, uses** □*noun* (yoos), *plural* **uses**

used *adjective* Not new; having been used by someone else: *a used car.*
used (yoozd) □*adjective*

useful *adjective* Capable of being used for some purpose; helpful: *a tool useful for drawing plans.*
use·ful (yoos′fəl) □*adjective*

useless *adjective* **1.** Of little or no worth or help: *a useless suggestion.* **2.** Having no result or effect: *It's useless to try to make her change her mind.*
use·less (yoos′lis) □*adjective*

usher *noun* A person who leads or takes people to their seats.
□ *verb* To act as an usher.
ush·er (ush′ər) □*noun, plural* **ushers** □*verb* **ushered, ushering, ushers**

usual *adjective* Common or ordinary; normal: *took her usual way home.* —See Synonyms at **ordinary.**
u·su·al (yŏo′zhŏo əl) □*adjective*

utensil *noun* A tool or container that is used especially in a kitchen: *cooking utensils.* —See Synonyms at **instrument.**
u·ten·sil (yŏo ten′səl) □*noun, plural* **utensils**

utensil

utility *noun* **1.** The ability or capacity to be useful. **2.** A company that provides a public service. Telephone, gas, and electric companies are utilities.
u·til·i·ty (yŏo til′i tē) □*noun, plural* **utilities**

utmost *adjective* Of the highest or greatest degree or amount: *a matter of the utmost importance.*
□*noun* The greatest possible effort or power: *gave her utmost to the job.*
ut·most (ut′mōst′) □*adjective* □*noun*

utter¹ *verb* **1.** To speak; say: *I did not utter a word.* **2.** To give out as a sound: *uttered a sigh of relief.*
ut·ter (ut′ər) □*verb* **uttered, uttering, utters**

utter² *adjective* Complete; total: *insisted on utter silence in the library.*
ut·ter (ut′ər) □*adjective*

utterance *noun* Something that is uttered.
ut·ter·ance (ut′ər əns) □*noun, plural* **utterances**

a	bat	ī	bite	ŏo	tool	*th*	feather
ā	make	î	fierce	ou	out	th	bath
â	dare	o	dot	u	nut	hw	wheat
ä	father	ō	no	û	turn	zh	measure
e	net	ô	law, for	ch	church	ə	about, open
ē	be	oi	soil	ng	ring		pencil, atom
i	dip	oo	look	sh	shade		circus

ANCIENT GREEK

The letter **V** has evolved from many forms of ancient writing. One of the earliest known examples is the Greek character shown above, which dates from almost 3,000 years ago. Over the years, artists and designers have created their own versions of the English letter **V**. Some of the more common examples seen today are shown below.

HANDWRITING	CALLIGRAPHY	MODERN SANS SERIF	MODERN SERIF	SCRIPT

---

v or **V**   *noun* The twenty-second letter of the English alphabet.
v or **V** (vē) ▢*noun, plural* **v's** or **V's**

vacant *adjective* Not occupied or filled; empty: *We found two vacant seats at the back of the room.* —See Synonyms at **empty.**
va·cant (vā′kənt) ▢*adjective*

vacation *noun* A period of rest from school, work, or other regular activities.
va·ca·tion (vā kā′shən) ▢*noun, plural* **vacations**

vaccinate *verb* To inoculate with a vaccine.
vac·ci·nate (vak′sə nāt′) ▢*verb* **vaccinated, vaccinating, vaccinates**

vaccination *noun* The act of giving a vaccine.
vac·ci·na·tion (vak′sə nā′shən) ▢*noun, plural* **vaccinations**

vaccine *noun* A preparation consisting of the weakened or dead germs of a disease that is used to inoculate a person against that disease. Vaccines are used against diseases such as measles and smallpox.
vac·cine (vak sēn′) ▢*noun, plural* **vaccines**

WORD HISTORY: **vaccine**

Vaccine comes from the Latin word for "cow." The first vaccine was prepared from a virus that causes a disease in cows.

---

vacuum *noun* **1.** A space that is completely empty of matter. **2.** A space that is almost completely empty of air. **3.** A vacuum cleaner. ▢*verb* To clean with a vacuum cleaner: *vacuum a rug.*
vac·u·um (vak′yōō əm *or* vak′yōōm) ▢*noun, plural* **vacuums** ▢*verb* **vacuumed, vacuuming, vacuums**

vacuum cleaner *noun* A machine for cleaning floors and furniture by sucking up dirt and dust.

vague *adjective* Not clear or distinct: *We could see only a vague shape in the dim light. She didn't have the vaguest idea of what to do next.*
vague (vāg) ▢*adjective* **vaguer, vaguest**

vain *adjective* **1.** Overly proud of oneself or one's appearance: *He is a vain, foolish man who takes hours to get dressed.* **2.** Without success: *I made a vain attempt to solve the problem.*
   in vain Without success: *We tried in vain to get his attention.*
vain (vān) ▢*adjective* **vainer, vainest**

valentine *noun* **1.** A card sent to someone one likes or loves on Valentine's Day. **2.** A person chosen to be one's sweetheart on Valentine's Day.
val·en·tine (val′ən tīn′) ▢*noun, plural* **valentines**

Valentine's Day *noun* February 14, celebrated as a day for sending valentines.

valiant *adjective* Courageous; brave: *She made a valiant effort to put out the fire.*
val·iant (val′yənt) ▢*adjective*

valid *adjective* **1.** Supported by facts or evidence; true: *His argument is valid. He doesn't have a valid reason for being late.* **2.** Being in force according to the law: *That license is only valid till the end of the month.*
val·id (**val′**id) □*adjective*

valley *noun* An area of low land between mountains or hills.
val·ley (**val′**ē) □*noun, plural* **valleys**

valuable *adjective* **1.** Worth a great deal of money: *a valuable antique.* **2.** Of great importance or use: *My past experience was valuable when I applied for a new job.*
□*noun* **valuables** Things one owns that are worth a great deal of money: *Our silverware and other valuables were locked away.*
val·u·a·ble (**val′**yo͞o ə bəl) □*adjective*
□*noun, plural* **valuables**

SYNONYMS: **valuable, priceless**

These adjectives mean worth a great deal of money: *a valuable diamond bracelet; a priceless antique.*

---

value *noun* The worth, importance, or usefulness of something: *An old, rusty car has little value. He places a great value on honesty.*
□*verb* **1.** To estimate the value of: *a rare book that was valued at a thousand dollars.* **2.** To think very highly of: *I value your friendship.* — See Synonyms at **appreciate.**
val·ue (**val′**yo͞o) □*noun, plural* **values** □*verb* **valued, valuing, values**

valve *noun* **1.** A device that controls the flow of liquids or gases. **2.** One of the two parts of the shell of an animal such as a clam, oyster, or scallop.
valve (valv) □*noun, plural* **valves**

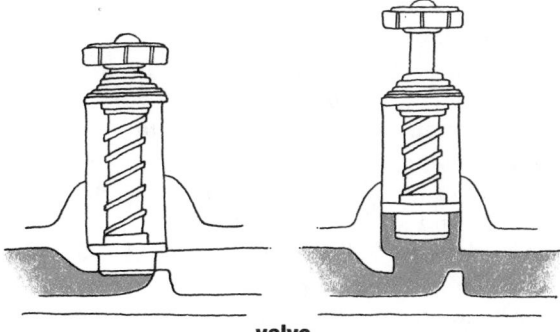

valve

van *noun* A covered truck for moving animals, furniture, and other goods.
van (van) □*noun, plural* **vans**

vandal *noun* Someone who destroys or damages property.
van·dal (**van′**dəl) □*noun, plural* **vandals**

vane *noun* **1.** A device that turns to show the direction of the wind. **2.** A thin, flat blade, as of a windmill or fan.
vane (vān) □*noun, plural* **vanes**

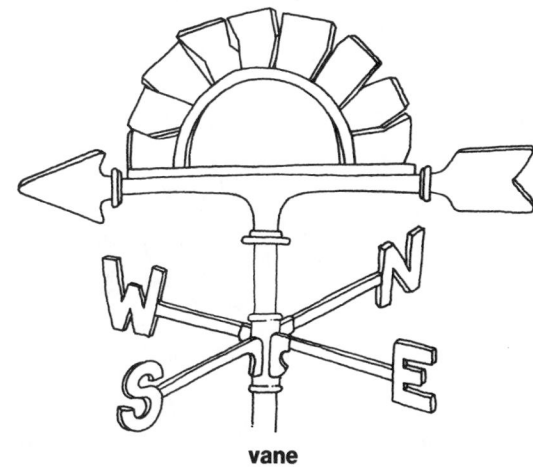

vane

vanilla *noun* A flavoring made from the dried seed pods of a tropical orchid. Vanilla is used in ice cream, cakes, and other sweets.
va·nil·la (və **nil′**ə) □*noun*

vanish *verb* To disappear; become invisible: *The plane vanished into the clouds.*
van·ish (**van′**ish) □*verb* **vanished, vanishing, vanishes**

vanity *noun* Too much pride in one's looks or ability; conceit.
van·i·ty (**van′**i tē) □*noun, plural* **vanities**

vapor *noun* Fine particles of matter in the air. Mist, steam, and smoke are all forms of vapor.
va·por (**vā′**pər) □*noun, plural* **vapors**

variable *adjective* Likely to change: *Weather is extremely variable in New England.*
var·i·a·ble (**vâr′**ē ə bəl) □*adjective*

variation *noun* **1.** A change from the normal or usual: *We made some variations in her recipe and produced a new dish.* **2.** Something that is similar to another thing, but with slight

a	bat	ī	bite	o͞o	tool	*th*	feather
ā	make	î	fierce	ou	out	th	bath
â	dare	o	dot	u	nut	hw	wheat
ä	father	ō	no	û	turn	zh	measure
e	net	ô	law, for	ch	church	ə	about, open
ē	be	oi	soil	ng	ring		pencil, atom
i	dip	oo	look	sh	shade		circus

changes: *The new dance is a variation of the waltz.*
var·i·a·tion (vâr′ē ā′shən) □*noun, plural* **variations**

variety *noun* **1.** Difference or change that keeps things from being dull: *There is not much variety in my job.* **2.** A number of different kinds within the same group: *He put a variety of vegetables in the salad.* **3.** Something that is different in kind: *new varieties of wheat.*
va·ri·e·ty (və rī′i tē) □*noun, plural* **varieties**

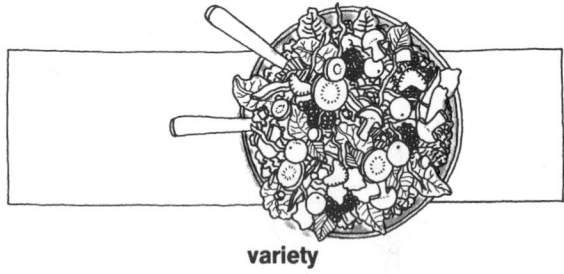

variety

various *adjective* **1.** Of different kinds: *many books on various subjects.* **2.** More than one; several: *I looked for the dress I wanted in various stores.*
var·i·ous (vâr′ē əs) □*adjective*

varnish *noun* A liquid that dries to leave a thin, hard, shiny, clear surface: *put a new coat of varnish on the floor.*
□*verb* To cover or coat with a varnish.
var·nish (vär′nish) □*noun, plural* **varnishes** □*verb* **varnished, varnishing, varnishes**

vary *verb* **1.** To be or become different: *The weather varies from day to day near the coast.* **2.** To make different; give variety to: *I try to vary my routine to avoid boredom.* —See Synonyms at **change.**
var·y (vâr′ē) □*verb* **varied, varying, varies**

vase *noun* A container that is usually deeper than it is wide and is used to hold flowers or as an ornament.
vase (vās *or* vāz *or* väz) □*noun, plural* **vases**

vase

vast *adjective* Very great in area, size, or amount: *a vast desert.*
vast (vast) □*adjective* **vaster, vastest**

vat *noun* A large tank or tub used for liquids.
vat (vat) □*noun, plural* **vats**

vault¹ *noun* A room or compartment with strong walls, used for keeping valuables safe: *She put her jewels in a vault at the bank.*
vault (vôlt) □*noun, plural* **vaults**

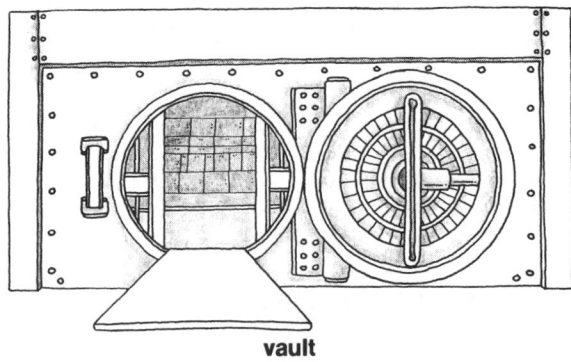

vault

vault² *verb* To jump or leap over: *The horse vaulted the fence.*
vault (vôlt) □*verb* **vaulted, vaulting, vaults**

veal *noun* The meat of a calf.
veal (vēl) □*noun*

vegetable *noun* A plant whose roots, leaves, flowers, or other parts are used as food. Turnips, cabbage, onions, potatoes, and broccoli are vegetables.
□*adjective* Of or made from vegetables: *Do you like vegetable soup?*
veg·e·ta·ble (vej′i tə bəl) □*noun, plural* **vegetables** □*adjective*

vegetarian *noun* A person that eats food from plants and does not eat meat.
veg·e·tar·i·an (vej′i târ′ē ən) □*noun, plural* **vegetarians**

vegetation *noun* Plants or plant life: *the thick vegetation of a fertile valley.*
veg·e·ta·tion (vej′i tā′shən) □*noun*

vehicle *noun* Something used for moving people or goods. Cars, trains, bicycles, airplanes, and ships are all vehicles.
ve·hi·cle (vē′i kəl) □*noun, plural* **vehicles**

veil *noun* **1.** A fine piece of fabric worn over the head and shoulders: *a bridal veil.* **2.** Something that covers or hides: *a veil of secrecy.*
□*verb* **1.** To cover with a veil: *Women veil their faces in some countries.* **2.** To hide or cover: *He tried to veil his disappointment with a grin.*

veil (vāl) □*noun, plural* **veils** □*verb* **veiled, veiling, veils**

veil

vein *noun* **1.** A blood vessel that carries blood to the heart from other parts of the body. **2.** One of the narrow tubes in an insect's wing or a leaf. **3.** A deposit of an ore or a mineral in the earth: *a vein of coal.* **4.** A streak of color in marble, wood, or other material: *pink marble with gray veins.* **5.** A mood: *He spoke in a cheerful vein.*
vein (vān) □*noun, plural* **veins**

velocity *noun* Speed or quickness of motion: *The velocity of the wind caused great damage.*
ve·loc·i·ty (və **los'**i tē) □*noun, plural* **velocities**

velvet *noun* A cloth with a smooth, thick pile. Velvet is made of silk, linen, or other materials.
vel·vet (**vel'**vit) □*noun, plural* **velvets**

vending machine *noun* A machine that delivers small items when one or more coins are put into a slot. Vending machines sell drinks, candy, stamps, and many other things.
vend·ing machine (**ven'**ding) □*noun*

vending machine

vendor *noun* Someone who sells goods: *There is a hot dog vendor on the corner.*
ven·dor (**ven'**dər) □*noun, plural* **vendors**

Venetian blind *noun* A window blind with many horizontal or vertical slats. The slats can be opened and closed and the blind can be raised or lowered.
Ve·ne·tian blind (və **nē'**shən) □*noun*

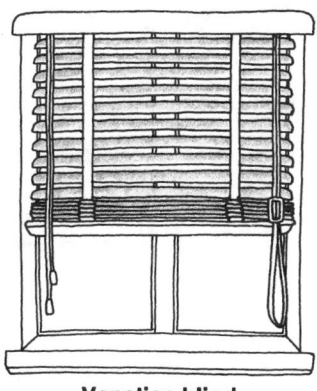

Venetian blind

venom *noun* The poison of certain snakes, spiders, or other creatures. It can be passed to a person or another animal through a bite or sting.
ven·om (**ven'**əm) □*noun, plural* **venoms**

vent *noun* An opening for gas, liquid, or vapor: *A vent in the attic permits hot air to escape.*
□*verb* To let out; express: *vented his anger by banging on the table.*
vent (vent) □*noun, plural* **vents** □*verb* **vented, venting, vents**

ventilation *noun* The circulation of air: *We opened the windows to get some ventilation.*
ven·ti·la·tion (ven'təl **ā'**shən) □*noun*

ventricle *noun* Either of the two chambers of the heart that pump blood into the arteries.
ven·tri·cle (**ven'**tri kəl) □*noun, plural* **ventricles**

ventriloquist *noun* Someone who can speak in such a way that the sound appears to come from a place other than the speaker's mouth

a bat	ī bite	o͞o tool	*th* feather
ā make	i fierce	ou out	th bath
â dare	o dot	u nut	hw wheat
ä father	ō no	û turn	zh measure
e net	ô law, for	ch church	ə about, open
ē be	oi soil	ng ring	pencil, atom
i dip	oo look	sh shade	circus

and lips: *The ventriloquist had a dummy named Harold.*
ven·tril·o·quist (ven tril′ ə kwist) □*noun, plural* **ventriloquists**

ventriloquist

venture *noun* A task or action that involves risks and possible danger: *a daring venture to rescue two captives from the enemy fort.*
□*verb* **1.** To take a risk with possible loss or danger: *He ventured his life to save the drowning boy.* **2.** To say in spite of the rash of criticism: *venture an opinion.*
ven·ture (ven′ chər) □*noun, plural* **ventures**
□*verb* **ventured, venturing, ventures**

Venus *noun* A planet of our solar system that is the second in order from the sun. Venus is brighter than any other natural object in the sky except the sun and the moon.
Ve·nus (vē′ nəs) □*noun*

veranda *noun* A porch or balcony with a roof.
ve·ran·da (və ran′ də) □*noun, plural* **verandas**

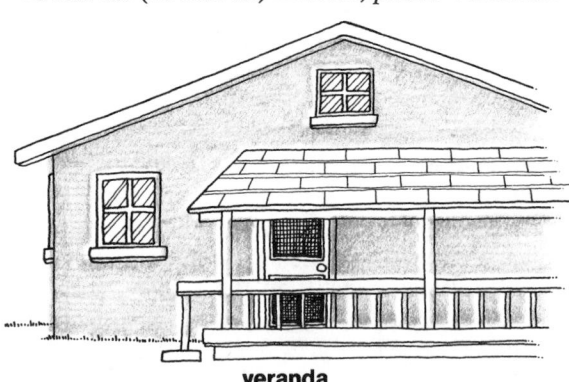
veranda

verb *noun* Any of a class of words that express an action or a state of being. For example, the words *be, run,* and *happen* are verbs.
verb (vûrb) □*noun, plural* **verbs**

verbal *adjective* Expressed in words; spoken: *All the students gave verbal reports on their projects.*
verb·al (vûr′ bəl) □*adjective*

verdict *noun* The decision made by a jury at the end of a trial: *The jury needed three hours to reach a verdict.*
ver·dict (vûr′ dikt′) □*noun, plural* **verdicts**

versatile *adjective* **1.** Able to do many things well: *a versatile student who does well in all subjects.* **2.** Having many different uses: *a versatile tool.*
ver·sa·tile (vûr′ sə til) □*adjective*

verse *noun* **1.** Words put together with rhythm or rhyme or both; poetry. **2.** One section or stanza of a poem or song: *a long poem with ten verses.* **3.** A short section of a chapter of the Bible.
verse (vûrs) □*noun, plural* **verses**

version *noun* **1.** A description or an account from one particular point of view: *Everyone had a different version of how the fire started.* **2.** A translation: *He has an Italian version of the Bible.*
ver·sion (vûr′ zhən) □*noun, plural* **versions**

vertebra *noun* Any of the small bones that make up the backbone.
ver·te·bra (vûr′ tə brə) □*noun, plural* **vertebras**

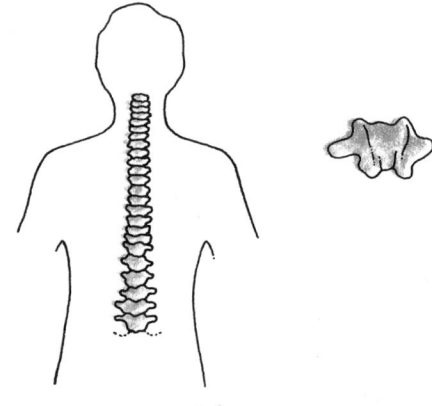
vertebra

vertebrate *noun* An animal that has a backbone. Fish, amphibians, reptiles, birds, and mammals are all vertebrates.
□*adjective* Having a backbone: *A whale is a vertebrate animal.*
ver·te·brate (vûr′ tə brāt′ *or* vûr′ tə brit) □*noun, plural* **vertebrates** □*adjective*

vertical *adjective* Straight up and down; upright: *The roof of our porch is supported by*

vertical posts.
ver·ti·cal (vûr′ti kəl) □*adjective*

very   *adverb* **1.** In a high degree; extremely: *It is very cold today.* **2.** Truly; indeed: *That is the very same car we saw yesterday.*
□*adjective* **1.** Absolute: *the very edge of the cliff.* **2.** Exactly the same; identical: *That is the very thing I was about to say.* **3.** Nothing more than; mere: *The very mention of his name frightened the boys.* **4.** Precise; exact: *The tree is in the very center of town.*
ver·y (ver′ē) □*adverb* □*adjective*

vessel   *noun* **1.** A ship or large boat. **2.** A hollow container, such as a cup, pitcher, or jar. **3.** A narrow tube in a body or a plant through which liquids flow: *a blood vessel.*
ves·sel (ves′əl) □*noun, plural* **vessels**

vest   *noun* A short, sleeveless jacket worn over a shirt or a blouse.
vest (vest) □*noun, plural* **vests**

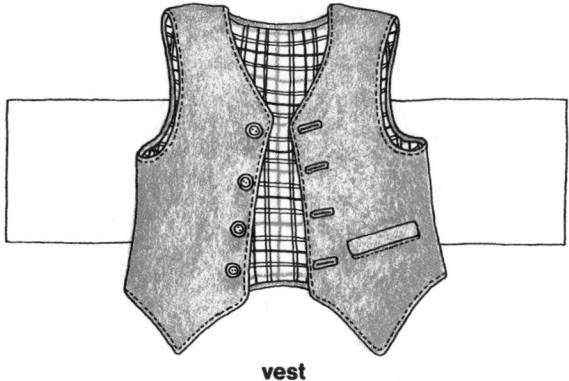

vest

veteran   *noun* **1.** Someone who has served in the armed forces. **2.** Someone who has had a great deal of experience: *He was a veteran of many political campaigns.*
□*adjective* Having had much experience.
vet·er·an (vet′ər ən) □*noun, plural* **veterans** □*adjective*

veterinarian   *noun* A doctor trained to treat animals.
vet·er·i·nar·i·an (vet′ər ə när′ē ən) □*noun, plural* **veterinarians**

veto   *noun* The right or power to keep a bill or measure from becoming a law.
□*verb* **1.** To use the power of veto: *The governor vetoed the new tax law.* **2.** To refuse to consent to; forbid: *My father vetoed my plan to get a job after school.*
ve·to (vē′tō) □*noun, plural* **vetoes** □*verb* **vetoed, vetoing, vetoes**

WORD HISTORY: veto

Veto is from a Latin word meaning "I forbid."

---

via   *preposition* By way of: *We drove home via the old road.*
vi·a (vī′ə) □*preposition*

vibrate   *verb* To move back and forth or from side to side.
vi·brate (vī′brāt′) □*verb* **vibrated, vibrating, vibrates**

vibration   *noun* A very rapid movement back and forth: *Vibrations from the explosion could be felt 50 miles away.*
vi·bra·tion (vī brā′shən) □*noun, plural* **vibrations**

vice-president   *noun* An officer who ranks just below a president and who takes the place of a president if it becomes necessary.
vice-pres·i·dent (vīs′prez′i dənt) □*noun, plural* **vice-presidents**

vice versa   *adverb* The other way around: *I helped him mow his lawn and vice versa.*
vi·ce ver·sa (vī′sə vûr′sə) □*adverb*

vicinity   *noun* The nearby or surrounding area: *There are many theaters and restaurants in the vicinity of his apartment.*
vi·cin·i·ty (vi sin′i tē) □*noun, plural* **vicinities**

vicious   *adjective* **1.** Full of spite; mean: *a vicious lie.* **2.** Marked by evil; wicked: *a vicious murder.* **3.** Savage and dangerous: *a vicious dog that attacked strangers.*
vi·cious (vish′əs) □*adjective*

victim   *noun* **1.** Someone that is harmed or killed: *Everyone contributed food and clothing to the victims of the fire.* **2.** Someone who suffers because of tricks or cheating: *I was the victim of a cruel joke.*
vic·tim (vik′tim) □*noun, plural* **victims**

victorious   *adjective* Being the winner in a battle, contest, or struggle: *He was the general of a victorious army.*
vic·to·ri·ous (vik tôr′ē əs) □*adjective*

a bat	ī bite	ōō tool	*th* feather
ā make	î fierce	ou out	th bath
â dare	o dot	u nut	hw wheat
ä father	ō no	û turn	zh measure
e net	ô law, for	ch church	ə about, open
ē be	oi soil	ng ring	pencil, atom
i dip	oo look	sh shade	circus

victory *noun* The winning of a battle, contest, or struggle; triumph.
vic·to·ry (vik′tə rē) ▢*noun, plural* **victories**

SYNONYMS: **victory, conquest, triumph**

These nouns mean the winning of a battle, contest, or struggle: *Being elected mayor was the greatest victory of her political career. The doctor developed a vaccine that was responsible for the conquest of polio. That famous general has many military triumphs to his credit.*

---

video *noun* The picture part of a television broadcast or of computer output.
vi·de·o (vid′ē ō) ▢*noun*

video cassette *noun* A videotape, as of a movie, that is contained in a cassette and that can be played back on a television set.

videodisc or **videodisk** *noun* A recording of sounds and pictures, as of a movie, that can be played back on a television set.
vid·e·o·disc or **vid·e·o·disk** (vid′ē ō disk′) ▢*noun, plural* **videodiscs** or **videodisks**

video game *noun* An electronic game in which images on a television screen are controlled by dials and buttons.

video game

videotape *noun* A special kind of magnetic recording tape used to record the picture and sound of movies and television programs.
videotape (vid′ē ō tāp′) ▢*noun, plural* **videotapes**

view *noun* **1.** The act of seeing something; sight: *Their first view of America was from the airplane.* **2.** Everything that can be seen from a particular place: *The house has a lovely view of the ocean.* **3.** The area that is as far as the eye can see: *The ship sailed out of our view.* **4.** An opinion; idea: *We all had different views on how to solve the problem.*

▢*verb* **1.** To look at: *view a movie.* **2.** To think about; regard: *She viewed the situation with great alarm.*
view (vyo͞o) ▢*noun, plural* **views** ▢*verb* **viewed, viewing, views**

viewpoint *noun* A way of thinking about something: *His viewpoint is quite different from mine.*
view·point (vyo͞o′point′) ▢*noun, plural* **viewpoints**

vigor *noun* Physical energy or strength: *We played with vigor and determination.*
vig·or (vig′ər) ▢*noun*

vigorous *adjective* Full of or done with vigor; lively: *a vigorous man who walks the ten miles to his office every day.*
vig·o·rous (vig′ər əs) ▢*adjective*

village *noun* A group of houses and buildings that is smaller than a town.
vil·lage (vil′ij) ▢*noun, plural* **villages**

villain *noun* Someone who is wicked or evil: *The villain of the story is a selfish old king.*
vil·lain (vil′ən) ▢*noun, plural* **villains**

vine *noun* A plant with a long stem that grows along the ground or climbs on something for support.
vine (vīn) ▢*noun, plural* **vines**

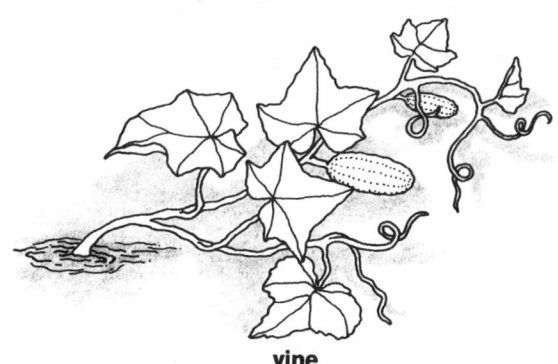

vine

vinegar *noun* A sour liquid that is made from fermented wine, cider, or other liquids. Vinegar is used in flavoring and preserving foods and in salad dressings.
vin·e·gar (vin′i gər) ▢*noun, plural* **vinegars**

WORD HISTORY: **vinegar**

Vinegar comes from French words that mean "sour wine."

---

vineyard *noun* A place where grapes are grown.

vine·yard (vin′yərd) ☐*noun, plural*
vineyards

vinyl *noun* A plastic material that is tough
and shiny, bends easily, and is used to make
such things as raincoats and phonograph records.
vi·nyl (vī′nəl) ☐*noun, plural* **vinyls**

viola *noun* A stringed musical instrument
that is similar to but larger than a violin.
vi·o·la (vē ō′lə) ☐*noun, plural* **violas**

viola

violate *verb* To fail to follow or obey; break:
Good citizens do not violate the law.
vi·o·late (vī′ə lāt′) ☐*verb* **violated, violating,**
violates

violence *noun* Very strong physical force:
Disagreements cannot be solved by the use of
violence.
vi·o·lence (vī′ə ləns) ☐*noun*

violent *adjective* **1.** Showing, having, or resulting from great physical force or rough action: *a violent storm.* **2.** Showing or having
strong feelings: *You must learn to control your*
violent temper.
vi·o·lent (vī′ə lənt) ☐*adjective*

violet *noun* A plant with small purple, pink,
yellow, or white flowers.
vi·o·let (vī′ə lit) ☐*noun, plural* **violets**

violet

violin *noun* A musical instrument that has
four strings and is played with a bow.
vi·o·lin (vī′ə lin′) ☐*noun, plural* **violins**

virgin *adjective* In the original or natural
state; not used or touched: *a virgin forest in*
which no trees have ever been cut.
vir·gin (vûr′jin) ☐*adjective*

virtue *noun* **1.** The condition of being morally good: *A person of virtue does not lie or*
steal. **2.** A particular example of moral goodness: *Kindness is a virtue.* **3.** A particular good
quality: *One virtue of our new house is that it's*
close to the school.
vir·tue (vûr′chōō) ☐*noun, plural* **virtues**

virus *noun* A form of living matter that is too
small to be seen through an ordinary microscope. Viruses cause diseases in human beings, animals, and plants. Measles, polio,
mumps, and the common cold are all caused
by viruses.
vi·rus (vī′rəs) ☐*noun, plural* **viruses**

vise *noun* A device with a pair of jaws that
can be opened and closed by means of a lever
or screw. A vise is used to hold something in
place so that it can be worked on.
vise (vīs) ☐*noun, plural* **vises**

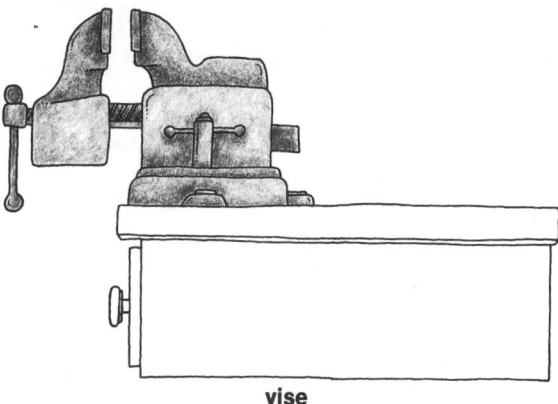
vise

visible *adjective* **1.** Capable of being seen:
The whole town is visible from the top of the
building. **2.** Easily seen or understood; clear:
He had no job and no visible means of support.
vis·i·ble (viz′ə bəl) ☐*adjective*

a bat	ī bite	ōō tool	th feather
ā make	î fierce	ou out	th bath
â dare	o dot	u nut	hw wheat
ä father	ō no	û turn	zh measure
e net	ô law, for	ch church	ə about, open
ē be	oi soil	ng ring	pencil, atom
i dip	oo look	sh shade	circus

vision *noun* **1.** The sense of sight; ability to see: *I wear glasses to correct my vision.* **2.** Unusual imagination and foresight: *She has the vision necessary to design the city of the future.* **3.** Something that is imagined: *He has visions of becoming President of the United States.*
vi·sion (vizh′ən) □*noun, plural* **visions**

visit *verb* To go or come to see for a while: *We have to visit our aunt tonight.*
□*noun* A short call or stay.
vis·it (viz′it) □*verb* **visited, visiting, visits**
□*noun, plural* **visits**

visitor *noun* Someone who visits.
vis·i·tor (viz′i tər) □*noun, plural* **visitors**

visor *noun* The part of a cap that sticks out in front and protects the eyes from sun, wind, or rain.
vi·sor (vī′zər) □*noun, plural* **visors**

visor

visual *adjective* Of, relating to, or used in seeing: *Certain visual handicaps can be corrected with glasses. The new space movie has fantastic visual effects.*
vis·u·al (vizh′ o͞o əl) □*adjective*

vital *adjective* **1.** Having to do with or needed for life: *The heart and lungs are vital organs.* **2.** Very important; essential: *The messenger brought vital information about the enemy's plans.* **3.** Full of life and energy. —See Synonyms at **necessary.**
vi·tal (vīt′əl) □*adjective*

vitamin *noun* Any of several substances that are needed for animals to continue living and growing in a normal way.
vi·ta·min (vī′tə min) □*noun, plural* **vitamins**

vivid *adjective* **1.** Very bright and strong: *The car is a vivid red.* **2.** Active; lively: *His paintings show that he has a vivid imagination.*
viv·id (viv′id) □*adjective*

vocabulary *noun* **1.** All the words of a language. **2.** All the words used by a particular person or group: *a book that helps students in-*crease *their vocabulary.* **3.** A list of words and phrases, usually in alphabetical order with definitions.
vo·cab·u·lar·y (vō kab′yə ler′ē) □*noun, plural* **vocabularies**

vocal *adjective* Of, relating to, or made by the voice: *The bark of a dog is a vocal sound.*
vo·cal (vō′kəl) □*adjective*

vocal cords *plural noun* A pair of bands of muscle in the larynx that stretch and vibrate when air from the lungs is forced between them to produce the sound of the voice.

voice *noun* **1.** The particular sound a person makes by using the mouth and vocal cords in speaking and singing: *I heard voices in the next room.* **2.** The ability to produce a sound with the mouth and vocal cords: *Have you ever lost your voice?* **3.** The right to express an opinion or choice: *Each student had a voice in making the plans for the trip.*
□*verb* To give expression to: *I intend to voice my complaints at the meeting.*
voice (vois) □*noun, plural* **voices** □*verb* **voiced, voicing, voices**

void *adjective* **1.** Having no legal force or effect: *The judge declared that the will was void.* **2.** Containing no matter; empty.
void (void) □*adjective*

volcano *noun* An opening in the crust of the earth that emits lava, dust, ash, and hot gases.
vol·ca·no (vol kā′nō) □*noun, plural*

WORD HISTORY: **volcano**

Volcano comes from the name of Vulcan, the Roman god of fire.

---

volleyball *noun* **1.** A game played between two teams that are separated by a net and hit a ball back and forth without letting it touch the ground. **2.** The ball used in this game.
vol·ley·ball (vol′ē bôl′) □*noun, plural* **volleyballs**

volt *noun* A unit of force for measuring an electric current.
volt (vōlt) □*noun, plural* **volts**

WORD HISTORY: **volt**

The *volt* is named after Alessandro Volta, an Italian scientist who invented an early kind of electric battery.

---

voltage *noun* The amount of force of an electric current, measured in volts.
volt·age (vōl′tij) □*noun, plural* **voltages**

volume *noun* **1.** A book. **2.** One book of a set: *The encyclopedia has ten volumes.* **3.** The measure of how much space an object takes up: *What is the volume of that bottle?* **4.** The force of sound; quality of being loud: *The sound increased in volume as we got closer.*
vol·ume (vol′yəm) □*noun, plural* **volumes**

WORD HISTORY: **volume**

Before the invention of books, rolls of paper or other material were used for writing. *Volume* comes from a Latin word meaning ''a roll for writing.''

---

voluntary *adjective* **1.** Made, done, or given of one's own free will; not required: *My decision to donate money to the library was a voluntary one.* **2.** Controlled by the will: *When you pick up a pencil, you use the voluntary muscles of the hand.*
vol·un·tar·y (vol′ən ter′ē) □*adjective*

volunteer *noun* **1.** Someone who does a job or gives service by free will and without pay: *Volunteers work every Monday to clean up the park. He works as a volunteer at the hospital.* **2.** Someone who enlists in the armed forces of his or her own free will.
□*adjective* Having to do with or made up of volunteers: *a volunteer fireman.*
□*verb* To give or offer of one's own free will: *I volunteered to help clean up after the party.*
vol·un·teer (vol′ən tîr′) □*noun, plural* **volunteers** □*adjective* □*verb* **volunteered, volunteering, volunteers**

vomit *verb* To bring up the contents of one's stomach through the mouth.
vom·it (vom′it) □*verb,* **vomited, vomiting, vomits**

vote *noun* **1.** The formal expression of choice or opinion, as in an election: *The team took a vote to elect a captain.* **2.** The right to vote: *Women in the United States did not have the vote until 1920.*
□*verb* **1.** To express one's choice by a vote: *I still haven't decided who is the best person to vote for.* **2.** To make available by a vote: *The town council voted money for a new park.*
vote (vōt) □*noun, plural* **votes** □*verb* **voted, voting, votes**

voter *noun* Someone who votes or has a right to vote.
vot·er (vō′tər) □*noun, plural* **voters**

vow *noun* A solemn promise or pledge: *We made a vow to stay friends forever.*
□*verb* To make a solemn promise or pledge: *I vowed never to reveal the secret.*
vow (vou) □*noun, plural* **vows** □*verb* **vowed, vowing, vows**

vowel *noun* **1.** A speech sound usually made by the breath passing through the mouth freely, without being cut off or blocked off. A vowel is usually the central or loudest part of a syllable. **2.** A letter that represents such a sound. The vowels in English are represented by *a, e, i, o, u,* and sometimes *y.*
vow·el (vou′əl) □*noun, plural* **vowels**

voyage *noun* A long journey to a distant place, made on a ship, aircraft, or spacecraft.
□*verb* To make a voyage: *He has voyaged all over the world.*
voy·age (voi′ij) □*noun, plural* **voyages** □*verb* **voyaged, voyaging, voyages**

vulgar *adjective* Having or showing very poor taste or manners: *vulgar language.*
vul·gar (vul′gər) □*adjective*

vulture *noun* Any of several large birds that usually have dark feathers and a bare head and neck. Vultures feed on the flesh of dead animals.
vul·ture (vul′chər) □*noun, plural* **vultures**

vulture

a	bat	ī	bite	o͞o	tool	*th*	feather
ā	make	î	fierce	ou	out	th	bath
â	dare	o	dot	u	nut	hw	wheat
ä	father	ō	no	û	turn	zh	measure
e	net	ô	law, for	ch	church	ə	about, open
ē	be	oi	soil	ng	ring		pencil, atom
i	dip	oo	look	sh	shade		circus

ANCIENT GREEK

The letter **W** has evolved from many forms of ancient writing. One of the earliest known examples is the Greek character shown above, which dates from almost 3,000 years ago. Over the years, artists and designers have created their own versions of the English letter **W.** Some of the more common examples seen today are shown below.

| HANDWRITING | CALLIGRAPHY | MODERN SANS SERIF | MODERN SERIF | SCRIPT |

---

w or **W** *noun* The twenty-third letter of the English alphabet.
w or **W** (**dub′**əl yōō′) ◻*noun, plural* **w's** or **W's**

wad *noun* **1.** A small, soft piece of material: *a wad of cotton; a wad of chewing gum.* **2.** A tight roll of paper or paper money.
◻*verb* To squeeze, roll, or crush into a wad: *He wadded up the note and threw it into the wastebasket.*
wad (wod) ◻*noun, plural* **wads** ◻*verb* **wadded, wadding, wads**

waddle *verb* To walk with short steps and a swaying body, as a duck does.
◻*noun* A swaying walk.
wad·dle (**wod′**əl) ◻*verb* **waddled, waddling, waddles** ◻*noun, plural* **waddles**

wade *verb* **1.** To walk in or through water, snow, or a similar substance that makes movement difficult: *We waded through the stream.* **2.** To move or make one's way through slowly and with difficulty: *I had to wade through the junk in the attic to find the photograph album.*
wade (wād) ◻*verb* **waded, wading, wades**

wafer *noun* A small, thin, crisp cookie or cracker.
wa·fer (**wā′**fər) ◻*noun, plural* **wafers**

waffle *noun* A light, crisp cake made of batter cooked in an appliance that presses a pattern of little squares into it.
waf·fle (**wof′**əl) ◻*noun, plural* **waffles**

wag *verb* To move or wave back and forth or up and down: *The dog wagged its tail.*
◻*noun* A wagging movement.
wag (wag) ◻*verb* **wagged, wagging, wags** ◻*noun, plural* **wags**

wage *noun* Payment made to a worker for work done; salary.
◻*verb* To take part in or carry on: *local residents waging a fight against the new highway.*
wage (wāj) ◻*noun, plural* **wages** ◻*verb* **waged, waging, wages**

wager *noun* A bet.
◻*verb* To make a wager; bet.
wa·ger (**wā′**jər) ◻*noun, plural* **wagers** ◻*verb* **wagered, wagering, wagers**

wagon *noun* **1.** A large vehicle with four wheels that is pulled by horses and used to carry loads. **2.** A small cart with wheels that can be pushed or pulled by hand.
wag·on (**wag′**ən) ◻*noun, plural* **wagons**

wail *verb* To make a long, loud cry because of sadness or pain: *The boy wailed when he broke the toy.*
◻*noun* A long cry or sound: *We lay awake listening to the wail of the wind.*
wail (wāl) ◻*verb* **wailed, wailing, wails** ◻*noun, plural* **wails**

waist *noun* **1.** The part of the human body between the ribs and the hips. **2.** The part of a garment that fits around the waist.
waist (wāst) ◻*noun, plural* **waists**

wait *verb* **1.** To stay somewhere until someone or something comes: *I'll wait for you at the corner.* **2.** To put off; delay; postpone: *She will be late so we won't wait dinner for her.*

3. To be put off or delayed: *It's raining so the picnic will have to wait until tomorrow.*
□*noun* A period of time spent in waiting: *a long wait at the dentist's office.*

wait on To serve or aid, as a waitress or a clerk in a store.
wait (wāt) □*verb* **waited, waiting, waits** □*noun, plural* **waits**

waiter *noun* A man who works in a restaurant serving food and drink to people.
wait·er (wā′tər) □*noun, plural* **waiters**

waitress *noun* A woman who works in a restaurant serving food and drink to people.
wait·ress (wā′tris) □*noun, plural* **waitresses**

wake[1] *verb* To stop or cause to stop sleeping; awaken: *I wake up at eight o'clock every day. My brother woke me up.*
□*noun* A watch kept over the body of a dead person.
wake (wāk) □*verb* **waked** or **woke, waked** or **woken, waking, wakes** □*noun, plural* **wakes**

wake[2] *noun* The track of waves left by something moving in the water.
wake (wāk) □*noun, plural* **wakes**

wake

waken *verb* To wake up: *When should I waken you tomorrow?*
wak·en (wā′kən) □*verb* **wakened, wakening, wakens**

walk *verb* **1.** To move or cause to move on foot at an easy pace: *walking to school; walk the dog.* **2.** To go over, across, or through on foot: *They walked the ranch from one end to the other.* **3.** To accompany on foot: *Let me walk you home.* **4.** In baseball, to go or allow to go to first base because the pitcher has thrown four balls.
□*noun* **1.** An act of walking: *He took a long walk in the woods.* **2.** The distance to be walked: *The walk to the bus stop is only two hundred yards.* **3.** A place set apart for walk-

ing: *There is a paved walk around the lake.*
walk (wôk) □*verb* **walked, walking, walks** □*noun, plural* **walks**

wall *noun* **1.** A solid structure that forms a side of a building or room, or that divides two areas. **2.** A structure made of brick, stone, wood, or other material that is used to divide, enclose, or protect. **3.** Something that looks or functions like a wall: *The soldiers ran into a wall of gunfire.*
□*verb* To divide, enclose, or shut off with a wall: *walled up the entrance to the old mine.*
wall (wôl) □*noun, plural* **walls** □*verb* **walled, walling, walls**

wallet *noun* A small, flat folding case for holding money, cards, and photographs.
wal·let (wol′it) □*noun, plural* **wallets**

wallpaper *noun* Paper printed in colors and patterns that is used to decorate walls.
□*verb* To cover with wallpaper.
wall·pa·per (wôl′pā′pər) □*noun, plural* **wallpapers** □*verb* **wallpapered, wallpapering, wallpapers**

walnut *noun* An edible nut that grows on a tall tree and has a hard, rough shell.
wal·nut (wôl′nut′) □*noun, plural* **walnuts**

WORD HISTORY: walnut

Walnut comes from an old English word that literally means "foreign nut."

---

walrus *noun* A large sea animal that lives in the Arctic and has tough, wrinkled skin and large tusks. Walruses are related to seals.
wal·rus (wôl′rəs) □*noun, plural* **walruses** or **walrus**

walrus

a	bat	ī	bite	o͞o	tool	*th*	feather
ā	make	î	fierce	ou	out	th	bath
â	dare	o	dot	u	nut	hw	wheat
ä	father	ō	no	û	turn	zh	measure
e	net	ô	law, for	ch	church	ə	about, open
ē	be	oi	soil	ng	ring		pencil, atom
i	dip	oo	look	sh	shade		circus

waltz *noun* **1.** A smooth, gliding dance done by two people to music having three beats to a measure. **2.** The music for this dance.
☐*verb* To dance a waltz.
waltz (wôltz) ☐*noun, plural* **waltzes** ☐*verb* **waltzed, waltzing, waltzes**

wampum *noun* Small beads made from polished shells and strung together into necklaces or belts. Wampum was once used by certain Native Americans as money.
wam·pum (wom′pəm) ☐*noun*

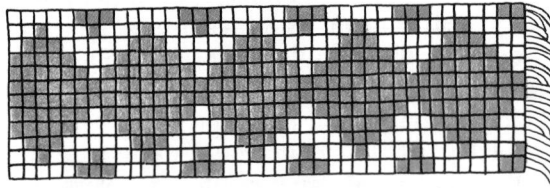

wampum
A design made with wampum

wand *noun* A thin rod or stick, especially one used by a magician.
wand (wond) ☐*noun, plural* **wands**

wander *verb* **1.** To move about with no aim or purpose: *I wandered through the store while I waited for my father.* **2.** To lose one's way: *The dog wandered away from the house and got lost.* **3.** To fail to pay attention: *His mind was wandering and he didn't hear his sister call to him.*
wan·der (won′dər) ☐*verb* **wandered, wandering, wanders**

want *verb* **1.** To have a wish for; desire: *She wants a new dress.* **2.** To have a need for; require: *The plants want water.*
☐*noun* A need: *She is in want of a job.*
want (wont) ☐*verb* **wanted, wanting, wants** ☐*noun, plural* **wants**

war *noun* **1.** Fighting or combat between two or more nations, states, or groups of people. **2.** A struggle or attack: *a war against poverty.*
☐*verb* To make a war.
war (wôr) ☐*noun, plural* **wars** ☐*verb* **warred, warring, wars**

ward *noun* **1.** A section or division of a hospital. **2.** A division of a city or town, especially an election district. **3.** Someone who is under the care and protection of a guardian or court.
ward (wôrd) ☐*noun, plural* **wards**

warden *noun* **1.** An official who makes sure that certain laws are obeyed: *a fire warden.* **2.** An official in charge of a prison.
war·den (wôr′dən) ☐*noun, plural* **wardens**

wardrobe *noun* **1.** All of a person's clothing. **2.** A large piece of furniture shaped like a closet for hanging or keeping clothes.
ward·robe (wôrd′rōb′) ☐*noun, plural* **wardrobes**

> *WORD HISTORY:* **wardrobe**
>
> *Wardrobe* comes from an old French word for a closet where clothes were stored. The French word was formed from words meaning "to guard a piece of clothing."

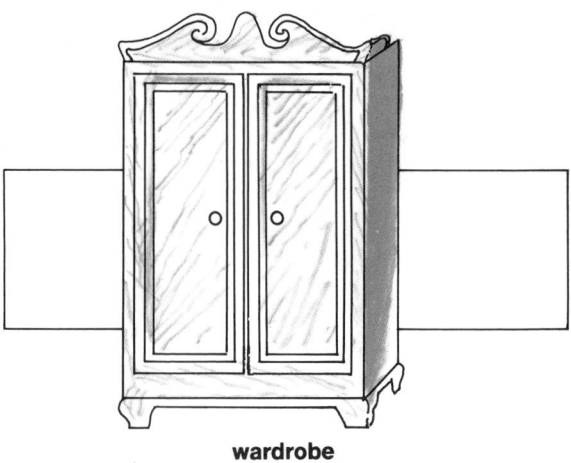

wardrobe

ware *noun* **1. wares** Goods for sale: *Many people displayed their wares at the county fair.* **2.** Pots, vases, and other things made from baked clay; pottery.
ware (wâr) ☐*noun, plural* **wares**

warehouse *noun* A large building where merchandise is stored.
ware·house (wâr′hous′) ☐*noun, plural* **warehouses**

warfare *noun* War or combat.
war·fare (wôr′fâr′) ☐*noun*

warlike *adjective* **1.** Quick to make war; hostile: *a warlike country.* **2.** Threatening war: *a warlike act.*
war·like (wôr′līk′) ☐*adjective*

warm *adjective* **1.** Somewhat hot; not cool or very hot: *warm weather; a glass of warm milk.* **2.** Having a feeling of heat: *We were warm and tired after the long walk.* **3.** Giving off or holding in heat: *a warm winter coat.* **4.** Friendly; kindly: *a warm greeting.*
☐*verb* To make or become warm or warmer; heat up: *The hot tea will warm you. The stew is warming in the oven.*
   warm up 1. To make or become warm or .

warmer; heat up: *Please warm up the rolls. They're in the oven and warmed up already.* **2.** To make or become ready to do something by exercising or practicing beforehand.
warm (wôrm) □*adjective* □*verb* **warmed, warming, warms**

warm-blooded *adjective* Having blood that stays at about the same temperature no matter how much the temperature of the surrounding air or water changes. Birds and mammals are warm-blooded.
warm·blood·ed (wôrm′ blud′ id) □*adjective*

warmth *noun* **1.** The condition or quality of being warm: *She felt the warmth of the sun as soon as she stepped outside.* **2.** The condition or quality of being friendly; kindness.
warmth (wôrmth) □*noun*

warn *verb* **1.** To tell of present or coming danger: *The radio bulletin warned that a blizzard was coming.* **2.** To advise or caution: *She warned us to be careful.*
warn (wôrn) □*verb* **warned, warning, warns**

warning *noun* A notice of coming danger given beforehand.
warn·ing (wôr′ ning) □*noun, plural* **warnings**

warrant *noun* **1.** An official written order that gives authority for doing something, such as making an arrest or search: *The police had a warrant to search the store for stolen goods.* **2.** A good reason for doing something: *She said I had no warrant for being angry.*
□*verb* **1.** To be or give a good reason for: *The boss said her good work warrants a promotion.* **2.** To guarantee: *My new watch is warranted for a year.*
war·rant (wôr′ ənt) □*noun, plural* **warrants**
□*verb* **warranted, warranting, warrants**

warrior *noun* Someone who fights or is experienced in fighting battles.
war·ri·or (wôr′ ē ər) □*noun, plural* **warriors**

warship *noun* A ship that is built and armed for use in battle.
war·ship (wôr′ ship′) □*noun, plural* **warships**

wart *noun* A small, hard lump that grows on the skin. It is caused by a virus.
wart (wôrt) □*noun, plural* **warts**

wary *adjective* **1.** Alert to danger; on guard: *The man was wary of strangers.* **2.** Showing great caution; careful: *Be wary of cars when you ride your bike.*
war·y (wâr′ ē) □*adjective* **warier, wariest**

was *verb* The first and third person singular past tense of the verb **be**: *I was away all week-*

end. *He was studying.*
was (woz *or* wuz) □*verb*

wash *verb* **1.** To clean with water or other liquid and often with soap: *wash your hands; wash a car.* **2.** To clean oneself, clothes, or other things with soap and water. **3.** To carry away or be carried away by moving water: *The rain washed the snow away.*
□*noun* **1.** The act of washing. **2.** The amount of clothes or linens that are to be or that have just been washed: *He did a wash yesterday.* **3.** A liquid used in cleansing or coating something: *Use this wash for your glasses.* **4.** A flow of water or the sound made by it: *He heard the wash of the ocean waves.*
wash (wosh) □*verb* **washed, washing, washes** □*noun, plural* **washes**

washer *noun* **1.** Someone or something that washes, especially a machine used to wash clothes or dishes. **2.** A small flat ring made of metal or rubber placed between a nut and a bolt to reduce friction and give a tighter fit.
wash·er (wosh′ ər) □*noun, plural* **washers**

washing machine *noun* A machine used for washing clothes and linens.
wash·ing machine (wosh′ ing) □*noun*

wasn't Contraction of "was not."
was·n't (woz′ ənt *or* wuz′ ənt)

wasp *noun* A flying insect with a narrow middle section. Wasps can give a painful sting.
wasp (wosp) □*noun, plural* **wasps**

wasp

waste *verb* **1.** To spend or use foolishly: *waste money; waste time.* **2.** To fail to use; lose: *waste an opportunity.* **3.** To wear away little by little: *The disease wasted his body.* **4.** To destroy completely: *The fire wasted the forest.*

a	bat	ī	bite	ōō	tool	*th*	feather
ā	make	î	fierce	ou	out	th	bath
â	dare	o	dot	u	nut	hw	wheat
ä	father	ō	no	û	turn	zh	measure
e	net	ô	law, for	ch	church	ə	about, open
ē	be	oi	soil	ng	ring		pencil, atom
i	dip	oo	look	sh	shade		circus

□*noun* **1.** An act of wasting: *Trying to get him to change his opinion is a waste of time.* **2.** Worthless material that is produced while making something. **3.** The material left over after food has been digested that is sent out of the body.

□*adjective* **1.** Left over or thrown away as worthless or useless: *waste materials.* **2.** Of, having to do with, or used for waste.

waste (wāst) □*verb* **wasted, wasting, wastes** □*noun, plural* **wastes** □*adjective*

SYNONYMS: **waste, squander**

These verbs mean to spend or use foolishly: *He drives a big car that wastes gas. She squandered her money on records and jewelry.*

---

wastebasket *noun* An open container to hold small items to be thrown out.
waste·bas·ket (wāst′bas′kit) □*noun, plural* **wastebaskets**

wasteful *adjective* Spending or using more than is needed: *a wasteful use of oil.*
waste·ful (wāst′fəl) □*adjective*

wasteland *noun* A lonely area with few plants or animals living on it.
waste·land (wāst′land′) □*noun, plural* **wastelands**

watch *verb* **1.** To look or look at: *We watched as she changed the flat tire. Did you watch the baseball game?* **2.** To be on the lookout: *Watch for your father.* **3.** To keep guard over: *The policeman watched the children cross the street.* **4.** To be careful about: *Watch what you are doing.*

□*noun* **1.** A small clock that can be carried in a pocket or worn on the wrist. **2.** The act of guarding: *I kept watch over the children while he went to the store.* **3.** Someone who guards or protects: *The night watch came on duty.*
watch (woch) □*verb* **watched, watching, watches** □*noun, plural* **watches**

watchdog *noun* A dog that is trained to guard property.
watch·dog (woch′dôg′) □*noun, plural* **watchdogs**

watchful *adjective* On the lookout; alert: *a watchful policeman patroling the street.*
watch·ful (woch′fəl) □*adjective*

watchman *noun* Someone whose job is to guard property, especially at night.
watch·man (woch′mən) □*noun, plural* **watchmen**

water *noun* The liquid that falls from the skies as rain and is found in rivers, oceans, lakes, and pools. It is a compound of hydrogen and oxygen.

□*verb* **1.** To supply with water: *water the lawn.* **2.** To give water to drink: *water a horse.* **3.** To produce a watery liquid, such as tears or saliva.
wa·ter (wô′tər) □*noun, plural* **waters** □*verb* **watered, watering, waters**

water buffalo *noun* A buffalo that lives in Africa and Asia and has large, spreading horns. Water buffaloes are used to pull or carry loads.

water buffalo

water color *noun* **1.** A paint that is made by mixing coloring material with water. **2.** A painting done with water colors. **3.** The art of painting with water colors.

watercress *noun* A plant that grows in water. Its leaves have a strong taste and are used in salads.
wa·ter·cress (wô′tər kres′) □*noun*

waterfall *noun* A stream of water that falls from a high place.
wa·ter·fall (wô′tər fôl′) □*noun, plural* **waterfalls**

waterfront *noun* **1.** Land that is at the edge of a body of water. **2.** The part of a city or town that is at the edge of the water and has docks for ships and boats.
wa·ter·front (wô′tər frunt′) □*noun, plural* **waterfronts**

water lily *noun* A water plant with broad, floating leaves and colorful flowers.

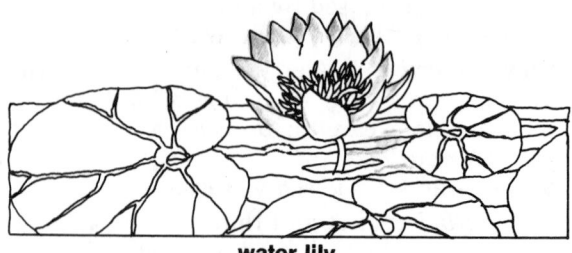

water lily

watermelon *noun* A very large melon with a hard, thick green rind. Its pink or reddish flesh is sweet and watery.
wa·ter·mel·on (wô′tər mel′ən) □*noun, plural* **watermelons**

water moccasin *noun* A poisonous snake that lives in swamps of the southern United States.

waterproof *adjective* Capable of keeping water from coming through: *waterproof shoes; a waterproof watch.*
□*verb* To make waterproof.
wa·ter·proof (wô′tər proof′) □*adjective* □*verb* **waterproofed, waterproofing, waterproofs**

watershed *noun* **1.** A ridge of high land that separates two different systems of rivers. **2.** The region from which a river, lake, or other body of water drains its water.
wa·ter·shed (wô′tər shed′) □*noun, plural* **watersheds**

water-ski *noun* Either of a pair of wide, short skis used for gliding over water while holding a rope attached to a motorboat.
□*verb* To glide over water on water-skis.
wa·ter·ski (wô′tər skē′) □*noun, plural* **water-skis** □*verb* **water-skied, water-skiing, water-skis**

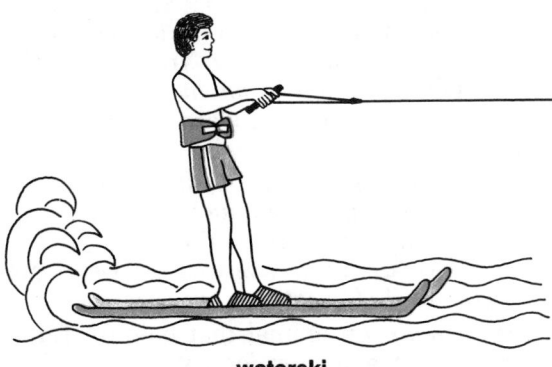

waterski

waterway *noun* A river, canal, or other body of water on which ships travel.
wa·ter·way (wô′tər wā′) □*noun, plural* **waterways**

water wheel *noun* A wheel that is turned by the power of water falling over it or flowing under it. Water wheels are used to drive machinery.

watery *adjective* **1.** Filled with or containing water or a similar liquid: *watery eyes.* **2.** Having too much water: *watery soup.*
wa·ter·y (wô′tə rē) □*adjective*

watt *noun* A unit of electrical power.
watt (wot) □*noun, plural* **watts**

WORD HISTORY: **watt**

The *watt* is named after James Watt, a Scottish inventor who developed the steam engine.

---

wave *verb* **1.** To move back and forth or up and down; flap or flutter: *flags waving in the wind.* **2.** To move a hand, arm, or something in the hand back and forth as a signal or greeting: *We waved hello as their car pulled up. He waved us away.* **3.** To fall or cause to fall in gentle curls: *Does she wave her hair?*
□*noun* **1.** A moving high point along the surface of water: *ocean waves.* **2.** A vibrating motion of energy or particles. Light, sound, heat, and x-rays travel in waves. **3.** An act of waving: *He signaled to me with a wave of his hand.* **4.** A curve or arrangement of gentle curls: *How do you get such nice waves in your hair?* **5.** A sudden increase: *a heat wave.*
wave (wāv) □*verb* **waved, waving, waves** □*noun, plural* **waves**

waver *verb* **1.** To move back and forth in an unsteady way: *The baby walked with wavering steps.* **2.** To be uncertain; falter: *she wavered between going to the movies with us or staying home.* **3.** To tremble or flicker: *The flame of the candle wavered.*
wa·ver (wā′vər) □*verb* **wavered, wavering, wavers**

wavy *adjective* Having waves or curves: *wavy hair; a wavy line.*
wav·y (wā′vē) □*adjective* **wavier, waviest**

wavy

a	bat	ī	bite	o͞o	tool	*th*	feather
ā	make	î	fierce	ou	out	th	bath
â	dare	o	dot	u	nut	hw	wheat
ä	father	ō	no	û	turn	zh	measure
e	net	ô	law, for	ch	church	ə	about, open
ē	be	oi	soil	ng	ring		pencil, atom
i	dip	oo	look	sh	shade		circus

wax¹ *noun* **1.** Any of various substances that are solid or soft and sticky, and that melt or become soft when heated. **2.** A substance like wax that is produced by bees. **3.** A substance like wax that is found in the ears. **4.** A substance containing wax that is used to polish floors, cars, furniture, and many other things. □*verb* To cover or polish with wax.
wax (waks) □*noun, plural* **waxes** □*verb* **waxed, waxing, waxes**

wax² *verb* To grow larger, as the moon does when it passes from new moon to full moon.
wax (waks) □*verb* **waxed, waxing, waxes**

way *noun* **1.** A method or means of getting or doing something: *We found a new way to solve the problem. Why did he treat us in such an unfriendly way?* **2.** A road or path: *the shortest way home.* **3.** Distance: *It's only a short way to the library.* **4.** A direction: *Which way did they go?* **5.** What one wants; wish: *a spoiled child who always gets her way.* **6.** A manner or feature: *In many ways it's the best idea we've come up with.*
□*adverb* Far: *The explosion came from way up the street.*
way (wā) □*noun, plural* **ways** □*adverb*

we *pronoun* The person who is speaking or writing, together with another person or persons: *We all went to the movies.*
we (wē) □*pronoun*

weak *adjective* **1.** Not having strength, power, or energy: *The illness left her tired and weak. That's a weak excuse that's hard to believe.* **2.** Likely to fail or break: *That chair has a weak leg and won't hold your weight.*
weak (wēk) □*adjective* **weaker, weakest**

weaken *verb* To make or become weak or weaker: *weaken tea with water. My legs weakened as I climbed the hill.*
weak·en (wē′kən) □*verb* **weakened, weakening, weakens**

weakly *adjective* Feeble; sick; weak: *a weakly child.*
□*adverb* In a weak way: *She spoke so weakly no one could hear her.*
weak·ly (wēk′lē) □*adjective* **weaklier, weakliest** □*adverb*

weakness *noun* **1.** The condition or quality of being weak: *I felt a weakness in my legs from the long walk.* **2.** A weak point; fault: *His biggest weakness is his laziness.* **3.** A special liking: *a weakness for spy novels.*
weak·ness (wēk′nis) □*noun, plural* **weaknesses**

wealth *noun* **1.** A great amount of money or valuable possessions; riches. **2.** A large amount: *Dictionaries contain a wealth of information.*
wealth (welth) □*noun*

wealthy *adjective* Having wealth; rich: *a wealthy nation; a wealthy family.*
wealth·y (wel′thē) □*adjective* **wealthier, wealthiest**

weapon *noun* **1.** Any instrument used to attack another or defend oneself from attack. Guns, clubs, and fists are weapons. **2.** Anything used to overcome or defeat: *a weapon against disease.*
wea·pon (wep′ən) □*noun, plural* **weapons**

wear *verb* **1.** To have or put on one's body: *He wore his new suit. She's wearing her mother's ring.* **2.** To have or show: *wear a smile.* **3.** To damage or remove by rubbing or use: *Water can wear away a stone.* **4.** To make or create through use or rubbing: *wear a hole in a rug.* **5.** To last even though used: *Her winter coat did not wear well.*
□*noun* **1.** The act of wearing or the condition of being worn: *clothes for evening wear.* **2.** Clothing: *men's wear.* **3.** Damage that comes from use or age: *I can't see any signs of wear on the furniture.* **4.** Service; use: *We got a lot of wear out of those clothes.*
  wear out 1. To use until no longer useful: *wear out a pair of shoes.* **2.** To tire or make exhausted: *It was a hard job that wore me out.*
wear (wâr) □*verb* **wore, worn, wearing, wears** □*noun*

weary *adjective* Very tired; fatigued: *Everyone was weary after the long trip.*
□*verb* To make or become tired.
wea·ry (wîr′ē) □*adjective* **wearier, weariest** □*verb* **wearied, wearying, wearies**

weasel *noun* An animal that has soft fur, a narrow body, and short legs. Weasels feed on small animals and birds.
wea·sel (wē′zəl) □*noun, plural* **weasels**

weasel

weather *noun* The condition of the atmosphere at a certain time and place: *hot weather that is perfect for the beach.*
weath·er (we*th*′ ər) ▢*noun*

weather vane *noun* A pointer that turns with the wind to show which way the wind is blowing.

weave *verb* **1.** To make by passing strands under and over other strands: *weave a blanket; weave straw baskets.* **2.** To spin a web, as a spider does. **3.** To move in and out, back and forth, or from side to side: *The motorcycle weaved through the traffic.*
▢*noun* A pattern or method of weaving: *a sweater with a tight weave.*
weave (wēv) ▢*verb* **wove** (**weaved** *for verb sense 3*), **woven** (**weaved** *for verb sense 3*), **weaving, weaves** ▢*noun, plural* **weaves**

web *noun* **1.** A network of fine, silky threads woven by a spider. **2.** Something made of parts that cross one another in a complicated manner: *a web of highways.* **3.** A fold of skin connecting the toes of ducks, frogs, and other animals.
web (web) ▢*noun, plural* **webs**

webbed *adjective* Having skin connecting the toes, such as of a duck or goose.
webbed (webd) ▢*adjective*

webbed
Webbed feet of a duck

web-footed *adjective* Having feet with webbed toes.
web-foot·ed (**web′ foot′** id) ▢*adjective*

wed *verb* **1.** To take a person as husband or wife; marry: *She wedded the boy next door.* **2.** To unite in marriage: *They were wed a year ago today.*
wed (wed) ▢*verb* **wedded, wed** or **wedded, wedding, weds**

we'd Contraction of "we had," "we should," and "we would."
we'd (wēd)

wedding *noun* **1.** A marriage ceremony. **2.** An anniversary of a marriage.
wed·ding (wed′ ing) ▢*noun, plural* **weddings**

wedge *noun* **1.** A block of wood, metal, or plastic that is wide at one end and tapers to a point at the other. Wedges are used to split apart, lift, or hold things. **2.** Something shaped like a wedge: *a wedge of cheese.*
▢*verb* **1.** To split apart or fix in place with a wedge: *I had to wedge the door open.* **2.** To crowd, push, or squeeze into a small space: *Everyone wedged into the elevator.*
wedge (wej) ▢*noun, plural* **wedges** ▢*verb* **wedged, wedging, wedges**

Wednesday *noun* The fourth day of the week, after Tuesday and before Thursday.
Wed·nes·day (wenz′ dē *or* wenz′ dā′) ▢*noun, plural* **Wednesdays**

WORD HISTORY: **Wednesday**

Wednesday was named after Woden, the chief god in old English mythology.

---

wee *adjective* **1.** Very little; tiny: *a wee kitten; a wee bit afraid.* **2.** Very early: *the wee hours.*
wee (wē) ▢*adjective*

weed *noun* A plant that grows where it is not wanted. Weeds are useless or harmful.
▢*verb* To remove weeds from: *weed a vegetable garden.*
   weed out To remove what is not wanted: *weeded out the poor swimmers from the team.*
weed (wēd) ▢*noun, plural* **weeds** ▢*verb* **weeded, weeding, weeds**

week *noun* **1.** A period of seven days in a row. **2.** The part of that period of seven days during which one works or goes to school.
week (wēk) ▢*noun, plural* **weeks**

weekday *noun* Any day of the week except Sunday and Saturday.
week·day (wēk′ dā′) ▢*noun, plural* **weekdays**

a	bat	ī	bite	o͞o	tool	*th*	feather
ā	make	î	fierce	ou	out	th	bath
â	dare	o	dot	u	nut	hw	wheat
ä	father	ō	no	û	turn	zh	measure
e	net	ô	law, for	ch	church	ə	about, open
ē	be	oi	soil	ng	ring		pencil, atom
i	dip	oo	look	sh	shade		circus

weekend *noun* The period of time from Friday evening through Sunday evening.
week·end (wēk'end') □*noun, plural* **weekends**

weekly *adjective* **1.** Happening, appearing, or to be paid once every week: *weekly meetings; a weekly allowance.* **2.** For a period of one week: *a weekly rate of pay.*
□*adverb* Every week; once a week: *He writes to me weekly.*
□*noun* A magazine or newspaper that is issued once a week.
week·ly (wēk'lē) □*adjective* □*adverb*
□*noun, plural* **weeklies**

weep *verb* To shed tears; cry: *She wept when she cut her finger.*
weep (wēp) □*verb* **wept, weeping, weeps**

weevil *noun* A beetle with a long snout that does great harm to plants and crops.
wee·vil (wē'vəl) □*noun, plural* **weevils**

weigh *verb* **1.** To use a scale to determine how heavy something is: *The veterinarian weighed the puppies.* **2.** To have a weight of: *She weighs three pounds more than I do.* **3.** To consider in a careful manner: *She weighed the facts carefully before deciding.*
  weigh down 1. To cause to bend under heavy weight: *Snow and ice weighed down the branches of the trees.* **2.** To be a burden to: *Troubles weighed down his spirits.*
  weigh on or **weigh upon** To be a burden to; oppress: *The lie he told is weighing on his conscience.*
weigh (wā) □*verb* **weighed, weighing, weighs**

weight *noun* **1.** The measure of how heavy a thing is: *My weight is 100 pounds.* **2.** The force of gravity pulling on an object: *Your weight on the moon would be less than your weight on earth.* **3.** A unit used for measuring this force: *Grams and kilograms are metric weights.* **4.** Something heavy: *I used a rock as a weight to keep the papers from flying away.* **5.** A load or burden: *His financial responsibilities are a great weight on his mind.* **6.** Importance; influence: *My teacher's advice has a lot of weight with me.*
weight (wāt) □*noun, plural* **weights**

weightless *adjective* **1.** Having little or no weight: *as weightless as a feather.* **2.** Experiencing little or no pull of gravity: *an astronaut weightless in space.*
weight·less (wāt'lis) □*adjective*

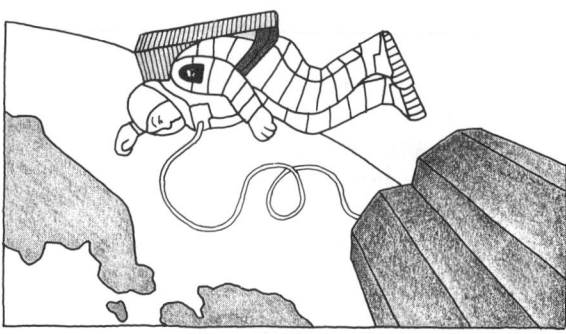
weightless

weird *adjective* Mysterious or strange: *I heard weird sounds coming from the forest.*
weird (wîrd) □*adjective* **weirder, weirdest**

welcome *verb* **1.** To greet in a warm and pleasant way: *She welcomed me with a hug.* **2.** To be willing or grateful to accept: *We welcomed the chance to stop working and rest for five minutes.*
□*noun* The act of welcoming: *a hearty welcome.*
□*adjective* **1.** Greeted or received with pleasure: *a welcome guest.* **2.** Free to have or use: *You are welcome to the book when I've finished it.* **3.** Used in the phrase *you're welcome* as a reply to *thank you.*
wel·come (wel'kəm) □*verb* **welcomed, welcoming, welcomes** □*noun, plural* **welcomes** □*adjective*

WORD HISTORY: **welcome**

A *welcome* was originally a visitor that you were particularly glad to see. The word comes from two old English words, the first meaning "pleasure" and the second meaning "guest."

---

weld *verb* To join two pieces of material by melting the area that is to be joined and then pressing the materials together.
weld (weld) □*verb* **welded, welding, welds**

welfare *noun* **1.** Health, happiness, or prosperity: *the welfare of her children.* **2.** Money or other kinds of help given to needy people by a government.
wel·fare (wel'fâr') □*noun*

well¹ *noun* **1.** A hole dug into the ground to get water, oil or gas. **2.** A natural spring or fountain. **3.** A source: *a well of information.*
well (wel) □*noun, plural* **wells**

well² *adverb* **1.** In a good or proper way; correctly: *He drives well. Does she dance well?*

2. To a sufficient degree: *I haven't slept well all week.* **3.** In a thorough way; completely: *Mix the paint well.* **4.** To a considerable degree: *It was well after midnight.*

□*adjective* **1.** In good health; not sick. **2.** All right; in good order: *All is well.* —See Synonyms at **healthy.**

□*interjection* **1.** A word used to express surprise or other sudden feelings: *Well! I never thought you would come.* **2.** A word used to begin a remark: *Well, I think you're wrong.*

well (wel) □*adverb* **better, best** □*adjective* □*interjection*

we'll Contraction of "we will" and "we shall."
we'll (wēl)

well-being *noun* Health and happiness; welfare.
well-be·ing (wel′bē′ing) □*noun*

well-known *adjective* Known to many people in many places: *a well-known actress.*
well-known (wel′nōn′) □*adjective*

went *verb* The past tense of the verb **go:** *I went to the movies.*
went (went) □*verb*

wept *verb* The past tense and past participle of the verb **weep:** *She wept over the lost dog. I could tell he had wept.*
wept (wept) □*verb*

were *verb* **1.** The second person singular past tense of the verb **be:** *You were not in your usual seat on the bus yesterday.* **2.** The first, second, and third person plural past tense of the verb **be:** *We were not at home yesterday. You were about to get yourselves into trouble. They were in the library.*
were (wûr) □*verb*

we're A contraction of "we are."
we're (wîr)

weren't A contraction of "were not."
were·n't (wûrnt *or* wûr′ənt)

west *noun* **1.** The direction in which the sun is seen setting in the evening. **2.** Often **West** A region in this direction, especially the part of the United States west of the Mississippi River.

□*adjective* **1.** Of, in, or toward the west: *the west end of town.* **2.** Coming from the west: *a west wind.*

□*adverb* In, from, or toward the west: *The road goes west of the lake.*

west (west) □*noun* □*adjective* □*adverb*

western *adjective* **1.** Of, in, or toward the west: *western mountains.* **2.** Coming from or

lying toward the west: *a western wind.*

□*noun* A book, movie, or television or radio program about frontier life in the western United States.

west·ern (wes′tərn) □*adjective* □*noun*, *plural* **westerns**

westward *adverb* To or toward the west: *We drove westward out of town.*

□*adjective* Moving to or toward the west: *the westward movement of the pioneers.*

west·ward (west′wərd) □*adverb* □*adjective*

wet *adjective* **1.** Covered, moistened, or soaked with a liquid. **2.** Rainy: *a long spell of wet weather.* **3.** Not yet dry or hardened: *wet paint; wet cement.*

□*verb* To make wet: *Wet the sponge before using it to wipe the table.*

wet (wet) □*adjective* **wetter, wettest** □*verb* **wet** *or* **wetted, wetting, wets**

we've Contraction of "we have."
we've (wēv)

whale *noun* A large sea mammal that resembles fish but breathes air.
whale (hwāl *or* wāl) □*noun*, *plural* **whales**

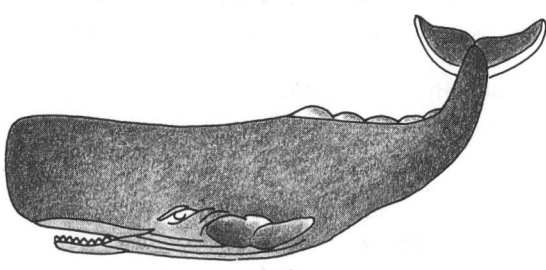

whale

whaler *noun* **1.** Someone who hunts whales. **2.** A ship used in whaling.
whal·er (hwā′lər *or* wā′lər) □*noun*, *plural* **whalers**

whaling *noun* The act or business of hunting whales.
whal·ing (hwā′ling *or* wā′ling) □*noun*

wharf *noun* A landing place at which ships may dock.
wharf (hwôrf *or* wôrf) □*noun*, *plural* **wharves** *or* **wharfs**

a	bat	ī	bite	o͞o	tool	*th*	feather
ā	make	î	fierce	ou	out	th	bath
â	dare	o	dot	u	nut	hw	wheat
ä	father	ō	no	û	turn	zh	measure
e	net	ô	law, for	ch	church	ə	about, open
ē	be	oi	soil	ng	ring		pencil, atom
i	dip	oo	look	sh	shade		circus

what *pronoun* **1.** Which thing or things: *What are we having for lunch?* **2.** That which; the thing that: *Listen to what I have to say.* □*adjective* **1.** Which one or ones of several or many: *What train do I take?* **2.** Whatever: *We repaired what damage had been done.* **3.** How great: *What fools we have been!* **4.** Used to ask a question about the nature or identity of someone or something: *What good will that do?* □*adverb* How: *What does it matter, after all?* □*interjection* A word used to express surprise: *What! More snow?*
what (hwot *or* hwut *or* wot *or* wut) □*pronoun* □*adjective* □*adverb* □*interjection*

whatever *pronoun* **1.** Anything at all: *Please do whatever you can to help.* **2.** No matter what: *Whatever you do, come early.* □*adjective* **1.** Of any number or kind; any: *Whatever help you need, we will give you.* **2.** Of any kind at all: *He was left with nothing whatever.*
what·ev·er (hwot ev′ ər *or* hwut ev′ ər *or* wot ev′ ər *or* wut ev′ ər) □*pronoun* □*adjective*

what's Contraction of "what is" and "what has."
what's (hwots *or* hwuts *or* wots *or* wuts)

wheat *noun* A kind of grass that bears grain and is an important source of food in all parts of the world. Wheat seeds are ground to make flour.
wheat (hwēt *or* wēt) □*noun*

wheel *noun* **1.** A disk or solid ring with spokes that rotate on an axle to move things or drive machines. **2.** Something that looks like, uses, or has a wheel: *a steering wheel on a car.* □*verb* **1.** To move or roll on wheels: *He wheeled the wagon out of the barn.* **2.** To turn suddenly: *she wheeled around and started to chase me.*
wheel (hwēl *or* wēl) □*noun, plural* **wheels** □*verb* **wheeled, wheeling, wheels**

wheelbarrow *noun* A small cart with one or two wheels in front and two straight handles at the back.
wheel·bar·row (hwēl′ bar′ō *or* wēl′ bar′ō) □*noun, plural* **wheelbarrows**

wheelchair *noun* A chair mounted on wheels so that it can be moved about with someone sitting in it. Wheelchairs are used by people who are sick or who cannot walk.
wheel·chair (hwēl′ châr′ *or* wēl′ châr′) □*noun, plural* **wheelchairs**

wheeze *verb* To breathe with difficulty, making a hoarse, whistling sound.
wheeze (hwēz *or* wēz) □*verb* **wheezed, wheezing, wheezes**

whelk *noun* A large sea snail with a spiral shell.
whelk (hwelk *or* welk) □*noun, plural* **whelks**

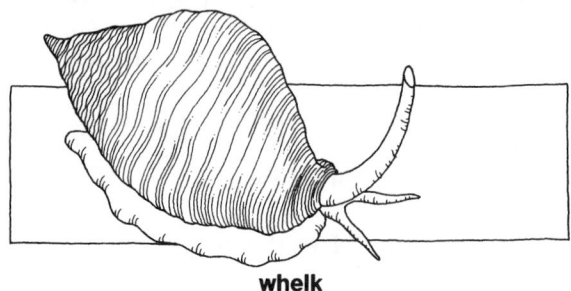
whelk

when *adverb* At what time: *When did they arrive? I don't know when to meet her.* □*conjunction* **1.** At the time that: *He came earlier, when everyone was still here.* **2.** As soon as: *Let me know when he calls.* **3.** Whenever: *She always arrives late when she has a music lesson.* **4.** Although: *He's watching television when he could be reading.* □*pronoun* What or which time: *Since when have you been giving the orders around here?*
when (hwen *or* wen) □*adverb* □*conjunction* □*pronoun*

whenever *adverb* When: *Whenever will they get here?* □*conjunction* **1.** At whatever time: *Come whenever you're ready.* **2.** Every time: *I smile whenever I think of her.*
when·ev·er (hwen ev′ ər *or* wen ev′ ər) □*adverb* □*conjunction*

where *adverb* **1.** At or in what place or position: *Where is your brother?* **2.** To what place or end: *Where did they go for vacation?* **3.** From what place or source: *Where did you get that idea?* □*conjunction* **1.** At or in what or which place: *I am going to my room, where I can study.* **2.** In or to a place in which or to which: *She lives where the weather is mild. I will go where you go.* **3.** Wherever: *Where there's smoke, there's fire.* **4.** But; on the contrary: *Mars has two moons, where Earth has only one.* □*pronoun* **1.** What or which place: *Where did they come from?* **2.** The place in, at, or to which: *This is where I found the puppy.*
where (hwâr *or* wâr) □*adverb* □*conjunction* □*pronoun*

whereabouts *adverb* Where or about where: *Whereabouts are my glasses?*
□*noun* The place where someone or something is: *Nobody knows the whereabouts of the old mine.*
where·a·bouts (hwâr′ə bouts′ *or* wâr′ə bouts′) □*adverb* □*noun*

whereupon *conjunction* Following which: *I got hungry, whereupon I made a sandwich.*
where·up·on (hwâr′ə pon′ *or* wâr′ə pon′) □*conjunction*

wherever *adverb* Where; in or to whatever place: *Wherever he goes, he is welcome.*
□*conjunction* In or to whatever place: *Sit wherever you wish.*
wher·ev·er (hwâr ev′ər *or* wâr ev′ər) □*adverb* □*conjunction*

whether *conjunction* 1. No matter if: *We will have dinner at six o'clock whether you are here or not.* 2. If: *We didn't know whether you were coming or not.*
wheth·er (hwe*th*′ər *or* we*th*′ər) □*conjunction*

whey *noun* The watery part of milk that separates from the curds when milk turns sour.
whey (hwā *or* wā) □*noun*

which *pronoun* 1. What one or ones: *Which is your house?* 2. The one or ones: *Take those which are yours.* 3. The thing or animal just mentioned: *The movie which I saw was in color.*
□*adjective* 1. What one or ones: *Which coat is yours?* 2. Being the thing just mentioned: *It started raining, at which point we left the park.*
which (hwich *or* wich) □*pronoun* □*adjective*

whichever *adjective* Being any one or ones: *Wear whichever dress you want.*
□*pronoun* Any one or ones: *Buy whichever you like best.*
which·ev·er (hwich ev′ər *or* wich ev′ər) □*adjective* □*pronoun*

whiff *noun* A puff or smell carried in the air: *a whiff of smoke; a whiff of fresh bread.*
whiff (hwif *or* wif) □*noun, plural* **whiffs**

while *noun* A period of time: *stay for a while.*
□*conjunction* 1. As long as; during the time that: *It rained while we were in the museum.* 2. Although: *He is fat while his brothers are thin.*
□*verb* To pass or spend pleasantly or in a relaxed way: *We whiled away the afternoon playing in the park.*
while (hwīl *or* wīl) □*noun* □*conjunction* □*verb* **whiled, whiling, whiles**

whim *noun* A sudden wish, desire, or idea: *She had a whim to buy a new dress.*
whim (hwim *or* wim) □*noun, plural* **whims**

whimper *verb* To cry with weak, broken sounds: *The child whimpered when his mother told him he couldn't go outside.*
□*noun* A low, broken sound.
whim·per (hwim′pər *or* wim′pər) □*verb* **whimpered, whimpering, whimpers** □*noun, plural* **whimpers**

whine *verb* To make a high, complaining sound: *The child whined that he was hungry.*
□*noun* A whimpering sound or complaint.
whine (hwīn *or* wīn) □*verb* **whined, whining, whines** □*noun, plural* **whines**

whinny *noun* A gentle neigh made by a horse.
□*verb* To make a gentle neighing sound, such as a horse does.
whin·ny (hwin′ē *or* win′ē) □*noun, plural* **whinnies** □*verb* **whinnied, whinnying, whinnies**

whip *noun* A rod that bends or that has a lash attached to one end.
□*verb* 1. To strike with a whip: *The cowboy whipped his horse to make him go faster.* 2. To move suddenly and quickly: *The dog whipped down the street.* 3. To beat cream, eggs, or other ingredients into a foam. 4. To defeat in a fight or contest; beat.
whip (hwip *or* wip) □*noun, plural* **whips** □*verb* **whipped, whipping, whips**

whippoorwill *noun* A brown North American bird with a call that sounds like its name.
whip·poor·will (hwip′ər wil′ *or* wip′ər wil′) □*noun, plural* **whippoorwills**

whir *verb* To move swiftly with a buzzing or humming sound: *The fan whirred softly.*
□*noun* A buzzing or humming sound.
whir (hwûr *or* wûr) □*verb* **whirred, whirring, whirs** □*noun, plural* **whirs**

whirl *verb* 1. To turn or cause to turn: *The helicopter blades whirled faster and faster.* 2. To turn suddenly, changing directions: *She whirled around when I called out to her.*

a	bat	ī	bite	o͞o	tool	*th*	feather
ā	make	î	fierce	ou	out	th	bath
â	dare	o	dot	u	nut	hw	wheat
ä	father	ō	no	û	turn	zh	measure
e	net	ô	law, for	ch	church	ə	about, open
ē	be	oi	soil	ng	ring		pencil, atom
i	dip	oo	look	sh	shade		circus

□*noun* A quick turn; a whirling, spinning movement.

whirl (hwûrl *or* wûrl) □*verb* **whirled, whirling, whirls** □*noun, plural* **whirls**

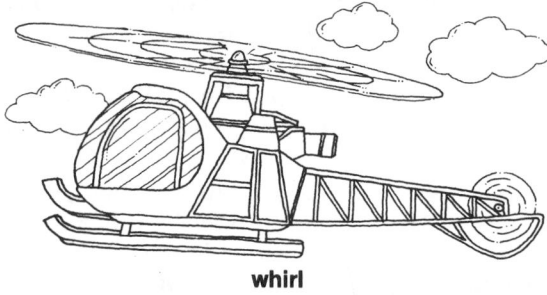

whirl

whirlpool *noun* A current of water that moves rapidly round and round.

whirl·pool (hwûrl′pool′ *or* wûrl′pool′) □*noun, plural* **whirlpools**

whirlwind *noun* A strong wind or current of air that turns round and round.

whirl·wind (hwûrl′wind′ *or* wûrl′wind′) □*noun, plural* **whirlwinds**

whisk *verb* **1.** To brush quickly and lightly: *I whisked the crumbs off the table.* **2.** To move or cause to move quickly: *Mom whisked me off to school.*

whisk (hwisk *or* wisk) □*verb* **whisked, whisking, whisks**

whisker *noun* **1. whiskers** The hair that grows on a man's face. **2.** A stiff, long hair growing near the mouth of certain animals, such as cats or rabbits.

whisk·er (hwisk′ər *or* wisk′ər) □*noun, plural* **whiskers**

whiskey *noun* An alcoholic drink made from corn, rye, barley, or other grains.

whis·key (hwis′kē *or* wis′kē) □*noun, plural* **whiskeys**

WORD HISTORY: **whiskey**

The word *whiskey* comes from Scotland. In the original language of Scotland the word means "water of life."

---

whisper *verb* To speak or say very softly: *She whispered the secret to me.*

□*noun* A soft, low sound: *I could hear whispers from the next room.*

whis·per (hwis′pər *or* wis′pər) □*verb* **whispered, whispering, whispers** □*noun, plural* **whispers**

whistle *verb* **1.** To make a clear, high sound by forcing air out through the teeth or through pursed lips. **2.** To make a sound like this: *The kettle whistles when the water boils. The wind whistled through the trees.* **3.** To signal or call by whistling: *The guard whistled for the car to stop.*

□*noun* **1.** A whistling sound or signal made by whistling: *We heard the whistle of the on-coming train.* **2.** A device that makes a whistling sound: *a policeman's whistle.*

whis·tle (hwis′əl *or* wis′əl) □*verb* **whistled, whistling, whistles** □*noun, plural* **whistles**

white *noun* **1.** The opposite of black; the color of snow. **2.** The white part of something: *the white of an egg.* **3.** A member of a race of people having light-colored skin.

□*adjective* **1.** Of or having the color white. **2.** Light in color: *the white meat of a chicken.* **3.** Having little color; pale: *He turned as white as a ghost.* **4.** Of or belonging to a race of people having light-colored skin. **5.** Pale gray or silvery: *The old man's hair was white.*

white (hwīt *or* wīt) □*noun, plural* **whites** □*adjective* **whiter, whitest**

white blood cell *noun* A colorless cell in the blood. Many white blood cells fight against infection by destroying disease germs.

whiten *verb* To make or become white or whiter.

whit·en (hwī′tən *or* wī′tən) □*verb* **whitened, whitening, whitens**

whitewash *noun* A thin liquid used to whiten walls and other surfaces.

white·wash (hwīt′wosh′ *or* wīt′wosh′) □*noun*

whitish *adjective* Somewhat white.

whit·ish (hwī′tish *or* wī′tish) □*adjective*

whittle *verb* **1.** To cut small bits or pieces from wood or other material with a knife: *She whittled the stick.* **2.** To make or shape something in this way: *He whittled a wooden horse for his grandson.*

whit·tle (hwit′əl *or* wit′əl) □*verb* **whittled, whittling, whittles**

whiz *verb* To move quickly with a buzzing sound: *The train whizzed along.*

whiz (hwiz *or* wiz) □*verb* **whizzed, whizzing, whizzes**

who *pronoun* **1.** What or which person or persons: *Who called?* **2.** That: *The boy who came yesterday left a note for you.*

who (hoo) □*pronoun*

who'd Contraction of "who would" and "who had."

who'd (hŏŏd)

whoever *pronoun* **1.** No matter who: *Whoever opened the safe was an expert.* **2.** Who: *Whoever invented such a thing?*

who·ev·er (hŏŏ ev′ ər) □*pronoun*

whole *adjective* Having all its parts; not divided: *The whole class is here. He read the whole book in two hours.*
□*noun* All of the parts of a thing: *Two halves make a whole.*

whole (hōl) □*adjective* □*noun, plural* **wholes**

SYNONYMS: whole, complete, entire

These adjectives mean including all parts or individuals: *The whole town is talking about the big fire. This is a complete deck of playing cards. She read the entire book in one night.*

---

whole number *noun* A number having no part that is a decimal or a fraction. The numbers 0, 2, 11, and 42 are whole numbers.

wholesale *noun* The sale of large quantities of goods to dealers.

whole·sale (hōl′ sāl′) □*noun, plural* **wholesales**

wholesome *adjective* **1.** Good for the health: *a simple but wholesome diet.* **2.** Having or showing good health.

whole·some (hōl′ səm) □*adjective*

who'll Contraction of "who will."

who'll (hŏŏl)

wholly *adverb* Entirely; completely: *He is wholly responsible for the accident.*

whol·ly (hō′ lē) □*adverb*

whom *pronoun* The objective case of **who**: *To whom did you give the letter? This is the girl whom I mentioned yesterday.*

whom (hŏŏm) □*pronoun*

whoop *noun* A loud cry or shout: *a whoop of joy.*
□*verb* To shout loudly: *The fans whooped when our team won the game.*

whoop (hŏŏp *or* hwŏŏp *or* wŏŏp) □*noun, plural* **whoops** □*verb* **whooped, whooping, whoops**

whooping crane *noun* A nearly extinct, large North American bird with long legs and black and white feathers.

whoop·ing crane (hŏŏ′ ping *or* hwŏŏ′ ping *or* wŏŏ′ ping) □*noun*

whooping crane

who's Contraction of "who is" and "who has."

who's (hŏŏz)

whose *pronoun* Belonging or relating to whom or which: *Whose car is this? The maple is a tree whose leaves turn red in the fall.*

whose (hŏŏz) □*pronoun*

why *adverb* For what reason or purpose: *Why won't you come with us?*
□*conjunction* Because of which; the reason for which: *I'll tell you why I don't want to go. Do you know the reason why he needs the money?*
□*interjection* A word used to show surprise, pleasure, or doubt: *Why, I'd love to go with you.*

why (hwī *or* wī) □*adverb* □*conjunction* □*interjection*

wick *noun* A cord or piece of twisted thread, such as in a candle or oil lamp that draws up the melted wax or oil to be burned.

wick (wik) □*noun, plural* **wicks**

wicked *adjective* Evil or morally bad; vicious: *a wicked witch who locked the princess in a tower.*

wick·ed (wik′ id) □*adjective*

wicker *noun* Thin twigs or branches that bend easily and are used especially to make baskets and furniture.

wick·er (wik′ ər) □*noun*

wide *adjective* **1.** Extending over or covering a large area from side to side: *a wide street; a wide table.* **2.** Having a certain distance from side to side: *a sheet of wallpaper 25 inches*

a bat	ī bite	ŏŏ tool	th feather
ā make	î fierce	ou out	th bath
â dare	o dot	u nut	hw wheat
ä father	ō no	û turn	zh measure
e net	ô law, for	ch church	ə about, open
ē be	oi soil	ng ring	pencil, atom
i dip	oo look	sh shade	circus

wide. **3.** Having a large amount: *a nursery with a wide selection of plants.* **4.** Far away from a certain place: *Every shot was wide of the target.*
□*adverb* **1.** Over a large area: *She has traveled far and wide during her lifetime.* **2.** To the full extent: *The dentist told me to open my mouth wide.*
wide (wīd) □*adjective* **wider, widest** □*adverb*

widen   *verb* To make or become wide or wider: *The river widens below the town.*
wid·en (wīd′ən) □*verb* **widened, widening, widens**

widespread   *adjective* **1.** Happening in many places or to a large number of people: *Concern about pollution is widespread in the country.* **2.** Spread out wide; fully open: *the widespread wings of a hawk in flight.*
wide·spread (wīd′spred′) □*adjective*

widow   *noun* A woman whose husband has died and who has not married again.
wid·ow (wid′ō) □*noun, plural* **widows**

widower   *noun* A man whose wife has died and who has not married again.
wid·ow·er (wid′ō ər) □*noun, plural* **widowers**

width   *noun* The distance of something from one side to the other: *The width of the kitchen is twelve feet.*
width (width) □*noun, plural* **widths**

wife   *noun* A woman who is married.
wife (wīf) □*noun, plural* **wives**

> **WORD HISTORY: wife**
>
> *Wife* comes from an old English word meaning ''woman.''

---

wig   *noun* A covering for the head made of real or artificial hair.
wig (wig) □*noun, plural* **wigs**

wiggle   *verb* To move or cause to move from side to side with short, quick motions: *The snake wiggled through the grass. Can you wiggle your toes?*
wig·gle (wig′əl) □*verb* **wiggled, wiggling, wiggles**

wigwam   *noun* A Native American dwelling made of poles covered with hides, bark, or other material.
wig·wam (wig′wom′) □*noun, plural* **wigwams**

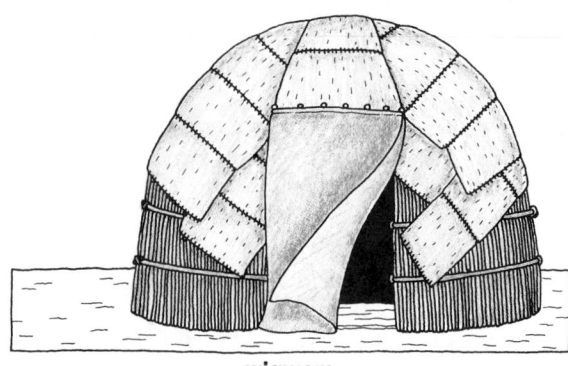

wigwam

wild   *adjective* **1.** Growing, living, or found in a natural state: *wild flowers; the wild animals of the jungle.* **2.** Not having discipline or control: *He was a wild boy who was always in trouble.* **3.** Strange; crazy: *His wild plans never work out.*
□*adverb* Not under control.
wild (wīld) □*adjective* **wilder, wildest** □*adverb*

wildcat   *noun* A lynx, bobcat, or other small, wild animal related to the domestic cat.
wild·cat (wīld′kat′) □*noun, plural* **wildcats**

wilderness   *noun* A wild place or region that is not lived in by people.
wil·der·ness (wil′dər nis) □*noun, plural* **wildernesses**

wildlife   *noun* Wild plants and animals that live in their natural surroundings.
wild·life (wīld′līf′) □*noun*

will¹   *noun* **1.** The power of mind to choose or control one's actions. **2.** Strong purpose; determination: *the will to win.* **3.** A legal document that says what a person wants done with his or her property after death.
□*verb* **1.** To use the power of the mind to bring about or do: *She willed herself to stay awake.* **2.** To give away one's property in a will: *He willed all his money to the university.*
will (wil) □*noun, plural* **wills** □*verb* **willed, willing, wills**

will²   *verb* **1.** Used to show future time: *She will be twenty next year.* **2.** Used to express an order: *You will do as you are told.* **3.** Used to express determination: *I will never go there again.*
will (wil) □*verb*

willful   *adjective* **1.** Said or done deliberately: *willful disobedience.* **2.** Obstinate or stubborn about having one's own way: *a willful, proud man.*
will·ful (wil′fəl) □*adjective*

willing *adjective* Ready to act or do: *He is willing to wait for hours if necessary.*
will·ing (wil′ing) ☐*adjective*

willow *noun* A tree with slender, flexible twigs and narrow leaves.
wil·low (wil′ō) ☐*noun, plural* **willows**

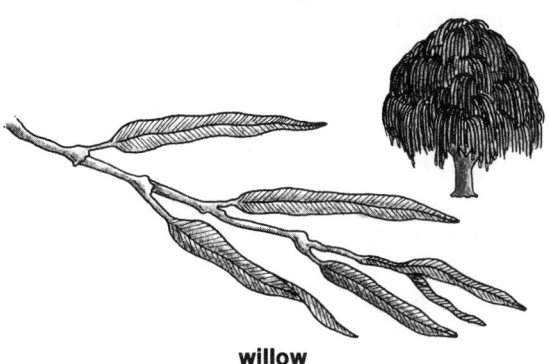

willow

wilt *verb* To become limp; droop: *The flowers wilted in the sun.*
wilt (wilt) ☐*verb* **wilted, wilting, wilts**

win *verb* **1.** To get victory in a contest or battle: *My brother's team won the game. Do you think she will win the election?* **2.** To gain through hard work: *She won fame as a scientist.*
☐*noun* A victory or triumph: *The hockey team started the year with six wins in a row.*
win (win) ☐*verb* **won, winning, wins** ☐*noun, plural* **wins**

wince *verb* To move back quickly from something that is painful, dangerous, or frightening: *We winced when the strange dog growled.*
wince (wins) ☐*verb* **winced, wincing, winces**

winch *noun* A machine for lifting or pulling something. It is made up of a drum and a long rope or chain with an object attached to it. When the drum is turned, the rope winds around it and lifts the object.
winch (winch) ☐*noun, plural* **winches**

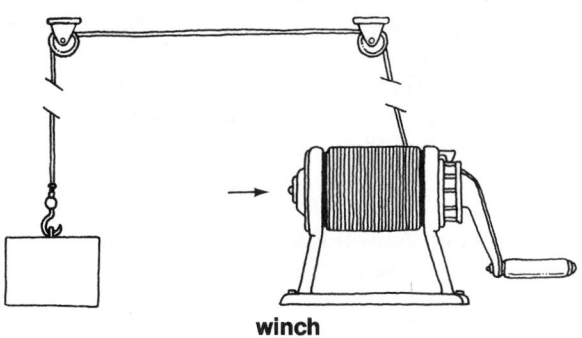

winch

wind¹ *noun* **1.** Air that moves over the earth. **2.** Breath: *She was out of wind after running all the way home.*
☐*verb* To cause to be out of breath: *All the running around winded the children.*
wind (wind) ☐*noun, plural* **winds** ☐*verb* **winded, winding, winds**

wind² *verb* **1.** To wrap around or on top of something: *Could you wind the rope around the pole please?* **2.** To move or cause to move first one way and then another: *The river winds through a deep valley.* **3.** To cause a clock or other device to work by turning or coiling the spring: *wind a watch.*
wind (wīnd) ☐*verb* **wound, winding, winds**

wind instrument *noun* A musical instrument that is played by blowing through it. Flutes and clarinets are wind instruments.

windmill *noun* A machine that uses the power of the wind to turn vanes set at the top. Windmills are used to grind grain and pump water.
wind·mill (wind′mil′) ☐*noun, plural* **windmills**

window *noun* An opening in a wall or ceiling that lets in air and light and is usually made of glass enclosed in a frame.
win·dow (win′dō) ☐*noun, plural* **windows**

WORD HISTORY: **window**

Window comes from an old Norse word that was formed from the words for "wind" and "eye."

---

windowpane *noun* A piece of glass in a window.
win·dow·pane (win′dō pān′) ☐*noun, plural* **windowpanes**

windpipe *noun* A tube that goes from the throat to the lungs and carries air to and away from the lungs.
wind·pipe (wind′pīp′) ☐*noun, plural* **windpipes**

windshield *noun* A sheet of glass or plastic at the front of an automobile, motorcycle, or other vehicle.

a bat	ī bite	ōō tool	th feather
ā make	î fierce	ou out	th bath
â dare	o dot	u nut	hw wheat
ä father	ō no	û turn	zh measure
e net	ô law, for	ch church	ə about, open
ē be	oi soil	ng ring	pencil, atom
i dip	oo look	sh shade	circus

wind·shield (**wind′**shēld′) □*noun, plural* **windshields**

windy *adjective* Having a great deal of wind: *a windy day.*
wind·y (**win′**dē) □*adjective* **windier, windiest**

wine *noun* An alcoholic beverage made of the fermented juice of grapes or other fruits.
wine (wīn) □*noun, plural* **wines**

wing *noun* **1.** One of the movable parts which a bird, bat, or insect uses in order to fly. **2.** A structure located on either side of an airplane. Wings lift the plane and support it on air during flight. **3.** A part that is attached to the main part of a structure: *A new wing was added to the museum.* **4. wings** An area at the side of a stage: *The next speaker was waiting in the wings.*
□*verb* **1.** To fly: *birds winging above the houses.* **2.** To wound slightly: *The bullet only winged him.*
wing (wing) □*noun, plural* **wings** □*verb* **winged, winging, wings**

winged *adjective* Having wings: *Flies and mosquitoes are winged insects.*
winged (wingd) □*adjective*

wingspread *noun* The distance between the tip of one wing to the tip of the other when they are spread wide: *the wingspread of an eagle.*
wing·spread (**wing′**spred′) □*noun, plural* **wingspreads**

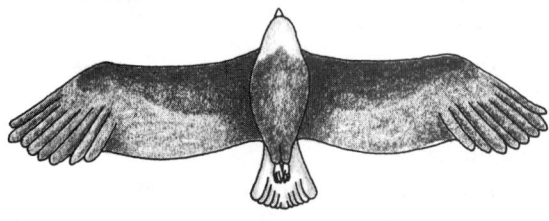

wingspread

wink *verb* To close and open one eye quickly: *She winked to show she understood.*
□*noun* **1.** The act of winking: *She gave me a wink as a signal.* **2.** A very short time: *If everyone helps the work will be done in a wink.*
wink (wingk) □*verb* **winked, winking, winks** □*noun, plural* **winks**

winner *noun* Someone or something that wins: *The winner of each race will get a prize.*
win·ner (**win′**ər) □*noun, plural* **winners**

winning *adjective* **1.** Successful or victorious: *the winning team.* **2.** Charming or attrac-

tive: *a winning smile.*
win·ning (**win′**ing) □*adjective*

winter *noun* The season of the year between fall and spring.
win·ter (**win′**tər) □*noun, plural* **winters**

wintergreen *noun* A plant that produces an oil used in medicine and for flavoring.
win·ter·green (**win′**tər grēn′) □*noun*

wintry *adjective* Of or like winter: *a wintry chill was in the air.*
win·try (**win′**trē) □*adjective* **wintrier, wintriest**

wipe *verb* **1.** To rub with something in order to clean or dry: *He wiped the table with a damp cloth. Please wipe your shoes on the mat.* **2.** To remove as if by rubbing: *I wiped the crumbs off the counter.*
  wipe out To destroy completely: *A sudden frost wiped out the whole crop.*
wipe (wīp) □*verb* **wiped, wiping, wipes**

wire *noun* **1.** A thin strand of metal made by stretching or drawing out a piece of metal. **2.** A telegram.
□*verb* **1.** To connect or fasten with a wire. **2.** To install or put in wires for electricity: *Who wired a new building?* **3.** To send a telegram: *I wired my answer to the office.*
wire (wīr) □*noun, plural* **wires** □*verb* **wired, wiring, wires**

wireless *adjective* Not using or having wires. Radio is a form of wireless communication because its signals are sent by waves that move through the air.
wire·less (**wīr′**lis) □*adjective*

wiring *noun* A system of wires that carries electricity: *He had completely new wiring put into the house.*
wir·ing (**wīr′**ing) □*noun*

wiry *adjective* **1.** Like wire: *wiry hair.* **2.** Thin but strong: *a wiry body.*
wir·y (**wīr′**ē) □*adjective* **wirier, wiriest**

wisdom *noun* Intelligence and good judgment in knowing what to do and what is good and bad and right and wrong.
wis·dom (**wiz′**dəm) □*noun*

wise *adjective* Having or showing good judgment and intelligence: *a wise person; a wise decision.*
wise (wīz) □*adjective* **wiser, wisest**

wish *noun* A strong desire for something: *He has always had a wish to meet the President.*
□*verb* **1.** To want something; desire: *The boy wished that he could have a dog.* **2.** To make or

express a wish.

wish (wish) ▢*noun, plural* **wishes** ▢*verb*
wished, wishing, wishes

wishbone　*noun* A bone with a shape like a V, located in front of the breastbone of a bird, such as a chicken or turkey. Two people often make wishes and grasp opposite ends of the bone, pulling until it breaks. According to tradition, the wish will be granted to the person left with the longer piece of bone.
wish·bone (wish′bōn′) ▢*noun, plural*
wishbones

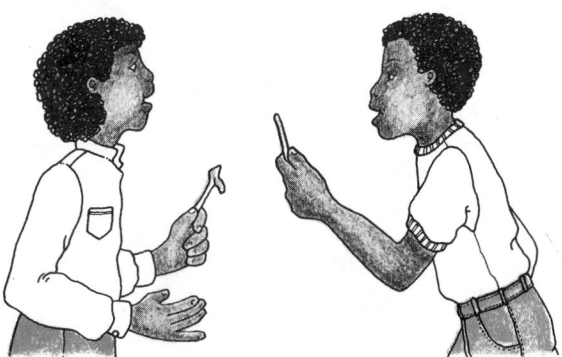

wishbone

wisteria　*noun* A climbing woody vine with hanging bunches of purple or white flowers.
wis·ter·i·a (wi stîr′ē ə) ▢*noun*

wistful　*adjective* Full of sad longing: *The lonely child had a wistful look on her face.*
wist·ful (wist′fəl) ▢*adjective*

wit　*noun* **1.** The ability to describe things, people, or situations in a clever, funny way. **2.** Someone having this ability. **3.** The ability to think and reason clearly: *She kept her wits about her and saved the animals from the burning barn.*
wit (wit) ▢*noun, plural* **wits**

witch　*noun* A woman who is thought to have magical powers.
witch (wich) ▢*noun, plural* **witches**

with　*preposition* **1.** In the company of: *with me.* **2.** In the possession of: *a clown with a red nose.* **3.** On the side of: *I'm with you all the way on this.* **4.** In spite of: *With all that talent, he still doesn't have a job.* **5.** Against: *He quarrels with everyone.* **6.** By means of: *Start the fire with flint and twigs.* **7.** Having or showing a feeling of: *He said good-by with great sadness.* **8.** At the same time as; during: *rising with the sun.* **9.** Because of; as a result of: *He was trembling with fear.* **10.** In proportion to:

Its height varies with its width. **11.** From: *She hates to part with money.* **12.** Between: *The company signed a contract with several bookstores.* **13.** In the care of: *You can leave your things with me.* **14.** In regard to: *I'm pleased with her report.*
with (wi*th* or with) ▢*preposition*

withdraw　*verb* **1.** To take away; remove: *We withdrew all our savings from the bank.* **2.** To take back: *She said I could use her bike, but then withdrew the offer.* **3.** To go away; remove oneself: *He withdrew from the race.*
with·draw (wi*th* drô′ or with drô′) ▢*verb*
withdrew, withdrawn, withdrawing,
withdraws

withdrawn　*verb* The past participle of **withdraw:** *Why has he withdrawn the invitation?* ▢*adjective* Shy or quiet; timid: *a withdrawn child with few friends.*
with·drawn (wi*th* drôn′ or with drôn′)
▢*verb* ▢*adjective*

withdrew　*verb* The past tense of **withdraw.**
with·drew (wi*th* drōō′ or with drōō′) ▢*verb*

wither　*verb* To dry up or cause to dry up; shrivel: *Plants will wither if they don't get enough water.*
with·er (wi*th*′ər) ▢*verb* **withered, withering,**
withers

within　*preposition* **1.** Inside of: *organs within the body.* **2.** Inside the limits of: *They were within ten miles of home.* **3.** Not going beyond: *within the law.*
▢*adverb* Inside; indoors: *He turned and went within.*
with·in (wi*th* in′ or with in′) ▢*preposition*
▢*adverb*

without　*preposition* **1.** Not having; lacking: *She was without the money to get home.* **2.** Not accompanied by: *There is no smoke without fire.* **3.** Outside.
▢*adverb* Outside.
with·out (wi*th* out′ or with out′)
▢*preposition* ▢*adverb*

withstand　*verb* To not give in to; resist or endure: *The enemy withstood our attack and fought bravely.*

a	bat	ī	bite	ōō	tool	*th*	feather
ā	make	i	fierce	ou	out	th	bath
â	dare	o	dot	u	nut	hw	wheat
ä	father	ō	no	û	turn	zh	measure
e	net	ô	law, for	ch	church	ə	about, open
ē	be	oi	soil	ng	ring		pencil, atom
i	dip	oo	look	sh	shade		circus

with·stand (with **stand'** *or* with **stand'**)
□*verb* **withstood, withstanding,
withstands**

withstood *verb* The past tense and past participle of **withstand:** *The old bike withstood years of abuse.*
with·stood (with **stood'** *or* with **stood'**)
□*verb*

witness *noun* **1.** Someone who has seen or heard something: *We were all witnesses of the great events of the day.* **2.** Someone who is called to testify before a court of law. **3.** Someone who is present at an event in order to confirm that the event took place.
□*verb* **1.** To be present at; see: *Did you witness the accident?* **2.** To sign a document as a witness: *witness a will.*
wit·ness (wit'nis) □*noun, plural* **witnesses**
□*verb* **witnessed, witnessing, witnesses**

witty *adjective* Clever and amusing: *a witty person; a witty remark.*
wit·ty (wit'ē) □*adjective* **wittier, wittiest**

wives *noun* The plural of **wife.**
wives (wīvz) □*noun*

wizard *noun* **1.** Someone who is thought to have magical powers; magician. **2.** Someone who has a certain skill: *She is a wizard at chess.*
wiz·ard (wiz'ərd) □*noun, plural* **wizards**

wk. An abbreviation for **week.**

wobble *verb* To move or cause to move unsteadily from side to side: *The table wobbles because one leg is shorter than the others.*
wob·ble (wob'əl) □*verb* **wobbled, wobbling, wobbles**

woe *noun* **1.** Deep sorrow or suffering; grief. **2.** Trouble: *the woes and sorrows of war.*
woe (wō) □*noun, plural* **woes**

woke *verb* A past tense of **wake:** *I woke up late every morning this week.*
woke (wōk) □*verb*

wolf *noun* A wild animal that is related to the dog. Wolves live mostly in northern regions and feed chiefly on the flesh of other animals.
□*verb* To eat quickly and greedily: *stop wolfing down your food.*
wolf (woolf) □*noun, plural* **wolves** □*verb*
wolfed, wolfing, wolfs

wolverine *noun* A wild animal having thick, dark fur and a bushy tail. Wolverines live in northern regions and feed on other animals.
wol·ver·ine (wool'və rēn') □*noun, plural*
wolverines

wolverine

wolves The plural of **wolf.**
wolves (woolvz) □*noun*

woman *noun* **1.** An adult female human being. **2.** Female human beings in general.
wom·an (woom'ən) □*noun, plural* **women**

WORD HISTORY: **woman**

Woman comes from an old English word made up of the words for "adult human female" and "human being." So *woman* originally meant "woman-person."

---

womb *noun* The organ in female mammals in which a baby is developed and nourished before birth.
womb (woom) □*noun, plural* **wombs**

women *noun* The plural of **woman.**
wo·men (wim'in) □*noun*

won *verb* The past tense and past participle of **win:** *We won first prize.*
won (wun) □*verb*

wonder *noun* **1.** A person, thing, or event that is unusual, surprising, or impressive: *The gigantic new skyscraper is a wonder.* **2.** The feeling caused by something unusual, surprising, or impressive: *We looked on with wonder as the man rescued the child from the sinking boat.*
□*verb* **1.** To feel awe and admiration: *We wondered at the sight of the huge plane flying low to the ground.* **2.** To be curious about: *I wonder what it's like to walk on the moon.*
won·der (wun'dər) □*noun, plural* **wonders**
□*verb* **wondered, wondering, wonders**

wonderful *adjective* **1.** Causing wonder; marvelous: *I bet it's wonderful to fly in a spaceship.* **2.** Very good: *a wonderful gift.*
won·der·ful (wun'dər fəl) □*adjective*

won't Contraction of "will not."
won't (wōnt)

wood *noun* **1.** The hard material that makes up the trunk and branches of trees and

bushes. Wood is used as fuel and for making buildings, furniture, paper, and many other things. **2. woods** A small area in which there are a great many trees; forest.
wood (wood) □*noun, plural* **woods**

woodchuck *noun* A North American animal with brownish fur and short legs; ground hog. Woodchucks dig burrows in the ground.
wood·chuck (wood′chuk′) □*noun, plural* **woodchucks**

woodcutter *noun* Someone whose job is to cut down trees or cut up wood.
wood·cut·ter (wood′kut′ər) □*noun, plural* **woodcutters**

wooded *adjective* Having trees or woods: *We play in a large wooded area behind the house.*
wood·ed (wood′id) □*adjective*

wooden *adjective* Made of wood.
wood·en (wood′n) □*adjective*

woodland *noun* A forest; woods.
wood·land (wood′lənd) □*noun, plural* **woodlands**

woodpecker *noun* A bird with a strong, pointed bill for drilling holes in trees in order to find insects to eat.
wood·peck·er (wood′pek′ər) □*noun, plural* **woodpeckers**

woodpecker

woodsman *noun* Someone who works or lives in the woods.
woods·man (woodz′mən) □*noun, plural* **woodsmen**

woodwind *noun* A musical instrument that is played by blowing air into it. In certain woodwinds, such as a clarinet, oboe, or bassoon, the sound is made when the breath causes a reed inside the mouthpiece to vibrate. In others, such as a flute or piccolo, the sound is made by blowing across an opening.

wood·wind (wood′wind′) □*noun, plural* **woodwinds**

woodwind

woodwork *noun* Something, such as the frame around a window, made of wood.
wood·work (wood′wûrk′) □*noun*

woody *adjective* **1.** Made of or containing wood: *a plant with a woody stem.* **2.** Covered with trees; wooded.
wood·y (wood′ē) □*adjective* **woodier, woodiest**

wool *noun* **1.** The thick, soft, curly hair of sheep and some other animals. **2.** Yarn, cloth, or clothing made of wool.
wool (wool) □*noun, plural* **wools**

woolen *adjective* Made of wool.
wool·en (wool′ən) □*adjective*

word *noun* **1.** A sound or group of sounds that has meaning and is a unit of speech. **2.** The written or printed letters that represent such a unit of speech. A sentence is made up of words. **3. words** A remark or short conversation: *a word of advice; only had time for a quick word before I left.* **4.** A promise: *He gave me his word that he'd help.* **5.** News or a message: *We've had no word from her in a month.* □*verb* To express in words: *Try to word your answers carefully.*

word for word Without changing or leaving out a word; exactly: *Tell me word for word what she said.*

a	bat	ī	bite	ōō	tool	*th*	feather
ā	make	î	fierce	ou	out	th	bath
â	dare	o	dot	u	nut	hw	wheat
ä	father	ō	no	û	turn	zh	measure
e	net	ô	law, for	ch	church	ə	about, open
ē	be	oi	soil	ng	ring		pencil, atom
i	dip	oo	look	sh	shade		circus

word (wûrd) □*noun, plural* **words** □*verb*
worded, wording, words

wording   *noun* The way something is said or written: *The wording of his instructions was not clear.*
word·ing (wûr′ding) □*noun*

wordy   *adjective* Using too many words: *a wordy explanation that took an hour.*
word·y (wûr′dē) □*adjective* **wordier, wordiest**

wore   *verb* The past tense of **wear**: *I wore my new suit to the dance.*
wore (wôr) □*verb*

work   *noun* **1.** The effort made to do or make something: *Cleaning a house is hard work.* **2.** What a person does to earn money; job or occupation: *A carpenter's work is building things out of wood.* **3.** A task: *We all have work to do.* **4.** Something that is made: *Everyone thought her new novel was her greatest work.* **5. works** The moving parts of a machine or device. —See Synonyms at **labor.**
□*verb* **1.** To put forth effort to do or make something: *I worked hard on my science project.* **2.** To have a job: *She works in a restaurant.* **3.** To function or cause to function in the proper way: *The toaster doesn't work. Please show me how to work this machine.*
    work out To do athletic exercises: *We work out together every morning.*
work (wûrk) □*noun, plural* **works** □*verb* **worked, working, works**

SYNONYMS: **work, job, occupation**
These nouns mean what a person does to earn money: *He found work in a steel mill. She has a job in a bookstore. She chose medicine as her occupation.*

---

workbench   *noun* A strong table or bench on which work is done. Workbenches are used by carpenters and other craftsmen.
work·bench (wûrk′bench′) □*noun, plural* **workbenches**

workbook   *noun* A book on a particular subject that has exercises and problems for a student to do.
work·book (wûrk′bŏŏk′) □*noun, plural* **workbooks**

worker   *noun* **1.** Someone who works: *How many workers are there on the farm?* **2.** A female ant, bee, or other insect that does most

of the work of a colony or hive and that cannot produce offspring.
work·er (wûr′kər) □*noun, plural* **workers**

workingman   *noun* Someone who does work in return for wages.
work·ing·man (wûr′king man′) □*noun, plural* **workingmen**

workman   *noun* **1.** A workingman. **2.** A person who is a skilled worker.
work·man (wûrk′mən) □*noun, plural* **workmen**

workmanship   *noun* **1.** The skill of a workman. **2.** The skill with which an object is made: *His work is noted for its fine workmanship.*
work·man·ship (wûrk′mən ship′) □*noun*

workout   *noun* Exercise or practice that makes a person more fit for activity: *Her skill and strength improved as a result of her daily workout at the gym.*
work·out (wûrk′out′) □*noun, plural* **workouts**

workout

workshop   *noun* A room or building where work is performed.
work·shop (wûrk′shop′) □*noun, plural* **workshops**

world   *noun* **1.** The earth: *Who was the first person to sail around the world?* **2.** A part of the earth: *The United States is in the western world.* **3.** All the people who live on earth: *The world wants peace.* **4.** A field or area of interest, activity, or knowledge: *the world of big business.* **5.** A large amount: *A vacation would do us all a world of good.* **6.** A heavenly body such as a planet: *Do you think that there is life on other worlds?*
world (wûrld) □*noun, plural* **worlds**

---

worm   *noun* Any of several kinds of animals having a soft, long body and no backbone. □*verb* **1.** To move by or as if by creeping or crawling: *The car wormed its way through the heavy traffic. He managed to worm out of trouble again.* **2.** To get from in a sly or sneaky way: *Don't try to worm the secret out of me.*
worm (wûrm) □*noun, plural* **worms** □*verb* **wormed, worming, worms**

worn   *verb* The past participle of **wear**: *Why haven't you worn your new shoes yet?* □*adjective* Damaged by wear or use: *The tires on the car are worn.*
worn (wôrn) □*verb* □*adjective*

worn-out   *adjective* **1.** No longer useful or in good condition: *a worn-out shirt.* **2.** Very tired; exhausted: *The men were worn-out after working all day.*
worn-out (wôrn′out′) □*adjective*

worry   *verb* **1.** To feel or cause to feel uneasy or anxious: *We worried about her until she phoned. Don't let his threats worry you.* **2.** To pull or tug at over and over: *The cat worried the string.* □*noun* Something that causes an uneasy feeling or anxiety: *Our biggest worry is that we'll be late for the train.*
wor·ry (wûr′ē) □*verb* **worried, worrying, worries** □*noun, plural* **worries**

worse   *adjective* **1.** The comparative of **bad**: *The situation is even worse than we thought it might be.* **2.** The comparative of **ill**: *Grandpa is worse and we think you should come home.* **3.** More inferior, such as in quality, condition, or effect: *She is an even worse speller than I am.* □*adverb* In a worse way: *I did worse on this test than on the last one.* □*noun* Something worse: *Her health has taken a turn for the worse.*
worse (wûrs) □*adjective* □*adverb* □*noun*

worship   *noun* Religious ceremonies and prayers in honor of God. □*verb* **1.** To honor and love as divine: *worship God.* **2.** To take part in a religious ceremony: *We worship in church every Sunday.* **3.** To love

or be devoted to: *The child worships his father.*
wor·ship (wûr′ship) □*noun* □*verb* **worshiped** or **worshipped, worshiping** or **worshipping, worships**

worst   *adjective* **1.** The superlative of **bad**: *He was the worst President we ever had.* **2.** The superlative of **ill**: *This is the worst health he has ever experienced.* **3.** Most inferior, such as in quality, condition, or effect: *the worst scrambled eggs I ever tasted.* □*noun* Someone or something that is worst: *That movie is the worst I ever saw.*
worst (wûrst) □*adjective* □*noun*

worth   *noun* **1.** The condition or quality that gives a person or thing value or importance: *the worth of a good reputation.* **2.** The value of something in money: *The worth of the house is $100,000.* **3.** The amount that a certain sum of money will buy: *We bought a dollar's worth of almonds.* □*adjective* **1.** Good enough to: *The new restaurant is worth trying.* **2.** Having the same value as; equal to: *an old book worth a hundred dollars.* **3.** Having wealth that amounts to: *Her family is worth a few million dollars.*
worth (wûrth) □*noun* □*adjective*

worthless   *adjective* Not useful or valuable: *a worthless piece of junk; worthless advice.*
worth·less (wûrth′lis) □*adjective*

worthwhile   *adjective* Valuable enough or important enough to spend effort, time, or money on: *a worthwhile project; a worthwhile sacrifice.*
worth·while (wûrth′hwīl′ or wûrth′wīl′) □*adjective*

worthy   *adjective* Having merit or value; good: *donated money to a worthy cause.*
wor·thy (wûr′thē) □*adjective* **worthier, worthiest**

would   *verb* **1.** Used to indicate something that is likely: *They would have arrived by now if they had left on time.* **2.** Used to express something that is preferred or wanted more than something else: *I would rather stay home tonight.* **3.** Used to indicate something planned or intended: *She said she would help.*

a	bat	ī	bite	oͦo	tool	*th*	feather
ā	make	î	fierce	ou	out	th	bath
â	dare	o	dot	u	nut	hw	wheat
ä	father	ō	no	û	turn	zh	measure
e	net	ô	law, for	ch	church	ə	about, open
ē	be	oi	soil	ng	ring		pencil, atom
i	dip	oo	look	sh	shade		circus

4. Used to make a request: *Would you help me move the sofa?*
would (wood) ▢*verb*

wouldn't Contraction of "would not."
would·n't (wood′ənt)

wound¹ *noun* An injury, especially one in which the skin is broken.
▢*verb* **1.** To injure or hurt by cutting, piercing, or breaking the skin: *He dropped the knife and wounded himself in the foot.* **2.** To hurt another's feelings: *The insulting remarks wounded her pride.*
wound (woond) ▢*noun, plural* **wounds**
▢*verb* **wounded, wounding, wounds**

wound² *verb* The past tense and past participle of **wind:** *I wound the watch.*
wound (wound) ▢*verb*

wove *verb* The past tense of **weave:** *She wove baskets for a living.*
wove (wōv) ▢*verb*

woven *verb* A past participle of **weave:** *We learned that she had woven the scarf herself.*
wo·ven (wō′vən) ▢*verb*

wow *interjection* A word used to express surprise or excitement: *Wow! She won!*
wow (wou) ▢*interjection*

wrap *verb* **1.** To cover or enclose by folding something around: *We wrapped the lettuce in a towel. Will you help me wrap the package?* **2.** To clasp or wind around: *She wrapped her arms around me.*
wrap (rap) ▢*verb* **wrapped, wrapping, wraps**

wrap

wrapper *noun* A piece of paper or other material that is used to cover something: *A candy wrapper.*
wrap·per (rap′ər) ▢*noun, plural* **wrappers**

wrapping *noun* Paper or other material used for wrapping or covering something.
wrap·ping (rap′ing) ▢*noun, plural* **wrappings**

wrath *noun* Very great anger; fury.
wrath (rath) ▢*noun, plural* **wraths**

wreak *verb* **1.** To express freely: *wreak one's anger.* **2.** To bring about; create: *The storm wreaked a trail of ruin and destruction along the coast.*
wreak (rēk) ▢*verb* **wreaked, wreaking, wreaks**

wreath *noun* A circle made of leaves, branches, or flowers that are tied or twisted together: *a Christmas wreath.*
wreath (rēth) ▢*noun, plural* **wreaths**

wreath

wreck *verb* To ruin or destroy: *The hurricane wrecked most of the ships in the harbor. His arrival wrecked all our plans.*
▢*noun* Something that has been wrecked: *That car is just an old wreck.*
wreck (rek) ▢*verb* **wrecked, wrecking, wrecks** ▢*noun, plural* **wrecks**

wreckage *noun* The remains of something wrecked: *Workers cleaned up the wreckage after the fire.*
wreck·age (rek′ij) ▢*noun, plural* **wreckages**

wren *noun* A small brown bird that holds its tail pointed upward.
wren (ren) ▢*noun, plural* **wrens**

wrench *noun* **1.** A sudden, hard twist or turn: *The drawer was stuck so I gave it a wrench to open it.* **2.** A tool with jaws, used for gripping and turning such things as nuts and bolts. —See Synonyms at **jerk.**
▢*verb* To pull or turn suddenly and with force: *wrenched the book away from her.*
wrench (rench) ▢*noun, plural* **wrenches** ▢*verb* **wrenched, wrenching, wrenches**

wrestle *verb* **1.** To force or try to force to the ground by grasping and tripping or throwing an opponent. **2.** To struggle with: *wrestled*

with a problem.
wres·tle (res′əl) ☐*verb* **wrestled, wrestling, wrestles**

wrestler *noun* Someone who wrestles.
wres·tler (res′lər) ☐*noun, plural* **wrestlers**

wrestling *noun* A sport in which two opponents wrestle with each other.
wres·tling (res′ling) ☐*noun*

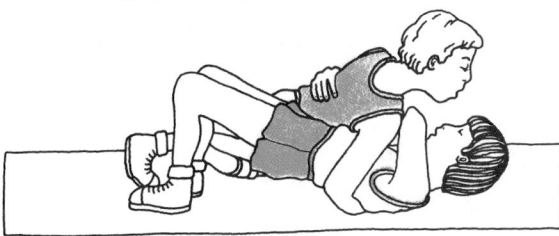
wrestling

wretched *adjective* **1.** Very unhappy or unfortunate: *I felt wretched when I heard the bad news.* **2.** Very poor in quality: *wretched working conditions.*
wretch·ed (rech′id) ☐*adjective*

wriggle *verb* **1.** To turn, twist, or move side to side with quick movements: *The dentist told me to stop wriggling and sit still.* **2.** To get into or out of a situation by clever means: *I tried to wriggle out of helping her wash the car.*
wrig·gle (rig′əl) ☐*verb* **wriggled, wriggling, wriggles**

wring *verb* **1.** To twist and squeeze to force water or other liquid out: *wring out a wet towel.* **2.** To force out liquid by twisting, squeezing, or pressing: *Wring the water out of the towel and hang it up.* **3.** To get by force: *I couldn't wring the secret out of her.* **4.** To hold tightly together and press or twist: *wring one's hands.*
wring (ring) ☐*verb* **wrung, wringing, wrings**

wring

wrinkle *noun* A small crease, ridge, or fold on a smooth surface: *You'll have to iron the wrinkles out of that shirt.*
☐*verb* To make or have wrinkles in: *He wrinkled the paper and threw it away.*
wrin·kle (ring′kəl) ☐*noun, plural* **wrinkles**
☐*verb* **wrinkled, wrinkling, wrinkles**

wrinkle

wrist *noun* The joint at which the hand and arm come together.
wrist (rist) ☐*noun, plural* **wrists**

wristwatch *noun* A watch worn around the wrist.
wrist·watch (rist′woch′) ☐*noun, plural* **wristwatches**

write *verb* **1.** To form letters, symbols, or words on a surface: *Write your name at the top of the paper.* **2.** To make up, as a story or poem; compose: *She has written four novels.* **3.** To send a letter or note to: *I write to my grandparents once a week.*
write (rīt) ☐*verb* **wrote, written, writing, writes**

writer *noun* Someone who writes, especially a person whose job is writing; author.
writ·er (rī′tər) ☐*noun, plural* **writers**

writing *noun* **1.** Letters or symbols written or printed on a surface: *Your writing is hard to read.* **2. writings** A collection of written works:

a bat	ī bite	oo tool	th feather
ā make	î fierce	ou out	th bath
â dare	o dot	u nut	hw wheat
ä father	ō no	û turn	zh measure
e net	ô law, for	ch church	ə about, open
ē be	oi soil	ng ring	pencil, atom
i dip	oo look	sh shade	circus

She has read all the writings of Shakespeare.
writ·ing (rī′ting) ▢*noun, plural* **writings**

written *verb* The past participle of **write:** *I haven't written my book report yet.*
writ·ten (rit′ən) ▢*verb*

wrong *adjective* **1.** Not correct; mistaken: *I sent the letter to the wrong address.* **2.** Bad or immoral: *It is wrong to lie.* **3.** Not fitting or suitable: *That color is wrong for you.* **4.** Not working or behaving properly: *Something is wrong with the car.* —See Synonyms at **false.**
▢*adverb* Incorrectly; mistakenly: *You did everything wrong.*
▢*noun* An unjust or immoral act: *You did a great wrong by lying to her.*
▢*verb* To treat unfairly or unjustly.
wrong (rông) ▢*adjective* ▢*adverb* ▢*noun, plural* **wrongs** ▢*verb* **wronged, wronging, wrongs**

wrote *verb* The past participle of **write:** *I wrote her a letter.*
wrote (rōt) ▢*verb*

wrung *verb* The past tense and past participle of **wring:** *Have you wrung out the clothes yet?*
wrung (rung) ▢*verb*

wry *adjective* Twisted or bent to one side: *He gave a wry smile.*
wry (rī) ▢*adjective* **wrier** or **wryer, wriest** or **wryest**

a	bat	ī	bite	o͞o	tool	*th*	feather
ā	make	î	fierce	ou	out	th	bath
â	dare	o	dot	u	nut	hw	wheat
ä	father	ō	no	û	turn	zh	measure
e	net	ô	law, for	ch	church	ə	about, open
ē	be	oi	soil	ng	ring		pencil, atom
i	dip	oo	look	sh	shade		circus

ANCIENT GREEK

The letter **X** has evolved from many forms of ancient writing. One of the earliest known examples is the Greek character shown above, which dates from almost 3,000 years ago. Over the years, artists and designers have created their own versions of the English letter **X**. Some of the more common examples seen today are shown below.

| HANDWRITING | CALLIGRAPHY | MODERN SANS SERIF | MODERN SERIF | SCRIPT |

---

x or **X** *noun* **1.** The twenty-fourth letter of the English alphabet. **2.** A mark made on a map, chart, or other drawing to show a place or location.
x or **X** (eks) □*noun, plural* **x's** or **X's**

Xerox A trademark for a machine or process that makes photographic copies of written or printed material.
Xe·rox (zîr oks′)

Xmas *noun* Christmas.
X·mas (kris′məs *or* eks′məs) □*noun, plural* **Xmases**

> ### WORD HISTORY: Xmas
>
> The character X in *Xmas* is not the letter *x* in the English alphabet. The X is the Greek letter named *chi*, which is the first letter in the Greek name for Christ. The symbol X has been used as an abbreviation for "Christ" for many centuries. *Xmas* is therefore an abbreviation for *Christmas*.

x-ray or **X-ray** *noun* **1.** A ray similar to a light ray that can go through substances that regular rays of light cannot go through. X-rays are used to take photographs of solid objects, such as bones, inside the body. **2.** A photograph made with x-rays: *an x-ray of a broken ankle.*
□*verb* To examine, photograph, or treat with x-rays: *The doctor will x-ray your arm to see if it is broken.*
x-ray or **X-ray** (eks′rā) □*noun, plural* **x-rays** or **X-rays** □*verb* **x-rayed** or **X-rayed, x-raying** or **X-raying, x-rays** or **X-rays**

> ### WORD HISTORY: x-ray
>
> Scientists and mathematicians often used the letter *x* as a symbol for something unknown. This symbol *x* is used in the word *x-ray* because the scientist who discovered x-rays did not completely understand them.

xylophone *noun* A musical instrument that is made up of two rows of wooden bars of varying lengths. A xylophone is played by striking the bars with small wooden mallets.
xy·lo·phone (zī′lə fōn′) □*noun, plural* **xylophones**

> ### WORD HISTORY: xylophone
>
> *Xylophone* comes from two Greek words, one meaning "wood" and the other meaning "sound."

xylophone

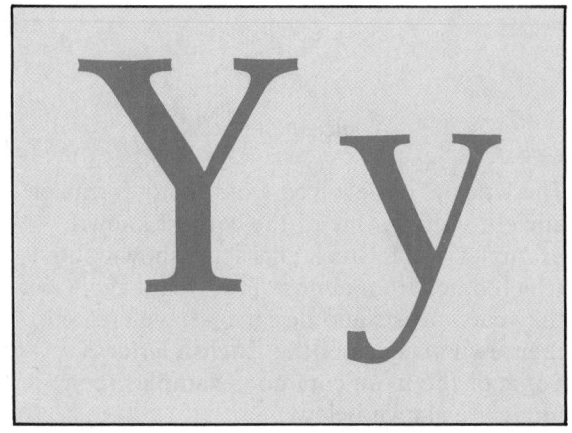

The letter **Y** has evolved from many forms of ancient writing. One of the earliest known examples is the Greek character shown above, which dates from almost 3,000 years ago. Over the years, artists and designers have created their own versions of the English letter **Y.** Some of the more common examples seen today are shown below.

HANDWRITING

CALLIGRAPHY

MODERN SANS SERIF

MODERN SERIF

SCRIPT

y or **Y** *noun* The twenty-fifth letter of the English alphabet.
y or **Y** (wī) ▢*noun, plural* **y's** or **Y's**

–y¹ A suffix that forms adjectives and means "full of" or "resembling": *dirty; watery.*

–y² A suffix that forms nouns and means "state or condition": *jealousy.*

–y³ A suffix that forms nouns and means "small one" or "dear one": *kitty; daddy.*

yacht *noun* A small ship used for pleasure trips or racing.
yacht (yät) ▢*noun, plural* **yachts**

WORD HISTORY: **yacht**

Yacht comes from an Old Dutch word that means "ship for chasing." The Dutch ships were used for chasing and capturing pirates.

---

yak *noun* An Asian animal with long hair and horns, important as a work animal and for its milk.
yak (yak) ▢*noun, plural* **yaks**

yak

yam *noun* **1.** The root of a climbing vine that grows in tropical climates. Yams are eaten as a vegetable or ground into flour. **2.** A reddish sweet potato.
yam (yam) ▢*noun, plural* **yams**

yank *verb* To pull with a sudden, jerking movement: *He yanked the magazine out of my hands.* —See Synonyms at **jerk.**
▢*noun* A sudden, sharp pull: *I gave a yank on the rope.*
yank (yangk) ▢*verb* **yanked, yanking, yanks** ▢*noun, plural* **yanks**

Yankee *noun* **1.** Someone born or living in New England. **2.** Someone from the northern part of the United States. **3.** Someone born or living in the United States.
Yan·kee (yang′kē) ▢*noun, plural* **Yankees**

yard¹ *noun* **1.** A unit of length equal to three feet or 36 inches. A yard equals 0.914 meter. **2.** A long pole attached crosswise to a mast to support a sail.
yard (yärd) ▢*noun, plural* **yards**

yard² *noun* **1.** A piece of ground near a house or other building. **2.** An enclosed area used for a certain kind of business or activity: *a lumber yard; a navy yard.*
yard (yärd) ▢*noun, plural* **yards**

yarn *noun* **1.** Wool or other fibers spun into long strands and used for knitting, weaving, or mending. **2.** A long tale of adventure.
yarn (yärn) ▢*noun, plural* **yarns**

yawn *verb* **1.** To open the mouth wide and breathe in deeply, usually because one is

sleepy or bored. **2.** To be open wide: *The entrance to the old mine yawned ahead of them.*
□*noun* The act of yawning.
yawn (yôn) □*verb* **yawned, yawning, yawns**
□*noun, plural* **yawns**

yawn

year *noun* **1.** The period of time during which the earth makes one complete revolution around the sun, equal to about 365¼ days. **2.** A period of twelve months. **3.** A period of time, often shorter than twelve months, used for a special activity: *the school year.*
year (yîr) □*noun, plural* **years**

yearly *adjective* **1.** Taking place once a year: *a yearly vacation.* **2.** For or during a single year: *yearly income.*
□*adverb* Once a year or every year: *We visit New York yearly.*
year·ly (yîr′lē) □*adjective* □*adverb*

yeast *noun* A fungus used in baking bread, brewing beer, and for other purposes.
yeast (yēst) □*noun, plural* **yeasts**

yell *verb* To shout or cry out loudly: *He yelled at me for not cleaning my room. The crowd yelled with excitement.*
□*noun* A loud shout or cry.
yell (yel) □*verb* **yelled, yelling, yells** □*noun, plural* **yells**

yellow *noun* **1.** The color of ripe lemons. **2.** The yolk of an egg.
□*adjective* Of the color yellow.
□*verb* To make or become yellow: *Paper yellows with age.*
yel·low (yel′ō) □*noun, plural* **yellows**
□*adjective* **yellower, yellowest** □*verb*
yellowed, yellowing, yellows

yellow jacket *noun* Any of several wasps with black and yellow markings.

yen *noun* A strong desire.
yen (yen) □*noun, plural* **yens**

yes *adverb* It is true: *Yes, I think you're right.*
□*noun* An answer that indicates agreement, approval, or support.
yes (yes) □*adverb* □*noun, plural* **yeses**

yesterday *noun* The day before today.
□*adverb* On the day before today: *I saw her yesterday.*
yes·ter·day (yes′tər dā′ *or* yes′tər dē) □*noun, plural* **yesterdays** □*adverb*

yet *adverb* **1.** At this time; now: *I can't leave yet.* **2.** Up to now; so far: *She hasn't arrived yet.* **3.** Besides; in addition: *She gave me yet another excuse.* **4.** Even; still more: *That story was sad, but I have a yet sadder one to tell.* **5.** Nevertheless: *She was young, yet wise.* **6.** At some future time: *I may yet change my mind.*
□*conjunction* Nevertheless; but despite this: *She looks happy, yet I know she's upset.*
yet (yet) □*adverb* □*conjunction*

yew *noun* An evergreen tree or shrub that has poisonous, flat dark-green needles and red berries. The tough wood of the yew is used for making archery bows.
yew (yōō) □*noun, plural* **yews**

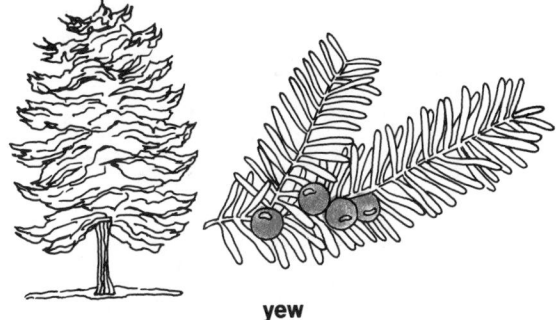

yew

yield *verb* **1.** To give forth; produce: *This tree will yield two bushels of apples.* **2.** To give up; surrender: *The general said his troops would never yield.* **3.** To give in: *I yielded to her arguments.* **4.** To give way to pressure or force: *We tried to beat down the door, but it would not yield.*

a bat	ī bite	ōō tool	*th* feather
ā make	î fierce	ou out	th bath
â dare	o dot	u nut	hw wheat
ä father	ō no	û turn	zh measure
e net	ô law, for	ch church	ə about, open
ē be	oi soil	ng ring	pencil, atom
i dip	oo look	sh shade	circus

□*noun* An amount produced: *a poor yield of wheat this year.*
yield (yēld) □*verb* **yielded, yielding, yields** □*noun, plural* **yields**

SYNONYMS: **yield, submit, surrender**

These verbs mean to give in or give up: *Even though I thought I was right, I yielded to his argument. You will have to submit to your father's decision. The enemy soldiers surrendered after a long fight.*

---

yogurt *noun* A sour tasting food resembling custard that is made from milk thickened by the action of bacteria.
yo·gurt (yō′gərt) □*noun*

yoke *noun* **1.** A bar with two pieces shaped like U's that fit around the necks of a pair of oxen or other animals so that they can pull a plow or a load. **2.** *plural* **yoke** or **yokes** A pair of animals joined by a yoke: *a yoke of oxen.* **3.** Part of a piece of clothing that fits closely around the neck and shoulders or over the hips.
□*verb* To join together with a yoke: *Yoke the oxen to the plow.*
yoke (yōk) □*noun, plural* **yokes** *or* yoke □*verb* **yoked, yoking, yokes**

yoke

yolk *noun* The yellow part of an egg.
yolk (yōk) □*noun, plural* **yolks**

yonder *adjective* At a distance; within sight but not near: *yonder meadow.*
□*adverb* In, to, or at that place; over there: *The town lies yonder across the river.*
yon·der (yon′dər) □*adjective* □*adverb*

you *pronoun* **1.** The person or persons spoken to: *You have very little time left. Are you sick?* **2.** A person in general; one; anyone: *You can never be too careful when you drive.*
you (yōō) □*pronoun*

you'd Contraction of "you had" or "you would."
you'd (yōōd)

you'll Contraction of "you will" or "you shall."
you'll (yōōl)

young *adjective* **1.** Not old or fully grown: *a young child.* **2.** At or near the beginning: *the young days of the settlement.* **3.** Having the qualities of young people: *an old woman with a young outlook on life.*
□*noun* Humans or animals in an early stage of development: *The young of many birds are covered with down when they hatch.*
young (yung) □*adjective* **younger, youngest** □*noun, plural* **young**

youngster *noun* A child or young person.
young·ster (yung′stər) □*noun, plural* **youngsters**

your *adjective* Belonging or relating to you: *Is this your house? Here's a list of your duties.*
your (yoor *or* yər) □*adjective*

you're Contraction of "you are."
you're (yoor *or* yər)

yours *pronoun* The one or ones belonging to you: *Is that hat yours? Use my car if yours hasn't been repaired.*
yours (yoorz) □*pronoun*

yourself *pronoun* Your own self: *You should not tire yourself. Keep it for yourself. You said it yourself.*
your·self (yoor self′ *or* yər self′) □*pronoun, plural* **yourselves**

youth *noun* **1.** The condition or quality of being young. **2.** The early time of life before one is an adult: *She spent her youth on a farm.* **3.** A boy or young man: *Her brother is a youth of sixteen.* **4.** Young people in general.
youth (yōōth) □*noun, plural* **youths**

youthful *adjective* **1.** Of or typical of a young person: *a youthful face.* **2.** Having or giving the look or quality of youth: *youthful clothing.*
youth·ful (yōōth′fəl) □*adjective*

you've Contraction of "you have."
you've (yōōv)

yo-yo *noun* A toy having two disks connected by a short axle. String is wound around the axle and one end is tied to a finger. When the yo-yo is thrown downward, the string unwinds, causing the yo-yo to spin. When the yo-yo reaches the end of the string, its spin causes it to climb back up the string, winding the string around the axle at the same time.
yo-yo (yō′yō′) □*noun, plural* **yo-yos**

yr. An abbreviation for **year.**

yucca   *noun* A plant that grows in dry regions of western and southern North America. It has stiff, pointed leaves and a large cluster of whitish flowers.
yuc·ca (yuk′ə) ▢*noun, plural* **yuccas**

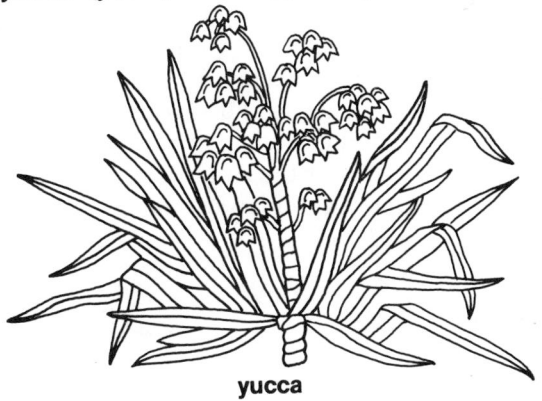

yucca

Yule or **yule**   *noun* Christmas or the Christmas season.
Yule or **yule** (yōōl) ▢*noun, plural* **Yules** or **yules**

yule log   *noun* A large log that it is customary to burn in the fireplace at Christmas.

Yuletide   *noun* The Christmas season.
Yule·tide (yōōl′tīd′) ▢*noun, plural* **Yuletides**

a bat	ī bite	ōō tool	*th* feather
ā make	î fierce	ou out	th bath
â dare	o dot	u nut	hw wheat
ä father	ō no	û turn	zh measure
e net	ô law, for	ch church	ə about, open
ē be	oi soil	ng ring	pencil, atom
i dip	oo look	sh shade	circus

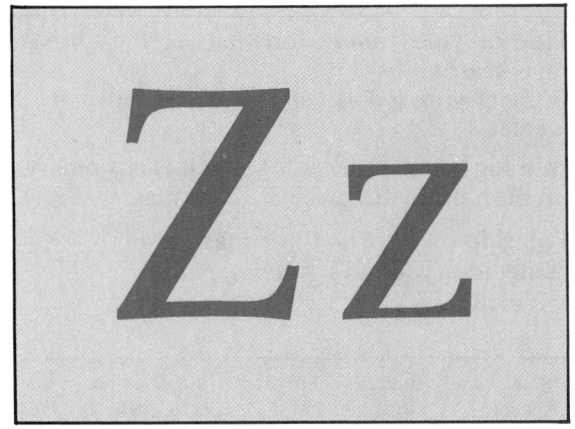

Z
ANCIENT GREEK

The letter **Z** has evolved from many forms of ancient writing. One of the earliest known examples is the Greek character shown above, which dates from almost 3,000 years ago. Over the years, artists and designers have created their own versions of the English letter **Z**. Some of the more common examples seen today are shown below.

Zz Zz	**Zz Zz**	**Zz Zz**	**Zz Zz**	*Zz Zz*
HANDWRITING	CALLIGRAPHY	MODERN SANS SERIF	MODERN SERIF	SCRIPT

z or **Z** *noun* The twenty-sixth letter of the English alphabet.
z or **Z** (zē) ▢*noun, plural* **z's** or **Z's**

zebra *noun* An African animal that is related to the horse. Its entire body is marked with black and whitish stripes.
ze·bra (zē′brə) ▢*noun, plural* **zebras**

zebra

zenith *noun* **1.** The point in the sky that is directly overhead. **2.** The highest or most important point: *the zenith of his career.*
ze·nith (zē′nith) ▢*noun, plural* **zeniths**

zero *noun* **1.** A number, written 0, that can be added to any other number without changing the value of the other number. **2.** The temperature marked by the numeral 0 on a thermometer. **3.** A point on a scale or other system of measurement that is marked by the numeral 0. **4.** Nothing.
▢*adjective* **1.** Of or at zero: *The temperature was zero.* **2.** None at all.
ze·ro (zîr′ō) ▢*noun, plural* **zeros** or **zeroes** ▢*adjective*

zigzag *noun* A line or course that moves in a series of short, sharp turns from one side or direction to another.
▢*verb* To move in or follow the form of a zigzag: *The road zigzags through the forest.*
zig·zag (zig′zag′) ▢*noun, plural* **zigzags** ▢*verb* **zigzagged, zigzagging, zigzags**

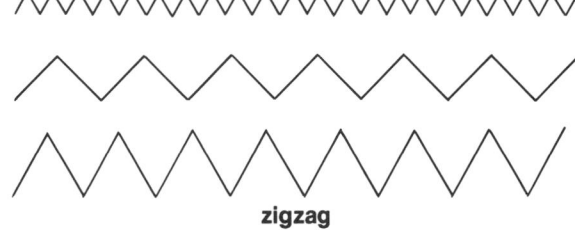

zigzag

zinc *noun* A chemical element that is a shiny bluish-white metal. Zinc is used in batteries and for coating iron.
zinc (zingk) ▢*noun*

zinnia *noun* A garden plant with flowers of various colors.
zin·ni·a (zin′ē ə) ▢*noun, plural* **zinnias**

zip *verb* To fasten or close with a zipper: *Zip up your jacket.*
zip (zip) ▢*verb* **zipped, zipping, zips**

Zip Code *noun* A numeral that identifies a postal delivery area in the United States, written after the address on a letter or package.

zipper *noun* A fastener that is made of two rows of teeth on separate edges that are made to lock and unlock by pulling a sliding tab up and down.
zip·per (**zip′**ər) □*noun, plural* **zippers**

zither *noun* A musical instrument that is made of a shallow, flat box with thirty to forty strings stretched over it. It is played by plucking the strings.
zith·er (**zith′**ər) □*noun, plural* **zithers**

zither

zodiac *noun* An imaginary band in the heavens that extends on both sides of the path traveled by the sun. It includes the paths traveled by the planets and the moon.
zo·di·ac (**zō′**dē ak′) □*noun*

zone *noun* **1.** A region or area that is divided or different from another one because of some special reason or use: *a hospital zone.* **2.** Any of the five regions into which the surface of the earth is divided according to climate and latitude.
□*verb* To divide into zones.
zone (zōn) □*noun, plural* **zones** □*verb* **zoned, zoning, zones**

zoo *noun* A park or other place where living animals are kept and shown.
zoo (zōō) □*noun, plural* **zoos**

zoological *adjective* Of or having to do with animals or zoology.
zo·o·log·i·cal (zō′ə **loj′**i kəl) □*adjective*

zoology *noun* The scientific study of animals.
zo·ol·o·gy (zō **ol′**ə jē) □*noun*

zoom *verb* **1.** To make or move with a loud, low buzzing or humming sound: *The car zoomed by.* **2.** To move or climb quickly; move quickly upward or downward: *The airplane zoomed into the sky. I zoomed down the stairs when she called me.*
zoom (zōōm) □*verb* **zoomed, zooming, zooms**

zucchini *noun* A long, narrow squash. Zucchini have thin, dark-green skin.
zuc·chi·ni (zōō **kē′**nē) □*noun, plural* **zucchini**

a	bat	ī	bite	ōō	tool	*th*	feather
ā	make	î	fierce	ou	out	th	bath
â	dare	o	dot	u	nut	hw	wheat
ä	father	ō	no	û	turn	zh	measure
e	net	ô	law, for	ch	church	ə	about, open
ē	be	oi	soil	ng	ring		pencil, atom
i	dip	oo	look	sh	shade		circus

Appendix

Table of Contents

Measurement Tables	752
Metric Conversion Chart	754
Events in United States History	755
Presidents of the United States	763
Chief Justices of the Supreme Court of the United States	764
Abbreviations	765
Manual Alphabet	766
Braille Alphabet	766
Roman Numeral Chart	767
Morse Code Chart	767
Geographic Lists	768
Map of North America	771
Map of the World	772
Map of the United States	774
Diagram of the Solar System	776
Photo Credits	778

Measurement Tables

THE METRIC SYSTEM

The metric system is a system of weights and measures based on the number 10. In the metric system the meter is the basic unit of length; the gram is the basic unit of weight; and the liter is the basic unit of volume. These are the most common prefixes added to the basic units of meter, gram, or liter:

kilo-   means 1,000
centi- means 1/100
milli- means 1/1000

The most commonly used abbreviations are:

mm = millimeter
cm = centimeter
m = meter
g = gram
kg = kilogram
ml = milliliter
l = liter
kl = kiloliter

Length

1 centimeter (cm) = 10 millimeters (mm)
1 meter (m) = 100 centimeters
1 kilometer (km) = 1,000 meters

Weight

1 kilogram (kg) = 1,000 grams (g)

Liquid Volume

1 liter (l) = 1,000 milliliters (ml)
1 kiloliter (kl) = 1,000 liters

THE U.S. CUSTOMARY SYSTEM

In the United States the customary system of measurement is still widely used, although the metric system is used by scientists and throughout most of the world. The most commonly used abbreviations in the customary system are:

in. = inch
ft. = foot
yd. = yard
mi. = mile
oz. = ounce
lb. = pound
c. = cup
pt. = pint
qt. = quart
gal. = gallon
pk. = peck
bu. = bushel

Length

1 foot (ft.) = 12 inches (in.)
1 yard (yd.) = 3 feet
1 mile (mi.) = 5,280 feet

Weight

1 pound (lb.) = 16 ounces (oz.)

Liquid Volume

1 pint (pt.) = 2 cups (c.)
1 quart (qt.) = 2 pints
1 gallon (gal.) = 4 quarts

Length

1 inch = 2.54 centimeters
1 foot = .3048 meter
1 yard = .9144 meter
1 mile = 1.6 kilometers

Weight

1 pound = 453.6 grams
2.2 pounds = 1 kilogram

Dry Measure

1 pint = .551 liter
1 quart = 1.1 liters
1 peck = 8.8 liters
1 bushel = 35.24 liters

Liquid Volume

1 pint = .473 liter
1 quart = .946 liter
1 gallon = 3.785 liters

Temperature

Fahrenheit		Celsius
32	Water freezes	0
212	Water boils	100
98.6	Normal body temperature	37

Metric Conversion Chart—Approximations

	When You Know	Multiply By	To Find
LENGTH	millimeters	0.04	inches
	centimeters	0.4	inches
	meters	3.3	feet
	meters	1.1	yards
	kilometers	0.6	miles
AREA	square centimeters	0.16	square inches
	square meters	1.2	square yards
	square kilometers	0.4	square miles
	hectares (10,000 m²)	2.5	acres
MASS AND WEIGHT	grams	0.035	ounces
	kilograms	2.2	pounds
	tons (100 kg)	1.1	short tons
VOLUME	milliliters	0.03	fluid ounces
	liters	2.1	pints
	liters	1.06	quarts
	liters	0.26	gallons
	cubic meters	35.3	cubic feet
	cubic meters	1.3	cubic yards
TEMPERATURE	Celsius temp.	9/5, +32	Fahrenheit temp.
	Fahrenheit temp.	−32, 5/9 × remainder	Celsius temp.
LENGTH	inches	2.5	centimeters
	feet	30.5	centimeters
	yards	0.9	meters
	miles	1.6	kilometers
AREA	square inches	6.5	square centimeters
	square feet	0.09	square meters
	square yards	0.8	square meters
	square miles	2.6	square kilometers
	acres	0.4	hectares
MASS AND WEIGHT	ounces	28	grams
	pounds	0.45	kilograms
	short tons (2,000 lb)	0.9	tons
VOLUME	fluid ounces	30	milliliters
	pints	0.47	liters
	quarts	0.95	liters
	gallons	3.8	liters
	cubic feet	0.03	cubic meters
	cubic yards	0.76	cubic meters

Events in United States History

Before 1492

For thousands of years before Columbus arrived, Native Americans lived in North and South America.

The Native American culture of the Aztecs reached a high level of development in art, architecture, mathematics, and astronomy. Their calendar was based on a year of 260 days.

1492

Christopher Columbus lands on San Salvador and discovers America.

Columbus shows riches from the New World to the Spanish court.

1513

Juan Ponce de León discovers and names Florida.

1522

Ferdinand Magellan sails around the world and gives Europeans a clear idea of where America is in relation to the rest of the world.

1565

The Spanish build a fort in St. Augustine, Florida. It is the first European settlement in what is now the United States.

1587

The first English child, Virginia Dare, is born in North America on Roanoke Island, Virginia.

1607

The English settle Jamestown, Virginia.

1620

The Pilgrims sail from England aboard the *Mayflower* and land in Plymouth, Massachusetts.

1634

Maryland is founded and is the first colony to allow freedom of religion.

Pilgrims Going to Church, a painting by George Henry Boughton.

755

1636
Harvard College, the first college in the American colonies, opens in Cambridge, Massachusetts.

1654
The first Jews arrive in New Amsterdam from Brazil.

1673
Jacques Marquette and Louis Joliet explore the Mississippi River.

1690
The *New England Primer* becomes the first elementary textbook to be published in the New World.

1773
Colonists dump tea into the Boston harbor as a protest against taxation, an event that is known as the Boston Tea Party.

The Spirit of '76, a painting by Archibald M. Willard.

During the Boston Tea Party, 342 chests of tea were dumped into Boston harbor by the colonists.

1775–1783
The American colonies fight Great Britain in the American Revolution.

1776
The Declaration of Independence proclaims that the British colonies are now the independent United States of America.

1781
Los Angeles, California, is founded.

1787
The Constitutional Convention meets in Philadelphia to write the Constitution of the United States.

1803
The Louisiana Purchase extends the western border of the United States to the Rocky Mountains.

1803–1805
Meriwether Lewis and William Clark lead a scientific expedition from the Missouri River to the Pacific Ocean. Their guide through the Rocky Mountains is a Native American woman named Sacajawea.

Sacajawea acted both as a guide and as an interpreter for Lewis and Clark.

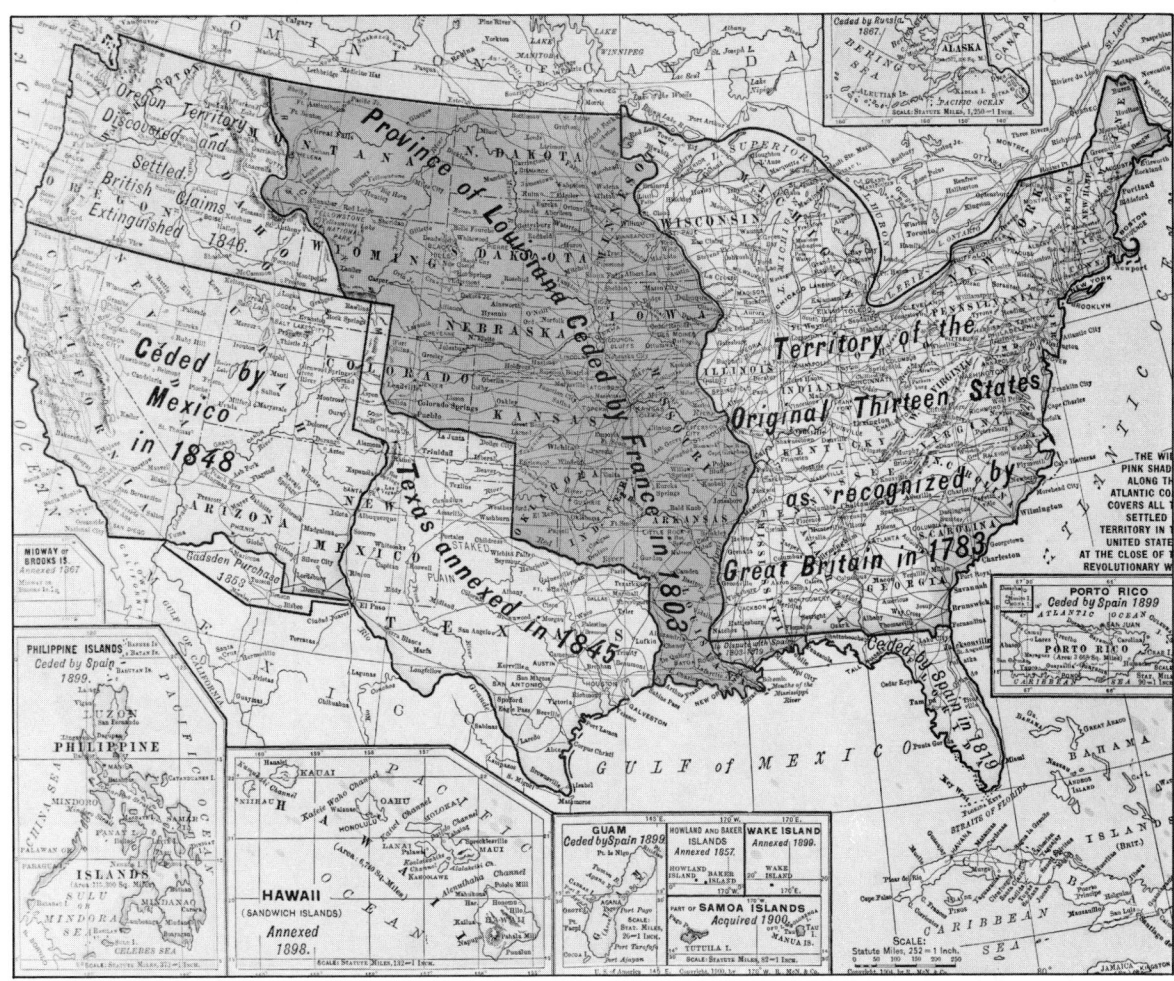

The Louisiana Purchase was bought from the French for 15 million dollars in 1803.

1812–1814
The United States fights England in the War of 1812.

1814
Francis Scott Key writes "The Star-Spangled Banner."

1844
Samuel F. B. Morse demonstrates his invention, the first telegraph.

1846–1848
The United States fights in the Mexican War.

1848
The First Women's Rights Convention meets in Seneca Falls, New York, and begins the movement for equal rights for women.

1849
Thousands of people head for California in the Gold Rush.

1861–1865
The Union Army fights the Confederate Army in the Civil War.

1869
The railroad joining the East and West coasts is completed.

A celebration took place when the last spike on the railroad linking the East and West coasts was driven at Promontory Point, near Ogden, Utah.

1876
Alexander Graham Bell invents the telephone.

1879
Thomas Edison invents the electric light bulb.

1898
The United States fights in the Spanish-American War, gaining Guam and Puerto Rico, and taking control of Hawaii.

1903
Orville and Wilbur Wright make the first airplane flight.

1908
Henry Ford introduces the Model T car.

The Wright brothers' first flight lasted only 12 seconds and covered a distance of 120 feet.

1909
Congress passes the Sixteenth Amendment, which requires all citizens to pay income tax.

1914
The Panama Canal opens to traffic, linking the Atlantic and Pacific oceans.

The Panama Canal took more than 16 years to complete.

1917–1918
The United States fights in World War I.

1920
The Nineteenth Amendment gives women the right to vote.

1927
Charles A. Lindbergh makes the first solo flight across the Atlantic Ocean from New York to Paris.

Charles Lindbergh's first solo trans-Atlantic flight took 33 hours and 39 minutes.

1929
The Stock Market crashes. Many people lose their savings and their jobs.

1932
Amelia Earhart becomes the first woman to fly alone across the Atlantic.

Amelia Earhart became the first woman to fly solo across the Atlantic Ocean.

1933
President Franklin D. Roosevelt introduces the New Deal, a series of programs to bring hope to the poor and unemployed.

This photograph taken by Dorothea Lange shows a farm mother and her children who were among those helped by the programs of President Franklin D. Roosevelt.

1941–1945
The United States fights in World War II.

1945

The first atomic bombs are dropped on the Japanese cities of Hiroshima and Nagasaki.

The United Nations is formed to settle disputes between nations and help keep peace in the world.

1946

ENIAC, the first electronic digital computer is invented.

ENIAC was much larger than the computers we use today.

1947

"Jackie" Robinson becomes the first black player in major-league baseball.

Jackie Robinson's highest batting average was .342.

1947

The transistor is invented and the age of modern electronics begins.

1950–1953

The United States fights in the Korean War.

1951

The Twenty-Second Amendment limits Presidents to two terms in office.

1952

The first hydrogen bomb is exploded on Bikini atoll in the Pacific Ocean.

1954

The Supreme Court rules that segregation in schools is unconstitutional.

1955–1956

Martin Luther King, Jr., leads a boycott of buses in Montgomery, Alabama, after Rosa Parks refuses to give up her seat on a segregated bus.

Dr. Martin Luther King, Jr., a leader in the fight for civil rights, was assassinated in 1968.

760

1958

The United States launches the satellite *Explorer I*, four months after the Soviet Union successfully put the first artificial satellite, *Sputnik I*, into orbit.

1959

Alaska and Hawaii become states.

1961

President John F. Kennedy creates the Peace Corps.

1962

John H. Glenn, Jr., becomes the first American astronaut to orbit the earth.

1963

President Kennedy is assassinated in Dallas, Texas.

1964

Congress passes the Civil Rights Act, which outlaws discrimination in jobs, schools, or elections on the basis of race, sex, religion, or national origin.

1964–1973

The United States fights in the Vietnam War.

1969

American astronauts walk on the moon.

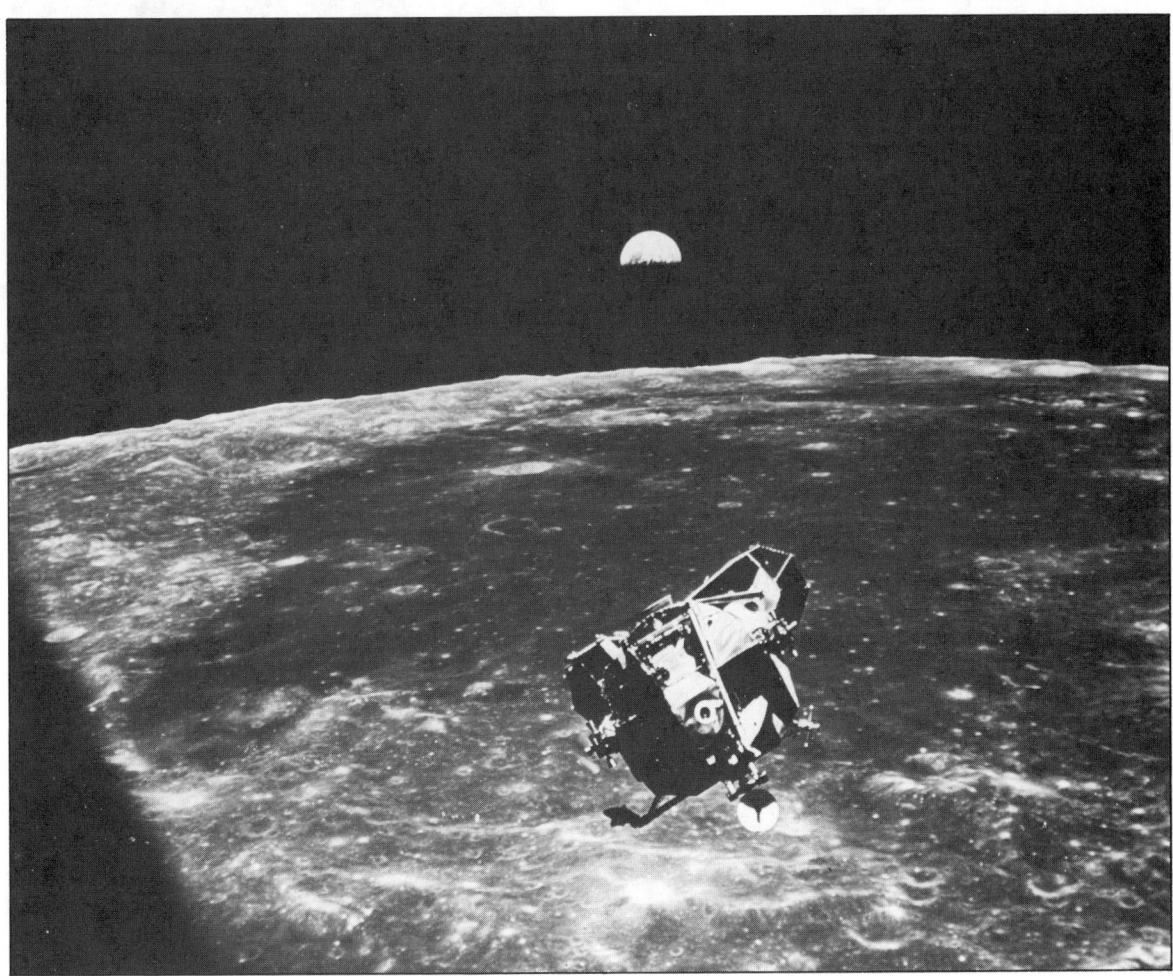

A view of the earth, as seen from the moon.

1971

The first microprocessor computer is invented and paves the way for inventions such as calculators and home computers.

1974

Richard M. Nixon becomes the first President to resign.

1976

The United States celebrates the Bicentennial, marking the two-hundredth anniversary of its independence.

Viking robot rockets land on Mars.

1981

Space shuttle *Columbia*, the world's first reusable spaceship, blasts off from Cape Canaveral, Florida.

Sandra Day O'Connor becomes the first woman justice on the Supreme Court.

1983

Dr. Sally K. Ride becomes the first American woman astronaut to go into space.

1986

The space shuttle *Challenger* explodes shortly after launch in the worst accident of the American space program.

1990

After 45 years, the Cold War between the United States and the Soviet Union is declared to be over.

1991

The United States fights in the Persian Gulf War.

1993

The orbiting Hubble Space Telescope is repaired and begins sending pictures of outer space that are ten times clearer than any telescope on the ground.

1995

The computer networks known as the Internet and World Wide Web provide a rapidly growing source of information for millions of people at school, work, and home.

Liftoff of the space shuttle *Columbia*, April 12, 1981.

The Hubble Space Telescope in orbit.

Using computers in the classroom.

Presidents of the United States

President	Term of Office	President	Term of Office
George Washington 1732–1799	1789–1797	Grover Cleveland 1837–1908	1885–1889
John Adams 1735–1826	1797–1801	Benjamin Harrison 1833–1901	1889–1893
Thomas Jefferson 1743–1826	1801–1809	Grover Cleveland 1837–1908	1893–1897
James Madison 1751–1836	1809–1817	William McKinley 1843–1901	1897–1901
James Monroe 1758–1831	1817–1825	Theodore Roosevelt 1858–1919	1901–1909
John Quincy Adams 1767–1848	1825–1829	William Howard Taft 1857–1930	1909–1913
Andrew Jackson 1767–1845	1829–1837	Woodrow Wilson 1856–1924	1913–1921
Martin Van Buren 1782–1862	1837–1841	Warren Gamaliel Harding 1865–1923	1921–1923
William Henry Harrison 1773–1841	1841	Calvin Coolidge 1872–1933	1923–1929
John Tyler 1790–1862	1841–1845	Herbert Clark Hoover 1874–1964	1929–1933
James Knox Polk 1795–1849	1845–1849	Franklin Delano Roosevelt 1882–1945	1933–1945
Zachary Taylor 1784–1850	1849–1850	Harry S. Truman 1884–1972	1945–1953
Millard Fillmore 1800–1874	1850–1853	Dwight David Eisenhower 1890–1969	1953–1961
Franklin Pierce 1804–1869	1853–1857	John Fitzgerald Kennedy 1917–1963	1961–1963
James Buchanan 1791–1868	1857–1861	Lyndon Baines Johnson 1908–1973	1963–1969
Abraham Lincoln 1809–1865	1861–1865	Richard Milhous Nixon 1913–1994	1969–1974
Andrew Johnson 1808–1875	1865–1869	Gerald Rudolph Ford Born 1913	1974–1977
Ulysses Simpson Grant 1822–1885	1869–1877	James Earl Carter Born 1924	1977–1981
Rutherford Birchard Hayes 1822–1893	1877–1881	Ronald Wilson Reagan Born 1911	1981–1989
James Abram Garfield 1831–1881	1881	George Herbert Walker Bush Born 1924	1989–1993
Chester Alan Arthur 1829–1886	1881–1885	William Jefferson Clinton Born 1946	1993–

Chief Justices of the Supreme Court of the United States

Chief Justice	Term of Office	Chief Justice	Term of Office
John Jay 1745–1829	1789–1795	Edward D. White 1845–1921	1910–1921
John Rutledge 1739–1800	1795	William H. Taft 1857–1930	1921–1930
Oliver Ellsworth 1745–1807	1796–1800	Charles E. Hughes 1862–1948	1930–1941
John Marshall 1755–1835	1801–1835	Harlan F. Stone 1872–1946	1941–1946
Roger B. Taney 1777–1864	1836–1864	Frederick M. Vinson 1890–1953	1946–1953
Salmon P. Chase 1808–1873	1864–1873	Earl Warren 1891–1974	1953–1969
Morrison R. Waite 1816–1888	1874–1888	Warren E. Burger 1907–1995	1969–1986
Melville W. Fuller 1833–1910	1888–1910	William H. Rehnquist 1924–	1986–

The United States Supreme Court.

Abbreviations

abbr	abbreviation	hr	hour	PA	Pennsylvania
AD	in the year of our Lord	ht	height	part	participle
adj	adjective	IA	Iowa	pkg	package
adv	adverb	ID	Idaho	pl	plural
AK	Alaska	i.e.	that is	p.m., PM	afternoon
AL	Alabama	IL	Illinois	PO	post office
a.m., AM	before noon	in	inch	pr	pair
Amer	America	IN	Indiana	PR	Puerto Rico
	American	Inc	incorporated	prep	preposition
amt	amount	interj	interjection	pres	president
anon	anonymous	Jan	January	pron	pronoun
ans	answer	Jr	junior	PS	postscript
Apr	April	kg	kilogram	pt	pint
AR	Arkansas	km	kilometer	PTA	Parent-Teacher Association
assn	association	KS	Kansas	PTO	Parent-Teacher Organization
asst	assistant	KY	Kentucky	qt	quart
atty	attorney	l	liter	rd	road
Aug	August	LA	Louisiana	Rev	reverend
ave	avenue	lb	pound	RFD	rural free delivery
AZ	Arizona	Lt	lieutenant	RI	Rhode Island
BC	before Christ	m	meter	rpm	revolutions per minute
bu	bushel		mile	RR	railroad
C	Celsius	MA	Massachusetts	rte	route
	centigrade	Maj	major	S	south
CA	California	Mar	March	Sat	Saturday
Can	Canada	MD	Maryland	SC	South Carolina
Capt	captain	ME	Maine	SD	South Dakota
cm	centimeter	Mex	Mexico	sec	second
Co	company	mg	milligram	Sept	September
CO	Colorado	mi	mile	sing	singular
Col	colonel	MI	Michigan	sq	square
conj	conjunction	min	minute	St	saint
ct	cent	ml	milliliter	Sun	Sunday
CT	Connecticut	mm	millimeter	tbsp	tablespoon
CZ	Canal Zone	MN	Minnesota	Thurs	Thursday
DC	District of Columbia	mo	month	TN	Tennessee
DE	Delaware	MO	Missouri	tsp	teaspoon
Dec	December	Mon	Monday	Tues	Tuesday
dept	department	mpg	miles per gallon	TX	Texas
doz	dozen	mph	miles per hour	UN	United Nations
Dr	doctor	MS	Mississippi	US	United States
DST	daylight saving time	mt	mountain	USA	United States of America
E	east	MT	Montana	UT	Utah
ea	each	n	noun	v	verb
e.g.	for example	N	north	VA	Virginia
esp	especially	NC	North Carolina	vb	verb
etc	et cetera	ND	North Dakota	VI	Virgin Islands
F	Fahrenheit	NE	Nebraska	vol	volume
Feb	February	NH	New Hampshire	VP	vice-president
FL	Florida	NJ	New Jersey	VT	Vermont
Fri	Friday	NM	New Mexico	W	west
ft	feet	no	number	WA	Washington
	foot	Nov	November	Wed	Wednesday
g	gram	NV	Nevada	WI	Wisconsin
GA	Georgia	NY	New York	wk	week
gal	gallon	Oct	October	wt	weight
gm	gram	OH	Ohio	WV	West Virginia
gov	governor	OK	Oklahoma	WY	Wyoming
govt	government	OR	Oregon	yd	yard
GU	Guam	oz	ounce	yr	year
HI	Hawaii	p	page		

Manual Alphabet

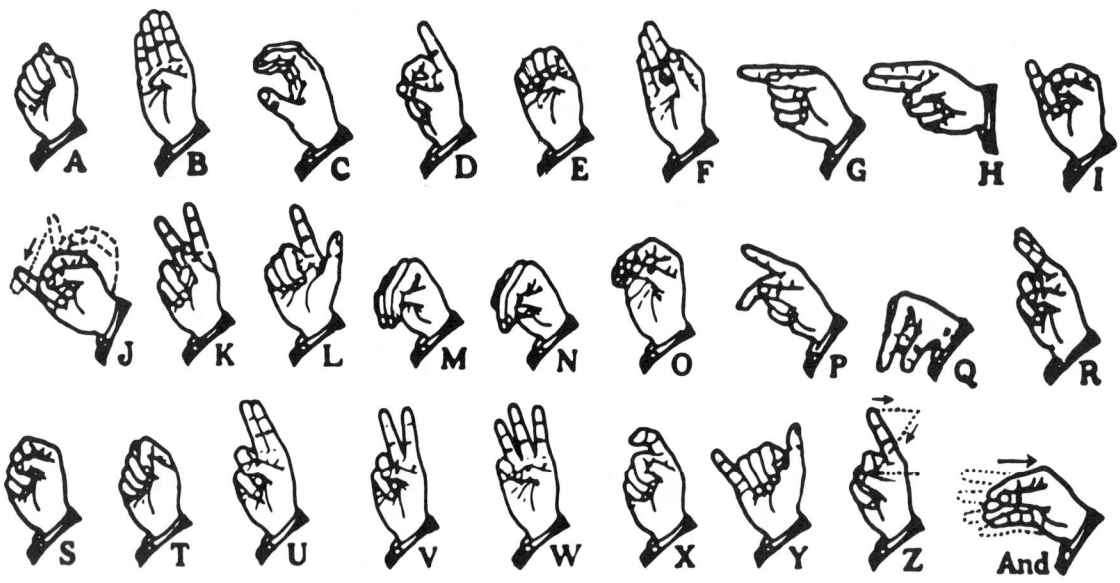

Braille Alphabet

a,1	b,2	c,3	d,4	e,5	f,6	g,7	h,8	i,9
● ○	● ○	● ●	● ●	● ○	● ●	● ●	● ○	○ ●
○ ○	● ○	○ ○	○ ●	○ ●	● ○	● ●	● ●	● ○
○ ○	○ ○	○ ○	○ ○	○ ○	○ ○	○ ○	○ ○	○ ○

j,0	k	l	m	n	o	p	q	r
○ ●	● ○	● ○	● ●	● ●	● ○	● ●	● ●	● ○
● ●	○ ○	● ○	○ ○	○ ●	○ ●	● ○	● ●	● ●
○ ○	● ○	● ○	● ○	● ○	● ○	● ○	● ○	● ○

s	t	u	v	w	x	y	z	&
○ ●	○ ●	● ○	● ○	○ ●	● ●	● ●	● ○	● ●
● ○	● ●	○ ○	● ○	● ●	○ ○	○ ●	○ ●	○ ●
● ○	● ○	● ●	● ●	● ○	● ●	● ●	● ●	● ●

			punctuation					
,	;	:	.	!	(	)	" ?	"
○ ○	○ ○	○ ○	○ ○	○ ○	○ ○	○ ○	○ ○	○ ○
● ○	● ○	● ○	● ○	● ○	● ●	● ●	● ○	○ ●
○ ○	● ○	● ○	● ○	● ●	● ●	● ●	● ●	● ●

apostrophe	numeral	hyphen	capital	numerical positions in the cell
○ ○	○ ●	○ ○	○ ○	1 ● ● 4
○ ○	○ ●	○ ○	○ ○	2 ● ● 5
● ○	● ●	● ●	○ ●	3 ● ● 6

766

Roman Numeral Chart

I	1	XV	15	XC	90
II	2	XVI	16	XCVIII	98
III	3	XVII	17	IC	99
IV	4	XVIII	18	C	100
V	5	XIX	19	CI	101
VI	6	XX	20	CC	200
VII	7	XXI	21	D	500
VIII	8	XXIX	29	DC	600
IX	9	XXX	30	CM	900
X	10	XL	40	M	1,000
XI	11	XLVIII	48	MDCLXVI	1666
XII	12	IL	49	MCMLXX	1970
XIII	13	L	50		
XIV	14	LX	60		

Morse Code Chart

A	· —	Q	— — · —	1	· — — — —	, (comma)	— — · · — —
B	— · · ·	R	· — ·	2	· · — — —	. (period)	· — · — · —
C	— · — ·	S	· · ·	3	· · · — —	?	· · — — · ·
D	— · ·	T	—	4	· · · · —	;	— · — · — ·
E	·	U	· · —	5	· · · · ·	:	— — — · · ·
F	· · — ·	V	· · · —	6	— · · · ·	/	— · · — ·
G	— — ·	W	· — —	7	— — · · ·	- (hyphen)	— · · · · —
H	· · · ·	X	— · · —	8	— — — · ·	apostrophe	· — — — — ·
I	· ·	Y	— · — —	9	— — — — ·	parenthesis	— · — — · —
J	· — — —	Z	— — · ·	0	— — — — —	underline	· · — — · —
K	— · —	Á	· — — · —				
L	· — · ·	Ä	· — · —				
M	— —	É	· · — · ·				
N	— ·	Ñ	— — · — —				
O	— — —	Ö	— — — ·				
P	· — — ·	Ü	· · — —				

Geographic Lists

The Continents and Oceans of the World

Continent	Ocean
Africa	Arctic
Antarctica	Atlantic
Asia	Indian
Australia	Pacific
Europe	
North America	
South America	

Highest Mountains in North America

Name (Country)	Approximate Height (feet/meters)
McKinley (U.S.)	20,320/6,096
Logan (U.S./Canada)	19,850/5,955
Orizaba (Mexico)	18,701/5,610
St. Elias (U.S./Canada)	18,008/5,402
Popocatépetl (Mexico)	17,887/5,366
Ixtacihuatl (Mexico)	17,342/5,203
Lucania (Canada)	17,147/5,144
King Peak (Canada)	16,971/5,091

The Provinces and Territories of Canada

Province or Territory	Capital
Alberta	Edmonton
British Columbia	Victoria
Manitoba	Winnipeg
New Brunswick	Fredericton
Newfoundland	Saint John's
Northwest Territories	Yellowknife
Nova Scotia	Halifax
Ontario	Toronto
Prince Edward Island	Charlottetown
Quebec	Quebec
Saskatchewan	Regina
Yukon Territory	Whitehorse

The States of the United States

State	Capital
Alabama	Montgomery
Alaska	Juneau
Arizona	Phoenix
Arkansas	Little Rock
California	Sacramento
Colorado	Denver
Connecticut	Hartford
Delaware	Dover
Florida	Tallahassee
Georgia	Atlanta
Hawaii	Honolulu
Idaho	Boise
Illinois	Springfield
Indiana	Indianapolis
Iowa	Des Moines
Kansas	Topeka
Kentucky	Frankfort
Louisiana	Baton Rouge
Maine	Augusta
Maryland	Annapolis
Massachusetts	Boston
Michigan	Lansing
Minnesota	Saint Paul
Mississippi	Jackson
Missouri	Jefferson City
Montana	Helena
Nebraska	Lincoln
Nevada	Carson City
New Hampshire	Concord
New Jersey	Trenton
New Mexico	Santa Fe
New York	Albany
North Carolina	Raleigh
North Dakota	Bismarck
Ohio	Columbus
Oklahoma	Oklahoma City
Oregon	Salem
Pennsylvania	Harrisburg
Rhode Island	Providence
South Carolina	Columbia
South Dakota	Pierre
Tennessee	Nashville
Texas	Austin
Utah	Salt Lake City
Vermont	Montpelier
Virginia	Richmond
Washington	Olympia
West Virginia	Charleston
Wisconsin	Madison
Wyoming	Cheyenne

The Nations of the World

Nation	Capital	Nation	Capital
Afghanistan	Kabul	Dominican Republic	Santo Domingo
Albania	Tiranë	Ecuador	Quito
Algeria	Algiers	Egypt	Cairo
Andorra	Andorra la Vella	El Salvador	San Salvador
Angola	Luanda	Equatorial Guinea	Malabo
Antigua and Barbuda	Saint John's	Eritrea	Asmara
Argentina	Buenos Aires	Estonia	Tallinn
Armenia	Yerevan	Ethiopia	Addis Ababa
Australia	Canberra	Fiji	Suva
Austria	Vienna	Finland	Helsinki
Azerbaijan	Baku	France	Paris
Bahamas	Nassau	Gabon	Libreville
Bahrain	Manama	Gambia	Banjul
Bangladesh	Dhaka	Georgia	Tbilisi
Barbados	Bridgetown	Germany	Berlin and Bonn
Belarus	Minsk	Ghana	Accra
Belgium	Brussels	Greece	Athens
Belize	Belmopan	Grenada	Saint George's
Benin	Porto-Novo	Guatemala	Guatemala City
Bhutan	Thimphu	Guinea	Conakry
Bolivia	Sucre and La Paz	Guinea-Bissau	Bissau
Bosnia and Herzegovina	Sarajevo	Guyana	Georgetown
Botswana	Gaborone	Haiti	Port-au-Prince
Brazil	Brasília	Honduras	Tegucigalpa
Brunei	Bandar Seri Begawan	Hungary	Budapest
		Iceland	Reykjavik
Bulgaria	Sofia	India	New Delhi
Burkina Faso	Ouagadougou	Indonesia	Jakarta
Burundi	Bujumbura	Iran	Tehran
Cambodia	Phnom Penh	Iraq	Baghdad
Cameroon	Yaoundé	Ireland	Dublin
Canada	Ottawa	Israel	Jersusalem
Cape Verde	Praia	Italy	Rome
Central African Republic	Bangui	Jamaica	Kingston
Chad	N'Djamena	Japan	Tokyo
Chile	Santiago	Jordan	Amman
China	Beijing	Kazakstan	Almaty
Colombia	Bogotá	Kenya	Nairobi
Comoros	Moroni	Kiribati	Bairiki
Congo	Brazzaville	Korea, North	Pyongyang
Costa Rica	San José	Korea, South	Seoul
Côte d'Ivoire (Ivory Coast)	Yamoussoukro and Abidjan	Kuwait	Kuwait
		Kyrgyzstan	Bishkek
Croatia	Zagreb	Laos	Vientiane
Cuba	Havana	Latvia	Riga
Cyprus	Nicosia	Lebanon	Beirut
Czech Republic	Prague	Lesotho	Maseru
Denmark	Copenhagen	Liberia	Monrovia
Djibouti	Djibouti	Libya	Tripoli
Dominica	Roseau	Liechtenstein	Vaduz

769

The Nations of the World, continued

Nation	Capital	Nation	Capital
Lithuania	Vilnius	San Marino	San Marino
Luxembourg	Luxembourg	São Tomé and Principe	São Tomé
Macedonia	Skopje	Saudi Arabia	Riyadh
Madagascar	Antananarivo	Senegal	Dakar
Malawi	Lilongwe	Seychelles	Victoria
Malaysia	Kuala Lumpur	Sierra Leone	Freetown
Maldives	Male	Singapore	Singapore
Mali	Bamako	Slovakia	Bratislava
Malta	Valletta	Slovenia	Ljubljana
Marshall Islands	Majuro	Solomon Islands	Honiara
Mauritania	Nouakchott	Somalia	Mogadishu
Mauritius	Port Louis	South Africa	Pretoria, Cape Town and Bloemfontein
Mexico	Mexico City		
Micronesia	Palikir	Spain	Madrid
Moldova	Chisinau	Sri Lanka	Colombo
Monaco	Monaco	Sudan	Khartoum
Mongolia	Ulan Bator	Suriname	Paramaribo
Morocco	Rabat	Swaziland	Mbabane
Mozambique	Maputo	Sweden	Stockholm
Myanmar (Burma)	Yangon (Rangoon)	Switzerland	Bern
Namibia	Windhoek	Syria	Damascus
Nauru	Yaren	Taiwan	Taipei
Nepal	Katmandu	Tajikistan	Dushanbe
Netherlands	Amsterdam and The Hague	Tanzania	Dar es Salaam
		Thailand	Bangkok
New Zealand	Wellington	Togo	Lomé
Nicaragua	Managua	Tonga	Nuku'alofa
Niger	Niamey	Trinidad and Tobago	Port of Spain
Nigeria	Abuja and Lagos	Tunisia	Tunis
Norway	Oslo	Turkey	Ankara
Oman	Muscat	Turkmenistan	Ashgabat
Pakistan	Islamabad	Tuvalu	Funafuti
Palau	Koror	Uganda	Kampala
Panama	Panama City	Ukraine	Kiev
Papua New Guinea	Port Moresby	United Arab Emirates	Abu Dhabi
Paraguay	Asunción	United Kingdom	London
Peru	Lima	United States of America	Washington, D.C.
Philippines	Manila	Uruguay	Montevideo
Poland	Warsaw	Uzbekistan	Tashkent
Portugal	Lisbon	Vanuatu	Vila
Qatar	Doha	Vatican City	
Romania	Bucharest	Venezuela	Caracas
Russia	Moscow	Vietnam	Hanoi
Rwanda	Kigali	Western Samoa	Apia
Saint Kitts and Nevis	Basseterre	Yemen	San'a
Saint Lucia	Castries	Yugoslavia	Belgrade
Saint Vincent and the Grenadines	Kingstown	Zaire	Kinshasa
		Zambia	Lusaka
		Zimbabwe	Harare

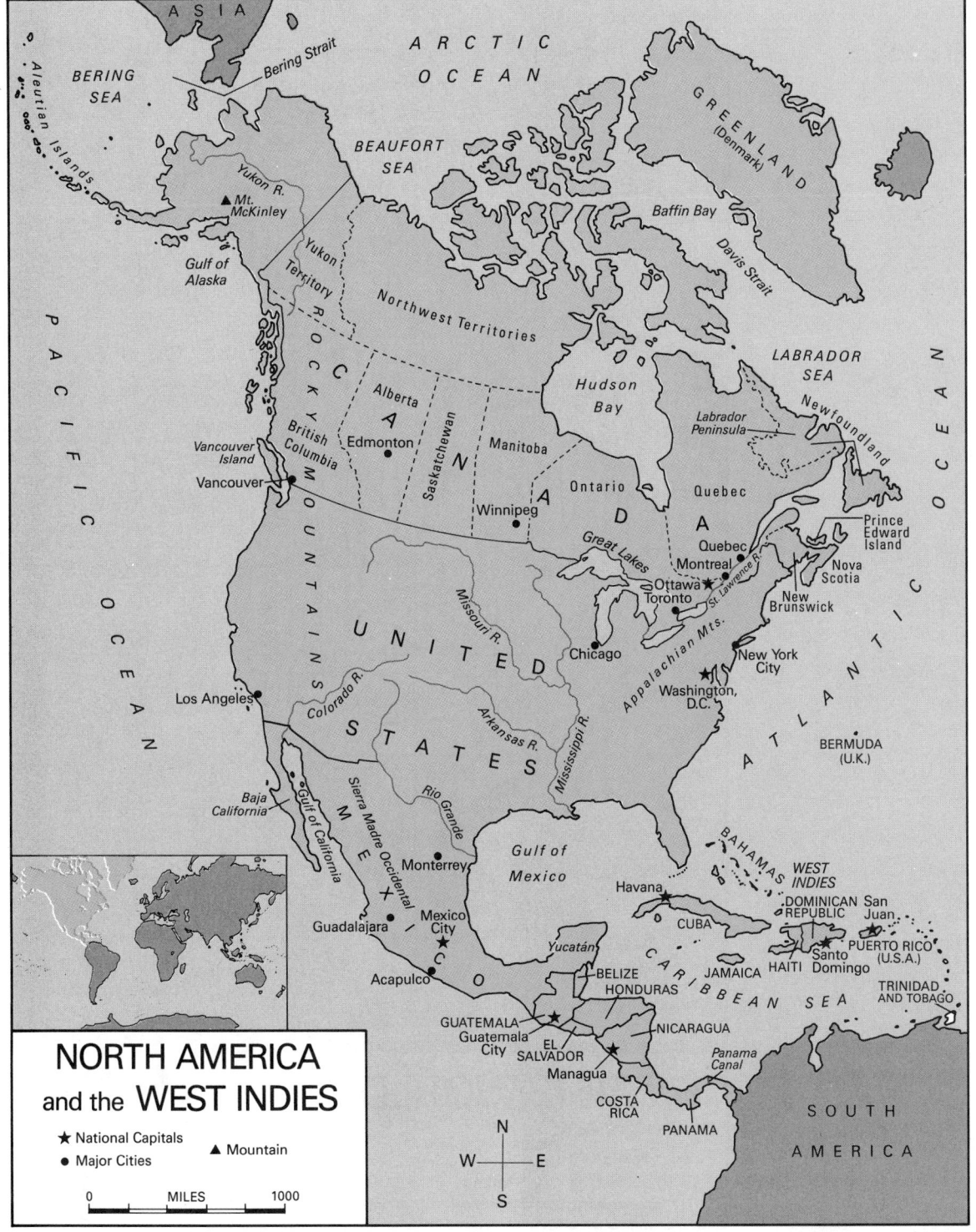

ARCTIC OCEAN

ASIA

BERING STRAIT

Aleutian Islands

BERING SEA

BEAUFORT SEA

Yukon R.
▲ Mt. McKinley

Gulf of Alaska

Yukon Territory

Northwest Territories

GREENLAND (Denmark)

Baffin Bay

Davis Strait

LABRADOR SEA

Hudson Bay

Labrador Peninsula

Newfoundland

Alberta

Edmonton

Saskatchewan

Manitoba

British Columbia

Vancouver Island

Vancouver

Ontario

Quebec

Prince Edward Island

C A N A D A

Great Lakes

Quebec
Montreal

St. Lawrence R.

Nova Scotia

Ottawa
Toronto

New Brunswick

Missouri R.

UNITED

Winnipeg

Chicago

Appalachian Mts.

New York City

Los Angeles

Colorado R.

STATES

Arkansas R.

Mississippi R.

Washington, D.C.

ATLANTIC OCEAN

BERMUDA (U.K.)

PACIFIC OCEAN

ROCKY MOUNTAINS

Baja California

Gulf of California

Sierra Madre Occidental

Rio Grande

Gulf of Mexico

BAHAMAS

WEST INDIES

Havana

CUBA

DOMINICAN REPUBLIC

San Juan

PUERTO RICO (U.S.A.)

Monterrey

M E X I C O

Guadalajara

Mexico City

Yucatán

JAMAICA

HAITI

Santo Domingo

TRINIDAD AND TOBAGO

Acapulco

CARIBBEAN SEA

BELIZE
HONDURAS

GUATEMALA
Guatemala City

EL SALVADOR

NICARAGUA

Managua

Panama Canal

COSTA RICA

PANAMA

SOUTH AMERICA

NORTH AMERICA and the WEST INDIES

★ National Capitals   ▲ Mountain

● Major Cities

N
W — E
S

0   MILES   1000

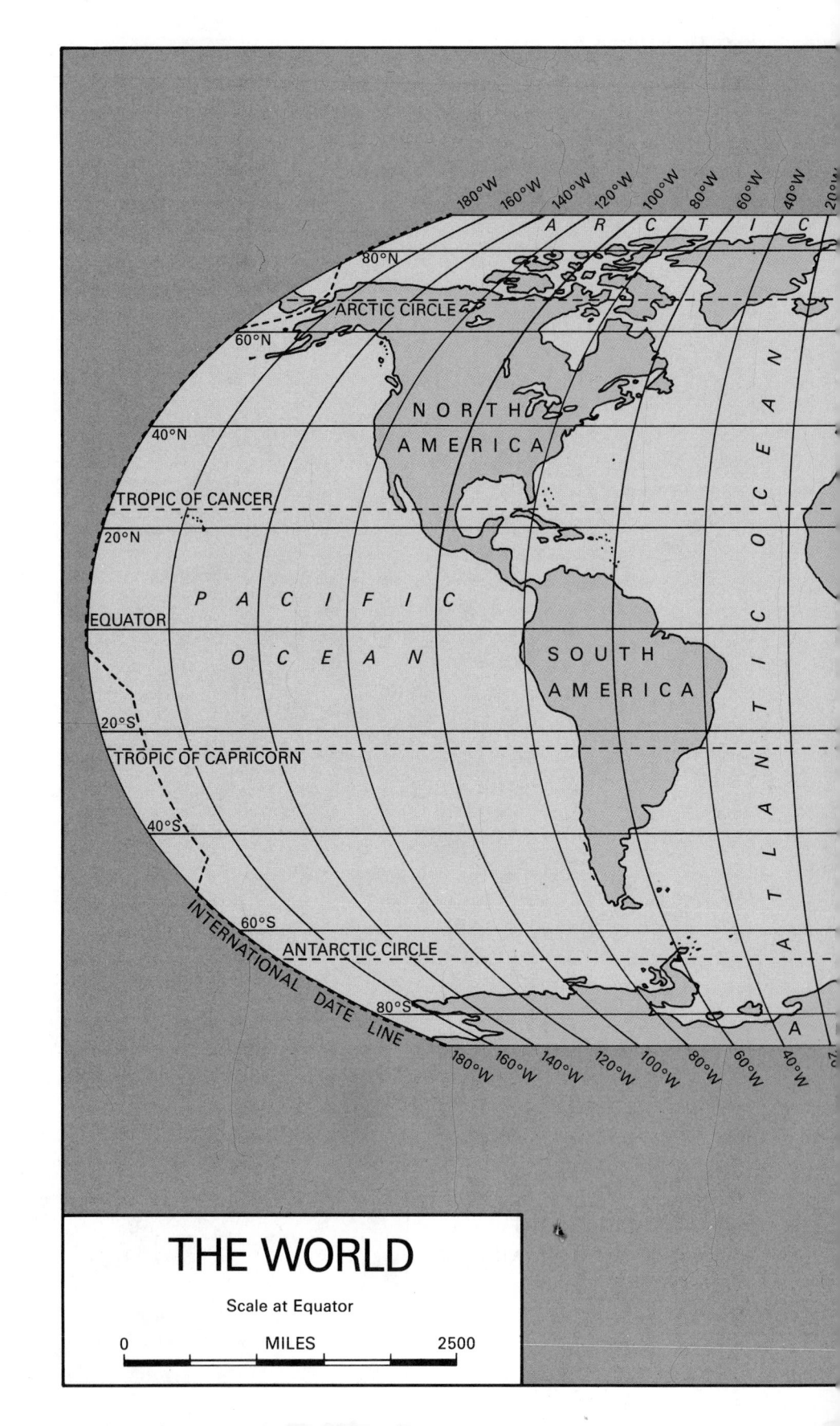

ARCTIC

180°W 160°W 140°W 120°W 100°W 80°W 60°W 40°W 20°W

80°N

ARCTIC CIRCLE

60°N

NORTH
AMERICA

40°N

TROPIC OF CANCER

20°N

EQUATOR

PACIFIC

OCEAN

ATLANTIC OCEAN

SOUTH
AMERICA

20°S

TROPIC OF CAPRICORN

40°S

60°S

INTERNATIONAL DATE LINE

ANTARCTIC CIRCLE

80°S

A

180°W 160°W 140°W 120°W 100°W 80°W 60°W 40°W

THE WORLD

Scale at Equator

0   MILES   2500

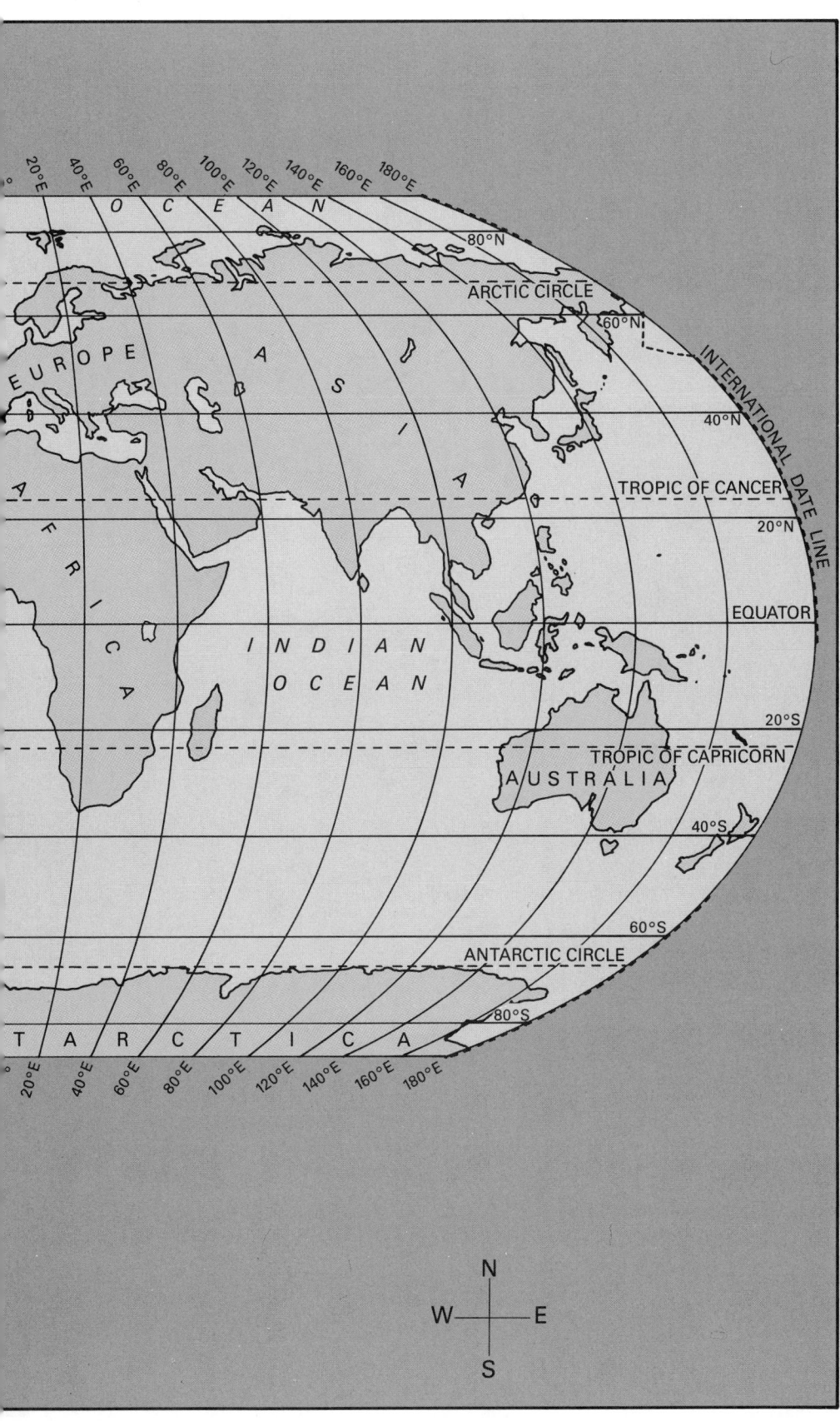

The United States

CANADA

MINNESOTA

Lake Superior

MICHIGAN

WISCONSIN

Minneapolis
Saint Paul

Madison
Milwaukee
Lansing
Detroit

Lake Michigan

Lake Huron

IOWA

Des Moines

Omaha

Lincoln

Chicago
Gary

ILLINOIS
INDIANA

Cleveland

OHIO

Columbus

Lake Erie

Lake Ontario

NEW YORK

Albany

PENNSYLVANIA

Philadelphia

Harrisburg

VERMONT

MAINE

Augusta

Portland

Montpelier

NEW HAMPSHIRE

Concord

MASSACHUSETTS

Boston

Hartford

Providence

RHODE ISLAND

CONNECTICUT

New York City

Trenton

NEW JERSEY

Wilmington

DELAWARE

Dover

Springfield
Indianapolis

WEST
VIRGINIA

Baltimore

Annapolis

MARYLAND

Washington, D.C.

Kansas City
Jefferson City
St. Louis

Topeka

MISSOURI

Louisville
Frankfort

KENTUCKY

Charleston

Ohio River

VIRGINIA

Richmond

ATLANTIC OCEAN

chita

Nashville

TENNESSEE

NORTH CAROLINA

Raleigh

Charlotte

Tulsa

lahoma City

Fort Smith

ARKANSAS

Memphis

Columbia

SOUTH
CAROLINA

MA

Little Rock

Mississippi River

MISSISSIPPI

Atlanta

ALABAMA
GEORGIA

Savannah

Dallas

Jackson
Montgomery

Austin

LOUISIANA

Baton Rouge

Mobile

Tallahassee

New Orleans

FLORIDA

Houston

N

W   E

S

Miami

Gulf of Mexico

miles

0 50 100 150 200 250

kilometers

0   100   200   300

⊗ National Capital

★ State Capital

● Major Cities

95°W 90°W 85°W 80°W 75°W 70°W 50°N

45°N

40°N

35°N

30°N

25°N

95°W 90°W 85°W 80°W 75°W

The Solar System

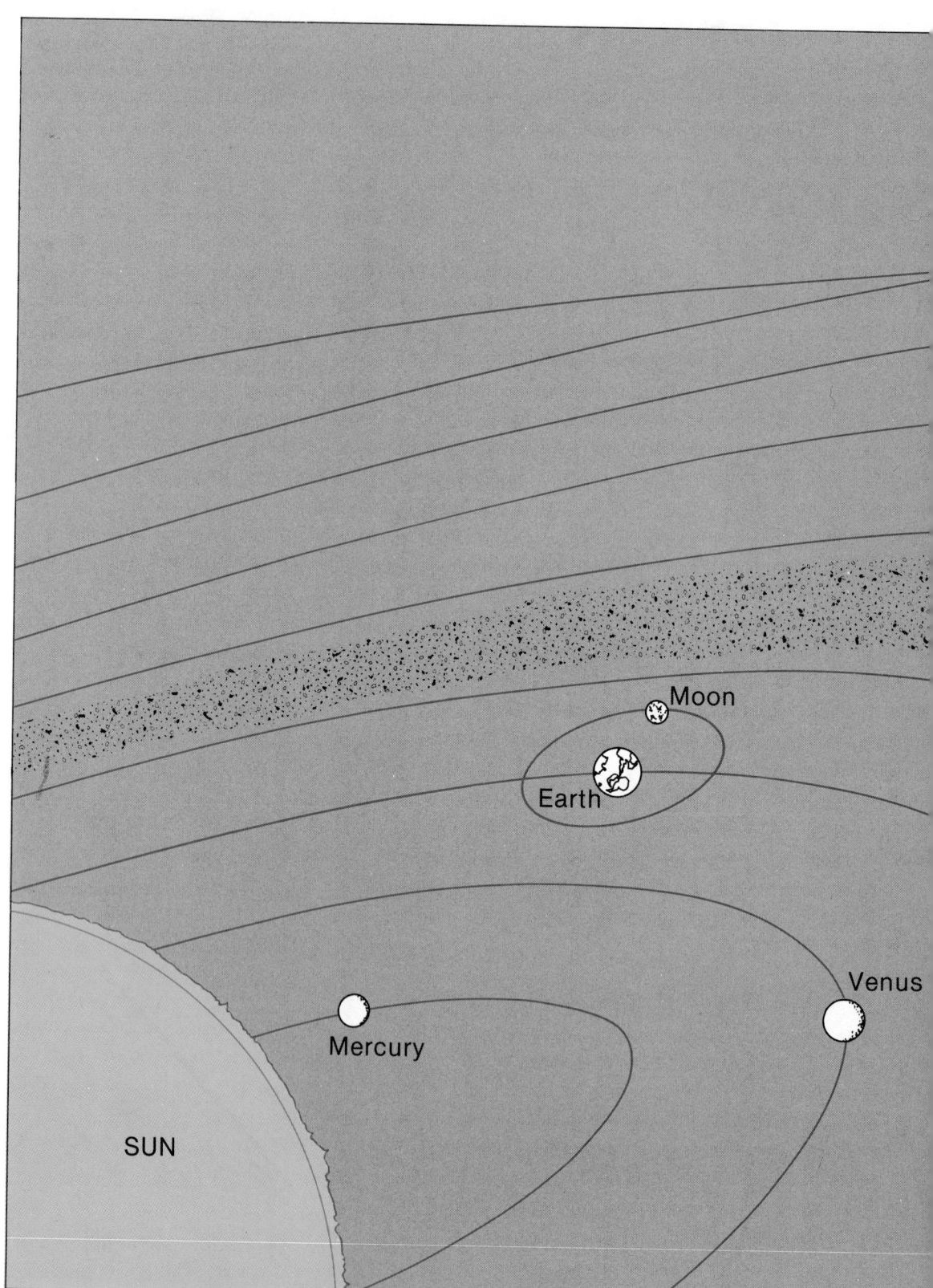

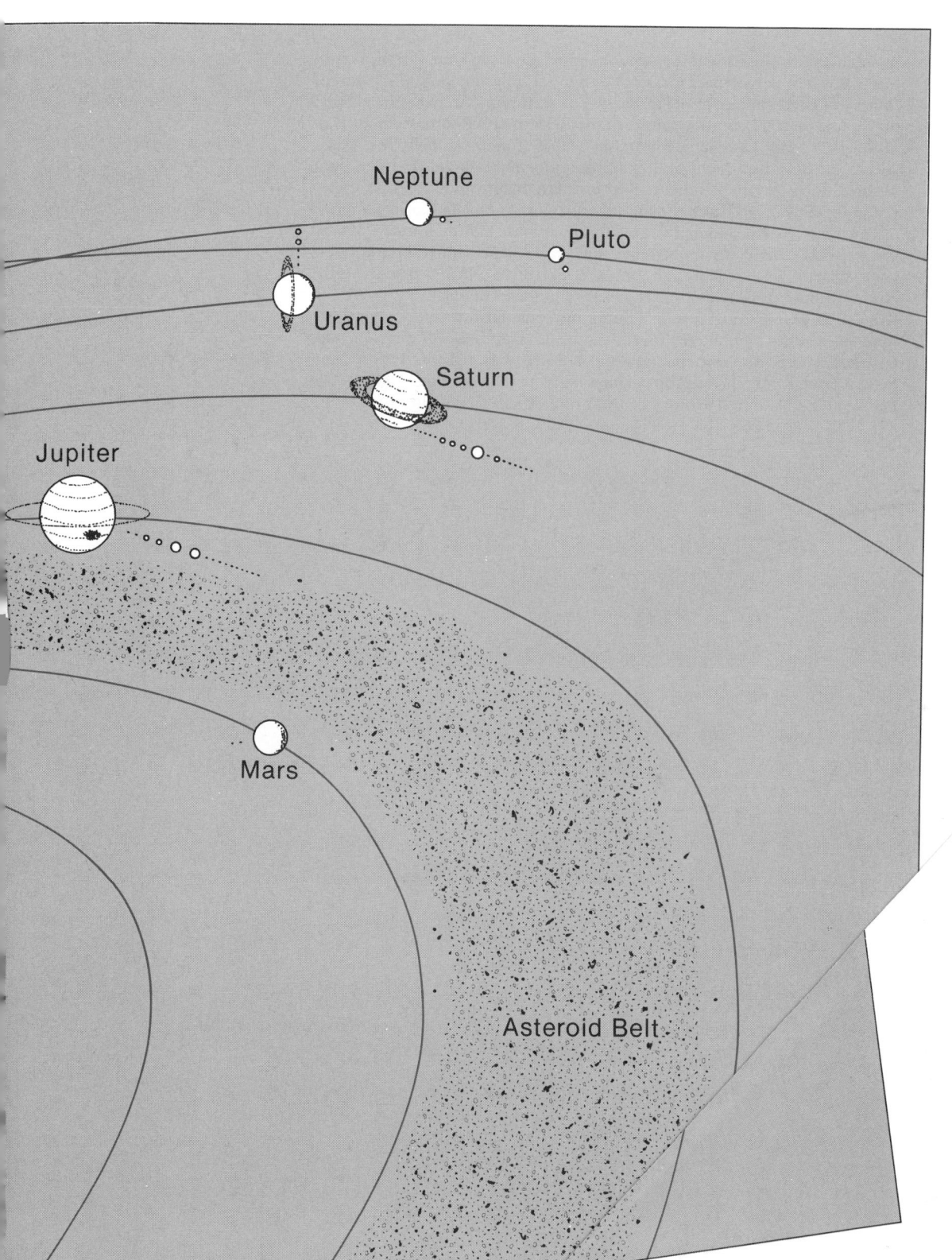

Neptune

Pluto

Uranus

Saturn

Jupiter

Mars

Asteroid Belt

Photo Credits

Aztec calendar, Museum of the American Indian, Heye Foundation; Columbus at Court of Barcelona, Library of Congress; "Pilgrims Going To Church," Library of Congress; Boston Tea Party, The Bettmann Archive, Inc.; "Spirit of '76," the original painting hangs in the Selectmen's Room of Abbot Hall, Marblehead, MA; Louisiana Purchase, The Bettmann Archive, Inc.; Sacajawea, The Bettmann Archive, Inc.; transcontinental railroad, The Bettmann Archive, Inc.; Wright Brothers, Smithsonian Institution; Panama Canal, Keystone View Co., Inc.; Charles Lindbergh, NASA; Amelia Earhart, Library of Congress; Dorothea Lange photo of mother and children, Library of Congress; ENIAC, The Bettmann Archive, Inc.; Jackie Robinson, Library of Congress; Martin Luther King, Jr., NAACP; earthrise, NASA; space shuttle, NASA; Hubble space telescope, NASA; computers, The Picture Cube/© Bob Kramer; Supreme Court justices, Supreme Court Historical Society; North America and the West Indies map, Jacques Chazaud; World map, Jacques Chazaud; United States map, copyright © 1986 by Houghton Mifflin Company. Adapted and reprinted by permission from the complete volume of "A People and a Nation: A History of the United States, 2nd edition."